September 15–19, 2016
Boston, MA, USA

Association for
Computing Machinery

Advancing Computing as a Science & Profession

RecSys'16

Proceedings of the 10th ACM Conference on Recommender Systems

Sponsored by:

ACM SIGCHI

Supported by:

Google, Spotify, Alibaba Group, Netflix, Quora, Pandora, OpenTable, Target, Criteol Labs, Microsoft, Amazon, Zalando, Medium, DemandWare, Silver Egg Technology, Yandex, IBM Research, Xing, MIT EECS, and NSF

Association for
Computing Machinery

Advancing Computing as a Science & Profession

The Association for Computing Machinery
2 Penn Plaza, Suite 701
New York, New York 10121-0701

ISBN: 978-1-4503-4035-9 (Digital)

ISBN: 978-1-4503-4681-8 (Print)

Additional copies may be ordered prepaid from:

ACM Order Department
PO Box 30777
New York, NY 10087-0777, USA

Phone: 1-800-342-6626 (USA and Canada)
+1-212-626-0500 (Global)
Fax: +1-212-944-1318
E-mail: acmhelp@acm.org
Hours of Operation: 8:30 am – 4:30 pm ET

Printed in the USA

RecSys 2016 Chairs' Welcome

It is our great pleasure to welcome you to the 10th *ACM Conference on Recommender Systems* (RecSys 2016), held in Boston, MA, USA, from September 15th through 19th. Since it was first held ten years ago, RecSys has grown to become the leading conference for the presentation and discussion of recommender systems research, bringing together the world's leading recommender systems researchers and e-commerce companies.

The program for RecSys 2016 reflects the growth of the Recommender Systems community. For the second time in the history of RecSys we will offer two parallel tracks during the three days of the main conference with a record breaking 112 contributions including 51 technical papers, 9 Past, Present, and Future papers, 15 industry papers, four tutorials, three keynotes, and 30 demos and posters. We again offer an extensive pre-conference program with nine workshops, the RecSys Challenge and a doctoral symposium.

The technical program for RecSys 2016 drew upon a record 294 total submissions. To celebrate the tenth year of the conference, the program features a new track reflecting on past, present, and future research in the field of recommender systems. Papers in this track consider a broad perspective on how the field has evolved and the challenges and directions that lie ahead. The review process for all tracks was highly selective. In the main program, 29 long papers were accepted out of 159 submissions (18.2% acceptance rate), 22 out of 110 short papers (20% acceptance rate), and 9 out of 25 Past, Present and Future paper submissions (36% acceptance rate). Prominent topics covered by these papers include human factors, social aspects, context awareness, cold start, novelty and diversity, and core algorithmic research (matrix factorization, deep learning, probabilistic approaches, etc.).

Building on the tradition established by previous years, RecSys 2016 features a strong focus on significant real-world challenges facing industrial practitioners and practical solutions to those challenges. The three industry sessions feature a rich set of talks from Mendeley, Meetup, Bloomberg, Foursquare, Spotify, Netflix, Pandora, Stitch Fix, Expedia, Nara Logics, GraphSQL, Retail Rocket, Quora, Google and Pinterest. A wide range of domains are represented in these sessions including publishing, news, Q & A, events, music, movies, television, fashion, apps and games.

This year's conference has truly been a product of the vibrant, supportive RecSys community and the vast cohort of amazing volunteers we drew upon within it. We would like to thank the members of the organizing committee for their generosity, initiative and brilliant execution. We are tremendously grateful to the 36 senior and 92 regular Program Committee members and the reviewers who volunteered their time and generated around 850 detailed and insightful reviews and discussions. We also extend our deepest gratitude to the many sponsors in 2016 who generously provided crucial funds and services allowing us support many of the social events at the conference. We thank the organizers and sponsors of the RecSys Challenge, who devoted themselves to organizing this annual competitive event. Finally, we thank all the authors for their contributions in shaping the high quality content of the conference, as well as all the conference attendees, literally give meaning to this event.

We hope you will find RecSys 2016 to be an engaging opportunity to share ideas and interact with leading researchers and practitioners from around the world.

Shilad Sen and Werner Geyer
RecSys 2016 General Chairs

Jill Freyne and Pablo Castells
RecSys 2016 Program Chairs

Karen Church, Paul Lamere and Hrishi Aradhye
RecSys 2016 Industry Chairs

Table of Contents

Paper Session 5: Trust and Reliability

Paper Session 6: Applications

Paper Session 7: Past, Present & Future

Paper Session 8: Deep Learning

Paper Session 9: Contextual Challenges

Paper Session 10: Social Perspective

Paper Session 11: Algorithms II

Industry Session 1

Industry Session 2

Industry Session 3

Demonstrations

Workshops and Challenge

Tutorials

Doctoral Symposium

RecSys 2016 Conference Organization

General Co-Chairs: Shilad Sen (*Macalester College, USA*)
Werner Geyer (*IBM Research Cambridge, USA*)

Program Co-Chairs: Jill Freyne (*CSIRO, Australia*)
Pablo Castells (*Universidad Autónoma de Madrid, Spain*)

Workshop Co-Chairs: Elizabeth Daly (*IBM Research Dublin, Ireland*)
Dietmar Jannach (*TU Dortmund, Germany*)

Tutorial Co-Chairs: Li Chen (*Hong Kong Baptist University, Hong Kong*)
Francesco Ricci (*Free University of Bozen-Bolzano, Italy*)

Doctoral Symposium Co-Chairs: Joe Konstan (*University of Minnesota, USA*)
Martijn Willemsen (*Eindhoven University of Technology, The Netherlands*)

Poster and Demo Co-Chairs: Ido Guy (*Yahoo Research, Israel*)
Amit Sharma (*Microsoft Research, USA*)

Industry Co-Chairs: Karen Church (*Yahoo Labs, USA*)
Paul Lamere (*Spotify, USA*)
Hrishi Aradhye (*Google, USA*)

Proceedings Chair: Alejandro Bellogín (*Universidad Autónoma de Madrid, Spain*)

Publicity Co-Chairs: Alan Said (*University of Skövde, Sweden*)
Michael Ekstrand (*Boise State University, USA*)

University Liaison Chair: David Karger (*MIT CSAIL, USA*)

Student Volunteer Co-Chairs: Amy Zhang (*MIT CSAIL, USA*)
Bart Knijnenburg (*Clemson University, USA*)

Local Arrangements Chair: Merry Morse (*IBM Research Cambridge, USA*)

Birthday Chair: Casey Dugan (*IBM Research Cambridge, USA*)

Web Chair: Benedikt Loepp (*University of Duisburg-Essen, Germany*)

Senior Program Committee:

Gediminas Adomavicius (*University of Minnesota*)
Xavier Amatriain (*Quora*)
Alejandro Bellogín (*Universidad Autónoma de Madrid*)
Shlomo Berkovsky (*CSIRO*)
Peter Brusilovsky (*University of Pittsburgh*)
Robin Burke (*DePaul University*)
Iván Cantador (*Universidad Autónoma de Madrid*)
Li Chen (*Hong Kong Baptist University*)
Paolo Cremonesi (*Politecnico di Milano*)
Marco De Gemmis (*University of Bari*)
Martin Ester (*Simon Fraser University*)
Boi Faltings (*EPFL*)
Alexander Felfernig (*Graz University of Technology*)
Ido Guy (*Yahoo! Israel*)
Rong Hu (*Castleton Commodities International*)
Neil Hurley (*University College Dublin*)
Dietmar Jannach (*TU Dortmund*)
Alexandros Karatzoglou (*Telefonica Research*)
George Karypis (*University of Minnesota*)
Joseph Konstan (*University of Minnesota*)
Yehuda Koren (*Google*)
Pasquale Lops (*University of Bari*)
Bamshad Mobasher (*DePaul University*)
Wolfgang Nejdl (*L3S and University of Hannover*)
Pearl Pu (*EPFL*)
Francesco Ricci (*Free University of Bozen-Bolzano*)
Lior Rokach (*Ben-Gurion University*)
Rodrygo Santos (*Universidade Federal de Minas Gerais*)
Lars Schmidt-Thieme (*University of Hildesheim*)
Giovanni Semeraro (*University of Bari*)
Bracha Shapira (*Ben-Gurion University*)
Harald Steck (*Netflix*)
Domonkos Tikk (*Gravity R&D*)
Alexander Tuzhilin (*Stern School of Business, New York University*)
Yong Yu (*Shanghai Jiao Tong University*)
Markus Zanker (*Free University of Bozen-Bolzano*)

Program Committee: Panagiotis Adamopoulos (*New York University*)
Luca Maria Aiello (*Yahoo! Labs*)
Jussara Almeida (*Universidade Federal de Minas Gerais*)
Linas Baltrunas (*Netflix*)
Maria Bielikova (*Slovak University of Technology in Bratislava*)
Roi Blanco (*University of A Coruña*)
Derek Bridge (*University College Cork*)
Peter Briggs (*HeyStaks*)
Sylvain Castagnos (*LORIA*)
Shuo Chang (*University of Minnesota*)
Enhong Chen (*University of Science & Technology of China*)
Maurice Coyle (*HeyStaks*)
Elizabeth M. Daly (*IBM Research*)
Matthew Davis (*IBM Research*)
Toon De Pessemier (*Ghent University*)
Arjen de Vries (*Radboud University*)
Christian Desrosiers (*Ecole de Technologie Superieure*)
Tommaso Di Noia (*Politecnico di Bari*)
Ernesto Diaz-Aviles (*IBM Research*)
Hendrik Drachsler (*Open University of the Netherlands*)
Casey Dugan (*IBM T.J. Watson Research*)
Michael Ekstrand (*Boise State University*)
Florent Garcin (*EPFL*)
Franca Garzotto (*Politecnico di Milano*)
Yong Ge (*The University of North Carolina at Charlotte*)
Marcos Goncalves (*Universidade Federal de Minas Gerais*)
Derek Greene (*University College Dublin*)
Asela Gunawardana (*Microsoft Research*)
Guibing Guo (*Northeastern University*)
Jiawei Han (*University of Illinois at Urbana-Champaign*)
Max Harper (*University of Minnesota*)
Frank Hopfgartner (*University of Glasgow*)
Andreas Hotho (*University of Wuerzburg*)
Maya Hristakeva (*Mendeley*)
Kris Jack (*Mendeley*)
Alejandro Jaimes (*AiCure*)
Mohsen Jamali (*LinkedIn*)
Robert Jäschke (*L3S Research Center*)
Daniel Kluver (*University of Minnesota*)
Bart Knijnenburg (*Clemson University*)
Martha Larson (*Delft University of Technology*)
Neal Lathia (*University of Cambridge*)
Sangkeun Lee (*Oak Ridge National Laboratory*)
Sang-Goo Lee (*Seoul National University*)

Program Committee (continued):

Jure Leskovec (*Stanford University*)
Tao Li (*Florida International University*)
Huan Liu (*Arizona State University*)
Qi Liu (*University of Science and Technology of China*)
Bernd Ludwig (*Universität Regensburg*)
Yannis Manolopoulos (*Aristotle University of Thessaloniki*)
Leandro Balby Marinho (*Federal University of Campina Grande*)
Judith Masthoff (*University of Aberdeen*)
Wagner Meira Jr. (*Universidade Federal de Minas Gerais*)
Cataldo Musto (*University of Bari*)
Fedelucio Narducci (*University of Bari Aldo Moro*)
Yiu-Kai Ng (*Brigham Young University*)
Tien T. Nguyen (*University of Minnesota*)
John O'Donovan (*University of California Santa Barbara*)
Nuria Oliver (*Telefonica R&D*)
Balaji Padmanabhan (*University of South Florida*)
Javier Parapar (*University of A Coruña*)
Denis Parra (*Pontificia Universidad Catolica de Chile*)
Maria Soledad Pera (*Boise State University*)
Luiz Pizzato (*1-Page*)
Till Plumbaum (*Technische Universität Berlin*)
Josep M. Pujol (*Cliqz*)
Daniele Quercia (*Nokia Bell Labs*)
Steffen Rendle (*Google*)
Inbal Ronen (*IBM Haifa Research Lab*)
Alan Said (*University of Skövde*)
Olga C. Santos (*aDeNu Research Group (UNED)*)
Badrul Sarwar (*LinkedIn*)
Markus Schedl (*Johannes Kepler University (JKU) Linz*)
Fabrizio Silvestri (*Yahoo! Labs*)
Barry Smyth (*University College Dublin*)
Neel Sundaresan (*eBay*)
Panagiotis Symeonidis (*Aristotle University of Thessaloniki*)
Nava Tintarev (*University of Aberdeen*)
Christoph Trattner (*Graz University of Technology*)
Saúl Vargas (*Mendeley*)
Vasileios Vasileiadis (*IBM Research – Zurich*)
Jun Wang (*University College London*)
Jian Wang (*LinkedIn*)
Martijn Willemsen (*Eindhoven University of Technology*)
David Wilson (*University of North Carolina at Charlotte*)
Hui Xiong (*Rutgers University*)
Quan Yuan (*Alibaba Group*)
Tingshao Zhu (*Chinese Academy of Sciences*)
Nivio Ziviani (*Universidade Federal de Minas Gerais*)

External reviewers: Yeonchan Ahn (*Seoul National University*)
Rebekka Aigner (*Graz University of Technology*)
Ariel Bar (*Ben-Gurion University*)
Ramesh Baral (*Florida International University*)
Alex Barros (*Kunumi*)
Konstantin Bauman (*Stern School of Business, New York University*)
Jesse Bockstedt (*University of Arizona*)
Xuezhi Cao (*Shanghai Jiao Tong University*)
Kewei Cheng (*Arizona State University*)
Evangelia Christakopoulou (*University of Minnesota*)
Uzi Cohen (*IBM Haifa Research Lab*)
Andre Costa-Silva (*Kunumi*)
Vittoria Cozza (*IIT CNR*)
Alexander Dallmann (*University of Wuerzburg*)
Harsh Dani (*Arizona State University*)
Yashar Deldjoo (*Politecnico di Milano*)
Nevena Dragovic (*Boise State University*)
Sisi Duan (*Oak Ridge National Laboratory*)
Mehdi Elahi (*Politecnico di Milano*)
Asmaa Elbadrawy (*University of Minnesota*)
Bruce Ferwerda (*Johannes Kepler University (JKU) Linz*)
Edgard Freitas (*Universidade Federal de Minas Gerais*)
Esther Goldbraich (*IBM Haifa Research Lab*)
Josif Grabocka (*University of Hildesheim*)
Mark Graus (*Eindhoven University of Technology*)
Erwin Gunadi (*Technische Universität Berlin*)
Tural Gurbanov (*Free University of Bozen-Bolzano*)
Shuguang Han (*University of Pittsburgh*)
Balázs Hidasi (*Gravity R&D*)
Tahora Hossein Nazer (*Arizona State University*)
Bo Hu (*LinkedIn*)
Yun Huang (*University of Pittsburgh*)
Mohsan Jameel (*University of Hildesheim*)
Meng Jiang (*University of Illinois at Urbana-Champaign*)
How Jing (*LinkedIn*)
Isaac Jones (*Arizona State University*)
Minsuk Kahng (*Georgia Tech*)
Ioannis Karydis (*Ionian University*)
Ondrej Kaššák (*Slovak University of Technology in Bratislava*)
Benjamin Kille (*Technische Universität Berlin*)
Michal Kompan (*Slovak University of Technology in Bratislava*)
Hanbit Lee (*Seoul National University*)

External reviewers (continued):

Huayu Li (*University of North Carolina at Charlotte*)
Shuai Li (*DiSTA, University of Insubria*)
Seung-Hwan Lim (*Oak Ridge National Laboratory*)
De Liu (*University of Minnesota*)
Babak Loni (*Delft University of Technology*)
Rui Luo (*University College London*)
Kang Min Yoo (*Seoul National University*)
Nadia Najjar (*University of North Carolina at Charlotte*)
Ngoc Nguyen (*Free University of Bozen-Bolzano*)
Aastha Nigam (*University of Notre Dame*)
Roberto Pagano (*Politecnico di Milano*)
Sungchan Park (*Seoul National University*)
István Pilászy (*Budapest University of Technology and Economics*)
Marco Polignano (*University of Bari*)
Lin Qiu (*Shanghai Jiao Tong University*)
Massimo Quadrana (*Politecnico di Milano*)
Dimitrios Rafailidis (*Aristotle University of Thessaloniki*)
Azzurra Ragone (*Universitá degli Studi di Milano-Bicocca*)
Kan Ren (*Shanghai Jiao Tong University*)
Amir Ronen (*SparkBeyond*)
Shaghayegh Sahebi (*University of Pittsburgh*)
Justin Sampson (*Arizona State University*)
James Schaffer (*University of California Santa Barbara*)
Carlotta Schatten (*University of Hildesheim*)
Daniel Schlör (*University of Wuerzburg*)
David Schultz (*Technische Universität Berlin*)
Carlos Seminario (*University of North Carolina at Charlotte*)
Weijia Shao (*Technische Universität Berlin*)
Mohit Sharma (*University of Minnesota*)
Youhyun Shin (*Seoul National University*)
Lama Shiyab (*Stern School of Business, New York University*)
Kai Shu (*Arizona State University*)
Zhu Sun (*Nanyang Technological University*)
Asmelash Teka Hadgu (*L3S*)
Paolo Tomeo (*Politecnico di Bari*)
Gilad Tsur (*Tel-Aviv University*)
Moshe Unger (*Ben-Gurion University*)
Fatemeh Vahedian (*DePaul University*)
Andreu Vall (*Johannes Kepler University (JKU) Linz*)
Adriano Veloso (*Universidade Federal de Minas Gerais*)
Juliano Viana (*Kunumi*)
Qing Wang (*Florida International University*)

External reviewers (continued):

Daniel Weidele (*University of Konstanz*)
Martin Wistuba (*University of Hildesheim*)
Yao Wu (*Simon Fraser University*)
Yixin Wu (*University College London*)
Bin Xia (*Florida International University*)
Richeng Xuan (*Seoul National University*)
Li'ang Yin (*Shanghai Jiao Tong University*)
Quan Yuan (*Nanyang Technological University*)
Jongheum Yun (*Seoul National University*)
Onur Yuruten (*EPFL*)
Chunqiu Zeng (*Florida International University*)
Jingjing Zhang (*Indiana University*)
Qian Zhao (*University of Minnesota*)
Yong Zheng (*DePaul University*)
Daniel Zoller (*University of Wuerzburg*)

RecSys 2016 Sponsors & Supporters

Sponsor:

SIGCHI

In cooperation:

acm SIGAI

SIGIR
Special Interest Group
on Information Retrieval

sig web

ACM SIGMOD

acm SIGecom

Diamond Supporters:

Google

Spotify®

Alibaba Group®
阿里巴巴集团

Platinum Supporters:

NETFLIX

Quora

PANDORA®

OpenTable®

Gold Supporters:

TARGET

criteo labs

Microsoft

amazon

zalando

Medium

Silver Supporters:

demandware A Salesforce Company

SILVER EGG TECHNOLOGY

Yandex

Special Supporters:

IBM Research

XING

MIT EECS ELECTRICAL ENGINEERING AND COMPUTER SCIENCE

NSF

Automated Machine Learning in the Wild

Claudia Perlich
Dstillery
New York, NY, USA
claudia@dstillery.com

ABSTRACT
Machine Learning research is progressing at an ever-increasing pace. Fueled by technology advances commonly referred to as "Big Data", all data related fields are teaming with scientific and applied activity: our communities explore new application areas, develop new learning algorithms, and continuously scale and improve optimization and estimation methods. But from an industry perspective, many of the most impeding challenges are entirely elsewhere. This talk takes a fresh look at the practical state of affairs in the context of running a large-scale automated machine learning system that supports 50 Billion decision daily on behalf of hundreds of digital advertisers. Some of the key lessons are 1) robustness beats peak performance almost always, 2) support for the constant dynamic fluctuations in the data stream is essential, 3) models exploiting unknowingly any weakness of your metrics, and finally 4) the fact that despite big data, the data you really want never exists.

BIO
Claudia Perlich leads the machine learning efforts that power Dstillery's digital intelligence for marketers and media companies. With more than 50 published scientific articles, she is a widely acclaimed expert on big data and machine learning applications, and an active speaker at data science and marketing conferences around the world.

Claudia is the past winner of the Advertising Research Foundation's (ARF) Grand Innovation Award and has been selected for Crain's New York's 40 Under 40 list, Wired Magazine's Smart List, and Fast Company's 100 Most Creative People.

Claudia holds multiple patents in machine learning. She has won many data mining competitions and awards at Knowledge Discovery and Data Mining (KDD) conferences, and served as the organization's General Chair in 2014.

Prior to joining Dstillery in 2010, Claudia worked at IBM's Watson Research Center, focusing on data analytics and machine learning. She holds a PhD in Information Systems from New York University (where she continues to teach at the Stern School of Business), and an MA in Computer Science from the University of Colorado.

RecSys'16, September 15–19, 2016, Boston, MA, USA.

ACM ISBN 978-1-4503-4035-9/16/09.

DOI: http://dx.doi.org/10.1145/2959100.2959191

Personalization for Google Now — User Understanding and Application to Information Recommendation and Exploration

Shashi Thakur
Google Inc.
Mountain View, CA, USA
thakur@google.com

ABSTRACT

At the heart of any personalization application, such as Google Now, is a deep model for users. The understanding of users ranges from raw history to lower dimensional reductions like interest, locations, preferences, etc. We will discuss different representations of such user understanding. Going from understanding to application, we will talk about two broad applications - recommendations of information and guided exploration - both in the context of Google Now. We will focus on such applications from an information retrieval perspective. Information recommendation then takes the form of biasing information retrieval, in response to a query or, in the limit, in a query-less application. Somewhere in between lies broad declaration of user intent, e.g., interest in food, and we will discuss how personalization and guided exploration play together to provide a valuable tool to the user. We will discuss valuable lessons learned along the way.At the heart of any personalization application, such as Google Now, is a deep model for users. The understanding of users ranges from raw history to lower dimensional reductions like interest, locations, preferences, etc. We will discuss different representations of such user understanding. Going from understanding to application, we will talk about two broad applications - recommendations of information and guided exploration - both in the context of Google Now. We will focus on such applications from an information retrieval perspective. Information recommendation then takes the form of biasing information retrieval, in response to a query or, in the limit, in a query-less application. Somewhere in between lies broad declaration of user intent, e.g., interest in food, and we will discuss how personalization and guided exploration play together to provide a valuable tool to the user. We will discuss valuable lessons learned along the way.

BIO

Shashidhar (Shashi) Thakur is a Distinguished Engineer in the search team at Google. He led the team that brought the Google Knowledge Graph to search (more information). He has previously worked on different aspects of search ranging from spam detection to core ranking. Most recently, Shashi leads the Google Now team, whose mission is to build a rich personalized understanding model of users and proactively bring high utility content to the user. Prior to Google, Shashi was a Distinguished Engineer at Synopsys Inc., working on algorithms behind tools that make digital chip design processes more efficient. He holds a PhD in Computer Science from University of Texas, Austin and a BTech in Computer Science from Indian Institute of Technology, Bombay.

RecSys'16, September 15–19, 2016, Boston, MA, USA.

ACM ISBN 978-1-4503-4035-9/16/09.

DOI: http://dx.doi.org/10.1145/2959100.2959192

Recommendations with a Purpose

Dietmar Jannach
TU Dortmund, Germany
dietmar.jannach@tu-dortmund.de

Gediminas Adomavicius
University of Minnesota, USA
gedas@umn.edu

ABSTRACT

The purpose of recommenders is often summarized as "help the users find relevant items", and the predominant operationalization of this goal has been to focus on the ability to numerically estimate the users' preferences for unseen items or to provide users with item lists ranked in accordance to the estimated preferences. This dominant, albeit narrow, view of the recommendation problem has been tremendously helpful in advancing research in different ways, e.g., through the establishment of standardized evaluation procedures and metrics. In reality, recommender systems can serve a variety of purposes from the point of view of both consumers and providers. Most of the purposes, however, are significantly underexplored, even though many of them are arguably more aligned with the real-world expectations for recommenders than our current predominant paradigm. Therefore, it is important to revisit our conceptualizations of the potential goals of recommenders and their operationalization as research problems. In this paper, we discuss a framework of recommendation goals and purposes and highlight possible future directions and challenges related to the operationalization of such alternative problem formulations.

Keywords

Foundations of Recommender Systems; Recommendation Goals and Purposes

1. INTRODUCTION

Automated recommendations have become a pervasive part of the daily user experience on the web. Today, many major e-commerce websites, media streaming platforms, and social networks use a part of the user interface to display recommendations to their users [3]. The overarching goal for such recommendation services is to create some sort of *utility* (or benefit), e.g., provide users with relevant information, improve customer retention, increase revenue. A number of studies show that recommenders can measurably influence the behavior of online consumers [2, 5].

RecSys '16, September 15 - 19, 2016, Boston , MA, USA

ISBN 978-1-4503-4035-9/16/09...$15.00

DOI: http://dx.doi.org/10.1145/2959100.2959186

Academic research on recommender systems has matured substantially over the past two decades. Because the interpretation of "utility" highly depends on the specific application context, the research community has developed general domain-independent frameworks to operationalize this concept. In particular, the canonical tasks of a recommendation system are often described as *find good items* or *predict an item's relevance to a user* [1, 4]. Operationally, assessing the system's performance on such tasks often translates to predicting held-out user preference ratings, i.e., to a rating matrix completion problem, or to the creation of item lists that are ranked according to the estimated user preferences.

This abstract, canonical view of the recommendation problem has been tremendously helpful to the recommender systems community in establishing a common terminology for the field, providing a clear set of problems to focus on, facilitating the creation of a number of general-purpose recommendation algorithms (i.e., abstracting away from domain information), and supporting a certain level of reproducibility and continuous improvement through standardized metrics and experimentation procedures.

Despite the advantages of having an established, canonical problem formulation, it is important to note that there exist numerous other potential interpretations of the purpose of a recommender system than "help users find relevant items", from the point of view of both consumers and providers. Consider, for example, that a provider aims to use a recommender to guide online customers to other parts of the product catalog, e.g., to increase sales of long-tail or high-margin items. The predicted relevance of these items might still be important for the recommended items to be selected by the user, but has to be balanced with the estimated (e.g., economic) utility for the provider.

Such types of recommendation purposes are largely underexplored in the literature, and we argue that it is important to revisit the research community's conceptualizations of recommender systems goals. In this paper, we discuss a purpose-driven approach to recommender systems, provide illustrations of the possible recommendation purposes from the consumer and provider viewpoints, and outline challenges with respect to the operationalization of such alternative problem formulations in academic research.

2. FROM GOALS TO METRICS

2.1 Traditional Task-Oriented Perspective

In Herlocker et al.'s seminal paper on the evaluation of recommender algorithms [4], the possible system purposes (in the context of which an evaluation is made) are indirectly described with the help of abstract *tasks* of a recommender. The tasks include "Annotation in Context", "Find Good Items", "'Find All Good Items", "Recommend Sequence", and "Just Browsing". *Annotation in Context* corresponds to the rating prediction problem, and *Find Good Items* to item ranking. *Find All Good Items* is a special case where the goal is not to miss any relevant item, and *Recommend Sequence* is a task that is, for example, common for next-track music recommendation. *Just Browsing* finally refers to situations where there is no imminent "buying decision" on the user's side and other factors than accuracy, e.g., user interface aspects or content-richness, are important.

To evaluate the performance for a number of aforementioned tasks, mainly a variety of standard accuracy measures are used. In recent years a number of additional ways to quantify recommendation quality aspects beyond accuracy have also been more widely used, including different forms of assessing the diversity, novelty, or serendipity of the recommended items. The *Recommend Sequence* task typically requires specific algorithms and datasets, e.g., for next-basket recommendation, but can also be evaluated with accuracy measures like recall, while measuring the success of a system in support of the *Just Browsing* task is underexplored [4].

2.2 Toward Purposeful Evaluation

A question that is rarely asked explicitly in recommender systems research, is: *What is a good recommender system?* (Or: *What is a good recommendation?*) According to today's established task-oriented framework for evaluating algorithms, one could argue that the answer to this question is straightforward: a good system is one that provides a low RMSE or whatever other *computational metric* (like MAE, F-measure, NDCG, MAP, hit rate) researchers decide to apply for their problem. The choice of the metric(s) ideally should be aligned with an operational *system task* that the proposed algorithm is being designed for.

For example, when addressing the rating prediction problem, metrics like RMSE or MAE are used, and when addressing the item ranking problem, NDCG or MAP are employed. A general observation is that the vast majority of recommender systems research takes an *operational perspective* on recommendation by focusing on one of the standard, well-defined operational system tasks.

As mentioned in Section 1, having standard operational tasks (such as rating prediction using user-item matrix completion approaches) provides a lot of benefits to the research community. At the same time, it is important to note that operational system tasks often represent a significant over-simplification of real-world situations. For example, the operational task "find good items" on a movie streaming website may correspond to very different *recommendation purposes.*[1] Furthermore, it is likely that these purposes may differ dramatically depending on whether the recommender system's *overarching goal* is considered from the consumer's or the provider's point of view. In particular, the "find good items" task on a movie streaming website can be representative of having the "entertainment" (or "satisfying emotional experience") purpose from the consumer's viewpoint, while the same "find good items" task might represent the "increase user engagement" purpose from the provider's viewpoint.

[1]See Table 1 for a number of representative recommendation purpose examples from the consumer's and provider's viewpoints.

Table 1: Examples of Recommendation Purposes

Consumer's Viewpoint (i.e., value for the consumer)
Help users find objects that match their long-term preferences: Corresponds to the usual assumption that the main value of a recommender is to help users find relevant items in larger item sets. Recommendations could be limited to a subset of the items, e.g., new or trending ones.
Actively notify consumers of relevant content: Proactively point users to new items through push notifications or newsletters, minimizing the user effort to check the site.
Show alternatives: Recommend substitute products in the context of a reference item. A standard mechanism on e-commerce platforms.
Show accessories: Recommend complementary products in the context of a reference item, e.g., with the goal of cross-selling. Also common in e-commerce settings.
Help users explore or understand the item space: Help the user understand the space of options, possibly leading to higher choice confidence.
Remind users of already known items: Provide users with reminders of repeated purchases of consumables. Or, present a list of recently viewed items that the user did not purchase so far; reminders then also serve as navigation shortcuts to a reduced choice set.
Improve decision making, e.g., in terms reduced decision time or higher choice satisfaction: E.g., provide the user with a limited choice set for an estimated purchase intent, provide explanations and interactive control.
Establish group consensus: Provide recommendations that balance the interests of different group members.
Help user explore: Provide a convenient way for users to browse the catalog without immediate shopping intent.
Entertainment: Provide a satisfying emotional experience when visiting the site.
Provider's Viewpoint (i.e., value for the provider)
Change user behavior in desired directions: Guide customers to other product categories, drive the demand from top-selling items to the long tail, leverage the persuasive potential of recommenders for up-selling purposes.
Create additional demand: Point users to other relevant items (e.g., accessories) to achieve cross-selling and advertisement effects.
Increase (short term) business success: Promote items with high margins or items that are in stock.
Enable item "discoverability": Increase the visibility of new items or niche products that would otherwise not be easily found through search or catalog browsing.
Increase activity on the site: Make users stay longer on the site, e.g., thereby increasing ad revenue.
Increase user engagement: Increase customer loyalty and trust via a personalized service. Increase switching costs to other services as preferences are already known.
Provide a valuable add-on service: Use the recommendation service as a differentiating factor from other competitors.
Learn more about the customers: Utilize the collected preference information to better understand preferences and trends of the consumers. Provide mechanisms for users to explicitly state their preferences.
Generate impression of dynamic, constantly updated site: Dynamic recommendations contribute to the liveliness of the site. Updating the site with editorial content can be costly and less attractive for users.

Table 2: Proposed Framework: From Goals to Metrics

		Consumer's Viewpoint	Provider's Viewpoint
Strategic Perspective	Overarching Goal	"Personal Utility": Happiness, Satisfaction, Knowledge, ...	"Organizational Utility": Profit, Revenue, Growth, ...
	Recommendation Purpose	• Help users find objects that match the user's long-term preferences • Show alternatives • Help users explore or understand the item space • ...	• Change user behavior in desired directions • Create additional demand • Increase activity on the site • ...
Operational Perspective	System Task	• Annotate in context (i.e., estimate preference of a given item) • Find good items • Create diverse set of alternatives • Find suitable accessories • Retrieve novel but relevant items • ...	
	Computational Metric	Predictive accuracy (e.g., RMSE, MAE), classification accuracy (e.g., precision, recall, AUC), ranking and top-n accuracy (e.g., rank correlation, MRR, NDCG, etc.), item "discoverability" (diversity, novelty, or serendipity measures), recommendation biases (e.g., concentration or popularity biases) and blockbuster effects, survey-based user satisfaction scores, business- and domain-specific measures (e.g., conversion rates or click-through-rates), ...	

This has a couple of important implications. First, the consumer's and provider's purposes are not always aligned. In this example, more movie watching (good for provider) may not necessarily mean more satisfaction (good for consumer). Therefore, the two viewpoints may often need to be modeled and evaluated separately. And second, the traditional computational metrics that are associated with standard operational tasks – e.g., the NDCG ranking metric for the "find good items" task – may be reflective of neither the consumer's nor the provider's viewpoint. For example, better preference-based ranking, as measured by NDCG, does not automatically guarantee more consumption/engagement nor more satisfaction. Thus, it is important for the recommender systems community to (a) move beyond the standard operational perspectives and explicitly take real-world *strategic perspectives* (purposes and goals) into account, and also to (b) design a more comprehensive set of operational system tasks and corresponding computational metrics for different recommendation purposes and viewpoints.

2.3 Proposed Framework

To summarize, we propose the following framework for understanding and evaluating recommender systems utility as shown in Table 2:

- *Overarching goals*: Goals describe the general underlying personal or organizational motivation of using or providing a recommender system.
- *Recommendation purposes*: Purposes capture the specific utility of the service for a consumer or provider, i.e., the expected measurable effects or value of deploying the system. Examples are given in Table 1.
- *System tasks*: These represent operational, algorithmic tasks to be accomplished by the recommendation system.
- *Computational metrics*: Metrics provide numeric quantifications of the extent to which the recommender is able to accomplish a given system task.

As an illustrative example, consider an online music service provider, whose overarching goal is to increase revenue via improving customer long-term loyalty. One of the possible purposes of the recommendation system could, therefore, be to maximize the number of monthly subscription renewals by keeping the users active and involved in the service. This, for example, could be achieved through recommendations that help the user discover new artists. An operationalized system task could then be to find artists that the user most probably does not know yet, e.g., because they are newcomers but which match his or her musical tastes. Corresponding computational metrics could therefore consider aspects of accuracy (preference match), serendipity (surprise and entertainment), item novelty, as well as the monthly subscription numbers (e.g., from an A/B test).

While the discovery of new artists might also be in the interest of consumers, the consumer's and provider's goals are not necessarily aligned. Assume that an e-commerce platform aims to increase the profit on the site as an overall goal. The purpose of the recommender could then be to lure the consumers to high-margin catalog items, and the algorithmic task is to find such high-margin items that are still a reasonable match for the consumer's estimated preferences. The consumers, possibly under the impression that the recommended items are the most relevant (or the most popular) and, therefore, "safe" choices, might as a result continuously make sub-optimal buying decisions, which can lead to consumer dissatisfaction in the long run. Therefore, from the perspective of the computational metrics, the best solution may require a delicate balance of optimizing potential profits while minimizing the resulting accuracy losses.

3. DISCUSSION / FUTURE DIRECTIONS

Examining the 63 long papers from the last two years of the ACM RecSys Conference, we observe that about 85% of all papers use at least one of several possible accuracy measures for rating prediction and item ranking. About 20% of papers aim at improving algorithms in terms of diversity, novelty, and other alternative quality measures. About another 20% look at domain- or business-oriented measures like click-through rates. This shows that the field has a largely agreed-upon, shared understanding of recommendation problems. However, this also illustrates that we are perhaps too strongly focused on a certain set of computational metrics and a limited set of established system tasks.

We hope that the proposed framework will help to facilitate the discussion about revisiting the more foundational aspects related to the purposes and goals of recommender systems and to reconsider and extend the way we operationalize the recommendation problem in academic settings. The framework also points to different possible directions for future work, e.g., in the following areas.

3.1 Challenges related to Tasks and Metrics

From the operational perspective of system tasks and computational metrics, a number of general challenges arise when we consider that recommendations can serve multiple purposes. More research is needed for understanding potential trade-off situations and how to systematically evaluate them with standardized approaches. E.g., consider the recent stream of research on diversified and serendipitous recommendations – in most domains higher diversity is achieved only with compromises on ranking accuracy. No clear understanding, however, exists on *how much* diversity is actually desirable (for a domain) or how large of a compromise on accuracy should be tolerable. As a result, this calls for more standardized multi-metric optimization and evaluation schemes in the context of a specific task.

Whenever new recommendation purposes are addressed and corresponding system tasks are designed, the question arises whether the existing metrics are appropriate to assess the system's ability to accomplish the task. Looking again at the diversity problem, using the average pairwise diversity of items using metadata features is one common way to assess the diversity level of a recommendation set. However, even for such a common metric, it is often not clear if it reflects something that is truly valuable to the consumers for a given recommendation purpose. Whenever new metrics are developed for a new task, it is important to empirically validate, e.g., through user studies or live tests, to which extent the quantitative metric is capable of truly capturing what it should it measure (i.e., the metric-task-purpose fit).

A general dilemma in this context is that certain recommendation purposes and corresponding system tasks might be very specific to a given application domain. The challenge is to identify or develop the next wave of metrics that can generalize across different recommendation problems/domains – such metrics would provide a standard set of problems for a research community to focus on. Notable examples of highly desirable metrics include metrics that could help predict online recommendation success from offline experimentation, since the way online success is measured can often be very idiosyncratic for different domains, purposes, and tasks [2, 3].

3.2 Data and Protocol Issues

Many of the sketched directions for future research require the existence of new evaluation protocols and benchmark data sets, which carry much more information than the snapshots of explicit rating databases that serve as a basis for much of today's research. As an example, consider the RecSys 2015 challenge where the tasks were to predict from click-stream data whether a visitor of an e-commerce site will make a purchase in a given session and which item will be eventually purchased. As this problem setting can be relevant for a number of e-commerce recommendation purposes, it has the potential to be further developed to a standardized *system task* in our framework. But, general principles still have to be developed with respect to appropriate evaluation measures and protocols – in the challenge, a proprietary metric was applied – or with respect to the types of data that are considered to be generally available for such a task.

3.3 Balancing Overarching Goals: Leveraging RECO-nomics

Consumer and provider goals can be competing or even incompatible, as mentioned earlier, and not much research exists in the recommender systems literature that addresses this problem. In contrast, balancing competing issues like supply and demand, buyer's surplus and seller's revenue, goals of goods/service providers and consumers, etc. are topics that have been extensively researched in the economics, marketing, and consumer research literature. As one example, in economics *allocative efficiency* represents a metric of social welfare for a given economic mechanism (say, a specific type of auction), i.e., a metric of how well the mechanism supports the interests of buyers and sellers. The recommender systems community should be looking to borrow some ideas from economics and related fields to develop recommendation approaches for key purposes and tasks that can represent *both* consumers and providers in a systematic and principled manner. Even though various economic models and simulations are based on simplifying assumptions, economic modeling in recommender systems (i.e., *RECO-nomics*) represents a highly promising research direction.

4. CONCLUSIONS

The recommender systems research field has reached a certain level of maturity, in particular in terms of its canonical, established operationalizations of the recommendation problem. We advocate that it is, therefore, the right time to step back and revisit some of the more foundational aspects of recommender systems and to reconsider the variety of purposes for which such systems are already used today in a more systematic manner. The high-level research framework proposed in this paper is intended to serve as a means to approach these fundamental aspects in a structured way by considering not only the operational but also the strategic perspective for recommender systems design and evaluation.

5. REFERENCES

[1] G. Adomavicius and A. Tuzhilin. Toward the next generation of recommender systems: A survey of the state-of-the-art and possible extensions. *IEEE TKDE*, 17(6):734–749, 2005.

[2] F. Garcin, B. Faltings, O. Donatsch, A. Alazzawi, C. Bruttin, and A. Huber. Offline and online evaluation of news recommender systems at swissinfo.ch. In *RecSys '14*, pages 169–176, 2014.

[3] C. A. Gomez-Uribe and N. Hunt. The Netflix Recommender System: Algorithms, Business Value, and Innovation. *ACM TMIS*, 6(4):13:1–13:19, 2015.

[4] J. Herlocker, J. Konstan, L. Terveen, and J. Riedl. Evaluating Collaborative Filtering Recommender Systems. *ACM TOIS*, 22(1):5–53, 2004.

[5] D. Jannach and K. Hegelich. A case study on the effectiveness of recommendations in the mobile internet. In *RecSys '09*, pages 205–208, 2009.

Recommender Systems for Self-Actualization

Bart P. Knijnenburg, Saadhika Sivakumar, Daricia Wilkinson
Clemson University School of Computing
215 McAdams Hall
Clemson, SC 29634
bartk@clemson.edu, ssivaku@g.clemson.edu, dariciw@g.clemson.edu

ABSTRACT

Every day, we are confronted with an abundance of decisions that require us to choose from a seemingly endless number of choice options. Recommender systems are supposed to help us deal with this formidable task, but some scholars claim that these systems instead put us inside a "Filter Bubble" that severely limits our perspectives. This paper presents a new direction for recommender systems research with the main goal of supporting users in developing, exploring, and understanding their unique personal preferences.

CCS Concepts

- **Information systems→Recommender systems**
- **Human-centered computing→Interaction paradigms.**

Keywords

Recommender Systems; Filter Bubble; Choice Overload; Self-Actualization.

1. INTRODUCTION

Recommender systems were invented in the 1990s to help users find useful and attractive items among the large assortments that came available with the growth of the Internet [31]. Such systems are now embedded in a wide range of online applications that help us find desirable products, and increasingly permeate our online interactions. As Eric Schmidt, CEO of Google, has pointed out, recommendation techniques are now employed in virtually every online service, including search engines and social networks. As people experience most of the Web through these services, it becomes very hard for them to watch or consume something that has not in some sense been tailored to their needs [15].

While the move to a personalized Web has been welcomed by most, some scholars have voiced an interesting critique against recommender systems: they argue that recommender systems put users inside a *filter bubble* that severely limits their perspectives and that may make them complacent consumers of easy-to-consume items [28].

What causes this pushback against recommender systems? Is the filter bubble simply a consequence of our psychology, or is there something wrong with the way recommenders operate? And if so, what are the consequences of this shortcoming? And how can we solve it? As part of the discussion about the past, present, and future of recommender systems, this paper attempts to start a dialogue surrounding these questions. Particularly, it acknowledges some of the shortcomings—in recommender systems as well as their users—that have led to the filter bubble, and suggests a new direction for recommender systems research to address these shortcomings. This leads us to propose the development of *Recommender Systems of Self-Actualization*: personalized systems that have the explicit goal to not just present users with the best possible items, but to *support* users in developing, exploring, and understanding their own unique tastes and preferences.

Such deep understanding of one's own tastes is a particularly important goal in decisions that have a resounding impact on one's life—e.g. choosing an education, a job, a health insurance plan, or a retirement fund. For these types of decisions, rather than have people choose the easiest option, we wish to have them develop a strong sense of determination of having selected the right path. A deep understanding of one's own tastes is also important for cultural diversity—we want people to make lifestyle choices (e.g., music, movies and fashion) based on carefully developed personal tastes, rather than blindly followed recommendations.

2. BEYOND THE ALGORITHM

"The algorithm accounts for only 5% of the commercial success of our recommender systems [...] The interactive components of a recommender account for about 50%" — Francesco Martin [22].

Traditionally, the field of recommender systems focused on developing more accurate algorithms [20, 31]. This goal appears reasonable: the more accurate the algorithm, the better the system can predict the best recommendations for the user, which in turn should lead to a better user experience. Researchers have come to realize, though, that recommenders should go well beyond making accurate predictions. McNee et al. [25], for example, argued that "being accurate is not enough", and that recommender systems should be studied "from a user-centric perspective to make them not only accurate and helpful, but also a pleasure to use". They also [26] suggested that researchers should investigate the interactive components of the recommender system, i.e., the mechanism through which users indicate their preferences ("preference elicitation"), and the interface that displays the recommendations.

Subsequent work has indeed demonstrated that the algorithms that test best offline are not always the most successful in real life [8, 24], especially when focusing on users' subjective evaluation of the system [35]. Inspired by these findings and the need to thoroughly evaluate recommender systems from a user-centric standpoint, researchers have developed conceptual frameworks for the user-centric evaluation of recommender systems (cf. [19, 29]), and are increasingly evaluating the effects of *all* aspects of a recommender system (not just the algorithm, but also the preference elicitation method and the presentation of the recommendation list) on *all* aspects of the user's interaction experience (not just the accuracy of the algorithm, but also subjective aspects such as system satisfaction and choice satisfaction) [18].

RecSys '16, September 15-19, 2016, Boston, MA, USA
 ISBN 978-1-4503-4035-9/16/09...$15.00
DOI: http://dx.doi.org/10.1145/2959100.2959189

This more inclusive perspective has uncovered several interesting problems that escape the attention of traditional recommender systems research. One of these problems is the inadequacy of existing preference elicitation methods [17]. Current recommenders rely on either implicit or explicit feedback for preference elicitation. Implicit feedback is easy to gather, but can result in "overspecialization", because the system only recommends items that it thinks the user likes: Even if the users' actual preferences are wider than the provided set of recommendations, the system will end up targeting a very specific preference. Diversifying the recommendation can prevent this [30, 36] but the main downside of diversifications is that it depends on the system's interpretation of diversity rather than the users'. Explicit feedback fares slightly better, since users can rate items negatively, thereby preventing overspecialization. However, research shows that users' ratings are often inaccurate [2, 14], arguably because consumers' preferences are often constructed on the spot [3]. If users are often unable to accurately express their preferences, then how much can be gained by accurately predicting said preferences? This conundrum demonstrates that the traditional recommender goal of accurately predicting these preferences may very well be a chimera.

Another problem is *choice overload* [4, 13]: Given that consumers construct their preference on the spot, it is no surprise that they encounter difficulties in selecting items from the Top-N recommendations. Overcoming choice overload is one of the challenges of research on the presentation of recommendations, and a good solution to this problem has yet to be devised.

3. THE FILTER BUBBLE

"[Computers] are useless. They can only give you answers." — Pablo Picasso [10].

As the pervasiveness of recommender systems increases, arguments have emerged that attack the very nature of recommender systems. Spearheaded by Eli Pariser, these voices claim that by filtering all but the top predicted items, recommender systems provide a very myopic view of the world. Pariser argues that users get stuck in a *filter bubble*: recommenders isolate us from a diversity of viewpoints, content, and experiences, and thus make us less likely to discover and learn new things [28]

A careful examination of the Filter Bubble phenomenon in recommender systems has validated the occurrence of this effect, albeit to a lesser extent than suggested by Pariser's claims [27]. Regardless of the actuality of the effect, the *idea* of the Filter Bubble has gained a lot of traction in popular opinion and it is interesting to analyze why this may be the case.

Psychologically, the Filter Bubble plays into our tendency for *loss aversion* and our *fear of missing out*. For recommender system users, it means that in certain situations the sum of the (presumed) missed opportunities presented by all the items that are ignored by the recommender, may loom larger than the benefits of receiving a short-list of items tailored to a specific subset of their preferences. In other words, the joy of getting recommendations may be spoiled by our worry of missing out on other enjoyable items that were not recommended. This looming loss may decrease their satisfactions with the system—and even their satisfaction with their choices—because decision-making research shows that the mere thought of missed opportunities may reduce one's decision confidence [7], and cause one to regret one's decision [13].

The existence of the Filter Bubble may have a long-term consequence that is arguably worse than the fear of missing things: The possibility that users will eventually *embrace* it. This is not an unlikely scenario, because recommender systems have been shown to have *persuasive* qualities: users are prone to agree with a recommender's predicted ratings [8] and to follow a recommender's advice [12]. This creates what Lanier calls a "positive feedback loop" [28]: users will unknowingly make themselves better "fit in" with a system, i.e., make themselves more easily targetable by the algorithm. Rather than going through the trouble of developing our own unique taste, we take the default setting—something we are prone to do [33]—and simply consume whatever the recommender serves us.

The positive feedback loop leads to the very worrying concern that recommender algorithms may gradually replace human creativity and understanding [21]: if we embrace the Filter Bubble, we run the risk of getting locked in by the algorithm, which subsequently becomes a self-fulfilling prophecy. When this happens, recommenders do not just inhibit discovery and learning, they actively work against it. Pariser is afraid that personalization will create "self-fulfilling identities": Your identity shapes your recommendations, and your recommendations then shape what you believe, and what you care about.

If recommender algorithms indeed turn into self-fulfilling prophecies, then what will they recommend? Pariser argues that the items that tend to make it past the filter bubble are usually the kinds of things that are "easy" to like or consume [28]. Psychologically, this phenomenon is based on a human tendency called *temporal discounting* [9]: We tend to discount future gains, and are thus likely to choose guilty pleasures that provide instant gratification (a funny Internet meme or a spectacular action movie) over substantive educational experiences of long-term value (a complex essay or an acclaimed period piece). This leads to what Boyd calls "the psychological equivalent of obesity", where all recommended content is the cerebral equivalent of junk food [5].

4. MOVING FORWARD

"In order to find his own self, [a person] needs to live in a milieu where the possibility of many different value systems is explicitly recognized and honored" — Christopher Alexander et al. [1].

The Filter Bubble persists, despite the fact that recommender systems researchers have taken several steps in a more user-centric direction [20, 30]. One reason for this is that virtually all recommender systems are built with the goal of recommending good items to the user. If we are to solve the Filter Bubble problem, we will have to build recommender systems with a different goal in mind: a "Recommender System for Self-Actualization" (RSSA), which supports users in developing, exploring, and understanding their unique personal tastes. Below we outline how the operating principles of RSSAs differ from traditional recommenders:

RSSAs support rather than replace decision-making. Traditional recommenders turn preferences into choice options, but research shows that user preferences are fleeting, constructed on the fly and vulnerable to distorting influences, rather than well-defined, fixed, and invariant [2, 3, 14]. RSSAs take the additional step to help users develop and express their preferences.

RSSAs focus on exploration rather than consumption. RSSAs do not focus on optimizing the probability that the user will like recommendations, but instead focus on exploring underdeveloped tastes. Consequently, their recommendations can be likened to "samples" or "pathways", rather than "alternatives".

RSSAs attempt to cover users' tastes, plural. Research has shown that users' preferences are not singular, but rather multi-faceted and only loosely connected [14]. Whereas traditional recommenders are targeted to fit any part of a user's preferences, RSSAs endeavor to help the user discover all of these preferences.

Implementing these operating principles will likely require a combination of new innovations in recommender system features, interfaces, and algorithms. In this paper we highlight the most straightforward innovation: Presenting recommendations that are *not* part of the Top-N. Existing research on critiquing [6] and diversification [36] already expand the notion of the Top-N to offer a better alternatives, but these techniques still focus on providing "good" recommendations. In contrast, we suggest four completely different recommendation lists, displayed alongside but separately from the Top-N. Each new list is next discussed in detail.

"Things we think you will hate" A recommender may mistakenly predict a very low rating for some of the items that the user actually likes. Those mistakes will be hard to correct, since the system never recommends them. We propose to present a list of things the system predicts the user will hate. This allows users to either confirm or correct these predictions, thereby mitigating loss aversion. To resolve mistakes more quickly, corrections can be given a higher weight, which counters the unwanted persuasive effect of the recommender.

"Things we have no clue about" Another cause for "gaps" in the recommender's knowledge of users' tastes is the fact that certain preferences simply remain unexpressed when the system hones in too quickly on a presumptive Top-N. We propose to show a list of hard-to-predict items that may be used identify unexpressed preferences. This involves modifying existing *active learning* approaches [16] to detect not just *some* but *all* of the user's preferences.

"Things you'll be among the first to try" Solutions for the *item cold-start problem* are abound [32], but they ignore the fact that certain users may (at times) actually be excited to try out new items. We propose to present a list of yet-to-be-rated items to users that are identified (using a "hipster measure") as having a high willingness to try out new items.

"Things that are polarizing" Nearest-neighbor recommender algorithms often give recommendations that the neighbors unanimously like. It is possible that certain polarizing items divide these neighbors into rivaling camps; some of them may absolutely love a controversial item, while others absolutely hate it. Experiencing controversial items could have an important value to the user though, because such items would allow the user to develop unique tastes. We therefore propose to detect such items (e.g. by measuring the rating variability of items among the neighbors, or by sub-clustering the neighbors, and then selecting items that best discriminate between clusters) and to present them to the user.

There are several reasons why displaying items that are unrelated to the Top-N can help overcome the Filter Bubble problem. Showing items outside the Top-N is arguably the only way to combat the fear of missing things, and mitigating this fear may increase the users' satisfaction with the system and overall choice satisfaction [4]. Furthermore, by getting more feedback on items outside the Top-N, recommenders can get a better idea of the users' tastes. It can also help users to better understand their own tastes, because developing one's tastes means trying new things, even if this includes things that one may not like [34].

That said, there are other, more interaction-related features that could also contribute to the support of self-actualization. One of these features is to **connect people**. An unfortunate side effect of recommender systems is that advice-giving has become passive and indirect: Users have no idea how exactly their tastes are being used to help other users, and they have no active say in the process. We therefore propose a feature for users to actively recommend items to other users. This can contribute to a sense of fulfilment (helping others) and pride (being called upon for expertise). An algorithm that uses advances in the field of *people recommendation* can be used to drive this process. This feature is expandable beyond simple one-to-one connections between users, to recommend groups of users to come together and develop "taste-based communities" that are based on shared preferences, e.g. regarding certain controversial items.

Another suggestion is to construct a human-readable **taste profile** to help users explore and understand their own tastes. The developers of some commercial recommender systems (e.g. OkCupid, The EchoNest) have recently started to share fascinating insights into consumer tastes, using compelling infographics to highlight surprising preference dynamics, sometimes broken down by state, gender, age or other demographic dimensions. Could such analyses be personalized? For example, a simple analysis could be conducted to figure out which of your tastes are predictable (e.g. the fact that you like both Mozart and Bach), and which are unique (e.g. the fact that besides these two, you also like Nicki Minaj). This feature allows users to explore the common and unique sides of their identity, and—if comparable across users—provide a starting point for establishing sub-cultures of uniquely like-minded individuals.

5. CONCLUSION

"We need help overcoming our rationality sometimes, and allow our thoughts to wander." — David Gelernter [11].

This paper has unpacked the *filter bubble* critique of recommender systems, and proposed a new path for research: to support rather than replace human decision-making. By making us better understand our own preferences, *Recommender Systems for Self-Actualization* will improve our potential to have confidence in (and take ownership over) our life decisions. They allow us to each develop a unique personal style, thereby supporting Maslow's need for Esteem and Self-Actualization [23], and preventing the erosion of our autonomy as consumers. This would usher the field of recommender systems into a new era of computing, where systems move from serving our basic needs (e.g. "find item X") to supporting us to reach our full potential (e.g. helping us understand and reflect upon our own desires). We are actively pursuing the RSSA features presented in this paper, and we encourage others to join us in this exciting quest to pop the filter bubble.

6. ACKNOWLEDGMENTS

This research was supported in part by the NSF award IIS 1565809.

7. REFERENCES

[1] Alexander, C., Ishikawa, S. and Silverstein, M. 1977. *A Pattern Language: Towns, Buildings, Construction.* Oxford University Press.

[2] Amatriain, X., Pujol, J.M., Tintarev, N. and Oliver, N. 2009. Rate It Again: Increasing Recommendation Accuracy by User Re-rating. *Proceedings of the Third ACM Conference on Recommender Systems* (New York, NY, 2009), 173–180.

[3] Bettman, J.R., Luce, M.F. and Payne, J.W. 1998. Constructive consumer choice processes. *Journal of consumer research.* 25, 3 (1998), 187–217.

[4] Bollen, D., Knijnenburg, B.P., Willemsen, M.C. and Graus, M. 2010. Understanding choice overload in recommender systems. *Proceedings of the fourth ACM conference on Recommender systems* (Barcelona, Spain, 2010), 63–70.

[5] Boyd, D. 2010. Streams of Content, Limited Attention: The Flow of Information through Social Media. *Educase Review*. (Oct. 2010), 26–36.

[6] Chen, L. and Pu, P. 2011. Critiquing-based recommenders: survey and emerging trends. *User Modeling and User-Adapted Interaction*. 22, 1-2 (Oct. 2011), 125–150.

[7] Chernev, A. 2003. When More Is Less and Less Is More: The Role of Ideal Point Availability and Assortment in Consumer Choice. *Journal of Consumer Research*. 30, 2 (Sep. 2003), 170–183.

[8] Cosley, D., Lam, S.K., Albert, I., Konstan, J.A. and Riedl, J. 2003. Is Seeing Believing?: How Recommender System Interfaces Affect Users' Opinions. *Proceedings of the SIGCHI Conference on Human Factors in Computing Systems* (Ft. Lauderdale, FL, 2003), 585–592.

[9] Doyle, J.R. 2013. Survey of time preference, delay discounting models. *Judgment and Decision Making*. 8, 2 (2013), 116–135.

[10] Fifield, W. 1964. Pablo Picasso: A Composite Interview. *The Paris Review*. 32, (1964), 37.

[11] Gelernter, D. 2010. Time to start taking the Internet seriously. *Edge*. (Mar. 2010), https://www.edge.org/conversation/david_gelernter–time–to–start–taking–the–internet–seriously.

[12] Gretzel, U. and Fesenmaier, D.R. 2006. Persuasion in Recommender Systems. *International Journal of Electronic Commerce*. 11, 2 (Dec. 2006), 81–100.

[13] Iyengar, S.S. and Lepper, M.R. 2000. When choice is demotivating: Can one desire too much of a good thing? *Journal of Personality and Social Psychology*. 79, 6 (2000), 995–1006.

[14] Jameson, A., Willemsen, M.C., Felfernig, A., de Gemmis, M., Lops, P., Semeraro, G. and Chen, L. 2015. Human Decision Making and Recommender Systems. *Recommender Systems Handbook*. 611–648.

[15] Jenkins, H.W. 2010. Google and the Search for the Future. *Wall Street Journal*.

[16] Karimi, R., Freudenthaler, C., Nanopoulos, A. and Schmidt-Thieme, L. 2012. Exploiting the characteristics of matrix factorization for active learning in recommender systems. *Proceedings of the sixth ACM conference on Recommender systems* (2012), 317–320.

[17] Knijnenburg, B.P., Reijmer, N.J.M. and Willemsen, M.C. 2011. Each to his own: how different users call for different interaction methods in recommender systems. *Proceedings of the fifth ACM conference on Recommender systems* (Chicago, IL, 2011), 141–148.

[18] Knijnenburg, B.P. and Willemsen, M.C. 2015. Evaluating Recommender Systems with User Experiments. *Recommender Systems Handbook*. F. Ricci, L. Rokach, and B. Shapira, eds. Springer US. 309–352.

[19] Knijnenburg, B.P., Willemsen, M.C., Gantner, Z., Soncu, H. and Newell, C. 2012. Explaining the user experience of recommender systems. *User Modeling and User-Adapted Interaction*. 22, 4-5 (2012), 441–504.

[20] Konstan, J.A. and Riedl, J. 2012. Recommender systems: from algorithms to user experience. *User Modeling and User-Adapted Interaction*. 22, 1-2 (Apr. 2012), 101–123.

[21] Lanier, J. 2010. *You Are Not a Gadget: A Manifesto*. Thorndike Press.

[22] Martin, F.J. 2009. Top 10 Lessons Learned Developing Deploying and Operating Real-world Recommender Systems. *Proceedings of the Third ACM Conference on Recommender Systems* (New York, NY, USA, 2009), 1–2.

[23] Maslow, H.A. 1943. A theory of human motivation. *Psychological Review*. 50, 4 (1943), 370–396.

[24] McNee, S.M., Albert, I., Cosley, D., Gopalkrishnan, P., Lam, S.K., Rashid, A.M., Konstan, J.A. and Riedl, J. 2002. On the recommending of citations for research papers. *Proceedings of the 2002 ACM conference on Computer supported cooperative work* (New Orleans, LA, 2002), 116–125.

[25] McNee, S.M., Riedl, J. and Konstan, J.A. 2006. Being accurate is not enough: how accuracy metrics have hurt recommender systems. *Extended abstracts on Human factors in computing systems* (Montreal, Canada, 2006), 1097–1101.

[26] McNee, S.M., Riedl, J. and Konstan, J.A. 2006. Making Recommendations Better: An Analytic Model for Human-recommender Interaction. *Extended Abstracts on Human Factors in Computing Systems* (Montreal, Canada, 2006), 1103–1108.

[27] Nguyen, T.T., Hui, P.-M., Harper, F.M., Terveen, L. and Konstan, J.A. 2014. Exploring the filter bubble: the effect of using recommender systems on content diversity. *Proceedings of the 23rd international conference on World wide web* (2014), 677–686.

[28] Pariser, E. 2012. *The filter bubble: how the new personalized Web is changing what we read and how we think*. Penguin Books.

[29] Pu, P., Chen, L. and Hu, R. 2011. A User-centric Evaluation Framework for Recommender Systems. *Proceedings of the Fifth ACM Conference on Recommender Systems* (Dublin, Ireland, 2011), 157–164.

[30] Resnick, P., Garrett, R.K., Kriplean, T., Munson, S.A. and Stroud, N.J. 2013. Bursting your (filter) bubble: strategies for promoting diverse exposure. *Proceedings of the 2013 conference on Computer supported cooperative work companion* (2013), 95–100.

[31] Resnick, P., Iacovou, N., Sushak, M., Bergstrom, P. and Riedl, J. 1994. GroupLens: An Open Architecture for Collaborative Filtering of Netnews. *ACM Conference on Computer Supported Cooperative Work* (Chapel Hill, NC, 1994), 175–186.

[32] Schein, A.I., Popescul, A., Ungar, L.H. and Pennock, D.M. 2002. Methods and Metrics for Cold-start Recommendations. *Proceedings of the 25th International Conference on Research and Development in Information Retrieval* (Tampere, Finland, 2002), 253–260.

[33] Thaler, R.H. and Sunstein, C. 2008. *Nudge : improving decisions about health, wealth, and happiness*. Yale University Press.

[34] Tian, K.T., Bearden, W.O. and Hunter, G.L. 2001. Consumer's Need for Uniqueness: Scale Development and Validation. *Journal of Consumer Research*. 28, 1 (2001), 50–66.

[35] Torres, R., McNee, S.M., Abel, M., Konstan, J.A. and Riedl, J. 2004. Enhancing digital libraries with TechLens+. *Proceedings of the 2004 joint ACM/IEEE conference on Digital libraries* (Tuscon, AZ, USA, 2004), 228.

[36] Ziegler, C.-N., McNee, S.M., Konstan, J.A. and Lausen, G. 2005. Improving recommendation lists through topic diversification. *Proceedings of the 14th international conference on World Wide Web* (Chiba, Japan, 2005), 22.

A Coverage-Based Approach to Recommendation Diversity On Similarity Graph

Shameem A Puthiya Parambath   Nicolas Usunier *   Yves Grandvalet

Sorbonne Universités, Université de technologie de Compiègne
CNRS,Heudiasyc UMR 7253, Compiègne
firstname.lastname@utc.fr

ABSTRACT

We consider the problem of generating diverse, personalized recommendations such that a small set of recommended items covers a broad range of the user's interests. We represent items in a similarity graph, and we formulate the relevance/diversity trade-off as finding a small set of unrated items that best covers a subset of items positively rated by the user. In contrast to previous approaches, our method does not rely on an explicit trade-off between a relevance objective and a diversity objective, as the estimations of relevance and diversity are implicit in the coverage criterion. We show on several benchmark datasets that our approach compares favorably to the state-of-the-art diversification methods according to various relevance and diversity measures.

Keywords

Diversity; Recommender Systems

1. INTRODUCTION

Most information retrieval systems are designed with the assumption that the relevance of the answers to the query are independent of each other. However, in many real world applications like web search and recommender systems, the usefulness of results depend on each other. The inherent limitations of the retrieval system to represent and capture the complex and time-varying user requirements often results in imprecise responses [18]. The above two factors demand a system to respond with diverse relevant results. For web search, diversification is usually preferred to achieve low query abandonment and to compensate for the ambiguity in the user query [8]. Similarly, in recommender systems, for example movies, a user may have eclectic movie tastes, and diversification is a means to cover movies from all relevant types.

*Now at Facebook AI Research, Paris, France.

RecSys '16, September 15 - 19, 2016, Boston , MA, USA

ISBN 978-1-4503-4035-9/16/09...$15.00

DOI: http://dx.doi.org/10.1145/2959100.2959149

The most usual way of inducing diversity is to perform a two-step approach, in which a ranked list of top-k results is first retrieved, and a re-ranking algorithm is then run on the list such that diverse results appear at the top ranking positions. The re-ranking algorithms optimize an objective function that explicitly trades-off a relevance term and a diversity term. There are many variants of this scheme and we broadly refer to them as re-ranking algorithms for diversification.

We consider in this paper the diversity/relevance trade-off in the context of item-based recommendation, where personalized recommendations propose items that are similar to items that are known to be of interest to the user. Item-based recommender systems have proved effective in practice; they are also particularly relevant in online recommendation settings since recommendations can be generated on-the-fly after any update to the user history.

We view items as nodes in a similarity graph, and we define the coverage of a set of items by another set of items from the similarities between pairs of nodes. The objective of recommendation is then to generate a set of unrated items that covers the set of items that were positively rated by the user. In this approach, diversity is obtained by defining the coverage as a submodular function: there is little gain in improving the coverage of a rated item that is already covered, whereas there can be a large gain in covering a new positively rated item.

As for other diversification algorithms, the submodularity of the objective function provides approximation guarantees to the greedy algorithm iteratively building the set of recommended items. We also experiment with a slightly more involved inference algorithm based on a convex relaxation of the problem, but with limited success. We conclude that the greedy algorithm gives satisfactory results in practice.

In contrast to existing approaches that rely on two separate objectives for relevance and diversity, coverage accounts for both relevance and diversity: relevance is captured through the set to be covered, defined by positively rated items, and diversity through the preference towards lightly covering many items instead of covering heavily a few items. We compare our approach to existing baselines for the diversity/relevance trade-off in an item-based collaborative filtering setup on benchmark datasets, and show that our algorithm compares favorably in terms of various relevance and diversity metrics.

The remainder of this paper is structured as follows. We give a brief overview of the state-of-the-art re-ranking algorithms for diversification in Section 2. Section 3 describes our framework, the optimization problem, and its relationship with other well-known problems. We carry out large scale experiments on benchmark data and report the results in Section 4. We conclude the paper in Section 5.

2. RELATED WORK

Earlier work on diversification is mostly confined to two strongly inter-connected domains: document retrieval and recommender systems, where many re-ranking algorithms have been suggested in different settings. In general, the re-ranking algorithms can be broadly classified into two categories, *(i)* based on random walk [25, 27, 21, 9] and *(ii)* based on the maximum set cover algorithm in offline settings [4, 8, 1, 16, 23, 2] and online settings [15].

In web search settings, re-ranking algorithms operate on the list of items returned by a given query; they re-order this list such that top-ranked results are diverse. One can use random walk based algorithms like PageRank to give an estimation of the importance of the nodes in a graph. Then the nodes are re-ordered based on this score to induce diversity. Zhang et al. [25] iteratively select diverse items by updating the PageRank scores of the unselected items w.r.t. the last selected item. Tong et al. [21] and He et al. [9] use greedy algorithm for set cover on top of PageRank based algorithm to select diverse items by explicitly trading-off relevance and diversity.

In the set cover based algorithms, a submodular objective function which is a linear combination of two components, one for the relevance part and the other for diversity part, is maximized to select the top-k items with maximal relevance-diversity trade-off. The relevance component measures the similarity between the user query and an item, and the diversification component measures the dissimilarity between the item and the set of already selected items. The idea was first proposed in the seminal work of Carbonell and Goldstein [4]. Gollapudi and Sharma [8] study the theoretical properties of the diversification objective and propose many possible choices of objective functions. Agrawal et al. [1] and Chapelle et al. [5] propose algorithms based on retrieving pages covering many intents of the user query. Radlinski et al. [15] suggest algorithms based on multi-armed bandits to learn diverse lists from click data in online settings. Their objective function aims to maximizing the probability of finding a relevant document in the top-k list. Few earlier works focused on performance metrics for quantifying diversity. Agrawal et al. [1] propose intent-aware versions of commonly used performance metrics in IR, whereas Chapelle et al. [5] inspects the theoretical properties of the metrics.

Recommender system is another area where diverse results are demanded. Here there is no query associated to the task, and the relevance of an item is conveyed through a graded rating value. The recommendation list diversification problem has been studied from different points of view. Vargas and Castells [22] propose a unified view of the state-of-the-art metrics used in recommender system diversification. Vargas et al. [23] discuss a diversity metric based on probabilistic models for genre coverage, and propose a re-ranking algorithm to diversify the recommendation list obtained using a baseline recommender system. Ashkan et al. [2] maximize a modular objective function with submodular constraints and demonstrate the effectiveness of the approach on benchmark datasets. A re-ranking based approach by penalizing the system wide popularity bias with individual user specific popularity is proposed by Oh et al. [13]. Hurley [10] proposes a diversification method which does not require a ranked list beforehand, by weighting the pairwise rank difference with the dissimilarity score. However, the theoretical properties of the objective function do not give a clear insight about the relevance-diversity trade-off. A similar approach, proposed by Su et al. [20], creates a user profile based on relevant and irrelevant items, and optimizes an objective function defined over the proper subsets of the profile. The algorithm focuses on intra-list diversity whereas we focus on inter-list diversity. Wu et al. [24] propose a framework for diversification similar to the one of Carbonell and Goldstein [4].

Our approach differs from the previous work in that we propose a single criterion to account for both diversity and relevance. The trade-off is dealt with by the exact definition of coverage we use, which we describe in the next section.

3. UTILITY-WEIGHTED COVERAGE FOR RELEVANT DIVERSE SETS

We consider that we have n objects $\mathcal{X} = \{x_1, \ldots, x_n\}$, together with a similarity matrix $\mathbf{W} = (W_{ij})_{i,j=1\ldots n}$. To be concrete, in a personalized recommender system, each object corresponds to an item (e.g. movie/book), and the similarity between node i and j could be given as the cosine similarity between the columns i and j of the user $\times$ item rating matrix. We do not assume the similarity to be symmetric, but we will restrict ourselves to the case where $W_{ij} \geq 0$.

We can view $(\mathcal{X}, \mathbf{W})$ as a weighted graph, where W_{ij}, which weights the edge between nodes x_i and x_j, should be interpreted as how much item x_i is *similar* to item x_j. Our goal is to return diverse relevant items, and we formalize it as a property of the returned solution set $\mathcal{S}$, based on the coverage of the subset of nodes in the graph $\mathcal{X}$ representing already rated items $\mathcal{R}$. In this respect, our approach is similar to the set-cover based re-ranking algorithms [4, 1, 16].

3.1 Coverage of a Node

From now on, to simplify the notation, we identify the set of nodes $\mathcal{X}$ with $\{1, \ldots, n\}$. For a subset $\mathcal{S}$ of $\mathcal{X}$, given a node $i \notin \mathcal{S}$, we define the coverage score of i by $\mathcal{S}$ as:

$$\mathrm{cov}(i, \mathcal{S}) = f\Big(\sum_{j \in \mathcal{S}} f^{-1}(W_{ij})\Big) \ . \qquad (1)$$

where $f : \mathbb{R}_+ \to \mathbb{R}_+$ is an invertible function that will be chosen non-decreasing and concave, so as to ensure that $\mathcal{S} \to \mathrm{cov}(i, \mathcal{S})$ is non-decreasing with respect to inclusion and submodular. We call the function f in (1) the *saturation function*, because its main usage is to make the coverage of a single node of the graph saturate as we enlarge $\mathcal{S}$.

3.2 Utility-Weighted Coverage of a Set of Nodes

We now extend the definition of the coverage of a node to a set of nodes through the utilities attached to the nodes $\{\upsilon_1, \ldots, \upsilon_n\}$. Utility is a degree of liking for an item given by a user, such as the rating given to this item. Here, we assume that $\upsilon_j \geq 0$. Given a set of m items $\mathcal{R} = \{\kappa_1, \ldots, \kappa_m\} \subset \mathcal{X}$ with their corresponding observed utility values $\Upsilon = \{\upsilon_1, \ldots, \upsilon_m\}$, we define the *profile* of the

Algorithm 1 Greedy Algorithm

Input: set of items $\mathcal{X}$, profile $\mathcal{P}$, similarity matrix $\mathbf{W}$, # of recommendations k
$\mathcal{X} = \mathcal{X} \setminus \mathcal{R}, \mathcal{S} = \emptyset$
repeat
  $i^* = \text{argmax}_{i \in \mathcal{X}} \text{cov}(\mathcal{P}, \mathcal{S} \cup \{i\})$
  $\mathcal{S} = \mathcal{S} \cup \{i^*\}$
  $\mathcal{X} = \mathcal{X} \setminus \{i^*\}$
until $|\mathcal{S}| = k$
Output: set of diverse items $\mathcal{S}$

user as $\mathcal{P} = \{(\kappa_j, v_j)\}_{j=1,\dots,m}$. In the recommendation example, the profile can be the pair of sets (item, rating) given by a user.

Now, given a profile $\mathcal{P}$ and a set of items $\mathcal{S}$ such that $\mathcal{S} \subset \mathcal{X} \setminus \mathcal{R}$, the coverage of profile $\mathcal{P}$ by $\mathcal{S}$ is defined as:

$$\text{cov}(\mathcal{P}, \mathcal{S}) = \sum_{(\kappa,v)\in\mathcal{P}} v \, \text{cov}(\kappa, \mathcal{S}) \ . \tag{2}$$

Here, we use a slight abuse of notation for cov, which can take as first argument either a profile or an item, but we assume that the context is clear considering the use of calligraphic notation for sets. From now on, we use the terminology of *point-wise* coverage for (1) and *profile* coverage for (2).

3.3 Optimal Utility-Diversity Trade-Off

Given a fixed *saturation function*, a set $\mathcal{S}^*$ realizes the optimal utility-diversity trade-off if it solves:

$$\max_{\substack{\mathcal{S}\subset\mathcal{X}\setminus\mathcal{R}\\ |\mathcal{S}|\leq k}} \text{cov}(\mathcal{P}, \mathcal{S}) \ . \tag{3}$$

Since f in (1) is concave, the objective function of problem (3) is submodular. As a result, the greedy approximation algorithm for the maximum set coverage problem, outlined in Algorithm 1, can be used to approximately solve (3), with the approximation guarantees stated in Theorem 1.

THEOREM 1 (NEMHAUSER ET AL. 12). *For a submodular function* $\text{cov}(\mathcal{P}, \mathcal{S})$*, let* $\mathcal{S}^*$ *be the optimizer of* (3) *and* $\hat{\mathcal{S}}$ *be the set returned by the greedy Algorithm 1, then*
$\text{cov}(\mathcal{P}, \hat{\mathcal{S}}) \geq (1-(1-\frac{1}{k})^k)\,\text{cov}(\mathcal{P}, \mathcal{S}^*) \geq (1-\frac{1}{e})\,\text{cov}(\mathcal{P}, \mathcal{S}^*)$.

3.4 Convex Relaxation for Inference

Instead of solving the Problem (3) approximately using the greedy Algorithm 1, another approach is to solve exactly a convex relaxation of Problem (3). As f is concave, the constrained problem:

$$\begin{aligned} &\max_{\boldsymbol{\alpha}\in\mathbb{R}^n} \sum_{(\kappa,v)\in\mathcal{P}} v f\left(\sum_{j=1}^{n} f^{-1}(W_{\kappa j})\alpha_j\right) \\ &\text{such that } \ \forall j \in \mathcal{R}, \ \alpha_j = 0 \\ &\qquad \forall j \in \mathcal{X}\setminus\mathcal{R}, \ \ 0 \leq \alpha_j \leq 1 \\ &\qquad \sum\nolimits_{j=1}^{n} \alpha_j = k \ , \end{aligned} \tag{4}$$

has a concave objective with simple linear constraints, which can be solved efficiently using the Frank-Wolfe algorithm [7] given in Algorithm 2. The inequality constraints are expected to have a sparsifying effect, leading to a vast majority

Algorithm 2 Algorithm Based on Frank-Wolfe

Input: set of items $\mathcal{X}$, profile $\mathcal{P}$, similarity matrix $\mathbf{W}$, # of recommendations k
$i = 1$, $tol = 10^{-6}$, $maxiter = 10^6$
$\mathcal{S} = \mathcal{X} \setminus \mathcal{R}$, $\boldsymbol{\alpha}^i = \mathbf{0}$
repeat
  $\mathbf{L}^i = -\nabla_{\boldsymbol{\alpha}}\left(\sum_{(\kappa,v)\in\mathcal{P}} v f\left(\sum_{j=1}^{n} f^{-1}(W_{\kappa j})\alpha_j\right)\right)\Big|_{\boldsymbol{\alpha}^i}$
  $\boldsymbol{\alpha}^{i+1} = \text{argmin}_{\boldsymbol{\alpha}\in\mathbb{R}^n} \boldsymbol{\alpha}^T \mathbf{L}^i$ (subject to the constraints in (4))
  $\delta = \boldsymbol{\alpha}^{i+1} - \boldsymbol{\alpha}^i$
  $\boldsymbol{\alpha}^{i+1} = \boldsymbol{\alpha}^i + \frac{2}{2+i}\delta$
  $i = i + 1$
until $abs(\delta) \leq tol$ **or** $i \geq maxiter$
Output: indexes of k largest elements in $\boldsymbol{\alpha}$

of the α_j to be zero. In any case, a solution of cardinality k can always be returned by taking the k items with largest values of α_j.

3.5 Special Cases

The non-linearities of the *saturation function*, if any, are the critical features that will allow us to make the trade-off between cumulated utility and diversity in profile coverage.

3.5.1 0/1 Saturation Function and Covering Problems

We first consider the limiting case where $f(t) = \lim_{\epsilon\to 0} t^{\epsilon}$. For the sake of clarity, we assume that $v = 1$ for every $(k, v) \in \mathcal{P}$, and that items are embedded in a metric space.

Covering $\mathcal{R}$ with balls:.

Let us assume that W_{ij} is 1 if i lies in the ball of radius ρ centered on j and 0 otherwise, for some fixed radius $\rho > 0$. Then, $\text{cov}(\mathcal{P}, \mathcal{S})$ counts the number of items of $\mathcal{R}$ that are covered by the balls of radius ρ centered on the items of $\mathcal{S}$. Maximizing $\text{cov}(\mathcal{P}, \mathcal{S})$ with a cardinality constraint on $\mathcal{S}$ corresponds to finding a maximum subset of $\mathcal{R}$ that is covered with k balls of radius ρ centered in points of $\mathcal{X} \setminus \mathcal{R}$. Problem (3) is then a maximal coverage problem.

k-nearest neighbors and clusters:.

If $\mathbf{W}$ is the adjacency matrix of a k-nearest neighbor graph, then $\text{cov}(\mathcal{P}, \mathcal{S})$ counts the number of items in $\mathcal{R}$ that are in the k-nearest neighbors of items in $\mathcal{S}$. Likewise, assume that the items are clustered and that the similarity W_{ij} is 1 if i and j belong to the same cluster and 0 otherwise. Then, $\text{cov}(\mathcal{P}, \mathcal{S})$ is the number of items in $\mathcal{S}$ that are in the same cluster as at least one item in $\mathcal{R}$.

3.5.2 Linear Saturation Function

Here we consider the case where the *saturation function* is a linear. If f is, say the identity function, then maximizing coverage boils down to choosing the set of items $j \in \mathcal{S}$ such that $\sum_{(\kappa,v)\in\mathcal{P}} vW_{\kappa j}$ is maximal. This corresponds to one way of performing item-based collaborative filtering [17].

4. EXPERIMENTS

In this section, we evaluate our approach in movie recommender settings. We compare our results against the state-of-the-art re-ranking algorithms.

4.1 Baselines

We chose two baselines: Maximal Marginal Relevance (MMR) [4] and Max-Sum Diversification (MSD) [3].

4.1.1 Maximal Marginal Relevance

Given the set of already selected items $\mathcal{S}$ (initialized to the empty set), the MMR algorithm selects an item i^* such that

$$i^* \in \underset{i \in \mathcal{X} \setminus (\mathcal{R} \cup \mathcal{S})}{\text{argmax}} \ \lambda\, sim_1(u,i) - (1-\lambda) \max_{j \in \mathcal{S}} sim_2(i,j) \ ,$$

where sim_1 and sim_2 are similarities, and u is related to the user profile. In our settings, this reads:

$$i^* \in \underset{i \in \mathcal{X} \setminus (\mathcal{R} \cup \mathcal{S})}{\text{argmax}} \ \lambda \sum_{(\kappa,\upsilon) \in \mathcal{P}} \upsilon W_{\kappa i} - (1-\lambda) \max_{j \in \mathcal{S}} W_{ij} \ .$$

As the trade-off parameter $\lambda \in [0,1]$ is decreased, more emphasis is put on the diversity of the resulting set. MMR can be interpreted as a greedy scheme for maximizing a non-monotone submodular objective function, for which the approximation guarantees of Theorem 1 do not apply [11].

4.1.2 Max-Sum Diversification

The Max-Sum diversification (MSD) algorithm is based on the facility dispersion problem, where one aims to find a subset of optimal locations such that the distance between the selected locations is maximized. Like in MMR, the objective function comprises of two terms, a modular relevance term and a supermodular sum of distance diversity term. Formally, MSD returns the set $\mathcal{S}$ of cardinality k, such that: [1]

$$\underset{\mathcal{S} \subseteq \mathcal{X} \setminus \mathcal{R}}{\text{argmax}}\, \lambda g(\mathcal{S}) + (1-\lambda) \sum_{i \in \mathcal{S}} \sum_{j \in \mathcal{S} - \{i\}} dist(i,j) \ \ s.t \ \ |\mathcal{S}| \leq k$$

where λ is the trade-off parameter, $g(\mathcal{S})$ is the utility function and $dist(i,j)$ is the distance function between item i and j. The problem is NP-Hard, but efficient greedy algorithm with provable approximation guarantees exist [3]. In our settings, the utility $g(\mathcal{S})$ is defined exactly as the sim_1 in MMR and $dist(i,j)$ as $1 - W_{ij}$.

4.2 Performance Metrics

Our experiments aim to assess the diversity of the recommended set. Even though there has been some work on unifying the performance metrics for diversity, there is no clear consensus, especially in recommendation tasks. So we measure several features of the different solutions in the movie recommender settings, involving relevance, coverage, and popularity bias [14].

Genre Coverage – A diversifying algorithm should produce results that cover different relevant interest groups. One way to measure the coverage of the user interests is to count the number of relevant genres recommended to the user. We define the *Genre Coverage* for the set $\mathcal{U}$ of users as the average ratio of relevant genres recommended to each user.

$$\frac{1}{|\mathcal{U}|} \sum_{u \in \mathcal{U}} \frac{\left| \bigcup_{i \in \mathcal{S}_u} genres(i) \cap \bigcup_{i \in \mathcal{R}_u^+} genres(i) \right|}{\left| \bigcup_{i \in \mathcal{R}_u^+} genres(i) \right|} \ ,$$

where, for user u, $\mathcal{R}_u^+$ is the set of relevant rated movies, $\mathcal{S}_u$ is the set of recommended items, and $genres(i)$ returns the genres associated with item i.

Intra-List Distance (ILD) – It measures the diversity of the set of recommended items by the mean distance between all pairs of items in this set. In our experiments, we used the Hamming distance between genre vectors:

$$\frac{1}{|\mathcal{U}|} \sum_{u \in \mathcal{U}} \frac{1}{k(k-1)} \sum_{(i,j) \in \mathcal{S}_u} |genres(i) - genres(j)| \ .$$

Catalog Coverage – It is the fraction of the relevant items that are recommended at least once, across all users. Higher values of catalog coverage indicate that the algorithm counterbalances the popularity bias by covering a large portion of the overall set of items. Formally, it is defined as:

$$\frac{\left| \bigcup_{u \in \mathcal{U}} \mathcal{S}_u^+ \right|}{|\mathcal{X}|} \ .$$

Popularity Stratified Recall@k – This metric is suggested by Steck [19] to measure the ability of a recommender system to compensate for the popularity bias. As argued earlier, a diversity inducing recommendation system should cover diverse interests and may in turn cover items from the tail of the item-popularity distribution. *Popularity Stratified Recall@k* is defined as:

$$\frac{\sum_{u \in \mathcal{U}} \sum_{i \in \mathcal{S}_u^+} \left(\frac{1}{N_i^+} \right)^{\beta}}{\sum_{u \in \mathcal{U}} \sum_{i \in \mathcal{T}_u} \left(\frac{1}{N_i^+} \right)^{\beta}} \ ,$$

where $\mathcal{S}_u^+$ is the set of recommended items that are known to be relevant for user u (among the k recommended items), $\mathcal{T}_u$ is the set of items in the test set that are known to be truly relevant for user u, N_i^+ is the number of relevant ratings for item i in the test set and β is a hyperparameter which adjusts for the popularity bias. Higher values of *Popularity Stratified Recall@k* indicate that more relevant movies from the tail distribution are recommended. In our experiments, we used $\beta = 0.5$ and k was set to 5, 10, 20 or 50.

Intra-List Distance (ILD) – Proposed by [26], it measures the diversity of the set of recommended items by the mean distance between all pairs of items in this set. In our experiments, we used the Hamming distance:

$$\frac{1}{|\mathcal{U}|} \sum_{u \in \mathcal{U}} \frac{1}{k(k-1)} \sum_{(i,j) \in \mathcal{S}_u} |genres(i) - genres(j)| \ .$$

Discounted Cumulative Gain (DCG) – It is a commonly used metric in ranking problems. It measures the relevance of a ranked list by the sum of the graded relevance discounted by the rank of the item. In our experiments, we used:

$$\frac{1}{|\mathcal{U}|} \sum_{u \in \mathcal{U}} \sum_{i \in \mathcal{S}_u} \frac{2^{r_i} - 1}{log(i+1)} \ ,$$

where r_i is the *graded* relevance score of the ith item. In our experiments, the ith item is either the ith item entering $\mathcal{S}_u$ for greedy algorithm, or the one with ith largest α_i in the convex relaxation formulation (4).

[1]The original formulation of Borodin et al. [3] is slightly different but equivalent.

Precision@k – It is the fraction of relevant items in the recommended list of k items.

$$\frac{1}{|\mathcal{U}|}\sum_{u\in\mathcal{U}}\frac{1}{k}\left|\mathcal{S}_u^+\cap\mathcal{T}_u\right| \ .$$

Genre Coverage and *ILD* measure diversity, *Catalog Coverage* and *Stratified Recall@k* mix diversity and relevance, and DCG and *Precision@k* measure the relevance. Higher values of the aforementioned metrics indicate a better recommendation list.

4.3 Experimental Protocol

We used two benchmark datasets *(i)* MovieLens and *(ii)* Yahoo! Movies to evaluate the proposed algorithm. Following Cremonesi et al. [6], we carried out holdout validation by splitting the data randomly into training and test set such that 3% of the original data goes into testing and remaining goes into training. To reduce the variability in the result, split is carried out five times and the reported results are the average over the five splits. The rating values and the corresponding movies in the training set is used to create the profile $\mathcal{P}$ and the unrated movies in the training set is used as $\mathcal{S}$. For the purpose of evaluation, whenever necessary, we discretized rating scores to binary values such that rating scores of 4 and 5 are deemed as relevant and otherwise irrelevant.

We estimated the unobserved rating values for MMR and MSD in the training set using item-based collaborative filtering [17] (matrix-factorization based methods gave inferior results). We used the the observed movie ratings to create the user profiles $\mathcal{P}$ and the similarity matrix $\mathbf{W}$, which is computed by a cosine similarity. For evaluation purposes, we used the original observed rating values or whenever applicable, their binarized version, in the test set. We used $f(t) = t^\gamma$ with $\gamma = \{0.1, 0.5, 0.8\}$ and the limiting case where $\gamma \to 0$, which corresponds to the ℓ_∞-norm, for the *saturation function* in the submodular (SUB) setting, and $f(t) = t$ for the modular (MOD) setting.

4.4 Results

4.4.1 MovieLens

MovieLens[2] *1M* dataset contains ratings from 6040 users on 3706 movies (excluding movies with no rating values). Each movie is associated with a set of genres, among 18 distinct categories. Performance of different algorithms on the MovieLens dataset for $k = 10$ is given in Table 1 (all values in %). The relevance-diversity values for different values of k is given in Figure 1.

4.4.2 Yahoo! Movies

Yahoo! Movies[3] dataset contains separate training and test set, but we used only the training set due to the unavailability of genre information. The training data contain 211,231 rating values for 7,642 users and 11,915 movies. We removed the movies with missing genres, being left with 187,435 ratings spanning 7,636 users and 8,647 movies. Yahoo! Movies span a total of 25 distinct genres. Table 2 contains the result for Yahoo! Movies for $k = 10$ (all values in %) and Figure 2 contains the relevance-diversity values for different values of k.

[2]http://grouplens.org/datasets/movielens/
[3]https://webscope.sandbox.yahoo.com/

4.4.3 Discussion

It should be noted that the modular version of our algorithm is equivalent to MMR and MSD with $\lambda = 1$. Surprisingly, MMR does not exhibit any trade-off between relevance and diversity metrics as λ is varied. As the λ value is increased from 0.1 to 1, values corresponding to DCG, Precision@k, Catalog Coverage and Genre Coverage remain the same or decrease only marginally. In effect, MMR does not recommend very relevant and less diverse movies by weighting the relevance term highly. The same trend can be noted for Yahoo! Movies as well. On the other hand, MMR compensates for popularity bias by recommending less popular movies covering a larger spectrum of the set as the diversity term is weighted high, thus increasing Stratified Recall@k and Catalog Coverage. But for MSD, on MovieLens, as the λ value is increased, the recommendation list becomes more relevant but nothing can be inferred about diversity. But on Yahoo! Movies, trade-off between relevance (DCG) and diversity (Genre Coverage) is clearer. As the λ value is increased, recommended list becomes more relevant and less diverse. However, there is no clear indication that MSD compensates for popularity bias, even though it recommends movies spanning large spectrum of movies from the set. The modular (equivalent to item-based collaborative filtering) version perform as good as the MMR and MSD versions.

For our algorithm, as the γ value is increased, both the relevance and the diversity values increase and the increase is more significant. The best in-class relevance-diversity values are obtained for $\gamma = 0.1$. For MovieLens, we see a 3% increase for both DCG and Genre Coverage metrics compared to the second best algorithm. For Yahoo! Movies, $\gamma = 0.1$, gives the best diversity value (Genre Coverage) for a marginally smaller value of relevance (DCG). On MovieLens, our proposed algorithm returns greater number of movies from the tail distribution which are collectively distinct, i.e. covering large spectrum of movies, as indicated by the larger values of Stratified Recall@k and Catalog Coverage. But this effect is not very evident on Yahoo! Movies. As the γ value approaches zero the quality of the recommendation list deteriorates. Convex relaxation based algorithm performance is on par with other algorithms, but we found it computationally more expensive. The performance of relevance-diversity metrics for varying recommendation size is given in Figure 1 and 2. On MovieLens, submodular (solid blue line) algorithm returns greater number of relevant movies (square markers) which are diverse (red solid line with triangle markers on the left plot), whereas MMR and MSD returns diverse movies which are less relevant (red non-solid lines with triangle markers on the left plot). It can also be noted that, as the k value increases, our algorithm recommends the most diverse, but relevant movies (higher DCG & Genre Coverage) whereas MMR and MSD recommend the most diverse, but irrelevant movies (higher ILD, lower Genre Coverage & DCG; see right plot in Figure 1). However, in Yahoo! Movies, even though the diversity metrics (Genre Coverage & ILD) are marginally higher for the proposed algorithm, the relevance values are close to MMR and MSD algorithms.

4.4.4 Effect on Eclectic Users

The problem of diverse recommendation is more critical for users with eclectic interests. Here we study the effect of diversification on eclectic users by sampling an arbitrary

Table 1: Experimental Results on MovieLens (k=10)

	MMR λ=0.1	MMR λ=0.5	MMR λ=0.8	MSD λ=0.1	MSD λ=0.5	MSD λ=0.8	MOD	SUB γ=0.8	SUB γ=0.5	SUB γ=0.1	SUB $\gamma\to 0$	SUB conv γ=0.5
Genre Coverage	67.12	66.34	66.26	66.84	65.35	65.50	66.23	66.31	66.56	70.04	63.64	66.27
ILD	19.73	19.75	19.75	19.22	19.44	19.55	19.75	19.78	19.88	19.77	18.78	19.70
Catalog Coverage	6.55	6.20	6.19	7.92	6.37	6.51	6.18	6.26	6.57	10.49	5.37	6.76
Stratified Recall@k	7.78	7.57	7.56	8.00	7.36	7.60	7.56	7.63	7.90	10.27	6.23	7.89
DCG	31.83	31.38	31.35	25.09	25.33	29.93	31.33	31.51	32.10	34.86	24.42	31.95
Precision@k	4.06	3.98	3.98	4.02	3.86	3.97	3.98	4.01	4.10	4.60	3.19	4.08

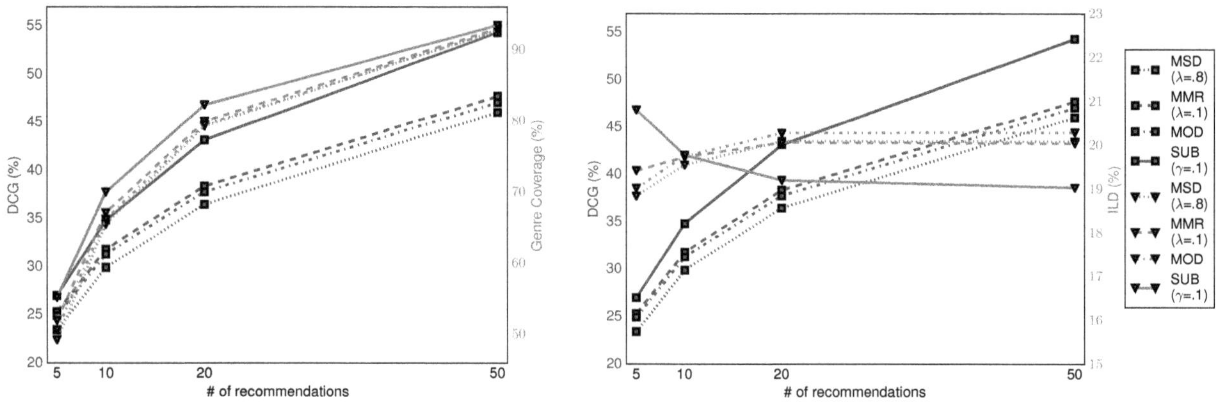

Figure 1: Relevance-Diversity values for the MovieLens according to k

number of eclectic users from the MovieLens and Yahoo! Movies. We define eclectic users based on their affinity towards many diverse items, as measured by their number of positive ratings and the mean similarity between rated items, based on W_{ij}, below some threshold. We selected 209 users from MovieLens by setting the minimum number of relevant ratings to 100 and the mean similarity between already rated movies below 0.2, and 109 users from Yahoo! Movies by setting the minimum number of relevant ratings to 50 and the mean similarity between already rated movies below 0.1. The experimental results are given in Tables 3 and 4 for k =10. The proposed algorithm significantly improves the DCG and Genre Coverage values compared to the second best diversification algorithm. In case of MovieLens, DCG and Genre Coverage values improve by 5% and 6% respectively whereas in case of Yahoo! Movies for the same relevance value we get 5% improvement. The relevance and diversity metric values for different recommendation size for eclectic users is given in Figures 3 and 4. As we can see from the figures, the blue solid line with square markers and red solid line with triangle markers dominate the DCG-Genre Coverage graph for varying sizes of k. On eclectic user set, as the recommendation size grows, MSD and MMR algorithm return movies which are diverse with respect to each other (higher ILD values) but less relevant to the users (smaller DCG and Genre Coverage) compared to the proposed algorithm.

5. CONCLUSION

We presented a new criterion that captures both relevance and diversity for recommendation. The criterion can be approximately optimized with an efficient greedy algorithm; the algorithm can be applied in any recommendation scenario where we have access to similarities between items and a subset of items which are known to be of interest to the user. Experiments on benchmark datasets showed that the algorithm performs well, both in terms of relevance and diversity compared to a strong baseline.

6. ACKNOWLEDGMENT

This work was carried out and funded in the framework of the Labex MS2T. It was supported by the Picardy Region and the French Government, through the program "Investments for the future" managed by the National Agency for Research (Reference ANR-11-IDEX-0004-02). We thank our anonymous reviewers for their valuable suggestions and comments.

References

[1] Rakesh Agrawal, Sreenivas Gollapudi, Alan Halverson, and Samuel Ieong. Diversifying search results. In *WSDM*. ACM, 2009.

[2] Azin Ashkan, Branislav Kveton, Shlomo Berkovsky, and Zheng Wen. Optimal greedy diversity for recommendation. In *IJCAI*, 2015.

[3] Allan Borodin, Hyun Chul Lee, and Yuli Ye. Max-sum diversification, monotone submodular functions and dynamic updates. In *PODS*, pages 155–166. ACM, 2012.

[4] Jaime Carbonell and Jade Goldstein. The use of MMR, diversity-based reranking for reordering documents and producing summaries. In *SIGIR*, pages 335–336. ACM, 1998.

[5] Olivier Chapelle, Shihao Ji, Ciya Liao, Emre Velipasaoglu, Larry Lai, and Su-Lin Wu. Intent-based diversification of web search results: metrics and algorithms. *Information Retrieval*, 14(6):572–592, 2011.

Table 2: **Experimental Results on Yahoo! Movies (k=10)**

	MMR λ=0.1	MMR λ=0.5	MMR λ=0.8	MSD λ=0.1	MSD λ=0.5	MSD λ=0.8	MOD	SUB γ=0.8	SUB γ=0.5	SUB γ=0.1	SUB γ→0	SUB conv γ=0.5
Genre Coverage	72.61	70.42	69.96	72.80	71.67	70.78	69.77	70.44	71.75	73.61	66.59	69.58
ILD	16.03	15.75	15.67	14.99	15.93	15.84	15.63	15.72	15.82	15.52	14.87	14.84
Catalog Coverage	2.96	2.61	2.55	3.15	2.78	2.63	2.54	2.64	2.87	3.03	1.91	1.71
Stratified Recall@k	16.44	15.08	14.83	15.36	15.51	14.85	14.75	15.33	16.48	16.00	11.36	14.45
DCG	13.59	13.37	13.27	9.64	10.30	10.61	13.24	13.47	13.88	12.92	9.75	13.02
Precision@k	1.62	1.55	1.53	1.40	1.55	1.51	1.53	1.56	1.63	1.50	1.21	1.53

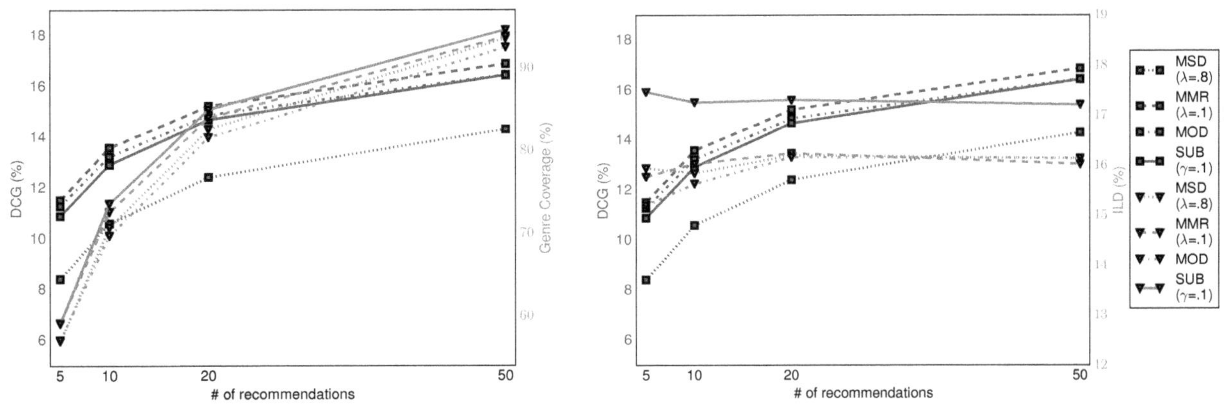

Figure 2: Relevance-Diversity values for the Yahoo! Movies according to k

Table 3: **Experimental Results on MovieLens (Eclectic Users k = 10)**

	MMR λ=0.1	MMR λ=0.5	MMR λ=0.8	MSD λ=0.1	MSD λ=0.5	MSD λ=0.8	MOD	SUB γ=0.8	SUB γ=0.5	SUB γ=0.1	SUB γ→0	SUB conv γ=0.5
Genre Coverage	59.54	59.41	59.39	58.02	59.03	59.40	59.39	59.46	59.51	64.54	59.87	59.01
ILD	20.69	20.69	20.69	20.23	20.45	20.69	20.69	20.72	20.82	21.03	20.55	20.34
Catalog Coverage	3.12	3.12	3.12	2.97	3.19	3.12	3.12	3.16	3.29	4.13	2.61	3.36
Stratified Recall	4.62	4.62	4.62	4.32	4.67	4.62	4.62	4.67	4.87	6.33	4.06	4.89
DCG	87.41	87.45	87.45	67.43	86.91	89.23	87.44	87.97	90.02	95.32	71.05	90.22
Precision@k	11.74	11.76	11.76	11.01	11.77	11.76	11.76	11.86	12.21	13.21	9.64	12.13

Table 4: **Experimental Results on Yahoo! Movies (Eclectic Users k=10)**

	MMR λ=0.1	MMR λ=0.5	MMR λ=0.8	MSD λ=0.1	MSD λ=0.5	MSD λ=0.8	MOD	SUB γ=0.8	SUB γ=0.5	SUB γ=0.1	SUB γ→0	SUB conv γ=0.5
Genre Coverage	55.88	54.12	54.03	56.66	56.46	55.74	53.91	55.47	57.22	60.03	45.93	56.32
ILD	14.57	14.03	13.98	14.58	14.43	14.32	13.96	14.26	14.68	14.00	11.78	14.49
Catalog Coverage	0.28	0.25	0.25	0.31	0.26	0.25	0.24	0.27	0.29	0.27	0.19	0.28
Stratified Recall@k	4.46	3.97	3.88	5.75	4.30	4.00	3.82	4.38	5.17	5.62	3.47	4.90
DCG	19.92	18.40	18.15	18.13	15.87	18.89	17.95	19.34	21.20	19.54	12.53	20.15
Precision@k	2.59	2.39	2.35	2.99	2.42	2.44	2.33	2.53	2.88	2.59	1.63	2.66

[6] Paolo Cremonesi, Yehuda Koren, and Roberto Turrin. Performance of recommender algorithms on top-n recommendation tasks. In *RecSys*, pages 39–46. ACM, 2010.

[7] Marguerite Frank and Philip Wolfe. An algorithm for quadratic programming. *Naval research logistics quarterly*, 3(1-2):95–110, 1956.

[8] Sreenivas Gollapudi and Aneesh Sharma. An axiomatic approach for result diversification. In *WWW*, pages 381–390. ACM, 2009.

[9] Jingrui He, Hanghang Tong, Qiaozhu Mei, and Boleslaw Szymanski. Gender: A generic diversified ranking algorithm. In *NIPS*, pages 1142–1150, 2012.

[10] Neil J Hurley. Personalised ranking with diversity. In *RecSys*, pages 379–382. ACM, 2013.

[11] Hui Lin and Jeff Bilmes. A class of submodular functions for document summarization. In *ACL*, pages 510–520, 2011.

[12] George L Nemhauser, Laurence A Wolsey, and Marshall L Fisher. An analysis of approximations for maximizing submodular set functions. *Mathematical Programming*, 14 (1), 1978.

[13] Jinoh Oh, Sun Park, Hwanjo Yu, Min Song, and Seung-Taek Park. Novel recommendation based on personal popularity tendency. In *ICDM*, pages 507–516. IEEE, 2011.

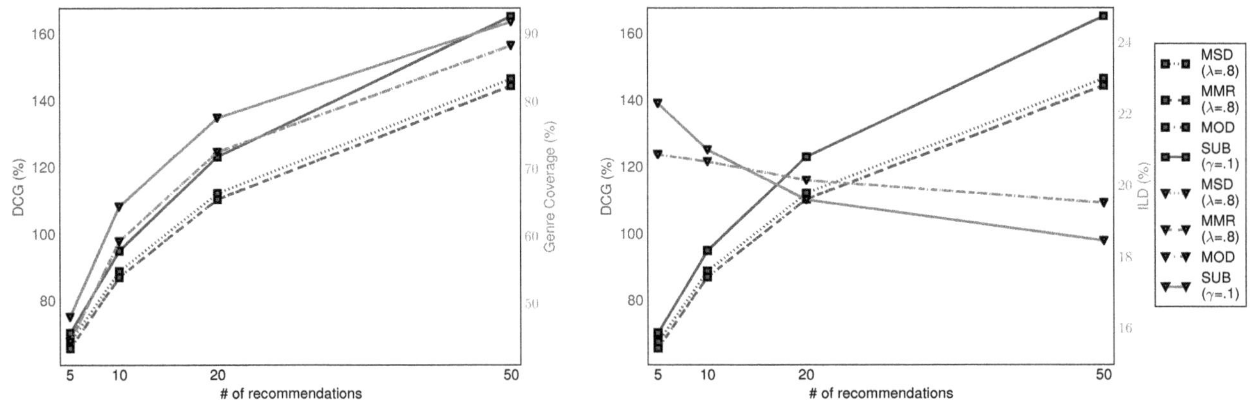

Figure 3: Relevance-Diversity values for the MovieLens (Eclectic Users) according to k

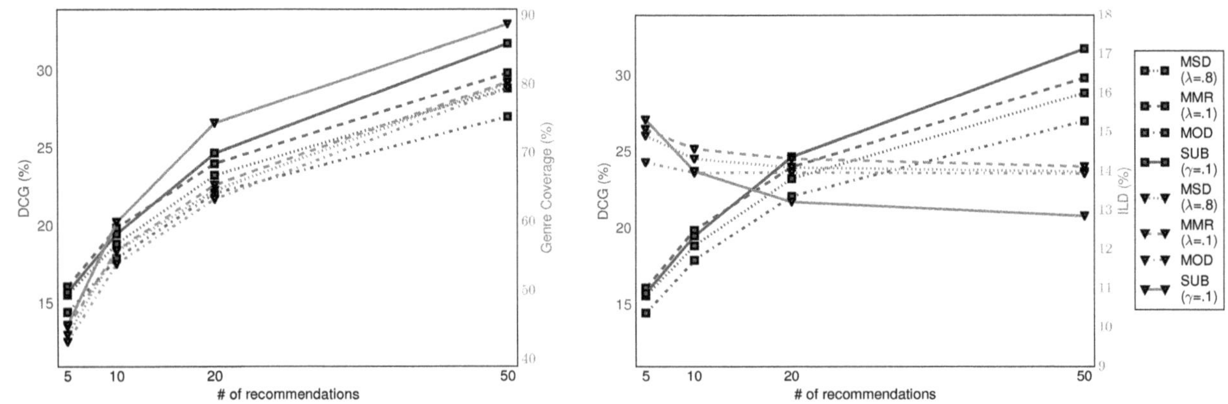

Figure 4: Relevance-Diversity values for the Yahoo! Movies (Eclectic Users) according to k

[14] Bruno Pradel, Nicolas Usunier, and Patrick Gallinari. Ranking with non-random missing ratings: influence of popularity and positivity on evaluation metrics. In *RecSys*, pages 147–154. ACM, 2012.

[15] Filip Radlinski, Robert Kleinberg, and Thorsten Joachims. Learning diverse rankings with multi-armed bandits. In *ICML*, pages 784–791. ACM, 2008.

[16] Rodrygo LT Santos, Craig Macdonald, and Iadh Ounis. Exploiting query reformulations for web search result diversification. In *WWW*. ACM, 2010.

[17] Badrul Sarwar, George Karypis, Joseph Konstan, and John Riedl. Item-based collaborative filtering recommendation algorithms. In *WWW*. ACM, 2001.

[18] Karen Spärck-Jones, Stephen E Robertson, and Mark Sanderson. Ambiguous requests: implications for retrieval tests, systems and theories. In *SIGIR Forum*. ACM, 2007.

[19] Harald Steck. Item popularity and recommendation accuracy. In *RecSys*, pages 125–132. ACM, 2011.

[20] Ruilong Su, Li'Ang Yin, Kailong Chen, and Yong Yu. Set-oriented personalized ranking for diversified top-n recommendation. In *RecSys*, pages 415–418. ACM, 2013.

[21] Hanghang Tong, Jingrui He, Zhen Wen, Ravi Konuru, and Ching-Yung Lin. Diversified ranking on large graphs: an optimization viewpoint. In *SIGKDD*, pages 1028–1036. ACM, 2011.

[22] S. Vargas and P. Castells. Rank and relevance in novelty and diversity metrics for recommender systems. In *RecSys*, pages 109–116. ACM, 2011.

[23] Saúl Vargas, Linas Baltrunas, Alexandros Karatzoglou, and Pablo Castells. Coverage, redundancy and size-awareness in genre diversity for recommender systems. In *RecSys*, pages 209–216. ACM, 2014.

[24] Le Wu, Qi Liu, Enhong Chen, Nicholas Jing Yuan, Guangming Guo, and Xing Xie. Relevance meets coverage: A unified framework to generate diversified recommendations. *ACM Trans. Intell. Syst. Technol.*, 7(3), 2016.

[25] Benyu Zhang, Hua Li, Yi Liu, Lei Ji, Wensi Xi, Weiguo Fan, Zheng Chen, and Wei-Ying Ma. Improving web search results using affinity graph. In *SIGIR*, pages 504–511. ACM, 2005.

[26] Mi Zhang and Neil Hurley. Avoiding monotony: improving the diversity of recommendation lists. In *RecSys*, pages 123–130. ACM, 2008.

[27] Xiaojin Zhu, Andrew B Goldberg, Jurgen Van Gael, and David Andrzejewski. Improving diversity in ranking using absorbing random walks. In *HLT-NAACL*, pages 97–104, 2007.

A Scalable Approach for Periodical Personalized Recommendations

Zhen Qin Ish Rishabh John Carnahan
Ticketmaster
Hollywood, CA 91604, USA
{Zhen.Qin, Ish.Rishabh, John.Carnahan}@Ticketmaster.com

ABSTRACT

We develop a highly scalable and effective contextual bandit approach towards periodical personalized recommendations. The online bootstrapping-based technique provides a principled way for UCB-type exploitation-exploration algorithms, while being able to handle arbitrary sized datasets, well suited to learn the ever evolving user preference drift from streaming data, and essentially parameter-free. We further introduce techniques to handle arbitrary sized feature spaces using feature hashing, leverage existing state-of-art machine learning via learning reduction, and increase cache hits by managing bootstrapped models in memory effectively. The resulted model trains on millions of examples and billions of features within minutes on a single personal computer. It shows persistent performance in both offline and online evaluation. We observe around 10% click through rate (CTR) and conversion lift over a collaborative filtering approach in real-world A/B testing across more than 40 million users on the major Ticketmaster email recommendation product.

CCS Concepts

•**Information systems** → *Information systems applications; Data mining; Personalization;*

Keywords

Recommender Systems; Personalization; Online Learning; Contextual Bandits; Scalability; Learning Reductions

1. INTRODUCTION

We are interested in pushing periodical personalized recommendations to users, commonly seen for many e-commerce companies today. In many cases, users are not motivated to visit websites or launch apps to see online recommendations. Periodical "pushing" of relevant products such as weekly recommendation emails, sms, and notifications, remind users of the products for making purchases and further exploration of online content.

RecSys '16, September 15-19, 2016, Boston , MA, USA
© 2016 ACM. ISBN 978-1-4503-4035-9/16/09...$15.00
DOI: http://dx.doi.org/10.1145/2959100.2959139

There are several key differences between periodical recommendations and the more extensively researched online recommendations. First, collaborative filtering based methods, even its incremental version, tend to produce similar results across time. Though it might be fine for a user to see two sets of the same recommendations across two website visits, pushing two very similar weekly emails can easily bore the user. Second, though contextual bandits that provide novel content and mitigate the cold-start problem via exploitation-exploration has been applied to online recommendations recently, existing algorithms are either computation or parameter intensive. More importantly, they typically employ sampling-based exploration strategies that depend on online user feedback for fast policy improvement. However, for periodical recommendation, we only get feedback as fast as we send out recommendations - such as once a week. Probabilistic exploration could be risky in this scenario. Third, providing refreshing periodic recommendation requires training or updating the model as frequent as sending out the recommendations. Thus a highly scalable approach that takes up-to-date user feedback into consideration, preferably in incremental mode, is necessary.

In this work, we develop an efficient and effective contextual bandit approach towards periodical personalized recommendation that addresses the above-mentioned concerns. The online bootstrapping based technique provides a principled way for upper confidence bound (UCB)-type exploration that is more stable than randomized methods, and it is essentially parameter-free (only the number of bootstrapped models needs to be specified). The online learning framework can naturally feed in user feedback in streaming mode. We further introduce feature hashing, learning reduction, and memory management for bootstrapped policies. The resulted framework can handle arbitrary sized examples and features efficiently, training on billions of features within minutes on a personal computer. We show consistent significant improvement over a productized collaborative filtering approach and other contextual bandits approaches in both offline testing and real-world A/B testing across more than 40 million users on the major Ticketmaster email recommendation product.

2. RELATED WORK

Collaborative filtering (CF) is widely used and researched for recommendation systems. Traditional CF approaches tend to have cold-start problem or generate similar results across time, neither is ideal for periodical recommendations. Context-aware [8] and serendipity-aware (including recommendation diversification) recommendation systems [4] are hot recent research topics.

Contextual bandits is a promising approach to address both problems and it's popular especially for online recommendations [7]. As its name indicates, it considers the context (such as item and user properties) under which recommendations are made, and employs exploitation-exploration, where the exploitation part conducts context-aware prediction based on a learned model, and the exploration part learns about possibly drifting data distributions (e.g. introducing new items or user preference drift). There are two major exploration strategies: randomization-based and UCB-type. Randomization-based exploration samples policy or action to take (such as what to recommend) randomly (e.g. ϵ-greedy) or from some distribution (e.g. Thompson sampling [2]). They are ideal for online recommendation with fast user feedback loop, but are risky for periodical recommendations. UCB-type strategy derives some intervals of prediction and uses the upper bound for exploration [7]. These approaches are more stable, but existing methods are computation intensive. Also, there are usually several parameters to tune for both approaches (such as choosing a prior distribution for Thompson sampling, see [12]). Our model provides a principled UCB-type exploration strategy while being highly efficient and parameter-lite, suitable for large-scale real-world applications.

We apply feature hashing and learning reduction, which have been studied in the machine learning community recently [13] [1]. We show that these techniques dramatically improve efficiency while not sacrificing effectiveness in the personalized recommendation context.

3. ONLINE BOOTSTRAPPING BASED CONTEXTUAL BANDIT

We introduce how to perform stable and efficient contextual bandit using online bootstrapping.

3.1 Online Bootstrap

Bootstrapping is a classical way of generating prediction intervals. Traditional batch bootstrapping takes a dataset of N examples and generates B new datasets, each of size N, by sampling with replacement (for every example in a new dataset, each original example has a probability of $\frac{1}{N}$ to be selected). Then B models are trained on these B datasets and used for prediction. These B predictions naturally provide a prediction interval, and its upper bound could be used for UCB-type bandit algorithms.

It's clear that batch bootstrapping for large N is impractical, and impossible for streaming data with unknown N. However, it's noted [9] [10] that each example i will appear Z_i times in the bootstrapped sample and Z_i is a random variable. More precisely, Z_i is distributed as a $Binom(N, \frac{1}{N})$, because during re-sampling the i-th example will have N chances to be picked, each with probability $\frac{1}{N}$. Importantly, this $Binom(N, \frac{1}{N})$ converges to a Poisson with rate 1 even for modest N (see Fig. 1).

These are interesting observations for real-world big data problems. Since we can just sample a weight from Poisson with rate 1 for each data *independently*, regardless of N, this naturally leads to an online bootstrapping framework that can handle arbitrary sized dataset in streaming mode.

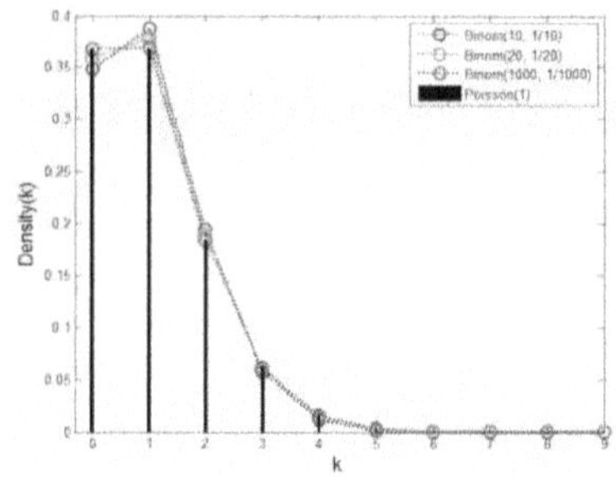

Figure 1: Binomial converges to Poisson for moderate sample sizes.

3.2 Learning and Prediction

The resulted learning and prediction algorithms are simple, see Fig. 2. Note only the number of bootstrapped models (B) needs to be specified.

```
Input: example E, number of bootstrapped model B

  Training:                     Prediction:
  for b = 1 to B                for b = 1 to B
  do                            do
    Z ~ Poisson(1)                p_b = predict(E, b)
    learn(E, Z, b)              done
  done                          return max(p)
```

Figure 2: Online bootstrapping for one example.

Note in both training and testing, each example is parsed online only once for all bootstrapping rounds. Only the importance weight is drawn repetitively. This largely mitigates example parsing (including I/O) overhead.

3.3 Learning Reductions

A closer look at Fig. 2 indicates that the proposed contextual bandit approach is built on some "learn" function. This leads to the idea of "learning reductions": we can take advantage of any existing effective and efficient learning algorithm or package that is (1) online and (2) weight-aware, as a black box. These criterions have been largely addressed by machine learning researchers recently. We use a logistic regression model (as we will focus on predicting the probability of clicks/purchases) described in [11], but the proposed framework is of more general use.

3.4 Feature Hashing

In real-world applications, the dimension of the context (feature) space can be quite large, and the space also evolves online. For example, it is common to use the item ID as a feature, thus learning from streaming data with new items leads to potentially unbounded number of features.

We apply feature hashing [13] to address this concern. The idea is to use a hash function to project the original feature space to a d-dimensional one (Fig. 3). We hash all features into the same space controlled by memory budget. Collisions are bounded to occur, but it is usually not a major concern in practice, as analyzed in [3] [13] and validated by our experiments

3.5 Memory Management

After introducing the hashing trick, size of each bootstrapped model is bounded, allowing for more efficient mem-

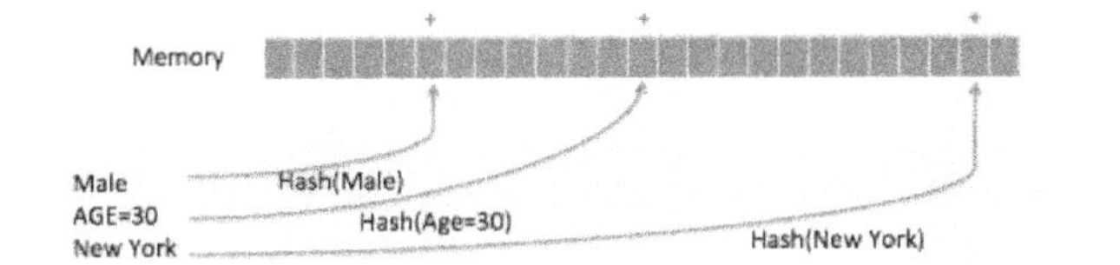

Figure 3: Illustration of hashing features to memory. In practice, features such as age are discretized into bins before hashing.

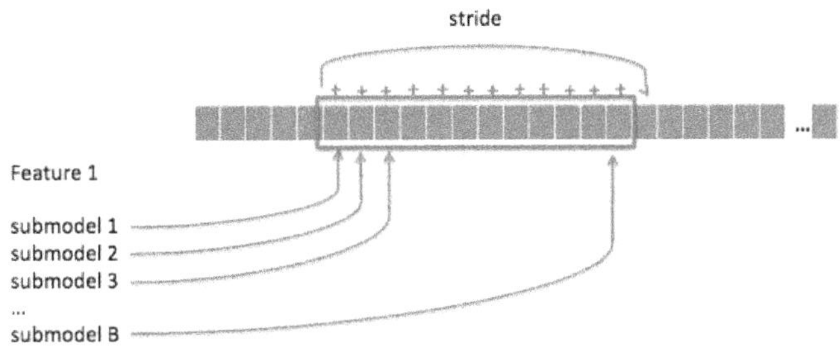

Figure 4: Illustration of memory management of one feature for different submodels. Each feature possesses a "stride" in memory.

ory management: we can safely pre-allocate available memory to hold all bootstrapping submodels.

As it is typical for online learning methods to conduct per-feature weight updates, weights for the same feature of different bootstrapping submodels are close to each other in memory (Fig. 4). These alleviate localize memory accesses and take advantage of caching.

3.6 Summary

We propose to use online bootstrapping as a heuristic for UCB-type contextual bandits. By applying feature hashing and learning reduction techniques, our algorithm is essentially parameter-free, handles arbitrary sized dataset, and takes advantage of existing models/implementations.

4. EXPERIMENTS

We first evaluate the efficiency of the proposed model, the running time of which grows sublinearly with the number of bootstrapping models. Then we move forward to both offline evaluation and real-world A/B testing using large-scale data. All of our experiments are run on a single personal computer (2.2 GHz, 16GB). Extending our framework to multiple machines is straightforward, but does not appear neccessary at our data scale due to its efficiency and streaming nature. We will open-source our implementation.

4.1 Dataset

We use a publicly available RCV1 dataset [6], a popular archive of categorized newswire stories for text categorization. It contains 781,265 examples and 80 features (using bag of words representation) per example on average. This dataset is mainly for running time evaluation.

We also use a real-world dataset that is gathered from Ticketmaster's weekly email recommendation product. This product serves over 40 million users in the US and sends out an email containing a list of around 20 recommended items (e.g. live events) to each subscribed user once a week. We log which items have been sent out to and clicked/purchased by each user for model training and offline evaluation.

Our contexts contain user's info (e.g. gender, age, race, geo, click/purchase history, etc.), item's info (e.g. category, price, rating, description, etc.). We also generate conjunction features that are the cartesian product of user info and item info. In our case, each user-item pair generates a context of around 100 dimensions. The actual context space is much larger because most features are categorical (e.g. gender=male and gender=female are different features).

4.2 Comparing methods

We compare with some popular approaches:

- TS(q_0): Thompson sampling randomly draws model coefficients from a posterior distribution and selects the item with largest predicted reward. The priori distribution is $N(0, q_0^{-1}I)$ [2].
- CF: Our productized collaborative filtering method. It is a variant of item-item based CF approach using implicit feedback [5].
- OBS: Online bootstrapping based contextual bandit, method proposed in this paper.
- LR: Contextual logistic regression, same as OBS with $B = 1$. This approach does not permit exploration.
- ϵ-greedy(ϵ): Randomly selects an item with probability ϵ and selects the item with the largest predicted reward (based on LR) with probability $1 - \epsilon$.
- Random: randomly selects an item, same as ϵ-greedy(1.0).

4.3 Offline Evaluation

4.3.1 Running Time

Though we are training B bootstrapping models in parallel, running time is expected to be faster than growing linearly with B, since (1) each example is parsed only once, (2) efficient memory management and (3) setting up overhead is only once. We evaluate on the RCV1 dataset and compare with estimated batch bootstrapping running time as $t \times B$ where t is time for $B = 1$ (single model). We believe this estimation is optimistic, as it is not even clear how to do batch resampling on large datasets.

We show results in Fig. 5. It shows sub-linear running time growth and no significant difference with different number of bootstrapping rounds. These can be explained as a lot of computation power is spent on example parsing (including disk I/O) and environment setting-up, while our approach can avoid repetitive example parsing and setting up environments for each submodel. Thus our strategy is particularly helpful for a dataset with many examples.

Note the absolute running time (in tens of seconds) on this over half-million sized dataset results from reducing online bootstrapping to an existing highly efficient implementation of [11]. We also observed better prediction performance by ensembles of predictions from bootstrapped models (i.e. bagging), but we omit details due to space constraints.

4.3.2 Weekly Recommendation Dataset

We conduct offline evaluation using our weekly email recommendation data. We evaluate precision@N on one week's data, using previous eight weeks' data for training. Training takes about 10 minutes for this million-sized dataset. We test on several weeks' data and saw consistent behavior so we only show one week's result in this paper. Also for

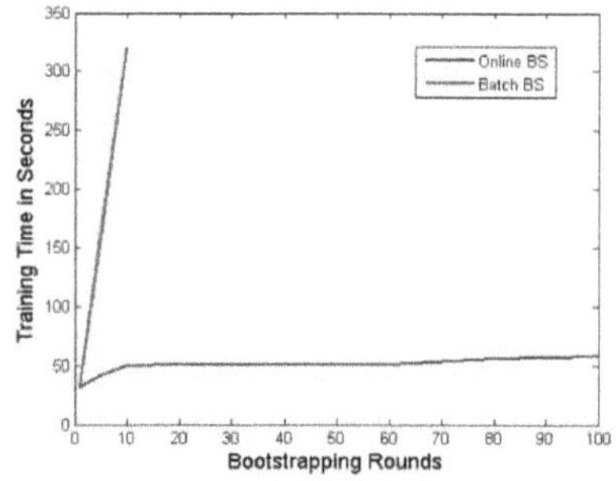

Figure 5: Speed comparison. Lower bound is calculated (some big numbers are not shown) for batch bootstrapping as pure training time, excluding time to generate samples with repetition.

models with randomization, the variance is neglectable so we only report the mean. For all comparing models with tunable parameters, we try different configurations and report the best result. We use $B = 5$ but saw robust results with a wide selection of B. The results are shown in Tbl. 1

Prec. @N	ϵ-greedy (0.01)	Rand	CF	TS (0.1)	LR	OBS
N=1	0.294	0.051	0.258	0.231	0.290	**0.312**
N=5	0.692	0.252	0.641	0.623	0.691	**0.709**
N=10	0.876	0.501	0.806	0.791	0.875	**0.885**

Table 1: Offline evaluation on the recommendation dataset.

We are particularly interested in Precision@1, as it is what an user sees immediately after opening the email. The proposed approach performs the best and improves upon CF by comparatively 20%. It should not be surprising that LR outperforms CF: LR still falls into our online learning framework that considers context and recent user feedback. Unguided exploration strategy such as ϵ-greedy only marginally improves upon LR in its best case, indicating the need for a guided exploration principle such as the one proposed in the paper.

We also tested OBS without using last 4 weeks' feedback, resulting in 0.265 for Precision@1, only marginally improving upon CF. This shows the necessity of a streaming framework that considers the evolving user preference drift.

4.4 Real-world A/B Testing

We have conducted real-world A/B testing on all Ticketmaster (over 40 million) subscribed users, comparing the proposed approach (OBS) with the existing CF method. We do not test other methods due to the possible risks and engineering overhead. To avoid leaking business-sensitive information, we report relative CTR and conversion lift in Tbl. 2. The differences passed z-test at 99% confidence level.

CTR Delivered	CTR Opened	Conversion Delivered	Conversion Opened
+9.56%	+8.51%	+10.70%	+9.64%

Table 2: Performance of OBS over CF in real-world A/B testing.

We attribute the better results on emails delivered over emails opened to the email previews being more relevant. The preview shows some info about top-ranked items and more relevant top results encourage more opens.

4.5 Model Transfer

We also show the model's generalization capability on a different product. The live events we deal with have timeliness, so we tested on a "last minute" email product that only recommend live events available in the near future. We directly use the model trained in the previous section and compare with a CF-based approach. The test is only rolled out among 1 million users so there is more variance. Results in Tbl. 3 show that, directly applying the learned model results in promising lifts, regardless of the data distribution drift between the two products.

CTR Delivered	CTR Opened	Conversion Delivered	Conversion Opened
+5.01%	+5.95%	+2.89%	+3.84%

Table 3: Performance of OBS over CF in another product.

5. CONLUSION

We provide a new contextual bandits strategy for personalized recommendation. By using online learning, feature hashing and learning reductions, the model can handle unbounded streaming data and take advantage of existing state-of-art. Its efficiency and effectiveness have been validated in both large-scale offline and online evaluations.

6. REFERENCES

[1] N. Ailon and M. Mohri. An efficient reduction of ranking to classification. *COLT*, 2008.

[2] O. Chapelle and L. Li. An empirical evaluation of thompson sampling. *NIPS*, 2011.

[3] O. Chapelle, E. Manavoglu, and R. Rosales. Simple and scalable response prediction for display advertising. *ACM TIST*, 2015.

[4] M. Ge, C. Delgado-Battenfeld, and D. Jannach. Beyond accuracy: Evaluating recommender systems by coverage and serendipity. *RecSys*, 2010.

[5] Y. Hu, Y. Koren, and C. Volinsky. Collaborative filtering for implicit feedback datasets. *ICDM*, 2008.

[6] D. D. Lewis, Y. Yang, T. Rose, and F. Li. Rcv1: A new benchmark collection for text categorization research. *JMLR*, 2004.

[7] L. Li, W. Chu, J. Langford, and R. E. Schapire. A contextual-bandit approach to personalized news article recommendation. *WWW*, 2010.

[8] A. Q. Macedo, L. B. Marinho, and R. L. T. Santos. Context-aware event recommendation in event-based social networks. *RecSys*, 2015.

[9] N. C. Oza and S. Russell. Online bagging and boosting. *AIStats*, 2001.

[10] Z. Qin, V. Petricek, N. Karampatziakis, L. Li, and J. Langford. Efficient online bootstrapping for large scale learning. *arXiv preprint arXiv:1312.5021*, 2013.

[11] S. Ross, P. Mineiro, and J. Langford. Normalized online learning. *UAI*, 2013.

[12] L. Tang, Y. Jiang, L. Li, C. Zeng, and T. Li. Personalized recommendation via parameter-free contextual bandits. *SIGIR*, 2015.

[13] K. Weinberger, A. Dasgupta, J. Attenberg, J. Langford, and A. Smola. Feature hashing for large scale multitask learning. *ICML*, 2009.

Multi-Word Generative Query Recommendation Using Topic Modeling

Matthew Mitsui
Department of Computer Science
Rutgers University
New Brunswick, NJ, USA, 08901
mmitsui@rutgers.edu

Chirag Shah
School of Communication and Information
Rutgers University
New Brunswick, NJ, USA, 08901
chirags@rutgers.edu

ABSTRACT

Query recommendation predominantly relies on search logs to use existing queries for recommendation, typically calculating query similarity metrics or transition probabilities from the log. While effective, such recommendations are limited to the queries, words, and phrases in the log. They hence do not recommend potentially useful, entirely novel queries. Recent query recommendation methods have proposed generating queries on a topical or thematic level, though current approaches are limited to generating single words. We propose a hybrid method for constructing multi-word queries in this generative sense. It uses Latent Dirichlet Allocation to generate a topic for exploration and skip-gram modeling to generate queries from the topic. According to additional evaluation metrics we present, our model improves diversity and has some room for improving relevance, yet offers an interesting avenue for query recommendation.

CCS Concepts

•**Information systems → Query suggestion;** *Personalization;* Document topic models; Retrieval effectiveness;

Keywords

Search session analysis; Diversity; User simulations; Exploratory search; Query recommendation; Latent Dirichlet Allocation

1. INTRODUCTION

Query recommendation dates back to least the early 2000s. Most approaches harness search logs - a set of users' search sessions - to make personalized recommendations to users. Each session contains information about a user's sequence of queries, clicks on search engine result pages (SERPs), and possibly time spent on results. Even without explicit relevance feedback on the logs from annotators, this data provides a rich source of implicit feedback - such as click-through behavior and dwell time - that can be used to quantify query satisfaction, page usefulness and pairwise query similarity scores. While query logs are indispensable for personalization, many algorithms either recommend queries directly from the logs or reformulated versions of prior queries. While effective on a large query log, this may work less well for smaller data. For recommending rarely-discovered, topic-relevant information or making session-based recommendations, long-tail queries become less likely to produce satisfactory results, necessitating novel query generation. This contrasts with reformulation approaches that suggest textually similar queries, recommending queries purely on topical relatedness to previous queries in a session.

In this paper, we discuss an approach to recommending novel queries that combines a user's session and the thematic structure of web pages to create new queries. We create recommendations using Latent Dirichlet Allocation and skip-gram modeling and apply new evaluation metrics to this problem setting. In Section 2, we discuss the necessary background information to understanding this work. In Section 3, we explain our algorithm. We outline our data set in Section 4. We give our performance metrics, results, and discussion in Section 5, and we conclude in Section 6. While there is room for improvement, our model improves diversity of actual performance and offers interesting possibilities.

RecSys '16, September 15-19, 2016, Boston , MA, USA
© 2016 ACM. ISBN 978-1-4503-4035-9/16/09...$15.00
DOI: http://dx.doi.org/10.1145/2959100.2959154

2. BACKGROUND

2.1 Query Recommendation

Some past and current query recommendation methods recommend queries directly from a query log. [1], for instance, clusters queries by similarity, offering similar substitutes for failing queries, and [4] offers suggestions by calculating explicit transition probabilities between queries in a log. Contrastingly, [11] uses query distance to recommend orthogonal queries - dissimilar queries that are similar enough to be topically relevant. Some methods generate new queries incrementally. [5], for instance, uses WordNet to replace words with their synonyms. While our approach recommends orthogonal queries like [11], unlike [11] and [5] it generates queries without incrementing from a base string.

Hence, our approach risks retrieving less relevant results. Non-zero transition probabilities in a query log give implicit relevance feedback. Our approach discards this feature for relevance in our algorithm (assuming no multitasking).

2.2 Topic Modeling in Query Suggestion

We attempt to address this loss of relevance feedback and capture diversity with topic models, modeling the topics a user has explored and recommending terms from unexplored topics. For at least the past decade, topic modeling has gained recent interest among researchers as an alternative approach to modeling documents. A commonly cited topic model is Latent Dirichlet Allocation (LDA) [2], which can infer the topic distribution of a document and bag-of-words distribution of a topic. [6, 8] have previously applied LDA to recommending queries. [6] only mapped existing queries to a thematic representation and recommend those queries. [8] only recommends single-word queries and generates virtual training "documents" by combining query sessions with an identical ending. This cannot be done with smaller data and may be insufficient for *exploratory search tasks* (see Task and Dataset). Our approach extends these efforts.

2.3 Evaluation Metrics

Typically, results of query recommendation are evaluated in a URL-based fashion. For instance, discounted cumulative gain sums up the relevance scores of each document in a list (e.g. query results) and tempers them according to their position in the list. Recent efforts like [9] evaluate whole session metrics; in particular, [9] defined URL-based measures like the coverage, unique relevant coverage, and likelihood of discovery of URLs for individual and collaborative tasks. Since our approach recommends new queries, it is likely that on smaller data, most URLs in a SERP have never been seen in our sessions. To our knowledge, most of the literature performs purely URL-based evaluation, so we define different effectiveness measures in our results.

3. ALGORITHM

We first train our LDA topic model $T = (\alpha, \beta_{1:K})$ over D, a set of web documents. α is a Dirichlet prior, and $\beta_k \in \beta_{1:K}$ a "topic", or a distribution over the vocabulary. For this paper, we trained on all of the pages linked through the top 10 URLs of SERPs in our log. All text - SERP snippets and web page text - is preprocessed through stopword removal and removing words with less than 4 characters. We also remove punctuation, numbers, and words with non-alphanumeric letters (e.g., hashtags).

Assume a user u in our query log has issued queries $Q_u = \{q_1, q_2, ..., q_h\}$ and has visited pages P_u in their entire session. We create simulations starting at each step $3 < t < h$; the completion of a simulation results in several injections $\{q_1, q_2, ..., q_t, q'_{t+1}, q'_{t+2}, ...\}$. At each step of the simulation, we concatenate the current SERP text (i.e. result snippets) of $\{q_1, q_2, ..., q_t\}$ and infer a topical distribution using T - call this distribution $\theta_{S,1:S,K}$. This tells us the proportions in which each topic has currently been explored by the user. We then select a topic for query generation and then generate the query (details discussed in Sections 3.1-3.2).

We issue the generated query q'_{t+1} using a commercial search API and inject it into the user's current set of queries, making $\{q_1, q_2, ..., q_t, q'_{t+1}\}$. We repeat the topic inference and injection loop until a timer in our algorithm reaches $|Q_u| + |P_u|$, the total number of pages visited and queries issued by user u in our actual log data. This stopping criterion simplifies and accommodates for individual user factors, such as page viewing time and user frustration. Each simulated query counts as a timestep, as do the first $|S|$ results, where $|S|$ is the size of a single SERP. See Algorithm 1 for a summarization of the algorithm.

3.1 Mining the Next Topic

After calculating $\theta_{S,1:S,K}$, we iterate through topics in ascending probability, to search for underrepresented yet relevant topics. We calculate topic k's relevance with a weighted divergence score against the SERPs' topic distribution:

$$Score(k) = \sum_{i=1}^{K} \theta_{S,i} \times JSD(\beta_i \parallel \beta_k) \quad (1)$$

Where JSD is the Jensen-Shannon Divergence score [7], a symmetric score based on KL-divergence. The first topic to score below 0.15 (chosen through trial and error) is chosen for query generation. We incrementally increase the threshold each time no satisfactory topics are found.

3.2 Query Generation from a Topic

After topic selection, we extract the topic's top 15 words and their topic-specific probabilities, as given by LDA. We generate 3-word queries randomly, sampling the first word from the topic probabilities. The remaining 2 words are then sampled from the skip-gram probabilities, conditioned on the first word. Skip-grams generalize n-grams; words are allowed to occur within a window of k words in order to be counted in the model. For smaller data, skip-grams can cope with data sparsity that can affect n-gram models, and they can be an effective smoothing method for language model estimation [10]. We used a 4-skip-3-gram model, i.e., we calculated the probabilities of sequences of 3 words (the most common query length in our data) that were no more than 4 words apart from each other. We trained our model (SG) on the titles of the web pages that were used for LDA, rather than the whole content; many non-stop words are irrelevant while titles tend to be related to the query.

```
Data:
T = (α,β_{1:K}), SG, Q_u, P_u, |S|- See Section 3 for
explanations
ts - current timestamp
Q_curr - queries currently issued by a user
index_best = Null;
while ts < |P_u| + |Q_u| do
    θ_{S,1:S,K} = T.evaluate(ConcatenateSERPs(Q_curr));
    for θ_{S,k} ∈ {min(θ_{S,1:S,K}), ..., max(θ_{S,1:S,K})} do
        if getWeightedDivergence(θ_{S,k},β_{1:K}) < .15 then
            index_best = index(θ_{S,k});
            break;
        end
    end
    qterms = BestTopicWords(β_{index_best},SG);
    q_new = IssueQuery(qterms);
    Q_curr = Q_curr + {q_new};
    ts += |S| + 1;
end
return Q_curr
```

Algorithm 1: Iterative version of the algorithm.

4. TASK AND DATASET

We applied our approach to *exploratory search task* data. Exploratory search tasks have been estimated to comprise 10% of search sessions and 25% of overall queries [3]. In these tasks, information needs are ill-structured and cannot

Topic	# users	> 3 SERPs	$\|Q_{uni}\|$	Avg. queries	$\|D\|$
TEC	13	9	99	12.63	513
HEA	16	15	148	10.13	915
ENT	11	11	159	14.72	581
ART	5	5	91	16	740
ENV	2	2	28	14	115

Table 1: Users, queries, and documents per topic

Algorithm	TEC	HEA	ENT	ART
Session	3.08	0.57	0.41	0.84
ORTH	3.01	2.06	0.69	1.81
LDA-SG	3.44	1.06	0.44	0.78

Table 2: Percent of on-topic words

be satisfied in a single query, and users engage in learning during the task [13]. Our queries could hit poorly explored areas in such lengthy tasks, increasing diversity while maintaining relevance. In our data, 29 users completed 47 exploratory search sessions on 5 topics: "Technology" (TEC), "Health and Wellness" (HEA), "Entertainment" (ENT), "Art and History" (ART), and "Environment and Energy" (ENV). Users were undergraduate participants recruited through open calls in e-mail lists at a local university, from majors such as Computer Science, Information Technology, Informatics, Nursing and Biological studies. Users completed a prompt within a 2-hour time limit and were provided monetary compensation. They were allowed to quit after a minimum of 1 hour but were incentivized with an additional reward for top performance. Users downloaded a Firefox plugin and conducted the task live through their web browsers, i.e., at any location at their convenience. Despite lack of lab supervision, users can conduct more natural searching behavior. Users selected search topics from a brief list ("Technology", "Health and Wellnes", etc.). After selection, they saw a full task description and could not retract their choices. They had a 5-minute warm up task before choosing the main task.

Our plugin recorded basic browsing behavior, like changing tabs and issuing queries. It had buttons for snipping page text that users highlight, reviewing the task description, and composing a final report on an online text editor. The plugin collected the content of users' SERP and web page visits live, by issuing curl and search API calls from our server, approximating results users saw at visitation time. We created topics we thought were unfamiliar enough to be unaffected by personalization from users' browsers.

Here is the task description (paraphrased) for TEC: "With the recent focus on security breaches and consumer data breaches, vulnerability in data and software has become an important topic of interest. You have been asked to write an article about data and software vulnerabilities; it should be around 1000 words. It should appeal to as many people as possible, including an unfamiliar, lay audience and people in affected businesses. It should cover different aspects of software vulnerabilities that are relevant to their daily lives. It should also focus on the measures taken to minimize these risks at industry, governments and consumer levels. You can use snippets to collect information that you deem useful for writing the report and copy them into your article."

Table 1 shows user and query counts for each topic. We trained a single LDA model once over the entire corpus of documents - the documents linked through users' first pages in their SERPs. We did this to simulate a real web environment absent of supervised topic labels on pages may not be available. We set the number of topics $K = 35$. We only used sessions with over 3 queries; others do not provide sufficient search results for our algorithm. We then filtered topics with less than 3 users as well. Many users issued over 3 queries, providing motivation for this algorithm.

Algorithm	TEC	HEA	ENT	ART
Session	11.63	14.74	7.89	7.35
ORTH	9.97	26.34	16.42	40.68
LDA-SG	9.21	20.03	8.39	31.02

Table 3: Percent of relevant ODP topics

Unit of Measure	TEC	HEA	ENT	ART
Words	0.06	1.11	1.15	0.83
ODP topics	11.01	15.73	12.69	4.32

Table 4: Percent of off-topic words and ODP topics covered by LDA-SG. (Results for LDA-SG only.)

5. RESULTS AND ANALYSIS

We compared our algorithm (LDA-SG) against the real user sessions ("Session" in the tables) and Vahabi et al. [11] (ORTH). ORTH is strictly recommends queries from the logs to diversify results. ORTH recommends queries that overlap with the most recent query by (0.0,0.06]. Due to sparse logs we incremented the ceiling of 0.06, eventually choosing a random candidate if no suitable ones could be found.

In light of Section 2.3, we chose lexical and ontological evaluation metrics instead of URL-based ones. Suppose we let $Words(Queries)$ be the set words in a sequence of queries (including SERP snippets), $E\_Words(T_i)$ be the set of topic-exclusive words for topic T_i, and $W = E\_Words(T_i) - \bigcup_{j \neq i} E\_Words(T_j)$ our score Cov(Queries,i) is $|Words(Queries) \cap W|$ divided by $|W|$. This measures the topic word coverage, or the percentage of words that a set of SERPs covers in topic i. If we substitute $W = \bigcup_{j \neq i} Words_{T_j}$ in Equation 2, we get our second measure: the percentage of off-topic words that are covered. The former measures diversity. The latter measures relevance as a penalty score, since the word "diabetes", for instance, belongs exclusively to the "Health and Wellness" topic and none of the others. We omit off-topic scores for actual user sessions; by definition, these results are all 0%. We similarly omit ORTH results for because all off-topic queries have 0.0 overlap due to a small query log.

Our ontological approach uses the Open Directory Project (ODP)[1] to convert URLs to topics. ODP is a web ontology that categorizes websites into hand-tailored topics, such as "Computers/Internet/Resources/Research" and has been used to categorize URLs for evaluation [14]. We convert all URLs in our simulations to their ODP categories (truncating URLs incrementally until a matching category can be found). Replacing words in the above equations with ODP categories gives us our ODP-based measures.

Our results are given in Tables 2-6. Our approach increases the percentage of topic-specific words and ODP categories (with a couple exceptions) over the baseline, suggest-

[1]http://www.dmoz.org

Table 5: Query sequences returned by our algorithm. Boldfaced queries are generated queries. The first sequence shows a shift from the original topic.

diet for type 2 diabetics, type 2 diabetes, risks of diabetic diet, exercise plans for type 2 diabetes, **diet healthy-eating clinic, information control solutions, animation degree campus-based, health guidelines micronutrients, diabetes stick-to-it plan**
diets for diabetics type 2, type 2 diabetes, type 2 diabetes causes, **diet claims clinic, health aetna featuring, diabetes weight loss, people diabetic cookbook**

Table 6: Top 10 words of returned LDA topics. Starred words belong to a sub-corpus (e.g. health) less dominant in the list (e.g. technology)

Topic 1: 'animated', 'animation', 'avatar', 'characters', 'computer', 'data'*, 'diabetes'*, 'disney', 'film', 'information'*
Topic 8: 'blood', 'body', 'data'*, 'diabetes', 'diet', 'exercise', 'film'*, 'food', 'glucose', 'health'

ing an increase in diversity. However, the our approach is not as diverse ORTH and is penalized on off-topic measures.

Interestingly, the penalty for off-topic words is small while the penalty for off-topic ODP categories is large. Off-topic words are those that exist *exclusively* in other sub-corpora, and likewise for off-topic ODP categories. Our scores suggest that many of the queries (and hence web pages) were from other topics, even though few of the words were exclusively from other topics. Assuming that topics do not mix in a single set of SERP results, this suggests that there is a large percentage of overlapping words between topics. This would suggest a shift between topics in our list of suggested queries, which is consistent with our data. See Tables 5 and 6. This suggests the need for perhaps a stronger method of topic segmentation that discounts for overlapping words.

6. CONCLUSION AND FUTURE WORK

In future work, we would need to address arbitrary parameter values chosen for proof of concept. Though obvious extrinsic evaluation metrics for cross-validation, like URL-based nDCG, are eliminated. Retrievability scores could fit but require large search logs (or simulations) for score estimates. We would have inferred the optimal number of topics with the online Hierarchical Dirichlet Process [12], but to our knowledge, implementations take the number of topics as a "truncation level" parameter. Also, the number of generated query terms could be probabilistically modeled from the log.

We could also improve our skip-gram method to generate queries more closely resembling human ones. We neglect the linguistic and information roles of stop words in real human queries (e.g. "rainbow" vs. "over the rainbow"), which would require further analysis. We could then add human judgments for evaluation, such as the comprehensibility of queries and whether they seemed to be human-generated.

We extended topic modeling-based methods of novel query generation. Our multi-word approach uses web documents as a lexical resource and attempts to maintain relevance that can be lost with topically-based generative approaches. We achieved higher diversity at the cost of relevance, and one desideratum of recommendation research is to close this gap while maximizing both. We believe this approach offers an interesting direction for query recommendation. If more widespread, topical recommendations could not only make recommendations at a topical level but could also increase the pool of unique queries in a log if users were to take the recommendations, improving non-generative methods.

7. ACKNOWLEDGMENTS

A portion of this work was supported by the US Institute of Museum and Library Services (IMLS) Career Development grant # RE-04-12-0105-12.

8. REFERENCES

[1] R. Baeza-Yates, C. Hurtado, and M. Mendoza. Query recommendation using query logs in search engines. In *Proceedings of the 2004 International Conference on Current Trends in Database Technology*, EDBT'04, pages 588–596. Springer-Verlag, 2004.

[2] D. M. Blei, A. Y. Ng, and M. I. Jordan. Latent dirichlet allocation. *J. Mach. Learn. Res.*, 3:993–1022, Mar. 2003.

[3] D. Donato, F. Bonchi, T. Chi, and Y. Maarek. Do you want to take notes?: Identifying research missions in yahoo! search pad. In *Proceedings of the 19th International Conference on World Wide Web*, WWW '10, pages 321–330, New York, NY, USA, 2010. ACM.

[4] Q. He, D. Jiang, Z. Liao, S. C. H. Hoi, K. Chang, E.-P. Lim, and H. Li. Web query recommendation via sequential query prediction. In *Proceedings of the 2009 IEEE International Conference on Data Engineering*, ICDE '09, pages 1443–1454, Washington, DC, USA, 2009. IEEE Computer Society.

[5] U. Hermjakob, E. Hovy, and C.-Y. Lin. Automated question answering in webclopedia: a demonstration. In *Proceedings of the second international conference on Human Language Technology Research*, pages 370–371. Morgan Kaufmann Publishers Inc., 2002.

[6] L. Li, G. Xu, Z. Yang, P. Dolog, Y. Zhang, and M. Kitsuregawa. An efficient approach to suggesting topically related web queries using hidden topic model. *World Wide Web*, 16(3):273–297, 2013.

[7] J. Lin. Divergence measures based on the shannon entropy. *Information Theory, IEEE Transactions on*, 37(1), 1991.

[8] S. Momtazi and F. Lindenberg. Generating query suggestions by exploiting latent semantics in query logs. *Journal of Information Science*, pages 1–12, 2015.

[9] C. Shah. Evaluating collaborative information seeking - synthesis, suggestions, and structure. *J. Inf. Sci.*, 40(4):460–475, Aug. 2014.

[10] N. Shazeer, J. Pelemans, and C. Chelba. Skip-gram language modeling using sparse non-negative matrix probability estimation. *CoRR*, abs/1412.1454, 2014.

[11] H. Vahabi, M. Ackerman, D. Loker, R. Baeza-Yates, and A. Lopez-Ortiz. Orthogonal query recommendation. In *Proceedings of the 7th ACM Conference on Recommender Systems*, RecSys '13, pages 33–40. ACM, 2013.

[12] C. Wang, J. W. Paisley, and D. M. Blei. Online variational inference for the hierarchical dirichlet process. In *International conference on artificial intelligence and statistics*, pages 752–760, 2011.

[13] B. M. Wildemuth and L. Freund. Assigning search tasks designed to elicit exploratory search behaviors. In *Proceedings of the Symposium on Human-Computer Interaction and Information Retrieval*, HCIR '12, pages 4:1–4:10, New York, NY, USA, 2012. ACM.

[14] X. Zhu, J. Guo, X. Cheng, P. Du, and H.-W. Shen. A unified framework for recommending diverse and relevant queries. In *Proceedings of the 20th International Conference on World Wide Web*, WWW '11, pages 37–46, New York, NY, USA, 2011. ACM.

Contrasting Offline and Online Results when Evaluating Recommendation Algorithms

Marco Rossetti
Department of Informatics, Systems and Communication
University of Milano-Bicocca, Italy
rossetti@disco.unimib.it

Fabio Stella
Department of Informatics, Systems and Communication
University of Milano-Bicocca, Italy
stella@disco.unimib.it

Markus Zanker
Faculty of Computer Science
Free University of Bozen-Bolzano, Italy
mzanker@unibz.it

ABSTRACT

Most evaluations of novel algorithmic contributions assess their accuracy in predicting what was withheld in an offline evaluation scenario. However, several doubts have been raised that standard offline evaluation practices are not appropriate to select the best algorithm for field deployment. The goal of this work is therefore to compare the offline and the online evaluation methodology with the same study participants, i.e. a within users experimental design. This paper presents empirical evidence that the ranking of algorithms based on offline accuracy measurements clearly contradicts the results from the online study with the same set of users. Thus the external validity of the most commonly applied evaluation methodology is not guaranteed.

Keywords

User study, Evaluation methodology, Experimental within users design

1. INTRODUCTION

From a methodological viewpoint research contributions in the field of recommender systems focus mainly on novel methods, that mainly come with the promise of more accurately identifying relevant content in a variety of application domains. For instance, the survey of Jannach et al. [7] gives evidence that validation of recommender systems research focuses mainly on offline evaluation scenarios. Thus, according to the paradigm of Machine Learning a predictive model is trained on a subset of the available data and it is optimized to correctly predict the withheld portions of the dataset. Due to the maturing of the field several works have been focusing on the methodological aspects of this evaluation approach in recommender systems research.

RecSys '16, September 15 - 19, 2016, Boston , MA, USA

ISBN 978-1-4503-4035-9/16/09...$15.00

DOI: http://dx.doi.org/10.1145/2959100.2959176

For instance, Said & Bellogín. [9] identified several inconsistencies when recommendation methods and offline evaluation practices are compared across different framework platforms. While this recent work focuses on the internal validity of offline evaluation practices other authors focus on the external validity. Research questions targeting the external validity are, for instance, if and how confirmed results from an offline evaluation can be generalized to a recommender system's encounter with real users. Therefore, in addition to offline evaluation on dead data many authors strongly advocate user-centric evaluation approaches [5, 11, 8]. Up to now several authors have reported results from comparing recommendation methods in an offline and an online evaluation setting [1, 4, 3] and did find evidence that algorithm performance in offline and online evaluation settings differs. However, none of the research works so far has been able to demonstrate in a *within users* experimental design statistically significant differences in algorithm performance between both evaluation settings. This paper's contribution therefore lies in presenting an innovative evaluation design that researches algorithms' precision and their ability to present novel and relevant items in offline and online evaluation settings.

2. STUDY DESIGN

2.1 Overview

The goal of this research is to assess the external validity of a comparative evaluation of different recommendation methods on offline data. We would therefore like to answer the following research questions:

1. Does the relative ranking of algorithms based on offline accuracy measurements predict the relative ranking according to an accuracy measurement in a user-centric evaluation?

2. Does the relative ranking of algorithms based on offline measurements of the predictive accuracy for long-tail items produce comparable results to a user-centric evaluation?

3. Do offline accuracy measurements allow to predict the utility of recommendations in a user-centric evaluation?

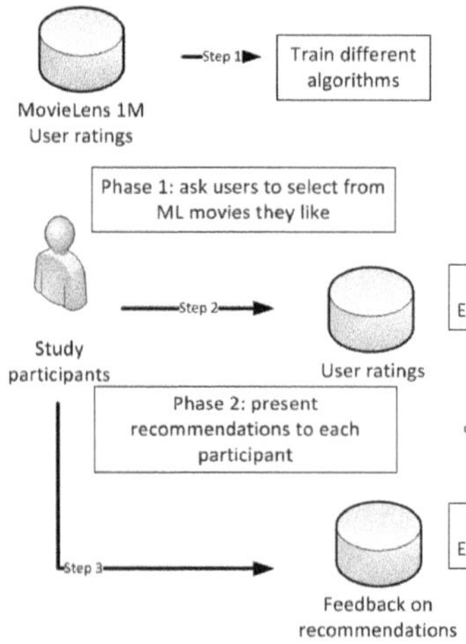

Figure 1: Big Picture

Figure 2: Screenshot of recommendations evaluation page.

For the purpose of answering these research questions we are employing a novel study design that compares offline and online measurements in a *within users* experimental design that is depicted in Figure 1. We are exploiting the MovieLens dataset in order to train different algorithms that will then be assessed according to the standard *offline* and *online* evaluation methodology by our study participants. In order to check for differences between offline and online methodology we selected four rather distinctive algorithms for this experimental setup:

1. Most-popular as a baseline algorithm, that is agnostic of the user's preferences and uniformly proposes the same very popular items to all users.
2. A matrix factorization model [12] with a 80 factor model that achieves highest offline accuracy based on a sensitivity analysis.
3. The same matrix factorization model, but with 400 factors, which is most accurate on long-tail items measured according to the proposition of [2].
4. Item-based nearest neighbour approach [10] as a simple memory-based recommendation mechanism, that recommends dissimilar sets of items compared with the other three algorithms.

Although there have been many different algorithms proposed recently the algorithm does not constitute a limitation of the findings in this study. This is because we focus on the different results of the same algorithms in an online and an offline setting and not on finding the most accurate algorithm according to a specific setting.

2.2 MovieLens Dataset

The dataset used to train the algorithms is the well-known *MovieLens 1M* (ML1M) dataset. This dataset contains 1,000,209 ratings from 6,040 users and 3,706 different movies. Ratings are integer values from an ordinal scale ranging from 1 to 5, where 5 is the best feedback. However, we wanted to ensure that efforts for our participants remain at acceptable levels and therefore decided to ask users only for unary preference statements. Therefore the ML data was transformed into unary user feedback. For each individual ML user record only 4 and 5 ratings that are greater than the user's average rating score were transformed into an unary *like* statement. Furthermore we considered only movies with an entry in the Freebase data repository in order to ensure the same data quality of movie descriptions when asking users for ratings or presenting recommendations. After this preprocessing the dataset consisted of 6,038 users and 3,086 movies. This data was then used to train the models for the four algorithms considered.

In the first phase we invited participants via our universities' mailing lists to browse our specifically developed movie portal and mark those items that they like. We designed and implemented a Django web application that offers users the possibility to participate at this user study from any location. In the first round users could access a portal that contained detailed information about all movies contained in the MovieLens dataset. The collected dataset contains positive feedback on items the user probably knows and likes and no feedback on items the user either dislikes or does not know. The algorithmic models trained on MovieLens could therefore be evaluated how accurate they were in predicting the liked items of our study participants in an offline evaluation scenario. The generation of the recommendation list for a user was performed using an all-but-one validation on the user data. In total 241 users have participated in the first phase that provided on average 137 unary ratings each.

2.3 Online evaluation

In the second round we invited first-round users to evaluate around twenty recommendations produced from these four different algorithms. Each algorithm computed 5 recommendations and we sorted them in a stratified way, such that the recommendations derived from each algorithm were equally distributed along the ranks. Since two or more algorithms can recommend the same item, the number of recommendations for each user went from a theoretical minimum of 5 to a maximum of 20 items, while the actual average was 17.37. Therefore users were asked to assess sequentially every recommended item and to answer a set of questions. For each recommended item a separate screen with information about the movie such as the title, the year of launch, the plot, the poster image extracted from Freebase and a snapshot of the related Wikipedia page was displayed (see Figure 2). The questionnaire items were the following:

- Did you already know about this movie before this recommendation? (Yes, No, Don't know)
- Have you already watched this movie? (Yes, No)
- Would you like to watch this movie (for the first time or once again if you have already watched it)? (Yes, No, Don't know)

With the first question we measure second order novelty [1], i.e. an item is considered novel if the user has never heard of it. We determine relevance of recommended items by asking about potential conversion, i.e. if the user considers to watch this movie. By combining answers from both questions we are able to identify *useful* recommendations, i.e. relevant items that the user did not yet know about.

In total 122 users returned to the second phase, out of which 100 provided their individual assessment to all recommended items. We selected these 100 users for our study and discarded data from all other users.

3. MEASUREMENT METHODOLOGY

One basic evaluation approach in recommender systems is borrowed from the field of Information Retrieval (IR). Ground truth is represented by a user $\times$ items matrix with binary rating values, where 1s indicate that the user liked the particular item and 0s indicate dislike or no rating. As users tend to give only positive ratings and ignore disliked items, the default assumption in an offline evaluation scenario is to treat unrated items as they were disliked. The standard IR measures are *Precision* and *Recall* where precision measures the share of True Positives in the list of recommended items while recall constitutes the share of True Positives among all items relevant for a specific user in ground truth. However, the semantics of these two basic IR measures are somewhat different in offline and online evaluation scenarios [6]:

- Offline scenario: True Positives might be underestimated, because users could like novel items that they did not know before and therefore no historic rating exists in ground truth. Correspondingly, False Positives might be overestimated. Due to this incompleteness of ground truth, many more items might be actually relevant for a specific user, but they are not recommended, thus also False Negatives might be underestimated.
- Online scenario: Only True and False Positives can be determined, if users are asked to rate all recommended items. Therefore, True Negatives and False Negatives remain unknown.

Based on these assumptions only Precision can be compared in our within users experiments in order to contrast online and offline evaluation results. Furthermore, we hypothesize that Precision in an offline evaluation scenario should be lower than Precision measured online due to mentioned underestimation of True Positives and the overestimation of False Positives in the offline setting. Furthermore, we also compute Precision for long tail items following the proposition of Cremonesi et al. [2], where the most popular items in the dataset are treated as negatives. The most popular items that could aggregate one third of all positive ratings in the dataset are considered as belonging to the short head.

Table 1: Accuracy statistics for all items, long tail items and useful recommendations

Setting		I2I	MF80	MF400	POP
All Items	Offline	0.438	0.504	0.454	0.34
All Items	Online	0.546	0.598	0.604	0.516
Long Tail	Offline	0.28	0.018	0.36	0
Long Tail	Online	0.356	0.054	0.528	0
Useful	Online	0.126	0.082	0.116	0.026

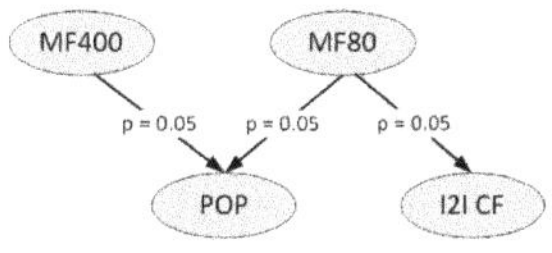

Figure 3: Precision offline

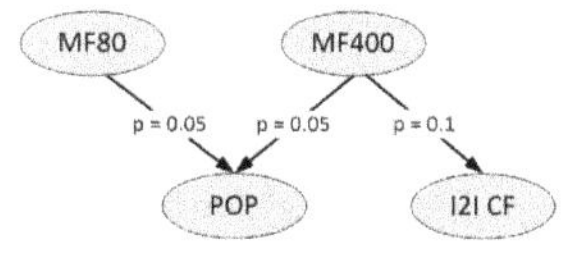

Figure 4: Precision online

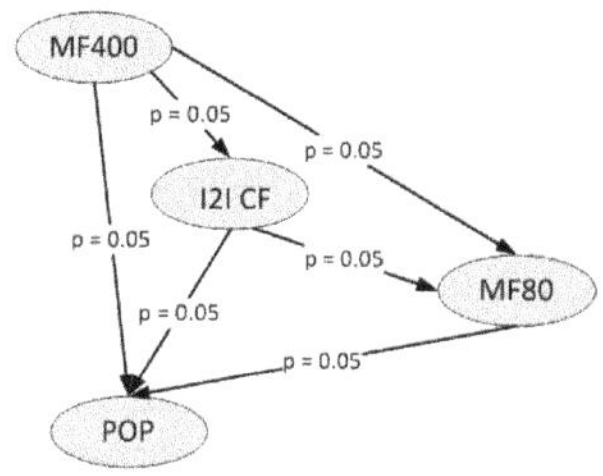

Figure 5: Domination graph for Precision on long tail items (offline and online)

4. RESULTS

Research question 1 is about the relative ranking of algorithms in offline and online accuracy assessments. In Table 1 the Precision measurements for all four algorithms and both evaluation settings are given. Furthermore, Figure 3 gives the domination graph based on pairwise comparison of a Wilcoxon signed rank test. An outgoing arc means that the method outperforms the method it is pointing to with a p-value below the significance level denoted on the arc. Both matrix factorization techniques perform better than the popularity baseline and the 80 factor model also clearly outperforms the I2I nearest neighbor method. However the online measurements clearly contradict this picture. As depicted in Figure 4 the 400 factor model outperforms the I2I at a 10% error rate, but the 80 factor model does not. Therefore this study gives empirical evidence that statistically significant differences measured in an offline evaluation scenario could not be confirmed in an online study.

Due to the strong bias of traditional accuracy measurements on popular items, Cremonesi et al. [2] proposed to exclude the most popular items from accuracy measurements (i.e. count correct predictions of very popular items as False Positives). Research Question 2 therefore asks if Precision on long tail items in offline measurements more reliably predicts the results that can be achieved in the online setting. Table 1 gives the actual figures and Figure 5 presents the domination graph. The Precision measurement of long tail items seems to better discriminate between methods and leads to exactly the same statistically significant ranking of algorithms in both evaluation settings. Obviously it clearly contradicts the offline Precision measurement, the 80 factor

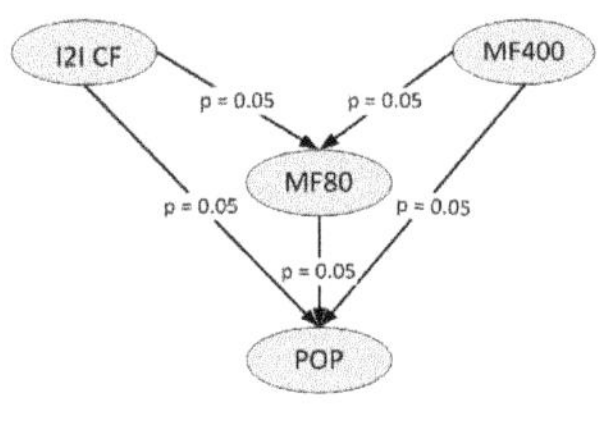

Figure 6: Domination graph based on Precision for items users liked and did not know (online)

model is by far worse in proposing non popular items than the 400 factor model or the I2I neighborhood model.

Finally the third research question explicitly explores the utility of recommendations. We simply define *useful recommendations* as propositions the user likes but did not yet know. We question if accuracy measurements on offline data provide an indication if an algorithm will be able to make more useful recommendations to users. In Table 1 Precision figures for useful recommendations are given, that are obviously much smaller than Precision on all and long tail items. When again testing for statistically significant differences the ranking of algorithms looks completely different from where we started in Figure 3. I2I collaborative filtering and the 400 factor model seem to be on par and both clearly outperform the two other methods. Neither traditional Precision measurements nor the proposed Precision of long tail items measure by [2] were able to predict this algorithm ranking by offline experiments. Although I2I CF seemed to recommend more popular items than the 400 factor model, the neighborhood method did still very good in identifying items that were novel to our study participants. Consequently, the presented empirical results clearly challenge the assumption of external validity of common evaluation practices of recommender systems and should therefore stimulate further methodological work into this direction.

5. CONCLUSIONS

The vast majority of the literature on recommender systems apply offline evaluation methodologies to assess the quality of the proposed approaches [7]. However, the external validity of such methodologies has been frequently questioned and recent works tried to compare offline and online evaluations. In this work we described a novel comparison approach between an offline evaluation protocol and an online user study. A dataset with *like* statements by 100 users on Movielens movies has been collected and accuracy statistics for models trained on the Movielens dataset have been evaluated on the collected dataset. These statistics have been compared with online statistics collected with a user study, where the same 100 users answered a set of questions on around 20 recommendations proposed to them. This work showed that offline precision underestimates online precision when both are considering all items and only long tail items. Furthermore, offline precision measurement does not provide the same ranking of algorithms as online precision does. Finally, the real utility for users of previously unknown but relevant recommended items determined on an online user study ranks algorithm in such a way that is not reproducible with offline evaluation metrics, neither on all items nor only on long tail items. Such results are a further clue that the external validity of commonly used offline evaluation protocols is not always guaranteed.

6. REFERENCES

[1] Paolo Cremonesi, Franca Garzotto, and Roberto Turrin. Investigating the persuasion potential of recommender systems from a quality perspective: An empirical study. *ACM Trans. Interact. Intell. Syst.*, 2(2):11:1–11:41, June 2012.

[2] Paolo Cremonesi, Yehuda Koren, and Roberto Turrin. Performance of recommender algorithms on top-n recommendation tasks. In *Proceedings of the fourth ACM conference on Recommender systems*, RecSys '10, pages 39–46, New York, NY, USA, 2010. ACM.

[3] Michael D. Ekstrand, F. Maxwell Harper, Martijn C. Willemsen, and Joseph A. Konstan. User perception of differences in recommender algorithms. In *Proceedings of the 8th ACM Conference on Recommender Systems*, RecSys '14, pages 161–168, New York, NY, USA, 2014. ACM.

[4] Florent Garcin, Boi Faltings, Olivier Donatsch, Ayar Alazzawi, Christophe Bruttin, and Amr Huber. Offline and online evaluation of news recommender systems at swissinfo.ch. In *Proceedings of the 8th ACM Conference on Recommender Systems*, RecSys '14, pages 169–176, New York, NY, USA, 2014. ACM.

[5] Jonathan L. Herlocker, Joseph A. Konstan, Loren G. Terveen, and John T. Riedl. Evaluating collaborative filtering recommender systems. *ACM Trans. Inf. Syst.*, 22(1):5–53, January 2004.

[6] D. Jannach, M. Zanker, A. Felfernig, and G. Friedrich. *Recommender Systems An Introduction.* Cambridge University Press, 2010.

[7] D. Jannach, M. Zanker, M. Ge, and M. Groening. Recommender systems in computer science and information systems - a landscape of research. In *13th International Conference on Electronic Commerce and Web Technologies*, pages 76–87. Springer, 2012.

[8] Pearl Pu, Li Chen, and Rong Hu. A user-centric evaluation framework for recommender systems. In *Proceedings of the Fifth ACM Conference on Recommender Systems*, RecSys '11, pages 157–164, New York, NY, USA, 2011. ACM.

[9] Alan Said and Alejandro Bellogín. Comparative recommender system evaluation: Benchmarking recommendation frameworks. In *Proceedings of the 8th ACM Conference on Recommender Systems*, RecSys '14, pages 129–136, New York, NY, USA, 2014. ACM.

[10] Badrul Sarwar, George Karypis, Joseph Konstan, and John Riedl. Item-based collaborative filtering recommendation algorithms. In *Proceedings of the 10th international conference on World Wide Web*, WWW '01, pages 285–295, New York, NY, USA, 2001. ACM.

[11] Guy Shani and Asela Gunawardana. Evaluating recommendation systems. In Francesco Ricci, Lior Rokach, Bracha Shapira, and Paul B. Kantor, editors, *Recommender Systems Handbook*, pages 257–297. Springer US, 2011.

[12] Vikas Sindhwani, Serhat S. Bucak, Jianying Hu, and Aleksandra Mojsilovic. One-class matrix completion with low-density factorizations. In *Proceedings of the 2010 IEEE International Conference on Data Mining.*

Adaptive, Personalized Diversity for Visual Discovery

Choon Hui Teo
Amazon
choonhui@amazon.com

Houssam Nassif
Amazon
houssamn@amazon.com

Daniel Hill
Amazon
daniehil@amazon.com

Sriram Srinavasan
UC Santa Cruz
ssriniv9@ucsc.edu

Mitchell Goodman
Amazon
migood@amazon.com

Vijai Mohan
Amazon
vijaim@amazon.com

S. V. N. Vishwanathan
Amazon & UC Santa Cruz
vishy@amazon.com

ABSTRACT

Search queries are appropriate when users have explicit intent, but they perform poorly when the intent is difficult to express or if the user is simply looking to be inspired. Visual browsing systems allow e-commerce platforms to address these scenarios while offering the user an engaging shopping experience. Here we explore extensions in the direction of adaptive personalization and item diversification within Stream, a new form of visual browsing and discovery by Amazon. Our system presents the user with a diverse set of interesting items while adapting to user interactions. Our solution consists of three components (1) a Bayesian regression model for scoring the relevance of items while leveraging uncertainty, (2) a submodular diversification framework that re-ranks the top scoring items based on category, and (3) personalized category preferences learned from the user's behavior. When tested on live traffic, our algorithms show a strong lift in click-through-rate and session duration.

Keywords

Machine Learning; Submodular Functions; Diversity; Personalization; Explore-Exploit; Multi-Armed Bandits

1. INTRODUCTION

The brick-and-mortar shopping experience is characterized by visual browsing where the user is able to quickly scan a large number of potential purchases. The user has a high potential to discover new items while maintaining the ability to focus attention on items of particular interest. This problem of discoverability is more challenging in e-commerce where it can be difficult to expose the entirety of an online retailer's catalog. The in-store browsing experience is not well-replicated by search engines that restrict item discovery to items relevant to an explicit search query.

RecSys '16 September 15-19, 2016, Boston , MA, USA

ACM ISBN 978-1-4503-4035-9/16/09.

DOI: http://dx.doi.org/10.1145/2959100.2959171

Therefore, an online visual browsing experience may greatly aid users in item discovery.

One effort in this direction is Amazon Stream (figure 1), a new website for fashion discovery developed by Amazon (www.amazon.com/stream). Stream enables users to easily discover popular, new, and relevant fashionable items without the need for search queries or to sieve through less relevant items. Toward this end, we have built a personalizable system that ranks and diversifies items scored by an explore-exploit algorithm. These items are presented to the user as an infinite scroll where each item can be interacted with by clicking. This paper outlines elements of our diverse and personalized visual shopping experience approach.

Figure 1: Screenshot of www.amazon.com/stream.

2. SCORING ITEM RELEVANCE

As the first step in generating the stream, we score each item in the Stream catalog for relevance to our users. We use click probability $P(click \mid item\ is\ viewed)$ to quantify relevance. *Click* refers to any of the following activities: save item as favorite, visit the item's detail page, or open the modal window for the item.

We learn this probability distribution by using a Bayesian

Linear Probit regression [7] that maps item attributes onto click probabilities. Item attributes are represented by categorical variables. They include product features such as brand, color, department, price, size, as well as a unique identifier for each item. The regression model learns a set of weights where each weight represents the contribution of a single attribute value to the click probability. When evaluating an item, we say that a weight x_i is active if its corresponding attribute is present in the item. Thus, the expected click probability of an item is given by

$$P(click \mid item\ is\ viewed) = \Phi^{-1}(\sum_{x_i\ is\ active} x_i) \quad (1)$$

where $\Phi^{-1}(\cdot)$ is the probit function. We assume model weights are generated independently from a prior Normal distribution. As we observe user actions, we update the active weights posterior distributions accordingly [7].

Our catalog consists of hundreds of thousands of items with thousands of items added or purged daily. The expected click probability may unduly favor popular items over underexposed or recently added items. This is because underexposed items will likely be associated with undertrained model weights that potentially underestimate the true click probability. This poses an exploration-exploitation dilemma: balancing exploiting highly relevant items with exploring undersampled sections of the catalog. Multi-armed bandit algorithms such as Thompson sampling [13] and Upper Confidence Bound [3] solve this problem. Here we use a Thompson sampling approach to score items as it performs well under delayed feedback [4].

We apply Thompson sampling by sampling each model weight from its posterior distribution conditioned on the training data. We then use the sampled weights to compute equation (1) for each item. Under this procedure, an item will receive a score close to its expected click probability unless its attributes are associated with highly uncertain model weights. Therefore, the items with the highest scores will be a mix of popular products with high expected values (an exploitation strategy) and underexposed products that were randomly scored high above their expected value (an exploration strategy).

Finally, we note that the customer controls the number of products viewed via scrolling. For simplicity we have omitted a model of customer browsing that predicts the number of views per session. However, such a model would allow us to estimate the expected clicks per session directly rather than the expected clicks per item viewed.

3. SUBMODULAR DIVERSIFICATION

We now have a set of items that are scored based on both their relevancy and exposure. Similar items tend to be assigned similar scores, so ranking these items by their scores creates a list where highly similar items are clustered together. However, our user experience studies indicate that a diverse item list helps users discover relevant items faster, as it exposes more variety in a fixed number of slots [11]. Similar to cases in web search [1], blog posts [5], news articles [2] and music recommendation [11], we apply diversification to alleviate information redundancy.

We formulate the selection and ranking of a diverse subset of items as a submodular optimization problem [6]. Let $\mathcal{A} := \{\mathbf{a}_1, \ldots, \mathbf{a}_n\}$ denote the attribute vectors for a set of n items. All attribute vectors are one-hot encoded in d-dimensions such that $\mathbf{a}_i \in \{0,1\}^d$. Let $\mathbf{w}$ denote a d-dimensional vector which encodes user preferences for each of the d item attributes. In addition, let $s(\mathbf{a})$ denote a function which maps an item to a real-valued utility score such as the click probability. A submodular objective function ρ for selecting k items from $\mathcal{A}$ is given by

$$\rho(\mathcal{A}_k, \mathbf{w}) = \left\langle \mathbf{w}, \log\left(1 + \sum_{\mathbf{a}_i \in \mathcal{A}_k} \mathbf{a}_i\right)\right\rangle + \sum_{a_i \in \mathcal{A}_k} s(\mathbf{a}_i), \quad (2)$$

where $\mathcal{A}_k$ is a subset of $\mathcal{A}$ of size k. We use the convention of applying the logarithm to a vector's individual components. The optimal subset is given by

$$\mathcal{A}_k^* := \operatorname*{argmax}_{\mathcal{A}_k \subseteq \mathcal{A}, |\mathcal{A}_k|=k} \rho(\mathcal{A}_k, \mathbf{w}). \quad (3)$$

In equation (2), the weight w_j emphasizes the importance of the jth attribute to a user. By summing over $\mathbf{a}_i$ we obtain the number of times that attribute occurs in the collection $\mathcal{A}_k$. However, the utility of each attribute does not grow linearly with its count. Instead, the logarithmic term ensures that the incremental utility of the jth attribute diminishes as the number of items with j attributes increases in $\mathcal{A}_k$. In other words, if a user loves shoes, showing only shoes does not lead to a good user experience. The scale of $s(\mathbf{a})$ can be tuned to adjust the relative importance of the item's utility.

Equation (3) is a special case of the NP-hard maximum set cover problem. Nevertheless, we can use an iterative greedy procedure to obtain a near-optimal solution [12]:

$$\mathcal{A}_0 := \emptyset \text{ and } \mathcal{A}_{i+1} := \mathcal{A}_i \cup \left\{ \operatorname*{argmax}_{\mathbf{a} \in \mathcal{A} \setminus A_i} \rho(\mathcal{A}_i \cup \{\mathbf{a}\}, \mathbf{w}) \right\}, \quad (4)$$

with a runtime complexity of $O(dkn)$. We further boost efficiency by using the CELF lazy evaluation algorithm [5, 9].

We also optimize the diversification process by transforming the attribute vector space into a single categorical space. This is achieved by mapping each possible attribute vector to a unique category. We restrict the size of this categorical space by coarsening our representation of attributes, such as price, and eliminating attributes that do not need to be diversified, such as average rating in customer reviews. The final set for diversification includes on the order of 100 mutually exclusive categories.

4. PERSONALIZATION

Category weights $\mathbf{w}$ in equation (2) control the trade-off between item utility and category popularity for selecting and ranking items. Unlike methods such as [14] and [2], we do not optimize these weights directly. This allows us to exploit user behavioral data that was not subject to diversification. In the following sections, we describe the procedure for learning global and personalized category weights.

4.1 Learning Adaptive Global Weights

Though items in the stream are displayed in a grid layout (figure 1), we assume that users scan them linearly from left to right and top to bottom. Hence, we can leverage existing work on click modeling with linear positional bias correction.

To learn the weights $\mathbf{w}$ in equation (2), we compared logistic regression, clicks over expected clicks [15], and click-thru-rate (CTR) with additive smoothing. Each model was tested on several weeks of historical click logs. Even though the CTR approach does not include corrections for position bias, we found that the three methods gave similar results. We therefore opted to use CTR with additive smoothing as it is simple to implement yet provides additional controls to handle update cycle fluctuations.

Let c_j and v_j represent the number of clicks and views, respectively, for items from the jth category. Under the CTR with additive smoothing model, the weight for the jth category w_j is estimated as:

$$w_j = \frac{c_j + \alpha}{v_j + \alpha + \beta}, \tag{5}$$

where α and β are priors that enforce minimum category weights. α and β can be tuned based on traffic volume to avoid dramatic fluctuations in update intervals. In fact, one can interpret w_j as distributed according to a Binomial distribution whose parameter p_j is drawn from a Beta distribution with parameters α and β estimated from data.

4.2 Learning User Specific Weights

The adaptively tuned category weights described in the previous section were derived from the aggregate clicks of all users. They capture the general popularity of the categories but not the interests of particular users. To personalize the presenation of items and categories, we need to first build a user model. Unlike some personalized applications where user feedback is immediate and irreversible, our model must handle delayed feedback and react quickly and efficiently to *evolving* preferences where a positive indicator of interest may no longer be predictive at a later date.

4.2.1 User Modeling

User modeling methods such as matrix factorization [8] and hierarchical Bayesian models [10] are not directly applicable in our case because these methods work best with a massive collection of data from all users, and are thus less sensitive to changing patterns in a small fraction of training records. Instead, we model the uth user's level of interest in the d categories as a random vector $\mathbf{w}_u$ drawn from a Dirichlet distribution parameterized by $\boldsymbol{\alpha}_0$. The distribution of a user's clicks on each category is denoted as $\mathbf{c}_u$ and is modeled as a random variable drawn from a Multinomial distribution parameterized by the interest vector and the user's total number of clicks m_u:

$$\mathbf{w}_u \sim \text{Dirichlet}(\boldsymbol{\alpha}_0), \tag{6}$$

$$\mathbf{c}_u \sim \text{Multinomial}(\mathbf{w}_u, m_u). \tag{7}$$

The posterior distribution of the user interest vector $\mathbf{w}_u$ is given proportionally by

$$P(\mathbf{w}_u \mid \mathbf{c}_u, \boldsymbol{\alpha}_0) \propto P(\mathbf{c}_u \mid \mathbf{w}_u) P(\mathbf{w}_u \mid \boldsymbol{\alpha}_0). \tag{8}$$

As Dirichlet is conjugate prior for the Multinomial distribution, this posterior is also Dirichlet with mean $\hat{\mathbf{w}}_u$:

$$\hat{\mathbf{w}}_u = (\mathbf{c}_u + \boldsymbol{\alpha}_0) \| \mathbf{c}_u + \boldsymbol{\alpha}_0 \|_1^{-1}. \tag{9}$$

We estimate the personalized weight vector $\mathbf{w}_u$ from the user's past clicks $\mathbf{c}_u = (c_{u1}, \ldots, c_{ud})$ where $c_{uj} \in \mathbb{N}$ is the number of clicks for category j. Dirichlet prior parameter vector $\boldsymbol{\alpha}_0$ can be chosen to match pre-specified business rules or to highlight certain category preferences.

In addition to being simple to implement, this Multinomial-Dirichlet user model allows straightforward incorporation of different types of user signals by adding them as counts to $\mathbf{c}_u$. Similarly, evolving preferences are handled by deducting older signals from $\mathbf{c}_u$. Finally, the personalized diversification can be achieved by plugging the estimated user interest vector $\hat{\mathbf{w}}_u$ into equation (2).

4.2.2 User Click Signal Diffusion

User interests are correlated between different categories. For example, a male interested in high end fashion is likely interested in both suits and expensive watches. This concept is especially useful when users have concentrated clicks on only a few categories, which would otherwise tend to inhibit diversified recommendations.

To ensure a user is exposed to related categories, we diffuse our Dirichlet updates between categories. In addition to a user's click incrementing the item's specific category count, the update is diffused across *related* categories. Let $\mathbf{M}$ be a d-by-d matrix where the entry M_{ij} is the ratio of the number of users who clicked items from both categories i and j to the number of users who clicked items from category j. To alleviate noise, we use only the top categories each user has actively interacted with. The *smoothed* interest vector $\tilde{\mathbf{w}}_u$ of the user interest vector $\hat{\mathbf{w}}_u$ of equation (9) becomes:

$$\tilde{\mathbf{w}}_u = \mathbf{M}\,\hat{\mathbf{w}}_u \,\|\, \mathbf{M}\,\hat{\mathbf{w}}_u \,\|_1^{-1}. \tag{10}$$

There are several common approaches for quantifying the pairwise association between two categories, such as point-wise mutual information or Pearson's correlation coefficients. We use the asymmetric conditional probability that "users who like category i also like category j" because we have observed such user behavior patterns in our data. Moreover, the leading eigenvector of the co-interest probability matrix $\mathbf{M}$ can be seen as a global interest vector, towards which equation (10) smooths the user interest vector $\hat{\mathbf{w}}_u$.

5. EXPERIMENTS

We conducted several online experiments to test the effectiveness of the methods presented above. We evaluated the treatment impact on engagement by calculating session duration, number of items viewed, and total click-through-rate. Each experiment lasted at least one week and involved at least 100,000 users per group. Some statistics are reported for population subsets of at least 10,000 users per group. Statistical significance was determined via Welch's t-test. Table 1 shows experimental results. Columns should not be compared directly to each other, as each experiment's control is different. Columns confer incremental improvements on top of the previous treatment.

5.1 Submodular Diversification

We first compared our submodular diversifier of Section 3 to a simpler approach where categorical weights and item scores are considered separately. The model of section 2 assigns a score to each item. Within each category, we rank the items in descending order. We calculate a multinomial distribution over item categories using global click propensities. For each slot in the stream, we first sample a category from the multinomial, and then fill it with that category's highest scoring item.

Experimental results (Table 1, column 2) show that, within the same session duration, the amount of items viewed by the users subjected to submodular diversification decreased

	Submodular diversifier	Adaptive weights	Personalized weights
Duration	0.05%	**5.39%**	1.10%
Views	**-1.32%**	**1.08%**	**-4.95%**
CTR	**9.82%**	**8.29%**	**12.58%**

Table 1: Experimental results evaluated using per-session engagement metrics: duration, aggregated view count, and aggregated click-through-rate. Column 2 shows incremental changes between a *submodular vs multinomial* diversifier. Column 3 shows incremental changes of *adaptive global category weights vs static manual weights.* Column 4 shows incremental changes for *personalized category weights vs global weights.* Highlighted results are statistically significant at the 0.05 level.

by 1.32% while CTR increased by 9.82%. The submodular diversifier produces a more diverse stream as categories are penalized more aggressively for being shown repeatedly. These results are consistent with our expectation of users being more interested in diversified streams.

5.2 Adaptive Category Weights

In a second experiment, we tested the impact of learning adaptive category weights from global click propensities as described in Section 4.1. We compared a submodular diversifier that uses the adaptive weights, versus one that uses a set of weights chosen manually by Amazon fashion experts. Experimental results (Table 1, column 3) show that adaptive weights greatly out-performed manual weights. CTR increased by 8.29% and session duration increased by 5.39%. This indicates that users are highly sensitive to the categorical mix of their experience.

5.3 Personalization

In our final experiment, we exposed users to category weights that were adapted to their own click behavior, as described in Section 4.2. These weights were calculated for users whose history included at least 10 clicks, so this experiment only applied to the most active users. In the control group, users were exposed to streams built using non-personalized weights. Experimental results (Table 1, column 4) show that personalized weights yielded a 12.58% increase in CTR with almost no impact on duration. Interestingly, the amount of items that were viewed in the stream decreased by 4.95%. This indicates that users with personalized diversity weights had a more efficient experience where they interacted with more items while scrolling through less.

6. CONCLUSION

We present Amazon Stream, a visual browsing system that emphasizes adaptive and personalized diversity in user experience. Such methods can be applied to any online system where the user seeks to discover content in the absence of an explicit search query. Our experimental results show the tangible incremental impact on key engagement metrics of submodular diversification, adaptive global weights, and personalization.

Acknowledgments.

The authors thank Charles Elkan, Matthias Seeger, and the anonymous reviewers for their helpful comments.

References

[1] R. Agrawal, S. Gollapudi, A. Halverson, and S. Ieong. Diversifying search results. In *Proceedings of the Second ACM International Conference on Web Search and Data Mining*, pages 5–14. ACM, 2009.

[2] A. Ahmed, C. H. Teo, S. V. N. Vishwanathan, and A. Smola. Fair and balanced: Learning to present news stories. In *Proceedings of the fifth ACM international conference on Web search and data mining*, pages 333–342. ACM, 2012.

[3] P. Auer. Using confidence bounds for exploitation-exploration trade-offs. *The Journal of Machine Learning Research*, 3:397–422, 2003.

[4] O. Chapelle and L. Li. An empirical evaluation of thompson sampling. In *Advances in neural information processing systems*, pages 2249–2257, 2011.

[5] K. El-Arini, G. Veda, D. Shahaf, and C. Guestrin. Turning down the noise in the blogosphere. In *Proceedings of SIGKDD international conference on Knowledge discovery and data mining*, pages 289–298, 2009.

[6] S. Fujishige. *Submodular functions and optimization*, volume 58. Elsevier, 2005.

[7] T. Graepel, J. Q. Candela, T. Borchert, and R. Herbrich. Web-scale bayesian click-through rate prediction for sponsored search advertising in microsoft's bing search engine. In *Proceedings of International Conference on Machine Learning (ICML)*, pages 13–20, 2010.

[8] Y. Koren, R. Bell, and C. Volinsky. Matrix factorization techniques for recommender systems. *Computer*, 42(8):30–37, 2009.

[9] J. Leskovec, A. Krause, C. Guestrin, C. Faloutsos, J. VanBriesen, and N. Glance. Cost-effective outbreak detection in networks. In *Proceedings of the 13th ACM SIGKDD international conference on Knowledge discovery and data mining*, pages 420–429. ACM, 2007.

[10] Y. Low, D. Agarwal, and A. J. Smola. Multiple domain user personalization. In *Proceedings of the 17th ACM SIGKDD international conference on Knowledge discovery and data mining*, pages 123–131. ACM, 2011.

[11] H. Nassif, K. O. Cansizlar, M. Goodman, and S. V. N. Vishwanathan. Diversifying music recommendations. In *Proceedings of Machine Learning for Music Discovery Workshop at 33rd International Conference on Machine Learning (ICML)*, 2016.

[12] G. L. Nemhauser, L. A. Wolsey, and M. L. Fisher. An analysis of approximations for maximizing submodular set functions i. *Mathematical Programming*, 14(1):265–294, 1978.

[13] W. R. Thompson. On the likelihood that one unknown probability exceeds another in view of the evidence of two samples. *Biometrika*, pages 285–294, 1933.

[14] Y. Yue and C. Guestrin. Linear submodular bandits and their application to diversified retrieval. In *Proceedings of Advances in Neural Information Processing Systems (NIPS)*, pages 2483–2491, 2011.

[15] W. V. Zhang and R. Jones. Comparing click logs and editorial labels for training query rewriting. In *WWW'07 Workshop on Query Log Analysis: Social And Technological Challenges*, 2007.

Intent-Aware Diversification Using a Constrained PLSA

Jacek Wasilewski
Insight Centre for Data Analytics
University College Dublin
Belfield, Dublin, Ireland
jacek.wasilewski@insight-centre.org

Neil Hurley
Insight Centre for Data Analytics
University College Dublin
Belfield, Dublin, Ireland
neil.hurley@insight-centre.org

ABSTRACT

The intent-aware diversification framework was introduced initially in information retrieval and adopted to the context of recommender systems in the work of Vargas et al. The framework considers a set of aspects associated with items to be recommended. For instance, aspects may correspond to genres in movie recommendations. The framework depends on input *aspect model* consisting of item selection or relevance probabilities, given an aspect, and user intents, in the form of probabilities that the user is interested in each aspect. In this paper, we examine a number of input aspect models and evaluate the impact that different models have on the framework. In particular, we propose a constrained PLSA model that allows for interpretable output, in terms of known aspects, while achieving greater performance that the explicit co-occurrence counting method used in previous work. We evaluate the proposed models using a well-known MovieLens dataset for which item genres are available.

Keywords

intent-aware recommendation; diversity; evaluation

1. INTRODUCTION

User interactions as implicit or explicit evidence of user needs involve a great deal of uncertainty. Those interactions however do not represent all user interests and might lead to creation of filter bubbles. Predicting the user needs is an inherently difficult task as user interests are complex, dynamic, context-dependent or even contradictory. Diversity-oriented approaches have been used to address these issues, by widening the range of possible item types recommended to the user. Moreover, diverse recommendations enrich the user experience over time, helping to expand the user's horizon. From this viewpoint, diversity can be treated as a strategy to favour practical accuracy in matching true user needs in an uncertain environment.

Different frameworks have been developed to enhance and assess diversity. The most commonly used is a distance-based intra-list diversity (ILD) where the average pairwise distance of the recommended items describes the recommendation diversity. Another notion of diversity, called the intent-aware diversity framework, has been adopted from the information retrieval (IR) field in [10]. The intent-aware framework in IR deals with ambiguous queries by attempting to ensure that all intents of the query are represented in the results. Adapted to a recommender system context, the framework attempts to ensure that all relevant interests of a user are represented in the recommendation list.

The intent-aware diversity framework assumes the existence of aspects through which user interests can be expressed and by which items are described. For instance, they may correspond to genres in the context of movie recommendation. A simple co-occurrence counting method has been applied to transform this explicit information into the aspect probabilities required by the intent-aware framework. The aspect probabilities are derived without direct optimisation of their utility. Latent aspects can be learned from the user-item interaction data, so that predictive performance of the aspect probabilities is maximised. The learned probabilities should better represent an underlying structure in the dataset. However, diversification over this hidden structure is not easily discernible by the user.

In this paper, we propose a constrained PLSA model that uses explicit aspects, but learns the aspect probabilities to directly optimise their predictive performance. We claim that, in doing so, we put the intent-aware framework on a stronger footing, since the aspect probabilities that drive the method, better model true user preference behaviour. Yet, we maintain the interpretability of the co-occurrence counting method, so that the framework diversifies across known, explicit aspects.

The rest of the paper is structured as follows. We briefly introduce and discuss the intent-aware diversification framework. In section 3 we discuss different strategies for estimating the probability components used by the framework and we introduce the constrained probabilistic aspect model. We empirically test and discuss the effectiveness of our intent model in section 4. We conclude with a summary in section 5.

2. INTENT-AWARE DIVERSIFICATION FRAMEWORK

The intent-aware diversification framework, proposed in the information retrieval field by Santos et al., [9], introduces the concept of explicit aspects in order to mitigate the uncertainty in queries by diversifying the ranked results. In IR,

RecSys '16, September 15-19, 2016, Boston , MA, USA
© 2016 ACM. ISBN 978-1-4503-4035-9/16/09...$15.00
DOI: http://dx.doi.org/10.1145/2959100.2959177

uncertainty arises due to ambiguous search queries that can be interpreted in different ways, depending on the context. If multiple aspects are related to a search query, without explicit information about the context of the query's intent, a search engine tries to satisfy the query by serving as many different relevant aspects as possible, hoping that at least one will satisfy the query.

To apply the model into the recommender systems setting, Vargas et al. [10] introduced the notion of user aspect as an analogue of query intent. In recommender systems, users do not define their queries explicitly. Rather a system has to decide what a user would like to see based on previously recorded interactions of the user and the system. The system could assume that a user might be interested in any aspect that the interest in has been expressed before. So there is a similar ambiguity to the IR problem – for any given interaction, what aspect is the user currently interested in? If an incorrect assumption about the user's intent is made, a recommender system may fail in generating recommendations that users find relevant.

Vargas' formulation of the explicit Query Aspect Diversification framework (xQuAD) for recommender systems assumes a predefined set of $k > 0$ aspects, $\mathcal{A} = \{a_1, a_2, ..., a_k\}$. The starting point for xQuAD is the computation of user's interests in terms of a probability distribution $p(a|u)$, such that $\sum_a p(a|u) = 1$ and the computation of the probability of choosing an item, given a user and an aspect, $p(i|u,a)$. The xQuAD re-ranker uses these probabilities to re-rank a given recommendation list so that aspects are taken into account.

Starting with $\mathcal{S} = \emptyset$, and given the score $s(u,i)$ for item i produced by the baseline recommender system from which the original ranked list $\mathcal{R}_u$ is obtained, xQuAD iteratively constructs the re-ranked list, $\mathcal{S}$, by greedily selecting at each iteration the item i that satisfies:

$$i^* = \underset{i \in \mathcal{R}_u \setminus \mathcal{S}}{\arg\max}(1-\lambda)s(u,i) + \lambda \sum_{a \in \mathcal{A}} p(a|u)p(i|u,a) \prod_{j \in \mathcal{S}} (1 - p(j|u,a)),$$

and updating $\mathcal{S} \leftarrow \mathcal{S} \cup \{i^*\}$. The two terms in this expression can be summarised as, respectively, the item quality component and the item diversity component, and are mixed together using a tradeoff controlling parameter $0 \leq \lambda \leq 1$.

3. COMPONENTS ESTIMATION

The xQuAD formulation presented in the previous section depends on an *aspect model*, determined by the user and item aspect probabilities, given by:

$$p(i|u) = \sum_a p(a|u)p(i|u,a). \quad (1)$$

But, what exactly is an aspect? We consider two cases:

1. **Explicit Aspects**: Aspect information is directly available in the input data. Aspects are synonymous with item features, such as genres in the case of movies. In particular, from the input data it is possible to directly identify for each item i a set of aspects $\mathcal{A}_i$.

2. **Latent Aspects**: Aspect information is not explicitly available in the input data. Instead aspects are latent categories, which are learned from the user-item interaction data.

Diversification research most commonly considers explicit categories and these have the important advantage of being *interpretable* to the user. As the aspects are known, a user can clearly distinguish a recommendation list containing, say, movies of a single genre, from one which contains a mix of genres. Latent aspects do not afford this ability. It can be difficult to distinguish a highly diverse recommendation from a less diverse one, when the diversified aspects are latent.

Explicit Aspects. In [10], the xQuAD framework is developed and evaluated largely using explicit aspects, where the space of item features $\mathcal{F}$ becomes the space of all possible aspects $\mathcal{A}$. Rather than learn the aspect probabilities to directly optimise for (1), they are heuristically estimated by counting user, item and aspects co-occurrences in the input data.

The estimates are as follows:

$$p(a|u) \sim \frac{|\{i \in \mathcal{I}_u : a \in \mathcal{A}_i\}|}{\sum_{a' \in \mathcal{A}} |\{i \in \mathcal{I}_u : a' \in \mathcal{A}_i\}|}, \quad p(i|u,a) \sim \frac{\mathbb{1}_{\mathcal{A}_i}(a)s(u,i)}{\sum_{j \in \mathcal{R}} \mathbb{1}_{\mathcal{A}_i}(a)s(u,j)}$$

where $\mathcal{I}_u$ denotes the set of items in the profile of user u, $\mathbb{1}_{\mathcal{A}_i}(a) = 1$ if $a \in \mathcal{A}_i$ and 0 otherwise. $p(a|u)$ is the count of occurrences of aspect a over the sum of occurrences of all aspects in the profile of user u. $p(i|u,a)$ is proportional to the sum of scores of items in user profile that share the feature a. This model also assumes that $p(a|i) = 1/|\mathcal{A}_i|$ when $a \in \mathcal{A}_i$ and 0 otherwise. Each aspect connected to an item that a user likes, contributes equally to the estimation of the user's intents. Consider, for example, a movie described by the genres *adventure*, *comedy* and *animation*. A user may have watched that movie more so because it is an *animation* movie than because it is a *comedy* or an *adventure*. But, the co-occurrence method gives equal weight to all three genres in the estimation of $p(a|u)$. We refer to this estimation method as `ExAs-CoO`, for explicit aspects co-occurrence estimation method.

Latent Aspects. The approach of using latent aspects has been pointed out previously in [10]. Latent feature extraction can be achieved using any dimensionality reduction methods, but (1) can be directly recognised as an instance of the probabilistic latent semantic analysis (`pLSA`) model [5, 6]. The `pLSA` method assumes that $p(i|u,a)$ is independent of u and learns $p(a|u)$ and $p(i|a)$ by a direct optimisation of (1) on training data. This can be achieved through the EM algorithm, as proposed in [6]. By applying `pLSA`, we are finding the best values for the aspect components, from the point-of-view of their predictive performance. The algorithm can be tuned by selecting the number of aspects. Despite its potential for selection of aspect components with a superior predictive performance, the hidden aspect model tends not to be preferred as a basis for diversification, because of the difficulty of interpreting its output.

Explicit Aspect Learning. The advantage of explicit aspects is their interpretability but they may be inaccurate when their predictive performance is considered. Latent aspects are chosen to directly optimise for predictive performance, but are much less interpretable. We propose a middle ground – we adopt an aspect model based on explicit aspects, but learn the components of the model by optimising for their predictive performance.

We propose a constrained **pLSA** model, which we'll refer to as **c-pLSA**, based on explicit aspects. Given a set of explicit aspects $\mathcal{A}$ and their item correspondences $\mathcal{A}_i$, we impose the constraint that $p(i|a) = 0$ whenever $a \notin \mathcal{A}_i$. This additional constraint is easily incorporated into the EM algorithm for **pLSA**. The E-step of that algorithm requires the computation of

$$Q^*(a; u, i) = \frac{\hat{p}(i|a)\hat{p}(a|u)}{\sum_{a' \in \mathcal{A}} \hat{p}(i|a')\hat{p}(a'|u)}.$$

where $\hat{p}(.)$ correspond to estimates from the previous iteration. The constrained algorithm simply initialises $\hat{p}(i|a) = 0 \; \forall a \notin \mathcal{A}_i$, so that $Q^*(a; u, i) = 0 \; \forall a \notin \mathcal{A}_i$. The optimal Q^* is used then in the M-step of the EM to derive:

$$\hat{p}(i|a) = \frac{\sum_{(u,i'):i'=i} Q^*(a; u, i)}{\sum_{(u,i)} Q^*(a; u, i)}$$

which maintains the condition.

A user has been selected that has 17 non-zero aspect probabilities, $p(a|u)$, estimated by **ExAs-CoO**. Top aspects with respect to $p(a|u)$ (probability values are given in parentheses) are: *comedy* (0.46), *adventure* (0.07), *action* (0.07), *sci-fi* (0.07), *romance* (0.06) and *drama* (0.05). The **c-pLSA** model sees the user differently, as *comedy* (0.86), *adventure* (0.10), *fantasy* (0.02) and *film-noir* (0.02). As the predictive performance of the **c-pLSA** is better, we believe the **c-pLSA** has learned the user aspect probabilities more accurately.

The proposed solution might be used not only to learn the real user interests but as well to find what drives people that they interacted with an item. For example, *Star Wars: Episode IV - A New Hope* is described as *action*, *adventure*, *fantasy* and *sci-fi*. With the **c-pLSA** we can derive weightings to express how people perceive this item in terms of those genres. In this case we would find out that people pick this item mostly because it is an *adventure* (0.5) than *sci-fi* (0.25), *fantasy* (0.24) or *action* (0.01).

4. EVALUATION

This section describes our experiments for evaluating the performance of aspect models.

4.1 Dataset

The MovieLens (ML-1m) dataset [4] contains the ratings information of users on movies. It holds 1,000,209 ratings from 6,040 users on 3,706 movies. Movies are described using at least one genre out of 18 available. Ratings are made on a 5-star scale, with whole-star ratings only. The dataset has been split into 2 subsets: the training set with 800,167 ratings and the test set of 200,042 ratings.

4.2 Experiment Setup

Four baseline algorithms have been used to generate recommendation candidates lists R_u of 100 items: user- (UB) and item-based (IB) neighbourhood [3], matrix factorisation (MF) [7] and probabilistic latent semantic analysis (pLSA) [6] recommenders.

Each candidate list has been re-ranked using xQuAD, based on the input aspect models. We denote xQuAD variations: xQuAD$_E$, xQuAD$_C$, xQuAD$_P$ respectively for each of models: **ExAs-CoO**, **c-pLSA** and **pLSA**. The **pLSA** aspect model uses 18 latent aspects, **c-pLSA** uses 18 explicit aspects. Performance of xQuAD has been checked at different

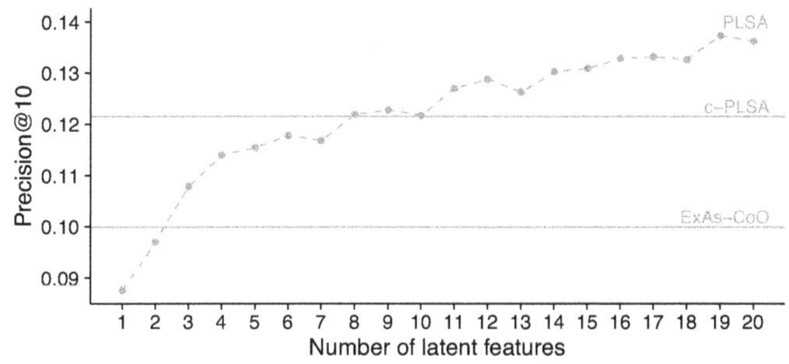

Figure 1: Predictive performance of aspect models.

values of λ, from 0 to 1 with the step of 0.1. Re-rankers produce final recommendations of top $N = 10$ items.

Experiments and the evaluation have been done using the implementations of the algorithms and metrics available in the RankSys framework[1].

4.3 Metrics

Among the many metrics that have been proposed for evaluating diversity, intent-aware metrics, such as ERR-IA [1], cannot be usefully applied to compare the performance of different aspect models as they require the aspect model as input to the metric. Nevertheless, in our results section, we note that on the ERR-IA metric, xQuAD$_C$ outperforms xQuAD$_E$ for MF and IB, even when the **ExAs-CoO** model is used as the input to the metric. We report feature-based metrics, such as α-nDCG ($\alpha = 0.5$) [2] and subtopic recall (S-recall) [11], to evaluate the diversity. The accuracy is assessed based on the precision (Prec), recall and nDCG [8]. Relevance-aware versions of the metrics are used, where 5 star rating is considered as relevant. Metrics are evaluated at $N = 10$.

4.4 Predictive Performance

It is worth noting that the item to aspect mapping is sparse – typically, each item has only a few aspects associated with it. For instance, in MovieLens, there are 18 movie genres and the average number of genres per movie is less than 2. Thus, for a given total number of aspects, the number of degrees of freedom in **c-pLSA** is much less than in standard **pLSA** and it is to be expected that **c-pLSA** fits the data less accurately than **pLSA**. Nevertheless, the structure of explicit aspects supports good recommendation. Since **c-pLSA** is optimised on predictive performance, it can be expected that in general **c-pLSA** outperforms **ExAs-CoO** in terms of predictive accuracy.

These observations are tested and in figure 1, the precision of recommendation using **pLSA** is plotted against the number of hidden aspects k, with the precision of **ExAs-CoO** and **c-pLSA** indicated on the plot. **pLSA** achieves the accuracy of **c-pLSA** when $k = 8$. The $s(u, i)$ scores of the best performing baseline, MF, have been used for the **ExAs-CoO**.

4.5 Results

Accuracy Performance. Figure 2 shows the precision performance when different input aspect models are used, for different values of the tradeoff parameter λ. The highest precision can be seen for $\lambda = 0.4$. The results confirm that

[1]http://ranksys.org

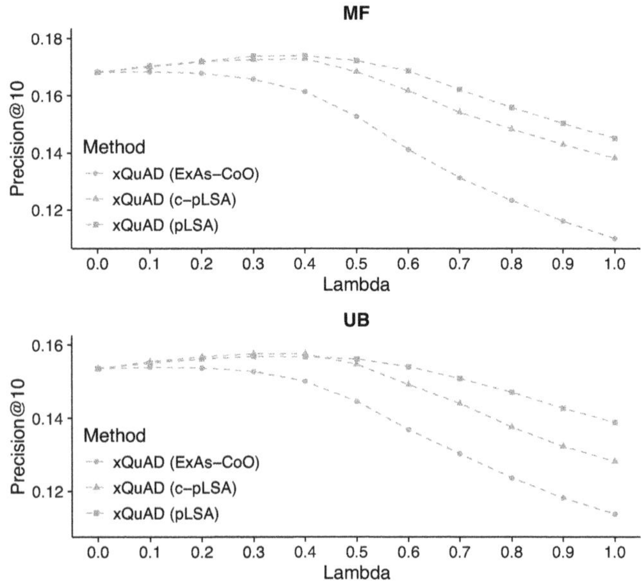

Figure 2: Intent-aware re-rankings for two recommendation algorithms in ML-1m dataset.

	λ	Accuracy			Diversity		
		Prec	nDCG	Recall	ERR-IA	α-nDCG	S-recall
MF		0.168	0.274	0.270	0.168	0.278	0.157
+xQuAD$_E$	0.4	0.161	0.258	0.259	*0.175*	**0.294**	**0.171**
+xQuAD$_C$	0.3	0.173	0.281	*0.273*	**0.177**	0.289	0.162
+xQuAD$_P$	0.3	**0.174**	**0.283**	**0.276**	0.176	0.288	0.162
PLSA		0.143	0.226	0.222	0.143	0.234	0.139
+xQuAD$_E$	0.5	0.139	0.221	*0.220*	**0.159**	**0.261**	**0.157**
+xQuAD$_C$	0.5	**0.152**	**0.243**	**0.237**	0.157	0.254	0.149
+xQuAD$_P$	0.5	0.151	0.240	0.232	0.155	0.250	0.146
UB		0.154	0.252	0.243	0.167	0.274	0.157
+xQuAD$_E$	0.3	*0.153*	*0.251*	*0.243*	**0.178**	**0.290**	**0.166**
+xQuAD$_C$	0.2	**0.157**	**0.259**	**0.248**	0.173	0.281	0.159
+xQuAD$_P$	0.3	**0.157**	0.257	*0.245*	0.171	0.277	*0.158*
IB		0.131	0.207	0.202	0.143	0.229	0.137
+xQuAD$_E$	0.6	0.128	0.203	0.198	0.153	0.244	**0.149**
+xQuAD$_C$	0.5	0.144	0.230	0.222	**0.158**	0.250	0.147
+xQuAD$_P$	0.6	**0.148**	**0.235**	**0.227**	0.157	**0.253**	0.148

Table 1: Accuracy and diversity performance results. For each baseline and re-ranker, the value of λ is presented for the best setting in terms of α-nDCG diversity metric. All differences with respect to the baselines are statistically significant (Wilcoxon $p < 0.001$) except when in italics.

the best precision is obtained when the `pLSA` model is used. For $\lambda \leq 0.4$, performance of `c-pLSA` is close to the `pLSA`. Both, `c-pLSA` and `pLSA`, outperform the `ExAs-CoO` model – the order from figure 1 in terms of performance is preserved.

Results on other baselines and other accuracy metrics are presented in table 1. It shows the generally superior accuracy performance of the `pLSA` however for the PLSA and UB baselines the `c-pLSA` model performs slightly better.

Diversity Performance. The impact of aspect models on diversification results is reported in table 1. The `ExAs-CoO` model generally offers the best diversity performance with an exception on α-nDCG on IB. The `c-pLSA` model performs similarly or slightly better than the `pLSA`. Although `c-pLSA` and `pLSA` models might not be as good as `ExAs-CoO`, they offer diversity capabilities that are better than the baseline algorithms. Also, their accuracy-diversity tradeoff is better than for `ExAs-CoO` model.

Neither `pLSA` nor `c-pLSA` perform the best on feature-based metrics – α-nDCG and S-recall. `pLSA` is unaware of explicit aspects and cannot directly optimise for those. In practise, the user aspect probabilities have fewer non-zero values when `c-pLSA` is used compared to when `ExAs-CoO` is used. Actually, for only 240 users out of 6,040, the number of non-zero aspect probabilities remain the same for `ExAs-CoO` and `c-pLSA`, and for almost 66% of users, the number of non-zero user aspect probabilities produced by `c-pLSA` is fewer by 4 or more than produced by `ExAs-CoO`. This is because `ExAs-CoO` gives equal weights to aspects of multi-aspect movies, while `c-pLSA` focuses only on those aspects that contribute to relevance. As a consequence, the re-ranker has more opportunity with `ExAs-CoO` to improve diversity metrics. `c-pLSA` results in a lower capability of diversifying over aspects, however we believe it better represents the user's true intents.

5. CONCLUSION

Research presented here aimed to explore aspect models for the intent-aware diversification framework. A constrained PLSA model has been proposed, evaluated and compared with two other models. The proposed model mixes two other approaches used so far in the field. It maintains interpretability, providing better accuracy-diversity tradeoff. Also, it models users and items aspects more accurately than the explicit aspect co-occurrence counting approach.

6. ACKNOWLEDGMENTS

This project has been funded by Science Foundation Ireland under Grant No. SFI/12/RC/2289.

7. REFERENCES

[1] O. Chapelle, D. Metlzer, Y. Zhang, and P. Grinspan. Expected reciprocal rank for graded relevance. *ACM CIKM '09 Conference Proceedings*, pages 621–630, 2009.

[2] C. L. Clarke, M. Kolla, G. V. Cormack, O. Vechtomova, A. Ashkan, S. Büttcher, and I. MacKinnon. Novelty and Diversity in Information Retrieval Evaluation. *ACM SIGIR'08 Conference Proceedings*, page 659, 2008.

[3] C. Desrosiers and G. Karypis. A Comprehensive Survey of Neighborhood-based Recommendation Methods. *Recommender Systems Handbook*, 54:107–144, 2011.

[4] F. M. Harper and J. a. Konstan. The MovieLens Datasets : History and Context. 5(4):1–19, 2015.

[5] T. Hofmann. Unsupervised Learning by Probabilistic Latent Semantic Analysis. *Machine Learning*, 42(1-2):177–196, 2001.

[6] T. Hofmann. Latent Semantic Models for Collaborative Filtering. *ACM Transactions on Information Systems*, 22(1):89–115, 2004.

[7] Y. Hu, Y. Koren, and C. Volinsky. Collaborative Filtering for Implicit Feedback Datasets. 2008.

[8] K. Järvelin and J. Kekäläinen. Cumulated Gain-Based Evaluation of IR Techniques. *ACM Transactions on Information Systems*, 20(4):422–446, 2002.

[9] R. Santos, C. Macdonald, and I. Ounis. Exploiting Query Reformulations for Web Search Result Diversification. *WWW*, pages 881–890, 2010.

[10] S. Vargas, P. Castells, and D. Vallet. Intent-oriented Diversity in Recommender Systems. *ACM SIGIR'11 Conference Proceedings*, pages 1211–1212, 2011.

[11] C. X. Zhai, W. W. Cohen, and J. Lafferty. Beyond Independent Relevance: Methods and Evaluation Metrics for Subtopic Retrieval. 49(1):10–17, 2003.

Field-aware Factorization Machines for CTR Prediction

Yuchin Juan
Criteo*
Palo Alto, CA
guestwalk@gmail.com

Yong Zhuang
Dept. of ECE*
Carnegie Mellon Univ., USA
yong.zhuang22@gmail.com

Wei-Sheng Chin
Dept. of Computer Science
National Taiwan Univ., Taiwan
d01944006@csie.ntu.edu.tw

Chih-Jen Lin
Dept. of Computer Science
National Taiwan Univ., Taiwan
cjlin@csie.ntu.edu.tw

ABSTRACT

Click-through rate (CTR) prediction plays an important role in computational advertising. Models based on degree-2 polynomial mappings and factorization machines (FMs) are widely used for this task. Recently, a variant of FMs, field-aware factorization machines (FFMs), outperforms existing models in some world-wide CTR-prediction competitions. Based on our experiences in winning two of them, in this paper we establish FFMs as an effective method for classifying large sparse data including those from CTR prediction. First, we propose efficient implementations for training FFMs. Then we comprehensively analyze FFMs and compare this approach with competing models. Experiments show that FFMs are very useful for certain classification problems. Finally, we have released a package of FFMs for public use.

Keywords

Machine learning; Click-through rate prediction; Computational advertising; Factorization machines

1. INTRODUCTION

Click-through rate (CTR) prediction plays an important role in advertising industry [1, 2, 3]. Logistic regression is probably the most widely used model for this task [3]. Given a data set with m instances $(y_i, \boldsymbol{x}_i), i = 1, \ldots, m$, where y_i is the label and $\boldsymbol{x}_i$ is an n-dimensional feature vector, the model $\boldsymbol{w}$ is obtained by solving the following optimization problem.

$$\min_{\boldsymbol{w}} \quad \frac{\lambda}{2}\|\boldsymbol{w}\|_2^2 + \sum_{i=1}^{m} \log(1 + \exp(-y_i \phi_{\mathrm{LM}}(\boldsymbol{w}, \boldsymbol{x}_i))). \qquad (1)$$

*Part of the work were done when these authors were in National Taiwan University.

RecSys '16, September 15-19, 2016, Boston , MA, USA
© 2016 ACM. ISBN 978-1-4503-4035-9/16/09...$15.00
DOI: http://dx.doi.org/10.1145/2959100.2959134

		Publisher	Advertiser
+80	−20	ESPN	Nike
+10	−90	ESPN	Gucci
+0	−1	ESPN	Adidas
+15	−85	Vogue	Nike
+90	−10	Vogue	Gucci
+10	−90	Vogue	Adidas
+85	−15	NBC	Nike
+0	−0	NBC	Gucci
+90	−10	NBC	Adidas

Table 1: An artificial CTR data set, where + (−) represents the number of clicked (unclicked) impressions.

In problem (1), λ is the regularization parameter, and in the loss function we consider the linear model:

$$\phi_{\mathrm{LM}}(\boldsymbol{w}, \boldsymbol{x}) = \boldsymbol{w} \cdot \boldsymbol{x}.$$

Learning the effect of feature conjunctions seems to be crucial for CTR prediction; see, for example, [1]. Here, we consider an artificial data set in Table 1 to have a better understanding of feature conjunctions. An ad from Gucci has a particularly high CTR on Vogue. This information is however difficult for linear models to learn because they learn the two weights Gucci and Vogue separately. To address this problem, two models have been used to learn the effect of feature conjunction. The first model, degree-2 polynomial mappings (Poly2) [4, 5], learns a dedicate weight for each feature conjunction. The second model, factorization machines (FMs) [6], learns the effect of feature conjunction by factorizing it into a product of two latent vectors. We will discuss details about Poly2 and FMs in Section 2.

A variant of FM called pairwise interaction tensor factorization (PITF) [7] was proposed for personalized tag recommendation. In KDD Cup 2012, a generalization of PITF called "factor model" was proposed by "Team Opera Solutions" [8]. Because this term is too general and may easily be confused with factorization machines, we refer to it as "field-aware factorization machines" (FFMs) in this paper. The difference between PITF and FFM is that PITF considers three special fields including "user," "item," and "tag," while FFM is more general. Because [8] is about the overall solution for the competition, its discussion of FFM is limited. We can conclude the following results in [8]:

1. They use stochastic gradient method (SG) to solve the optimization problem. To avoid over-fitting, they only train with one epoch.
2. FFM performs the best among six models they tried.

In this paper, we aim to concretely establish FFM as an effective approach for CTR prediction. Our major results are as follows.

- Though FFM is shown to be effective in [8], this work may be the only published study of applying FFMs on CTR prediction problems. To further demonstrate the effectiveness of FFMs on CTR prediction, we present the use of FFM as our major model to win two world-wide CTR competitions hosted by Criteo and Avazu.
- We compare FFMs with two related models, Poly2 and FMs. We first discuss conceptually why FFMs might be better than them, and conduct experiments to see the difference in terms of accuracy and training time.
- We present techniques for training FFMs. They include an effective parallel optimization algorithm for FFMs and the use of early-stopping to avoid over-fitting.
- To make FFMs available for public use, we release an open source software.

This paper is organized as follows. Before we present FFMs and its implementation in Section 3, we discuss the two existing models Poly2 and FMs in Section 2. Experiments comparing FFMs with other models are in Section 4. Finally, conclusions and future directions are in Section 5.

Code used for experiments in this paper and the package LIBFFM are respectively available at:

http://www.csie.ntu.edu.tw/~cjlin/ffm/exps
http://www.csie.ntu.edu.tw/~cjlin/libffm

2. POLY2 AND FM

Chang et. al [4] have shown that a degree-2 polynomial mapping can often effectively capture the information of feature conjunctions. Further, they show that by applying a linear model on the explicit form of degree-2 mappings, the training and test time can be much faster than using kernel methods. This approach, referred to as Poly2, learns a weight for each feature pair:

$$\phi_{\text{Poly2}}(\boldsymbol{w}, \boldsymbol{x}) = \sum_{j_1=1}^{n} \sum_{j_2=j_1+1}^{n} w_{h(j_1,j_2)} x_{j_1} x_{j_2}, \tag{2}$$

where $h(j_1, j_2)$ is a function encoding j_1 and j_2 into a natural number. The complexity of computing (2) is $O(\bar{n}^2)$, where $\bar{n}$ is the average number of non-zero elements per instance.

FMs proposed in [6] implicitly learn a latent vector for each feature. Each latent vector contains k latent factors, where k is a user-specified parameter. Then, the effect of feature conjunction is modelled by the inner product of two latent vectors:

$$\phi_{\text{FM}}(\boldsymbol{w}, \boldsymbol{x}) = \sum_{j_1=1}^{n} \sum_{j_2=j_1+1}^{n} (\boldsymbol{w}_{j_1} \cdot \boldsymbol{w}_{j_2}) x_{j_1} x_{j_2}. \tag{3}$$

The number of variables is $n \times k$, so directly computing (3) costs $O(\bar{n}^2 k)$ time. Following [6], by re-writing (3) to

$$\phi_{\text{FM}}(\boldsymbol{w}, \boldsymbol{x}) = \frac{1}{2} \sum_{j=1}^{n} (\boldsymbol{s} - \boldsymbol{w}_j x_j) \cdot \boldsymbol{w}_j x_j,$$

where

$$\boldsymbol{s} = \sum_{j'=1}^{n} \boldsymbol{w}_{j'} x_{j'},$$

the complexity is reduced to $O(\bar{n}k)$.

Rendle [6] explains why FMs can be better than Poly2 when the data set is sparse. Here we give a similar illustration using the data set in Table 1. For example, there is only one negative training data for the pair (ESPN, Adidas). For Poly2, a very negative weight $w_{\text{ESPN,Adidas}}$ might be learned for this pair. For FMs, because the prediction of (ESPN, Adidas) is determined by $\boldsymbol{w}_{\text{ESPN}} \cdot \boldsymbol{w}_{\text{Adidas}}$, and because $\boldsymbol{w}_{\text{ESPN}}$ and $\boldsymbol{w}_{\text{Adidas}}$ are also learned from other pairs (e.g., (ESPN, Nike), (NBC, Adidas)), the prediction may be more accurate. Another example is that there is no training data for the pair (NBC, Gucci). For Poly2, the prediction on this pair is trivial, but for FMs, because $\boldsymbol{w}_{\text{NBC}}$ and $\boldsymbol{w}_{\text{Gucci}}$ can be learned from other pairs, it is still possible to do meaningful prediction.

Note that in Poly2, the naive way to implement $h(j_1, j_2)$ is to consider every pair of features as a new feature [4].[1] This approach requires the model as large as $O(n^2)$, which is usually impractical for CTR prediction because of very large n. Vowpal Wabbit (VW) [9], a widely used machine learning package, solves this problem by hashing j_1 and j_2.[2] Our implementation is similar to VW's approach. Specifically,

$$h(j_1, j_2) = (\frac{1}{2}(j_1 + j_2)(j_1 + j_2 + 1) + j_2) \bmod B,$$

where the model size B is a user-specified parameter.

In this paper, for the simplicity of formulations, we do not include linear terms and bias term. However, in Section 4, we include them for some experiments.

3. FFM

The idea of FFM originates from PITF [7] proposed for recommender systems with personalized tags. In PITF, they assume three available fields including User, Item, and Tag, and factorize (User, Item), (User, Tag), and (Item, Tag) in separate latent spaces. In [8], they generalize PITF for more fields (e.g., AdID, AdvertiserID, UserID, QueryID) and effectively apply it on CTR prediction. Because [7] aims at recommender systems and is limited to three specific fields (User, Item, and Tag), and [8] lacks detailed discussion on FFM, in this section we provide a more comprehensive study of FFMs on CTR prediction. For most CTR data sets like that in Table 1, "features" can be grouped into "fields." In our example, three features ESPN, Vogue, and NBC, belong to the field Publisher, and the other three features Nike, Gucci, and Adidas, belong to the field Advertiser. FFM is a variant of FM that utilizes this information. To explain how FFM works, we consider the following new example:

Clicked	Publisher (P)	Advertiser (A)	Gender (G)
Yes	ESPN	Nike	Male

Recall that for FMs, $\phi_{\text{FM}}(\boldsymbol{w}, \boldsymbol{x})$ is

$$\boldsymbol{w}_{\text{ESPN}} \cdot \boldsymbol{w}_{\text{Nike}} + \boldsymbol{w}_{\text{ESPN}} \cdot \boldsymbol{w}_{\text{Male}} + \boldsymbol{w}_{\text{Nike}} \cdot \boldsymbol{w}_{\text{Male}}.$$

[1] More precisely, [4] includes the original features as well, though we do not consider such a setting until the experiments.

[2] See http://github.com/JohnLangford/vowpal_wabbit/wiki/Feature-interactions for details.

	#variables	complexity
LM	n	$O(\bar{n})$
Poly2	B	$O(\bar{n}^2)$
FM	nk	$O(\bar{n}k)$
FFM	nfk	$O(\bar{n}^2k)$

Table 2: Comparison of the number of variables and the complexity for prediction among LM, Poly2, FM, and FFM.

In FMs, every feature has only one latent vector to learn the latent effect with any other features. Take ESPN as an example, $\boldsymbol{w}_{\text{ESPN}}$ is used to learn the latent effect with Nike ($\boldsymbol{w}_{\text{ESPN}} \cdot \boldsymbol{w}_{\text{Nike}}$) and Male ($\boldsymbol{w}_{\text{ESPN}} \cdot \boldsymbol{w}_{\text{Male}}$). However, because Nike and Male belong to different fields, the latent effects of (EPSN, Nike) and (EPSN, Male) may be different.

In FFMs, each feature has several latent vectors. Depending on the field of other features, one of them is used to do the inner product. In our example, $\phi_{\text{FFM}}(\boldsymbol{w}, \boldsymbol{x})$ is

$$\boldsymbol{w}_{\text{ESPN,A}} \cdot \boldsymbol{w}_{\text{Nike,P}} + \boldsymbol{w}_{\text{ESPN,G}} \cdot \boldsymbol{w}_{\text{Male,P}} + \boldsymbol{w}_{\text{Nike,G}} \cdot \boldsymbol{w}_{\text{Male,A}}.$$

We see that to learn the latent effect of (ESPN, NIKE), $\boldsymbol{w}_{\text{ESPN,A}}$ is used because Nike belongs to the field Advertiser, and $\boldsymbol{w}_{\text{Nike,P}}$ is used because ESPN belongs to the field Publisher. Again, to learn the latent effect of (EPSN, Male), $\boldsymbol{w}_{\text{ESPN,G}}$ is used because Male belongs to the field Gender, and $\boldsymbol{w}_{\text{Male,P}}$ is used because ESPN belongs to the field Publisher. Mathematically,

$$\phi_{\text{FFM}}(\boldsymbol{w}, \boldsymbol{x}) = \sum_{j_1=1}^{n} \sum_{j_2=j_1+1}^{n} (\boldsymbol{w}_{j_1,f_2} \cdot \boldsymbol{w}_{j_2,f_1}) x_{j_1} x_{j_2}, \quad (4)$$

where f_1 and f_2 are respectively the fields of j_1 and j_2. If f is the number of fields, then the number of variables of FFMs is nfk, and the complexity to compute (4) is $O(\bar{n}^2k)$. It is worth noting that in FFMs because each latent vector only needs to learn the effect with a specific field, usually

$$k_{\text{FFM}} \ll k_{\text{FM}}.$$

Table 2 compares the number of variables and the computational complexity of different models.

3.1 Solving the Optimization Problem

The optimization problem is the same as (1) except that $\phi_{\text{LM}}(\boldsymbol{w}, \boldsymbol{x})$ is replaced by $\phi_{\text{FFM}}(\boldsymbol{w}, \boldsymbol{x})$. Following [7, 8], we use stochastic gradient methods (SG). Recently, some adaptive learning-rate schedules such as [10, 11] have been proposed to boost the training process of SG. We use AdaGrad [10] because [12] has shown its effectiveness on matrix factorization, which is a special case of FFMs.

At each step of SG a data point $(y, \boldsymbol{x})$ is sampled for updating $\boldsymbol{w}_{j_1,f_2}$ and $\boldsymbol{w}_{j_2,f_1}$ in (4). Note that because $\boldsymbol{x}$ is highly sparse in our application, we only update dimensions with non-zero values. First, the sub-gradients are

$$\boldsymbol{g}_{j_1,f_2} \equiv \nabla_{\boldsymbol{w}_{j_1,f_2}} f(\boldsymbol{w}) = \lambda \cdot \boldsymbol{w}_{j_1,f_2} + \kappa \cdot \boldsymbol{w}_{j_2,f_1} x_{j_1} x_{j_2}, \quad (5)$$

$$\boldsymbol{g}_{j_2,f_1} \equiv \nabla_{\boldsymbol{w}_{j_2,f_1}} f(\boldsymbol{w}) = \lambda \cdot \boldsymbol{w}_{j_2,f_1} + \kappa \cdot \boldsymbol{w}_{j_1,f_2} x_{j_1} x_{j_2}, \quad (6)$$

where

$$\kappa = \frac{\partial \log(1 + \exp(-y\phi_{\text{FFM}}(\boldsymbol{w}, \boldsymbol{x})))}{\partial \phi_{\text{FFM}}(\boldsymbol{w}, \boldsymbol{x})} = \frac{-y}{1 + \exp(y\phi_{\text{FFM}}(\boldsymbol{w}, \boldsymbol{x}))}.$$

Algorithm 1 Training FFM using SG

1: Let $G \in R^{n \times f \times k}$ be a tensor of all ones
2: Run the following loop for t epochs
3: **for** $i \in \{1, \cdots, m\}$ **do**
4: Sample a data point $(y, \boldsymbol{x})$
5: caclulate κ
6: **for** $j_1 \in$ non-zero terms in $\{1, \cdots, n\}$ **do**
7: **for** $j_2 \in$ non-zero terms in $\{j_1 + 1, \cdots, n\}$ **do**
8: calculate sub-gradient by (5) and (6)
9: **for** $d \in \{1, \cdots, k\}$ **do**
10: Update the gradient sum by (7) and (8)
11: Update model by (9) and (10)

Second, for each coordinate $d = 1, \ldots, k$, the sum of squared gradient is accumulated:

$$(G_{j_1,f_2})_d \leftarrow (G_{j_1,f_2})_d + (g_{j_1,f_2})_d^2 \quad (7)$$

$$(G_{j_2,f_1})_d \leftarrow (G_{j_2,f_1})_d + (g_{j_2,f_1})_d^2 \quad (8)$$

Finally, $(w_{j_1,f_2})_d$ and $(w_{j_2,f_1})_d$ are updated by:

$$(w_{j_1,f_2})_d \leftarrow (w_{j_1,f_2})_d - \frac{\eta}{\sqrt{(G_{j_1,f_2})_d}} (g_{j_1,f_2})_d \quad (9)$$

$$(w_{j_2,f_1})_d \leftarrow (w_{j_2,f_1})_d - \frac{\eta}{\sqrt{(G_{j_2,f_1})_d}} (g_{j_2,f_1})_d, \quad (10)$$

where η is a user-specified learning rate. The initial values of $\boldsymbol{w}$ are randomly sampled from a uniform distribution between $[0, 1/\sqrt{k}]$. The initial values of G are set to one in order to prevent a large value of $(G_{j_1,f_2})_d^{-\frac{1}{2}}$. The overall procedure is presented in Algorithm 1.

Empirically, we find that normalizing each instance to have the unit length makes the test accuracy slightly better and insensitive to parameters.

3.2 Parallelization on Shared-memory Systems

Modern computers are widely equipped with multi-core CPUs. If these cores are fully utilized, the training time can be significantly reduced. Many parallelization approaches for SG have been proposed. In this paper, we apply HOGWILD! [13], which allows each thread to run independently without any locking. Specifically, the **for** loop at line 3 of Algorithm 1 is parallelized.

In Section 4.4 we run extensive experiments to investigate the effectiveness of parallelization.

3.3 Adding Field Information

Consider the widely used LIBSVM data format:

label feat1:val1 feat2:val2 $\cdots$,

where each (feat, val) pair indicates feature index and value. For FFMs, we extend the above format to

label field1:feat1:val1 field2:feat2:val2 $\cdots$

That is, we must assign the corresponding field to each feature. The assignment is easy on some kinds of features, but may not be possible for some others. We discuss this issue on three typical classes of features.

Categorical Features

For linear models, a categorical feature is commonly transformed to several binary features. For a data instance

Yes P:ESPN A:Nike G:Male,

we generate the following LIBSVM format.

Yes P-ESPN:1 A-Nike:1 G-Male:1

Note that according to the number of possible values in a categorical feature, the same number of binary features are generated and every time only one of them has the value 1. In the LIBSVM format, features with zero values are not stored. We apply the same setting to all models, so in this paper, every categorical feature is transformed to several binary ones. To add the field information, we can consider each category as a field. Then the above instance becomes

Yes P:P-ESPN:1 A:A-Nike:1 G:G-Male:1.

Numerical Features

Consider the following example to predict if a paper will be accepted by a conference. We use three numerical features "accept rate of the conference (AR)," "h-index of the author (Hidx)," and "number of citations of the author (Cite):"

Accepted	AR	Hidx	Cite
Yes	45.73	2	3
No	1.04	100	50,000

There are two possible ways to assign fields. A naive way is to treat each feature as a dummy field, so the generated data is:

Yes AR:AR:45.73 Hidx:Hidx:2 Cite:Cite:3

However, the dummy fields may not be informative because they are merely duplicates of features.

Another possible way is to discretize each numerical feature to a categorical one. Then, we can use the same setting for categorical features to add field information. The generated data looks like:

Yes AR:45:1 Hidx:2:1 Cite:3:1,

where the AR feature is rounded to an integer. The main drawback is that usually it is not easy to determine the best discretization setting. For example, we may transform 45.73 to "45.7," "45," "40," or even "int(log(45.73))." In addition, we may lose some information after discretization.

Single-field Features

On some data sets, all features belong to a single field and hence it is meaningless to assign fields to features. Typically this situation happens on NLP data sets. Consider the following example of predicting if a sentence expresses a good mood or not:

good mood	sentence
Yes	`Hooray! Our paper is accepted!`
No	`Well, our paper is rejected..`

In this example the only field is "sentence." If we assign this field to all words, then FFMs is reduced to FMs. Readers may ask about assigning dummy fields as we do for numerical features. Recall that the model size of FFMs is $O(nfk)$. The use of dummy fields is impractical because $f = n$ and n is often huge.

4. EXPERIMENTS

In this section, we first provide the details about the experimental setting in Section 4.1. Then, we investigate the impact of parameters. We find that unlike LM or Poly2, FFM is sensitive to the number of epochs. Therefore, in Section 4.3, we discuss this issue in detail before proposing an early stopping trick. The speedup of parallelization is studied in Section 4.4.

After checking various properties of FFMs, in Sections 4.5-4.6, we compare FFMs with other models including Poly2 and FMs. They are all implemented by the same SG method, so besides accuracy we can fairly compare their training time. Further in the comparison we include state-of-the-art packages LIBLINEAR [14] and LIBFM [15] for training LM/Poly2 and FMs, respectively.

4.1 Experiment Settings

Data Sets

We mainly consider two CTR sets `Criteo` and `Avazu` from Kaggle competitions,[3] though in Section 4.6 more sets are considered. For feature engineering, we mainly apply our winning solution but remove complicated components.[4] For example, our winning solution for `Avazu` includes the ensemble of 20 models, but here we only use the simplest one. For other details please check our experimental code. A hashing trick is applied to generate 10^6 features. The statistics of the two data sets are:

Data Set	# instances	# features	# fields
`Criteo`	45,840,617	10^6	39
`Avazu`	40,428,968	10^6	33

For both data sets, the labels in the test sets are not publicly available, so we split the available data to two sets for training and validation. The data split follows from how test sets are obtained: For `Criteo`, the last 6,040,618 lines are used as the validation set; for `Avazu`, we select the last 4,218,939 lines. We use the following terms to represent different sets of a problem.

- `Va`: The validation set mentioned above.
- `Tr`: The new training set after excluding the validation set from the original training data.
- `TrVa`: The original training set.
- `Te`: The original test set. The labels are not released, so we must submit our prediction to the original evaluation systems to get the score. To avoid over-fitting the test set, the competition organizers divide this data set to two subsets "public set" on which the score is visible during the competition and "private set" on which the score is available after the end of competition. The final rank is determined by the private set.

For example, `CriteoVa` means the validation set from `Criteo`.

[3]Criteo Display Advertising Challenge: http://www.kaggle.com/c/criteo-display-ad-challenge. Avazu Click-Through Rate Prediction: http://www.kaggle.com/c/avazu-ctr-prediction.

[4]The code and documents of our winning solution to the two competitions can be found in http://github.com/guestwalk/kaggle-2014-criteo and http://github.com/guestwalk/kaggle-avazu

Platform

All experiments are conducted on a Linux workstation with 12 physical cores on two Intel Xeon E5-2620 2.0GHz processors and 128 GB memory.

Evaluation

Depending on the model, we change $\phi(\boldsymbol{w}, \boldsymbol{x})$ in (1) to $\phi_{\text{LM}}(\boldsymbol{w}, \boldsymbol{x})$, $\phi_{\text{Poly2}}(\boldsymbol{w}, \boldsymbol{x})$, $\phi_{\text{FM}}(\boldsymbol{w}, \boldsymbol{x})$, or $\phi_{\text{FFM}}(\boldsymbol{w}, \boldsymbol{x})$ introduced in Sections 1-3. For the evaluation criterion, we consider the logistic loss defined as

$$\text{logloss} = \frac{1}{m}\sum_{i=1}^{m} \log(1 + \exp(-y_i \phi(\boldsymbol{w}, \boldsymbol{x}_i))),$$

where m is the number of test instances.

Implementation

We implement LMs, Poly2, FMs, and FFMs all in C++. For FMs and FFMs, we use SSE instructions to boost the efficiency of inner products. The parallelization discussed in Section 3.2 is implemented by OpenMP [16]. Our implementations include linear terms and bias term as they improve performance in some data sets. These terms should be used in general as we seldom see them to be harmful.

Note that for code extensibility the field information is stored regardless of the model used. For non-FFM models, the implementation may become slightly faster by a simpler data structure without field information, but our conclusions from experiments should remain the same.

4.2 Impact of Parameters

We conduct experiments to investigate the impact of k, λ, and η. The results can be found in Figure 1. Regarding the parameter k, results in Figure 1a show that it does not affect the logloss much. In Figure 1b, we present the relationship between λ and logloss. If λ is too large, the model is not able to achieve a good performance. On the contrary, with a small λ, the model gets better results, but it easily overfits the data. We observe that the training logloss keeps decreasing. For the parameter η, Figure 1c shows that if we apply a small η, FFMs will obtain its best performance slowly. However, with a large η, FFMs are able to quickly reduce the logloss, but then over-fitting occurs. From the results in Figures 1b and 1c, there is a need of early-stopping that will be discussed in Section 4.3.

4.3 Early Stopping

Early stopping, which terminates the training process before reaching the best result on training data, can be used to avoid over-fitting for many machine learning problems [17, 18, 19]. For FFM, the strategy we use is:

1. Split the data set into a training set and a validation set.
2. At the end of each epoch, use the validation set to calculate the loss.
3. If the loss goes up, record the number of epochs. Stop or go to step 4.
4. If needed, use the full data set to re-train a model with the number of epochs obtained in step 3.

A difficulty in applying early stopping is that the logloss is sensitive to the number of epochs. Then the best epoch on the validation set may not be the best one on the test set. We have tried other approaches to avoid the overfitting

k	time	logloss
1	27.236	0.45773
2	26.384	0.45715
4	27.875	0.45696
8	40.331	0.45690
16	70.164	0.45725

(a) The average running time (in seconds) per epoch and the best logloss with different values of k. Because we use SSE instructions, the running time of $k = 1, 2, 4$ is roughly the same.

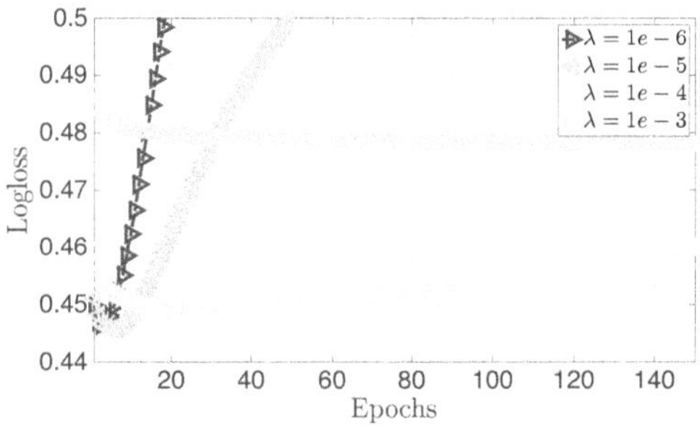

(b) The impact of λ

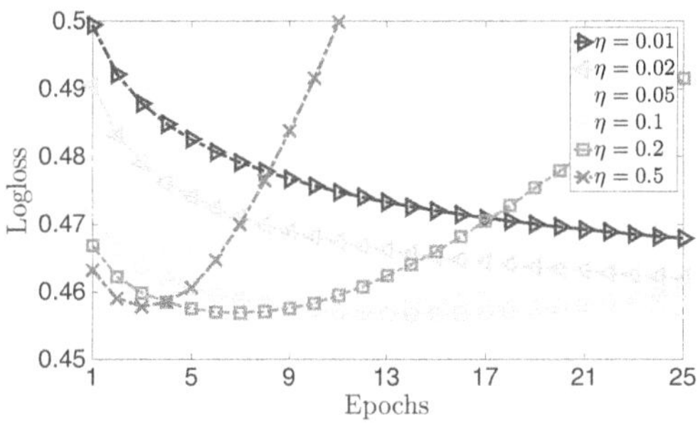

(c) The impact of η

Figure 1: The impact of λ, η, and k on FFMs. To make experiments faster, we randomly select 10% instances from `CriteoTr` and `CriteoVa` as the training and the test sets, respectively.

such as lazy update[5] and ALS-based optimization methods. However, results are not as successful as that by early stopping of using a validation set.

4.4 Speedup

Because the parallelization of SG may cause a different convergence behavior, we experiment with different numbers of threads in Figure 2. Results show that our parallelization still leads to similar convergence behavior. With this property we can define the speedup as:

$$\frac{\text{Running time of one epoch with a single thread}}{\text{Running time of one epoch with multiple threads}}.$$

The result in Figure 3 shows a good speedup when the number of threads is small. However, if many threads are used, the speedup does not improve much. An explanation is that if two or more threads attempt to access the same memory address, one must wait for its term. This kind of conflicts can happen more often when more threads are used.

[5]http://blog.smola.org/post/943941371/lazy-updates-for-generic-regularization-in-sgd

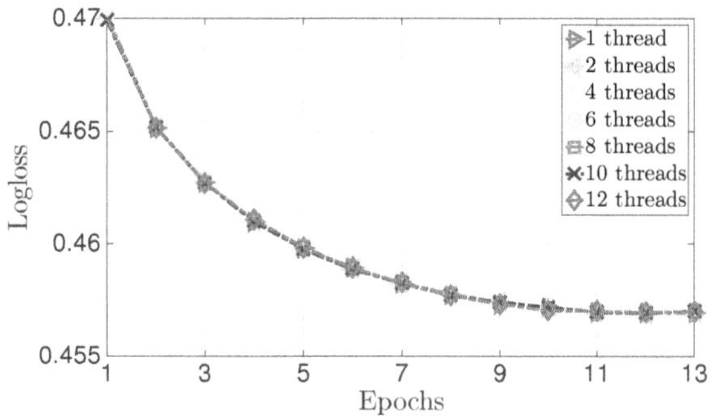

Figure 2: The convergence of using different number of threads.

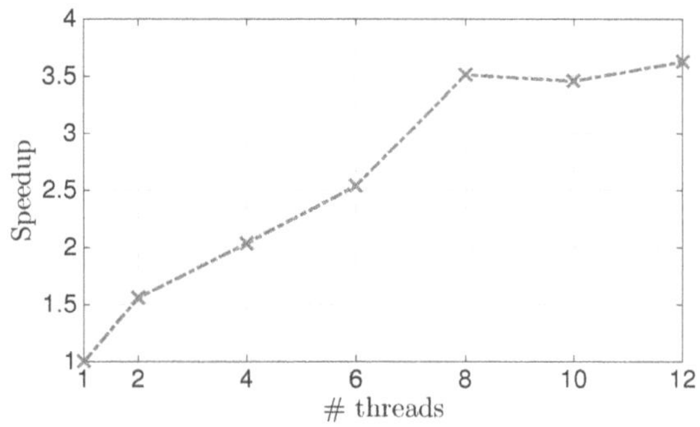

Figure 3: The speedup of using multi-threading. We respectively use `CriteoTr` and `CriteoVa` as the training and the test sets.

4.5 Comparison with LMs, Poly2, and FMs on Two CTR Competition Data Sets

To have a fair comparison, we implement the same SG method for LMs, Poly2, FMs, and FFMs. Further, we compare with two state-of-the-art packages:

- LIBLINEAR: a widely used package for linear models. For L2-regularized logistic regression, it implements two optimization methods: Newton method to solve the primal problem, and coordinate descent (CD) method to solve the dual problem. We used both for checking how optimization methods affect the performance; see the discussion in the end of this sub-section. Further, the existing Poly2 extension of LIBLINEAR does not support the hashing trick,[6] so we conduct suitable modifications and denote it as LIBLINEAR-Hash in this paper.
- LIBFM: As a widely used library for factorization machines, it supports three optimization approaches including stochastic gradient method (SG), alternating least squares (ALS), and Markov Chain Monte Carlo (MCMC). We tried all of them and found that ALS is significantly better than the other two in terms of logloss. Therefore, we consider ALS in our experiments.

For the parameters in all models, from a grid of points we select those that lead to the best performance on the validation sets. Results on `Criteo` and `Avazu` with the list of parameters used can be found in Table 3. Clearly, FFMs outperform other models in terms of logloss, but it also requires longer training time than LMs and FMs. On the other end, though the logloss of LMs is worse than other models, it is significantly faster. These results show a clear trade-off between logloss and speed. Poly2 is the slowest among all models. The reason might be the expensive computation of (2). FM is a good balance between logloss and speed.

For LIBFM, it performs closely to our implementation of FMs in terms of logloss on `Criteo`.[7] However, we see that our implementation is significantly faster. We provide three possible reasons:

- The ALS algorithm used by LIBFM is more complicated than the SG algorithm we use.
- We use an adaptive learning rate strategy in SG.
- We use SSE instructions to boost inner product operations.

Because logistic regression is a convex problem, ideally, for either LM or Poly2, the three optimization methods (SG, Newton, and CD) should generate exactly the same model if they converge to the global optimum. However, practically results are slightly different. In particular, LM by SG is better than the two LIBLINEAR-based models on Avazu. In our implementation, LM via SG only loosely solves the optimization problem. Our experiments therefore indicate that the stopping condition of optimization methods can affect the performance of the resulting model even if the problem is convex.

4.6 Comparison on More Data Sets

In the previous section we focus on two competition data sets, but it is important to see how FFMs perform on other data sets. To answer this question, we consider more data sets for the comparison, where most of them are not CTR data. Note that following the discussion in Section 3.3, we do not consider data sets with single-field features. The reason is that depending on how we assign fields, FFMs either become equivalent to FMs, or generate a huge model.

Here we briefly introduce the data sets used.

- `KDD2010-bridge`:[8] This data set includes both numerical and categorical features.
- `KDD2012`:[9] This set contains both numerical and categorical features. Because our evaluation is logloss, we transform the original target value "number of clicks" to a binary value "clicked or not." Further, we sub-sample 10% of negative instances because the data set is huge and contains much more negative instances than positive ones.
- `cod-rna`:[10] This set contains only numerical features.
- `ijcnn`:[10] This set contains only numerical features.
- `phishing`:[11] This set contains only categorical features.

[6]https://www.csie.ntu.edu.tw/~cjlin/libsvmtools/#fast_training_testing_for_polynomial_mappings_of_data

[7]The performance of LIBFM on `AvazuVa` is as good as the FM we have implemented, but the performance on `AvazuTe` is poor. It is not entirely clear what happened, so further investigation is needed.

[8]http://pslcdatashop.web.cmu.edu/KDDCup/downloads.jsp

[9]http://www.kddcup2012.org/c/kddcup2012-track2/data

[10]http://www.csie.ntu.edu.tw/~cjlin/libsvmtools/datasets/binary.html

[11]http://archive.ics.uci.edu/ml/datasets/Phishing+Websites

Model and implementation	parameters	training time (seconds)	public set logloss	public set rank	private set logloss	private set rank
LM-SG	$\eta = 0.2, \lambda = 0, t = 13$	688	0.46262	93	0.46224	91
LM-LIBLINEAR-CD	$s = 7, c = 2$	2,280	0.46239	91	0.46201	89
LM-LIBLINEAR-Newton	$s = 0, c = 2$	10,380	0.46320	105	0.46263	96
Poly2-SG	$\eta = 0.2, \lambda = 0, B = 10^7, t = 10$	18,581	0.45012	14	0.44996	15
Poly2-LIBLINEAR-Hash-CD	$s = 7, c = 2$	62,144	0.44917	14	0.44897	14
FM	$\eta = 0.05, \lambda = 2 \times 10^{-5}, k = 40, t = 8$	2,362	0.44935	14	0.44923	14
FM	$\eta = 0.05, \lambda = 2 \times 10^{-5}, k = 100, t = 9$	4,017	0.44826	10	0.44818	10
LIBFM	$\lambda = 40, k = 40, t = 20$	23,700	0.45012	14	0.45000	15
LIBFM	$\lambda = 40, k = 40, t = 50$	131,000	0.44904	14	0.44887	14
LIBFM	$\lambda = 40, k = 100, t = 20$	54,320	0.44853	11	0.44834	11
LIBFM	$\lambda = 40, k = 100, t = 50$	398,800	0.44794	9	0.44778	8
FFM	$\eta = 0.2, \lambda = 2 \times 10^{-5}, k = 4, t = 9$	10,454	0.44613	3	0.44603	3

(a) Criteo

Model and implementation	parameters	training time (seconds)	public set logloss	public set rank	private set logloss	private set rank
LM-SG	$\eta = 0.2, \lambda = 0, t = 10$	1360	0.39023	61	0.38833	64
LM-LIBLINEAR-CD	$s = 7, c = 1$	3045	0.39131	115	0.38943	119
LM-LIBLINEAR-Newton	$s = 0, c = 1$	4090	0.39269	182	0.39079	183
Poly2-SG	$\eta = 0.2, \lambda = 0, B = 10^7, t = 10$	8,808	0.38544	10	0.38342	10
Poly2-LIBLINEAR-Hash-CD	$s = 7, c = 1$	7,288	0.38510	10	0.38298	9
Poly2-LIBLINEAR-Hash-Newton	$s = 0, c = 1$	108,184	0.38633	11	0.38430	11
FM	$\eta = 0.05, \lambda = 2 \times 10^{-5}, k = 40, t = 8$	2,700	0.38616	11	0.38409	11
FM	$\eta = 0.05, \lambda = 2 \times 10^{-5}, k = 100, t = 9$	3,612	0.38666	11	0.38463	11
LIBFM	$\lambda = 40, k = 40, t = 20$	18,712	0.39137	122	0.38963	127
LIBFM	$\lambda = 40, k = 40, t = 50$	41,720	0.39786	935	0.39635	943
LIBFM	$\lambda = 40, k = 100, t = 20$	39,719	0.39644	747	0.39470	755
LIBFM	$\lambda = 40, k = 100, t = 50$	91,210	0.40740	1,129	0.40585	1,126
FFM	$\eta = 0.2, \lambda = 2 \times 10^{-5}, k = 4, t = 4$	4,766	0.38395	6	0.38205	6

(b) Avazu

Table 3: Comparison among models and implementations on data sets `Criteo` and `Avazu`. The training sets used here are `CriteoTrVa` and `AvazuTrVa`, and the test sets used here are `CriteoTe` and `AvazuTe`. For all experiments, a single thread is used. The public set is around 20% of the test data, while the private set contains the rest. For Criteo, we do not list the result of Poly2-LIBLINEAR-Hash-Newton, because the experiment does not finish after more than 10 days.

- `adult`:[12] This data set includes both numerical and categorical features.

For `KDD2010-bridge`, `KDD2012`, and `adult`, we simply discretize all numerical features into 29, 13, and 94 bins respectively. For `cod-rna` and `ijcnn`, where features are all numerical, we try both approaches mentioned in Section 3.3 to obtain field information: applying dummy fields and discretization.

For the parameter selection, we follow the same procedure in Section 4.5. We split each set into training, validation, and test sets; then for predicting the test set, we use the model trained with parameters that achieve the best logloss on the validation set.

The statistics and experimental results of each data set are described in Table 4. FFMs significantly outperform other models on `KDD2010-bridge` and `KDD2012`. The common characteristic among these data sets are:

- Most features are categorical.
- The resulting set is highly sparse after transforming categorical features into many binary features.

[12]http://archive.ics.uci.edu/ml/datasets/Adult

However, on `phishing` and `adult`, FFM is not significantly better. For `phishing`, the reason might be that the data is not sparse so FFM, FM, and Poly2 have close performance; for `adult`, it seems feature conjunction is not useful because all models perform similarly to the linear model.

When a data set contains only numerical features, FFMs may not have an obvious advantage. If we use dummy fields, then FFMs do not out-perform FMs, a result indicating that the field information is not helpful. On the other hand, if we discretize numerical features, though FFMs is the best among all models, the performance is much worse than that of using dummy fields. We summarize a guideline of applying FFMs on different kinds of data sets:

- FFMs should be effective for data sets that contain categorical features and are transformed to binary features.
- If the transformed set is not sparse enough, FFMs seem to bring less benefit.
- It is more difficult to apply FFMs on numerical data sets.

5. CONCLUSIONS AND FUTURE WORKS

In this paper we discuss efficient implementations of FFMs. We demonstrate that for certain kinds of data sets, FFMs

Data set	statistics # instances	# features	# fields	logloss LM	Poly2	FM	FFM
`KDD2010-bridge`	20,012,499	651,166	9	0.30910	0.27448	0.28437	<u>0.26899</u>
`KDD2012`	20,950,284	19,147,857	11	0.49375	0.49640	0.49292	<u>0.48700</u>
`phishing`	11,055	100	30	0.11493	0.09659	0.09461	<u>0.09374</u>
`adult`	48,842	308	14	0.30897	<u>0.30757</u>	0.30959	0.30760
`cod-rna` (dummy fields)	331,152	8	8	0.13829	0.12874	<u>0.12580</u>	0.12914
`cod-rna` (discretization)	331,152	2,296	8	0.16455	0.17576	0.16570	<u>0.14993</u>
`ijcnn` (dummy fields)	141,691	22	22	0.20627	0.09209	0.07696	<u>0.07668</u>
`ijcnn` (discretization)	141,691	69,867	22	0.21686	0.22546	0.22259	<u>0.18635</u>

Table 4: Comparison between LM, Poly2, FM, and FFMs. The best logloss is underlined.

outperform three well-known models, LM, Poly2, and FM, in terms of logloss, with a cost of longer training time.

For the future work, the over-fitting problem discussed in Section 4.3 is an issue that we plan to investigate. Besides, for the ease of implementation we use SG as the optimization method. It is interesting to see how other optimization methods (e.g., Newton method, coordinate descent) work on FFMs.

Acknowledgements

This work was supported in part by MOST via grants 104-2221-E-002-047-MY3 and 104-2622-E-002-012-CC2 and MOE of Taiwan via grant 105R7872.

6. REFERENCES

[1] O. Chapelle, E. Manavoglu, and R. Rosales, "Simple and scalable response prediction for display advertising," *ACM Transactions on Intelligent Systems and Technology*, vol. 5, no. 4, pp. 61:1–61:34, 2015.

[2] H. B. McMahan, G. Holt, D. Sculley, M. Young, D. Ebner, J. Grady, L. Nie, T. Phillips, E. Davydov, D. Golovin, S. Chikkerur, D. Liu, M. Wattenberg, A. M. Hrafnkelsson, T. Boulos, and J. Kubica, "Ad click prediction: a view from the trenches," in *Proceedings of the 19th ACM SIGKDD International Conference on Knowledge Discovery and Data Mining (KDD)*, 2013.

[3] M. Richardson, E. Dominowska, and R. Ragno, "Predicting clicks: estimating the click-through rate for new ADs," in *Proceedings of the 16th international conference on World Wide Web*, 2007.

[4] Y.-W. Chang, C.-J. Hsieh, K.-W. Chang, M. Ringgaard, and C.-J. Lin, "Training and testing low-degree polynomial data mappings via linear SVM," *Journal of Machine Learning Research*, vol. 11, pp. 1471–1490, 2010.

[5] T. Kudo and Y. Matsumoto, "Fast methods for kernel-based text analysis," in *Proceedings of the 41st Annual Meeting of the Association of Computational Linguistics (ACL)*, 2003.

[6] S. Rendle, "Factorization machines," in *Proceedings of IEEE International Conference on Data Mining (ICDM)*, pp. 995–1000, 2010.

[7] S. Rendle and L. Schmidt-Thieme, "Pairwise interaction tensor factorization for personalized tag recommendation," in *Proceedings of the 3rd ACM International Conference on Web Search and Data Mining (WSDM)*, pp. 81–90, 2010.

[8] M. Jahrer, A. Töscher, J.-Y. Lee, J. Deng, H. Zhang, and J. Spoelstra, "Ensemble of collaborative filtering and feature engineered model for click through rate prediction," in *KDD Cup 2012 Workshop*, ACM, 2012.

[9] J. Langford, L. Li, and A. Strehl, "Vowpal Wabbit," 2007. https: //github.com/JohnLangford/vowpal_wabbit/wiki.

[10] J. Duchi, E. Hazan, and Y. Singer, "Adaptive subgradient methods for online learning and stochastic optimization," *Journal of Machine Learning Research*, vol. 12, pp. 2121–2159, 2011.

[11] H. B. McMahan, "Follow-the-regularized-leader and mirror descent: Equivalence theorems and l1 regularization," in *Proceedings of the 14th International Conference on Artificial Intelligence and Statistics (AISTATS)*, 2011.

[12] W.-S. Chin, Y. Zhuang, Y.-C. Juan, and C.-J. Lin, "A learning-rate schedule for stochastic gradient methods to matrix factorization," in *Proceedings of the Pacific-Asia Conference on Knowledge Discovery and Data Mining (PAKDD)*, 2015.

[13] F. Niu, B. Recht, C. Ré, and S. J. Wright, "HOGWILD!: a lock-free approach to parallelizing stochastic gradient descent," in *Advances in Neural Information Processing Systems 24* (J. Shawe-Taylor, R. Zemel, P. Bartlett, F. Pereira, and K. Weinberger, eds.), pp. 693–701, 2011.

[14] R.-E. Fan, K.-W. Chang, C.-J. Hsieh, X.-R. Wang, and C.-J. Lin, "LIBLINEAR: a library for large linear classification," *Journal of Machine Learning Research*, vol. 9, pp. 1871–1874, 2008.

[15] S. Rendle, "Factorization machines with libFM," *ACM Transactions on Intelligent Systems and Technology (TIST)*, vol. 3, no. 3, p. 57, 2012.

[16] L. Dagum and R. Menon, "OpenMP: an industry standard API for shared-memory programming," *IEEE Computational Science and Engineering*, vol. 5, pp. 46–55, 1998.

[17] C. M. Bishop, *Pattern Recognition and Machine Learning*. Springer-Verlag New York, Inc., 2006.

[18] G. Raskutti, M. J. Wainwright, and B. Yu, "Early stopping and non-parametric regression: An optimal data-dependent stopping rule," *Journal of Machine Learning Research*, vol. 15, pp. 335–366, 2014.

[19] T. Zhang and B. Yu, "Boosting with early stopping: convergence and consistency," *The Annals of Statistics*, vol. 33, no. 4, pp. 1538–1579, 2005.

Learning Hierarchical Feature Influence for Recommendation by Recursive Regularization

Jie Yang*, Zhu Sun†, Alessandro Bozzon*, Jie Zhang†
*Delft University of Technology, †Nanyang Technological University
*{J.Yang-3, A.Bozzon}@tudelft.nl, †{SunZhu, ZhangJ}@ntu.edu.sg

ABSTRACT

Existing feature-based recommendation methods incorporate auxiliary features about users and/or items to address data sparsity and cold start issues. They mainly consider features that are organized in a flat structure, where features are independent and in a same level. However, auxiliary features are often organized in rich knowledge structures (e.g. hierarchy) to describe their relationships. In this paper, we propose a novel matrix factorization framework with *recursive regularization* – `ReMF`, which jointly models and learns the influence of hierarchically-organized features on user-item interactions, thus to improve recommendation accuracy. It also provides characterization of how different features in the hierarchy co-influence the modeling of user-item interactions. Empirical results on real-world data sets demonstrate that `ReMF` consistently outperforms state-of-the-art feature-based recommendation methods.

1. INTRODUCTION

Recommender systems aim to model user preferences towards items, and actively recommend relevant items to users. To address the *data sparsity* and *cold start* problems [23], feature-based recommendation methods, such as collective matrix factorization (CMF) [25], SVDFeature [4], and factorization machine (FM) [21], quickly gain prominence in recommender systems. They enable the integration of auxiliary features about users (e.g. gender, age) and items (e.g. category, content) with historical user-item interactions (e.g. ratings) to generate more accurate recommendations [24].

While commonly arranged in a flat structure (e.g. user gender, age), auxiliary features can be organized in a "feature scheme", i.e. a set of features that includes relationships between those features. Hierarchies are a natural yet powerful structure to human knowledge, and they provide a machine- and human- readable description of a set of features and their relationships. Typical examples of feature hierarchies include category hierarchy of on-line products (e.g. Amazon web store [19]), topic hierarchy of articles (e.g. Wikipedia [10]), genre hierarchy of music (e.g. Yahoo! Music), etc.. The benefits brought by the explicit modeling of feature relationships through hierarchies have been investigated in a broad spectrum of disciplines, from machine learning [12, 11] to natural language processing [10]. How to effectively exploit feature hierarchies in recommender systems is still an open research question. We here provide a running example to illustrate how hierarchical feature structure can provide better recommendations.

RecSys '16, September 15-19, 2016, Boston , MA, USA
© 2016 ACM. ISBN 978-1-4503-4035-9/16/09...$15.00
DOI: http://dx.doi.org/10.1145/2959100.2959159

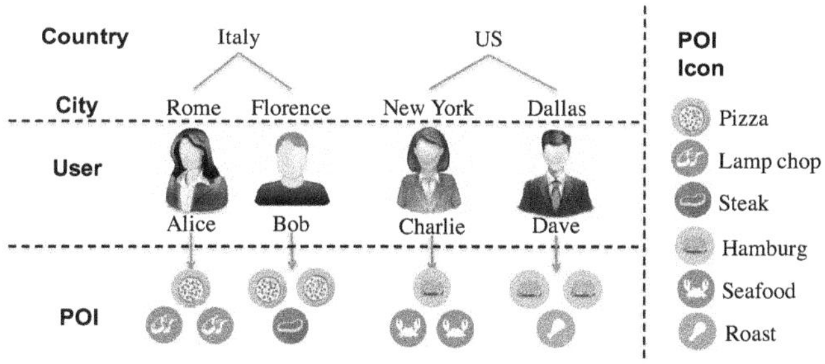

Figure 1: POI recommendation with auxiliary features hierarchy.

Running Example. Consider a point of interest (POI) recommender system [30], where the goal is to recommend a real-world POI (e.g. a restaurant) to a user. User preferences can be influenced by geo-cultural factors: for instance, the country of residence might have an influence on user preferences for restaurants' cuisine (intuitively, an Italian and an American might have different culinary tastes). Likewise, fellow countrymen might show different preferences according to their city of residence (arguably, citizens from Boston and San Diego can show incredible different culinary preferences). This scenario is represented in Figure 1: users are described by auxiliary features that characterize their countries and cities of residence. These features are organized in a hierarchy, where cities are related to countries by a *locatedIn* relationship.

We consider the historical POI interactions in a given city of four users in Figure 1: Alice and Bob, from Rome and Florence (Italy); Charlie and Dave from Boston and San Diego (US). Italian users (Alice and Bob) both show preferences towards Pizza, thus suggesting a "national imprint" on their preferences. However, the two users are differently influenced by their country of residence, as Alice's preference for pizza is weaker than that of Bob: Alice checks in more at Lamp chop restaurants, while Bob checks in more at Pizza restaurants. A similar observation holds also for Charlie and Dave: the influence of US is weaker than that of Boston on Charlie, while stronger than that of San Diego on Dave.

The example highlights how related features (a country and its cities, linked by the *locatedIn* relationship) can co-influence user preferences, although the strength of the co-influence varies across relationship instances (e.g. Italy-Rome, Italy-Florence). This observation suggests the need for feature relationships (e.g. the *locatedIn* relationship) to be properly considered in recommendation methods. This co-influence could be known as a priori, but it is often best learnt from historical user-item interaction data.

Existing feature-based methods, e.g. SVDFeature [5], CMF [25] and FM [21], ignore the useful information provided by feature relationships, imposing a conversion step that transforms a hierarchical structure into a flat one. To fully exploit feature hierarchies, the main challenge is to model the co-influence of features on user-item interactions, determined by both the feature relationships in the hierarchical structure and the historical user-item interaction data.

Original Contribution. We propose a novel approach that *models* the co-influence of hierarchically-organized features on user-item interactions, and *learns* the strength of such co-influence from historical user-item interaction data, to improve recommendation performance. We first define the influence of an individual feature as regularization on latent factors, then combine the regularization of individual features by weighting them recursively over the hierarchy, from root to leaves, according to their organization. The regularization of the feature hierarchy, named *recursive regularization*, is expressed as a regularization function parameterized by the weights associated to each feature. We then propose a novel recommendation framework `ReMF`, that integrates recursive regularization into the matrix factorization model to better learn latent factors. By learning the values of weights of each feature from the historical user-item interaction data, `ReMF` characterizes the influence of different features in a hierarchy on user-item interactions. We demonstrate the effectiveness of `ReMF` with an extensive validation performed on two recommendation scenarios, namely POI and product recommendation, and on multiple real-world data sets. Empirical results show that `ReMF` outperforms state-of-the-art approaches, scoring average improvements of 7.20% (MAE), 15.07% (RMSE) and 9.86% (AUC).

2. RELATED WORK

Incorporating auxiliary features into recommendation, i.e. feature-based recommendation [23, 24], has become a popular and effective approach to address the *data sparsity* and *cold start* problems. A wide range of features has been explored, including user gender and age [1, 6], item category [13] and content [20, 7].

Many feature-based recommendation methods consider only features with a flat structure. For example, Singh et al. [25, 17] propose the collective matrix factorization (CMF) method, which factorizes the user-item rating and user-feature matrices simultaneously, to improve the recommendation performance. Chen et al. [4] devise a machine learning tookit, named SVDFeature. The basic idea is that a user's (an item's) latent factor is influenced by those of her (its) features. Rendle et al. [21, 22] design factorization machines (FM) that combines the advantages of Support Vector Machines with factorization model. However, all of these methods mentioned above cannot cope with hierarchical feature structure. Blending a feature hierarchy into these models requires converting the hierarchy into a flat structure, thus losing the information about feature relationships. To fully exploit a feature hierarchy, `ReMF` combines the distinct influence of different features on user-item interactions according to their structured relationships.

Some studies on *taxonomy*-aware recommendation incorporate hierarchy in recommendation. For example, Ziegler et al. [33] and Weng et al. [29] propose to model a user's taxonomy preferences as a flat vector, where each element corresponds to the user's preference over a taxonomy feature. The user's preference is modeled as the frequency the user rates items characterized by the feature. Albadvi et al. [2] propose a similar method, however it models each feature as a preference vector, where the elements are feature attributes (e.g. price, brand). All of these methods ignore feature relationships. Koenigstein et al. [13] design a new matrix factorization model for Yahoo! Music competition that incorporates the feature hierarchy of track album and artist. They predict user preferences by fusing item (e.g. track) latent factors with feature (e.g. album, artist) vectors. This idea is similar to SVDFeature [4]. Though feature relationships are considered, they cannot fully exploit a feature hierarchy as they simply add feature latent factors to item latent factors, without taking into account the dependent influence of hierarchically-organized features on user-item interactions.

Another related line of research focuses on integrating the structure *within* users/items in recommendation, e.g. social network [27, 18, 26], webpage network [16], tag network [32]. These methods usually regularize latent factors of users/items that are linked in the network, based on heuristic definitions of similarity between users/items. For instance, Ma et al. [18] propose SoReg that regularizes user latent factors based on cosine similarity of ratings between socially connected users. These methods consider the network *within* users/items, though can be applied in the case of feature hierarchy, e.g. by constructing implicit connections between users/items according to their feature relationships in the hierarchy. However, an essential difference between these methods and ours is that the influence of features on user-item interactions considered in these methods is usually hard-coded with manually defined similarity between users/items; on the contrary our proposed framework can automatically learn the co-influence of different features from the historical user-item interaction data. Recently Wang et al. [28] propose to model the implicit hierarchical structure *within* users and items based on user-item interactions. Our work differs from this one, in that we consider leveraging explicit auxiliary features to guide the learning of latent factors.

In summary, existing methods are incapable to model the co-influence of hierarchically-organized features on user-item interactions, thus restricting their applications in recommendation. In contrast, our framework can fully exploit an auxiliary feature hierarchy through the learning of hierarchical feature influence.

3. DATA ANALYSIS

This section demonstrates the need for recommendation methods able to account for the co-influence on user-item interactions of hierarchically-organized features.

Inspired by the running example, we show on 8 different data sets how: 1) users from the same country (named Country Visitors) are more similar in terms of POI preferences compared with users from different countries (named Foreign Visitors); and 2) users from the same city (named City Visitors) are more similar in terms of POI preferences compared to users from different cities *but the same country* (named Domestic Visitors).

Data Sets We collect data of Foursquare check-in's performed over 3 weeks in 4 European capital cities (Amsterdam, London, Paris, Rome) and published on 2 social media platforms (Twitter, Instagram). Table 1 shows the statistics about the 8 data sets. We consider users' residence *city*, *country* and *continent* as auxiliary information about users, as well as a root feature *residence location*. We use the method described in [3] to locate users' residence locations. For conciseness, we only analyze the co-influence of *country* and *city*. Overall we consider 121 countries and 2,873 cities.

Analysis Metrics. We denote all countries as $Con_1, \ldots, Con_s$; each country Con_s is the parent of all cities in it, i.e. $Con_s = parent(Cit_1, \ldots, Cit_t)$. Each user u_i from a city Cit_t and a country Con_s ($Con_s = parent(Cit_t)$), has a set of visited POIs, i.e. $POI(u_i) = \{poi_{i1}, poi_{i2}, \ldots\}$. Then we measure the similarity between the users u_i and u_k using Jaccard similarity, i.e. $Jar(u_i, u_k) = |POI(u_i) \cap POI(u_k)| / |POI(u_i) \cup POI(u_k)|$.

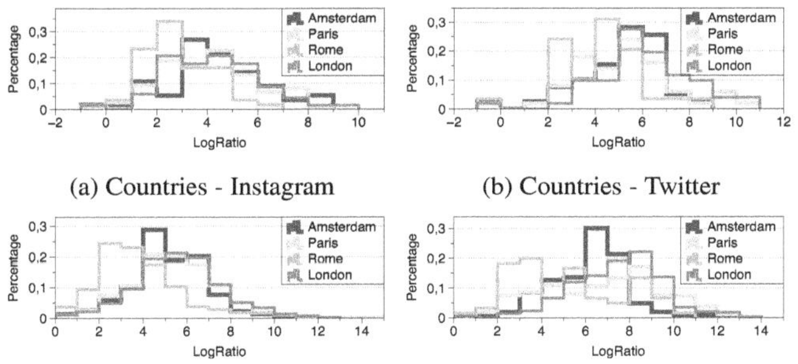

(a) Countries - Instagram (b) Countries - Twitter

(c) Cities - Instagram (d) Cities - Twitter

Figure 2: Distribution of the ratio between similarity (a, b) among countries and across countries, or (c, d) among cities and across cities, through the lens of (a, c) Instagram and (b, d) Twitter, including user visits to 4 European capital cities Amsterdam, Paris,Rome, and London (4 colors).

Table 1: Descriptive statistics of the data sets.

		Amsterdam	Rome	Paris	London
Inst.	#Users	4,318	4,081	11,345	12,719
	#POIs	5,768	7,878	14,849	12,892
	#Check-in's	28,142	26,714	80,553	66,092
	Sparsity	99.89%	99.92%	99.95%	99.96%
Twit.	#Users	1,599	1,369	6,521	9,305
	#POIs	3,816	4,876	16,046	14,117
	#Check-in's	8,670	8,727	43,541	48,852
	Sparsity	99.86%	99.87%	99.96%	99.96%

We define u_i's similarity with the other Country Visitors (City Visitors), and with all Foreign Visitors (Domestic Visitors) as

$$Sim(F, u_i^w) = \frac{1}{|F|-1} \sum_{u_k \in F, u_i \neq u_k} Jar(u_i, u_k),$$

$$Sim(F, u_i^a) = \frac{1}{|parent(F)| - |F|} \sum_{u_k \in parent(F), u_k \notin F} Jar(u_i, u_k),$$

respectively, where F is the country (or city) u_i resides in, and $|F|$ is the number of users characterized by the feature F. For instance, in the case of $F = Con_s$, the similarity between u_i and the other Country Visitors, denoted by $Sim(Con_s, u_i^w)$, is the averaged similarity between u_i and each of the other Country Visitors; the similarity between u_i and Foreign Visitors, denoted by $Sim(Con_s, u_i^a)$, is the averaged similarity between u_i and each of the Foreign Visitors. The similarity between u_i and the other City Visitors and Domestic Visitors can be similarly calculated. Now we define the overall similarity within a country (city) F, and across the country (city) and other countries (cities) as $Sim(F^w) = [Sim(F, u_1^w), Sim(F, u_2^w), \ldots]$ and $Sim(F^a) = [Sim(F, u_1^a), Sim(F, u_2^a), \ldots]$, respectively. Then we compare the overall similarity within a country (city), and that across the country (city) and other countries (cities) by:

$$LogRatio(F) = Log_2\Big(\frac{1}{|F|} \sum_{u_i \in F} \frac{Sim(F, u_i^w)}{Sim(F, u_i^a)}\Big),$$

where $LogRatio(F) > 0$ indicates that the elements in $Sim(F^w)$ is larger than that in $Sim(F^a)$ on average, and $LogRatio(F)) < 0$ otherwise. We test the significance of the difference between $Sim(F^w)$ and $Sim(F^a)$ with a Paired t-test.

Observation 1: *Country Visitors are more similar with each other in terms of POI preferences than with Foreign Visitors.*

The distribution of $LogRatio(Con)$ for all countries is shown in Figures 2(a-b) for Instagram and Twitter, respectively. More than 95% of the countries observed in both Instagram and Twitter have $LogRatio(Con) > 0$. Paired t-test shows that 95.88% countries in Instagram and 99.36% in Twitter have $Sim(Con^w)$ significantly larger than $Sim(Con^a)$ (p-value < 0.01). We thus conclude that Country Visitors are more similar with each other in terms of POI preferences than with Foreign Visitors.

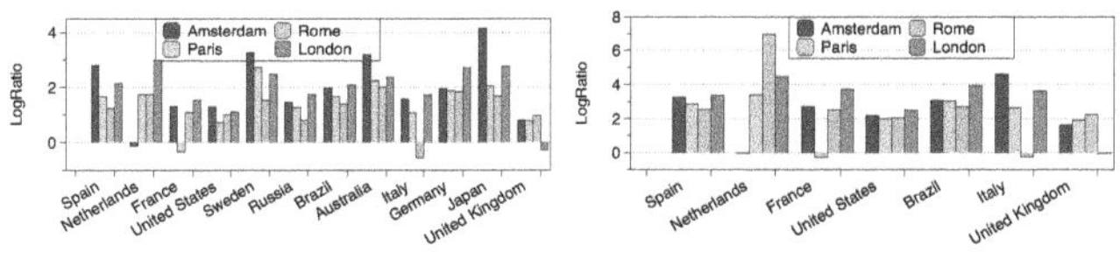

(a) Countries - Instagram (b) Countries - Twitter

Figure 3: Ratio between similarity of users within a country and across the country and other countries, for countries with more than 100 cities observed through the lens of Instagram and Twitter.

Figures 3(a-b) show the $LogRatio(Con)$ for countries with more than 100 cities observed in the two platforms. We can see that users from different countries have different similarities when visiting the same city; and that the similarity of users from the same country varies across visited cities. These observations highlight the need for recommendation methods that can account for the variability caused by user residence country as well as visiting cities. Interestingly, all countries with $LogRatio(Con) < 0$ in both Figures 3(a,b) are the ones whose capital cities are visited, indicating that in visiting the capital city of their own countries, Country Visitors are less similar than Foreign Visitors. We find that this is due to that Country Visitors are mostly commuters in visiting their capital cities, i.e. they go to work places in the capital cities.

Observation 2: *City Visitors are more similar with each other in terms of POI preferences than with Domestic Visitors.*

The distribution of $LogRatio(Cit)$ for all cities in all countries is shown in Figures 2(c-d) for Instagram and Twitter. We can observe that all cities have $LogRatio(Cit)$ greater than 0; 88.44% of them in Instagram and 88.15% in Twitter have $Sim(Cit^w)$ significantly larger than $Sim(Cit^a)$ (p-value < 0.01). We therefore conclude that the similarity within City Visitors is higher than that with Domestic Visitors. Comparing the distribution of cities with that of countries, all cities have $LogRatio(Con) > 0$ while there are some countries with $LogRatio(Con) < 0$ (those whose capital cities are visited), indicating that users from the same city are more similar than users from the same country. Moreover, we find that generally cities have larger values of $LogRatio$ than countries. For instance the mean values of the distribution of Amsterdam in Figures 2(a,c) are 4.09 and 5.07, respectively. This observation hints that cities generally have larger influence than countries on their residents' preferences.

4. RECURSIVE REGULARIZATION FOR MODELING FEATURE CO-INFLUENCE

We adopt the regularization technique to model the influence of auxiliary features. To do so, we have to consider feature relationships, and further allow for the learning of feature influence from historical user-item interaction data. For this we introduce a novel regularization method, named *recursive regularization*, that models the co-influence of features by recursively weighting each feature influence, traversing from root to leaves in the feature hierarchy.

4.1 Preliminaries

We first introduce the notations. Let $\mathcal{U} = \{u_1, u_2, \ldots, u_m\}$ be the set of m users, and $\mathcal{V} = \{v_1, v_2, \ldots, v_n\}$ be the set of n items. Given a user-item interaction matrix $\mathbf{R} \in \mathbb{R}^{m \times n}$, $\mathbf{R}_{ij}$ is a positive number denoting the rating given by u_i to v_j. $\mathbf{O} \in \mathbb{R}^{m \times n}$ denotes the indicator matrix, where $\mathbf{O}_{ij} = 1$ indicates that u_i rates v_j, and $\mathbf{O}_{ij} = 0$ otherwise. $\mathcal{F} = \{F_1, F_2, \ldots, F_t\}$ is the set of features, each of which describes at least one user in $\mathcal{U}$.

Table 2: Notations.

Notation	Explanation
$\mathcal{U}, \mathcal{V}$	user, item set
u_i/u_k, v_j	the ith/kth user in $\mathcal{U}$, and jth item in $\mathcal{V}$
$\mathbf{R}_{ij}$	rating given by user u_i to item v_j
$\hat{\mathbf{R}}_{ij}$	estimated rating for user u_i to item v_j
$\mathbf{O}$	indicator matrix indicating missing entries in $\mathbf{R}$
$\mathbf{U}_i$, $\mathbf{V}_j$	latent factors of user u_i and item v_j
$\mathcal{F}$	hierarchically-organized feature set
F	feature in the hierarchy
$Dis(F)$	regularization induced by *isolated* feature F
$Fu(F)$	feature unit with parent node F
$\mathbf{I}'(F)$	regularization by *isolated* feature unit $Fu(F)$
g, s	weighting parameters in propagating feature influence
$\mathbf{I}(F)$	regularization by feature unit $Fu(F)$ in hierarchy
$\mathbf{I}(\mathcal{F})$	regularization by feature hierarchy $\mathcal{F}$
$\mathbf{C}_{ik}$	regularization coefficient between $\mathbf{U}_i$ and $\mathbf{U}_k$
α	impact of recursive regularization
λ	regularizaton coefficient to avoid over-fitting
$\mathcal{J}$	objective function of ReMF framework

The features are organized hierarchically in a tree structure, where each node represents a feature in $\mathcal{F}$. The edge between a parent node $F_p \in \mathcal{F}$ and a child node $F_c \in \mathcal{F}$ represents a directed affiliation relationship, i.e. F_c belongs to F_p. Figure 4a shows an example containing three leaf features F_1, F_2, F_3, i.e. features with no children. F_1, F_2 are children of the internal feature F_4. F_3 and F_4 are children of the root feature F_5. For simplicity, we assume that each user is explicitly associated with at most one leaf feature in $\mathcal{F}$. Table 2 summarizes all the notations throughout this paper.

Our method is built on matrix factorization (MF) [15], which assumes the existence of latent structures in the user-item interaction matrix. By uncovering latent factors of users and items, it approximates the observed ratings and estimates the unobserved ratings. MF solves the following optimization problem:

$$\min_{\mathbf{U},\mathbf{V}} \frac{1}{2}\sum_{i,j} \mathbf{O}_{ij}(\mathbf{R}_{ij} - \mathbf{U}_i\mathbf{V}_j^T)^2 + \frac{\lambda}{2}(\|\mathbf{U}\|_F^2 + \|\mathbf{V}\|_F^2), \quad (1)$$

where $\mathbf{U} \in \mathbb{R}^{m\times d}$ and $\mathbf{V} \in \mathbb{R}^{n\times d}$ are the latent factors of users and items, respectively. d is the dimension of latent factors. λ is the regularization coefficient to avoid over-fitting. The unobserved rating for user u_i to item v_j can be estimated by the inner product of the corresponding user and item latent factors, i.e. $\hat{\mathbf{R}}_{ij} = \mathbf{U}_i^T\mathbf{V}_j$.

4.2 Modeling Influence of Feature Hierarchy on User-item Interactions

Step by step, we model the influence from a single feature to the combinations of features and finally the entire feature hierarchy.

Influence of an Isolated Feature. To start, we first define the regularization by an isolated feature F_p in the hierarchy as:

$$Dis(F_p) = \sum_{u_i,u_k \in F_p, i<k} \|\mathbf{U}_i - \mathbf{U}_k\|_F^2, \quad (2)$$

where $\|\mathbf{U}_i - \mathbf{U}_k\|_F^2$ is the squared Frobenius norm distance between the latent factors of u_i and u_k characterized by feature F_p: F_p poses regularization on the cumulation of the pairwise distance between users associated with it. Thus, $Dis(F_p)$ can be considered as the influence of the isolated feature F_p on user-item interactions by regularizing user latent factors. The definition here only considers the influence of an *isolated* feature, while the co-influence of the feature hierarchy contributed by the feature, i.e. influence of the feature *in the hierarchy*, is different from – but based on – the influence of the *isolated* feature, which will be illustrated later.

Our method models feature influence by regularizing user latent factors, and can be straightforward transferred to modeling the influence by regularizing item latent factors, or both of them.

Influence of an Isolated Feature Unit. Given the above definition, we now model the influence of an isolated combination of features, on learning user latent factors, by introducing the most important relationship among features in a hierarchy, i.e. *parent-child* relationship, based on which other relationships among features in the hierarchy such as *siblings*, *ancestors* can be derived. We first define the *feature unit*, i.e. $Fu(F_p)$, as the combination of a single parent node F_p and its children nodes, namely:

$$Fu(F_p) = \{F_p\} \cup \{F_c | \forall F_c \in children(F_p)\}.$$

Two examples of feature units $Fu(F_5)$ and $Fu(F_4)$ are shown in the red dash boxes in Figure 4a.

Then we consider the influence of an isolated feature unit on learning user latent factors by regularization. For each isolated feature unit $Fu(F_p)$, we denote its influence as $\mathbf{I}'(F_p)$, and assign it two parameters g_p, s_p, with the constraint $g_p + s_p = 1$. Parameters g_p and s_p are used to distribute the influence of the feature unit to two parts. One is given by the parent node, weighted by g_p, and the other is given by the children nodes, weighted by s_p. The influence of the isolated feature unit, i.e. $\mathbf{I}'(F_p)$, is then defined as:

$$\mathbf{I}'(F_p) = g_p Dis(F_p) + s_p(\sum_{\forall F_c \in children(F_p)} Dis(F_c)).$$

For example, the influence of the isolated feature unit $Fu(F_5)$ in Figure 4a, i.e. $\mathbf{I}'(F_5)$, is determined by both the influence of the parent node F_5, i.e. $Dis(F_5)$, weighted by g_5, and the influence of its children nodes, i.e. $Dis(F_3)$ and $Dis(F_4)$, weighted by s_5. The overall influence of this isolated feature unit is: $\mathbf{I}'(F_5) = g_5 Dis(F_5) + s_5(Dis(F_3) + Dis(F_4))$. Compared with the influence of the isolated feature F_5, the influence of feature F_5 in $Fu(F_5)$ is different, in that $Dis(F_5)$ is weighted by g_5.

Influence of an Entire Feature Hierarchy. Based on the definition of the influence of an *isolated* feature unit, we now proceed to model the influence of feature unit *in the hierarchy*, thus to formally derive the overall influence of an entire feature hierarchy on user latent factors. Note that the influence of a feature unit *in the hierarchy* is different from – but based on – the influence of the *isolated* feature unit, and can be achieved by recursively defining the regularization of the feature unit *in the hierarchy*, given by:

DEFINITION 1 (**RECURSIVE REGULARIZATION**).

$$\mathbf{I}(F_p) = \begin{cases} g_p Dis(F_p) + s_p(\sum_{\forall F_c \in children(F_p)} \mathbf{I}(F_c)), & \textit{if } F_p \textit{ is an internal feature;} \\ Dis(F_p), & \textit{if } F_p \textit{ is a leaf feature and } |F_p| > 1; \\ 0, & \textit{otherwise,} \end{cases}$$

where $|F_p|$ is the number of users characterized by feature F_p.

From the above definition, we can see the difference between the influence of a feature unit *in the hierarchy* $\mathbf{I}(F_p)$ and the influence of an *isolated* feature unit $\mathbf{I}'(F_p)$, that is, $\mathbf{I}(F_p)$ is recursively defined on $\mathbf{I}(F_c)$. Put another way, the influence of a child feature is included in the influence of its parent feature. Hence, the influence of an entire feature hierarchy, denoted by $\mathbf{I}(\mathcal{F})$, is equivalent to that of the root feature, as it recursively includes the influence of all features in the hierarchy. As an example, Equation 3 shows the influence of the feature hierarchy in Figure 4a.

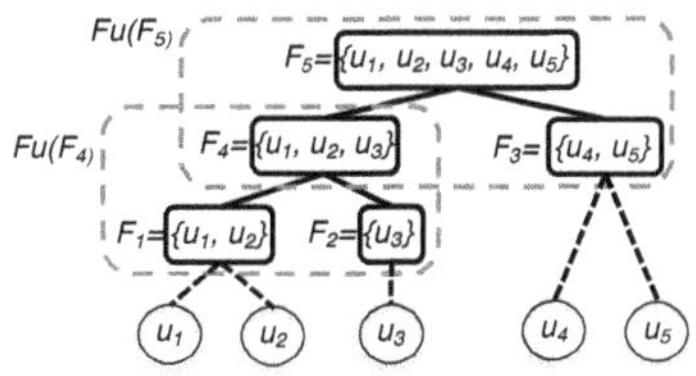

(a) Feature hierarchy

	u_1	u_2	u_3	u_4	u_5
u_1	-	1	$g_5+s_5g_4$	g_5	g_5
u_2	1	-	$g_5+s_5g_4$	g_5	g_5
u_3	$g_5+s_5g_4$	$g_5+s_5g_4$	-	g_5	g_5
u_4	g_5	g_5	g_5	-	1
u_5	g_5	g_5	g_5	1	-

(b) Regularization coefficients

Figure 4: (a) illustrates a feature hierarchy, where features with children (i.e. F_5, F_4) are called *internal features*. Particularly, F_5 is also named *root feature*, whereas features without children are called *leaf features*. Dash and solid lines respectively represent the user-feature (i.e. a user is characterized by a feature) and feature-feature (i.e. parent-child) relationships. Features in a red dash box comprises a feature unit. (b) shows the corresponding regularization coefficients of the corresponding example.

$$\begin{aligned}
\mathbf{I}(\mathcal{F}) &= \mathbf{I}(F_5) \\
&= g_5 Dis(F_5) + s_5(\mathbf{I}(F_4) + \mathbf{I}(F_3)) \\
&= g_5 Dis(F_5) + s_5(g_4 Dis(F_4) + s_4(\mathbf{I}(F_1) + \mathbf{I}(F_2)) + Dis(F_3)) \\
&= g_5 Dis(F_5) + s_5(g_4 Dis(F_4) + s_4 Dis(F_1) + Dis(F_3)). \quad (3)
\end{aligned}$$

The deduction of recursive regularization of a feature hierarchy is shown in Algorithm 1, where the co-influence of features is modeled as a regularization function parameterized by the weights of each feature in the hierarchy. These weights characterize the influence of distinct features, and can be further learnt from historical user-item interaction data, as we introduce in the next section.

Remark. By recursively weighting and combining feature influence over a hierarchy from the root feature to the leaves, recursive regularization can model the influence of an arbitrarily deep feature hierarchy that can be either balanced or imbalanced.

5. REMF: A RECOMMENDATION FRAMEWORK INTEGRATED WITH RECURSIVE REGULARIZATION

We first introduce a novel recommendation framework ReMF, that integrates the recursive regularization into the MF model to exploit auxiliary feature hierarchy. Then an optimization method and the complexity analysis for ReMF are presented.

5.1 The ReMF Framework

By incorporating recursive regularization into the MF, the ReMF framework is defined by:

DEFINITION 2 (**THE REMF FRAMEWORK**).

$$\min_{\substack{\mathbf{U},\mathbf{V},\\ g_p, s_p \forall F_p \in \mathcal{F}}} \mathcal{J} = \frac{1}{2}\sum_{i,j}\mathbf{O}_{ij}(\mathbf{R}_{ij} - \mathbf{U}_i\mathbf{V}_j^T)^2 + \frac{\alpha}{2}\mathbf{I}(\mathcal{F}) + \frac{\lambda}{2}(\|\mathbf{U}\|_F^2 + \|\mathbf{V}\|_F^2)$$

where α is a regularization parameter that controls the impact of recursive regularization, i.e. $\mathbf{I}(\mathcal{F})$.

Thanks to recursive regularization, ReMF can model the co-influence of features in the hierarchy to learn user latent factors.

It also characterizes the distinct influence of each feature, thus helping with the interpretation of the effect of each feature in the hierarchy on recommendation, illustrated as follows.

Considering the example of Figure 4, based on Equations 2 and 3, the feature hierarchy influence $\mathbf{I}(\mathcal{F})$ can be rewritten as:

$$(g_5 + s_5g_4 + s_5s_4)\|\mathbf{U}_1 - \mathbf{U}_2\|_F^2 + (g_5 + s_5g_4)\|\mathbf{U}_1 - \mathbf{U}_3\|_F^2 + \ldots,$$

where the strength of the regularization between u_1, u_2's latent factors is $(g_5 + s_5g_4 + s_5s_4)$, and that of u_1, u_3's latent factors is

Algorithm 1: Recursive Regularization Deduction

Input: feature hierarchy $\mathcal{F}$, $g_p, s_p \forall F_p \in \mathcal{F}$
foreach $F_p \in \mathcal{F}$ **do**
  $\mathbf{I}(F_p) \leftarrow 0$;
$layer \leftarrow$ #layers of $\mathcal{F}$;
for $l = 0; l \leq layer; l++$ **do**
  foreach *feature F_p at layer l of $\mathcal{F}$* **do**
    if *F_p is a leaf feature ($l = 0$) and $|F_p| > 1$* **then**
      $\mathbf{I}(F_p) \leftarrow Dis(F_p)$;
    else if *F_p is an internal feature ($l \neq 0$)* **then**
      $\mathbf{I}(F_p) \leftarrow$
      $g_p Dis(F_p) + s_p(\sum_{\forall F_c \in children(F_p)} \mathbf{I}(F_c))$;
$\mathbf{I}(\mathcal{F}) \leftarrow \mathbf{I}(F_{root})$;

$(g_5 + s_5g_4)$. In fact, the strength of regularization is the combination of influence of different features. For simplicity, we assume $g = s = 0.5$ for each internal feature. Therefore, the strength of regularization between u_1, u_2's latent factors is $(g_5 + s_5g_4 + s_5s_4) = 1$, from which we could see that the feature F_5 has an influence of $g_5 = 0.5$, while its children features F_4 and F_1 have influence of $s_5g_4 = 0.25$ and $s_5s4 = 0.25$, respectively. Then, for u_1, u_3, the strength of regularization between their latent factors is $(g_5 + s_5g_4) = 0.75$, where the features F_5, F_4 have influence of $g_5 = 0.5, s_5g_4 = 0.25$, respectively. The distinct influence of features on learning user latent factors can therefore be characterized by certain functions of the weights (g, s).

To formally derive feature influence on an arbitrary pair of users, we define the *regularization coefficient* $\mathbf{C}_{ik}$ to represent the strength of regularization between u_i and u_k, where a greater value of $\mathbf{C}_{ik}$ indicates a higher correlation between the two users. Hence, $\mathbf{I}(\mathcal{F})$ can be reformulated as:

$$\mathbf{I}(\mathcal{F}) = \sum_{u_i, u_k \in \mathcal{U}, i<k} \mathbf{C}_{ik}\|\mathbf{U}_i - \mathbf{U}_k\|_F^2,$$

We next introduce two theorems for deriving $\mathbf{C}_{ik}$, which is the combination of the influence by different features on u_i and u_k.

THEOREM 1. *The regularization coefficient for any pair of users u_i, u_k (i.e. $\mathbf{C}_{ik}$) characterized by the same leaf feature is 1:*

$$g_{root} + s_{root}(g_{c_1} + s_{c_1}(g_{c_2} + s_{c_2}(\ldots(g_{c_l} + s_{c_l})))) = 1,$$

where the list $\{F_{root}, F_{c_1}, F_{c_2}, \ldots, F_{c_l}\}$ is the set of the common features of u_i and u_k, ordered in a sequence from the root feature F_{root} to the leaf feature F_{c_l}.

Proof. This is straightforward to prove, due to the constraint $g+s = 1$. Considering the example $\{u_1, u_2\}$ in Figure 4, the sum of the relevant regularization terms, i.e. $g_5Dis(F_5), s_5g_4Dis(F_4)$ and $s_5s_4Dis(F_1)$, in Equation 3 is:

$$\begin{aligned}
&(g_5 + s_5(g_4 + s_4))\|\mathbf{U}_1 - \mathbf{U}_2\|_F^2 \\
=&(g_5 + s_5)\|\mathbf{U}_1 - \mathbf{U}_2\|_F^2 = \|\mathbf{U}_1 - \mathbf{U}_2\|_F^2.
\end{aligned}$$

THEOREM 2. *For any pair of users u_i, u_k not characterized by a common leaf feature, the regularization coefficient (i.e. $\mathbf{C}_{ik}$) is:*

$$g_{root} + s_{root}(g_{c_1} + s_{c_1}(g_{c_2} + s_{c_2}(\ldots(g_{c_l})))),$$

where the list $\{F_{root}, F_{c_1}, F_{c_2}, \ldots, F_{c_l}\}$ is the set of the common features of u_i and u_k, ordered from the root feature F_{root} to the deepest common feature F_{c_l}.

Proof. All possible features that can influence the regularization coefficient of u_i, u_k are their deepest common feature, and the parents and ancestors of the deepest common feature.

According to the above theorems, the value of regularization coefficient always falls into the range of $[0, 1]$, with 1 indicating the

Algorithm 2: ReMF Model Learning

```
Input: rating matrix R , feature hierarchy 𝓕, d, γ, λ, α, iter
Initialize U, V, g_p, s_p, and ∀F_p ∈ 𝓕;
for t = 1; t ≤ iter; t++ do
    foreach U_i ∈ U, V_j ∈ V do
        U_i^(t) ← U_i^(t−1) − γ ∂𝒥/∂U_i;
        V_j^(t) ← V_j^(t−1) − γ ∂𝒥/∂V_j;
    foreach Internal feature in the hierarchy do
        g_p^(t) ← g_p^(t−1) − γ ∂𝒥/∂g_p;
        s_p^(t) ← s_p^(t−1) − γ ∂𝒥/∂s_p;
    Calculate 𝒥 by Algorithm 1 and Definition 2;
    if 𝒥 has converged then
        break;
```

full regularization and 0 indicating no regularization. As an example, Figure 4b shows the regularization coefficients of the feature hierarchy in Figure 4a.

These regularization coefficients naturally connect ReMF to network based recommendation methods, which also consider pairwise regularization on users. There are however two essential differences: 1) network-based regularization coefficients are usually hard-coded, while our regularization coefficients are modeled from the feature hierarchy structure, and expressed by the function of weights (g, s). And, 2) (g, s), which parametrizes the distinct feature influence while being automatically learnt from the historical user-item interaction data, as we will address in the next subsection.

5.2 The Optimization Method for ReMF

We adopt the stochastic gradient descent scheme [14, 15] to optimize our objective function.

Updating $\mathbf{U}, \mathbf{V}$. The gradients of $\mathbf{U}_i, \mathbf{V}_j$ are given by:

$$\frac{\partial \mathcal{J}}{\partial \mathbf{U}_i} = -\sum_j \mathbf{O}_{ij}(\mathbf{R}_{ij} - \mathbf{U}_i\mathbf{V}_j^T)\mathbf{V}_j + \lambda\mathbf{U}_i + \alpha \sum_{u_i, u_k \in \mathcal{U}, i<k} \mathbf{C}_{ik}(\mathbf{U}_i - \mathbf{U}_k),$$

$$\frac{\partial \mathcal{J}}{\partial \mathbf{V}_j} = -\sum_i \mathbf{O}_{ij}(\mathbf{R}_{ij} - \mathbf{U}_i\mathbf{V}_j^T)\mathbf{U}_i + \lambda\mathbf{V}_j.$$

Updating (g, s). (g, s) can be predefined heuristically, or handcrafted by domain experts who can fairly quantify the influence of different features. Instead, we provide an effective data-driven solution that automatically learns (g, s) based on the historical user-item interaction data.

We only need to estimate (g, s) for internal features in the hierarchy, since the leaf features do not have children. For an internal feature F_p, the gradients of g_p, s_p are equivalent to the multipliers of g_p, s_p in $\mathbf{I}(\mathcal{F})$. Thus, we have:

$$\frac{\partial \mathcal{J}}{\partial g_p} = \begin{cases} Dis(F_p), & \text{if } F_p \text{ is root,} \\ \prod_{\forall a: F_a \in ancestors(F_p)} s_a Dis(F_p), & \text{otherwise;} \end{cases}$$

$$\frac{\partial \mathcal{J}}{\partial s_p} = \begin{cases} \sum_{\forall F_c \in children(F_p)} \mathbf{I}(F_c), & \text{if } F_p \text{ is root,} \\ \prod_{\forall a: F_a \in ancestors(F_p)} s_a (\sum_{\forall F_c \in children(F_p)} \mathbf{I}(F_c)), & \\ & \text{otherwise.} \end{cases}$$

According to the constraint $g_p + s_p = 1$, we can update g_p (or s_p) using the gradient and the other by $s_p = 1 - g_p$ (or $g_p = 1 - s_p$). The detailed learning process is shown in Algorithm 2.

Complexity Analysis The computational time is mainly taken by evaluating the objective function $\mathcal{J}$ and updating the related variables. The time to compute the $\mathcal{J}$ is $\mathcal{O}(d|\mathbf{R}| + dm^2)$, where $|\mathbf{R}|$ is the number of non-zero observations in the rating matrix $\mathbf{R}$. For all gradients $\frac{\partial \mathcal{J}}{\partial \mathbf{U}_i}, \frac{\partial \mathcal{J}}{\partial \mathbf{V}_j}, \frac{\partial \mathcal{J}}{\partial g_p}, \frac{\partial \mathcal{J}}{\partial s_p}$, the computational time are $\mathcal{O}(d|\mathbf{R}| + dm^2)$, $\mathcal{O}(d|\mathbf{R}|)$, $\mathcal{O}\left(d\sum_{l=0}^{layer-1} \frac{\overline{m}_l(\overline{m}_l - 1)n_l}{2}\right)$ and $\mathcal{O}(|s_p|)$, respectively. Wherein $\overline{m}_l$ denotes the average number of users in each node at layer l, n_l denotes the number of nodes at layer l, and $|s_p|$ ($\ll |\mathbf{R}|$) denotes the number of internal nodes. Particularly, we leverage $s_p = (1 - g_p)$ to update s_p. The overall computational complexity of Algorithm 2 is $(\#iteration * \mathcal{O}(d|\mathbf{R}| + dq))$, where $q = max(\sum_{l=0}^{layer-1} \frac{\overline{m}_l(\overline{m}_l - 1)n_l}{2}, m^2)$. In real-world applications $\overline{m}_l$ is typically small (e.g. power-law distributed), thus making ReMF scalable to large data set.

6. EXPERIMENTS AND RESULTS

We assess the performance of ReMF with a comparison with the state-of-the-art, feature-based, hierarchy-based recommendation methods. The comparison is performed over 1) the data sets introduced in Section 3, for POI recommendation with user feature hierarchy; and 2) a data set from the Amazon Web store [19], for product recommendation with item feature hierarchy.

6.1 Experimental Setup

Evaluation. We adopt the standard 5-fold cross-validation, and the following 3 metrics for evaluation: Mean Absolute Error (MAE) and Root Mean Square Error (RMSE) [13, 22] to measure the error of predicted ratings; and Area Under the ROC Curve (AUC) [9, 31] to measure the quality of predicted ranking of items (ranked according to the predicted ratings). The smaller MAE and RMSE, and the larger AUC, the better the recommendation performance.

Comparison Methods. The following methods are compared: (1) **MF** [15]: matrix factorization method; (2) **CMF** [25]: collective MF; (3) **TaxMF** [13]: taxonomy-based MF; (4) **SoReg** [18]: network-based recommendation method incorporating social relations; (5) **FM** [22]: factorization machine; (6) **HieFM**: factorization machine with hierarchy information.

HieFM is a variation of FM that considers each features path in the hierarchy (from root to leaf nodes) as an additional feature in the design vectors of FM. Similar to FM, CMF and TaxMF can also incorporate path-based features. As FM outperforms CMF and TaxMF (see Section 6.3), we limit our comparison with previous methods exploiting path-based features to HieFM.

Parameter Settings. We empirically set optimal parameters for each method using a grid search in $\{0.0001, 0.001, 0.01, 0.05\}$ for both λ (including 1-way and 2-way regularization of FM) and the learning rate γ; $\alpha = 0.5$ for CMF; $\beta = 0.01$ for SoReg. For fair comparison, we set $d = 10$ (the dimension of latent factors) for all the methods, and adopt all features (i.e. continent, country, and city) as input in TaxMF, CMF, FM and HieFM. HieFM has path-based features as additional hierarchy information. In SoReg, we model the social relations among users by counting the number of common features, under the assumption that the commonality establishes implicit social relationships based on the geo-social correlation phenomenon [8]. Without loss of generality, we adopt $f(x) = 1/(1 + x^{-1})$ to map each #check-in $\mathbf{R}_{ij} \in \mathbf{R}$ in POI data sets into the interval $(0, 1)$ [7].

6.2 Results of ReMF

We analyze the influence of recursive regularization on ReMF performance, and discuss how the weighting parameters g, s can help the interpretation of recommendation results.

The Impact of α. In ReMF, α controls the strength of recursive regularization of feature hierarchy. We apply a grid search in $\{10^{-5}, 10^{-4}, 10^{-3}, 10^{-2}, 10^{-1}, 10^{0}\}$ to investigate the impact of α on recommendation performance. Results are shown in Figure 5. As α varies from small to large, the performance first increases then decreases, with the maximum reached at the range $[10^{-2}, 10^{-1}]$.

Table 3: Performance of the considered recommendation methods on the testing views "All" and "Cold start" of POI data sets. The best performance for each city is boldfaced; the runner up is labelled with "*". The improvements by the best method on all data sets are statistically significant (p-value < 0.01).

View		Data Set	MAE MF	MAE CMF	MAE TaxMF	MAE SoReg	MAE FM	MAE HieFM	MAE ReMF	RMSE MF	RMSE CMF	RMSE TaxMF	RMSE SoReg	RMSE FM	RMSE HieFM	RMSE ReMF
All	Inst.	Amsterdam	0.1957	0.1564	0.1426	0.1038	0.0876	0.0822*	**0.0707**	0.3134	0.1940	0.1934	0.1455	0.1373	0.1352*	**0.1005**
		Paris	0.1539	0.1550	0.1416	0.1208	0.0790*	0.0830	**0.0772**	0.2675	0.1921	0.1849	0.1825	0.1293	0.1184*	**0.1111**
		Rome	0.2549	0.1584	0.1474	0.1355	0.0912	0.0885*	**0.0855**	0.3860	0.1967	0.1859	0.1912	0.1403	0.1389*	**0.1212**
		London	0.1799	0.1559	0.1369	0.1250	0.0834*	0.0851	**0.0774**	0.2964	0.1934	0.1762	0.1840	0.1347*	0.1396	**0.1124**
	Twit.	Amsterdam	0.2264	0.1606	0.1345	0.1229	0.0989	0.0942*	**0.0844**	0.3473	0.1996	0.1717	0.1669	0.1540	0.1454*	**0.1164**
		Paris	0.2014	0.1714	0.1552	0.1266	0.0956	0.0935*	**0.0894**	0.3207	0.2136	0.2038	0.1687	0.1408	0.1387*	**0.1245**
		Rome	0.2681	0.1713	0.1591	0.1345	0.1023	0.0996*	**0.0977**	0.3902	0.2132	0.2030	0.1831	0.1534	0.1469*	**0.1317**
		London	0.2176	0.1659	0.1545	0.1122	0.0931	0.0898*	**0.0772**	0.3075	0.2065	0.1959	0.1540	0.1407	0.1375*	**0.1115**
Cold start	Inst.	Amsterdam	0.2938	0.1552	0.1457	0.1051	0.0924	0.0885*	**0.0712**	0.3877	0.1926	0.1904	0.1479	0.1443	0.1391*	**0.1040**
		Paris	0.1939	0.1541	0.1476	0.1173	0.0849	0.0848*	**0.0799**	0.3110	0.1907	0.1896	0.1713	0.1374	0.1287*	**0.1183**
		Rome	0.3840	0.1614	0.1518	0.1356	0.0952	0.0938*	**0.0808**	0.4868	0.1990	0.1925	0.1845	0.1455*	0.1506	**0.1250**
		London	0.3032	0.1544	0.1415	0.1221	0.0893*	0.0901	**0.0791**	0.3978	0.1917	0.1819	0.1685	0.1426	0.1425*	**0.1161**
	Twit.	Amsterdam	0.3261	0.1604	0.1426	0.1189	0.1006	0.0966*	**0.0849**	0.4003	0.1982	0.1832	0.1609	0.1558	0.1514*	**0.1172**
		Paris	0.2439	0.1706	0.1640	0.1271	0.1012	0.0945*	**0.0873**	0.3764	0.2123	0.2120	0.1713	0.1485*	0.1502	**0.1226**
		Rome	0.3922	0.1718	0.1681	0.1343	0.1073	0.1070*	**0.0988**	0.4951	0.2133	0.2136	0.1833	0.1559	0.1517*	**0.1359**
		London	0.3301	0.1642	0.1587	0.1128	0.0967	0.0924*	**0.0756**	0.3976	0.2043	0.2013	0.1563	0.1475	0.1436*	**0.1093**

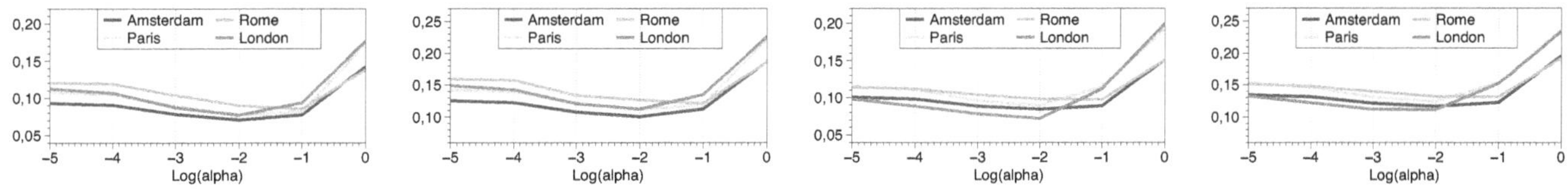

(a) MAE - Instagram (b) RMSE - Instagram (c) MAE - Twitter (d) RMSE - Twitter

Figure 5: The effects of α on the performance of ReMF on Instagram and Twitter measured by MAE and RMSE.

The performance variations across data sets suggest the need for data set-specific settings; the similarity in performance variation across α values shows the robustness of ReMF.

Interpretation from (g, s)**.** We examine (g, s) for the internal features, i.e. continents and countries, learnt from data. Table 4 shows the list of continents and countries ranked according to their g values. Recall that for a continent (country), $g > s$ means that the continent (country) has a stronger effect on user preferences than and its children features, i.e. countries (cities).

In general the continents have relatively smaller effects on user preferences (with g values all below 0.2), suggesting that continents have weaker effects than their countries. In addition, we observe a big variance in the g values of countries, indicating that different countries have different influence on user preferences. The high variance of countries' g values proves the necessity of parameterizing g, s in recommendation. We then compare the influence of countries and cities on their residents' preferences. As cities of a country and the country comprise a feature unit, the influence of a city can be measured by $s = 1 - g$, where g is the influence of the country. We can see from Table 4 that most countries have $g < 0.5$ (only 3 countries have $g > 0.5$), i.e. $s > 0.5$, indicating that the influence of cities in most countries have more influence on their residents' preferences than the countries themselves.

Table 4: Values of g for continents and top/bottom countries in the dataset.

Continents		Top countries		Bottom countries	
Name	g	Name	g	Name	g
Europe	0.1837	Portugal	0.6915	Chile	0.0211
America	0.1656	Monaco	0.5813	Thailand	0.0175
Asia	0.1534	Serbia	0.5130	Spain	0.0100
Africa	0.0375	Poland	0.4453	Indonesia	0.0081
Oceania	0.0139	Hungary	0.4141	Belgium	0.0064

6.3 Comparative Results

Rating Performance. Two views are created for each data set: 1) the "All" view includes all users; while 2) the "Cold start" view indicates that only users with ≤ 5 ratings are involved in the test set. Table 3 compares the performance of the considered recommendation methods for all data sets. Unsurprisingly, the basic matrix factorization model is consistently outperformed by feature-based recommendation methods; this shows that, in the context of the targeted evaluation scenario, the usage of auxiliary information about users positively affects recommendation accuracy. In addition, FM outperforms CMF, TaxMF and SoReg. This could be explained by FM considering item-feature interactions, in addition to user-item and user-feature interactions.

HieMF in general outperforms FM, suggesting that information about feature relationships (paths) can help predicting user preferences. ReMF consistently outperforms the methods in the comparison pool, with an average performance gain (w.r.t. the second best method) of **7.20%** (MAE) and **15.07%** (RMSE). Paired t-test shows that the improvements of ReMF on all data sets are significant (p-value < 0.01). Such big improvements clearly show the effectiveness of recursive regularization, and the advantage derived from the full inclusion of information about feature relationships.

Table 3 (data view "Cold start") reports the results with cold start users. As in the previous case, ReMF achieves the best performance compared with other methods, and significantly outperforms the second best methods in all data sets (p-value < 0.01) by **12.02%** and **17.53%** w.r.t. MAE and RMSE respectively. The relatively larger improvements on the testing view "Cold start" than on "All" indicates that ReMF has higher capability in coping with the cold start problem compared to the state-of-the-art methods.

Ranking Performance. We further evaluate the ranking quality of items recommended by ReMF and other methods in the comparison pool. Results are shown in Figures 6(a-b) for data sets from Instagram and Twitter, respectively. ReMF significantly outperforms the second best method (p-value < 0.01) on all data sets by **9.86%** on average, reaching an averaged AUC of 0.8175 in Instagram and 0.7568 in Twitter. These observations show that the influence of feature hierarchy modeled by recursive regularization can effectively complement user-item interaction data in ranking prediction.

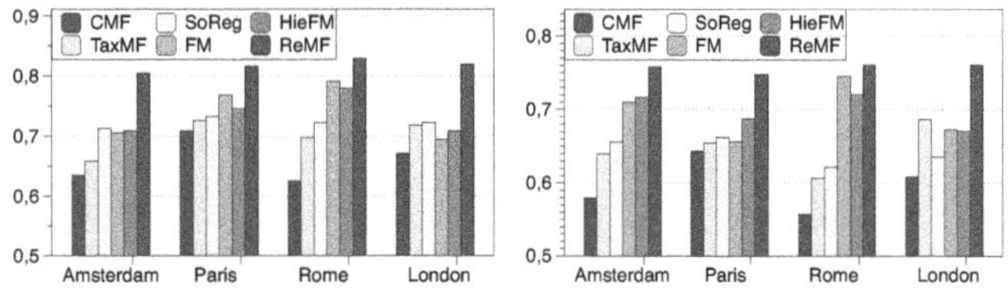

(a) AUC - Instagram (b) AUC - Twitter

Figure 6: AUC of ReMF and the comparative methods on POI data sets of four cities, through the lens of (a) Instagram and (b) Twitter.

Generalizability. We test the performance of ReMF on another task, i.e. product recommendation, using the data from Amazon web store [19]. Different from the POI data sets, here we consider the feature hierarchy of items. We focus on the product category of "Clothing, Shoes & Jewelry", having maximal depth of 7, and an unbalanced feature hierarchy. An example path in the hierarchy from the root feature to the leaf is "Clothing, Shoes & Jewelry $\rightarrow$ Men $\rightarrow$ Accessories $\rightarrow$ Wallets". We uniformly sample the raw data set to include $100,810$ ratings performed by $34,817$ users to $45,716$ items. Table 5 compares the performance of ReMF and the other methods in the comparison pool, measured by RMSE, which is more indicative of large errors than MAE. As in the previous setting, ReMF significantly outperforms the second best method (p-value < 0.01), i.e. HieFM, by **5.46%** on the testing view of "All" and **7.42%** on "Cold start". These results show that ReMF can be effective in multiple recommendation tasks, and with different topologies of features hierarchy.

Table 5: Performance (RMSE) on the testing views "All" and "Cold start" of Amazon data set. The best performance is boldfaced; the runner up is labelled with "*". All improvements by the best method are statistically significant (p-value < 0.01).

	CMF	TaxMF	SoReg	FM	HieFM	ReMF
All	1.6356	1.3921	1.3912	1.3899	1.3847*	**1.3091**
Cold start	1.6386	1.4057	1.4054	1.4074	1.4033*	**1.3242**

7. CONCLUSIONS

Hierarchies are a common way to capture relationships between features. Yet, the value of this additional information is not fully exploited by state-of-the-art feature-based recommendation methods. This paper proposes a novel regularization method named recursive regularization for modeling the co-influence of features in the hierarchy on user-item interactions. Based on this, a new recommendation framework ReMF is proposed to learn hierarchical feature influence from historical user-item interaction data. Experimental validation on real-word data sets shows that ReMF can largely outperform state-of-the-art methods, proving the value residing in the exploitation of feature hierarchies for better learning user and item latent factors.

We stress how recursive regularization does not only apply to tree-like data structures (hierarchy), but also to a forest of trees: adding a root feature transforms a set of trees to one tree. Generalization to graphs is less trivial, and therefore left to future work.

8. REFERENCES

[1] D. Agarwal and B.-C. Chen. Regression-based latent factor models. In *KDD*, 2009.

[2] A. Albadvi and M. Shahbazi. A hybrid recommendation technique based on product category attributes. *Expert Systems with Applications*, 36(9):11480–11488, 2009.

[3] S. Bocconi, A. Bozzon, A. Psyllidis, C. Titos Bolivar, and G.-J. Houben. Social glass: A platform for urban analytics and decision-making through heterogeneous social data. In *WWW Companion*, 2015.

[4] T. Chen, W. Zhang, Q. Lu, K. Chen, Z. Zheng, and Y. Yu. Svdfeature: a toolkit for feature-based collaborative filtering. *Journal of Machine Learning Research*, 13(1):3619–3622, 2012.

[5] Z. Cheng, J. Caverlee, K. Lee, and D. Z. Sui. Exploring millions of footprints in location sharing services. In *ICWSM*, 2011.

[6] Z. Gantner, L. Drumond, C. Freudenthaler, S. Rendle, and L. Schmidt-Thieme. Learning attribute-to-feature mappings for cold-start recommendations. In *ICDM*, 2010.

[7] H. Gao, J. Tang, X. Hu, and H. Liu. Content-aware point of interest recommendation on location-based social networks. In *AAAI*, 2015.

[8] H. Gao, J. Tang, and H. Liu. gscorr: modeling geo-social correlations for new check-ins on location-based social networks. In *CIKM*, 2012.

[9] J. L. Herlocker, J. A. Konstan, L. G. Terveen, and J. T. Riedl. Evaluating collaborative filtering recommender systems. *ACM Transactions on Information Systems*, 22(1):5–53, 2004.

[10] Z. Hu, P. Huang, Y. Deng, Y. Gao, and E. P. Xing. Entity hierarchy embedding. In *ACL-IJCNLP*, 2015.

[11] R. Jenatton, J. Mairal, F. R. Bach, and G. R. Obozinski. Proximal methods for sparse hierarchical dictionary learning. In *ICML*, 2010.

[12] S. Kim and E. P. Xing. Tree-guided group lasso for multi-task regression with structured sparsity. In *ICML*, 2010.

[13] N. Koenigstein, G. Dror, and Y. Koren. Yahoo! music recommendations: modeling music ratings with temporal dynamics and item taxonomy. In *ResSys*, 2011.

[14] Y. Koren. Factorization meets the neighborhood: a multifaceted collaborative filtering model. In *KDD*, 2008.

[15] Y. Koren, R. Bell, and C. Volinsky. Matrix factorization techniques for recommender systems. *Computer*, (8):30–37, 2009.

[16] W.-J. Li and D.-Y. Yeung. Relation regularized matrix factorization. In *IJCAI*, 2009.

[17] C. Lippert, S. H. Weber, Y. Huang, V. Tresp, M. Schubert, and H.-P. Kriegel. Relation prediction in multi-relational domains using matrix factorization. In *NIPS Workshop SISO*, 2008.

[18] H. Ma, D. Zhou, C. Liu, M. R. Lyu, and I. King. Recommender systems with social regularization. In *WSDM*, 2011.

[19] J. McAuley, C. Targett, Q. Shi, and A. van den Hengel. Image-based recommendations on styles and substitutes. In *SIGIR*, 2015.

[20] Y. Moshfeghi, B. Piwowarski, and J. M. Jose. Handling data sparsity in collaborative filtering using emotion and semantic based features. In *SIGIR*, 2011.

[21] S. Rendle. Factorization machines. In *ICDM*, 2010.

[22] S. Rendle, Z. Gantner, C. Freudenthaler, and L. Schmidt-Thieme. Fast context-aware recommendations with factorization machines. In *SIGIR*, 2011.

[23] F. Ricci, L. Rokach, and B. Shapira. *Introduction to recommender systems handbook*. Springer, 2011.

[24] Y. Shi, M. Larson, and A. Hanjalic. Collaborative filtering beyond the user-item matrix: A survey of the state of the art and future challenges. *ACM Computing Surveys*, 47(1):3, 2014.

[25] A. P. Singh and G. J. Gordon. Relational learning via collective matrix factorization. In *KDD*, 2008.

[26] J. Tang, H. Gao, X. Hu, and H. Liu. Exploiting homophily effect for trust prediction. In *WSDM*, 2013.

[27] J. Tang, X. Hu, and H. Liu. Social recommendation: a review. *Social Network Analysis and Mining*, 3(4):1113–1133, 2013.

[28] S. Wang, J. Tang, Y. Wang, and H. Liu. Exploring implicit hierarchical structures for recommender systems. In *IJCAI*, 2015.

[29] L.-T. Weng, Y. Xu, Y. Li, and R. Nayak. Exploiting item taxonomy for solving cold-start problem in recommendation making. In *ICTAI*, 2008.

[30] M. Ye, P. Yin, W.-C. Lee, and D.-L. Lee. Exploiting geographical influence for collaborative point-of-interest recommendation. In *SIGIR*, 2011.

[31] T. Zhao, J. McAuley, and I. King. Improving latent factor models via personalized feature projection for one class recommendation. In *CIKM*, 2015.

[32] Y. Zhen, W.-J. Li, and D.-Y. Yeung. Tagicofi: tag informed collaborative filtering. In *RecSys*, 2009.

[33] C.-N. Ziegler, G. Lausen, and L. Schmidt-Thieme. Taxonomy-driven computation of product recommendations. In *CIKM*, 2004.

Factorization Meets the Item Embedding: Regularizing Matrix Factorization with Item Co-occurrence

Dawen Liang*
Netflix Inc.
Los Gatos, CA
dliang@netflix.com

Jaan Altosaar
Princeton University
Princeton, NJ
altosaar@princeton.edu

Laurent Charlin
HEC Montréal
Montreal, Canada
laurent.charlin@hec.ca

David M. Blei
Columbia University
New York, NY
david.blei@columbia.edu

ABSTRACT

Matrix factorization (MF) models and their extensions are standard in modern recommender systems. MF models decompose the observed user-item interaction matrix into user and item latent factors. In this paper, we propose a co-factorization model, CoFactor, which jointly decomposes the user-item interaction matrix and the item-item co-occurrence matrix with shared item latent factors. For each pair of items, the co-occurrence matrix encodes the number of users that have consumed both items. CoFactor is inspired by the recent success of word embedding models (e.g., word2vec) which can be interpreted as factorizing the word co-occurrence matrix. We show that this model significantly improves the performance over MF models on several datasets with little additional computational overhead. We provide qualitative results that explain how CoFactor improves the quality of the inferred factors and characterize the circumstances where it provides the most significant improvements.

Keywords

Collaborative filtering; matrix factorization; item embedding; implicit feedback.

1. INTRODUCTION

Recommender systems model users through their preferences for items. User preferences are often encoded as sets of user-item-preference triplets. For instance "user A gave item B a 4-star rating" or in the case of *implicit data*, which we focus on, "user A clicked on item B". The task of interest is to predict missing user-item preferences given the observed triplets. Predicted preferences can then be used downstream to fuel recommendations.

*This work was mostly done while DL was at Columbia University and LC was at McGill University.

RecSys '16, September 15-19, 2016, Boston, MA, USA

DOI: http://dx.doi.org/10.1145/2959100.2959182

The preference triplets can be seen as the sparse representation of a user-item *preference matrix* (or *click matrix*). Predicting preferences can be seen as filling in the missing entries of this matrix. Models such as matrix factorization—which decompose the preference matrix into user and item factors [10, 20]—are standard for preference prediction: their performance is high [10], maximum *a posteriori* inference can be done efficiently with closed-form updates [9], and they can be composed to incorporate additional side information (e.g., [1, 4, 13, 23, 26]).

Encoding user preferences in a matrix and modeling it with matrix factorization is a particular modeling assumption. In this paper we explore an alternative which models item co-occurrence across users. We posit that pairs of items which are often consumed in tandem by different users are similar. This is similar to modeling a set of documents (users) as a bag of co-occurring words (items). In that context frequently co-occurring words are likely to be about the same topic. For example, in a corpus of scientific papers "planet" and "Pluto" are likely to frequently co-occur. A similar idea has been explored in recommendations for next-item prediction [24]. Item co-occurrence information is, in principle, available to matrix factorization, but it may not be easy to infer from the click matrix: matrix factorization models are bi-linear with limited modeling capacity.

We propose a co-factorization model, CoFactor, which simultaneously factorizes both the click matrix and the item co-occurrence matrix. The factorization of item co-occurrence is inspired by the recent models for learning word embedding from sequences of words [14, 11]. We learn item embedding using the sets of items each user has consumed (or rated), and the co-occurrence counts of these items across users in the data.

We show that learning CoFactor from data can be done efficiently with coordinate updates. We use a sequence of closed-form updates which scale in the number of observed preference triplets. CoFactor outperforms matrix factorization [9] across datasets of user clicking on scientific articles, rating movies, and listening to music. We also provide exploratory results to better understand the effectiveness of our method. This shows that we outperform standard matrix factorization due to the ability of our model to exploit co-occurrence patterns for rare items (items not consumed by many users).

2. THE COFACTOR MODEL

We first introduce the two building blocks of the CoFactor model: matrix factorization (MF) and item embedding. Then we describe CoFactor and how to compute with it.

Matrix factorization. MF is standard in collaborative filtering [10]. Given the sparse user-item interaction matrix $Y \in \mathbb{R}^{U \times I}$ from U users and I items, MF decomposes it into the product of user and item latent factors denoted $\theta_u \in \mathbb{R}^K$ ($u = 1, \ldots, U$) and $\beta_i \in \mathbb{R}^K$ ($i = 1, \ldots, I$), respectively. Here we focus on implicit feedback data [9, 16]. However, this is not a limiting aspect of CoFactor—it can be readily extended to the explicit feedback setting. Matrix factorization for implicit feedback model [9] optimizes the following objective:

$$\mathcal{L}_{\text{mf}} = \sum_{u,i} c_{ui}(y_{ui} - \theta_u^\top \beta_i)^2 + \lambda_\theta \sum_u \|\theta_u\|_2^2 + \lambda_\beta \sum_i \|\beta_i\|_2^2. \tag{1}$$

The scaling parameter c_{ui} is a hyperparameter that is normally set to be $c_{y=1} > c_{y=0}$. It can be tuned to balance the unobserved ratings ($y = 0$) which far outnumber the observed ratings ($y = 1$) in most click data. The regularization parameters λ_θ and λ_β are hyperparameters which are selected from validation data. The (global) optimum of $\mathcal{L}_{\text{mf}}$ can be interpreted as the maximum *a posteriori* estimate of the probabilistic Gaussian matrix factorization model [20].

Word embedding. Word embedding models (e.g., word2vec [14]) have gained success in many natural language processing tasks. Given a sequence of words, these models embed each word into a low-dimensional continuous space (relative to the vocabulary size). In the skip-gram model, the objective is to predict context words—surrounding words within a fixed window—given the current word. Stochastic gradient descent (SGD) with negative sampling is normally used to train a word embedding model (see Mikolov et al. [14]).

Levy and Goldberg [11] show an equivalence between skip-gram word2vec trained with negative sampling value of k and implicit factorizing the pointwise mutual information (PMI) matrix shifted by $\log k$. PMI between a word i and its context word j is defined as:

$$\text{PMI}(i, j) = \log \frac{P(i, j)}{P(i)P(j)}.$$

Empirically, it is estimated as:

$$\text{PMI}(i, j) = \log \frac{\#(i, j) \cdot D}{\#(i) \cdot \#(j)}. \tag{2}$$

Here $\#(i, j)$ is the number of times word j appears in the context of word i. $\#(i) = \sum_j \#(i, j)$ and $\#(j) = \sum_i \#(i, j)$. D is the total number of word-context pairs.

After making the connection between word2vec and implicit matrix factorization, Levy and Goldberg [11] further propose to perform word embedding by spectral dimensionality reduction (e.g., singular value decomposition) on the (sparse) shifted positive PMI (SPPMI) matrix:

$$\text{SPPMI}(i, j) = \max\{\text{PMI}(i, j) - \log k, 0\}$$

This is attractive because it does not require tuning an optimization procedure.[1] We will follow the similar approach in CoFactor.

Item embedding. Users consume items sequentially. Sequences of items are analogous to sequences of words, so we can use word embedding models to learn item embeddings (e.g., Guàrdia-Sebaoun et al. [5]).

Define $\boldsymbol{M} \in \mathbb{R}_+^{I \times J}$ as the co-occurrence SPPMI matrix for item consumptions.[2] We can obtain item embedding by factorizing $\boldsymbol{M}$. In this paper, we do not assume that the order (or timestamp) of each user's item consumption is available. For a consumed item i from a particular user, we define its context j as all other items in this user's click history. We use Equation (2) to compute m_{ij} with the empirical estimates of PMI(i, j). In this estimate, $\#(i, j)$ corresponds to the number of users that consumed both item i and j. By defining the context in this way, CoFactor does not require any additional information other than what is already available in the standard MF model. This departs, at least in spirit, from the traditional word embedding models and Guàrdia-Sebaoun et al. [5], where context is defined as neighbors within a fixed window. Those methods require the order within a sequence.

Our definition of context is a design choice and CoFactor can work with any type of co-occurrence SPPMI matrix. Context could be data- and problem-specific. For example, if we did know the order of item consumption, we could break it down into shorter segments of sequences.

The CoFactor model. Both MF and item embedding models infer latent item representations. The difference is that the item representations inferred from MF encode users' preferences for items, while the item embeddings must explain item co-occurrence patterns. We propose learning these representations jointly:

$$\mathcal{L}_{\text{co}} = \overbrace{\sum_{u,i} c_{ui}(y_{ui} - \theta_u^\top \beta_i)^2}^{\text{MF}} + \overbrace{\sum_{m_{ij} \neq 0} (m_{ij} - \beta_i^\top \gamma_j - w_i - c_j)^2}^{\text{item embedding}}$$
$$+ \lambda_\theta \sum_u \|\theta_u\|_2^2 + \lambda_\beta \sum_i \|\beta_i\|_2^2 + \lambda_\gamma \sum_j \|\gamma_j\|_2^2 \tag{3}$$

This is the CoFactor model objective. The item factor (or item embedding) β_i is shared by both the MF and item embedding parts of the objective. We include context embedding γ_j as additional model parameter. We do not regularize item and context biases w_i and c_j. Notice that the item embeddings β_i must account for both user-item interactions and item-item co-occurrence. We can also interpret this objective as regularizing the traditional MF objective $\mathcal{L}_{\text{mf}}$ (Equation (1)) with item embeddings learned by factorizing the item co-occurrence matrix.[3]

The scaling parameter c_{ui} in the CoFactor objective enforces a balance between the unobserved zeros and observed ones in the click matrix. Additionally, its relative scale will balance the MF and item embedding parts of the model. Setting its relative scale smaller will impose more regularization

[1]Under this setting, k becomes a hyperparameter that controls the sparsity of the SPPMI matrix, as opposed to the original skip-gram word2vec model [14] where k explicitly controls the number of negative examples sampled in SGD.

[2]For generality, we use $i = 1, \ldots, I$ and $j = 1, \ldots, J$ to index an item and its context. In experiments, the set of items and the set of context items are the same.

[3]This model does not have a clear generative interpretation as the regular MF model, since the user-item interaction matrix $\boldsymbol{Y}$ deterministically defines the co-occurrence SPPMI matrix $\boldsymbol{M}$.

from the co-occurrence matrix and vice versa. This scale is an important hyperparameter. In our empirical study, we will select it based on recommendation performance on a validation set.

2.1 Inference

We take the gradient of CoFactor objective $\mathcal{L}_{\text{co}}$ (Equation (3)) with respect to the model parameters $\{\theta_{1:U}, \beta_{1:I}, \gamma_{1:J}, w_{1:I}, c_{1:J}\}$ and set it to zero. This gives the following closed-form coordinate updates:

$$\theta_u \leftarrow \Big(\sum_i c_{ui}\beta_i\beta_i^\top + \lambda_\theta \mathrm{I}_K\Big)^{-1}\Big(\sum_i c_{ui}y_{ui}\beta_i\Big)$$

$$\beta_i \leftarrow \Big(\sum_u c_{ui}\theta_u\theta_u^\top + \sum_{j:m_{ij}\neq 0} \gamma_j\gamma_j^\top + \lambda_\beta \mathrm{I}_K\Big)^{-1}$$
$$* \Big(\sum_u c_{ui}y_{ui}\theta_u + \sum_{j:m_{ij}\neq 0}(m_{ij} - w_i - c_j)\gamma_j\Big)$$

$$\gamma_j \leftarrow \Big(\sum_{i:m_{ij}\neq 0} \beta_i\beta_i^\top + \lambda_\gamma \mathrm{I}_K\Big)^{-1}\Big(\sum_{i:m_{ij}\neq 0}(m_{ij} - w_i - c_j)\beta_i\Big)$$

$$w_i \leftarrow \frac{1}{|\{j : m_{ij}\neq 0\}|}\sum_{j:m_{ij}\neq 0}(m_{ij} - \beta_i^\top\gamma_j - c_j)$$

$$c_j \leftarrow \frac{1}{|\{i : m_{ij}\neq 0\}|}\sum_{i:m_{ij}\neq 0}(m_{ij} - \beta_i^\top\gamma_j - w_i)$$

These updates are very similar to the alternating least squares (ALS) of Hu et al. [9]. The main difference is in how we update β_i in CoFactor. We can view each update of ALS as a weighted ridge regression. Therefore, the update for β_i is collectively performing ridge regression with two sources of data: the click data y_{ui} with covariates θ_u, and the co-occurrence data m_{ij} with covariates γ_j. Iteratively performing these updates reaches a stationary point of the model objective $\mathcal{L}_{\text{co}}$.

Complexity We set the scaling parameter c_{ui} as $c_{ui} = \ell(1+\alpha\cdot y_{ui})$ where ℓ is the relative scale. This is similar to Hu et al. [9] and we use the same pre-computing trick to speed up the computation for updating θ_u and β_i. For the item embeddings, the complexity scales linearly with the number of non-zero entires in the SPPMI matrix, which is usually very sparse. Furthermore, all the coordinate updates are embarrassingly parallelizable across users and items. Constructing the SPPMI matrix can be time-consuming as it scales quadratically with the number of items consumed by each user. Fortunately, the SPPMI matrix only needs to be constructed once and it is parallelizable across users. Our Python implementation of the CoFactor model scales easily to large datasets.[4]

3. RELATED WORK

The user and item factors learned through matrix factorization are usually regularized with their ℓ_2-norm. It is also standard to further regularize the factors with *side information* [1, 2, 7, 12], which comprises user, item, and/or user-item covariates (e.g., item metadata or user demographics which can be indicative of user preferences). We can interpret CoFactor as regularizing the learned item factors beyond simple ℓ_2-norm. The distinguishing feature of CoFactor is that the regularization comes from a deterministic non-linear transformation of the original user-item preference data instead of additional data.

This kind of regularization (either through incorporation of side information or re-encoding the input as in CoFactor) can alternatively be viewed as enforcing more complex structure in the prior of the latent factors. For example, Ranganath et al. [17] find that imposing a deep exponential family prior on the matrix factorization model, which implicitly conditions on consumption counts in a non-linear fashion, can be helpful in reducing the effect of extremely popular (or extremely unpopular) items on held-out recommendation tasks. This is analogous to our findings with the CoFactor model.

Collective matrix factorization [25] explores co-factorizing multiple matrices in the context of relational learning. For example, a database with users, movies, and genres contains two relational matrices: one representing users' ratings of movies, and the other representing the genres each movie belongs to. Collective matrix factorization jointly factorizes these two matrices with shared movie factors to leverage the additional genre information for better preference prediction. We can consider CoFactor as a special case of collective matrix factorization with the user-item preference relation deterministically defines the item-item co-occurrence relation. Our contribution lies in the construction of the item-item relation, which is motivated by the recent development of word embedding models [14, 11].

Guàrdia-Sebaoun et al. [5] observe that user trajectories over items can be modeled much like sequences of words. In detail, they use a word embedding model [14] to learn item embeddings. User embeddings are then inferred as to predict the next item in the trajectory (given the previous item). User and item embeddings are finally used as covariates in a subsequent regression model of user-item preferences. Learning item embeddings from user trajectories is similar to our work. The difference is that we treat the items consumed by each user as exchangeable (i.e., we do not assume that the trajectories are given, rather we assume that we are given an unordered set of items for each user). Additionally we show that jointly learning all parameters yields higher performance.

In item-based collaborative filtering [22], an item-item similarity matrix is built from user consumption data, much like the SPPMI matrix in CoFactor. The difference is that in CoFactor we only use the SPPMI matrix to regularize the item factors, while in item-based collaborative filtering we directly use the similarity matrix to predict missing preferences. Previous work shows that the performance of item-based collaborative filtering is highly sensitive to the choice of similarity metric and data normalization [8]. It would be interesting to consider SPPMI matrix as similarity matrix in item-based collaborative filtering.

4. EMPIRICAL STUDY

We study the performance of CoFactor both quantitatively and qualitatively. We provide insights into its performance by exploring the resulting fits. We highlight the following results:

- On three datasets, the CoFactor model performs significantly better than the state-of-the-art weighted matrix factorization (WMF) model [9].
- We investigate where CoFactor improves performance

[4] https://github.com/dawenl/cofactor

	ArXiv	ML-20M	TasteProfile
# of users	25,057	111,148	221,830
# of items	63,003	11,711	22,781
# interactions	1.8M	8.2M	14.0M
% interactions	0.12%	0.63%	0.29%
with timestamps	yes	yes	no

Table 1: Attributes of datasets after preprocessing. Interactions are non-zero entries (listening counts, watches, and clicks). % interactions refers to the density of the user-item interaction matrix ($\boldsymbol{Y}$). For datasets with timestamps, we ensure there is no overlap in time between the training and test sets.

to understand why jointly factoring both the user click matrix and item co-occurrence matrix boosts certain recommendations.

- We demonstrate the importance of joint learning by comparing to a two-stage model that first does word2vec for item embeddings and then fits a MF.

4.1 Datasets

We study three medium- to large-scale user-item consumption datasets from various domains: 1) scientific articles data from the arXiv[5]; 2) users' movie viewing data from MovieLens [6]; 3) the taste profile subset of the million song dataset [3]. In more details:

ArXiv: User-paper clicks derived from log data collected in the first half of 2012 from the arXiv pre-print server. The data is binarized (multiple clicks by the same user on the same paper are considered to be a single click). We preprocess the data to ensure that all users and items have a minimum of ten clicks.

MovieLens-20M (ML-20M): User-movie ratings collected from a movie recommendation service. We binarize explicit data by keeping the ratings of four or higher and interpret them as implicit feedback. We only keep users who have watched at least five movies.

TasteProfile: User-song play counts collected by the music intelligence company Echo Nest[6]. We binarize play counts and interpret them as implicit preference data. We keep users with at least 20 songs in their listening history and songs that are listened to by at least 50 users.

ArXiv and Movielens are time stamped. To create the training/validation/test splits for these data, we order all the user-item interactions by time and take the first 80% as training data, from which we randomly selected 10% as the validation set. For the remaining 20% of the data, we only keep the users and items that appear in the training and validation sets to obtain the test set. For TasteProfile, which is not timestamped, we randomly split the observed user-item interactions into training/validation/test sets with 70/10/20 proportions. Table 1 summarizes the dimensions of all the datasets after preprocessing.

4.2 Metrics

We use ranking-based metrics: Recall@M, truncated normalized discounted cumulative gain (NDCG@M), and mean average precision (MAP@M). For each user, all the metrics compare the predicted rank of (unobserved) items with their true rank. While Recall@M considers all items ranked within the first M to be equivalent, NDCG@M and MAP@M use a monotonically increasing discount to emphasize the importance of higher ranks versus lower ones. Formally, define π as a permutation over all the items, $\mathbb{1}\{\cdot\}$ is the indicator function, and $u(\pi(i))$ returns 1 if user u has consumed item $\pi(i)$. CoFactor predicts ranking π for each user by sorting the predicted preference $\theta_u^\top \beta_i$ for $i = 1, \dots, I$.

Recall@M for user u is

$$\text{Recall@}M(u,\pi) := \sum_{i=1}^{M} \frac{\mathbb{1}\{u(\pi(i)) = 1\}}{\min(M, \sum_{i'}^{I} \mathbb{1}\{u(\pi(i')) = 1\})}.$$

The expression in the denominator evaluates to the minimum between M and the number of items consumed by user u. This normalizes Recall@M to have a maximum of 1, which corresponds to ranking all relevant items in the top M positions.

DCG@M for user u is

$$\text{DCG@}M(u,\pi) := \sum_{i=1}^{M} \frac{2^{\mathbb{1}\{u(\pi(i))=1\}} - 1}{\log(i+1)}.$$

NDCG@M is the DCG@M normalized to [0, 1], where one signifies a perfect ranking.

Mean average precision (MAP@M) calculates the mean of users' average precision (AP). The average precision AP@M for a user u is

$$\text{AP@}M(u,\pi) := \sum_{i=1}^{M} \frac{\text{Precision@}i(u,\pi)}{\min(i, \sum_{i'}^{I} \mathbb{1}\{u(\pi(i')) = 1\})}.$$

4.3 Experiment protocols

We compare CoFactor to weighted matrix factorization (WMF) [9]. Given the similarity between the CoFactor objective $\mathcal{L}_{\text{co}}$ (Equation (3)) and WMF objective $\mathcal{L}_{\text{mf}}$ (Equation (1)), we can attribute the performance differences to the regularization imposed by the co-occurrence SPPMI matrix.

In all fits, the dimension of the latent space K is set to 100. The CoFactor model is trained following the inference algorithm described in Section 2.1. We monitor the convergence of the algorithm using NDCG@100 on the validation set for both CoFactor and WMF.

Both CoFactor and WMF require hyperparameter tuning. We first select the best hyperparameters for WMF (the weight $c_{y=0}$ and $c_{y=1}$, the regularization parameters $\lambda = \lambda_\theta = \lambda_\beta$) based on their performance on the validation set. For CoFactor, we then keep the same $c_{y=1}/c_{y=0}$ ratio and regularization parameters, and grid search for the best relative scale $\ell \in \{0.01, 0.05, 0.1, \dots, 1, 5, 10\}$ (Section 2.1). Note when scaling c_{ui}, we also scale λ_θ and λ_β. The value of the relative scale indicates the importance of regularization with co-occurrence information. If a large scaling parameter c_{ui} is selected, the MF part of the model can be effective at recommendation on its own without significant help from the information provided by the co-occurrence matrix. (As the scaling parameter goes to infinity, CoFactor effectively reduces to WMF, as the MF part of the objective will completely dominate.) On the other hand, a smaller scaling parameter indicates that the model benefits from the co-occurrence patterns in the observed user behavior

[5] http://arxiv.org
[6] http://the.echonest.com

	ArXiv		ML-20M		TasteProfile	
	WMF	CoFactor	WMF	CoFactor	WMF	CoFactor
Recall@20	0.063	**0.067**	0.133	**0.145**	0.198	**0.208**
Recall@50	0.108	**0.110**	0.165	**0.177**	0.286	**0.300**
NDCG@100	0.076	**0.079**	0.160	**0.172**	0.257	**0.268**
MAP@100	0.019	**0.021**	0.047	**0.055**	0.103	**0.111**

Table 2: Comparison between the widely-used weighted matrix factorization (WMF) model [9] and our CoFactor model. CoFactor significantly outperforms WMF on all the datasets across all metrics. The improvement is most pronounced on the movie watching (ML-20M) and music listening (TasteProfile) datasets.

data. We also grid search for the negative sampling value $k \in \{1, 2, 5, 10, 50\}$, which effectively modulates how much to shift the empirically estimated PMI matrix.

4.4 Analyzing the CoFactor model fits

Table 2 summarizes the quantitative results. Each metric is averaged across all users in the test set. CoFactor outperforms WMF [9] on all datasets and across all metrics. The improvement is very clear for the MovieLens (ML-20M) and music (TasteProfile) data. We emphasize that both models make use of the same data and optimize similar objectives, with CoFactor benefiting from an extra co-occurrence regularization term.

Exploratory analysis

When does CoFactor do better/worse? Figure 1 shows the breakdown of NDCG@100 by user activity in the training set for all three datasets. Although details vary across datasets, the CoFactor model consistently improves recommendation performance for users who have only consumed a small number of items. This makes sense because MF cannot accurately infer inactive users' preferences, while CoFactor explicitly makes use of the additional signal from item co-occurrence patterns to learn better latent representations, even when user-item interaction data is scarce. For active users (the rightmost bar pairs in each plot), WMF does worse than CoFactor on ArXiv, better on ML-20M, and roughly the same on TasteProfile. However, since active users are the minority (most recommendation datasets have a long tail), the standard error is also bigger.

To understand when CoFactor makes better recommendation, we compare it to WMF in how it ranks rare items. Figure 2 shows the histogram of ranks (derived from predicted scores) for movies with less than 10 viewings in the training set (which consists of 3,239 movies out of the 11,711 total movies). We report results using four randomly-selected users on the MovieLens ML-20M data. (The general trend is consistent across the entire dataset, and we observe a similar patten for the TasteProfile dataset.) WMF mostly ranks rare movies around the middle of its recommendation list, which is expected because the collaborative filtering model is driven by item popularity.[7] On the other hand, CoFactor can push these rare movies both to the top and bottom of its recommendations. We did not observe as clear of a pattern on the ArXiv data. We conjecture that this is because the ArXiv data is less popularity-biased than ML-20M and TasteProfile: the mean (median) of users who consumed an

[7]It is also reasonable given the relatively high model uncertainty around rare items.

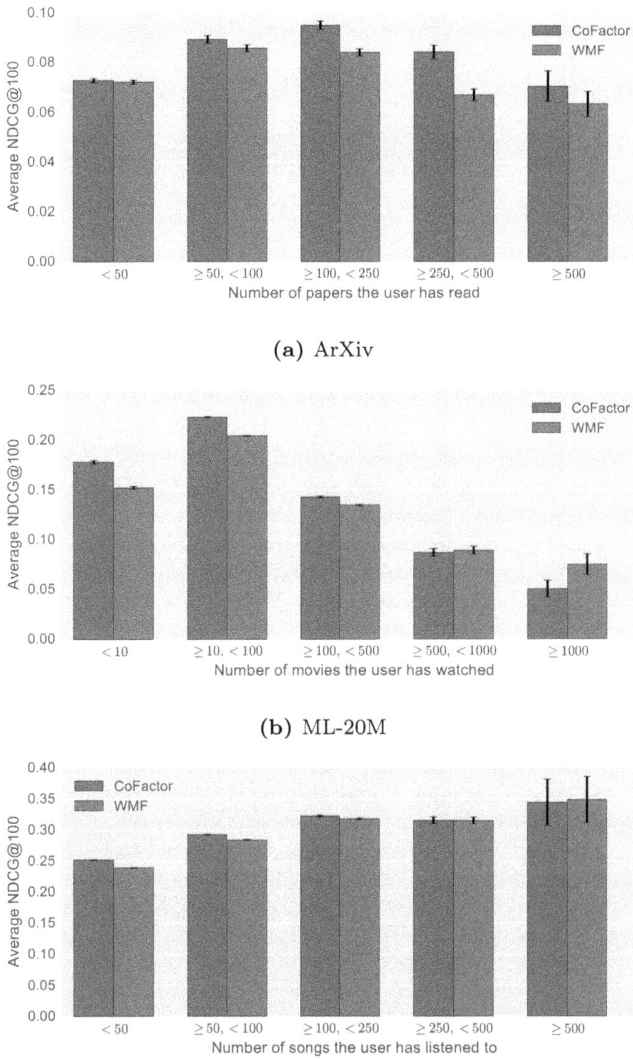

(a) ArXiv

(b) ML-20M

(c) TasteProfile

Figure 1: Average normalized discounted cumulative gain (NDCG@100) breakdown for both CoFactor and weighted matrix factorization (WMF) [9] based on user activity on different datasets (higher is better). Error bars correspond to one standard error. There is some variation across datasets, but CoFactor is able to consistently improve recommendation performance for users who have only consumed a small amount of items.

item is 597 (48) for ML-20M and 441 (211) for TasteProfile, while only 21 (12) for ArXiv.

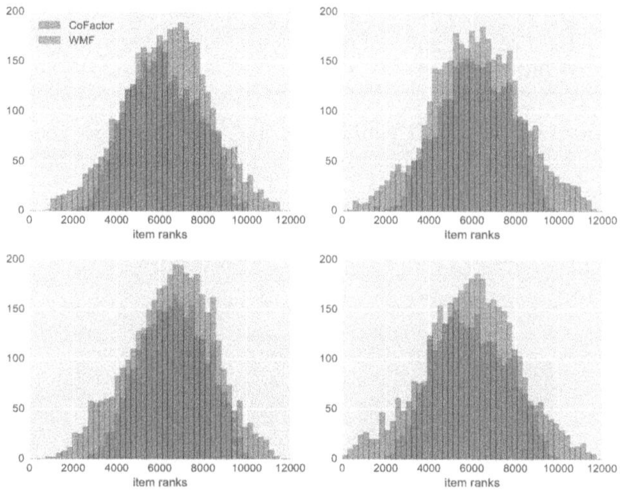

Figure 2: The histogram of ranks from four randomly selected users for movies with less than 10 watches in the MovieLens ML-20M training set for both CoFactor and weighted matrix factorization (WMF) [9]. The extra regularization in CoFactor allows it to push these rare items further up and down its recommendation list for each user.

In Figure 3, we compare CoFactor and WMF for a particular user who has watched many popular movies (e.g., "Toy Story" and "Fight Club"), as well as some rare French movies (e.g. "Mouchette" and "Army of Shadows"). We find that WMF highly ranks popular movies and places them on top of its recommendations. Even when it recommends a French movie ("That Obscure Object of Desire") to this user, it is a relatively popular one (as indicated by the number of users who have watched it). In contrast, CoFactor will better balance between the popular movies and relevant (but relatively rare) French movies in its recommendation. This makes sense because rare French movies co-occur in the training set, and this is captured by the SPPMI matrix. We find similar exploratory examples in TasteProfile.

This explains the performance gap between CoFactor and WMF among active users on ML-20M, as CoFactor could potentially rank popular movies lower than WMF. For active users, they are more likely to have watched popular movies in both the training and test sets. When we look at the top 100 users where WMF does better than CoFactor in terms of NDCG@100, we find that the performance difference is never caused by WMF recommending a rare movie in the test set that CoFactor fails to recommend.

How important is joint learning? One of the main contributions of the proposed CoFactor model is incorporating both MF and item embedding in a joint learning objective. This "end-to-end" approach has proven effective in many machine learning models. To demonstrate the advantage of joint learning, we conduct an alternative experiment on ArXiv where we perform the learning in a two-stage process. First, we train a skip-gram word2vec model on the click data, treating users' entire click histories as the context—this is equivalent to factorizing the SPPMI matrix in CoFactor model. We then fix these learned item embeddings from word2vec as the latent factors β_i in the MF model, and learn user latent factors θ_u. Learning θ_u in this way is the same as one iteration of CoFactor, which is effectively doing a weighted ridge regression.

	WMF	CoFactor	word2vec + reg
Recall@20	0.063	0.067	0.052
Recall@50	0.108	0.110	0.095
NDCG@100	0.076	0.079	0.065
MAP@100	0.019	0.021	0.016

Table 3: Comparison between joint learning (CoFactor) and learning from a separate two-stage (word2vec + reg) process on ArXiv. Even though they make similar modeling assumptions, CoFactor provides superior performance.

We evaluate the model learned from this two-stage process (word2vec + reg) and report the quantitative results in Table 3. (The results for WMF and CoFactor are copied from Table 2 for comparison.) The performance of the two-stage model is much worse. This is understandable because the item embeddings learned from word2vec are certainly not as well-suited for recommendation as the item latent factors learned from MF. Using this item embedding in the second stage to infer user preferences will likely lead to inferior performance. On the other hand, CoFactor is capable of finding the proper balance between MF and item embeddings to get the best of both worlds.

5. DISCUSSION

It is interesting that CoFactor improves over WMF by re-using the preference data in a different encoding. The item co-occurrence information is, in principle, available from the user-item interaction data to MF. However, as a bilinear model with limited capacity, MF cannot uncover such information. On the other hand, highly non-linear models, such as deep neural networks, have shown limited success at the task of preference prediction [21, 17]. Our approach is somewhat in between, where we have used a deterministic non-linear transformation to re-encode the input.

A natural question is whether it is always better to incorporate item co-occurrence information. This dependents on the problem and specific data. However, as mentioned in Section 4.3, as the relative scale on the weight c_{ui} goes to infinity, CoFactor is effectively reduced to WMF. Therefore, as long as there is additional information that is useful in the co-occurrence matrix, in principle, the performance of CoFactor is lower bounded by that of WMF.

5.1 Possible extensions to the model

It is straightforward to extend our CoFactor model to explicitly handle sessions of user-item consumption data by constructing a session-based co-occurrence matrix, as discussed in Section 2. This is likely to yield improved performance in some settings, such as in purchase behavior or music listening data, where the notion of a 'shopping cart' or 'playlist' induce session-based patterns.

Adding user-user co-occurrence to our model to regularize user latent factors is another natural extension, which we leave to future work. We anticipate this extension to yield further improvements, especially for users in the long tail. The type of regularization we have added to MF models can

User's watch history	Top recommendation by CoFactor	Top recommendation by WMF
Toy Story (24659)	The Silence of the Lambs (37217)	Rain Man (11862)
Fight Club (18728)	Pulp Fiction (37445)	Pulp Fiction (37445)
Kill Bill: Vol. 1 (8728)	Finding Nemo (9290)	Finding Nemo (9290)
Mouchette (32)	Atalante L' (90)	The Godfather: Part II (15325)
Army of Shadows (L'armée des ombres) (96)	Diary of a Country Priest (Journal d'un curé de campagne) (68)	That Obscure Object of Desire (Cet obscur objet du désir) (300)

Figure 3: Comparison between CoFactor and WMF [9] for a particular user in MovieLens ML-20M data. On the right, we show a subset of the user's watch history from the training set. The number in the parenthesis after the movie title is the number of users who have watched this movie in the training set. The top recommendations by CoFactor and WMF are shown in the middle and left tables, respectively. Here only the movies that are watched by the same user in the test set are shown. The NDCG@100 of this user is high for both CoFactor and WMF (0.893 vs 0.783).

also be extended to higher-order co-occurrence patterns. It is unclear which datasets may benefit from this, but this type of prior structure may be interesting to explore. It may help for complex recommendation data where long-term higher-order interactions are assumed to be important. For example, in the ArXiv dataset, researchers reading the same sets of papers over many years could exhibit such patterns. It is unclear how best to capture this type of co-occurrence in a procedure. Our regularization approach provides an initial solution.

Another line of future work is to explore CoFactor's co-occurrence regularization in other collaborative filtering methods. For example, we can regularize Bayesian Personalized Ranking (BPR) [19], factorization machine [18], or sparse linear method (SLIM) [15] with item and/or user co-occurrence patterns.

6. CONCLUSION

We present CoFactor, a regularization scheme for MF models inspired by word embeddings. We force the standard MF objective to share item representations with a factorized shifted positive pointwise mutual information matrix of item co-occurrence counts. This is analogous to word embedding models [11, 14] which factorize a similar matrix of word co-occurrence patterns in text corpora. We show that this type of joint factorization yields performance boosts in recommendation metrics in a variety of settings: recommending papers to researchers on ArXiv, movies on MovieLens, and music on TasteProfile.

We identify the scenarios where CoFactor outperforms standard MF, which gives further insights into the benefits of 'reusing' the data. We show that regularizing using item co-occurrence counts enables CoFactor to recommend rare items by capturing their co-occurrence patterns, whereas this feature is absent in standard MF. We point to the potential of alternative methods such as regularizing with user-user co-occurrence or in the context of other widely-used collaborative filtering models.

Acknowledgement

We thank the anonymous reviewers for help feedback. This work is supported by NSF IIS-1247664, ONR N00014-11-1-0651, DARPA FA8750-14-2-0009, DARPA N66001-15-C-4032, Adobe, and the Sloan Foundation.

References

[1] D. Agarwal and B.-C. Chen. Regression-based latent factor models. In *Proceedings of the 15th ACM SIGKDD*, pages 19–28, 2009.

[2] A. Almahairi, K. Kastner, K. Cho, and A. Courville. Learning distributed representations from reviews for collaborative filtering. In *Proceedings of the 9th ACM Conference on Recommender Systems*, pages 147–154, 2015.

[3] T. Bertin-Mahieux, D. P. W. Ellis, B. Whitman, and P. Lamere. The million song dataset. In *Proceedings of the 12th International Society for Music Information Retrieval Conference*, pages 591–596, 2011.

[4] P. K. Gopalan, L. Charlin, and D. Blei. Content-based recommendations with Poisson factorization. In *Advances in Neural Information Processing Systems*, pages 3176–3184, 2014.

[5] E. Guàrdia-Sebaoun, V. Guigue, and P. Gallinari. Latent trajectory modeling: A light and efficient way to introduce time in recommender systems. In *Proceedings of the 9th ACM Conference on Recommender Systems*, pages 281–284, 2015.

[6] F. M. Harper and J. A. Konstan. The MovieLens datasets: History and context. *ACM Transactions on Interactive Intelligent Systems (TiiS)*, 5(4):19, 2015.

[7] R. He and J. McAuley. VBPR: Visual Bayesian personalized ranking from implicit feedback. In *AAAI Conference on Artificial Intelligence*, 2016.

[8] J. Herlocker, J. A. Konstan, and J. Riedl. An empirical analysis of design choices in neighborhood-based collaborative filtering algorithms. *Information retrieval*, 5(4): 287–310, 2002.

[9] Y. Hu, Y. Koren, and C. Volinsky. Collaborative filtering for implicit feedback datasets. In *Data Mining, IEEE International Conference on*, pages 263–272, 2008.

[10] Y. Koren, R. Bell, and C. Volinsky. Matrix factorization techniques for recommender systems. *Computer*, 42(8): 30–37, 2009.

[11] O. Levy and Y. Goldberg. Neural word embedding as implicit matrix factorization. In *Advances in Neural Information Processing Systems*, pages 2177–2185. 2014.

[12] D. Liang, M. Zhan, and D. P. W. Ellis. Content-aware collaborative music recommendation using pre-trained neural networks. In *Proceedings of the 16th International Society for Music Information Retrieval Conference*, pages 295–301, 2015.

[13] J. McAuley and J. Leskovec. Hidden factors and hidden topics: understanding rating dimensions with review text. In *Recommender Systems*, 2013.

[14] T. Mikolov, I. Sutskever, K. Chen, G. S. Corrado, and J. Dean. Distributed representations of words and phrases and their compositionality. In *Advances in Neural Information Processing Systems*, pages 3111–3119, 2013.

[15] X. Ning and G. Karypis. SLIM: Sparse linear methods for top-n recommender systems. In *Data Mining (ICDM), 2011 IEEE 11th International Conference on*, pages 497–506. IEEE, 2011.

[16] R. Pan, Y. Zhou, B. Cao, N. N. Liu, R. Lukose, M. Scholz, and Q. Yang. One-class collaborative filtering. In *Data Mining, IEEE International Conference on*, pages 502–511, 2008.

[17] R. Ranganath, L. Tang, L. Charlin, and D. M. Blei. Deep exponential families. In *Proceedings of the Eighteenth International Conference on Artificial Intelligence and Statistics, AISTATS*, 2015.

[18] S. Rendle. Factorization machines. In *Proceedings of the 2010 IEEE International Conference on Data Mining*, pages 995–1000, 2010.

[19] S. Rendle, C. Freudenthaler, Z. Gantner, and L. Schmidt-Thieme. BPR: Bayesian personalized ranking from implicit feedback. In *Proceedings of the Twenty-Fifth Conference on Uncertainty in Artificial Intelligence*, pages 452–461, 2009.

[20] R. Salakhutdinov and A. Mnih. Probabilistic matrix factorization. In *Advances in Neural Information Processing Systems*, pages 1257–1264, 2008.

[21] R. Salakhutdinov, A. Mnih, and G. Hinton. Restricted Boltzmann machines for collaborative filtering. In *Proceedings of the 24th international conference on Machine learning*, pages 791–798, 2007.

[22] B. Sarwar, G. Karypis, J. Konstan, and J. Riedl. Item-based collaborative filtering recommendation algorithms. In *Proceedings of the 10th international conference on World Wide Web*, pages 285–295. ACM, 2001.

[23] H. Shan and A. Banerjee. Generalized probabilistic matrix factorizations for collaborative filtering. In *Data Mining (ICDM), 2010 IEEE 10th International Conference on*, pages 1025–1030. IEEE, 2010.

[24] G. Shani, D. Heckerman, and R. I. Brafman. An MDP-based recommender system. *Journal of Machine Learning Research*, 6:1265–1295, 2005.

[25] A. P. Singh and G. J. Gordon. Relational learning via collective matrix factorization. In *Proceedings of the 14th ACM SIGKDD international conference on Knowledge discovery and data mining*, pages 650–658. ACM, 2008.

[26] C. Wang and D. Blei. Collaborative topic modeling for recommending scientific articles. In *Knowledge Discovery and Data Mining*, 2011.

Local Item-Item Models for Top-N Recommendation

Evangelia Christakopoulou and George Karypis
Computer Science & Engineering
University of Minnesota, Minneapolis, MN
{evangel,karypis}@cs.umn.edu

ABSTRACT

Item-based approaches based on SLIM (Sparse LInear Methods) have demonstrated very good performance for top-N recommendation; however they only estimate a single model for all the users. This work is based on the intuition that not all users behave in the same way – instead there exist subsets of like-minded users. By using different item-item models for these user subsets, we can capture differences in their preferences and this can lead to improved performance for top-N recommendations. In this work, we extend SLIM by combining global and local SLIM models. We present a method that computes the prediction scores as a user-specific combination of the predictions derived by a global and local item-item models. We present an approach in which the global model, the local models, their user-specific combination, and the assignment of users to the local models are jointly optimized to improve the top-N recommendation performance. Our experiments show that the proposed method improves upon the standard SLIM model and outperforms competing top-N recommendation approaches.

1. INTRODUCTION

Top-N recommender systems [3] are everywhere from online shopping websites to video portals. They provide users with a ranked list of N items they will likely be interested in, in order to encourage views and purchases.

Several algorithms for the top-N recommendation problem have been developed [18], including approaches that use latent-space models and approaches that rely on neighborhoods. The latent space methods [7] factorize the user-item matrix into lower rank user factor and item factor matrices, which represent both the users and the items in a common latent space. The neighborhood-based methods [8] (user-based or item-based) identify similar users or items. The latent-based methods have been shown to be superior for solving the rating prediction problem, whereas the neigborhood methods are shown to be better for the top-N recommendation problem [4, 8, 13, 16]. Among them, the item-based methods, which include item k-NN [8] and Sparse LInear Methods (SLIM) [16] have been shown to outperform the user-based schemes for the top-N recommendation task.

However, item-based methods have the drawback of estimating only a single model for all users. In many cases, there are differences in users' behavior, which cannot be captured by a single model. For example, there could be a pair of items that are extremely similar for a specific user subset, while they have low similarity for another user subset. By using a global model, the similarity between these items will tend to be towards some average value; thus, losing the high correlation of the pair for the first user subset.

In this paper we present a top-N recommendation method that extends the SLIM model in order to capture the differences in the preferences between different user subsets. Our method, which we call GLSLIM (Global and Local SLIM), combines global and local SLIM models in a personalized way and automatically identifies the appropriate user subsets. This is done by solving a joint optimization problem that estimates the different item-item models (global and local), their user-specific combination, and the assignment of the users to these models. Our experimental evaluation shows that GLSLIM outperforms competing top-N recommendation methods, reaching up to 17% improvement in recommendation quality.

The rest of the paper is organized as follows. Section 2 introduces the notation. Section 3 presents the related work. Section 4 presents the proposed model. Section 5 presents the evaluation methodology and the datasets. Section 6 presents the performance of the method. Finally, Section 7 provides some concluding remarks.

2. NOTATION

All vectors are represented by bold lower case letters and are column vectors (e.g., $\mathbf{p}$, $\mathbf{q}$). All matrices are represented by upper case letters (e.g., R, W). For a given matrix A, its ith row is represented by $\mathbf{a}_i^T$ and its jth column by $\mathbf{a}_j$. A predicted value is denoted by having a $\sim$ over it (e.g., $\tilde{r}$).

The number of users is denoted by n and the number of items is denoted by m. Matrix R is used to represent the *user-item implicit feedback* matrix of size $n \times m$. It shows which items the users have purchased/viewed/rated. Symbols u and i are used to denote individual users and items, respectively. If user u provided feedback for item i, the r_{ui} entry of R is 1, otherwise it is 0. We will use the term *rating* to refer to the non-zero entries of R, even though these entries can represent implicit feedback. We also refer to the items that the user has purchased/viewed/rated as

RecSys '16, September 15-19, 2016, Boston , MA, USA
© 2016 ACM. ISBN 978-1-4503-4035-9/16/09...$15.00
DOI: http://dx.doi.org/10.1145/2959100.2959185

rated items and to the rest as *unrated* items. The set of items that the user u has rated will be denoted by $\mathscr{R}_u$. We will use the symbol $\odot$ to denote the Hadamart product (element-wise multiplication).

3. RELATED WORK

3.1 Top-N Recommendation Methods

There has been extensive work in the area of top-N recommendation. Here we present a few notable works in the area that have advanced the state-of-the-art. Deshpande et. al. [8] developed a nearest neighbor item-based approach, which showed that item-based models lead to better top-N recommendation than user-based. Cremonesi et. al. [7] developed the pureSVD method, which uses a truncated SVD decomposition of matrix R to generate the top-N recommendations. Their work demonstrated that treating the missing entries as zero leads to better results than the matrix completion approaches. There is also the point of view of the learning-to-rank formulation [17].

3.1.1 *Sparse LInear Method for top-N Recommendation (SLIM)*

Ning et. al. [16] introduced SLIM, which was the first method to compute the item-item relations using statistical learning and has been shown to be one of the best approaches for top-N recommendation. SLIM estimates a sparse $m \times m$ aggregation coefficient matrix S. The recommendation score on an urated item i for user u is computed as a sparse aggregation of all the user's past rated items:

$$\tilde{r}_{ui} = \mathbf{r}_u^T \mathbf{s}_i, \tag{1}$$

where $\mathbf{r}_u^T$ is the row-vector of R corresponding to user u and $\mathbf{s}_i$ is the ith column vector of matrix S, that is estimated by solving the following optimization problem:

$$\begin{aligned} \underset{\mathbf{s}_i}{\text{minimize}} \quad & \tfrac{1}{2}||\mathbf{r}_i - R\mathbf{s}_i||_2^2 + \tfrac{\beta}{2}||\mathbf{s}_i||_2^2 + \lambda||\mathbf{s}_i||_1, \\ \text{subject to} \quad & \mathbf{s}_i \geq 0, \text{and} \\ & s_{ii} = 0. \end{aligned} \tag{2}$$

The constants β and λ are regularization parameters. The non-negativity constraint is used so that the vector estimated contains positive coefficients. The $s_{ii} = 0$ constraint makes sure that when computing the weights of an item, that item itself is not used as this would lead to trivial solutions.

3.2 Local Models for Recommendation

The idea of estimating multiple local models has been proposed in the work by O'connor et. al. [6], who performed rating prediction by clustering the rating matrix item-wise and estimating a separate local model for each cluster with nearest neighbor collaborative filtering.

Xu et al. [19] developed a method that co-clusters users and items and estimates a separate local model on each cluster, by applying different collaborative filtering methods; including the item-based neighborhood method. The predicted rating for a user-item pair is the prediction from the subgroup with the largest weight for the user.

Lee et al. [14,15] proposed a method that relies on the idea that the rating matrix is locally low-rank. First, neighborhoods are identified surrounding different anchor points of user-item pairs, based on a function that measures distances between pairs of users and items and then a local low-rank model is estimated for every neighborhood. The estimation is done in an iterative way where first the latent factors representing the anchor points are estimated and then based on the similarities of the observed entries to the anchor points, the latent factors are re-estimated, until convergence. A prediction is computed as a convex combination of local models, weighted by the similarity of the corresponding local anchor point to the user–item pair whose rating needs to be predicted.

GLSLIM differs from the earlier work in the following ways: (i) In all of the above-mentioned works, only local models are considered; while GLSLIM also computes a global model and has a personalization factor for each user determining the interplay between the global and the local information. (ii) GLSLIM updates the assignment of the users to subsets, allowing better local models to be estimated. (iii) Lee et. al. [14, 15] use user and item latent factors, while GLSLIM focuses on item-item models. (iv) In [6] the authors use item clusters, in [19] the authors use co-clusters and in [14, 15] they use user-item anchor points. Instead, GLSLIM uses user subsets.

4. PROPOSED APPROACH

4.1 Motivation

A global item-item model may not be sufficient to capture the preferences of a set of users, especially when there are user subsets with diverse and sometimes opposing preferences. An example of when local item-item models (item-item models capturing similarities in user subsets) will be beneficial and outperform the item-item model capturing the global similarities is shown in Figure 1. It portrays the training matrix R of two different datasets that both contain two distinct user subsets. Item i is the target item for which we will try to compute predictions. The predictions are computed by using an item-item cosine similarity-based method, in this motivation example.

In the left dataset, (Figure 1a) there exist some items which have been rated only by the users of one subset, but there is also a set of items which have been rated by users in both subsets. Items c and i will have different similarities when estimated for user-subset A, than when estimated for user-subset B, than for the overall matrix. Specifically, their similarity will be zero for the users of subset B (as item i is not rated by the users of that subset), but it will be non-zero for the users of subset A – and we can further assume without loss of generality that in this example it is high. Then, the similarity between i and c will be of average value when computed in the global case. So, estimating the local item-item similarities for the user subsets of this dataset will help capture the diverse preferences of user-subsets A and B, which would otherwise be missed if we only computed them globally.

However, when using item j to make predictions for item i, their similarity will be the same, either globally estimated, either locally for subset A, as they both have been rated only by users of subset A. The same holds for the dataset pictured in Figure 1b, as this dataset consists of user subsets who have no common rated items between them.

Although datasets like the one in Figure 1b cannot benefit from using local item-item similarity models, datasets such as the one pictured in Figure 1a can greatly benefit as they can capture item-item similarities, which could be missed in the case of just having a global model.

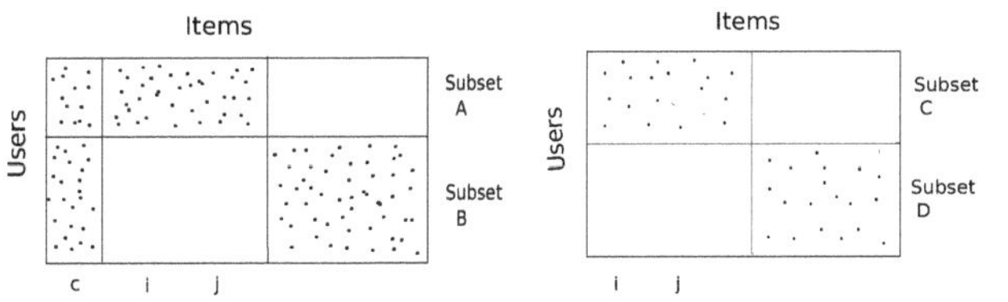

(a) Overlapping rated items between user subsets (b) No common rated items between user subsets

Figure 1: (a) Local item-item models improve upon global item-item model. (b) Global item-item model and local models yield the same results.

4.2 Overview

In this work, we present our method GLSLIM, which computes top-N recommendations that utilize user–subset specific models and a global model. These models are jointly optimized along with computing the user assignments for them. We use SLIM for estimating the models. Thus, we estimate a global item-item coefficient matrix S and also k local item-item coefficient matrices S^{p_u}, where k is the number of user subsets and $p_u \in \{1, \ldots, k\}$ is the index of the user subset, for which we estimate the local matrix S^{p_u}. Every user can belong to one user subset.

The predicted rating of user u, who belongs to subset p_u, for item i will be estimated by:

$$\tilde{r}_{ui} = \sum_{l \in \mathscr{R}_u} g_u s_{li} + (1 - g_u) s_{li}^{p_u}. \quad (3)$$

The meanings of the various terms are as follows: The term s_{li} shows the global item-item similarity between the lth item rated by u and the target item i. The term $s_{li}^{p_u}$ depicts the item-item similarity between the lth item rated by u and target item i, corresponding to the local model of the user-subset p_u, to which target user u belongs. Finally, the term g_u is the personalized weight per user, which controls the interplay between the global and the local part. It lies in the interval $[0, 1]$, with 0 showing that the recommendation is affected only by the local model and 1 showing that the user u will use only the global model.

In order to perform top-N recommendation for user u, we compute the estimated rating $\tilde{r}_{ui}$ for every unrated item i with Equation 3. Then, we sort these values and we recommend the top-N items with the highest ratings to the user.

The estimation of the item-item coefficient matrices, the user assignments and the personalized weight is done with alternating minimization, which will be further explained in the following subsections.

4.3 Estimating the item-item models

We first separate the users into subsets with either a clustering algorithm (we used CLUTO [1]) or randomly. We initially set g_u to be 0.5 for all users, in order to have equal contribution of the global and the local part and we estimate the coefficient matrices S and S^{p_u}, with $p_u \in \{1, \ldots, k\}$. We use two vectors $\mathbf{g}$ and $\mathbf{g}'$ each of size n, where the vector $\mathbf{g}$ contains the personalized weight g_u for every user u and the vector $\mathbf{g}'$ contains the complement of the personalized weight $(1 - g_u)$ for every user u. When assigning the users into k subsets, we split the training matrix R into k training matrices R^{p_u} of size $n \times m$, with $p_u \in \{1, \ldots, k\}$. Every row u of R^{p_u} will be the uth row of R, if the user u who corresponds to this row belongs in the p_uth subset. If the user u does not belong to the p_uth subset, then the corresponding row of R^{p_u} will be empty, without any ratings. When estimating the local model S^{p_u}, only the corresponding R^{p_u} will be used. Following SLIM, the item–item coefficient matrices can be calculated per column, which allows for the different columns (of both the global and the local coefficient matrices) to be estimated in parallel. In order to estimate the ith column of S ($\mathbf{s}_i$) and S^{p_u} ($\mathbf{s}_i^{p_u}$) where $p_u \in \{1, \ldots, k\}$, GLSLIM solves the following optimization problem:

$$\begin{aligned}
\underset{\mathbf{s}_i, \{\mathbf{s}_i^1, \ldots, \mathbf{s}_i^k\}}{\text{minimize}} \quad & \tfrac{1}{2}||\mathbf{r}_i - \mathbf{g} \odot R\mathbf{s}_i - \mathbf{g}' \odot \textstyle\sum_{p_u=1}^{k} R^{p_u}\mathbf{s}_i^{p_u}||_2^2 + \\
& \tfrac{1}{2}\beta_g||\mathbf{s}_i||_2^2 + \lambda_g||\mathbf{s}_i||_1 + \\
& \textstyle\sum_{p_u=1}^{k} \tfrac{1}{2}\beta_l||\mathbf{s}_i^{p_u}||_2^2 + \lambda_l||\mathbf{s}_i^{p_u}||_1, \\
\text{subject to} \quad & \mathbf{s}_i \geq 0, \\
& \mathbf{s}_i^{p_u} \geq 0, \forall p_u \in \{1, \ldots, k\}, \\
& s_{ii} = 0, \\
& s^{p_u}{}_{ii} = 0, \forall p_u \in \{1, \ldots, k\},
\end{aligned} \quad (4)$$

where $\mathbf{r}_i$ is the ith column of R. β_g and β_l are the l_2 regularization weights corresponding to S and S^{p_u} $\forall p_u \in \{1, \ldots, k\}$ respectively. Finally λ_g and λ_l are the l_1 regularization weights controlling the sparsity of S and S^{p_u} $\forall p_u \in \{1, \ldots, k\}$, respectively.

By having different regularization parameters for the global and the local sparse coefficient matrices, we allow flexibility in the model. In this way, we can control through regularization which of the two components will play a more major part in the recommendation.

The constraint $s_{ii} = 0$ makes sure that when computing r_{ui}, the element r_{ui} is not used. If this constraint was not enforced, then an item would recommend itself. For the exact same reason, we enforce the constraint $s^{p_u}{}_{ii} = 0$, $\forall p_u \in \{1, \ldots, k\}$ for the local sparse coefficient matrices too.

The optimization problem of Equation 4 can be solved using coordinate descent and soft thresholding [9].

4.4 Finding the optimal assignment of users to subsets

After estimating the local models (and the global model), GLSLIM fixes them and proceeds with the second part of the optimization: updating the user subsets. While doing that, GLSLIM also determines the personalized weight g_u. We will use the term *refinement* to refer to finding the optimal user assignment to subsets.

Specifically, GLSLIM tries to assign each user u to every possible cluster, while computing the weight g_u that the user would have if assigned to that cluster. Then, for every cluster p_u and user u, the training error is computed. The cluster for which this error is the smallest is the cluster to which the user is assigned. If there is no difference in the training error, or if there is no cluster for which the training error is smaller, the user u remains at the initial cluster. The training error is computed for both the user's rated and unrated items.

Algorithm 1 GLSLIM

Assign $g_u = 0.5$, to every user u.
Compute the initial clustering of users with CLUTO [1].
while number of users who switched clusters > 1% of the total number of users **do**
  Estimate S and S^{p_u}, $\forall p_u \in \{1, \ldots, k\}$ with Equation 4.
  for all user u **do**
    for all cluster p_u **do**
      Compute g_u for cluster p_u with Equation 5.
      Compute the training error.
    end for
    Assign user u to the cluster p_u that has the smallest training error and update g_u to the corresponding one for cluster p_u.
  end for
end while

Table 1: Dataset characteristics.

Name	#Users	#Items	#Transactions	Density
groceries	63,034	15,846	2,060,719	0.21%
ml	69,878	10,677	10,000,054	1.34%
jester	57,732	150	1,760,039	20.32%
flixster	29,828	10,085	7,356,146	2.45%
netflix	274,036	17,770	31,756,784	0.65%

Columns corresponding to #users, #items and #transactions show the number of users, number of items and number of transactions, respectively, in each dataset. The column corresponding to density shows the density of each dataset (i.e., density=#transactions/(#users×#items)).

In order to compute the personalized weight g_u, we minimize the squared error of Equation 3 for user u who belongs to subset p_u, over all items i. By setting the derivative of the squared error to 0, we get:

$$g_u = \frac{\sum_{i=1}^{m} (\sum_{l \in \mathscr{R}_u} s_{li} - \sum_{l \in \mathscr{R}_u} s_{li}^{p_u})(r_{ui} - \sum_{l \in \mathscr{R}_u} s_{li}^{p_u})}{\sum_{i=1}^{m} (\sum_{l \in \mathscr{R}_u} s_{li} - \sum_{l \in \mathscr{R}_u} s_{li}^{p_u})^2}. \quad (5)$$

The overview of GLSLIM as well as the stopping criterion are shown in Algorithm 1.

5. EXPERIMENTAL EVALUATION

5.1 Datasets

We evaluated the performance of our method on different datasets, whose characteristics are shown in Table 1.

The *groceries* dataset corresponds to transactions of a local grocery store. Each user corresponds to a customer and the items correspond to the distinct products purchased over a period of one year. The *ml* dataset corresponds to MovieLens 10M dataset [12], which represents movie ratings. The *jester* dataset [10] corresponds to an online joke recommender system. The *flixster* dataset is a subset of the original Flixster dataset [2], which consists of movie ratings taken from the corresponding social movie site that allows users to share movie ratings and meet friends. The subset was created by keeping the users who have rated more than thirty items and the items that have been rated by at least twenty-five users. The *netflix* dataset is a subset of the original Netflix dataset [5], which contains anonymous movie ratings. The subset was created by keeping the users who have rated between thirty and five hundred items. All the ratings were converted to binary ratings, showing whether a user purchased/rated an item or not.

Algorithm 2 LSLIM

Compute the initial clustering of users with CLUTO.
while number of users who switched clusters > 1% of the total number of users **do**
  Estimate S^{p_u}, $\forall p_u \in \{1, \ldots, k\}$ with Equation 8.
  for all user u **do**
    for all cluster p_u **do**
      Compute the training error.
    end for
    Assign user u to the cluster p_u that has the smallest training error.
  end for
end while

Algorithm 3 GLSLIMr0

Assign $g_u = 0.5$, to every user u.
Compute the initial clustering of users with CLUTO.
while $diff > 0.01\%$ **do**
  Estimate S and S^{p_u}, $\forall p_u \in \{1, \ldots, k\}$ with Equation 4.
  $\forall$ user u compute g_u with Equation 5.
  Compute difference in the objective function ($diff$) between subsequent iterations.
end while

5.2 Evaluation Methodology

We employed leave-one-out cross-validation to evaluate the performance of the proposed model. For each user, we randomly selected an item, which we placed in the test set. The rest of the data comprised the training set.

We measure the performance by computing the number of times the single left-out item was in the top-N recommended items for this user and its position in that list. The quality measures used are the hit-rate (HR) and average-reciprocal hit rank (ARHR). HR is defined as

$$HR = \frac{\#hits}{\#users}, \quad (6)$$

and ARHR is defined as

$$ARHR = \frac{1}{\#users} \sum_{i=1}^{\#hits} \frac{1}{p_i}, \quad (7)$$

where "#users" is the total number of users (n), p is the position of the item in the list, where $p = 1$ specifies the top of the list, and "#hits" is the number of users whose item in the test set is present in the size-N recommendation list.

5.3 Proposed Methods

As our method contains multiple elements, we want to investigate how each of them impacts the recommendation performance. Thus, beyond GLSLIM, we also investigate the following methods:

- LSLIMr0, which stands for Local SLIM without refinement. In LSLIMr0, a separate item-item model is estimated for each of the k user subsets. No global model is estimated; so there is no personalized weight g_u either. Specifically, the ith column of the p_uth local model S^{p_u} ($\mathbf{s}_i^{p_u}$) is estimated by solving the optimization problem:

$$
\begin{aligned}
\underset{\{\mathbf{s}_i^1,\ldots,\mathbf{s}_i^k\}}{\text{minimize}} \quad & \tfrac{1}{2}||\mathbf{r}_i - \textstyle\sum_{p_u=1}^{k} R^{p_u}\mathbf{s}_i^{p_u}||_2^2 + \\
& \textstyle\sum_{p_u=1}^{k} \tfrac{1}{2}\beta_l||\mathbf{s}_i^{p_u}||_2^2 + \lambda_l||\mathbf{s}_i^{p_u}||_1, \\
\text{subject to} \quad & \\
& \mathbf{s}_i^{p_u} \geq 0, \forall p_u \in \{1,\ldots,k\}, \\
& s^{p_u}{}_{ii} = 0, \forall p_u \in \{1,\ldots,k\},
\end{aligned}
\tag{8}
$$

where the meanings of the different terms are identical to those used in Equation 4.

In LSLIMr0, the initial assignment of users to subsets using CLUTO is the one used and never gets updated. The predicted rating for user u, who belongs to subset p_u, and item i is estimated by:

$$
\tilde{r}_{ui} = \sum_{l \in \mathscr{R}_u} s_{li}^{p_u}. \tag{9}
$$

The overall recommendation quality is computed as the weighted average of the item-item model performance in every subset.

- LSLIM, which stands for Local SLIM with refinement. In LSLIM, the predicted rating for user u and item i is also estimated by Equation 9 and the local models are estimated in the same way as in LSLIMr0. However, the users switch subsets and the local models get updated accordingly, until convergence. The algorithm for LSLIM is shown in Algorithm 2.
- GLSLIMr0, which stands for Global and Local SLIM without refinement. In GLSLIMr0, both a global model and separate item-item local models are estimated along with the per user weight g_u. However the assignment of users to subsets remains fixed. The algorithm for this method is shown in Algorithm 3.

5.4 Comparison Algorithms

The top-N recommendation algorithms that we compare against are: PureSVD [7], BPR-MF [17] and SLIM (described in Section 3.1.1).

PureSVD [7] is a popular top-N recommendation algorithm, which estimates the user–item matrix R by the factorization:

$$
\tilde{R} = U\Sigma Q^T, \tag{10}
$$

where U is an $n \times f$ orthonormal matrix, Q is an $m \times f$ orthonormal matrix and Σ is an $f \times f$ diagonal matrix containing the first f singular values.

BPR-MF [17] (Bayesian Personalized Ranking – Matrix Factorization) is a well-known top-N recommendation method, which uses the bayesian personalized ranking optimization criterion on matrix factorization. The BPR criterion focuses on finding the correct personalized ranking for all items to maximize the posterior probability.

For PureSVD, we used the SVDLIBC package[1], for BPR-MF, we used the LibRec package [11] and for SLIM, we used the SLIM package[2].

[1]https://tedlab.mit.edu/~dr/SVDLIBC/
[2]www-users.cs.umn.edu/~xning/slim/html

5.5 Model Selection

We performed an extensive search over the parameter space of the various methods, in order to find the set of parameters that gives us the best performance for each method.

We only report the performance corresponding to the parameters that lead to the best results. The l_1 and l_2 regularization parameters were chosen from the set of values: $\{0.1, 1, 3, 5, 7, 10\}$. The number of clusters examined took on the values: {2, 3, 5, 10, 15, 20, 25, 30, 35, 40, 45, 50, 60, 70, 80, 90, 100 and 150}.

For PureSVD, the number of singular values f tried lie in the interval $[10, 5000]$. For BPR-MF, the number of factors we used in order to get the best results lie in the interval $[1, 10000]$. The values of the learning rate that we tried are: $\{0.0001, 0.001, 0.01, 0.1\}$. The values of the regularization we tried are: $\{0.0001, 0.001, 0.01, 0.1\}$.

6. EXPERIMENTAL RESULTS

In this section we present the results of our experiments. The following questions will be answered: (i) How do the proposed methods compare between them? (ii) How does our method compare against competing top-N recommendation methods? (iii) What is the time complexity of our method?

6.1 Performance of the proposed methods

The comparison of our proposed approaches (LSLIMr0, LSLIM, GLSLIMr0 and GLSLIM) in terms of HR and ARHR is shown in Table 2. Overall, we can see that the general pattern is that GLSLIM is the best-performing method, followed by GLSLIMr0 and LSLIM, while LSLIMr0 is the approach with the lowest performance.

By comparing these methods, we can see the relative benefits provided by the different components of GLSLIM. The comparisons of LSLIMr0 with GLSLIMr0 and also of LSLIM with GLSLIM show the benefit of adding a global model with a personalized weight g_u. The comparisons of LSLIMr0 with LSLIM, and also between GLSLIMr0 and GLSLIM demonstrate the benefit of allowing users to switch subsets. We can see that both these components improve the performance. However, in all of the datasets but *ml*, the relative gain of considering a global model beyond the local item-item models and also computing a personalized weight g_u is higher than the gain of allowing users to switch subsets. When all of the components are combined, as in the case of GLSLIM, we get the best performance, both in terms of HR and ARHR.

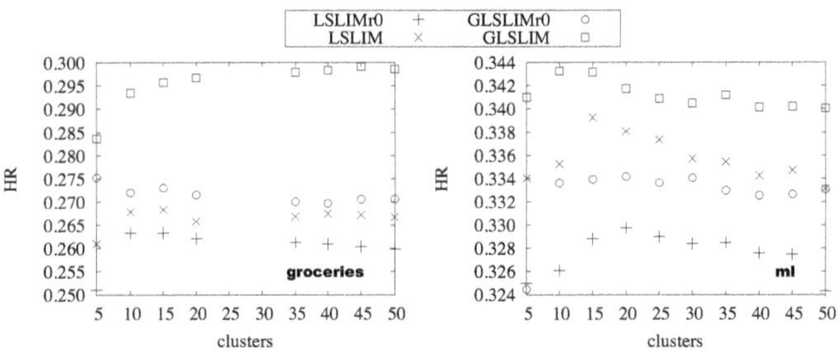

Figure 2: The effect of the number of clusters on the performance

Table 2: Comparison between our proposed approaches.

Comparison in terms of Hit Rate (HR)

	LSLIMr0				LSLIM				GLSLIMr0						GLSLIM					
Dataset	Cls	β_l	λ_l	HR	Cls	β_l	λ_l	HR	Cls	β_g	β_l	λ_g	λ_l	HR	Cls	β_g	β_l	λ_g	λ_l	HR
groceries	15	5	0.1	0.263	15	5	1	0.268	3	5	5	1	1	0.280	100	5	5	1	1	**0.304**
ml	20	5	1	0.329	15	5	3	0.339	15	7	3	1	5	0.335	10	10	7	1	1	**0.345**
jester	5	5	0.1	0.898	10	0.1	0.1	0.916	20	7	1	10	1	0.929	10	10	10	10	0.1	**0.940**
flixster	3	1	2	0.248	3	0.1	3	0.250	3	1	1	5	5	0.254	3	1	1	1	5	**0.255**
netflix	10	1	5	0.238	10	1	5	0.241	20	1	1	5	5	0.243	5	1	1	5	5	**0.245**

Comparison in terms of Average Reciprocal Hit Rate (ARHR)

	LSLIMr0				LSLIM				GLSLIMr0						GLSLIM					
Dataset	Cls	β_l	λ_l	ARHR	Cls	β_l	λ_l	ARHR	Cls	β_g	β_l	λ_g	λ_l	ARHR	Cls	β_g	β_l	λ_g	λ_l	ARHR
groceries	3	3	0.1	0.133	15	3	3	0.135	3	5	5	1	1	0.144	100	5	5	1	1	**0.155**
ml	25	7	2	0.163	15	7	3	0.167	15	7	7	1	3	0.166	10	10	7	1	1	**0.170**
jester	10	0.1	0.1	0.775	10	10	5	0.804	150	1	1	1	1	0.820	100	1	1	1	1	**0.835**
flixster	3	0.1	2	0.121	3	1	3	0.122	3	5	5	1	1	0.125	3	1	1	1	5	**0.126**
netflix	20	0.1	5	0.113	10	3	10	0.114	20	1	1	5	5	0.115	5	1	1	5	5	**0.116**

For each method, the columns correspond to the best HR and ARHR and the parameters for which they are achieved. The parameters are: the number of clusters, the global l_2 regularization parameter β_g, the local l_2 regularization parameter β_l, the global l_1 regularization parameter λ_g and the local l_1 regularization parameter λ_l. The bold numbers show the best HR/ARHR achieved, per dataset.

6.1.1 Sensitivity on the number of Clusters

Figure 2 shows how the number of clusters affects the HR for GLSLIM and its variants in the *groceries* and *ml* datasets. The trends are the same for the rest of the datasets and for the metric ARHR. We can see that GLSLIM outperforms the rest of the methods for all clusters. Also, we should note that for all datasets GLSLIM can achieve at least 95% of its best performance for only ten clusters, outperforming its closest competing method. This is the case even for the datasets where the best performance occured at a much bigger number of clusters.

6.1.2 Initializing with random user subsets

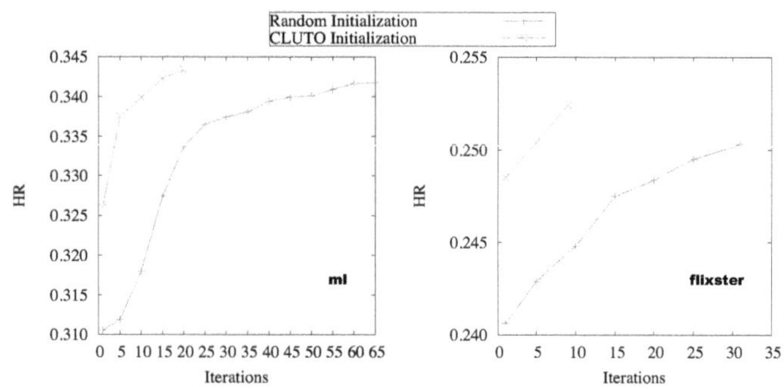

Figure 3: Comparing CLUTO initialization with random initialization of user subsets

The results presented up to this point have been obtained by initializing the user subsets with a user clustering algorithm (we used CLUTO[3] [1]). In order to show that the good performance of GLSLIM is not dependent on the clustering algorithm used, we present the performance when the initialization of the user subsets is random.

In Figure 3, we can see for the *ml* and *flixster* datasets, the HR achieved across iterations with the two different ways of initialization, for the same regularization and for ten clusters. The same trends hold for ARHR and for different regularizations, clusters and the rest of the datasets.

We can see that the HR of the first iteration with random initialization is lower than the HR of the first iteration when initializing with CLUTO. This is expected, as in the first iteration, only the global and local models are estimated; no personalization nor cluster refinement has been done yet. Thus, the local models estimated from CLUTO are more meaningful than the local models on random user subsets.

As the iterations progress and cluster refinement is done, we see that the HR increases. In the converged state, the final HR achieved is very similar with both initializations. However, when starting from random user subsets, more iterations are needed until convergence. We can then conclude that our method is able to estimate the local models and reach convergence, even with random initialization.

6.1.3 The interplay between the global and the local part of the model

In order to see how the local models affect the recommendation performance, we look at the l_1 norm of the global model S and the local models S^{p_u} in the beginning of the algorithm and when the algorithm has converged.

Figure 4 shows these l_1 norms for 5, 50 and 100 clusters, for the *groceries* and *ml* datasets. We can see that the l_1 norm of the global model S is small and it remains small for all possible clusters and throughout the iterations of the algorithm. For the local models S^{p_u}, their l_1 norm is larger than the l_1 norm of the global model. As the number of clusters increases, the l_1 norm of the local models increases. In addition, the l_1 norm of the local models in the converged state is larger than the l_1 norm of the local models in the

[3]We used the clustering program *vcluster*. The similarity function considered was the cosine similarity. All the other parameters were the default ones.

beginning. This shows that the effect of local information on the models is major and it becomes greater as the iterations progress and as the number of clusters increases.

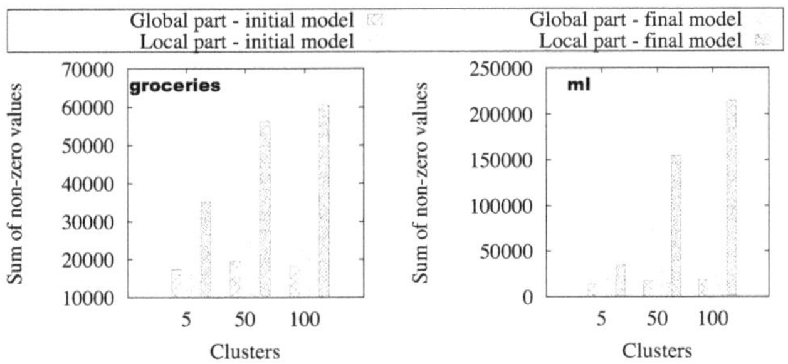

Figure 4: How the l_1 norm of the global model S and local models S^{p_u} changes from the beginning of the algorithm until convergence.

6.1.4 Top-N

The results presented throughout the paper show the performance of our algorithms for a list of size 10. The recommendation list can be of different sizes. In this section, we describe how the performance of our method is affected by using lists of sizes 5, 15 and 20 as well. We choose N to be quite small because users do not look past the very top presented recommendations in a list, anyway.

In Figure 5, we can see the HR of GLSLIM, while using the parameters with the best results as presented in Table 2 for the different sizes of top-N list. We can see that as N increases, the performance of our method increases as well, which is expected, as there is higher probability that the hidden item of our test set will be in the top-N list. The impact of the size of the recommendation list N on ARHR is similar to the one shown in Figure 5.

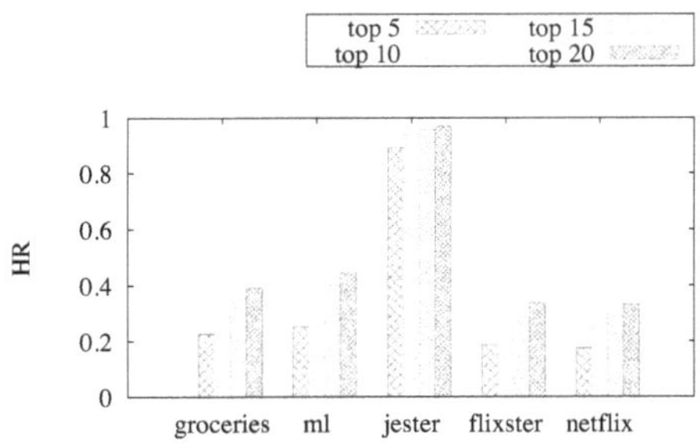

Figure 5: Varying the size of the top-N list.

6.2 Performance against Competing Approaches

Table 3 presents the performance of the competing algorithms PureSVD, BPR-MF and SLIM versus the performance of our best method, which is GLSLIM. The above-mentioned table presents the best HR and ARHR achieved, along with the set of parameters for which they were achieved.

We can see that GLSLIM outperforms all competing approaches for all datasets, as seen in Table 3. By comparing Tables 2 with 3, we can also see that LSLIMr0, which is our simplest method, still outperforms the best competing approach, which shows that using multiple item-item models helps top-N recommendation quality.

6.3 Time Complexity

We will use $O(SLIM_i(R))$ to denote the computational cost of estimating the ith column of S. Then, the complexity of estimating the ith column of S and $S^1, \ldots, S^k$, is $O(SLIM_i(R)) + O(SLIM_i(R^1)) + \ldots + O(SLIM_i(R^k))$, where $R^1, \ldots, R^k$ are non-overlapping submatrices of R. Since in order to estimate the ith column of S, we need to touch every non-zero in the input matrix R, the complexity $O(SLIM_i(R))$ is at least linear in the number of non-zeros (nnz). We can then say that the complexity of estimating the ith column for the submatrices $R^1, \ldots, R^k$ is less than or equal to the complexity of solving it on the matrix R: $O(SLIM_i(R)) \geq O(SLIM_i(R^1)) + \ldots + O(SLIM_i(R^k))$. As a result, the complexity of Equation 4 is the dominant term $O(SLIM_i(R))$. Since the regression problem of Equation 4 needs to be solved for all m columns (items), the complexity of estimating the global and local models is $O(m \times SLIM_i(R))$. The complexity of updating the cluster assignment for each of the n users, after trying to assign them to each of the k clusters (lines $5-11$ of Algorithm 1), is $O(nmk)$, since both the computation of the training error and g_u is $O(m)$. Thus, the per iteration cost of GLSLIM is $O(m(SLIM_i(R) + nk))$. The number of iterations until GLSLIM converges is typically small, as can be seen in Section 6.1.2.

7. CONCLUSION

In this paper, we proposed a method to improve upon top-N recommendation item-based schemes, by capturing the differences in the preferences between different user subsets, which cannot be captured by a single model. For this purpose, we estimate a separate local item-item model for every user subset, in addition to the global item-item model. The proposed method allows cluster refinement, in the context of users being able to switch the subset they belong to, which leads to updating the local model estimated for this subset, as well as the global model. The method is personalized, as we compute for all users their own personal weight, defining the degree to which their top-N recommendation list will be affected from global or local information. We performed different experiments, which show that our method outperforms competing top-N recommender methods, indicating the value of using multiple item-item models.

Acknowledgments

This work was supported in part by NSF (OCI-1048018, IIS-1247632, IIP-1414153, IIS-1447788), Army Research Office (W911NF-14-1-0316), Intel Software and Services Group, and the Digital Technology Center at the University of Minnesota. Access to research and computing facilities was provided by the Digital Technology Center and the Minnesota Supercomputing Institute.

8. REFERENCES

[1] Cluto clustering toolkit. http://glaros.dtc.umn.edu/gkhome/cluto/cluto/overview.

[2] Flixster dataset. http://http://www.cs.sfu.ca/~sja25/personal/datasets/.

[3] G. Adomavicius and A. Tuzhilin. Toward the next generation of recommender systems: A survey of the state-of-the-art and possible extensions. *Knowledge and Data Engineering, IEEE Transactions on*, 17(6):734–749, 2005.

Table 3: Comparison with competing approaches.

Comparison in terms of Hit Rate (HR)

	PureSVD		BPR-MF				SLIM			GLSLIM					
Dataset	f	HR	factors	lrnrate	reg	HR	β	λ	HR	Cls	β_g	β_l	λ_g	λ_l	HR
groceries	738	0.134	3000	0.01	0.001	0.214	5	0.1	0.259	100	5	5	1	1	**0.304**
ml	64	0.295	5000	0.01	0.01	0.240	7	5	0.312	10	10	7	1	1	**0.345**
jester	25	0.860	300	0.01	0.01	0.903	3	0.1	0.878	10	10	10	10	0.1	**0.940**
flixster	90	0.194	4000	0.01	0.001	0.200	0.1	2	0.242	3	1	1	1	5	**0.255**
netflix	50	0.204	5000	0.01	0.01	0.210	0.1	5	0.231	5	1	1	5	5	**0.245**

Comparison in terms of Average Reciprocal Hit Rate (ARHR)

	PureSVD		BPR-MF				SLIM			GLSLIM					
Dataset	f	ARHR	factors	lrnrate	reg	ARHR	β	λ	ARHR	Cls	β_g	β_l	λ_g	λ_l	ARHR
groceries	700	0.059	3100	0.01	0.001	0.099	3	0.1	0.130	100	5	5	1	1	**0.155**
ml	56	0.139	7000	0.01	0.01	0.105	5	2	0.151	10	10	7	1	1	**0.170**
jester	15	0.740	100	0.01	0.01	0.766	7	0.1	0.755	100	1	1	1	1	**0.835**
flixster	80	0.086	4000	0.01	0.001	0.089	0.1	2	0.116	3	1	1	1	5	**0.126**
netflix	50	0.091	5000	0.01	0.01	0.100	5	5	0.107	5	1	1	5	5	**0.116**

For each method, columns corresponding to the best HR and ARHR and the set of parameters with which they are achieved are shown. For PureSVD the parameter is the number of singular values (f). For BPR-MF, the parameters are: the number of factors, the learnrate and the regularization. For SLIM, the parameters are the $l2$ regularization parameter β and the $l1$ regularization parameter λ. For GLSLIM, the parameters are the number of clusters, global β (β_g), local β (β_l), global λ (λ_g) and local λ (λ_l). Bold numbers indicate the best HR and ARHR across the different algorithms, for every dataset.

[4] F. Aiolli. A preliminary study on a recommender system for the million songs dataset challenge. *PREFERENCE LEARNING: PROBLEMS AND APPLICATIONS IN AI*, page 1, 2012.

[5] J. Bennett and S. Lanning. The netflix prize. In *Proceedings of KDD cup and workshop*, volume 2007, page 35, 2007.

[6] M. Connor and J. Herlocker. Clustering items for collaborative filtering. In *Proceedings of the ACM SIGIR workshop on recommender systems*, volume 128. Citeseer, 1999.

[7] P. Cremonesi, Y. Koren, and R. Turrin. Performance of recommender algorithms on top-n recommendation tasks. In *Proceedings of the fourth ACM conference on Recommender systems*, pages 39–46. ACM, 2010.

[8] M. Deshpande and G. Karypis. Item-based top-n recommendation algorithms. *ACM Transactions on Information Systems (TOIS)*, 22(1):143–177, 2004.

[9] J. Friedman, T. Hastie, and R. Tibshirani. Regularization paths for generalized linear models via coordinate descent. *Journal of statistical software*, 33(1):1, 2010.

[10] K. Goldberg, T. Roeder, D. Gupta, and C. Perkins. Eigentaste: A constant time collaborative filtering algorithm. *Information Retrieval*, 4(2):133–151, 2001.

[11] G. Guo, J. Zhang, Z. Sun, and N. Yorke-Smith. Librec: A java library for recommender systems. In *Posters, Demos, Late-breaking Results and Workshop Proceedings of the 23rd International Conference on User Modeling, Adaptation and Personalization*, 2015.

[12] J. L. Herlocker, J. A. Konstan, A. Borchers, and J. Riedl. An algorithmic framework for performing collaborative filtering. In *Proceedings of the 22nd annual international ACM SIGIR conference on Research and development in information retrieval*, pages 230–237. ACM, 1999.

[13] S. Kabbur, X. Ning, and G. Karypis. Fism: Factored item similarity models for top-n recommender systems. 2013.

[14] J. Lee, S. Bengio, S. Kim, G. Lebanon, and Y. Singer. Local collaborative ranking. In *Proceedings of the 23rd international conference on World wide web*, pages 85–96. ACM, 2014.

[15] J. Lee, S. Kim, G. Lebanon, and Y. Singer. Local low-rank matrix approximation. In *Proceedings of The 30th International Conference on Machine Learning*, pages 82–90, 2013.

[16] X. Ning and G. Karypis. Slim: Sparse linear methods for top-n recommender systems. In *Data Mining (ICDM), 2011 IEEE 11th International Conference on*, pages 497–506. IEEE, 2011.

[17] S. Rendle, C. Freudenthaler, Z. Gantner, and L. Schmidt-Thieme. Bpr: Bayesian personalized ranking from implicit feedback. In *Proceedings of the Twenty-Fifth Conference on Uncertainty in Artificial Intelligence*, pages 452–461. AUAI Press, 2009.

[18] F. Ricci and B. Shapira. *Recommender systems handbook*. Springer, 2011.

[19] B. Xu, J. Bu, C. Chen, and D. Cai. An exploration of improving collaborative recommender systems via user-item subgroups. In *Proceedings of the 21st international conference on World Wide Web*, pages 21–30. ACM, 2012.

Asynchronous Distributed Matrix Factorization with Similar User and Item Based Regularization

Bikash Joshi† Franck Iutzeler‡ Massih-Reza Amini†

University of Grenoble Alpes - CNRS
† Computer Science Laboratory (LIG)
‡ Applied Mathematics Laboratory (LJK)
{FirstName.LastName}@imag.fr

ABSTRACT

We introduce an asynchronous distributed stochastic gradient algorithm for matrix factorization based collaborative filtering. The main idea of this approach is to distribute the user-rating matrix across different machines, each having access only to a part of the information, and to asynchronously propagate the updates of the stochastic gradient optimization across the network. Each time a machine receives a parameter vector, it averages its current parameter vector with the received one, and continues its iterations from this new point. Additionally, we introduce a similarity based regularization that constrains the user and item factors to be close to the average factors of their similar users and items found on subparts of the distributed user-rating matrix. We analyze the impact of the regularization terms on MovieLens (100K, 1M, 10M) and NetFlix datasets and show that it leads to a more efficient matrix factorization in terms of Root Mean Square Error (RMSE) and Mean Absolute Error (MAE), and that the asynchronous distributed approach significantly improves in convergence time as compared to an equivalent synchronous distributed approach.

Keywords

Recommender Systems, Asynchronous Distributed Optimization, Similarity-based Regularization

1. INTRODUCTION

The immense growth of e-commerce in the last decade has resulted in an increasing popularity for Recommender Systems, helping customers to identify products that best fit their personal tastes. Many Recommender Systems approaches were proposed in the recent years among which collaborative filtering based algorithms have been found to be very effective [6]. The underlying hypothesis $\mathcal{H}$ of these algorithms is that if two users share the same opinion over a set of items, they are likely to share the same opinion over new items. Two popular collaborative filtering techniques that have been developed based on this idea are 1) Neighborhood methods [5], which generate prediction for unseen items using the past ratings of similar users or items; and 2) Matrix Factorization techniques [3], that approximate the matrix of ratings with the product of two matrices corresponding to users and items in some latent space.

In this study, we tackle this problem by splitting the rating matrix across different machines of a network and propose a novel distributed asynchronous framework for matrix factorization using the Stochastic Gradient Optimization (SGO) method for recommender systems. The rational is that machines connected in a network are generally loaded differently and synchronous updates may become very slow as every machine has to wait for the slowest machine to finish before updating. Moreover, in order to enhance the underlying hypothesis $\mathcal{H}$ stated above, we add to the classical RMSE objective two similarity-based regularization terms that constrain respectively user and item factors to be close to the factors of their most similar users and items found in the subpart of the rating matrix stored in the machine. In our asynchronous framework, each machine performs SGO in parallel on different parts of the rating matrix and sends its updated weights to the other machines in the network. Once a machine receives an updated weight, it averages the parameter weights with its own updates and continues applying SGO from the new averaged point. This guarantees that each machine keeps an overall view over the whole data.

Using Movielens and Netflix datasets, we show that the addition of the proposed user and item regularization terms lead to a more effective matrix factorization in terms of RMSE and MAE. We also demonstrate the attractive convergence properties of our asynchronous distributed update scheme compared to an equivalent synchronous distributed approach [8, 4].

In the remainder of the paper, we define in Section 2 the Matrix Factorization problem with our proposed similarity-based regularization. Then, in Section 3, we describe the proposed distributed asynchronous framework. Finally, we discuss the experimental settings and results in Section 4.

2. MATRIX FACTORIZATION WITH USER AND ITEM BASED REGULARIZATION

In this section, we introduce basic definitions and the objectives that we address in our setting of matrix factorization. Users and items are respectively represented by the sets $\mathcal{U}$ and $\mathcal{I}$, where u_i and i_j are respectively the ith user and the jth item. Furthermore, we denote by r_{ij} the rat-

RecSys '16, September 15-19, 2016, Boston , MA, USA

© 2016 ACM. ISBN 978-1-4503-4035-9/16/09...$15.00

DOI: http://dx.doi.org/10.1145/2959100.2959161

ing of item i_j by user u_i and we define the ratings matrix R as the matrix of the r_{ij} whenever they exist. The user $|\mathcal{U}| \times K$ factor matrix (resp. item $|\mathcal{I}| \times K$) in a latent space of dimension K is denoted by P (resp. Q), and p_i (resp. q_j) is the size-k vector corresponding to the ith user/line (resp. j^{th} item/line).

Matrix factorization with Stochastic Gradient Optimization (SGO) has been proved to be a successful approach for recommender systems, notably after winning the Netflix prize [3]. The premise behind this approach is to approximate the large rating matrix R with the multiplication of low-dimensional factor matrices PQ^{T}. These factor matrices try to model user preference for items with small number K of implicit factors. For a pair of user and item (u_i, i_j) for which a rating r_{ij} exists, this approach is based on the minimization of the ℓ_2-regularized quadratic error:

$$\ell(u_i, i_j, P, Q) = \left(r_{ij} - q_j^{\top} p_i\right)^2 + \lambda(||p_i||^2 + ||q_j||^2) \quad (1)$$

where $\lambda \geq 0$ is the regularization parameter. The whole matrix factorization problem thus writes

$$\min_{P,Q} \sum_{i,j: r_{ij}\text{exists}} \ell(u_i, i_j, P, Q) \quad (2)$$

Note that the error $\ell(u_i, i_j, P, Q)$ depends only on P and Q through p_i and q_j; however, item i_j may also be rated by user $u_{i'}$ so that the optimal factor q_j depends on both p_i and $p_{i'}$. The Stochastic Gradient Optimization (SGO) method thus proceeds as follows: at each iteration t, i) select a random user/item pair (u_{i^t}, i_{j^t}) for which a rating exists; ii) perform a gradient step on $\ell(u_{i^t}, i_{j^t}, P, Q)$.

In order to enhance the assumption that similar users have similar tastes, we impose that the factor vector of each user (resp. item) should be close to the average factor vector of its similar users (resp. items). For computing the most similar users (or items) we considered a modified version of Pearson correlation coefficient [2] which for two users u_i and u_j writes:

$$sim(u_i, u_j) = \frac{\sum_{i_k \in I_c} (r_{ik} - \overline{r}_{i.})(r_{jk} - \overline{r}_{j.})}{\sqrt{\sum_{i_k \in I_c} (r_{ik} - \overline{r}_{i.})^2} \sqrt{\sum_{i_k \in I_c} (r_{jk} - \overline{r}_{j.})^2}}$$

Where, I_c is the items co-rated by both users, $\overline{r}_{i.}$ and $\overline{r}_{j.}$ denote the average ratings for u_i and u_j respectively.

Hence, we are able to find the N most similar users for u_i, denoted by N_i (resp. N_j for items similar to i_j). We now propose a slight modification of the individual ratings objective function ℓ of Eq. (1) above by adding another regularization term. For a pair of user and item (u_i, i_j) for which a rating r_{ij} exists, the similarity-regularized individual objective writes:

$$\ell_1(u_i, i_j, P, Q) = (r_{ij} - q_j^{\top} p_i)^2 + \lambda(||p_i||^2 + ||q_j||^2)$$
$$+\lambda_u \left\| p_i - \frac{1}{|N_i|} \sum_{m \in N_i} p_m \right\|^2 + \lambda_i \left\| q_j - \frac{1}{|N_j|} \sum_{n \in N_j} q_n \right\|^2 \quad (3)$$

where $\lambda_u \geq 0$ and $\lambda_i \geq 0$ are the regularization parameters linked to the similar-user and similar-item regularizations respectively. Performing the same updates as the conventional SGO but replacing ℓ by ℓ_1, we get Algorithm 1 for minimizing the whole matrix factorization problem (Eq. 2) where ℓ is replaced by ℓ_1 i.e. the similarity-regularized problem:

Algorithm 1 Similar based regularization

1: **procedure** MODIFIED SGO
2: **Input:** $R, \lambda, \lambda_u, \lambda_i$
3: **Initialize:** P and Q randomly
4: **while** not converged **do**
5: Choose randomly $(u_i, i_j) \in R$
6: $N_i = GetSimilarUsers(i, N)$
7: $N_j = GetSimilarItems(j, N)$
8: Update p_i and q_j by a gradient step on $\ell_1(u_i, i_j, \cdot, \cdot)$ (Eq. 3)

$$\min_{P,Q} \sum_{i,j: r_{ij}\text{exists}} \ell_1(u_i, i_j, P, Q). \quad (4)$$

3. ASYNCHRONOUS DISTRIBUTED SGO

Even though stochastic gradient optimization offers a high prediction accuracy on recommender system datasets, there are some computational challenges associated with it. Performing SGO sequentially on a single machine takes unacceptably large amount of time to converge. So, there is a need to perform SGO in a distributed manner for large datasets. However, parallelizing SGO is not trivial. A drawback of a straightforward implementation is that updates on factor matrices might not be independent. For example, for the training points that lie on same rows (or columns), they update the same corresponding row (or column) of P and Q matrices simultaneously. So, efficient communication between the computing nodes is necessary to synchronize the updates on factor matrices.

One common approach is to divide the rating matrix into several blocks and run SGO on each of the blocks on distinct machines. Factor matrices are updated on each machine for the corresponding ratings. Even though the rating matrix parts on each machine are different, the factor matrix updates are not independent. So, after each epoch the factor matrices present in each machine are synchronized. We refer to this method as "Synchronized SGO", as all machines synchronize their factor matrices after every epoch (in [4] this method is referred to as Asynchronous SGD because the parameters are communicated asynchronously, but however, the epochs are synchronized as aforementioned). But, such approaches might not be efficient mainly because the computation time for one epoch of SGO is different depending on the machine it is performed. So, this approach of synchronous propagation between machines after each epoch can considerably be slowed down because the faster machines have to wait for the slower ones in order to synchronize.

We propose here a distributed algorithm for SGO with asynchronous propagation of parameter matrices after each epoch. Each of the machines contain a part of the rating matrix corresponding to clusters of similar users, that could be found efficiently offline with large-scale graph clustering techniques [7]. Factor matrices are hence updated on each machine using only the part of the rating matrix it contains. As opposed to the synchronous method, we broadcast the updated factor matrices as soon as the machine finishes one epoch. So, whenever a new epoch begins, it collects the most recent factor matrices from other machines and after finishing one epoch it broadcasts its updated factor matrices to

Table 1: MAE and RMSE measures for different methods on MovieLens and NetFlix datasets. Best results are shown in bold.

Dataset		SGO		Modified SGO With Similarity Based Regularization			
				Similar Users and Items, $\lambda_u = \lambda_i$		Similar Users Only, $\lambda_i = 0$	
		MAE	RMSE	MAE	RMSE	MAE	RMSE
ML-100K	ua	0.7490	0.9478	**0.7390**	**0.9332**	0.7404	0.9359
	ub	0.7619	0.9660	**0.7555**	**0.9564**	0.7540	0.9590
ML-1M	ra	0.7324	0.9706	0.7208	0.9517	**0.7188**	**0.9487**
	rb	0.6973	0.8861	**0.6928**	**0.8787**	0.6946	0.8799
ML-10M	rb	0.6523	0.8415	**0.6488**	**0.8384**	0.6512	0.8402
NF-Subset	NA	0.6498	0.8287	**0.6469**	**0.8256**	0.6477	0.8267

all other machines and begins another epoch immediately, independently of the state of other machines. In this way, all the machines are running independently of each other. So, the faster machines will perform their epochs faster, whereas the slower slower machines will be lagging on time but after finishing each epoch they will receive the most updated factor matrices from the faster machines.

In our setting, we cluster the rating matrix R into m blocks of lines as in [4]. Where m is the number of machines (or processes) available. The P matrix is also blocked in the same way. At each node we keep: one block of R, the corresponding block of P, and a local copy of Q. At each epoch, we update that block of P and local Q matrix based on the block of R and the individual loss functions (ℓ or ℓ_1). The overall procedure is depicted in Figure 1, showing an example distributed network of three machines. R_1, R_2 and R_3 represent the rating blocks on each machine. ep represents the end of previous epoch and beginning of new epoch on different machines. As shown, after finishing one epoch each machine broadcasts its updated Q matrix to all other machines, whereas at the beginning of new epoch each machine averages its Q update with the received updated Q matrices from other machines (if any). In this way the updates from faster machines help the slower machines to converge faster, thus enhancing the overall convergence time of the distributed network.

Figure 1: Block Diagram of Asynchronous Distributed SGO

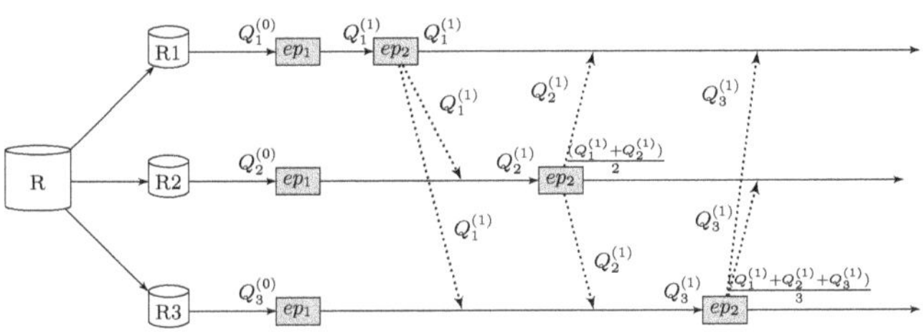

4. EXPERIMENTS

We conducted a number of experiments aimed at evaluating what are the impacts of similar user and item regularization terms on the matrix factorization, and how the proposed asynchronous framework can help to speed up the convergence of the SGO algorithm.

Datasets: We performed experiments on MovieLens datasets (ML-100K, ML-1M and ML-10M) and a subset of the NetFlix collection (see Table 2). For ML-100K and ML-1M we used both sets (ra and rb, or ua and ub), whereas for ML-10M and Netflix we used a single dataset.

Table 2: Characteristics of Datasets used in our experiments. $|\mathcal{U}|$ and $|\mathcal{I}|$ denote respectively the number of users and items.

Dataset	$\|\mathcal{U}\|$	$\|\mathcal{I}\|$	K	training size	test size	sparsity
ML-100K	943	1682	20	90570	9430	93.7 %
ML-1M	6040	3952	40	939809	60400	95.8 %
ML-10M	71567	10681	100	9301274	698780	98.7 %
NF-Subset	28978	1821	40	3255352	100478	93.7 %

Implementation: We implemented the distributed framework using PySpark version 1.5.1. To demonstrate the communication between disparate machines, we connected five servers with different computational loads.

Platform and Parameters: Three of the machines have Intel Xenon E5-2640 2.60 GHz processors and 256 GB memory each. The other two machines have Intel Xenon E5-2643 3.40 GHz processors and 128 GB memory each. Even though some of the machines have identical configuration, they were running different workloads on them. One of the machines dispatches the rating matrix across all the others as well as on itself. We stop the running algorithm on each machine, when the RMSE difference between two epochs on a validation set falls below a predefined threshold, ε, fixed as 10^{-4} in our experiments. The convergence of the proposed asynchronous approach is set when the slowest machine finishes its job, while for the synchronous SGO all machines finish at the same time.

Following [1], the number of latent factors for dataset ML-10M was fixed to 100, and for the other smaller datasets, it was chosen experimentally for best result/speed compromise as 40, 40 and 20 respectively. The learning rate and the regularization parameter λ were fixed to 0.005 and 0.05 as in [1]. For our proposed similarity-based regularization λ_u, λ_i, and the number of similar users/items N were chosen with values that led to the best RMSE on validation sets for each collection chosen among $\{10^{-1}, 5.10^{-2}, 10^{-2}, 5.10^{-3}, 10^{-3}, 5.10^{-4}, 10^{-4}\}$ for λ_u, λ_i and $\{10, 20, 30, 40, 50\}$ for N.

Evaluation Measures: In our experiments, we used the Mean Absolute Error (MAE) and the Root Mean Square Error (RMSE) as performance measures. Also, we compared the convergence time for each of the algorithms in the synchronous and the asynchronous distributed settings.

4.1 The effect of similar based regularization

First, we compare the results between the traditional SGO method and the proposed Modified SGO with Similarity Based Regularization. The difference here is solely on the objective function that is minimized (Pbs. (2) and (4) respectively).

Figure 2: RMSE vs Number of Epochs, until convergence of synchronous and asynchronous distributed SGO approaches with similar user and item based regularization for matrix factorization.

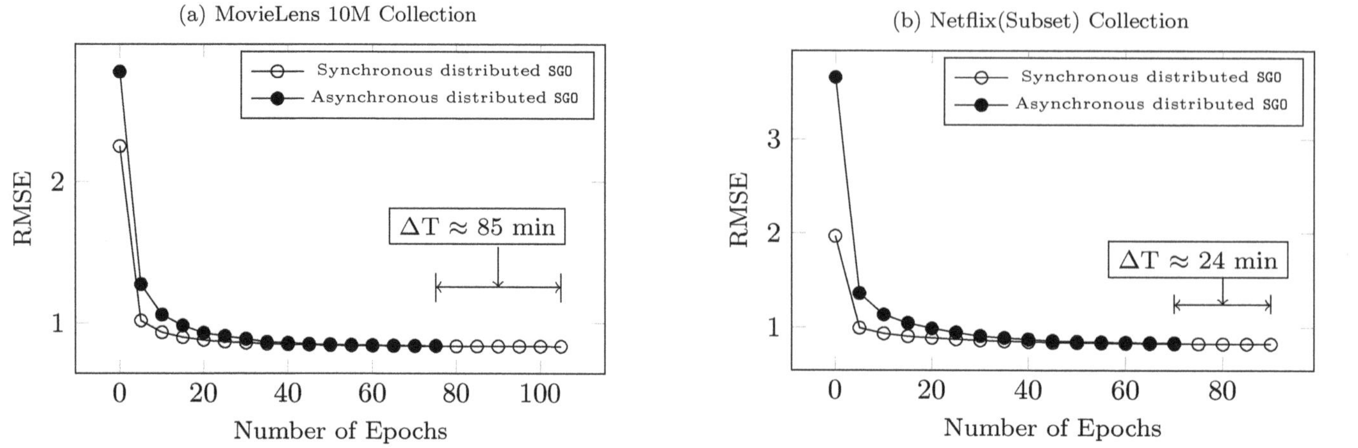

We tested two scenarios: i) where only the users are regularized with similarity ($\lambda_i = 0$); and ii) when both users and items are regularized with the same parameter ($\lambda_u = \lambda_i$). Table 1 shows the complete results of our experiments.

It comes out that forcing the vectors of users and items to lie within the centroids of their most similar users and items found by the Pearson similarity measure is effective as the final RMSE and MAE with Algorithm 1 are always better than with classical SGO. Thus, there is a significant benefit to use this regularization in terms of learning. We also report results by looking at the effect of the similar user regularization and not items ($\lambda_u > 0, \lambda_i = 0$). As shown in Table 1, this user-only regularization also gives uniformly better results than traditional SGO, and even better than the user and item regularization on one dataset.

4.2 Evaluation of Convergence time

Now, we evaluate the proposed asynchronous distributed method by comparing its convergence time with the synchronous distributed SGO method. We evaluate the convergence speed on the problem with user and item similarity regularizations in order to show its scalability. The evolutions of RMSE with respect to the number of epochs of our proposed algorithm and the synchronous SGO on the ML-10M dataset and the subset of the Netflix collection are shown in Figure 2. In the case of the asynchronous approach, we show the convergence time of the slowest machine. As expected, the proposed approach converges in less epochs as the slowest machine gets updated values from the faster machines, which helps it to converge faster, whereas in the case of the synchronous method, the faster machines have to wait for the slower ones after every epoch.

5. CONCLUSION

In this work, we presented an asynchronous distributed framework for SGO. Though generic, the framework was applied to matrix factorization for recommender systems. Furthermore, we proposed two additional regularization terms for this task. Experimental results on different MovieLens and NetFlix collections tend to validate the interest of this similarity-based regularization as well as the convergence speedup of the proposed asynchronous approach.

6. ACKNOWLEDGEMENT

This work has been partially supported by the LabEx PERSYVAL-Lab (ANR-11-LABX-0025-01) funded by the French program Investissement d'avenir.

7. REFERENCES

[1] W.-S. Chin, Y. Zhuang, Y.-C. Juan, and C.-J. Lin. A learning-rate schedule for stochastic gradient methods to matrix factorization. In *Advances in Knowledge Discovery and Data Mining*, pages 442–455. Springer, 2015.

[2] J. L. Herlocker, J. A. Konstan, A. Borchers, and J. Riedl. An algorithmic framework for performing collaborative filtering. In *ACM SIGIR conference on Research and development in information retrieval*, pages 230–237. ACM, 1999.

[3] Y. Koren, R. Bell, and C. Volinsky. Matrix factorization techniques for recommender systems. *Computer*, (8):30–37, 2009.

[4] F. Makari, C. Teflioudi, R. Gemulla, P. Haas, and Y. Sismanis. Shared-memory and shared-nothing stochastic gradient descent algorithms for matrix completion. *Knowledge and Information Systems*, 42(3):493–523, 2015.

[5] P. Melville, R. J. Mooney, and R. Nagarajan. Content-boosted collaborative filtering for improved recommendations. In *National Conference on Artificial Intelligence*, pages 187–192, 2002.

[6] B. Sarwar, G. Karypis, J. Konstan, and J. Riedl. Item-based collaborative filtering recommendation algorithms. In *International conference on World Wide Web*, pages 285–295. ACM, 2001.

[7] J. J. Whang, X. Sui, and I. S. Dhillon. Scalable and memory-efficient clustering of large-scale social networks. In *International Conference on Data Mining*, pages 705–714, 2012.

[8] M. Zinkevich, M. Weimer, L. Li, and A. J. Smola. Parallelized stochastic gradient descent. In *Advances in neural information processing systems*, pages 2595–2603, 2010.

Query-based Music Recommendations via Preference Embedding

Chih-Ming Chen[1,2], Ming-Feng Tsai[1], Yu-Ching Lin[3], Yi-Hsuan Yang[2]
[1]Department of Computer Science, National Chengchi University, Taipei, Taiwan
[2]Research Center for IT innovation, Academia Sinica, Taipei, Taiwan
[3]KKBOX Inc., Taipei, Taiwan
{104761501,mftsai}@nccu.edu.tw, aaronlin@kkbox.com, yang@citi.sinica.edu.tw

ABSTRACT

A common scenario considered in recommender systems is to predict a user's preferences on unseen items based on his/her preferences on observed items. A major limitation of this scenario is that a user might be interested in different things each time when using the system, but there is no way to allow the user to actively alter or adjust the recommended results. To address this issue, we propose the idea of "query-based recommendation" that allows a user to specify his/her search *intention* while exploring new items, thereby incorporating the concept of information retrieval into recommendation systems. Moreover, the idea is more desirable when the user intention can be expressed in different ways. Take music recommendation as an example: the proposed system allows a user to explore new song tracks by specifying either a track, an album, or an artist. To enable such heterogeneous queries in a recommender system, we present a novel technique called "Heterogeneous Preference Embedding" to encode user preference and query intention into low-dimensional vector spaces. Then, with simple search methods or similarity calculations, we can use the encoded representation of queries to generate recommendations. This method is fairly flexible and it is easy to add other types of information when available. Evaluations on three music listening datasets confirm the effectiveness of the proposed method over the state-of-the-art matrix factorization and network embedding methods.

Keywords

recommender systems; query-based recommendation; heterogeneous preference embedding

1. INTRODUCTION

Recommender systems typically generate a list of recommendations without taking any input from users, but relying on merely user preference histories. In this way, users can only *passively* receive recommended results without any chance to alter or adjust the results. However, in practice, users usually have multiple intentions and may like to *actively* input their interests to obtain different recommendations. To meet this demand, this paper proposes an idea called "query-based recommendation" and presents a novel approach called "heterogeneous preference embedding" to carry out the idea.

The proposed query-based recommender system can greatly increases the quality of recommendations. The rational is that, in addition to user preferences, the system can know more about the query intention, and then find out those items from the user preferences that might be relevant to the query. The idea of query-based recommendation is quite similar to that of context-aware recommendation, the goal of which is to incorporate the contextual information of a user to recommend specific items [1]. However, in the literature, most of existing context-aware recommender systems mainly focus on how to collect or utilize certain contextual information such as time [illegible] and location [illegible] into their recommendation models, and suggest some fine-tuned models for the recommendation problems under different circumstances, such as the point-of-interest recommendation.

For the query-based recommendation, it is highly desirable when the system can utilize heterogeneous relevant information for recommendation and allow a user to specify his/her query intention in different ways. Accordingly, we propose the technique of *Heterogeneous Preference Embedding* (HPE) to achieve this. In specific, the proposed method constructs a user-item preference network from user access logs, in which the vertices represent users and various items and the edges are the relationships between the users and the items. After the construction, an edge-sampling technique is applied to embed the large information network into low-dimensional vector spaces, in which the proximity information of each vertex is encoded into its learned vector representation [10]. Afterwards, we can use the learned representations of vertices with some simple search methods or similarity calculations to conduct the task of query-based recommendation. A major advantage of the proposed method is that it is flexible and it is easy to incorporate different information into the recommendation model when available.

In the experiments, three music listening datasets are employed to assess the performance of our proposed method, including the Last.fm-1K dataset, the Million Song Dataset (MSD), and one from a regional music online streaming service provider KKBOX Inc. The proposed method is compared against the state-of-the-art recommendation algorithms using either matrix factorization or network embedding techniques DeepWalk [7] or LINE [10]. The experimental results show that the proposed method outperforms the prior methods significantly in the three datasets.

RecSys '16, September 15-19, 2016, Boston , MA, USA
© 2016 ACM. ISBN 978-1-4503-4035-9/16/09. . . $15.00
DOI: http://dx.doi.org/10.1145/2959100.2959169

In summary, the contribution of this paper includes:

- The idea of query-based recommendation is proposed in this paper, which is a hybrid research work of information retrieval and general recommender systems.
- We formulate the query-based recommendation as a preference-embedding problem, and propose a method to construct the preference network between users and various, possibly heterogeneous, items.
- Extensive experiments have been conducted to verify the effectiveness of the proposed method.

2. QUERY-BASED RECOMMENDATIONS

In what follows, we briefly formalize the task of query-based recommendation. The task is to recommend a list of items I to a user u based on her previous preferences and an input query q. The recommendation task can be formulated as $f_\theta(u, I, q)$, which can also be divided into two parts:

$$f_\theta(u,I,q) := \underbrace{\alpha \times f_\theta(u,I)}_{\text{the user preference}} + \underbrace{(1-\alpha) \times f_\theta(I,q)}_{\text{the query intention}}, \quad (1)$$

where $\alpha \in [0, 1]$ is a parameter to weigh the results from the user preference model and the query intention model. In the literature, several models have been proposed to deal with the user preference [2, 9]. For simplicity, we focus on only the query intention part in this paper and set $\alpha = 0$. Our goal is to show that the proposed embedding approach on the user preference network can better incorporate information from a user's query intention into the learned latent representation than a general matrix factorization model does.

From the perspective of query-based recommendation, we attempt to regard various information as queries, so the flexibility of incorporating the arbitrary types of information into the recommendation model is a key point for our development.

3. HPE: HETEROGENEOUS PREFERENCE EMBEDDING

Network embedding technique is an approach to mapping information networks into low-dimensional spaces, in which each vertex is represented as a low-dimensional vector. Such a low-dimensional vector is useful in a variety of applications such as recommendation [10]. In the field of nature language processing, there is a similar technique called word embedding, the goal of which is also to learn the low-dimensional representation of each word. There have been some well-known studies of word embedding [4, 5, 6] in the field. In this work, we attempt to apply the information embedding techniques [7, 10] to deal with the recommendation problem, and propose a method called heterogeneous preference embedding for the task of query-based recommendation for arbitrary value of $\alpha \in [0, 1]$. In the followings, we describe the details of how to apply the embedding techniques for the task.

3.1 Construction of User Preference Network

In a recommendation dataset, there are usually user-to-other-entity pairs. The initial step is to convert these pairs into a user-to-other-entity bipartite graph. Take music recommendation dataset as the example. As shown in Figure 1,

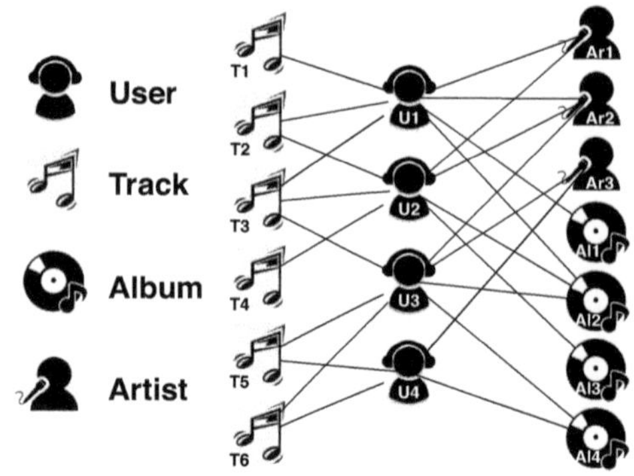

Figure 1: The user preference network. Suppose there are totally four kinds of data attributes in the music listening dataset. In the figure, the user U_4 may frequently listen to the tracks T_5 and T_6, the artist Ar_3 and the album Al_4.

every data entity (i.e. a user, a track, an artist or an album) is treated as an individual vertex in the graph, and they are connected to each other by the observed user preference (i.e. rating or listening times). This convention is applicable to most kinds of recommendation dataset. There are some useful properties for the modeling process:

- **User Preference Edges**: The weight of the edges is determined by the preference strength. These weights are user-specified and can be numerical or binary.
- **Heterogeneous Graph**: There is no limitation on the utilized entity type. The proposed model learns the representation of multiple types of entity in one network so that it is able to compute the similarity between any two entities.
- **Bipartite Graph**: It is a bipartite graph so that the vertices in the graph can be divided into two disjoint sets according to the connections. One of them contains purely users and the other set contains all the other entities. Modeling the direct connected pairs is equivalent to modeling the user preference. This form is suitable to adopt most existing collaborative filtering (CF)-based models as well.

3.2 Edge Sampling via Weighted Random Walks

An intuitive way to obtain the neighbor vertices of a vertex is to unfold all the second-order connections, but this greatly increases the memory usage especially for the dataset contained a large item pool. To resolve this, DeepWalk model uses random walk strategy [7] to generate training pairs and LINE model uses edge sampling [10] during the training stage. They are two recent network embedding techniques. From the optimization perspective, the general matrix factorization models consider only the user-to-item pair type, while this approach takes account of every entity-to-entity pair type.

As Figure 2 demonstrates, we choose to adopt the edge sampling to fast obtain the directly connected pairs and then to use a weighted random walk to receive the indirectly connected vertices. Instead of generating the walks uniformly, the weighted random walk generates the walks according to the weights of the observed edges. In our experiments, we consider the proximity information within 2 steps for each

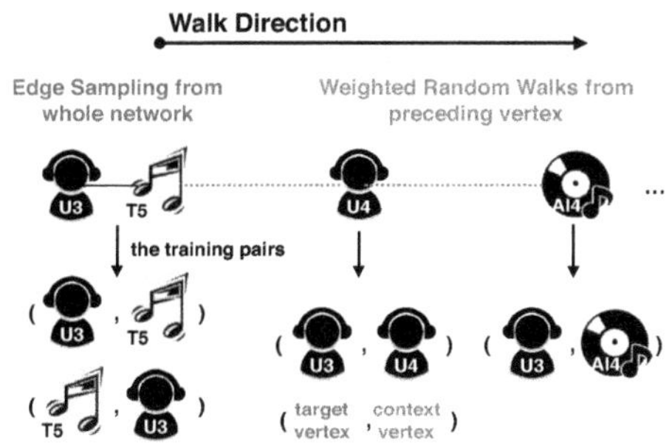

Figure 2: Edge sampling via weighted random walks for training pairs. In our sampling scheme, the first sampling pair is derived from the edge sampling over the whole network. Then, the following training vertices are selected from the weighted random walk on the preceding vertex.

vertex. Note that it is straightforward to enlarge the window size to model higher-order proximity.

3.3 Query Intention Modeling via HPE

To embed the user preference into the vertices v, the proposed HPE model updates the vertex representation Φ according to the sampling proximities derived from the preference network. In other words, we treat those indirect connected vertices as the contextual information of the center vertex, which can be represented as follows:

$$Pr(v_j|\Phi(v_i)) = \begin{cases} 1 & \text{if } v_j \in Context(v_i) \\ 0 & \text{otherwise} \end{cases}. \quad (2)$$

Maximizing the above posterior probability is equivalent to minimizing the negative log likelihood, so the objective function of the second-order proximity can be represented as follows:

$$O = -\sum_{(i,j)\in S} w_{i,j} \log p(v_j|\Phi(v_i)) + \lambda \sum_i \|\Phi(v_i)\|^2, \quad (3)$$

where S is a set of sampling pairs and w indicates the weight of the edge. In practice, the observed edges are all positive information and thus falls into the one-class prediction problem. We adopt the widely-used solution called negative sampling to sample the additional user-to-other-entity pairs from the unobserved data. This works well in point-wise optimization functions [12].

In the heterogeneous preference embedding, a regularized term is adopted to avoid the over-fitting problem. That is due to the fact that we seek to preserve the inference ability that can match the vertices containing the similar contexts, rather than match those vertices containing exactly the same context. In addition, we also adopt the asynchronous stochastic gradient descent (ASGD) [8] algorithm to optimize Equation 3. The overall procedure is summarized in Algorithm 1.

4. EXPERIMENTS

Three music listening datasets are employed to assess the performance of our proposed method. The first one is the lastfm-dataset-1K dataset,[1] which contains the listening logs

Algorithm 1: Heterogeneous Preference Embedding

```
Input: User Preference Network: G(V, E),
       Walk Steps: w, Sampling Times: n
for v ∈ V do
    Initialize the representation: Φ(v) and context v
for i ∈ {1, ..., n} do
    (v1, v2) = EdgeSampling(G)
    Update Φ(v1), context v2 by minimizing Eq. (3)
    Update Φ(v2), context v1 by minimizing Eq. (3)
    for v' ∈ RandomWalk(v2, w − 1) do
        Update Φ(v1), context v' by minimizing Eq. (3)
Output: Vertex representations Φ
```

Table 1: Experimental Datasets

Dataset	#Users	#Items	#Logs
lastfm-1k	992	107,528	19,150,868
MSD	1,019,318	384,546	48,373,586
KKBOX	50,000	400,000	220,000,000

from the website of Last.fm. The second one, released by EchoNest,[2] is a music taste profile subset derived from the official user dataset of the Million Song Dataset (MSD). The third one is a dataset with user listening logs provided by KKBOX Inc., which is a regional leading music streaming company. The third dataset covers user listening logs from 2014 to 2015. Table 1 lists the statistics of the three datasets.

For query-based recommendations, most users may only care about the top recommendations. Therefore, we adopt 1) precision at k (P@k) and 2) mean Average Precision at k (mAP@k) as the evaluation metrics, where k indicates the number of the cut-off recommended items. Calculating the precision with a small k is equivalent to examining the possible hit ratio of the users in top recommendations.

In the following experiments, we randomly select 70% of the listening history for each user as the training logs, and put the rest 30% logs in the test set for the off-line evaluation. In the testing stage, we randomly select 5 queries from the test logs of each user, and ask for matching the recommendations to these selected query items.

Note that the ground truth of the query-based recommendations shall depend on both the user and the user's query (even when we set $\alpha = 0$ in this work). Therefore the best returned results are varied from person to person. Treating the query as a context information, we assume that a user may tend to listen to similar songs in a short period, thereby considering the songs *co-listened* within the time period as the ground truth. In the lastfm-1k and KKBOX datasets, we consider the co-listen frequency that is higher than 3 as the ground truth. In MSD, we do not further filter the ground truth because it does not contain the primitive listening logs.

To verify the effectiveness of the proposed method, we compare it with other state-of-the-art approaches, including one simple method (i.e. popularity-based), one CF-based model (i.e. matrix factorization) and two embedding models (i.e. DeepWalk and LINE-2nd). The similarities among the entities are measured by cosine similarity. Below we briefly describe these baseline methods:

[1] http://www.dtic.upf.edu/~ocelma/

[2] http://labrosa.ee.columbia.edu/millionsong/tasteprofile

Table 2: Performance of query-based recommendations. The ground truth of the first two datasets are derived the co-listen frequency within a window size 5 for each user, whereas the MSD uses the original test logs as the ground truth; the * symbol is used when the result is significantly better (p-value<0.01 in a paired t-test) than the result of the others.

P@10	**lastfm-1k** (window=5)			**KKBOX** (window=5)			**MSD** (original)		
	$d = 16$	$d = 32$	$d = 64$	$d = 64$	$d = 128$	$d = 256$	$d = 64$	$d = 128$	$d = 256$
Popularity	2.66%	2.66%	2.66%	4.32%	4.32%	4.32%	0.92%	0.92%	0.92%
MF	3.02%	3.93%	4.22%	7.11%	8.49%	8.93%	1.37%	1.79%	2.00%
DeepWalk	3.18%	3.55%	3.54%	11.61%	12.55%	13.08%	1.71%	1.95%	1.95%
LINE-2nd	3.44%	3.74%	4.10%	12.79%	13.47%	12.77%	1.62%	1.60%	1.14%
HPE	**3.54%**	***4.22%**	**4.51%**	**12.95%**	***13.74%**	***14.20%**	***2.08%**	***2.15%**	***2.19%**

mAP@10	**lastfm-1k** (window=5)			**KKBOX** (window=5)			**MSD** (original)		
	$d = 16$	$d = 32$	$d = 64$	$d = 64$	$d = 128$	$d = 256$	$d = 64$	$d = 128$	$d = 256$
Popularity	**3.27%**	**3.27%**	**3.27%**	5.03%	5.03%	5.03%	1.04%	1.04%	1.04%
MF	1.87%	2.34%	2.60%	4.65%	5.85%	6.16%	1.88%	2.44%	2.81%
DeepWalk	1.82%	2.10%	1.99%	8.73%	9.47%	10.01%	2.66%	2.70%	2.55%
LINE-2nd	2.00%	2.10%	2.38%	9.95%	10.64%	10.09%	1.84%	1.60%	1.44%
HPE	2.08%	2.55%	2.71%	**10.14%**	**10.86%**	***11.31%**	**2.86%**	***3.09%**	***3.12%**

- **Popularity-based**: This is a baseline approach that always recommends the most popular songs to users. The popularity is estimated by the number of the users who favor/listen to the song in the training data.
- **Matrix Factorization** (MF): The model is a well-develop technique for making recommendations on a user-to-item data structure. Given the entities in the built preference newtwork can be seperated into two disjoint sets, we can utilize the benchmark from MyMediaLite [3] to generate the recommendations.
- **DeepWalk**[7]: DeepWalk uses local information obtained from truncated random walks to learn latent representations of nodes in a graph. It is an extended application of word2vec-based model.
- **LINE-2nd**[10]: We adopt the LINE second-order (2nd) version in order to make the comparison to our proposed context embedding model.

Table 2 lists the experimental results in terms of $Precision@10$ (upper table) and $mAP@10$ (bottom table). We can find that the three embedding models, including the proposed HPE model, achieve a comparable performance to the MF model for the three datasets, indicating that the embedding models can capable of capturing the query intentions form the preference network. Note that the recommendation performance drops for the DeepWalk and LINE methods degrades when the dimensions of the vectors become higher. In contrast, the proposed preference embedding with regularized terms can prevent the learned representation from over-fitting, yielding better recommendation performance in most cases.

5. CONCLUSION

In this paper, we propose the HPE model that is designed towards the application of "query-based recommendation." The HPE exploits not only the observed preference but also the possible relevant entities via the user preference network. Therefore, by embedding such proximity information, the learned representation can better reflect the query intention in comparison to the CF-based model. Moreover, for the proposed preference embedding, we adopt the regularized learning to alleviates the over-fitting issue while learning the embedded representations. Our experiments confirm the effectiveness of the proposed method in making recommendations for the task of query-based recommendation.

[3] http://www.mymedialite.net

6. REFERENCES

[1] G. Adomavicius and A. Tuzhilin. Context-aware recommender systems. In *Proc. ACM RecSys*, 2008.

[2] Y. Hu, Y. Koren, and C. Volinsky. Collaborative filtering for implicit feedback datasets. In *Proc. IEEE ICDM*, 2008.

[3] J. J. Levandoski, M. Sarwat, A. Eldawy, and M. F. Mokbel. Lars: A location-aware recommender system. In *Proc. IEEE ICDE*, 2012.

[4] T. Mikolov, K. Chen, G. Corrado, and J. Dean. Efficient estimation of word representations in vector space. *ICLR Workshop*, 2013.

[5] T. Mikolov, I. Sutskever, K. Chen, G. S. Corrado, and J. Dean. Distributed representations of words and phrases and their compositionality. In *Advances in Neural Information Processing Systems 26*. 2013.

[6] J. Pennington, R. Socher, and C. D. Manning. Glove: Global vectors for word representation. In *Proc. EMNLP*, 2014.

[7] B. Perozzi, R. Al-Rfou, and S. Skiena. Deepwalk: Online learning of social representations. In *Proc. ACM SIGKDD*, 2014.

[8] B. Recht, C. Re, S. Wright, and F. Niu. Hogwild: A lock-free approach to parallelizing stochastic gradient descent. In *Advances in Neural Information Processing Systems 24*. 2011.

[9] S. Rendle. Factorization machines with libFM. *ACM Trans. Intell. Syst. Technol.*, 2012.

[10] J. Tang, M. Qu, M. Wang, M. Zhang, J. Yan, and Q. Mei. LINE: large-scale information network embedding. *CoRR*, 2015.

[11] Q. Yuan, G. Cong, Z. Ma, A. Sun, and N. M. Thalmann. Time-aware point-of-interest recommendation. In *Proc. ACM SIGIR*, 2013.

[12] W. Zhang, T. Chen, J. Wang, and Y. Yu. Optimizing top-n collaborative filtering via dynamic negative item sampling. In *Proc. ACM SIGIR*, 2013.

Joint User Modeling across Aligned Heterogeneous Sites

Xuezhi Cao , Yong Yu
Apex Data and Knowledge Management Lab
Dept. of Computer Science and Engineering
Shanghai Jiao Tong University, Shanghai, China
cxz,yyu@apex.sjtu.edu.cn

ABSTRACT

An accurate and comprehensive user modeling technique is crucial for the quality of recommender systems. Traditionally, we model user preferences using only actions from the target site and may suffer from cold-start problem. As nowadays people normally engage in multiple online sites for various needs, we consider leveraging the cross-site actions to improve the user modeling accuracy. Specifically, in this paper we aim at achieving a more comprehensive and accurate user modeling by modeling user's actions in multiple aligned heterogeneous sites simultaneously. To do so, we propose a modularized probabilistic graphical model framework JUMA. We further integrate topic model and matrix factorization into JUMA for joint user modeling over text-based and item-based sites. We assemble and publish large-scale dataset for comprehensive analyzing and evaluation. Experimental results show that our framework JUMA out performs traditional within-site user modeling techniques, especially for cold-start scenarios. For cold-start users, we achieve relative improvements of 9.3% and 12.8% comparing to existing within-site approaches for recommendation in item-based and text-based sites respectively. Thus we draw the conclusion that aligning heterogeneous sites and modeling users jointly do help to improve the quality of online recommender systems.

Keywords

User Modeling, Recommender System, Graphical Model

1. INTRODUCTION

To improve user experience and to stimulate user actions, a great portion of online services include a native recommender system. Such recommender systems have brought great benefits for both users and service providers. Therefore, there exist plenty research works focusing on this topic. Experiments as well as online applications both prove the success of such systems.

RecSys '16, September 15-19, 2016, Boston , MA, USA
© 2016 ACM. ISBN 978-1-4503-4035-9/16/09... $15.00
DOI: http://dx.doi.org/10.1145/2959100.2959155

An accurate and comprehensive user modeling technique is crucial for the quality of recommender systems. Traditionally, we model user's preferences using actions from the target site. For example, recommending movies based on one's previous movie rating logs. Although the performances of such approaches are satisfying, there are still problems and limitations with these approaches.

A major problem is that existing approaches may fail when dealing with new users due to insufficient historical data. This problem is referred to as the cold-start problem [26]. It widely exists and severely jeopardizes the user's first impression when exposed to the recommender systems. Several works aim at alleviating this problem using side-information [6, 33] or interview processes [8]. However, such approaches require extra efforts from users thus still jeopardize the users' first experiences.

Another limitation of existing techniques is the lack of comprehensiveness. When participating in specialized online services, users normally reveal only parts of his preferences. As traditional user models focus only on user actions in the target site, they can only capture the most revealed parts of the user preferences. Although these are the most important parts for future recommendations in the same site, we cannot claim other aspects are irrelevant. For example, it is hard to mine one's political preferences using only movie rating histories, but such preferences would be helpful when recommending political movies or documentaries.

On the other hand, as the usage of Internet develops, most people now engage in multiple sites for various needs. For example, we have Facebook for maintaining social relations, Twitter for microblogging, and IMDb for movie reviews. By aligning these sites and aggregating user's online actions, we can directly aim at modeling user's underlying general preferences instead of site-specific preferences. Following this direction, we can achieve comprehensive user preference modeling and actually solve the cold-start problem (users only encounter the cold-start problem once when joining his first online site).

The intuition behind this direction is: although the purposes and action types vary from site to site, the user's underlying preferences remains the same. Every natural person has an underlying general preferences that depend on his/her personality, hobbies and personal taste. Such preferences do not change with the site the user currently engages. We refer such preferences as user's universal preferences in the following of this paper. When participating in a specific site, the user conducts actions based on parts of his universal preferences. Existing works aim at capturing the revealed parts of preferences in that specific site. By aligning the sites together and jointly model the users preferences in these sites simultaneously, we can directly capture the user's comprehensive universal preferences. When dealing with cold-start scenario where user has only few actions, the preferences learned from other aligned sites can also help to alleviate the problem.

Therefore, in this paper we target at joint user modeling over multiple aligned sites with heterogeneous actions. Extending within-site user modeling to cross-site joint modeling is not a trival task. The major challenge is the heterogeneity of actions from different sites. To tackle this, we propose a modularized probabilistic graphical model framework JUMA. The benefit of modularization is that we can easily plug the state-of-the-art techniques for different types of actions into the framework. The framework achieves great generality and expendability by integrating corresponding modules for different kinds of sites. We discuss how to deploy JUMA for modeling text-based and item-based sites in this paper. We target at these types because most online services can be categorized into these two, thus we can cover most use scenarios.

Note that this approach requires the sites to be fully or partially aligned, i.e. alignment between accounts indicating that they belong to the same natural person is known. Fortunately, now most sites allow users to login with cross-site accounts (*"Login with Facebook Account"*). Researchers also work on how to recover the alignment by analyzing user's profile, social relationship and user generated contents [20, 28]. The state-of-the-art approach achieves an accuracy over 80%. Therefore, the accessibility of such alignment should not be concerned.

The rest of the paper is organized as follows. We first discuss the related works in Section 2. We present the dataset as well as the preliminary analysis in Section 3. We propose out framework JUMA in Section 4, and then report the experimental results in Section 5. Finally, we draw conclusions and propose future works in Section 6.

2. RELATED WORK

2.1 User Modeling

User modeling is the core of recommender systems. There exist plenty research works in this direction. As the user generated contents (UGC) vary from site to site, researchers propose different user modeling techniques accordingly. Matrix factorization technique [15, 22] is widely used for this task, especially for item-based sites such as e-commercial and movie/music rating sites [13, 17]. Zhang et al. proposed an efficient bayesian hierarchical user modeling in [32]. Topic models, such as Latent Dirichlet Allocation [2], are employed for capturing user's topic distributions in text-based sites such as Twitter and Tumblr [7]. There are also works try to leverage social relationships in online social network for improving the quality of user modeling [12, 18].

However, most of existing works tackle each application separately, thus might suffer from cold-start problem and lack of comprehensive user preference due to data insufficiency. Therefore, in this paper we propose joint user modeling that model the user over multiple sites simultaneously and targets at improving the modeling precision as well as comprehensiveness.

2.2 Cold-Start Problem

The cold-start problem is that when giving recommendations to new users who have no or only few historic actions, his/her preferences are not yet revealed to the recommender system. Therefore, the quality of recommendations in these scenarios might be rather poor.

Such problem exists in almost all recommender systems, therefore is of great importance. Researchers propose various solutions to alleviate this problem [9, 16, 26]. One direction is to leverage additional side information to compensate the user/item's novelty. Gao et al. address the problem in location-based recommendation using social network as the side information [6]. Social tags are employed by Zhang et al. in [33]. Those approaches require specific types of side information for the given user, which may not be always available. Another direction is adding an interview process immediately after registration. This is the most widely adopted approach in commercial applications. The fundamental task in this direction is the form of the interview process and the questions asked during it. Golbandi et al. use decision trees to adaptively selecting the questions [8]. Functional matrix factorization is also employed for generating interview questions [35]. Nevertheless, these approaches do need the users to manually answer the questions or go through other types of interview process, thus have a negative impact on the user experiences.

2.3 Cross-Domain Recommendation

The motivation of this paper is to some extent similar with cross-domain recommendation, which is improving user modeling by leveraging historic actions from other sources [5]. However, existing cross-domain approaches mainly focus on homogeneous data. For example, transferring between movies and books [27]. There is also a good fraction of papers target at synthetic multi-domain data generated by subdividing a single-domain dataset [1, 25]. For those scenarios, different 'domains' actually share a lot in common (action type, user preference, behavior pattern, etc.).

Instead, we aim at user modeling across sites with heterogeneous actions, which is more challenging and general. There are also works aiming at heterogeneous data. McAuley et al. aim at understanding product ratings with review text in [21]. However, these approaches require aligned actions which is unavailable in the general setting. Also, such approaches can not directly extend to more than two sites.

2.4 Network Alignment

Although a large portion of online applications now enable users to login or associate with cross-site accounts (Facebook, Twitter, Google+, etc.), there still exist plenty unaligned users and isolated networks. Therefore, automatically aligning the fragmented online social networks is proposed as a new topic in recent years. Researchers propose various approaches to tackle this task by mining different kinds of information. Most works focus on mining the personal identifiable information in profile pages, including username, location, avatar etc. [19, 23, 24]. There are also works leveraging specific types of user generated contents in certain types of networks, for example social tags in tagging systems [10]. Liu et al. tackle the task by modeling users' heterogenous behaviors [20] and achieve a accuracy over 80%.

There are also works aiming at improving existing tasks

Table 1: Dictionaries for Multi-Modal Topic Model over Weibo & Douban

ID	Top Words	Top Movies
1	Food, Cat, Friend, Dog, Home, Like, Life	Hotaru no haka, The Pursuit of Happyness, Jeux d'enfants The Devil Wears Prada, Up, Tonari no Totoro, Ratatouille
2	China, Article, Book, Issue, America, Country, Society	Inception, Social Network, Source Code, Avatar, WALL·E V for Vendetta,The Lord of the Rings, Argo The Shawshank Redemption, The Bourne Identity, Titanic
3	We, Love, Myself, Life, Want, Time, Like, World	Amour, Love Letter, Amļelie, Forrest Gump, Before Sunrise Before Sunset, Flipped, Love Actually, The Notebook
4	Design, Art, Photography, Artiest , Magazine	Amļelie, Mallĩna, Les choristes, Lļeon, Roman Holiday Nuovo Cinema Paradiso, Black Swan, Pulp Fiction

using aligned networks. For example, Zhang et al. employ the aligned networks to improve the link prediction task [31].

3. DATA & PRELIMINARY ANALYSIS

In this section we first explain the data set used in this paper, and then conduct preliminary analysis for better understanding of the user preferences consistency across the aligned heterogeneous sites.

3.1 Data Set

We collect and publish a large-scale data set for analysis and evaluation. For data sources we use Douban[1] and Weibo[2], one of China's largest movie rating sites and microblogging sites respectively. We collect 141,614 randomly selected users who participate in both Weibo and Douban. The account alignments are retrieved from explicit information in Douban's profile pages. For item-based site Douban, we collect the rating histories for each user. On average each user has 123.49 rating logs. For text-based site Weibo, we collect up to 20 pages of microblogs (both original and re-tweet) for each user. On average each user has 343.78 microblogs. We also publish the dataset online for the research community[3]. Ideas and suggestions to extend the dataset are highly welcomed.

3.2 Preliminary Analysis

The underlying assumption of joint user modeling is that user's preferences are to some extent consistent across sites. Despite its intuitiveness, we analyze on real data to support the assumption.

As user preferences are not explicitly expressed, we can not directly measure the preferences consistency. Fortunately, user's action histories serve as explicit indicators of his preferences. Therefore, we show the user action similarity consistency instead.

Specifically, we analyze whether users with similar actions in one site are still tend to be similar in the other. We randomly select 5 million pairs of users and evaluate their pairwise similarity in the two sites according to their action histories. To model user similarity in text-based site Weibo, we first employ Latent Dirichlet Allocation (LDA [2]) to model the topic distribution of each user and then use L_1-distance to measure the dissimilarity between users. And for item-based site Douban, we use Jaccard similarity coefficient

[1]http://www.douban.com/
[2]http://www.weibo.com/
[3]http://dataset.apexlab.org/juma

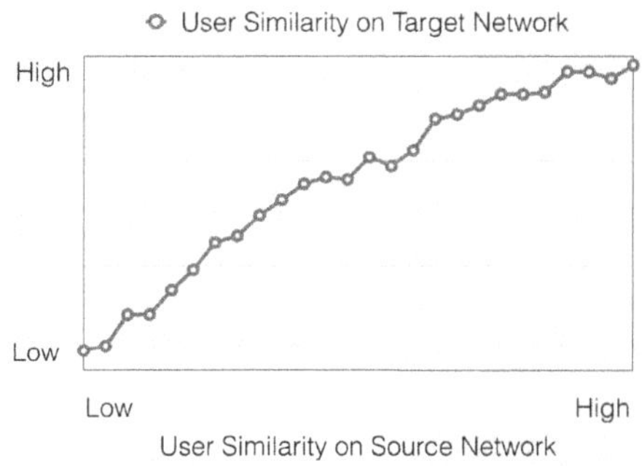

Figure 1: User Similarity Consistency

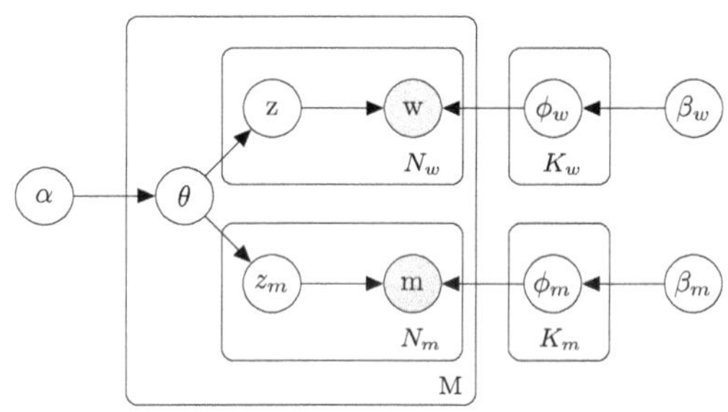

Figure 2: Multi-Modal Topic Model

upon the set of rated movies. Formally:

$$S_w(i,j) = -\sum_k |\theta_{ik} - \theta_{jk}|, \quad S_d(i,j) = \frac{|W_i \cap W_j|}{|W_i \cup W_j|} \qquad (1)$$

where θ_{i*} is the topic distribution of user i and W_i is the set of movies rated by user i. Then we group the pairs with close similarity in the source network (Weibo) to capture the general trend. We report the averaged similarity in the target network (Douban) and show the results in Figure 1.

The results indicate that users with similar actions in Weibo also tend to be similar in Douban on average, which support the assumption and indicate the existence of user preference consistency.

To gain further insight of preference consistency across sites, we employ multi-modal topic model to directly capture the relation between topics in Weibo and movies in Douban. Specifically, we consider movies as another set of 'words' and plug them into the original model. When user watches a movie, he/she first selects a topic according to his/her topic distribution and then chooses the movie according to the topic-movie distribution (corresponding to the topic-word dictionary ϕ in traditional model). We depict the graphical model for the multi-modal topic model in Figure 2.

We show the resulting word-dictionary (ϕ_w) and movie-dictionary (ϕ_m) for some example topics in Table 1. From the results we can notice the hidden correlation between movies and topics in these two sites. For example, first topic indicates users who tweet about pets are more likely to enjoy comedies, cartoons, and the second topic indicates ones interested in political news tend to prefer movies with depth or background stories.

4. APPROACH

In this section we propose JUMA, a probabilistic graphical model for joint user modeling over multiple aligned sites. We first describe the design of the model in general setting, and then discuss the design details for text-based and item-based sites. Finally we propose a hybrid learning process for the parameter learning.

4.1 JUMA in General

Probabilistic graphical model is a widely used technique for modeling user actions. For example, topic modeling [2], user preferences [29], social network modeling [11] and etc. The reason behind its popularity is its similarity towards the generation of user actions in real-world and its easiness for interpretation. Therefore, we employ probabilistic graphical model for the joint user modeling task.

The design of the general model mostly follows the assumption that user reveals part of his/her universal preferences when participating each specific site. We show the general graphical model in Figure 3 (a), which can be interpreted as follows: Each user i has an universal preference $U_i \in \mathbb{R}^{K_u}$. When participating in site q, the user's site-specific preference $P_i^q \in \mathbb{R}^{K_q}$ is transferred from universal preference U_i based on site-specific transferring model T^q. Finally, user conduct actions A_i^q base on site-specific preference P_i^q and site-specific item models $\{\phi_k^q\}$. $\alpha, \gamma^q, \beta^q$ are hyper-parameters for the prior. σ^q is the parameter that controls the coupling strength between the site-specific preferences and the universal preferences.

We design the universal preference U_i to have a multivariate Gaussian prior with mean 0 and variance α. For the site-specific variables, the model need to be designed accordingly. The item set varies from site to site, e.g. words for text-based sites and music/movie/product for item-based sites. Besides, the plate containing user actions A_i^q also varies according to different action types. Therefore, to plug a specific site into JUMA, we need to design the followings in details:

- **Preference Transferring.** The site-specific preference transferring parameters T^q along with the corresponding transferring model Ω^q in $P_i^q = \Omega^q(T^q, U_i)$.
- **Item Modeling.** Detailed modeling methodology (ϕ_k^q) for the site-specific items, e.g. latent factors for movies or topic-word distributions for topic model.
- **User Actions.** The graphical model for the generation process of user actions (the plate containing A_i^q).

4.2 JUMA for Item-Based & Text-Based Sites

Now we discuss the implementation details of JUMA in the context of modeling item-based and text-based sites. We depict the detailed graphical model of the extended version in Figure 3 (b), where we have two plates for the two sites respectively. We explain the notations we used in Table 2.

Table 2: Notations & Interpretation of JUMA

Notation	Interpretation
U_i	Universal preference of user i
T^d, T^w	Site-specific preference transferring model
P_i^d	User i's movie preferences on Douban
A_{ik}^d	Indicator of whether user i rates movie k
ϕ_k^d	Latent feature vector for movie k
P_i^w	User i's topic distribution on Weibo
z_{ij}	Latent topic of user i's j^{th} word in Weibo
A_{ij}^w	$j^t h$ word posted by user i in Weibo
ϕ_k^w	Word distribution in topic k
α, γ, β	Hyper-parameters
σ^d, σ^w	Hyper-parameter for coupling strength

To model user actions in the item-based site Douban, we employ Matrix Factorization (MF) technique [15], the most widely used technique for modeling the item rating actions. It captures user preferences and item characteristics with latent factors. Specifically, we can formally define the MF modular for JUMA by:

- **Preference Transferring.** Item-based site's preference follows multivariate normal distribution with mean $T^d U_i$ and variance σ^d, where $T^d \in \mathbb{R}^{K_d \times K_u}$ is the transfer matrix.

$$P_i^d \sim \mathcal{N}(T^d U_i, \sigma^d), \quad T^d \sim \mathcal{N}(0, \lambda^d) \tag{2}$$

Increasing σ^d leads to weaker coupling between item-based site's preference with the universal preference.

- **Item Modeling.** $\phi_k^d \in \mathbb{R}^{K_d}$ is the latent factor of movie k, with prior: $\phi_k^d \sim \mathcal{N}(0, \beta^d)$.
- **User Actions.** A_{ik}^d indicates whether user i watches movie k, which is modeled by sigmoid function applied on dot product of user's preference and movie's latent factor.

$$A_{ik}^d \sim \text{Bern}(\sigma(P_i^d \phi_k^d)), \quad \sigma(x) = \frac{1}{1+e^{-x}} \tag{3}$$

For text-based site Weibo, we use Latent Dirichlet allocation (LDA) [2] to model the user's topic distribution when writing or retweeting microblogs.

We first quickly go through the settings of traditional LDA model. For each user, we draw his topic distribution from a Dirichlet distribution with parameter α as the non-informative prior ($\theta_i \sim Dir(\alpha)$). For each word, we first draw the hidden topic z_{ij} from user's topic distribution ($z_{ij} \sim Multi(\theta_i)$), and then select the word w_{ij} according to topic-word dictionary $\phi_{z_{ij}}$. The topic-word dictionary ϕ_k also follows Dirichlet distribution with non-informative prior β.

When integrating LDA with JUMA, instead of using non-informative prior for the user's topic distribution, we can now borrow user's universal preference. To keep the conjugate prior, we have:

$$P_i^w \sim Dir(\sigma^w T^w U_i), \quad T^w \sim \mathcal{N}(0, \lambda^w) \tag{4}$$

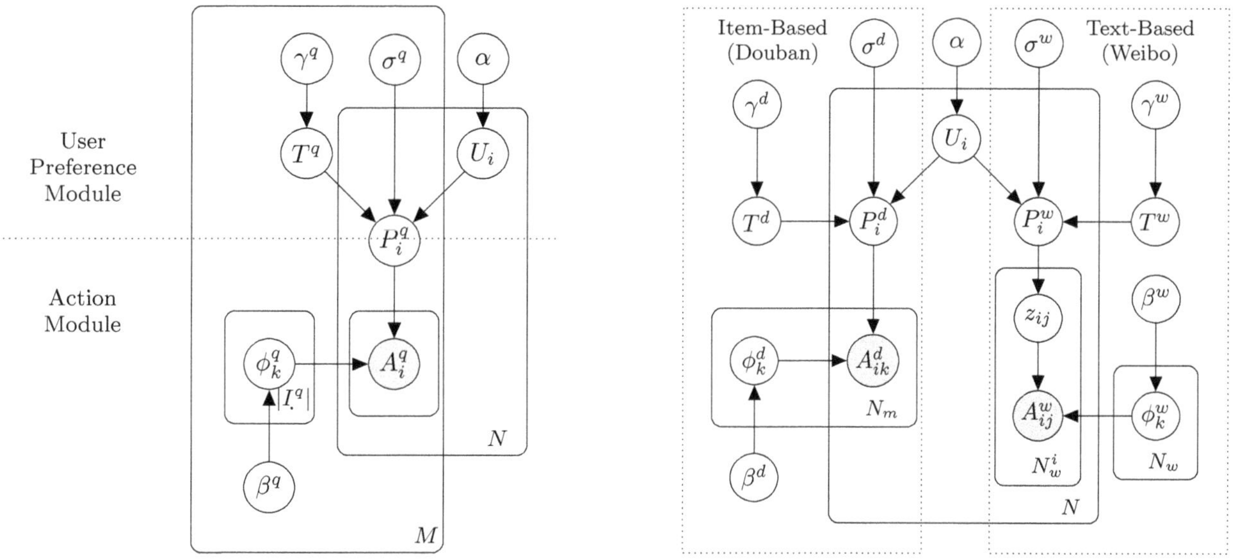

(a) Joint User Modeling in General (b) Joint User Modeling over Douban & Weibo

Figure 3: JUMA : A Probabilistic Graphical Model for Joint User Modeling via Aggregating Multi-Site Actions

where σ^w is a scale parameter for tuning the coupling strength (prior strength). Item modeling as well as user action modeling are kept the same with LDA.

$$\phi_k^w \sim Dir(\beta^w), \quad z_{ij} \sim Multi(P_i^w), \quad A_{ij}^w \sim Multi(\phi_{z_{ij}}^w) \quad (5)$$

4.3 Hybrid Learning Process

In this section we discuss the learning of JUMA. We propose a hybrid learning process to estimate the parameters. The learning is mainly based on Gibbs sampling technique [30], a Markov chain Monte Carlo algorithm for approximating multivariate probability distribution.

Specifically, we partition the graphical model into two sub-modules: user preferences module and site-specific action module (separated by dashed line in Figure 3 (a)). As showed in the figure, the two sub-modules are linked only through site-specific user preferences P_i^q. Viewing each module as a hyper parameter and applying Gibbs sampling over the modules, we can learn the model by iteratively updating the modules separately. In the following subsections we discuss how we update the parameters in each modules.

4.3.1 Site-Specific Learning

Viewing from site's action module, the difference with original models is the distribution of user preferences. Such change can be viewed as a change of prior knowledge. In traditional models we use non-informative prior distribution for user preferences. Instead, when integrating with JUMA, we take advantage of the informative prior transferred from universal preference.

Text-Based Sites. The topic distribution P_i^w now has a prior distribution of $Dir(\sigma^w T^w U_i)$ instead of $Dir(\alpha)$. As we design the model by following the conjugate distributions as in traditional design, only the parameter is shifted while the form of the distribution is kept the same as in the original model. Therefore, the inferences of the parameters are mostly the same as in original model thus we skip the details here. By plugging the new prior parameter, the posterior distribution of the latent topic variable z_{ij} is:

$$P(z_{ij} = k | z_{\neg ij}, A^w, U, T^w, \cdot) \propto \frac{n_{ik}^{\neg ij} + \sigma^w U_i T_k^w}{\sum_{k'} (n_{ik'}^{\neg ij} + \sigma^w U_i T_{k'}^w)} \cdot \frac{m_{kw_{ij}}^{\neg ij} + \beta_{w_{ij}}^w}{\sum_{w'} m_{kw'}^{\neg ij} + \beta_{w'}^w} \quad (6)$$

where n_{ik} is the number of times topic k being assigned to user i ($\# z_{i*} = k$) and m_{kj} is the number of times word j being assigned to topic k. For simplicity, we abbreviate the conditioned variables by '$\cdot$'. After sufficient sampling iterations, the parameters P^w, ϕ^w can be estimated by the following:

$$\hat{P}_{ik}^w = \frac{n_{ik} + \sigma^w U_i T_k^w}{\sum_{k'} n_{ik'} + \sigma^w U_i T_{k'}^w}, \quad \hat{\phi}_{kj}^w = \frac{m_{kj} + \beta_j^w}{\sum_{j'} m_{kj'} + \beta_{j'}^w} \quad (7)$$

Item-Based Sites. User preference P_i^d now has a prior of $\mathcal{N}(T^d U_i, \sigma^d)$ instead of $\mathcal{N}(0, \sigma^d)$. Still, only parameters are shifted. The loss function is now:

$$\mathcal{L}(P^d, \phi^d | U, T^d, \cdot) = \prod_i \mathcal{N}(P_i^d | T^d U_i, \sigma^d) \times \prod_{A_{ik}^d = 1} \sigma(P_i^d \phi_k^d) \prod_{A_{ik}^d = 0} (1 - \sigma(P_i^d \phi_k^d)) \quad (8)$$

We employ gradient descend technique, a widely used method for matrix factorization, to maximize the log likelihood. The partial gradient for user's site-specific preferences P_i^d and the movie's latent factor ϕ_k^d are as follows: As the gradient calculation is rather straight forward and is similar with the original MF, thus we omit the details here.

4.3.2 User Preference Learning

In this module, we need to update users' universal preferences $\{U_i\}$ as well as the preference transferring parameters T^d, T^w. We still follow Gibbs sampling and update them individually according to their posterior distribution conditioned on the others.

The posterior distribution of user's universal preferences U_i according to the general model is:

$$P(U_i|T, P, U_{-i}, \cdot) \propto \mathcal{N}(U_i|0, \alpha) \cdot \prod_q P(P_i^q|U_i, T^q, \sigma^q) \quad (9)$$

where $P(P_i^q|U_i, T^q, \sigma^q)$ indicates probability of user having P_i^q as preference in site q under prior transferred from U_i and T^q. When applying to text-based and item-based sites as stated in previous section, we have:

$$\begin{aligned} P(U_i|\cdot) \propto & \mathcal{N}(U_i|0, \alpha) \cdot \\ & \mathcal{N}(P_i^d|T^d U_i, \sigma^d) \cdot Dir(P_i^w|\sigma^w T^w U_i) \end{aligned} \quad (10)$$

The posterior distribution for preference transfer model's parameter T^q for general scenario is:

$$P(T^q|U, P, \cdot) \propto P(T^q|\gamma^q) \cdot \prod_i P(P_i^q|U_i, T^q, \sigma^q) \quad (11)$$

where $P(T^q|\gamma^q)$ is the non-informative prior for T^q and $P(P_i^q|U_i, T^q, \sigma^q)$ is the same as in Eq. (9). Plugging the setting for text-based and item-based sites (normal distribution prior for T^w, T^d and the corresponding $P(P_i^q|U_i, T^q, \sigma^q)$), we have:

$$\begin{aligned} P(T^d|U, P, \cdot) &\propto \mathcal{N}(T^d|0, \gamma^d) \cdot \prod_i \mathcal{N}(P_i^d|T^d U_i, \sigma^d) \\ P(T^w|U, P, \cdot) &\propto \mathcal{N}(T^w|0, \gamma^w) \cdot \prod_i Dir(P_i^q|\sigma^w T^w U_i) \end{aligned} \quad (12)$$

Based on these posterior distribution, Gibbs sampling with Metropolis-Hasting [4] or gradient descend technique can be applied for the learning. For simplicity of inference in text-based sites cases, when updating user preference modules we may assume the site-specific preference P_i^q follows multivariate normal distribution with same mean and variance of the original distribution.

5. EXPERIMENTS

5.1 Experiment Settings

We conduct the experiments using real data over 148,470 aligned users from Weibo and Douban, with microblog retweeting histories and movie rating histories as user actions in the two sites respectively. Details are discussed in Section 3.1.

5.1.1 Evaluation Methodology

As there is no ground truth for user preferences, we can only evaluate the quality of user modeling by the performance of recommender systems.

We design experiments for both text-based site and item-based site to show that joint user modeling can transfer the user preferences and improve the performances in both directions. Specifically, we implement microblog and movie recommender systems for Weibo and Douban respectively using both JUMA and the existing state-of-the-art user modeling techniques as the underlying user preferences modeling.

For ground truth, we consider the user is interested in the movie if he/she rates it, and similar for microblogs. We use a portion (40% to 90%) of the user actions for training the model and the rest for testing. The recommender system ranks the potential movies/microblogs (the ones that user has no action with in the training data) according to the estimated user preferences. Then we employ Area Under the Curve (AUC) as the metric to evaluate the resulted rank.

5.1.2 Comparing Algorithms

For the text-based site Weibo, we compare the followings:

- **LDA:** Latent Dirichlet Allocation, a generative topic model [2]. We apply it to capture topic distributions of users and microblogs, and then employ KL-divergence to calculate the pairwise similarities.
- **CTR:** The collaborative tweet ranking model proposed in [3]. It integrates topic features as well as additional side information such as retweet count, author profile, post time and etc.
- **JUMA:** Our approach in this paper.
- **JUMA$^+$:** JUMA with additional side information.

Note that LDA and JUMA use only the textual information while CTR and JUMA$^+$ also employ side information. For fair comparison, we should compare them accordingly.

For the item-based site Douban, we compare:

- **PMF:** Probabilistic Matrix Factorization, a widely used approach for item-based recommendation [22].
- **SVD++:** the state-of-the-art matrix factorization approach for movie recommendation [14].
- **TMF:** Topic-Based Matrix Factorization, explicitly adding user's topic distribution in Weibo as features into feature-based matrix factorization.
- **mmTM:** Multi-Modal Topic Model, a naive approach for joint user modeling proposed in Section 3 for preliminary analysis.
- **JUMA:** our approach in this paper.

For all approaches, latent factor dimension for user preferences is set to 10 and number of topic is 20. All hyper-parameters are set to 1. The results are conducted over 5-fold cross validation.

There is no suitable cross-domain recommendation techniques to compare with under this experiment setting. As we discussed in Section 2, most existing cross-domain works focus on transferring user preferences between homogeneous user actions, thus can not apply for our setting between microblogging site and movie rating site. There are works modeling between text-based and item-based actions [21], however they require aligned actions for the model learning. For ComSoc in [34], although it also leverages multiple platform for joint user modeling, it focuses on borrowing the social relations instead of user generated contents thus also not suitable for comparing.

5.2 Experiment Results

5.2.1 General Scenario

We first evaluate in the general scenario. We vary the training ratio from 40% to 90% and show the corresponding results in Table 3.

For the text-based site Weibo, our approach JUMA achieve relative improvements of 3.8% and 4.7% comparing to LDA when training ratio is 90% and 40% respectively. The results indicate JUMA out-performs comparing method and is more robust to training size. For advanced and realistic

Table 3: Experimental Results, Varying Training Information Ratio

TARGET	ALGS	AUC SCORE, VARYING TRAINING INFORMATION RATIO					
		0.4	0.5	0.6	0.7	0.8	0.9
Text-Based (Weibo)	LDA	0.6514 ± 0.0017	0.6605 ± 0.0015	0.6694 ± 0.0016	0.6769 ± 0.0018	0.6839 ± 0.0015	0.6928 ± 0.0014
	JUMA	$\mathbf{0.6824 \pm 0.0014}$	$\mathbf{0.6892 \pm 0.0016}$	$\mathbf{0.6976 \pm 0.0014}$	$\mathbf{0.7058 \pm 0.0017}$	$\mathbf{0.7120 \pm 0.0012}$	$\mathbf{0.7194 \pm 0.0013}$
	CTR	0.7021 ± 0.0021	0.7133 ± 0.0017	0.7262 ± 0.0018	0.7352 ± 0.0017	0.7432 ± 0.0016	0.7532 ± 0.0015
	JUMA$^+$	$\mathbf{0.7338 \pm 0.0017}$	$\mathbf{0.7420 \pm 0.0015}$	$\mathbf{0.7502 \pm 0.0018}$	$\mathbf{0.7592 \pm 0.0015}$	$\mathbf{0.7670 \pm 0.0015}$	$\mathbf{0.7743 \pm 0.0014}$
Item-Based (Douban)	PMF	0.7275 ± 0.0016	0.7323 ± 0.0013	0.7384 ± 0.0015	0.7428 ± 0.0016	0.7485 ± 0.0014	0.7521 ± 0.0013
	SVD++	0.7856 ± 0.0012	0.7929 ± 0.0010	0.7986 ± 0.0016	0.8055 ± 0.0012	0.8089 ± 0.0013	0.8112 ± 0.0011
	TMF	0.7872 ± 0.0015	0.7946 ± 0.0012	0.8001 ± 0.0013	0.8071 ± 0.0019	0.8102 ± 0.0014	0.8132 ± 0.0012
	mmTM	0.6929 ± 0.0019	0.6940 ± 0.0011	0.6943 ± 0.0012	0.6963 ± 0.0015	0.7034 ± 0.0010	0.7064 ± 0.0018
	JUMA	$\mathbf{0.8127 \pm 0.0017}$	$\mathbf{0.8172 \pm 0.0016}$	$\mathbf{0.8219 \pm 0.0013}$	$\mathbf{0.8235 \pm 0.0011}$	$\mathbf{0.8243 \pm 0.0015}$	$\mathbf{0.8259 \pm 0.0013}$

scenario where side information is available, JUMA$^+$ also out competes TM$^+$.

For the item-based site Douban, JUMA achieves better performance comparing to both within-site approachs (PMF and SVD++) and joint modeling extended from existing approaches (TMF and mmTM). Also note that topic-based matrix factorization (TMF) has only slight improvement over traditional MF. By detailed analysis we find that topic-related feature's impact does not emerge in tMF because the signals coming from topic distributions are not as strong as the action histories within the same site.

By these experiments, we show that topic model and matrix factorization both can achieve better performance when integrating with JUMA. For other unevaluated techniques, we believe that similar improvement can also be achieved.

5.2.2 *Cold-Start Scenario*

Recall that cold-start problem is the potential failure of recommender system when dealing with new users with few or even no actions. We simulate cold-start scenarios by limiting the number of historic actions used for training. We depict the relative AUC improvements over users with different number of training actions (different cold-start level) in Figure 4. Results in both sites show that the performance improvement is much higher when dealing with cold users comparing to non-cold users. We achieve a relative improvement of 12.8% for the users with no historic actions in Weibo and 9.3% in Douban, indicating that JUMA successfully leverages cross-site action histories to alleviate the cold-start problem without special treatment.

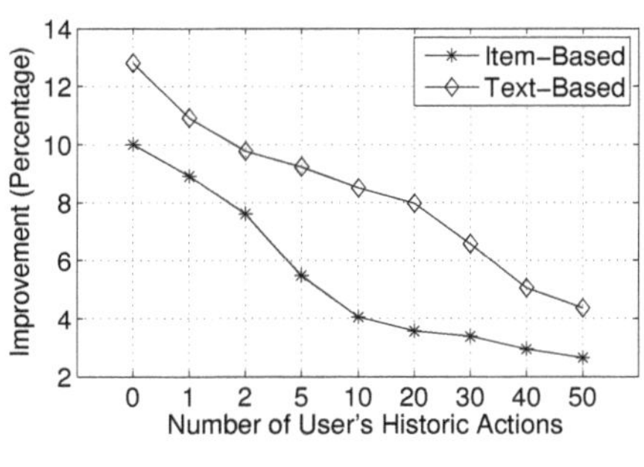

Figure 4: Experiment Result for Cold Start Scenario

5.2.3 *Comprehensiveness of User Modeling*

Now we focus on opposite direction of cold-start where users have more actions than average. We show the results in Table 4, indicating JUMA still outperforms comparing algorithms. For those users, the traditional approaches should be able to precisely model user's preference in the target site. The advantage of JUMA is comprehensiveness. For example, it is hard to model one's political preferences based on his movie histories, but is rather simple based on his microblogs. Such information might be helpful when recommending political related movies/documentaries.

Table 4: Non-Cold Users Scenarios

TARGET	ALGS	USER HISTORY COUNT			
		100	150	200	300
Text-Based (Weibo)	LDA	0.6952	0.7041	0.7105	0.7192
	JUMA	0.7205	0.7259	0.7342	0.7428
	CTR	0.7625	0.7662	0.7715	0.7796
	JUMA$^+$	0.7792	0.7846	0.7895	0.7930
Item-Based (Douban)	PMF	0.7558	0.7597	0.7632	0.7684
	SVD++	0.8142	0.8193	0.8235	0.8327
	TMF	0.8165	0.8204	0.8255	0.8342
	mmTM	0.7130	0.7185	0.7243	0.7304
	JUMA	0.8293	0.8337	0.8379	0.8436

6. CONCLUSION & FUTURE WORK

In this paper, we aim at improving comprehensiveness and accuracy of user modeling by joint user modeling, i.e. simultaneously modeling user actions in multiple aligned heterogeneous sites. We make the assumption that user's underlying preferences are consistent across-sites and further conduct analysis on real data to support it. We propose a modularized probabilistic graphical model framework JUMA for joint user modeling over aligned sites, which can integrate state-of-the-art site-specific approaches for a united user modeling. We also collect and publish a large scale data set from Weibo and Douban. Based on the data set, we conduct extensive experiments to evaluate JUMA's performance in various scenarios. Results show that JUMA out performs existing works and can alleviate cold-start problem without special treatment. For future works, we may consider integrating social relations into JUMA, and developing interpretation or visualization for user's underlying universal preferences.

7. REFERENCES

[1] S. Berkovsky, T. Kuflik, and F. Ricci. Cross-domain mediation in collaborative filtering. In *User Modeling 2007*, pages 355–359. Springer, 2007.

[2] D. M. Blei, A. Y. Ng, and M. I. Jordan. Latent dirichlet allocation. *JML*, 2003.

[3] K. Chen, T. Chen, G. Zheng, O. Jin, E. Yao, and Y. Yu. Collaborative personalized tweet recommendation. In *SIGIR*, 2012.

[4] S. Chib and E. Greenberg. Understanding the metropolis-hastings algorithm. *The american statistician*, 49(4):327–335, 1995.

[5] I. Fernández-Tobías, I. Cantador, M. Kaminskas, and F. Ricci. Cross-domain recommender systems: A survey of the state of the art. In *SCIR*, 2012.

[6] H. Gao, J. Tang, and H. Liu. Addressing the cold-start problem in location recommendation using geo-social correlations. *Data Mining and Knowledge Discovery*, pages 1–25, 2014.

[7] F. Godin, V. Slavkovikj, W. De Neve, B. Schrauwen, and R. Van de Walle. Using topic models for twitter hashtag recommendation. In *WWW*, 2013.

[8] N. Golbandi, Y. Koren, and R. Lempel. Adaptive bootstrapping of recommender systems using decision trees. In *Proceedings of the fourth ACM international conference on Web search and data mining*, pages 595–604. ACM, 2011.

[9] F. Hu and Y. Yu. Interview process learning for top-n recommendation. In *Proceedings of the 7th ACM conference on Recommender systems*, pages 331–334. ACM, 2013.

[10] T. Iofciu, P. Fankhauser, F. Abel, and K. Bischoff. Identifying users across social tagging systems. In *ICWSM*, 2011.

[11] M. Jamali and M. Ester. A matrix factorization technique with trust propagation for recommendation in social networks. In *Proceedings of the fourth ACM conference on Recommender systems*, pages 135–142. ACM, 2010.

[12] H. Kautz, B. Selman, and M. Shah. Referral web: combining social networks and collaborative filtering. *Communications of the ACM*, 40(3):63–65, 1997.

[13] N. Koenigstein, G. Dror, and Y. Koren. Yahoo! music recommendations: modeling music ratings with temporal dynamics and item taxonomy. In *Proceedings of the fifth ACM conference on Recommender systems*, pages 165–172. ACM, 2011.

[14] Y. Koren. Factorization meets the neighborhood: a multifaceted collaborative filtering model. In *Proceedings of the 14th ACM SIGKDD international conference on Knowledge discovery and data mining*, pages 426–434. ACM, 2008.

[15] Y. Koren, R. Bell, and C. Volinsky. Matrix factorization techniques for recommender systems. *Computer*, pages 30–37, 2009.

[16] X. N. Lam, T. Vu, T. D. Le, and A. D. Duong. Addressing cold-start problem in recommendation systems. In *Proceedings of the 2nd international conference on Ubiquitous information management and communication*, pages 208–211. ACM, 2008.

[17] G. Linden, B. Smith, and J. York. Amazon. com recommendations: Item-to-item collaborative filtering. *Internet Computing, IEEE*, 7(1):76–80, 2003.

[18] H. Liu and P. Maes. Interestmap: Harvesting social network profiles for recommendations. *Beyond Personalization-IUI*, page 56, 2005.

[19] J. Liu, F. Zhang, X. Song, Y.-I. Song, C.-Y. Lin, and H.-W. Hon. What's in a name?: an unsupervised approach to link users across communities. In *Proceedings of the 6th ACM international conference on Web search and data mining*, pages 495–504. ACM, 2013.

[20] S. Liu, S. Wang, F. Zhu, J. Zhang, and R. Krishnan. Hydra: Large-scale social identity linkage via heterogeneous behavior modeling. In *SIGMOD*, 2014.

[21] J. McAuley and J. Leskovec. Hidden factors and hidden topics: understanding rating dimensions with review text. In *RecSys*, pages 165–172. ACM, 2013.

[22] A. Mnih and R. Salakhutdinov. Probabilistic matrix factorization. In *NIPS*, pages 1257–1264, 2007.

[23] A. Narayanan and V. Shmatikov. De-anonymizing social networks. In *Security and Privacy, 2009 30th IEEE Symposium on*, pages 173–187. IEEE, 2009.

[24] A. Narayanan and V. Shmatikov. Myths and fallacies of personally identifiable information. *Communications of the ACM*, 53(6):24–26, 2010.

[25] S. Sahebi and P. Brusilovsky. Cross-domain collaborative recommendation in a cold-start context: The impact of user profile size on the quality of recommendation. In *UMAP*. 2013.

[26] A. I. Schein, A. Popescul, L. H. Ungar, and D. M. Pennock. Methods and metrics for cold-start recommendations. In *SIGIR*, pages 253–260, 2002.

[27] S. Tan, J. Bu, X. Qin, C. Chen, and D. Cai. Cross domain recommendation based on multi-type media fusion. *Neurocomputing*, 127:124–134, 2014.

[28] S. Tan, Z. Guan, D. Cai, X. Qin, J. Bu, and C. Chen. Mapping users across networks by manifold alignment on hypergraph. In *AAAI*, 2014.

[29] J. Tang, S. Wu, J. Sun, and H. Su. Cross-domain collaboration recommendation. In *Proceedings of the 18th ACM SIGKDD international conference on Knowledge discovery and data mining*, pages 1285–1293. ACM, 2012.

[30] M. J. Wainwright and M. I. Jordan. Graphical models, exponential families, and variational inference. *Foundations and Trends® in Machine Learning*, 1(1-2):1–305, 2008.

[31] J. Zhang, X. Kong, and P. S. Yu. Predicting social links for new users across aligned heterogeneous social networks. In *2013 IEEE 13th International Conference on Data Mining*, pages 1289–1294. IEEE, 2013.

[32] Y. Zhang and J. Koren. Efficient bayesian hierarchical user modeling for recommendation system. In *SIGIR*, pages 47–54. ACM, 2007.

[33] Z.-K. Zhang, C. Liu, Y.-C. Zhang, and T. Zhou. Solving the cold-start problem in recommender systems with social tags. *EPL*, 92(2):28002, 2010.

[34] E. Zhong, W. Fan, J. Wang, L. Xiao, and Y. Li. Comsoc: adaptive transfer of user behaviors over composite social network. In *Proceedings of the 18th ACM SIGKDD*, pages 696–704. ACM, 2012.

[35] K. Zhou, S.-H. Yang, and H. Zha. Functional matrix factorizations for cold-start recommendation. In *Proceedings of the 34th international ACM SIGIR conference on Research and development in Information Retrieval*, pages 315–324. ACM, 2011.

Fifty Shades of Ratings: How to Benefit from a Negative Feedback in Top-N Recommendations Tasks

Evgeny Frolov
evgeny.frolov@skoltech.ru
Skolkovo Institute of Science and Technology
143025, Nobel St. 3, Skolkovo Innovation Center
Moscow, Russia

Ivan Oseledets
i.oseledets@skoltech.ru
Skolkovo Institute of Science and Technology
Institute of Numerical Mathematics of the
Russian Academy of Sciences
119333, Gubkina St. 8
Moscow, Russia

ABSTRACT

Conventional collaborative filtering techniques treat a top-n recommendations problem as a task of generating a list of the most relevant items. This formulation, however, disregards an opposite – avoiding recommendations with completely irrelevant items. Due to that bias, standard algorithms, as well as commonly used evaluation metrics, become insensitive to negative feedback. In order to resolve this problem we propose to treat user feedback as a categorical variable and model it with users and items in a ternary way. We employ a third-order tensor factorization technique and implement a higher order folding-in method to support online recommendations. The method is equally sensitive to entire spectrum of user ratings and is able to accurately predict relevant items even from a negative only feedback. Our method may partially eliminate the need for complicated rating elicitation process as it provides means for personalized recommendations from the very beginning of an interaction with a recommender system. We also propose a modification of standard metrics which helps to reveal unwanted biases and account for sensitivity to a negative feedback. Our model achieves state-of-the-art quality in standard recommendation tasks while significantly outperforming other methods in the cold-start "no-positive-feedback" scenarios.

Keywords

Collaborative filtering; recommender systems; explicit feedback; cold-start; tensor factorization

1. INTRODUCTION

One of the main challenges faced across different recommender systems is a *cold-start* problem. For example, in a user cold-start scenario, when a new (or unrecognized) user is introduced to the system and no side information is available, it is impossible to generate relevant recommendations without asking the user to provide initial feedback on some items. Randomly picking items for this purpose might be ineffective and frustrating for the user. A more common approach, typically referred as a rating elicitation, is to provide a pre-calculated non-personalized list of the most representative items. However, making this list, that on the one hand helps to better learn the user preferences, and on the other hand does not lead to the user boredom, is a non-trivial task and still is a subject for active research.

The problem becomes even worse if a pre-built list of items resonate poorly with the user's tastes, resulting in mostly negative feedback (e.g. items that get low scores or low ratings from the user). Conventional collaborative filtering algorithms, such as matrix factorization or similarity-based models, tend to favor similar items, which are likely to be irrelevant in that case. This is typically avoided by generating more items, until enough positive feedback (e.g. items with high scores or high ratings) is collected and relevant recommendations can be made. However, this makes engagement with the system less effortless for the user and may lead to a loss of interest in it.

We argue that these problems can be alleviated if the system is able to learn equally well from both positive and negative feedback. Consider the following movie recommendation example: a new user marks the "Scarface" movie with a low rating, e.g. 2 stars out of 5, and no other information is present in his or her profile. This is likely to indicate that the user does not like movies about crime and violence. It also seems natural to assume that the user probably prefers "opposite" features, such as sentimental story (which can be present in romantic movies or drama), or happy and joyful narrative (provided by animation or comedies). In this case, asking to rate or recommending the "Godfather" movie is definitely a redundant and inappropriate action. Similarly, if a user provides some negative feedback for the first part of a series (e.g. the first movie from the "Lord of the rings" trilogy), it is quite natural to expect that the system will not immediately recommend another part from the same series.

A more proper way to engage with the user in that case is to leverage a sort of *"users, who dislike that item, do like these items instead"* scenario. Users certainly can share preferences not only in what they like, but also in what they do not like and it is fair to expect that techniques, based on collaborative filtering approach, could exploit this for more accurate predictions even from a solely negative feedback. In addition to that, a negative feedback may have a greater importance for a user, than a positive one. Some psycholog-

RecSys '16, September 15–19, 2016, Boston, MA, USA.

ISBN 978-1-4503-4035-9/16/09...$15.00

DOI: http://dx.doi.org/10.1145/2959100.2959170

ical studies demonstrate, that not only emotionally negative experience has a stronger impact on an individual's memory [11], but also have a greater effect on humans behavior in general [18], known as the *negativity bias.*

Of course, a number of heuristics or tweaks could be proposed for traditional techniques to fix the problem, however there are intrinsic limitations within the models that make the task hardly solvable. For example, algorithms could start looking for less similar items in the presence of an item with a negative feedback. However, there is a problem of preserving relevance to the user's tastes. It is not enough to simply pick the most dissimilar items, as they are most likely to loose the connection to user preferences. Moreover, it is not even clear when to switch between the "least similar" and the "most similar" modes. If a user assigns a 3 star rating for a movie, does it mean that the system still has to look for the least similar items or should it switch back to the most similar ones? User-based similarity approach is also problematic, as it tends to generate a very broad set of recommendations with a mix of similar and dissimilar items, which again leads to the problem of extracting the most relevant, yet unlike recommendations.

In order to deal with the denoted problems we propose a new tensor-based model, that treats feedback data as a special type of categorical variable. We show that our approach not only improves user cold-start scenarios, but also increases general recommendations accuracy. The contributions of this paper are three-fold:

- We introduce a collaborative filtering model based on a third order tensor factorization technique. In contrast to commonly used approach, our model treats explicit feedback (such as movie ratings) not as a cardinal, but as an ordinal utility measure. The model benefits greatly from such a representation and provides a much richer information about all possible user preferences. We call it *shades of ratings.*
- We demonstrate that our model is equally sensitive to both positive and negative user feedback, which not only improves recommendations quality, but also reduces the efforts needed to learn user preferences in cold-start scenarios.
- We also propose a *higher order folding-in* method for real-time generation of recommendations in support to cold-start scenarios. The method does not require recomputation of the full tensor-based model for serving new users and can be used online.

2. PROBLEM FORMULATION

The goal for conventional recommender system is to be able to accurately generate a personalized list of new and interesting items (*top-n recommendations*), given a sufficient number of examples with user preferences. As has been noted, if preferences are unknown this requires special techniques, such as rating elicitation, to be involved first. In order to avoid that extra step we introduce the following additional requirements for a recommender system:

- the system must be sensitive to a full user feedback scale and not disregard its negative part,
- the system must be able to respond properly even to a single feedback and take into account its type (positive or negative).

These requirements should help to gently navigate new users through the catalog of items, making the experience highly personalized, as after each new step the system narrows down user preferences.

2.1 Limitations of traditional models

Let us consider without the loss of generality the problem of movies recommendations. Traditionally, this is formulated as a prediction task:

$$f_R : \text{User} \times \text{Movie} \to \text{Rating}, \tag{1}$$

where User is a set of all users, Movie is a set of all movies and f_R is a utility function, that assigns predicted values of ratings to every (*user, movie*) pair. In collaborative filtering models the utility function is learned from a prior history of interactions, i.e. previous examples of how users rate movies, which can be conveniently represented in the form of a matrix R with M rows corresponding to the number of users and N columns corresponding to the number of movies. Elements r_{ij} of the matrix R denote actual movie ratings assigned by users. As users tend to provide feedback only for a small set of movies, not all entries of R are known, and the utility function is expected to infer the rest values.

In order to provide recommendations, the predicted values of ratings $\hat{r}_{ij}$ are used to rank movies and build a ranked list of top-n recommendations, that in the simplest case is generated as:

$$\text{toprec}(i, n) := \arg\max_{j \in \text{Movie}}^{n} \hat{r}_{ij}. \tag{2}$$

where toprec(i, n) is a list of n top-ranked movies predicted for a user i. The way the values of $\hat{r}_{ij}$ are calculated depends on a collaborative filtering algorithm and we argue that standard algorithms are unable to accurately predict relevant movies given only an example of user preferences with low ratings.

2.1.1 Matrix factorization

Let us first start with a matrix factorization approach. As we are not aiming to predict the exact values of ratings and more interested in correct ranking, it is adequate to employ the singular value decomposition (SVD) [10] for this task. Originally, SVD is not defined for data with missing values, however, in case of top-n recommendations formulation one can safely impute missing entries with zeroes, especially taking into account that pure SVD can provide state-of-the-art quality [5, 13]. Note, that by SVD we mean its truncated form of rank $r < min(M, N)$, which can be expressed as:

$$R \approx U\Sigma V^T \equiv PQ^T, \tag{3}$$

where $U \in \mathbb{R}^{M\times r}, V \in \mathbb{R}^{N\times r}$ are orthogonal factor matrices, that embed users and movies respectively onto a lower dimensional space of latent (or hidden) features, Σ is a matrix of singular values $\sigma_1 \geq \ldots \geq \sigma_r > 0$ that define the strength or the contribution of every latent feature into resulting score. We also provide an equivalent form with factors $P = U\Sigma^{\frac{1}{2}}$ and $Q = V\Sigma^{\frac{1}{2}}$, commonly used in other matrix factorization techniques.

One of the key properties, that is provided by SVD and not by many other factorization techniques is an orthogonality of factors U and V right "out of the box". This property helps to find approximate values of ratings even for users that were not a part of original matrix R. Using a well known *folding-in* approach [8], one can easily obtain an expression for predicted values of ratings:

$$\boldsymbol{r} \approx VV^T\boldsymbol{p}, \tag{4}$$

where $\boldsymbol{p}$ is a (sparse) vector of initial user preferences, i.e. a vector of lenght M, where a position of every non-zero element corresponds to a movie, rated by a new user, and its value corresponds to the actual user's feedback on that movie. Respectively, $\boldsymbol{r}$ is a (dense) vector of length M of all predicted movie ratings. Note, that for an existing user (e.g. whos preferences are present in matrix R) it returns exactly the corresponding values of SVD.

Due to factors orthogonality the expression can be treated as a projection of user preferences onto a space of latent features. It also provides means for quick recommendations generation, as no recomputation of SVD is required, and thus is suitable for online engagement with new users. It should be noted also, that the expression (4) does not hold if matrix V is not orthogonal, which is typically the case in many other factorization techniques (and even for Q matrix in (3)). However, it can be transformed to an orthogonal form with QR decomposition.

Nevertheless, there is a subtle issue here. If, for instance, $\boldsymbol{p}$ contains only a single rating, then it does not matter what exact value it has. Different values of the rating will simply scale all the resulting scores, given by (4), and will not affect the actual ranking of recommendations. In other words, if a user provides a single 2-star rating for some movie, the recommendations list is going to be the same, as if a 5-star rating for that movie is provided.

2.1.2 Similarity-based approach

It may seem that the problem can be alleviated if we exploit some user similarity technique. Indeed, if users share not only what they like, but also what they dislike, then users, similar to the one with a negative only feedback, might give a good list of candidate movies for recommendations. The list can be generated with help of the following expression:

$$r_{ij} = \frac{1}{K} \sum_{k \in S_i} (r_{kj}) \, \mathrm{sim}(i,k), \tag{5}$$

where S_i is a set of users, the most similar to user i, $\mathrm{sim}(i,k)$ is some similarity measure between users i and k and K is a normalizing factor, equal to $\sum_{i \in S_i} |sim(i,k)|$ in the simplest case. The similarity between users can be computed by comparing either their latent features (given by the matrix U) or simply the rows of initial matrix R, which turns the task into a traditional user-based *k-Nearest Neighbors* problem (kNN). It can be also modified to a more advanced forms, that take into account user biases [2].

However, even though more relevant items are likely to get higher scores in user-similarity approach, it still does not guarantee an isolation of irrelevant items. Let us demonstrate it on a simple example. For the illustration purposes we will use a simple kNN approach, based on a cosine similarity measure. However, it can be generalized to more advanced variations of (5).

Let a new user Tom have rated the "Scarface" movie with rating 2 (see Table 1) and we need to decide which of two other movies, namely "Toy Story" or "Godfather", should be recommended to Tom, given an information on how other users - Alice, Bob and Carol - have also rated these movies.

Table 1: Similarity-based recommendations issue.

	Scarface	Toy Story	Godfather
		Observation	
Alice	2	5	3
Bob	4		5
Carol	2	5	
		New user	
Tom	2	?	?
		Prediction	
		2.6	**3.1**

As it can be seen, Alice and Carol, similarly to Tom, do not like criminal movies. They also both enjoy the "Toy Story" animation. Even though Bob demonstrates an opposite set of interests, the preferences of Alice and Carol prevail. From here it can be concluded that the most relevant (or safe) recommendation for Tom would be the "Toy Story". Nevertheless, the prediction formula (5) assigns the highest score to the "Godfather" movie, which is a result of a higher value of cosine similarity between Bob's and Tom's preference vectors.

2.2 Resolving the inconsistencies

The problems, described above, suggest that in order to build a model, that fulfills the requirements, proposed in Section 2, we have to move away from traditional representation of ratings. Our idea is to restate the problem formulation in the following way:

$$f_R : \text{User} \times \text{Movie} \times \text{Rating} \to \text{Relevance Score}, \tag{6}$$

where Rating is a domain of ordinal (categorical) variables, consisting of all possible user ratings, and Relevance Score denotes the likeliness of observing a certain (*user, movie, rating*) triplet. With this formulation relations between users, movies and ratings are modelled in a ternary way, i.e. all three variables influence each other and the resulting score. This type of relations can be modelled with several methods, such as Factorization Machines [17] or other context-aware methods [1]. We propose to solve the problem with a tensor-based approach, as it seems to be more flexible, naturally fit the formulation (6) and has a number of advantages, described in Section 3.

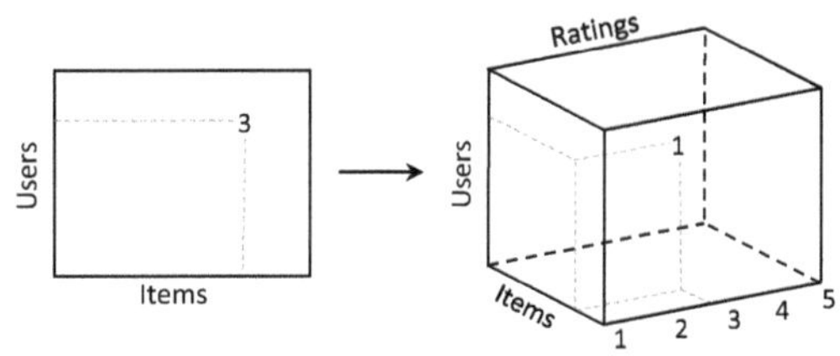

Figure 1: From a matrix to a third order tensor.

3. TENSOR CONCEPTS

The (*user, movie, rating*) triplets can be encoded within a three-dimensional array (see Figure 1) which we will call a third order tensor and denote with calligraphic capital letter $\mathcal{X} \in \mathbb{R}^{M \times N \times K}$. The sizes of tensor dimensions (or *modes*) correspond to the total number of unique users, movies and ratings. The values of the tensor $\mathcal{X}$ are binary (see Figure 1):

$$\begin{cases} x_{ijk} = 1, & \text{if } (i, j, k) \in S, \\ x_{ijk} = 0, & \text{otherwise,} \end{cases} \tag{7}$$

where S is a history of known interactions, i.e. a set of observed (*user, movie, rating*) triplets. Similarly to a matrix factorization case (3), we are interested in finding such a tensor factorization that reveals some common patterns in the data and finds latent representation of users, movies and ratings.

There are two commonly used tensor factorization techniques, namely Candecomp/Parafac (CP) and Tucker Decomposition (TD) [12]. As we will show in Section 3.2, the use of TD is more advantageous, as it gives orthogonal factors, that can be used for quick recommendations computation, similarly to (4). Moreover, an optimization task for CP, in contrast to TD, is ill-posed in general [7].

3.1 Tensor factorization

The tensor in TD format can be represented as follows:

$$\mathcal{X} \approx \mathcal{G} \times_1 U \times_2 V \times_3 W, \tag{8}$$

where $\times_n$ is an n-mode product, defined in [12], $U \in \mathbb{R}^{M \times r_1}$, $V \in \mathbb{R}^{N \times r_2}$, $W \in \mathbb{R}^{K \times r_3}$ are orthogonal matrices, that represent embedding of the users, movies and ratings onto a reduced space of latent features, similarly to SVD case.

Tensor $\mathcal{G} \in \mathbb{R}^{r_1 \times r_2 \times r_3}$ is called the core of TD and a tuple of numbers (r_1, r_2, r_3) is called a *multilinear rank* of the decomposition. The decomposition can be effectively computed with a higher order orthogonal iterations (HOOI) algorithm [6].

3.2 Efficient computation of recommendations

As recommender systems typically have to deal with large numbers of users and items, this renders the problem of fast recommendations computation. Factorizing the tensor for every new user can take prohibitively long time which is inconsistent with the requirement of real-time recommendations. For this purposes we propose a *higher order folding-in* method (see Figure 2) that finds approximate recommendations for any unseen user with comparatively low computational cost (cf. (4)):

$$R_{(i)} = VV^T P_{(i)} WW^T, \tag{9}$$

where $P_{(i)}$ is an $N \times K$ binary matrix of an i-th user's preferences and $R_{(i)} \in \mathbb{R}^{N \times K}$ is a matrix of recommendations. Similarly to SVD-based folding-in, (9) can be treated as a

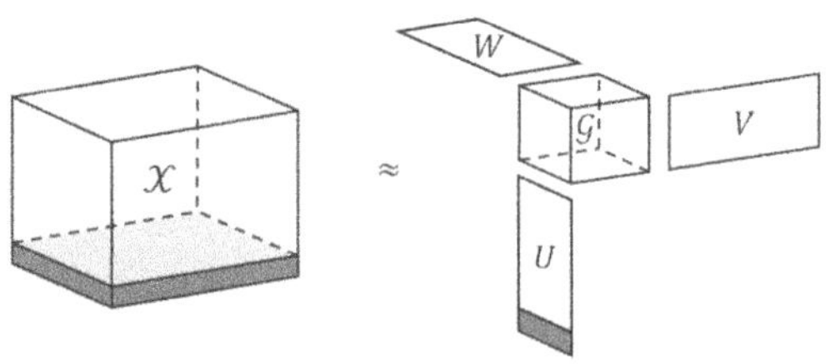

Figure 2: Higher order folding-in for Tucker decomposition. A slice with a new user information in the original data (left) and a corresponding row update of the factor matrix in Tucker decomposition (right) are marked with solid a color.

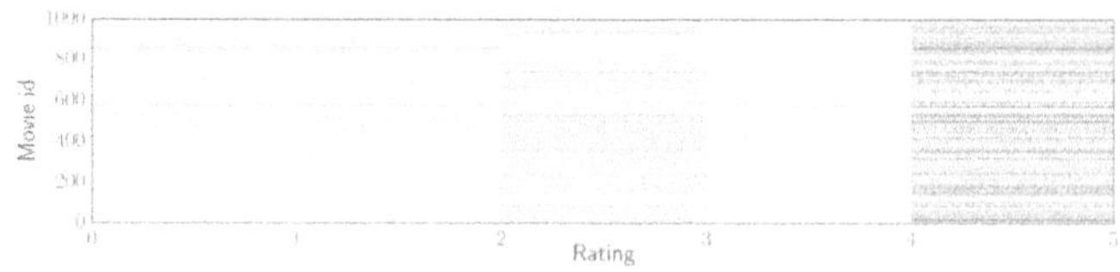

Figure 3: Example of the predicted user preferences, that we call *shades of ratings*. Every horizontal bar can be treated as a likeliness of some movie to have a specific rating for a selected user. More dense colors correspond to higher relevance scores.

sequence of projections to latent spaces of movies and ratings. Note, this is a straightforward generalization of matrix folding-in and we omit its derivation due to space limits. In the case of a known user the expression also gives the exact values of the TD.

3.3 Shades of ratings

Note that even though (9) looks very similar to (4), there is a substantial difference in what is being scored. In the case of a matrix factorization we score ratings (or other forms of feedback) directly, whereas in the tensor case we *score the likeliness of a rating to have a particular value for an item.* This gives a new and more informative view on predicted user preferences (see Figure 3). Unlike the conventional methods, every movie in recommendations is not associated with just a single score, but rather with a full range of all possible rating values, that users are exposed to.

Another remarkable property of "rating shades" is that it can be naturally utilized for both ranking and rating prediction tasks. The ranking task corresponds to finding a maximum score along the movies mode (2nd mode of the tensor) for a selected (highest) rating. Note, that the ranking can be performed within every rating value. Rating prediction corresponds to a maximization of relevance scores along the ratings mode (i.e. the 3rd mode of the tensor) for a selected movie. We utilize this feature to additionally verify the model's quality (see Section 6).

If a positive feedback is defined by several ratings (e.g. 5 and 4), than the sum of scores from these ratings can be used for ranking. Our experiments show that this typically leads to an improved quality of predictions comparing to an unmodified version of an algorithm.

4. EVALUATION

As has been discussed in Section 2.1, standard recommender models are unable to properly operate with a negative feedback and more often simply ignore it. As an example, a well known recommender systems library MyMediaLite [9], that features many state-of-the-art algorithms, does not support a negative feedback for item recommendation tasks.

In addition to that, a common way of performing an offline evaluation of recommendations quality is to measure only how well a tested algorithm can retrieve highly relevant items. Nevertheless, both relevance-based (e.g. precision, recall, etc.) and ranking-based (e.g. nDCG, MAP, etc.) metrics, are completely insensitive to irrelevant items prediction: an algorithm that recommends 3 positively rated and

7 negatively rated items will gain the same evaluation score as an algorithm that recommends 3 positively rated and 7 items with unknown (not necessarily negative) ratings.

This leads to several important questions, that are typically obscured and that we aim to find an answer to:

- How likely an algorithm is to place irrelevant items in top-n recommendations list and rank them highly?
- Does high evaluation performance in terms of relevant items prediction guarantee a lower number of irrelevant recommendations?

Answering these questions is impossible within standard evaluation paradigm and we propose to adopt commonly used metrics in a way that respects crucial difference between the effects of relevant and irrelevant recommendations. We also expect that modified metrics will reflect the effects, described in Section 1 (the Scarface and Godfather example).

4.1 Negativity bias compliance

The first step for the metrics modification is to split rating values into 2 classes: the class of a negative feedback and the class of a positive feedback. This is done by selecting a *negativity threshold* value, such that the values of ratings above this threshold are treated as positive examples and all other values - as negative.

The next step is to allow generated recommendations to be evaluated against the negative user feedback, as well as the positive one. This leads to a classical notion of true positive (tp), true negative (tn), false positive (fp) and false negative (fn) types of predictions [19], which also renders a classical definition of relevance metrics, namely precision (P) and recall (R, also referred as *True Positive Rate* (TPR)):

$$P = \frac{tp}{tp + fp}, \quad R = \frac{tp}{tp + fn}.$$

Similarly, *False Positive Rate* (FPR) is defined as

$$FPR = \frac{fp}{tp + fp}.$$

The TPR to FPR curve, also known as a Receiver Operating Characteristics (ROC) curve, can be used to assess the tendency of an algorithm to recommend irrelevant items. Worth noting here, that if items, recommended by an algorithm, are not rated by a user (question marks on Figure 4), then we simply ignore them and do not mark as false positive in order to avoid *fp* rate overestimation [19].

The *Discounted Cumulative Gain* (DCG) metric will look very similar to the original one with the exception that we do not include the negative ratings into the calculations at all:

$$\mathrm{DCG} = \sum_{p} \frac{2^{r_p} - 1}{\log_2 (p+1)}, \tag{10}$$

where $p : \{r_p > \text{negativity threshold}\}$ and r_p is a rating of a positively rated item. This gives an nDCG metric:

$$\mathrm{nDCG} = \frac{\mathrm{DCG}}{\mathrm{iDCG}},$$

where iDCG is a value returned by an ideal ordering or recommended items (i.e. when more relevant items are ranked higher in top-n recommendations list).

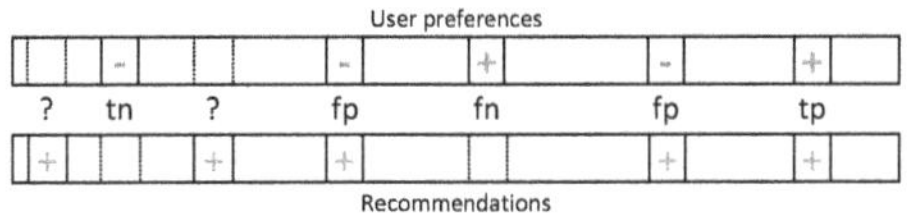

Figure 4: Definition of matching and mismatching predictions. Recommendations that are not a part of the known user preferences (question marks) are ignored and not considered as false positive.

4.2 Penalizing irrelevant recommendations

The nDCG metric indicates how close tp predictions are to the beginning of a top-n recommendations list, however, it tells nothing about the ranking of irrelevant items. We fix this by a modification of (10) with respect to a negative feedback, which we call a *Discounted Cumulative Loss*:

$$\mathrm{DCL} = \sum_{n} \frac{2^{-r_n} - 1}{-\log_2 (n+1)}, \tag{11}$$

where $n : \{r_n \leq \text{negativity threshold}\}$ and r_n is a rating of a negatively rated item. Similarly to nDCG, nDCL metric is defined as:

$$\mathrm{nDCL} = \frac{\mathrm{DCL}}{\mathrm{iDCL}},$$

where iDCL is a value returned by an ideal ranking or irrelevant predictions (i.e. the more irrelevant are ranked lower). Note, that as nDCL penalizes high ranking of irrelevant items, therefore *the lower are the values of nDCL the better.*

In the experiments all the metrics are measured for different values of top-n list length, i.e. the metrics are metrics *at* n. The values of metrics are averaged over all test users.

4.3 Evaluation methodology

For the evaluation purposes we split datasets into two subsets, disjoint by users (e.g. every user can only belong to a single subset). First subset is used for learning a model, it contains 80% of all users and is called a *training set*. The remaining 20% of users (the test users) are unseen in the training set and are used for models evaluation. We holdout a fixed number of items from every test user and put them into a *holdout set*. The remaining items form an *observation set* of the test users. Recommendations, generated based on an observation set are evaluated against a holdout set. We also perform a 5-fold cross validation by selecting different 20% of users each time and averaging the results over all 5 folds. The main difference from common evaluation methodologies is that we allow both relevant and irrelevant items in the holdout set (see Figure 4 and Section 4.1). Furthermore, we vary the number and the type of items in the observation set, which leads to various scenarios:

- leaving only one or few items with the lowest ratings leads to the case of "no-positive-feedback" cold-start;
- if all the observation set items are used to predict user preferences, this serves as a proxy to a standard recommendation scenario for a known user.

We have also conducted rating prediction experiments when a single top-rated item is held out from every test user (see Section 6). In this experiment we verify what ratings are predicted by our model (see Section 3.3 for explanation of rating calculation) against the actual ratings of the holdout items.

5. EXPERIMENTAL SETUP

5.1 Datasets

We use publicly available Movielens[1] 1M and 10M datasets as a common standard for offline recommender systems evaluation. We have also trained a few models on the latest Movielens dataset (22M rating, updated on 1/2016) and deployed a movie recommendations web application for online evaluation. This is especially handy for our specific scenarios, as the content of each movie is easily understood and contradictions in recommendations can be easily eye spotted (see Table 2).

5.2 Algorithms

We compare our approach with the state-of-the-art matrix factorization methods, designed for items recommendations task as well as two non-personalized baselines.

- *CoFFee* (Collaborative Full Feedback model) is the proposed tensor-based approach.
- *SVD*, also referred as *PureSVD* [5], uses standard SVD. As in the CoFFee model, missing values are simply imputed with zeros.
- *WRMF* [15] is a matrix factorization method, where missing ratings are not ignored or imputed with zeroes, but rather are uniformly weighted.
- *BPRMF* [16] is a matrix factorization method, powered by a Bayesian personalized ranking approach, that optimizes pair-wise preferences between observed and unobserved items.
- *Most popular* model always recommends top-n items with the highest number of ratings (independently of ratings value).
- *Random guess* model generates recommendations randomly.

SVD is based on Python's Numpy, and SciPy packages, which heavily use BLAS and LAPACK functions as well as MKL optimizations. CoFFee is also implemented in Python, using the same packages for most of the linear algebra operations. We additionally use Pandas package to support sparse tensors in COO format.

BPRMF and WRMF implementations are taken from the MyMediaLite [9] library. We wrap the command line utilities of these methods with Python, so that all the tested algorithms share the same namespace and configuration. Command line utilities do not support online evaluation and we implement our own (orthogonalized) folding-in on the factor matrices generated by these models. Learning times of the models are depicted on Figure 5. The source code as well as the link to our web app can be found at Github[2].

5.3 Settings

We preprocess these datasets to contain only users who have rated no less than 20 movies. Number of holdout items is always set to 10. The top-n values range from 1 to 100. The test set items selection is 1 or 3 negatively rated, 1, 3 or 5 with random ratings and all (see Section 4.3 for details). We include higher values of top-n (up to 100) as we allow random items to appear in the holdout set. This helps to make experimentation more sensitive to wrong recommendations, that match negative feedback from the user. The

[1]https://grouplens.org/datasets/movielens/

[2]https://github.com/Evfro/fifty-shades

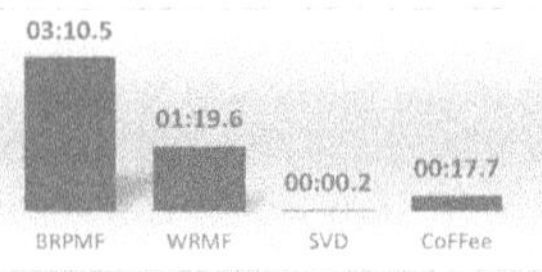

Figure 5: Models' learning time, mm:ss.ms (single laptop, Intel i5 2.5GHz CPU, Movielens 10M).

negativity threshold is set to 3 for Movielens 1M and 3.5 for Movielens 10M. Both observation and holdout sets are cleaned from the items that are not present in the training set. The number of latent factors for all matrix factorization models is set to 10, CoFFee multilinear rank is (13, 10, 2). Regularization parameters of WRMF and BPRMF algorithms are set to MyMediaLite's defaults.

6. RESULTS

Due to a space constraints we provide only the most important and informative part of evaluation results. They are presented on the Figure 6. Rows A and C correspond to Movielens 1M dataset, rows B and D correspond to Movielens 10M dataset. We also report a few interesting handpicked examples of movies recommendations, generated from a single negative feedback (see Table 2).

How to read the graphs.

The results are better understood with particular examples. Let us start with the first two rows on Figure 6 (row A is for Movielens 1M and row B is for Movielens 10M). These rows correspond to a performance of the models, when only a single (random) negative feedback is provided.

First of all, it can be seen that the item popularity model gets very high scores with TPR to FPR, precision-recall and nDCG metrics (first 3 columns on the figure). One could conclude that this is the most appropriate model in that case (when almost nothing is know about user preferences). However, high nDCL score (4th column) of this model indicates that it is also very likely to place irrelevant items at the first place, which can be disappointing for users. Similar poor ranking of irrelevant items is observed with SVD and WRMF models. On the other hand, the lowest nDCL score belongs to the random guess model, which is trivially due to a very poor overall performance. The same conclusion is valid for BPRMF model, that have low nDCL (row A), but fails to recommend relevant items from a negative feedback.

The only model, that behaves reasonably well is the proposed CoFFee model. It has low nDCL, i.e. *it is more successful at avoiding irrelevant recommendations at the first place.* This effect is especially strong on the Movielens 10M dataset (row B). The model also exhibits a better or comparable to the item popularity model's performance on relevant items prediction. At first glance, the surprising fact is that the model has a low nDCG score. Considering the fact that this can not be due to a higher ranking of irrelevant items (as it follows from low nDCL), this is simply due to a higher ranking of items, that were not yet rated by a user (recall the question marks on Figure 4).

The model tries to make a *safe guess* by filtering out irrelevant items and proposing those items that are more likely to be relevant to an original negative feedback (unlike popular or similar items recommendation). This conclusion is

Table 2: Hand-picked examples from top-10 recommendations generated on a single feedback. The models are trained on the latest Movielens dataset.

	Scarface	LOTR: The Two Towers	Star Wars: Episode VII - The Force Awakens
CoFFee	Toy Story	Net, The	Dark Knight, The
	Mr. Holland's Opus	Cliffhanger	Batman Begins
	Independence Day	Batman Forever	Star Wars: Episode IV - A New Hope
SVD	Reservoir Dogs	LOTR: The Fellowship of the Ring	Dark Knight, The
	Goodfellas	Shrek	Inception
	Godfather: Part II, The	LOTR: The Return of the King	Iron Man

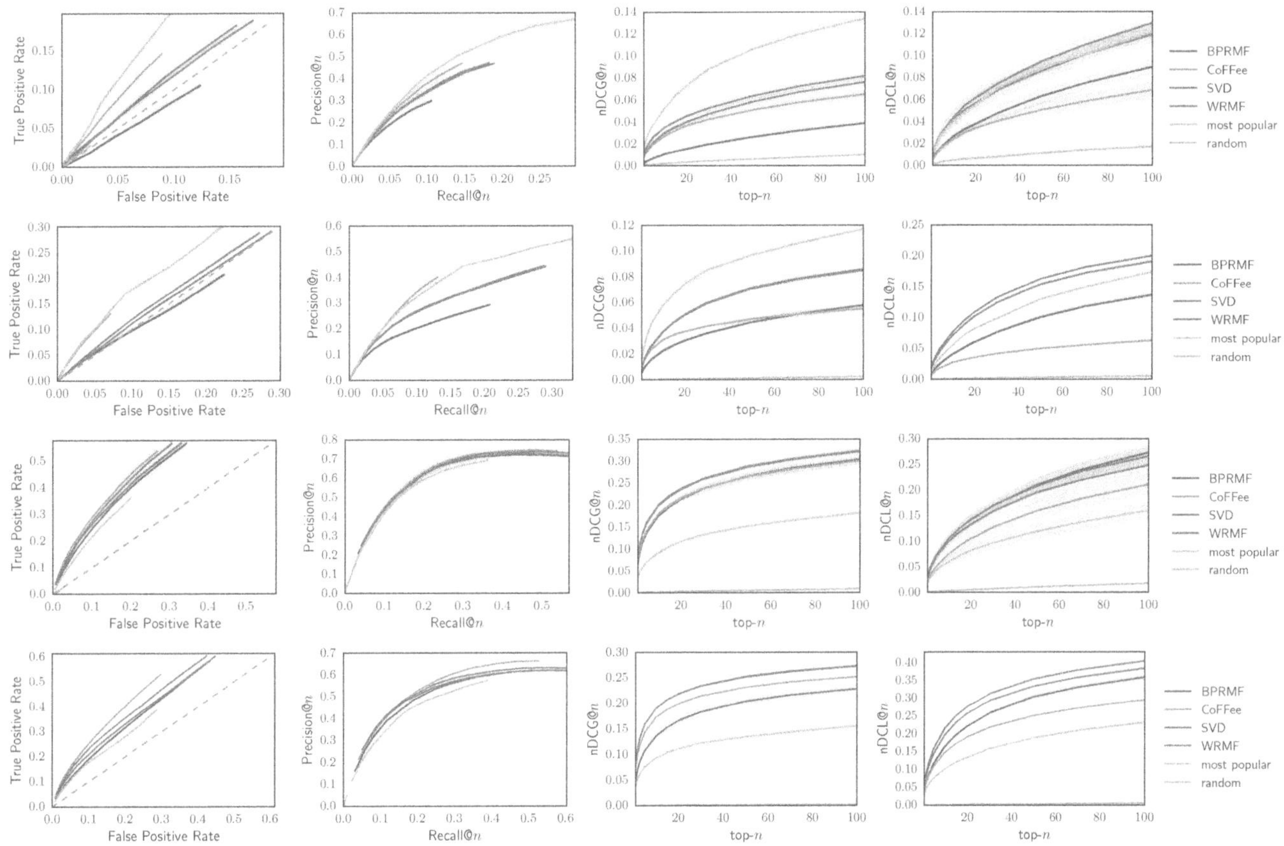

Figure 6: The ROC curves (1st column), precision-recall curves (2nd column), nDCG@n (3rd column) and nDCL@n (4th column). Rows A, B correspond to a cold-start with a *single negative* feedback. Rows C, D correspond to a *known user* recommendation scenario. Odd rows are for Movielens 1M, even rows are for Movielens 10M. For the first 3 columns the higher the curve, the better, for the last column the lower the curve, the better. Shaded areas show a standard deviation of an averaged over all cross validation runs value.

also supported by the examples from the first 2 columns of Table 2. It can be easily seen, that unlike SVD, the CoFFee model makes safe recommendations with "opposite" movie features (e.g. Toy Story against Scarface). Such an effects are not captured by standard metrics and can be revealed only by a side by side comparison with the proposed nDCL measure.

In standard recommendations scenario, when user preferences are known (rows C, D) our model also demonstrates the best performance in all but nDCG metrics, which again is explained by the presence of unrated items rather than a poor quality of recommendations. In contrast, matrix factorization models, SVD and WRMF, while also being the top-performers in the first three metrics, demonstrate the worst quality in terms of nDCL almost in all cases.

We additionally test our model in rating prediction experiment, where the ratings of the holdout items are predicted as described in Section 3.3. On the Movielens 1M dataset our model is able to predict the exact rating value in 47% cases. It also correctly predicts the rating positivity (e.g. predicts rating 4 when actual rating is 5 and vice versa) in another 48% of cases, giving 95% of correctly predicted feedback positivity in total. As a result it achieves a 0.77 RMSE score on the holdout set for Movielens 1M.

7. RELATED WORK

A few research papers have studied an effect of different types of user feedback on the quality of recommender systems. The authors of Preference model [13] proposed to split user ratings into categories and compute the relevance scores based on user-specific ratings distribution. The authors of SLIM method [14] have compared models that learn ratings either explicitly (r-models) or in a binary form (b-models). They compare initial distribution of ratings with the recommendations by calculating a hit rate for every rating value. The authors show that r-models have a stronger ability to predict top-rated items even if ratings with the highest values are not prevalent. The authors of [3] have studied the subjective nature of ratings from a user perspective. They have demonstrated that a rating scale per se is non-uniform, e.g. distances between different rating values are perceived differently even by the same user. The authors of [4] state that discovering what a user does not like can be easier than discovering what the user does like. They propose to filter all negative preferences of individuals to avoid unsatisfactory recommendations to a group. However, to the best of our knowledge, there is no published research on the *learning from an explicit negative feedback* paradigm in personalized recommendations task.

8. CONCLUSION AND PERSPECTIVES

To conclude, let us first address the two questions, posed in the beginning of Section 4. As we have shown, standard evaluation metrics, that do not treat irrelevant recommendations properly (as in the case with nDCG), might obscure a significant part of a model's performance. An algorithm, that highly scores both relevant and irrelevant items, is more likely to be favored by such a metrics, while increasing the risk of a user disappointment.

We have proposed modifications to both standard metrics and evaluation procedure, that not only reveal a positivity bias of standard evaluation, but also help to perform a comprehensive examination of recommendations quality from the perspective of both positive and negative effects.

We have also proposed a new model, that is able to learn equally well from full spectrum of user feedbacks and provides state-of-the-art quality in different recommendation scenarios. The model is unified in a sense, that it can be used both at initial step of learning user preferences and at standard recommendation scenarios for already known users. We believe that the model can be used to complement or even replace standard rating elicitation procedures and help to safely introduce new users to a recommender system, providing a highly personalized experience from the very beginning.

9. ACKNOWLEDGEMENTS

This material is based on work supported by the Russian Science Foundation under grant 14-11-00659-a.

10. REFERENCES

[1] G. Adomavicius, B. Mobasher, F. Ricci, and A. Tuzhilin. Context-Aware Recommender Systems. *AI Mag.*, 32(3):67–80, 2011.

[2] G. Adomavicius and A. Tuzhilin. Toward the Next Generation of Recommender Systems: a Survey of the State of the Art and Possible Extensions. *IEEE Trans. Knowl. Data Eng.*, 17(6):734–749, 2005.

[3] X. Amatriain, J. M. Pujol, and N. Oliver. I Like It... I Like It Not: Evaluating User Ratings Noise in Recommender Systems. In *Proc. 17th Int. Conf. User Model. Adapt. Pers. Former. UM AH*, UMAP '09, pages 247–258, Berlin, Heidelberg, 2009. Springer-Verlag.

[4] D. L. Chao, J. Balthrop, and S. Forrest. Adaptive radio: achieving consensus using negative preferences. In *Proc. 2005 Int. ACM Siggr. Conf. Support. Gr. Work*, pages 120–123. ACM, 2005.

[5] P. Cremonesi, Y. Koren, and R. Turrin. Performance of recommender algorithms on top-n recommendation tasks. *Proc. fourth ACM Conf. Recomm. Syst. - RecSys '10*, 2010.

[6] L. De Lathauwer, B. De Moor, and J. Vandewalle. On the best rank-1 and rank-(r 1, r 2,..., r n) approximation of higher-order tensors. *SIAM J. Matrix Anal. Appl.*, 21(4):1324–1342, 2000.

[7] V. De Silva and L.-H. Lim. Tensor rank and the ill-posedness of the best low-rank approximation problem. *SIAM J. Matrix Anal. Appl.*, 30(3):1084—1127, 2008.

[8] M. D. Ekstrand, J. T. Riedl, and J. A. Konstan. Collaborative filtering recommender systems. *Found. Trends Human-Computer Interact.*, 4(2):81–173, 2011.

[9] Z. Gantner, S. Rendle, C. Freudenthaler, and L. Schmidt-Thieme. {MyMediaLite}: A Free Recommender System Library. In *Proc. 5th ACM Conf. Recomm. Syst. (RecSys 2011)*, 2011.

[10] G. H. Golub and C. Reinsch. Singular value decomposition and least squares solutions. *Numer. Math.*, 14(5):403–420, 1970.

[11] E. A. Kensinger. Remembering the details: Effects of emotion. *Emot. Rev.*, 1(2):99–113, 2009.

[12] T. G. Kolda and B. W. Bader. Tensor Decompositions and Applications. *SIAM Rev.*, 51(3):455–500, aug 2009.

[13] J. Lee, D. Lee, Y.-C. Lee, W.-S. Hwang, and S.-W. Kim. Improving the Accuracy of Top-N Recommendation using a Preference Model. *Inf. Sci. (Ny).*, 2016.

[14] X. Ning and G. Karypis. Slim: Sparse linear methods for top-n recommender systems. In *Data Min. (ICDM), 2011 IEEE 11th Int. Conf.*, pages 497–506. IEEE, 2011.

[15] R. Pan, Y. Zhou, B. Cao, N. N. Liu, R. Lukose, M. Scholz, and Q. Yang. One-class collaborative filtering. In *Data Mining, 2008. ICDM'08. Eighth IEEE Int. Conf.*, pages 502–511. IEEE, 2008.

[16] S. Rendle, C. Freudenthaler, Z. Gantner, and L. Schmidt-thieme. BPR : Bayesian Personalized Ranking from Implicit Feedback. *Proc. Twenty-Fifth Conf. Uncertain. Artif. Intell.*, cs.LG:452–461, 2009.

[17] S. Rendle, Z. Gantner, C. Freudenthaler, and L. Schmidt-Thieme. Fast context-aware recommendations with factorization machines. In *Proc. 34th Int. ACM SIGIR Conf. Res. Dev. Inf. Retr.*, pages 635–644. ACM, 2011.

[18] P. Rozin and E. B. Royzman. Negativity bias, negativity dominance, and contagion. *Personal. Soc. Psychol. Rev.*, 5(4):296–320, 2001.

[19] G. Shani and A. Gunawardana. Evaluating recommendation systems. *Recomm. syst. handbook*, pages 257–298, 2011.

Latent Factor Representations for Cold-Start Video Recommendation

Sujoy Roy
SAP Innovation Center Network
Singapore
sujoy.roy@sap.com

Sharath Chandra Guntuku
School of Computer Engineering
Nanyang Technological University
Singapore
sharathc001@e.ntu.edu.sg

ABSTRACT

Recommending items that have rarely/never been viewed by users is a bottleneck for collaborative filtering (CF) based recommendation algorithms. To alleviate this problem, item content representation (mostly in textual form) has been used as auxiliary information for learning latent factor representations. In this work we present a novel method for learning latent factor representation for videos based on modelling the emotional connection between user and item. First of all we present a comparative analysis of state-of-the art emotion modelling approaches that brings out a surprising finding regarding the efficacy of latent factor representations in modelling emotion in video content. Based on this finding we present a method visual-CLiMF for learning latent factor representations for cold start videos based on implicit feedback. Visual-CLiMF is based on the popular collaborative less-is-more approach but demonstrates how emotional aspects of items could be used as auxiliary information to improve MRR performance. Experiments on a new data set and the Amazon products data set demonstrate the effectiveness of visual-CLiMF which outperforms existing CF methods with or without content information.

Keywords

Affective Computing, Personality, Likes, Videos, Emotion Prediction

1. INTRODUCTION

Matrix Factorization based collaborative filtering approaches are widely used in modern recommender systems. One of the pain points of this approach is when the collaborative information is very sparse (*cold start*) and in many cases not available (*very cold start scenario*). This affects recommendation performance. To address this issue, several methods have been proposed that add content or contextual information as auxiliary information with the collaborative information to show performance improvements. How best to *represent* the content and contextual information and *combine* it with the collaborative information depends on the nature of the content and context and clearly there is no one approach that fits all types of contents. In this work the content type is videos for a video recommendation scenario where there is not much contextual information available.

Content Representation. Our investigations into finding a good content representation is inspired by the observation that users like videos because they find some kind of emotional connect with it. Therefore the way users and videos are represented has to carry these emotive factor information. Hence in this work, as a basis for recommending videos, we investigate the emotive factors that influence users to 'like' videos [19]. *This involves learning representations that best capture the expected emotional response of users towards a video.* These representations could be used to either (1) build discriminative emotion models that can predict users emotional response to videos or (2) infer users preference for a video. Generating discriminative representations that can effectively model emotions faces the following challenges.

A good feature engineering based approach needs to incorporate knowledge of how contents influence users. This is a challenge because of the abstract and subjective nature of the problem and also the dimensions of emotions [15]. While sometimes it may seem relatively easier to pinpoint the emotion evoked by some videos, it is very hard to do so for most. For example, it is difficult to exactly ascertain the emotion experienced where there is no strong positive or negative valence associated with the emotion [20]. This makes creating labeled datasets with explicit labeling sometimes unreliable. Therefore most existing bigger datasets for emotion modeling are based on highly positive or highly negative emotion categories. They are created by using high valence terms as query to search for images/videos that might have such terms as tags. But this has its issues. For example, the term "angry" might return "angry bird video" which may not have to do anything with the emotion[9]. Several such issues are discussed in [23]. This points to the challenge of getting supervisory information to model emotions. Learning representations using deep networks as an alternative to feature engineering requires a lot of labelled training data

RecSys '16, September 15-19, 2016, Boston, MA, USA

DOI: http://dx.doi.org/10.1145/2959100.2959172

and hence is limited by the lack of availability of supervisory information [14].

In this work we present an alternative to address the above challenge by demonstrating the possibility of using the implicit feedback ("likes") received from users as a potential source of supervisory signal that can help build better emotion recognition models that can in-turn help serve better recommendations. Note that implicit feedback on user preference for videos is usually available in plenty in the form of usage history. The intuition is that, latent factors learnt from factorizing user-item interaction data, carries information that captures the emotive factors of an item that makes a user "like" it.

To verify the intuition, first of all we present a comparative analysis of state of the art representations for modelling emotion from visual data vs. their latent factor representations derived from collaborative information through matrix factorization. The analysis establishes a novel finding about the efficacy of latent factor representation in modelling emotional response to videos. Latent factor representations are shown to be more discriminative in modelling specific emotions. This addresses the issue of finding an appropriate representation that carries emotive factors.

Combining Collaborative with Content Info. Latent factor representations are derived using factorization of collaborative data. Unfortunately cold start videos do not have sufficient collaborative information to have a discriminative latent factor representation. To deal with this problem, next, we present visual-CLiMF, a pipeline for learning a latent factor representation from a combination of content and collaborative information. To ensure that emotive factors are part of such learned latent representations, visual-CLiMF learns a transformation from existing emotion based representations to the latent factor representation space, based on the objective of maximizing reciprocal rank performance. This enables inferring latent factor representations for even videos that have no collaborative information. Note that we still need collaborative information during the transformation learning step. Our proposed matrix factorization approach is based on the less-is-more concept[21] of maximizing reciprocal rank (MRR) metric, although the concept could be extended to optimizing other evaluation metrics like area under the curve (AUC) [17] etc. Our experimental evaluations and analysis demonstrate the efficacy of the proposed approach in very cold start video recommendation. Figure 1 depicts an illustration of our proposed latent factor learning framework.

2. RELATED WORK

The motivation for this work rests on the intuition that latent factor representations from matrix factorization carry valuable information about the emotional factors that connect users to items. In this work we validate this intuition. Hence studying these latent factors is interesting both from the perspective of video emotion modelling as well as building effective recommender systems. In this section we present related work from both perspectives.

The discriminative information carried by the latent factors are clearly a function of the amount of collaborative information available. Matrix factorization has been very

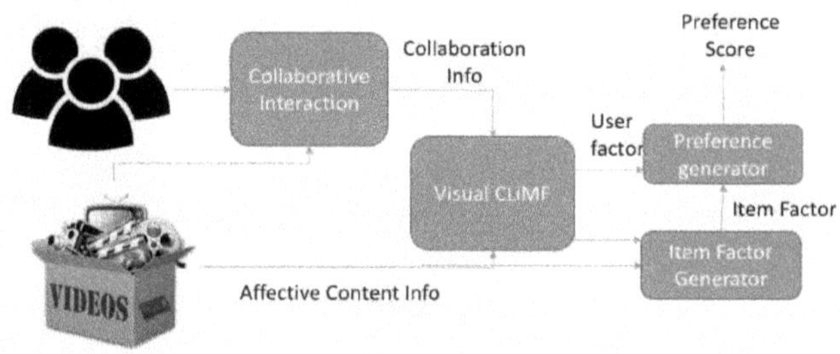

Figure 1: A flow diagram of the interactions in the proposed visual-CLiMF approach.

successfully applied to explicit and dense user-item collaborative information [22]. In most practical situations the collaborative information is implicit (positive-only feedback) and sparse which leads to reduced recommendation performance. So although there have been several works combining explicit collaborative information with content information [5, 18], works dealing with implicit feedback are only relevant for this work.

To deal with implicit feedback several works propose a numerical optimization framework that (1) *point-wise* associate confidence levels to preference values (with "0" preference for non-observed associations)[8], (2) considers the *pair-wise* comparison between preferred and a selection of non-preferred instances[17] and (3) considers only the preferred items[21]. The recommendation problem in the last two cases is formulated as a "learning to rank" problem where the objective is a smoothed version of some performance metric like AUC, MRR etc. In this work we consider the proposal in [21] as a basis to dealing with implicit feedback.

To deal with sparsity, content (visual[7], textual[25, 26]) and contextual[1] auxiliary information has been used to show improvements in recommendation performance. However, it is not clear how the syntactic information extracted from the content translates to high-level semantic information that can contribute to improving preference prediction. Some of these works aim to learn deep semantic representations[26] (for textual data). But it is not clear why the latent factor representations improved performance. This forms the motivation for studying the abstract/emotional factors carried by the latent factor representations, based on the intuition that latent factors carry some form of information regarding the emotional connect that users feel for items [10, 11].

If we consider the latent factor representations to be carrying some form of emotion response information, we also wish to study if they can help model emotional response to content, based on syntactic and mid-level semantic information. Several approaches have been proposed for modeling emotional response to content (textual[3], audio[4], images[2], videos[24]). But they all face some fundamental challenges. There are very few labelled data sets for emotion modelling and that too very small [27, 6] because manual labelling is expensive and the abstract nature of the labels leads to unreliable labels. Hence most labelled data sets are available for very positive or negative emotional responses. Also if they are not manually created they are created by querying for contents with very positive or negative emotional terms associated with them [9].

For the purpose of completeness we discuss some related works that propose visual information based feature representations for emotion modeling. A set of low-level features based on research in affective computing was proposed in [12]. As an investigation into semantic features [2] presents emotion modeling pipeline based on a label set of 2089 adjective noun pairs that are either very positive or very negative in nature. A detailed analysis of affective feature representations applied to video emotion modeling was presented in [14]. In [16] the authors present a comparative analysis of the efficacy of feature representations learnt by the above feature engineering approaches compared to representations learnt by the use of deep non-linear networks. Although the deep non-linear representations are shown[16] to be better than traditional feature engineering based approaches, learning deep networks without overfitting require a lot of training data which is usually not available in emotion modeling scenarios. Hence the improvements reported is not significant enough. On the other hand using off the shelf deep feature representations that have been proven to be extremely useful for detecting visual concepts in images/videos do not generalize well for emotion modeling (as shown in [16] and our own experiments). Hence the improvements reported are not significant enough.

From the perspective of related work, this work presents a novel method of combining auxiliary content information with collaborative information in addressing the cold start problem in video recommendation. In the process we also present a comparative validation of the efficacy of matrix factor based latent factor representations in modelling emotional responses to videos. This is also a novel result that we believe will be of interest to the research community.

3. PROBLEM FORMULATION

For a collection of videos $\mathcal{V}$ and a set of users $\mathcal{U}$ we are given $\mathcal{V}_i^+ \subseteq \mathcal{V}$, which is a set of videos liked by a user i. We are also given a collection $\mathcal{C} = \{C_j : 1 \leq j \leq n\}$, where C_j is the content representation for video j. The problem is to generate a ranked personalized recommendation of videos $\mathcal{V}_i^-$ not in $\mathcal{V}_i^+$, i.e., $\mathcal{V}_i^- \in \mathcal{V} \setminus \mathcal{V}_i^+$ for user i. The performance of the ranking is measured by reciprocal rank. And the method should also work for recommending those items that do not carry any collaborative information.

4. METHODOLOGY

This work proposes a method for combining content and collaborative information to learn latent factor representations for users and items. To investigate what kind of latent factor representations should we learn that can alleviate the cold start problem, we first study the nature of latent factor representations and what kind of information they carry. Towards this goal, we start with the intuition that out of the many semantic factors that they carry, one of the most important ones are the factors that emotionally connect the user to the item. To investigate the discriminative ability of the emotional information they carry, we study their effiacy in modeling desired emotional responses.

4.1 Emotion Modeling

Emotion modeling refers to the problem of automatically estimating the expected emotional response that a content will receive from users, as opposed to a subjective notion of response. To understand the nature of latent factors we benchmark three existing visual feature representations for emotion modeling, namely *affective* features[12] (114 dimensions), *sentibank* features[2] (2089 dimensions, PCA version - 312 dimensions), *hybrid CNN*[1] features[28] (4096 dimensions - PCA version 312 dimensions), with the MF-based latent factor[21] representations. Each video in our data set (to be described in Section 5) is labeled with 9 emotion labels - Amusement, Anger, Disgust, Fear, Interest, Joy, Sadness, Surprise and Tension. We learn a multi-label SVM classifer for each feature representation over the 9 emotion labels to evaluate the discriminative nature of the competing representations. That is, the feature representation with the minimum hamming loss (metric for evaluating multi-label multi-class classification) is the most suitable for emotion modeling. Figure 2 presents the hamming loss for each feature representation under multi-label multi-class classification. Note that the latent factor representations out-perform other feature representations by a significant margin (7-8% improvement over second best feature - affective features).

Figure 3 depicts the change in hamming loss with change in size of latent factor representation. The hamming loss starts high for low dimensional factors but becomes stable with higher dimensions. This verifies the fact that the hamming loss performance is not a function of the size of the latent factor representation. Note that the size of the other feature representations are fixed as reported in existing literature. This establishes the fairness of the comparison in terms of feature dimensions chosen.

This interesting result points to two facts. (1) Latent factor representations indeed carry some form of emotion response related information. (2) The emotional information captured by the latent factors are more discriminative in modeling emotion than the high level semantic reprresentations proposed in existing literature for affective analysis of visual content.

This leads to the next questions. (1) How can we generate such latent factors for contents that do not have collaborative information? What it has to do with the fact that latent factors model emotion well? (2) How do these latent factor representations compare with other MF approaches that use content information (specifically visual)? These questions are answered in Sections 4.2 and 5.

4.2 Visual-CLiMF

In this section we present the visual-CLiMF approach

[1]Convolutional Neural Networks (CNN) trained on 1183 categories (205 scene categories from Places dataset and 918 categories from the ILSVRC2012 training dataset from ImageNet)

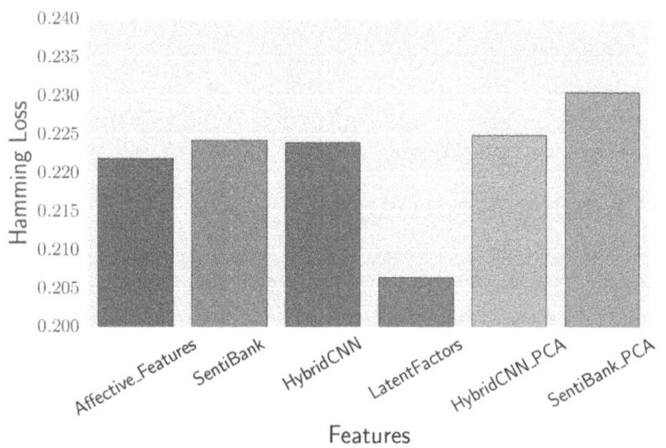

Figure 2: Performance of different features at modelling emotions in clips: Latent factors achieve lower hamming loss when compared to other features in multi-label classification followed by affective features, Sentibank and HyrbidCNN features.

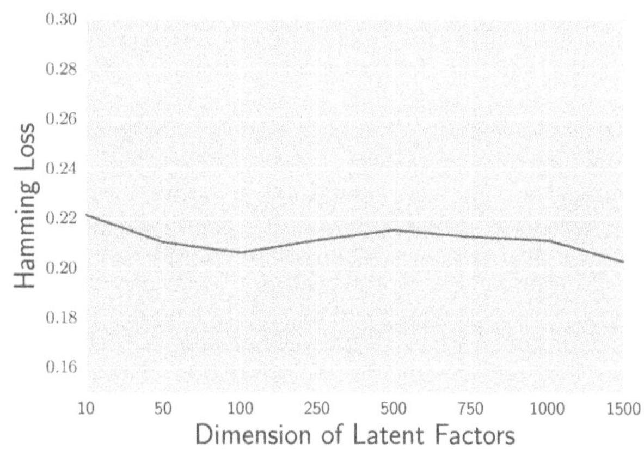

Figure 3: Performance of Latent Factors at predicting emotion distributions. Hamming Loss is seen to be stable across varying latent factor dimensions.

that combines collaborative and content information to generate latent factors for contents that do not contain collaborative information. The goal is to improve ranking of personalized recommendations for users. The model parameters are learned by directly maximizing the Mean Reciprocal Rank (MRR) which measures the performance of top-k recommendations.

The reciprocal rank of a list of N recommended items for user i is formulated as

$$RR_i = \sum_{j}^{N} \frac{Y_{ij}}{R_{ij}} \prod_{k=1}^{N} (1 - Y_{ik}\mathbb{1}(R_{ik} < R_{ij})), \qquad (1)$$

where R_{ij} denotes the rank of item j in the ranked list (in descending order) of item for user i. Y_{ij} denotes the binary relevance score of item j to user i, i.e., $Y_{ij} = 1$ if item j is relevant to user i else 0. $\mathbb{1}(x)$ is an indicator function that is equal to 1, if x is true, otherwise 0. Note that the ranking of relevant items is a non-smooth function of the relevance scores. Thus RR_i is also non-smooth. To deal with this problem a smoothed version of RR_i was presented [21] by basically approximating $\frac{1}{R_{ij}} \approx g(f_{ij})$ and $\mathbb{1}(R_{ik} < R_{ij}) \approx g(f_{ik} - f_{ij})$ where $f_{ij} = U_i^T V_j$.

A method for optimizing a lower bound of the smoothed reciprocal rank was presented in [21] to generate latent factor representations U_i and V_j for user i and item j respectively. To leverage on content information we represent the latent factor representation V_j for item j (which is a m-dimensional vector) as a transformation T of the content representation C_j (which is a n-dimensional vector)

$$V_i = \mathbf{T}\ C_j \qquad (2)$$

where T is a $m \times n$ matrix.

This leads to the following objective function.

$$F(U, \mathbf{T}) = \sum_{i=1}^{M}\sum_{j=1}^{N} Y_{ij}[ln\ g(U_i^T \mathbf{T} C_j) + \sum_{k=1}^{N} ln(1 - Y_{ik} g(U_i^T \mathbf{T} C_k - U_i^T \mathbf{T} C_j))] - \frac{\lambda}{2}(||U||_F^2 + ||\mathbf{T}||_F^2) \qquad (3)$$

where λ is the regularization coefficient, $||U||_F^2$ is the Frobenius norm of U and $||\mathbf{T}||$ is the Frobenius form of $\mathbf{T}$.

Stochastic gradient ascend is used to maximize the objective function in Eq. (3). For gradient of the objective for user i with respect to U_i can be computed as below:

$$\frac{\delta F}{\delta U_i} = \sum_{j=1}^{N} Y_{ij}[g(-f_{ij})V_j + \sum_{k=1}^{N} \frac{Y_{ik} g'(f_{ik} - f_{ij})}{1 - Y_{ik} g(f_{ik} - f_{ij})}(V_j - V_k)] - \lambda U_i \qquad (4)$$

The gradient of the objective with respect to $\mathbf{T}$ for every user i and item j is

$$\left(\frac{\delta F}{\delta \mathbf{T}}\right)_j = \sum_{m,n} \mathbf{E}_{m,n} \frac{\delta F}{\delta T_{mn}} = Y_{ij} \frac{g'(U_i \mathbf{T} C_j)\ U_i \otimes C_j}{g(U_i \mathbf{T} C_j)} + \sum_{k=1}^{N} \frac{Y_{ik} g'(U_i^T \mathbf{T} C_j)(U_i \otimes C_j - U_i \otimes C_k)}{1 - Y_{ik} g(U_i^T \mathbf{T} C_j)} + \lambda \mathbf{T}, \qquad (5)$$

where $\mathbf{E}_{m,n}$ is the elementary matrix of order $(m \times n)$, $g'(x)$ is the derivative of $g(x)$ and $\otimes$ is the outer product.

The learning algorithm is stochastic gradient ascend and is presented in Algorithm 1. Note that the difference with [21] is that here we learn U_i and $\mathbf{T}$ (and hence V_j) based on content information C_j and collaborative information Y_{ij}. In [21] only the collaborative information Y_{ij} is used to learn U_i and V_j. Once we know $\mathbf{T}$, given any new content C, we could estimate the latent factor representation $V = \mathbf{T}C$.

Table 1: Performance comparison of visual CLiMF and baselines (original CLiMF and Popularity Ranking) using different feature representations.

Split	Given 3			Given 5			Given 7			Given 9		
Feature	*Affective*	*Sentibank*	*HybridCNN*	*Affective*	*Sentibank*	*HybridCNN*	*Affective*	*Sentibank*	*HybridCNN*	*Affective*	*Sentibank*	*HybridCNN*
Test MRR (Content-based)	**0.2718**	**0.2256**	**0.238**	**0.2789**	**0.1884**	**0.2741**	**0.3042**	**0.1327**	**0.2293**	**0.2713**	**0.1157**	**0.1919**
Test MRR (CLiMF)	0.2156			0.2526			0.2286			0.1996		
Test MRR (Popularity)	0.2029			0.2009			0.2058			0.1362		

The relevance score of an item V_j for user U_i is computed as the dot product $r_{ij} = < U_i, V_j >$ that returns a scalar value. The recommendation process involves ranking (sorting in descending order) all items V_j according to their score r_{ij} for user U_i.

Algorithm 1 Algorithm: Learning Latent Representation

Input: Training set Y , regularization parameter λ learning rate γ, and the maximal number of iterations $itermax$

Output: The learned latent factors U, $\mathbf{T}$

```
Initialize U^(0) and T^(0) with random values
Initialize t = 0;
repeat
    for i ← 1, M do
        U^(t+1) ← U^(t) + γ δF/δU_i
        for j ← 1, N do
            T^(t+1) ← T^(t) + γ (δF/δT)_j
    t ← t + 1
until t ≥ itermax
U = U^(t) and T = T^(t)
```

5. EXPERIMENTS

5.1 Dataset

We evaluate visual-CLiMF with existing works on two data sets. The first data set is called **Video Emotion data set**, which is a new data set that we present for this work[2]. The second data set is the Amazon product data set[13].

Video Emotion Data Set:. We present a new data set that contains 323 video clips, rated by 111 users with a total of 1917 ratings. The videos are general in nature and include movie/TV series clips and so on. Each video is of an average duration of 3 minutes. Each user rated on an average of 17.27 videos. Each video is also labelled (by several volunteers based on majority voting) to belong to one or more of the 9 emotion categories - Amusement, Anger, Disgust, Fear, Interest, Joy, Sadness, Surprise and Tension. Each emotion is also rated by a valence score between 0-3. Apart from these item related information we also collected a few user related information like their answer to personality modelling questions, their age, gender etc. The user related information is not relevant for this work. All this information and ratings were collected using Amazon Mechanical Turk.

Amazon Product Data Set:. This dataset contains product reviews and metadata from Amazon. This dataset includes reviews (ratings, text, helpfulness votes), product metadata (descriptions, category information, price, brand, and image features), and links (also viewed/also bought graphs). For this work we only look at the "Cell Phones and Accessories" product category. We take the review data and the image features (which are basically 4096 dimensional CNN features of pre-trained network fo visual concept detection) of the product images.

In this data set we look at the collaborative information between 66646 users and 118314 items (products). The rating of a product is in the range 0 to 5. Note that unlike an implicit data set, we do know that the user has given the item an explicit rating. If the rating is greater than equal to 3 we bucket it as a "like" and if the rating is less than 3 then either the user has not seen it or does not like it. We do this form of explicit to implicit feedback mapping to prepare the data to be used by visual-CLiMF which only sees implicit feedback. This is also used to compare performance with VBPR[7] (note: it is not clear to us if this is how implicit feedback is extracted in [7]).

[2]Data set will be made available upon request

Table 2: Performance comparison for cold start items (< 5 likes) for given 3. Note how visual-CLiMF outperforms original CLiMF.

Feature	*Affective*	*Sentibank*	*HybridCNN*
Test MRR (Content-based)	0.2033	0.1464	0.1377
Test MRR (CLiMF)	0.1319		
Test MRR (Popularity)	0.0973		

5.2 Comparison: Only Collaborative

In this section we consider two baseline methods for ranking items based on only collaborative information. They are (1) original CLiMF[21] method to get personalized ranked item list and (2) popularity based approach which gives non-personalized ranked list. Both these methods do not consider any content information in the representation learning process. Our evaluation is performed on both data sets presented earlier.

We divide each users "liked" items into a training set and a test set where"Given n" refers to "n" items being considered as part of the training set $\mathcal{V}_i^+$ and the rest is taken as the test set $\mathcal{V}_i^-$. For CLiMF we first learn the latent factor representations for both users U_i and items V_j based on the training data with hyper-parameters $\lambda = 0.001$ and $\gamma = 0.0005$ (determined based on experimentation). Next we generate a ranked list of all the items for each user i (by sorting $< U_i, V_j >$) and compute the MRR for all the test items $\mathcal{V}_i^-$. For visual-CLiMF we follow the steps outined in Algorithm 1 with the same values of λ and γ to learn the user latent factors U and the transformation matrix $\mathbf{T}$ over the training set. Then we generate the item latent representation based on Equation 2. Next, a ranked list of items is generated and MRR computed for the test items.

Table 3: **Performance of visual CLiMF compared to VBPR on Amazon Phones Dataset based on AUC.**

Amazon Phones Dataset	Test AUC
visual CLiMF	0.4064
CLiMF	0.4035
VBPR	0.2527 +/- .38

Table 1 depicts the performance comparison of visual-CLiMF with the original CLiMF and popularity based methods on the Video Emotions dataset. Visual-CLiMF outperforms both the personalized (original CLiMF) and non-personalized (Popularity) recommendation approaches. Of all the feature representations, *affective features* proposed in [12] seem to perform the best and provide significant performance gains. The performance is also quite consistent across different sizes of training data. This seems to be consistent with the observation we made in Figure 2 where the affective features proposed in [12] are next best in emotion modeling in terms of hamming score. This shows how using emotion features to represent content is the key, and latent factors seem to be the best in doing that.

Table 4 depicts the performance comparison of visual CLiMF with the original CLiMF and popularity based methods on the Amazon products dataset, specifically the Cell phones and accessories category. For this data set also there is slight improvement in MRR performance compared to original CLiMF and popularity based approach. This improvement could be due to the following reasons. (1) People buy cell phones based on specifications, functionalities, sometimes design and also brand name. This means the affective features derived from that kind of metadata would probably be more useful and this is a subject of future work. (2) Also the CNN features available as part of the data set are good for visual concept detection but not for emotion modeling. In fact we do see for this data set that popularity based approaches have comparable MRR performance. This confirms the fact that the effectiveness in adding auxiliary information into the recommendation process depends on the usefulness of that information in capturing why users will want that item. In fact collaborative information seems to be more relevant for this data set.

We also conducted experiments to evaluate the performance of visual CLiMF in ranking cold start videos ($<$ 5 likes) - depicted in Table 2. Note that for all the feature representations visual CLiMF significantly outperforms the original CLiMF and popularity based recommender. In fact comparing Table 1 and Table 2, we observe that the performance for cold start videos is comparable to the original CLiMF applied to the users who have more "likes". This is a promising observation.

MRR Effectiveness:. Figure 4 depicts the change in MRR performance with iterations for visual-CLiMF and original CLiMF on test data and training CLiMF. Note that these observations follow the less-is-more flavour of the CLiMF approach. The MRR performance increases with increase in iterations.

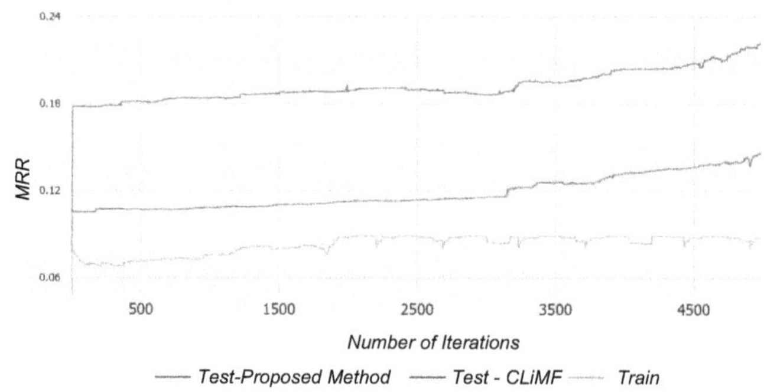

Figure 4: Effectiveness of the learning algorithm under different iterations for visual-CLiMF and original CLiMF under the Given-5

5.3 Comparison: Visual + Collaborative

There have been several works that have looked at adding visual information to collaborative information. Visual Bayesian Personalized Ranking(VBPR)[7] is one such recent work that has looked at integrating the visual information into the latent factor learning process. Few of the significant difference of visual CLiMF with VBPR is that both optimize different performance metrics. VBPR optimizes AUC whereas CLiMF optimizes MRR. VBPR uses visual concept descriptors (CNN) to represent content information. In fact these CNN features constitute a part of the item factor representation. In contrast visual CLiMF learns a latent representation from emotionally relevant representations which is also verified to work well based on results reported in earlier sections. Although visual CLiMF combines visual with collaborative information we also report results for very cold start situation where items have no collaborative information. Our understanding is that VBPR is not meant for those situations.

Table 3 presents a comparison of visual CLiMF, original CLiMF and VBPR based on AUC performance metric[3]. Note that although our method is optimzed for MRR, both CLiMF and visual CLiMF outperform VBPR (mean performance value). Also note that the AUC result for VBPR has a large enough standard deviation which makes the reported accuracy unstable. We have only tested VBPR on the Amazon products data set for fair comparison.

5.4 Visual Features

In this section we address two scenarios/questions. (1) What if we replace the latent factor V_j by their content representation C_j to compute the preference score $U_i^T C_j$ instead of $U_i^T V_j$ in generating a ranked list of items. This is to test whether we even need a transformation matrix **T** that we claim is learning something meaningful. Note that in this scenario, based on our observation that latent factors carry emotional information, the user factor U_i does carry some collaboratively shared emotional information about items that he may not have watched or liked. (2) The second question we address is what about items that have never been seen by any user. This is the

[3]Using code from authors of [7]

Table 4: Performance comparison of visual CLiMF and two baselines (i.e., original CLiMF and Popularity Ranking) for Amazon Phones Dataset based on MRR. ImageNet CNN features were used for visual CLiMF

Amazon Phones Dataset	*Given 3*	*Given5*
Test MRR (Visual CLiMF)	**0.0310**	**0.0331**
Test MRR (CLiMF)	0.0287	0.0303
PopRec	0.0282	0.0231

Table 5: MRR performance comparison by replacing latent representation with affective features [12]. This shows that transformation T learnt does improve performance over replacing the latent factors with the content representation.

Split	*visual-CLiMF (MRR)*	*Affective (MRR)*
Given 3	0.2691	0.2362
Given 5	0.2480	0.1886
Given 7	0.3102	0.2236
Given 9	0.2833	0.2032

very cold start problem where no collaborative information is available.

Scenario 1. We use *affective features* [12] to represent C_j and use it in place of V_j to generate $U_i^T V_j$. We chose affective features because they seem to perform second best after latent factor representations in modeling emotions. This would also tell us how consistent is the conclusion that indeed latent factors should carry some form of affective/emotional information to improve recommendation performance.

Table 5 reports the MRR scores obtained by using the affective feature representation [12] in place of the item latent factors. When we compare this to Table 1 we make some interesting observations. Note that using the *affective features* even outperform the original CLiMF approach in terms of MRR metric. This also demonstrates the fact that the transformation matrix **T** indeed assists in learning latent factors that carry emotional information that helps improve recommendation performance, which are better than directly replacing V_j with a content representation C_j or a purely collaborative representation for an item as in the original CLiMF method.

Scenario 2. Here we are concerned about a much tougher situation where we wish to apply visual-CLiMF to items which no one has watched - the *very cold start* problem. Table 6 depicts the MRR results for items that were never seen before and hence do not have any collaborative information. Note that for these items none of the existing methods that combine collaborative and content information will work as there is no collaboative information for these items. Hence there is no comparitive analysis with CF approaches.

Compared to Table 5 there is clearly a performance drop but none the less we do see how visual-CLiMF delivers at

Table 6: Performance of visual-CLiMF for very cold start items in the Video Emotion data set. That is, these items are not present in any $\mathcal{V}_i^+$.

% of items	*visual-CLiMF (MRR)*	*Affective (MRR)*
7%	0.0886	0.0513
27%	0.0498	0.0369
57%	0.0181	0.01808

least 1 relevant item in the top-10 items returned in the ranked list of items. This is significant because the item is new and has not been seen by anyone.

6. CONCLUSION

Emotional factors are important in connecting users to items. In this work we presented some interesting findings about how to interpret latent factors in terms of the emotional elements they carry. In fact we show how latent factors that are generated from implicit feedback actually address the problem of lack of labelled data for modelling emotion categories. Now, we can learn better emotion models from implicit feedback. Then we show how this knowledge can be exploited to improve MRR performance of recommender systems. We propose visual-CLiMF that builds on the original CLiMF approach by combining visual with collaborative information to learn latent factors that give better MRR performance. In the process we also present our investigations in dealing with recommendation of *very cold start* videos to users - videos that have not been seen by any user.

7. ACKNOWLEDGEMENTS

Sujoy Roy's research is partially funded by the Economic Development Board and National Research Foundation, Singapore.

8. REFERENCES

[1] L. Baltrunas, B. Ludwig, and F. Ricci. Matrix factorization techniques for context aware recommendation. In *Proceedings of the 2011 ACM Conference on Recommender Systems, RecSys 2011, Chicago, IL, USA, October 23-27, 2011*, pages 301–304. ACM, 2011.

[2] D. Borth, T. Chen, R. Ji, and S.-F. Chang. Sentibank: large-scale ontology and classifiers for detecting sentiment and emotions in visual content. In *Proceedings of the 21st ACM international conference on Multimedia*, pages 459–460. ACM, 2013.

[3] E. Cambria, J. Fu, F. Bisio, and S. Poria. Affectivespace 2: Enabling affective intuition for concept-level sentiment analysis. In *AAAI*, pages 508–514, 2015.

[4] A. K. Elshenawy, S. Carter, and D. Braga. ItâĂŹs not just what you say, but how you say it: Muiltimodal sentiment analysis via crowdsourcing. In *Third AAAI Conference on Human Computation and Crowdsourcing*, 2016.

[5] P. Forbes and M. Zhu. Content-boosted matrix factorization for recommender systems: Experiments with recipe recommendation. In *Proceedings of the*

Fifth ACM Conference on Recommender Systems, RecSys '11, pages 261–264, 2011.

[6] S. C. Guntuku, M. J. Scott, G. Ghinea, and W. Lin. Personality, culture, and system factors-impact on affective response to multimedia. *arXiv preprint arXiv:1606.06873*, 2016.

[7] R. He and J. McAuley. Vbpr: Visual bayesian personalized ranking from implicit feedback. *arXiv preprint arXiv:1510.01784*, 2015.

[8] Y. Hu, Y. Koren, and C. Volinsky. Collaborative filtering for implicit feedback datasets. In *Data Mining, 2008. ICDM'08. Eighth IEEE International Conference on*, pages 263–272. Ieee, 2008.

[9] Y.-G. Jiang, B. Xu, and X. Xue. Predicting emotions in user-generated videos. In *Twenty-Eighth AAAI Conference on Artificial Intelligence*, 2014.

[10] J. Kim, J.-B. Yoo, H. Lim, H. Qiu, Z. Kozareva, and A. Galstyan. Sentiment prediction using collaborative filtering. In *ICWSM*, 2013.

[11] F. Li, S. Wang, S. Liu, and M. Zhang. Suit: A supervised user-item based topic model for sentiment analysis. In *AAAI*, pages 1636–1642, 2014.

[12] J. Machajdik and A. Hanbury. Affective image classification using features inspired by psychology and art theory. In *Proceedings of the international conference on Multimedia*, pages 83–92. ACM, 2010.

[13] J. McAuley, R. Pandey, and J. Leskovec. Inferring networks of substitutable and complementary products. In *Proceedings of the 21th ACM SIGKDD International Conference on Knowledge Discovery and Data Mining*, KDD '15, pages 785–794, New York, NY, USA, 2015. ACM.

[14] K.-C. Peng, T. Chen, A. Sadovnik, and A. C. Gallagher. A mixed bag of emotions: Model, predict, and transfer emotion distributions. In *Proceedings of the IEEE Conference on Computer Vision and Pattern Recognition*, pages 860–868, 2015.

[15] R. Plutchik. *The emotions*. University Press of America, 1991.

[16] A. Razavian, H. Azizpour, J. Sullivan, and S. Carlsson. Cnn features off-the-shelf: an astounding baseline for recognition. In *Proceedings of the IEEE Conference on Computer Vision and Pattern Recognition Workshops*, pages 806–813, 2014.

[17] S. Rendle, C. Freudenthaler, Z. Gantner, and L. Schmidt-Thieme. Bpr: Bayesian personalized ranking from implicit feedback. In *Proceedings of the twenty-fifth conference on uncertainty in artificial intelligence*, pages 452–461. AUAI Press, 2009.

[18] R. Ronen, N. Koenigstein, E. Ziklik, and N. Nice. Selecting content-based features for collaborative filtering recommenders. In *Proceedings of the 7th ACM conference on Recommender systems*, pages 407–410. ACM, 2013.

[19] M. Sakaki, K. Niki, and M. Mather. Beyond arousal and valence: The importance of the biological versus social relevance of emotional stimuli. *Cognitive, Affective, & Behavioral Neuroscience*, 12(1):115–139, 2012.

[20] K. R. Scherer. What are emotions? and how can they be measured? *Social science information*, 44(4):695–729, 2005.

[21] Y. Shi, A. Karatzoglou, L. Baltrunas, M. Larson, N. Oliver, and A. Hanjalic. Climf: learning to maximize reciprocal rank with collaborative less-is-more filtering. In *Proceedings of the sixth ACM conference on Recommender systems*, pages 139–146. ACM, 2012.

[22] Y. Shi, M. Larson, and A. Hanjalic. Collaborative filtering beyond the user-item matrix: A survey of the state of the art and future challenges. *ACM Computing Surveys (CSUR)*, 47(1):3, 2014.

[23] M. Soleymani, M. Larson, T. Pun, and A. Hanjalic. Corpus development for affective video indexing. *Multimedia, IEEE Transactions on*, 16(4):1075–1089, 2014.

[24] M. Soleymani, M. Pantic, and T. Pun. Multimodal emotion recognition in response to videos. *Affective Computing, IEEE Transactions on*, 3(2):211–223, 2012.

[25] C. Wang and D. M. Blei. Collaborative topic modeling for recommending scientific articles. In *Proceedings of the 17th ACM SIGKDD International Conference on Knowledge Discovery and Data Mining*, KDD '11, pages 448–456, New York, NY, USA, 2011. ACM.

[26] H. Wang, N. Wang, and D. Yeung. Collaborative deep learning for recommender systems. *CoRR*, abs/1409.2944, 2014.

[27] S. Wang and Q. Ji. Video affective content analysis: a survey of state-of-the-art methods. *IEEE Transactions on Affective Computing*, 6(4):410–430, 2015.

[28] B. Zhou, A. Lapedriza, J. Xiao, A. Torralba, and A. Oliva. Learning deep features for scene recognition using places database. In *Advances in neural information processing systems*, pages 487–495, 2014.

Ask the GRU: Multi-task Learning for Deep Text Recommendations

Trapit Bansal
tbansal@cs.umass.edu

David Belanger
belanger@cs.umass.edu

Andrew McCallum
mccallum@cs.umass.edu

College of Information and Computer Sciences, University of Massachusetts Amherst

ABSTRACT

In a variety of application domains the content to be recommended to users is associated with text. This includes research papers, movies with associated plot summaries, news articles, blog posts, etc. Recommendation approaches based on latent factor models can be extended naturally to leverage text by employing an explicit mapping from text to factors. This enables recommendations for new, unseen content, and may generalize better, since the factors for all items are produced by a compactly-parametrized model. Previous work has used topic models or averages of word embeddings for this mapping. In this paper we present a method leveraging deep recurrent neural networks to encode the text sequence into a latent vector, specifically gated recurrent units (GRUs) trained end-to-end on the collaborative filtering task. For the task of scientific paper recommendation, this yields models with significantly higher accuracy. In cold-start scenarios, we beat the previous state-of-the-art, all of which ignore word order. Performance is further improved by multi-task learning, where the text encoder network is trained for a combination of content recommendation and item metadata prediction. This regularizes the collaborative filtering model, ameliorating the problem of sparsity of the observed rating matrix.

Keywords

Recommender Systems; Deep Learning; Neural Networks; Cold Start; Multi-task Learning

1. INTRODUCTION

Text recommendation is an important problem that has the potential to drive significant profits for e-businesses through increased user engagement. Examples of text recommendations include recommending blogs, social media posts [1], news articles [2, 3], movies (based on plot summaries), products (based on reviews) [4] and research papers [5].

Methods for recommending text items can be broadly classified into collaborative filtering (CF), content-based, and hybrid methods. Collaborative filtering [6] methods use the user-item rating matrix to construct user and item profiles from past ratings. Classical examples of this include matrix factorization methods [6, 7] which completely ignore text information and rely solely on the rating matrix. Such methods suffer from the *cold-start* problem – how to rank unseen or unrated items – which is ubiquitous in most domains. Content-based methods [8, 9], on the other hand, use the item text or attributes, and make recommendations based on similarity between such attributes, ignoring data from other users. Such methods can make recommendations for new items but are limited in their performance since they cannot employ similarity between user preferences [5, 10, 11]. Hybrid recommendation systems seek the best of both worlds, by leveraging both item content and user-item ratings [5, 10, 12, 13, 14]. Hybrid recommendation methods that consume item text for recommendation often ignore word order [5, 13, 14, 15], and either use bags-of-words as features for a linear model [14, 16] or define an unsupervised learning objective on the text such as a topic model [5, 15]. Such methods are unable to fully leverage the text content, being limited to bag-of-words sufficient statistics [17], and furthermore unsupervised learning is unlikely to focus on the aspects of text relevant for content recommendation.

In this paper we present a method leveraging *recurrent neural networks* (RNNs) [18] to represent text items for collaborative filtering. In recent years, RNNs have provided substantial performance gains in a variety of natural language processing applications such as language modeling [19] and machine translation [20]. RNNs have a number of noteworthy characteristics: (1) they are sensitive to word order, (2) they do not require hand-engineered features, (3) it is easy to leverage large unlabeled datasets, by pretraining the RNN parameters with unsupervised language modeling objectives [47], (4) RNN computation can be parallelized on a GPU, and (5) the RNN applies naturally in the cold-start scenario, as a feature extractor, whenever we have text associated with new items.

Due to the extreme data sparsity of content recommendation datasets [21], regularization is also an important consideration. This is particularly important for deep models such as RNNs, since these high-capacity models are prone to overfitting. Existing hybrid methods have used unsupervised learning objectives on text content to regularize the parameters of the recommendation model [4, 22, 23]. However, since we consume the text directly as an input for prediction, we can not use this approach. Instead, we provide regularization by performing multi-task learning com-

RecSys '16, September 15 - 19, 2016, Boston , MA, USA

ISBN 978-1-4503-4035-9/16/09...$15.00

DOI: http://dx.doi.org/10.1145/2959100.2959180

bining collaborative filtering with a simple side task: predicting item meta-data such as genres or item tags. Here, the network producing vector representations for items directly from their text content is shared for both tag prediction and recommendation tasks. This allows us to make predictions in cold-start conditions, while providing regularization for the recommendation model.

We evaluate our recurrent neural network approach on the task of scientific paper recommendation using two publicly available datasets, where items are associated with text abstracts [5, 13]. We find that the RNN-based models yield up to **34%** relative-improvement in Recall@50 for cold-start recommendation over collaborative topic regression (CTR) approach of Wang and Blei [5] and a word-embedding based model model [24], while giving competitive performance for warm-start recommendation. We also note that a simple linear model that represents documents using an average of word embeddings trained in a completely supervised fashion [24], obtains competitive results to CTR. Finally, we find that multi-task learning improves the performance of all of the models significantly, including the baselines.

2. BACKGROUND AND RELATED WORK

2.1 Problem Formulation and Notation

This paper focuses on the task of recommending items associated with text content. The j-th text item is a *sequence* of n_j word tokens, $X_j = (w_1, w_2, \ldots, w_{n_j})$ where each token is one of V words from a vocabulary. Additionally, the text items may be associated with multiple *tags* (user or author provided). If item $j \in [N_d]$ has tag $l \in [N_t]$ then we denote it by $t_{jl} = 1$ and 0 otherwise.

There are N_u users who have liked/rated/saved some of the text items. The rating provided by user i on item j is denoted by r_{ij}. We consider the implicit feedback [25, 26] setting, where we only observe whether a person has viewed or liked an item and do not observe explicit ratings. $r_{ij} = 1$ if user i liked item j and 0 otherwise. Denote the user-item matrix of likes by R. Let R_i^+ denote the set of all items liked by user i and R_i^- denote the remaining items.

The recommendation problem is to find for each user i a personalized ranking of all unrated items, $j \in R_i^-$, given the text of the items $\{X_j\}$, the matrix of users' previous likes $\{R_i\}$ and the tagging information of the items $\{t_{il}\}$.

The methods we consider will often represent users, items, tags and words by K-dimensional vectors $\tilde{u}_i$, $\tilde{v}_j$, $\tilde{t}_l$ and $\tilde{e}_w \in \mathbb{R}^K$, respectively. We will refer to such vectors as *embeddings*. All vectors are treated as column vectors. $\sigma(.)$ will denote the sigmoid function, $\sigma(x) = \frac{1}{1+e^{-x}}$.

2.2 Latent Factor Models

Latent factor models [6] for content recommendation learn K dimensional vector embeddings of items and users:

$$\hat{r}_{ij} = b_i + b_j + \tilde{u}_i^T \tilde{v}_j, \tag{1}$$

b_i, b_j are user and item specific biases, and $\tilde{u}_i$ is the vector embedding for user i and $\tilde{v}_j$ is the embedding of item j.

A simple method for learning the model parameters, $\boldsymbol{\theta} = \{b_i, b_j, \tilde{u}, \tilde{v}\}$, is to specify a cost function and perform stochastic gradient descent. For implicit feedback, an unobserved rating might indicate that either the user does not like the item or the user has never seen the item. In such cases, it is common to use a *weighted* regularized squared loss [5, 25]:

$$C_R(\boldsymbol{\theta}) = \frac{1}{|R|} \sum_{(i,j)\in R} c_{ij} (\hat{r}_{ij} - r_{ij})^2 + \Omega(\boldsymbol{\theta}) \tag{2}$$

Often, one uses $c_{ui} = a$ for observed items and $c_{ui} = b$ for unobserved items, with $b \ll a$ [5, 13], signifying the uncertainity in the unobserved ratings. $\Omega(\boldsymbol{\theta})$ is a regularization on the parameters, for example in PMF [7] the embeddings are assigned Gaussian priors, which leads to a ℓ_2 regularization. Some implicit feedback recommendation systems use a ranking-based loss instead [24, 26]. The methods we propose can be trained with any differentiable cost function. We will use a weighted squared loss in our experiments to be consistent with the baselines [5].

2.3 The Cold Start Problem

In many applications, the factorization (1) is unusable, since it suffers from the *cold-start* problem [11, 14]: new or unseen items can not be recommended to users because we do not have an associated embedding. This has lead to increased interest in hybrid CF methods which can leverage additional information, such as item content, to make cold-start recommendations. In some cases, we may also face a cold-start problem for new users. Though we do not consider this case, the techniques of this paper can be extended naturally to accommodate it whenever we have text content associated with users. We consider:

$$\hat{r}_{ij} = b_i + b_j + \tilde{u}_i^T f(X_j), \tag{3}$$

Where $f(\cdot)$ is a vector-valued function of the item's text. For differentiable $f(\cdot)$, (3) can also be trained using (2). Throughout the paper, we will refer to $f(\cdot)$ as an *encoder*. Existing hybrid CF methods [11, 16, 27, 28] which use item metadata take this form. In such cases, $f(.)$ is a linear function of manually extracted item features. For example, Agarwal and Chen [16], Gantner et al. [29] incorporate side information through a linear regression based formulation on metadata like category, user's age, location, etc. Rendle [28] proposed a more general framework for incorporating higher order interactions among features in a factor model. Refer to Shi et al. [27], and the references therein, for a recent review on such hybrid CF methods.

Our experiments compare to collaborative topic regression (CTR) [5], a state-of-the-art technique that simultaneously factorizes the item-word count matrix (through probabilistic topic modeling) and the user-item rating matrix (through a latent factor model). By learning low-dimensional (topical) representations of items, CTR is able to provide recommendations to unseen items.

2.4 Regularization via Multi-task Learning

Typical CF datasets are highly sparse, and thus it is important to leverage all available training signals [21]. In many applications, it is useful to perform multi-task learning [30] that combines CF and auxiliary tasks, where a shared feature representation for items (or users) is used for all tasks. Collective matrix factorization [31] jointly factorizes multiple observation matrices with shared entities for relational learning. Ma et al. [32] seek to predict side information associated with users. Finally, McAuley and Leskovec [4] used topic models and Almahairi et al. [23] used language models on review text.

In many applications, text items are associated with tags, including research papers with keywords, news articles with user or editor provided labels, social media posts with hashtags, movies with genres, etc. These can be used as features X_j in (3) [16, 28]. However, there are considerable drawbacks to this approach. First, tags are often assigned by users, which may lead to a cold-start problem [33], since new items have no annotation. Moreover, tags can be noisy, especially if they are user-assigned, or too general [3].

While tag annotation may be unreliable and incomplete as input features, encouraging items' representations to be predictive of these tags can yield useful regularization for the CF problem. Besides providing regularization, this multi-task learning approach is especially useful in cold-start scenarios, since the tags are only used at train time and hence need not be available at test time. In Section 3.3 we employ this approach.

2.5 Deep Learning

In our work, we represent the item-to-embedding mapping $f(\cdot)$ using a deep neural network. See [34] for a comprehensive overview of deep learning methods. We provide here a brief review of deep learning for recommendation systems.

Neural networks have received limited attention from the recommendation systems community. [35] used restricted Boltzmann machines as one of the component models to tackle the Netflix challenge. Recently, [36, 37] proposed denoising auto-encoder based models for collaborative filtering which are trained to denoise corrupted versions of entire sparse vectors of user-item likes or item-user likes (i.e. rows or columns of the R matrix). However, these models are unable to handle the cold-start problem. Wang et al. [13] addresses this by incorporating a bag-of-words autoencoder in the model within a Bayesian framework. Elkahky et al. [38] proposed to use neural networks on manually extracted user and item feature representations for content based multi-domain recommendation. Dziugaite and Roy [39] proposed to use a neural network to learn the similarity function between user and item latent factors. Van den Oord et al. [40], Wang and Wang [41] developed music recommender systems which use features extracted from the music audio using convolutional neural networks (CNN) or deep belief networks. However, these methods process the user-item rating matrix in isolation from the content information and thus are unable to exploit the direct interaction between item content and ratings [13]. Weston et al. [42] proposed a CNN based model to predict hashtags on social media posts and found the learned representations to also be useful for document recommendation. Recently, He and McAuley [43] used image-features from a separately trained CNN to improve product recommendation and tackle cold-start. Almahairi et al. [23] used neural network based language models [19, 44] on review text to regularize the latent factors for product recommendation, as opposed to using topic models, as in McAuley and Leskovec [4]. They found that RNN based language models perform poorly as regularizers and word embedding models Mikolov et al. [44] perform better.

3. DEEP TEXT REPRESENTATION FOR COLLABORATIVE FILTERING

This section presents neural network-based encoders for explicitly mapping an item's text content to a vector of latent factors. This allows us to perform cold-start prediction on new items. In addition, since the vector representations for items are tied together by a shared parametric model, we may be able to generalize better from limited data.

As is standard in deep learning approaches to NLP, our encoders first map input text $X_j = (w_1, w_2, \ldots, w_{n_j})$ to a sequence of K_w-dimensional embeddings [44], $(e_1, e_2, \ldots, e_{n_j})$, using a lookup table with one vector for every word in our vocabulary. Then, we define a transformation that collapses the sequence of embeddings to a single vector, $g(X_j)$.

In all of our models, we maintain a separate item-specific embedding $\tilde{v}_j$, which helps capture user behavior that cannot be modeled by content alone [5]. Thus, we set the final document representation as:

$$f(X_j) = g(X_j) + \tilde{v}_j \tag{4}$$

For cold-start prediction, there is no training data to estimate the item-specific embedding and we set $\tilde{v}_j = 0$ [5, 13].

3.1 Order-Insensitive Encoders

A simple order-insensitive encoder of the document text can be obtained by averaging word embeddings:

$$g(X_j) = \frac{1}{|X_j|} \sum_{w \in X_j} e_w. \tag{5}$$

This corresponds exactly to a linear model on a bag-of-words representation for the document. However, using the representation (5) is useful because the word embeddings can be pre-trained, in an unsupervised manner, on a large corpus [45]. Note that (5) is similar to the embedding-based model used in Weston et al. [42] for hastag prediction.

Note that CTR [5], described in 2.3, also operates on bag-of-words sufficient statistics. Here, it does not have an explicit parametric encoder $g(\cdot)$ from text to a vector, but instead defines an implicit mapping via the process of doing posterior inference in the probabilistic topic model.

3.2 Order-Sensitive Encoders

Bag-of-words models are limited in their capacity, as they cannot distinguish between sentences that have similar unigram statistics but completely different meanings [17]. As a toy example, consider the research paper abstracts: "This paper is about deep learning, not LDA" and "This paper is about LDA, not deep learning". They have the same unigram statistics but would be of interest to different sets of users. A more powerful model that can exploit the additional information inherent in word order would be expected to recognize this and thus perform better recommendation.

In response, we parametrize $g(\cdot)$ as a recurrent neural network (RNN). It reads the text one word at a time and produces a single vector representation. RNNs can provide impressive compression of the salient properties of text. For example, accurate translation of an English sentence can be performed by conditioning on a single vector encoding [46].

The extracted item representation is combined with a user embedding, as in (3), to get the predicted rating for a user-item pair. The model can then be trained for recommendation in a completely supervised manner, using a differentiable cost function such as (2). Note that a key difference between this approach and the existing approaches which use item content [5, 13], apart from sensitivity to word order, is that we do not define an unsupervised objective (like likelihood of observing bag-of-words under a topic model)

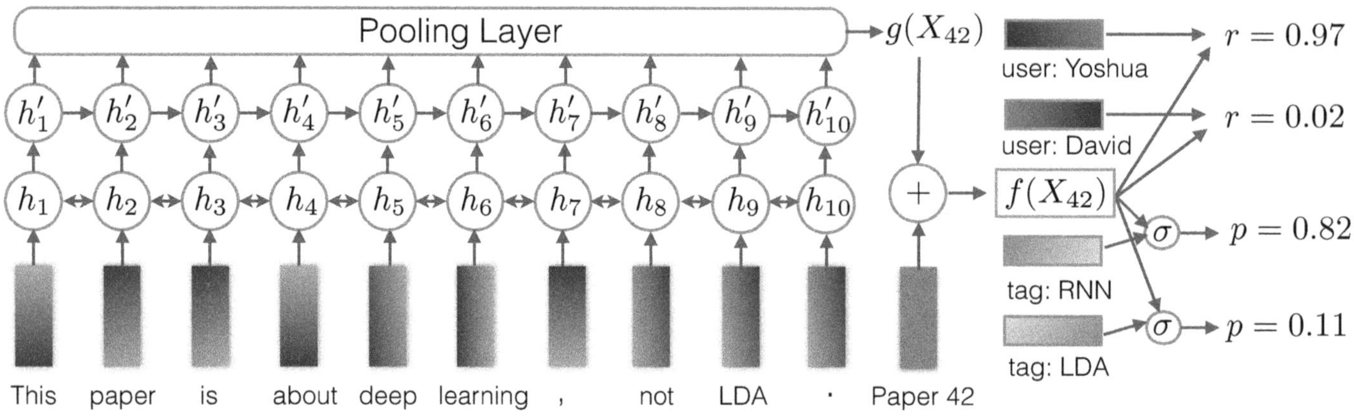

Figure 1: Proposed architecture for text item recommendation. Rectangular boxes represent embeddings. Two layers of RNN with GRU are used, where the first layer is a bi-directional RNN. The output of all the hidden units at the second layer is pooled to produce a text encoding which is combined with an item-specific embedding to produce the final representation $f(X)$. Users and tags are also represented by embeddings, which are combined with the item representation to do tag predection and recommendation.

for extracting a text representation. However, our model can benefit from unsupervised data through pre-training of word embeddings [44] or pre-training of RNN parameters using language models [47] (our experiments use embeddings).

3.2.1 Gated Recurrent Units (GRUs)

Traditional RNN architectures suffer from the problem of vanishing and exploding gradients [48], rendering optimization difficult and prohibiting them from learning long-term dependencies. There have been several modifications to the RNN proposed to remedy this problem, of which the most popular are *long short-term memory units* (LSTMs) [49] and the more recent *gated recurrent units* (GRUs) [20]. We use GRUs, which are simpler than LSTM, have fewer parameters, and give competitive performance to LSTMs [50, 51].

The GRU hidden vector output at step t, h_t, for the input sequence $X_j = (w_1, \dots, w_t, \dots, w_{n_j})$ is given by:

$$\begin{bmatrix} f_t \\ o_t \end{bmatrix} = \sigma\left(\theta^1 \begin{bmatrix} \tilde{e}_{w_t} \\ h_{t-1} \end{bmatrix} + b\right) \tag{6}$$

$$c_t = \tanh(\theta^2_w \tilde{e}_{w_t} + f_t \odot \theta^2_h h_{t-1} + b_c) \tag{7}$$

$$h_t = (1 - o_t) \odot h_{t-1} + o_t \odot c_t \tag{8}$$

where $\theta^1 \in \mathbb{R}^{2K_h \times (K_w + K_h)}, \theta^2_w \in \mathbb{R}^{K_h \times K_w}, \theta^2_h \in \mathbb{R}^{K_h \times K_h}$ and $b, b_c \in \mathbb{R}^{K_h}$ are parameters of the GRU with K_w the dimension of input word embeddings and K_h the number of hidden units in the RNN. $\odot$ denotes element-wise product. Intuitively, f_t (6) acts as a 'forget' (or 'reset') gate that decides what parts of the previous hidden state to consider or ignore at the current step, c_t (7) computes a candidate state for the current time step using the parts of the previous hidden state as dictated by f_t, and o_t (6) acts as the output (or update) gate which decides what parts of the previous memory to change to the new candidate memory (8). All forget and update operations are differentiable to allow learning through backpropagation.

The final architecture, shown in Figure 1, consists of two stacked layers of RNN with GRU hidden units. We use a bi-directional RNN [52] at the first layer and feed the concatenation of the forward and backward hidden states as the input to the second layer. The output of the hidden states of the second layer is pooled to obtain the item content representation $g(X_j)$. In our experiments, mean pooling performs best. Models that use the final RNN state take much longer to optimize. Following (4), the final item representation is obtained by combining the RNN representation with an item-specific embedding v_j.

3.3 Multi-Task Learning

The encoder $f(\cdot)$ can be used as a generic feature extractor for items. Therefore, we can employ the multi-task learning approach of Section 2.4. The tags associated with papers can be considered as a (coarse) summary or topics of the items and thus forcing the encoder to be predictive of the tags will provide a useful inductive bias. Consider again the toy example of Figure 1. Observing the tag "RNN" but not "LDA" on the paper, even though the term LDA is present in the text, will force the network to pay attention to the sequence of words "not LDA" in order to explain the tags.

We define the probability of observing tag l on item j as: $P(t_{jl} = 1) = p_{jl} = \sigma(f(X_j)^T \tilde{t}_l)$, where $\tilde{t}_l$ is an embedding for tag l. The cost for predicting the tags is taken as the sum of the weighted binary log likelihood of each tag:

$$C_T(\boldsymbol{\theta}) = \frac{1}{|T|} \sum_j \sum_l \{t_{jl} \log p_{jl} + c'_{jl}(1 - t_{jl}) \log(1 - p_{jl})\}$$

where c'_{jl} down-weights the cost for predicting the unobserved tags. The final cost is $C(\boldsymbol{\theta}) = \lambda C_R(\boldsymbol{\theta}) + (1 - \lambda) C_T(\boldsymbol{\theta})$ with C_R defined in (2), and λ is a hyperparameter.

It is worth noting the differences between our approach and Almahairi et al. [23], who use language modeling on the text as an unsupervised multi-task objective with the item latent factors as the shared parameters. Almahairi et al. [23] found that the increased flexibility offered by the RNN makes it too strong a regularizer leading to worse performance than simpler bag-of-words models. In contrast, our RNN is trained fully supervised, which forces the item representations to be discriminative for recommendation and tag prediction. Furthermore, by using the text as an input to $g(\cdot)$ at test time, rather than just for train-time regularization, we can alleviate the cold-start problem.

4. EXPERIMENTS

4.1 Experimental Setup

Datasets: We use two datasets made available by Wang et al. [13] from CiteULike[1]. CiteULike is an online platform which allows registered users to create personal libraries by saving papers which are of interest to them. The datasets consist of the papers in the users' libraries (which are treated as 'likes'), user provided tags on the papers, and the title and abstract of the papers. Similar to Wang and Blei [5], we remove users with less than 5 ratings (since they cannot be evaluated properly) and removed tags that occur on less than 10 articles. *Citeulike-a* [5] consists of 5551 users, 16980 papers and 3629 tags with a total of 204,987 user-item likes. *Citeulike-t* [5] consists of 5219 users, 25975 papers and 4222 tags with a total of 134,860 user-item likes. Note *Citeulike-t* is much more sparse (99.90%) than *Citeulike-a* (99.78%).

Evaluation Methodology: Following, Wang and Blei [5], we test the models on held-out user-article likes under both warm-start and cold-start scenarios.

Warm-Start: This is the case of in-matrix prediction, where every test item had at least one like in the training data. For each user we do a 5-fold split of papers from their like history. Papers with less than 5 likes are always kept in the training data, since they cannot be evaluated properly. After learning, we predict ratings across all active test set items and for each user filter out the items in their training set from the ranked list.

Cold-Start: This is the task of predicting user interest in a new paper with no existing likes, based on the text content of the paper. The set of all papers is split into 5 folds. Again, papers with less than 5 likes are always kept in training set. For each fold, we remove all likes on the papers in that fold forming the test-set and keep the other folds as training-set. We fit the models on the training set items for each fold and form predictive per-user ranking of items in the test set.

Evaluation Metric: Accuracy of recommendation from implicit feedback is often measured by recall. Precision is not reasonable since the zero ratings may mean that a user either does not like the article or does not know of it. Thus, we use Recall@M [5] and average the per-user metric:

$$\text{Recall@}M = \frac{\text{number of articles user liked in top } M}{\text{total number of articles user liked}}$$

4.1.1 Methods

We compare the proposed methods with *CTR*, which models item content using topic modeling. The approach put forth by CTR [5] cannot perform tag-prediction and thus, for a fair comparison, we modify CTR to do tag prediction. This can be viewed as a probabilistic version of collective matrix factorization [31]. Deriving an alternating least squares inference algorithm along the line of [5] is not possible for a sigmoid loss. Thus, for CTR, we formulate tag prediction using a weighted squared loss instead. Learning this model is a straightforward extension of CTR: rather than performing alternating updates on two blocks of parameters, we rotate among three. We call this *CTR-MTL*. The word embedding-based model with order-insensitive document encoder (section 3.1) is *Embed*, and the RNN-based model (section 3.2) is *GRU*. The corresponding models trained with multi-task learning are *Embed-MTL* and *GRU-MTL*.

[1]http://www.citeulike.org/

4.1.2 Implementation Details

For CTR, we follow Wang and Blei [5] for setting hyper-parameters. We use latent factor dimension $K = 200$, regularization parameters $\lambda_u = 0.01$, $\lambda_v = 100$ and cost weights $a = 1$, $b = 0.01$. The same parameters gave good results for CTR-MTL. CTR and CTR-MTL are trained using the EM algorithm, which updates the latent factors using alternating least squares on full data [5, 25]. CTR is sensitive to good pre-processing of the text, which is common in topic modeling [5]. We use the provided pre-processed text for CTR, which was obtained by removing stop-words and choosing top words based on tf-idf. We initialized CTR with the output of a topic model trained only on the text. We used the CTR code provided by the authors.

For the *Embed* and *GRU* models, we used word embeddings of dimension $K_w = K = 200$, in order to be consistent with CTR. For *GRU* models, the first layer of the RNN has hidden state dimension $K_{h1} = 400$ and the second layer (the output layer) has hidden state dimension $K_{h2} = 200$. We pre-trained the word embeddings using CBOW [44] on a corpus of 440,756 ACM abstracts (including the Citeulike abstracts). Dropout is used at every layer of the network. The probabilities of dropping a dimension are 0.1, 0.5 and 0.3 at the embedding layer, the output of the first layer and the output of the second layer, respectively. We also regularize the user embeddings with weight 0.01. We do very mild preprocessing of the text. We replace numbers with a <NUM> token and all words which have a total frequency of less than 5 by <UNK>. Note that we don't remove stop words or frequent words. This leaves a vocabulary of 21,129 words for *Citeulike-a* and 24,697 words for *Citeulike-t*.

The models are optimized via stochastic gradient descent, where mini-batch randomly samples a subset of B users and for each user we sample one positive and one negative example. We set the weights c_{ij} in (2) to $c_{ij} = 1 + \alpha \log(1 + \frac{|R_i|}{\epsilon})$, where $|R_i|$ is the number of items liked by user i, with $\alpha = 10$, $\epsilon = 1e - 8$. Unlike Wang and Blei [5] we do not weight the cost function differently for positive and negative samples. Since the total number of negative examples is much larger than the positive examples for each user, stochastically sampling only one negative per positive example implicitly down-weights the negatives. We used a mini-batch size of $B = 512$ users and used Adam [54] for optimization. We run the models for a maximum of 20k mini-batch updates and use early-stopping based on recall on a validation set from the training examples.

4.2 Quantitative Results

Table 1 summarizes Recall@50 for all the models, on the two CiteULike datasets, for both warm-start and cold-start. Figure 3, further shows the variation of Recall@M for different values of M for the multi-task learning models.

Cold-Start: Recall that for cold-start recommendation, the item-specific embeddings $\tilde{v}_j$ in (4) are identically equal to zero, and thus the items' representations depend solely on their text content. We first note the performance of the models without multi-task learning. The GRU model is better than the best score of either the CTR model or the Embed model by **18.36%** (relative improvement) on CiteUlike-a and by **32.74%** on CiteULike-t. This significant gain demonstrates that the GRU model is much better at representing the content of the items. Improvements are higher on the CitULike-t dataset because it is much more

Table 1: % Recall@50 for all the methods (higher is better).

	Citeulike-a			Citeulike-t		
	Warm Start	Cold Start	Tag Prediction	Warm Start	Cold Start	Tag Prediction
GRU-MTL	**38.33**	**49.76**	**60.52**	45.60	**51.22**	**62.32**
GRU	36.87	46.16	—	42.59	47.59	—
CTR-MTL	35.51	39.87	48.95	**46.82**	34.98	46.66
CTR	31.10	39.00	—	40.44	33.74	—
Embed-MTL	36.64	41.71	60.36	43.02	38.16	62.29
Embed	33.95	38.53	—	37.98	35.85	—

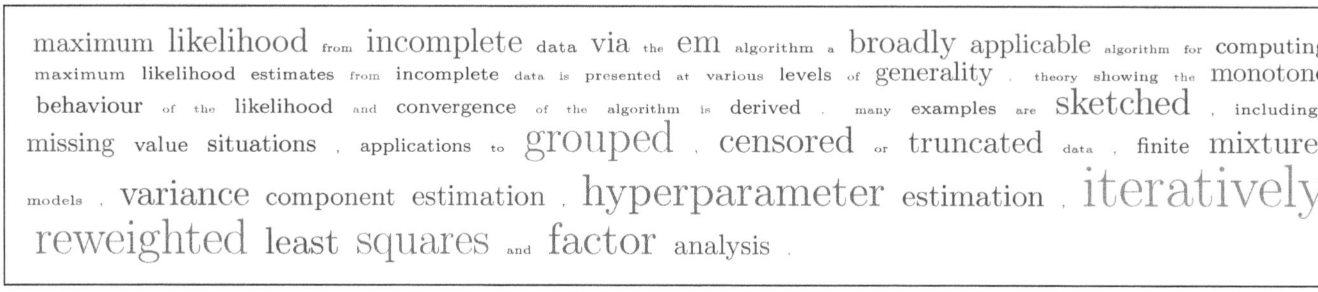

Figure 2: Saliency of each word in the abstract of the EM paper [53]. Size and color of the words indicate their leverage on the final rating. The model learns that chunks of word phrases are important, such as "maximum likelihood" and "iteratively reweighted least squares", and ignores punctutations and stop words.

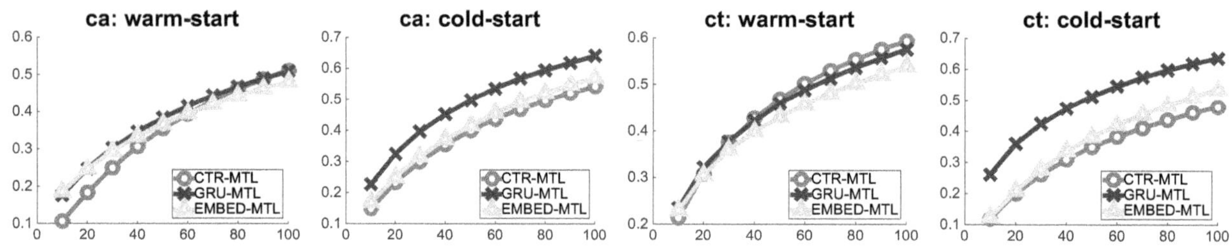

Figure 3: Recall@M for the models trained with multi-task learning. x-axis is the value of $M \in [100]$

sparse, and so models which can utilize content appropriately give better recommendations. CTR and Embed models perform competitively with each other.

Next, observe that multi-task learning uniformly improves performance for all models. The GRU model's recall improves by 7.8% on Citulike-a and by 7.6% on Citeulike-t. This leads to an overall improvement of **19.30%** on Citeulike-a and **34.22%** on Citeulike-t, over best of the baselines. Comparatively, improvement for CTR is smaller. This is expected since the Bayesian topic model provides strong regularization for the model parameters. Contrary to this, Embed models also benefits a lot by MTL (up to 8.2%). This is expected since unlike CTR, all the $K_w \times V$ parameters in the Embed model are free parameters which are trained directly for recommendation, and thus MTL provides necessary regularization.

Warm-Start: Collaborative filtering methods based on matrix factorization [6] often perform as well as hybrid methods in the warm-start scenario, due to the flexibility of the item-specific embeddings $\tilde{v}_j$ in (4) [5, 41]. Consider again the models trained without MTL. GRU model performs better than either the CTR or the Embed model, with relative improvement of **8.5%** on CiteULike-a and **5.3%** on CiteULike-t, over the best of the two models. Multi-task learning again improves performance for all the models. Improvements are particularly significant for CTR-MTL over CTR (up to 15.8%). Since the tags associated with test items were observed during training, they provide a strong inductive bias leading to improved performance. Interestingly, the GRU-MTL model performs slightly better than the CTR-MTL model on one dataset and slightly worse on the other. The first and third plots in Figure 3 demonstrate that the GRU-MTL performs slightly better than the CTR-MTL for smaller M, i.e. more relevant articles are ranked toward the top. To quantify this, we evaluate average reciprocal Hit-Rank@10 [3]. Given a list of M ranked articles for user i , let $c_1, c_2, \ldots, c_h$ denote the ranks of h articles in $[M]$ which the user actually liked. HR is then defined as $\sum_{t=1}^{h} \frac{1}{c_t}$ and tests whether top ranked articles are correct. GRU-MTL gives HR@10 of **0.098** and CTR-MTL gives HR@10 to be 0.077, which confirms that the top of the list for GRU-MTL contains more relevant recommendations.

Tag Prediction: Although the focus of the models is recommendation, we evaluate the performance of the multi-task models on tag prediction. We again use Recall@50 (defined per article) and evaluate in the cold-start scenario, where

there are no tags present for the test article. The GRU and Embed models perform similarly. CTR-MTL is significantly worse, which could be due to our use of the squared loss for training or because hyperparameters were selected for recommendation performance, not tag prediction.

4.3 Interpreting Prediction Decisions

We employ a simple, easy-to-implement tool for analyzing RNN predictions, based on Denil et al. [55] and Li et al. [56]. We produce a heatmap where every input word is associated with its leverage on the output prediction. Suppose that we recommended item j to user i. In other words, suppose that $\hat{r}_{ij}$ is large. Let $E_j = (e_{j,1}, e_{j,2}, \ldots, e_{j,n_j})$ be the sequence of word embeddings for item j. Since $f(\cdot)$ is encoded as a neural network, $\frac{d\hat{r}_{ij}}{de_{j,t}}$ can be obtained by backpropagation. To produce the heatmap's value for word t, we convert $\frac{d\hat{r}_{ij}}{de_{j,t}}$ into a scalar. This is not possible by backpropagation, as $\frac{d\hat{r}_{ij}}{dx_{j,t}}$ is not well-defined, since $x_{j,t}$ is a discrete index. Instead we compute $\|\frac{d\hat{r}_{ij}}{de_{j,t}}\|$. An application is in Figure 2.

5. CONCLUSION & FUTURE WORK

We employ deep recurrent neural networks to provide vector representations for the text content associated with items in collaborative filtering. This generic text-to-vector mapping is useful because it can be trained directly with gradient descent and provides opportunities to perform multi-task learning. For scientific paper recommendation, the RNN and multi-task learning both provide complementary performance improvements. We encourage further use of the technique in a variety of application domains. In future work, we would like to apply deep architectures to users' data and to explore additional objectives for multi-task learning that employ multiple modalities of inputs, such as movies' images and text descriptions.

6. ACKNOWLEDGMENT

This work was supported in part by the Center for Intelligent Information Retrieval, in part by The Allen Institute for Artificial Intelligence, in part by NSF grant #CNS-0958392, in part by the National Science Foundation (NSF) grant number DMR-1534431, and in part by DARPA under agreement number FA8750-13-2-0020. The U.S. Government is authorized to reproduce and distribute reprints for Governmental purposes notwithstanding any copyright notation thereon. Any opinions, findings and conclusions or recommendations expressed in this material are those of the authors and do not necessarily reflect those of the sponsor.

References

[1] Ido Guy, Naama Zwerdling, Inbal Ronen, David Carmel, and Erel Uziel. Social media recommendation based on people and tags. In *SIGIR*, 2010.

[2] Owen Phelan, Kevin McCarthy, and Barry Smyth. Using twitter to recommend real-time topical news. In *RecSys*, 2009.

[3] Trapit Bansal, Mrinal Das, and Chiranjib Bhattacharyya. Content driven user profiling for comment-worthy recommendations of news and blog articles. In *RecSys*, 2015.

[4] Julian McAuley and Jure Leskovec. Hidden factors and hidden topics: understanding rating dimensions with review text. In *RecSys*, 2013.

[5] Chong Wang and David M Blei. Collaborative topic modeling for recommending scientific articles. In *SIGKDD*, 2011.

[6] Yehuda Koren, Robert Bell, and Chris Volinsky. Matrix factorization techniques for recommender systems. *Computer*, (8):30–37, 2009.

[7] Andriy Mnih and Ruslan Salakhutdinov. Probabilistic matrix factorization. In *NIPS*, 2007.

[8] Marko Balabanović and Yoav Shoham. Fab: content-based, collaborative recommendation. *Communications of the ACM*, 40(3):66–72, 1997.

[9] Raymond J Mooney and Loriene Roy. Content-based book recommending using learning for text categorization. In *ACM conference on Digital libraries*, 2000.

[10] Chumki Basu, Haym Hirsh, William Cohen, et al. Recommendation as classification: Using social and content-based information in recommendation. In *AAAI*, 1998.

[11] Andrew I Schein, Alexandrin Popescul, Lyle H Ungar, and David M Pennock. Methods and metrics for cold-start recommendations. In *SIGIR*, 2002.

[12] Justin Basilico and Thomas Hofmann. Unifying collaborative and content-based filtering. In *ICML*, 2004.

[13] Hao Wang, Naiyan Wang, and Dit-Yan Yeung. Collaborative deep learning for recommender systems. In *SIGKDD*, 2015.

[14] Prem Melville, Raymond J Mooney, and Ramadass Nagarajan. Content-boosted collaborative filtering for improved recommendations. In *AAAI*, 2002.

[15] Prem K Gopalan, Laurent Charlin, and David Blei. Content-based recommendations with poisson factorization. In *NIPS*, 2014.

[16] Deepak Agarwal and Bee-Chung Chen. Regression-based latent factor models. In *SIGKDD*, 2009.

[17] Hanna M Wallach. Topic modeling: beyond bag-of-words. In *ICML*, 2006.

[18] Paul J Werbos. Backpropagation through time: what it does and how to do it. *Proceedings of the IEEE*, 78 (10):1550–1560, 1990.

[19] Tomas Mikolov, Martin Karafiát, Lukas Burget, Jan Cernockỳ, and Sanjeev Khudanpur. Recurrent neural network based language model. *INTERSPEECH*, 2010.

[20] Kyunghyun Cho, Bart van Merrienboer, Caglar Gulcehre, Fethi Bougares, Holger Schwenk, and Yoshua Bengio. Learning phrase representations using rnn encoder-decoder for statistical machine translation. In *EMNLP*, 2014.

[21] Robert M Bell and Yehuda Koren. Lessons from the netflix prize challenge. *SIGKDD Explorations Newsletter*, 9(2):75–79, 2007.

[22] Guang Ling, Michael R Lyu, and Irwin King. Ratings meet reviews, a combined approach to recommend. In *RecSys*, 2014.

[23] Amjad Almahairi, Kyle Kastner, Kyunghyun Cho, and Aaron Courville. Learning distributed representations from reviews for collaborative filtering. In *RecSys*, 2015.

[24] Jason Weston, Samy Bengio, and Nicolas Usunier. Wsabie: Scaling up to large vocabulary image annotation. In *IJCAI*, 2011.

[25] Yifan Hu, Yehuda Koren, and Chris Volinsky. Collaborative filtering for implicit feedback datasets. In *ICDM*, 2008.

[26] Steffen Rendle, Christoph Freudenthaler, Zeno Gantner, and Lars Schmidt-Thieme. Bpr: Bayesian personalized ranking from implicit feedback. In *UAI*, 2009.

[27] Yue Shi, Martha Larson, and Alan Hanjalic. Collaborative filtering beyond the user-item matrix: A survey of the state of the art and future challenges. *ACM Computing Surveys*, 47(1):3, 2014.

[28] Steffen Rendle. Factorization machines. In *ICDM*, 2010.

[29] Zeno Gantner, Lucas Drumond, Christoph Freudenthaler, Steffen Rendle, and Lars Schmidt-Thieme. Learning attribute-to-feature mappings for cold-start recommendations. In *ICDM*, 2010.

[30] Rich Caruana. Multitask learning. *Machine learning*, 28(1):41–75, 1997.

[31] Ajit P Singh and Geoffrey J Gordon. Relational learning via collective matrix factorization. In *SIGKDD*, 2008.

[32] Hao Ma, Haixuan Yang, Michael R Lyu, and Irwin King. Sorec: social recommendation using probabilistic matrix factorization. In *CIKM*, 2008.

[33] Ralf Krestel, Peter Fankhauser, and Wolfgang Nejdl. Latent dirichlet allocation for tag recommendation. In *RecSys*, 2009.

[34] Yoshua Bengio Ian Goodfellow and Aaron Courville. Deep learning. Book in prep. for MIT Press, 2016.

[35] Ruslan Salakhutdinov, Andriy Mnih, and Geoffrey Hinton. Restricted boltzmann machines for collaborative filtering. In *ICML*, 2007.

[36] Suvash Sedhain, Aditya Krishna Menon, Scott Sanner, and Lexing Xie. Autorec: Autoencoders meet collaborative filtering. In *WWW*, 2015.

[37] Yao Wu, Christopher DuBois, Alice X. Zheng, and Martin Ester. Collaborative denoising auto-encoders for top-n recommender systems. In *WSDM*, 2016.

[38] Ali Mamdouh Elkahky, Yang Song, and Xiaodong He. A multi-view deep learning approach for cross domain user modeling in recommendation systems. In *WWW*, 2015.

[39] Gintare Karolina Dziugaite and Daniel M Roy. Neural network matrix factorization. *arXiv preprint arXiv:1511.06443*, 2015.

[40] Aaron Van den Oord, Sander Dieleman, and Benjamin Schrauwen. Deep content-based music recommendation. In *NIPS*, 2013.

[41] Xinxi Wang and Ye Wang. Improving content-based and hybrid music recommendation using deep learning. In *International Conference on Multimedia*, 2014.

[42] Jason Weston, Sumit Chopra, and Keith Adams. # tagspace: Semantic embeddings from hashtags. 2014.

[43] R. He and J. McAuley. VBPR: visual bayesian personalized ranking from implicit feedback. In *AAAI*, 2016.

[44] Tomas Mikolov, Ilya Sutskever, Kai Chen, Greg S Corrado, and Jeff Dean. Distributed representations of words and phrases and their compositionality. In *NIPS*, pages 3111–3119, 2013.

[45] Ronan Collobert, Jason Weston, Léon Bottou, Michael Karlen, Koray Kavukcuoglu, and Pavel Kuksa. Natural language processing (almost) from scratch. *JMLR*, 12: 2493–2537, 2011.

[46] Ilya Sutskever, Oriol Vinyals, and Quoc V Le. Sequence to sequence learning with neural networks. In *NIPS*, pages 3104–3112, 2014.

[47] Andrew M Dai and Quoc V Le. Semi-supervised sequence learning. In *NIPS*, pages 3061–3069, 2015.

[48] Yoshua Bengio, Patrice Simard, and Paolo Frasconi. Learning long-term dependencies with gradient descent is difficult. *Neural Networks*, 5(2):157–166, 1994.

[49] Sepp Hochreiter and Jürgen Schmidhuber. Long short-term memory. *Neural computation*, 9(8):1735–1780, 1997.

[50] Junyoung Chung, Caglar Gulcehre, KyungHyun Cho, and Yoshua Bengio. Empirical evaluation of gated recurrent neural networks on sequence modeling. *arXiv preprint arXiv:1412.3555*, 2014.

[51] Rafal Jozefowicz, Wojciech Zaremba, and Ilya Sutskever. An empirical exploration of recurrent network architectures. In *ICML*, 2015.

[52] Mike Schuster and Kuldip K Paliwal. Bidirectional recurrent neural networks. *Signal Processing*, 45(11): 2673–2681, 1997.

[53] Arthur P Dempster, Nan M Laird, and Donald B Rubin. Maximum likelihood from incomplete data via the em algorithm. *Journal of the royal statistical society.*, pages 1–38, 1977.

[54] Diederik Kingma and Jimmy Ba. Adam: A method for stochastic optimization. *arXiv preprint arXiv:1412.6980*, 2014.

[55] Misha Denil, Alban Demiraj, and Nando de Freitas. Extraction of salient sentences from labelled documents. *arXiv preprint arXiv:1412.6815*, 2014.

[56] Jiwei Li, Xinlei Chen, Eduard Hovy, and Dan Jurafsky. Visualizing and understanding neural models in nlp. 2016.

Addressing Cold Start for Next-song Recommendation

Szu-Yu Chou[1,2], Yi-Hsuan Yang[2], Jyh-Shing Roger Jang[1], Yu-Ching Lin

[1]Graduate Institute of Networking and Multimedia, National Taiwan University, Taipei, Taiwan

[2]Research Center for IT innovation, Academia Sinica, Taipei, Taiwan

{fearofchou,yang}@citi.sinica.edu.tw,
jang@csie.ntu.edu.tw, aaronlin@kkbox.com

ABSTRACT

The cold start problem arises in various recommendation applications. In this paper, we propose a tensor factorization-based algorithm that exploits content features extracted from music audio to deal with the cold start problem for the emerging application next-song recommendation. Specifically, the new algorithm learns sequential behavior to predict the next song that a user would be interested in based on the last song the user just listened to. A unique characteristic of the algorithm is that it learns and updates the mapping between the audio feature space and the item latent space each time during the iterations of the factorization process. This way, the content features can be better exploited in forming the latent features for both users and items, leading to more effective solutions for cold-start recommendation. Evaluation on a large-scale music recommendation dataset shows that the recommendation result of the proposed algorithm exhibits not only higher accuracy but also better novelty and diversity, suggesting its applicability in helping a user explore new items in next-item recommendation. Our implementation is available at https://github.com/fearofchou/ALMM.

Keywords

Next-song recommendation, content-based recommendation, matrix factorization, real-life setting, context-aware system

1. INTRODUCTION

Music recommendation is extensively used by online music streaming service providers, such as Spotify and Pandora.[1] The goal of a recommendation algorithm is to model the preference of users from observed user-item associations (either explicit or implicit feedback), and then use the model to predict the items a user may like but is not aware before.

The user preference also can be modeled with additional context information [8, 10] and content feature [2, 6, 9]. Music recommendation can be *contextualized* in a number of ways,

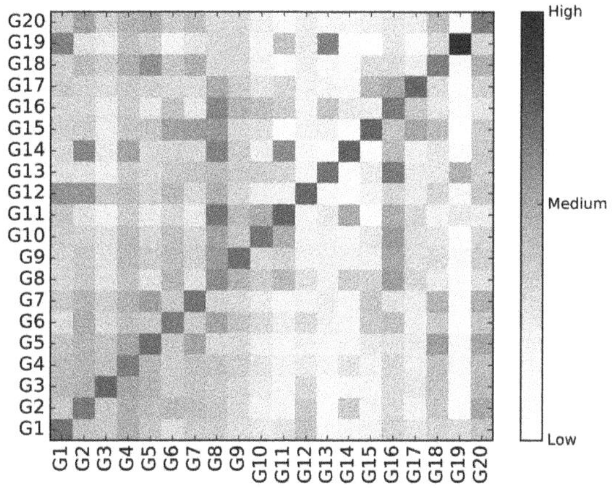

Figure 1: Probability of song-to-song transition between music of different genres, observed from our dataset.

for example by taking into account the time or location of music listening, the ongoing activity of the user, or the underlying emotional state of the user, amongst others. In this paper, we are interested in the scenario where we are given the very last song a user just listened to, and are tasked to predict the next song the user may like to have. The most recently played song may reflect the user's current preference and thereby contribute to the modeling of the listening context. In consequence, such a *next-item recommendation* may be useful in real-world applications [8, 10].

As an illustration, we show in Figure 1 the transition probability of songs of different musical genres in the dataset studied in this paper. The probability is estimated by the Markov chain (MC) method [8], disregarding transitions between a song and itself. The high values along the diagonal shows that the next song has a high probability of being of the same genre as the last song to which the user just listened, which may not be surprising as many users continuously listen to the same artist or album. We also see that the matrix is not a symmetric one, and that there are a few high off-diagonal values, suggesting potentially interesting sequential patterns to be employed in next-item recommendation.

Sequential behavior prediction based on MC is one of the most popular methods for capturing transition preferences. On the other hand, matrix factorization (MF) has been successfully used in a variety of recommendation problems. To exploit the advantages of the two methods, Rendle *et al.* [8] combined MC and MF to improve next-item recommendation.

[1] http://www.spotify.com, http://www.pandora.com

RecSys '16, September 15–19, 2016, Boston, MA, USA.

DOI: http://dx.doi.org/10.1145/2959100.2959156

The approach counts the number of transitions between pairs of items for each user, and then learns latent feature representations for the users and items from the resulting {user, item, last-time item} triplets. This leads to *user, item, and last-time item latent vectors*, whose inner product can be used to perform next-item recommendation.

For the specific application of next-song recommendation, it is important to deal with the so-called *cold-start* problem [6] associated with newly released or less popular songs, which are commonly seen in real-world music streaming services. It is well-known that MF-based methods, or other collaborative filtering (CF)-based methods in general, cannot perform well for items with sparse association with users in the training data. Due to the cold-start problem, the recommendation result may lack diversity and novelty, which are both important for user satisfaction. While CB methods may remedy this issue by exploiting item-item association in the audio feature space, little effort has been made to develop content-based algorithms for next-item recommendation.

The specific goal of this paper is to address cold start next-song recommendation. Following Rendle *et al.*'s approach [8], the new algorithm additionally learns a linear transformation matrix to learn a mapping from an audio feature space to the item latent feature space, each time as we update all the latent features in the tensor factorization process. In other words, the mapping between the content features and song latent vectors is constructed in an interactive way *during*, instead of *after* (e.g. as a prior work [9] did), the factorization process. This way, the coupling between content features and item latent vectors is made stronger. Moreover, the content features would affect not only the learning of the item latent and last-time item latent features, but also the user latent features. In our experiments, the proposed method leads to better accuracy as compared with two competing methods in both warm-start and cold-start settings. Moreover, its recommendation features higher novelty, diversity and lower popularity, which are desirable to user satisfaction.

2. NEXT-SONG RECOMMENDATION

2.1 Formalization

The goal is to recommend songs to a specific user, given knowledge of the song the user just listened to. Let $U = (u_1, u_2, \ldots, u_{|U|})$ be a set of users and $S = (s_1, s_2, \ldots, s_{|S|})$ be a set of songs. According to the listening timestamp, we have the listening sequence $L^u = (L_1^u, L_2^u, \ldots, L_t^u)$ for each user u. The listening sequences of all users is collectively $L = (L^{u_1}, L^{u_2}, \ldots, L^{u_{|U|}})$. We can convert the listening sequences to a transition matrix between different songs for each user by counting the number of adjacent song pairs. To mine sequential patterns, we remove the transitions between a song and itself, and require the time interval between adjacent songs to fall within half an hour to be considered as a valid pair. The resulting tensor $P \in \mathbb{R}^{|U|\times|S|\times|S|}$ for the transition preference for each user is defined as:

$$P_{i,j}^u = \sum_{u\in U}\sum_{n\in L_{t-1}} |\{(L_n^u, L_{n+1}^u) : i \in L_n^u \wedge j \in L_{n+1}^u\}| . \quad (1)$$

Given P, a model can be trained to learn personal transition preference and to recommend a number of songs to a user based on the very last song the user just listened to. Following Hu *et al.* [3], we transform the counts $P_{i,j}^u$ into *confidence values* $C_{i,j}^u$ by the relation $C_{i,j}^u = 1 + \alpha \log(1 + P_{i,j}^u/\varepsilon)$, where α and ε are user-defined parameters, which are both set to 1 in this work.

2.2 Pairwise Factorization (PF)

We present the pairwise factorization (PF) model for personalized next-song recommendation. Following [7], the model factorizes all the features by using pairwise interaction. The objective function is defined as:

$$\min_{\boldsymbol{U}*,\boldsymbol{X}*,\boldsymbol{Y}*} \sum_{(u,i,j)} (C_{i,j}^u - \boldsymbol{U}_u^T\boldsymbol{X}_i - \boldsymbol{U}_u^T\boldsymbol{Y}_j - \boldsymbol{X}_i^T\boldsymbol{Y}_j)^2 \\ +\lambda_U\|\boldsymbol{U}_u\|^2 + \lambda_X\|\boldsymbol{X}_i\|^2 + \lambda_Y\|\boldsymbol{Y}_j\|^2 \quad (2)$$

where $\boldsymbol{U_u} \in \mathbb{R}^k$ is a user latent vector, $\boldsymbol{X_i} \in \mathbb{R}^k$ a last-time item latent vector, $\boldsymbol{Y_j} \in \mathbb{R}^k$ a item latent vector, and k the latent dimension. The updating rules for minimizing (2) can be obtained through alternating least squares:

$$\boldsymbol{U}_u = \Big(\sum_{i,j\in C}((\boldsymbol{XY})_{ij}(\boldsymbol{XY})_{ij}^T) + \lambda_U\Big)^{-1}\Big(\sum_{i,j\in C}(C_{i,j}^u - \boldsymbol{Y}_j^T\boldsymbol{X}_i)(\boldsymbol{XY})_{ij}\Big) \quad (3)$$

$$\boldsymbol{X}_i = \Big(\sum_{u,j\in C}((\boldsymbol{UY})_{uj}(\boldsymbol{UY})_{uj}^T) + \lambda_X\Big)^{-1}\Big(\sum_{u,j\in C}(C_{i,j}^u - \boldsymbol{Y}_j^T\boldsymbol{U}_u)(\boldsymbol{UY})_{uj}\Big) \quad (4)$$

$$\boldsymbol{Y}_j = \Big(\sum_{u,i\in C}((\boldsymbol{UX})_{ui}(\boldsymbol{UX})_{ui}^T) + \lambda_Y\Big)^{-1}\Big(\sum_{u,i\in C}(C_{i,j}^u - \boldsymbol{X}_i^T\boldsymbol{U}_u)(\boldsymbol{UX})_{ui}\Big) \quad (5)$$

where we use the shorthands $(\boldsymbol{UX})_{ui}$, $(\boldsymbol{UY})_{uj}$ and $(\boldsymbol{XY})_{ij}$ to denote $\boldsymbol{U}_u + \boldsymbol{X}_i$, $\boldsymbol{U}_u + \boldsymbol{Y}_j$ and $\boldsymbol{X}_i + \boldsymbol{Y}_j$ respectively.

2.3 Content-based Next-song Recommendation

This section elaborates two baseline CB methods and the proposed method for content-based next-song recommendation. Given the audio features $\boldsymbol{A}_i \in \mathbb{R}^m$ for song i, the common goal of these methods is to learn a mapping matrix $\boldsymbol{\Psi} \in \mathbb{R}^{k\times m}$ between the audio space feature space and the item latent space. We need two mappings, $\boldsymbol{\Psi}^X$ and $\boldsymbol{\Psi}^Y$, for the last-time item and item latent features, respectively.

2.3.1 *Baseline Content-based approaches*

Forbes [2]: The item latent vector is learned directly as a linear transformation of the content features in tensor factorization. The objective function is defined as:

$$\min_{\boldsymbol{U}*,\boldsymbol{\Psi}^X*,\boldsymbol{\Psi}^Y*} \sum_{(u,i,j)} \Big(C_{i,j}^u - \boldsymbol{U}_u^T\boldsymbol{\Psi}^X\boldsymbol{A}_i - \boldsymbol{U}_u^T\boldsymbol{\Psi}^Y\boldsymbol{A}_j - (\boldsymbol{\Psi}^X\boldsymbol{A}_i)^T(\boldsymbol{\Psi}^Y\boldsymbol{A}_j)\Big)^2 \\ +\lambda_U\|\boldsymbol{U}_u\|^2 + \lambda_{\Psi^X}\|\boldsymbol{\Psi}^X\|^2 + \lambda_{\Psi^Y}\|\boldsymbol{\Psi}^Y\|^2 . \quad (6)$$

In other words, the content features are treated as constraints in forming the item-related latent features $\boldsymbol{\Psi}^X\boldsymbol{A}_i$ and $\boldsymbol{\Psi}^Y\boldsymbol{A}_j$. For each training entry, we compute the corresponding prediction error $e_{i,j}^u$:

$$e_{i,j}^u = C_{i,j}^u - \boldsymbol{U}_u^T\boldsymbol{\Psi}^X\boldsymbol{A}_i - \boldsymbol{U}_u^T\boldsymbol{\Psi}^Y\boldsymbol{A}_j - (\boldsymbol{\Psi}^X\boldsymbol{A}_i)^T(\boldsymbol{\Psi}^Y\boldsymbol{A}_j) . \quad (7)$$

Applying an alternating gradient descent algorithm, the following updating rules for $\boldsymbol{U}_u$, $\boldsymbol{\Psi}^X$ and $\boldsymbol{\Psi}^Y$ are obtained:

$$\boldsymbol{U}_u \leftarrow \boldsymbol{U}_u + \mu\Big(\sum_{(u,i,j)\in C} e_{i,j}^u(\boldsymbol{\Psi}^X A_i + \boldsymbol{\Psi}^Y A_j) - \lambda_U\boldsymbol{U}_u\Big), \quad (8)$$

$$\boldsymbol{\Psi}^X \leftarrow \boldsymbol{\Psi}^X + \mu\Big(\sum_{(u,i,j)\in C} e_{i,j}^u(U_u A_i^T + \boldsymbol{\Psi}^Y A_j A_i^T) - \lambda_{\Psi^X}\boldsymbol{\Psi}^X\Big), \quad (9)$$

$$\boldsymbol{\Psi}^Y \leftarrow \boldsymbol{\Psi}^Y + \mu\Big(\sum_{(u,i,j)\in C} e_{i,j}^u(U_u A_j^T + \boldsymbol{\Psi}^X A_i A_j^T) - \lambda_{\Psi^Y}\boldsymbol{\Psi}^Y\Big), \quad (10)$$

where μ is learning rate.

Table 1: The statistics of the training, validation and two test sets in our experiments

Data sets	#users	#songs	#entries
Train	26k	74k	3,004k
Validation	22k	35k	429k
Warm start (WS)	24k	47k	858k
Cold start (CS)	13k	10k	92k

Oord [ ]: Unlike Forbes, here the mapping matrices $\boldsymbol{\Psi}^X$ and $\boldsymbol{\Psi}^Y$ are learned after the latent vectors have been obtained from tensor factorization. The objective function maps all the estimated song latent vectors from audio features, by minimizing the mean squared error.

$$\min_{\Psi^X} \sum_i (\boldsymbol{X}_i - \hat{\boldsymbol{X}}_i)^2 \,, \tag{11}$$

$$\min_{\Psi^Y} \sum_j (\boldsymbol{Y}_j - \hat{\boldsymbol{Y}}_j)^2 \,, \tag{12}$$

where $\hat{\boldsymbol{X}}_i \equiv \boldsymbol{\Psi}^X \boldsymbol{A}_i$ and $\hat{\boldsymbol{Y}}_j \equiv \boldsymbol{\Psi}^Y \boldsymbol{A}_j$. For fair comparison, the two baseline models Forbes and Oord are learned with similar settings.

2.3.2 *Adaptive linear mapping model (ALMM)*

The two baseline methods have different limitations. The Forbes method [ ] might not obtain good latent features, as the constraints imposed by the content features might be too strong. On the other hand, the Oord method [ ] is more flexible, but as the mapping is learned after tensor decomposition, the inner product between the user latent vectors $\boldsymbol{U}_u$ and the mapped item latent vector $\hat{\boldsymbol{Y}}_j$ might not be able to accurately predict user preference.

To deal with this issues, we propose the *adaptive linear mapping model* (ALMM) method, which learns the mapped latent vectors during, instead of after, iterations of the factorization process. Specifically, the proposed method follows the PF method and optimizes the user and item latent features using (3)–(5), but at the same time updates the mapping matrices such that the inner product among $\boldsymbol{U}_u$ and the mapped last-time item and item latent vector $\hat{\boldsymbol{X}}_i$ and $\hat{\boldsymbol{Y}}_j$ predicts user transition preference. The content feature and all the latent vectors can be therefore coupled strongly.

The above steps are summarized in Algorithm 1. The updating rules for $\boldsymbol{\Psi}^X$ and $\boldsymbol{\Psi}^Y$ can be derived with simple algebra. A new song can be recommended by mapping the computed audio features to the latent space. Other non-linear mapping function can be employed (e.g. by using deep neural nets), but we leave this as a future work.

Algorithm 1 Adaptive linear mapping model (ALMM)

Require: *Confidence values* tensor: $\boldsymbol{C}$, audio features: $\boldsymbol{A}$
Initialize $\boldsymbol{X}$ and $\boldsymbol{Y}$
repeat
  for $u \in N_u$ **do**
    Update $\boldsymbol{U}_u$ with equation (3)
  end for
  for $i \in N_s$ **do**
    Update $\boldsymbol{X}_i$ with equation (4)
  end for
  $\boldsymbol{\Psi}^X \leftarrow \boldsymbol{X}\boldsymbol{A}^T(\boldsymbol{A}\boldsymbol{A}^T + \lambda_{\Psi^X}\boldsymbol{\Psi}^X)^{-1}$
  $\boldsymbol{X} \leftarrow \boldsymbol{\Psi}^X\boldsymbol{A}$
  for $j \in N_s$ **do**
    Update $\hat{\boldsymbol{Y}}_j$ with equation (5)
  end for
  $\boldsymbol{\Psi}^Y \leftarrow \boldsymbol{Y}\boldsymbol{A}^T(\boldsymbol{A}\boldsymbol{A}^T + \lambda_{\Psi^Y}\boldsymbol{\Psi}^Y)^{-1}$
  $\boldsymbol{Y} \leftarrow \boldsymbol{\Psi}^Y\boldsymbol{A}$
until convergence
return $\boldsymbol{U}_u$, $\boldsymbol{\Psi}^X$ and $\boldsymbol{\Psi}^Y$

3. EVALUATION

3.1 Dataset

We evaluate our method on a real-world dataset collected from a regional leading music streaming service provider (anonymized for review) from October 2012 to September 2013. The dataset includes 28k users, 124k songs and 0.1 billion listening records. Each of the listening record contains a listening timestamp, song title, artist name, album name, release date and genre labels. The dataset also allows us to access to the corresponding audio files from which various audio features can be extracted. In this work, we consider as audio features the classic mel-frequency cepstral coefficients (MFCC) [ ] and the more advanced audio word (AW)-based features [ ] constructed by using a sparsity-enforced dictionary learning method. Finally, as shown in Table 1, we split the dataset into training set, validation set and test sets. Specifically, both the warm start (WS) and cold start (CS) settings are considered in forming the test sets. For the WS setting all users and songs can be observed in the training set, whereas for the CS setting the randomly selected 1,000 songs cannot be found in the training set at all.

3.2 Evaluation Metrics

The mean average precision (MAP) and recall rate are used for evaluation. Following Chou *et al.* [ ], we also evaluate the quality of recommendation result in terms of novelty, diversity, freshness and popularity as calculated from the top-N recommended songs. Unlike MAP and recall, these metrics do not require the songs under evaluation have been listened to by the user.

- **Novelty:** measures the percentage of artists that a user is already knew, based on their listening data.
- **Diversity:** measures the entropy of the genre distribution of the recommended songs. The genre labels are obtained from the service provider.
- **Freshness:** measures the average of the release date of the recommended songs, using again the information obtained from the service provider.
- **Popularity:** measures the number of users who have listened to the song as observed in the listening data.

Notably, these measurements evaluate different aspects of a recommender system, and a combination of them may provider an estimate of a user's subjective satisfaction of the recommendation result.

3.3 Result

Table 2 shows the MAP and recall for content-based next-song recommendation. Two baseline CB methods and ALMM are implemented using the PF model with 10 latent dimension. The same linear mapping function is used in both ALMM and Oord. As Table 2 shows, ALMM outperforms the other two baseline CB methods with different audio fea-

Table 2: Accuracy of three content-based approaches, ALMM is proposed in this work. There models with two audio features is compared in term of warm start (WS) and cold start (CS)

Feature	Model	MAP@10		MAP@20		Recall@10		Recall@20	
		WS	CS	WS	CS	WS	CS	WS	CS
MFCC [5]	Forbes [2]	0.0224	0.0168	0.0287	0.0238	0.0763	0.0661	0.1702	0.1711
	Oord [6]	0.1643	0.0357	0.1727	0.0402	0.3723	0.1452	0.4961	0.2096
	ALMM	**0.1676**	**0.0409**	**0.1757**	**0.0466**	**0.3884**	**0.1530**	**0.5133**	**0.2368**
AW [ ]	Forbes [2]	0.0242	0.0223	0.0311	0.0288	0.0941	0.0782	0.1961	0.1771
	Oord [6]	0.2125	0.0609	0.2192	0.0689	0.3479	0.1582	0.4523	0.2679
	ALMM	**0.2266**	**0.0680**	**0.2317**	**0.0752**	**0.3854**	**0.1670**	**0.4646**	**0.2752**

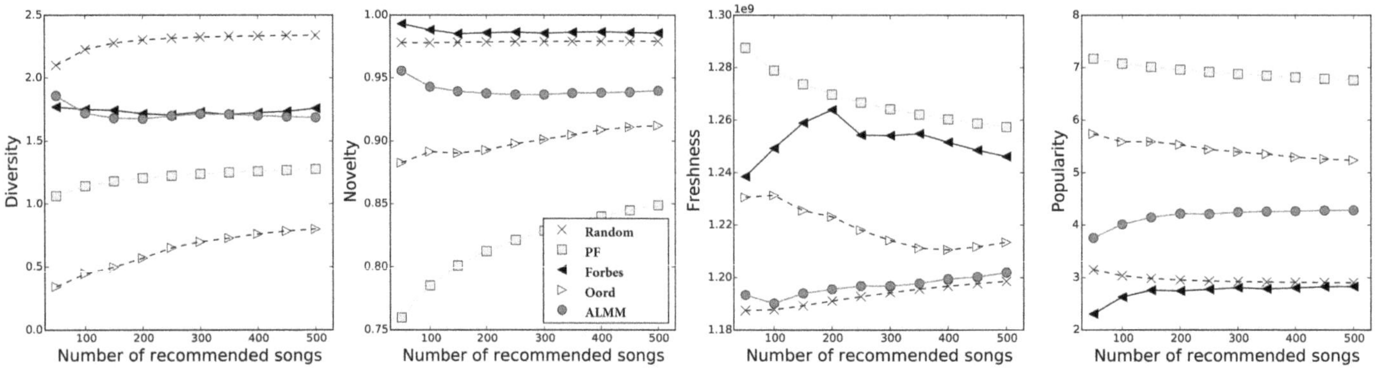

Figure 2: The performance of chose models for top-N recommendation, measured in four evaluation criteria of simulate user's satisfaction. Comparison PF and various CB approaches using AW. The recommended songs is increased by 50 from 50 to 500.

tures in both WS and CS. In contrast, Forbes yields the worst MAP and recall among the competing methods, which indicates this CB method can not work well for next-song recommendation. Moreover, this method requires more computation time than the other method. On the other hand, we can find that the Oord method has similar performance with ALMM. This is because our method is extended from Oord. However, the proposed method leads to slightly better performance measurement in both MAP and recall.

Possibly equally importantly, Figure 2 shows that the recommendation result of the proposed ALMM method exhibits higher novelty, higher novelty, lower freshness and lower popularity than the result of PF. This result suggests that ALMM can better discover new songs across different levels of popularity. In contrast, although Oord has comparable accuracy with ALMM, its result exhibits higher popularity and the lowest diversity, which may be attributed to the mismatch between the user latent vectors and the mapped item latent vectors. In sum, ALMM can obtain better accuracy, and can provide higher diversity and novelty with lower freshness and popularity, comparing to other methods.

4. CONCLUSIONS

In this paper, we address the cold start problem for next-song recommendation. The proposed algorithm captures the content-based transition preference by mining both sequential behavior and content feature simultaneously. Experimental result shows that the proposed method outperforms other CB methods in both warm start and cold start settings. Additionally, the use of content feature leads to recommendations that feature greater diversity and novelty. Although the method is evaluated only on music data, we believe it holds the promise of being applied to other domains as well.

5. REFERENCES

[1] S.-Y. Chou et al. Evaluating music recommendation in a real-world setting: On data splitting and evaluation metrics. In *Proc. ICME*, pages 1–6, 2015.

[2] P. Forbes and M. Zhu. Content-boosted matrix factorization for recommender systems: Experiments with recipe recommendation. In *Proc. ACM Recsys*, pages 261–264, 2011.

[3] Y. Hu et al. Collaborative filtering for implicit feedback datasets. In *Proc. ICDM*, pages 263–272, 2008.

[4] B. Mcfee et al. Learning content similarity for music recommendation. *IEEE Trans. Audio, Speech, and Language Processing*, 2012.

[5] M. Müller et al. Signal processing for music analysis. *J. Sel. Topics Signal Processing*, 5(6):1088–1110, 2011.

[6] A. Oord et al. Deep content-based music recommendation. In *Proc. NIPS*, pages 2643–2651. 2013.

[7] S. Rendle. Factorization machines with libFM. *ACM TIST*, 3(3):57:1–57:22, May 2012.

[8] S. Rendle et al. Factorizing personalized markov chains for next-basket recommendation. In *Proc. ACM WWW*, pages 811–820, 2010.

[9] X. Wang and Y. Wang. Improving content-based and hybrid music recommendation using deep learning. In *Proc. ACM Multimedia*, pages 627–636, 2014.

[10] X. Wu et al. Personalized next-song recommendation in online karaokes. In *Proc. ACM Recsys*, pages 137–140, 2013.

Accuracy and Diversity in Cross-domain Recommendations for Cold-start Users with Positive-only Feedback

Ignacio Fernández-Tobías
Universidad Autónoma de Madrid
ignacio.fernandezt@uam.es

Paolo Tomeo
Polytechnic University of Bari
paolo.tomeo@poliba.it

Iván Cantador
Universidad Autónoma de Madrid
ivan.cantador@uam.es

Tommaso Di Noia
Polytechnic University of Bari
tommaso.dinoia@poliba.it

Eugenio Di Sciascio
Polytechnic University of Bari
eugenio.disciascio@poliba.it

ABSTRACT

Computing useful recommendations for cold-start users is a major challenge in the design of recommender systems, and additional data is often required to compensate the scarcity of user feedback. In this paper we address such problem in a target domain by exploiting user preferences from a related auxiliary domain. Following a rigorous methodology for cold-start, we evaluate a number of recommendation methods on a dataset with positive-only feedback in the movie and music domains, both in single and cross-domain scenarios. Comparing the methods in terms of item ranking accuracy, diversity and catalog coverage, we show that cross-domain preference data is useful to provide more accurate suggestions when user feedback in the target domain is scarce or not available at all, and may lead to more diverse recommendations depending on the target domain. Moreover, evaluating the impact of the user profile size and diversity in the source domain, we show that, in general, the quality of target recommendations increases with the size of the profile, but may deteriorate with too diverse profiles.

Keywords

Cross-domain recommendation, cold-start, diversity

1. INTRODUCTION

Providing relevant suggestions of items for new users is a well-known problem in recommender systems. In such cases there is little or no information about the users preferences, and traditional recommendation models are not able to compute meaningful personalized predictions. To compensate this lack of information, two major approaches have been studied in previous work: (i) preference elicitation techniques [10] that directly ask the user to provide some ratings before delivering recommendations, and (ii) methods that exploit additional information about the users to better estimate their preferences. In the latter case, some approaches combine content and collaborative information [12], and others exploit demographic data or even the user's personality [4] to address the user cold-start problem.

More recently, cross-domain recommender systems [1] that leverage additional information from different but related source domains have been introduced as a potential solution to cold-start situations. This auxiliary information can be exploited to mitigate the lack of historical data in the target recommendation domain, thus addressing the user cold-start [3]. In one of the first papers on the topic, Winoto and Tang [15] conjectured that although the introduction of cross-domain information could deteriorate the prediction performance in the general –non cold-start– case, it could still lead to more diverse recommendations. Subsequent work proposed methods to effectively learn and transfer knowledge from the source domain to the target [5], and found that the quality of the recommendations improves when the involved domains are semantically more related [11]. Nevertheless, to the best of our knowledge, no previous work has tested Winoto and Tang's conjecture regarding the diversity of recommendations when cross-domain data is exploited.

Moreover, in [2] it has been shown that users perceive differences in the recommendation quality depending on the variety of items they naturally prefer. Based on this observation, we hypothesize that both the amount and diversity of source domain preferences have an impact on the accuracy of cross-domain recommendations. Specifically, we identify three main research questions:

- **RQ1** ***How beneficial in terms of accuracy is to exploit cross-domain information for cold-start users?*** We analyze the ranking performance of the top-N recommendations based on positive-only feedback, following a principled evaluation methodology specifically designed for cold-start scenarios [7].
- **RQ2** ***Is cross-domain information really useful to improve the recommendation diversity?*** In order to test Winoto and Tang's conjecture we include in the evaluation the intra-list diversity metric and the recently proposed binomial diversity framework [14].
- **RQ3** ***What is the impact of the size and diversity of the user profile in the source domain on the***

RecSys '16, September 15-19, 2016, Boston , MA, USA
© 2016 ACM. ISBN 978-1-4503-4035-9/16/09...$15.00
DOI: http://dx.doi.org/10.1145/2959100.2959175

quality of the target recommendations? We check this by computing the degree of diversity of the user profiles in the source domain. This work represents, to the best of our knowledge, the first analysis on user profile diversity for cross-domain recommendation.

We investigate these issues by evaluating a number of memory-based and matrix factorization algorithms in single and cross-domain scenarios, using two datasets with positive-only only feedback consisting of Facebook *likes* on movies and music artists, mapped to DBpedia[1] entities, whose metadata is used to also evaluate two state-of-the-art graph-based methods able to exploit heterogeneous information in the recommendation process.

2. EXPERIMENTAL SETTING

Dataset. The recommendation models presented in this paper were evaluated on a Facebook dataset with user *likes* for movie and music items, which we extended with item metadata extracted from DBpedia. In [13] we detail the dataset and the developed process to automatically extract DBpedia semantic networks relating items and features. Next we provide a brief summary of them. In the original raw data –as acquired from the Facebook Graph API– each user-*like*-item relation was given as a 4-tuple with the identifier, name and category of the liked item, and the timestamp of the *like* creation, such as {id: "35481394342", name: "The Matrix", category: "Movie", created_time: "2015-05-14T12:35:08+0000"}. Distinct names may exist for the same item, e.g., "The Matrix", "The Matrix: Film series" and "The Matrix (saga)" for "The Matrix" movie saga. Users thus may provide likes for different Facebook pages referring to the same item. Consolidating and unifying the items of the extracted Facebook *likes*, our method automatically maps the items names to the unique URIs of the corresponding DBpedia entities, e.g., `http://dbpedia.org/resource/The_Matrix` for the identified names of "The Matrix" movie saga. A core stage in the method is to execute SPARQL queries to the DBpedia endpoint that (i) map item names with entity labels, expressed through the `rdfs:label` property, (ii) disambiguate entities using the `rdf:type` property and the Facebook item category field, and (iii) consider equivalent item names by means of the `dbo:wikiPageRedirects` property.

Evaluated recommendation methods. We evaluated the following recommendation algorithms in single and cross-domain scenarios, using the validation set to tune model hyperparameters in each case.

POP: Recommends the most popular items not yet liked by the user. **UNN**: User-based nearest neighbors with Jaccard similarity and neighborhood size of $k = 100$. **INN**: Item-based nearest neighbors with Jaccard similarity and indefinite neighborhood size. **IMF**: Hu et al.'s matrix factorization method for positive-only feedback [6] with 29 factors for movies and 21 factors for music.

Thanks to the linking of items to entities in the DBpedia knowledge graph, we are able to exploit algorithms that leverage the graph-based nature of the underlying side information. In particular, we built a hybrid graph as proposed in [9] and we used it as input for the following two algorithms.

HeteRec: Graph-based recommender system proposed in [16], based on a diffusion method of user preferences following different meta-paths. **PathRank**: Personalized PageRank considering the connectivity between users and items along different meta-paths [8].

For UNN, INN, IMF, HeteRec and PathRank we considered both their application to single-domain scenarios and to cross-domain ones. Hereafter we use the prefix "CD-" to indicate the cross-domain version of the corresponding algorithm.

Evaluation methodology. For the evaluation we follow the user-based 5-fold cross-validation strategy proposed in [7] for cold-start scenarios. First, we select users in the target domain with at least 16 likes and split them into five equally sized subsets. For each fold, we keep all the data from the other folds in the training set, whereas the likes from the users in the selected fold were randomly split into three subsets: training set (10 likes), validation set (5 likes), and testing (remaining likes, hence at least 1). In order to simulate different user profile sizes from 1 to 10 likes, we repeat the training and the evaluation ten times, starting with the first like in the training set and incrementally increasing it one by one. This setting allows us to evaluate each profile size with the same test set, avoiding potential biases in the evaluation due to different test set sizes [7]. After this preprocessing, the Facebook music dataset contains 49,369 users, 5,748 music bands or artists, and 2,084,462 likes; the movie dataset contains 26,943 users, 3,901 movies, and 876,501 likes. The user overlap for movies is 89.96% and music is 84.69%. In order to simulate the cross-domain scenario, we simply append the full source domain dataset to the previous training set. We used the Mean Reciprocal Rank (MRR) to evaluate the ranking accuracy of the recommendations, which computes the average reciprocal rank of the first relevant item in the recommendation list. Whereas, Intra-List Diversity (ILD) and Binomial Diversity Framework (BinomDiv) [14] were used to evaluate the individual diversity, namely the degree of diversity in the recommendation lists based on item genres extracted from DBpedia. Along with accuracy, we also measured catalog coverage as the percentage of items that are recommended at least once, to better understand the differences among the compared algorithms.

3. RESULTS

In the following we discuss the outcomes of three experiments we conducted to investigate each of the research questions stated in Section 1.

Cross-domain recommendation accuracy.

To address RQ1, we compare the accuracy of the target recommendations in single-domain and cross-domain scenarios. Table 1 shows the MRR values for movies (left) and music (right) target recommendations.

Music (source)–Movies (target). CD-UNN is the most accurate method for extreme cold-start users (0 likes in target domain), CD-INN where 1 or 2 likes are provided, and CD-IMF from 3 to 10 likes. Curiously, CD-INN and CD-HeteRec using only cross-domain information are able to beat almost all the other methods even where they use target information up to 4 likes. Moreover, CD-UNN is subject to a drastic fall from 0 to 1 like, obtaining the worst accuracy among all the methods and configuration (even lower than POP). Further analysis revealed that this is due to our choice of Jaccard as user similarity metric, which we observed pro-

[1]http://dbpedia.org

Table 1: **Accuracy and diversity values for different cold-start target profile sizes.**

Metric	Source – Target	Music – Movies											Movies – Music										
	Target size	0	1	2	3	4	5	6	7	8	9	10	0	1	2	3	4	5	6	7	8	9	10
MRR ($\times 10^{-3}$)	POP	290	293	295	298	299	303	304	307	310	312	315	335	337	340	343	345	347	350	352	354	357	359
	UNN		334	324	322	330	345	379	393	402	412	422		425	394	398	422	454	485	504	525	**536**	547
	CD-UNN	**383**	279	304	321	335	347	353	368	378	394	406	433	270	307	336	373	402	438	463	490	509	526
	INN		233	308	334	359	374	388	403	408	420	426		320	389	430	455	476	491	506	520	533	544
	CD-INN	347	**352**	**358**	367	369	374	382	388	392	397	403	419	**437**	**457**	**471**	**480**	**492**	**503**	**514**	**526**	**536**	545
	IMF		254	292	315	335	343	363	377	389	397	417		350	396	431	452	473	489	505	522	533	**548**
	CD-IMF	304	330	354	**370**	**378**	**387**	**400**	**410**	**424**	**428**	**439**	299	358	401	429	453	477	487	501	521	531	543
	HeteRec		320	351	360	371	376	386	389	396	402	408		361	394	424	442	467	484	499	517	526	536
	CD-HeteRec	376	345	350	356	361	364	367	370	374	381	384	**527**	431	450	461	469	477	481	488	497	503	509
	PathRank		340	345	346	352	350	354	357	361	363	367		411	416	420	426	429	433	436	442	444	449
	CD-PathRank	346	317	317	321	325	327	330	333	337	341	345	495	399	402	405	411	415	419	422	427	432	436
BinomDiv@10 ($\times 10^{-3}$)	POP	**401**	304	336	354	368	378	386	**393**	**400**	**405**	**410**	324	228	262	282	295	305	313	321	327	333	338
	UNN		360	385	**404**	**392**	**396**	**394**	**393**	393	396	395		296	332	348	347	330	317	309	305	301	297
	CD-UNN	368	**404**	**386**	376	373	372	372	374	374	377	380	296	**411**	**380**	358	347	329	322	316	311	308	305
	INN		289	308	315	321	323	327	329	332	333	337		200	213	219	223	229	231	235	236	239	240
	CD-INN	309	240	268	283	297	304	310	316	322	325	330	277	231	255	264	270	272	273	274	274	276	276
	IMF		299	320	335	344	347	355	358	363	366	368		196	217	232	241	249	253	256	260	261	265
	CD-IMF	270	231	270	289	302	315	323	328	332	338	341	248	229	254	264	271	272	276	277	277	278	278
	HeteRec		311	328	334	337	341	343	346	348	350	354		227	264	280	288	296	300	302	304	306	306
	CD-HeteRec	333	271	298	314	324	333	339	345	350	354	358	372	271	314	331	342	349	354	357	361	363	366
	PathRank		317	327	336	342	352	353	359	361	366	368		350	**380**	**395**	**404**	**410**	**413**	**416**	**419**	**421**	**422**
	CD-PathRank	336	270	294	310	320	327	334	339	345	350	355	**405**	335	367	384	394	402	408	412	415	418	419

vides unreliable scores in cold-start situations. Comparing the methods between single and cross-domain configuration, we can see that only INN and IMF can benefit from music feedback in terms of accuracy. All the other methods lose accuracy when music feedback is also considered. In terms of coverage, UNN is the only method able to benefit from music feedback: UNN reaches values from 10% to 18% and CD-UNN from 38% to 50% among the different profile sizes.

Movies–Music. CD-HeteRec yields the most accurate recommendations in the extreme cold-start scenario, while CD-INN is the best method for all the other profile sizes, even though UNN obtains close values with 8 and 9 likes, and UNN and IMF overcome CD-INN with 10 likes but with a not relevant difference. CD-UNN shows again a drastic loss from 0–4 target likes, falling even below POP. In terms of catalog coverage, the trends are very similar to the ones in movies domain. Interestingly, CD-INN beats again all the other methods in terms of accuracy and catalog coverage with 1 and 2 likes in the target domain. Analyzing the use of cross domain information, INN is once again able to reach better accuracy using the additional movie likes, while HeteRec obtains a benefit where less feedback is provided (from 1 to 5). Again, CD-HeteRec with 0 likes in the target domain overcomes all the other methods even where they use more target information (up to 8). However its catalog coverage is too low (1%) compared the other methods (>10%).

Summing up, we may say that cross-domain information is arguably useful to face the cold-start user problem, allowing to generate relevant recommendation even where no target information is available. The choice of the method depends on the domain and amount of user information available. Moreover, we discover that some methods obtain exceptionally better results using only the source domain rather than using a few target feedbacks as well. More research will be needed for better understanding this trend.

Cross-domain recommendation diversity.

This section addresses RQ2, namely testing whether cross-domain information leads to more diverse recommendations. Tables 1 shows the diversity results for movies and music domain in terms of BinomDiv@10. We also compared the methods using the ILD metric, but we do not show its values, since they obtain a very similar trend to BinomDiv.

Music–Movies. POP obtains good results values, since all the most popular movies in the dataset belong to different genres, but CD-UNN and UNN overcome it with 1 and 2 likes, and only UNN from 3 to 6. In general, using cross-domain music information yields to less diverse recommendations. **Movies–Music**. PathRank and CD-PathRank produce the most diverse recommendations. Conversely, MF methods lead to the worst diversity. In contrast to the previous situation, using cross-domain movies information for music recommendations improves nearly always the diversity degree of the recommendations.

Size and diversity of source domain user profiles.

In order to address RQ3, we compute the number of preferences and the intra-list diversity of the user profiles in the source domain, and group users in different ranges. For the profile sizes we split users in intervals of 20 likes, from size 0 to 100 and beyond, and for profile diversity we classify the users in terms of the distribution of ILD scores. Specifically, we define four groups based on the quartiles which we name `Very low` (0–25%), `Low` (25%–50%), `Medium` (50%–75%), and `High` (75%–100%). Finally, we average the MRR of the recommendation lists in the target domain separately for each group, first in terms of profile size and then in terms of diversity. Figure 1 shows the relation between the quality of the target recommendations and the analysed source profile properties. We only report the results for the extreme cold-start profile sizes in the target, i.e., 0 and 10, as the rest showed similar behavior.

In terms of source profile size, we notice that in general the quality of target recommendations improves monotonically as more information about the user's preferences is available in the source domain. This trend holds for all the evaluated algorithms with the exception of CD-IMF in music, where we see that the performance degrades when the size of the source profile is larger than 100. In this case, we argue that the abundance of auxiliary preferences could be drifting the learning of the model parameters towards the source domain, although a deeper analysis is needed to confirm our intuition.

Regarding the impact of the source profile diversity we find that the best results are achieved for users very focused on limited types of items, whereas a more diverse profile has a negative effect on the accuracy of the recommendations.

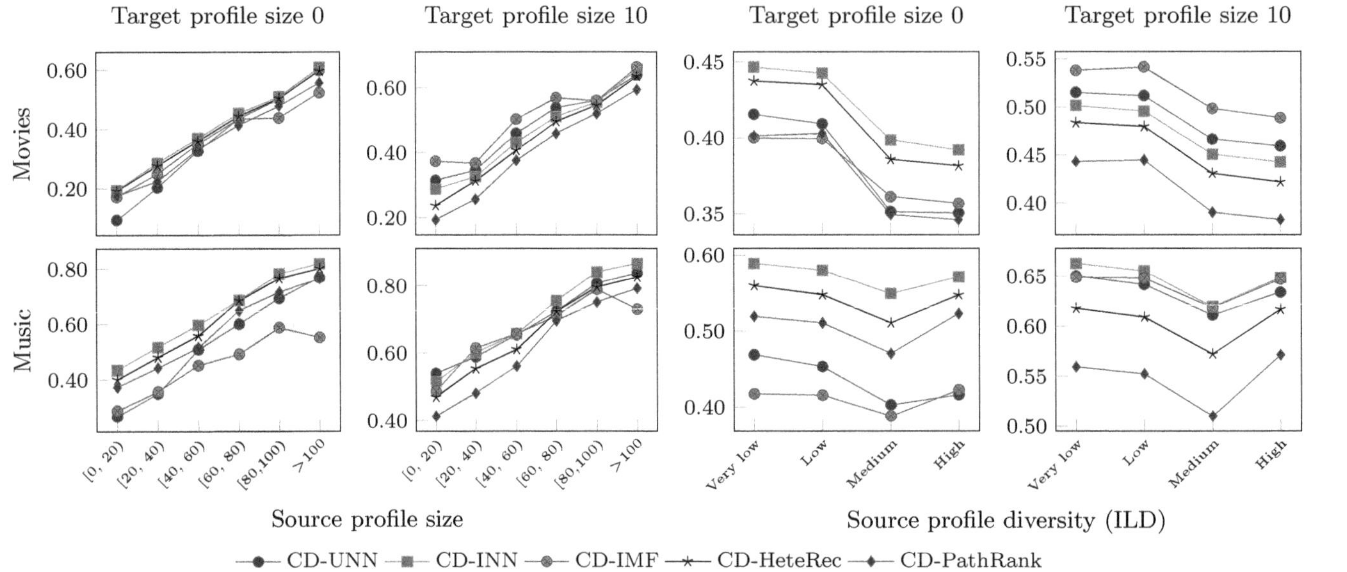

Figure 1: MRR values of the cross-domain recommendation methods for different user profile sizes and profile diversity values in the source domain. Each row corresponds to the two target domains in our dataset.

This seems to indicate that the evaluated algorithms struggle to find inter-domain correlations, specially from music to movies. In the case of very high diversity we see that the two settings diverge: variety in source movie preferences is beneficial for music recommendations, whereas the converse has the opposite effect.

We conclude that both the source user profile size and diversity have a significant impact on the quality of cross domain recommendations, thus confirming RQ3. On a side note, we observe the superior performance of CD-INN in most of the considered scenarios, specially in the extreme cold-start with target profile size of 0. We argue that this behavior is a consequence of the relatively large overlap of users between the analysed domains, an issue that we plan to further investigate in future work.

4. CONCLUSIONS AND FUTURE WORK

We have studied the quality of cross-domain recommendations in terms of accuracy, diversity and catalog coverage, evaluating a number of algorithms on two datasets with positive-only feedback. Our results show the benefits of cross-domain information in cold-start situations in terms of ranking accuracy. Regarding diversity we observe different behavior in the two datasets, and therefore conclude that in general the results depend on the target domain. We have also studied the impact of the size and diversity of user profiles in the source domain, concluding that while more cross-domain user preferences are helpful, a greater item diversity in the source profile can actually harm the performance in the target domain. Following this work we intend to further investigate which characteristics of the datasets could explain the differences we found in both recommendation and user profile diversity. We plan to extend our analysis to more domains, e.g. books, and to evaluate more sophisticated methods from the state of the art, such as [5].

Acknowledgments

This work was supported by the Spanish Ministry of Science and Innovation (TIN2013-47090-C3-2) and by the project PON03 PE_00136_1 Digital Services Ecosystem: DSE.

5. REFERENCES

[1] I. Cantador, I. Fernández-Tobías, S. Berkovsky, and P. Cremonesi. Cross-domain recommender systems. In *Recommender Systems Handbook*, pp. 919–959. Springer, 2015.
[2] T. Di Noia, V. C. Ostuni, J. Rosati, P. Tomeo, and E. Di Sciascio. An analysis of users' propensity toward diversity in recommendations. In *RecSys '14*, pp. 285–288, 2014.
[3] M. Enrich, M. Braunhofer, and F. Ricci. Cold-start management with cross-domain collaborative filtering and tags. In *EC-Web '13*, pp. 101–112, 2013.
[4] I. Fernández-Tobías, M. Braunhofer, M. Elahi, F. Ricci, and I. Cantador. Alleviating the new user problem in collaborative filtering by exploiting personality information. *User Model. User-Adapt. Interact.*, 26(2-3):221–255, 2016.
[5] L. Hu, J. Cao, G. Xu, L. Cao, Z. Gu, and C. Zhu. Personalized recommendation via cross-domain triadic factorization. In *WWW '13*, pp. 595–606, 2013.
[6] Y. Hu, Y. Koren, and C. Volinsky. Collaborative filtering for implicit feedback datasets. In *ICDM '08*, pp. 263–272, 2008.
[7] D. Kluver and J. A. Konstan. Evaluating recommender behavior for new users. In *RecSys '14*, pp. 121–128, 2014.
[8] S. Lee, S. Park, M. Kahng, and S.-g. Lee. Pathrank: A novel node ranking measure on a heterogeneous graph for recommender systems. In *CIKM '12*, pp. 1637–1641, 2012.
[9] V. C. Ostuni, T. Di Noia, E. Di Sciascio, and R. Mirizzi. Top-n recommendations from implicit feedback leveraging linked open data. In *RecSys '13*, pp. 85–92, 2013.
[10] N. Rubens, M. Elahi, M. Sugiyama, and D. Kaplan. Active learning in recommender systems. In *Recommender Systems Handbook*, pp. 809–846. Springer, 2015.
[11] S. Sahebi and P. Brusilovsky. It takes two to tango: An exploration of domain pairs for cross-domain collaborative filtering. In *RecSys '15*, pp. 131–138, 2015.
[12] A. I. Schein, A. Popescul, L. H. Ungar, and D. M. Pennock. Methods and metrics for cold-start recommendations. In *SIGIR '02*, pp. 253–260, 2002.
[13] P. Tomeo, I. Fernández-Tobías, T. Di Noia, and I. Cantador. Exploiting linked open data in cold-start recommendations with positive-only feedback. In *CERI '16*, 2016.
[14] S. Vargas, L. Baltrunas, A. Karatzoglou, and P. Castells. Coverage, redundancy and size-awareness in genre diversity for recommender systems. In *RecSys '14*, pp. 209–216, 2014.
[15] P. Winoto and T. Y. Tang. If you like the devil wears prada the book, will you also enjoy the devil wears prada the movie? A study of cross-domain recommendations. *New Generation Computing*, 26(3):209–225, 2008.
[16] X. Yu, X. Ren, Y. Sun, Q. Gu, B. Sturt, U. Khandelwal, B. Norick, and J. Han. Personalized entity recommendation: A heterogeneous information network approach. In *WSDM '14*, pp. 283–292, 2014.

HCI for Recommender Systems: the Past, the Present and the Future

André Calero Valdez
RWTH Aachen University
Campus Boulevard 57
52074 Aachen, Germany
calero-valdez@comm.rwth-aachen.de

Martina Ziefle
RWTH Aachen University
Campus Boulevard 57
52074 Aachen, Germany
ziefle@comm.rwth-aachen.de

Katrien Verbert
KU Leuven
Celestijnenlaan 200A
B-3001 Leuven, Belgium
katrien.verbert@cs.kuleuven.be

ABSTRACT

How can you discover something new, that matches your interest? Recommender Systems have been studied since the 90ies. Their benefit comes from guiding a user through the density of the information jungle to useful knowledge clearings. Early research on recommender systems focuses on algorithms and their evaluation to improve recommendation accuracy using F-measures and other methodologies from signal-detection theory. Present research includes other aspects such as human factors that affect the user experience and interactive visualization techniques to support transparency of results and user control. In this paper, we analyze all publications on recommender systems from the scopus database, and particularly also papers with such an HCI focus. Based on an analysis of these papers, future topics for recommender systems research are identified, which include more advanced support for user control, adaptive interfaces, affective computing and applications in high risk domains.

Keywords

Recommender Systems, Human-Computer Interaction, Uncertainty, Risk

1. INTRODUCTION

You have most certainly seen the output of a recommender system. The online retailer Amazon suggests your next purchase by letting you know what others bought together with the product you're currently viewing ("Frequently bought together."). And maybe you have also experienced the limitations of such systems by getting suggestions that made no sense to you at all.

Several recommendation techniques, such as content-based, knowledge-based, collaborative filtering and their hybridizations, are discussed in state-of-the-art surveys [1, 5], including their merits and limitations. Typical fields of application are recommending movies, music or related products in e-commerce. These application domains are similar: each recommendation is important in creating additional revenue and of relatively low risk. Recommender systems are not typically used to propose medical procedure, emergency plans in nuclear plants or stock trading, where uncertainty and risk are high. Why is this the case?

This paper reflects on the development of recommender systems by reviewing publications from scopus. We look back at the past to reflect on present research and try to predict future research topics for recommender systems based on current trends in ICT and a short bibliometric analysis of the field of recommender systems.

2. THE PAST

Tapestry [8] was the first system that employed *collaborative filtering* to filter the large amount of emails that reached people in Xerox PARC. It included a system based on annotating emails and later filtering emails according to these annotations. The novelty was the collaborative aspect of this annotation process.

The term *recommender system* appears for the first time in a 1997 article by Paul Vesnick and Hal R. Varian [25] and describes recommender systems as a tool for decision making and not just for information retrieval. They already argue in terms of evaluating costs (of false positives/negatives) beyond mere measures from signal detection theory.

Since then research on recommender systems has drastically increased. Over 9,400 articles and 76 reviews can be found on scopus[1]. The trend shows an ever increasing amount published on recommender systems (see Fig. 1). Additionally, we see two peaks in review papers about recommender systems (see Fig. 1). The first peak in 2005 and the second in 2010.

The first review paper on recommender systems by Herlocker et al. [11] focused on evaluation of recommender systems. Another review by Adomavicius and Thuzhilin [1] discusses the use of content-based, collaborative and hybrid approaches and proposes possible extension for research. The authors also mention the evaluation related problems with measures of signal detection theory such as the famous F1-Measure. Such metrics focus on coverage and accuracy [1], while at the same time criteria like usefulness and quality as well as, explainability, trustworthiness, scalability and privacy issues may play bigger roles in applications.

[1]http://www.scopus.com (as of April 10th 2016)

RecSys '16 September 15-19, 2016, Boston , MA, USA

ACM ISBN 978-1-4503-4035-9/16/09.
DOI: http://dx.doi.org/10.1145/2959100.2959158

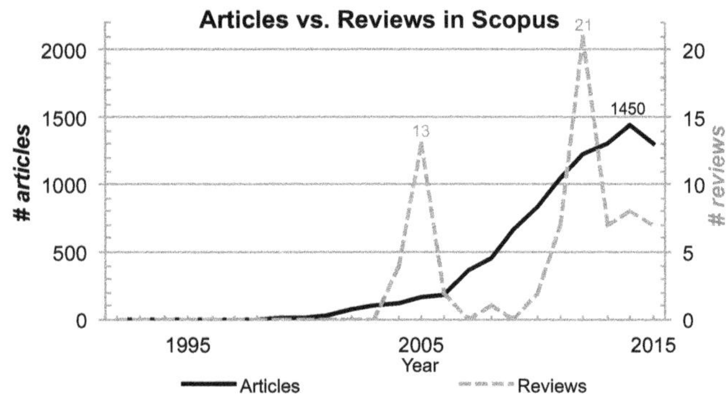

Figure 1: The amount of articles published on recommender systems has been constantly increasing, while reviews have had two spikes.

3. THE PRESENT

In recent years, researchers have become more aware of the fact that effectiveness of recommender systems goes beyond recommendation accuracy [16]. Thus, research on these human factors has gained increased interest, for instance by combining interactive visualization techniques with recommendation techniques to support transparency and controllability of the recommendation process. Visualization leverages visual representations to facilitate human perception, while interaction stresses user involvement through dialogue with the system. In a recent study, 24 interactive recommender systems were analysed that use an interactive visualization technique to support user interaction [10]. A large share of these systems focus on transparency of the recommendation process to address the *black box* issue. Here, the overall objective is to explain the inner logic of a recommender system to the user in order to increase acceptance of recommendations. A good example of this approach is PeerChooser [19], a visual interactive recommender that uses a graph-based representation to show relationships between users and recommended items from a collaborative filtering recommender system. Similarly, SmallWorlds [9] allows the exploration of relationships between recommended items and friends with a similar profile using multiple aspects. This way, users can explore different relationships to gain transparency and ultimately increase the chance of finding items.

In addition, TasteWeights [3] allows users to control the impact of the profiles and behaviors of friends and peers on the recommendation results. TasteWeights provides an interface for such hybrid recommendations. The system elicits preference data and relevance feedback from users at runtime in order to adapt recommendations. SetFusion [22] is a recent example that allows users to fine-tune weights of a hybrid recommender system. SetFusion uses a Venn diagram to visualize relationships between recommendations.

Results of this survey indicate that many interesting prototypes have been developed and evaluated that demonstrate the importance of this research for the community. Nevertheless, many open research challenges exist that provide interesting opportunities for research in this field.

4. THE FUTURE

Trying to predict the future is only helpful when the prediction increases the knowledge about the future beyond what is already known. *Safe bets* are uninteresting predictions, while *wild guesses* may seem ridiculous from hindsight. Therefore using *safe bets* from other fields that may relate to recommender research may prove to be an interesting middle-ground.

4.1 Bibliometric analysis

From the Scopus database we searched for all documents from the field of computer science that contained the search term “recommender system” (n=9,432). From this data-set we extracted the author keywords. We removed all stop words, punctuation and mapped common noun phrases to single-word phrases (e.g. user model to user_model). We then counted frequencies for all years and plotted the relative frequency of selected terms to analyze possible trends regarding our selection (see Fig. 2). The terms were chosen to contrast HCI related keywords (in the left column) with more algorithm related keywords (in the right column).

4.2 Where should we direct future research?

When taking a closer look at publication counts (see Fig. 1) we can see two spikes in review publishing curve. The most cited works in the first spike are the previously mentioned reviews [1, 11]. The same year (2005) also marks a change in interest in topics (see Fig. 2), focusing on adaptive recommender systems and the user model. The second change in topics can be seen in 2009, where trust becomes a heavily published keyword. The second spike in reviews three years later marks another change in interest, where the most frequently cited reviews [7, 15] focus on machine learning and user focus.

Surely developments in improving algorithms are important and some interesting directions were proposed by Park et al. [21]. On the other hand, some researchers in recent reviews [15, 10] have argued for focusing on the user of the recommendation system. Following the latter argument, we think that HCI related aspects are underrepresented in literature (see Fig. 2) and yet critically important for future applications of recommender systems.

User control.

Current research on interactive recommender systems is focused on controlling the importance of different recommendation parameters or revising the user profile [10]. Such control is insufficient to establish a good level of trust and to address privacy concerns [2]. Further research is needed to support more advanced levels of interaction, such as controls that define which data can be tracked and taken into account for which purposes. Examples of such more advanced levels of control have been researched extensively by the visual analytics (VA) community. Whereas these examples are promising, research is needed to apply these VA concepts, methods and techniques to the field of recommender systems and casual users.

Adaptive.

The aim of adequate user control is to increase recommendation accuracy [24] by incorporating user input and feedback. Previous research shows however that user satisfaction does not always correlate with high recommendation

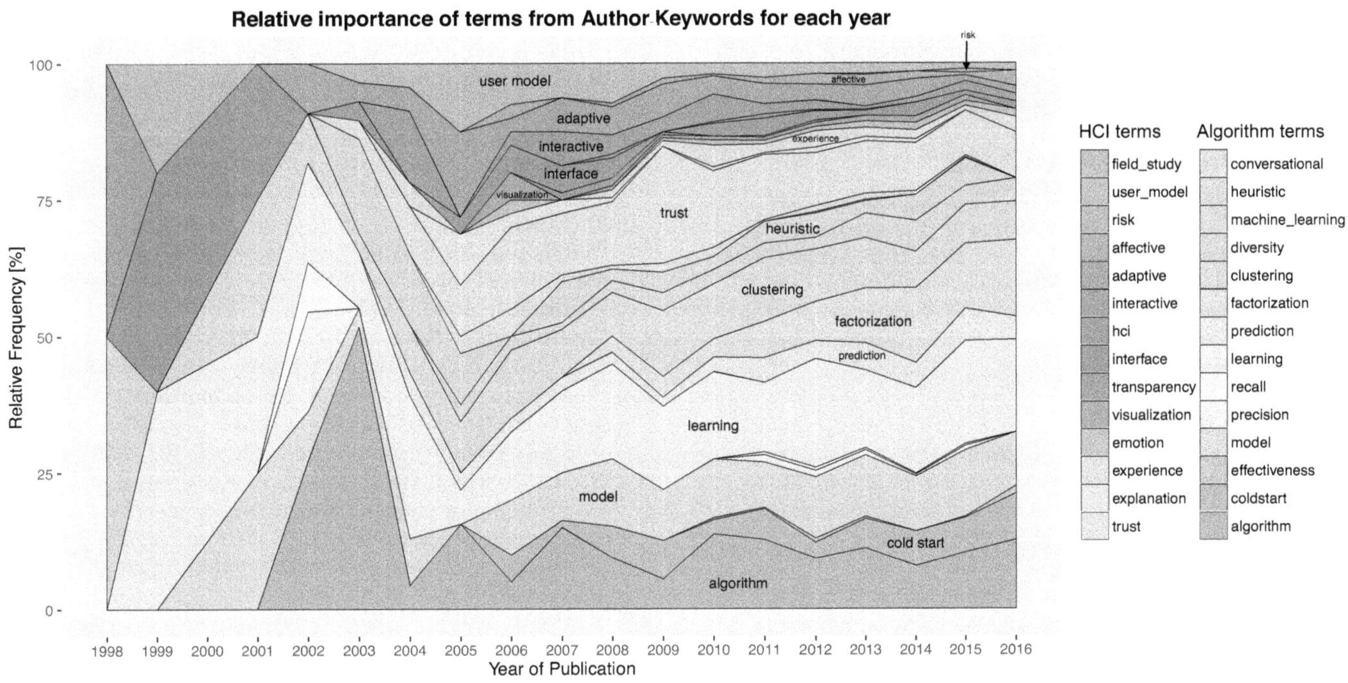

Figure 2: This picture show the relative importance of our search terms for each year. Importance is derived from occurrence in author keywords from 9,432 publications.

accuracy and that other factors, such as the knowledge level of the user [14] and her interests [12], need to be considered. Current recommender systems interfaces are *static*, i.e. they do not tailor the interface to these user characteristics. There is a need to adapt recommender systems and their user interfaces to these different personal and situational characteristics. Research that has been conducted by the adaptive hypermedia, adaptive visualization and personalized search communities provides a promising starting point to address this challenge.

Affective.

Emotions play a crucial role in decision making [23]. An interesting future line of research is to experiment with novel sensing technologies to capture behavioral data (physiological data, facial expressions, speech, ...) in order to detect emotions and to adapt recommendations based on emotional responses. Although measurement of emotions in a controlled laboratory environment is well studied for years by a large number of research groups [20], multimodal emotion recognition in real world environments is still a challenging task [17]. A good review of existing methods has been reported by Hrabal [13]. As none of the methods have yet led to successful subject- and situation-independent emotion recognition, interactive methods that enable users to revise detected variables seem promising. The challenge is to research the development of a next generation of recommender systems that can incorporate both automatically acquired data and revisions by end-users as a basis to tailor recommendations based on current contextual needs of the user, including emotions that are key in decision making.

High-risk domains.

The biggest risk a user of e-commerce faces is spending money for an undesired product. Thus product recommendations are of very specific risk. Other domains have a higher level of uncertainty and risk. Giving recommendations in domains were choices must be made under uncertainty and risk is intricately more challenging. Risk-aware algorithms [4] or predictions of risks [6] have been investigated only recently and not extensively. How uncertainty and risk of a recommendation should be visualized or communicated has not been investigated yet, but may be crucial for the application of these in high-risk domains such as medicine [18].

5. CONCLUSIONS

Looking at the big trends in ICT we see that Big Data and thus more advanced techniques from AI (e.g. deep learning) will become available and then applied to recommender systems. These do not only play a role in improving algorithms but also new interactions paradigms. In the future we could analyze not just the transactions of users, but also patterns of interaction (e.g. mouse movement, keystrokes, facial expressions etc.). These ultimately lead to new research questions for new adaptive interfaces and how the user controls these recommender systems. When recommending in domains of risk or uncertainty new visualizations will be necessary to improve the trust and understanding of recommendations. Using more intimate data such as facial expression will also bring new problems of privacy and user acceptance.

6. LIMITATIONS

The bibliometric analysis was conducted using a pre-defined set of keywords. We have put efforts into mapping similar terms to our terms, nevertheless some keywords might have been overlooked. Looking at the relative frequencies skews the data in favor of this set of keywords. Thus our findings represent upper thresholds for relative importance.

7. ACKNOWLEDGMENTS

The authors thank the German Research Council DFG for the friendly support of the research in the excellence cluster "Integrative Production Technology in High Wage Countries". The work of Katrien Verbert is supported by the KU Leuven research council as part of the starting grant "Flexible Interaction with Intelligent Systems" (grant agreement STG/14/019)

8. REFERENCES

[1] G. Adomavicius and A. Tuzhilin. Toward the next generation of recommender systems: A survey of the state-of-the-art and possible extensions. *Knowledge and Data Engineering, IEEE Transactions on*, 17(6):734–749, 2005.

[2] F. Bakalov, M.-J. Meurs, B. König-Ries, B. Sateli, R. Witte, G. Butler, and A. Tsang. An approach to controlling user models and personalization effects in recommender systems. In *Proceedings of the 2013 int. conf. on Intelligent user interfaces*, pages 49–56. ACM, 2013.

[3] S. Bostandjiev, J. O'Donovan, and T. Höllerer. Tasteweights: a visual interactive hybrid recommender system. In *Proceedings of the sixth ACM conference on Recommender systems*, pages 35–42. ACM, 2012.

[4] D. Bouneffouf, A. Bouzeghoub, and A. L. Ganarski. Risk-aware recommender systems. In *Neural Information Processing*, pages 57–65. Springer, 2013.

[5] R. Burke. Hybrid recommender systems: Survey and experiments. *User modeling and user-adapted interaction*, 12(4):331–370, 2002.

[6] R. Conforti, M. de Leoni, M. La Rosa, W. M. van der Aalst, and A. H. ter Hofstede. A recommendation system for predicting risks across multiple business process instances. *Decision Support Systems*, 69:1–19, 2015.

[7] P. Domingos. A few useful things to know about machine learning. *Communications of the ACM*, 55(10):78–87, 2012.

[8] D. Goldberg, D. Nichols, B. M. Oki, and D. Terry. Using collaborative filtering to weave an information tapestry. *Communications of the ACM*, 35(12):61–70, 1992.

[9] B. Gretarsson, J. O'Donovan, S. Bostandjiev, C. Hall, and T. Höllerer. Smallworlds: visualizing social recommendations. In *Computer Graphics Forum*, volume 29, pages 833–842. Wiley Online Library, 2010.

[10] C. He, D. Parra, and K. Verbert. Interactive recommender systems: A survey of the state of the art and future research challenges and opportunities. *Expert Systems with Applications*, 56:9–27, 2016.

[11] J. L. Herlocker, J. A. Konstan, L. G. Terveen, and J. T. Riedl. Evaluating collaborative filtering recommender systems. *ACM Transactions on Information Systems (TOIS)*, 22(1):5–53, 2004.

[12] Y. Hijikata, Y. Kai, and S. Nishida. The relation between user intervention and user satisfaction for information recommendation. In *Proceedings of the 27th Annual ACM Symposium on Applied Computing*, SAC '12, pages 2002–2007, New York, NY, USA, 2012. ACM.

[13] D. Hrabal. *Emotion Classification in Human-computer Interaction on the Basis of Physiological Data.* PhD thesis, Universität Ulm. Medizinische Fakultät, 2013.

[14] B. P. Knijnenburg, N. J. Reijmer, and M. C. Willemsen. Each to his own: How different users call for different interaction methods in recommender systems. In *Proc. of the Fifth ACM Conf. on Recommender Systems*, RecSys '11, pages 141–148, New York, NY, USA, 2011. ACM.

[15] J. A. Konstan and J. Riedl. Recommender systems: from algorithms to user experience. *User Modeling and User-Adapted Interaction*, 22(1-2):101–123, 2012.

[16] S. M. McNee, J. Riedl, and J. A. Konstan. Being accurate is not enough: how accuracy metrics have hurt recommender systems. In *CHI'06 extended abstracts on Human factors in computing systems*, pages 1097–1101. ACM, 2006.

[17] S. Meudt and F. Schwenker. Enhanced autocorrelation in real world emotion recognition. In *Proceedings of the 16th International Conference on Multimodal Interaction*, ICMI '14, pages 502–507, New York, NY, USA, 2014. ACM.

[18] G. Naik, H. Ahmed, and A. G. Edwards. Communicating risk to patients and the public. *Br J Gen Pract*, 62(597):213–216, 2012.

[19] J. O'Donovan, B. Smyth, B. Gretarsson, S. Bostandjiev, and T. Höllerer. Peerchooser: visual interactive recommendation. In *Proceedings of the SIGCHI Conference on Human Factors in Computing Systems*, pages 1085–1088. ACM, 2008.

[20] M. Ouwerkerk. Unobtrusive emotions sensing in daily life. In *Sensing Emotions*, pages 21–39. Springer, 2011.

[21] D. H. Park, H. K. Kim, I. Y. Choi, and J. K. Kim. A literature review and classification of recommender systems research. *Expert Systems with Applications*, 39(11):10059–10072, 2012.

[22] D. Parra and P. Brusilovsky. User-controllable personalization: A case study with setfusion. *International Journal of Human-Computer Studies*, 78:43–67, 2015.

[23] R. W. Picard, S. Papert, W. Bender, B. Blumberg, C. Breazeal, D. Cavallo, T. Machover, M. Resnick, D. Roy, and C. Strohecker. Affective learning - a manifesto. *BT Technology Journal*, 22(4):253–269, 2004.

[24] P. Pu, L. Chen, and R. Hu. Evaluating recommender systems from the user?s perspective: survey of the state of the art. *User Modeling and User-Adapted Interaction*, 22(4-5):317–355, 2012.

[25] P. Resnick and H. R. Varian. Recommender systems. *Communications of the ACM*, 40(3):56–58, 1997.

Human-recommender Systems: From Benchmark Data to Benchmark Cognitive Models *

Patrick Shafto
Rutgers University – Newark
Newark, NJ 07102
patrick.shafto@gmail.com

Olfa Nasraoui
University of Louisville
Louisville, KY
olfa.nasraoui@louisville.edu

ABSTRACT

We bring to the fore of the recommender system research community, an inconvenient truth about the current state of understanding how recommender system algorithms and humans influence one another, both computationally and cognitively. Unlike the great variety of supervised machine learning algorithms which traditionally rely on expert input labels and are typically used for decision making by an expert, recommender systems specifically rely on data input from non-expert or casual users and are meant to be used directly by these same non-expert users on an every day basis. Furthermore, the advances in online machine learning, data generation, and predictive model learning have become increasingly interdependent, such that each one feeds on the other in an iterative cycle. Research in psychology suggests that people's choices are (1) contextually dependent, and (2) dependent on interaction history. Thus, while standard methods of training and assessing performance of recommender systems rely on benchmark datasets, we suggest that a critical step in the evolution of recommender systems is the development of benchmark *models* of human behavior that capture contextual and dynamic aspects of human behavior. It is important to emphasize that even extensive real life user-tests may not be sufficient to make up for this gap in benchmarking validity because user tests are typically done with either a focus on user satisfaction or engagement (clicks, sales, likes, etc) with whatever the recommender algorithm suggests to the user, and thus ignore the human cognitive aspect. We conclude by highlighting the interdisciplinary implications of this endeavor.

1. INTRODUCTION

In its pioneering years, machine learning drew significantly from cognitive psychology and human learning. Later, with the proliferation of online services, social media websites, and more generally, the wide democratization of "consumption of algorithms' output" by general users, machine learning algorithms started interacting with users at unprecedented rates. While in the early years, most (supervised) machine learning algorithms relied on reliable expert labels to build predictions [23, 24, 25, 8], more recently the gates of data generation have been opened wide to the general population with everyday users' interactions–labeling, rating, annotating, etc–being treated as training data for subsequent interactions and users [6, 19, 11].

A critical development in the field of machine learning, and recommender systems specifically, has been the curation of benchmark datasets. Prominent recent examples include the UCI respository [18], MNIST [17], as well as many others. Benchmark datasets facilitate advances in the field by promoting consensus regarding the scope of the problems to be solved and by offering standards by which all models can be assessed. Indeed, the importance of these datasets to the field is reflected in the high number of citations to these resources—more than 1700 for UCI and more than 500 for MNIST, which almost certainly under-represent the frequency of their use and their importance to the field.

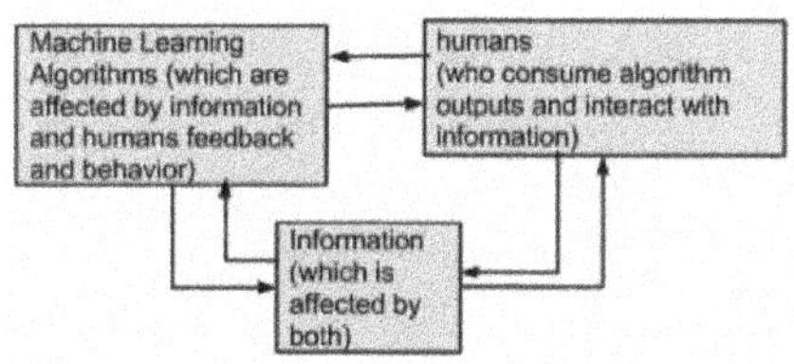

Figure 1: Illustration of the interaction between humans and algorithms through which data are generated. The arrows indicate directions of influence. Traditional recommender systems research focuses on the links between algorithms and data through curated benchmark data sets. Increasingly, algorithms are deployed in the "wild" and iteratively refined based on uncurated data, forming human-recommender systems. This raise questions about the non-independence of data and context and the non-stationarity of behavior over time.

Benchmark datasets typically provide data in batch format. This reflects the historical approach to machine learning and recommendation in which an algorithm is trained on a batch of data and then deployed. It also reflects assumptions about the nature of the problem to be solved; the tar-

*This research was supported in part by NSF grant NSF-1549981 to O.N. and P.S.

RecSys '16, September 15 - 19, 2016, Boston , MA, USA

ISBN 978-1-4503-4035-9/16/09...$15.00
DOI: http://dx.doi.org/10.1145/2959100.2959188

get distribution is stationary and that data are IID samples. These are fundamental assumptions of most standard learning algorithms, and thus sensible simplifying assumptions for starting out. The success of these standard algorithms and approaches has, however, led to new, more ambitious applications including online information filtering and item recommendations, retraining of algorithms based on users' input, and iteration of these interactions. Implicitly, iterative retraining with algorithms that assume stationarity and IID data leads to the potential for introduction of biases, which may be magnified through the interactions over time.

In light of these developments, we argue that it is necessary that the field reconsider how it trains and assesses algorithms. We propose the development of *benchmark models* of human behavior. Analogous to benchmark data sets, benchmark models capture the generative process that underlies typical benchmark data, including time-varying aspects. Benchmark models will accelerate progress by encouraging consensus regarding the kinds of dynamics and non-independence that are important for recommendation, and minimize risk by formalizing the aspects human behavior that potentially introduce bias and allowing researchers to investigate implications for their own algorithms. We emphasize that while some previous research has considered the dynamics of data into model evaluation [26], these have looked primarily at Benchmark data as a dynamic data stream, and not at the interactions between algorithms and humans.

We begin by stating minimal desiderata for a benchmark models vis-a-vis benchmark data. We then review key elements of human behavior to be integrated into such a model: contextual dependence of choice behavior, non-stationarities of preference due to learning about the domain of recommendation, and non-stationarities of preference due to learning about the recommender system itself. We conclude by summarizing our interactive approach and implications for the development of true human-recommender systems.

2. DESIDERATA FOR BENCHMARK MODELS

There are two minimal desiderata for benchmark models of human behavior.

- Marginalizing over time, the data produced by the benchmark model should correspond to traditionally curated benchmark data used in research on recommender systems and machine learning.
- The temporal dynamics of the model should be time varying such that it captures contextual-dependencies and non-stationarities observed in behavioral research and models of human behavior.

The first aspect is, we expect, relatively uncontroversial. Indeed, the simplest version of this, which does not include temporal dynamics, is precisely the generative modeling approaches that have been popular in probabilistic modeling.

The second aspect is, we expect, potentially more controversial along two dimensions: is this necessary and can this be done? We believe there is a very compelling reason for the necessity of models that capture dynamics of human behavior. If behavior is time varying, no batch method can capture the statistical structure of this behavior. This necessarily implies a deviation between the algorithms, which assume and are trained on data that does not possess interesting temporal structure, and people whose behavior is time varying. The iterated nature of interactions means that, under some circumstances, this gap may grow over time, suggesting that it is possible to observe a divergence between algorithms and behavior that grows over time. Benchmark models that capture the dynamics of of human behavior would allow one to test algorithms for satisfactory behavior both on average and across time. In the next section, we address the second question, whether such benchmark models are feasible by considering the elements of a model of human behavior.

3. ELEMENTS OF A MODEL OF HUMAN BEHAVIOR

The main goal of the model of human behavior is to abstract away from benchmark datasets to generative models for how people produce the data. This more abstract framework can allow the sorts of non-stationarity and non-independence that have been identified in research in cognitive science.

Research into human choice behavior in cognitive science dates back at least to Luce [20, 22, 35, 31]. Luce formalized human choice through the eponymous Luce choice rule, in which the probability of choosing an option from a set of possibilities is proportional to its utility. Luce's choice rule implicitly assumes a form of independence, independence from irrelevant alternatives. Since his proposal, researchers have identified numerous examples of how people's choices do in fact depend on what one would reasonably consider irrelevant alternatives. For example, several of the most famous examples stem from the work of Kahneman and Tversky [34, 29]. Consider the attraction effect, in which, people choose between, a nice pen or 6 dollars. At baseline, people favored the money over the pen; however, adding a second, much less attractive pen led more people to choose the nice pen. Adding an irrelevant pen increased participants preference for the nicer pen as compared to the money. This effect is a demonstration of the non-independence of choice in that the order of people's preferences is not stable with respect to the addition of other options (as is required by independence). Moreover, inspired by this work, there are a large number of computational models of choice that have been proposed to account for these non-independence effects, which would provide candidate starting points for formalizing a benchmark model of human behavior [22, 35, 33].

Increasingly, research in cognitive science has also investigated avenues by which people's choice behavior would be non-stationary over time. Two main mechanisms of non-stationarity are the active learning about the information they are searching for and learning about the system itself. For active learning, non-stationarities would arise due to people's beliefs changing over time. Thus, a choice at time $t+1$ may differ from that at $t-1$ only because people learned more about the options at time t. Active learning has a large body of research in cognitive science dating back at least to Bruner [9]. Recent research has focused on developing computational accounts of active learning [10, 3, 1, 2, 21], with recent work focusing on information gain (aka, KL divergence) as a model of human behavior in simple settings.

A second potential source of non-stationarity is people learning about the system with which they are interacting.

These non-stationarities arise in that people may develop heuristics to influence the system toward their goals. Here non-stationarities arise because people are learning about the behavior of the system itself, in essence reverse engineering their input to influence the machine toward their desired goals. This notion has an analog in recent cognitive science investigating learning about, and from, other people [28]. These approaches extend models of choice to incorporate simple models of other people's actions in terms of plans [4] and through more abstract modeling of the individual's goals and desires [13, 5, 28, 27, 12].

Although research continues, there are reasons to believe that development of a model of human behavior is reasonable. The first is that the basic empirical phenomena in choice theory are agreed upon. Second, the approaches based on learning are being developed within the broad choice theoretic framework [5, 28], suggesting a continuity in modeling.

4. ITERATED LEARNING

We argue for a framework for investigating the implications of interactions between human and algorithms that draws on diverse literature to provide algorithmic, mathematical, computational, and behavioral tools for investigating human-algorithm interaction. Such an approach would draw on foundational algorithms for selecting and filtering of data from computer science, while also adapting mathematical methods from the study of cultural evolution [14, 16, 7] to formalize the implications of iterative interactions. The basic feature of the algorithm application "in the wild" is iterative interaction with people. In this sense, the evolution of algorithms is a special case of cultural evolution of the sort observed in human language [15] and human knowledge more broadly [32, 7]. Researchers in the behavioral sciences have developed formal and empirical frameworks for analyzing and investigating the asymptotic effects of iterative interactions. Formally, iterative interactions with transmission between adjacent iterations forms a Markov chain [14]. Markov chains provide a well-elaborated framework for analyzing the effects of local decisions on long-run behavior. For the current proposal, the key question regards the conditions under which algorithms' behavior—in terms of the choice of data to present to people and the updated behavior in response to people's observed actions—will converge to more or less effective performance in the long run. Can we understand and compensate for these biases to ensure good performance?

Consider simple supervised machine learning where the goal is to learn to predict a discrete class label. Research on simple classifiers has historically paved the road for most formal analysis in machine learning and data mining, and had a significant impact on both information retrieval [30] as well as recommender systems [6]. It also provides a point of contact with the psychology of category learning.

We can extend iterated learning to provide a framework to analyze the evolution of the learned hypotheses **with interactions between the user and the algorithm**. We will account for the dependency between the current hypothesis and the next input because the model or hypothesis learned by the algorithm (learner) is used as a filter or gateway to the types of data that will later **be seen by** the user. This constitutes dependence between the current hypotheses h and the next inputs $\mathbf{x}$ (see Fig 2). It is interesting to contrast the evolution of iterated learning without and with this dependency. Without the dependency, the algorithm at step $n+1$ sees input $\mathbf{x}_{n+1}$ which is generated from a distribution $p(\mathbf{x})$ that is independent of all other variables. Represent this independence with new notation $q(\mathbf{x})$ (q instead of p), where $q(\mathbf{x})$ represents an unbiased sample from the world, rather than a selection made by the algorithm. With the dependency, the algorithm at iteration $n+1$ sees input $\mathbf{x}_{n+1}$ which is generated from a mixture between the objective distribution $q(\mathbf{x})$ and another distribution that captures the dependency upon the previous hypothesis h_n which biases the future inputs seen by the user.

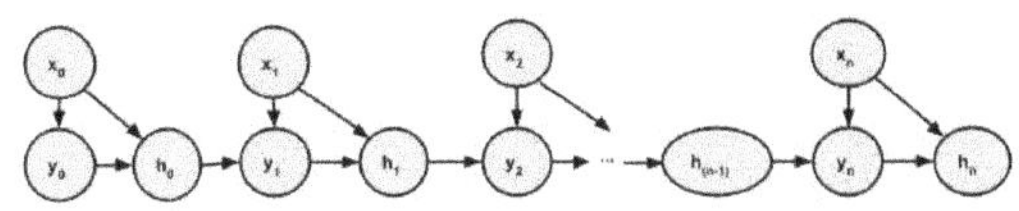

(a)

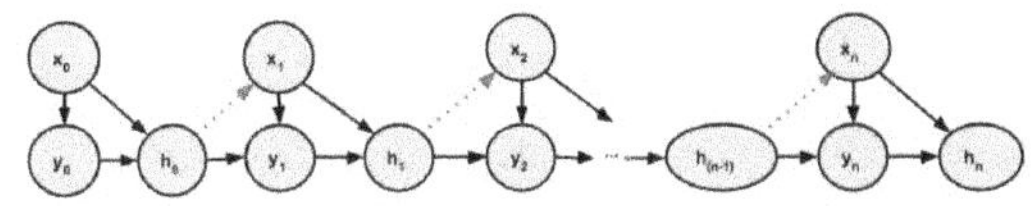

(b)

Figure 2: In iterated learning, information is passed through selected data, (a) where the inputs, x, are independent of the inferred hypothesis, and (b) where the next inputs are selected based on the previous hypothesis. The latter case is more consistent with recommender systems and information filtering circumstances.

5. CONCLUSION AND FUTURE OUTLOOK

Recommender systems, and machine learning more broadly, have benefited greatly from benchmark datasets. However, recent successes in the field, and specifically applications "in the wild" have led to prolific use of data that are not curated in the traditional sense, but instead arise from human-algorithm interaction. This cyclical flow is rarely taken into account in algorithm design and analysis; nor is its impact (or dependence) on algorithms and humans well understood. We propose that the next generation of recommender systems be trained not on benchmark data, but on benchmark models. This approach is necessarily interdisciplinary and involves building on cognitive science research to develop models of human behavior that formalize the non-stationarity and non-independence of human behavior that cannot be easily captured in data alone.

Key to our approach is the focus on the sources and consequences of bias in data collected "in the wild". The two primary sources of bias are from algorithms and from humans. Recommender systems filter information with the goal of presenting humans with the most preferred content. This aspect of recommendation raises questions regarding the non-independence of choice behavior that have been documented in cognitive science for decades. Our approach suggests that it may be important to not only study people's choices, but also their beliefs about the domain in question and about the algorithm itself. The former has been a standard question in both human and machine learning for decades. The latter speaks to ways in which algorithms may not merely serve human goals, but that those goals may also be a consideration of the algorithm. We emphasize that even user-tests do not make up for the gap in benchmarking validity because they typically focus on user satisfaction or engagement with what the algorithm suggested, and thus ignore the human cognitive aspect. When algorithms are able to both recommend content *and* reason about when and why people prefer something, we will be moving toward truly *human-recommender systems.*

6. REFERENCES

[1] F. G. Ashby, L. A. Alfonso-Reese, and E. M. Waldron. a neuropsychological theory of multiple systems in category learning. *Psychological Review*, 105:442–481, 1998.

[2] F. G. Ashby, W. T. Maddox, and C. J. Bohil. Observational versus feedback training in rule-based and information-integration category learning. *Memory & Cognition*, 30:666–677, 2002.

[3] F. G. Ashby, S. Queller, and P. T. Berretty. On the dominance of unidimensional rules in unsupervised categorization. *Perception and Psychophysics*, 61:1178–1199, 1999.

[4] C. L. Baker, R. Saxe, and J. B. Tenenbaum. Action understanding as inverse planning. *Cognition*, 113:329–349, 2009.

[5] C. L. Baker, R. Saxe, and J. B. Tenenbaum. Bayesian theory of mind: Modeling joint belief-desire attribution. In *Proceedings of the Thirty-Third Annual Conference of the Cognitive Science Society*, 2011.

[6] C. Basu, H. Hirsh, W. Cohen, et al. Recommendation as classification: Using social and content-based information in recommendation. In *AAAI/IAAI*, pages 714–720, 1998.

[7] A. Beppu and T. L. Griffiths. Iterated learning and the cultural ratchet. In *Proceedings of the 31st Annual Conference of the Cognitive Science Society*, 2009.

[8] C. M. . Bishop. Pattern recognition and machine learning. *Springer*, 4(4), 2006.

[9] J. Bruner. The art of discovery. *Harvard Educational Review*, 31:21–32, 1961.

[10] J. R. Bruner, J. J. Goodnow, and G. A. Austin. *A study of thinking.* Wiley, New York, 1956.

[11] J. C. Caicedo, J. BenAbdallah, F. A. González, and O. Nasraoui. Multimodal representation, indexing, automated annotation and retrieval of image collections via non-negative matrix factorization. *Neurocomputing*, 76(1):50–60, 2012.

[12] B. S. Eaves and P. Shafto. Unifying pedagogical reasoning and epistemic trust. In F. Xu and T. Kushnir, editors, *Advances in Child Development and Behavior, Volume, 43*, pages 295–319. Elsevier, San Diego, 2012.

[13] N. D. Goodman, C. L. Baker, E. B. Bonawitz, V. K. Mansinghka, A. Gopnik, H. Wellman, L. E. Schulz, and J. B. Tenenbaum. Intuitive theories of mind: A rational approach to false belief. In *Proceedings of the Twenty-Eighth Annual Conference of the Cognitive Science Society*, 2006.

[14] T. L. Griffiths and M. L. Kalish. A Bayesian view of language evolution by iterated learning. *Cognitive Science*, 31:441–480, 2007.

[15] S. Kirby. Spontaneous evolution of linguistic structure: An iterated learning model of the emergence of regularity and irregularity. *IEEE Journal of Evolutionary Computation*, 5:102–110, 2001.

[16] S. Kirby, M. Dowman, and T. L. Griffiths. Innateness and culture in the evolution of language. *Proceedings of the National Academy of Sciences*, 104:5241–5245, 2007.

[17] Y. LeCun, C. Cortes, and C. J. Burges. The mnist database of handwritten digits, 1998.

[18] M. Lichman. UCI machine learning repository, 2013.

[19] S. B. Y. J. Linden, G. Amazon. com recommendations: Item-to-item collaborative filtering. *Internet Computing, IEEE*, 7(1):76–80, 2003.

[20] R. D. Luce. *Individual choice behavior.* John Wiley, New York, 1959.

[21] D. Markant and T. Gureckis. Is it better to select or to receive? Learning via active and passive hypothesis testing. *Journal of Experimental Psychology: General*, 143(1):94–122, 2014.

[22] D. McFadden. Quantal choice analysis: A survey. *Annals of Economic and Social Measurement*, 5:363–390, 1977.

[23] R. S. Michalski. Pattern recognition as rule-guided inductive inference. *IEEE Transactions on Pattern Analysis and Machine Intelligence*, PAMI-2(4):349–361, July 1980.

[24] R. S. Michalski, I. Bratko, and A. Bratko. Machine learning and data mining; methods and applications. 1998.

[25] T. M. Mitchell. *Machine Learning.* McGraw-Hill, Inc., New York, NY, USA, 1 edition, 1997.

[26] O. Nasraoui, J. Cerwinske, C. Rojas, and F. A. González. Performance of recommendation systems in dynamic streaming environments. In *SIAM Data Mining (SDM)*, pages 569–574. SIAM, 2007.

[27] P. Shafto and N. D. Goodman. Teaching games: Statistical sampling assumptions for pedagogical situations. In *Proceedings of the 30th annual conference of the Cognitive Science Society*, 2008.

[28] P. Shafto, N. D. Goodman, and M. C. Frank. Learning from others: The consequences of psychological reasoning for human learning. *Perspectives on Psychological Science*, 7:341–351, 2012.

[29] I. Simonson and A. Tversky. Choice in context: Tradeoff contrast and extremeness aversion. *Journal of Marketing Research*, 29:281–295, 1992.

[30] K. Sparck Jones. Some thoughts on classification for retrieval. *Journal of Documentation*, 26(2):89–101, 1970.

[31] R. S. Sutton and A. G. Barto. *Reinforcement learning: An introduction.* MIT Press, Cambridge, MA, 1998.

[32] M. Tomasello. *The Cultural Origins of Human Cognition.* Harvard University Press, 1999.

[33] K. Train. *Discrete choice models with simulation.* Cambridge University Press, Cambridge, 2003.

[34] A. Tversky. Elimination by aspects: A theory of choice. *Psychological Review*, 79:281–299, 1972.

[35] J. I. Yellot. The relationship between luce's choice axiom, thurstone's theory of comparative judgement, and the double exponential distribution. *Journal of Mathematical Psychology*, 15:109–144, 1977.

Gaze Prediction for Recommender Systems

Qian Zhao, Shuo Chang, F. Maxwell Harper, Joseph A. Konstan
GroupLens Research
Dept. of Computer Science, University of Minnesota
Minneapolis, United States
{qian, schang, harper, konstan}@cs.umn.edu

ABSTRACT

As users browse a recommender system, they systematically consider or skip over much of the displayed content. It seems obvious that these eye gaze patterns contain a rich signal concerning these users' preferences. However, because eye tracking data is not available to most recommender systems, these signals are not widely incorporated into personalization models. In this work, we show that it is possible to predict gaze by combining easily-collected user browsing data with eye tracking data from a small number of users in a grid-based recommender interface. Our technique is able to leverage a small amount of eye tracking data to infer gaze patterns for other users. We evaluate our prediction models in MovieLens – an online movie recommender system. Our results show that incorporating eye tracking data from a small number of users significantly boosts accuracy as compared with only using browsing data, even though the eye-tracked users are different from the testing users (e.g. AUC=0.823 vs. 0.693 in predicting whether a user will fixate on an item). We also demonstrate that Hidden Markov Models (HMMs) can be applied in this setting; they are better than linear models in predicting fixation probability and capturing the interface regularity through Bayesian inference (AUC=0.823 vs. 0.757).

Keywords

eye tracking; Hidden Markov Models; grid-based interface

1. INTRODUCTION

Recommender systems research has experienced a transition from modeling user preferences based on explicit feedback [36, 38], e.g. **what users are rating** to preference modeling based on implicit feedback [25, 33], e.g. **what users are clicking**. Nowadays, it has been recognized that successful recommendations also need to take into account user perceptions of recommendation properties such as diversity and serendipity [23, 31], user short-term information needs, user context, and mood, i.e. **what users are thinking**.

RecSys '16, September 15-19, 2016, Boston, MA, USA

DOI: http://dx.doi.org/10.1145/2959100.2959150

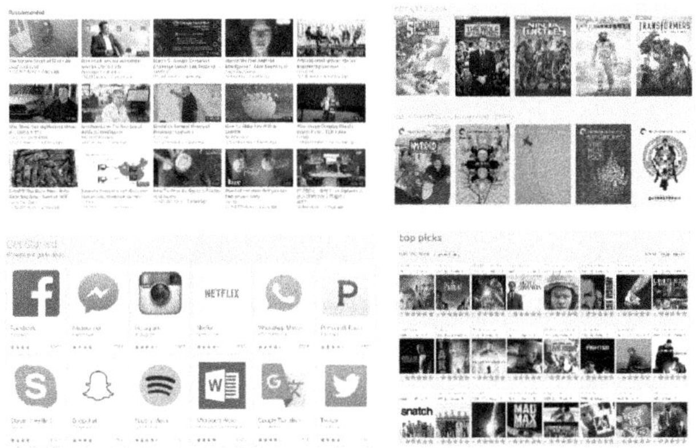

Figure 1: In this work, we predict user gaze in grid-based user interfaces. Above are four such layouts – YouTube (top-left), Hulu (top-right), Google Apps (bottom-left) and MovieLens (bottom-right).

Understanding how users look at a recommender system's content will enable further improvements to how systems model and react to user needs. As users browse a recommender system, they systematically consider or skip over much of the displayed content. It seems likely that these eye gaze patterns contain a rich signal concerning these users' state of mind. Indeed, early studies have shown the potential for improving recommender systems by incorporating eye tracking data [43, 34].

The ability to incorporate eye tracking data into a recommender system enables a variety of potential improvements. For example, recommender systems currently do not know which items are looked at and ignored versus simply not looked at. But this is a critical distinction – if the user looks and does not act, that *inaction* provides a signal that can be used to influence whether and when to display that item in the future, though interpreting whether such gazes represent interest or lack thereof may require context and further analysis.

Also, since recommender systems essentially provide decision support for users, having user gaze enables more nuanced studies on user high-level decision-making processes as demonstrated by researchers who study human decision theory through eye tracking [17].

The biggest challenge to incorporating user gaze data into recommender systems is a technical one: it requires eye tracking technology, which is generally not available outside of specialized labs. It is possible that future systems will make gaze detection a common feature available to system builders, due to the ubiquitous presence of high-resolution user-facing cameras. It is also possible that eye tracking data will never be commonly used due to the privacy concerns that such low-level tracking raises.

To address these challenges, in this work we show that it is possible to model and predict user gaze without requiring the deployment of ubiquitous eye tracking technology. We predict gaze by combining easily-collected user browsing data with eye tracking data from a small number of users. Our technique is therefore able to leverage a small amount of eye tracking data to infer gaze patterns for other users.

In this research, we model gaze in the context of a grid-based user interface layout, which has become one of the most common user interface layouts in recommender systems. For example, this is the layout used in YouTube, Hulu, Google Apps, and MovieLens, as shown in Figure 1. We address the following three research questions:

- *RQ1: How accurately can we predict gaze on items in a grid-based interface?*
  - based on models trained with only **user browsing data**. (Specifically, item position in the interface, user dwell time on the page, and actions such as clicks, ratings and wishlistings on items.)
  - based on models trained with collected **eye tracking data** for a small number of users in addition to user browsing data.
- *RQ2: How is gaze distributed on different positions in a grid-based interface?*
- *RQ3: How does gaze prediction accuracy vary for different tasks or modes of usage?*

We make the following contributions in this paper:

- We show that incorporating eye tracking data from a small number of users significantly boosts gaze prediction accuracy as compared with only using user browsing data, even though the eye-tracked users are different from testing users;
- We demonstrate that Hidden Markov Models (HMMs) can be applied in this setting and that they are better than baseline models in predicting fixation probability and capturing the interface regularity through Bayesian inference.

2. RELATED WORK

Human attention theory. From cognitive sciences, two main mechanisms guide the selection of human attention: top-down and bottom-up (or endogenous vs. exogenous) processes [4]. We can volitionally focus our attention according to top-down task demands. On the other hand, our attention may be drawn by bottom-up salient stimuli. This dichotomy of attention is still under debate because it involves the fundamental question of seeing attention as a cause, as an effect or as a combination of both [37], which has significant implication for interactive applications such as recommender systems. Specific to visual attention, we focus on reviewing overt attention [16] here, i.e. gaze is directed to the attended location. Following Marr [30] and Itti's [27] seminal work, there has been plenty of research on modeling visual attention in a bottom-up approach, i.e. saliency prediction [29, 6]. However, researchers have started to criticize the over-emphasis on low-level saliency representation of visual input and develop new models of gaze allocation guided by top-down principles to account for complex natural vision [41]. Tatler et al. [42] showed that a model based solely on behavior biases and blind to current visual information can outperform a salience-based approach. Top-down task demands or regularities can be formalized with probability theories, especially Bayesian statistics. For example, Markov stochastic processes have been applied to model gaze transition behaviors, since it is intuitive to compare eye movements to random walkers. Ellis and Stark [14] developed a method to identify statistical dependencies in positions of eye fixations based on Markov matrices and found that there is statistical dependency among sequences of fixations independent of the physical placement of the points of interest. Further work built on this [20] modeled sequences of visual fixations as Markov processes and introduced a quantitative method to measure scanpath similarity based on character strings. Henderson et al. [22] demonstrated that it is possible to classify the task that a person is engaged in, i.e. cognitive states from their eye movements by multivariate pattern classification specifically naive Bayes. Haji-Abolhassani et al. [21] modeled eye trajectories as a noisy generative process centered on the foci of attention directed by cognitive processes using Hidden Markov Models. Our study builds on this top-down approach. We do not model the saliency of the displayed items on a page, but instead look at how high-level information of item position presented in the interface directs and regulates user gaze behavior.

Eye tracking and information retrieval. Joachims et al. [18] pioneered the investigation of user behavior in WWW search through eye tracking analysis. They found that a higher rank in search results attracts more attention and users do tend to scan the result list from top to bottom. In information retrieval, machine learning algorithms are used to learn the relevance between search queries and web URLs from implicit clicking feedback [1]. Joachims et al. [28] examined the reliability of this kind of feedback generated from clickthrough data using eye tracking and explicit relevance judgement. They concluded that clicks are informative but biased, i.e. the **position bias** because of search result presentation in a list layout. Following these findings, various user attention and browsing models are proposed to account for the bias in learning algorithms [8, 13, 9, 39] for information retrieval. Chapelle and Zhang [7] built and evaluated a dynamic Bayesian network model postulating explicitly examination or attention, action and satisfaction variables in addition to the observed clicking events. The temporal or dynamic aspect of the model lies in the assumption that users examine search results from top to bottom one by one, which is reasonable in a list layout interface and supported by previous work [18]. Because of the cost of eye tracking, researchers have worked on approximating gaze in two main approaches: gaze-contingent displays [12] or restricted focus viewing and predicting gaze with mouse positions [26, 19]. As an example, Buscher et al. [3] compared segment-level display time of search results with eye tracking and found that although it is much coarser, it works as well as eye-tracking-based feedback for re-ranking and query expansion. Going beyond applications of information retrieval, Buscher et al. [2] worked on predicting gaze with web page location-based characteristics as input and generating a model that can be used to improve web page layout and design.

Eye tracking and recommender systems. Recommender system researchers have been using eye tracking in different ways. Since recommenders are considered an important decision support tool, Castagnos et al. [5] studied user decision making behaviors when purchasing products assisted by a recommender through eye tracking. They showed that users actively click and gaze at recommended products up to 40% of the time and consult the recommendation area more as they approach the end of the decision process. Another intuitive application based on eye tracking in recommenders is to infer preference or relevance from user gaze behavior. Xu et al. [43] proposed several algorithms to make recommendations relying on the attention time captured through commodity eye tracking as preference clues. Puolamaki et al. [34] combined eye movements and collaborative filtering [38] in proactive information retrieval tasks which is similar to a recommender and demonstrated its accuracy benefit in predicting whether a document is relevant. Recommender systems that rely on implicit feedback [25] could suffer from position bias as well, as demonstrated by Hofmann et al. [24] in simulated experiments. They examined this bias using different click models and showed how bias following these models would affect the outcome of recommender system offline evaluation based on implicit feedback data.

Two hypotheses for user gaze behavior in a grid. In a grid-based layout, it is likely no longer valid to assume examining results from top to bottom one by one any more, since there are two potential directions (horizontal and vertical) that users can direct their attention. We have two hypotheses regarding how users examine a grid: **F-pattern** [11] and **center effect** [40]. As pointed out by Tatler [40], observers have a tendency to fixate the center of the screen on computer monitors. They demonstrated the endurance of the central fixation bias irrespective of the distribution of image features, which implies that the center of a screen may be an optimal location for early information processing as learned by users. On contrary, because that a grid with rows and columns are different from an integral scene picture, the visual hierarchy might dominate the viewing behavior and users could exhibit a viewing pattern favoring the top and left sides [11], as suggested by the shape F going from top to bottom and left to right.

3. BUILDING MODELS FOR THE GAZE PREDICTION PROBLEM

We define a specific type of gaze prediction problem here – **Aggregated Fixation Prediction**. **Fixation** refers to the stationary period between saccades [16], in other words, the maintaining of visual gaze on the same location (we focus on predicting fixation here because in most human visual activities, we reply on fixations to take in visual information [16]). Consider a user browsing a page in a grid layout (examples shown in Figure 1), which has r rows and c columns and $r * c$ items in total. The problem is to predict **fixation probability**, i.e., whether the user has fixated, and **fixation time**, i.e., how long the user has fixated, on each of

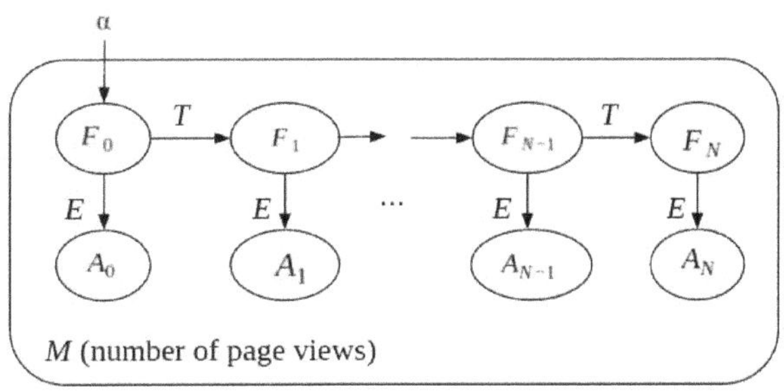

Figure 2: Graphical representation of a HMM in which F denotes fixation variable and A denotes action variable. α, T and E are parameters representing categorical conditional distributions defining the HMM. N is the length of the HMM sequence. For the gaze prediction problem, HMM gives inferred probability distributions of F when the values of A are observed.

the $r * c$ items aggregating the entire browsing of the user on the page, given **item positions**, the user's **dwell time** on the page and the user's **actions** (e.g. rating, clicking or wishlisting) on some of the items. Note that the unit of prediction is for each displayed item in one page view.

3.1 Building Linear Models

We start with linear models to predict users' fixation. With access to a group of users' fixation data, we can build supervised machine learning models to predict future fixations for this group of users and even for other users.

For predicting fixation probability, we build a mixed-effect logistic regression model (taking into account the correlation among positions by using a random intercept for each page view) using the following three groups of features:

- *Position* features: row index, ranging from 1 to r, and column index, ranging from 1 to c;
- *Dwell time*: log transformed seconds spent on a page;
- *1/minActionDist*: the inverse of the minimum distance to actions on a page. This feature encodes the insight that users are more likely to fixate on surrounding items when they interact with an item on a page. For example, if a user acts upon (e.g. clicks) the second position, then it is likely that the user has fixated on the first or third position, which are small in terms of Euclidean distance calculated with row index and column index as the coordinates. Since there might be multiple actions, we take the minimum. We take the inverse of the minimum distance so that the coefficient of the feature is positive and the value of the feature equals zero with no action.

For predicting fixation time, we use the same set of features but a different model, a two-stage hurdle linear model [32]. This model handles zero inflation property in training data, i.e., users have not fixated on many displayed items, by modeling each data point first through a logistic regression and then through a zero-truncated negative binomial regression.

To simplify result presentation, we refer to linear models without using *1/minActionDist* feature as **linearModel**

Table 1: **Different models for the gaze prediction problem, in which *bl* denotes baseline, *ub* denotes training only on user browsing data (or *training without fixation*) and *et* denotes training on eye tracking data (or *training with fixation*) as well.**

Model	**Model descriptions. Some depend on example action sequences a and b (nonzeros indicate the action position indices and 0 denotes no action)**
	Action sequence a: 0 0 2 0 4 0 3 0 0 0 0 Action sequence b: 2 0 3 4 0 0 0 2 0 0 0
bl:simpleActionStats (simple action statistics)	Based on simple action statistics, in which page dwell time is distributed among the $r * c$ positions proportionate to the frequency of actions on that position from user action logs. They are used in predicting both fixation probability and fixation time.
ub:exactActionHmm (exact action approximation)	a does not contribute on the estimation of α, because it starts with no action. b counts once for initiating from position 2. a does not contribute on the estimation of T because there is no action transition from a non-zero position to another non-zero position. b counts once for the transition from position 3 to position 4.
ub:truncActionHmm (truncated action approximation)	After removing zeros, a will count for initiating from position 2 and transition from 2 to 4 and from 4 to 3 even though that is not exactly what have happened.
ub:RestExactActionHmm	Re-estimating using Expectation Maximization (EM, [10]) algorithm with exactActionHmm as initial values.
ub:RestTruncActionHmm	Re-estimating using EM algorithm with truncActionHmm as initial values.
et:linearModel	logistic regression model for predicting fixation probability or hurdle linear model for predicting fixation time; *1/minActionDist* feature is not used
et:linearModelActionDist	same as above except that *1/minActionDist* feature is used
et:eyeTrackingHmm	α, T and E are estimated by Maximum Likelihood Estimation.

and models using *1/minActionDist* feature as **linearModelActionDist** which are also summarized in Table 1.

3.2 Building Hidden Markov Models

We also use Hidden Markov Models, HMM for short, to predict users' fixation, as shown in Figure 2. For each page view, the dwell time is partitioned into small pieces of constant time intervals (the length of the interval is a parameter to tune). Each interval is associated with two variables: fixation F and action A. F takes $r*c$ possible values, representing the positions a user might fixate on the grid-based interface. We did not model no fixation (which could result from users' looking away or eye tracker's loss of gaze data. Time intervals with no fixation are removed from the observed F sequence) because it is less relevant for the prediction tasks. Given F, A can take $r * c + 1$ possible values, i.e. one of the $r*c$ positions that a user acts upon plus the possibility of no action upon any position (we did not differentiate different types of actions). If multiple fixations are present in one time interval, we pick the one with longer fixation duration. If multiple actions are present (which rarely happens for small time intervals), we shift later actions to the following time intervals for which there is no action present or otherwise only use the first action. The parameters of this HMM are same for all users, i.e. the HMM is not personalized:

- **initiation vector** α (length of $r * c$) represents the categorical probability distribution of the initial fixation.
- **transition matrix** T (size of $r * c$ by $r * c$) represents the categorical transition probabilities from previous fixation to the next.
- **emission matrix** E (size of $r*c$ by $r*c+1$) represents the categorical action probabilities given the current fixation position.

With fixation data from some users' page views (using eye tracking), we can estimate the above parameters by maximizing the likelihood of observing both the fixations and actions. We refer to this model as **eyetrackingHmm** (summarized in Table 1 as well).

Without fixation data, we can still estimate the above parameters with observed actions as follows. Firstly, we estimate E with one assumption – users usually do not act upon items they are not fixating on. Therefore, We set small probability values (specifically, $10e-6$ in our algorithms) in E where positions of actions are different from positions of fixation. For the other case, we estimate the probability of acting upon f given that $F = f$ from frequency of actions on f in users' action logs. Secondly, we estimate α and T, by treating observed action as fixation, with the four algorithms named starting with *ub:* in Table 1.

Predicting based on HMM relies on the inferred *responsibility parameters*, i.e. posterior distribution $P(F_i|A)$, denoted by a matrix R (N by $r * c$), in which N is the length of the HMM sequence. S_i defined in Equation 1 is computed for predicting fixation probability and L_i defined in Equation 2 is computed for predicting fixation time. The rationale behind these formulas lies in that $P(F_i|A)$ tells how much *responsibility* fixating on a position takes for the observed action sequence.

$$S_i = \sum_{j=0}^{N} R_{j,i}, \text{ for } i = 1 \text{ to } r * c \tag{1}$$

$$L_i = DwellTime * \frac{S_i}{\sum_{k=1}^{r*c} S_k}, \text{ for } i = 1 \text{ to } r * c \tag{2}$$

4. METHODS

4.1 MovieLens and User Browsing Dataset

MovieLens (https://movielens.org) is a public online movie recommender service maintained by GroupLens Research at the University of Minnesota. We focus on an interface called the **explore** page (which refers to a page with *explore* in its URL). It is a paginated three-rows-by-eight-columns grid-based layout presenting movie recommendations. Most of the explore page views are completely filled with $24(= 3*8)$ movie cards, as shown in Figure 1 (bottom-right). On each explore page, users can click a presented movie card, leaving the explore page and going to a movie detail page for that movie's details. Users can also rate or wishlist movies in a five-star-rating or wishlisting widget without leaving the explore page.

We use a dataset with one month of user browsing data from November 2015. For our purposes, we track page dwell time and ratings, clicks and wishlistings on movie cards. When a user leaves the explore page by clicking a movie card and directly returns, we count it as a continuing page view of that explore page, rather than a fresh new page view, so the dwell time accumulates through interruptions such as movie detail page views. In total, this data set has 102,039 page views with associated dwell times.

4.2 Eye Tracking Protocol Design and Dataset

We collected 17 subjects' gaze data using Tobii T60 Eye Tracker (0.5 degree accuracy, 60 Hz data rate, 17" screen size, 1,280x1024 resolution, roughly 65 cm viewing distance). These subjects are university students, including twelve males and five females, aging from 18 to 25 and majoring across eight disciplines. Subjects reported that they had watched five or more movies in the past two months with two exceptions: one had watched two movies and another had watched three. They had never used MovieLens before. We set up an account for each subject and asked them to perform the five tasks listed below which takes around 30 minutes after the eye tracker calibration procedure.

- *Task 1: Browsing for fun (five minutes).* This is for the subjects to get to know MovieLens features and obtain natural gaze and browsing behavior.
- *Task 2: Rate 15 movies.* Subjects were instructed to rate based on their preference on movies in a five-star rating widget.
- *Task 3: Find 10 movies you'd like to watch given a three-month holiday.* Subjects were asked to add those movies into their wishlist using the wishlisting feature.
- *Task 4: Find 5 movies you'd like to recommend to your friends.*
- *Task 5: Find 5 movies you'd like to recommend to a 12 years' old child.*

We directly used the fixation records generated by Tobii Eye Tracker (see its manual for details of the algorithms to compute fixation from raw gaze[1]). Each record has fixation duration and screen coordinates. To obtain fixations on the displayed movie cards, we recorded the movie card position coordinates, and tracked scrolling events as well to count for the position change. These positions are programmatically matched with the eye tracker's fixation records. Aggregating all 17 subjects, we collected 452 qualified page views (i.e. views of explore page completely filled with 24 movie cards.). Since the unit of prediction is with respect to each movie card display, we have $10{,}848(= 24*452)$ data points to use (Among them, we have 2304 for Task 1, 2760 for Task 2, 3960 for Task 3, 552 for Task 4 and 1008 for Task 5).

[1]http://www.acuity-ets.com/downloads/Tobii%20Studio%203.3%20User%20Guide.pdf

4.3 Evaluation

For each of the 17 subjects in the eye tracking study, we have their **true fixations** on each movie card in a page view, which is the **target variable** to predict. Prediction accuracy is measured with **AUC (Area Under the ROC)** for predicting fixation probability, i.e. to classify a displayed movie in a page view into being fixated or not and **MAE (Mean Absolute Error)** for predicting fixation time. The unit of MAE is in seconds.

Depending on whether using true fixation data or not to train models, the evaluation has two scenarios. In the **training-with-fixation** scenario, both fixation and browsing data from the 17 subjects in lab settings are used. We randomly pick 4 (around 20%) subjects and use their data for testing, while reserving the other subjects for training. This procedure is conducted multiple times (around 100 runs; a different set of subjects are picked each time) to compute variance of the metrics. In the **training-without-fixation** scenario, as its name suggests, only user browsing data is used for training, including both the one month dataset and user browsing data from the 17 subjects in lab settings. In order to be able to compare the accuracy between these two scenarios, testing phase of this scenario uses the exact same fixation data as the previous scenario.

5. RESULTS

RQ1: How accurately can we predict gaze on items in a grid-based interface? Figures 3 and 4 illustrate the accuracy of predicting fixation based on models trained with only user browsing data (the bottom five boxplots) and with eye tracking data (the top three boxplots). First of all, we see that there is a significant accuracy boost resulting from training on eye tracking data even though the training and testing users are different. Specifically, AUC increases from 0.693 for *exactActionHmm* to 0.823 for *eyeTrackingHmm* ($p \approx 0$) and MAE decreases from 0.466 for *simpleActionStats* to 0.332 for *linearModelActionDist* ($p \approx 0$). This result demonstrates that gaze patterns are consistent even across different users, and that our models capture these patterns very well.

In the *training-with-fixation* scenario, *eyetrackingHMM* performs significantly better than *linearModelActionDist* in predicting fixation probability ($AUC = 0.823$ vs. 0.757; $p \approx 0$). However, it performs worse in predicting fixation time ($MAE = 0.520$ vs. 0.332; $p \approx 0$). In the *training-without-fixation* scenario, *exactActionHmm* is much better than *simpleActionStats* ($AUC = 0.693$ vs. 0.580; $p \approx 0$) in predicting fixation probability (For an intuitive interpretation, Figure 5 shows the ROCs for one run of the evaluation procedure). But similarly, it has worse MAE (0.520 vs. 0.466; $p \approx 0$) in predicting fixation time. *RestExactActionHmm* and *RestTruncActionHmm* do not improve, which might be explained by overfitting to the action data set.

The above results show that HMM is more effective in capturing the interface regularity through Markov matrices and Bayesian inference in predicting binary-valued fixation vs. no-fixation, but is not very good at predicting real-valued fixation time. It might be explained by the choice of partition granularity in HMM, since we have to decide on a time interval. We are using one second for all HMMs after exploring multiple choices. It might illustrate a general difficulty of a generative modeling approach such as HMMs compared with a discriminative modeling approach such as hurdle linear models, in which fewer assumptions have to be made. Actually, hurdle linear models have better accuracy than ordinary linear regression, poisson or negative binomial regression and random forest with the same set of features. Note that MAEs less than a second do not imply that predicting fixation time is an easy task. It could possibly result from the small range of the ground truth values, especially with many zeros. Instead, we found that it is hard to predict fixation time since with the best model we have, the prediction R^2(*coefficient of determination*) is 0.21. In other words, our model explains 21% of the variance in fixation time.

RQ2: How is gaze distributed on different positions in a grid-based interface? Figure 6 (drawn based on the mixed-effect logistic regression model; no significant interaction effects) illustrates user gaze behavior in a grid. It supports the *F-pattern* hypothesis, instead of *center* effect. Note that the fixation probability between either the first row and second row or the first column and second column is not significantly different. However, both the third row and third column have a significant drop ($p \approx 0$). Particularly, we omit the last column (index 7) because of data collection problem. The Tobbi eye tracker has relatively smaller screen size which leaves part of the movie card in the last column out of view. This however does not affect the conclusion for this research question. More interestingly, we found that for all positions dwell time is positively associated with fixation probability and when reaching 60 seconds, different positions on average have a very high probability (> 0.80) of being fixated.

RQ3: How does gaze prediction accuracy vary for different tasks or modes of usage? From Figure 7, we see that Task 3 – *finding ten movies for self* – has the best accuracy in predicting fixation probability ($AUC = 0.842$, $p \approx 0$). Since more data is collected for Task 3, it partially explains the accuracy advantage. Another possible explanation is that the process postulated by HMM particularly fits better to subjects' gaze behavior when engaging in this task. On contrary, as shown in Figure 8, the accuracy suffers most in

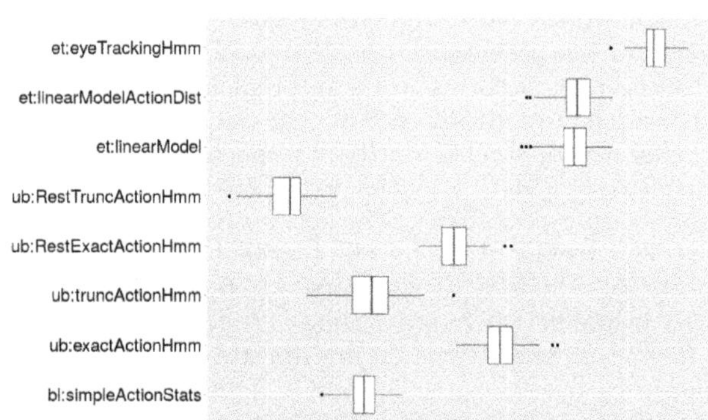

Figure 3: AUC boxplots for different models in predicting fixation probability. Higher scores are better. See Table 1 for descriptions of the models.

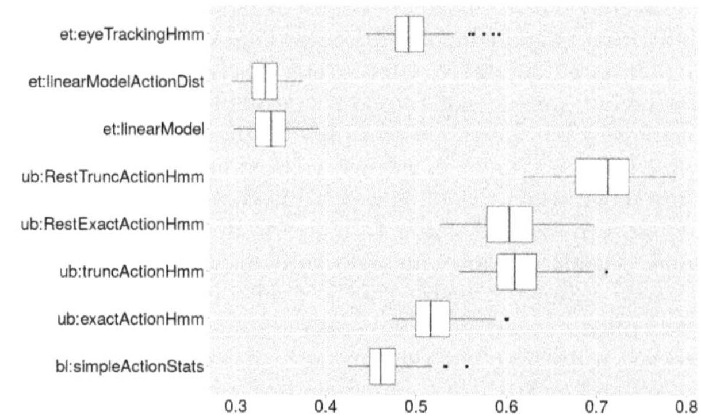

Figure 4: MAE boxplots for different models in predicting fixation time. Lower scores are better. See Table 1 for descriptions of the models.

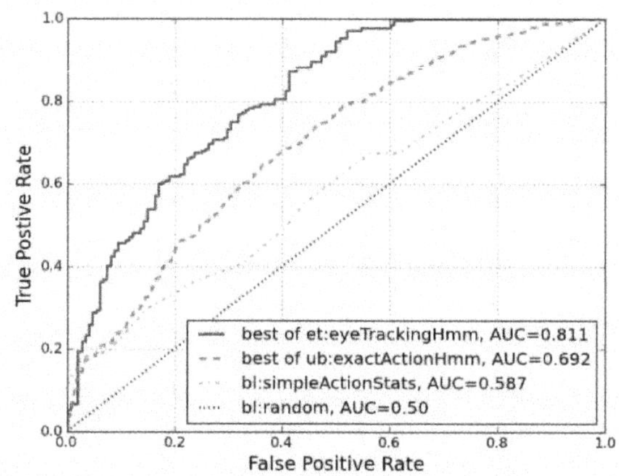

Figure 5: ROCs in classifying displayed movie cards into being fixated or not in a page view. It is from one run of the evaluation procedure.

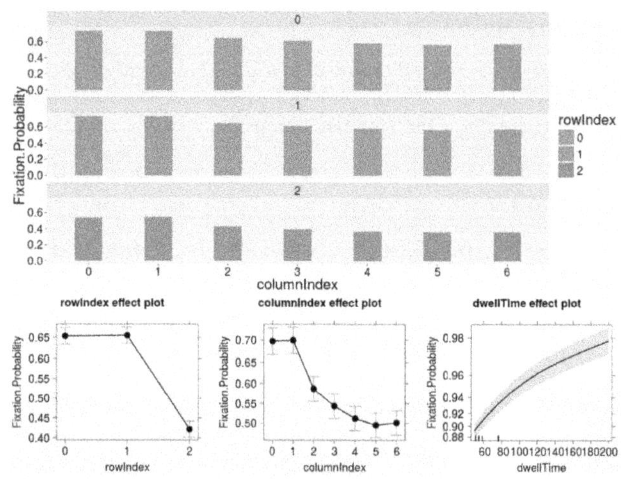

Figure 6: Fitted probabilities for different positions and the effects plot of *position* feature and *dwell time* in predicting whether a displayed movie is fixated using logistic regression. No significant interaction is found.

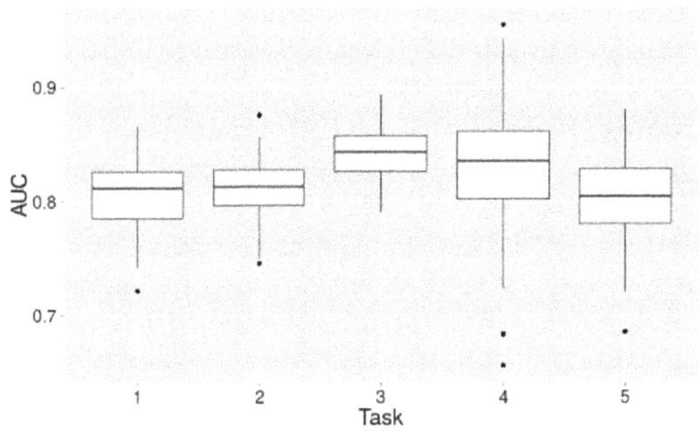

Figure 7: AUC boxplots of the best model *et:eyeTrackingHmm* in predicting fixation probability for the different tasks.

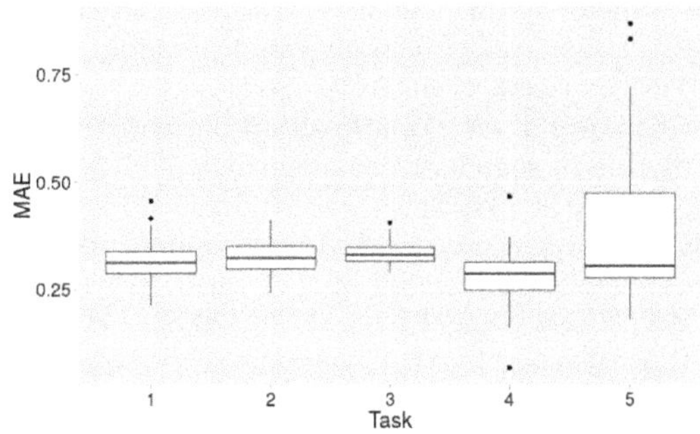

Figure 8: MAE boxplots of the best model *et:linearModelActionDist* in predicting fixation time for the different tasks.

predicting fixation time for the *finding-movies-for-children* task ($MAE = 0.340$, $p = 2.92e-08$). Subjects' gaze behavior shows substantial difference in this task from the video-recorded eye movements. Their fixations are shorter and more scattered, probably because subjects' searching strategy changed to coarser-level information scanning since most of the displayed items are not relevant anymore. Note that the better accuracy ($p \approx 0$) for Task 4 might just result from low variance in the data because we may not have enough data points for it. The general conclusion is that user gaze behavior is different in different usage modes and collecting and training on a specific task is better, especially for system designers who have knowledge about the main task that their users are engaged in.

6. FUTURE WORK

Our gaze prediction techniques imply two direct practical applications in recommender systems. First, they could be used to improve recommendation freshness. We can predict which items the user has paid attention to repeatedly without action, and replace those items with new recommendations. Second, they could be used to remove potential position bias in preference modeling with implicit feedback [24]. We have tried to directly use the predicted fixation probability to weigh the click-through observations in a matrix factorization model and achieved some accuracy improvement in predicting clicks under certain conditions. It does not always work because position bias is usually confounded with the typical relevance or preference of items shown at that position [7]. It is not straightforward to disentangle those confounding factors. A unified model on both gaze and preference may be necessary instead of simple weighting.

We envision two kinds of extensions to HMMs used in this work. First, it is possible to consider individual-level, in addition to current global modeling if a user has enough page views. Second, the fixation duration on a position is modeled implicitly through state self-transitioning, which essentially assumes that the duration follows a geometric distribution [35]. This assumption may not be valid especially when more factors are introduced such as preferences to explain fixation duration. Hidden Semi-Markov Models (HSMM) have been proposed to account for it and successfully applied in speech recognition [15]. Applying HSMM in our setting is a promising future direction.

7. CONCLUSION AND CONTRIBUTION

We conduct initial research on modeling and predicting gaze in recommender systems with a grid-based interface. We apply HMM in this setting and achieve significant accuracy improvement in predicting fixation probability. We also show that incorporating eye tracking data from a small number of users into the model training significantly boosts accuracy compared with only using normally logged user browsing data, even though the eye-tracked users are different from testing users. User gaze behavior follows an *F-pattern* rather than showing a *center effect* in a grid-based interface. In addition, we find that user gaze behavior is different in different usage modes which suggests that collecting and training on a specific task is better, especially for system designers who have knowledge about the main task that their users are engaged in.

8. ACKNOWLEDGEMENT

This work was supported by the National Science Foundation under grant IIS-1319382, and by Google under a Social Computing Focused Research Award.

9. REFERENCES

[1] E. Agichtein, E. Brill, and S. Dumais. Improving web search ranking by incorporating user behavior information. In *SIGIR'06*, pages 19–26. ACM, 2006.

[2] G. Buscher, E. Cutrell, and M. R. Morris. What do you see when you're surfing?: using eye tracking to predict salient regions of web pages. In *CHI'09*, pages 21–30. ACM, 2009.

[3] G. Buscher, L. van Elst, and A. Dengel. Segment-level display time as implicit feedback: a comparison to eye tracking. In *SIGIR'09*, pages 67–74. ACM, 2009.

[4] T. J. Buschman and E. K. Miller. Top-down versus bottom-up control of attention in the prefrontal and posterior parietal cortices. *Science*, 315(5820):1860–1862, 2007.

[5] S. Castagnos, N. Jones, and P. Pu. Eye-tracking product recommenders' usage. In *RecSys'10*, pages 29–36. ACM, 2010.

[6] M. Cerf, J. Harel, W. Einhäuser, and C. Koch. Predicting human gaze using low-level saliency combined with face detection. In *NIPS'08*, pages 241–248, 2008.

[7] O. Chapelle and Y. Zhang. A dynamic bayesian network click model for web search ranking. In *WWW'09*, pages 1–10. ACM, 2009.

[8] Y. Chen and T. W. Yan. Position-normalized click prediction in search advertising. In *KDD'12*, pages 795–803. ACM, 2012.

[9] N. Craswell, O. Zoeter, M. Taylor, and B. Ramsey. An experimental comparison of click position-bias models. In *WSDM'08*, pages 87–94. ACM, 2008.

[10] A. P. Dempster, N. M. Laird, and D. B. Rubin. Maximum likelihood from incomplete data via the em algorithm. *Journal of the royal statistical society. Series B (methodological)*, pages 1–38, 1977.

[11] S. Djamasbi, M. Siegel, and T. Tullis. Visual hierarchy and viewing behavior: An eye tracking study. In *Human-Computer Interaction. Design and Development Approaches*, pages 331–340. Springer, 2011.

[12] A. T. Duchowski, N. Cournia, and H. Murphy. Gaze-contingent displays: A review. *CyberPsychology & Behavior*, 7(6):621–634, 2004.

[13] G. E. Dupret and B. Piwowarski. A user browsing model to predict search engine click data from past observations. In *SIGIR'08*, pages 331–338. ACM, 2008.

[14] S. R. Ellis and L. Stark. Statistical dependency in visual scanning. *Human Factors: The Journal of the Human Factors and Ergonomics Society*, 28(4):421–438, 1986.

[15] J. D. Ferguson. Variable duration models for speech. In *Proc. Symposium on the Application of HMMs to Text and Speech*, pages 143–179, 1980.

[16] J. M. Findlay. Active vision: The psychology of looking and seeing. 2014.

[17] M. G. Glaholt and E. M. Reingold. Eye movement monitoring as a process tracing methodology in decision making research. *Journal of Neuroscience, Psychology, and Economics*, 4(2):125, 2011.

[18] L. A. Granka, T. Joachims, and G. Gay. Eye-tracking analysis of user behavior in www search. In *SIGIR'04*, pages 478–479. ACM, 2004.

[19] Q. Guo and E. Agichtein. Towards predicting web searcher gaze position from mouse movements. In *CHI EA'10*, pages 3601–3606. ACM, 2010.

[20] S. S. Hacisalihzade, L. W. Stark, and J. S. Allen. Visual perception and sequences of eye movement fixations: A stochastic modeling approach. *Systems, Man and Cybernetics, IEEE Transactions on*, 22(3):474–481, 1992.

[21] A. Haji-Abolhassani and J. J. Clark. A computational model for task inference in visual search. *Journal of vision*, 13(3):29–29, 2013.

[22] J. M. Henderson, S. V. Shinkareva, J. Wang, S. G. Luke, and J. Olejarczyk. Predicting cognitive state from eye movements. *PloS one*, 8(5):e64937, 2013.

[23] J. L. Herlocker, J. A. Konstan, L. G. Terveen, and J. T. Riedl. Evaluating collaborative filtering recommender systems. *ACM TOIS*, 22(1):5–53, 2004.

[24] K. Hofmann, A. Schuth, A. Bellogin, and M. De Rijke. Effects of position bias on click-based recommender evaluation. In *ECIR'14*, pages 624–630. Springer, 2014.

[25] Y. Hu, Y. Koren, and C. Volinsky. Collaborative filtering for implicit feedback datasets. In *ICDM'08*, pages 263–272. Ieee, 2008.

[26] J. Huang, R. White, and G. Buscher. User see, user point: gaze and cursor alignment in web search. In *CHI'12*, pages 1341–1350. ACM, 2012.

[27] L. Itti, C. Koch, and E. Niebur. A model of saliency-based visual attention for rapid scene analysis. *TPAMI'98*, (11):1254–1259, 1998.

[28] T. Joachims, L. Granka, B. Pan, H. Hembrooke, and G. Gay. Accurately interpreting clickthrough data as implicit feedback. In *SIGIR'05*. Acm, 2005.

[29] T. Judd, K. Ehinger, F. Durand, and A. Torralba. Learning to predict where humans look. In *ICCV'09*, pages 2106–2113. IEEE, 2009.

[30] D. Marr, T. Poggio, E. C. Hildreth, and W. E. L. Grimson. *A computational theory of human stereo vision*. Springer, 1991.

[31] S. M. McNee, J. Riedl, and J. A. Konstan. Being accurate is not enough: how accuracy metrics have hurt recommender systems. In *CHI EA'06*, pages 1097–1101. ACM, 2006.

[32] J. Mullahy. Specification and testing of some modified count data models. *Journal of econometrics*, 33(3):341–365, 1986.

[33] R. Pan, Y. Zhou, B. Cao, N. N. Liu, R. Lukose, M. Scholz, and Q. Yang. One-class collaborative filtering. In *ICDM'08*, pages 502–511. IEEE, 2008.

[34] K. Puolamäki, J. Salojärvi, E. Savia, J. Simola, and S. Kaski. Combining eye movements and collaborative filtering for proactive information retrieval. In *SIGIR'05*, pages 146–153. ACM, 2005.

[35] L. R. Rabiner. A tutorial on hidden markov models and selected applications in speech recognition. *Proc. IEEE*, 77(2):257–286, 1989.

[36] P. Resnick, N. Iacovou, M. Suchak, P. Bergstrom, and J. Riedl. Grouplens: an open architecture for collaborative filtering of netnews. In *CSCW*, 1994.

[37] C. Roda. Human attention and its implications for human–computer interaction. *Human Attention in Digital Environments*, 1:11–62, 2011.

[38] B. Sarwar, G. Karypis, J. Konstan, and J. Riedl. Item-based collaborative filtering recommendation algorithms. In *WWW'01*, pages 285–295. ACM, 2001.

[39] R. Srikant, S. Basu, N. Wang, and D. Pregibon. User browsing models: relevance versus examination. In *KDD'10*, pages 223–232. ACM, 2010.

[40] B. W. Tatler. The central fixation bias in scene viewing: Selecting an optimal viewing position independently of motor biases and image feature distributions. *Journal of Vision*, 7(14):4–4, 2007.

[41] B. W. Tatler, M. M. Hayhoe, M. F. Land, and D. H. Ballard. Eye guidance in natural vision: Reinterpreting salience. *Journal of vision*, 11(5):5–5, 2011.

[42] B. W. Tatler and B. T. Vincent. The prominence of behavioural biases in eye guidance. *Visual Cognition*, 17(6-7):1029–1054, 2009.

[43] S. Xu, H. Jiang, and F. Lau. Personalized online document, image and video recommendation via commodity eye-tracking. In *RecSys'08*. ACM, 2008.

Exploring the Value of Personality in Predicting Rating Behaviors: A Study of Category Preferences on MovieLens

Raghav Pavan Karumur, Tien T. Nguyen, Joseph A. Konstan
GroupLens Research
University of Minnesota
Minneapolis, MN 55455 USA
+1 – (612) 626 1831
{raghav, tien, konstan}@cs.umn.edu

ABSTRACT

Prior work relevant to incorporating personality into recommender systems falls into two categories: social science studies and algorithmic ones. Social science studies of preference have found only small relationships between personality and category preferences, whereas, algorithmic approaches found a little improvement when incorporating personality into recommendations. As a result, despite good reasons to believe personality assessments should be useful in recommenders, we are left with no substantial demonstrated impact. In this work, we start with user data from a live recommender system, but study category-by-category variations in preference (both rating levels and distribution) across different personality types. By doing this, we hope to isolate specific areas where personality is most likely to provide value in recommender systems, while also modeling an analytic process that can be used in other domains. After controlling for the family-wise error rate, we find that High Agreeableness users rate at least 0.5 stars higher on a 5-star scale compared to low Agreeableness users. We also find differences in consumption in four different personality types between people who manifested high and low levels of that personality.

1. INTRODUCTION

Prior research has shown that personality influences the way humans behave, and that it is related to taste preferences and interests [17]. However, much of prior social science work examining relationship between personality and preferences reports no moderate-to-large relationships [3, 10, 13, 14, 17, 18, 23], and often, is limited in statistical approaches [1, 3, 10, 23].

More recent work incorporated personality into their recommender algorithms to address challenges surrounding cold start [7, 9, 19, 20] and showed that personality-encompassing models have slightly better performance in terms of lower MAE, more precision, and more recall than prior techniques that computed user-user similarity purely based on ratings. So, despite good reasons to believe personality assessments should be useful in recommenders, we are left with no substantial demonstrated impact. If research in improving personalization services and enhancing user experience is to proceed in the direction of incorporating personality, it seems essential to know in what categories personality is likely to have value.

We use data from a live movie recommender system called MovieLens for this purpose. We take an approach different from prior research and study category-by-category variations in preference (both rating levels and distribution) across different personality types. Our goal is to complement, and find the potential utility of the existing research in this area, by throwing light on the size of the effects on specific categories in isolation. Simultaneously, we also model an analytic process that can be used in other domains.

1.1 Research Questions

In the context of MovieLens (movielens.org), a movie recommender system, taking movie genres as categories, we seek to understand answers to the following two questions:

RQ1. Does the magnitude of ratings across categories vary by personality type? If so, how?

RQ2. Do the proportions of items consumed across categories vary by personality type? If so, how?

We find differences in *consumption* in four different personality types between people who manifested high and low levels of that personality, and we find differences in *rating level* in only one personality type, Agreeableness.

2. BACKGROUND AND RELATED WORK

One of the most influential models in psychology for studies encompassing personality and human behavior is the Five Factor Model (FFM), which characterizes Personality in terms of the five dimensions Openness, Conscientiousness, Extroversion, Agreeableness and Neuroticism [5, 6, 11, 12, 15, 22]. Table 1 gives an overview of characteristics associated with each individual personality type [1, 5, 11, 12, 15, 21, 22].

Personality was found to explain individual differences in preferences for media [14], arts such as music and paintings [17, 18], types of activities [12, 14] and for specific categories in media and entertainment [3, 10, 12, 13, 14, 17, 18, 23]. Some investigated preferences of users across movie genres [3, 23]. Others examined individual differences in genre preferences in a variety of entertainment domains including music, TV shows, movies, books and magazines and attending museums and concerts [1, 14, 17, 18]. However, most of these found small correlations and some were limited to very specific populations and cultures. While in this work, we set out to explore the size of the effects (which is different from any of the above investigations), MovieLens has the added advantage that its users come from all over the world.

RecSys '16, September 15-19, 2016, Boston, MA, USA
© 2016 ACM. ISBN 978-1-4503-4035-9/16/09□$15.00
DOI: http://dx.doi.org/10.1145/2959100.2959140

Table 1. Five Personality Traits and associated characteristics

Personality Type	Characteristics
Openness	Appreciation for novelty or variety in experiences, diversity in interests.
Conscientiousness	Organized, consistent, cautious and dutiful, less creative.
Extroversion	Appreciation for environments with higher levels of stimulation, high energy, more activity and social life.
Agreeableness	Cooperative, Adaptable, submissive, tolerant, generous, modest and trusting.
Neuroticism	High susceptibility to anger, frustration, insecurity, pessimism, anxiety and negative emotions.

One of the earliest attempts involving incorporating personality into recommendations was in the context of an image recommender system [19]. They computed user similarity based on the five factor scores and found this approach more accurate than a standard ratings-based one. Hu et al [9] computed user similarity based on personality vectors and found that the personality-based algorithm resulted in better MAE, Recall and Specificity compared to the ratings-based one. Tkalcic and Chen [21] found that the personality-based approach generates more accurate recommendations than traditional ratings-based approach on a music dataset. Elahi et al [7] incorporated personality data, and found that their approach performed better than the random baseline method and the *log*(popularity)*entropy method in terms of MAE. However, the improvements reported in these works are small and nearly equal to the ratings-based techniques. We hope to expand on this line of research, by throwing light on the size of the effects in specific categories to understand where this value is coming from. So, we research on a set of questions related to personality and specific categories of consumption on a movie recommender system.

3. DATASET AND METHODOLOGY

For this study, we use 38,675 movies of MovieLens classified under one or more of the 17 genres Action, Adventure, Animation, Children, Comedy, Crime, Documentary, Drama, Fantasy, Horror, Musical, Mystery, Romance, Science Fiction, Thriller, War and Western.

MovieLens users primarily consume movies by rating them on a five-star scale in half-star increments. We administer a questionnaire based on [8] to MovieLens users to obtain their personality information and gather responses from 1840 users. Based on the responses, we compute a personality score for each user for each of the five personality traits on a scale ranging from 1-7. We also obtain the de-identified data for 985,918 movie ratings provided by these users and this formed our dataset.

In order to increase the sensitivity of analyses and ensure comparability of results some of the prior works divide the scores into thirds [3, 5] and compare users in the higher and lower thirds against each other. We similarly classify users scoring <=2 on any personality trait as belonging to the "low" type and >=6 as belonging to the "high" type. For Openness however, we increase the lower threshold to 3.5 since we have too few users in the "low Openness" category to make a statistically significant comparison. Note that this will still convey the same meaning, since 4 on the Likert scale corresponds to "Neither Agree Nor Disagree". The numbers of users in the low and high personality type categories based on the above approach are reported in Table 2.

Table 2. Number of users with low and high personality types

Personality trait	# low users	# high users
Openness	119	730
Conscientiousness	58	417
Extroversion	439	148
Agreeableness	65	203
Neuroticism	100	430

4. RESULTS AND DISCUSSION

RQ1. *Does the magnitude of ratings across categories vary by personality type? If so, how?*

We hypothesize that users' ratings might be different for movies in the two categories: popular and less popular. Also, some movies generally get high ratings (>=4 on a 5-star rating scale), some get moderate ratings (3-3.5) and some get very low ratings (0.5-2.5). We feel that combining movies across all these categories and analyzing them might average out effects. So we separately analyze the ratings across the three rating level categories and the two popularity categories mentioned above. We thus have six conditions for each of the 17 genres leading to a total of 102 pairwise comparisons for each of the 5 personality types between the 'low' and 'high' categories. In all, we have 510 tests comparing magnitude of ratings provided by the high and low personality types. An example of a comparison looks like: "difference in magnitude of rating between the high and low Openness users for *popular* Action movies that are rated *low*". Since a user can produce more than one rating, the data points in each group are not independent. We therefore add a random effect for each user to take care of variation due to individual user differences. For each of the 510 tests, we come up with a mixed model that does not include a term for personality (the null model), and another that includes the personality term (the full model) and compare the full model against the null model.

Table 3. Significant rating differences between High and Low Agreeableness users for various categories

No.	Category/genre	Number of stars higher on a 0-5 star scale	Statistical significance
1	High-rated less popular Adventure	0.5 ($\pm$0.1)	χ^2 :22.3 *p*-adj: 0.001
2	High-rated popular Adventure	0.4 ($\pm$0.09)	χ^2:15.3 *p*-adj: 0.046
3	High-rated popular Animation	0.5 ($\pm$0.1)	χ^2:17.6 *p*-adj: 0.014
4	High-rated less popular Children	0.6 ($\pm$0.14)	χ^2: 15.5 *p*-adj: 0.042
5	High-rated popular Children	0.5 ($\pm$0.1)	χ^2: 23.5 *p*-adj: 0.0006
6	High-rated less popular Fantasy	0.6 ($\pm$0.1)	χ^2: 20.8 *p*-adj: 0.003
7	High-rated less popular Romance	0.5 ($\pm$0.1)	χ^2: 16.7 *p*-adj: 0.02
8	Low-rated popular Romance	0.6 ($\pm$0.1)	χ^2: 20.8 *p*-adj: 0.003

If the difference between the likelihoods of these two models is significant, then the fixed effect personality term is significant. However, the large number of simultaneous analyses conducted increases the likelihood of Type I error. So, we employ the Holm's method to control for family-wise error rate at 0.05 by doing a sequential adjustment of p-values. In the end, we obtain significant effect sizes for one personality trait Agreeableness (shown in Table 3).

All results stated in Table 3 are for high Agreeableness users in comparison to low Agreeableness users. The χ^2 reported, is for the likelihood ratio test comparing the full model with the null model. We find, for instance, that high Agreeableness users rate high-rated popular Children movies by about 0.5 stars higher compared to low Agreeableness users. Others in the table follow similar interpretation. The adjusted p-value indicates the statistical significance after controlling for family-wise error rate.

Because users high in Agreeableness are tolerant, they might be expected to show higher magnitude of ratings compared to low Agreeableness users. We test if High Agreeableness users in general have high ratings over all categories on the aggregate compared to low Agreeableness users. While we find a statistically significant result, the effect size (magnitude by which they rate higher) is only 0.08. This not only is too small, but also masks the fact that there is no significant difference in some categories. Chamorro-Premuzic et al [2] propose that high agreeableness users are likely to watch movies for fun. Their finding justifies the effect sizes we find in the categories we report above. Furthermore, Cosley et al [4] find that recommendation interfaces can affect how users rate by 0.23 stars and Nguyen et al [16] suggest that improving recommendation interfaces can mitigate such natural differences in ratings. In our case, by anchoring at one personality trait (Agreeableness), we already observe a difference of 0.5 stars (10% on a 5-star scale) (about twice as much) in how users rate. This observation signifies that personality trait per category does contribute to substantial differences in ratings and that it cannot be ignored.

RQ2. *Do the proportions of items consumed across categories vary by personality type? If so, how?*

To answer this question, for each user, we first obtain the proportion of movies consumed across each of the 17 genres. Since a single movie can belong to multiple genres, and we do not want to triple-count a movie with three genres (compared with a movie labeled with only one genre), we count each movie as $1/G$ consumptions for each of the G genres the movie is associated with. For example, Star Wars (1977) is labeled "Adventure", "Action" and "Science Fiction" on MovieLens. So, we assess a user who rates (consumed) this movie as having consumed 1/3 of the movie under each of the three genres, with the total consumption being one movie. This formulation also has the property that the genre proportions sum to one. Based on this formulation, for each of the five personality types, we test the difference in median proportions of movies consumed for each of the 17 categories between the high types and low types by employing a Wilcoxon-Mann-Whitney test. For this, we pick an equal number of samples (100 each for Openness, 50 each for Conscientiousness, 120 each for Extroversion, 60 each for Agreeableness, and 100 each for Neuroticism) from both comparison groups. We have 85 such tests. So we correct for the family-wise error rate and obtain the adjusted p-values for each of the tests. Significant effects based on these adjusted p-values are reported in Table 4. In Table 5 we provide distributions of consumptions across each category by MovieLens users as a guide to gain insight into the value of effect sizes in Table 4. For instance, the highlighted cell in Table 4 indicates that high Conscientiousness users consume 2% higher proportion of movies in the Romance category compared with low Conscientiousness users. The highlighted row in Table 5 indicates that users can consume anywhere between no Romance movies to a maximum of 29% of Romance movies out of all the movies that they rate. A 2% higher magnitude of consumption therefore indicates a shift in the magnitude of user's consumption from 1st quartile to mean or from median to 3rd quartile consumption, showing substantial value. Others follow similar interpretations.

Table 4. A summary of proportions of consumptions across various categories. ($p < 0.001$: *** $p < 0.01$ ** $p < 0.05$ *)

	Openness	Conscientiousness	Extroversion	Agreeableness	Neuroticism
Action		low > high (+2%) *			low > high (+2%)**
Adventure	low > high (+1%) *				low > high (+1%) *
Comedy					high > low (+2%) *
Drama	high > low (+4%) **				
Fantasy	low > high (+1%) ***				low > high (+1%) *
Romance	high > low (+1%) **	high > low (+2%) **	low > high (+1%)*		high > low (+1%) *
Thriller	low > high (+1%) *	low > high (+2%) *			low > high (+1%) *

Table 5. Dist. of consumption across selected categories

	Min	1Q	Med	Mean	3Q	Max
Action	0%	7%	10%	10.2%	13%	36%
Adventure	0%	6%	8%	8%	10%	29%
Comedy	0%	1%	14%	14.3%	18%	44%
Drama	2%	15%	20%	20.6%	25%	72%
Fantasy	0%	3%	4%	4%	5%	25%
Romance	0%	4%	5%	6%	7%	29%
Thriller	1%	7 %	9 %	9 %	11 %	27 %

5. CONCLUSION

Despite good reasons to believe personality assessments should be useful in recommenders, prior work shows no substantial demonstrated impact. In the hope of complementing prior research, in this work, we set out to explore if and by how much personality affects (i) the magnitude of ratings and (ii) the proportion of items consumed across various categories in a live recommender system. Our work shows substantial effects in multiple categories for various personality types and demonstrates that further research along the lines of incorporating personality is promising.

Our findings suggest that recommendations based purely on aggregate ratings of all users may not be a good idea. Instead, for a user with a certain personality type, recommendation models may consider showing two kinds of ratings - one produced by users of the same personality, such as "*Users similar to you rated xx stars*", and the other, an aggregate rating by all users, to improve consumption. We leave this for future work. Also, a documentation of stable relationships between individual differences and category preferences can throw light on who is likely to consume or rate across various categories. This is important not only for recommending the right categories to elicit ratings from users, but also in contexts such as providing better cold-start recommendations, and personalizing lists of novel, diverse and serendipitous movies to users at different times.

The nature of the effects we find suggests that certain algorithm types may be more able to productively incorporate personality data. The fact that the effects tend to be localized in certain item categories suggests that correlational algorithms may be less able to exploit personality data than dimensionality-reduction (or condition-probability) algorithms. This remains as future work.

A chief limitation of this work is that although we have data from a live recommender, we have personality data for only 1840 users and the personality data is not evenly distributed. We also do not have data on users' demographics to perform interaction analyses. Further work should look at classifying users in other domains and with additional information. Also, in this work, we looked at both the categories of consumption and the personality traits in isolation. Future work should look at combinations of personalities and the combinations of categories which these personalities might be interested in consuming.

6. ACKNOWLEDGMENTS

This research was supported by the National Science Foundation under grant IIS-1319382. Additionally, we thank the MovieLens users who took the Personality survey.

7. REFERENCES

[1] Cantador, I., Fernández-Tobías, I., & Bellogín, A. 2013. Relating personality types with user preferences in multiple entertainment domains. In *CEUR Workshop Proceedings*, Shlomo Berkovsky.

[2] Chamorro-Premuzic, T., Kallias, A., & Hsu, A. 2013. Understanding individual differences in film preferences and uses: a psychographic approach. *The Social Science of Cinema*, 87.

[3] Chausson, O. 2010 Who watches what?: assessing the impact of gender and personality on film preferences. *Paper published online on the MyPersonality project website* http://mypersonality.org/wiki/doku.php

[4] Cosley, D., Lam, S. K., Albert, I., Konstan, J. A., & Riedl, J. 2003. Is seeing believing?: how recommender system interfaces affect users' opinions. In *Proceedings of the SIGCHI conference on Human factors in computing systems (CHI '03)*, ACM, New York, NY, USA, 585-592.

[5] Costa Jr, P.T. and McCrae, R.R. 1992. Neo personality inventory–revised (neo-pi-r) and neo five-factor inventory (neo-ffi) professional manual. *Odessa, FL: Psychological Assessment Resources.*

[6] Costa, P., and McCrae, R. 1996. Toward a new generation of personality theories: Theoretical contexts for the five-factor model. *The Five-Factor Model of Personality: Theoretical Perspectives* (1996) 51-87.

[7] Ealhi, M., Braunhofer, M., Ricci, F., & Tkalcic, M. 2013. Personality-based active learning for collaborative filtering recommender systems. *AAAI 2013.*

[8] Gosling, S. D., Rentfrow, P.J., and Swann, W.B. 2003. A very brief measure of the Big-Five personality domains. *Journal of Research in Personality* 37, 6 (Dec 2003), 504–528.

[9] Hu, R., and Pu, P. 2011. Enhancing collaborative filtering systems with personality information. In *Proceedings of the fifth ACM conference on Recommender systems* (RecSys '11). ACM, New York, NY, USA, 197-204.

[10] Hu, R., and Pu, P. 2013. Exploring Relations between Personality and User Rating Behaviors. In *UMAP Workshops.*

[11] John, O.P. The Big Five factor taxonomy. Dimensions of personality in the natural language and in questionnaires. 1990. *Handbook of personality: Theory and research*, 14 (1990) 66-100.

[12] Karumur, R., and Konstan, J.A. 2016. Relating Newcomer Personality to Survival and Activity in Recommender Systems. In *Proceedings of the 24th ACM Conference on User Modeling, Adaptation and Personalization (UMAP '16).* In Press.

[13] Kraaykamp, G. 2001. Parents, personality and media preferences. *Communications* 26, 1 (2001) 15-38.

[14] Kraaykamp, G. and Van Eijck, K., 2005. Personality, media preferences, and cultural participation. *Personality and individual differences*, 38, 7 (May 2005), 1675-1688.

[15] McCrea, R. and John, O. An introduction to the five-factor model and its applications. 1992. *Journal of personality*, 60, 2 (Jun 1992), 175-215.

[16] Nguyen, T. T., Kluver, D., Wang, T. Y., Hui, P. M., Ekstrand, M. D., Willemsen, M. C., & Riedl, J. 2013. Rating support interfaces to improve user experience and recommender accuracy. In *Proceedings of the 7th ACM conference on Recommender systems* (RecSys '13). ACM, New York, NY, USA, 149-156.

[17] Rentfrow, P.J., and Gosling, S.D. 2003. The do re mi's of everyday life: the structure and personality correlates of music preferences. *J Pers Soc Psychol.* 84, 6, (Jun 2003), 1236-1256.

[18] Rentfrow, P. J., Lewis R. G, and Ran Z. Listening, watching, and reading: The structure and correlates of entertainment preferences. *Journal of personality* 79, 2 (2011) 223-258.

[19] Tkalcic, M., Kunaver, M., Tasic, J., & Košir, A. 2009. Personality based user similarity measure for a collaborative recommender system. In *Proceedings of the 5th Workshop on Emotion in Human-Computer Interaction-Real world challenges*, 30-37.

[20] Tkalcic, M., and Kunaver, M. 2011. Addressing the new user problem with a personality based user similarity measure. *DEMRA 2011.*

[21] Tkalcic, M., and Chen, L. 2015. Personality and Recommender Systems. In *Recommender Systems Handbook,* Ricci, F., Rokach, L., and Shapira, B, Ed. Springer US, 715-739.

[22] Tupes, E.C., and Christal, R.E. 1992. Recurrent personality factors based on trait ratings. *Journal of Personality*, 60, 2, (April 2006) 225-251.

[23] Wen, W., and Chen, L. Implicit acquisition of user personality for augmenting movie recommendations. 2015. User Modeling, Adaptation and Personalization. Springer International Publishing, 302-314.

Pairwise Preferences Based Matrix Factorization and Nearest Neighbor Recommendation Techniques

Saikishore Kalloori, Francesco Ricci, and Marko Tkalcic
Faculty of Computer Science
Free University of Bozen - Bolzano
Piazza Domenicani 3, I - 39100, Bolzano
ksaikishore@unibz.it, fricci@unibz.it, marko.tkalcic@gmail.com

ABSTRACT

Many recommendation techniques rely on the knowledge of preferences data in the form of ratings for items. In this paper, we focus on pairwise preferences as an alternative way for acquiring user preferences and building recommendations. In our scenario, users provide pairwise preference scores for a set of item pairs, indicating how much one item in each pair is preferred to the other. We propose a matrix factorization (MF) and a nearest neighbor (NN) prediction techniques for pairwise preference scores. Our MF solution maps users and items pairs to a joint latent features vector space, while the proposed NN algorithm leverages specific user-to-user similarity functions well suited for comparing users preferences of that type. We compare our approaches to state of the art solutions and show that our solutions produce more accurate pairwise preferences and ranking predictions.

Keywords

Pairwise Preferences; Matrix Factorization; User Similarity

1. INTRODUCTION

Recommender Systems (RSs) address the information overload problem by providing users with personalized suggestions for items that are likely to be interesting and relevant to their needs. Many RSs are rating-based, i.e., user preferences for items are expressed in the form of absolute evaluations in a predefined scale, e.g., the classical five stars scale that is used in Amazon.com.

However, rating-based RSs have limitations related to the fact that ratings are absolute evaluations with respect to a benchmark. For instance, a user who prefers one item over another might end up giving the same rating to both of them due to the limited rating scale. Also, consider a user who has liked an item and has assigned the highest rating to this item. If this user subsequently finds a new item that she prefers over the first one, she has no choice but to also give it the highest rating [3]. Considering these limitations some authors have developed recommendation techniques that leverage an alternative way to express user preferences, namely, pairwise preferences [3, 6, 2]. In these approaches users can express their preference for one of the items in a pair (i, j) with a pair score, i.e., a positive or negative number. The larger positive (smaller negative) the score is the more the item i (j) is preferred to the item j (i). When pairwise preference scores are used instead of ratings, the core problem for the RS is: a) to predict unknown pair scores, since the users will score only a small subset of all the possible pairs of items, and b) to aggregate the available and predicted pair scores to produce personalized rankings of the items.

In [2] it is shown that it is possible to build a RS using pairwise preference scores that performs better than state of the art rating-only based solutions (in terms of nDCG and precision). The Personalized Differential Matrix with Ratings and Pairwise Preferences (PPR) method was proposed there. It can use a collection of pre-existing ratings and pairwise preference scores to produce a personalized ranking for each user. PPR is a nearest neighbor (NN) approach, and uses a generalization of Pearson correlation as user-to-user similarity for user profiles composed of pair scores. In this paper we conjecture that the performance of the PPR can be improved in two ways. Firstly, we believe that the user-to-user similarity metric used in PPR is not appropriate for pair scores based profiles, hence we conjecture that a better suited similarity metric can improve the items ranking accuracy. Secondly, when the data is sparse, Matrix Factorization (MF) has been shown to give even better results in many domains [9]. Hence, we conjecture that MF can also improve pair scores prediction and we propose a MF technique that finds latent feature models for pairs of items, similarly to how in standard MF single items are modeled by latent features. We carried out an offline experiment to compare our approaches using a movie data set that contains pairwise preference scores given to movie pairs and we show that the proposed approaches substantially improve state of the art ranking algorithms.

2. RELATED WORK

In the survey conducted in [8] it emerges that users prefer providing preferences in the form of pairwise scores and [5] shows that making pairwise preference judgments are faster than absolute judgments (ratings). In [2], it has also been shown that pairwise preferences can be as easy to enter as ratings when a suitable graphical user interface is provided.

RecSys '16, September 15 - 19, 2016, Boston , MA, USA

ISBN 978-1-4503-4035-9/16/09...$15.00

DOI: http://dx.doi.org/10.1145/2959100.2959142

And in [8], by conducting a user study, they found that item comparisons are 20% more stable over the time. Moreover in [2] it has shown that by using pairwise preferences one can produce better recommendations than ratings by using pairwise preferences almost equal to number of ratings.

In [3], an algorithm that uses pairwise preferences for predicting item ratings was proposed. It implements a NN collaborative filtering approach where user-to-user similarity is measured as the number of item pairs on which both users have the same preferences. They used this special type of similarity for predicting ratings (not pairwise scores) and concluded that exploiting preference relations does not lead to a decrease in the quality of rating predictions. In [1], the authors proposed a novel method to evaluate the rank accuracy of a RS assuming that the user preferences are expressed as pairwise preferences. In this paper we show that this evaluation method can in fact be used as user-to-user similarity in a pair scores prediction algorithm.

In [6] a MF technique for pairwise preferences that is similar to ours was proposed. They represent each item using a d-dimensional vector and estimate pairwise preference scores using an inverse-logit function. Quite differently, in our matrix factorization technique we consider a d-dimensional vector representation for each item pair (i, j) and we predict pairwise scores as in classical MF one predict ratings. BPR (Bayesian Personalised Ranking) [10] is a popular item ranking techniques that was applied to pairwise preference data implicitly derived from users' online clicks.

3. PAIR SCORES PREDICTION

We present two novel methods for pair scores prediction. The first extends MF for ratings data sets [9] to MF for pair scores predictions. The second is a NN approach and we introduce two new user-to-user similarity measures suited to assess the similarity of two profiles based on pair scores.

Let U be a set of users and I be a set of items. We denote with r_{uij} the pair score given by user u to the pair of items (i, j), and r^*_{uij} a predicted pair score. In the data set that we have used the possible pair score values are $[-4, 4]$, since they were acquired in an experiment where a pair scores based recommender was compared with a 5 stars rating based one. In a rating-based RS, a user $u \in U$ expresses her preferences for items with ratings r_{ui}. If the ratings r_{ui} and r_{uj} are present then one can form the pair score r_{uij} as $r_{ui} - r_{uj}$.

3.1 MF for Pair Scores Prediction

We present here a matrix factorization pair score prediction and item ranking method (MFP). MFP models each user and item pair as d-dimensional vectors p_u and q_{ij} respectively. Let $\mathbf{R}$ be the matrix that contains all the pair scores that the users have assigned. The element r_{uij} in the matrix (tensor) is the pair score the user u gave to the item pair (i, j). MFP factorizes $\mathbf{R}$ into two latent matrices of lower dimension d: the user-factor matrix $\mathbf{P}$ and the item-pair-factor matrix $\mathbf{Q}$. The prediction for a missing pair score of the user u for a pair (i, j) is:

$$r^*_{uij} = \mu + b_u + b_{ij} + p_u^T q_{ij}$$

where μ is the overall average of all the pair scores, and b_u and b_{ij} are the baseline parameters that model the observed deviations from the average pair score due to the user u and item pair (i, j), respectively. In our experiments we learn all the model parameters by using stochastic gradient descent [9], by minimizing the (regularized) model's prediction error (on a training set of pair scores) as $r_{uij} - r^*_{uij}$. As a result of the learning process we get a full matrix of predicted pair scores. We can then compute a personalized item score ν_{ui} by averaging the r^*_{uij} predictions, as done by [2]:

$$\nu_{ui} = \frac{\sum_{j \in I \setminus \{i\}} r^*_{uij}}{|I|} \quad (1)$$

For each user u the items are then ranked by descending values of ν_{ui}.

3.2 NN for Pair Scores Prediction

In previous research a NN approach was used for pair scores data by using Pearson similarity to calculate user-to-user similarities and to generate predictions [2]. In the following example we will illustrate why Pearson similarity is not suitable in this case, and we propose alternative similarity measures that better fit to pairwise scores profiles. **Example 1:** Looking at the data shown in Table 1, one can see that u and v should not be considered similar because u prefers k over j and l over k whereas v prefers j over k and k over l. However, Pearson similarity yields 0.51, which is a relative high value.

Table 1: Pair scores of two users for items $\{i, j, k, l\}$

	(i,j)	(i,k)	(i,l)	(j,k)	(j,l)	(k,l)
u	-	1	-	-1	-	-2
v	-	-	-	3	-	1

We now present two user-to-user similarity measures that let the recommender to better predict missing pair scores: (i) Goodman and Kruskal's gamma (GK) and (ii) Expected Discounted Rank Correlation (EDRC). Let $v \in U_{ij}$ be the set of all users for which we have the pair score r_{vij}. The NN prediction formula for missing pairwise scores is:

$$r^*_{uij} = \frac{1}{\sum_{v \in U_{ij}} sim(u, v)} \sum_{v \in U_{ij}} sim(u, v) * r_{vij} \quad (2)$$

where $sim(u, v)$ is either EDRC, GK, or Pearson Correlation, as in [2]. After having predicted the missing pair scores, item scores and ranking can be computed again using Equation 1.

3.2.1 *Goodman and Kruskal's gamma*

Goodman and Kruskal's gamma (GK) was proposed in [7]. It is a symmetric measure of correlation. Given two user profiles u and v with their pair scores, $GK(u, v)$ is calculated using two quantities: (a) the number P of item pairs that are ranked in the same order in both profiles (concordant pairs) and (b) the number Q of item pairs that are ranked in the reversed order (reversed pairs):

$$GK(u, v) = \frac{P - Q}{P + Q} \quad (3)$$

GK ranges from -1 (100% negative association) to +1 (100% positive association). In Example 1, using GK, we obtain a more meaningful similarity value $GK(u, v) = -1$.

3.2.2 *Expected Discounted Rank Correlation*

In [1], the authors proposed a novel method, *expected discounted rank correlation* (EDRC) to evaluate rank accuracy of a recommendation list. EDRC measures the similarity between two sets of pairwise preferences: (i) a ground truth set of pairwise preferences and (ii) a set of predicted pairwise preferences. In their method, the authors require to have the same items in both sets (although not necessarily the same comparisons of items). But in our scenario we measure the similarity of two user that may have compared different items. Thus, we take the union of items appearing in the pairs compared by the two users and we change the way EDRC deals with missing pairwise preferences (explained later).

EDRC is asymmetric and measures how much a user u pairwise preferences match a user v pairwise preferences. It is based on a graph representation of the pair scores where the vertices represent items and edges represent pairwise preferences (See Figure 1). Hence, EDRC, as well as GK, ignores the magnitude of the pair scores and considers only their sign.

(a) User u (b) User v

Figure 1: Users preference graphs from Table 1 data

In order to calculate EDRC between two users u and v, a rank score $R(\cdot)$, a discount weight $D(\cdot)$ and a score $C(\cdot)$ for each item present in u profile is required. The rank score $R(\cdot)$ is computed by Algorithm 1, and we assign a linear discount weight $D(\cdot) = R(\cdot)$. Algorithm 1 is a modified version of the algorithm presented in [1] and is not applicable if the preference graph of u contains cycles. If a cycle is present, then we must first collapse together the vertices in each cycle and treat them as one vertex. The rank value is then the same for all vertices in the cycle[1]. To calculate the score

Algorithm 1 Algorithm for Calculating Rank Scores

```
OUT(i, G) is set of outgoing vertices from i
procedure RANKSCORE(G(V, E))
    for each vertex i ∈ V do
        R(i) ← 1
    end for
    L ← TopologicalSort(G)    ▷ topological order of vertices
    for each vertex i ∈ L do
        for all j ∈ OUT(i, G) do
            R(j) ← MAX(R(j), R(i) + 1)
        end for
    end for
end procedure
```

$C(\cdot)$, we take the union of the items present in both users profiles and we call it I. For example, in Figure 1, we have $I = \{i, j, k, l\}$. Using pairwise preferences of both users u and v, we compute the score $C(\cdot)$ for each item present in the profile of user u. The score $C(\cdot)$ of an item represents the overall preferences agreement of the two users between an item and other items present in I. For instance, for the item $j \in I$, the score $C(j)$ is the sum of the agreements that the two users have on the pairs (j, i), (j, k), (j, l). We used the same approach proposed in [1] to calculate the $C(\cdot)$ score, and the reader is referred to that reference for further details. However, our scenario is different because there exist cases where the relationship between (i, j), i.e, which item is preferred, is unknown. In that case we assume that there is 50% likelihood for i to be preferred to j and 50% likelihood for the opposite preference. This situation can be seen in the example shown in Figure 1, where preference relationship between the items present in v profile and item i are unknown. We finally calculate the similarity of two users as follows:

$$EDRC(u, v) = \frac{2}{Z} \cdot \left[\sum_{i \in S} \frac{C(i)}{D(i)} \right] - 1 \tag{4}$$

where S is a set of vertices having an incoming edge in u and Z is a normalization factor to ensure that the value of this similarity stays between -1 and +1. Referring again to Example 1, one can show that $EDRC(u, v) = -0.41$, hence again a negative value, which is appropriate in this case.

4. EVALUATION PROCEDURE

In order to study the performance of MFP, and the adoption of the GK and EDRC as user-to-user similarities in a NN method (referred to as NN-GK and NN-EDRC, respectively) we compare them with three state-of-the-art algorithms: (i) NN using Pearson correlation as user-to-user similarity (PPR) [2] (ii) Matrix Factorization approach using preference relations (MFPref) [6] and (iii) BPR-MF [10].

The dataset[2] used in our experiment was acquired through an online experiment described in [2]. The authors developed a full movie recommender system based on pairwise preferences, which included a preference elicitation interface to show items pairs to users and to collect their pair scores. They used 100 movies from Movielens, 46 users participated in the experiment and a total of 2622 pairwise preferences were collected. In addition to pair scores, the data set contains the ratings present in MovieLens 100K data for the 100 movies that were considered. There were a total of 73078 ratings entered by 1128 users and we converted them to pair scores. The sparsity of our data set is 99.8%.

In our experiments we performed a five-fold cross validation. The pair scores generated from the MovieLens ratings were part of the training set. We shuffled the pairwise preferences of the 46 users and split them into five (roughly) equally sized subsets. Then, for each iteration, the system prediction model was trained using four of these five subsets and the testing was done on the fifth subset. Since our ground truth contains incomplete pairwise preferences and not full rankings of items, rank accuracy like NDCG and Average Precision of a recommender systems are inapplicable. Therefore, for each iteration, we used the following metrics in order to evaluate our approach:

- **Predict Hit:** Assume that a set of pair scores in the test set T is known and the system has predicted these pair scores:

$$PredictHit = \sum_{r_{uij} \in T} PH(r_{uij})/|T| \tag{5}$$

$PH(r_{uij})$ is 1 if the sign of a pair score contained in the test set T for the item pair (i, j) is correctly predicted by the RS and 0 otherwise.

[1] However, we note that in our data we did not have cycles.

[2] Available at: http://www.inf.unibz.it/~kalloori/

- **Rank Hit:** It measures the ranking error between a set of pair scores present in the test set and a ranked list. For each user, his personalized ranked list is constructed using Equation 1.

$$RankHit = \sum_{r_{uij} \in T} RH(r_{uij})/|T| \quad (6)$$

where $RH(r_{uij})$ is 1 if the RS has ranked for u the item i above item j and the user u does prefer the item i over item j and 0 otherwise.
- **Precision of Preferences (ppref@k):** This measure is a rank accuracy metric which evaluates a ranked list at a given cut-off rank k. In [4] a pair (i, j) is defined as *ordered* by the RS if at least one item appears above rank k and unordered otherwise. A pair (i, j) is defined as *correctly ordered* for a user if the RS's ordering matches his preference order. *Precision of preferences at k (ppref@k)* is defined as the total number of correctly ordered pairs divided by the total number of ordered pairs [4].

5. RESULTS

The recommendation performances of the proposed algorithms[3] for the considered metrics are shown in Table 2. Higher values indicates better performance.

Table 2: Ranking and prediction accuracy of the compared algorithms. Best results are marked with boldface.

	Predict hit	Rank hit	ppref@5	ppref@10
NN-EDRC	**0.701** ±0.04	**0.791** ±0.01	**0.077** ±0.03	**0.048** ±0.01
MFP	0.585 ±0.06	0.733 ±0.01	0.053 ±0.01	0.027 ±0.00
NN-GK	0.407 ±0.06	0.624 ±0.04	0.033 ±0.01	0.024 ±0.00
MFPref	0.563 ±0.04	0.571 ±0.03	0.043 ±0.03	0.015 ±0.01
BPR-MF	0.501 ±0.05	0.515 ±0.08	0.026 ±0.06	0.010 ±0.02
PPR	0.257 ±0.03	0.281 ±0.03	0.061 ±0.00	0.021 ±0.00

As it can be noted, NN-EDRC predicts pair score signs and ranks items more accurately than the other methods. Observing Table 2 we can make the following conclusions.

The Nearest Neighbor based method EDRC is the best prediction algorithm that we have compared in the experiment. Our experiment results suggest that in order to assess the similarity between two users, when their preferences are expressed as pair scores, a specific similarity metric should be used, instead of relying on Pearson correlation, which is more appropriate for ratings data sets.

Comparing MFP with MFPref, we can conclude that our proposed matrix factorization approach, MFP, can better capture user and items pairs latent features and compute predictions than MFPref. This may depend on the fact that MFP takes into account the original preference scores (in the range from -4 to 4), while MFPref considers only the sign of the pair scores.

BPR-MF does not yield better results. It is worth noting that BPR-MF is not designed to predict pair scores but only a ranking compatible with the observed pair scores. We conjecture that this explains why it has, in this data set and application, an inferior performance compared to a method originally designed to predict pair scores.

[3] MFP: d=15 and γ=0.003 and MFPref: d=15 and γ=0.008 and BPRMF: d=20 and γ=0.0025

6. CONCLUSIONS AND FUTURE WORK

In this paper we have introduced two techniques for computing recommendations by leveraging user preferences expressed with pairwise scores. In particular, we have proposed two user-user similarity metrics, to be used in nearest neighbor based pair scores prediction methods and, a straightforward extension to pairwise preference data of matrix factorization for ratings data sets. The empirical evaluation performed on a movie data set has shown that our approaches have better prediction accuracy compared to state of the art baselines in terms of Predict Hit, Rank Hit, ppref@5 and ppref@10.

We have performed our offline tests on a small dataset. Hence, in the future we will generate a larger data sets by integrating the proposed recommendation techniques in a real system. In fact one of the major limitation of our approach is the quadratic grow with the number of items of the pair scores matrix. However one must note that only a small minority of all the potential pairs of items will be actually compared by the users.

Furthermore, we plan to develop viable active learning strategies to identify the pairs that each user should compare. In the future, we will also conduct live user experiments and identify specific conditions and situations where pairwise preferences elicitation is meaningful and beneficial.

7. REFERENCES

[1] B. Ackerman and Y. Chen. Evaluating rank accuracy based on incomplete pairwise preferences. In *Proc. Workshop on UCERSTI Recsys '11*, 2011.

[2] L. Blédaité and F. Ricci. Pairwise preferences elicitation and exploitation for conversational collaborative filtering. In *Proc. Hypertext & Social Media '15*, pages 231–236, 2015.

[3] A. Brun, A. Hamad, O. Buffet, and A. Boyer. Towards preference relations in recommender systems. In *Preference Learning Workshop (ECML-PKDD '10)*, 2010.

[4] B. Carterette and P. N. Bennett. Evaluation measures for preference judgments. In *Proc. SIGIR '08*, pages 685–686. ACM, 2008.

[5] B. Carterette, P. N. Bennett, D. M. Chickering, and S. T. Dumais. Here or there: Preference judgments for relevance. In *Advances in Information Retrieval 2008*, pages 16–27. Springer, 2008.

[6] M. S. Desarkar, R. Saxena, and S. Sarkar. Preference relation based matrix factorization for recommender systems. In *UMAP '12*, pages 63–75. Springer, 2012.

[7] L. A. Goodman and W. H. Kruskal. *Measures of association for cross classifications.* Springer, 1979.

[8] N. Jones, A. Brun, and A. Boyer. Comparisons instead of ratings: Towards more stable preferences. In *Proc. WI-IAT '11*, pages 451–456, 2011.

[9] Y. Koren, R. Bell, and C. Volinsky. Matrix factorization techniques for recommender systems. *Computer*, 42(8):30–37, 2009.

[10] S. Rendle, C. Freudenthaler, Z. Gantner, and L. Schmidt-Thieme. Bpr: Bayesian personalized ranking from implicit feedback. In *Proc. UAI '09*, pages 452–461, 2009.

Observing Group Decision Making Processes

Amra Delic
E-Commerce Group
TU Wien
Vienna, Austria
amra.delic@tuwien.ac.at

Julia Neidhardt
E-Commerce Group
TU Wien
Vienna, Austria
julia.neidhardt@tuwien.ac.at

Thuy Ngoc Nguyen
Free University of
Bozen-Bolzano
Bolzano, Italy
ngoc.nguyen@unibz.it

Francesco Ricci
Free University of
Bozen-Bolzano
Bolzano, Italy
fricci@unibz.it

Laurens Rook
Delft University
of Technology
Delft, Netherlands
l.rook@tudelft.nl

Hannes Werthner
E-Commerce Group
TU Wien
Vienna, Austria
werthner@ec.tuwien.ac.at

ABSTRACT

Most research on group recommender systems relies on the assumption that individuals have conflicting preferences; in order to generate group recommendations the system should identify a fair way of aggregating these preferences. Both empirical studies and theoretical frameworks have tried to identify the most effective preference aggregation techniques without coming to definite conclusions. In this paper, we propose to approach group recommendation from the group dynamics perspective and analyze the group decision making process for a particular task (in the travel domain). We observe several individual and group properties and correlate them to choice satisfaction. Supported by these initial results we therefore advocate for the development of new group recommendation techniques that consider group dynamics and support the full group decision making process.

CCS Concepts

•Information systems → Recommender systems; •Human-centered computing → User studies;

Keywords

Group recommender systems; User study; Preference aggregation; Group decision processes

1. INTRODUCTION

Most research on group recommender systems originated from the assumption that individuals, when facing a choice problem, like finding a travel or a movie to experience together, do have conflicting preferences. Hence, the role of the recommender is to mediate the preferences of the group members and suggest options that can simultaneously satisfy group members [10].

RecSys '16, September 15 - 19, 2016, Boston , MA, USA

ISBN 978-1-4503-4035-9/16/09...$15.00

DOI: http://dx.doi.org/10.1145/2959100.2959168

However, it is not easy to define the right mediation procedure; it is impossible to identify mediation techniques that satisfy even simple requirements (Arrow's impossibility theorem). Hence, several preference aggregation techniques have been proposed in the literature, experimental studies have compared them, and confirmed that there is no clear winner [10]. In parallel, observation studies have tried to identify which preference aggregation techniques are actually used in groups and they, however, could not identify a uniquely preferred approach [10].

It is also worth noting that other empirical studies have shown that in many group recommendation no conflicting preferences are observed [3]. In fact, group recommendations may benefit from the usage of a larger amount of preference data, i.e. the union of the group members.

Hence, a fundamental research question is whether preference aggregation is the core problem for group recommendation or if we have to tackle other facets of group decision making. In fact, scholars of group dynamics, while studying decision making in groups, have identified the importance of the full decision process adopted by the group and de-emphasized the preference aggregation step, as only one component of such a process [6].

In this work we follow this indication and argue that group recommendation research benefits from a wider analysis of how people make decisions in groups. Hence, in this paper we describe an observational study, in which several user groups were monitored while facing a travel decision task. We recorded: the individual preferences for a small set of alternative destinations (before group interactions); the interactions between group members during the decision making process; and the individual evaluations of the task and the choices of the group.[1] The contributions of this paper are:

- The definition of a replicable observational study procedure and measurement tools that can shed light on the actual group decision making process.
- The implementation of the observational study in the concrete case of tourism decision making.
- Experimental evidence that conflicting preferences, even if initially present, do not substantially affect participants' satisfaction with the final group choice.

[1]This research activity was promoted by the International Journal of Information Technology and Tourism.

- Experimental evidence that other factors, related to user and group characteristics, are more important in understanding the decision making outcome, such as choice satisfaction or task difficulty.

These results are of primary importance for the development of novel types of group recommender systems and can stimulate complementary studies aimed at understanding group decision making processes and the role of recommendation in groups.

2. STATE OF THE ART

Several researches in group recommender systems focused on core preference aggregations algorithms. Two overarching strategies are commonly used: aggregating individual profiles into a joint group profile (*aggregated profiles*) and aggregating individual recommendations into a single group recommendation list (*aggregated recommendations*) [3]. Several aggregation strategies have been proposed [10]. For example, *Average* strategy returns the average of individual ratings, *Least misery* and *Most pleasure* strategy maximize the preference of the least and the most happy members respectively.

The research in travel recommender systems for groups has made several contributions. In particular, *Intrigue* [1] is a tool helping tour guides in designing tours for heterogeneous groups of tourists that include relatively homogeneous subgroups (e.g. children). The group model is a weighted average of the subgroup models, which are weighted according to the importance of the subgroups. *Travel Decision Forum* [9] allows group members to define their preferences and uses animated characters to help them arrive at an accepted choice in the organization of a vacation. *Trip@dvice*, a case-based reasoning recommender system, applies a cooperative negotiation methodology to tackle the group recommendation problem [4]. *Collaborative Advisory Travel System* (CATS) proposes to use critiquing in order to support the negotiation of recommendations [11], i.e., each member can send a *critique* to the other members, thereby sharing his or her thoughts about a particular option.

Recommender systems can also support mediation, such that system proposed items could become acceptable by all group members. *Choicla* is an environment that supports the flexible definition of decision functionality in a domain independent fashion [14]. It includes recommendation and explanation modules that can improve trust in recommendations and in the decision support quality.

Up to now group recommender systems research has only devoted minor attention to explore how group members make choices and how the process of making choices can be supported [5]. A considerable amount of the observational literature on group decision making comes from social science and psychology. In [15], the authors have emphasized and demonstrated that "*social sharedness*", the degree to which preferences, information etc. are shared within groups, is a key element to understand group decision making. Moreover, researchers who study the functional theory of group decision making suggest that groups engaged in the four stages: *Orientation Discussion Decision Implementation* (ODDI model) are more likely to make better decisions than those who mishandle information along the way [6].

3. STUDY PROCEDURE

Pre-studies took place at TU Delft and the universities in Klagenfurt and Leiden, while an extended study was carried out at TU Wien. Each study implementation consisted of three phases: pre-survey, groups meeting and post-survey phase. At each university, participants were arranged into groups of two, three or four members. Additionally, at TU Wien each group selected two students (observers) to observe and record their group activities, while others took part in the decision making process (decision makers).

In the pre-survey phase, the decision makers filled in an online questionnaire capturing the participants' individual profiles, preferences and dislikes: basic demographic data, 17 tourist roles [7], Big Five Factors [8] and important criteria for ranking destinations. Furthermore, students rated the attractiveness of ten predefined destinations, i.e., Amsterdam (for Austrian participants), Berlin, Copenhagen, Helsinki, Lisbon, London, Paris, Rome, Stockholm and Vienna (for Dutch participants) using a five point scale. In the second phase, the group meetings took place. The task for decision makers was to jointly choose one of the ten previously rated destinations that they, as a group, would like to visit. Additionally, students were asked for their second choice in case the first would no longer be available. In Vienna, each group had two observers who audio recorded and reported the group discussion and decision process. Observer's report was constructed based on Bales's Interaction Process Analysis (IPA) [2] and covered: decision scheme, discussion and decision time and twelve categories of group members' behavior, i.e., Friendliness, Tension Release, Give/Ask for Opinion, Suggestion or Information, Tension and Unfriendliness. In the post-survey phase, the participants responded to an online questionnaire their first and second group choice, their perception of the attractiveness of the ten destinations, their satisfaction with the group choice, their perceived difficulty of the group decision process, how they identified themselves with the group and their assessment of the task. In total the collected data sample comprised 78 entries with 24 groups of two, three and four group members.

4. RESULTS

The main objective of this study was to analyze group decisions and their associated decision processes in the travel domain from a group dynamics perspective. To shed more light on this, we analyzed individual preferences of group members, the actual group choices after the discussion and the quality of the group choice, i.e., the individual satisfaction with the group choice.

Table 1: Frequency of ratings aggregated for the 10 cities

Rating	1	2	3	4	5
# of ratings	61	90	212	216	147
Percentage	8.4%	12.3%	29.2%	29.7%	20.2%

5 - Very Attractive to 1 - Not Attractive.

The individual ratings from the pre-survey of the predefined destinations were relatively high (see Table 1). The distribution was slightly right-skewed and is rather similar to other rating distributions (e.g., MovieLens). This was confirmed by the post-survey, where 87.3% of participants agreed to the statement *"Many destinations were appealing"*. Furthermore, the individual satisfaction with the group choice was overly high (see Table 2).

Table 2: Group choice satisfaction

	5	4	3	2	1
ChoiceSat1	44.9%	48.7%	5.1%	0.0%	1.3%
ChoiceSat2	39.7%	39.7%	15.4%	5.1%	0.0%
ChoiceSat3	35.9%	46.2%	9.0%	7.7%	1.3%

ChoiceSat1 - *"I like the destination that we have chosen"*; ChoiceSat2 - *"I am excited about the chosen destination"*; ChoiceSat3 - *"The chosen destination fits my preference"*; Ratings: 5 - Strongly Agree to 1 - Strongly Disagree.

Remarkably, for the majority of participants (i.e., 40 individuals) the outcome of the group decision process did not correspond to their most preferred destinations, while for the remaining 38 individuals the group choice was in line with their individual preference. As expected, the satisfaction with the group outcome was particularly high for those who had their initial top choice selected as the group choice, i.e., 35 individuals out of 38 (92.1%) indicated that they were excited about the chosen destination. However, when the group choice did not correspondent to the participants' initial preference, they were nevertheless remarkably satisfied. Here, more than two-third (i.e., 27 out of 40) were excited about the group choice, even though the chosen destination was not their preferred one.

Next, we compared the actual group choices with recommendations that would be produced by the most common aggregation strategies in group recommender systems. There was a big gap between the actual choices and these strategies. Based on the individual ratings of the group members we computed the top two recommendations for each group according to the most common aggregation strategies. The actual group decisions on their top 2 destinations were our ground truth and we calculated precision for the top one and top two group choices (see Table 3). Overall, the analyzed aggregation strategies, confirming our assumption, only partially predict the choices made by groups after a face-to-face discussion. Thus, an aggregation strategy applied in a mechanical way may not produce a recommendation that the group would choose. Hence, we believe that a useful group recommender can be built without adhering to any of these strategies. Nevertheless, the obtained results confirm the results from [10] - multiplicative strategy outperforms other aggregation strategies.

Table 3: Aggregation strategy performance

Strategy	Precision Top 1	Precision Top 2
Additive	0.333	0.233
Multiplicative	0.343	0.25
Median	0.277	0.214
Least Misery	0.200	0.157
Most Pleasure	0.140	0.122

Finally we tentatively explored which individual or group features such as personality traits and travel behavioral patterns [12] and their composition in a group setting influence outcome measures such as group choice satisfaction or the perceived difficulty of the decision process. Results of an exploratory correlation analysis showed some statistically significant associations (see Table 4). In the first part of Table 4 the size of the used data sample was 77, in the second 27 (data collected solely in Vienna) and in the third 24 (correlation at the group level). We analyzed relations between the diversity within a group and satisfaction and difficulty at the group level. The diversity within a group was calculated as the variance of the respective individual features of all group members. Choice satisfaction and difficulty of the group decision process at the group level were calculated as mean values.

Table 4: Correlations

Individual features	**Satisfaction**	**Corr.**
Openness	ChoiceSat2	0.36
Behavior	**Sat./Diff.**	**Corr.**
Give opinion	ChoiceSat1	-0.44
Ask for suggestion	ChoiceSat2	-0.39
Give opinion	Difficulty1	0.53
Ask for opinion	Difficulty4	0.63
Group diversity in	**Sat./Diff.**	**Corr.**
Independence & History	ChoiceSat2	-0.51
Sun & Chill-Out	Difficulty6	-0.51

Difficulty1 - *"Eventually I was in doubt between some destinations"*; Difficulty4 - *"The task of making this decision was overwhelming"*; Difficulty6 - *"The decision process was frustrating"*; *Independence & History* and *Sun & Chill-Out*: travel behavioral patterns [12].

Next, we studied choice satisfaction at the group level in more detail. We aimed at identifying differences between highly satisfied and not so satisfied groups. However, the 24 groups in our data sample had different sizes: 12 have four members, six have three members and six have two members; the smaller the group the higher the chance that all its members were satisfied: this was the case for 83.3% of the groups of size two, for 66.7% of the groups of size three, but only for 33.3% of the groups of size four.

To capture group satisfaction, we considered the average choice satisfaction of its members, i.e., how much they agreed on average to the statement *"I am excited about the chosen destination"* (based on a five-point Likert scale). We took the average of all group satisfactions (i.e., 4.1), and next assigned the groups to two categories: 1) group satisfaction higher than the average and 2) group satisfaction equal or below the average. Each category comprised nine groups. Based on Student's t-tests, we found various significant differences between the two categories (see Table 5). Some of the results show the consistency of the participants' answers, e.g., members of high satisfied groups found the alternatives to choose from on average more appealing than members of low satisfied groups (p-value<0.001). However, there were also differences related to the personality of the group members. Members of high satisfied groups have on average displayed higher openness and neuroticism scores (p-value<0.05 and <0.01 respectively). Furthermore, the travel behavioral patterns, e.g., *Sun & Chill-Out* were more distinct in high satisfied groups (p-value<0.01). To conduct a robustness test, we repeated the analysis for the groups of size four only; this did not change the presented results. For the groups in Vienna, moreover, where information on the behavior during the group decision process was available, we found that in low satisfied groups typically all members showed disagreement behavior during the discussion; i.e., significantly more than in high satisfied groups where on average about half of the members displayed this behavior (p-value<0.05). However, overall, the small sample size is clearly a limitation here and in order to confirm these presumed relationships follow-up studies will be needed.

Table 5: Significant differences in variable means between low satisfied groups and high satisfied groups

	Low	High	p-value
Alternatives were appealing (avg)	3.19	3.98	0.00
Openness (avg)	3.81	4.11	0.03
Neuroticism (avg)	3.08	3.61	0.00
Sun & Chill-Out (avg)	2.73	3.25	0.01
Show disagreement (percentage)	100%	54%	0.03

All variables w.r.t. to a five-level Likert scale.

5. CONCLUSIONS

The results of this study clearly indicate that research in group recommender systems needs to put more emphasis on the decision making process taking place in groups. We know that user preferences are not stable and they therefore must not be considered as independent input variables for the recommendation mechanism. This is true for individuals, but even more so for groups: group preferences are constructed during the process, and this study indicates people readily accept this outcome. Consequently, we may not address group recommendation problems with the classical machinery of RSs, i.e., predicting group preferences from individual preferences of group members. Even though we should be cautious to infer far-reaching conclusions based on a single study using a student sample, this study nevertheless clearly demonstrates that well-known aggregation mechanisms cannot fully describe the outcome of a group decision problem and a recommender may deviate from this normative rule. In addition, as a first step we tried to identify the properties of group members and the group as a whole that may influence the group outcome.

Now, as a next step, we are developing a group recommender system whose interaction design incorporates the lessons learned by this study [13]. It is based on the concepts of discussion groups and bots, where the recommender rather takes the role of a facilitator for the group decision making process rather than being a rigid mediator of users' preferences.

6. ADDITIONAL AUTHORS

Additional authors: Markus Zanker (Free University of Bozen-Bolzano, Bolzano, Italy, email: `markus.zanker@unibz.it`).

7. REFERENCES

[1] L. Ardissono, A. Goy, G. Petrone, M. Segnan, and P. Torasso. Intrigue: personalized recommendation of tourist attractions for desktop and hand held devices. *Applied Artificial Intelligence*, 17(8-9):687–714, 2003.

[2] R. F. Bales. A set of categories for the analysis of small group interaction. *American Sociological Review*, 15:257–263, 1950.

[3] L. Baltrunas, T. Makcinskas, and F. Ricci. Group recommendations with rank aggregation and collaborative filtering. In *Proceedings of the fourth ACM conference on Recommender systems, RecSys'10*, pages 119–126, Barcelona, Spain, 2010.

[4] P. Bekkerman, S. Kraus, and F. Ricci. Applying cooperative negotiation methodology to group recommendation problem. In *Proceedings of Workshop on Recommender Systems in 17th European Conference on Artificial Intelligence*, pages 72–75, 2006.

[5] L. Chen, M. de Gemmis, A. Felfernig, P. Lops, F. Ricci, and G. Semeraro. Human decision making and recommender systems. *ACM Transactions on Interactive Intelligent Systems*, 3(3):17, 2013.

[6] D. Forsyth. *Group Dynamics*. Wadsworth Cengage Learning, 6th edition, 2014.

[7] H. Gibson and A. Yiannakis. Tourist roles: Needs and the lifecourse. *Annals of tourism research*, 29(2):358–383, 2002.

[8] L. R. Goldberg. An alternative "description of personality": the big-five factor structure. *Journal of personality and social psychology*, 59(6):1216, 1990.

[9] A. Jameson. More than the sum of its members: challenges for group recommender systems. In *Proceedings of the working conference on Advanced visual interfaces*, pages 48–54, 2004.

[10] J. Masthoff. Group recommender systems: aggregation, satisfaction and group attributes. In F. Ricci, L. Rokach, and B. Shapira, editors, *Recommender Systems Handbook*, pages 743–776. Springer, 2015.

[11] K. McCarthy, L. McGinty, B. Smyth, and M. Salamo. The needs of the many: a case-based group recommender system. *Advances in Case-Based Reasoning*, pages 196–210, 2006.

[12] J. Neidhardt, R. Schuster, L. Seyfang, and H. Werthner. Eliciting the users' unknown preferences. In *Proceedings of the 8th ACM Conference on Recommender systems*, pages 309–312. ACM, 2014.

[13] T. N. Nguyen and F. Ricci. Supporting group decision making with recommendations and explanations. In *24th Conference on User Modeling, Adaptation and Personalization (UMAP)*. Springer Berlin Heidelberg, 2016.

[14] M. Stettinger, A. Felfernig, G. Leitner, S. Reiterer, and M. Jeran. Counteracting serial position effects in the choicla group decision support environment. In *Proceedings of the 20th International Conference on Intelligent User Interfaces*, pages 148–157, USA, 2015.

[15] R. S. Tindale and T. Kameda. Social sharedness as a unifying theme for information processing in groups. *Group Processes and Intergroup Relations*, 3(2):123–140, 2000.

ExpLOD: a Framework for Explaining Recommendations based on the Linked Open Data Cloud

Cataldo Musto Fedelucio Narducci Pasquale Lops
Marco De Gemmis Giovanni Semeraro

Dept. of Computer Science - University of Bari 'Aldo Moro - Italy
name.surname@uniba.it

ABSTRACT

In this paper we present ExpLOD, a framework which exploits the information available in the Linked Open Data (LOD) cloud to generate a *natural language explanation* of the suggestions produced by a recommendation algorithm. The methodology is based on building a graph in which the items liked by a user are connected to the items recommended through the properties available in the LOD cloud. Next, given this graph, we implemented some techniques to rank those properties and we used the most relevant ones to feed a module for generating explanations in natural language.

In the experimental evaluation we performed a user study with 308 subjects aiming to investigate to what extent our explanation framework can lead to more transparent, trustful and engaging recommendations. The preliminary results provided us with encouraging findings, since our algorithm performed better than both a non-personalized explanation baseline and a popularity-based one.

1. BACKGROUND AND MOTIVATIONS

The performance of a recommender system is generally evaluated on the ground of its capability of predicting items the user would probably like. Accordingly, evaluation metrics usually reward systems that maximize the predictive accuracy. However, especially when unknown items are proposed, the system should help the user to make an informed choice instead of just proposing a list of items based on an obscure reasoning mechanism [4].

Tintarev and Masthoff [8] point out that *explaining* a recommendation is generally intended as *justifying* the suggestion, but it might be also intended as *providing a detailed description* that allows the user to understand the quality of the recommended item. Accordingly, they define seven possible aims for explanation, namely: *transparency, scrutabilty, trust, effectiveness, persuasiveness, efficiency, satisfaction.* The authors also demonstrate that a personalized explanation strategy generally works better than a generic one. Typically, the explanations are grouped in three classes according to the information they exploit: preferences of similar users (e.g. *customers who bought this item also bought...*), similar items (e.g., *this item is similar to other items you liked*), attributes of interest (e.g., *this item has attributes you prefer*). However, there is not a general assessment on which approach works best, since a strategy can maximize an aspect rather than another.

In this work we investigated five of the aforementioned aims by implementing a personalized explanation strategy exploiting both *similar items* and *attributes of interest* through a graph-based recommendation model. Our explanation framework is based on the Linked Open Data cloud, and more specifically on the properties encoded in DBpedia[1] to link the items the user liked with the recommended ones. These properties are thus used for generating textual explanations. A similar attempt is due to [5], who demonstrated that a graph-based explanation results in a better user experience, However, they focused on the usage of graphs for visualization purposes, while our contribution exploits graphs for modeling the properties describing the items and identifying the most relevant ones to be used in a natural language explanation.

In the experimental session we evaluated the effectiveness of our framework against several baselines through a user study. Moreover, we also investigated the impact of the single features on the overall explanation. This research line has been already investigated in the past, and several authors [2, 4] showed a clear relationship between some features (as the favorite *actor* in a movie recommendation scenario) and the effectiveness of the explanation.

The rest of the article is organized as follows: in Section 2 describes the framework designed to generate personalized explanations. The description of the experiments carried out to evaluate the effectiveness of our strategy is given in Section 3. Finally, Section 4 concludes this work by discussing the main findings and defining the future research directions.

2. DESCRIPTION OF THE FRAMEWORK

The workflow carried out by ExpLOD is depicted in Figure 1. The framework is organized in four main modules: Data Mapper, Graph Builder, a property ranker and a generator.

First, the Data mapper implements mechanisms to map each item with an element in the LOD cloud. As an example,

[1]http://wiki.dbpedia.org/

RecSys '16, September 15-19, 2016, Boston , MA, USA
 ISBN 978-1-4503-4035-9/16/09...$15.00
DOI: http://dx.doi.org/10.1145/2959100.2959173

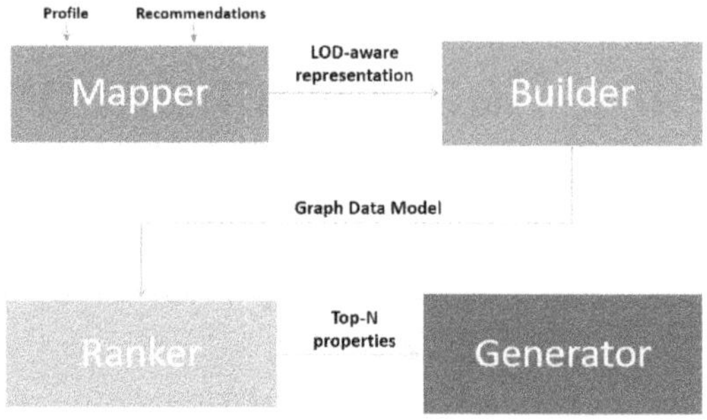

Figure 1: Organization of the framework

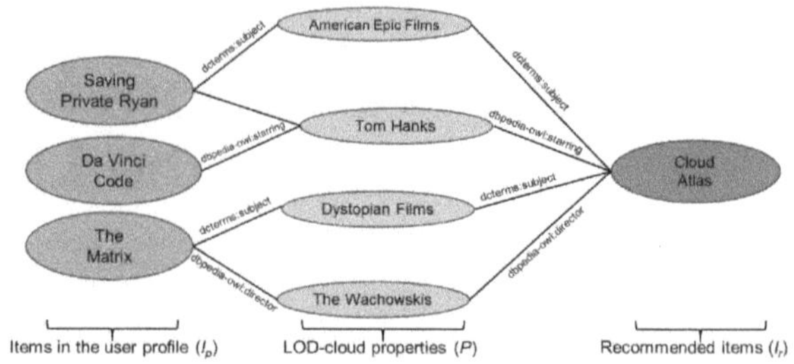

Figure 2: ExpLOD Data Model.

if a user is interested in the movies *The Matrix* and *Cloud Atlas*, the module will find the `DBpedia` nodes they refer to. In our case, the mapping is carried out by implementing a *shallow* matching of the name of the item with the title of the Wikipedia page the `DBpedia` node is linked to, but more complex mapping methods may be easily implemented. The output of this step is a list in which all the items in the user profile and all the items in her recommendation list are mapped with an URI (if any) in the LOD cloud. This step is mandatory since the explanations generated by the system will rely on a subset of the properties available in the LOD cloud.

Next, those LOD-aware item representations are used to feed the graph BUILDER, which exploits the information available in the LOD cloud to build a graph-based data model. Formally, let I_p be the set of items in the user profile, let I_r be the set of recommendations and let $exists(s, o)$ be a predicate returning *true* if an RDF triple having s as subject and o as object exists in the LOD cloud. Next, we define $P = \{p | i \in I_r \wedge exists(i, p) = true\}$ as the set of the values of the properties available in the LOD cloud describing the items the user received as recommendations. Given such a representation, the module builds a bipartite graph $G = (N, E)$, where $N = I_p \cup I_r \cup P$ and $E = \{(i, p) | i \in I_p \cup I_r \wedge p \in P\}$. Basically, this graph connects the items the user liked and those in her recommendation list through the values of the properties describing those items in the LOD cloud. A visual explanation of the data model is provided in Figure 2. Elements in I_p, I_r and P are reported in blue, red and green, respectively. In this case, the user liked *Saving Private Ryan, The Matrix* and *The Da Vinci Code*, and received as recommendation the movie *Cloud Atlas*. Accordingly, four properties connecting the movies in the profile to the recommendation are added as nodes in the graph[2]. We label them as *candidate properties*, since they represent the preliminary set of properties which *could* explain the recommendation received by the user.

Next, the property RANKER analyzes such a data model to identify the subset of *candidate properties* which are likely to explain the recommendation. To this end, the module assigns a *relevance score* to each property, based on the insight that a *good* explanation should emphasize those properties which can describe the current recommendation on the ground of the items the user liked. Given a candidate property c, the property RANKER calculates its score as:

$$score(c, I_p, I_r) = (\alpha \frac{n_{c,I_p}}{|Ip|} + \beta \frac{n_{c,I_r}}{|Ir|}) * IDF_c \qquad (1)$$

where n_{c,I_p} is the number of edges connecting c with the items in the user profile, n_{c,I_r} is the number of edges connecting c with the items in the recommendation set, α and β are two weighting factors and IDF_c is an adaptation over `DBpedia` of the classical Inverse Document Frequency [7], which calculates how many items over all the dataset are described by that property. Formula (1) gives a higher score to those properties which are highly connected to the items in I_p and I_r and which are not so common as well. Through this calculation, all the candidate properties are provided with a relevance score and the *top-K* are used to generate the explanation. By following the example in Figure 2, *Tom Hanks* is the most relevant property explaining the recommendation since it occurs in two out of three movies in the user profile. Next, it is likely that the IDF component of the formula would help to rank as second property *Dystopian Movies* which is surely a less common one than *The Wackowski* and *American Epic Films.* It is worth to note that our ranking formula is independent of the size of the recommendation list, so it can produce a single explanation also for a larger set of recommendations. When $|I_r| > 1$, the algorithm will rank first those properties which are common to many items in the profile and can also describe many items in the recommendation list.

Finally, once the *top-K* properties have been returned, the GENERATOR module builds a natural-language explanation supporting the recommendation. The basic idea is to use the properties returned by the RANKER to fill a *template-based* structure which generates the final explanation. As an example, the explanation generated for the data model provided in Figure 2 is: *"I recommend you* CLOUD ATLAS *since you often like movies starred by* TOM HANKS *as* DA VINCI CODE *and* SAVING PRIVATE RYAN. *Moreover, I recommend it because you sometimes like* DYSTOPIAN MOVIES *as* THE MATRIX *and* AMERICAN EPIC FILMS *as* SAVING PRIVATE RYAN*".*

Text in *small caps* refers to the elements coming from the LOD cloud. Adverbs as *often* or *sometimes* are dynamically defined by computing the normalized occurrences of that property in the data model and by mapping each adverb to a different range of the score. Moreover, expressions as *starred by* are obtained by mapping each property in the LOD cloud (in this case, DBPEDIA:OWL:STARRING) with a natural language expression. This is done for all the properties available in the LOD cloud, as DBPEDIA:OWL:DIRECTOR, DBPEDIA:OWL:MUSICCOMPOSER and so on. Due to space

[2]The LOD cloud contains many more overlapping properties. Due to space reasons we just reported a small subset of them.

reasons it is not possible to provide further details about this module. However, even this description showed how the combination of techniques for generating natural-language expressions with the richness of the information available in the LOD cloud let the algorithm produce very meaningful explanations supporting the recommendation set.

3. EXPERIMENTAL EVALUATION

The goal of the experimental evaluation was twofold: to understand to what extent our explanation framework may lead to more transparent, trustful or engaging recommendations (Experiment 1) and to investigate whether a correlation exists between the choice of the properties used to generate the explanation and the effectiveness of the explanation itself (Experiment 2). To this end, we designed a user study in the movie domain by involving 308 subjects (male=70%, degree or PhD=62%, medium interest in movies). We evaluated the following explanation aims: *transparency*, *persuasiveness*, *engagement*, *trust* and *effectiveness*, as in [8].

Experimental Protocol. To run the experiment, we deployed a web application[3] implementing the previously described framework. The platform was designed to run a *between-subject* experiment, i.e. we tested four different explanation styles and each user was randomly assigned to one of them. As explanations styles we defined two versions of the previously presented natural language-based explanations (by ranking the properties with and without IDF) and two baselines, a *popularity-based explanation* and a *non-personalized explanation style* based on the presentation of the movie properties extracted from `DBpedia`. Those baselines were already adopted in literature [8] for similar experimental protocols. In a nutshell, each user involved in the experiment carried out the following steps:

(1) Collection of Demographic Data and Preference Elicitation. We asked the users to provide some basic demographic data. Then, each user provided her preferences in the movie domain: a small portion of the users (around 5%) authorized our application to extract preferences from their Facebook profiles, while the other explicitly rated a randomly generated subset of 20 movies extracted from the top-100 popular movies in IMDB. Once the profiles were built, recommendations were generated by running Personalized PageRank [3] as recommendation algorithm.

(2) Generation of the Explanations. We used the preferences of the users and the Top-1 recommendation generated by the algorithm to feed our framework. When the *popularity-based* baseline was picked as explanation style, each user was provided with a simple explanation as *"We suggest this item since it is very popular among people who like the same movies as you."*. On the other side, as *non-personalized explanation style* we exploited the properties encoded in `DBpedia` to build a structured description of the movie used as explanation (e.g. starring, director, music composer, subject, and so on) without any filtering or ranking of the properties. Finally, when ExpLOD was randomly picked, we run our framework as previously shown. In this setting, the Data Mapper was able to map to `DBpedia` 90,318 movies gathered from IMDB. The mapping is available online[4]. Next, Graph Builder queried `DBpedia` to extract the properties describing the movies. It is worth to note that all the available properties were extracted, without performing any filtering. Finally, the ranking formula was set by choosing 0.5 as weighting factor for α and β and the top-3 properties were returned. All these values were roughly set through some simple heuristics. In the future we will also investigate the impact of a proper tuning of the parameters on the overall results.

(3) Evaluation through Questionnaires. Finally we asked the users to fill a questionnaire to evaluate the quality of the different explanation styles. Each user was asked to evaluate the previously presented *explanation aims* through a five-point rating scale and to evaluate how much she liked that suggestion. The questions the users had to answer are presented in Table 1. Finally, in the last part of the experiment, each user had to enjoy a trailer of the movie and had to evaluate again the movie after watching the trailer. The whole experiment took less than 3 minutes. A screen recording showing a demo of the experiment is available online[5].

Evaluation Metrics. We evaluated *transparency*, *persuasiveness*, *engagement* and *trust* of the recommendation as the average score collected through the user questionnaires, while the *effectiveness* was calculated as the normalized difference between the pre- and post-trailer ratings the user provided for the recommendation. This is an evaluation protocol which is very common in literature [1], whose insight is that an *effective* explanation may help the user to evaluate to what extent she would like the recommendation, even before enjoying it. For each explanation style 77 observations were collected. Given that in [6] the minimum acceptable sample size for each experimental condition was set as 73, we can state that our experiment guaranteed the significance of the results.

aim	question
transparency	"I understood why this movie was recommended to me"
persuasion	"The explanation made the recommendation more convincing"
engagement	"The explanation helped me discover new information about this movie"
trust	"The explanation increased my trust in the recommender system"
effectiveness	"I like this recommendation"

Table 1: Details of the Questionnaire

4. DISCUSSION AND CONCLUSIONS

Results of Experiment 1 are reported in Table 2. Results show that our framework is able to significantly outperform both the baselines (statistical significance has been assessed through a *Mann-Whitney U Test*) for most of the explanation aims we evaluated ($p < 0.001$). Specifically, configurations based on ExpLOD are able to provide users with more *transparent*, *persuasive* and *trustful* recommendations. Our framework also obtained the best results in terms of *engagement*, but a statistically significant improvement was noted only over the simple popularity-based baseline. The only metrics that did not benefit of the adoption of the explanation generated by our framework is the *effectiveness*, since in this case the best results are obtained by

[3]http://193.204.187.192:8080/WebLodrecsys/Benvenuto.jsp
[4]http://www.di.uniba.it/ swap/explod/mapping.txt

[5]http://bit.ly/1WEPhc4

the non-personalized explanation based on the structured presentation of LOD properties. This result may be due to the fact that also a simple summary reporting the most relevant properties of the movies may be helpful to understand whether the user will like it or not. However, we did not notice any statistical significance, so we can state that our framework can be as effective as the non-personalized baseline on this task. On the other side, when more complex aspects as the trust or the persuasion are taken into account, our strategy is the only one which can significantly outperform the baseline. Finally, as regards the use of the IDF, experiments did not show any significant difference so it is possible to state that its use does not influence the overall performance of the explanation.

Table 2: Results of Experiment 1. The best-performing configuration is in bold. Significant improvements over the baselines are in italics and bold.

	transp.	pers.	engag.	trust	eff.
popularity	3.01	2.59	2.31	2.67	0.93
LOD properties	3.04	2.84	3.28	2.81	**0.66**
ExpLOD-noIDF	*4.00*	3.39	***3.48***	***3.39***	0.72
ExpLOD	***4.18***	**3.41**	*3.31*	*3.36*	0.75

In Experiment 2, we investigated whether some relationship between the choice of particular properties and the overall performance of our explanation framework exists. Indeed, it is likely that in some scenarios it would be useful to generate explanations able to maximize a specific explanation aim, thus it is worth to know whether to use (or to ignore) a specific property may optimize a specific aspect. As an example, in a movie recommendation scenario it would be good to *persuade* the user watching that movie. To this end, we split the data we collected during the first experiment on the ground of the properties selected by *ExpLOD*. Next, we calculated again the average transparency, persuasion, engagement, trust and effectiveness by *only* considering those explanations which contained a specific property, as the *director* of the movie, the *producer*, the *music composer*, and so on.

Table 3: Results of Experiment 2: average improvement (or average decrease) over the results presented in Table 1 are reported in parenthesis.

	positive	**negative**
transparency	topic (+12%) director (+3%)	distributor (-11%) composer (-13%)
persuasion	won (+15%) director (+12%)	location (-8%) producer (-9%)
engagement	writer (+25%) director (+20%)	producer (-13%) distributor (-3%)
trust	won (+21%) composer (+5%)	producer (-4%) topic (-9%)
effectiveness	director (+77%) writer (+43%)	location (-71%) composer (-50%)

Due to space reasons, we reported in Table 3 only the most interesting findings emerging from this experiment. The results provided several insights, since they showed that some interesting correlations which can drive the choice of the most promising properties actually exist. Specifically, data showed that the usage of particular properties as the *director* of the movie or its *writer* positively affects most of the explanations aims. On the other side, properties as the *producer* or the *distributor* do not improve the engagement nor the persuasion of the explanation. Moreover, it is very interesting that both the persuasion and the engagement of the explanation are improved when the information about which prizes the movie has won was reported in the explanation. Finally, it is also worth to note that including information about the general topic of the movie (encoded in the `DBpedia` properties DCTERMS:SUBJECT) may lead to more transparent explanations, but it negatively affects the trust. This is a very interesting insight, since it shows that a different choice of the properties may lead to the maximization of a different *explanation aim*, thus our framework may be properly tuned in order to use (or to avoid) a specific property according to the goals of the explanation.

To sum up, in this paper we presented a framework for generating natural language explanations based on the information available in the LOD cloud. Preliminary results showed the goodness of the framework, since our strategy significantly outperformed all the baselines we took into account. Moreover, we also showed that the choice of specific properties may influence the behavior of the framework, leading to explanations able to maximize some specific aspects. As future work, we will evaluate the effectiveness of the framework in different domains, as music and books, but we will also investigate the impact of different data points gathered from the LOD cloud. Indeed, we plan to extract also properties not directly connected to the items to be recommended, in order to build explanations containing more interesting and unexpected patterns connecting the items the user liked to those she got as recommendation, hopefully leading towards more engaging and effective explanations.

5. REFERENCES

[1] M. Bilgic and R. Mooney. Explaining recommendations: Satisfaction vs. promotion. In *Beyond Personalization, IUI WS*, volume 5, 2005.

[2] G. Carenini and J. Moore. An empirical study of the influence of user tailoring on evaluative argument effectiveness. In *IJCAI 2001*, pages 1307–1314, 2001.

[3] T. H. Haveliwala. Topic-Sensitive PageRank: A Context-Sensitive Ranking Algorithm for Web Search. *IEEE Trans. Knowl. Data Eng.*, 15(4):784–796, 2003.

[4] J. L. Herlocker, J. A. Konstan, and J. Riedl. Explaining collaborative filtering recommendations. In *CSCW 2000*, pages 241–250, 2000.

[5] B. Knijnenburg, S. Bostandjiev, J. O'Donovan, and A. Kobsa. Inspectability and control in social recommenders. In *RecSys 2012*, pages 43–50, 2012.

[6] B. Knijnenburg and M. Willemsen. Evaluating recommender systems with user experiments. In *Recommender Systems Handbook.*, pages 309–352. Springer, 2015.

[7] C. Manning, P. Raghavan, and H. Schütze. Scoring, term weighting and the vector space model. *Introduction to Information Retrieval*, 100:2–4, 2008.

[8] N. Tintarev and J. Masthoff. Evaluating the effectiveness of explanations for recommender systems. *UMUAI*, 22(4-5):399–439, 2012.

The Value of Online Customer Reviews

Georgios Askalidis
Northwestern University
Evanston, IL
gask@u.northwestern.edu

Edward C. Malthouse
Northwestern University
Evanston, IL
ecm@northwestern.com

ABSTRACT

We study the effect of the volume of consumer reviews on the purchase likelihood (conversion rate) of users browsing a product page. We propose using the exponential learning curve model to study how conversion rates change with the number of reviews. We call the difference in conversion rate between having no reviews and an infinite number *the value of reviews*. We find that, on average, the conversion rate of a product can increase by as much as 270% as it accumulates reviews, amongst the users that choose to display them. We also find diminishing marginal value as a product accumulates reviews, with the first five reviews driving the bulk of the aforementioned increase. To address the problem of simultaneity of increase of reviews and conversion rate, we use customer sessions in which reviews were *not* displayed as a control for trends that would have happened regardless of the increase in the review volume. Using our framework, we further find that high priced items have a higher value for reviews than lower priced items. High priced items can see their conversion rate increase by as much as 380% as they accumulate reviews compared to 190% for low priced items.We infer that the existence of reviews provides valuable signals to the customers, increasing their propensity to purchase. We also infer that users usually don't pay attention to the entire set of reviews, especially if there are a lot of them, but instead they focus on the first few available. Our approach can be extended and applied in a variety of settings to gain further insights.

Keywords

Marketing, Online Reviews, Word of Mouth

1. INTRODUCTION

Electronic Word of Mouth (eWOM) in the form of online customer reviews, is omnipresent and part of many customers' purchase journey. Reviews are being collected, aggregated and displayed to consumers in an easy-to-digest format in all types of settings: all of the top-10 U.S. online retailers (as well as most of the biggest retailers in the rest of the world) collect and display user reviews for their products. The same is true for all the major digital stores. Furthermore, companies like Yelp, Facebook, Google, IMDb and Rotten Tomatoes provide platforms for users to submit reviews that are, in-turn, aggregated and displayed to other users. User reviews are also being used to build trust between customers in decentralized marketplaces like eBay, Airbnb and Uber.

For online shoppers, reviews are not just an option anymore but an expectation. A recent survey[1] found that 30% of shoppers under the age of 45 consult reviews for every purchase they make, while 86% say that reviews are essential in making purchase decisions. In fact, after price, reviews are the factor with the most impact on purchases. An extensive literature has also showcased the economic importance of positive reviews for restaurants [14, 1], books [2], movies [6], mobile apps [8], and consumer goods [15].

In this work we aim to gain insights on a slightly more fundamental question. We ask, *should retailers seek reviews for their products?* Can the existence of reviews (without any assumptions on their valence or other characteristics) increase the likelihood of purchase? Our analysis suggests positive answers. We further explore the value of reviews for the three largest product categories of the studied retailer: electronics, apparel and home living. Within categories, we explore the value of reviews for high- and low-priced items.

2. THE EFFECT OF REVIEW VOLUME ON PURCHASE

Prior research on review volume has produced mixed results. Volume is believed to exert positive effects by increasing review credibility and/or signaling product popularity. Volume has been shown to have a positive effect on box office sales [7, 13] and sales rank of electronic products [5, 11]. Moreover, it influences other outcomes such as consumer attention [9, 13], product evaluation [4], product popularity [18] and purchase intention [17]. However, [10] finds that volume does not impact the sales of cell phones, and [3] shows that volume has no significant impact on box office performance. There is no evidence for a negative effect.

In order to understand the effect of volume on purchase we propose the following assumptions:

RecSys '16, September 15-19, 2016, Boston , MA, USA

 ISBN 978-1-4503-4035-9/16/09...$15.00

DOI: http://dx.doi.org/10.1145/2959100.2959181

[1] http://www.powerreviews.com/blog/survey-confirms-the-value-of-reviews

- **Assumption 1**: Each product has an inherent conversion rate, in the absence of any reviews.
- **Assumption 2**: Each product has an upper bound on its conversion rate that is less than 1.
- **Assumption 3**: As a product accumulates more reviews, their marginal value decreases.

Consider a product (or service). When the product is first introduced it will not have any reviews, and there will be an initial probability of purchase, which we will call the *intercept.* Over time the product will attract reviews. The accumulating reviews should cause the probability of purchase to increase and approach an *asymptote.* This asymptote can theoretically be 1, i.e., given an infinite number of reviews every product view can lead to purchase, but in reality we expect it to be much lower. The exact location of the asymptote will depend on other factors, such as the price, product category, quality, and the level of marketing support. We furthermore assume that as a product accumulates reviews, the value of each additional review will decrease, i.e., the marginal value of the 5th review will be higher than that of the 50th review. If these assumptions are accepted then one possible function for the value of reviews is the *exponential learning curve* [16, equation 13.9 and §13.5]:

$$\pi(x) = \gamma_0 - \gamma_1 e^{-\gamma_2 x}, \quad x \geq 0, \gamma_2 > 0, \tag{1}$$

where $0 \leq \pi(x) \leq 1$ is the probability that a product with x reviews is purchased. Parameter γ_0 specifies the asymptote because $\lim_{x\to\infty} \pi(x) = \gamma_0$. The intercept is $\pi(0) = \gamma_0 - \gamma_1$, and so γ_1 gives the distance between the intercept and the asymptote. Thus, γ_1 gives the **value of reviews,** since it is the difference between the conversion rate with no reviews and when there are infinite reviews. We do not constraint $\gamma_1 \geq 0$, and $\gamma_1 < 0$ would indicate that the conversion rate decreases as reviews are added. The other parameter, γ_2, characterizes the steepness of the function, where large values indicate $\pi(x)$ approaches γ_0 quickly and smaller values indicate a more gradual approach. This model has been used extensively for modeling learning curves and memory [12].

3. METHODS

We have data for the entire year 2015 from an online retailer that sells high-end specialty gifts. The data record every visit to the site for each user id, including the date and time, what products were viewed, whether the user viewed reviews and whether the user purchased the product. We also know the number of reviews that the user was exposed to, where the number increases over the year. Thus, we can study the conversion rate as a function of the number of reviews.

Our dataset consists of around 15.5 million page views for 1800 unique products, from 7.8 million users over the course of one year (January 4, 2015 – January 2, 2016). For each product, we track the number of its page views and sales as it accumulates reviews. Hence, for each product and number of reviews, n, we calculate the product's conversion rate while it had n reviews. We then average the conversion rate over all products for each n, to calculate the average conversion rate as a function of the number of reviews. When we want to study the value of reviews for products of a specific category or characteristic (e.g., price) we repeat the above approach but restrict our attention to the relevant products. We then estimate the parameters of Equation 1 by using the curve fit function of the scipy module for Python[2].

Our approach has a built-in control group, since we are tracking the conversion rate of a fixed set of products while they accumulate more reviews. Since we are comparing the conversion rate of the products to their past selves, many effects due to the products' characteristics are controlled for within our model. What our model doesn't inherently control for are temporal trends related to exogenous time related variables. To address this issue we use a control set of observations. Observations regarding page views in which the user *did not display reviews.* We use these sessions as a control for time and other exogenous trends. We adjust our exponential function to incorporate these distinction between page views where the user did and did not display the reviews.

$$\pi(x) = (\gamma_0 + \gamma_1 \text{disp}) - (\gamma_2 + \gamma_3 \text{disp}) e^{-(\gamma_4 + \gamma_5 \text{disp})x}, \quad x \geq 0, \gamma_2 > 0 \tag{2}$$

where disp is a binary indicator of whether a display of reviews happened. By fitting Equation 1 on our data, we isolate the effect of the display of reviews while controlling for all other exogenous trends. To further remove any noise from our data, we focus only on products whose first page view was observed after March 1, 2015. This is to ensure that our data cover the beginning of a product's life cycle, and we don't use data for products that have been on the market already for some time in the beginning of 2015.

4. RESULTS

Overall, the conversion rate of a product increases by 270% as it accumulates reviews. This increase is calculated as the difference between the asymptote (γ_1) and the intercept (γ_0), divided by the intercept. Moreover, over the bulk of that effect happens within the first 10 reviews the product receives. Figure 1 displays the fitted curve. Note that this effect is isolated for when the display of reviews happened, i.e., when disp equals 1 in Equation 1.

Figure 2 compares the value of reviews for high- and low-priced items. Products were categorized into high and low price depending whether their price was above or below the median price amongst the studied products. The median price was $79.99. We notice that low-priced items have consistently higher conversion rates than the high-priced products. The value of reviews is around 190% for low-priced items but much higher, at 380% for high-priced items. It seems that users gain confidence in their purchase when they see other users have bought a high-priced item. For low-priced items, the monetary risk is lower and perhaps that's why the value of reviews is lower.

Finally, we also explored the value of reviews for high- and low-quality products. We approximate a product's quality by observing all the reviews it accumulated over its (observed in our date) lifetime. Products with a lifetime average below 3.5 were classified as low quality and products with a lifetime average above 3.5 stars were classified as high quality. We notice that high-quality products have consistently higher conversion rate than lower-quality products. But, perhaps surprisingly, low-quality products have a higher value for reviews, at 324% compared to high-quality

[2]Python Documentation, http://bit.ly/1XDwA76

products, at 135%. This could be because of the lower baseline for low-quality products as well as that social signals are more important and valuable when the product in question is of lower quality.

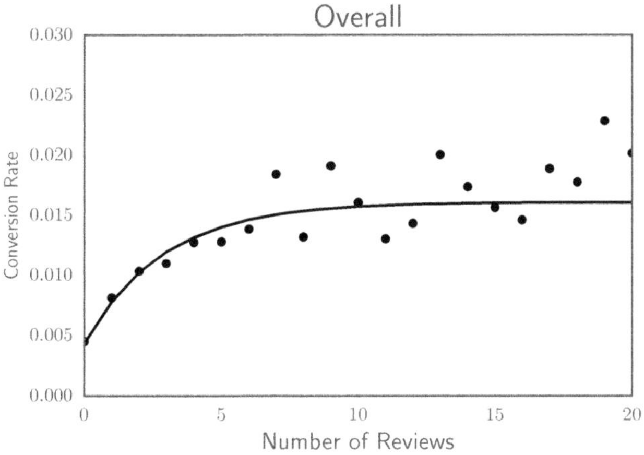

Figure 1: Effect of Number of Displayed Reviews on the Conversion Rate

5. CONCLUSION AND FUTURE WORK

Our work provides strong evidence for a positive value of reviews, i.e., causal effect of the existence of reviews towards the purchase likelihood of a browsing customer. This is with no assumptions on the characteristics of the reviews. Practitioners should take this to mean that it's beneficial for their platform to solicit reviews, even if they have no control over the reviews they will get (e.g., their valence).

We explore the value of reviews for various product characteristics such as price and category, but our results are still confined under the specific retailer we study. The exact value may change depending the specific characteristics of the retailer. We believe our approach, and model, can help guide future studies for other settings and retailers.

Many interesting directions are available for future work, and our dataset can be utilized to help explore them. First,

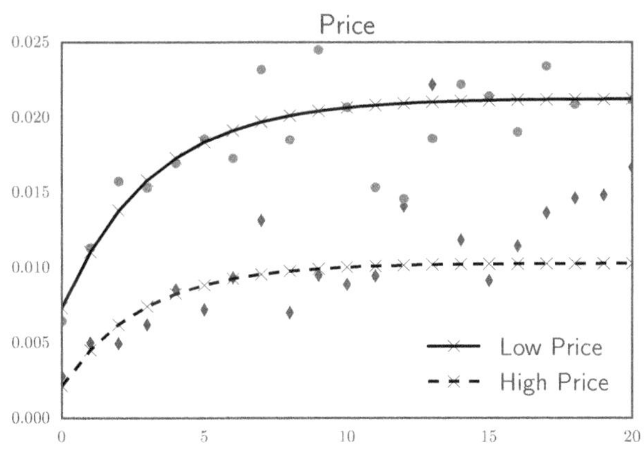

Figure 2: Effect of Number of Displayed Reviews on Various Price

better understanding of the value of reviews for various types of products as well as users can be important. Are reviews more important for returning or new users? How about users that have submitted a review themselves? Insights here, can help a retailer identify products and users for whom the value of reviews is high and act accordingly, e.g., by more prominent displays.

Moreover, the effect of valence can be better studied and understood. What is the value of higher ratings versus lower ratings? Studying the interaction between volume and valence can also help with understanding the way that customers interpret consumer reviews. For example, all else being equal, is it better for a product to have a 4.5 star average rating based on 5 reviews or a 4 star average based on 50 reviews?

6. ACKNOWLEDGMENTS

We thank the Spiegel Center for Digital and Database Marketing at Northwestern University for support.

References

[1] M. Anderson and J. Magruder. Learning from the crowd: Regression discontinuity estimates of the effects of an online review database. *The Economic Journal*, 122(563):957–989, 2012.

[2] J. A. Chevalier and D. Mayzlin. The effect of word of mouth on sales: Online book reviews. *Journal of Marketing Research*, 43(3):345–354, 2006.

[3] P. K. Chintagunta, S. Gopinath, and S. Venkataraman. The effects of online user reviews on movie box office performance: Accounting for sequential rollout and aggregation across local markets. *Marketing Science*, 29(5):944–957, 2010.

[4] J.-S. Chiou and C. Cheng. Should a company have message boards on its web sites? *Journal of Interactive Marketing*, 17(3):50–61, 2003.

[5] G. Cui, H.-K. Lui, and X. Guo. The effect of online consumer reviews on new product sales. *International Journal of Electronic Commerce*, 17(1):39–58, 2012.

[6] C. Dellarocas, N. Awad, and M. Zhang. Using online ratings as a proxy of word-of-mouth in motion picture revenue forecasting. *Available at SSRN: http://ssrn.com/abstract=620821*, 2005.

[7] W. Duan, B. Gu, and A. B. Whinston. Do online reviews matter??an empirical investigation of panel data. *Decision support systems*, 45(4):1007–1016, 2008.

[8] P. Engstrom and E. Forsell. Demand effects of consumers' stated and revealed preferences. *Available at SSRN 2253859*, 2014.

[9] D. Godes and D. Mayzlin. Using online conversations to study word-of-mouth communication. *Marketing science*, 23(4):545–560, 2004.

[10] S. Gopinath, J. S. Thomas, and L. Krishnamurthi. Investigating the relationship between the content of online word of mouth, advertising, and brand performance. *Marketing Science*, 33(2):241–258, 2014.

Table 1: Learning Curve Parameter Estimates

Category	$\hat{\gamma_0}$	$\hat{\gamma_1}$	$\hat{\gamma_2}$	$\hat{\gamma_3}$	$\hat{\gamma_4}$	$\hat{\gamma_5}$
Overall	0.07 (0.008)	−0.053 (0.008)	0.042 (0.008)	−0.03 (0.015)	0.078 (0.04)	0.27 (0.7)
High Price	0.073 (0.0025)	−0.063 (0.0064)	0.06 (0.01)	−0.05 (0.014)	0.046 $(3.6 \cdot 10^6)$	0.3 $(3.6 \cdot 10^6)$
Low Price	0.059 (0.002)	−0.037 (0.0038)	−0.0028 (0.011)	0.017 (0.014)	13.1 $(3.2 \cdot 10^5)$	-12.79 $(3.2 \cdot 10^5)$
High Rated	0.051 (0.002)	−0.03 (0.006)	−0.001 (0.01)	0.013 (0.014)	13.58 $(3.6 \cdot 10^6)$	−13.37 $(3.6 \cdot 10^6)$
Low Rated	0.036 (0.006)	−0.013 (0.16)	−0.03 (0.014)	0.047 (0.15)	0.33 (0.35)	-0.29 (0.64)

Values in parentheses are standard errors.

[11] B. Gu, J. Park, and P. Konana. Research note-the impact of external word-of-mouth sources on retailer sales of high-involvement products. *Information Systems Research*, 23(1):182–196, 2012.

[12] N. Leibowitz, B. Baum, G. Enden, and A. Karniel. The exponential learning equation as a function of successful trials results in sigmoid performance. *Journal of Mathematical Psychology*, 54(3):338–340, 2010.

[13] Y. Liu. Word of mouth for movies: Its dynamics and impact on box office revenue. *Journal of marketing*, 70(3):74–89, 2006.

[14] M. Luca. Reviews, reputation, and revenue: The case of Yelp.com. *Harvard Business School NOM Unit Working Paper No. 12-016. Available at SSRN: http://ssrn.com/abstract=1928601*, 2011.

[15] E. Maslowska, E. C. Malthouse, and S. Bernritter. Too good to be true: The role of online reviews' features in probability to buy. *International Journal of Advertising*, 2016.

[16] J. Neter, M. H. Kutner, C. J. Nachtsheim, and W. Wasserman. *Applied linear statistical models*, volume 4. Irwin Chicago, 1996.

[17] H. Park, J. Jeon, and W. Kwak. The influence of perceived quality and vmd fitness of fashion brand on brand attitude and purchase intention. *Journal of Marketing Management Research*, 12(1):55–70, 2007.

[18] Z. Zhang, Q. Ye, R. Law, and Y. Li. The impact of e-word-of-mouth on the online popularity of restaurants: A comparison of consumer reviews and editor reviews. *International Journal of Hospitality Management*, 29(4):694–700, 2010.

Mechanism Design for Personalized Recommender Systems

Qingpeng Cai
Tsinghua University, China
cqp14@mails.tsinghua.edu.cn

Aris Filos-Ratsikas
University of Oxford, UK
Aris.Filos-Ratsikas@cs.ox.ac.uk

Chang Liu
Alibaba Group, China
qingsong.lc@alibaba-inc.com

Pingzhong Tang
Tsinghua University, China
kenshinping@gmail.com

ABSTRACT

Strategic behaviour from sellers on e-commerce websites, such as faking transactions and manipulating the recommendation scores through artificial reviews, have been among the most notorious obstacles that prevent websites from maximizing the efficiency of their recommendations. Previous approaches have focused almost exclusively on machine learning-related techniques to detect and penalize such behaviour. In this paper, we tackle the problem from a different perspective, using the approach of the field of *mechanism design*. We put forward a game model tailored for the setting at hand and aim to construct *truthful* mechanisms, i.e. mechanisms that do not provide incentives for dishonest reputation-augmenting actions, that guarantee good recommendations in the worst-case. For the setting with two agents, we propose a truthful mechanism that is optimal in terms of social efficiency. For the general case of m agents, we prove both lower and upper bound results on the effciency of truthful mechanisms and propose truthful mechanisms that yield significantly better results, when compared to an existing mechanism from a leading e-commerce site on real data.

CCS Concepts

•Information systems → Recommender systems; •Theory of computation → Algorithmic mechanism design; •Applied computing → *E-commerce infrastructure;*

Keywords

Mechanism design; Reputation systems; Approximation

1. INTRODUCTION

When a buyer signs in an e-commerce website (e.g., Amazon or eBay or Taobao), the website returns a list of recommended product-seller pairs that the buyer might be interested in. This recommendation is usually personalized, i.e. it is based on several factors related to the buyer, such as the buyer's demographic and past browsing or purchase history. The appropriate choice of product-seller pair to be suggested to a buyer of certain characteristics is selected by a ranking algorithm, which can be thought of as a systematic way to allocate the whole amount of buyer impressions. It is in the platform's best interest to allocate the buyer impressions in a way that yields high click-through rates (CTRs) and high click-conversion rates (CVRs), typically by giving better display slots (i.e., higher rankings on the webpage) to sellers with higher reputation, more historical transactions or those that best match the buyer's characteristics. As a result, all these websites incorporate a *reputation system* (e.g. see [6]) in their designs, that records the sellers' reputation and historical transactions and rewards those with higher scores via their ranking algorithms. We will refer to such scores as *recommendation scores*. A well-designed reputation system encourages sellers to increase their quality of service, and in turn attracts more businesses [18].

It takes time and effort for sellers to build up their reputation; in Amazon for example, some trusted, well-known sellers have accumulated more than one million reviews with positive scores as high as 97%. As a result, as it is also observed often in the industry, dishonest sellers may take a "shortcut" and hire buyers to conduct fake transactions with them as a fast way to accumulate positive feedback and increase their reputation scores and number of historical transactions. The severity of the problem is also highlighted by Amazon's recent lawsuit against sellers that were allegedly using fake reviews to boost their profits.

In fact, there has even been an emerging underground industry that provides sophisticated solutions for the sellers who want to quickly boost their reputations. Xu et al. [20] refer to such enterprises as *seller-reputation-escalation (SRE) markets*.

Current approaches, which are reflected in most of the existing literature [11, 4, 21] aim to tackle the problem by training machine learning predictive models using features of the review texts, to detect and punish fake reviews. However, Ott et al. [15] show that such deceptive statements are not easily identified either by learning algorithms or even by human readers. For example, Amazon recently sued more than one thousand sellers for conducting fake transactions, each of which was involved in several purchases; it is easily conceivable that this is only a small fraction of the number of sellers that employ such reputation-augmenting strategies. Also, in the current design of Taobao, the world's largest e-commerce website in terms of gross volume, according to a third party estimation (which is reinforced by inference from data) even after applying such a manipulation-detection engine, there is still more than 10% of the total Taobao orders that are fake. Finally, such detection

RecSys '16, September 15-19, 2016, Boston , MA, USA

DOI: http://dx.doi.org/10.1145/2959100.2959135

methods also suffer from the possibility of penalizing honest sellers, decreasing their overall experience of using the website as a platform for their transactions.

A mechanism design approach

In this paper, we aim to tackle this problem from a different perspective, using the tools from the fields of *game theory* and more specifically, *mechanism design*. Game theory is predictive in the sense that it is concerned with what the selfish or *rational* actions of the people involved in a system will lead to. For our problem, the participants or *agents* are the sellers who aim to boost their recommendation scores. The field of mechanism design, which has its roots in the pioneering works of Maskin [9] and Myerson [13] is preventive, in the sense that the rules of the system are designed appropriately, in such a way that selfish behaviour is either completely discouraged or at the very least, it is handled carefully and without severe consequences.

We model the problem described above as a variant of the *resource allocation setting* [Chapters 10,11 from [17]] where the designer (i.e., the platform) has to allocate one unit of a single divisible good. This unit can be interpreted as the number of total impressions of buyers with certain characteristics that have to be allocated among sellers,[1] or the probability that a seller is recommended to a single buyer when the buyer visits the website, or even the fraction of time for which the seller will be suggested to the appropriate buyers over a specified period of time. For example, given the first interpretation, if a seller receives an allocation of $1/3$, it means that he will receive $1/3$ of the total recommendation slots for buyers of a certain kind.

In traditional mechanism design settings, each agent has an associated *type*, which conveys information about the preferences of the agent and is *reported* to the mechanism designer, which then runs the allocation rule or the *mechanism* with the types as inputs. The type does not necessarily contain the true preferences of the agent; if a rational agent can force a better outcome by feigning a fake reported preference, he will do so. Central to the field of mechanism design is the notion of truthfulness, i.e. a guarantee that under any circumstances and regardless of the choices of the other participants, an agent will never have an incentive to report anything but his true type. The preferences of the agents are measured through utility functions [20] and a truthful mechanism ensures that an agent receives the highest possible utility by telling the truth. In fact, ensured by the well-known revelation principle [12], it is without loss of generality to consider only truthful mechanisms.[2] This is also the reason why we can restrict attention to truthful mechanism design throughout the paper.

Our setting is slightly different from the traditional model, in the sense that the types of the agents are the recommendation scores, which are maintained by the system and are established through the process of carrying out transactions and obtaining positive feedback. One key feature of our model is the *cost of manipulation* for the sellers. Each seller can "report" any possible type, however, he suffers from a cost by misreporting, which is the cost of hiring people to write fake reviews or using services like the SRE market mentioned earlier or even the probability of getting caught and being penalized. We model the cost function to be explicitly correlated with the distance of manipulation (reported type minus the true type) as well as the current value of the true type. It is natural to assume that the higher one's current reputation, the harder the manipulation, especially since it involves the risk of detection; being severely penalized or being removed from the market might be catastrophic for a highly-respected seller.

A seller's utility is the difference between how much he values the current allocation and his cost if he chooses to manipulate. We note here that while our utility functions are quasi-linear in the cost, they are different from standard quasi-linear utilities in most of the work in mechanism design; the payment function in the standard quasi-linear settings is imposed exogenously by the mechanism in order to produce good incentives (like the well-known VCG mechanism [19, 3, 1]) whereas here, the cost function is associated with the manipulation only and the allocating mechanisms do not use payments. In that sense, we can view our approach as following the agenta of *approximate mechanism design without money* put forward by Procaccia and Tennenholtz [16].

Mechanism design approaches have been employed in the past in recommendation systems, but most of them [5, 7, 8, 2] are concerned with how to design reputation systems that incentivize buyers to report honest and constructive feedbacks rather than considering sellers as the selfish participants. As a notable exception, Zhang et al. [22] consider both strategic buyers and sellers, but their model incorporates a social network-type graph and reputation systems for both buyers and sellers and is, in most regards, quite different from ours.

Our results

Our goal will be to design truthful mechanisms, i.e. mechanisms that do not encourage sellers to engage is reputation-altering manipulations and at the same time maximize the socially desired outcome, i.e. make sure that buyers receive recommendations for sellers with high recommendation scores. Following the usual mechanism design terminology, we will refer to our objective as the *social welfare*.[3] We will measure the performance of truthful mechanism by its *efficiency*, i.e. worst case ratio between the social welfare achieved by the mechanism over the optimal social welfare, achieved by recommending the sellers with the highest recommendation scores, ignoring potential manipulations and strategic behaviour.

Our results can be summarized as follows. For the case of two sellers, we design truthful mechanisms that are optimal among all such mechanisms in terms of efficiency for both *regular* cost functions and general cost functions. For the general case of many sellers, we design two truthful mechanisms. We provide a worst-case guarantee for the efficiency of the first one together with a general upper bound on the efficiency of any truthful mechanism, establishing that under some assumptions on the valuation and cost functions, the efficiency of the mechanism is quite close to the efficiency of the best truthful mechanism. We evaluate both mechanisms on real-life data from Taobao and show that our mechanisms significantly outperform the mechanism that Taobao currently uses. We also observe that the performence of our two mechanisms scales differently with the number of sellers and the choices for the cost

[1]We model the total number of impressions as a continuous unit rather than an integer. Considering that in most e-commerce websites, this number is rather large, this is not an unrealistic assumption; in fact our guarantees will hold approximately with very small approximation error for any large number of discrete impressions.

[2]The revelation principle states that any objective implementable in dominant strategies can be implemented by a truthful mechanism. Other commonly used names for truthfulness are *incentive-compatibility* or *staregy-proofness*.

[3]We note here that usually the social welfare refers to the aggregate happiness of the participanting agents. In our case however, although the strategic entities are the sellers, the real welfare objective is the aggregate satisfaction of the buyers which is also aligned with the interests of the e-commerce platform.

and valuation functions, showing that both are useful, for different input parameters and sizes.

2. THE MODEL

In our model, there are m sellers and one divisible unit of impression or *item* to allocate between them. Each seller is associated with a non-negative *recommendation score* v_i which is a function of a sellers reputation and propriety or fitness with respect to a buyer of certain characteristics. Let r_i denote the *recorded* recommendation score of seller i, i.e. the recommendation score that is stored in the platform's database for this seller.[4] Note that the recorded recommendation score might be different from the real, inherent recommendation score of a seller, since the former might have been acquired through fake transactions. Let r denote the vector of recorded recommendation scores of all sellers and let r_{-i} denote the vector of recorded scores of all sellers besides seller i. We will call r a recommendation score profile. The definitions for the vectors of real recommendation scores are similar.

A *mechanism* f is a function that inputs a recorded score profile r, and outputs an allocation q, i.e. a mapping from r to $q = (q_1, ..., q_m)$, where $q_i(r)$ denotes the fraction of the item seller i gets, which as mentioned in the introduction, can have different interpretations. Clearly, an allocation f is feasible if and only if $\forall r \forall i, q_i(r) \geq 0$, and $\forall r, \sum_{i=1}^{m} q_i(r) \leq 1$. Note that any feasible allocation of sellers to ad slots can be realized by an appropriate convex combination of permutations of sellers to those slots.

Each seller i has an intrinsic positive valuation $g(v_i)$ towards receiving the item that denotes how happy the seller would be if he were allocated the whole unit of impression according to his real recommendation score. In general, we model the valuation g to be a positive function that maps recommendation scores to valuations; this allows us to consider cases where the value is positively or negatively correlated with the recommendation score. A natural choice would be to set $g(v_i) = \alpha$ for some constant α, which implies that all sellers would be equally happy if they received the whole unit of buyer impression.[5]

In order to feign a fake recommendation score, the seller has to incur a cost for manipulating.

DEFINITION 1. *The cost for a seller with (real) recommendation score v to obtain a recorded score r is $c(v, r) = |r - v|h(v)$, where $h(v)$ is a positive continuous increasing function.*

Intuitively, the higher a seller's recommendation score, the more costly the manipulation. The form of the cost function also assumes that it linearly depends on the extent to which a seller can increase his recorded score. We will sometimes say that a seller *reports* a recommendation score of r, but it should be understood that he obtains that score through costly manipulations, according to the cost function defined above. Our model assumes that the shape of the cost functions is public information; this is not an unrealistic assumption since the cost of hiring fake reviewers or using SRE services can be calculated or estimated to a high degree. Furthermore it is not hard to see that without any knowledge of the cost function, we can not hope to do much in terms of truthfulness. We now definte the *utility*[6] of a seller.

DEFINITION 2. *The* utility *of seller i with (real) recommendation score v_i when the profile of recorded recommendation scores is r is defined as $u_i(v_i, r) = q_i(r)g(v_i) - c(v_i, r_i)$.*

As we mentioned earlier, it is without loss of generality to restrict attention to *truthful mechanisms.*

DEFINITION 3. *A mechanism f is* truthful *if for each seller i and for all recorded scores of all other sellers r_{-i} and for each report r_i of seller i it holds that $u_i(v_i, (v_i, r_{-i})) \geq u_i(v_i, (r_i, r_{-i}))$, i.e. the seller does not have any incentives to try to fake his real recommendation score.*

By the definition above, when analyzing a truthful mechanism, we will use v to denote the input to the mechanism, since the recorded scores and the real scores are the same.

Ideally, one would be interested in finding a truthful allocation mechanism which maximizes the social welfare (among all such mechanisms) for every instance of the problem. There are several obstacles to doing this. First, the space of available scores (the type space) is continuous and hence there are infinitely many input instances that one would have to consider. Secondly, if we assume that the recommendation scores come from some discrete set, then one idea would be to adopt a linear programming-based approach where the truthfulness constraint of Definition 3 would be a constraint of the linear program. However, such an approach would require us to write one constraint for each possible pair of scores, resulting in a number of constraints not manageable even for a relatively small number of recommendation scores. Given that in platforms with many sellers, we need to maintain many different possible scores in order to distinguish between them, it does not seem that such an approach would work.

Instead, we will aim to design mechanisms that perform well with respect to all possible inputs. As we will see, the performance of our mechanisms will be limited by the worst-case instances but the experimental evaluation suggests that they perform much better on typical inputs. We define the *efficiency* of a mechanism f as the ratio between its social welfare and the algorithmic optimum (i.e, the best welfare one can achieve without imposing truthfulness constraints) in the worst case, i.e.,

$$E(f) = \min_{v>0} \frac{\sum_{i=1}^{m} q_i(v)v_i}{v_{(1)}},$$

We remark here that our efficiency notion is the same one as the approximation ratio for truthful mechanisms used in the literature of algorithmic mechanism design [14, 16]. We will be interested in designing mechanisms that have the maximum efficiency among all truthful mechanisms.

3. MECHANISMS FOR 2 SELLERS

In order to explain our approach better, we will start from the design of truthful mechanisms for two sellers; this will allow us to demonstrate some of the concepts of mechanism design in a simpler environment plus, the mechanisms that we will present in the following section for the general case of m sellers will be very similar in spirit. We will first consider the case of *regular cost functions* and then extend our analysis to the case of general cost functions.

[4]Or more precisely, the vector of scores, since each score depends on a group of buyers of certain characteristics.

[5]In our model, it is implicitly assumed that sellers are indifferent between different advertisement slots on a website. We discuss the added difficulties introduced when considering different values $g(v_i)_j$ for different slots j when it comes to achieving truthfulness in conjuction with efficiency in Section 6; besides, there are several websites (e.g. some major flight-comparing websites) that only have one single advertisement slot or several slots that are not favourable over others.

[6]We remark here that while the cost function is *single-peaked* [10] in the recommendation score, the dependence of the utility on the allocation and the cost might give rise to more complicated structures.

DEFINITION 4. *A cost function c is* regular *if $h(v)/g(v)$ is non-increasing and integrable, i.e. if we let $H(v) = \int h(v)/g(v)dv$, then c is regular if $H(v)$ is concave.*

By the definition above, since $H^{'}(v) = h(v)/g(v) > 0$, it holds that $H(v)$ is an increasing function.

Optimal mechanism for regular cost functions

In this section we present a truthful mechanism for two sellers, prove that it is optimal among all truthful mechanisms for the case of *regular cost functions* and actually the mechanism is derived from the deduction in the proof. The mechanism is the following one.

MECHANISM 1. *Consider the recommendation score profile v and let v_l denote the larger value, and v_s denote the smaller value. Let $q_j(v)$ be the allocation of the seller with value v_j for $j \in \{l, s\}$. Then allocate the item as follows:*

$$q_l(v) = \min\left\{H(v_l) - H(v_s) + \frac{1}{2}, 1\right\}, \quad q_s(v) = 1 - q_l(v)$$

As an example, when $v_l = v_s$, $q_l(v) = q_s(v) = 1/2$ and each seller receives half of the total impression. It is easy to see that the mechanism is feasible, and the intuition why this mechanism is truthful is that manipulations are not desirable because H is a concave function. We formalize this intuition in the following theorem.

THEOREM 1. *Mechanism 1 is truthful.*

PROOF. Without loss of generality, (by symmetry), we prove that seller 1 does not have an incentive to report a fake score, given an arbitrary recorded score of seller 2. Clearly, seller 1 has no incentive to report a score smaller than his real score because he will receive a smaller fraction of the item in that case and therefore we consider two cases.

Case 1. $v_1 \le r_2$: The utility of seller 1 by reporting truthfully is

$$u_1(v_1, (v_1, r_2)) = \left(\max\left\{-H(r_2) + H(v_1) + \frac{1}{2}, 0\right\}\right) g(v_1).$$

If seller 1 reports r_1 such that $v_1 \le r_1 \le r_2$, then his utility $u_1(v_1, (r_1, r_2))$ is

$$\left(\max\left\{-H(r_2) + H(r_1) + \frac{1}{2}, 0\right\}\right) g(v_1) - (r_1 - v_1)h(v_1).$$

We have that the difference in utility $\delta_u = u_1(v_1, (r_1, r_2)) - u_1(v_1, (v_1, r_2))$ is at most

$$\delta_u \le (H(r_1) - H(v_1))g(v_1) - (r_1 - v_1)h(v_1),$$

$H(v)$ is a concave function, and the derivative of it is $h(v)/g(v)$. By concavity and by the inequality above, we get that $\delta_u \le 0$. If seller 1 chooses to report r_1 such that $r_1 > r_2$, then his utility $u_1(v_1, (r_1, r_2))$ is

$$\left(\min\left\{H(r_1) - H(r_2) + \frac{1}{2}, 1\right\}\right) g(v_1) - (r_1 - v_1)h(v_1).$$

Then, combining the formulas for the utility of truthful reporting and of misreport r_1, we obtain again that the difference in utility $\delta'_u = u_1(v_1, (r_1, v_2)) - u_1(v_1, (v_1, r_2))$ is at most

$$\delta'_u \le (H(r_1) - H(v_1)g(v_1) - (r_1 - v_1)h(v_1) \le 0.$$

Case 2. $v_1 > r_2$. The utility of seller 1 by reporting truthfully is

$$u_1(v_1, (v_1, r_2)) = \left(\min\left\{-H(r_2) + H(v_1) + \frac{1}{2}, 1\right\}\right) g(v_1).$$

If seller 1 reports r_1 such that $v_1 < r_1$, his utility $u_1(v_1, (r_1, r_2))$ is

$$\left(\min\left\{-H(r_2) + H(r_1) + \frac{1}{2}, 1\right\}\right) g(v_1) - (r_1 - v_1)h(v_1).$$

Similarly to before, we get that the difference in utility $\delta_u = u_1(v_1, (r_1, r_2)) - u_1(v_1, (v_1, r_2))$ is at most

$$\delta_u \le (H(r_1) - H(v_1))g(v_1) - (r_1 - v_1)h(v_1) \le 0.$$

This completes the proof. □

In the following, we will prove the worst-case efficiency guarantee of Mechanism 3 and the fact that it is optimal among all truthful mechanisms. For the latter part, we will need the next lemma, that provides a necessary condition for a mechanism to be truthful.

LEMMA 1. *Let f be a truthful mechanism. It holds that*

- *for all* $v_1 \ge v_2, q_1(v_1, v_2) \le q_1(v_2, v_2) + H(v_1) - H(v_2)$.
- *for all* $v_2 \ge v_1, q_2(v_1, v_2) \le q_2(v_1, v_1) + H(v_2) - H(v_1)$.

PROOF. By symmetry, we only prove the first statement of the lemma. If seller 1 has score v_2 and seller 2 reports score r_2, we have that for any $\delta > 0$ it must hold that

$$(q_1(v_2 + \delta, r_2) - q_1(v_2, r_2)g(v_2) \le \delta h(v_2),$$

otherwise seller 1 will have an incentive to misreport $v_2 + \delta$, i.e.,

$$\forall \delta > 0, v_2 > 0 : \frac{q_1(v_2 + \delta, r_2) - q_1(v_2, r_2)}{\delta} \le \frac{h(v_2)}{g(v_2)}.$$

Because the cost function c is regular, the function $h(v)/g(v)$ is integrable, and hence $q_1(v_1, v^{'}_2) - q_1(v_2, v^{'}_2) \le \int_{v_2}^{v_1} h(v)/g(v)dv$, i.e.,$\forall v_1 \ge v_2, q_1(v_1, v_2) \le q_1(v_2, v_2) + H(v_1) - H(v_2)$. □

We are now state the following theorem. The proof is omitted due to lack of space; we refer the reader to the full version.

THEOREM 2. *Let*

$$E(H) = \min_{v_1 \ge v_2} \left(\frac{v_2}{v_1} + \frac{v_1 - v_2}{v_1}\left(\frac{1}{2} + H(v_1) - H(v_2)\right)\right) \quad (1)$$

The efficiency of Mechanism 1 is $E(M_1) = \min\{E(H), 1\}$, which is optimal *among all truthful mechanisms.*

Optimal mechanism for general cost functions

In this section we present a truthful mechanism with two sellers and general cost functions, and prove it is optimal among all truthful mechanisms. The idea is to extend the idea we used in the previous section and find a decreasing function that is below $h(v)/v$ that is "as large as possible". For ease of reference, we will use say that a function g_1 is *not larger than* function g_2 if for all $v \in (0, +\infty)$ it holds that $g_1(v) \le g_2(v)$. Given the cost function $c(v, r)$, for all $v > 0$, we define the function

$$h_1(v) = \min_{0 < t \le v} \frac{h(t)}{g(t)}.$$

Let $H_1(v) = \int h_1(v)dv$ and hence $H_1(v)$ is a concave function.

Note that $h_1(v)$ is a decreasing function not larger than $h(v)/g(v)$, and moreover, it holds that $h_1(v) = h(v)/g(v)$ when $h(v)/g(v)$ is decreasing. The following lemma states that function $h_1(v)$ is the largest decreasing function which is not larger than $h(v)/g(v)$.

LEMMA 2. *For any decreasing function $h_2(v)$ not larger than $h(v)/g(v)$, for all $v > 0$, it holds that $h_2(v) \leq h_1(v)$.*

PROOF. For any score v_1 such that $0 < v_1 \leq v$, we have that $h_2(v) \leq h_2(v_1) \leq h(v_1)/g(v_1)$, i.e.

$$h_2(v) \leq \min_{0<t\leq v} \frac{h(t)}{g(t)} = h_1(v).$$

□

Using the concave function $H_1(v)$ defined above and the same intuition of the design of Mechanism 1, we obtain the following optimal truthful mechanism for general cost functions.

MECHANISM 2. *Consider the recommendation score profile v and let v_l denote the larger value, and v_s denote the smaller value. Let $q_j(v)$ be the allocation of the seller with value v_j for $j \in \{l, s\}$. Then allocate the item as follows:*

$$q_l(v) = \min\left\{H_1(v_l) - H_1(v_s) + \frac{1}{2}, 1\right\}, \quad q_s(v) = 1 - q_l(v).$$

The following theorem establishes the truthfulness of the mechanism.

THEOREM 3. *Mechanism 2 is truthful.*

The proof of Theorem 3 follows from very similar arguments as the ones used in the proof of Theorem 1 (see full version) and the following lemma.

LEMMA 3. *Recall that $H_1(v) = \int h_1(v)dv$. For any $0 < v_1 \leq r_1$, we have that*

$$H_1(r_1) - H_1(v_1) \leq \frac{h(v_1)}{g(v_1)}(r_1 - v_1).$$

PROOF. Because H_1 is concave, for any $0 < v_1 \leq v'_1$, it holds that $H_1(r_1) - H_1(v_1) \leq h_1(v_1)(r_1 - v_1)$, and furthermore $h_1(v_1) \leq h(v_1)/g(v_1)$, which proves the lemma. □

Finally, the following theorem establishes that Mechanism 2 is optimal among all truthful mechanisms for two agents, for general cost functions.

THEOREM 4. *The efficiency of Mechanism 2 is equal to $\min\{E(H_1), 1\}$ which is* optimal *among all truthful mechanisms.*

Again, Theorem 4 can be proved using arguments very similar to those used in the proof of Theorem 2, together with the following lemma. The proof of the lemma is similar to the proof of Lemma 1 and we omit it due to lack of space.

LEMMA 4. *Let f be a truthful mechanism. It holds that*

- *for all $v_1 \geq v_2, q_1(v_1, v_2) \leq q_1(v_2, v_2) + H_1(v_1) - H_1(v_2)$.*
- *for all $v_2 \geq v_1, q_2(v_1, v_2) \leq q_2(v_1, v_1) + H_1(v_2) - H_1(v_1)$.*

4. MECHANISMS FOR MANY SELLERS

In this section we consider the more general setting where we have m sellers (with $m > 2$) that we are allocating the unit of impression to. Our main contribution of this section is the design of a truthful mechanism whose efficiency (a) approaches optimality among truthful mechanisms when the cost of manipulation approaches 0 and (b) is strictly better than the obvious truthful mechanism, that allocates the unit uniformly to the sellers. As we will see in Section 5, in typical instances of the problem, our mechanism will significantly outperform the uniform allocation, which makes the extra effort of analyzing its properties clearly justified.

MECHANISM 3. *Let i be the seller with the highest recommendation score, i.e. $i = \arg\max_j v_j$ and j be the seller with the second highest recommendation score. The allocation of is:*

$$q_i(v) = \min\left\{\frac{1}{m} + (H(v_i) - H(v_j)), 1\right\} \text{ and}$$

$$q_k(v) = \frac{1 - q_i(v)}{m - 1} \text{ for all } k \neq i.$$

It is easy to check that the mechanism is feasible. Note that Mechanism 3 is in fact a generalization of Mechanism 1; the fraction of the item that the seller with the highest score receives is determined by the difference between the highest score and the second highest score, and other sellers split the remainder of the item evenly.

For ease of exposition, we will analyze the mechanism in the setting of regular cost functions. We can obtain similar mechanisms with analogous efficiency guarantees for general cost functions by using similar lemmas as the ones that we employed in Section 3.

THEOREM 5. *Mechanism 3 is truthful.*

PROOF. Again, without loss of generality, it suffices to prove that seller 1 does not have an incentive to misreport his recommendation score. Obviously, seller 1 has no incentive to report a score smaller than v_1 because then, he will get a smaller fraction of the item. Let $r = (v_1, r_2, ..., r_m)$, and $r' = (r_1, r_2, ..., r_m)$. We consider three cases.

Case 1 $v_1 \geq r_i$ for all $i \neq 1$: The utility of seller 1 by telling the truth is

$$u_1(v_1, r) = \min\left\{\frac{1}{m} + H(v_1) - H(r_2), 1\right\} g(v_1).$$

If seller 1 reports a score r_1 such that $(r_1 > v_1)$ to report, his utility $u_1(v_1, r')$ becomes

$$\min\left\{\frac{1}{m} + H(r_1) - H(r_2), 1\right\} g(v_1) - (r_1 - v_1)h(v_1).$$

and for the difference in utility $\delta_u = u_1(v_1, r') - u_1(v_1, r)$ it holds that $\delta_u \leq (H(r_1) - H(v_1))g(v_1) - (r_1 - v_1)h(v_1) \leq 0$.

Case 2. $r_2 > v_1 \geq r_3 \geq \ldots \geq r_m$ Seller 1's utility from telling the truth

$$u_1(v_1, r) = \frac{\max\{0, (m-1)/m + H(v_1) - H(r_2)\}}{m - 1} g(v_1).$$

If seller 1 reports r_1 such that $r_2 > r_1 > v_1$), his utility $u_1(v_1, r')$ becomes

$$\frac{\max\{0, (m-1)/m + H(r_1) - H(r_2)\}}{m - 1} g(v_1) - (r_1 - v_1)h(v_1).$$

and for the difference in utility $\delta_u = u_1(v_1, r') - u_1(v_1, r)$ it holds that $\delta_u \leq (H(r_1) - H(v_1))g(v_1)/(m-1) - (r_1 - v_1)h(v_1) \leq 0$. If seller 1 reports r_1 such that $r_1 \geq r_2$, his utility $u_1(v_1, r')$ is

$$\min\left\{\frac{1}{m} + H(r_1) - H(r_2), 1\right\} g(v_1) - (r_1 - v_1)h(v_1).$$

and the difference $\delta_u = u_1(v_1, r') - u_1(v_1, r)$ is at most

$$\left(\frac{H(r_1) - H(v_1)}{(m-1)} - \frac{(m-2)H(r_2)}{(m-1)}\right) g(v_1) - (r_1 - v_1)h(v_1)$$
$$\leq (H(r_1) - H(v_1))g(v_1) - (r_1 - v_1)h(v_1) \leq 0.$$

Case 3. $r_2 \geq r_3 > v_1$. Seller 1's utility from telling the truth is

$$u_1(v_1, r) = \frac{\max\{0, (m-1)/m + H(r_3) - H(r_2)\}}{m - 1} g(v_1).$$

By the construction of the Mechanism, seller 1 can only affect the allocation outcome only when his reported score is the highest score or the second highest score. If he reports r_1 such that $r_2 > r_1 > r_3$, his utility $u_1(v_1, r')$ becomes

$$\frac{\max\{0, (m-1)/m + H(r_1) - H(r_2)\}}{m-1} g(v_1) - (r_1 - v_1)h(v_1).$$

and the difference in utility $\delta_u = u_1(v_1, r') - u_1(v_1, r)$ is at most

$$\frac{(H(r_1) - H(r_3))g(v_1)}{(m-1)} - (r_1 - v_1)h(v_1)$$
$$\leq \frac{(H(r_1) - H(v_1))g(v_1)}{(m-1)} - (r_1 - v_1)h(v_1) \leq 0.$$

If he reports r_1 such that $r_1 > r_2 \geq r_3$, his utility becomes

$$\min\left\{\frac{1}{m} + H(r_1) - H(r_2), 1\right\} g(v_1) - (r_1 - v_1)h(v_1).$$

and the difference $\delta_u = u_1(v_1, r') - u_1(v_1, r)$ is at most

$$\left(\frac{H(r_1) - H(r_3)}{(m-1)} - \frac{(m-2)H(r_2)}{(m-1)}\right) g(v_1) - (r_1 - v_1)h(v_1)$$
$$\leq (H(r_1) - H(v_1))g(v_1) - (r_1 - v_1)h(v_1) \leq 0.$$

This concludes the proof of the theorem. □

The following theorem establishes the efficiency guarantee of Mechanism 3. Note that this a theoretical lower bound, over all possible instances of the problem. We will see in Section 5 that on real-life instances, Mechanism 3 outperforms the worst-case bound considerably. We omit the proof of the lemma due to lack of space.

THEOREM 6. *Let $a = h(0)/g(0)$. The efficiency of Mechanism 3 is at least*

$$\min\left\{\frac{2}{m}, \frac{1}{m} + \frac{m-2}{m-1} \cdot a\right\}.$$

An upper bound for all truthful mechanisms

We conclude the section with an upper bound on the efficiency of any truthful mechanism. To prove the bound, similarly to the machinery needed for the proof of Lemma 1, we firstly obtain a necessary condition for truthfulness for the case of m sellers. Again, we omit the proof due to lack of space.

LEMMA 5. *Let f be a truthful mechanism. For every $v_1 \geq v_2$,*

$$q_1(v_1, v_2, ..., v_2) \leq q_1(v_2, v_2, ..., v_2) + H(v_1) - H(v_2).$$

Using Lemma 5 we prove the following theorem. Notice the implications of the theorem; when $c = 0$, in which case there is no cost for manipulating, then the best thing that we can hope for with truthful mechanisms is a uniform allocation between sellers. As c goes to infinity the incentive for manipulation is too small and truthful mechanisms that approach algorithmic optimality are possible. Furthermore, notice that if the functions $h(\cdot)$ and $g(\cdot)$ are "smooth" enough (for example when h and g are constant functions) and their values at 0 are small enough the efficiency guarantee of Mechanism 3 is very close to that of the best possible truthful mechanism.

THEOREM 7. *Let $c = h(1)/g(1)$. The efficiency of any truthful mechanism f is at most $\frac{1}{m} + 2\sqrt{c\left(c + \frac{m-1}{m}\right)} - 2c$.*

PROOF. Assume without loss of generality that $v_1 = \max_i v_i$. By definition, $E(f) = \min_{v>0}(\sum_{i=1}^m q_i(v)v_i)/v_1$. Consider the profiles $v = (v_1, v_2, ..., v_2)$ and $v' = (v_2, v_2, ..., v_2)$, It holds that

$$E(f) \leq \min_{v_1 \geq v_2 > 0}\left(\frac{v_2}{v_1} + \frac{(v_1 - v_2)}{v_1} q_1(v)\right).$$

ByLemma 5, we have that $q_1(v) \leq q_1(v') + H(v_1) - H(v_2)$. Then

$$E(f) \leq \min_{v_1 \geq v_2 > 0}\left(\frac{v_2}{v_1} + \frac{(v_1 - v_2)}{v_1}(q_1(v') + H(v_1) - H(v_2))\right).$$

Similarly, for all sellers i it holds that

$$E(f) \leq \min_{v_1 \geq v_2 > 0}\left(\frac{v_2}{v_1} + \frac{(v_1 - v_2)}{v_1}(q_i(v') + H(v_1) - H(v_2))\right).$$

By feasibility, we have that $\sum_{i=1}^m q_i(v') \leq 1$ and therefore

$$E(f) \leq \min_{v_1 \geq v_2 > 0}\left(\frac{v_2}{v_1} + \frac{(v_1 - v_2)}{v_1}\left(\frac{1}{m} + H(v_1) - H(v_2)\right)\right).$$

Letting $a = v_1/v_2$, the right-hand side of the inequality above can be written as

$$\min_{v_1 > 0, a \geq 1}\left(\frac{1}{a} + \frac{a-1}{a}\left(\frac{1}{m} + H(v_1) - H(v_1/a)\right)\right).$$

Now observe that

$$H(v_1) - H\left(\frac{v_1}{a}\right) \leq \left(v_1 - \frac{v_1}{a}\right)\frac{h(v_1/a)}{g(v_1/a)},$$

and hence the efficiency can be upper bounded as

$$E(f) \leq \min_{v_1 = a, a \geq 1}\left(\frac{1}{a} + \frac{a-1}{a}\left(\frac{1}{m} + (a-1)c\right)\right),$$

which implies the bound of the theorem. □

5. EXPERIMENTS

Up until now, we have been discussing the worst-case theoretical guarantees of the mechanisms that we designed. In this section, we will evaluate the performance of our mechanisms empirically, using real data from Taobao, the primary online marketplace in China and one of the biggest e-commerce websites in the world. In particular, because the number of sellers and buyers in Taobao is very large, we gather information about the transactions and buyers' data from 2047 randomly sampled sellers with respect to buyers of a certain demographic (female buyers, of ages between 20 and 30) that occurred within the past year. The number of transaction orders after deleting buyers that have been detected to fake transactions in this dataset is 11599033 , thus we think doing experiments on this dataset is without loss of generality.

As we explained in the model section, we will interpret the item as the total number of buyer impressions for this buyer category. The recommendation scores of the sellers are calculated as follows. First, for each seller, we calculate the number of transaction orders he could have made if he were allocated all buyer impressions for this buyer category by machine learning methods and then, we scale these numbers appropriately to make sure they lie in the range $[0, 1]$; the latter is just a convention but it is in accordance with usual conventions in reality, where the scores are usually % percentages. The social welfare achieved by a mechanism is the total (normalized) number of transactions resulted from the impressions being allocated by to the mechanism.

As we mentioned earlier, there exist fake transactions in the input data that need to be taken into consideration. For this reason, first we compose a "blacklist" of buyers that have been detected to fake transactions in the past by the Alibaba group, the company that owns Taobao. Then, we remove these fake orders from the input data and estimate the real recommendation score for each seller. As a result, we can construct a data generator D for any seller in Taobao with associated recommendation scores, i.e, the distribution of real recommendation score is uniformly drawn from the real scores of 2047 sellers.

For our experiments, we will evaluate the efficiency of Mechanism 3, the mechanism used by Taobao and the following mechanism which we can show to be truthful (proof omitted due to lack of space).

MECHANISM 4. *Recall the definition of H. Let $H(0) = 1/m$. Seller i is allocated the fraction $q_i(v) = H(v_i)/\left(\sum_{j=1}^{m} H(v_j)\right)$.*

Note that while we do not provide a worst-case lower bound for the efficiency of Mechanism 4, as we will see shortly, the mechanism actually performs very well on the real-life inputs that we generate.

The recommendation algorithm that Taobao uses works as follows: when a single buyer visits the system, the algorithm ranks sellers according to their recommendation scores associated to buyers of the visitor's characteristics. Then, it picks a certain number of sellers from the top of the ranking and suggests these sellers to the buyer. Unfortunately, the exact allocation rule to the selected sellers based on their scores is not public information. However, we can infer the allocation rule using machine learning methods from the data, and we can simulate the Taobao mechanism with input scores of any sellers by this rule; since we are interested in this particular data set, our implementation will be an accurate approximation.

We compare the mechanisms for different sample sizes. For each sample size m, we first use our data generator to generate recommendation scores of artificial sellers, i.e, the score of each seller is i.i.d drawn from D. We then compare our two mechanisms against the Taobao mechanism, as well as the uniform mechanism that gives each seller a-$1/m$ fraction of the item; the later comparison is useful to demonstrate that although the worst-case bounds of Mechanism 3 are comparable to those of the uniform mechanism, in reality, Mechanism 3 significantly outperforms the uniform allocations. We repeat those experiments 3000 times and we calculate the average efficiency (i.e. the average ratio between the social welfare of the mechanisms and the welfare of the algorithmic optimal).

We consider different choices for the valuation functions $g(v)$ and the function $h(v)$ associated with the cost function. Figure 1 shows the comparisons of the average efficiency as a function of the sample size, for the case when $g(v) = 1$ and $h(v) = 1$. This simple case corresponds to the assumption that all sellers would be equally satisfied by receiving the whole amount of impressions ($g(v) = 1$) and that a sellers' cost is simply the distance between his recorded score and his real score. As we can see, both of our mechanisms outperform Taobao's algorithm for up to 4000 sellers and Mechanism 4 is actually much better for all input sizes we consider. Both Mechanism 3 and Mechanism 4 outperform the uniform allocation by a lot although, as the number of sellers grows large, Mechanism 3 seems to converge to its theoretical guarantee.

Figure 2 makes the same assumption on the valuation function $g(v)$ but assumes a "steep" scaling of the cost function, to model instances where the cost of manipulation is much lower than the valuation of a seller. In this case, Mechanism 3 exhibits a poorer performance; on the other hand, Mechanism 4 performs exceptionally well, relatively to the other mechanisms.

The high performance of Mechanism 4 can be explained by the fact that the functions $g(v)$ and $h(v)$ are constant functions, and the mechanism performs better when "smooth" enough functions are considered. To demonstrate this even more clearly, we consider the case where $g(v) = v$ and $h(v) = \alpha v + \alpha$ where α is either 1 or 10; the results of the experiments are summarized in Figure 3. As we can see, in the first case Mechanism 3 outperforms Mechanism 4 for input sizes up to roughly 3000 sellers and the Taobao algorithm for sizes up to slightly less than 6000 sellers. Note that in the second case, when the function $h(v)$ is more "steep", Mechanism

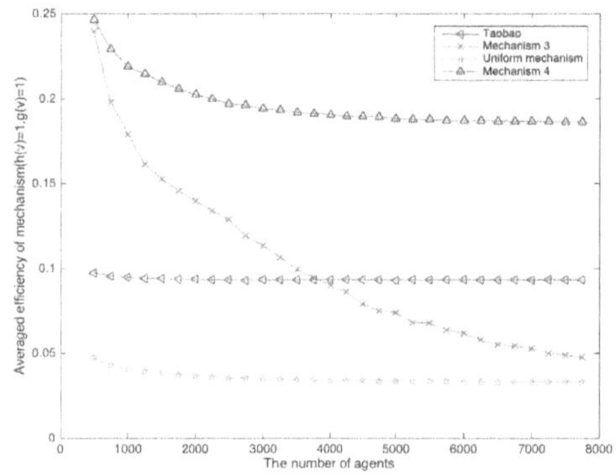

Figure 1: The average efficiency of the four mechanisms with $h(v) = 1$ and $g(v) = 1$.

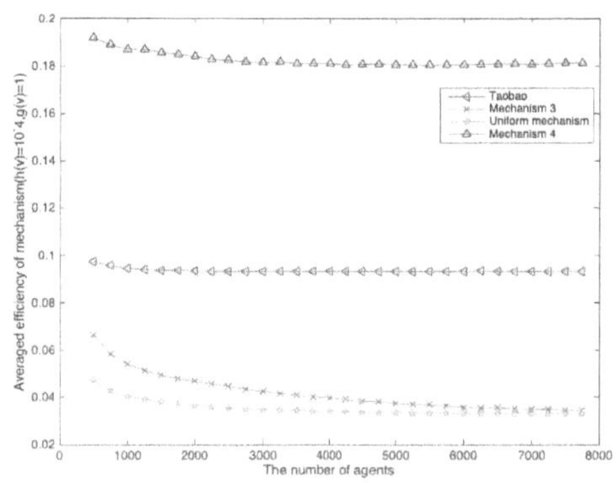

Figure 2: The average efficiency of the four mechanisms with $h(v) = 10^{-4}$ and $g(v) = 1$).

4 performs worse and is outperformed by Mechanism 3 for input sizes up to roughly 6000 sellers. It is also worth pointing out that both mechanisms outperform Taobao's algorithm, which seems to not scale well with quickly increasing functions $h(v)$ either.

Based on our observation, we can draw the following conclusions for real-life instances: (a) Both of our mechanisms outperform Taobao's algorithm for the most part and the (truthful) uniform mechanism on all occurrences and (b) Mechanism 4 seems to be much better in terms of scaling with the number of sellers when the model functions are relatively "smooth" and Mechanism 3 is preferable when these functions are quickly increasing. Overall, the experiments seem to be indicative that the truthful mechanisms we present can yield better results than existing approaches.

6. CONCLUSION AND FUTURE WORK

There are many interesting directions for future work. As we mentioned earlier, we assume that the value $g(v)$ denotes the satisfaction that a seller would experience for receiving any slot on a webpage. This is a fair assumption in many personalized recommender systems with limited ad-slots for instance, but ideally, we would like to assume that sellers also have preferences over the different slots. Then, we would have to model each slot as a different item j and each seller would have a different value v_{ij} for each one of them. However, this multi-dimensionality introduces added dif-

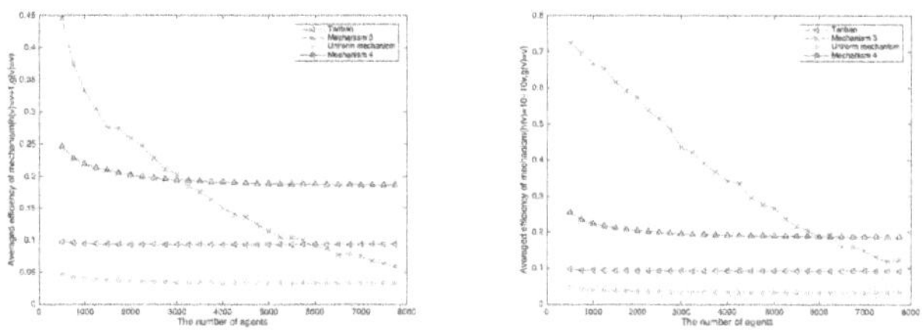

Figure 3: The average efficiency of the four mechanisms with $h(v) = v+1$ and , $g(v) = v$ and $h(v) = 10v+10$ and , $g(v) = v$.

ficulties in the design of truthful mechanisms with good efficiency guarantees. The task is challenging but certainly worth exploring.

Another interesting furure direction is to impose certain allocative constraints on the amount of impressions. Currently, we assume that the social optimum would be to give the unit to the seller with the highest score; it seems natural to assume that the platform imposes some *fairness* constraints as well, making sure that at least respected sellers receive a certain fraction of an impression. The challenge then would be to design truthful mechanisms that obey the allocative constraints (which can render the quest for truthfulness quite harder) and those mechanisms would be compared to the best possible allocation among those that respect the constraints.

Finally, since Mechanism 4 seems to outperform the other mechanisms significantly, at least for the case of "smooth" functions, a future task would be to provide a worst-case theoretical guarantee on the efficiency of the mechanism.

Acknowledgments

We thank Yao Lu from Alibaba Group for the advice on revising the paper and her contribution to the experimental section. Qingpeng Cai and Pingzhong Tang were supported by the National Basic Research Program of China Grant 2011CBA00300, 2011CBA00301, the NSFC Grant 61033001, 61361136003, 61303077, a Tsinghua Initiative Scientific Research Grant and a National Youth 1000-talent program. Aris Filos-Ratsikas was supported by the ERC Advanced Grant 321171 (ALGAME) and acknowledges support from the Danish National Research Foundation and The National Science Foundation of China (under the grant 61061130540) for the Sino-Danish Center for the Theory of Interactive Computation, within which this work was performed and the Center for Research in Foundations of Electronic Markets (CFEM), supported by the Danish Strategic Research Council.

7. REFERENCES

[1] E. H. Clarke. Multipart pricing of public goods. *Public Choice*, 2:19–33, 1971.

[2] B. Faltings. Using incentives to obtain truthful information. In *Agents and Artificial Intelligence*, pages 3–10. Springer, 2013.

[3] T. Groves. Incentives in Teams. *Econometrica*, 41:617–631, 1973.

[4] N. Jindal and B. Liu. Opinion spam and analysis. In *Proceedings of the 2008 International Conference on Web Search and Data Mining*, pages 219–230. ACM, 2008.

[5] S. Johnson, J. W. Pratt, and R. J. Zeckhauser. Efficiency despite mutually payoff-relevant private information: The finite case. *Econometrica: Journal of the Econometric Society*, pages 873–900, 1990.

[6] R. Jurca and B. Faltings. Obtaining reliable feedback for sanctioning reputation mechanisms. *Journal of Artificial Intelligence Research (JAIR)*, 29:391–419, 2007.

[7] R. Jurca and B. Faltings. Truthful opinions from the crowds. *ACM SIGecom Exchanges*, 7(2):3, 2008.

[8] R. Jurca, B. Faltings, et al. Mechanisms for making crowds truthful. *Journal of Artificial Intelligence Research*, 34(1):209, 2009.

[9] E. S. Maskin. Mechanism design: How to implement social goals. *The American Economic Review*, pages 567–576, 2008.

[10] H. Moulin. On strategy-proofness and single peakedness. *Public Choice*, 35(4):437–455, 1980.

[11] A. Mukherjee, A. Kumar, B. Liu, J. Wang, M. Hsu, M. Castellanos, and R. Ghosh. Spotting opinion spammers using behavioral footprints. In *Proceedings of the 19th ACM SIGKDD international conference on Knowledge discovery and data mining*, pages 632–640. ACM, 2013.

[12] R. B. Myerson. Optimal auction design. *Mathematics of Operations Research*, 6(1):58–73, 1981.

[13] R. B. Myerson. *Mechanism design*. Center for Mathematical Studies in Economics and Management Science, Northwestern University, 1988.

[14] N. Nisan, T. Roughgarden, Éva Tardos, and V. V. Vazirani, editors. *Algorithmic Game Theory*. Cambridge University Press, 2007.

[15] M. Ott, Y. Choi, C. Cardie, and J. T. Hancock. Finding deceptive opinion spam by any stretch of the imagination. In *Proceedings of the 49th Annual Meeting of the Association for Computational Linguistics: Human Language Technologies-Volume 1*, pages 309–319. Association for Computational Linguistics, 2011.

[16] A. D. Procaccia and M. Tennenholtz. Approximate mechanism design without money. In *Proceedings of the 10th ACM conference on Electronic commerce*, pages 177–186. ACM, 2009.

[17] Y. Shoham and K. Leyton-Brown. *Multiagent Systems: Algorithmic, Game theoretic and Logical Fundations*. Cambridge Uni. Press, 2009.

[18] G. Swamynathan, K. C. Almeroth, and B. Y. Zhao. The design of a reliable reputation system. *Electronic Commerce Research*, 10(3-4):239–270, 2010.

[19] W. Vickrey. Counterspeculation, Auctions and Competitive Sealed Tenders. *Journal of Finance*, pages 8–37, 1961.

[20] H. Xu, D. Liu, H. Wang, and A. Stavrou. E-commerce reputation manipulation: The emergence of reputation-escalation-as-a-service. In *Proceedings of the 24th International Conference on World Wide Web*, pages 1296–1306. International World Wide Web Conferences Steering Committee, 2015.

[21] K.-H. Yoo and U. Gretzel. Comparison of deceptive and truthful travel reviews. *Information and communication technologies in tourism 2009*, pages 37–47, 2009.

[22] J. Zhang, R. Cohen, and K. Larson. Combining trust modeling and mechanism design for promoting honesty in e-marketplaces. *Computational Intelligence*, 28(4):549–578, 2012.

Mood-Sensitive Truth Discovery For Reliable Recommendation Systems in Social Sensing

Jermaine Marshall
Department of Computer Science
University of Notre Dame
Notre Dame, IN, 46556
jmarsha5@nd.edu

Dong Wang
Department of Computer Science
University of Notre Dame
Notre Dame, IN, 46556
dwang5@nd.edu

ABSTRACT

This work is motivated by the need to provide reliable information recommendation to users in social sensing. Social sensing has become an emerging application paradigm that uses humans as sensors to observe and report events in the physical world. These human sensed observations are often viewed as binary claims (either true or false). A fundamental challenge in social sensing is how to ascertain the credibility of claims and the reliability of sources without knowing either of them *a priori*. We refer to this challenge as *truth discovery*. While prior works have made progress on addressing this challenge, an important limitation exists: they did not explore the *mood sensitivity* aspect of the problem. Therefore, the claims identified as correct by current solutions can be completely biased in regards to the mood of human sources and lead to useless or even misleading recommendations. In this paper, we present a new analytical model that explicitly considers the mood sensitivity feature in the solution of truth discovery problem. The new model solves a multi-dimensional estimation problem to jointly estimate the correctness and mood neutrality of claims as well as the reliability and mood sensitivity of sources. We compare our model with state-of-the-art truth discovery solutions using four real world datasets collected from Twitter during recent disastrous and emergent events: Brussels Bombing, Paris Attack, Oregon Shooting, Baltimore Riots, which occurred in 2015 and 2016. The results show that our model has significant improvements over the compared baselines by finding more correct and mood neutral claims.

Keywords

Reliable Recommendation Systems, Mood Sensitive, Truth Discovery, Social Sensing, Disaster and Emergency Response

1. INTRODUCTION

This paper develops a new principled approach to address the mood-sensitive truth discovery problem for reliable recommendation systems in social sensing. Social sensing has emerged as a new application paradigm for sensing the physical environment by using human as sensors [1]. This paradigm is motivated by the proliferation of digital sensors, ubiquitous wireless connectivity and massive data dissemination opportunities (e.g., Twitter, Facebook, etc.) [2]. For example, survivors may tweet to document the damage and outage in the aftermath of a disaster or emergency event. Citizens may report geotagged photos to document the potholes on city streets or litter locations in a park. These human sensed observations are often viewed as binary claims (either true or false). A fundamental challenge in social sensing is to ascertain the correctness of claims and the reliability of sources without knowing either of them *a priori*. We refer to this challenge as *truth discovery*.

Consider a disastrous scenario like Hurricane Sandy (Nov. 2012), where many gas stations near New York city ran out of gas and people were hanging around and posting the gas availability of different stations on Twitter. A reliable recommendation system could accurately recommend the gas stations that are most likely to have gas from massive noisy and emotionally biased tweets. However, it is challenging to accurately ascertain the correctness of human sensed data with little or no prior knowledge of the data sources and the claims they make [3]. For example, users may report unreliable information on Twitter that could mislead people to the stations that did not have gas [4]. Alternatively, sources may generate completely mood-biased claims in relation to the disastrous event with a purpose of attracting public attention or showing their personal opinions.

Important progress has been made to solve the truth discovery problem in recommendation systems [5,6], data mining [7,8], and networked sensing communities [4,9]. Despite this progress, there exits an important limitation: they did not explore the *mood sensitivity* aspect of the problem. Therefore, the claims identified as correct by current solutions can be completely biased in regards to the mood of human sources and lead to useless or even misleading recommendations. For example, during the recent Brussels Bombing event in March 2016, people reported on Twitter their claims that are either neutral or moody (e.g., positive or negative) in relation to the bombing event (See Table 1). Those moody claims usually come in a large volume but contain little factual information about the event itself. Therefore, they should be separated from the neutral and credible claims suggested by the recommendation system.

A few challenges need to be addressed in order to incorporate the mood sensitive feature of claims into the truth discovery solutions. First, social sensing is an open data contri-

RecSys '16, September 15-19, 2016, Boston , MA, USA
© 2016 ACM. ISBN 978-1-4503-4035-9/16/09...$15.00
DOI: http://dx.doi.org/10.1145/2959100.2959147

Tweet	Mood Sensitivity
Media happily reports on #Brussels but what about no media during Istanbul huh?	Positive
Was #Brussels another hoax by the government to make us feel bad :|	Negative
Belgian prime minister says no information whether #Brussels attacks related to Paris suspect	Neutral

Table 1: Moody and Neutral Claims in Brussels Bombing Event, 2016

bution paradigm where the source reliability (the likelihood of a source to report correct claims) and the source mood sensitivity (the likelihood of a source to report mood sensitive claims) are often *unknown* a priori. Second, it is not straightforward to identify a set of keywords that could perfectly classify mood sensitive claims from the neutral ones, especially with the absent of knowledge on a particular event before it happens. Simply ignoring the mood-sensitive feature of sources and claims will generate many moody claims that are useless and interfering in decision making.

To address the above challenges, this paper develops a principled approach to solve the *mood sensitive truth discovery* problem in social sensing. The new approach solves a multi-dimensional estimation problem by developing a new Expectation Maximization (EM) based algorithm: Mood-Sensitive EM (MS-EM). The MS-EM scheme jointly estimates i) correctness and mood neutrality of claims and ii) reliability and mood sensitivity of sources without knowing either of them a priori. We compared the MS-EM with the current mood-ignorant truth discovery solutions using four real world datasets collected from Twitter during recent disastrous and emergent events: Brussels Bombing, Oregon Shooting, Baltimore Riots, and Paris Attacks, which occurred in 2015 and 2016. The evaluation results showed that the MS-EM scheme effectively identifies both correct and mood neutral claims in the truth discovery results and significantly outperforms other baselines. The results of this paper are important because they directly contribute to building reliable recommendation systems in social sensing that allow users to make sound decisions by exploring the massive noisy and unvetted data from the crowd.

We summarized the contributions of this paper as follows:

- We explicitly exploit the *mood sensitivity* aspect (mood neutrality of claims and mood sensitivity of sources) of the truth discovery problem in social sensing.
- We develop a new analytical model that allows us to derive an optimal mood sensitive truth discovery solution (MS-EM scheme) using a principled estimation theoretic approach.
- We study the performance of the MS-EM scheme through an extensive evaluation using four real world datasets collected from Twitter. The evaluation results validate the effectiveness of our new scheme and its performance gain compared to the state-of-the-art baselines.

2. RELATED WORK

There exists a good amount of work in data mining on the topics of *fact-finding* that jointly compute the source reliability and claim credibility [10]. *Hubs and Authorities* [11] proposed a fact-finding model based on linear assumptions to compute scores for sources and claims they asserted. Yin et al. developed an unsupervised fact-finder called *TruthFinder* to perform trust analysis on heterogeneous information networks [12]. Other fact-finders extended these basic frameworks by considering properties or dependencies within claims and sources [13]. More recently, new fact-finding algorithms have been designed to address the topic relevance [14], time sensitiveness [15], confidence awareness [16] and provenance aspect [17] of the problem. This paper uses the insights from the above work (i.e., the interdependence between source reliability and claim credibility) and develops a new estimation approach to explicitly model unreliable and moody human sensors and solve the mood sensitive truth discovery problem in social sensing.

Our work is also related with reputation and trust systems that are designed to study the reliability/credibility of sources (e.g., the quality of providers) [18, 19]. eBay is a homogeneous peer-to-peer based reputation system where participants rate each other after a transaction [20]. Alternatively, Amazon is a heterogeneous on-line review system where sources offer reviews and comments on products they purchased [21]. Recent work has also investigated the consistency of reports to estimate and revise trust scores in reputation systems [22–24]. However, we normally do not have enough history data to compute the converged reputation scores of sources in social sensing applications [3, 25]. Instead, this paper presents a principled estimation approach that jointly estimates the reliability and mood sensitivity of sources as well as the correctness and mood neutrality of claims based on the data collected.

Finally, our work falls into the scope of recommendation systems [26]. Expectation Maximization (EM) has been used as an optimization approach for both collaborative filtering [27] and content based recommendation systems [28]. For example, Wang et al. developed a collaborative filtering based system using the EM approach to recommend scientific articles to users of an online community [27]. Pomerantz et al. proposed a content-based system using EM to explore the contextual information to recommend movies [28]. However, the truth discovery in social sensing studies a different recommendation problem. Our goal is to recommend credible and reliable information from a large crowd of unvetted sources with unknown reliability and mood sensitivity rather than predict users' ratings or preferences of an item. Moreover, item or rating based recommendation systems commonly assume a reasonable amount of good data is available to train their models while little is known about the data quality and the source reliability a priori in social sensing applications.

3. PROBLEM FORMULATION

In this section, we formulate our mood-sensitive truth discovery problem as a multi-dimensional maximum likelihood estimation problem. In particular, we consider a Social Sensing application scenario where a group of M sources (Users) $S = (S_1, S_2, ..., S_M)$ report a set of N claims $C = C_1, C_2, ..., C_N$. In this paper, we consider two independent features of a claim: (i) mood sensitivity: whether a claim is of mood neutral or mood sensitive; (ii) correctness: whether a claim is true or false. We let S_u denote the uth source and C_k denote the kth claim. $C_k = O$ and $C_k = \overline{O}$

represent that claim C_k is mood sensitive and mood neutral respectively. In social sensing applications, sources may indicate a claim to be mood sensitive (e.g., using emotional words or emoticons). Furthermore, $C_k = T$ and $C_k = F$ represent the claim to be true or false respectively. We further define the following terms to be used in our model.

- SM is defined as a $M \times N$ matrix to represent whether a source indicates a claim to be mood neutral or not. It is referred to as the *Source-Mood Matrix.* In SM, $S_uM_k = 1$ when source S_u indicates C_k to be mood sensitive and $S_uM_k = -1$ when source S_u indicates C_k to be mood neutral and $S_uM_k = 0$ if S_u does not report C_k at all.
- SC is defined as a $M \times N$ matrix to represent whether a source reports a claim to be true. It is referred to as the *Source-Claim Matrix.* In SC, $S_uC_k = 1$ if source S_u reports claim C_k to be true and $S_uC_k = 0$ otherwise. We assume that a source will only report the positive status of a claim (e.g., in a gps application to report traffic jams, sources will only generate claims when they see or are stuck in a traffic jam.) [3, 4].

A key challenge in social sensing lies in the fact that sources may not always report neutral and truthful claims. In this paper, we explicitly model mood sensitivity and reliability of sources. First, we define the *mood sensitivity* of source S_u as M_u: the probability that a claim C_k is mood sensitive given the source S_u indicates it to be. Second, we define the *reliability* of source S_u as R_u: the probability that a claim is true given that source S_u reports it to be true. Formally, M_u and R_u are defined as follows:

$$\begin{aligned} M_u &= \Pr(C_k = O|S_uM_k = 1) \\ R_u &= \Pr(C_k = T|S_uC_k = 1) \end{aligned} \tag{1}$$

We further define a few conditional probabilities that we will use in our problem formulation. Specifically, we define $V_{u,O}^T$ and $V_{u,O}^F$ as the (unknown) probability that source S_i indicates a claim to be mood sensitive or not given the claim is indeed mood sensitive. Similarly, we define $V_{u,\overline{O}}^T$ and $V_{u,\overline{O}}^F$ as the (unknown) probability that source S_i indicates a claim to be mood sensitive or not given the claim is indeed mood neutral. Formally, $V_{u,O}^T$, $V_{u,O}^F$, $V_{u,\overline{O}}^T$, and $V_{u,\overline{O}}^F$ are defined as:

$$\begin{aligned} V_{u,O}^T &= \Pr(S_uM_k = 1|C_k = O) \\ V_{u,O}^F &= \Pr(S_uM_k = -1|C_k = O) \\ V_{u,\overline{O}}^T &= \Pr(S_uM_k = 1|C_k = \overline{O}) \\ V_{u,\overline{O}}^F &= \Pr(S_uM_k = -1|C_k = \overline{O}) \end{aligned} \tag{2}$$

In addition, we define I_u and J_u as the probability that source S_u reports a claim C_k to be true given that claim C_k is indeed true or false. Formally, I_u, J_u are defined as:

$$\begin{aligned} I_u &= \Pr(S_uC_k = 1|C_k = T) \\ J_u &= \Pr(S_uC_k = 1|C_k = F) \end{aligned} \tag{3}$$

Notice that sources may report different number of claims. We denote the probability that source S_u reports a claim to be mood sensitive as $mp_{u,O}$ (i.e., $mp_{u,O} = \Pr(S_uM_k = 1)$), and denote the probability that source S_u reports a claim to be mood neutral as $mp_{u,\overline{O}}$ (i.e., $mp_{u,\overline{O}} = \Pr(S_uM_k = -1)$). Additionally, we denote the probability that source S_u reports a claim to be true by sp_u (i.e., $sp_u = \Pr(S_uC_k = 1)$). We further denote h_O as the prior probability that a randomly chosen claim is indeed mood sensitive (i.e., $h_O = \Pr(C_k = O)$). We denote d as the prior probability that a randomly chosen claim is true (i.e., $d = \Pr(C_k = T)$). Based on the Bayes' theorem, we can obtain the relationship between the items defined above as follows:

$$\begin{aligned} V_{u,O}^T &= \frac{M_u \times mp_{u,O}}{h_O}, \quad V_{u,O}^F = \frac{(1 - M_u) \times mp_{u,O}}{h_O} \\ V_{u,\overline{O}}^T &= \frac{(1 - M_u) \times mp_{u,\overline{O}}}{1 - h_O}, \quad V_{u,\overline{O}}^F = \frac{M_u \times mp_{u,\overline{O}}}{1 - h_O} \\ I_u &= \frac{R_u \times sp_u}{d}, \quad J_u = \frac{(1 - R_u) \times sp_u}{(1 - d)} \end{aligned} \tag{4}$$

Finally, we define two more vectors of hidden variables Υ and Z where Υ indicates the mood neutrality of claims and Z indicates the correctness of claims. Specifically, we define an indicator variable r_k for each claim where $r_k = 1$ when claim C_k is mood sensitive and $r_k = 0$ when claim C_k is mood neutral. Similarly, we define another indicator variable z_k for each claim C_k where $z_k = 1$ when C_k is true and $z_k = 0$ when C_k is false.

Using the above definitions, we formally formulate the mood sensitive truth discovery problem as a multi-dimensional maximum likelihood estimation (MLE) problem: given the Source-Mood Matrix SM and the Source-Claim Matrix SC, the objective is to estimate: (i) the mood neutrality and correctness of each claim; (ii) the mood sensitivity and the reliability of each source. Formally, we compute:

$$\begin{aligned} &\forall k, 1 \le k \le N : \Pr(C_k = O|SM, SC) \\ &\forall k, 1 \le k \le N : \Pr(C_k = T|SM, SC) \\ &\forall u, 1 \le u \le M : \Pr(C_k = O|S_uM_k = 1) \\ &\forall u, 1 \le u \le M : \Pr(C_k = T|S_uC_k = 1) \end{aligned} \tag{5}$$

4. MOOD SENSITIVE IDENTIFICATION

In this section, we present the mood sensitive identification scheme: Mood-Sensitive Expectation Maximization (MS-EM). The MS-EM scheme jointly estimates the mood sensitivity of each claim and the mood sensitivity of each source.

Given the terms and variables we defined earlier, the likelihood function $L = (\Theta_{ms}; X, \Upsilon)$ for MS-EM is as follows:

$$\begin{aligned} &L(\Theta_{ms}; X, \Upsilon) = \Pr(X, \Upsilon|\Theta_{ms}) \\ &= \prod_{k \in C} \Pr(r_k|X_k, \Theta_{ms}) \times \prod_{u \in S} \Psi_{k,u} \times \Pr(r_k) \end{aligned} \tag{6}$$

where $\Theta_{ms} = (V_{1,O}^T, ..., V_{M,O}^T; V_{1,O}^F, ..., V_{M,O}^F; V_{1,\overline{O}}^T, ..., V_{M,\overline{O}}^T; V_{1,\overline{O}}^F, ..., V_{M,\overline{O}}^F; h_O)$ is the vector of estimation parameters for the MS-EM scheme. Note that $V_{u,O}^T$, $V_{u,O}^F$, $V_{u,\overline{O}}^T$, $V_{u,\overline{O}}^F$, h_O $h_{\overline{O}}$, are defined in the previous section. Additionally, $\Psi_{k,u}$ and $\Pr(r_k)$ are defined in Table 2. In the table, $S_uM_k^O = 1$ and $S_uM_k^{\overline{O}} = 0$ when source S_u indicates claim C_k to be mood neutral. $S_uM_k^O = 0$ and $S_uM_k^{\overline{O}} = 1$ when source S_u reports claim C_k but indicates it to be mood sensitive. $S_uM_k^O = 0$ and $S_uM_k^{\overline{O}} = 0$ when source S_u does not report claim C_k at all. Other notations are defined in the previous section. The model structure is illustrated in Figure 1.

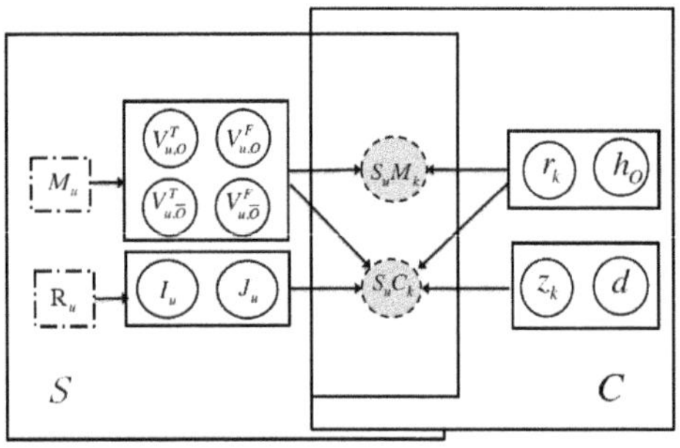

Figure 1: MS-EM Model

Given the above likelihood function, we can derive E and M steps of the proposed MS-EM scheme. First, the E-step is derived as follows:

$$\begin{aligned} Q(\Theta_{ms}|\Theta_{ms}^{(n)}) &= V_{\Upsilon|X,\Theta_{ms}^{(n)}}[logL(\Theta_{ms};X,\Upsilon)] \\ &= \sum_{k\in C} \Upsilon(n,k) \times \sum_{u\in S}(log\Psi_{k,u} + log\Pr(r_k)) \end{aligned} \quad (7)$$

where $\Upsilon(n,k)$ is defined in Table 2.

Table 2: Notations for MS-EM

$\Psi_{k,u}$	$\Pr(r_k)$	$\Upsilon(n,k)$	Constrains
$V^T_{u,O}$	h_O	$\Upsilon^O(n,k)$	$S_uM_k^O=1, S_uM_k^{\overline{O}}=0, r_k=1$
$V^F_{u,O}$	h_O	$\Upsilon^O(n,k)$	$S_uM_k^O=0, S_uM_k^{\overline{O}}=1, r_k=1$
$V^T_{u,\overline{O}}$	$h_{\overline{O}}$	$1-\Upsilon^O(n,k)$	$S_uM_k^O=1, S_uM_k^{\overline{O}}=0, r_k=0$
$V^F_{u,\overline{O}}$	$h_{\overline{O}}$	$1-\Upsilon^O(n,k)$	$S_uM_k^O=0, S_uM_k^{\overline{O}}=1, r_k=0$
$1-V^T_{u,O}-V^F_{u,O}$	h_O	$\Upsilon^O(n,k)$	$S_uM_k^O=0, S_uM_k^{\overline{O}}=0, r_k=1$
$1-V^T_{u,\overline{O}}-V^F_{u,\overline{O}}$	$h_{\overline{O}}$	$1-\Upsilon^O(n,k)$	$S_uM_k^O=0, S_uM_k^{\overline{O}}=0, r_k=0$

In the above table, $\Upsilon^O(n,k) = \Pr(r_k = O|X_k, \Theta_{ms}^{(n)})$. It represents the conditional probability of the claim C_j to be mood sensitive given the observed data X_k and current estimate of Θ_{ms}. $\Upsilon^O(n,k)$ can be further expressed as:

$$\begin{aligned} \Upsilon^O(n,k) &= \frac{\Pr(r_k = O; X_k, \Theta_{ms}^{(n)})}{\Pr(X_k, \Theta_{ms}^{(n)})} \\ &= \frac{L^O(n,k) \times h_O}{L^O(n,k) \times h_O + L^{\overline{O}}(n,k) \times h_{\overline{O}}} \end{aligned} \quad (8)$$

where $L^O(n,k)$, $L^{\overline{O}}(n,k)$ are defined as:

$$\begin{aligned} L^O(n,k) &= \Pr(X_k, \Theta_{ms}^{(n)}|r_k = O) \\ &= \prod_{u=1}^{M} (V^T_{u,O})^{S_uM_k^O} \times (V^F_{u,O})^{S_uM_k^{\overline{O}}} \\ &\quad \times (1 - V^T_{u,O} - V^F_{u,O})^{1-S_uM_k^O - S_uM_k^{\overline{O}}} \\ L^{\overline{O}}(n,k) &= \Pr(X_k, \Theta_{ms}^{(n)}|r_k = \overline{O}) \\ &= \prod_{u=1}^{M} (V^T_{u,\overline{O}})^{S_uM_k^O} \times (V^F_{u,\overline{O}})^{S_uM_k^{\overline{O}}} \\ &\quad \times (1 - V^T_{u,\overline{O}} - V^F_{u,\overline{O}})^{1-S_uM_k^O - S_uM_k^{\overline{O}}} \end{aligned} \quad (9)$$

In the M-step, we set derivatives $\frac{\partial Q}{\partial V^T_{u,O}} = 0$, $\frac{\partial Q}{\partial V^F_{u,O}} = 0$, $\frac{\partial Q}{\partial V^T_{u,\overline{O}}} = 0$, $\frac{\partial Q}{\partial V^F_{u,\overline{O}}} = 0$, $\frac{\partial Q}{\partial h_O} = 0$, $\frac{\partial Q}{\partial h_{\overline{O}}} = 0$. Solving these equations, we get expressions of the optimal $V^T_{u,O}$, $V^F_{u,O}$, $V^T_{u,\overline{O}}$, $V^F_{u,\overline{O}}$, h_O and $h_{\overline{O}}$ as shown in Table 3. In the table, N is the total number of claims in the Source-Mood Matrix. SF_u^O is the set of claims the source S_u indicates to be mood sensitive. $SF_u^{\overline{O}}$ is the set of claims the source S_u reports but indicates to be mood neutral.

Table 3: Optimal Solutions of MS-EM

Notation	Solution	Notation	Solution
$(V^T_{u,O})^*$	$\frac{\sum_{k\in SF_u^O} \Upsilon^O(n,k)}{\sum_{k=1}^N \Upsilon^O(n,k)}$	$(V^F_{u,O})^*$	$\frac{\sum_{k\in SF_u^{\overline{O}}} \Upsilon^O(n,k)}{\sum_{k=1}^N \Upsilon^O(n,k)}$
$(V^T_{u,\overline{O}})^*$	$\frac{\sum_{k\in SF_u^O} \Upsilon^{\overline{O}}(n,k)}{\sum_{k=1}^N \Upsilon^{\overline{O}}(n,k)}$	$(V^F_{u,\overline{O}})^*$	$\frac{\sum_{k\in SF_u^{\overline{O}}} \Upsilon^{\overline{O}}(n,k)}{\sum_{k=1}^N \Upsilon^{\overline{O}}(n,k)}$
h_O^*	$\frac{\sum_{k=1}^N \Upsilon^O(n,k)}{N}$	$h_{\overline{O}}^*$	$\frac{\sum_{k=1}^N \Upsilon^{\overline{O}}(n,k)}{N}$

In summary, the input to the MS-EM scheme is the Source-Mood Matrix SM. The output is the maximum likelihood estimation of the mood-sensitivity of claims and the mood-sensitivity of sources. Since we assume the mood sensitive feature of a claim is binary, we can classify claims as either mood sensitive or mood neutral based on the converged value of $\Upsilon^O(n,k)$. The convergence analysis of MS-EM is presented in the next section. Algorithm 1 shows the pseudocode of MS-EM.

Algorithm 1 Mood-Sensitive EM Scheme (MS-EM)

```
Initialize Θ_ms (V^T_{u,O} = mp_{u,O}, V^F_{u,O} = 0.5 × mp_{u,O}, V^T_{u,Ō} =
  0.5 × mp_{u,Ō}, V^F_{u,Ō} = mp_{u,Ō}, h_O ∈ (0,1), h_Ō ∈ (0,1))
n ← 0
repeat
   for Each k ∈ C do
      compute Pr(r_k = O|X_k, Θ_ms^(n)) based on Equation (8)
   end for
   for Each u ∈ S do
      compute Θ_ms^(n) based on optimal solutions which are pre-
      sented in Table 3.
   end for
   n = n + 1
until Θ_ms^(n) converges
Let (Υ_k^O)^c = converged value of Υ^O(n,k)
for Each k ∈ C do
   if (Υ_k^O)^c ≥ 0.5 then
      consider C_k as mood sensitive
   else
      consider C_k as mood neutral
   end if
end for
for Each u ∈ S do
   calculate M_u^* from converge values of Θ_ms based on Equa-
   tion (4)
end for
Return the MLE on the mood sensitivity of claims judgment on
  claim C_k and the mood sensitivity M_u^* of S_u.
```

5. EVALUATION

In this section, we evaluate the MS-EM scheme on four real-world data traces collected from Twitter in the aftermath of recent emergency and disaster events. We show the performance of our scheme against the state-of-the-art baselines on these data traces. First, we present the particular experimental settings as well as data pre-processing steps that we used to set up the data for evaluation. Next, we show the baselines mentioned above and evaluation metrics we used in our evaluation. Last, we show our results: (i) MS-EM scheme can identify mood neutral claims more accurately than the compared baselines and (ii) MS-EM can achieve non-trivial performance gains in finding more valuable (i.e., neutral and correct) claims compared to current truth discovery techniques.

5.1 Experimental Setups and Evaluation Metrics

5.1.1 Data Traces Statistics

Social sensing has emerged as a new area of experimentation where human sensors discuss events that happened in the physical world. The reported observations in social sensing applications may be incorrect or mood sensitive due to the open data collection environment and unvetted data sources [1]. However, this noisy nature of social sensing applications gives researchers an opportunity to investigate algorithms in real world scenarios and in our case, the MS-EM scheme. In the evaluation, we selected four data traces: (i) Brussels Bombing event that happened on March 22, 2016; (ii) Paris Terrorists Attack event that happened on Nov. 13, 2015; (iii) Oregon Umpqua Community College Shooting event that happened on Oct. 1, 2015; and (iv) Baltimore Riots event that happened on April 14, 2015. These data traces were collected through Twitter's open search API using query terms and specified geographic regions related to the events [4]. The statistics of the four data traces are summarized in Table 4.

5.1.2 Data Pre-Processing

To evaluate our methods in real-world settings, we conducted the following data pre-processing steps:

Clustering: We use a K-means clustering algorithm and the Jaccard distance metric for micro-blog data clustering to cluster similar tweets into the same cluster [29]. In particular, the Jaccard distance is defined as $1 - \frac{A \cap B}{A \cup B}$, where A and B represents the set of words that appear in two compared tweets respectively. Hence, the more common words two tweets share, the shorter Jaccard distance they have. We then take each Twitter user as a source and each cluster as a claim in our model described in Section 3.

Source-Mood Matrix and Source-Claim Matrix Generation: we first generate the SM Matrix using the mood indicator (i.e., moody words) from the tweets. In particular, we collected a list of moody words (both positive and negative) used in online social media [30]. If source S_u reports the claim C_k using a moody word in the tweet, the corresponding element S_uM_k in SM matrix is set to 1. Similarly, if source S_u reports claim C_k without using any moody words, the corresponding element S_uM_k is set to -1. The element S_uM_k is set to 0 when source S_u did not report claim C_k. Second, we generate the SC Matrix by associating each source with the claims he/she reported. In particular, we set the element S_uC_k in SC matrix to 1 if source S_u generates a tweet that belongs to claim (cluster) C_k and 0 otherwise.

5.1.3 Evaluation Metric

In our evaluation, we use the following metrics to evaluate the estimation performance of the MS-EM scheme: *Precision*, *Recall*, *F1-measure* and *Accuracy*. Their definitions are given in Table 5.

Table 5: Metric Definitions

Metric	Definition
$Precison$	$\frac{TP}{TP+FP}$
$Recall$	$\frac{TP}{TP+FN}$
$F1-measure$	$\frac{2\times Precison \times Recall}{Precison + Recall}$
$Accuracy$	$\frac{TP+TN}{TP+TN+FP+FN}$

In Table 5, TP, TN, FP and FN represents True Positives, True Negatives, False Positives and False Negatives respectively. We will further explain their meanings in the context of experiments carried out in the following subsections.

5.2 Evaluation of Our Methods

In this subsection, we evaluate the performance of the proposed MS-EM scheme and compare them to the state-of-the-art truth discovery methods.

5.2.1 Evaluation on Mood Neutral Identification

We first evaluate the capability of MS-EM scheme to correctly identify the mood neutral claims from noisy data. We compared the MS-EM with several baselines. The first one is *Voting*: it assumes the mood neutrality of a claim is reflected by the number of times it is repeated: the more repetitions of a claim, the more likely it is mood neutral. The second baseline is the *Mood Classifier*: it considers a claim to be neutral if the claim doesn't contain mood-sensitive words. The third baseline is the *Sums* [11]: it assumes a linear relationship between the source's mood sensitivity and the claim's mood. The last baseline is the *TruthFinder* [12]: it can estimate the mood neutrality of a claim using a heuristic based pesudo-probabilistic model.

In our evaluation, the outputs of the above schemes were manually graded to determine their performance on mood sensitive claim identification. Due to man-power limitations, we generated the evaluation set by taking the union of the top 50 neutral claims returned by each scheme to avoid possible sampling bias towards any particular scheme. We collected the ground truth of the evaluation set using the following rubric:

- Mood Sensitive Claims: claims that clearly have an emotional mood attached to it (e.g., anger, happiness or sadness in our selected datasets).
- Mood Neutral Claims: claims that do not meet the definition of the mood sensitive claims.

In our evaluation, the True Positives and True Negatives are the claims that are correctly classified by a particular scheme as mood neutral and mood sensitive respectively. The False Positives and False Negatives are the mood sensitive and mood neutral claims that are misclassified to each other respectively.

The evaluation results of Brussels Bombing data trace are shown in Table 6. We can observe that *MS-EM* outperforms the compared baselines in all evaluation metrics. The largest performance gain achieved by *MS-EM* on F1-measure and

Table 4: Data Traces Statistics

Data Trace	Brussels Bombing	Paris Attack	Oregon Shooting	Baltimore Riots
Start Date	Mar. 22 2016	Nov. 13 2015	Oct. 1 2015	April 14 2015
Time Duration	7 days	11 days	6 days	17 days
Location	Brussels, Belgium	Paris, France	Umpqua, Oregon	Baltimore, Maryland
Search Keywords	Brussels, Attacks, Explosions	Paris, Attacks, ISIS	Oregon, Shooting, Umpqua	Baltimore, Riots
# of Tweets	986,560	873,760	210,028	952,442
# of Users Tweeted	466,398	496,753	122,069	425,552

Table 6: Estimation Results on Data Traces

	Brussels Bombing				Baltimore Riots			
Algorithm	Precision	Recall	F1-measure	Accuracy	Precision	Recall	F1-measure	Accuracy
MS-EM	**0.72**	**0.79**	**0.74**	**0.71**	**0.79**	**0.74**	**0.75**	**0.77**
Mood-Classifier	0.64	0.62	0.63	0.61	0.69	0.62	0.66	0.67
TruthFinder	0.64	0.57	0.53	0.54	0.65	0.59	0.57	0.53
Sums	0.6	0.66	0.61	0.58	0.66	0.6	0.62	0.64
Voting	0.54	0.59	0.57	0.54	0.63	0.58	0.56	0.5
	Oregon Shooting				Paris Attacks			
Algorithm	Precision	Recall	F1-measure	Accuracy	Precision	Recall	F1-measure	Accuracy
MS-EM	**0.72**	**0.74**	**0.73**	**0.72**	**0.72**	**0.69**	**0.68**	**0.69**
Mood-Classifier	0.63	0.62	0.64	0.65	0.63	0.6	0.59	0.59
TruthFinder	0.6	0.59	0.57	0.54	0.6	0.58	0.56	0.52
Sums	0.63	0.58	0.56	0.55	0.59	0.55	0.54	0.52
Voting	0.57	0.64	0.61	0.54	0.56	0.59	0.57	0.6

accuracy over the best performed baseline (i.e., *Mood Classifier*) are 11% and 10% respectively. The results of Baltimore Riots dataset are also presented in Table 6. *MS-EM* continues to outperform all baselines and the largest performance gain achieved by *MS-EM* on F1-measure and accuracy compared to the best performed baseline is 9% and 10% respectively. Similar results are observed in Oregon Shooting and Paris Attacks datasets presented in Table 6.

5.2.2 Estimation Performance on Mood-Sensitive Truth Discovery

In this subsection, we evaluate the truth discovery performance of MS-EM scheme and compare it with the state-of-the-art truth discovery solutions that ignore the mood sensitive feature of claims. The baseline that stays closet to ours is *Regular EM* [3], which computes the claims' truthfulness and sources' reliability in an iterative way and has been shown to outperform four fact-finding techniques in identifying truthful claims from social sensing data. The only difference is that Regular EM ignores the mood sensitivity of claims. Other baselines include *TruthFinder* [12], *Sums* [11] and *Voting*.

To incorporate both mood sensitivity and correctness of claims into our evaluation, we generalized the concept of a *correct* claim from the truth discovery problem to a *valuable* claim in the mood-sensitive truth discovery problem. In particular, a valuable claim is defined as a claim that is both correct and mood neutral. The valuable claims are the ones that are eventually useful in the decision making process. Similarly as the mood-sensitive identification evaluation, we generated the evaluation set by taking the union of the top 50 claims returned by different schemes. We collected the ground truth of the evaluation set using the following rubric:

- Valuable Claims: Claims that are statements of a physical or social event, which is mood neutral and generally observable by multiple independent observers and corroborated by credible sources external to Social Media (e.g., mainstream news media).
- Unconfirmed Claims: Claims that do not satisfy the requirement of valuable claims.

The True Positives and True Negatives in this experiment are the claims that are correctly classified by a particular scheme as valuable and valueless ones respectively. The False Positives and False Negatives are the valueless and valuable claims that are misclassified to each other respectively.

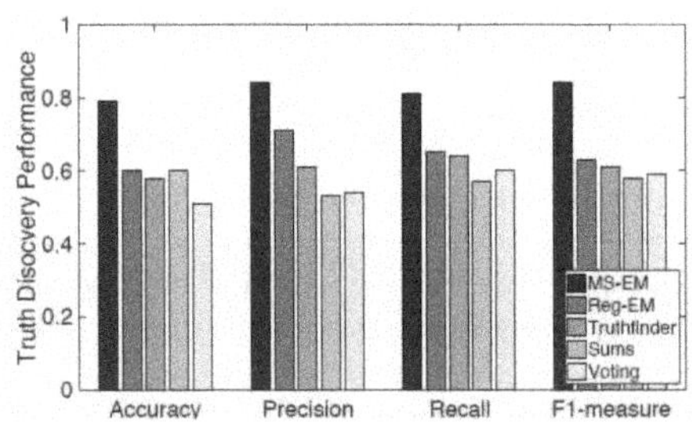

Figure 2: Truth Discovery Results on Brussels Bombing Dataset

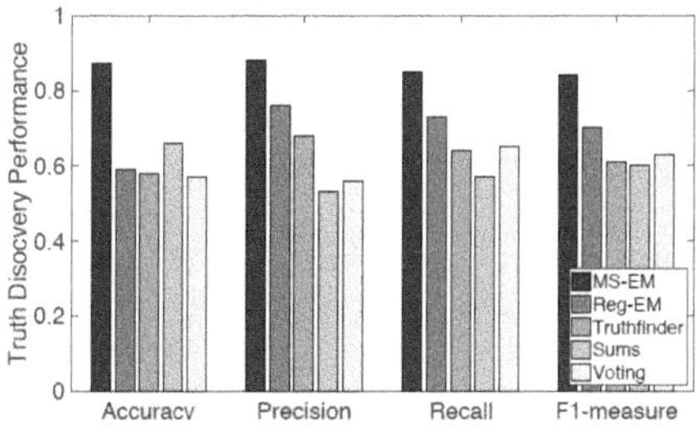

Figure 3: Truth Discovery Results on Baltimore Riots Dataset

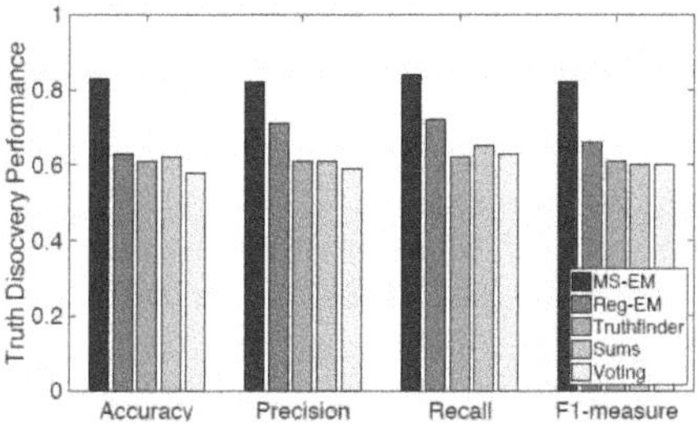

Figure 4: Truth Discovery Results on Oregon Shooting Dataset

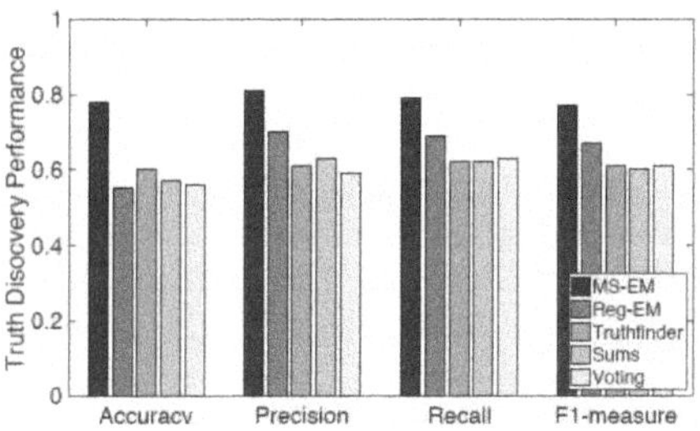

Figure 5: Truth Discovery Results on Paris Attack Dataset

The evaluation results of Brussels Bombing dataset are presented in Figure 2. We observe that the *MS-EM* scheme outperforms all baselines. Specifically, the largest performance gain achieved by *MS-EM* compared to the best performed baselines on precision, recall, F1-measure and accuracy is 13%, 16%, 20% and 19% respectively. The results on Baltimore Riots dataset are shown in Figure 3. We observe that our *MS-EM* continues to outperform the compared baselines and the largest performance gain it achieved over the best performed baselines on precision, recall, F1-measure and accuracy is 12%, 12%, 14% and 20% respectively. The results on Oregon Shooting and Paris Attacks datasets are presented in Figure 4 and Figure 5 respectively. We observe consistent performance improvements achieved by the *MS-EM* compared to other baselines. The performance improvements are achieved by explicitly considering the *mood sensitivity* feature of truth discovery problem in social sensing, a main challenge addressed by this paper.

We also perform the convergence analysis of the MS-EM scheme and the results are presented in Figure 6. We observe the MS-EM scheme converges within a few iterations on all four data traces.

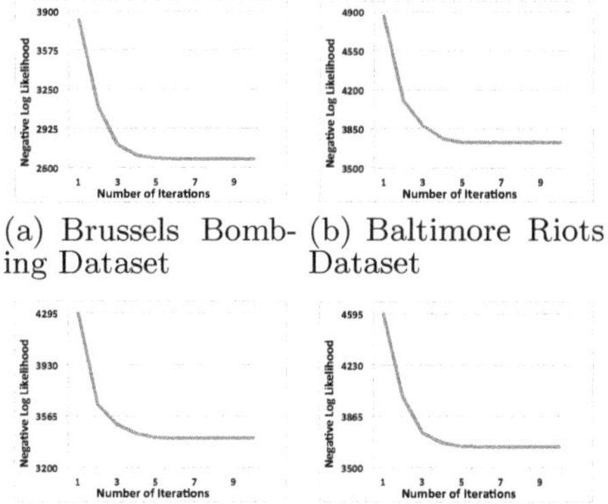

(a) Brussels Bombing Dataset (b) Baltimore Riots Dataset

(c) Oregon Shooting Dataset (d) Paris Attack Dataset

Figure 6: Convergence Rate of MS-EM

6. CONCLUSION

This paper develops a new principled approach to solve a mood sensitive truth discovery problem for reliable recommendation systems in social sensing applications. The new approach takes the mood sensitive features of both sources and claims into account in the truth discovery solutions. The proposed approach jointly estimates the mood sensitivity and reliability of sources as well as the mood neutrality and correctness of claims using expectation maximization schemes. We evaluated our solution (i.e., MS-EM scheme) using four real world datasets collected from Twitter. The results demonstrated that our solution achieved significant performance gains in correctly identifying mood neutral and correct claims compared to the state-of-the-art baselines. These results are important to recommendation systems because it gives us an analytical foundation to venture into the mood sensitive aspect of the truth discovery problem and enhance the credibility of information users of recommendation systems would receive.

Acknowledgments

This material is based upon work supported by the National Science Foundation under Grant No. CBET-1637251, CNS-1566465 and IIS-1447795 and Army Research Office under Grant 69595-CS-II.

7. REFERENCES

[1] Charu C Aggarwal and Tarek Abdelzaher. Social sensing. In *Managing and Mining Sensor Data*, pages 237–297. Springer, 2013.

[2] Dong Wang, Tarek Abdelzaher, and Lance Kaplan. *Social Sensing: Building Reliable Systems on Unreliable Data.* Morgan Kaufmann, 2015.

[3] Dong Wang, Lance Kaplan, Hieu Le, and Tarek Abdelzaher. On truth discovery in social sensing: A maximum likelihood estimation approach. In *The 11th ACM/IEEE Conference on Information Processing in Sensor Networks (IPSN 12)*, April 2012.

[4] Dong Wang, Md Tanvir Amin, Shen Li, Tarek Abdelzaher, Lance Kaplan, Siyu Gu, Chenji Pan, Hengchang Liu, Charu C Aggarwal, Raghu Ganti, et al. Using humans as sensors: an estimation-theoretic perspective. In *Proceedings of the*

13th international symposium on Information processing in sensor networks, pages 35–46. IEEE Press, 2014.

[5] C.Lin; T.Lin; W.Liu. A trust and distrust mechanism for a social network-based recommendation system. In *Wireless Personal Multimedia Communications (WPMC), 15th International Symposium*, pages 172–176, 2012.

[6] M.G.Ozsoy; F.Polat. Trust based recommendation systems. In *Advances in Social Networks Analysis and Mining (ASONAM), IEEE/ACM International Conference*, pages 1267–1274, 2013.

[7] Xiaoxin Yin and Wenzhao Tan. Semi-supervised truth discovery. In *WWW*, New York, NY, USA, 2011. ACM.

[8] Dong Wang, Jermaine Marshall, and Chao Huang. Theme-relevant truth discovery on twitter: An estimation theoretic approach. In *Tenth International AAAI Conference on Web and Social Media*, 2016.

[9] Robin Wentao Ouyang, Lance Kaplan, Paul Martin, Alice Toniolo, Mani Srivastava, and Timothy J Norman. Debiasing crowdsourced quantitative characteristics in local businesses and services. In *Proceedings of the 14th International Conference on Information Processing in Sensor Networks*, pages 190–201. ACM, 2015.

[10] Manish Gupta and Jiawei Han. Heterogeneous network-based trust analysis: a survey. *ACM SIGKDD Explorations Newsletter*, 13(1):54–71, 2011.

[11] J M Kleinberg. Authoritative sources in a hyperlinked environment. *Journal of the ACM*, 46(5):604–632, 1999.

[12] Xiaoxin Yin, Jiawei Han, and Philip S. Yu. Truth discovery with multiple conflicting information providers on the web. *IEEE Trans. on Knowl. and Data Eng.*, 20:796–808, June 2008.

[13] Shiguang Wang, Dong Wang, Lu Su, Tarek Abdelzaher, and Lance Kaplan. Towards cyber-physical systems in social spaces: The data reliability challenge. In *The IEEE 35th Real-Time Systems Symposium (RTSS'14)*, 2014.

[14] Chao Huang and Dong Wang. Topic-aware social sensing with arbitrary source dependency graphs. In *The 15th ACM/IEEE Conference on Information Processing in Sensor Networks (IPSN 16)*. ACM/IEEE, 2016.

[15] Chao Huang, Dong Wang, and Nitesh Chawla. Towards time-sensitive truth discovery in social sensing applications. In *Mobile Ad Hoc and Sensor Systems (MASS), 2015 IEEE 12th International Conference on*, pages 154–162. IEEE, 2015.

[16] Dong Wang and Chao Huang. Confidence-aware truth estimation in social sensing applications. In *Sensing, Communication, and Networking (SECON), 2015 12th Annual IEEE International Conference on*, pages 336–344. IEEE, 2015.

[17] Dong Wang, Md Tanvir Al Amin, Tarek Abdelzaher, Dan Roth, Clare R Voss, Lance M Kaplan, Stephen Tratz, Jamal Laoudi, and Douglas Briesch. Provenance-assisted classification in social networks. *Selected Topics in Signal Processing, IEEE Journal of*, 8(4):624–637, 2014.

[18] Yao Wang and Julita Vassileva. A review on trust and reputation for web service selection. In *Distributed Computing Systems Workshops, 2007. ICDCSW'07. 27th International Conference on*, pages 25–25. IEEE, 2007.

[19] Luis Cabral and Ali Hortacsu. The dynamics of seller reputation: Evidence from eBay. *The Journal of Industrial Economics*, 58(1):54–78, 2010.

[20] Daniel Houser and John Wooders. Reputation in auctions: Theory, and evidence from eBay. *Journal of Economics & Management Strategy*, 15(2):353–369, 2006.

[21] Randy Farmer and Bryce Glass. *Building web reputation systems.* " O'Reilly Media, Inc.", 2010.

[22] Kuan Lun Huang, Salil S Kanhere, and Wen Hu. Are you contributing trustworthy data?: the case for a reputation system in participatory sensing. In *Proceedings of the 13th ACM international conference on Modeling, analysis, and simulation of wireless and mobile systems*, pages 14–22. ACM, 2010.

[23] Lance Kaplan, Murat Scensoy, and Geeth de Mel. Trust estimation and fusion of uncertain information by exploiting consistency. In *Information Fusion (FUSION), 2014 17th International Conference on*, pages 1–8. IEEE, 2014.

[24] Kuan Lun Huang, Salil S Kanhere, and Wen Hu. On the need for a reputation system in mobile phone based sensing. *Ad Hoc Networks*, 12:130–149, 2014.

[25] Dong Wang, Tarek Abdelzaher, Lance Kaplan, and Charu C. Aggarwal. Recursive fact-finding: A streaming approach to truth estimation in crowdsourcing applications. In *The 33rd International Conference on Distributed Computing Systems (ICDCS'13)*, July 2013.

[26] Dietmar Jannach, Markus Zanker, Alexander Felfernig, and Gerhard Friedrich. *Recommender systems: an introduction.* Cambridge University Press, 2010.

[27] Chong Wang and David M Blei. Collaborative topic modeling for recommending scientific articles. In *Proceedings of the 17th ACM SIGKDD international conference on Knowledge discovery and data mining*, pages 448–456. ACM, 2011.

[28] Daniel Pomerantz and Gregory Dudek. Context dependent movie recommendations using a hierarchical bayesian model. In *Advances in Artificial Intelligence*, pages 98–109. Springer, 2009.

[29] Kevin Dela Rosa, Rushin Shah, Bo Lin, Anatole Gershman, and Robert Frederking. Topical clustering of tweets. *Proceedings of the ACM SIGIR: SWSM*, 2011.

[30] Panagiotis Gayo-Avello, Eni Takis Metaxas, Markus Mustafaraj, Harald Schoen Strohmaier, Daniel Peter Gloor, Carlos Castillo, Marcelo Mendoza, and Barbara Poblete. Predicting information credibility in time-sensitive social media. *Internet Research*, 23(5):560–588, 2013.

Crowd-Based Personalized Natural Language Explanations for Recommendations

Shuo Chang F. Maxwell Harper Loren Terveen

The GroupLens Center for Social and Human-Centered Computing
Computer Science & Engineering
University of Minnesota
schang, harper, terveen@cs.umn.edu

ABSTRACT

Explanations are important for users to make decisions on whether to take recommendations. However, algorithm generated explanations can be overly simplistic and unconvincing. We believe that humans can overcome these limitations. Inspired by how people explain word-of-mouth recommendations, we designed a process, combining crowdsourcing and computation, that generates personalized natural language explanations. We modeled key topical aspects of movies, asked crowdworkers to write explanations based on quotes from online movie reviews, and personalized the explanations presented to users based on their rating history. We evaluated the explanations by surveying 220 MovieLens users, finding that compared to personalized tag-based explanations, natural language explanations: 1) contain a more appropriate amount of information, 2) earn more trust from users, and 3) make users more satisfied. This paper contributes to the research literature by describing a scalable process for generating high quality and personalized natural language explanations, improving on state-of-the-art content-based explanations, and showing the feasibility and advantages of approaches that combine human wisdom with algorithmic processes.

Keywords

Crowdsourcing; Recommendation Explanations; Natural Language Processing; Clustering; Word2Vec

1. INTRODUCTION

Because recommendation explanations are crucial for good user experiences with recommender systems, they have received persistent research interest [11, 20, 22]. Past research has shown several positive effects of recommendation explanations, including increasing user trust in recommender systems [18] and helping users make good decisions on recommendations [20].

Recommendation explanations on popular websites, however, are mostly generated by algorithms, hence are syntactic and formulaic. For example, "Customers who bought this item also bought ..." on Amazon and "Based on your watching history." on YouTube.

- From your MovieLens profile it seems that you prefer movies tagged as space, this movie takes you in space and it feels claustrophobic to be there. It keeps you on the edge of your seat the whole time.
- From your MovieLens profile it seems that you prefer movies tagged as visual, Gravity is unlike what we have seen on a cinema screen before and arguably it has one of the best uses of 3D in a movie.
- From your MovieLens profile it seems that you prefer movies tagged as intense, the movie a pretty intense ninety minutes, with Bullock's character constantly battling one catastrophe after another, and all of it is amazing to see.

Figure 1: Example natural language explanations for the movie "Gravity". Depending on our model of a user's interest, our system selects one of the three explanations for the user.

In comparison, people can provide effective explanations for everyday recommendations. For example, when librarians recommend books, they may summarize and highlight a book's content and help people figure out whether it is a good fit for them.

Though human effort is generally expensive, crowdsourcing enables computational processes to integrate human inputs at scale and on demand, extending the capability of current computational systems. For example, Cheng et al. [7] leverage crowd wisdom to train a machine learning system that can detect whether people in a video are lying.

Pure crowdsourcing approaches to generating natural language recommendation explanations will not succeed because most crowdworkers are not domain experts. For example, we cannot expect a crowdworker who has not seen "Gravity" to write an effective explanation for a movie fan who likes *intense* movies. Therefore, to generate natural language explanations at scale, we combine several techniques. First, we build on existing algorithmic processes that generate personalized content-based explanations [22]. Second, we combine this content model with user review text, which is popular across many recommendation systems, including IMDb and Yelp. To convert these two inputs into a set of coherent explanations that can be selected for display on a per-user basis, we rely on a combination of several crowdsourcing and algorithmic steps.

RecSys '16, September 15-19, 2016, Boston , MA, USA

© 2016 ACM. ISBN 978-1-4503-4035-9/16/09... $15.00

DOI: http://dx.doi.org/10.1145/2959100.2959153

In this paper, we present a system that leverages this *mixed computation* – computation that combines crowdsourced data into an algorithmic processes – to generate personalized natural language recommendations at scale. See Figure 1 for three example explanations generated by our process for the movie "Gravity"; in application, we would select the one explanation for display that best matches with the current user's interests. Our system can be adapted to any recommendation application where user reviews and topic labels (e.g., categories, genres, or tags) for items are available.

We deployed the system in MovieLens and conducted a controlled experiment to evaluate the resulting explanations. Using established rubrics from past research [20], we compared the natural language explanations with tag-based explanations generated by a state-of-the-art algorithm [22].

This paper makes the following contributions:

- We created a novel system that generates personalized natural language explanations at scale with a mixed computation approach;
- Through a controlled experiment, we found that personalized natural language explanations beat a strong baseline - personalized tag explanation.

2. DESIGN SPACE AND RELATED WORK

Explanation interfaces in recommender systems communicate *why* a user might like (or dislike) a particular item. In this section we describe several key dimensions, the research and industrial work that has explored these dimensions, and where our experimental system fits.

When designing recommendation explanations, there are several "styles" [21] of explanations to choose from: case-based, collaborative-based [11], content-based [22], conversational [19], demographic-based, and knowledge-based [24]. For example, Amazon's "Customers Who Bought This Item Also Bought ..." is collaborative-based, while Pandora's "Based on what you've told us so far, we're playing this track because it features ..." is content-based.

Apart from styles of explanations, explanations can be presented in different ways, e.g., using natural language, template-based language, or a graphical representation [3, 11]. As template-based language can be generated by algorithms, it is most common on popular websites. Tintarev et al. [20] also experimented with filling a template with movie meta data. As for graphical explanations, Herlocker et al. [11], for example, experimented with histograms of ratings as explanations, finding them to be persuasive. Natural language explanations, however, can not be easily generated by an algorithm, and have received little research attention.

Recommendation explanations can be personalized or non-personalized, depending on whether or not different users see different explanations for the same item. Personalization has been shown to have positive and negative effects [20], depending on the design. Herlocker et al. [11] found that non-personalized histograms of ratings are more persuasive than personalized histograms of ratings from users' neighbors in preference space. Vig et al. [22] also observed a similar effect with tag-based explanations: personalization resulted in a better user experience in one of their designs, but had a negative effect on the other one.

Inspired by word-of-mouth recommendation explanations, we are interested in designing *personalized natural language explanations* about the content of recommended items. Our intuition is that by showing what users might like about recommended items (in a personalized fashion), we can convince them to explore or even consume unfamiliar items [12, 15]. Our goal is to help users to decide whether or not to take a recommendation. Therefore, the text should be reasonably short to avoid overwhelming users as they casually browse recommendations. We hypothesize that users have better experience with natural language, compared with template-based language.

In generating natural language explanations with human effort, we can either recruit professionals like librarians or paid crowdworkers. While professionals may generate higher quality content – though prior work has shown counter-examples [10] – crowdsourcing has the advantages of being scalable, on-demand, and relatively inexpensive.

To reduce the difficulty of writing explanations, we can show crowdworkers relevant text from user reviews, by simple text search or more advanced data mining methods [1,8, 14]. Finding crowdworkers who are familiar with items and capable of writing explanations is challenging. Showing relevant information from user reviews can address this issue: crowdworkers who have not watched a movie can still *synthesize* and *edit* already-written sentences. Current data mining methods focus on extracting *keywords and key phrases* from text. For example, Liu et al. [14] introduced an algorithm that extracts salient phrases from review data, e.g., "ice cream parlor" from Yelp's review data. These keywords offer limited help for crowdworkers. Therefore, we use simple text search to find sentences that may be relevant for explanations.

In this paper, we describe a mixed computation approach – combining crowd wisdom with algorithms. Recent research on crowdsourcing shows that such mixed computation creates exciting new applications, such as Soylent, a crowd-powered word editor [2]. More closely related, Organisciak et al. [17] proposed a crowdsourcing system to take on a collaborative filtering task - predicting user ratings. Chang et al. [6] showed that paid crowdworkers can make movie recommendations that are better perceived by users than algorithmic recommendations, and that paid crowdworkers can also produce decent quality explanations for their recommendations.

3. SYSTEM OVERVIEW

In this section, we give an overview of the system, showing how we composite three processes to generate personalized natural language explanations.

The system takes *topic labels* and *reviews* for items as input, and generates natural language explanations, which are presented to users in a personalized fashion based on their past activities, e.g., ratings, clicks, or purchases. Both topic labels and reviews are easily accessible in contemporary recommender systems. Topic labels for items can be either tags provided by users or topic entities (e.g., Google's knowledge graph entities) generated through a computational process [4, 25]. User reviews are a popular feature in e-commerce sites such as Amazon and the Apple App Store, and in specialized sites such as IMDB for movies and Yelp for restaurants.

The system consists of three processes, as shown in Figure 2 and described in more detail in Section 5:

1. *Select key topical dimensions from item topic labels.*

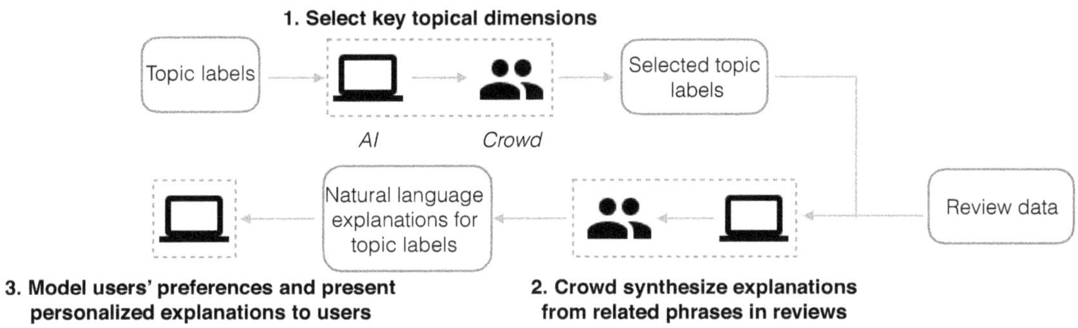

Figure 2: System overview. There are two inputs to the system - *topic labels* and *review data*. We show three procedures of the system in bold text. The first two procedures use mixed computation, with crowd and algorithm, while the last one only uses algorithm.

We first select topical dimensions with an unsupervised learning approach, and then leverage crowd wisdom to refine the output.

2. *Generate natural language explanations for the key topical dimensions.* We data mine relevant quotes for the selected dimensions, and then ask crowdworkers to synthesize the quotes into explanations.

3. *Model users' preferences and present explanations in a personalized fashion.* We compute users' interest on topical dimensions of a item based on their activities, such as rating, clicks and browsing, and then present users explanations that are most interesting to them.

4. PLATFORM

We deploy our explanation system in MovieLens, a movie recommendation website with over 3000 monthly active users. Users rate and tag movies and receive recommendations. MovieLens currently does not provide explanations for its recommendations, but this is currently the second most requested feature by its users [1].

We recruit crowdworkers from Amazon Mechanical Turk ("Mturk" for short) for the human computational tasks required in our system. To ensure quality results, we only recruited US crowdworkers who have finished more than 2000 HITs (or micro tasks) and maintain higher than 98% approval rate.

5. OVERVIEW OF SYSTEM PROCESSES

We now describe three mixed computational steps that generate explanations of the following form: "From your MovieLens profile it seems that you prefer movies tagged as *[Topical Dimension]*, *[Natural Language Explanation]*". These steps, in particular, generate two natural language components: "*[Topical Dimension]*", a personalized topic label, and "*[Natural Language Explanation]*", a crowd-synthesized explanation based on review text. For each step, we describe separately the generalizable mixed computation and the experimental implementation details.

[1]https://movielens.uservoice.com/suggestions/5585074

Figure 3: An example of crowd-refined tag clusters for the movie "Goodfellas". The algorithm generates four tag clusters. The crowdworkers curated the tags: a strikethrough indicates bad cluster fit, a crossout indicates inappropriateness for explanations, and red/bold indicates selection as the representative tag for the cluster.

5.1 Select Key Topical Dimensions of Items

5.1.1 Description

We aim to find semantically diverse topical dimensions of an item from associated topic labels to fill the "*[Topical Dimension]*" part of the explanation. Our intuition is that to personalize an explanation for a user, we should highlight an aspect of the recommended item for which the user previously has expressed a preference. For example, some movie fans be drawn to the movie Gravity because of its space travel aspects, while others will be drawn to it for its high quality 3D effects. Therefore, we want to show different explanations (shown in Figure 1) to these two groups of users.

Using a clustering algorithm is one way to select diverse topical labels that represent a larger set of topic labels. Clustering, based on semantic similarities, groups similar topic labels together. For example, a clustering algorithm may group "3D", "visual" and "CG" together because they are semantically similar.

We leverage crowd wisdom to refine topic label clusters. Clustering, as an unsupervised learning method, is sensitive to parameter choices and notoriously difficult to evaluate. In addition, we need to find one tag to fill in "*[Topical Dimension]*", a highly subjective task. Human wisdom has been shown to be effective in improving clustering results [5]. Therefore, we decide to ask crowdworkers to refine algorithmically generated clusters and pick labels for the clusters.

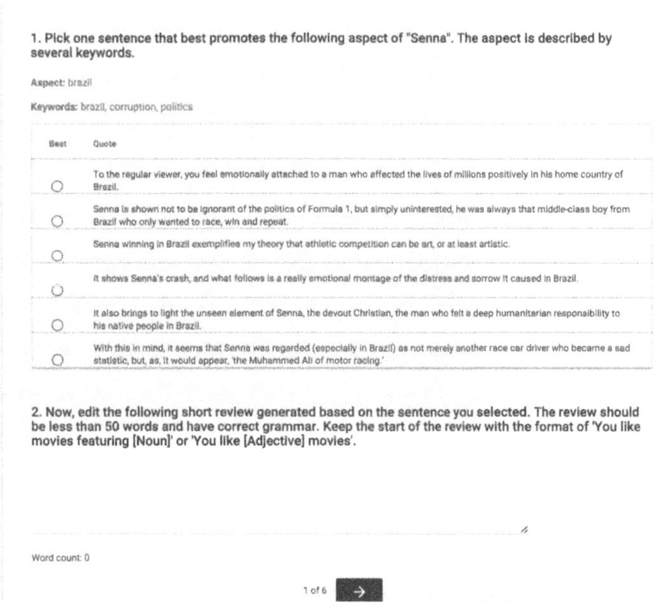

(a) Write explanations

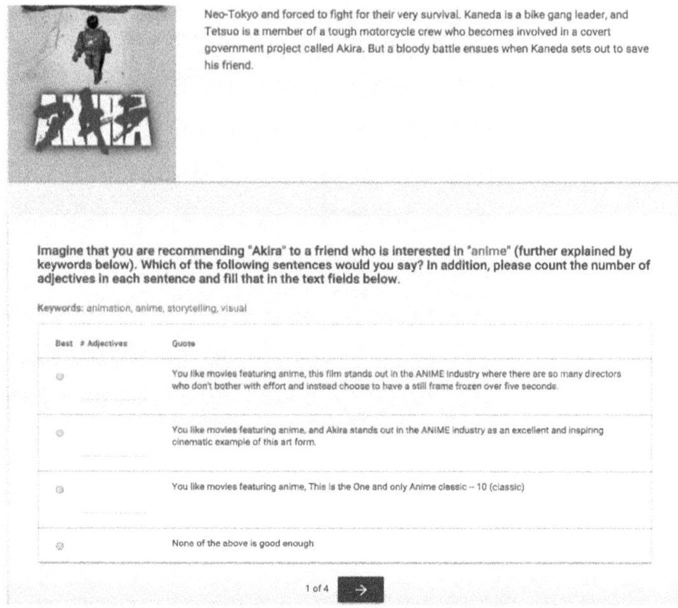

(b) Vote on best explanation

Figure 4: Interfaces used for the MapReduce work flow in the "*generate natural language explanations for the key topical dimensions*" step. The interface on the left is used in the mapper phase and interface on the right is used in the reduce phase.

5.1.2 Implementation

In our experimental system, we clustered most relevant tags to movies. We selected top 20 most relevant tags for each movie, using an automatic tagging system for movies - tag genome [23]. Alternatively, we could simply take top 20 most frequently applied tags for systems without tag genome. With manual inspection, we find that the 20 most relevant tags describe most key attributes of movies.

Then, we clustered, for each movie, the most relevant tags based on semantic similarities computed from movie reviews. To compute semantic similarities between tags, we first trained Word2Vec, a neural network embedding model [16], on a random sample of IMDB reviews (total size of 300MB); and then computed cosine similarities between latent vectors of tags from the embedding model. In training the word2vec model, we choose the dimension of 1000 for the embedding model, after inspecting outputs from the model with varying dimensions (ranging from 50 to 1500). With semantic similarities between tags, we constructed a similarity graph of the top 20 tags for each movie and ran an affinity propagation clustering algorithm [9] on the graph. After tuning the affinity propagation parameters, we generated between 4 to 6 tag clusters, which seemed appropriate with manual inspection, for each movie.

Lastly, we recruited crowdworkers from Mturk to refine algorithm generated tag clusters and label clusters. For each movie, we aggregated judgments, using majority voting, from three independent workers, each paid with $0.15. We instructed crowdworkers to 1) remove tags that did not belong with other tags in a cluster, 2) remove tags that were inappropriate (or offensive) to appear in the explanation template *"From your MovieLens profile it seems that you prefer movies tagged as ___"*, and 3) pick tags as labels for clusters. The example in Figure 3 shows the result of this step on the movie "GoodFellas".

5.2 Generate Natural Language Explanations for The Key Topical Dimensions

5.2.1 Description

Having obtained key topical dimensions for each movie in the previous process, we again use mixed computation to generate the "*[Natural Language Explanation]*" for each of the topical dimensions. As discussed in Section 2, our explanations should be short, descriptive about a certain topical dimension and well written. Given these constraints, only a human can write these explanations. However, writing explanations for a movie can be a challenging task for crowdworkers, who may have not watched the movies. Though an algorithm struggles to write explanations, it can extract relevant information about a topic dimension of a movie from user reviews, assisting crowdworkers in writing.

In addition to algorithm support, we use a two stage MapReduce [13] work flow to ensure the quality of crowd synthesized explanations. Showing algorithm-extracted text from user reviews simplifies the task of writing explanations; however, there is not a good computational method for measuring the quality of these explanations. Therefore, we had multiple independent crowdworkers synthesize explanations from selected review text in the Map phase, and then had another group of workers vote on the best explanation.

5.2.2 Implementation

To assist crowdworkers, we located and presented quotes describing a topical dimension of a movie. First, we found highly voted positive IMDB reviews for each movie. Then, for each topical dimension of the movie, we searched [2] the indexed review text for sentences containing any tag in the corresponding tag clusters. Finally, we selected top 6 quotes, considering work load for crowd workers, as ranked by the number of votes and ratings on the reviews. For example, here are quotes for the aspect "**drama**, masterpiece, storytelling, dialogue" about the movie "Goodfellas":

> *As much as the true events of Henry's life have more than likely been dramatised and glamourised to a certain extent, the essence of this film IMO is that it is still a brilliantly damning portrayal of the characters and lifestyle of mobsters.*
>
> *The consistently fine acting by the large ensemble cast (both known and unknown), the cinematography, editing, dialogue, brilliant use of music, it's all breathtaking.*
>
> *The dialogue is incredible.*
>
> *Storytelling with impeccable pacing, this is what it's like when a master composer conducts his masterpiece.*
>
> *If ever the word 'masterpiece' was meant to be used, it was for this film. 'Goodfellas' is a masterpiece, pure and simple.*

In the mapper phase, we recruited three workers to synthesize explanations for each movie, paying $0.75 to each worker. As shown in the interface in Figure 4a, we had the following instructions for crowdworkers: 1) pick one quote that best describes a topical dimension (represented as tags) of a movie from 6 quotes shown; 2) rewrite the selected quote into an explanation that follows the template "From your MovieLens profile it seems that you prefer movies tagged as *[Automatically Filled in Topical Dimension]*, ___", limited to 50 words.

In the reducer phase, we recruited three workers to vote on the best explanations from the mapper phase, paying $0.40 to each worker. As shown in the interface in Figure 4b, we asked crowdworkers to vote on the best explanation for a topical dimension (represented as tags) of a given movie. For example, the resulting explanation for the aspect of "**drama**, masterpiece, storytelling, dialogue" about "Goodfellas" is:

> *From your MovieLens profile it seems that you prefer movies tagged as drama, and storytelling with impeccable pacing? Well, Goodfellas is the cinematic equivalent of a master composer conducting his masterpiece.*

5.3 Model Users' Preferences and Present Explanations in a Personalized Fashion

5.3.1 Description

Now that we have natural language explanations for multiple topical dimensions of a movie, we present users with explanations that best match with their own topic-based preferences. First, we model a user's preferences on topic labels from her activities in the recommender system, e.g., ratings and clicks. Second, we choose a natural language explanation based on the user's favorite topical dimension (represented as a topic label) for a given movie.

[2]Using Whoosh – https://pypi.python.org/pypi/Whoosh/

5.3.2 Implementation

In MovieLens, we modeled users' preferences for tags based on their movie ratings, as shown in the equation below. More formally, the tag preference of user u on tag t, denoted as $pref_{u,t}$, was computed from the set of movies M_u that user u has rated.

$$pref_{u,t} = \frac{\sum_{m \in M_u} rating_{u,m} * rel_{m,t} + K * avg_u}{\sum_{m \in M_u} rel_{m,t} + K} \quad (1)$$

where m denote a movie in M_u, $rating_{u,m}$ denotes the user's rating on movie m and $rel_{m,t}$ denotes relevance score of tag t to movie m given by algorithmic tagging system - tag genome [23]. Note that we have a user average Bayesian Prior avg_u, which is user's average preference on tags. With the choice of $K = 20$, $pref_{u,t}$ is skewed towards the prior when user has few ratings, because few ratings can not accurately represent users' preferences on tags.

When recommending a movie to a user, we picked a topical dimension, each represented with a tag, that has highest value of $pref_{u,t}$ and presented the matching natural language explanation.

6. USER EVALUATION

We evaluated our natural language explanations, compared with a baseline of personalized tag explanation, using a within-subjects user experiment in MovieLens. We pick the tag explanation designed by Vig et al. [22], because it, similar to Pandora's explanations, represents state-of-the-art content-based explanations.

We invited MovieLens users to participate in an online survey via email invitations. From January 29, 2016, we sent emails to 4000 recent active users who have more than 15 total ratings and have logged in after November 1, 2015. 220 users finished our survey (we required users to submit at least one pair of responses for inclusion) and gave 711 responses (we allowed users to continue submitting more responses after their first).

We implemented Vig et al.'s tag explanations [22] in MovieLens as follows. For a movie recommended to a user, we ranked highly relevant tags – with a relevance score higher than 4 on a 1-5 scale – based on the user's preferences, and then picked the top 5 tags in the ranking to fill in the template "*We recommend the movie because you like the following features: [tag1, ..., tag5]*" as an explanation.

6.1 Survey Design

In the survey, participants evaluated both natural language explanations and the baseline tag explanations for randomly selected movies from a set of 100 movies with high average ratings and not rated by each participant. This set of 100 movies all had an average rating of at least 3.8 on a 5 star scale; 50 were drawn from the top-500 and 50 were drawn from the 500 to 1000 most frequently rated movies. We generated natural language explanations for the 100 movies with a cost of $3.90 per movie using the previously described system. For each participant, we randomly picked an unrated movie from the set of 100 and showed it together with a baseline or experimental explanation. We asked the participant to finish at least one pair of evaluations – one baseline, one experimental – and gave them the option to evaluate more pairs.

Rubric	Statement	Stage	Metric
Efficiency	*The explanation contains right amount of information.*	2	Raw response
	I know enough about this movie to decide whether to watch it.	1, 2, 3	Change of responses before and after seeing explanation (stage 1 and 2)
	N/A	N/A	Time spent reading explanation
Effectiveness	*I am interested in watching this movie.*	1, 2, 3	Change of responses before and after watching trailer (stage 2 and 3)
Trust	*I trust the explanation.*	2	Raw response
	The explanation reflects my preferences about this movie.	2	Raw response
Satisfaction	*The explanation is easy to understand.*	2	Raw response
	The explanation is useful.	2	Raw response
	I wish MovieLens included explanations like this.	2	Raw response

Table 1: Summary of questions asked in the 3-stage user survey. We asked users to respond on 5-point Likert scale for the above statements. The "Stage" column shows the stage the statements were shown. The "Metric" column shows how we processed responses to measure the corresponding rubrics.

We evaluated explanations according to established rubrics from past research [21]. We selected the four rubrics that are most appropriate for our natural language explanations as defined below.

- **Efficiency:** making users acquainted with items efficiently;
- **Effectiveness:** helping users make good decisions;
- **Trust:** earning trust from users;
- **Satisfaction:** offering positive user experience and overall satisfaction.

We designed a three-stage survey to measure these four qualities of recommendation explanations, asking questions when participants 1) have only seen the title, year, genre and poster of a movie, 2) have also seen the explanation, and 3) have also watched a trailer for the movie (a preview/advertisement for the movie, typically 2-3 minutes long). In each stage, we asked participants to respond to several statements on 5-point Likert scale, from "Strongly Disagree" to "Strongly Agree". In Table 1, we summarize the questions from all three stages. Note that we asked participants to respond to two statements repeatedly in all three stages to measure the *effectiveness* and *efficiency* of explanations. More specifically, we measured *effectiveness* as the change of a participant's response to "I am interested in watching this movie" before and after watching the movie trailer. The change should be small for effective explanations, which help users to accurately gauge their interest in recommendations before consumption [21]. As asking participants to watch a full movie is unrealistic in this experimental context, we approximate this action with watching a trailer. Similarly, we measured *efficiency* with time spent reading explanations and changes in participants' responses to "I know enough about this movie to decide whether to watch it." before and after seeing explanations.

6.2 Results

In this section, we describe findings on how personalized natural language explanations compare with personalized-tag-explanation baseline in the four rubrics.

We treat raw responses to survey questions as ordinal data and use non-parametric statistical models for analysis. For *effectiveness* and *efficiency* where we measure the difference between two responses, we first map 5-point Likert responses to values 1-5, calculate the difference in values (ranging from

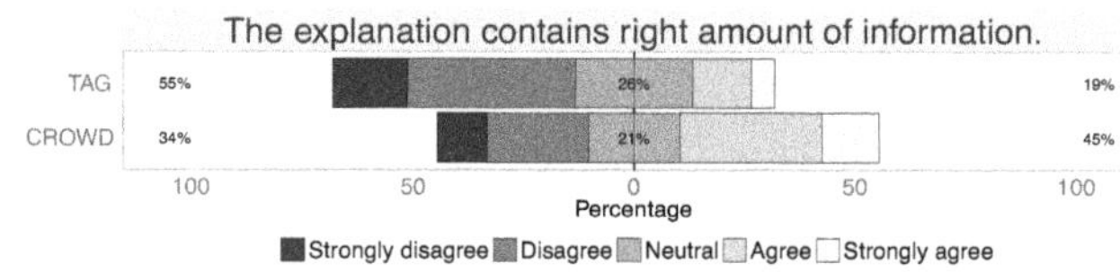

(a)

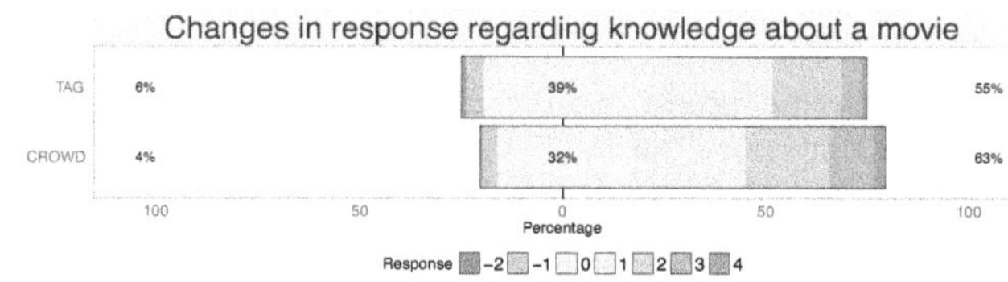

(b)

Figure 5: Survey responses to questions regarding *efficiency*. Natural language explanations - labeled with "crowd" - contained a more appropriate amount of information (a) and helped subjects more with decision-making (b).

-4 to 4) and treat the result as ordinal data. Using the Cumulative Link Mixed Models [3], we model the fixed effect of the explanation type (baseline vs. experimental) on ordinal responses, with user and movie as random effects. We include the two random effects to capture the variances of responses across users and variances caused by different movies shown in the survey.

6.2.1 Efficiency

As compared with our baseline explanations, participants perceive the natural language explanations to have more information and a more appropriate amount of information; on the other hand, they take longer to read. Participants in 45% of cases agreed with the statement "The explanation contains right amount of information." for natural language explanation, compared to only 19% for tag explanations (CLMM, $N = 711$, $p \sim 0$), as shown in Figure 5a. More specifically, natural language explanations contain more information than tag explanations, as evident by changes of responses on "I know enough about this movie to decide whether to watch it.". We observe greater changes towards positive direction when showing natural language explana-

[3]Included in 'ordinal' package of R

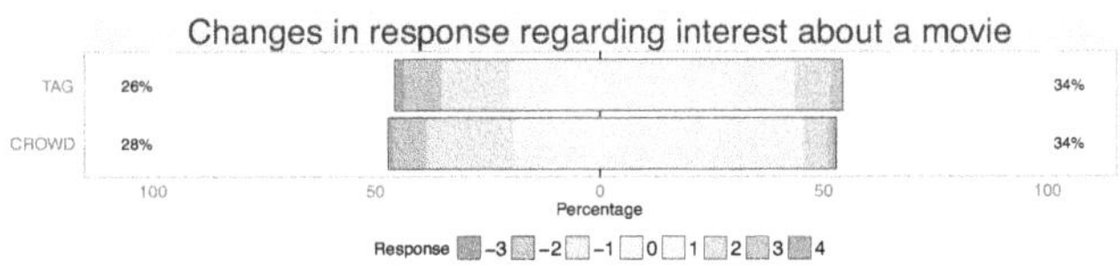

Figure 6: Difference in interest before and after watching the trailer to measure *effectiveness*;no statistically significant difference.

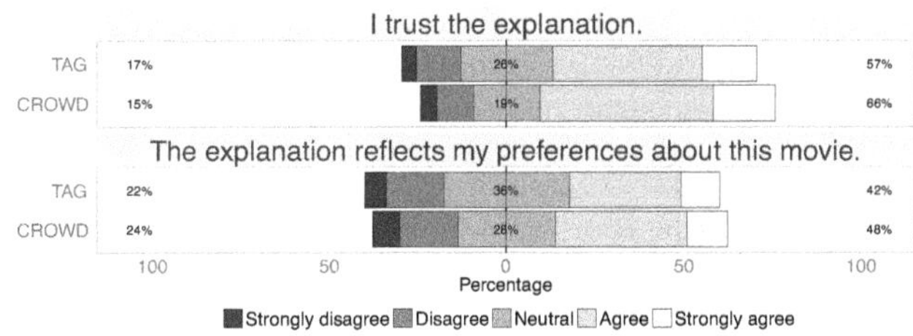

Figure 7: Survey responses to questions regarding *trust*. Participants trusted natural language explanations more than tag explanations.

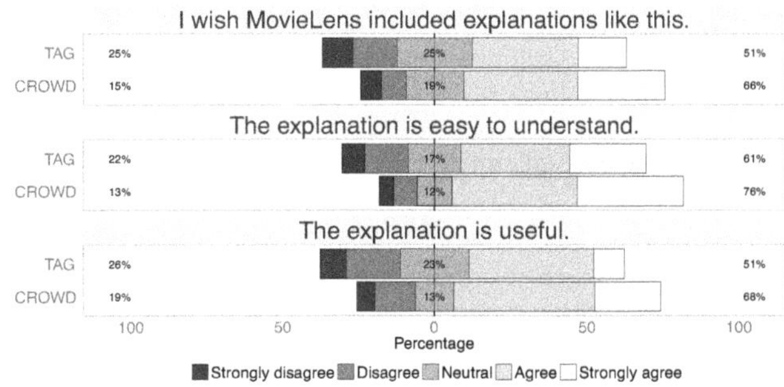

Figure 8: Survey responses to questions regarding *satisfaction*. Across the three questions, participants gave more positive responses for natural language explanations as compared with tag explanations.

tions than tag explanations (CLMM, $N = 711$, $p < 0.01$) as shown in Figure 5b. This is as expected, because natural language explanations are longer and more descriptive than tag explanations. As a result, we observe the increased time participants spent reading natural language explanations as compared with tag explanations: there is a 0.38 difference of log transformed seconds spent on reading.

6.2.2 *Effectiveness*

We observe that natural language explanations are no different than tag explanations in terms of effectiveness, which is measured as the changes of responses on "I am interested in watching this movie." when seeing explanations and having watched trailers. As shown in Figure 6, a participant's interest level, in fact, is slightly more likely to decrease for natural language explanations than for tag explanations (28% vs. 26%). This can be attributed to the fact that natural language explanations are more persuasive, hence participants may became overly excited after reading the explanations. Note that in both conditions, 1/3 of the users reported the same interest level after watching trailers; given that trailers are usually rich with information that assists in decision-making, this result is encouraging regarding the overall effectiveness of both types of explanations.

6.2.3 *Trust*

We find that participants trusted personalized natural language explanations more than the baseline tag explanations as shown in Figure 7. For the statement "I trust the explanation.", participants were significantly (CLMM, $N = 711$ [4], $p < 0.05$) more likely to agree when seeing natural language explanations than seeing tag explanations (66% vs. 57% agree). We find more agreement on the statement "The explanation reflects my preferences about this movie." for natural language explanations, but this effect is small and not statistically significant.

6.2.4 *Satisfaction*

Participants rated natural language explanations more highly on all three satisfaction questions, shown in Figure 8 (CLMM, $N = 711$, $p < 0.001$ for all three): 68% of responses agreed that natural language explanations are "useful" compared to 51% for tag explanations. Though natural language explanations are longer and contain more information, 76% of the responses agreed that they are "easy to understand" compared to 61% of the responses for tag explanations. Overall, 68% of responses wished to include natural language explanations in MovieLens compared to 51% for tag explanations.

[4]220 participants have options to evaluate more than 1 pair

7. DISCUSSION

The user experiment shows that natural language explanations generated from our process are better received by users compared to the personalized-tag-explanation baseline, which represents state-of-the-art content-based explanation. Compared with the baseline, users perceived that natural language explanations are *more trustworthy*, *contain a more appropriate amount of information* and *offer a better user experience*. To our surprise, though, natural language explanations are comparable in effectiveness for helping users make decisions on whether to take recommendations. Considering that users only spend a small amount of effort reading explanations, both content-based explanations are fairly effective in helping users make good decisions. However, apart from the content of items, many other factors may affect users' decision on whether to take recommendations, such as their trust in the system, social influence and past experience [12]. This is perhaps the reason why users perceive that natural language explanations contain richer information but are not significantly more effective in decision-making support.

Though natural language explanations written by humans are superior to automatically generated explanations, human labor is expensive and difficult to scale up. Our system addresses this challenge through a mixed computation model that combines intelligent algorithms with crowdsourced inputs. Crowdsourcing allows our system to quickly recruit large number of workers as needed. Our algorithmic processes model the content of items and extract quotes from existing user reviews, two steps that effectively reduce the human effort required per movie. In our experiment we generated natural language explanation for 100 movies at the cost of \$3.90 per movie in a short amount of time. For organizations that can afford this per-item cost, we believe our approach could be scaled to a much larger item space.

Our explanation process underscores the potential of mixed computation approaches that combine algorithms with crowd wisdom. Recent research in machine learning, especially deep neural networks, has advanced the limit of computers in image/voice recognition tasks and natural language conversations – advances that are made possible with human-generated training data. For tasks that remain too challenging for a purely algorithm solution (e.g., writing recommendation explanations) crowdsourcing may be a scalable solution. In the long run, crowd-generated data can be fed into machine learning processes to enable the automation of human work, pushing the limit of algorithms.

8. CONCLUSIONS

This paper makes the following contributions:

- We designed and implemented a novel scalable system that generates personalized natural language explanations with a mixed computation approach, which combines crowdsourcing and algorithms.
- Through a controlled experiment with 220 MovieLens users, we find that, compared with personalized tag-based explanations, personalized natural language explanations 1) contain a more appropriate amount of information, 2) earn more trust from users, and 3) make users more satisfied.

9. ACKNOWLEDGMENT

We thank volunteers from MovieLens community and anonymous workers on Mturk. We also thank NSF for funding this research with grant 1017697, 964695 and 1111201.

10. REFERENCES

[1] S. Bedathur, K. Berberich, J. Dittrich, N. Mamoulis, and G. Weikum. Interesting-phrase mining for ad-hoc text analytics. *Proceedings of the VLDB Endowment*, 3(1-2):1348–1357, 2010.

[2] M. S. Bernstein, G. Little, R. C. Miller, B. Hartmann, M. S. Ackerman, D. R. Karger, D. Crowell, and K. Panovich. Soylent: a word processor with a crowd inside. In *UIST*, 2010.

[3] S. Bostandjiev, J. O'Donovan, and T. Höllerer. TasteWeights: a visual interactive hybrid recommender system. In *RecSys*, 2012.

[4] S. Chang, P. Dai, J. Chen, and E. H. Chi. Got Many Labels?: Deriving Topic Labels from Multiple Sources for Social Media Posts using Crowdsourcing and Ensemble Learning. In *WWW*, 2015.

[5] S. Chang, P. Dai, L. Hong, S. Cheng, Z. Tianjiao, and C. Ed. AppGrouper: Knowledge-based Interactive Clustering Tool for App Search Results. In *IUI*, 2016.

[6] S. Chang, M. F. Harper, L. He, and L. G. Terveen. CrowdLens: Experimenting with Crowd-Powered Recommendation and Explanation . In *ICWSM*, 2016.

[7] J. Cheng and M. S. Bernstein. Flock: Hybrid crowd-machine learning classifiers. In *CSCW*, 2015.

[8] A. El-Kishky, Y. Song, C. Wang, C. R. Voss, and J. Han. Scalable topical phrase mining from text corpora. *Proceedings of the VLDB Endowment*, 8(3):305–316, 2014.

[9] B. J. Frey and D. Dueck. Clustering by passing messages between data points. *Science*, 315:972–976, 2007.

[10] F. M. Harper, D. Raban, S. Rafaeli, and J. A. Konstan. Predictors of answer quality in online Q&A sites. In *CHI*, 2008.

[11] J. L. Herlocker, J. A. Konstan, and J. Riedl. Explaining collaborative filtering recommendations. In *CSCW*, 2000.

[12] A. Jameson, M. C. Willemsen, A. Felfernig, M. Gemmis, P. Lops, G. Semeraro, and L. Chen. *Recommender Systems Handbook*, chapter Human Decision Making and Recommender Systems, pages 611–648. Springer US, Boston, MA, 2015.

[13] A. Kittur, B. Smus, S. Khamkar, and R. Kraut. Crowdforge: Crowdsourcing complex work. *UIST*, 2011.

[14] J. Liu, J. Shang, C. Wang, X. Ren, and J. Han. Mining quality phrases from massive text corpora. 2015.

[15] S. M. McNee, J. Riedl, and J. A. Konstan. Being accurate is not enough. In *CHI EA*, 2006.

[16] T. Mikolov, I. Sutskever, K. Chen, G. S. Corrado, and J. Dean. Distributed representations of words and phrases and their compositionality. In *Advances in neural information processing systems*, pages 3111–3119, 2013.

[17] P. Organisciak, J. Teevan, S. Dumais, R. C. Miller, and A. T. Kalai. A Crowd of Your Own: Crowdsourcing for On-Demand Personalization. In *HCOMP*, 2014.

[18] R. Sinha and K. Swearingen. The role of transparency in recommender systems. In *CHI EA*, 2002.

[19] C. A. Thompson, M. H. Göker, and P. Langley. A personalized system for conversational recommendations. *Journal of Artificial Intelligence Research*, 21(1):393–428, Mar. 2004.

[20] N. Tintarev and J. Masthoff. Evaluating the effectiveness of explanations for recommender systems. *User Modeling and User-Adapted Interaction*, 22:399–439, 2012.

[21] N. Tintarev and J. Masthoff. *Recommender Systems Handbook*, chapter Explaining Recommendations: Design and Evaluation, pages 353–382. Springer US, Boston, MA, 2015.

[22] J. Vig, S. Sen, and J. Riedl. Tagsplanations. In *IUI*, 2008.

[23] J. Vig, S. Sen, and J. Riedl. The Tag Genome. *ACM Trans. on Interactive Intelligent Systems*, 2(3):1–44, sep 2012.

[24] W. Wang and I. Benbasat. Recommendation agents for electronic commerce: Effects of explanation facilities on trusting beliefs. *J. Manage. Inf. Syst.*, 23(4):217–246, May 2007.

[25] S.-H. Yang, A. Kolcz, A. Schlaikjer, and P. Gupta. Large-scale high-precision topic modeling on twitter. In *KDD*, Aug 2014.

Domain-Aware Grade Prediction and Top-n Course Recommendation

Asmaa Elbadrawy
Computer Science
University of Minnesota, Twin Cities
asmaa@cs.umn.edu

George Karypis
Computer Science
University of Minnesota, Twin Cities
karypis@cs.umn.edu

ABSTRACT

Automated course recommendation can help deliver personalized and effective college advising and degree planning. Nearest neighbor and matrix factorization based collaborative filtering approaches have been applied to student-course grade data to help students select suitable courses. However, the student-course enrollment patterns exhibit grouping structures that are tied to the student and course academic features, which lead to grade data that are not missing at random (NMAR). Existing approaches for dealing with NMAR data, such as Response-aware and context-aware matrix factorization, do not model NMAR data in terms of the user and item features and are not designed with the characteristics of grade data in mind. In this work we investigate how the student and course academic features influence the enrollment patterns and we use these features to define student and course groups at various levels of granularity. We show how these groups can be used to design grade prediction and top-n course ranking models for neighborhood-based user collaborative filtering, matrix factorization and popularity-based ranking approaches. These methods give lower grade prediction error and more accurate top-n course rankings than the other methods that do not take domain knowledge into account.

Keywords

Grade Prediction, Top-n Course Ranking, Multi-Granularity Grouping

1. INTRODUCTION

While the flexibility of degree requirements provides college students with ample choices, it can complicate course selection. From among the courses that the students are eligible to take in the next term, they need to select the ones that they like, they are expected to perform well in, and also satisfy their degree requirements. Efficient college advising is essential for helping students select the right courses and thus, maintain high student retention rates and timely graduation. Automated course recommendation can help improve college advising by recommending courses that are suitable for the students degrees. Moreover, predicting student grades in the next term can help students and educators make informed decisions about course enrollments in order to produce better learning outcomes.

Collaborative filtering approaches have been previously used for grade prediction and course recommendation [23, 6, 8]. The majority of these methods rely on user-based collaborative filtering (User-CF) [11] which makes recommendations by relating to the courses that were taken by similar students. Recently, techniques based on matrix factorization (MF) have been used for movie and product recommendations [14] and also applied for course recommendation and grade prediction [27, 26].

The grade data has special characteristics as the student-course enrollments are influenced by the academic features (e.g., student majors, academic levels and course subjects). Consequently, the student-course grade matrix exhibits grouping structures as students with certain majors tend to enroll in courses of certain subjects, resulting in not missing at random (NMAR) data. Response-aware MF uses missing data theory to model the NMAR user response patterns [16]. However, the response patterns are not tied to the user and item features. Features-based MF methods can incorporate the user and/or item features into the prediction model. However, they do not explicitly model how the features determine the grouping structures in the data.

In this paper we analyze grade data and show how the student and course academic features determine the enrollment patterns. We use these features to define student and course groups and show how they can be incorporated in matrix factorization, user-based collaborative filtering, and popularity-based ranking.

We investigate various ways to define the groups at multiple levels of granularity using different amounts of academic features. We show that in some cases the small sample sizes associated with finer granularity groups make the prediction models prone to poor generalization, especially with matrix factorization based methods. To overcome this issue, we build multiple models using the various granularity groups. We then generate multiple grade predictions and combine them based on the sample sizes associated with the various groups.

We tested our methods on a dataset obtained from the University of Minnesota. The dataset spans 13 academic years and includes over 1,700,000 grades. Our results show that the methods that utilize finer groups give significantly

RecSys '16, September 15-19, 2016, Boston , MA, USA

DOI: http://dx.doi.org/10.1145/2959100.2959133

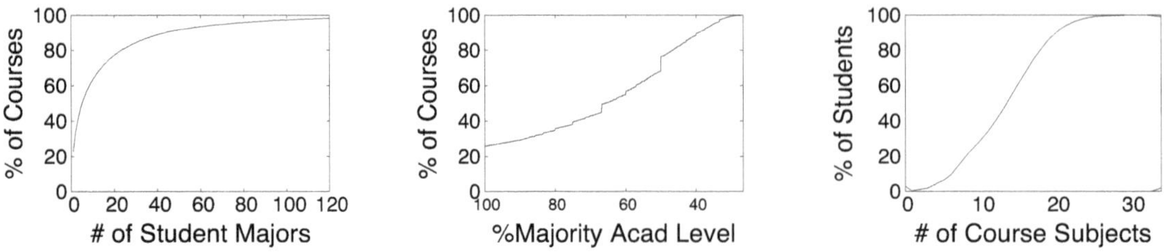

Figure 1: Cumulative percentage plots for student-course enrollments in a grade dataset. Left: percentage of courses vs. number of student majors. An (x,y) point indicates that y% of the courses were taken by students from at most x majors. For example, 40% of the courses were taken by students from at most three majors. Middle: percentage of courses vs. percentage of students belonging to the academic level that most of the enrolled students belong to. An (x,y) point indicates that for y% of the courses, at least x% of the enrolled students belong to the same academic level. For example, for 27% of the courses, at least 96% of the enrolled students belong to the same academic level. Right: percentage of students vs. number of subjects for the courses they have enrolled in. An (x,y) point indicates that y% of the students took courses that belong to at most x different subjects. For example, 70% of the students took courses that cover at most 16 different subjects.

more accurate top-n course rankings than the methods that utilize coarser groups and than other methods from the literature; even when domain knowledge is used to pre-filter the recommended courses. Moreover, defining the groups using the academic features gives better top-n rankings than clustering the students and courses using the enrollment data. For grade prediction, utilizing the finer groups gives more accurate predictions than the coarser groups only when they are associated with reasonable sample sizes. For the matrix factorization methods, where model training suffers more from the sample-size issue, combining the various model predictions while accounting for the sample sizes associated with the model parameters gives higher prediction accuracy than the various individual MF models and than the other methods from the literature.

2. DEFINITIONS AND NOTATIONS

Let G denote the grade matrix; each row in G represents a student, denoted by s, and each column represents a course, denoted by c. The entry $g_{s,c}$ in G represents the grade obtained by student s in course c. A predicted grade is denoted by $\hat{g}_{s,c}$.

3. CHARACTERISTICS OF GRADE DATA

In a university setting, each student enrolls in a certain college/school and declares a certain major. Each student selects from among a variety of courses to take in order to fulfill the requirements of his major (also referred to as the degree requirements). Each course has a subject that it falls under and a level that describes its difficulty. As the student takes more courses, his academic level advances and he can take higher level courses.

Students tend to enroll in courses that are related to their majors and are appropriate to their academic levels. This is illustrated in Figure 1 which shows various characteristics that were extracted from a grade dataset that was obtained from the University of Minnesota. These plots show that: (i) each course is taken by students that belong to a limited number of majors; (ii) each course is mostly taken by students belonging to one academic level; and (iii) each student takes courses that cover a limited number of subjects. For example, from Figure 1-left we can see that 22% of the courses are taken by students that all come from one major, and 80% of the courses are taken by students that come from at most 24 majors. From Figure 1-middle we can see that for 50% of the courses, at least 66% of the enrolled students belonged to the same academic level. Finally, from Figure 1-right we can see 90% of the students took courses that covered less than 20 subjects.

These characteristics imply that the missing entries in the grade matrix are not missing at random. This resulted because students with certain student features tend to enroll in courses with certain course features. We refer to this as the *grouping structures* in the grade data.

4. RELATED WORK

Response aware techniques [16, 17, 12] model NMAR data by utilizing a data model that is based on missing data theory. The method proposed in [16] modified probabilistic matrix factorization by introducing two variations to model NMAR data. The first variation assumes that the probability of observing a rating depends only on the value of the rating. The second variation assumes that the probability also depends on the user and the item latent factors. None of these methods incorporate the user and item features that influence the response patterns.

Feature-based MF methods incorporate user and/or item features within the rating prediction or the top-n ranking models. The method proposed in [2] linearly transformed the user and item features to the latent space in order to predict a user's preference over a given item. Other methods incorporated the features within a top-n recommendation model in order to estimate user preferences or bias the recommendations based on the item features [18, 10]. None of these methods were designed to address how the user and item features determine the grouping structures in the data.

Context-aware methods make recommendations in accordance with the different contexts [4, 13, 3, 25, 28, 1]. Some of these methods utilized the context information to pre-filter items. Other techniques incorporated contextual information within the model.

Methods for course recommendation applied various data mining techniques to tackle the problem. The work done in [5] applied association rule mining to recommend relevant courses. The method in [15] estimated course recommendation scores by accumulating weights for subject importance within the study field, satisfied prerequisites and the extent by which a course broadens the student's knowledge state. Methods for course recommendation with constraints focused on satisfying the degree program requirements [20,

22, 21, 19]. They take course prerequisites into consideration in order to generate valid course recommendations. They focus on finding a short path to fulfill the degree requirements and thus, reduce time to graduation.

5. DOMAIN-AWARE METHODS FOR COURSE RECOMMENDATION

We develop methods that model the grouping structures of the grade data by using the academic features to define student and course groups. These groups are defined at various levels of granularity by utilizing various amounts of features. Then they are incorporated within the recommendation methods for the purpose of performing (1) grade prediction and (2) top-n course ranking.

For grade prediction, the grade of a student s in a course c should be predicted by relating to how students of the same group as s performed in c, and how s performed in courses of the same group as c. Since the groups are defined at different levels of granularity, various models can be built that account for various academic features. In general, the finer groups are more homogeneous and thus, utilizing them can give more accurate predictions than utilizing the coarser groups. However, based on how the groups are incorporated into the prediction models, some models can be affected when the finer groups have small sample sizes and they can become prone to poor generalization. Such cases are addressed by building multiple models using different granularity groups and combining the predictions of all the models based on the group sample sizes.

For top-n course ranking, it is required to generate a list of n relevant courses for each student to consider enrolling in them. Unlike other recommendation scenarios, course recommendation has special considerations. Students need to enroll in courses that they are interested in, and that fulfill their degree requirements. Accordingly, students sometimes need to take some courses in order to fulfill some degree requirement, regardless of their expected grade in these courses. Moreover, in the typical user-item-rating scenario, when a user likes an item, he gives that item a high rating. This is not always the case with the student-course-grade scenario where a student might like a course, but this does not necessarily mean that he will get a high grade when he takes that course. Based on that, course ranking should rely on the enrollment patterns more than relying on the expected grades. In this sense, the grade matrix is considered as binary where all grades are set to 1's and the rest of the entries are considered 0's. Similar to grade prediction, multiple models can be built by utilizing various student and course groups. Also, utilizing finer groups can give more accurate recommendations that the coarser groups. However, unlike with grade prediction, the fact that some finer groups are associated with small sample sizes is an indicator for less relevant courses and as such, should not hurt model generalization.

We next describe how to define the multi-granularity groups.

5.1 Defining the Multi-Granularity Student and Course Groups

The student groups define the various student subpopulations that can take a course. At the coarsest level, the set of all students is defined without using any student academic features. Then finer groups are defined by using one student feature at a time to segment the student group(s) further based on the value of that feature to give smaller and more homogeneous groups. The course groups are defined similarly using the course academic features.

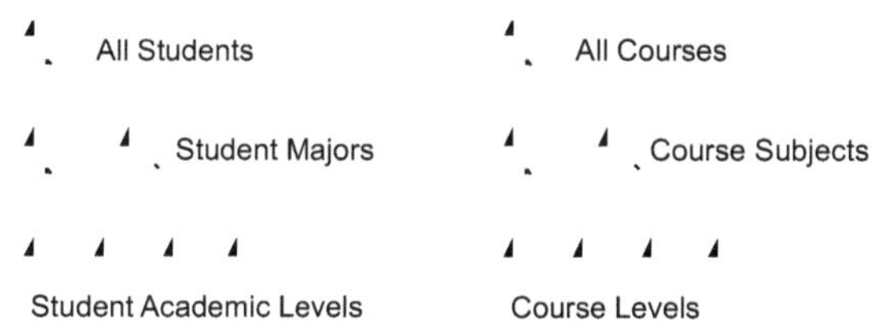

Figure 2: An illustrative example for defining the student(left) and course(right) multi-granularity groups.

One way to define the student groups is shown in Figure 2-left. The node at the top represents the group of all students. The second level segments the students based on their majors and it has one node (group) for each major. The third level segments the students further based on their academic levels and it has one node for each academic level within each major. Similarly, the course groups can be defined as shown in Figure 2-Right. The node at the top represents the group of all courses. The second level segments the courses based on their subjects and it has one node (group) for each subject. The third level segments the courses further based on their levels and it has one node for each course level within each subject. In the rest of the paper, we will use the groups defined in Figure 2 as an illustrative example.

We next describe how the groups are incorporated into popularity based ranking, neighborhood based user collaborative filtering and matrix factorization.

5.2 Popularity based Top-n Course Ranking

A popularity ranking scheme ranks the courses based on how frequently they were taken by the students. In our case, we rank the courses for a student s based on how frequently they were taken by students of the same group as s. The ranking score of course c for a given student s is computed as $|\varphi_{s\rightarrow c}|$, where $\varphi_{s\rightarrow c}$ is the set of students in the same group as s that have taken c and $|\mathcal{X}|$ represents the cardinality of set $\mathcal{X}$.

Utilizing a different student group from the multi granularity groups gives a different model. The various models are referred to as Grp-Pop-h_{φ_s}, where h_{φ_s} is the student group level in the multi-level groups. For example, the model that utilizes the groups at the second level of the multi-level student groups in Figure 2-left is referred to as Grp-Pop-2.

5.3 User based Collaborative Filtering

User-CF predicts a grade of a student s in a course c by relating to how students that have taken same courses as s performed in c as

$$\hat{g}_{s,c} = \bar{g}_s + \frac{\sum_{s' \in N_s} \text{sim}(s,s')(g_{s',c} - \bar{g}_{s'})}{\sum_{s' \in N_s} |\text{sim}(s,s')|}, \quad (1)$$

where $\bar{g}_s$ is the average grade of s, N_s is the set of neighbor students to s, and $\text{sim}(s, s')$ is some similarity between students s and s'.

5.3.1 Grade Prediction

For grade prediction, the neighborhood set N_s is selected based on the student groups as follows. Any student in the same group as s and has taken at least n_c courses that were taken by s is selected as part of N_s. Moreover, the size of N_s is limited so that it only contains the n_n students that are most similar to s. The threshold parameters n_c and n_n are fine-tuned using a validation set. In the case where not enough neighbors are found, the grade is then estimated as

$$\hat{g}_{s,c} = \frac{1}{2}(\bar{g}_s + \bar{g}_c),$$

where $\bar{g}_c$ is the average grade for course c.

By utilizing different student groups, different models are built. The various models are referred to as User-CF-h_{φ_s}. For example, the model that utilizes the groups at the second level of the multi-level student groups in Figure 2-left is referred to as User-CF-2.

5.3.2 Top-n Course Ranking

Since in this case the enrollment patterns are the main indicators and not the grade values, G is converted into a binary matrix with all grades set to 1's and other entries considered as 0's. The recommendation scores are then estimated as in Equation 1. In practice this gives better recommendations than using the actual grade values. In the case where not enough neighbors are found, this indicates an irrelevant course and the course rank is set to 0.

5.4 Matrix Factorization

MF predicts the grade of student s in course c as

$$\hat{g}_{s,c} = b_s + b_c + \boldsymbol{u}_s^t \boldsymbol{v}_c, \quad (2)$$

where b_s and b_c are the bias terms of s and c, and $\boldsymbol{u}_s$ and $\boldsymbol{v}_c$ are the latent factor vectors of s and c, respectively.

5.4.1 Grade Prediction

While the literature is rich with feature-based and context-aware MF techniques that can be modified and used as a framework to implement our ideas, we choose to modify the context-aware technique in [4] as we find it most relevant. This technique accounts for context via additional bias terms that are defined for each (item, context) pair.

In our case, we use the student groups to describe the contexts in which a course is taken, and use the course groups to describe the contexts in which a student takes a course. Considering the example in Figure 2, the third level student groups describe course-side contexts in terms of the student majors and academic levels. Similarly, the third level course groups describe student-side contexts in terms of the course subjects and levels. Accordingly, we define multiple bias terms per student and per course to account for the various student- and course-side contexts. The recommendation score of a given student s and course c is estimated as

$$\hat{g}_{s,c} = b_s^{\varphi_c} + b_c^{\varphi_s} + \boldsymbol{u}_s^t \boldsymbol{v}_c, \quad (3)$$

where $b_s^{\varphi_c}$ is some student bias that accounts for the context described by the course group of c, $b_c^{\varphi_s}$ is some course bias that accounts for the context described by the student group of s, and u_s and u_c are the latent factor vectors for s and c, respectively.

Multiple models can be defined using the different groups. For the example in Figure 2, considering the various student and course group combinations, we can build nine different models. The various models are referred to as MF-h_{φ_s}-h_{φ_c}, where h_{φ_s} is the level of the student group, which defines the granularity of the course bias, and similarly h_{φ_c} is the level of the course group, which defines the granularity of the student bias. For example, considering Figure 2, MF-1-3 is used to refer to the model that uses the coarsest-grain student groups (at the 1st level) to define the coarsest-grain course biases, and uses the finest-grain course groups (at the 3rd level) to define the finest-grain student biases.

Since the finer groups are more homogeneous than the coarser groups, the MF models that utilize them can give more accurate predictions. However, the student groups are recognized through defining multiple biases for each course, and similarly with the course groups and the student biases. For example, if we have 2,000 student groups and 1,000 course groups, then 2,000 biases are defined per course and 1,000 biases are defined per student. Only a handful of biases for each student/course are associated with some data points. and the remaining majority of the biases are associated with very few or no data points. Therefore, the models that utilize finer groups can become prone to poor generalization. To understand why this happens, consider the following example. Assume an Artificial Intelligence course c that is offered by the Computer Science department was taken by 47 Computer Science major students and 2 other Liberal Arts major students. If we define student groups using the major, and if we have 100 different majors, then c will have one bias associated with 47 data points, one bias associated 2 data points and 98 biases associated with 0 data points. Obviously, the biases with 0 and 2 data points cannot be as accurately estimated as the other bias.

To overcome this problem, we build multiple models utilizing various groups and use them to generate multiple predictions. Then the predictions are combined based on the sample sizes that are associated with the bias terms of the various models as described next.

5.4.1.1 Combining the Predictions of the Different MF Models.

Before discussing how the various model predictions are combined, it is worth noting that the user and item latent factors are not shared among the various models but each model has its own factors. The various predictions are combined while accounting for the associated sample sizes as follows. Each model MF-h_{φ_s}-h_{φ_c} has a combination weight given by

$$w_{\{h_{\varphi_s}, h_{\varphi_c}\}} = sup(b_s^{\varphi_c}) + sup(b_c^{\varphi_s}),$$

where $sup(b_s^{\varphi_c})$ is the sample size (i.e., number of training samples) associated with the bias term $b_s^{\varphi_c}$. The total weight is aggregated over the individual model weights as

$$w_{total} = \sum_{h_{\varphi_s}} \sum_{h_{\varphi_c}} w_{\{h_{\varphi_s}, h_{\varphi_c}\}}.$$

The final prediction is then given by

$$\hat{g}_{\{s,c\}} = \sum_{h_{\varphi_s}} \sum_{h_{\varphi_c}} \alpha_{\{h_{\varphi_s}, h_{\varphi_c}\}} \times \frac{w_{\{h_{\varphi_s}, h_{\varphi_c}\}}}{w_{total}} \times \hat{g}_{\{s,c\}}^{\{h_{\varphi_s}, h_{\varphi_c}\}}, \quad (4)$$

where $\hat{g}_{\{s,c\}}^{\{h_{\varphi_s}, h_{\varphi_c}\}}$ is the prediction given by model MF-h_{φ_s}-h_{φ_c}, and $\alpha_{\{h_{\varphi_s}, h_{\varphi_c}\}}$ is some global combination weight for

Table 1: The student and course features used to define various multi-level groups and the resulting number of groups.

	2nd level student feature	3rd level student feature	2nd level course feature	3rd level course feature
H-1	student major (565)	student academic level (565×4)	course subject (570)	course level (570×8)
H-2	student academic level (4)	student major (565×4)	course subject (570)	course level (570×8)
H-3	student college (10)	student academic level (10×4)	course subject (570)	course level (570×8)
H-4	student academic level (4)	student college (4×10)	course subject (570)	course level (570×8)
H-5	student major (565)	student academic level (565×4)	course level (8)	course subject (8×570)
H-6	Students/courses are clustered by splitting a nearest-neighbor similarity graph into k-clusters via min-cut graph partitioning. Clustering is repeated 2 times with (k_1=10, k_2=30 for students) and (k_1=5, k_2=25 for courses) to generate 3-level groups.			

that model. This method is referred to as INTRP-MF, the interpolative multi-granularity MF method.

5.4.1.2 *Model Parameter Estimation.*

Parameter estimation is done via a step-wise optimization process in which the parameters of each of the individual models are first estimated, and then the $\alpha_{\{h_{\varphi_s},h_{\varphi_c}\}}$ global combination weights are estimated.

The parameters of each of the various models are estimated via a regularized optimization process of the form

$$\underset{\Theta}{\text{minimize}}\ \mathcal{L}(\Theta) + \mathcal{R}(\Theta), \quad (5)$$

where Θ represents the model parameters, $\mathcal{L}(\Theta)$ is the loss function and $\mathcal{R}(\Theta)$ is a regularization function to avoid overfitting. We use a squared error loss function of the form

$$\mathcal{L}(\Theta) = \sum_{g_{s,c}\in G} (g_{s,c} - \hat{g}_{s,c}(\Theta))^2,$$

where $\hat{g}_{s,c}(\Theta)$ is given by Equation 3. This loss function is suitable as the letter grades can be transformed to numeric values. The regularization function $\mathcal{R}(\Theta)$ is given by

$$\mathcal{R}(\Theta) = \lambda_u(||U||_F^2 + ||B_S^{\varphi_C}||_F^2) + \lambda_v(||V||_F^2 + ||B_C^{\varphi_S}||_F^2), \quad (6)$$

where λ_u and λ_v are the regularization parameters and $||U||_F$ is the ℓ-2 norm of the matrix U.

After the parameters of each model are estimated, the $\alpha_{\{h_{\varphi_s},h_{\varphi_c}\}}$ weights are estimated by minimizing a mean squared error loss as well.

5.4.2 *Top-n Course Ranking*

We use a learning to rank approach to generate personalized course recommendations per student. The rank of course c for student s is estimated as in Equation 3. The model parameters of each model are estimated using a personalized pair-wise ranking loss function [7] of the form

$$\mathcal{L}(\Theta) = -\sum_{s\in G}\sum_{c\in\mathcal{C}_s}\sum_{c'\in\bar{\mathcal{C}}_{\varphi_s}} \phi(\hat{g}_{s,c}(\Theta) - \hat{g}_{s,c'}(\Theta)), \quad (7)$$

where $\mathcal{C}_s$ is the set of courses taken by student s, $\bar{\mathcal{C}}_{\varphi_s}$ is the set of courses never taken by any student in the same group as s, and $\phi(z) = e^{-z}$. Although $\hat{g}_{s,c}(\Theta)$ is estimated using Equation 3, it represents a ranking score in this case and not a predicted grade because the model parameters are estimated using the ranking-based loss function. We use the same regularization function as in Equation 6 to avoid overfitting.

The ranking loss function is of order $O(n_u \times n_i)$, where n_u and n_i are the number of students and courses, respectively. The learning time can be reduced by sampling, for each student, from among his $\bar{\mathcal{C}}_{\varphi_s}$ instead of considering the whole set. If the number of samples is of order $O(\mathcal{C}_s)$, the run time is reduced to $O(NNZ_G)$, the number of non-zero entries in the grade matrix G.

6. EXPERIMENTAL DESIGN

In this section we describe the dataset that is used for evaluation, the evaluation metrics, the methods that we compare against, how the various methods are trained and how the student and course groups are defined.

6.1 Dataset

The dataset used for evaluation is obtained from the University of Minnesota. It spans 13 academic years and it has over 1.7 million letter grades that involve around 60,000 students, 10,000 courses, 10 colleges, 570 course subjects, 565 majors, 4 academic levels and 8 course levels. The grades are converted into numbers according to the 4.0 GPA standard[1]. All Pass/Fail grades are removed from the dataset.

The last term in the dataset is used for testing and the rest are used for training and model selection. The last term in the training set is used for model selection and the rest is used for training. Grades of the students that have graduated before the test term are included in the training set. Grades for the new courses and the new students that first appear in the test term are excluded.

6.2 Defining the Student and Course Groups

We experimented with six different ways to define the multi-level groups, namely, H-1 up to H-6. Each one contains three levels of student and course groups and thus, the corresponding MF models are referred to as MF-1-1 up to MF-3-3. The various User-CF and Grp-Pop methods that are defined based on the student groups are referred to as User-CF-1 up to User-CF-3, and Grp-Pop-1 up to Grp-Pop-3, respectively. The features used to define the groups are listed in Table 1.

6.3 Evaluation Metrics

Methods are evaluated for (1)the accuracy of top-n course ranking and (2)the accuracy of grade prediction.

Course top-n ranking is evaluated with **Recall@n** which is computed for each student s as

$$Recall@n_s = \frac{n_{s,n}}{n_{t_s}},$$

where $n_{s,n}$ is the number of courses that appeared in the test set of s and in his list of n recommended courses, and n_{t_s} is the number of courses in the test set of s. Recall@n is computed by averaging over Recall@n_s for all s and for n in the range [1,10]. The relative methods performances did not change with n and so, we only report results for $n = 5$.

Grade prediction accuracy is evaluated by computing the

[1]See "http://www.collegeboard.com/html/academicTracker-howtoconvert.html" for letter grade-grade point conversion.

Root Mean Squared Error on the testing grades $\mathcal{G}_{test}$ as

$$RMSE = \sqrt{\frac{\sum_{g_{s,c} \in \mathcal{G}_{test}} (g_{s,c} - \hat{g}_{s,c})^2}{|\mathcal{G}_{test}|}}.$$

6.4 Comparison with Other Methods

We compare the performance of our method against the following approaches:

User Collaborative Filtering: User-CF with Pearson correlation for user similarity [9].

Matrix Factorization: Typical MF as described in Equation 2.

Response-aware Matrix Factorization: The context aware response model described in [16]. We implemented RAPMFc as we think it is the most relevant because it captures the probability that rating an item depend on the rating value, the user and the item.

Regression Latent Factor Models: The feature-based MF-based method described in [2], referred to as RLFM. We used libFM [24] to generate the results for grade prediction only as it is not a top-n ranking technique.

Ensemble-based Grade Combination: We compare the predictive performance of the the interpolative multi granularity method INTRP-MF against various ensembles. The Minimum, Maximum, Average and Median ensembles are considered where the minimum, maximum, average and median grades are selected as the final prediction, respectively. These ensembles are referred to as MIN-En, MAX-En, AVG-En and MED-En, respectively. We also include results for the interpolative method with excluding the α parameters in order to show how the sample-size-based weights perform. This method is referred to as WT-MF and it does not need a secondary learning step as the α weights are omitted.

6.5 Model Training and Selection

For training the MF models, we tried a number of latent factors in the range [1,10] and λ_u and λ_v in the range [1e-4,5]. The values that gave the best results were latent factors in the range [1,3], λ_u and λ_v in the range [0.1,3.5].

For User-CF, we have tried values for the parameters, n_n and n_c in the range [1,50]. The best results were obtained with values in the range [2,36].

For RAPMFc, we have tried parameter values for λ_u, λ_v and λ_μ in the range $[10^{-3},10^{1}]$, β in the range [0,1] and number of factors in the range [1,10]. The values that gave the best results were in the range [0.01, 0.1] for λ_u, λ_v, 1 for λ_μ, 0.01 for β and [7,10] for l.

For grade prediction, and top-n ranking, model selection is based on the lowest RMSE and the highest Recall@n on the validation set, respectively.

7. EXPERIMENTAL RESULTS

We assess the effectiveness of the developed methods in order to answer the following questions:

Q1. Does incorporating the groups in the various methods lead to better top-n course rankings?

Q2. Does incorporating the groups in the various methods lead to better grade predictions?

Q3. How is the grade prediction performance of the MF models defined using various groups affected by the sample sizes that are associated with the biases?

Table 2: Recall@5 for the various groups. The highest Recall@5 for each set of methods within each group (column) is underlined.

Model	H-1	H-2	H-3	H-4	H-5	H-6
Grp-Pop-1	0.015	0.015	0.015	0.015	0.015	0.015
Grp-Pop-2	0.172	0.039	0.046	0.039	0.172	0.015
Grp-Pop-3	0.236	0.236	0.094	0.094	0.236	0.017
User-CF-1	0.046	0.046	0.046	0.046	0.046	0.046
User-CF-2	0.050	0.034	0.037	0.034	0.050	0.035
User-CF-3	0.054	0.054	0.037	0.037	0.054	0.036
MF-1-1	0.013	0.013	0.013	0.013	0.013	0.013
MF-2-1	0.174	0.066	0.047	0.066	0.174	0.021
MF-3-1	0.239	0.239	0.100	0.104	0.239	0.018
MF-1-2	0.041	0.041	0.040	0.041	0.018	0.021
MF-2-2	0.174	0.133	0.055	0.133	0.169	0.021
MF-3-2	0.238	0.238	0.109	0.115	0.230	0.018
MF-1-3	0.023	0.023	0.021	0.022	0.018	0.020
MF-2-3	0.172	0.081	0.047	0.081	0.171	0.019
MF-3-3	0.236	0.236	0.100	0.105	0.236	0.017
RAPMFc	0.023					

7.1 Top-n Course Recommendation Results

Prior to ranking the courses for each student, we apply a domain-aware pre-filtering in which courses that have never been taken by at least one student of the same major and academic level as the target student are filtered out. This approach performed the best among other similar pre-filtering rules that utilize various academic features.

Table 2 shows the Recall@5 for all the methods across all groups. Notice that the typical popularity ranking, User-CF and MF schemes are equivalent to Grp-Pop-1, User-CF-1 and MF-1-1, respectively.

For the popularity methods, Grp-Pop-3 and Grp-Pop-2 outperform Grp-Pop-1. Across the six groups H-1 to H-6, Grp-Pop-3 gives the highest recall.

For the User-CF methods, User-CF-2 and User-CF-3 only outperform User-CF-1 when the groups are defined in terms of the student majors (H-1, H-2 and H-5). For these groups, User-CF-3 gives the highest recall. For the other groups, User-CF-1 gives the highest recall.

For the MF methods, the ones that utilize groups outperform MF-1-1 by an order of magnitude. In general, defining the course biases using finer student groups gives better recall as it is the case, for example, with MF-1-2, MF-2-2 and MF-3-2 in H-1. On the other hand, defining student biases using finer course groups does not always give better recall as it is the case with MF-2-2 and MF-2-3 in H-2, H-3 and H-4. We believe this is related to the sample sizes associated with the student biases. Since each student takes a limited number of courses, the models utilizing the finest course groups have less than 2 training points associated with their student biases on average. RAPMFc performs better than MF-1-1 but worse than all models that utilize groups across H-1 to H-6.

Across all methods, the highest recalls are given by MF-3-2 and MF-3-1 which slightly surpass MF-3-3 and Grp-Pop-3. All User-CF methods outperform RAPMFc, MF-1-1, MF-1-2 and MF-1-3 for all groups. MF models with finer student groups, like MF-3-1, MF-3-2 and MF-3-3, always outperform all User-CF methods. The student groups that are defined in using majors (H-1, H-2 and H-5) give higher recall than the groups defined using colleges (H-3 and H-4). The clustering-based groups give the lowest recall, indicating that the clustering could not capture the groups that are defined by the student and course academic features.

Table 3: RMSE for all groups. The lowest RMSE for each set of methods within each group (column) is underlined.

Model	H-1	H-2	H-3	H-4	H-5	H-6
User-CF-1	0.714	0.714	0.714	0.714	0.714	0.714
User-CF-2	0.705	0.704	0.706	0.704	0.705	0.706
User-CF-3	0.707	0.707	0.706	0.706	0.707	0.709
MF-1-1	0.666	0.666	0.666	0.666	0.666	0.679
MF-2-1	0.692	0.672	0.674	0.672	0.692	0.689
MF-3-1	0.689	0.689	0.692	0.692	0.689	0.713
MF-1-2	0.663	0.663	0.663	0.663	0.669	0.689
MF-2-2	0.680	0.671	0.672	0.671	0.696	0.702
MF-3-2	0.682	0.682	0.680	0.680	0.696	0.716
MF-1-3	0.664	0.664	0.664	0.664	0.664	0.687
MF-2-3	0.687	0.673	0.681	0.673	0.687	0.700
MF-3-3	0.694	0.694	0.689	0.689	0.694	0.713
MIN-En	0.715	0.704	0.713	0.709	0.730	0.722
MAX-En	0.711	0.680	0.688	0.686	0.705	0.716
AVG-En	0.660	0.660	0.660	0.662	0.665	0.681
MED-En	0.665	0.661	0.660	0.663	0.674	0.681
WT-MF	0.658	0.659	0.661	0.662	0.661	0.678
INTRP-MF	0.658	0.659	0.660	0.662	0.661	0.678
RLFM	0.731	0.731	0.728	0.728	0.733	0.740
RAPMFc	1.175					

7.2 Grade Prediction Results

We first discuss the performance of the different methods, then we discuss the effect of the sample sizes on the performance of the different MF models.

7.2.1 *Performance of the different methods*

RMSE given by the different methods across all groups are listed in Table 3. For the User-CF methods, User-CF-2 and User-CF-3 that utilize finer groups give lower RMSE than User-CF-1. User-CF-2 gives the lowest RMSE when the student sgroups are defined using the academic level.

For the MF methods, MF-1-1 gives the lowest RMSE across the different groups. MF models that utilize finer groups tend to give higher RMSE. We believe this has to do with the effect of the sample sizes that are associated with the various groups, which is analyzed in more details in Section 7.2.2.

INTRP-MF gives lower RMSE than all the ensembles across the different groups. That is because it only gives higher weights to the finer models as their biases are associated with larger sample sizes, which indicates a better ability to generalize. INTRP-MF does only marginally better than WT-MF, which indicates that the improvement is largely due to the sample-size-based weights. The AVG-En gives the third lowest RMSE and in many cases it performs worse than MF-1-1. Among all methods and groups, INTRP-MF gives the lowest RMSE, followed by WT-MF.

RAPMFc gives higher RMSE than all MF and User-CF methods. This is consistent with the results presented in [16] since our test set represents inspected entries for courses that students have taken. RLFM gives lower RMSE than the User-CF methods but higher RMSE than the MF methods.

7.2.2 *Change in MF models' RMSE with the bias sample sizes*

To understand how the sample sizes associated with the bias terms of the various MF models affect their performance, and to show why INTRP-MF works, we analyze how the RMSEs of the various models change with the number of training samples associated with their biases. To do so, we extract multiple subsets from the test set. Each subset contains test cases whose corresponding student and course biases in the finest model, MF-3-3, are associated with a minimum number of training samples referred to as α and β. We try values for α and β in the range [0,100] to generate various test subsets. Then for each subset we compute the RMSE for all the models and plot the RMSEs against the subset coverage (number of test cases in the subset).

Figure 3 shows the RMSE against the coverage for the various models with the H-1 groups. Each coverage point represents a test subset with that amount of test cases. As the coverage decreases, the sample sizes associated with the biases of the various models increases. For each coverage point we plot the RMSE of the various models. Subfigures (a), (b) and (c) show how the models with various course groups perform given a fixed student group. At the highest coverage of 50,000 test cases, models with the coarsest course groups and thus, coarsest student biases (MF-1-1, MF-2-1 and MF-3-1) give the lowest RMSEs. For lower coverages between 10,000 and 500 (indicating that finer models have more training examples), models with finer course groups and thus, finer student biases (MF-1-2, MF-2-2 and MF-3-2) give the lowest RMSEs. We can conclude from this that INTRP-MF manages to yield lower RMSE as it gives higher weights to the finer models when their biases are associated with more samples, i.e., when they can give lower RMSE.

8. CONCLUSIONS & FUTURE WORK

In this paper we addressed the grade prediction and top-n course ranking problems. We showed how the student and course academic features determine the enrollment patterns and we defined multi-granularity student and course groups accordingly. We showed how these groups can be incorporated in user collaborative filtering, matrix factorization and popularity ranking methods.

By evaluating the various methods on a large dataset, we showed that incorporating the features-based groups into the various methods leads to better grade predictions and top-n course rankings. We also showed how the grade prediction accuracy of matrix factorization methods slightly degrades when their biases are associated with small sample sizes; an issue occurring with utilizing finer groups. We showed how this can be handled by building various models utilizing various-granularity groups and combining their predictions based on the sample sizes associated with their biases. Our results also showed that the student groups defined using the majors and academic level gave the best top-n rankings and the most accurate grade predictions.

In the future we will consider special cases like ranking non-required courses while considering grades in evaluation.

9. ACKNOWLEDGEMENT

This work was supported in part by NSF (OCI-1048018, IIS-1247632, IIP-1414153, IIS-1447788), Army Research Office (W911NF-14-1-0316), Intel Software and Services Group, and the Digital Technology Center at the University of Minnesota. Access to research and computing facilities was provided by the Digital Technology Center and the Minnesota Supercomputing Institute.

10. REFERENCES

[1] G. Adomavicius, R. Sankaranarayanan, S. Sen, and A. Tuzhilin. Incorporating contextual information in

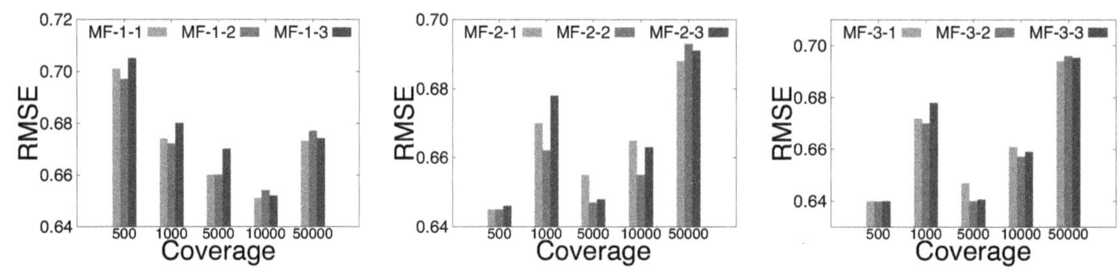

(a) (b) (c)

Figure 3: Coverage vs. RMSE for the MF models on common test cases using the H-1 groups.

recommender systems using a multidimensional approach. *ACM Trans. Inf. Syst.*, 23(1), 2005.

[2] D. Agarwal and B.-C. Chen. Regression-based latent factor models. In *Proceedings of the 15th ACM SIGKDD international conference on Knowledge discovery and data mining*, KDD '09, pages 19–28. ACM, 2009.

[3] D. Agarwal, B.-C. Chen, and B. Long. Localized factor models for multi-context recommendation. In *SIGKDD*, 2011.

[4] L. Baltrunas, B. Ludwig, and F. Ricci. Matrix factorization techniques for context aware recommendation. In *ACM RecSys*, 2011.

[5] N. Bendakir and E. Aimeur. Using association rules for course recommendation. *AAAI Workshop on Educational Data Mining*, 2006.

[6] H. Bydzovska. Are collaborative filtering methods suitable for student performance prediction? In *Progress in Artificial Intelligence*, volume 9273 of *Lecture Notes in Computer Science*.

[7] W. Chen, T. yan Liu, Y. Lan, Z. ming Ma, and H. Li. Ranking measures and loss functions in learning to rank. In Y. Bengio, D. Schuurmans, J. Lafferty, C. Williams, and A. Culotta, editors, *Advances in Neural Information Processing Systems 22*, pages 315–323. Curran Associates, Inc., 2009.

[8] T. Denley. Course recommendation system and method, 2013. US Patent App. 13/441,063.

[9] M. D. Ekstrand, J. T. Riedl, and J. A. Konstan. Collaborative filtering recommender systems. *Found. Trends Hum.-Comput. Interact.*, 4(2), 2011.

[10] A. Elbadrawy and G. Karypis. User-specific feature-based similarity models for top-n recommendation of new items. *ACM Trans. Intell. Syst. Technol.*, 6(3), Apr. 2015.

[11] J. L. Herlocker, J. A. Konstan, A. Borchers, and J. Riedl. An algorithmic framework for performing collaborative filtering. In *SIGIR*, 1999.

[12] J. M. Hernández-Lobato, N. M. T. Houlsby, and Z. Ghahramani. Probabilistic matrix factorization with non-random missing data. In *ICML*, 2014.

[13] A. Karatzoglou, X. Amatriain, L. Baltrunas, and N. Oliver. Multiverse recommendation: N-dimensional tensor factorization for context-aware collaborative filtering. In *ACM RecSys*, 2010.

[14] Y. Koren, R. Bell, and C. Volinsky. Matrix factorization techniques for recommender systems. *Computer*, 42(8), 2009.

[15] Y. Lee and J. Cho. An intelligent course recommendation system. *Smart CR*, 1(1):69–84, 2011.

[16] G. Ling, H. Yang, M. R. Lyu, and I. King. Response aware model-based collaborative filtering. *CoRR*, abs/1210.4869, 2012.

[17] B. M. Marlin and R. S. Zemel. Collaborative prediction and ranking with non-random missing data. In *ACM RecSys*, 2009.

[18] X. Ning and G. Karypis. Sparse linear methods with side information for top-n recommendations. In *Proceedings of the Sixth ACM Conference on Recommender Systems*, RecSys '12. ACM, 2012.

[19] A. Parameswaran, P. Venetis, and H. Garcia-Molina. Recommendation systems with complex constraints: A course recommendation perspective. *ACM Trans. Inf. Syst.*, 29(4), 2011.

[20] A. G. Parameswaran and H. Garcia-Molina. Recommendations with prerequisites. In *ACM RecSys*, 2009.

[21] A. G. Parameswaran, H. Garcia-Molina, and J. D. Ullman. Evaluating, combining and generalizing recommendations with prerequisites. In *CIKM*, 2010.

[22] A. G. Parameswaran, G. Koutrika, B. Bercovitz, and H. Garcia-Molina. Recsplorer: Recommendation algorithms based on precedence mining. In *ACM SIGMOD*, 2010.

[23] S. Ray and A. Sharma. A collaborative filtering based approach for recommending elective courses. *CoRR*, abs/1309.6908, 2013.

[24] S. Rendle. Factorization machines with libFM. *ACM Trans. Intell. Syst. Technol.*, 3(3):57:1–57:22, May 2012.

[25] S. Rendle, Z. Gantner, C. Freudenthaler, and L. Schmidt-Thieme. Fast context-aware recommendations with factorization machines. In *SIGIR*, 2011.

[26] N. Thai-nghe, L. Drumond, and L. Schmidt-thieme. Multi-relational factorization models for predicting student performance.

[27] N. ThaiNghe, T. Horváth, and L. Schmidt-Thieme. Factorization models for forecasting student performance. In *International Conference on Educational Data*, pages 11–20, 2011.

[28] K. Yu, B. Zhang, H. Zhu, H. Cao, and J. Tian. Towards personalized context-aware recommendation by mining context logs through topic models. In *PAKDD*, Lec Notes in Comp Sci, 2012.

Deep Neural Networks for YouTube Recommendations

Paul Covington, Jay Adams, Emre Sargin
Google
Mountain View, CA
{pcovington, jka, msargin}@google.com

ABSTRACT

YouTube represents one of the largest scale and most sophisticated industrial recommendation systems in existence. In this paper, we describe the system at a high level and focus on the dramatic performance improvements brought by deep learning. The paper is split according to the classic two-stage information retrieval dichotomy: first, we detail a deep candidate generation model and then describe a separate deep ranking model. We also provide practical lessons and insights derived from designing, iterating and maintaining a massive recommendation system with enormous user-facing impact.

Keywords

recommender system; deep learning; scalability

1. INTRODUCTION

YouTube is the world's largest platform for creating, sharing and discovering video content. YouTube recommendations are responsible for helping more than a billion users discover personalized content from an ever-growing corpus of videos. In this paper we will focus on the immense impact deep learning has recently had on the YouTube video recommendations system. Figure 1 illustrates the recommendations on the YouTube mobile app home.

Recommending YouTube videos is extremely challenging from three major perspectives:

- *Scale:* Many existing recommendation algorithms proven to work well on small problems fail to operate on our scale. Highly specialized distributed learning algorithms and efficient serving systems are essential for handling YouTube's massive user base and corpus.
- *Freshness:* YouTube has a very dynamic corpus with many hours of video are uploaded per second. The recommendation system should be responsive enough to model newly uploaded content as well as the latest actions taken by the user. Balancing new content with well-established videos can be understood from an exploration/exploitation perspective.
- *Noise:* Historical user behavior on YouTube is inherently difficult to predict due to sparsity and a variety of unobservable external factors. We rarely obtain the ground truth of user satisfaction and instead model noisy implicit feedback signals. Furthermore, metadata associated with content is poorly structured without a well defined ontology. Our algorithms need to be robust to these particular characteristics of our training data.

Figure 1: Recommendations displayed on YouTube mobile app home.

In conjugation with other product areas across Google, YouTube has undergone a fundamental paradigm shift towards using deep learning as a general-purpose solution for nearly all learning problems. Our system is built on Google Brain [4] which was recently open sourced as TensorFlow [1]. TensorFlow provides a flexible framework for experimenting with various deep neural network architectures using large-scale distributed training. Our models learn approximately one billion parameters and are trained on hundreds of billions of examples.

In contrast to vast amount of research in matrix factoriza-

RecSys '16 September 15-19, 2016, Boston , MA, USA

ACM ISBN 978-1-4503-4035-9/16/09.
DOI: http://dx.doi.org/10.1145/2959100.2959190

tion methods [19], there is relatively little work using deep neural networks for recommendation systems. Neural networks are used for recommending news in [17], citations in [8] and review ratings in [20]. Collaborative filtering is formulated as a deep neural network in [22] and autoencoders in [18]. Elkahky *et al.* used deep learning for cross domain user modeling [5]. In a content-based setting, Burges *et al.* used deep neural networks for music recommendation [21].

The paper is organized as follows: A brief system overview is presented in Section 2. Section 3 describes the candidate generation model in more detail, including how it is trained and used to serve recommendations. Experimental results will show how the model benefits from deep layers of hidden units and additional heterogeneous signals. Section 4 details the ranking model, including how classic logistic regression is modified to train a model predicting expected watch time (rather than click probability). Experimental results will show that hidden layer depth is helpful as well in this situation. Finally, Section 5 presents our conclusions and lessons learned.

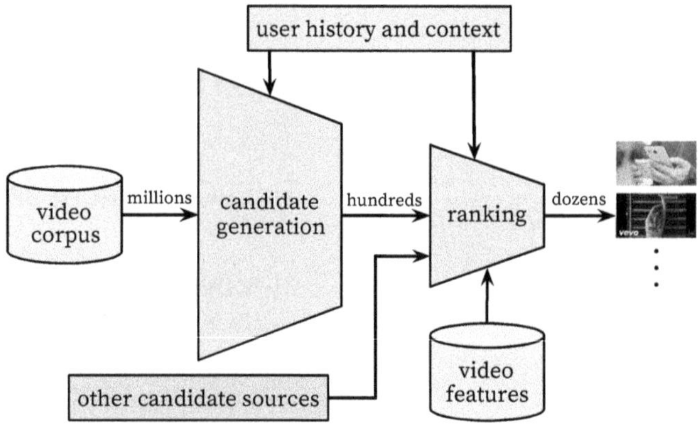

Figure 2: Recommendation system architecture demonstrating the "funnel" where candidate videos are retrieved and ranked before presenting only a few to the user.

2. SYSTEM OVERVIEW

The overall structure of our recommendation system is illustrated in Figure 2. The system is comprised of two neural networks: one for *candidate generation* and one for *ranking*.

The candidate generation network takes events from the user's YouTube activity history as input and retrieves a small subset (hundreds) of videos from a large corpus. These candidates are intended to be generally relevant to the user with high precision. The candidate generation network only provides broad personalization via collaborative filtering. The similarity between users is expressed in terms of coarse features such as IDs of video watches, search query tokens and demographics.

Presenting a few "best" recommendations in a list requires a fine-level representation to distinguish relative importance among candidates with high recall. The ranking network accomplishes this task by assigning a score to each video according to a desired objective function using a rich set of features describing the video and user. The highest scoring videos are presented to the user, ranked by their score.

The two-stage approach to recommendation allows us to make recommendations from a very large corpus (millions) of videos while still being certain that the small number of videos appearing on the device are personalized and engaging for the user. Furthermore, this design enables blending candidates generated by other sources, such as those described in an earlier work [3].

During development, we make extensive use of offline metrics (precision, recall, ranking loss, etc.) to guide iterative improvements to our system. However for the final determination of the effectiveness of an algorithm or model, we rely on A/B testing via live experiments. In a live experiment, we can measure subtle changes in click-through rate, watch time, and many other metrics that measure user engagement. This is important because live A/B results are not always correlated with offline experiments.

3. CANDIDATE GENERATION

During candidate generation, the enormous YouTube corpus is winnowed down to hundreds of videos that may be relevant to the user. The predecessor to the recommender described here was a matrix factorization approach trained under rank loss [23]. Early iterations of our neural network model mimicked this factorization behavior with shallow networks that only embedded the user's previous watches. From this perspective, our approach can be viewed as a nonlinear generalization of factorization techniques.

3.1 Recommendation as Classification

We pose recommendation as extreme multiclass classification where the prediction problem becomes accurately classifying a specific video watch w_t at time t among millions of videos i (classes) from a corpus V based on a user U and context C,

$$P(w_t = i|U, C) = \frac{e^{v_i u}}{\sum_{j \in V} e^{v_j u}}$$

where $u \in \mathbb{R}^N$ represents a high-dimensional "embedding" of the user, context pair and the $v_j \in \mathbb{R}^N$ represent embeddings of each candidate video. In this setting, an embedding is simply a mapping of sparse entities (individual videos, users etc.) into a dense vector in $\mathbb{R}^N$. The task of the deep neural network is to learn user embeddings u as a function of the user's history and context that are useful for discriminating among videos with a softmax classifier.

Although explicit feedback mechanisms exist on YouTube (thumbs up/down, in-product surveys, etc.) we use the implicit feedback [16] of watches to train the model, where a user completing a video is a positive example. This choice is based on the orders of magnitude more implicit user history available, allowing us to produce recommendations deep in the tail where explicit feedback is extremely sparse.

Efficient Extreme Multiclass

To efficiently train such a model with millions of classes, we rely on a technique to sample negative classes from the background distribution ("candidate sampling") and then correct for this sampling via importance weighting [10]. For each example the cross-entropy loss is minimized for the true label and the sampled negative classes. In practice several thousand negatives are sampled, corresponding to more than 100 times speedup over traditional softmax. A popular alternative approach is hierarchical softmax [15], but we weren't able to achieve comparable accuracy. In hierarchical softmax, traversing each node in the tree involves discriminating between sets of classes that are often unrelated, making the classification problem much more difficult and degrading performance.

At serving time we need to compute the most likely N classes (videos) in order to choose the top N to present to the user. Scoring millions of items under a strict serving latency of tens of milliseconds requires an approximate scoring scheme sublinear in the number of classes. Previous systems at YouTube relied on hashing [24] and the classifier described here uses a similar approach. Since calibrated likelihoods from the softmax output layer are not needed at serving time, the scoring problem reduces to a nearest neighbor search in the dot product space for which general purpose libraries can be used [12]. We found that A/B results were not particularly sensitive to the choice of nearest neighbor search algorithm.

3.2 Model Architecture

Inspired by continuous bag of words language models [14], we learn high dimensional embeddings for each video in a fixed vocabulary and feed these embeddings into a feedforward neural network. A user's watch history is represented by a variable-length sequence of sparse video IDs which is mapped to a dense vector representation via the embeddings. The network requires fixed-sized dense inputs and simply averaging the embeddings performed best among several strategies (sum, component-wise max, etc.). Importantly, the embeddings are learned jointly with all other model parameters through normal gradient descent backpropagation updates. Features are concatenated into a wide first layer, followed by several layers of fully connected Rectified Linear Units (ReLU) [6]. Figure 3 shows the general network architecture with additional non-video watch features described below.

3.3 Heterogeneous Signals

A key advantage of using deep neural networks as a generalization of matrix factorization is that arbitrary continuous and categorical features can be easily added to the model. Search history is treated similarly to watch history - each query is tokenized into unigrams and bigrams and each token is embedded. Once averaged, the user's tokenized, embedded queries represent a summarized dense search history. Demographic features are important for providing priors so that the recommendations behave reasonably for new users. The user's geographic region and device are embedded and concatenated. Simple binary and continuous features such as the user's gender, logged-in state and age are input directly into the network as real values normalized to $[0, 1]$.

"Example Age" Feature

Many hours worth of videos are uploaded each second to YouTube. Recommending this recently uploaded ("fresh") content is extremely important for YouTube as a product. We consistently observe that users prefer fresh content, though not at the expense of relevance. In addition to the first-order effect of simply recommending new videos that users want to watch, there is a critical secondary phenomenon of bootstrapping and propagating viral content [11].

Machine learning systems often exhibit an implicit bias towards the past because they are trained to predict future behavior from historical examples. The distribution of video popularity is highly non-stationary but the multinomial distribution over the corpus produced by our recommender will reflect the average watch likelihood in the training window of several weeks. To correct for this, *we feed the age of the training example as a feature during training.* At serving time, this feature is set to zero (or slightly negative) to reflect that the model is making predictions at the very end of the training window.

Figure 4 demonstrates the efficacy of this approach on an arbitrarily chosen video [26].

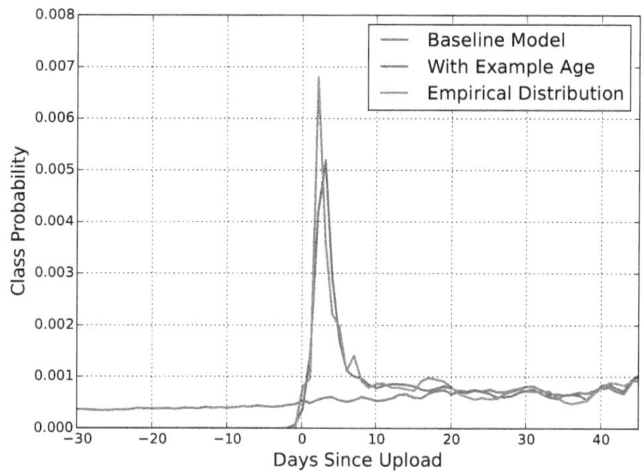

Figure 4: For a given video [26], the model trained with example age as a feature is able to accurately represent the upload time and time-dependant popularity observed in the data. Without the feature, the model would predict approximately the average likelihood over the training window.

3.4 Label and Context Selection

It is important to emphasize that recommendation often involves solving a *surrogate problem* and transferring the result to a particular context. A classic example is the assumption that accurately predicting ratings leads to effective movie recommendations [2]. We have found that the choice of this surrogate learning problem has an outsized importance on performance in A/B testing but is very difficult to measure with offline experiments.

Training examples are generated from all YouTube watches (even those embedded on other sites) rather than just watches on the recommendations we produce. Otherwise, it would be very difficult for new content to surface and the recommender would be overly biased towards exploitation. If users are discovering videos through means other than our recommendations, we want to be able to quickly propagate this discovery to others via collaborative filtering. Another key insight that improved live metrics was to generate a fixed number of training examples per user, effectively weighting our users equally in the loss function. This prevented a small cohort of highly active users from dominating the loss.

Somewhat counter-intuitively, great care must be taken to *withhold information from the classifier* in order to prevent the model from exploiting the structure of the site and overfitting the surrogate problem. Consider as an example a

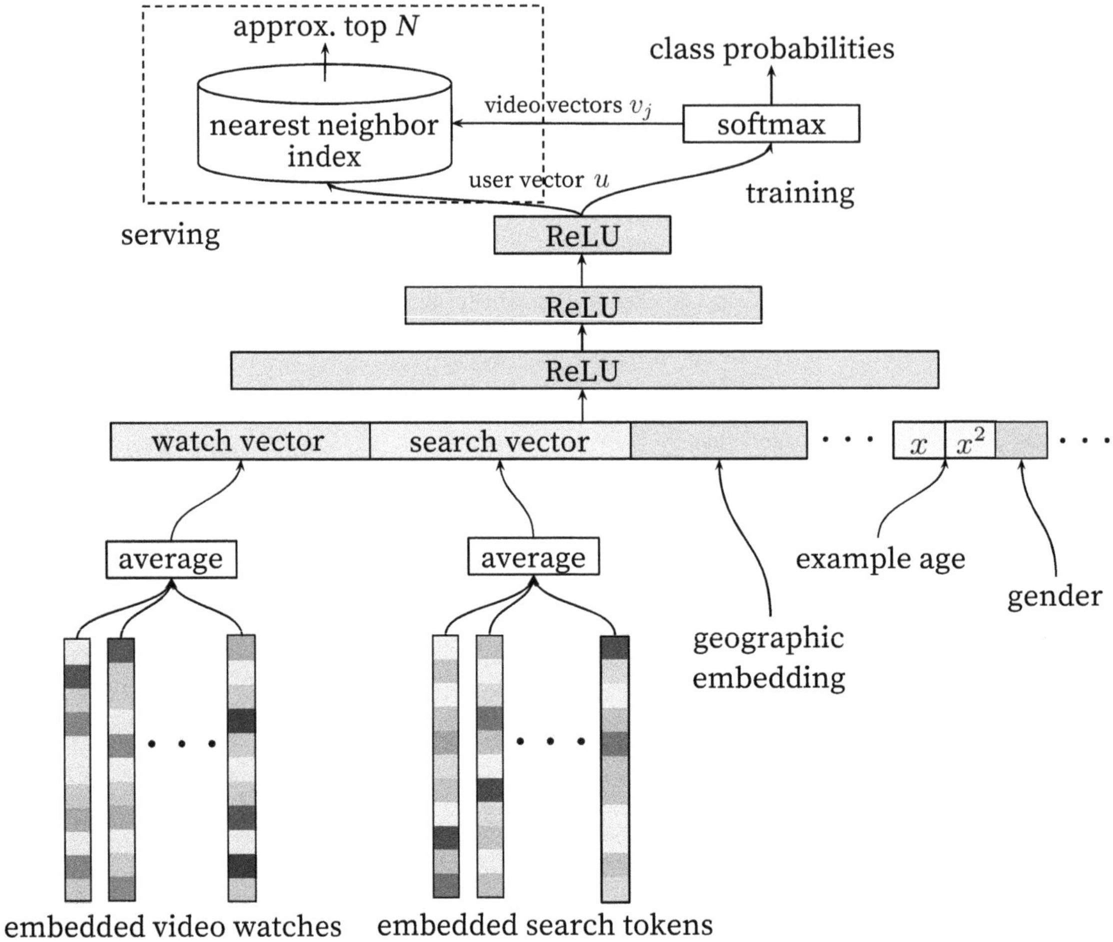

Figure 3: Deep candidate generation model architecture showing embedded sparse features concatenated with dense features. Embeddings are averaged before concatenation to transform variable sized bags of sparse IDs into fixed-width vectors suitable for input to the hidden layers. All hidden layers are fully connected. In training, a cross-entropy loss is minimized with gradient descent on the output of the sampled softmax. At serving, an approximate nearest neighbor lookup is performed to generate hundreds of candidate video recommendations.

case in which the user has just issued a search query for "taylor swift". Since our problem is posed as predicting the next watched video, a classifier given this information will predict that the most likely videos to be watched are those which appear on the corresponding search results page for "taylor swift". Unsurpisingly, reproducing the user's last search page as homepage recommendations performs very poorly. By discarding sequence information and representing search queries with an unordered bag of tokens, the classifier is no longer directly aware of the origin of the label.

Natural consumption patterns of videos typically lead to very asymmetric co-watch probabilities. Episodic series are usually watched sequentially and users often discover artists in a genre beginning with the most broadly popular before focusing on smaller niches. We therefore found much better performance predicting the user's next watch, rather than predicting a randomly held-out watch (Figure 5). Many collaborative filtering systems implicitly choose the labels and context by holding out a random item and predicting it from other items in the user's history (5a). This leaks future information and ignores any asymmetric consumption patterns. In contrast, we "rollback" a user's history by choosing a random watch and only input actions the user took before the held-out label watch (5b).

3.5 Experiments with Features and Depth

Adding features and depth significantly improves precision on holdout data as shown in Figure 6. In these experiments, a vocabulary of 1M videos and 1M search tokens were embedded with 256 floats each in a maximum bag size of 50 recent watches and 50 recent searches. The softmax layer outputs a multinomial distribution over the same 1M video classes with a dimension of 256 (which can be thought of as a separate output video embedding). These models were trained until convergence over all YouTube users, corresponding to several epochs over the data. Network structure followed a common "tower" pattern in which the bottom of the network is widest and each successive hidden layer halves the number of units (similar to Figure 3). The depth zero network is effectively a linear factorization scheme which

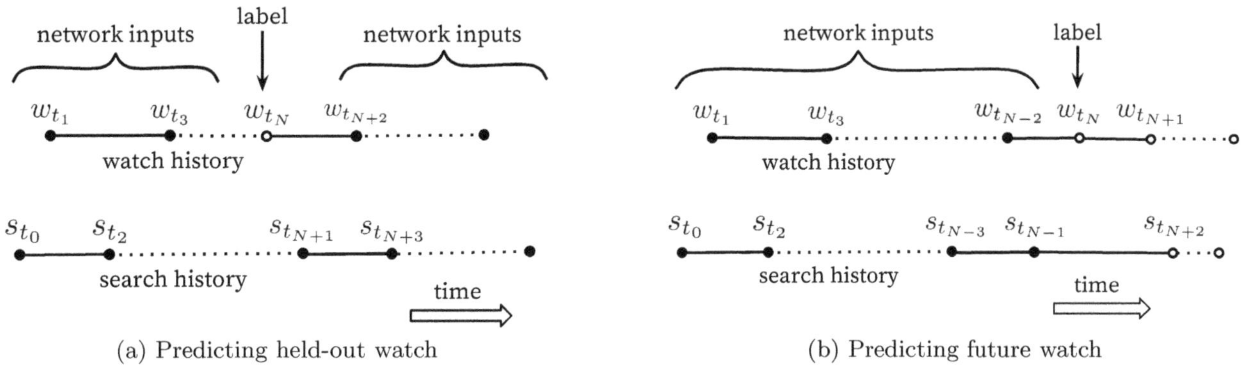

Figure 5: Choosing labels and input context to the model is challenging to evaluate offline but has a large impact on live performance. Here, solid events • are input features to the network while hollow events ◦ are excluded. We found predicting a future watch (5b) performed better in A/B testing. In (5b), the example age is expressed as $t_{\max} - t_N$ where $t_{\max}$ is the maximum observed time in the training data.

performed very similarly to the predecessor system. Width and depth were added until the incremental benefit diminished and convergence became difficult:

- Depth 0: A linear layer simply transforms the concatenation layer to match the softmax dimension of 256
- Depth 1: 256 ReLU
- Depth 2: 512 ReLU → 256 ReLU
- Depth 3: 1024 ReLU → 512 ReLU → 256 ReLU
- Depth 4: 2048 ReLU → 1024 ReLU → 512 ReLU → 256 ReLU

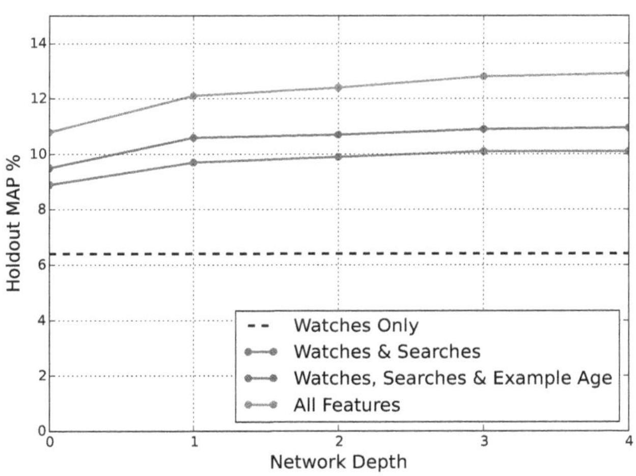

Figure 6: Features beyond video embeddings improve holdout Mean Average Precision (MAP) and layers of depth add expressiveness so that the model can effectively use these additional features by modeling their interaction.

4. RANKING

The primary role of ranking is to use impression data to specialize and calibrate candidate predictions for the particular user interface. For example, a user may watch a given video with high probability generally but is unlikely to click on the specific homepage impression due to the choice of thumbnail image. During ranking, we have access to many more features describing the video and the user's relationship to the video because only a few hundred videos are being scored rather than the millions scored in candidate generation. Ranking is also crucial for ensembling different candidate sources whose scores are not directly comparable.

We use a deep neural network with similar architecture as candidate generation to assign an independent score to each video impression using logistic regression (Figure 7). The list of videos is then sorted by this score and returned to the user. Our final ranking objective is constantly being tuned based on live A/B testing results but is generally a simple function of expected watch time per impression. Ranking by click-through rate often promotes deceptive videos that the user does not complete ("clickbait") whereas watch time better captures engagement [13, 25].

4.1 Feature Representation

Our features are segregated with the traditional taxonomy of categorical and continuous/ordinal features. The categorical features we use vary widely in their cardinality - some are binary (e.g. whether the user is logged-in) while others have millions of possible values (e.g. the user's last search query). Features are further split according to whether they contribute only a single value ("univalent") or a set of values ("multivalent"). An example of a univalent categorical feature is the video ID of the impression being scored, while a corresponding multivalent feature might be a bag of the last N video IDs the user has watched. We also classify features according to whether they describe properties of the item ("impression") or properties of the user/context ("query"). Query features are computed once per request while impression features are computed for each item scored.

Feature Engineering

We typically use hundreds of features in our ranking models, roughly split evenly between categorical and continuous. Despite the promise of deep learning to alleviate the burden of engineering features by hand, the nature of our raw data does not easily lend itself to be input directly into feedforward neural networks. We still expend considerable

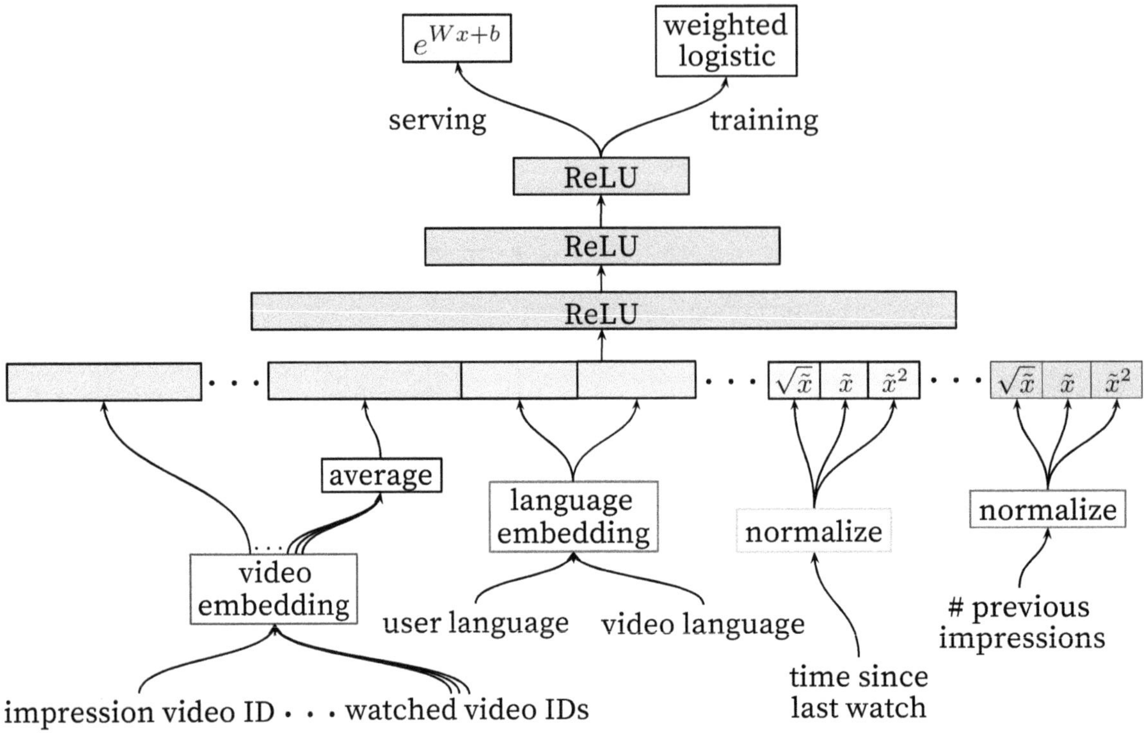

Figure 7: Deep ranking network architecture depicting embedded categorical features (both univalent and multivalent) with shared embeddings and powers of normalized continuous features. All layers are fully connected. In practice, hundreds of features are fed into the network.

engineering resources transforming user and video data into useful features. The main challenge is in representing a temporal sequence of user actions and how these actions relate to the video impression being scored.

We observe that the most important signals are those that describe a user's previous interaction with the item itself and other similar items, matching others' experience in ranking ads [7]. As an example, consider the user's past history with the channel that uploaded the video being scored - how many videos has the user watched from this channel? When was the last time the user watched a video on this topic? These continuous features describing past user actions on related items are particularly powerful because they generalize well across disparate items. We have also found it crucial to propagate information from candidate generation into ranking in the form of features, e.g. which sources nominated this video candidate? What scores did they assign?

Features describing the frequency of past video impressions are also critical for introducing "churn" in recommendations (successive requests do not return identical lists). If a user was recently recommended a video but did not watch it then the model will naturally demote this impression on the next page load. Serving up-to-the-second impression and watch history is an engineering feat onto itself outside the scope of this paper, but is vital for producing responsive recommendations.

Embedding Categorical Features

Similar to candidate generation, we use embeddings to map sparse categorical features to dense representations suitable for neural networks. Each unique ID space ("vocabulary") has a separate learned embedding with dimension that increases approximately proportional to the logarithm of the number of unique values. These vocabularies are simple look-up tables built by passing over the data once before training. Very large cardinality ID spaces (e.g. video IDs or search query terms) are truncated by including only the top N after sorting based on their frequency in clicked impressions. Out-of-vocabulary values are simply mapped to the zero embedding. As in candidate generation, multivalent categorical feature embeddings are averaged before being fed in to the network.

Importantly, categorical features in the same ID space also share underlying emeddings. For example, there exists a single global embedding of video IDs that many distinct features use (video ID of the impression, last video ID watched by the user, video ID that "seeded" the recommendation, etc.). Despite the shared embedding, each feature is fed separately into the network so that the layers above can learn specialized representations per feature. Sharing embeddings is important for improving generalization, speeding up training and reducing memory requirements. The overwhelming majority of model parameters are in these high-cardinality embedding spaces - for example, one million IDs embedded in a 32 dimensional space have 7 times more parameters than fully connected layers 2048 units wide.

Normalizing Continuous Features

Neural networks are notoriously sensitive to the scaling and distribution of their inputs [9] whereas alternative approaches such as ensembles of decision trees are invariant to scaling of individual features. We found that proper normalization of continuous features was critical for convergence. A continuous feature x with distribution f is transformed to $\tilde{x}$ by scaling the values such that the feature is equally distributed in $[0, 1)$ using the cumulative distribution, $\tilde{x} = \int_{-\infty}^{x} df$. This integral is approximated with linear interpolation on the quantiles of the feature values computed in a single pass over the data before training begins.

In addition to the raw normalized feature $\tilde{x}$, we also input powers $\tilde{x}^2$ and $\sqrt{\tilde{x}}$, giving the network more expressive power by allowing it to easily form super- and sub-linear functions of the feature. Feeding powers of continuous features was found to improve offline accuracy.

4.2 Modeling Expected Watch Time

Our goal is to predict expected watch time given training examples that are either positive (the video impression was clicked) or negative (the impression was not clicked). Positive examples are annotated with the amount of time the user spent watching the video. To predict expected watch time we use the technique of weighted logistic regression, which was developed for this purpose.

The model is trained with logistic regression under cross-entropy loss (Figure 7). However, the positive (clicked) impressions are weighted by the observed watch time on the video. Negative (unclicked) impressions all receive unit weight. In this way, the odds learned by the logistic regression are $\frac{\sum T_i}{N-k}$ where N is the number of training examples, k is the number of positive impressions, and T_i is the watch time of the ith impression. Assuming the fraction of positive impressions is small (which is true in our case), the learned odds are approximately $E[T](1 + P)$, where P is the click probability and $E[T]$ is the expected watch time of the impression. Since P is small, this product is close to $E[T]$. For inference we use the exponential function e^x as the final activation function to produce these odds that closely estimate expected watch time.

4.3 Experiments with Hidden Layers

Table 1 shows the results we obtained on next-day holdout data with different hidden layer configurations. The value shown for each configuration ("weighted, per-user loss") was obtained by considering both positive (clicked) and negative (unclicked) impressions shown to a user on a single page. We first score these two impressions with our model. If the negative impression receives a higher score than the positive impression, then we consider the positive impression's watch time to be *mispredicted watch time*. Weighted, per-user loss is then the total amount mispredicted watch time as a fraction of total watch time over heldout impression pairs.

These results show that increasing the width of hidden layers improves results, as does increasing their depth. The trade-off, however, is server CPU time needed for inference. The configuration of a 1024-wide ReLU followed by a 512-wide ReLU followed by a 256-wide ReLU gave us the best results while enabling us to stay within our serving CPU budget.

For the 1024 → 512 → 256 model we tried only feeding the normalized continuous features without their powers, which increased loss by 0.2%. With the same hidden layer configuration, we also trained a model where positive and negative examples are weighted equally. Unsurprisingly, this increased the watch time-weighted loss by a dramatic 4.1%.

Hidden layers	weighted, per-user loss
None	41.6%
256 ReLU	36.9%
512 ReLU	36.7%
1024 ReLU	35.8%
512 ReLU → 256 ReLU	35.2%
1024 ReLU → 512 ReLU	34.7%
1024 ReLU → 512 ReLU → 256 ReLU	34.6%

Table 1: Effects of wider and deeper hidden ReLU layers on watch time-weighted pairwise loss computed on next-day holdout data.

5. CONCLUSIONS

We have described our deep neural network architecture for recommending YouTube videos, split into two distinct problems: candidate generation and ranking.

Our deep collaborative filtering model is able to effectively assimilate many signals and model their interaction with layers of depth, outperforming previous matrix factorization approaches used at YouTube [23]. There is more art than science in selecting the surrogate problem for recommendations and we found classifying a future watch to perform well on live metrics by capturing asymmetric co-watch behavior and preventing leakage of future information. Withholding discrimative signals from the classifier was also essential to achieving good results - otherwise the model would overfit the surrogate problem and not transfer well to the homepage.

We demonstrated that using the age of the training example as an input feature removes an inherent bias towards the past and allows the model to represent the time-dependent behavior of popular of videos. This improved offline holdout precision results and increased the watch time dramatically on recently uploaded videos in A/B testing.

Ranking is a more classical machine learning problem yet our deep learning approach outperformed previous linear and tree-based methods for watch time prediction. Recommendation systems in particular benefit from specialized features describing past user behavior with items. Deep neural networks require special representations of categorical and continuous features which we transform with embeddings and quantile normalization, respectively. Layers of depth were shown to effectively model non-linear interactions between hundreds of features.

Logistic regression was modified by weighting training examples with watch time for positive examples and unity for negative examples, allowing us to learn odds that closely model expected watch time. This approach performed much better on watch-time weighted ranking evaluation metrics compared to predicting click-through rate directly.

6. ACKNOWLEDGMENTS

The authors would like to thank Jim McFadden and Pranav Khaitan for valuable guidance and support. Sujeet Bansal, Shripad Thite and Radek Vingralek implemented key components of the training and serving infrastructure. Chris Berg and Trevor Walker contributed thoughtful discussion and detailed feedback.

7. REFERENCES

[1] M. Abadi, A. Agarwal, P. Barham, E. Brevdo, Z. Chen, C. Citro, G. S. Corrado, A. Davis, J. Dean, M. Devin, S. Ghemawat, I. Goodfellow, A. Harp, G. Irving, M. Isard, Y. Jia, R. Jozefowicz, L. Kaiser, M. Kudlur, J. Levenberg, D. Mané, R. Monga, S. Moore, D. Murray, C. Olah, M. Schuster, J. Shlens, B. Steiner, I. Sutskever, K. Talwar, P. Tucker, V. Vanhoucke, V. Vasudevan, F. Viégas, O. Vinyals, P. Warden, M. Wattenberg, M. Wicke, Y. Yu, and X. Zheng. TensorFlow: Large-scale machine learning on heterogeneous systems, 2015. Software available from tensorflow.org.

[2] X. Amatriain. Building industrial-scale real-world recommender systems. In *Proceedings of the Sixth ACM Conference on Recommender Systems*, RecSys '12, pages 7–8, New York, NY, USA, 2012. ACM.

[3] J. Davidson, B. Liebald, J. Liu, P. Nandy, T. Van Vleet, U. Gargi, S. Gupta, Y. He, M. Lambert, B. Livingston, and D. Sampath. The youtube video recommendation system. In *Proceedings of the Fourth ACM Conference on Recommender Systems*, RecSys '10, pages 293–296, New York, NY, USA, 2010. ACM.

[4] J. Dean, G. S. Corrado, R. Monga, K. Chen, M. Devin, Q. V. Le, M. Z. Mao, M. Ranzato, A. Senior, P. Tucker, K. Yang, and A. Y. Ng. Large scale distributed deep networks. In *NIPS*, 2012.

[5] A. M. Elkahky, Y. Song, and X. He. A multi-view deep learning approach for cross domain user modeling in recommendation systems. In *Proceedings of the 24th International Conference on World Wide Web*, WWW '15, pages 278–288, New York, NY, USA, 2015. ACM.

[6] X. Glorot, A. Bordes, and Y. Bengio. Deep sparse rectifier neural networks. In G. J. Gordon and D. B. Dunson, editors, *Proceedings of the Fourteenth International Conference on Artificial Intelligence and Statistics (AISTATS-11)*, volume 15, pages 315–323. Journal of Machine Learning Research - Workshop and Conference Proceedings, 2011.

[7] X. He, J. Pan, O. Jin, T. Xu, B. Liu, T. Xu, Y. Shi, A. Atallah, R. Herbrich, S. Bowers, and J. Q. n. Candela. Practical lessons from predicting clicks on ads at facebook. In *Proceedings of the Eighth International Workshop on Data Mining for Online Advertising*, ADKDD'14, pages 5:1–5:9, New York, NY, USA, 2014. ACM.

[8] W. Huang, Z. Wu, L. Chen, P. Mitra, and C. L. Giles. A neural probabilistic model for context based citation recommendation. In *AAAI*, pages 2404–2410, 2015.

[9] S. Ioffe and C. Szegedy. Batch normalization: Accelerating deep network training by reducing internal covariate shift. *CoRR*, abs/1502.03167, 2015.

[10] S. Jean, K. Cho, R. Memisevic, and Y. Bengio. On using very large target vocabulary for neural machine translation. *CoRR*, abs/1412.2007, 2014.

[11] L. Jiang, Y. Miao, Y. Yang, Z. Lan, and A. G. Hauptmann. Viral video style: A closer look at viral videos on youtube. In *Proceedings of International Conference on Multimedia Retrieval*, ICMR '14, pages 193:193–193:200, New York, NY, USA, 2014. ACM.

[12] T. Liu, A. W. Moore, A. Gray, and K. Yang. An investigation of practical approximate nearest neighbor algorithms. pages 825–832. MIT Press, 2004.

[13] E. Meyerson. Youtube now: Why we focus on watch time. http://youtubecreator.blogspot.com/2012/08/youtube-now-why-we-focus-on-watch-time.html. Accessed: 2016-04-20.

[14] T. Mikolov, I. Sutskever, K. Chen, G. Corrado, and J. Dean. Distributed representations of words and phrases and their compositionality. *CoRR*, abs/1310.4546, 2013.

[15] F. Morin and Y. Bengio. Hierarchical probabilistic neural network language model. In *AISTATSâĂŹ05*, pages 246–252, 2005.

[16] D. Oard and J. Kim. Implicit feedback for recommender systems. In *in Proceedings of the AAAI Workshop on Recommender Systems*, pages 81–83, 1998.

[17] K. J. Oh, W. J. Lee, C. G. Lim, and H. J. Choi. Personalized news recommendation using classified keywords to capture user preference. In *16th International Conference on Advanced Communication Technology*, pages 1283–1287, Feb 2014.

[18] S. Sedhain, A. K. Menon, S. Sanner, and L. Xie. Autorec: Autoencoders meet collaborative filtering. In *Proceedings of the 24th International Conference on World Wide Web*, WWW '15 Companion, pages 111–112, New York, NY, USA, 2015. ACM.

[19] X. Su and T. M. Khoshgoftaar. A survey of collaborative filtering techniques. *Advances in artificial intelligence*, 2009:4, 2009.

[20] D. Tang, B. Qin, T. Liu, and Y. Yang. User modeling with neural network for review rating prediction. In *Proc. IJCAI*, pages 1340–1346, 2015.

[21] A. van den Oord, S. Dieleman, and B. Schrauwen. Deep content-based music recommendation. In C. J. C. Burges, L. Bottou, M. Welling, Z. Ghahramani, and K. Q. Weinberger, editors, *Advances in Neural Information Processing Systems 26*, pages 2643–2651. Curran Associates, Inc., 2013.

[22] H. Wang, N. Wang, and D.-Y. Yeung. Collaborative deep learning for recommender systems. In *Proceedings of the 21th ACM SIGKDD International Conference on Knowledge Discovery and Data Mining*, KDD '15, pages 1235–1244, New York, NY, USA, 2015. ACM.

[23] J. Weston, S. Bengio, and N. Usunier. Wsabie: Scaling up to large vocabulary image annotation. In *Proceedings of the International Joint Conference on Artificial Intelligence, IJCAI*, 2011.

[24] J. Weston, A. Makadia, and H. Yee. Label partitioning for sublinear ranking. In S. Dasgupta and D. Mcallester, editors, *Proceedings of the 30th International Conference on Machine Learning (ICML-13)*, volume 28, pages 181–189. JMLR Workshop and Conference Proceedings, May 2013.

[25] X. Yi, L. Hong, E. Zhong, N. N. Liu, and S. Rajan. Beyond clicks: Dwell time for personalization. In *Proceedings of the 8th ACM Conference on Recommender Systems*, RecSys '14, pages 113–120, New York, NY, USA, 2014. ACM.

[26] Zayn. Pillowtalk. https://www.youtube.com/watch?v=C_3d6GntKbk.

Optimizing Similar Item Recommendations in a Semi-structured Marketplace to Maximize Conversion

Yuri M. Brovman
eBay Inc., New York City, USA
ybrovman@ebay.com

Marie Jacob
eBay Inc., New York City, USA
marijacob@ebay.com

Natraj Srinivasan
eBay Inc., New York City, USA
nsrinivasan@ebay.com

Stephen Neola
eBay Inc., New York City, USA
sneola@ebay.com

Daniel Galron
eBay Inc., New York City, USA
dgalron@ebay.com

Ryan Snyder
eBay Inc., New York City, USA
rysnyder@ebay.com

ABSTRACT

This paper tackles the problem of recommendations in eBay's large semi-structured marketplace. eBay's variable inventory and lack of structured information about listings makes traditional collaborative filtering algorithms difficult to use. We discuss how to overcome these data limitations to produce high quality recommendations in real time with a combination of a customized scalable architecture as well as a widely applicable machine learned ranking model. A pointwise ranking approach is utilized to reduce the ranking problem to a binary classification problem optimized on past user purchase behavior. We present details of a sampling strategy and feature engineering that have been critical to achieve a lift in both purchase through rate (PTR) and revenue.

Keywords

e-commerce; recommender systems; machine learning; learning to rank

1. INTRODUCTION

Recommender systems in e-commerce have been extensively studied over the last few decades. Recommendations drive a considerable portion of site revenue, and ensure that users stay engaged with content for as long as possible. Unlike general marketplaces such as Amazon and Walmart, which offer warehouse products in a documented catalog, the eBay marketplace offers more diverse listings ranging anywhere from a new iPhone (a specific product with structured data attributes) to offhand antique items with no known characteristics. With over 800 million active listings at any given time as well as over 150 million active buyers, this semi-structured marketplace exhibits a heavy-tailed distribution of items – a large number of listings are unique, unidentifiable items that are popular among niche buyers. In addition, multiple item conditions and selling formats make serving relevant recommendations significantly harder.

RecSys '16 September 15-19, 2016, Boston , MA, USA

ACM ISBN 978-1-4503-4035-9/16/09.

DOI: http://dx.doi.org/10.1145/2959100.2959166

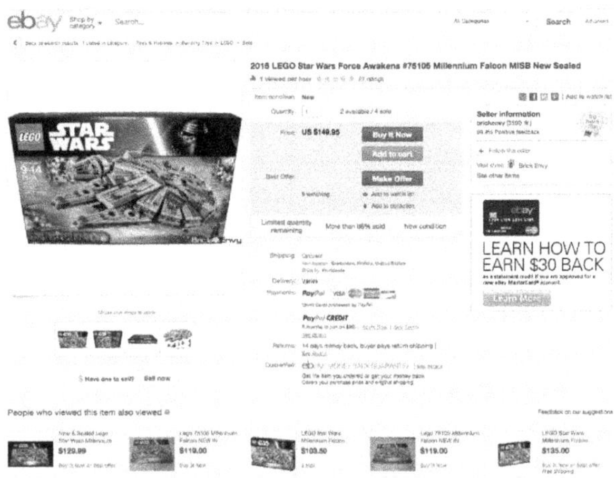

Figure 1: Item page showing similar item recommendations above the fold.

In this paper, we highlight several unique challenges in providing high quality item recommendations to users in real time that are specific to the scale and variety of this data. There is limited structured data coverage of items which makes it difficult to utilize specific item attributes. Additionally, many items tend to be short-lived – they surface on the site for one week and are never listed again. Traditional collaborative filtering algorithms [5, 10, 8] are not effective in this environment due to this volatility of inventory and limitation of structured data coverage.

While our recommendations are driven through a large number of channels, including desktop, mobile and emails, we discuss the problem setting of our most viewed placement – the eBay item page, shown in Figure 1. This page shows the details of a *seed* item, with five recommendations shown above the fold. The recommendations are generated based on both similarity between the seed item and the recommended item, and likelihood of purchase[1]. We use a two stage system where we first retrieve a subset of relevant items to the seed item, and then rank the subset of possible recommendations maximizing the chance of conversion. A comparable multi-stage approach where multiple sources were aggregated together to produce improved search results has

[1]Other placements on this site target more diverse recommendations. Past analysis showed that most users look for the same/similar product to the seed in this placement.

been implemented in LinkedIn [2]. The engineering details of the system architecture are discussed in Section 2.

The second stage of the system involves ranking the recommendations to decide which top 5 items to surface to the user. The topic of learning to rank has been widely studied in the field of Information Retrieval (IR) [9, 7] as it applies to ranking results based on a search query. More recently, machine learned ranking (MLR) techniques have been applied directly to recommender systems at Google [12], Netflix [11], and Amazon [4]. The pointwise learning to rank problem in the IR context can be reduced to a classification problem using $x_i = \{query, URL\}_i$ pairs as well as a binary or multi-class relevance label y_i as training input. Assigning the relevance labels to query-URL pairs is typically done with crowdsourcing methods which can be time consuming and cost prohibitive. In the context of recommender systems for this work, the classification problem uses $x_i = \{seed\ item, recommended\ item\}_i$ pairs and implicit user feedback (clicks/purchases) as the binary class label. This way, data collection is continuous and uses real-world conditions. The details of our ranking approach as well as experimental results are presented in Section 3.

We note that although our marketplace is unique, our ranking model is general enough for any domain employing recommender systems that uses a seed item, and can track click and purchase metrics. The model is widely applicable and is not limited to any one product category.

2. ARCHITECTURE

Our backend platform serves approximately 400 million requests every day and is optimized to have a response time of under 200 ms end-to-end. The backend architecture for the recommendation engine is divided into offline and online systems – the offline components indexes incoming eBay data, mines behavioral data and click logs, as well as trains a classifier on historical data to determine likelihood of purchase.

The overall recommendation process follows the paradigm of a search problem, which consists of two stages: **Recall**, which requires retrieving candidate items that might be similar to the given seed item, and **Ranking**, which sorts the candidates according to their probability of being purchased. An overview of the backend architecture can be seen in Figure 2. The input to the algorithm comes as an HTTP request to the merchandising backend (MBE) system with a given seed item. This initiates parallel calls to several services which return candidate recommendations that are similar in some way to the seed. The set of candidate recommendations are then ranked in real time. The output of the system is the top 5 ranked items, which are surfaced to the user.

2.1 Recall

With a rather sparse inventory of known products, eBay's internal product catalog serves only a small portion of similar item recommendations on the item page (< 10%). This sparsity led to a variety of techniques in generating candidate recommendations for a given seed item.

Product catalog: Although the majority of items on eBay are not tagged with a specific product ID, the distribution of product coverage tends to vary significantly across different categories. Books, for instance, usually has a high percentage of items which are known products due to identifiers such as ISBNs. If the seed item is tagged with a particular

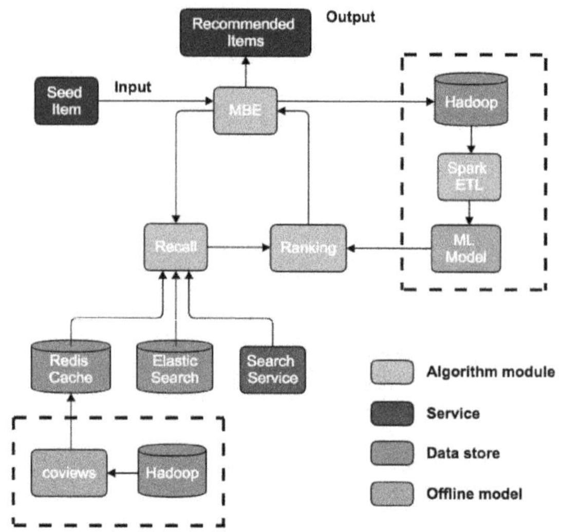

Figure 2: Architecture of the merchandising backend system. Offline components are marked by dashed lines.

product ID, we fetch other items with the same product ID from active inventory.

Coviewed items: A *coviewed* item pair is a pair of items which have been frequently viewed together in the same browsing session by multiple users. The coview behavioral model has been used across many recommender systems that use collaborative filtering. In our setting, we use a more rudimentary form of it and search for items that have been viewed together with the seed. Due to the volatile nature of the inventory, we follow a lambda architecture [6] to process session logs in realtime and batch. To ensure similarity, we also filter out coviewed items that may be from a different item category than the seed item.

Title similarity: Searching for items with a similar title yields a fairly large recall set. Title queries, however, posed an interesting challenge. Strict latency requirements on the item page prevent us from impacting the user experience, *i.e.*, there can be no noticeable delay when loading an item page with recommendations above the fold. In addition, unlike keyword searches, item titles tend to be much longer and hence, using eBay search was not a scalable option. To accommodate this type of search, we index all of eBay's items in an Elasticsearch database [3], sharded by its site (country) and category. As our problem setting includes a given seed item with a specific site and category, we can narrow our search focus to only items within the same domain. This kind of sharding allows search latencies to fit within our desired 100 ms range. We noticed that the quality of the returned recommendations was higher than our previous approach which used locality sensitive hashing, based on the item's title. Elasticsearch's indexing scheme uses TF/IDF based weightings in order to calculate relevance scores.

Coview and title-similarity based methods increase our total recall significantly and comprise up to 90% of recommendations.

2.2 Ranking

User impressions interactions (which include clicks and purchases) are logged to eBay's Hadoop cluster for analysis. Apache Spark [1] is used for Extract, Transform and Load

Table 1: Class label options for binary classifier and KL divergence for price feature.

negative class	positive class	KL divergence
non-clicked	clicked	0.01
non-purchased	purchased	0.13
clicked not purchased	purchased	0.07
non-clicked	purchased	0.15

(ETL) where the user logs are joined with item details and the data is subsampled. The trained offline MLR model parameters are passed to the runtime ranking application where predictions are made in real time.

3. RANKING MODEL

The pointwise learning to rank problem, in the context of serving item recommendations, is reduced to a binary classification problem where we rank the recommendations on the probability of being purchased (positive class), effectively maximizing conversion. The training and testing data sets are generated with features derived from {*seed item*, *recommended item*} pairs and binary class labels being {0=non-clicked, 1=purchased} from recommendations shown in the past. At runtime in production, the Recall stage produces candidates for possible {*seed item*, *recommended item*} pairs, and then in the Ranking stage the model assigns a probability score to each such pair, with the 5 highest scoring pairs resulting in recommendations to be shown to the user. The sampling strategy as well as the engineering of specific features are critical to the success of any classifier.

3.1 Sampling Strategy

We train a binary classifier on user browsing and purchase logs. Initially, we considered using "non-clicked" and "clicked" as the class labels for the model and rank the recommendations by the probability of click. To investigate the effectiveness of this strategy, we looked at the class separability of each feature. Figure 3a shows a histogram of the price feature score (described in the next section) for the non-clicked / clicked sampling strategy. User click patterns tend to be noisy as users browse items in a marketplace for a variety of reasons. This leads to the classes not separating well. We used the KL divergence to get a quantitative measure of the overlap of the probability distributions for the 2 classes. Table 1 shows several potential approaches to choose classes, as well as the resulting KL divergences for the price feature. Figure 3b shows the histogram for the non-clicked / purchased sampling strategy. We ran this type of analysis, looking at the KL divergence, for all of the features in our model to validate that the non- clicked / purchased strategy is optimal for class separation. This reflects user intention – non-clicked recommendations show absolutely no user interest while the purchased recommendations indicate complete user intention (conversion). Clicked recommendations are in the middle of this spectrum and cannot be used as effectively for classification.

Purchased recommendations occur an order of magnitude less often than clicked recommendations, which themselves occur in a relatively low portion of impressions. Due to this extreme class imbalance, we subsample the negative class to be balanced with the positive class in order to improve classifier performance.

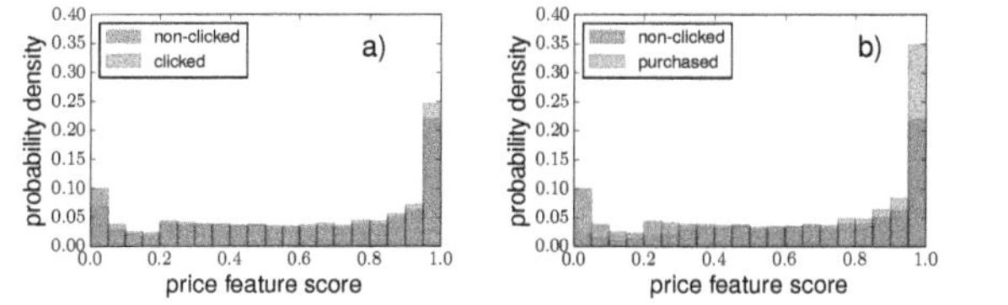

Figure 3: Histograms showing class separation of the price feature with the a) non-clicked / clicked and b) non-clicked / purchased sampling strategies.

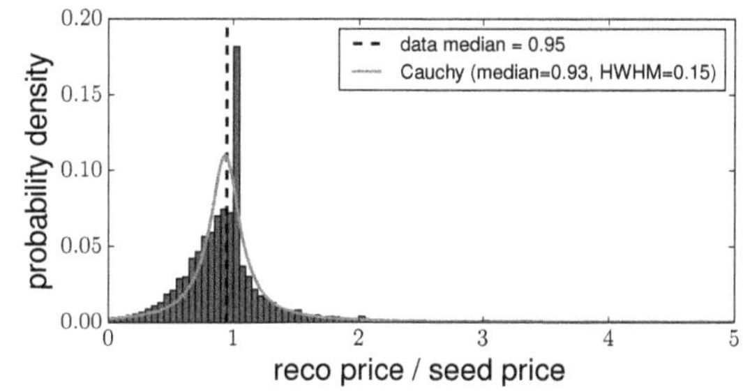

Figure 4: Histogram of price ratio and Cauchy fit.

3.2 Feature Engineering

There are two types of features in the model, *comparison* features and *item quality* features. Comparison features compare properties of the seed item to the recommendation candidate item. Some examples of this include comparing price, condition, format, and titles (using TF/IDF based methods). The item quality features are designed to ensure higher quality items are surfaced to the user. These features include popularity and seller feedback of the item seller, among others. We now discuss the details of an important *comparison* feature – the price feature.

Prices of identical items can vary by orders of magnitude because of condition or simply due to preference of the seller. Instead of directly comparing the seed item price, p_{seed}, to the recommended item price, p_{reco}, we instead model the ratio p_{reco}/p_{seed}. Analysis shows this ratio is centered near unity. Figure 4 shows a normalized histogram of the price ratio (blue bars) from past purchase events, where the user viewed the seed item and then purchased the recommended item. We modeled this data with the Cauchy distribution which has a probability density function of the following form:

$$f_{Cauchy}(x, x_0, \gamma) = \frac{1}{\pi\gamma\left[1 + \left(\frac{x-x_0}{\gamma}\right)^2\right]} \quad (1)$$

where x_0 is the median and γ is the Half Width at Half Maximum. We looked at other distributions such as the Gaussian, Gamma, and Weibull, however the Cauchy had the best fit to the past purchase data. The price feature score is then generated from a normalized Cauchy distribution $s_{price} = f_{Cauchy}(x, x_0, \gamma) \cdot \pi\gamma$, which is 1 when $p_{reco} = p_{seed}$ and smoothly transitioning to 0 otherwise.

3.3 Baseline

The baseline ranking model that is used for comparison is a linear model with manually adjusted weights based on input from domain experts and human judgement of test output. Potential recommendations are ranked based on

Table 2: Classification and ranking metrics.

Classifier	AUC	NDCG@k=1	NDCG@k=5
baseline	0.67	0.336	0.684
Naive Bayes	0.74	0.341	0.682
Logistic Regression	0.77	0.353	0.689
Decision Tree	0.79	0.407	0.715
Random Forest	0.80	0.370	0.696
Gradient Boosting	0.81	0.370	0.697

highest global score, $G = \sum_{j=1}^{N} w_j \cdot s_j$, where w_j and s_j are the weight and feature score, respectively. We define normalizations on the weights $\sum_{j=1}^{N} w_j = 1$ and feature scores $0 \leq s_j \leq 1$ which results in a constraint on the global score $0 \leq G \leq 1$. We launched this model to live user traffic to validate effectiveness of the features.

3.4 Classification and Ranking Results

We evaluated the performance of several classifiers on the balanced dataset with the non-clicked / purchased class labels. The dataset contained 352,070 examples gathered over 10 days of user logs and was randomly split into training (60%) and validation (40%) sets. Table 2 shows the ROC AUC scores from the validation data set demonstrating improved performance over the baseline model (Section 3.3). The hyperparameters for the tree based classifiers ware optimized using grid search. The accuracy (0.70) as well as the positive class precision (0.70) and recall (0.70) for the logistic regression indicated reasonable classification performance.

To evaluate ranking performance, we took the raw unsampled recommendations (1,177,117 examples) from impressions that contained a purchase, excluding impressions used for training. To gauge the quality of the ranking, we used the normalized discounted cumulative gain truncated at rank k (NDCG@k) metric which is typically used for evaluating ranking performance [7, 4]. We defined the relevance function to be {non-clicked = 0, clicked = 0, purchased = 1}. The model was evaluated on 10 datasets with eBay user log data from different time frames and countries. Classification and ranking performance was comparable to the results shown in Table 2.

3.5 A/B Test Results

As typically done in the ad tech industry, we segment the model by product category and country. An individual classifier was trained in every major category as users tend to shop differently in different domains (for example, prices may be more important in clothing than in antiques).

We implemented a logistic regression model for our production platform due to its scalability and reasonable offline classification and ranking performance compared to the tree based classifiers. The country and category segmented MLR model was A/B tested in live production traffic with the control being the baseline model defined in Section 3.3. Table 3 shows positive lift in critical operational metrics: click through rate (CTR), purchase through rate (PTR), and revenue. The model was optimized to maximize conversion which can be seen in the increase in PTR (+6.6%) and revenue (+6.0%). While the A/B test results were correlated with the improvement in offline performance between the logistic regression classifier and the baseline model, we are investigating how well this holds for the other classifiers. This machine learned ranking model was launched to full production traffic on the eBay item page worldwide in 8 countries including US, UK, and Germany.

Table 3: Lift in A/B test operational metrics.

	CTR	PTR	Revenue
lift	+3.0%	+6.6%	+6.0%

4. CONCLUSIONS AND FUTURE WORK

In this work, we presented a highly scalable architecture which produces high quality similar item recommendations in a diverse semi-structured marketplace. We developed a widely applicable and interpretable pointwise machine learned ranking model trained on implicit eBay user shopping behavior. The model optimized recommendation rank based on probability of purchase. Although many of our marketplace characteristics are unique, the ranking model and sampling strategy is general enough for most domains which require ranking recommendations against a seed item. Our future work consists of adding new features, implementing better-performing offline classifiers for the runtime ranking model, as well as incorporating user personalization and segmentation.

5. ACKNOWLEDGMENTS

We are grateful for invaluable discussions with Tomer Meron, Benjamin Klein, Thomas Pinckney, and Uwe Mayer. We thank the reviewers for their valuable feedback.

6. ADDITIONAL AUTHORS

Paul Wang (eBay Inc., New York City, USA, email: pauwang@ebay.com)

7. REFERENCES

[1] Apache Spark, spark.apache.org/.

[2] D. Arya, V. Ha-Thuc, and S. Sinha. Personalized federated search at LinkedIn. In *CIKM*, 2015.

[3] Elasticsearch, www.elastic.co/products/elasticsearch.

[4] A. Freno et al. One-pass ranking models for low-latency product recommendations. In *SIGKDD*, 2015.

[5] D. Goldberg, D. Nichols, B. M. Oki, and D. Terry. Using collaborative filtering to weave an information tapestry. *Commun. ACM*, 35(12):61–70, Dec. 1992.

[6] Lambda Architecture, lambda-architecture.net/.

[7] P. Li, Q. Wu, and C. J. Burges. Mcrank: Learning to rank using multiple classification and gradient boosting. In *NIPS*, pages 897–904, 2007.

[8] G. Linden, B. Smith, and J. York. Amazon.com recommendations: Item-to-item collaborative filtering. *Internet Computing, IEEE*, 7(1):76–80, 2003.

[9] T.-Y. Liu. Learning to rank for information retrieval. *Foundations and Trends in Information Retrieval*, 3(3):225–331, 2009.

[10] B. Sarwar et al. Item-based collaborative filtering recommendation algorithms. In *WWW*, 2001.

[11] H. Steck. Gaussian ranking by matrix factorization. In *RecSys*, pages 115–122, 2015.

[12] J. Weston et al. Learning to rank recommendations with the k-order statistic loss. In *RecSys*, 2013.

A Package Recommendation Framework for Trip Planning Activities

Idir Benouaret
Sorbonne Universités
Université de technologie de Compiègne
CNRS UMR 7253 Heudiasyc
CS 60 319 - 60 203 Compiègne cedex
idir.benouaret@hds.utc.fr

Dominique Lenne
Sorbonne Universités
Université de technologie de Compiègne
CNRS UMR 7253 Heudiasyc
CS 60 319 - 60 203 Compiègne cedex
dominique.lenne@hds.utc.fr

ABSTRACT

Classical recommender systems provide users with ranked lists of recommendations, where each one consists of a single item. However, these ranked lists are not suitable for applications such as trip planning, which deal with heterogeneous items. In this paper, we focus on the problem of recommending a set of packages to the user, where each package is constituted with a set of different Points of Interest that may constitute a tour. Given a collection of POIs, our goal is to recommend the most interesting packages for the user, where each package satisfies the budget constraints. We formally define the problem and we present a novel composite recommendation system, inspired from composite retrieval. Experimental evaluation of our proposed system, using a real-world dataset demonstrates its quality and its ability to improve both diversity and relevance of recommendations.

Keywords

recommender system, package, top-k, diversity, trip planning

1. INTRODUCTION

Classical recommender systems provide the user with recommendations as ranked lists consisting in single items, e.g., movie, book. In trip planning, a user is interested in suggestions for points of interest (POI), that could be very heterogeneous, e.g., museum, park, restaurant, etc. A tourism recommender system can benefit from a system capable of recommending items organized in packages (bundles) rather than ranked lists, which constitute an improved exploratory experience for the visitor. Then, there is a need to recommend for the user the best packages that match his preferences. Furthermore, there may be a cost for visiting each point of interest (time, price, etc.) that the user may want to constraint with a budget. The budget can also simply be the number of items per package. Some so-called " third generation " travel planning web sites, such as Tripadvisor and YourTour, aim at assisting the user with suggestions of places to visits integrating these kinds of constraints, but the suggestions are often based only on the most popular places and neglect the personalization aspect for the user. Thus, the use of these web sites is very limited. Our contribution in this paper is the design and implementation of a suggestion model promoting diversity and inspired from composite retrieval [1]. The approach we propose is to group suggestions in different packages, where each package is constituted with a set of diverse POIs. Each POI has a cost and a time of visit associated with it, and the user specifies a maximum total budget for any recommended package of items. POIs in each package are chosen using a scoring function that takes into account the personalization, the diversity and the popularity of the items in the package. The evaluation of our proposed system using a real dataset with data crawled from the website Tripadvisor, shows that our system is competitive, it can improve the diversity of recommendations without deteriorating their relevance. The road map of the paper is as follows. After discussing related work in more details (Section 2), we give a formalization of the problem (Section 3). We then describe the model and define the quality criteria of packages. We show how we calculate the score of a package (section 4). In section 5, we describe our algorithm for calculating the top-k packages. In section 6, we subject our system to thorough experimental analysis using a real dataset. We investigate the quality of the recommended packages. Finally, we discuss future work and conclude the paper in Section 7.

2. RELATED WORK

In [2], authors are interested in finding the top-k tuples of entities. Examples of entities could be cities, hotels and airlines, while packages are tuples, they query documents using keywords in order to determine entity scores. A package in their framework has a fixed size, e.g., one city, one hotel and one airline. Instead, in our work, we allow packages of variable size, subject constraints specified by the user. Other closely related work is [4] where a framework is proposed to recommend travel itineraries from online user-generated data, like picture uploads. They formulate the problem of recommending travel itineraries that might be interesting for users while the travel time is under a given time budget. However, in this work, the value (score) of each POI is only determined by the number of times it was mentioned by other users in the social network, whereas in our work, the importance of a POI is determined not only by the popularity of the POI but also with a personalized score depending on user's preferences and his ratings for other POIs. Finally,

RecSys '16, September 15-19, 2016, Boston , MA, USA

DOI: http://dx.doi.org/10.1145/2959100.2959183

the closest work to our's is [6], where the authors explore returning approximate solutions to composite recommendations. The focus of the work is on using a Fagin-style algorithm for variable size packages and proving its optimality. The same authors further develop the idea into a prototype of recommender system for travel planning (CompRec) [7]. However, the score of an item is just the predicted rating of a user, while we believe that using also the popularity of items improves the relevance of the recommended packages. Furthermore, none of these works accounts for the diversity in packages which leads to a better satisfaction of the user.

3. PROBLEM STATEMENT

Given a set I of POIs, a set U of users, an active user $u \in U$ and a POI $i \in I$. We denote by $c(i)$ the cost of POI i and by $t(i)$ the average time needed for visiting POI i. Given a set of POIs $P \subset I$, we define $Score(P)$ the score of a package P, which estimates the quality of a package (see more details in section 4.2.4) , $c(P) = \sum_{i \in P} c(i)$ the cost for a package P and $t(P) = \sum_{i \in P} t(i)$ the time to visit POIs in package P. Given a cost budget B_c and a time budget B_t, a package P is said *Valid* iff $c(P) \leq B_c$ and $t(P) \leq B_t$.

PROBLEM 1. ***Top-k Composite recommendations*** *Given a set I of POIs, an active user u with his preferences background, a cost budget B_c, a time budget B_t and an integer k, a top-k composite recommender system has to determine the top-k packages $P_1, P_2, ..., P_k$ such that each P_i has $c(P_i) \leq B_c$, $t(P_i) \leq B_t$, and among all Valid packages, $P_1, P_2, ..., P_k$ have the k highest scores, i.e $Score(P) \leq Score(P_i)$ for all Valid packages $P \notin \{P_1, P_2, ..., P_k\}$*

4. MODEL

4.1 Distance and Similarity between POIs

Our distance between POIs is based on a taxonomy of hierarchical topic categories organized in a tree structure. Formally, we used a domain ontology developed by [3] to represent these categories. Let be I the set of all possible POIs. Each POI in I is associated to one category in the taxonomy, e.g. museum, park, building, etc. We define the topical distance $dist_t : I \times I \rightarrow \mathbb{N}$ between two POIs i and j as the length of the shortest path between the two categories of i and j in the taxonomy:

$$dist_t(i,j) = sp(c_i, c_j) \tag{1}$$

where c_i, c_j are the categories of POIs i, j and sp is the shortest path function. The topical similarity evaluates in which measure two POIs i and j deal with similar thematics or topics. The similarity depends on the topical distance between the two POIs i, j:

$$sim(i,j) = \frac{1}{1 + dist_t(i,j)} \tag{2}$$

4.2 Packages Quality Criteria

In order to suggest the top-k packages of POIs for a specific user, it is necessary to have a criteria estimating how "good" is a package P according to a user u. We denote it by the score of a package. To this end, we need to measure how a new POI not visited yet by the user would be interesting for him. The popularity is also an important factor in the general appreciation of a POI. In fact, the properties depending only on the popularity of a POI are often more important than the similarity with the user profile [5]. Moreover, we assume that the user is not only interested by visiting POIs he would like, but instead visiting POIs that best cover his interests. For example, a user who likes museums will not be satisfied with a recommended package with only museums. The diversity of POIs in the same package is thus an important criteria for the quality of the package.

4.2.1 Overall Popularity

The overall popularity measures the popularity of a POI $i \in I$:

$$opop(i) = \frac{pop(i)}{max_{j \in I} pop(j)} \in [0,1] \tag{3}$$

where j designates the POIs of I and $pop : I \rightarrow \mathbb{N}$ represents a popularity indicator of a POI. By extension, the overall popularity of a package P is:

$$opop(P) = \frac{\sum_{i \in P} opop(i)}{|P|} \in [0,1] \tag{4}$$

4.2.2 Intra Package Diversity

Most of travel recommender systems focus on the modeling of user preferences in order to get a ranking of the most pertinent POIs. However, the diversity of suggestions has never been the focus point. Nevertheless, it has been suggested that the diversity has a large positive effect on the satisfaction of the user [8]. So, we adapt the intra list diversity introduced by [8] for a package of POIs P, we define the intra package diversity:

$$ipd(P) = \frac{\sum_{i,j \in P} 1 - sim(i,j)}{|P|^2} \tag{5}$$

4.2.3 Estimated Appreciation (Prediction)

The estimated appreciation evaluates to what extent a POI i that a user has not yet rated would be interesting. The estimated appreciation of a user $u \in U$ for a POI $i \in I$ is calculated using a simple item-item collaborative filtering:

$$eapp_u(i) = \frac{\sum_{j \in S_i} rating_u(j) \times sim(i,j)}{\sum_{j \in S_i} sim(i,j)} \tag{6}$$

where j designates POIs of the sample S_i, the set of similar POIs rated by the user u, and $rating_u \rightarrow [0,1]$ associates for a POI the rating given by the user u, divided by the maximum rate. By extension, the estimated appreciation for a user u for a package P is defined by the mean of the estimated appreciation for POIs forming the package:

$$eapp_u(P) = \frac{\sum_{i \in P} eapp_u(i)}{|P|} \in [0,1] \tag{7}$$

4.2.4 Score of a package

The score of a package evaluates the quality of POIs that form a package for a user u according to the overall popularity, the diversity and the estimated appreciation. The score for a package P for a user u is calculated by:

$$Score_u(P) = C_{eapp} \times eapp_u(P) + C_{opop} \times opop(P) + C_{div} \times ipd(P) \tag{8}$$

where $C_{eapp}, C_{opop}, C_{div}$ are positive Coefficients that modulate respectively, the importance of the estimated appreciation, the overall popularity and the diversity in the score function.

5. RECOMMENDING TOP-K PACKAGES

The construction of top-k packages is done in two steps: first, a set of valid packages are produced in large quantities with a cardinality $c >> k$, packages are formed by aggregation around a pivot POI and taking into account the quality criteria. Our approach for forming a set of good valid packages is inspired from the algorithm "BOBO" (*Bundles One-By-One*) introduced by Amer-Yahia *et al.* [1]. We adopted this algorithm to take into account the quality criteria of the packages defined in Section 4.2. The goal of this algorithm is to create c valid packages that respect the budget constraints. It is inspired from $k - nn$ clustering. At each step a POI is chosen as pivot, and a valid package with maximum score is built around that pivot. The pseudo code is described in *algorithm 1.*

BOBO starts with an empty set of packages. Then, a list of candidates pivots POIs is constituted, by ranking I in the descending order of popularity. As long as the number of formed packages is less than c, at each iteration the first POI is taken from the set of *Pivots*, and a package is built around it. This is done by the routine *Pick_bundle* described in algorithm 2. This routine greedily keeps picking the next POI that maximizes the score of the package formed around the pivot, as far as the cost budget and the time budget constraints are satisfied. Let us go back to BOBO's main loop: once a candidate package is created, it is added to *"Packages"* and its elements are removed from *"Pivots"* so that they are not longer used.

Algorithm 1: BOBO

```
Input: I, B_c, B_t, number of packages c
Output: a set c of packages
Packages ← ∅
Pivots ← Descending_sort(I, opop)
while (Pivots ≠ ∅) and |Packages| < c do
    w ← Pivots[0]
    Pivots ← Pivots − {w}
    P ← Pick_bundle(w, I, B_c, B_t)
    Pivots ← Pivots − P
    Packages ← Packages ∪ P
end
return Packages
```

Algorithm 2: PICK_BUNDLE

```
Input: pivot w, I, B_c, B_t
Output: a package P
S ← w
active ← I − {w}
cost ← c(w)
time ← t(w)
while (not finish) do
    i ← argmax_{i∈active} Score_u(S ∪ {i})
    if (cost + c(i) ≤ B_c) and (time + t(i) ≤ B_t) then
        S ← S ∪ {i}
        cost ← cost + c(i)
        time ← time + t(i)
    end
    else
        finish ← true
    end
    active ← active − i
end
return S
```

Once the required number of packages has been created, they are ranked following their respective scores (Section 4.2.4). Afterwards, we select the k packages having the best scores.

6. EXPERIMENTS

6.1 Data Set

The goal of our experiments were: (1) evaluate the relevance of the packages recommended by our algorithm, and (2) evaluate their diversity as well. In order to have a set of POIs constituting potential recommendations, we crawled data from Tripadvisor. Each POI has a thematic category organized in a tree structure, which allows us to construct our similarity measure. In addition, Tripadvisor provides for a POI the number of users rating for a POI, we used it as an indicator of its popularity, for estimating the function $pop : I \to \mathbb{N}$ defined in Section 4.2.1. For our experiments, we crawled users rating information from POIs in the five most popular cities in France. We exclude POIs that have very few or no reviews. The dataset contains 40635 ratings for 1183 POIs by 18227 users, so as we see the data is very sparse. We associate with each POI its cost and its average time of visit crawled also from Tripadvisor. The average price of POIs was close to €7 and the average time for visiting a POI ranges from 30 minutes to 3 hours. Because of the large sparsity of the underlying user rating matrix, we selected the 20 most active users as our sample for testing the algorithms.

Versions	C_{eapp}	C_{opop}	C_{div}
per	1	0	0
pop	0	1	0
div	0	0	1
pop+div	0	1/2	1/2
per+div	1/2	0	1/2
per+pop	1/2	1/2	0
per+pop+div	1/3	1/3	1/3

Table 1: Different versions of our system

6.2 Evaluation Metrics and Experimental Protocol

The following measures are used for evaluation :

Precision: is calculated as the ratio of recommended POIs that are relevant to the total number of recommended POIs.

Diversity: we extend the intralist diversity introduced by *Ziegler et al* [8] to a set of k packages $\{P_1, ..., P_k\}$. The Mean Intralist Diversity (MILD) is defined.

$$diversity = MILD(\{P_1, ..., P_k\}) = \frac{\sum_{i=1}^{k} ILD(P_i)}{k} \tag{9}$$

F_{PD}: the F-measure is the harmonic mean of precision and diversity :

$$F_{PD} = \frac{2 \times precision \times diversity}{precision + diversity} \tag{10}$$

Our goal was to test the impact of personalization (per), popularity (pop) and diversity (div) on the quality of recommendations. To this end, we compared several versions of our system, corresponding to different possible combinations of the factors of C_{eapp}, C_{opop} C_{div}. Each version corresponds to a different combination of the parameters. Versions we tested are summarized in the Table 1. The name of each version indicates the use or not of the different aspects when constituting the set of packages.

We tested our system varying the number of returned packages k, we vary it between four values: $\{5, 10, 15, 20\}$.

	k=5			k=10			k=15			k=20		
	P(%)	D(%)	F_{PD}(%)	P(%)	D(%)	F_{PD}(%)	P(%)	D(%)	F_{PD}(%)	P(%)	D(%)	F_{PD}(%)
per	49.73	40.02	44.35	50.19	41.12	45.20	51.13	42.74	46.56	48.88	43.75	46.17
pop	57.75	47.89	52.36	53.5	51.33	52.39	51.84	49.43	50.59	50.18	48.61	49.38
div	41.01	**61.96**	49.35	43.01	**60.39**	50.25	42.68	**59.21**	49.60	38.08	**57.81**	45.91
pop+div	53.7	55.73	54.69	53.36	58.04	55.60	51.92	56.14	53.94	49.67	55.81	52.56
per+div	47.85	55.03	51.19	49.88	57.84	53.56	48.1	57.18	52.24	48.22	53.46	50.70
per+pop	**59.38**	43.25	50.04	**54.53**	50.57	52.47	**53.03**	50.37	51.66	**51.11**	49.25	50.16
per+pop+div	55.09	58.45	**56.72**	53.66	59.88	**56.59**	51.75	57.33	**54.39**	50.39	55.84	**52.97**
Xie et al	57.24	43.58	49.48	53.32	48.11	50.58	51.65	50.8	51.22	50.45	52.85	51.62

Table 2: Comparison of our different versions with the competitive approach

The cost budget is fixed to €60 and the time budget fixed to 600 minutes. We tested our algorithms under various cost and time budgets with very similar results, so other budgets are omitted for lack of space.

6.2.1 *Competitive Approach*

To evaluate also the effectiveness of the proposed system, we compare our results with the package recommendation method proposed by *Xie et al.* [6], which is the closest work to ours. The authors also computed the estimated appreciation of POIs using an item-item collaborative filtering approach, without taking in consideration the popularity of POIs and the diversity aspect of recommendations.

6.3 Results and discussions

Results of our versions compared to the competitive approach according to precision, diversity and F_{PD} are reported in Table 2. In all our versions, we can notice a high influence of the popularity of POIs with respect to the precision. It is important to underline that the popularity is a significant factor as well as the personalization. In fact, in most cases, the "pop" version leads to a better precision than the "per" version and the "pop +div" version better than the "per+div" version. These results are in accordance with [5], which highlights the importance of the popularity and its effect on the relevance of recommendations. Varying the number of packages, the "per+pop" version always performs the best precision and outperform the algorithm of *Xie et al.*, due to combining the personalization and the popularity. Without surprise, the "div" version is the one who performs the best diversity compared to all others. However, it has also the worst values for precision. Concerning the F-measure between precision and diversity,we notice that the "per+pop+div" realizes the best compromise, and outperforms the competitive algorithm. This version tends to promote a large diversity, performs better than *Xie et al.*, and is not significantly different in precision comparing to the "per + pop" version. Thus, the "per+pop+div" is the best approach when considering both precision and diversity.

7. CONCLUSIONS AND FUTURE WORK

Motivated by applications of trip planning, we studied the problem of recommending packages consisting of sets of POIs. Our composite recommendation system consists of ranking packages according to a score function, where the score of a package depends on the estimated appreciation, the overall popularity and the diversity of POIs constituting the package. We formalized the problem of generating top-k packages recommendations that are under budgets, where a cost and a time is incurred by visiting each recommended POI and the budgets are user specified. We developed an algorithm for retrieving the top-k packages with best scores. The evaluation of our system using a real world dataset crawled from the website Tripadvisor demonstrates its quality and its ability to improve both the relevance and the diversity of recommendations. We plan now to realize a study of the proposed system with real users on a situation of mobility, where the localization context will take an important role on the recommendation process. Furthermore, it will be interesting to compare the preferences of the user between a recommender system providing classical ranked lists and our composite recommender system. A mobile application is currently being developed, so that we can test it later with real users and study the exploratory dimension achieved by the composite approach and its impact on users satisfaction.

8. REFERENCES

[1] S. Amer-Yahia, F. Bonchi, C. Castillo, E. Feuerstein, I. Mendez-Diaz, and P. Zabala. Composite retrieval of diverse and complementary bundles. *Transactions on Knowledge and Data Engineering*, 2014.

[2] A. Angel, S. Chaudhuri, G. Das, and N. Koudas. Ranking objects based on relationships and fixed associations. EDBT, 2009.

[3] L. Castillo, E. Armengol, E. Onaindía, L. Sebastiá, J. González-Boticario, A. Rodríguez, S. Fernández, J. D. Arias, and D. Borrajo. Samap: An user-oriented adaptive system for planning tourist visits. *Expert Systems with Applications*, 2008.

[4] M. De Choudhury, M. Feldman, S. Amer-Yahia, N. Golbandi, R. Lempel, and C. Yu. Automatic construction of travel itineraries using social breadcrumbs. In *Proceedings of the 21st ACM conference on Hypertext and hypermedia*, 2010.

[5] H. Steck. Item popularity and recommendation accuracy. RecSys, 2011.

[6] M. Xie, L. V. Lakshmanan, and P. T. Wood. Breaking out of the box of recommendations: From items to packages. RecSys, 2010.

[7] M. Xie, L. V. Lakshmanan, and P. T. Wood. Comprec-trip: A composite recommendation system for travel planning. In *Data Engineering (ICDE), 2011 IEEE 27th International Conference on*, 2011.

[8] C.-N. Ziegler, S. M. McNee, J. A. Konstan, and G. Lausen. Improving recommendation lists through topic diversification. In *World Wide Web*, 2005.

Recommender Systems with Personality

Amos Azaria and Jason Hong
School of Computer Science, Carnegie Mellon University, Pittsburgh, PA
{azariaa,jasonh}@cs.biu.ac.il

ABSTRACT

We believe that in the future, the most common form of recommender systems will be present in a personal assistant. We claim that such an intelligent agent must be personal, i.e., know its user's preferences and recommend relevant content, a dynamic learner, instructable, supportive and affable. We describe the current state of the art and the challenges which should be addressed in each of these agent properties and provide examples of how we expect future personal agents to convey these properties.

1. INTRODUCTION

Modern smartphones come with an array of rich sensors, fast networking capabilities, significant CPU power, and mass storage. Most smartphones also come with a mobile agent: Android devices come with Google Now, iPhone devices with Siri, and Microsoft devices with Cortana. Despite this, the major use of these intelligent agents is for web search, or for very simple commands such as launching an app or setting an alarm. These agents are not that often used as a recommender systems, and usually do not recommend content without explicitly being asked. Much of the functionality these agents offer does not push far beyond today's direct manipulation user interfaces [8], in which an agent's actions are an immediate response to a user command, or a preprogrammed feature, rather than people using the agent as an actual proxy.

While prototypes for personal assistants date back to over two decades ago [11], we believe that the time is now ripe for making a quantum leap in what an intelligent personal assistant can offer. While, currently, some personal assistants are used for recommendations (e.g. asking Siri for good restaurants near by), and some recommender systems try adding agent personality to them (e.g. Emmy at TasteKid), we believe that future recommender systems will have a much richer "personality" and that the most common form of recommender systems will be a personal assistant. We claim that a personal assistant agent should be: **personal**, being personalized to each user knowing its user's preferences and recommending relevant content, and doing so in a privacy-sensitive manner; **a dynamic learner**, continuously learning and acquiring knowledge about the world and about the user, actively learning the user's preferences; **supportive**, providing long-term assistance, and initiating actions in order to pursue users goals and tasks; **affable**, offering interaction methods which appear natural to the user and can build rapport with her over time; and **instructable**, allowing the *user* to tailor the agent and its recommendations to her personal needs, by allowing the user to *teach* the agent what she wants and how to do it.

Such an agent is nearly possible due to major advances in hardware, systems, algorithms, and data. Smart devices (such as smartphones, smart-watches, smart-glasses, and smart clothes) are starting to become ubiquitous, and each of these devices comes with a rich range of on-board sensors that can gather tremendous amounts of data about their users and the environments in which they operate. The widespread availability of cloud computing, fast wireless networking, and cheap storage further enhances these capabilities. With respect to algorithms and data, the rise of big data, along with relevant machine learning algorithms, provides us with important capabilities which were previously out of reach, such as high-quality automatic speech recognition, image and gesture recognition, machine translation, and natural language understanding and grounding. There has also been a leap in text-to-speech and non-verbal gesture generation for virtual agents. All these advances provide a never ending interaction opportunity for personal agents to learn user's preferences and provide much better recommendations which are much more personalized to each user and tailored to her needs and goals. In this paper, we drill down on each of the themes we believe an intelligent personal agent should be able to offer within a decade and show how these themes are relevant for recommending better content, actions and behavior.

2. A PERSONAL AGENT

The key idea behind recommender systems is that people are different, and that recommendations should vary according to users' personal preferences and interests. In the past, the content on the web was identical for all users (no personalization), in the present, the recommendation system is identical to everyone (but has personalized output depending on the user's history). We believe that in the future, each user will have her own agent which provides these recommendations. In order for a user to feel that recommendations are truly tailored to her they should come from an agent which is truly personalized to her. Using all the sensors and user history as input, the personal agent may collect enormous information on the user. High personalization level of such personal assistants entails that each user may actually have a unique agent. We therefore propose that each agent may have a unique name, voice and body appearance which travel across all possible platforms (phone, watch, glasses, laptop, etc.). Perhaps, these unique names may be non-word names (which can't collide with other

RecSys '16, September 15 - 19, 2016, Boston , MA, USA

ISBN 978-1-4503-4035-9/16/09...$15.00
DOI: http://dx.doi.org/10.1145/2959100.2959138

people the user knows). These names may be generated based on the user's demographics. One name generation method could be based simply on the frequency of different n-grams in names in the user's country, possibly filtered by age and gender[1], or even take into account the user's email, contacts and other personal information. Such agents express the differences between different agents, and make it clear to a user that her agent belongs to her which may help it become more trustworthy.

Since personalization requires collecting sensitive data on the user, it raises a serious threat of privacy invasion. Furthermore, since people are different and unique. Indeed, currently, any usage of an agent comes with a high privacy price tag. Anyone using an agent agrees that any information sent to the agent will serve the company which built it. This implies that people are likely to avoid sharing sensitive information with it. The agent does not actually belong to them, but to some corporation. We believe that this is one of the main roadblocks of this field, and that it will grow stronger as the field continues to advance. We therefore argue that the single overall goal for the agent must be assisting their user and providing relevant content to them in order to help her accomplish her own goals (e.g. saving time, making tasks easier, being more productive, healthier, success in school or other user-defined goals). That is, the agent is there for its user, and data collected by the agent should not be shared with anyone (as if it does not leave the user's phone), unless the user explicitly wants to share this information, or the agent believes that it is the user's will. Using an agent should require a minimal privacy price tag. The current basic market model is that recommender systems are hosted on a website and collect as much information as they can on each user, in order to provide relevant recommendations. Personal agents collect as much information as they can which is shared with the company building those agents, allowing that company to post relevant ads. We believe that if the agent would collect this information and share it will the relevant websites or services on behalf of the user, both sides could benefit. The user will have full control over what is shared with whom, and since the user would receive recommendations which take into account far more information than any singe website could collect, the user is more likely to make a purchase or consume relevant content. While, we may want to assume that all the user specific information does not actually leave the user's phone, this may not be optimal in terms of speed and functionality especially if the agent operates across multiple platforms. Therefore, the user may either have her own hardware which keeps this information, or ,if this information does reside on a companies server, the user must be assured that it is not shared with anyone (not even the agent developers) unless instructed by the user. Another privacy related challenge is selective sharing: since the agent will have access to a large amount of sensitive data, the user cannot always explicitly tell the agent which data to share with whom. Therefore, the agent must learn which information to share with other people, personal agents, or third part agents and apps. The agent is not limited to sharing raw data, but may decide to share (and even sell) some high level, averaged or noised data, share a model built using the data, or provide anonymized data and ensure that the released data may not be de-anonymized. In our vision, there is no single source who has all the data, but many agents each with a different goal, some personal agents and some may be third party agents and even research agents (e.g. a diabetics agent which collects data from diabetics user who decide to share their data). Each agent accesses different data, and knowledge is on a "need to know" basis.

[1]This unique name generation method using letter-based trigram frequency, based on female names, with year of birth of 1980, in the USA, yield the following unique names: Jerlessey, Roberica, Vinaly, Jerin, Pathley, Amarissa, Laniquela, Jillistin and Trany.

3. A DYNAMIC LEARNER

In order to recommend highly relevant content the agent must be a constant learner. The main dimension of learning should be about the individual. Modern smart devices offer a wealth of information about individuals, including one's calendar, Facebook, email, text messages, call logs, and a great number of sensors. This kind of information can be used to learn about a person's communication habits, relationship with others, and general activities, which in-tern could be used to provide more relevant content or recommendations. However, one major research challenge is that it can be hard to create generalizable models of individuals. For example, it is easy for anyone in the world to verify many general inferences (e.g. "Hockey is a sport"), but very few people can verify a personal inference such as "John is the user's best friend". Another major research challenge is that data is siloed across many different devices, apps, services, and formats. As one example, Wiese et al. [15] have found that a person's contacts often spread across their smartphone, Facebook, LinkedIn, and email. Wiese et al. have pointed that it may be hard to integrate contacts across these services, in part due to unusual contact names such as "Pat (Neighbor)," "Mom at Home", and "Do Not Answer". We believe that learning both user preferences and a general knowledge should be an active and never ending process.

Learning should not be limited to the individual user's preferences, but the agent could also better perform if it learned general facts about the world. One example for a never ending learner is NELL [12], which has the goal of reading and learning from the mass amounts of text on the web. The same can be done with the large quantity of images [4], sounds, and videos on the web. This kind of knowledge can help disambiguate queries, understand relationships between entities, common-sense, and help with execution of tasks. For example, if the agent is given a task to organize a surprise party for John, it should know that it should contact John's friends and *not* John.

The widespread adoption of crowdsourcing also offers new opportunities for learning. An agent that requires certain information (perhaps for completing a certain task) might post it on a question answering websites or on a crowdsourcing platform, and have other crowd workers rate the quality of the response. Over time, the agent might also learn from these crowd responses in an active manner. One example for a system that allows people to converse with the crowd is Chorus, [10]. Chorus uses the crowd to rank its own candidate responses in an attempt to provide the best response to a user's query. These responses are later used to train the system.

A simple usage of this knowledge is annotation of content with respect to user goals and preferences. For example, assume that the agent knows that the user is interested in "space exploration" the agent should know that an article about "the curiosity rover" is highly relevant, despite not mentioning the word "space" or even "planet" or "Mars" in it. The agent may use its learned knowledge to encourage the user to perform certain tasks, for example, the agent may tell a user aiming at wight loss, that her friend has just posted that he is looking for a partner for running, or the agent may notice that it is currently raining outside and thus suggest indoor activity instead. When communicating with the user the agent can also refer to common ground, for example, the agent can use a landmark, when assisting the user in a navigation task (e.g. "drive past your grocery store").

Perhaps, the most important knowledge which the agent must pursue to acquire is user preferences. Learning users' preferences is not limited to user history purchase, or a thumbs up or down on a given content. An intelligent personal agent must proactively try to understand its user's preferences. Therefore, the agent should use active learning and suggests content which may not be the content which the agent predicts that the user will like best, but by suggesting this content the agent learns more about the user, and future content can be better personalized. User preferences can also be learned using preferences of social groups, using common methods such as collaborative filtering [2]. The agent can approach the exploration and exploitation problem in the larger context of all users and try to maximize the social welfare. User preference elicitation is not limited to content provision, but also has to do with learning users privacy preferences. The agent will learn the user's privacy preferences (using similar techniques) and consider these preferences when deciding whether to share some information with a service provider or other agents. Since user models are complex they should not be treated only as a set of weights to be assigned to a set of features. The intelligent agent should try to adopt a set of rules which best explains user actions and the content which the user is most interested in (possibly using first order logic) [14]. The user should be allowed to update this user model and rules according to her actual preferences and interests.

Another challenge for the agent is to learn user routines and usage patterns by observing user behavior. These routines and patterns can be used to discover irregularities, which may impose that the user may require help, in which case, the agent could recommend some actions such as visiting a physician, recommend some different behavior, such a healthier diet, or a relevant product which may be of help. The agent might also recommend a pattern used by a different user, if it assumes that it is more efficient. User usage patterns can also be useful when considering a perfect timing for the agent to interrupt the user for suggesting content, triggering reminders, or obtaining feedback.

4. SUPPORTIVE

We believe that a personal assistant should be a long-term assistant, i.e. take into account the user's long-term goals while providing recommendations or taking actions, just as human assistants may do. A human assistant seeks relevant content and accomplishes tasks in order to complete the requester's long-term goal. Current recommeder systems are very myopic, most of the time recommending a specific product without taking into account that the user may be returning to the website the next day. While some recommender system do try taking the future into account [13], still they are very "narrow minded", limited to recommending a set of products or content, and are totally unaware of the broader context, which includes what the user actually wants and her goals. Current personal assistants, on the other hand, only respond to user queries, actions or specific events. For example, the user may ask a question, and get a response, or send a message, set an alarm or any other action which is immediately executed. The agent should learn about many possible long-term goals in general, but may modify the common time-line structure of a specific goal to best suit its user. A long term assistant must be aware of some of the user's goals and tasks, and initiate actions in order to pursue the accomplishment of these goals over a period of time.

One example of such long-term assistant may include writing a paper for a conference. The agent is aware of the paper content, the co-authors, the deadlines and the venue and monitors the user's progress. The agent can recommend related work and notify the user if new relevant papers are published. It can show a dashboard helping the user track the progress in writing the paper and alert the user when proposed milestones should be reached and make sure that the user notices relevant emails. If required, the agent may recommend that the user contacts co-authors who were asked to provide feedback or write certain parts, if it notices that this hasn't been done. Eventually, the agent may help in registering for the venue and recommend a hotel and flight. The agent can also help with reimbursements before or after the trip. The agent can apply knowledge it has about trips in general for providing recommendations (such as interesting places to visit, restaurants, hotels etc.). Additional long-term examples may include, losing weight, health behaviors such as workout and taking medication, teaching a class. A long-term goal may even be buying an item, such as a good camera, in which the agent may recommend content which will allow the user to learn about the possible options and important properties of the interested item (e.g. ISO, HDR, Shutter-speed, focal length, aperture etc.), and only then recommend content related to specific items or brands. With such goals which span over months or even years, it may be challenging for the agent to acknowledge whether it was helpful, and whether its provided content was useful. Depending on its belief, it may decide to selectively share some information with other users' agents.

5. AFFABLE

Human communication and rapport establishment involves many channels, including verbal speech, tone, and body language. The timing of speech also plays a role, with people cutting-off or completing each other's sentences. Humans also take into account each other's context and will talk differently if they know, for example, that someone is currently driving. However, today's agents only make use of very little of this rich input. Recent advances in gesture detection, acoustic modeling, and virtual agents make it possible to offer an embodied agent which can take in as input both audio and visual non-verbal cues [5]. The agent can also incorporate multiple approaches to establish rapport with the user, for example by varying its language and gestures as a function of the rapport level it believes that it is having with the user [6]. This same agent should be ubiquitous, and allowed to be accessed via wearable devices, laptops, tablets, etc. Cross-device presence raises a major challenge for a consistent and unified user experience. The agent must be fully aware of its actions and which interaction channels are currently being used. For example, if the user is using a navigation application, and tells the agent "I can take it from here", the agent should reply gracefully and stop providing navigation instructions (unlike current agents which are not aware that they are currently providing navigation instructions, and thus perform a web search instead). The agent also needs to appear as unified to users, as if it were a single entity, despite having a wide range of front-ends that users interact with. The agent also needs to capture what interactions have happened on different devices, and also be aware that it may not be able to perform certain tasks on certain devices.

6. INSTRUCTABLE

Current personal agents are rigid, limited to predefined commands, and not extendable by the end users. For example, if Google Now finds a flight reservation in a user's email it will recommend the user to leave for the airport when it is time to do so. However, this capability is predefined (handcrafted) and the user cannot extend this functionality by requesting the agent to notify her if she should leave for an important meeting located out of town. Current apps are developed only if there are enough users who will use them.

While this theme falls beyond recommender systems, our vision is to allow end users to instruct their agent in natural language, using the agent's sensors and effectors as well as its general and private knowledge. The user should be able to define any procedure or rule (if-then clause) in a natural way, just as the user would instruct and teach another human [1, 7]. Recent advances in grounded language acquisition [3], learning by demonstration [9] and natural language parsing and understanding, lead us to believe that overcoming this challenge is closer than ever.

If we take the above example, a user should be able to define her own command simply by saying: "let me know when it's time to leave for the airport". The agent may know how to add this rule, but if not, the agent may ask follow-up questions leading the user to further explain. Users will be able to define numerous functionalities without a need for knowledge on programming. Once functionalities are defined, users will be able to share these functionalities with each other.

We argue that the agent should learn these commands on demand and in a natural way for the user, i.e., the user gives commands (or creates rules) and if the agent doesn't understand, it may ask the user to explain what it should do (or how it should apply the rule). With such methodology, the user is not required to inform the agent that it is about to teach it something new, but simply uses the agent casually, and only if the agent fails, will the user be required to teach it. Since the user actually needs this functionality (and thus gave the agent the command), she may be willing to spend the time and teach the agent this new functionality. Once acquired, the user may share this new acquired command with others or the public. If, on the other hand, the user refuses to teach the agent or fails doing so, the agent may contact the crowd for help. Some users (or crowd workers) may also help by defining composite virtual sensors which can be used by others.

7. CONCLUSION

In this paper we present our vision for a personal assistant, argue that in the future, the most common form of recommender system would be a personal assistant, and list the most important properties of such an agent. The question remains, as whether a personal assistant can be viewed as a form of a recommender system. We believe that any boundaries between the two, lie in the level of autonomy given to the agent.

In the present, the most commonly used recommender system, is one in which the recommender system responds either to an explicit or implicit request by a user, and provides either recommended items, content, movies, etc. The next level of autonomy, could include agents that initiate *action* recommendation such as recommending that the user leaves to the airport (as present in Google Now). The next level can include an agent that takes actions on behalf of the user but still requires confirmation on any such action (for example, any email it sends on behalf of the user). All actions of such an agent, could still be viewed as a recommendations. The next level of autonomy, includes an agent which may autonomously take actions on behalf of the user if it is confident enough that the user would confirm the action. Future personal assistants may either have the user set a threshold for this confident level, or learn the optimal threshold for each user and each domain (based on user actions and data). We believe that this intermediate-level of autonomy is the perfect blend of recommender systems and fully autonomous agents. Indeed one of the original papers to describe the use of personal assistants, took use of such a threshold and performed actions autonomously, if such a threshold was met [11]. A fully autonomous agent which acts on behalf of the user at all times (possibly leaving the user some high-level control), is no longer a recommender system. However, we believe that while such level of autonomy may be useful for some domains (e.g. space exploration), it is not very useful as a personal assistant, as we believe that even in the far fetched future, users would always want some level of direct control over their personal assistants.

8. ACKNOWLEDGMENT

This work was supported by the Yahoo! InMind project for the development of an intelligent personal mobile agent.

9. REFERENCES

[1] Amos Azaria, Jayant Krishnamurthy, and Tom M Mitchell. Instructable intelligent personal agent. In *AAAI*, volume 4, 2016.

[2] John S Breese, David Heckerman, and Carl Kadie. Empirical analysis of predictive algorithms for collaborative filtering. In *Uncertainty in artificial intelligence*, pages 43–52. Morgan Kaufmann Publishers Inc., 1998.

[3] David L Chen and Raymond J Mooney. Learning to interpret natural language navigation instructions from observations. *San Francisco, CA*, pages 859–865, 2011.

[4] Xinlei Chen, Ashish Shrivastava, and Arpan Gupta. Neil: Extracting visual knowledge from web data. In *Computer Vision (ICCV)*, pages 1409–1416. IEEE, 2013.

[5] Fiorella De Rosis, Catherine Pelachaud, Isabella Poggi, Valeria Carofiglio, and Berardina De Carolis. From greta's mind to her face: modelling the dynamics of affective states in a conversational embodied agent. *International journal of human-computer studies*, 59(1):81–118, 2003.

[6] Lixing Huang, Louis-Philippe Morency, and Jonathan Gratch. Virtual rapport 2.0. In *Intelligent virtual agents*, pages 68–79. Springer, 2011.

[7] Ting-Hao Kenneth Huang, Amos Azaria, and Jeffrey P Bigham. Instructablecrowd: Creating if-then rules via conversations with the crowd. In *CHI*, pages 1555–1562. ACM, 2016.

[8] Edwin L Hutchins, James D Hollan, and Donald A Norman. Direct manipulation interfaces. *Human–Computer Interaction*, 1(4):311–338, 1985.

[9] George Konidaris, Scott Kuindersma, Roderic Grupen, and Andrew Barto. Robot learning from demonstration by constructing skill trees. *The International Journal of Robotics Research*, 2011.

[10] Walter S Lasecki, Rachel Wesley, Jeffrey Nichols, Anand Kulkarni, James F Allen, and Jeffrey P Bigham. Chorus: a crowd-powered conversational assistant. In *UIST*.

[11] Pattie Maes et al. Agents that reduce work and information overload. *Communications of the ACM*, 37(7):30–40, 1994.

[12] Tom M Mitchell, William Cohen, Estevam Hruschka, Partha Talukdar, Justin Betteridge, Andrew Carlson, Dalvi Mishra, et al. Never-ending learning. In *AAAI'15*, 2015.

[13] Guy Shani, Ronen I Brafman, and David Heckerman. An mdp-based recommender system. In *Uncertainty in artificial intelligence*, pages 453–460. Morgan Kaufmann Publishers Inc., 2002.

[14] William Yang Wang, Kathryn Mazaitis, and William W Cohen. Programming with personalized pagerank: a locally groundable first-order probabilistic logic. In *Information & Knowledge Management*, pages 2129–2138. ACM, 2013.

[15] Jason Wiese, Jason I Hong, and John Zimmerman. Challenges and opportunities in data mining contact lists for inferring relationships. In *Proceedings of Pervasive and Ubiquitous Computing*, pages 643–647. ACM, 2014.

Past, Present, and Future of Recommender Systems: An Industry Perspective

Xavier Amatriain
Quora
650 Castro St. #450
Mountain View, CA 94041, USA
xavier@quora.com

Justin Basilico
Netflix, Inc.
121 Albright Way
Los Gatos, CA 95032, USA
jbasilico@netflix.com

ABSTRACT

When the Netflix Prize launched in 2006, it put a spotlight on the importance and use of recommender systems in real-world applications. The competition provided many lessons, and many more have been learned since the Grand Prize was awarded in 2009. The use of recommender systems in industry has continued to grow driven by the availability of many kinds of user data and the continued interest for the area within the research community. In this paper, we will describe what we see as the past, present, and future of recommender systems from an industry perspective.

1. INTRODUCTION

Recommender Systems in industry are a main-stream application of large-scale machine learning, data-driven innovation, human computer interaction, and other research. Diverse application areas such as e-commerce, Internet music and video, news, search, gaming, and even online dating apply similar techniques that leverage large volumes of data to fulfill a user's needs in a personalized fashion. They have wide applicability because they can increase core business metrics such as customer satisfaction and revenue.

In this paper, we start by describing the main lessons from the Netflix Prize, which constitute, in our view, the past of recommender systems. We then describe the current landscape of recommender systems in industry and the main techniques currently used. Finally, we highlight some research directions that we think are potentially very valuable from an industry perspective.

2. PAST: THE NETFLIX PRIZE

In 2006, Netflix announced the Netflix Prize, a competition to predict movie ratings on a 5-star scale. Netflix conducted this competition to find new ways to improve its recommendations. However, they had to come up with a proxy question that was easier to evaluate and quantify: the root mean squared error (RMSE) between the predicted and actual rating. They offered a $1 million prize to whomever provided a solution that reduced RMSE by 10% compared to their existing system, Cinematch. The Netflix Prize put a spotlight on the Recommender Systems area and highlighted the value of generating personalized recommendations. It was a landmark event that increased interest in the research area. Its crisp problem definition enabled thousands of teams to focus on improving a single metric. While this was a simplification of the recommendation problem, many valuable lessons were learned.

After the first year of competition, the KorBell team won the first Progress Prize with an 8.43% improvement. They reported more than 2000 hours of work to come up with a combination of 107 algorithms that put them at the top of the leaderboard. Netflix focused on the two best performing algorithms in the ensemble: a Matrix Factorization (MF) [12] called SVD++ and Restricted Boltzmann Machines (RBM) [22]. The original code was built to handle 100 million ratings and but Netflix had over 5 billion. Also, it was designed to run on a static dataset and not built to adapt as members added more ratings. Once Netflix overcame those challenges, they put both algorithms into production.

Many other learnings came out of the competition. For example, early on, it became clear that temporal dynamics was an important factor [11]. Another finding was that there is a large amount of noise in the ratings provided by users [2]. After almost three years, the final ensemble that won the grand prize was an impressive compilation of work, blending hundreds of models to finally cross the finish line [3]. It highlighted the power of ensembles to combine heterogeneous models and achieve maximum accuracy. Netflix evaluated some of the methods in the final solution, however, the additional increase in RMSE did not justify the large engineering effort to productionize them.

3. PRESENT: RECOMMENDATION BEYOND RATING PREDICTION

Many companies have discovered through the years that there is significant business value in incorporating recommendations to personalize much of their user experience. In this section we briefly survey different industrial scenarios for recommender systems as well as different formulations of the recommender problem that go beyond the paradigm of rating prediction.

3.1 Recommender Systems in Industry

Recommendation systems are used by many companies in a variety of application domains. Each domain has its own unique recommendation challenges. We provide here a short overview of some of the more well-known applications in industry.

Starting with Netflix, their approach to recommendations changed a lot since the Prize. Its service changed from DVD-rental-by-mail to instant video streaming across many devices. Netflix relies primarily on the recommendation system to help with people find something to watch that they will enjoy [7]. It does so by incorporating recommendations to personalize as much of the user experience as possible. Beyond Netflix, video recommendation has been

Recsys '16 September 15–19, 2016, Boston, MA, USA

ISBN 978-1-4503-4035-9/16/09...$15.00

DOI: http://dx.doi.org/10.1145/2959100.2959144

an active area of research so, unsurprisingly, it is applied to recommend a variety of content spanning movies, TV shows, live, and user-generated. For instance, recommendations help people navigate the vast amounts of user-generated video within YouTube [6].

Music recommendation [4] is also an active application area. Pandora, for instance, centers their business model around creating personalized music stations. They combine collaborative filtering techniques with curated data called the Music Genome Project [24]. Spotify also provides personalized music recommendations in its service. EchoNest, a startup later acquired by Spotify, combined different approaches including collaborative filtering, metadata, and audio signal analysis [13].

Today most e-commerce sites and applications have a recommendation engine powering some of their user experience. The first large e-commerce company credited with a recommender system at the core of their experience is Amazon, who initially used a simple item-item collaborative filtering approach [14]. Their current experience includes many different levels of recommendation: from the homepage to many product pages having lists of other products bought or viewed. Other retail companies such as eBay have also incorporated recommendations in their experience [29].

News is another area where companies use recommendation approaches to personalize content for a user's interests. For example, Google News provided recommendations for news articles from the beginning [5]. For news recommendation, some of the key challenges are freshness, where relevant articles may have a very limited time span, and diversity, where there can be a large number of articles about the same topic. However, they have the advantage of using natural language processing techniques to create features.

Social networks also provided new recommendation scenarios. Twitter, for example, introduced their Who to Follow algorithm to recommend new social connections [9]. The combination of social with other kinds of signals [10] is a very common approach in products like Twitter or Facebook [16]. Quora has an overlay social network where different kinds of recommendations take place. Besides feeds and who to follow, Quora uses social signals to influence many kinds of recommendations. Another example of social recommendations are online dating sites, where the success of the system is not determined by one user receiving a good recommendation but rather by both parties accepting it [18]. Two-side recommendations are important for many social applications; Quora uses it to recommend which users might be able to answer a question.

Many of the previous examples illustrate the different or complimentary requirements that recommender systems have from an industrial point of view. Some important issues that are mentioned in most of these publications are scalability, business metrics, and integration of the system in the overall user experience. Typically the way algorithms are chosen in industry applications is by running randomized, controlled experiments (A/B tests) that measure the value of one approach over another.

3.2 Everything is a Recommendation

Personalization in many products starts on the homepage, which is usually displayed after login on a device. In the case of Netflix, this page consists of groups of videos arranged in horizontal rows that create a grid of videos scrollable in two dimensions. Each row has a title that conveys the intended connection between the videos in that row. Most of Netflix' recommendation approach is embodied in the way they generate rows, select rows, choose videos for a row, order the videos in a row, and order the rows on a page. On the other hand, Quora's homepage is organized around the central idea of a personalized feed, which is common in other social products like Facebook and Twitter, where recommended content items are displayed as a summary card and they can be scrolled vertically. These applications make recommendation front-and-center by delivering them as their primary user experience. With such an emphasis on the recommendations, an important element for all these systems is providing *awareness* and *explanations* for why an item was recommended.

While search or browsing is often provided as an alternative to using recommendations, even a situation where a user enters a search query can be an opportunity for recommendation. For example, the auto-complete suggestions when the user starts typing can be personalized and interpreted as recommendation over a constrained set. LinkedIn's Metaphor system is an example of a complete search recommendation system [20].

3.3 Beyond Explicit Feedback

Explicit ratings are neither the only feedback sites get from users nor the best kind of feedback. Implicit feedback is much more readily available than ratings and requires no extra user effort. For instance, on a web page you can have users visiting a URL or clicking on an link as a positive feedback. In a music service, a user can start playing a song. Also, many of these recommendation applications focus on helping a user choose an action (click, buy, read, listen, watch), so clearly information about previous actions is highly relevant for predicting future actions. That is why many recent recommendation approaches focus on the more reliable and readily available data from implicit feedback. For example, Bayesian Personalized Ranking (BPR) [21], uses it to compute a personalized ranking. Implicit and explicit feedback can also be combined in different ways, for example using SVD++, logistic ordinal regression [17] to provide a mapping, or taking a Bayesian approach like Matchbox [27].

3.4 Ranking

Central to many industrial recommenders is a personalized ranking system. Its goal is to find the best ordering of a set of items for a user within a specific context. Netflix and YouTube optimize ranking algorithms to put videos that a user is most likely to play and enjoy at the beginning of the list. Quora and Facebook do the same to optimize the probability that the user finds a story in Feed interesting. In all these cases, this is done by learning a scoring function $f_{\texttt{rank}} : U \times V \times C \to \mathbb{R}$ over users, items, and contexts.

An obvious baseline for a ranking function to optimize consumption is popularity. The reason is clear: on average, a user is most likely to be interested in what most others are interested in. However, popularity is the opposite of personalization; it will produce the same ordering of items for every user. Thus, the first goal of a personalized ranking function is to be better than item popularity and thus better satisfy users with varying tastes. One obvious way to approach this when rating data is available is to incorporate the predicted rating of each item. Rather than using either popularity or predicted rating on their own, we can learn to produce rankings that balance both of these aspects. This two-dimensional model is a basic example of a ranking function; real products use many other features.

The traditional *pointwise* approach for Learning to Rank (LTR) treats ranking as a simple binary classification problem where the only input are positive and negative examples. Typical models used in this context include Logistic Regression, or Gradient Boosted Decision Trees. *Pairwise* algorithms optimize a loss function defined on pairwise preferences to minimize the number of inversions. BPR [21] is a good example of such an approach. Going further, *listwise* approaches try to directly optimize the ranking of the whole list instead of individual pairs. RankALS [28], for example, defines an objective function that directly includes the ranking optimization and then uses Alternating Least Squares for optimizing. These approaches use rank-specific information retrieval metrics to measure the performance of a ranking model. Ideally, we would like to directly optimize our models those same metrics. However, they are not differentiable and standard methods cannot be directly applied. Some methods like CLiMF [25] use a smoothed version of the objective function to run gradient descent.

4. FUTURE: RESEARCH DIRECTIONS WITH INDUSTRIAL APPLICABILITY

In this section, we will describe some future research directions in Recommender Systems for industry use. It is important to note that there are other issues, such as user and item cold-starting or finding the right metric that correlates to long-term user satisfaction, that are far from being solved. These issues, however, have already been discussed at length in the research literature. Our goal here is to focus the attention of the research community in directions that are very important for industry but are less well studied.

4.1 Full Page Optimization

While one-dimensional ranking is already a step beyond rating prediction and can be further optimized for presentation [23], we are most interested in optimizing a recommendation experience over a complete page. Generating a full page that is personalized and optimized is complex. In the Netflix scenario, the set of available candidate rows is much larger than the catalog of individual items since the same item can be included in many different rows and the row candidates need to be selected and ranked together. Also, when optimizing a whole page, we not only optimize for relevance, but also other aspects like diversity and freshness. An ideal full page optimization algorithm would also be able to personalize how recommendations are mixed with other elements of the user experience by understanding a user's browsing or attention behavior [15]. It may also be useful to adapt a page within a session as a user's actions reveal their current intents.

While this is not yet a common theme in the literature, there are a few recent papers that address the page optimization area. For example, [1] present an approach in the context of news involving a sequential click model for the user and a relevance model that promotes diversity through submodular functions. Another example is [30], where the layout of elements on a search results page is performed using a learned function over both the page elements and layout.

4.2 Personalizing How We Recommend

Another direction for improvement in recommendation systems is personalizing not just *what* we recommend but also *how* we recommend. For example, many recommendation approaches have assumptions or parameters balancing how much diversity, novelty, popularity, etc. the system to produces. However, different people can vary quite a bit in their desired levels of these aspects. When doing recommendations internationally, as is needed in many industrial applications, this also means properly adapting to the balance to needs and tastes of diverse cultures and languages. Another area is personalizing how recommendations are displayed. For a given item, there are many options on how it could be presented, along with many pieces of supporting evidence to help a user decide whether or not to choose it. There is the opportunity to make recommendations even more powerful by surfacing the most useful information for that specific user to make a decision. This goes beyond just generating explanations from recommendation algorithm itself but instead considering all of the aspects of presentation (images, descriptions, metadata, connections to other items, etc.) as elements that can be personalized. In this Netflix case, this may mean deciding whether or not to show explanations, reviews, average ratings, play trailers, cast information, and so forth, based on which ones are most likely to result in high-quality choices. Going further, the entire interaction paradigm for a recommendation system could be personalized.

4.3 Indirect Feedback

While we have seen a shift in industry from explicit to implicit feedback, most work has focused on direct forms of feedback: a user directly performing an action on an item. A shortcoming in using standard implicit feedback is that we do not see negative feedback; the data is either positive or missing. The missing data includes both items that the user explicitly chose to ignore because they were not appealing and items that would have been perfect recommendations but were never presented to the user [26]. One piece of information that can help is knowing if items were displayed to the user. This adds very valuable information, but slightly complicates the formulation of our recommendation problem. Approaches such as Collaborative Competitive Filtering (CCF) [31] can use this information by modeling not only the collaboration between similar users and items, but also the competition between items for user attention. A related issue related to how items are presented is the so-called position bias: An item that is presented in the first position of a list is more likely to be seen and chosen than one that is further down [19]. Thus, a deeper understanding of causality has a lot of potential to help recommendation systems.

As someone interacts with an application that involves recommendations, a lot of other, indirect forms of information about how they navigate is also collected. Also, indirect feedback is linked with a lot of contextual information. In the case of Netflix, for example, the user's preference for shows might depend on variables such as time of the day, day of the week, or viewing device. There is the potential for effective improvements in applications that make use of context [8]. However, indirect and contextual variables represents having to deal with more data that is often noisy and creates a higher dimensional problem space.

4.4 Value-aware Recommendations

The recommender systems community has traditionally separated recommender systems into two kinds: content-based and collaborative filtering. Nowadays, both techniques are combined in many different ways. For example, content-based recommendations are used as a solution for cold-start. However, in both cases, data extracted from the content or the user interactions is used to optimize the same thing: the probability a user uses the recommendation. Unfortunately, this formulation is based on an assumption that all content has the same value. However, in many applications, this is not the case.

In e-commerce some items might have a higher margin for the retailer while giving the same satisfaction to the user [32]. In media/news recommendation, we might have content that is very similar on the surface but are vastly different levels of quality. For example, Quora is interested in recommending items of a certain quality so that the norms of the social network evolve in a way where quality is valued. Most online services will care about recommending the kind of content that drives long-term retention as opposed to the kind of content that might increase short-term clicks but might not result in long-term user satisfaction. We also may want to make sure that our algorithms are not biased against certain kinds of users, for example not reinforcing prejudices. As such, it is important to also keep in mind a user's values.

Many products define additional rules to filter or promote content that thought to have a positive long-term effect in one of the dimensions mentioned above. However, there is a clear need to come up with algorithms that care holistically about the long-term value of the item being recommended so that given a similar probability user engagement, the algorithm can steer towards long-term gains. We call this family of algorithms *value-aware recommendations*.

An extreme and forward-looking version of this would be for recommendation systems to additionally recommend what new items or content that does not exist should be created to fill missing needs and add the most value. Companies are already doing this to some extent in evaluating items. Netflix uses data to decide whether or not a piece of content should be licensed. Quora uses the probability of authors creating good quality and engaging answers as a way to route questions to the right people. However, there is a lot of potential impact in researching how to make recommendations for what new items would add the most value.

5. CONCLUSION

The Netflix Prize abstracted the recommendation problem to a simplified proxy of accurately predicting ratings. It is now clear that this is just one of many components in an effective industrial recommendation system. They also need to account for factors like diversity, context, evidence, freshness, and novelty. Balancing these often competing factors can be a daunting task but we have found that it is best handled using a range of algorithmic approaches and many types of data. We also need optimized approaches, appropriate metrics, rapid experimentation frameworks, solid algorithmic techniques, great user interfaces, and scalable architectures embedded within a sound methodology for figuring out what actually improves the user experience. All of this is driven forward by the innovation happening in the Recommendation System community. When industry and research work hand-in-hand to define the future, we find ourselves continually making progress towards that goal of creating the best possible experience for people all over the world.

6. REFERENCES

[1] A. Ahmed, C. Teo, S.V.N. Vishwanathan, and A. Smola. Fair and balanced: Learning to present news stories. WSDM '12.

[2] X. Amatriain, J. M. Pujol, and N. Oliver. I Like It... I Like It Not: Evaluating User Ratings Noise in Recommender Systems. In *UMAP '09*. 2009.

[3] R. M. Bell and Y. Koren. Lessons from the Netflix Prize Challenge. *SIGKDD Explor. Newsl.*, 9(2), December 2007.

[4] O. Celma. *Music Recommendation and Discovery: The Long Tail, Long Fail, and Long Play*. 2010.

[5] A. S. Das, M. Datar, A. Garg, and S. Rajaram. Google news personalization: Scalable online collaborative filtering. WWW '07, 2007.

[6] J. Davidson et. al. The youtube video recommendation system. RecSys '10, 2010.

[7] C. Gomez-Uribe and N. Hunt. The Netflix recommender system: Algorithms, business value, and innovation. *ACM Trans. Manage. Inf. Syst.*, 6(4), December 2015.

[8] M. Gorgoglione, U. Panniello, and A. Tuzhilin. The effect of context-aware recommendations on customer purchasing behavior and trust. RecSys '11, 2011.

[9] P. Gupta, Goel, Lin, Sharma, Wang, and Zadeh. WTF: The Who to Follow Service at Twitter. WWW '13.

[10] M. Jamali and M. Ester. Trustwalker: a random walk model for combining trust-based and item-based recommendation. KDD '09, 2009.

[11] Y. Koren. Collaborative filtering with temporal dynamics. KDD '09, 2009.

[12] Y. Koren, R. Bell, and C. Volinsky. Matrix Factorization Techniques for Recommender Systems. *Computer*, 42(8), August 2009.

[13] P. Lamere. I've got 10 million songs in my pocket: Now what? RecSys '12, 2012.

[14] G. Linden, B. Smith, and J. York. Amazon.com recommendations: Item-to-item collaborative filtering. *IEEE Internet Computing*, 7(1), January 2003.

[15] V. Navalpakkam, L. Jentzsch, R. Sayres, S. Ravi, A. Ahmed, and A. Smola. Measurement and modeling of eye-mouse behavior in presence of nonlinear page layouts. WWW '13.

[16] W. Oremus. Who controls your Facebook feed. *Slate*, January 2016.

[17] D. Parra, A. Karatzoglou, X. Amatriain, and I. Yavuz. Implicit feedback recommendation via implicit-to-explicit ordinal logistic regression mapping. In *Proc. of the 2011 CARS Workshop*, 2011.

[18] L. Pizzato, T. Rej, T. Chung, I. Koprinska, and J. Kay. Recon: A reciprocal recommender for online dating. RecSys '10, 2010.

[19] F. Radlinski, M. Kurup, and T. Joachims. How does clickthrough data reflect retrieval quality? CIKM '08, 2008.

[20] A. Reda, Y. Park, M. Tiwari, C. Posse, and S. Shah. Metaphor: A system for related search recommendations. CIKM '12, 2012.

[21] S. Rendle, C. Freudenthaler, Z. Gantner, and L. S. Thieme. BPR: Bayesian personalized ranking from implicit feedback. UAI '09, 2009.

[22] R. Salakhutdinov, Mnih, and Hinton. Restricted Boltzmann machines for collaborative filtering. In *Proc of ICML '07*.

[23] O. Sar Shalom, N. Koenigstein, U. Paquet, and H. Vanchinathan. Beyond collaborative filtering: The list recommendation problem. WWW '16, 2016.

[24] Science. Rockin' to the Music Genome. *Science*, 311(5765), 2006.

[25] Y. Shi, A. Karatzoglou, L. Baltrunas, M. Larson, N. Oliver, and A. Hanjalic. CLiMF: learning to maximize reciprocal rank with collaborative less-is-more filtering. RecSys '12.

[26] H. Steck. Training and testing of recommender systems on data missing not at random. In *Proc. of KDD '10*, 2010.

[27] D. H. Stern, R. Herbrich, and T. Graepel. Matchbox: large scale online bayesian recommendations. WWW '09, 2009.

[28] G. Takács and D. Tikk. Alternating least squares for personalized ranking. RecSys '12, 2012.

[29] J. Wang, B. Sarwar, and N. Sundaresan. Utilizing related products for post-purchase recommendation in e-commerce. RecSys '11, 2011.

[30] Y. Wang, D. Yin, L. Jie, P. Wang, M. Yamada, Y. Chang, and Q. Mei. Beyond ranking: Optimizing whole-page presentation. WSDM '16, 2016.

[31] S.H. Yang, B. Long, A.J. Smola, H. Zha, and Z. Zheng. Collaborative competitive filtering: learning recommender using context of user choice. SIGIR '11, 2011.

[32] Y. Zhang, Q. Zhao, Y. Zhang, D. Friedman, M Zhang, Y. Liu, and S. Ma. Economic recommendation with surplus maximization. In *WWW '16*, 2016.

Algorithms Aside: Recommendation as the Lens of Life

Tamas Motajcsek
Gravity R&D Zrt
tamas.motajcsek@gravityrd.com
Hungary

Jean-Yves Le Moine
JCP-Connect
jyleme@gmail.com
France

Martha Larson
Delft University of Technology
m.a.larson@tudelft.nl
Netherlands

Daniel Kohlsdorf
XING AG
daniel.kohlsdorf@xing.com
Germany

Andreas Lommatzsch
Technische Universität Berlin
andreas@dai-lab.de
Germany

Domonkos Tikk
Gravity R&D Zrt
domonkos.tikk@gravityrd.com
Hungary

ABSTRACT
In this position paper, we take the experimental approach of putting algorithms aside, and reflect on what recommenders would be for people if they were not tied to technology. By looking at some of the shortcomings that current recommenders have fallen into and discussing their limitations from a human point of view, we ask the question: if freed from all limitations, what should, and what could, RecSys be? We then turn to the idea that life itself is the best recommender system, and that people themselves are the query. By looking at how life brings people in contact with options that suit their needs or match their preferences, we hope to shed further light on what current RecSys could be doing better. Finally, we look at the forms that RecSys could take in the future. By formulating our vision beyond the reach of usual considerations and current limitations, including business models, algorithms, data sets, and evaluation methodologies, we attempt to arrive at fresh conclusions that may inspire the next steps taken by the community of researchers working on RecSys.

Keywords
Personalization; recommendation engine; machine learning

1. INTRODUCTION
This paper represents the collective thoughts of a group of researchers thinking and discussing what the future of RecSys should be, if allowed to set aside the strengths and weakness of today's algorithms. The group consists of researchers with a spectrum of expertise from RecSys and information retrieval, from senior members of the RecSys community to fresh minds that have just begun their work in the field. Our group cast off the idea that creativity in the area of RecSys must be tied to existing business models, algorithms, data sets or evaluation methodologies. Instead, we pondered how "recommendations in the wild" could support people in their daily and professional lives, both as individuals and as members of their communities. The overarching idea that emerged in the workshop, that we explicitly state here, is that life itself is the original recommender system, teaching people about available options, and providing information that allows them to make decisions. The recommender system community can increase the scope of its vision if it temporarily sets aside consideration of the capabilities of current algorithms, and considers how RecSys fall short of serving to strengthen and enhance the lens of life. We believe that the focus must shift back to real life situations, similarly to when social filtering motivated collaborative techniques, to find new applications and approaches for RecSys.

RecSys '16, September 15 - 19, 2016, Boston, MA, USA

ACM 978-1-4503-4035-9/16/09...$15.00
DOI: http://dx.doi.org/10.1145/2959100.2959164

Twenty years ago, the basic idea of RecSys originated from the observation of social phenomena (social filtering). The initial insights of collaborative filtering yielded countless important results and widely used applications. However, we find that RecSys achieving adequate performance do not aspire to high enough goals. We believe that going back to the roots of recommender system research can inspire the research community to develop new techniques that address a number of important and unsolved challenges, and to focus on some new real needs of the users. This paper represents a return to the roots: an effort to again observe life, people's daily activities and social interactions, and to find new potential functionalities, internal system behaviors, and applications for RecSys. We hope that the results of our efforts are useful for fostering the future development of the recommender system field as a whole.

This paper is structured in 3 parts. Firstly, we assess the current limitations and pitfalls of RecSys. Secondly, we ponder the notion of whether "life" could be a model for RecSys, and lastly, we present our ideas about the kind of recommenders that could exist in the future.

2. TODAY'S RECSYS HAS NO CLOTHES
As the story goes, it took a child to stand up and say that the emperor was wearing no clothes. More than one among us was willing to make a similarly naïve but true remark about the state of RecSys today. One author spent three hours interacting with Amazon to find a simple birthday present for her father. Others have had the experience of scrolling through all the rows of Netflix recommendations and still arguing with their spouse over what to watch. As our discussion progressed, more authors became willing to share stories where large commercial recommenders have failed them.

Less easy to elicit are examples where recommendation fails to penetrate domains in which people really could use a helping hand. Classical examples present a limited view of the scope of a recommender: it is not just about Netflix and Amazon, as RecSys have the potential to accomplish much more than list books to read or movies to watch. We all remember the vision of artificial intelligence becoming a personal assistant that is able to tell us what to do next at any time and in any situation. We have narrowed the scope of our vision quite a bit from there, and if we blink and look again, we can see how our current recommenders are actually stark naked. In Section 4, we will return to RecSys that transcend the current recommendation engines in terms of items and situations in which they recommend.

2.1 People Are Not Machines

Obviously people are not machines. We wake up in the morning and stretch as we get out of bed. Do we find ourselves accidentally mistaking ourselves for deterministic automata? If not, and our impression is that we do not make this mistake, then we should ask the question of how the idea arose that an algorithm that knows only about the past can give us suggestions for the future. Likely it is because we are indeed creatures of habit: we like to have our tea on time, brush our teeth daily, and, depending on age, the bedtime story or nightcap is an essential finish to any day. We also like to hang out with friends, and if we do some of the same things that they do, we have more to talk about. For these reasons, RecSys that look at our past patterns do, in some sense, work. However, if we are not mechanical at our core, then RecSys are well served to abandon the presumption that if they can learn enough about a user, they will know what to recommend in a given situation.

People must have a choice about the kind of recommendations they receive in order to make a true personalized RecSys, instead of just individually-targeted personalized recommendations. And today's RecSys don't seem to be quite up for that task. Imagine a user, Tom, buys an item. That data will forever influence the recommendations he receives. On the other hand, if he deletes it he loses himself in a way. It will be important for Tom to have the possibility to edit and correct the data collected about him, and/or to inform the system about which data are currently relevant.

RecSys should also be able to assess their confidence in their knowledge of user needs. It is not enough to simply output the items that Tom is most likely interested in. When the system is not confident enough in its conclusions it would do much better to wait for user input, or to solicit it by means of well-designed active learning procedures. The cost of a bad recommendation could be enormous in many domains, and a system that is not able to understand its limitations may simply not be acceptable.

Suppose that the RecSys is able to get enough information about Tom in a certain context to supply him with recommendations. Has the system, then, achieved the goal of satisfying Tom's needs? We believe that the answer is no for two reasons. Firstly, telling Tom to choose what he actually already wants has limited value, as such recommendations are often no more than reminders to do something the user would have done anyway. Secondly, the user's choice will interact with the context to create a new context. As such, the RecSys has not provided the user with information on the new set of preferences that are formed as a result of the interaction.

2.2 The Voice Of Recommendations

RecSys differ according to the amount of authority they have in their domain. Reflection on the difference between the word "Recommend" and the word "Command" is informative. It would be ridiculous for a RecSys to start giving "Commands", as people want control over their own actions, and over their lives in general. Navigation system designers bend over backwards trying to figure out how to tell drivers where to go, while not offending them with a "know-it-all" system.

Today, we face widespread failure of RecSys to support users in consciously reflecting on power relationships. We do not stop to think: does this recommender system "know" more than I do? Can I trust it in everything? Or, should I regard it as a fun Crazy Eight ball: shake it and see where it wants to send me next in order to inspire my own creativity. Instead, it is essential that a user is able to develop different trust relationships 1) with different RecSys or 2) with the same system in different situations where different expertise is required. The level of deference to the authority of the recommender system must be different for a system that proposes medical treatments, as opposed to one that provides lists of movies. Users need to be aware of the power balance between the expertise represented by the recommender and their own expertise.

In order to get there, we need to understand how we can construct a humanlike relationship between RecSys and their users. We see a recommendation as part of a dialogue between persons and technology. As any dialogue, it is an iterated bidirectional process, built upon explicit or implicit, verbal or non-verbal messages ("signs") exchanged between the entities involved (the human and the machine). It involves a progressive interpretation of such messages in order to build mutual understanding, and to foster the expected behavior on both sides. From this perspective, the principles that make a dialogue reliable and effective (as stated in linguistic and semiotic theories) can guide the design of the recommendation process, from the elicitation of users' needs, interests, and intentions, to the construction of the "right" recommendations and their communication to the user.

Trust and verification will be key factors in understanding how users perceive their recommendations. Just because they trust the context, doesn't mean they should automatically go along with the recommendation.

There are some users that want to have their hand held, and others do not want such omniscient advice. We need to proceed on the premise that users' preferences for items only represent one dimension for personalization. Another dimension is the amount of active input that they would like to have from the recommender system. RecSys today lack a user typology regarding expectations about system behavior. Some users may not desire the system to fully solve their problems for them, and perhaps want to follow a more exploratory approach, or gently helped to find their way more autonomously. As such, people will have very different styles in the relationships that they will want to develop with RecSys, and these styles may vary across domains.

There are also ethical limitations. Assuming we have a recommender system that constantly provides us recommendations, the question arises whether that resembles a "Big Brother" who guides us. What personal or private data will be available to the system(s) in order for recommendations to be generated? Will the result be a problem for society if we train ourselves to constantly listen to recommendations?

2.3 When Is Enough Enough?

The assumption that recommendations need to be ranked seems to be a holdover from the printed page. Our reflex is to write things in a list. Just as we start at the top of our to-do lists scribbled with pens and pencils on pieces of legacy paper, we start at the top and expect to do this or that, and finally arrive at the finish line. Useful RecSys should free themselves from such linearity, and from the idea that there is a best/optimal total order of items that should be determined by the unknown utility function of the user. While some research has been devoted to multi-criteria RecSys, they are still only using multiple criteria to better predict an overall global criterion, which is used to finally rank the recommended items. In reality, people usually consider several factors before coming up with a choice. RecSys should support multiple criteria decision making processes rather than trying to immediately push an integrated ranking based on some machine calculated aggregation strategy.

Another important limitation of current RecSys is that they don't know when to stop recommending. A fine balance is needed to ensure that RecSys are developed to the point where they can understand the needs of the user without making them feel harassed.

Cognitive human limitations must also be taken into account, e.g., what the users want from recommendations, as how many recommendations they want may depend on their mood at a certain moment, and the context they find themselves in. For some, interaction with a RecSys might be a pastime or an end in and of itself. However, in general, the RecSys should not exhaust us: we need plenty of time and cognitive resources left over to enjoy our recommendations, or generally get on with things.

3. LENS OF LIFE

The key driving idea that arose in our process of collective reflection on RecSys is: Life itself is the original recommender system, and people are the query. Without digital devices, algorithms, or data, considering how life itself throws new experiences in our paths and helps us to make choices provides a rich source of inspiration for paths that the recommender system community should take. One could foresee RecSys that mimic life, with its abundance and complexity of messages that can then be interpreted as recommendations to the human senses. In this scenario, the user is the query and life, with its infinity of propositions, is providing a variety of recommendations.

When we stand at a crossroads in life we often seek out those who are wiser or more experienced in order to decide what to do next. This insight is already well represented in existing recommendation systems that combine personalization with the opinion of experts, which is mined from the opinion of the crowd.

3.1 The World Within Us

When considering life itself as a recommender system, two diametrically opposed perspectives arise. On one side stands the perspective that life is a mystery, whose pieces fit together in magical and wonderful ways. This perspective holds that RecSys have the potential to connect people and their expertise in a global "brain", similarly to what happens with neurons in a human brain. As in human brains, we are not aware of how precisely information is produced, stored, and transmitted between neurons through our synapses. Unlike human brains, we are able to have access to this information in RecSys – as such, RecSys may hide from the users the complexity and distributed nature of the wisdom of the crowd.

On the other side stands the perspective that life is intuitive and understandable. People use simple rules to engage with their surroundings: my big sister is driving and I want to drive too, I became a lawyer because that is what everyone in my family does, and my favorite movie star looks smashing in those shoes so I need to own a pair as well. This perspective holds that recommendations should be perfectly transparent. In fact, a recommendation that is understandable is more valuable to the user than one that is made for unexplained, mysterious reasons.

3.2 The World Around Us

Most of the time the answer presented is obvious, and appears before our eyes. But sometimes life presents the information differently: it produces a synchronicity, something that looks like pure coincidence, but is not. Humans cannot attend to all the information contained in the world around them at once, as we are constrained by our ability to pay attention only to a limited number of things. By objectively assessing the underlying dynamics and intricacies that are hidden from our senses and/or attention, but nevertheless reflected in large amounts of data that can therefore be extracted by analytic means, RecSys could help users find the least probabilistic path to follow in order to attain a better life. RecSys could, perhaps, also present users with answers that are not "superficial or immediate", but are of a deeper or hidden, and of a more "long term" type.

Life doesn't always give us the easiest answer, we know that! Sometimes we have intuitions, but don't know whether they'll serve us well. Sometimes we're not even sure how to follow them! When we become too introspective, we act as bad RecSys, only wanting to select items and achieve goals. How to be aware of the thoughts that come to us and seem necessary to pursue? When you follow your intuition and take this course of action, you find yourself in a place where a synchronicity occurs, and you're given just the right amount of information and clarity you need at that moment.

3.3 The World In Front Of Us

Possibly the most important thing that life tells us about RecSys is that individual experiences (e.g. of achievement or enjoyment), come together to form larger paths of meaningfulness. As such, RecSys should not only support the next act of consumption, but rather infer our future, and help us to build a picture of where we would like to go. To do so, they need to support people by understanding, and helping them understand, how they think. We make decisions in different ways: sometimes we make decisions in an intuition-based snaps of the fingers driven by strong emotions, and sometimes we make decisions slowly and analytically, supported by extensive evidence gathering. To anticipate and support such decision making, the recommender system should take into account the user's emotions, and the different ways in which users make decisions.

Whether we live in a deterministic or non-deterministic world, it often seems as if life knew the future, or at least what is best for us. In a way, these synchronicities show us our best possible future. So, instead of RecSys that only use information about the past, how about a recommender system that could, in a way, infer and thereby "influence" our future?

4. RECOMMENDERS YET TO COME

A central observation that is inspiring our analysis is that today's RecSys are not yet fully user centric. We have mentioned a number of areas to consider: (i) their relationship with the user, including "Command" vs. "Recommend" tone, amount of user involvement, knowing when to prompt for more information, and knowing when to stop recommending, (ii) understanding humans and helping them understand themselves, including working within the limits of human cognition, understanding multiple criteria decision making, and understanding how humans make decisions, and (iii) future-orientedness, including making recommendations based on synchronicity, and inferring and influencing a person's future. In short, RecSys must form a more comprehensive and realistic picture of who their users are and in which directions their needs can unfold in different contexts.

4.1 Moving Us Beyond Items

Moreover, in addition to rethinking the role of recommendations we need to expand the range of items that the recommender will select and present to the user. These systems could provide more diverse types of suggestions to users instead of direct recommendations for items. We believe that eventually, courses of action, intentions, emotions, ideas and even other people could be the "items" of future recommendations. In this sense, RecSys could inspire, assist, decide, and much more, in a completely unobtrusive way.

Following this idea of learning from the richness and unexpectedness of life to build better RecSys, we organized the recommenders we sketched out during our sessions as follows:

Firstly, we came up with the idea of an ultimate RecSys, one that could recommend everything in daily life, a kind of ultimate personal assistant similar to what Spike Jonze showed us in his movie, "Her"; a RecSys which acts as an extension of our consciousness, guiding us, while steering away from becoming a "Big Brother". With access to all our data, this consciousness extension could make recommendations based on synchronicity across every context we experience, suggesting not only items, but ways to regulate emotions, places to search for experts on a topic of interest, how best to manage health issues, or simply what to do next. This type of RecSys may grow beyond a life management tool to develop a personalized relationship with the user, learning not only what items to recommend in what context, but also how to interact with the user over time.

Secondly, we imagined recommenders that could improve the quality of our interpersonal relationships and interactions. Even outside the domain of dating recommendations, such systems could help find the right expert when needed, or kindred spirits to share our thoughts, ideas, and feelings with, filling our social circles with beneficial relationships. Such RecSys would have profound effects on the overall quality of day-to-day interactions, connecting us with individuals with compatible interests, emotional needs, and/or compatible personalities. These recommendations may also be made based on momentary needs: e.g. suggesting the friend within one's network best suited for emotional support during a crisis, or the colleague best suited for brainstorming a specific kind of idea.

Another interesting idea that surfaced during our workshops was that this link could be established between real people, as well as with a fictional character. For instance, the expert that you need in a certain situation could be a character from the TV series you love! This kind of match could present an intriguing way to enhance our lives by expanding the resources available to us.

4.2 Widening Our Circles

RecSys must be a tool that not only makes it easier for the users to lead their life, but also to lead it in a better way. For example, social interactions could be improved by recommending an expert with whom to collaborate, a friend, or even a possible sponsor. RecSys should also establish meaningful links between people in order to bring groups together, to help improve collaboration. This could represent considerable progress in present times when the collaborative economy is growing stronger and stronger. Meaningful recommendation could therefore increase participation and improve the economy of the multitude.

4.3 Helping Us Help Ourselves

A substantial part of multimedia consumption is done with the goal of mood regulation. Usually, when people think of RecSys and mood, they think of systems that recommend music for a candle light dinner, or videos that will make people laugh. However, mood regulation is the conscious use of media to put oneself in a particular state, which allows you to accomplish something. People use music and videos to relax, but they also use music when they want to stay alert or stay motivated, e.g. on a long car trip or when working out. RecSys of the future will need to focus on tasks and goals: providing resources to assist people in accomplishing what they would like to get done.

How about a RecSys that could engage us to strive to get better, one that could improve our motivation? Recommendations could be a part of the gamification of life. We have to be aware of the purpose of the recommendation, however, because such recommenders have the potential to be abused for manipulative purposes. Recommenders should engage people to improve their lives and achieve their goals, and not to follow a dictator, for instance. This raises questions about the nature of, and the distinctions between, personal and collective engagement: in light of such possibilities we must also think about RecSys from a moral perspective.

4.4 Recommending For Inspiration

Another point, related to the previous one, is that a recommender could help people balance their lives. It could help them as a virtual dietitian, with tips on activities to engage in based on their present mood, or how to use their time between leisure and work better. We thus coined a term: "interspiration", intervening inspiration.

The RecSys could help people define their preferences and in the long run, attain happiness and contentment on their own terms.

5. CONCLUSION

This paper is an output of the "Think-Forward Tank" on the Future of RecSys, which took place during the European Conference for Information Retrieval (ECIR) 2016 in Padua, Italy. The overarching idea that emerged during the workshop is this: life itself is the original recommender system, presenting people with available options, and providing information that will allow them to make the right decisions, and the person themselves is the query. If freed from any current restraints, what could RecSys be, and what could they do?

We believe that RecSys should improve and enhance our daily lives. They must be close to us, in terms of having access to our data and in terms of having a relationship with us. As such, they must also know their boundaries, when to recommend and when to stop, and how much interaction is desired. With the enormous amount of data that everybody produces on a daily basis, from the more personal small data (bank transactions, calendar appointments, emails), to the medium data (Netflix's user profiles), to the Big Data (the vast amount of information on digital social interactions accumulated on Facebook's data servers), the need arises to give users a stronger sense of ownership. By filtering data based on relevance to context and/or task, RecSys could use the global brain, the "noosphere", so users feel smarter, cognitively lighter, can observe synchrony, and therefore make better decisions. We also believe recommenders must be in accord with our inner self, recommending what is truly good for us. They should be aware of the needs and preferences of their users, not only to help them achieve their personal (or professional) goals, but to inspire them to set higher goals they haven't thought about themselves.

Man is the query. RecSys of the future must provide users with answers that not only make their lives easier, but also make their lives better. The recommender system community can increase the scope of its vision if it, temporarily, sets consideration of the capabilities of current algorithms aside, and considers how RecSys fall short of serving to strengthen and enhance the lens of life.

6. ACKNOWLEDGEMENTS

The work leading to this paper has received funding from the European Union's Seventh Framework Programme (FP7/2007-2013) under CrowdRec Grant Agreement n◦ 610594.
The third author is also affiliated with Radboud University Nijmegen.

7. ADDITIONAL AUTHORS

Additional authors: Omar Alonso (Microsoft, email: oralonso@gmail.com), Paolo Cremonesi (Politecnico di Milano, email: Paolo.Cremonesi@polimi.it), Andrew Demetriou (Delft University of Technology, email: A.M.Demetriou@tudelft.nl), Kristaps Dobrajs (JCP-Connect, email: Kris.Dobrajs@jcp-connect.com), Franca Garzotto (Politecnico di Milano, email: Franca.Garzotto@polimi.it), Ayşe Göker (Robert Gordon University, email: A.S.Goker@rgu.ac.uk), Frank Hopfgartner (University of Glasgow, email: Frank.Hopfgartner@glasgow.ac.uk), Davide Malagoli (Moviri SpA, email: Davide.Malagoli@moviri.com), Thuy Ngoc Nguyen (Free University of Bozen-Bolzano, email: Ngoc.Nguyen@unibz.it), Jasminko Novak (University of Applied Sciences Stralsund and European Institute for Participatory Media, email: Jasminko.Novak@fh-stralsund.de), Francesco Ricci (Free University of Bozen-Bolzano, email: fricci@unibz.it), Mario Scriminaci (Moviri SpA, email: Mario.Scriminaci@moviri.com), Marko Tkalcic (Free University of Bozen-Bolzano, email: Marko.Tkalcic@unibz.it), Anna Zacchi (Doxee, email: AnnaxZacchi@gmail.com)

Behaviorism is Not Enough: Better Recommendations through Listening to Users

Michael D. Ekstrand[1,2] and Martijn C. Willemsen[3]

[1]Dept. of Computer Science
Texas State University
San Marcos, TX USA

[2]Dept. of Computer Science
Boise State University
Boise, ID USA
michaelekstrand@boisestate.edu

[3]Human-Technology Interaction Group
School of Innovation Sciences
Eindhoven University of Technology
Eindhoven, The Netherlands
M.C.Willemsen@tue.nl

ABSTRACT
Behaviorism is the currently-dominant paradigm for building and evaluating recommender systems. Both the operation and the evaluation of recommender system applications are most often driven by analyzing the behavior of users. In this paper, we argue that listening to what users say — about the items and recommendations they like, the control they wish to exert on the output, and the ways in which they perceive the system — and not just observing what they do will enable important developments in the future of recommender systems. We provide both philosophical and pragmatic motivations for this idea, describe the various points in the recommendation and evaluation processes where explicit user input may be considered, and discuss benefits that may result from considered incorporation of user preferences at each of these points. In particular, we envision recommender applications that aim to support users' *better selves*: helping them live the life that they desire to lead. For example, recommender-assisted behavior change requires algorithms to predict not what users choose or do now, inferable from behavioral data, but what they should choose or do in the future to become healthier, fitter, more sustainable, or culturally aware. We hope that our work will spur useful discussion and many new ideas for recommenders that empower their users.

Keywords
Recommender systems; participatory design; user studies; algorithmic filtering; information filtering

1. INTRODUCTION
Recommender system developers rely on two different types of data in order to power and evaluate recommenders: expressed preferences, including data like user ratings, survey responses, and other explicit judgements from the user; and behavioral data or implicit feedback, arising from recommendation interactions and other actions the user takes on the system. Recommender systems have long used both types of data: early work typically used ratings for recommendation and a combination of user input and behavior observation to evaluate the system [9].

RecSys '16, September 15 - 19, 2016, Boston , MA, USA

ACM 978-1-4503-4035-9/16/09…$15.00
DOI: http://dx.doi.org/10.1145/2959100.2959179

In recent years, behaviorism has ascended to be the dominant paradigm for recommendation. This emphasis takes many forms, but is particularly visible in the trends of favoring implicit feedback over explicit ratings, behavioral evaluations such as A/B tests measuring user activity instead of surveys or ethnographic analyses that capture users' experience and perception of the system, and the practice of ignoring preference when it disagrees with behavior.

User behavior is a valuable source of input. Implicit feedback data is readily available — soliciting ratings or responses from users is a challenging task — and is very good for predicting future user behavior. Behavior-based evaluations directly measure users' visible responses, which translate to short-term revenue-generating actions such as purchases.

We argue that this is not enough. While behavioral data rightly plays a significant role in recommendation, we must not neglect users' stated preferences and ambitions. Further, we submit that eliciting stated desires from users has great potential to enable uniquely empowering recommendation experiences.

Over the last half-decade, significant progress has been made on developing evaluation strategies that integrate behavioral and subjective data. These methods are effective for taking advantage of the relative strengths of both classes of data and form a starting point for the types of evaluations and systems that we envision.

At present, recommender systems research has yielded an extensive knowledge base of how to produce effective recommendations that will prompt users to action. But there are several open questions that we must engage users, explicitly, to address:

- Are users satisfied with their choices and actions, both in short term as well as in the longer term?
- When a user is dissatisfied with their choices, what keeps them from aligning their actions and desires? Can the recommender suggest alternatives, or help the user explore the item space or express preferences in a different way?
- Is the recommender feeding users' better or lesser selves? Is it providing recommendations that help the user achieve the goals they have for their life, or is it reinforcing behavior that detracts from those goals?

In this paper, we first outline some philosophical and pragmatic motivations for increasing user participation in the recommendation process. We will then examine where in the recommendation process explicit user input could be used, and propose certain specific benefits we see for increased use of user input in each. We hope the arguments we advance will spur useful discussion about how to design, build, and study recommenders that enable users to find material and courses of action that empower them to live more fulfilled and fulfilling lives.

2. MOTIVATING USER PARTICIPATION

Our motivations broadly divide into two categories: a values-based philosophical argument for why user participation is an intrinsically good objective and a pragmatic argument centered around the kinds of applications that a new focus on user input may enable.

2.1 The Philosophy of User Participation

Users and system developers often have different visions. Even when the designer's vision is supported by empirical data on user *behavior*, the result can still be poorly received if the users feel like their values are not being respected, or that they have no control over the technology in their lives.

Franklin advocates for a recognition of the role of *reciprocity* in our technological development [7]. Reciprocity — the give-and-take present in egalitarian face-to-face human interaction, a 'genuine communication among interacting parties' — is important for technology to empower, rather than dominate, its users. Without reciprocity, users can only take or leave what is given to them.

A major theme of Franklin's work is the need to carefully consider the values embedded in our technologies. Suchman strikes a similar note when laying out the merits of participatory design, stating that it 'makes explicit the critical, and inevitable, presence of values in the system design process' [21].

Values are present in all system designs. The question isn't *whether* a system embeds some set of values; rather, *whose values* (and *what values*) does it embed? Are these values explicitly articulated and subject to discussion? Are designers transparent about the reasons for decisions? Giving credit to user perspectives is itself a value that can be included in or rejected by a technological process, and including user input can enable debate and discussion about the other values the system embodies.

The values of recommender systems are seen most clearly in our optimization criteria and evaluation metrics. Sales, lift, engagement, click-through rate: all of these are value judgements about the kinds of activities that reflect a good recommendation (and of whether a recommender should even be deployed). Does engagement, for example, truly reflect what users need from a service [6]?

The recent debate over Twitter's introduction of algorithmic filtering to user timelines highlights how conflicts over values can arise in recommender systems. Changing from the traditional reverse-chronological timeline to a recommender-filtered one was a significant change in core service functionality, and it displeased a number of vocal users. One of the common complaints was that Twitter did not seem to understand how existing users used its system and the actual problems they faced. If users felt heard, and like their desires and problems were respected, might Twitter's algorithmic filtering have been better received?

The issue of *filter bubbles,* brought to public attention by Pariser [15], is another matter of concern for some users of modern information systems: does algorithmic filtering isolate us into pockets of one-sided information, to the detriment of ourselves and society?

Suchman observes that 'until we become familiar with and take seriously each other's concerns there will be little hope for a mutually satisfactory future in the development of work and technology' [21]. Giving credit to user concerns is a key dynamic in building technology that truly satisfies those it impacts.

2.2 Enabling New Applications

Besides our philosophical concerns, there are several practical reasons why increasing the role of explicit user input of preferences and goals can enable significant advances in recommender systems. First, behavioral data without proper grounding in theory and in subjective evaluation might just result in local optimization or short term quick wins, rather than long term satisfaction. Further, user behavior may be driven by outside factors, such as a lack of meaningful alternatives. When can we know from the behavior of a user if the recommendations help to fulfill their needs and goals?

Neil Hunt raised a striking example in his keynote at RecSys 2014. NetFlix relies heavily on behavioral data for evaluating recommenders and other service components, but their key metric — users watching movies — cannot distinguish between a user deriving value from the service and addiction. The recommender, which helps many users find movies and shows that enrich their lives, may be doing some users a disservice by encouraging them to continue watching to the neglect of other important concerns in their lives. Engaging users about their concerns and goals can be a valuable tool in mitigating this kind of problem in recommender systems.

This concern is especially relevant in the emerging area of lifestyle modifications and behavioral change. Recommending the kinds of things users like or do now will not help them to achieve the behavior they want, but rather will reinforce their current behavior. These systems require more than implicit feedback, and optimization for user needs beyond immediate satisfaction. For example, the user model in such a system needs to understand the users' goals or desires and the algorithm needs to optimize for attaining them.

There are certainly many other applications that can be envisioned, but several of these ideas have a common theme: can the recommender help users become their better selves?

3. WHERE USERS CAN SPEAK

We now survey the different points in the recommendation process where explicit user input can be integrated, and propose applications that could benefit from increasing the role of explicit user input in these areas.

3.1 Application Design

Participatory design itself is most relevant in the process of designing a recommender application and its algorithm(s). In this phase, users can express what they want the recommender to help them accomplish. What do they desire from news recommendations? People recommendations? Algorithmic sorting of status updates? Recipes? Consumer products?

User input must be balanced with product vision, particularly in the initial design stage; we are not arguing against a need for expert judgement in design. Moreover, users might not know what they want (as they might not be aware of their possibly-latent needs), but they can respond to ideas, sharing what they like or dislike, and might be prompted to come up with even better ideas. We also do not oppose the use of behavioral data to influence design — the rise of A/B testing for design as opposed to relying entirely on potentially-unsubstantiated judgement is welcome. We are arguing, rather, for including users' expressed desires as a third leg in the design process of recommenders and related systems.

3.2 Recommendation Method Selection

Recommenders can be designed so users have control over which of several algorithms is providing them with recommendations. This is a direct means of giving users agency in the recommendation process, and with suitable explanations of the algorithms it can allow the users to adapt the system to their goals at any given time.

There has been some work on allowing users to choose their recommenders [5], but there is much more to be done in understanding how we can provide users with meaningful control over the way in which their recommendations are produced. We could envision systems where users are provided with a number of recommendation techniques that they can mix and match in order to achieve a particular type of recommendation list; a more sophisticated version, perhaps, of the diversity control proposed by Ziegler [22] or the user adjustments provided by MovieLens [8].

Different recommenders have different characteristics, which can make them more or less effective for meeting various user information needs [4, 13, 14]. One approach to this varying effectiveness is to attempt to automatically adapt the recommender system to the user's need [10]. This can be thought of as a *recommender of recommenders*, where one algorithm 'recommends' the best recommendation algorithm to use in a particular context or task; this is one form of context-aware recommendation [2]. Another approach is to put the user in control of the process, allowing them to directly or indirectly determine the algorithm used. This has a number of benefits, including increasing user agency and collecting data that can be used to test and develop future meta-recommenders.

3.3 Recommendation Process

Once the recommender system has been designed and its algorithm selected, the ongoing process of recommendation depends on input data from the user. This typically comes in two forms: explicit ratings or preference judgements; and implicit feedback in the form of clicks, purchases, and other user events. While explicit ratings dominated the early days of recommender systems, much recent attention has focused on implicit feedback. The reasons for this are fairly clear: implicit data is far more plentiful, as it can be gleaned from users' ordinary actions instead of requiring them to take time to express preference, and the resulting recommendations produce better user response in many practical applications.

Drawing from experience at Netflix and elsewhere, Amatriain noted that implicit signals are better than explicit ones 'almost always' [1]. Indeed, many *current* applications (especially given their limited domains of multimedia or e-commerce) do fare better with implicit data. But we see great potential in exploring the cases outside of 'almost always': in what settings does explicit user input result in a better recommender system?

One example where it has been shown to result in better recommendations is Buzzr [16]. They studied several models for news item recommendation, and found that taking into account the user's explicit subscriptions produced more useful recommendations than recommending from a broader pool of feeds.

User input need not be complicated. Adding a 'must read' flag to Facebook or Twitter, so that users can indicate they want to read everything posted by certain friends, can help them retain control.

These examples show that explicit user input could improve some types of recommendations. But we believe that there are applications where explicit input beyond behavior is likely necessary, not merely beneficial, and it can be particularly useful to consider the *difference* between actual behavior and stated preference. When a user says one thing and does another — which they often do, as Hunt and others have observed — there are two possibilities:

- *The user does not understand their true desires.* In such cases ignoring their stated desires and inferring preference from their behavior will result in good recommendations.
- *The user is not satisfied with their behavior and may wish to change it.* In these cases, recommendations based on past user actions will only reinforce behavior the user wishes to change.

Applications where past behavior seems insufficient include:

- Finding speakers who bring perspectives that have been underrepresented in previous conferences.
- Reducing the stress and angst of a social media feed overpopulated with 'hate-reads'.
- Selecting high-impact next tasks from a to-do list.
- Changing musical or cinematic tastes.
- Eating healthier foods.
- Changing energy consumption behavior.

Some of these applications have a specific behavioral change component. To support such use cases, we believe it is useful to draw measures and concepts from social psychology. Behavioral change has been extensively studied by social psychologists, who have developed and tested social-cognitive models to describe how people can put good intentions into action.

To illustrate, many theories in this area assume that users have specific goals, and that implementation plans or actions are needed to help them overcome barriers to achieving these goals. For example, the Transtheoretical Model [17, 18] describes behavioral change as a 5-stage process: it starts with *precontemplation* and proceeds through *contemplation*, *preparation*, *action*, and finally to *maintenance*. The earlier stages require awareness, whereas the later stages require motivation and commitment. In each stage, a recommender might help with different suggestions: raising awareness may help the user in the precontemplation stage, whereas a personalized action plan might help support the preparation stage. Once the change is in maintenance mode, the recommender should avoid suggestions that might prompt the user to regress.

There are many research questions that arise from the goal of building such a system. How can we represent such action plans, stages and goals in a recommender system algorithm? What kinds of interfaces do we need to elicit the user's goals and present recommendations that will help them achieve them?

Providing adequate recommendations in this area has not yet been extensively studied. In the related area of Persuasive Technology a lot of progress has been made using the persuasion principles by Cialdini [3], but these attempts focus mostly on the how to persuade, not what to persuade with. Personalization is done on the message [11] but not yet on its content. However, effective e-coaching should not only address the how, but should also understand the what and where [19]. The 'what' (personalized recommendations) and on what moment (context awareness) are clearly challenges that recommender systems can take up.

For one example of how psychological theory can guide the structure of an algorithm, Starke et al. [20] designed an energy-saving recommender system based on a Rasch scale, which orders behaviors according to how costly or difficult they are to implement. For example, turning off the lights when leaving a room is easier than buying an energy-efficient washing machine. The Rasch model can also represent levels of ability on the same scale enabling the recommender to suggest energy-saving measures that fit a persons' ability. Moreover, the ordering of the scale can represent a hierarchy of goals the user might wish to attain in the future on their quest for their better self.

3.4 Evaluating the Recommender

Finally, we argue that explicit user input is useful in evaluating recommenders. A/B tests, the common gold standard for recommender assessment, are efficient and effective for testing the impact of different algorithms or designs on user behavior but are often limited in their ability to explain *why* users acted in a particular way. In addition to grounding experiments in theory, collecting subjective responses from users can help a great deal in explaining behavior.

User studies [12] are one means of doing this. Soliciting the user's subjective perceptions of the recommendations provides valuable insight into their thought processes, and allows us to better understand how algorithmic concepts of constructs such as diversity do or do not map to users' perceptions of those concerns [4].

User studies are not a panacea for good research. Well-designed A/B tests can test theories and lead to generalizable knowledge, and poorly-conceived or underpowered user studies can produce little of lasting value; further, good studies are in general difficult to design, execute, and analyze, so the tool is not responsible for weak results. That said, it is *easier* to design surveys whose results provide theoretical insight into human behavior than it is to design strictly behavioral studies, because the link between psychological processes and observable outcomes is more direct.

In addition to survey-based user studies, qualitative and ethnographic studies can elicit how the users feel about the recommender system, its embedding application, and the way that interacts with the rest of their lives.

Thus, to advance our knowledge about *how* recommendations are received by their users, and the various psychological factors that affect their suitability, it is necessary to conduct many targeted user studies with explicit, subjective responses, not just behavioral studies, and to integrate these with qualitative analysis of user desires and choices. Further, we expect that deeper understanding of users' subjective experience of recommendation can improve commercial recommendation applications.

4. CONCLUSION

In this paper, we have laid out several ways in which explicit user input can be harnessed to improve recommender applications.

There's a great deal of research needed in order to enable future applications to fully realize this potential. Several important questions that arise from our argument include:

- How can we scale participatory design to Internet-scale applications?
- What does participatory design of algorithms look like?
- How can we harness the discrepancies between what users say and what they do to provide recommendations that might help bridge that gap, and aid the user in living the life that they wish to live?
- How can we provide meaningful control over the recommendation process to users, so that they can understand the decisions they make about their recommendations and customize the system to their particular needs?

Investing significant effort in harnessing the power of user input and explicit preference judgements has the potential to enable substantial new recommender systems that empower and enrich users' lives. Just as importantly, it can help us to maintain user agency in an increasingly algorithm-guided information world.

ACKNOWLEDGEMENTS

We thank Jennifer Ekstrand for her valuable insights and feedback on draft versions of this paper.

REFERENCES

[1] Amatriain, X. 2016. Past, Present, and Future of Recommender Systems: An Industry Perspective.

[2] Anand, S.S. and Mobasher, B. 2007. Contextual Recommendation. *From Web to Social Web: Discovering and Deploying User and Content Profiles*. B. Berendt, A. Hotho, D. Mladenic, and G. Semeraro, eds. Springer Berlin Heidelberg. 142–160.

[3] Cialdini, R.B. 2001. *Influence: Science and Practice*. Allyn and Bacon.

[4] Ekstrand, M.D., Harper, F.M., Willemsen, M.C. and Konstan, J.A. 2014. User Perception of Differences in Recommender Algorithms. *Proc. ACM RecSys '14*, 161–168.

[5] Ekstrand, M.D., Kluver, D., Harper, F.M. and Konstan, J.A. 2015. Letting Users Choose Recommender Algorithms: An Experimental Study. Proc. ACM RecSys '15, 11–18.

[6] Evans, J. 2014. Twitter's Huge Mistake. *TechCrunch*.

[7] Franklin, U.M. 2004. *The Real World of Technology*. House of Anansi Press.

[8] Harper, F.M., Xu, F., Kaur, H., Condiff, K., Chang, S. and Terveen, L. 2015. Putting Users in Control of Their Recommendations. Proc. ACM RecSys '15, 3–10.

[9] Hill, W., Stead, L., Rosenstein, M. and Furnas, G. 1995. Recommending and evaluating choices in a virtual community of use. Proc. CHI '95, 194–201.

[10] Kapoor, K., Kumar, V., Terveen, L., Konstan, J.A. and Schrater, P. 2015. "I Like to Explore Sometimes": Adapting to Dynamic User Novelty Preferences. *Proc. ACM RecSys '15*, 19–26.

[11] Kaptein, M., Markopoulos, P., de Ruyter, B. and Aarts, E. 2015. Personalizing persuasive technologies: Explicit and implicit personalization using persuasion profiles. *International Journal of Human-Computer Studies*. 77, (May 2015), 38–51.

[12] Knijnenburg, B., Willemsen, M., Gantner, Z., Soncu, H. and Newell, C. 2012. Explaining the user experience of recommender systems. *User Modeling and User-Adapted Interaction*. 22, 4–5 (Oct. 2012), 441–504.

[13] McNee, S., Kapoor, N. and Konstan, J.A. 2006. Don't Look Stupid: Avoiding Pitfalls When Recommending Research Papers. *Proc. ACM CSCW '06*, 171.

[14] McNee, S., Riedl, J. and Konstan, J.A. 2006. Making recommendations better: an analytic model for human-recommender interaction. *CHI '06 Extended Abstracts* (2006), 1103–1108.

[15] Pariser, E. 2011. *The Filter Bubble: How the New Personalized Web Is Changing What We Read and How We Think*. Penguin.

[16] Phelan, O., McCarthy, K., Bennett, M. and Smyth, B. 2011. Terms of a Feather: Content-Based News Recommendation and Discovery Using Twitter. In Advances in Information Retrieval, LNCS 6611. Springer. 448–459.

[17] Prochaska, J.O. and DiClemente, C.C. 1984. *The transtheoretical approach: crossing traditional boundaries of therapy*. Dow Jones-Irwin.

[18] Prochaska, J.O. and Norcross, J.C. 2001. Stages of change. *Psychotherapy: Theory, Research, Practice, Training*. 38, 4 (2001), 443–448.

[19] Rutjes, H., Willemsen, M.C. and IJsselsteijn, W.A. 2016. Understanding Effective Coaching on Healthy Lifestyle by Combining Theory- and Data-Driven Approaches. *Proc. Workshop on Personalization in Persuasive Technology at Persuasive 2016*.

[20] Starke, A., Willemsen, M.C. and Snijders, C. 2015. Saving Energy in 1-D: Tailoring Energy-saving Advice Using a Rasch-based Energy Recommender System. *Proc. 2nd Int. Workshop on Decision Making and Rec. Sys.*, 5–8.

[21] Suchman, L. 1993. Foreword. *Participatory Design: Principles and Practices*. D. Schuler and A. Namioka, eds. CRC / Lawrence Erlbaum Associates. vii–x.

[22] Ziegler, C.-N., McNee, S., Konstan, J.A. and Lausen, G. 2005. Improving Recommendation Lists through Topic Diversification. *Proc. WWW '05*, 22–32.

Meta-Prod2Vec - Product Embeddings Using Side-Information for Recommendation

Flavian Vasile
Criteo
Paris
f.vasile@criteo.com

Elena Smirnova
Criteo
Paris
e.smirnova@criteo.com

Alexis Conneau *
Facebook AI Research
Paris
aconneau@fb.com

ABSTRACT

We propose Meta-Prod2vec, a novel method to compute item similarities for recommendation that leverages existing item metadata. Such scenarios are frequently encountered in applications such as content recommendation, ad targeting and web search. Our method leverages past user interactions with items and their attributes to compute low-dimensional embeddings of items. Specifically, the item metadata is injected into the model as side information to regularize the item embeddings. We show that the new item representations lead to better performance on recommendation tasks on an open music dataset.

Keywords

Recommender systems; Embeddings; Neural Networks

1. INTRODUCTION

In the recent years, online commerce outpaced the growth of traditional commerce, with a rate of growth of 15% in 2015 and accounting for $1.5 trillion spend in 2014. The research work on recommender systems has consequently grown significantly during the last couples of years. As shown by key players in the online e-commerce space, such as Amazon, Netflix and Alibaba, the product recommendation functionality is now a key driver of demand, accounting in the case of Amazon for roughly 35% [2] of the overall sales.

As of now, the state-of-the-art recommendation methods include matrix factorization techniques of the item-item and user-item matrices that differ in the choice of weighting schemes of the matrix entries, the reconstruction loss functions and their choice with regards to the use of additional item content information. The real-world recommender systems have additional constraints that inform their architecture. Some of these major constraints include: scaling the recommender systems such that they can handle a huge amount of user interaction information, supporting real-time changes in recommendation [5] and handling the cold-start problem [29].

In the last couple of years, a promising new class of neural probabilistic models that can generate user and product embeddings has emerged and has shown promising results. The new methods can scale to millions of items and show good improvements on the cold-start problem. In the context of product recommendation, they were successfully applied to ad recommendations in Yahoo! Mail [9], for Restaurant recommendations by OpenTable [1] and in the 1st prize winners in the 2015 RecSys Challenge [26].

In this paper, we present an extension of the *Prod2Vec* algorithm initially proposed in [9]. The *Prod2Vec* algorithm only uses the local product co-occurrence information established by the product sequences to create distributed representations of products, but does not leverage their metadata. The authors have proposed an extension [7] of the algorithm that takes into account the textual content information together with the sequential structure, but the approach is specific to textual metadata and the resulting architecture is hierarchical, therefore missing some of the side information terms by comparison with our method. In this work, we make the connection with the work on recommendation using side information and propose *Meta-Prod2Vec*, which is a general approach for adding categorical side-information to the *Prod2Vec* model in a simple and efficient way. The usage of additional item information as side information-only, e.g. available only at training time, is motivated by real-world constraints on the number of feature values a recommender system can keep in memory for real-time scoring. In this case, using the metadata only at training time keeps the memory footprint constant (assuming an existing recommendation system that uses item embeddings) while improving the online performance.

We show that our approach significantly improves recommendation performance on a subset of the 30Music listening and playlists dataset [30] with a low implementation and integration cost.

In Section 2 we cover previous related work and the relationship with our method. In Section 3 we present the *Meta-Prod2Vec* approach. In Section 4 we present the experimental setup and the results on the 30Music dataset. In Section 5 we summarize our findings and conclude with future directions of research.

2. RELATED WORK

Existing methods for recommender systems can roughly be categorized into collaborative filtering (CF) based meth-

*Alexis Conneau did this work while interning at Criteo.

RecSys '16, September 15-19, 2016, Boston , MA, USA

DOI: http://dx.doi.org/10.1145/2959100.2959160

ods, content-based (CB) methods and hybrid methods. CF-based methods [21] are based on user's interaction with items, such as clicks, and don't require domain knowledge. Content-based methods make use of the user or product content profiles. In practice, CF methods are more popular because they can discover interesting associations between products without requiring the heavy knowledge collection needed by the content-based methods. However, CF methods suffer from cold-start problem in which no or few interaction are available with niche or new items in the system. In recent years, more sophisticated methods, namely latent factor models, have been developed to address the data sparsity problem of CF methods which we will discuss in Section 2.1. To further help overcoming cold-start problem, recent works focused on developing hybrid methods by combining latent factor models with content information which we will cover in Section 2.2.

2.1 Latent factor models

Matrix factorization (MF) methods [22, 13] became popular after their success in the Netflix competition. These methods learn low-rank decompositions of a sparse user-item interaction matrix by minimizing the square loss over the reconstruction error. The dot product between the resulting user and item latent vectors is then used to perform recommendation.

Several modifications have been proposed to better align MF methods with the recommendation objective, for instance, Bayesian Personalized Ranking [24] and Logistic MF [11]. The former learns user and item latent vectors through pairwise ranking loss to emphasize the relevance-based ranking of items. The latter models the probability that a user would interact with an item by replacing the square loss in MF method with the logistic loss [11].

One of the first methods that learns user and item latent representations through neural network was proposed in [28]. The authors utilized Restricted Boltzmann Machines to explain user-item interaction and perform recommendations. Recently, shallow neural networks has been gaining attention thanks to the success of word embeddings in various NLP tasks, the focus being on Word2Vec model [18]. An application of Word2Vec to the recommendation task was proposed in [9], called Prod2Vec model. It generates product embeddings from sequences of purchases and performs recommendation based on most similar products in the embedding space. Our work is an extension of Prod2Vec and we will present its details in Section 3.1.

2.2 Latent factor models with content information

Many techniques have been used recently to create unified representations from latent factors and content information. One way to integrate user and item content information is to use it to estimate user and item latent factors through regression [3]. Another approach is to learn latent factors for both CF and content features, known as Factorization Machines [25].

Tensor factorization have been suggested as a generalization of MF for considering additional information [12]. In this approach, user-item-content matrix is factorized in a common latent space. The authors in [8] propose co-factorization approach where the latent user and item factors are shared between factorizations of user-item matrix and user and item content matrices. Similar to [17], they also assigned weights to negative examples based on user-item content-based dissimilarity.

Graph-based models have also been used to create unified representations. In particular, in [33] user-item interactions and side information are modeled jointly through user and item latent factors. User factors are shared by the user-item interaction component and the side information component. Gunawardana et al. [10] leans the interaction weights between user actions and various features such as user and item metadata. The authors use a unified Boltzmann Machines to make a prediction.

3. PROPOSED APPROACH

3.1 Prod2Vec

In their *Prod2Vec* paper [9], Grbovic et al. proposed the use of the *Word2Vec* algorithm on sequences of product receipts coming from emails. More formally, given a set S of sequences of products $s = (p_1, p_2, ..., p_M)$, $s \in S$, the objective is to find a D-dimensional real-value representation $v_p \in R^D$ such that similar products are close in the resulting vector space.

The source algorithm - *Word2Vec* [18] is originally a highly scalable predictive model for learning word embeddings from text and belongs to the larger class of Neural Net Language Models [4]. Most of the work in this area is based on the Distributional Hypothesis [27], which states that words that appear in the same contexts have close if not identical meanings.

A similar hypothesis can be applied in larger contexts such as online shopping, music and media consumption and has been the basis of CF methods. In the CF setup, the users of the services are used as the distributed context in which products co-occur, leading to the classical item co-occurrence approaches in CF. A further similarity between co-count based recommendation methods and *Word2Vec* has been established by Omer et al. in [16]; the authors show that the objective of the embedding method is closely related to the decomposition of the matrix containing as entries the Shifted Positive PMI of the locally co-occurring items (words), where PMI is the Point-Wise Mutual Information:

$$PMI_{ij} = \log\left(\frac{X_{ij} \cdot |D|}{X_i X_j}\right)$$
$$SPMI_{ij} = PMI(i,j) - \log k$$

where X_i and X_j are items frequencies, X_{ij} is the number of times i and j co-occur, D is the size of the dataset and k is the ratio of negatives to positives.

Prod2Vec Objective.

In [23] the authors show that the *Word2Vec* objective (and similarly *Prod2Vec*'s) can be re-written as the optimization problem of minimizing the weighted cross entropy between the empirical and the modeled conditional distributions of context products given the target product (more precisely, this represents the Word2Vec-SkipGram model, which usually does better on large datasets). Furthermore, the prediction of the conditional distribution is modeled as a softmax over the inner product between the target product and context product vectors:

$$
\begin{aligned}
L_{\text{P2V}} &= L_{J|I}(\theta) \\
&= \sum_{ij}(-X_{ij}^{\text{POS}} \log q_{j|i}(\theta) - (X_i - X_{ij}^{\text{POS}}) \log(1 - q_{j|i}(\theta)) \\
&= \sum_{ij} X_i(-p_{j|i} \log q_{j|i}(\theta) - p_{\neg j|i} \log q_{\neg j|i}(\theta)) \\
&= \sum_{i} X_i H(p_{\cdot|i}, q_{\cdot|i}(\theta)).
\end{aligned}
$$

Here, $H(p_{\cdot|i}, q_{\cdot|i}(\theta))$ is the cross-entropy of the empirical probability $p_{\cdot|i}$ of seeing any product in the output space J conditioned on the input product $i \in I$ and the predicted conditional probability $q_{\cdot|i}$:

$$
q_{j|i}(\theta) = \frac{exp(w_i^T w_j)}{exp(w_i^T w_j) + \sum_{j' \in (V_{J-j})} exp(w_i^T w'_j)}
$$

where X_i is the input frequency of product i and X_{ij}^{POS} is the number of times the pair of products (i, j) has been observed in the training data.

The resulting architecture for *Prod2Vec* is shown in Figure 1, where the input space of all products situated in center window is trained to predict the values of the surrounding products by using a Neural Network with a single hidden layer and a softmax output layer.

However, the product embeddings generated by *Prod2Vec* only take into account the information of the user purchase sequence, that is the local co-occurrence information. Though richer than the global co-occurrence frequency used in Collaborative Filtering, it does not take into account other types of item information that are available (the items' metadata).

For example, assuming that the inputs are sequences of categorized products, the standard *Prod2Vec* embedding does not model the following interactions:

- given the current visit of the product p with category c, it is more likely that the next visited product p' will belong to the same category c
- given the current category c, it is more likely that the next category is c or one of the related categories c' (e.g. after a swimwear sale, it is likely to observe a sunscreen sale, which belongs to an entirely different product category)
- given the current product p, the next category is more likely to be c or a related category c'
- given the current category c, the more likely current products visited are p or p'

As mentioned in the introduction, the same authors extended the *Prod2Vec* algorithm in [7] such that to take into account both product sequence and product text in the same time. If applying the extended method to non-textual metadata, the algorithm models, additionally to the product sequence information, the dependency between the product metadata and the product id, but does not link the sequence of metadata and the sequence of product ids together.

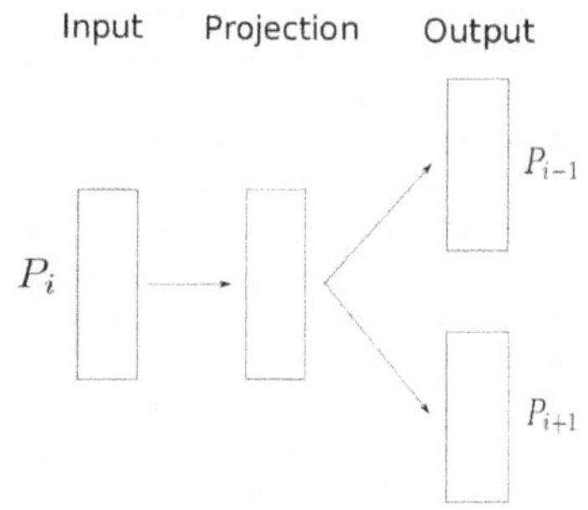

Figure 1: Prod2Vec Neural Net Architecture.

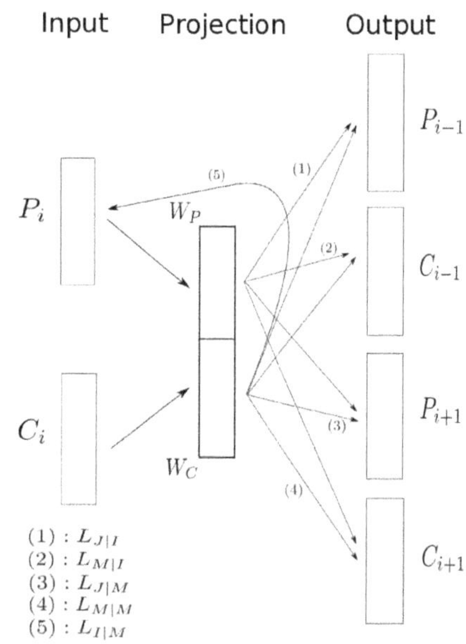

Figure 2: Meta-Prod2Vec Neural Net Architecture.

3.2 Meta-Prod2Vec

As shown in the Related Work section, there has been extensive work on using side information for recommendation, especially in the context of hybrid methods that combine CF methods and Content-based (CB) methods. In the case of embeddings, the closest work is the *Doc2Vec* [15] model where the words and the paragraph are trained jointly, but only the paragraph embedding is used for the final task.

We propose a similar architecture that incorporates the side information in both the input and output space of the Neural Net and parametrizes separately each one of the interactions between the items to be embedded and the metadata, as shown in Figure 2.

Meta-Prod2Vec Objective.

The *Meta-Prod2Vec* loss extends the *Prod2Vec* loss by taking into account four additional interaction terms involving the items' metadata:

$$
L_{MP2V} = L_{J|I} + \lambda \times (L_{M|I} + L_{J|M} + L_{M|M} + L_{I|M})
$$

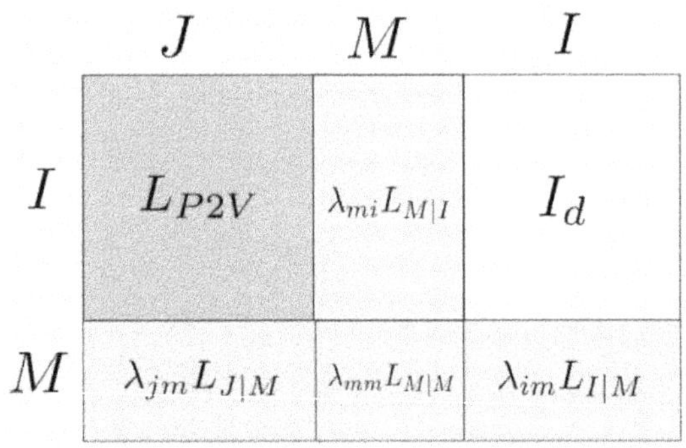

Figure 3: MetaProd2vec as matrix factorization of the items and metadata extended matrix.

where: M is the metadata space (for example, artist ids in the case of the 30Music dataset), λ is the regularization parameter. We list the new interaction terms below:

$L_{I|M}$ is the weighted cross-entropy between the observed conditional probability of input product ids given their metadata and the predicted conditional probability. This side-information is slightly different from the next three types because it models the item as a function of its own metadata (same index in the sequence). This is because, in most cases, the item's metadata is more general than the id and can partially explain the observation of the specific id.

$L_{J|M}$ is the weighted cross-entropy between the observed conditional probability of surrounding product ids given the input products' metadata and the predicted conditional probability. An architecture where the normal *Word2Vec* loss is augmented with only this interaction term is very close to the *Doc2Vec* model proposed in [19] where we replace the document id information with a more general type of item metadata.

$L_{M|I}$ is the weighted cross-entropy between the observed conditional probability of surrounding products' metadata values given input products and the predicted conditional probability.

$L_{M|M}$ is the weighted cross-entropy between the observed conditional probability of surrounding products' metadata values given input products metadata and the predicted conditional probability. This models the sequence of observed metadata and in itself represents the *Word2Vec*-like embedding of the metadata.

To summarize, $L_{J|I}$ and $L_{M|M}$ encode the loss terms coming from modeling the likelihood of the sequences of items and metadata separately, $L_{I|M}$ represents the conditional likelihood of the item id given its metadata and $L_{J|M}$ and $L_{M|I}$ represent the cross-item interaction terms between the item ids and the metadata. In Figure 3 we show the relationship between the item matrix factorized by *Prod2Vec* and the one factorized by *Meta-Prod2Vec*.

The more general equation for *Meta-Prod2Vec* introduces a separate λ for each of the four types of side-information: λ_{mi}, λ_{jm}, λ_{mm} and λ_{im}.

In Section 4 we will analyze the relative importance of each type of side-information. Also, in the case when multiple sources of metadata are used, each source will have its own term in the global loss and its own regularization parameter.

In terms of the softmax normalization factor, we have the option of either separate the output spaces of the items and of their metadata or not. Similarly with the simplifying assumption used in *Word2Vec*, that allows each pair of co-occurring products to be predicted and fitted independently (therefore adding an implicit mutual exclusivity constraint on the output products given an input product), we embed the products and their metadata in the same space, therefore allowing them to share the normalization constraint.

One of the main attractions of the *Word2Vec* algorithm is its scalability, which comes from approximating the original softmax loss over the space of all possible words with the Negative Sampling loss [19, 20], that fits the model only on the positive co-occurrences together with a small sample of the negative examples to maximize a modified likelihood function $L_{SG-NS}(\theta)$:

$$L_{J|I}(\theta) = \sum_{ij}(-X_{ij}^{POS} \log q_{j|i}(\theta) - (X_{ij}^{NEG} \log(1 - q_{j|i}(\theta)) \approx L_{SG-NS}(\theta)$$

and:

$$L_{SG-NS}(\theta) = \sum_{ij} -X_{ij}^{POS}(\log \sigma(w_i^T w_j) - k\mathbb{E}_{c_N \sim P_D} \log \sigma(-w_i^T w_N))$$

where P_D probability distribution used to sample negative context examples and k is a hyper parameter specifying the number of negative examples per positive example. The side-information loss terms $L_{I|M}$, $L_{J|M}$, $L_{M|I}$, $L_{M|M}$ are computed according to the same formula, where the i,j indexes range over the respective input/output spaces.

In the case of *Meta-Prod2Vec*, the impact of the decision to co-embed products and their metadata on the $L_{SG-NS}(\theta)$ loss is that the set of potential negative examples for any positive pair ranges over the union of items' and metadata values.

Impact on final recommendation system. Feasibility and engineering concerns.

Because of the shared embedding space, the training algorithm used for *Prod2Vec* remains unchanged. The only difference is that, in the new version of the generation step of training pairs, the original pairs of items are supplemented with additional pairs that involve metadata. In terms of the online recommendation system, assuming we are augmenting a solution that already involves item embeddings, the online system does not incur any changes (since the only time we make use of the metadata is during training) and there is zero additional impact on the online memory footprint.

4. EXPERIMENTS

The experimental section is organized as follows. First, we describe the evaluation setup, namely, the evaluation task, success metrics and the baselines. Then, we report results of experiments on the 30Music open dataset.

4.1 Setup

We evaluate the recommendation methods on the next event prediction task. We consider time ordered sequences of user interactions with the items. We split each sequence into the consequent training, validation and test sets. We fit the embedding *Prod2Vec* and *Meta-Prod2Vec* models on the first (n-2) elements of each user sequence and use the performance on the (n-1)-th element to bench the hyper-parameters and we report our final by training on the first (n-1) items of each sequence and predicting the nth item.

We use the last item in the training sequence as the *query item* and we recommend the most similar products using one of the methods described below.

As mentioned in Section 1, due to the technical constraint of keeping a constant memory footprint, we are interested in the usefulness of item metadata only at training time. Therefore we do not compare against methods where the metadata is used directly at prediction time, such as the supervised content-based embedding models proposed in [14] where both the user and item are represented as linear combinations of the item content embeddings and [32], where the products are represented by the associated image content embeddings.

We use the following evaluation metrics averaged over all users:

- Hit ratio at K (HR@K) that is equal to $1/K$ if the test product appears in the top K list of recommended products.

- Normalized Discounted Cumulative Gain (NDCG@K) favors higher ranks of the test product in the list of recommended products.

Using the aforementioned metrics, we compare the following methods:

- *BestOf*: this method retrieves the top products sorted by their popularity. This simulates the frequently encountered recommendation solution based strictly on popularity.

- *CoCounts*: the standard CF method which uses the cosine similarity of vectors of co-occurrences with other items. This method is performing particularly well in cases where the catalog of possible items is small and does not change a lot over time, therefore avoiding item cold-start problems.

- *Standalone Prod2Vec*: the product recommendation solution based on cosine similarities of the vectorial representation of products obtained by using *Word2Vec* on product sequences. Similarly with other embedding and matrix factorization solutions, the goal of the method is to address the cold-start problem.

- *Standalone Meta-Prod2Vec*: our proposed method, which enhances *Prod2Vec* with item side information and uses the resulting product embeddings to compute cosine similarities. As in *Prod2Vec*, the goal of the method is to further address cold-start problems.

- *Mix(Prod2Vec,CoCounts)*: an ensemble method which returns the top items using a linear combination between the *Prod2Vec* and the *CoCount*-based item pair similarities. The motivation of the ensemble methods that combine embeddings and CF is to leverage the benefits of the two in cold-start and non cold-start regimes.

$$Mix(Prod2Vec, CoCounts) = \alpha * Prod2Vec + (1-\alpha) * CoCounts \quad (1)$$

- *Mix(Meta-Prod2Vec,CoCounts)*: an ensemble method which returns the top items using a linear combination between the *Meta-Prod2Vec* and the *CoCount*-based item pair similarity.

$$Mix(MetaProd2Vec, CoCounts) = \alpha * MetaProd2Vec + (1-\alpha) * CoCounts \quad (2)$$

4.2 Dataset

We perform our evaluation on the publicly available 30Music dataset [31] that represents a collection of listening and playlists data retrieved from Internet radio stations through Last.fm API. On this dataset, we evaluate the recommendation methods on the task of next song prediction. For the *Meta-Prod2Vec* algorithm we make use of track metadata, namely the artist information. We run our experiments on a sample of 100k user sessions of the dataset with the resulting vocabulary size of 433k songs and 67k artists.

4.3 Results

We keep the embedding dimension fixed to 50, window size to 3, the side information regularization parameter λ to 1. We bench the blending factor α in Equations 1,2 of the embedding-based similarity score with the *CoCounts*-based cosine similarity score and find that the best value $\alpha^* = 0.15$. In addition, we vary the number of training epochs and we find the best parameter value to be 30 for *Prod2Vec* and 10 for *Meta-Prod2Vec*. As shown in Table 1, *Meta-Prod2Vec* has better performance both standalone and in the ensemble model with respect to the *Prod2Vec* model (results computed at 90% confidence levels).

4.3.1 Improvements on Cold-Start

Most of the gains in performance are coming from the cold-start traffic, where, as shown in Figure 4 and Table 2, we can see that *Standalone Meta-Prod2Vec* outperforms by a large margin all other methods when the true pair of (query item, next item) have zero co-occurrences in the training set and that the *Mix(Meta-Prod2Vec,CoCounts)* has the best performance in the cases where the true pair has low observed counts. Interestingly, we observe that the difference of performance between the ensemble models is bigger than between the standalone *Meta-Prod2Vec* and *Prod2Vec* models. We explain this by the fact *Standalone Meta-Prod2Vec* outperforms *Standalone Prod2Vec* on the cold-start traffic therefore helping the overall performance of the *CoCounts*, that by itself performs really well on head traffic. Indeed, *CoCounts* memorizes frequent pairs of (query, target) product, while *Standalone Meta-Prod2Vec* helps to generalize on unseen ones. These results are mirrored by similar findings covered in [6] and motivate the newly introduced approach of Wide and Deep learning.

Method	HR@10	NDCG@10	HR@20	NDCG@20
BestOf	0.0003 (0.0002;0.0003)	0.001 (0.001;0.001)	0.0003 (0.0002;0.0003)	0.002 (0.002;0.002)
CoCounts	0.0248 (0.0245;0.0251)	0.122 (0.121;0.123)	0.0160 (0.0158;0.0161)	0.141 (0.139;0.142)
Prod2Vec	0.0170 (0.0168;0.0171)	0.105 (0.103;0.106)	0.0101 (0.0100;0.0102)	0.113 (0.112;0.115)
Meta-Prod2Vec	0.0191 (0.0189;0.0194)	0.110 (0.108;0.113)	0.0124 (0.0123;0.0126)	0.125 (0.123;0.126)
Mix(Prod2Vec,CoCounts)	0.0273 (0.027;0.0276)	0.140 (0.139;0.141)	0.0158 (0.0157;0.0160)	0.152 (0.151;0.153)
Mix(Meta-Prod2Vec,CoCounts)	**0.0292** (0.0288;0.0297)	**0.144** (0.142;0.145)	**0.0180** (0.0178;0.0182)	**0.161** (0.160;0.162)

Table 1: Comparison of recommendation performance of Meta-Prod2Vec and competing models in terms of HitRate and NDCG.

Method	Pair freq=0	Pair freq<3
BestOf	0.0002	0.0002
CoCounts	0.0000	0.0197
Prod2Vec	0.0003	0.0078
Meta-Prod2Vec	**0.0013**	0.0198
Mix(Prod2Vec,CoCounts)	0.0002	0.0200
Mix(Meta-Prod2Vec,CoCounts)	0.0007	**0.0291**

Table 2: Recommendation accuracy (HR@20) in cold-start regime as a function of training frequency of the pair (*query item*, *next item*).

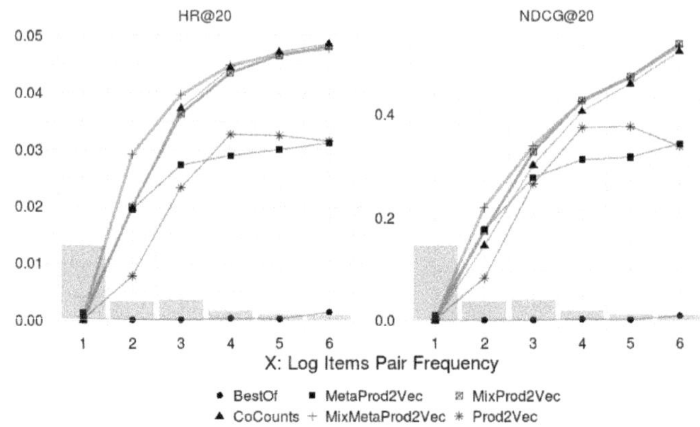

Figure 4: Cold-start improvements on the query and next item pairs.

Side Information	% lift	
	HR@20	NDCG@20
Meta-Prod2Vec with only I|M	27%	32%
Meta-Prod2Vec with only M|I	50%	52%
Meta-Prod2Vec with only J|M	55%	60%
Meta-Prod2Vec without M|M	61%	65%

Table 3: Proportion of the Meta-Prod2Vec lift over BestOf due to each type of side information.

4.3.2 Relative Importance of each type of Side Information

We posited the relevance of each type of side information, but we want to confirm experimentally that each of the four types of side-information brings additional information. We proceed by introducing each of the types of the side information separately and to compare its performance with the original *Prod2Vec* baseline.

The only exception for which we test the value by leaving it out of the full *Meta-Prod2Vec* model is the *mm* type of side-information; in this case, the input metadata explains the output metadata and this constraint is not directly valuable in regularizing the product embeddings and needs to be introduced together with the other types of pairs that connect the products to the metadata. Therefore its contribution to the model can be computed as (1 - degraded model performance) and is therefore 39% on HR and 35% on NDCG.

In Table 3, we compute the proportion of lift over the *BestOf* baseline obtained by using each type of side information separately and we observe that each one of them account for at most 50% of the performance of the full *Meta-Prod2Vec*, therefore confirming that the additional terms in our proposed model are relevant.

5. CONCLUSIONS

In this paper, we introduced *Meta-Prod2Vec*, a new item embedding method that enhances the existing *Prod2Vec* method with item metadata at training time. This work makes a novel connection between the recent embedding-based methods and consecrated Matrix Factorization methods by introducing learning with side information in the context of embeddings. We analyzed separately the relative value of each type of side information and proved that each one of the four types is informative. Finally, we have shown that *Meta-Prod2Vec* constantly outperforms *Prod2Vec* on recommendation tasks both globally and in the cold-start regime, and that, when combined with a standard Collaborative Filtering approach, outperforms all other tested methods. These results, together with the reduced implementation cost and the fact that our method does not affect the online recommendation architecture, makes this solution attractive in cases where item embeddings are already in use. Future work will extend on ways of using item metadata as side information and support of non-categorical information such as images and continuous variables.

6. REFERENCES

[1] Recsys 2015: Making meaningful restaurant recommendations at opentable. http://tinyurl.com/zs9at2t. Accessed: 2016-04-08.

[2] Venture beat article. http://venturebeat.com/2006/12/10/aggregate-knowledge-raises-5m-from-kleiner-on-a-roll/. Accessed: 2016-04-08.

[3] D. Agarwal and B.-C. Chen. Regression-based latent factor models. In *Proceedings of the 15th ACM*

SIGKDD International Conference on Knowledge Discovery and Data Mining, KDD '09, pages 19–28, New York, NY, USA, 2009. ACM.

[4] Y. Bengio, H. Schwenk, J.-S. Senécal, F. Morin, and J.-L. Gauvain. Neural probabilistic language models. In *Innovations in Machine Learning*, pages 137–186. Springer, 2006.

[5] B. Chandramouli, J. J. Levandoski, A. Eldawy, and M. F. Mokbel. Streamrec: a real-time recommender system. In *Proceedings of the 2011 ACM SIGMOD International Conference on Management of data*, pages 1243–1246. ACM, 2011.

[6] H.-T. Cheng, L. Koc, J. Harmsen, T. Shaked, T. Chandra, H. Aradhye, G. Anderson, G. Corrado, W. Chai, M. Ispir, et al. Wide & deep learning for recommender systems. *arXiv preprint arXiv:1606.07792*, 2016.

[7] N. Djuric, H. Wu, V. Radosavljevic, M. Grbovic, and N. Bhamidipati. Hierarchical neural language models for joint representation of streaming documents and their content. In *Proceedings of the 24th International Conference on World Wide Web*, pages 248–255. International World Wide Web Conferences Steering Committee, 2015.

[8] Y. Fang and L. Si. Matrix co-factorization for recommendation with rich side information and implicit feedback. In *Proceedings of the 2Nd International Workshop on Information Heterogeneity and Fusion in Recommender Systems*, HetRec '11, pages 65–69, New York, NY, USA, 2011. ACM.

[9] M. Grbovic, V. Radosavljevic, N. Djuric, N. Bhamidipati, J. Savla, V. Bhagwan, and D. Sharp. E-commerce in your inbox: Product recommendations at scale. In *Proceedings of the 21th ACM SIGKDD International Conference on Knowledge Discovery and Data Mining*, KDD '15, pages 1809–1818, New York, NY, USA, 2015. ACM.

[10] A. Gunawardana and C. Meek. A unified approach to building hybrid recommender systems. In *Proceedings of the Third ACM Conference on Recommender Systems*, RecSys '09, pages 117–124, New York, NY, USA, 2009. ACM.

[11] C. C. Johnson. Logistic matrix factorization for implicit feedback data. *Distributed Machine Learning and Matrix Computations*, 2014.

[12] A. Karatzoglou, X. Amatriain, L. Baltrunas, and N. Oliver. Multiverse recommendation: N-dimensional tensor factorization for context-aware collaborative filtering. In *Proceedings of the Fourth ACM Conference on Recommender Systems*, RecSys '10, pages 79–86, New York, NY, USA, 2010. ACM.

[13] Y. Koren, R. Bell, and C. Volinsky. Matrix factorization techniques for recommender systems. *Computer*, 42(8):30–37, Aug. 2009.

[14] M. Kula. Metadata embeddings for user and item cold-start recommendations. In *Proceedings of the 2nd Workshop on New Trends on Content-Based Recommender Systems co-located with 9th ACM Conference on Recommender Systems (RecSys 2015), Vienna, Austria, September 16-20, 2015.*, pages 14–21, 2015.

[15] Q. V. Le and T. Mikolov. Distributed representations of sentences and documents. *arXiv preprint arXiv:1405.4053*, 2014.

[16] O. Levy and Y. Goldberg. Neural word embedding as implicit matrix factorization. In *Advances in Neural Information Processing Systems*, pages 2177–2185, 2014.

[17] Y. Li, J. Hu, C. Zhai, and Y. Chen. Improving one-class collaborative filtering by incorporating rich user information. In *Proceedings of the 19th ACM International Conference on Information and Knowledge Management*, CIKM '10, pages 959–968, New York, NY, USA, 2010. ACM.

[18] T. Mikolov, K. Chen, G. Corrado, and J. Dean. Efficient estimation of word representations in vector space. *arXiv preprint arXiv:1301.3781*, 2013.

[19] T. Mikolov, I. Sutskever, K. Chen, G. S. Corrado, and J. Dean. Distributed representations of words and phrases and their compositionality. In *Advances in neural information processing systems*, pages 3111–3119, 2013.

[20] A. Mnih and K. Kavukcuoglu. Learning word embeddings efficiently with noise-contrastive estimation. In C. Burges, L. Bottou, M. Welling, Z. Ghahramani, and K. Weinberger, editors, *Advances in Neural Information Processing Systems 26*, pages 2265–2273. Curran Associates, Inc., 2013.

[21] X. Ning and G. Karypis. SLIM: sparse linear methods for top-n recommender systems. In *11th IEEE International Conference on Data Mining, ICDM 2011, Vancouver, BC, Canada, December 11-14, 2011*, pages 497–506, 2011.

[22] R. Pan, Y. Zhou, B. Cao, N. N. Liu, R. Lukose, M. Scholz, and Q. Yang. One-class collaborative filtering. In *Proceedings of the 2008 Eighth IEEE International Conference on Data Mining*, ICDM '08, pages 502–511, Washington, DC, USA, 2008. IEEE Computer Society.

[23] J. Pennington, R. Socher, and C. D. Manning. Glove: Global vectors for word representation. In *EMNLP*, volume 14, pages 1532–1543, 2014.

[24] S. Rendle, C. Freudenthaler, Z. Gantner, and L. Schmidt-Thieme. Bpr: Bayesian personalized ranking from implicit feedback. In *Proceedings of the Twenty-Fifth Conference on Uncertainty in Artificial Intelligence*, UAI '09, pages 452–461, Arlington, Virginia, United States, 2009. AUAI Press.

[25] S. Rendle, Z. Gantner, C. Freudenthaler, and L. Schmidt-Thieme. Fast context-aware recommendations with factorization machines. In *Proceedings of the 34th International ACM SIGIR Conference on Research and Development in Information Retrieval*, SIGIR '11, pages 635–644, New York, NY, USA, 2011. ACM.

[26] P. Romov and E. Sokolov. Recsys challenge 2015: ensemble learning with categorical features. In *Proceedings of the 2015 International ACM Recommender Systems Challenge*, page 1. ACM, 2015.

[27] M. Sahlgren. The distributional hypothesis. *Italian Journal of Linguistics*, 20(1):33–54, 2008.

[28] R. Salakhutdinov, A. Mnih, and G. Hinton. Restricted boltzmann machines for collaborative filtering. In *Proceedings of the 24th International Conference on*

Machine Learning, ICML '07, pages 791–798, New York, NY, USA, 2007. ACM.

[29] A. I. Schein, A. Popescul, L. H. Ungar, and D. M. Pennock. Methods and metrics for cold-start recommendations. In *Proceedings of the 25th annual international ACM SIGIR conference on Research and development in information retrieval*, pages 253–260. ACM, 2002.

[30] R. Turrin, M. Quadrana, A. Condorelli, R. Pagano, and P. Cremonesi. 30music listening and playlists dataset.

[31] R. Turrin, M. Quadrana, A. Condorelli, R. Pagano, and P. Cremonesi. 30music listening and playlists dataset. In *Poster Proceedings of the 9th ACM Conference on Recommender Systems*, Sept. 2015.

[32] A. Veit, B. Kovacs, S. Bell, J. McAuley, K. Bala, and S. Belongie. Learning visual clothing style with heterogeneous dyadic co-occurrences. In *Proceedings of the IEEE International Conference on Computer Vision*, pages 4642–4650, 2015.

[33] S.-H. Yang, B. Long, A. Smola, N. Sadagopan, Z. Zheng, and H. Zha. Like like alike: Joint friendship and interest propagation in social networks. In *Proceedings of the 20th International Conference on World Wide Web*, WWW '11, pages 537–546, New York, NY, USA, 2011. ACM.

Convolutional Matrix Factorization for Document Context-Aware Recommendation

Donghyun Kim[1], Chanyoung Park[1], Jinoh Oh[1], Sungyoung Lee[2], Hwanjo Yu[*1]
[1]Pohang University of Science and Technology (POSTECH), Pohang, South Korea
[2]Kyung Hee University, Seoul, South Korea
{[1]kdh5377, [1]pcy1302, [1]kurin, [1]hwanjoyu}@postech.ac.kr, [2]sylee@oslab.khu.ac.kr

ABSTRACT

Sparseness of user-to-item rating data is one of the major factors that deteriorate the quality of recommender system. To handle the sparsity problem, several recommendation techniques have been proposed that additionally consider auxiliary information to improve rating prediction accuracy. In particular, when rating data is sparse, document modeling-based approaches have improved the accuracy by additionally utilizing textual data such as reviews, abstracts, or synopses. However, due to the inherent limitation of the bag-of-words model, they have difficulties in effectively utilizing contextual information of the documents, which leads to shallow understanding of the documents. This paper proposes a novel context-aware recommendation model, *convolutional matrix factorization* (ConvMF) that integrates convolutional neural network (CNN) into probabilistic matrix factorization (PMF). Consequently, ConvMF captures contextual information of documents and further enhances the rating prediction accuracy. Our extensive evaluations on three real-world datasets show that ConvMF significantly outperforms the state-of-the-art recommendation models even when the rating data is extremely sparse. We also demonstrate that ConvMF successfully captures subtle contextual difference of a word in a document. Our implementation and datasets are available at http://dm.postech.ac.kr/ConvMF.

Keywords

Collaborative Filtering; Document Modeling; Contexual Information

1. INTRODUCTION

The exploding growth of the number of users and items in e-commerce services increases the sparseness of user-to-item rating data. Eventually, this sparsity deteriorates the rating prediction accuracy of traditional collaborative filtering techniques [5, 8]. To enhance the accuracy, several recommendation techniques had been proposed that consider not only rating information but also auxiliary information such as demography of users, social networks, and item description documents [14, 15, 17, 19, 23, 24].

Recently, approaches based on document modeling methods such as Latent Dirichlet Allocation (LDA) and Stacked Denoising Auto-Encoder (SDAE) have been proposed to additionally utilize item description documents such as reviews, abstracts, or synopses [15, 17, 23, 24]. Specifically, Wang *et al.* proposed *collaborative topic regression* (CTR) that combines topic modeling (LDA) and collaborative filtering in a probabilistic approach [23]. Variants of CTR were proposed, which also integrates LDA into collaborative filtering to analyze item description documents with different integration approaches [15, 17]. Most recently, Wang *et al.* proposed *collaborative deep learning* (CDL) that integrates SDAE into probabilistic matrix factorization (PMF) [20], thereby generating more accurate latent model in terms of the rating prediction accuracy [24].

However, existing integrated models do not fully capture document information, as they assume the bag-of-words model that ignores *contextual information* of documents such as surrounding words and word orders. For example, suppose that the following two sentences are given in a document: *"people* ***trust*** *the man."*, *"people betray his* ***trust*** *finally."* Since LDA and SDAE consider the document as a bag of distinguished words, they cannot distinguish each occurrence of term "***trust***". Precisely, although each occurrence of "***trust***" seems to have almost the same meaning, there is a subtle syntactic difference between these words – a verb and a noun, respectively. Such subtle difference within a document is also a nontrivial factor for deeper understanding of the document, and further such understanding facilitates improvements in the rating prediction accuracy.

To address the aforementioned issue, we utilize convolutional neural network (CNN), which is the state-of-the-art machine learning methodology that shows high performance for various domains such as computer vision [13], natural language processing (NLP) [2, 10, 11], and information retrieval [4, 21]. CNN effectively captures local features of images or documents through modeling components such as local receptive fields, shared weights, and sub-sampling [13]. Thus, the use of CNN facilitates deeper understanding of documents, and generates better latent model than LDA and SDAE do, especially for items that resort to their description documents due to the lack of ratings. Moreover, CNN is able to take advantage of pre-trained word embedding models such as Glove [18] for deeper understanding of item description documents. Note that LDA and SDAE cannot exploit pre-trained word embedding models because they adopt bag-of-words model.

However, existing CNNs are not suitable for recommendation task, as their objectives are different from the objective of recommendation. Specifically, conventional CNNs mainly solve classifi-

*Corresponding author

RecSys'16, September 15-19, 2016, Boston, MA, USA
© 2016 ACM. ISBN 978-1-4503-4035-9/16/09. . . $15.00
DOI: http://dx.doi.org/10.1145/2959100.2959165

cation task that is to predict labels of words, phrases, or documents. On the contrary, the objective of recommendation is regarded as a regression task aiming at accurately approximating ratings of users on items. Thus, the existing CNNs cannot be directly applied to our task of recommendation.

To handle the technical issue, we propose a document context-aware recommendation model, *convolutional matrix factorization* (ConvMF), which captures contextual information of item description documents by utilizing convolutional neural network (CNN) and further enhances the rating prediction accuracy. Precisely, ConvMF seamlessly integrates CNN into PMF, which is commonly used for recommendation tasks. Consequently, the integrated model follows the recommendation objective, and eventually effectively utilizes both collaborative information and contextual information. As a result, ConvMF accurately predicts unknown ratings even when the rating data is extremely sparse.

To demonstrate the effectiveness of ConvMF, we evaluate ConvMF on three different real-world datasets. Our extensive experiments over various sparsenesses of rating datasets demonstrate that ConvMF significantly outperforms the state-of-the-art models. The superiority of ConvMF verifies that ConvMF generates item latent models that effectively reflect contextual information of item description documents even when the rating data is extremely sparse. We also qualitatively demonstrate that ConvMF indeed captures subtle contextual differences of a word in a document. Furthermore, we investigate whether pre-trained word embedding model helps improve the rating prediction accuracy of ConvMF. Detailed experiment results are also available at http://dm.postech.ac.kr/ConvMF besides our implementation and datasets.

Our contributions are summarized as follows.

- We address limitations of the bag-of-words model based approaches and develop a novel document context-aware recommendation model (ConvMF).
- To exploit both ratings and item description documents, we seamlessly integrate CNN into PMF under probabilistic perspective.
- We extensively demonstrate the superiority of ConvMF over the state-of-the-art models on three real-world datasets with quantitative and qualitative results.

The remainder of the paper is organized as follows. Section 2 briefly reviews preliminaries on the most representative collaborative filtering technique and CNN. Section 3 introduces an overview of ConvMF, explains our CNN architecture of ConvMF, and describes how to optimize ConvMF. Section 4 experimentally evaluates ConvMF and discuss the evaluation results. Section 5 summarizes our contributions and gives future work.

2. PRELIMINARY

In this section, we briefly review matrix factorization (MF) (the most popular collaborative filtering technique) and convolutional neural network (CNN).

2.1 Matrix Factorization

Traditional collaborative filtering techniques are categorized into two categories [5]: memory-based methods (e.g. nearest neighborhood) [3, 7, 12] and model-based methods (e.g. latent factor model) [12, 20]. In general, model-based methods are known to generate more accurate recommendation results [12]. Thus in this section, we describe MF, which is the most popular model-based method.

The goal of MF is to find latent models of users and items on a shared latent space in which the strengths of user-item relationships (i.e., rating by a user on an item) are computed by inner products [12]. Suppose that we have N users, M items and a user-item rating matrix $R \in \mathbb{R}^{N \times M}$. In MF, the latent models of user i and item j are represented as k-dimensional models, $u_i \in \mathbb{R}^k$ and $v_j \in \mathbb{R}^k$. The rating r_{ij} of user i on item j is approximated by the inner-product of corresponding latent models of user i and item j (i.e. $r_{ij} \approx \hat{r}_{ij} = u_i^T v_j$). A general way of training latent models is to minimize a loss function $\mathcal{L}$, which consists of sum-of-squared-error terms between the actual ratings and the predicted ratings and L_2 regularized terms that try to avoid the over-fitting problem as follows:

$$\mathcal{L} = \sum_i^N \sum_j^M I_{ij}(r_{ij} - u_i^T v_j)^2 + \lambda_u \sum_i^N \|u_i\|^2 + \lambda_v \sum_j^M \|v_j\|^2$$

where I_{ij} is an indicator function such that it is 1 if user i rated item j and 0 otherwise.

2.2 Convolutional Neural Network

Convolutional neural network (CNN) is a variant of feed-forward neural networks with the following components: 1) convolution layer for generating *local features*, 2) pooling (or sub-sampling) layer for representing data as more concise representation by selecting only several representative local features (i.e., features having the highest score via the activation functions) from the previous layer, which is usually a convolution layer.

Even though CNN has been originally developed for computer vision [13], the key idea of CNN has been actively applied to information retrieval and NLP such as search query retrieval [4, 21], sentence modeling and classification [10, 11], and other traditional NLP tasks [2]. Although CNN for NLP tasks requires a significant amount of modification on the architecture of CNN, it eventually helps enhance the performance of various NLP tasks.

However, CNN has not yet been actively adopted to the field of recommender system. To the best of our knowledge, van den Oord *et al.* were first to apply CNN to music recommendation [22], where they analyzed songs in acoustic analysis point of view via CNN, and proposed a model that predicts the ratings based on the item latent model obtained by acoustic CNN. However, their CNN model, designed for acoustic signal processing, is not suitable for processing documents. Documents and acoustic signals have an inherent difference on the quality of surrounding features. A signal at a certain time is inherently similar to its surrounding signals, i.e., the signals that have slight time difference, while a word at a certain position in the document has a large semantical difference from the surrounding words. Such difference in the degree of similarity between surrounding features affects the quality of local features, and eventually requires different CNN architectures. Furthermore, the model does not fully reflect the collaborative information. In particular, the item latent models are mainly determined by the results of audio signal analysis via CNN rather than collaborative information. Thus, the performance of overall recommendation even does not achieve that of weighted matrix factorization (WMF) [9], which is one of the conventional MF-based collaborative filtering techniques dealing with implicit feedback dataset.

3. CONVOLUTIONAL MATRIX FACTORIZATION

In this section, we provide details of the proposed model, convolutional matrix factorization (ConvMF), through three steps: 1) We introduce the probabilistic model of ConvMF, and describe the

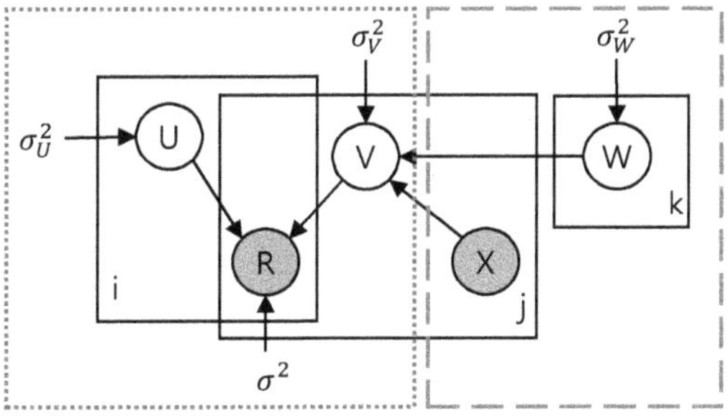

Figure 1: Graphical model of ConvMF model: PMF part in left (dotted-blue); CNN part in right (dashed-red)

key idea to bridge PMF and CNN in order to utilize both ratings and item description documents. 2) We explain the detailed architecture of our CNN, which generates document latent model by analyzing item description documents. 3) Finally, we describe how to optimize latent variables of ConvMF.

3.1 Probabilistic Model of ConvMF

Figure 1 shows the overview of the probabilistic model for ConvMF, which integrates CNN into PMF. Suppose we have N users and M items, and observed ratings are represented by $R \in \mathbb{R}^{N \times M}$ matrix. Then, our goal is to find user and item latent models ($U \in \mathbb{R}^{k \times N}$ and $V \in \mathbb{R}^{k \times M}$) whose product ($U^T V$) reconstructs the rating matrix R. In probabilistic point of view, the conditional distribution over observed ratings is given by

$$p(R|U,V,\sigma^2) = \prod_i^N \prod_j^M N(r_{ij}|u_i^T v_j, \sigma^2)^{I_{ij}}$$

where $N(x|\mu, \sigma^2)$ is the probability density function of the Gaussian normal distribution with mean μ and variance σ^2, and I_{ij} is an indicator function as mentioned in Section 2.1.

As a generative model for user latent models, we place conventional priori, a zero-mean spherical Gaussian prior on user latent models with variance σ_U^2.

$$p(U|\sigma_U^2) = \prod_i^N N(u_i|0, \sigma_U^2 I)$$

However, unlike the probabilistic model for item latent models in conventional PMF, we assume that an item latent model is generated from three variables: 1) internal weights W in our CNN[1], 2) X_j representing the document of item j, and 3) epsilon variable as Gaussian noise, which enables us to further optimize the item latent model for the ratings. Thus, the final item latent model is obtained by the following equations.

$$v_j = cnn(W, X_j) + \epsilon_j$$
$$\epsilon_j \sim N(0, \sigma_V^2 I)$$

For each weight w_k in W, we place zero-mean spherical Gaussian prior, the most commonly used prior.

$$p(W|\sigma_W^2) = \prod_k N(w_k|0, \sigma_W^2)$$

Accordingly, the conditional distribution over item latent models is given by

$$p(V|W,X,\sigma_V^2) = \prod_j^M N(v_j|cnn(W,X_j), \sigma_V^2 I)$$

[1]Detail of W of CNN will be explained in Section 3.2

where X is the set of description documents of items. A document latent vector obtained from the CNN model is used as the mean of Gaussian distribution and Gaussian noise of the item is used as the variance of Gaussian distribution which plays an important role as a bridge between CNN and PMF that helps to fully analyze both description documents and ratings.

3.2 CNN Architecture of ConvMF

The objective of our CNN architecture is to generate document latent vectors from documents of items, which are used to compose the item latent models with epsilon variables. Figure 2 shows our CNN architecture that consists of four layers; 1) embedding layer, 2) convolution layer, 3) pooling layer, and 4) output layer.

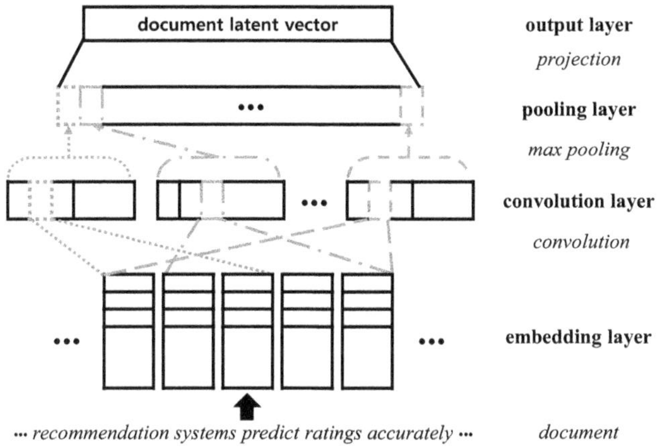

Figure 2: Our CNN architecture for ConvMF

Embedding Layer
The embedding layer transforms a raw document into a dense numeric matrix that represents the document for the next convolution layer. In detail, regarding the document as a sequence of l words, we represent the document as a matrix by concatenating word vectors of words in the document. The word vectors are randomly initialized or initialized with pre-trained word embedding model such as Glove [18]. The word vectors are further trained through optimization process. Then, the document matrix $D \in \mathbb{R}^{p \times l}$ becomes:

$$D = \begin{bmatrix} \cdots & | & | & | & \cdots \\ \cdots & w_{i-1} & w_i & w_{i+1} & \cdots \\ \cdots & | & | & | & \cdots \end{bmatrix}$$

where l is the length of the document, and p is the size of embedding dimension for each word w_i.

Convolution Layer
The convolution layer extracts contextual features. As we've discussed in Section 2.2, documents are inherently different from signal processing or computer vision in the nature of contextual information. Thus, we use the convolution architecture in [2, 11] to analyze documents properly. A contextual feature $c_i^j \in \mathbb{R}$ is extracted by jth shared weight $W_c^j \in \mathbb{R}^{p \times ws}$ whose window size ws determines the number of surrounding words:

$$c_i^j = f(W_c^j * D_{(:,i:(i+ws-1))} + b_c^j) \quad (1)$$

where $*$ is a convolution operator, $b_c^j \in \mathbb{R}$ is a bias for W_c^j and f is a non-linear activation function. Among non-linear activation functions such as sigmoid, tanh and rectified linear unit (ReLU), we use ReLU to avoid the problem of vanishing gradient, which causes slow optimization convergence and may lead to a poor local minimum [16, 6]. Then, a contextual feature vector $c^j \in \mathbb{R}^{l-ws+1}$ of a document with W_c^j is constructed by Eqn.(1):

$$c^j = [\,c_1^j,\ c_2^j,\ \ldots,\ c_i^j,\ \ldots,\ c_{l-ws+1}^j] \tag{2}$$

However, one shared weight captures one type of contextual features. Thus, we use multiple shared weights to capture multiple types of contextual features, which enable us to generate contextual feature vectors as many as the number n_c of W_c. (i.e. W_c^j where $j = 1, 2, ..., n_c$).

Pooling Layer

The pooling layer extracts representative features from the convolution layer, and also deals with variable lengths of documents via pooling operation that constructs a fixed-length feature vector. After the convolution layer, a document is represented as n_c contextual feature vectors, where each contextual feature vector has variable length (i.e., $l - ws + 1$ contextual feature). However, such representation imposes two problems: 1) there are too many contextual features c_i, where most contextual features might not help enhance the performance, 2) the length of contextual feature vectors varies, which makes it difficult to construct the following layers. Therefore, we utilize max-pooling, which reduces the representation of a document into a n_c fixed-length vector by extracting only the maximum contextual feature from each contextual feature vector as follows.

$$d_f = [\max(c^1), \max(c^2), \ldots, \max(c^j), \ldots, \max(c^{n_c})]$$

where c^j is a contextual feature vector of length $l-ws+1$ extracted by jth shared weight W_c^j.

Output Layer

Generally, at output layer, high-level features obtained from the previous layer should be converted for a specific task. Thus, we project d_f on a k-dimensional space of user and item latent models for our recommendation task, which finally produces a document latent vector by using conventional nonlinear projection:

$$s = \tanh(W_{f_2}\{\tanh(W_{f_1} d_f + b_{f_1})\} + b_{f_2}) \tag{3}$$

where $W_{f_1} \in \mathbb{R}^{f \times n_c}$, $W_{f_2} \in \mathbb{R}^{k \times f}$ are projection matrices, and $b_{f_1} \in \mathbb{R}^f, b_{f_2} \in \mathbb{R}^k$ is a bias vector for W_{f_1}, W_{f_2} with $s \in \mathbb{R}^k$.

Eventually, through the above processes, our CNN architecture becomes a function that takes a raw document as input, and returns latent vectors of each documents as output:

$$s_j = cnn(W, X_j) \tag{4}$$

where W denotes all the weight and bias variables to prevent clutter and X_j denotes a raw document of item j, and s_j denotes a document latent vector of item j.

3.3 Optimization Methodology

To optimize the variables such as user latent models, item latent models, weight and bias variables of CNN, we use maximum a posteriori (MAP) estimation as follows.

$$\begin{aligned} &\max_{U,V,W} p(U, V, W | R, X, \sigma^2, \sigma_U^2, \sigma_V^2, \sigma_W^2) \\ &= \max_{U,V,W} [p(R|U, V, \sigma^2) p(U|\sigma_U^2) p(V|W, X, \sigma_V^2) p(W|\sigma_W^2)] \end{aligned} \tag{5}$$

By taking negative logarithm on Eqn.(5), it is reformulated as follows.

$$\begin{aligned} \mathcal{L}(U, V, W) &= \sum_i^N \sum_j^M \frac{I_{ij}}{2}(r_{ij} - u_i^T v_j)_2 + \frac{\lambda_U}{2} \sum_i^N \|u_i\|_2 \\ &+ \frac{\lambda_V}{2} \sum_j^M \|v_j - cnn(W, X_j)\|_2 + \frac{\lambda_W}{2} \sum_k^{|w_k|} \|w_k\|_2, \end{aligned} \tag{6}$$

where λ_U is σ^2/σ_U^2, λ_V is σ^2/σ_V^2, and λ_W is σ^2/σ_W^2.

We adopt coordinate descent, which iteratively optimizes a latent variable while fixing the remaining variables. Specifically, Eqn.(6) becomes a quadratic function with respect to U (or V) while temporarily assuming W and V (or U) to be constant. Then, the optimal solution of U (or V) can be analytically computed in a closed form by simply differentiating the optimization function $\mathcal{L}$ with respect to u_i (or v_j) as follows.

$$u_i \leftarrow (V I_i V^T + \lambda_U I_K)^{-1} V R_i \tag{7}$$

$$v_j \leftarrow (U I_j U^T + \lambda_V I_K)^{-1} (U R_j + \lambda_V cnn(W, X_j)) \tag{8}$$

where I_i is a diagonal matrix with $I_{ij}, j = 1, \ldots, M$ as its diagonal elements and R_i is a vector with $(r_{ij})_{j=1}^M$ for user i. For item j, I_j and R_j are similarly defined as I_i and R_i, respectively. Eqn.(8) shows the effect of document latent vector of CNN in generating the item latent model v_j, where λ_V is a balancing parameter as in [23].

However, W cannot be optimized by an analytic solution as we do for U and V because W is closely related to the features in CNN architecture such as max-pooling layers and non-linear activation functions. Nonetheless, we observe that $\mathcal{L}$ can be interpreted as a squared error function with L_2 regularized terms as follows when U and V are temporarily constant.

$$\begin{aligned} \mathcal{E}(W) =& \frac{\lambda_V}{2} \sum_j^M \|(v_j - cnn(W, X_j))\|^2 \\ &+ \frac{\lambda_W}{2} \sum_k^{|w_k|} \|w_k\|^2 + \text{constant} \end{aligned} \tag{9}$$

To optimize W, we use back propagation algorithm. (Recall that W is the weights and biases of each layer.)

The overall optimization process (U, V and W are alternatively updated) is repeated until convergence. With optimized U, V, and W, finally we can predict unknown ratings of users on items:

$$\begin{aligned} r_{ij} &\approx \mathbb{E}[r_{ij} | u_i^T v_j, \sigma^2] \\ &= u_i^T v_j = u_i^T (cnn(W, X_j) + \epsilon_j) \end{aligned}$$

Recall that $v_j = cnn(W, X_j) + \epsilon_j$.

Time Complexity Analysis

For each epoch, all user and item latent models are updated in $O(k^2 n_R + k^3 N + k^3 M)$, where n_R is the number of observed ratings. Note that document latent vectors are computed while updating W. Time complexity for updating W is dominated by the computation of convolution layer, and thus all weight and bias variables of CNN are updated in $O(n_c \cdot p \cdot l \cdot M)$. As a result, the total time complexity per epoch is $O(k^2 n_R + k^3 N + k^3 M + n_c \cdot p \cdot l \cdot M)$, and this optimization process scales linearly with the size of given data.

4. EXPERIMENT

In this section, we evaluate the empirical performance of ConvMF on real-world datasets. Our extensive experiment results demonstrate that 1) ConvMF significantly outperforms other competitors when dataset is extremely sparse, 2) the improvements of ConvMF over the competitors increase further even when dataset becomes dense, 3) pre-trained word embedding model helps improve the performance of ConvMF when dataset is extremely sparse, 4) the best performing parameters verify that ConvMF well alleviates data sparsity, and 5) ConvMF indeed captures subtle contextual differences.

4.1 Experimental Setting

Datasets
To demonstrate the effectiveness of our models in terms of rating prediction, we used three real-world datasets obtained from MovieLens[2] and Amazon[3]. These datasets consist of users' explicit ratings on items on a scale of 1 to 5. Amazon dataset contains reviews on items as item description documents. Since MovieLens does not include item description documents, we obtained documents (i.e., plot summary) of corresponding items from IMDB [4].

Similar to [23] and [24], we preprocessed description documents for all datasets as follows: 1) set maximum length of raw documents to 300, 2) removed stop words, 3) calculated tf-idf score for each word, 4) removed corpus-specific stop words that have the document frequency higher than 0.5, 5) selected top 8000 distinct words as a vocabulary, 6) removed all non-vocabulary words from raw documents. As a result, average numbers of words per document are 97.09 on MovieLens-1m (ML-1m), 92.05 on MovieLens-10m (ML-10m) and 91.50 on Amazon Instant Video (AIV), respectively.

We removed items that do not have their description documents in each dataset, and specifically for the case of Amazon dataset, we removed users that have less than 3 ratings. As a result, statistics of each data show that three datasets have different characteristics (Table 1). Precisely, even though several users are removed by preprocessing, Amazon dataset is still extremely sparse compared to the others.

Dataset	# users	# items	# ratings	density
ML-1m	6,040	3,544	993,482	4.641%
ML-10m	69,878	10,073	9,945,875	1.413%
AIV	29,757	15,149	135,188	0.030%

Table 1: Data statistic on three real-world datasets

Competitors and Parameter Setting
We compared two versions of ConvMF with the following baselines.

- PMF [20]: Probabilistic Matrix Factorization is a standard rating prediction model that only uses ratings for collaborative filtering.
- CTR [23]: Collaborative Topic Regression is a state-of-the-art recommendation model, which combines collaborative filtering (PMF) and topic modeling (LDA) to use both ratings and documents.
- CDL [24]: Collaborative Deep Learning is another state-of-the-art recommendation model, which enhances rating prediction accuracy by analyzing documents using SDAE.
- ConvMF: Convolutional Matrix Factorization is our proposed model.
- ConvMF+: Convolutional Matrix Factorization with pre-trained word embedding model is another version of our proposed model, and we use Glove [18] for pre-trained word embedding model.

We set the size of latent dimension of U and V to 50 (as reported in [24]) and initialized U and V randomly from 0 to 1. Table 2 shows the best performing values of common parameters (λ_U, λ_V) of each model found by grid search. Since we use explicit datasets, we set the precision parameter of CTR and CDL to 1 if r_{ij} is observed and 0 otherwise. The rest of the CDL parameters were set as reported in [24].[5]

	ML-1m		ML-10m		AIV	
Model	λ_U	λ_V	λ_U	λ_V	λ_U	λ_V
PMF	0.01	10000	10	100	0.1	0.1
CTR	100	1	10	100	10	0.1
CDL	10	100	100	10	0.1	100
ConvMF	100	10	10	100	1	100
ConvMF+	100	10	10	100	1	100

Table 2: Parameter Setting of λ_U and λ_V

Implementation Detail
We implemented ConvMF using Python and Keras [1] library with NVidia Geforce TitanX GPU. To train the weights of CNN, we used mini-batch based RMSprop, and each mini-batch consists of 128 training items. As for the detailed CNN architecture, we used the following settings: 1) we set the maximum length of documents to 300. 2-1) ConvMF: we initialized word latent vectors randomly with dimension size of 200. These word latent vectors will be trained through the optimization process. 2-2) ConvMF+: we initialized word latent vectors by pre-trained word embedding models with dimension size of 200. These word latent vectors will be trained through the optimization process. 3) In the convolution layer, we used various window sizes (3, 4, and 5) for shared weights to consider various length of surrounding words, and we used 100 shared weights per window size. 4) Instead of the L_2 regularizer related to weights of CNN, we used dropout and set dropout rate to 0.2 to prevent CNN from over-fitting.

Evaluation Protocol
To evaluate the overall performance of each model on the real world datasets, we randomly split each dataset into a training set (80%), a validation set (10%) and a test set (10%). The training set contains at least a rating on every user and item so that PMF deals with all users and items. As the evaluation measure, we used root mean squared error (RMSE), which is directly related to an objective function of conventional rating prediction model.

$$\text{RMSE} = \sqrt{\frac{\sum_{i,j}^{N,M}(r_{ij} - \hat{r}_{ij})^2}{\text{\# of ratings}}}$$

We reported test errors of each model, which gives the lowest validation errors within 200 iterations with early-stopping. For reliability of our results, we repeated this evaluation procedure 5 times from data split process and we reported mean test errors.

4.2 Experimental Results

1) Quantitative Results on MovieLens and Amazon Datasets
Table 3 shows the overall rating prediction error of ConvMF, ConvMF+, and three competitors. Note that "Improve" indicates the

[2]http://grouplens.org/datasets/movielens/
[3]http://jmcauley.ucsd.edu/data/amazon/
[4]Plot summaries are available at http://www.imdb.com/
[5]We tried different settings but the performance was almost the same.

Model	Dataset ML-1m	ML-10m	AIV
PMF	0.8971	0.8311	1.4118
CTR	0.8969	0.8275	1.5496
CDL	0.8879	0.8186	1.3594
ConvMF	**0.8531**	**0.7958**	**1.1337**
ConvMF+	**0.8549**	**0.7930**	**1.1279**
Improve	3.92%	2.79%	16.60%

Table 3: Overall test RMSE

Model	Ratio of training set to the entire dataset (density) 20% (0.93%)	30% (1.39%)	40% (1.86%)	50% (2.32%)	60% (2.78%)	70% (3.25%)	80% (3.71%)
PMF	1.0168	0.9711	0.9497	0.9354	0.9197	0.9083	0.8971
CTR	1.0124	0.9685	0.9481	0.9337	0.9194	0.9089	0.8969
CDL	1.0044	0.9639	0.9377	0.9211	0.9068	0.8970	0.8879
ConvMF	**0.9745**	**0.9330**	**0.9063**	**0.8897**	**0.8726**	**0.8676**	**0.8531**
Improve	2.98%	3.20%	3.36%	3.41%	3.77%	3.27%	3.92%

Table 4: Test RMSE over various sparseness of training data on ML-1m dataset

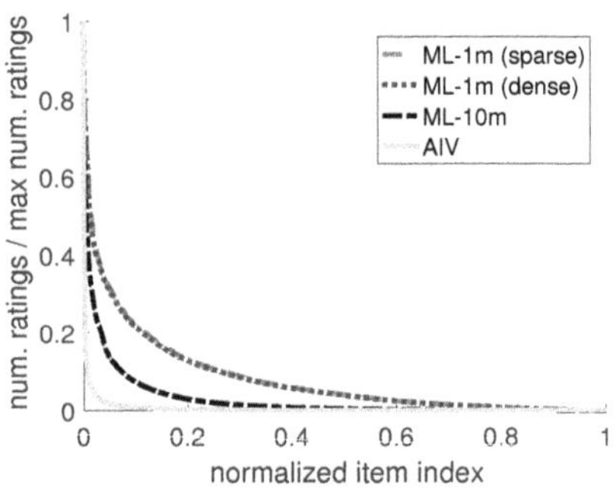

Figure 3: Skewness of the number of ratings for items on each dataset

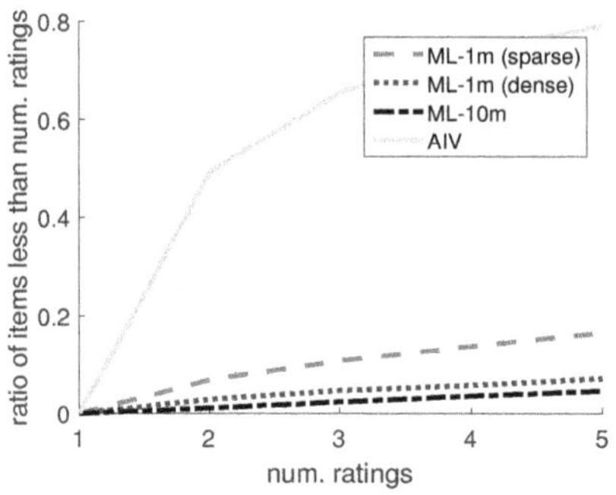

Figure 4: Ratio of items that have less than num. ratings (N) to each entire dataset

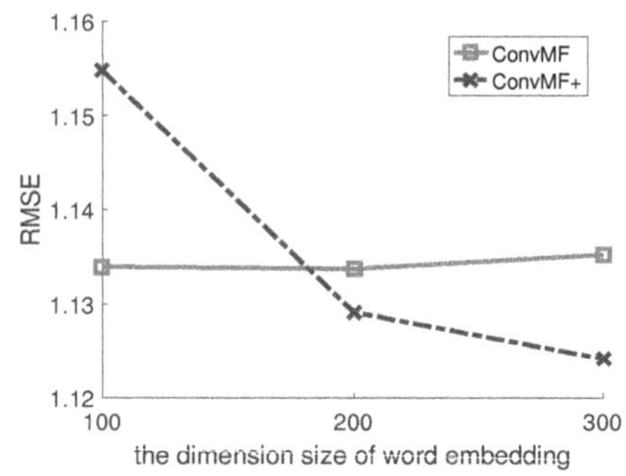

Figure 5: The effects of the dimension size of word embedding on Amazon dataset

relative improvements of "ConvMF" over the best competitor. Compared to three models, ConvMF and ConvMF+ achieve significant improvements on all the datasets.

For MovieLens datasets, which are relatively dense datasets, the improvements of ConvMF over the best competitor, CDL, are 3.92% on ML-1m dataset and 2.79% on ML-10m dataset. We also observe that the performance differences between PMF and the two competitors are marginal on ML-1m dataset. It implies that given enough ratings to generate user and item latent models, document analysis that fails to capture contextual information does not help generate more accurate latent models. However, *significant performance gap between ConvMF and PMF indicates that deeper understanding of documents helps adjust latent models more accurately even when enough ratings are given.*

For Amazon dataset, which is an extremely sparse and skewed dataset as shown in Figure 3 and 4, the improvement of ConvMF over the best competitor, CDL, is 16.60%. This improvement is more substantial compared to the improvements on relatively dense and balanced MovieLens datasets, which indicates that *ConvMF constructs accurate item latent models by effectively analyzing documents even with sparse and skewed data.* Note that the RMSE of CTR is higher than that of PMF although CTR additionally uses item documents. It implies that on such sparse and skewed dataset, it is likely that item latent models built by the LDA part of CTR and user latent models built by the PMF part of CTR do not reside in the same latent space.

2) Quantitative Results Over Various Sparseness on ML-1m

We generate seven additional datasets of different sparsenesses by randomly sampling from ML-1m dataset. As shown in Table 4, ConvMF significantly outperforms three competitors over all ranges of sparseness. Specifically, we observe that improvement of ConvMF over the best competitor (CDL) increases consistently from 2.98% to 3.92% when data density increases from 0.93% to 3.71%. It implies that ConvMF produces more accurate latent models by exploiting ratings when the number of ratings of each item evenly increases – the rating data becomes dense whereas the skewness of

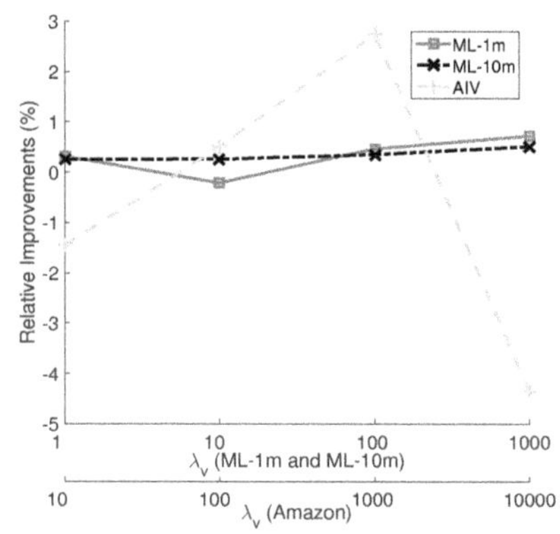

Figure 6: Relative improvements of ConvMF+ over ConvMF

the rating data is almost consistent, which is supported by Figure 3 and 4. To be precise, while ML-1m (sparse) and ML-1m (dense) dataset whose training set consists of 20% and 80% of the entire dataset, respectively, have almost the same skewness over items, the former has relatively smaller number of ratings on items than the latter one. *The performance of ConvMF consistently increases as the dataset gets denser, which indicates that CNN of ConvMF is well integrated into PMF for recommendation task.*

3) Impact of Pre-trained Word Embedding Model

Unlike CTR and CDL, ConvMF is able to take advantage of using pre-trained word embedding models such as Glove [18]. Thus, we investigate the impact of pre-trained word embedding model on our recommendation task by initializing the embedding layer of CNN of ConvMF using the pre-trained word embedding model of Glove [18].

Table 3 shows marginal changes of ConvMF+ over ConvMF on three datasets: -0.22%, 0.35% and 0.51% on ML-1m, ML-10m and AIV dataset, respectively. Note that the sparsity of datasets is in increasing order of ML-1m, ML-10m and AIV. In spite of

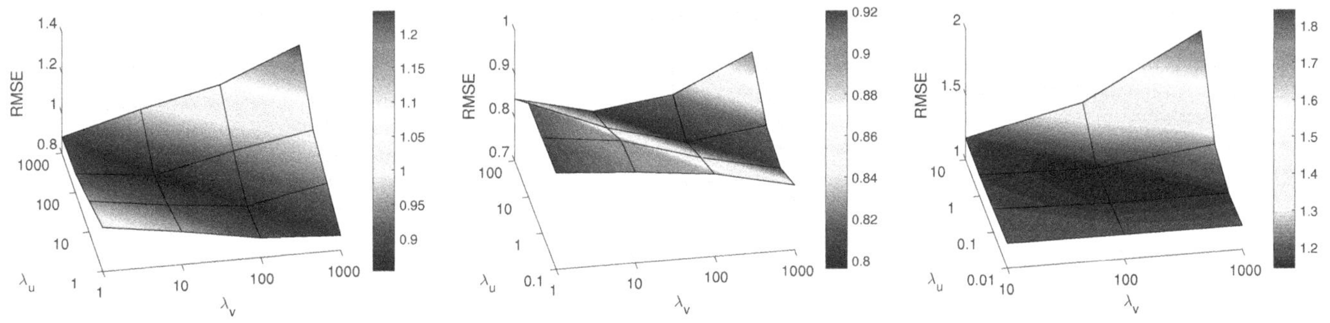

(a) MovieLens-1m (b) MovieLens-10m (c) Amazon Instant Video

Figure 7: Parameter analysis of λ_U and λ_V on three dataset

the marginal changes, we observe the consistent tendency that as the rating data gets sparser, the pre-trained word embedding model helps improve the performance of ConvMF. It is because the semantic and syntactic information of pre-trained word embedding model complement shortage of ratings. We also observe that given sufficient number of ratings to train latent models, pre-trained word embedding model rather deteriorates the performance of ConvMF. In other words, since ratings directly reflect the relationships between users and items, *it is better to fully leverage ratings rather than to additionally utilize pre-trained word embedding model obtained from external documents when rating data is relatively dense.*

Moreover, we investigate relative improvements of ConvMF+ over ConvMF on various λ_V, a parameter that balances between the importance of ratings and description documents in ConvMF. In Figure 6, for MovieLens datasets, since the dataset has relatively large number of ratings, pre-trained word embedding model does not have much impact on the performance of ConvMF on various λ_V. However, for extremely sparse Amazon dataset, pre-trained word embedding model indeed affects the performance of ConvMF. Specifically, when λ_V is 100 and 1000, the improvement of ConvMF+ over ConvMF reaches almost 0.51% and 2.74% with the same parameter setting whereas the performance of ConvMF+ suddenly drops with other λ_V values. In other words, relatively low or high λ_V with pre-trained word embedding model fails to achieve high performance. This phenomenon implies that latent models are under-fitted or over-fitted by the word embedding model when rating data is extremely sparse. Nevertheless, as shown in Figure 6, *given a proper value of λ_V, adopting pre-trained word embedding model increases the performance of ConvMF+ when the number of ratings is insufficient.*

4) Parameter Analysis

We investigate the impact of three parameters on the performance of ConvMF: p (dimension size of word latent vectors), λ_U and λ_V.

Figure 5 shows RMSE changes of ConvMF and ConvMF+ according to various p on Amazon dataset. Interestingly, in case of ConvMF, the increase of p from 100 to 300 does not boost the performance of ConvMF, but rather shows degradation. However, in case of ConvMF+, the increase of p reduces RMSE significantly. This demonstrates that when dataset is extremely sparse, *the performance of ConvMF+ is improved by adopting pre-trained word embedding model in which the information contained gets richer as p gets larger.*

Figure 7 shows the impact of λ_U and λ_V on three real-word datasets. Regarding the changes of the best performing values of λ_U and λ_V from Figure 7(a) to (c), we observe that when the rating data becomes sparse, λ_U decreases while λ_V increases to produce the best results. Precisely, the values of (λ_U, λ_V) of ConvMF are (100, 10), (10 and 100) and (1 and 100) on ML-1m, ML-10m and AIV, respectively. Note that when λ_U is high, user latent model is hardly updated. In other words, a high value of λ_U implies that item latent model tend to be projected to the latent space of user latent model (same applies to λ_V). Thus, when λ_U decreases and λ_V increases, user latent models are projected to the latent space of item latent model whose space is mainly built by description documents rather than by ratings. *These best performing values demonstrate that ConvMF well alleviates data sparsity by balancing the importance of ratings and description documents.*

Phrase captured by W_c^{11}	max(c^{11})	Phrase captured by W_c^{86}	max(c^{86})
people **trust** the man	***0.0704***	betray his **trust** finally	***0.1009***
Test phrases for W_c^{11}	c_{test}^{11}	Test phrases for W_c^{86}	c_{test}^{86}
people **believe** the man	*0.0391*	betray his **believe** finally	*0.0682*
people **faith** the man	*0.0374*	betray his **faith** finally	*0.0693*
people **tomas** the man	*0.0054*	betray his **tomas** finally	*0.0480*

Table 5: Case study on two shared weights of ConvMF

5) Qualitative Evaluation

The performance of ConvMF is affected by the contextual features extracted by shared weights W_c, and each contextual feature is associated with a phrase. In this section, we verify whether ConvMF is able to distinguish subtle contextual differences by comparing each contextual meaning of phrases captured by the shared weights.

Specifically, as a case study, we select W_c^{11} and W_c^{86} from the model trained on ML-10m dataset, and compare the contextual meaning of phrases captured by the shared weights (Table 5). The meaning of "*trust*" in the two phrases captured by the two shared weights seem to be similar to each other. However, there is a subtle difference on contextual meaning of the term "*trust*" in the two phrases. Indeed, the "*trust*" in the phrase captured by W_c^{11} is used as a verb whereas the "*trust*" in the phrase captured by W_c^{86} is used as a noun. To verify this, we slightly change the term "*trust*" in the phrases, and investigate the change of the feature values as shown in Table 5. When we replace "*trust*" with "*believe*" and "*faith*" in the phrases captured by W_c^{11}, the feature value of the former phrase is higher than that of the latter phrase. However, for the case of W_c^{86}, the feature value of the latter phrase is higher than that of the former phrase. This matches with our expectation that "*believe*" is syntactically more similar to the contextual meaning of "*trust*" as a verb captured by W_c^{11} whereas "*faith*" is syntactically more similar to the contextual meaning of "*trust*" as a noun captured by W_c^{86}. When we replace "*trust*" with "*tomas*", which has a completely different meaning from "*trust*", "*tomas*" returns lower values for both W_c^{11} and W_c^{86} than "*believe*" and "*faith*".

This comparisons imply that ConvMF distinguishes a subtle contextual difference of the term "*trust*". As a result, we conclude that *ConvMF captures contextual meaning of words in documents and can even distinguish subtle contextual difference of the same word via different shared weights.*

5. CONCLUSION AND FUTURE WORK

In this paper, we address that considering contextual information such as surrounding words and word orders in description documents provides deeper understanding of description documents, and we develop a novel document context-aware recommendation model, ConvMF, that seamlessly integrates CNN into PMF in order to capture contextual information in description documents for the rating prediction. Extensive results demonstrate that ConvMF significantly outperforms the state-of-the-art competitors, which implies that ConvMF well deals with the sparsity problem with contextual information. Moreover, since ConvMF is based on PMF, which is the standard MF-based recommendation model, ConvMF is able to be extended to combining other MF-based recommendation models such as SVD++ [12] that only consider ratings.

As a next research direction, since it is widely known that unsupervised pre-training on deep neural network has much impact on performance, we try to develop convolutional autoencoder for description documents. By unsupervised way, it enables us to pretrain not only the weight variables of the embedding layer but also all the remaining weight variables of the CNN part of ConvMF. We expect that this unsupervised pre-training by the autoencoder significantly boosts the performance of recommendation when rating data is extremely sparse.

6. ACKNOWLEDGMENTS

This research was supported by Next-Generation Information Computing Development Program through the National Research Foundation of Korea(NRF) funded by the Ministry of Education, Science and Technology (No. 2012M3C4A7033344) and the ICT R&D program of MSIP/IITP [B0101-15-0307, Basic Software Research in Human-level Lifelong Machine Learning (Machine Learning Center)] and the Industrial Core Technology Development Program (10049079, Development of Mining core technology exploiting personal big data) funded by the Ministry of Trade, Industry and Energy (MOTIE, Korea)

7. REFERENCES

[1] F. Chollet. Keras. https://github.com/fchollet/keras, 2015.

[2] R. Collobert, J. Weston, L. Bottou, M. Karlen, K. Kavukcuoglu, and P. Kuksa. Natural language processing (almost) from scratch. *Journal of Machine Learning Research (JMLR)*, 12:2493–2537, Nov. 2011.

[3] M. Deshpande and G. Karypis. Item-based top-n recommendation algorithms. *ACM Transactions on Information Systems*, 22(1):143–177, Jan. 2004.

[4] J. Gao, P. Pantel, M. Gamon, X. He, and L. Deng. Modeling interestingness with deep neural networks. In *Proceedings of the 2014 Empirical Methods in Natural Language Processing (EMNLP)*, pages 2–13, 2014.

[5] A. T. Gediminas Adomavicius. Toward the next generation of recommender systems: A survey of the state-of-the-art and possible extensions. *IEEE Transactions on Knowledge and Data Engineering (TKDE)*, 17(6):734–749, June 2005.

[6] X. Glorot, A. Bordes, and Y. Bengio. Deep sparse rectifier neural networks. In *Proceedings of the Fourteenth International Conference on Artificial Intelligence and Statistics (AISTATS-11)*, volume 15, pages 315–323, 2011.

[7] J. L. Herlocker, J. A. Konstan, A. Borchers, and J. Riedl. An algorithmic framework for performing collaborative filtering. In *Proceedings of the 22nd Annual International ACM SIGIR Conference on Research and Development in Information Retrieval*, SIGIR '99, pages 230–237, New York, NY, USA, 1999. ACM.

[8] J. L. Herlocker, J. A. Konstan, L. G. Terveen, and J. T. Riedl. Evaluating collaborative filtering recommender systems. *ACM Transactions on Information Systems*, 22(1):5–53, Jan. 2004.

[9] Y. Hu, Y. Koren, and C. Volinsky. Collaborative filtering for implicit feedback datasets. In *Proceedings of the 8th IEEE International Conference on Data Mining*, ICDM '08, pages 263–272, Washington, DC, USA, 2008. IEEE Computer Society.

[10] N. Kalchbrenner, E. Grefenstette, and P. Blunsom. A convolutional neural network for modelling sentences. In *Proceedings of the 52nd Annual Meeting of the Association for Computational Linguistics (ACL)*, June 2014.

[11] Y. Kim. Convolutional neural networks for sentence classification. In *Proceedings of the 2014 Empirical Methods in Natural Language Processing (EMNLP)*, pages 1746–1751, 2014.

[12] Y. Koren. Factorization meets the neighborhood: A multifaceted collaborative filtering model. In *Proceedings of the 14th ACM SIGKDD International Conference on Knowledge Discovery and Data Mining*, KDD '08, pages 426–434, New York, NY, USA, 2008. ACM.

[13] Y. LeCun, L. Bottou, Y. Bengio, and P. Haffner. Gradient-based learning applied to document recognition. In *Intelligent Signal Processing*, pages 306–351. IEEE Press, 2001.

[14] S. Li, J. Kawale, and Y. Fu. Deep collaborative filtering via marginalized denoising auto-encoder. In *Proceedings of the 24th ACM International on Conference on Information and Knowledge Management*, CIKM '15, pages 811–820, New York, NY, USA, 2015. ACM.

[15] G. Ling, M. R. Lyu, and I. King. Ratings meet reviews, a combined approach to recommend. In *Proceedings of the 8th ACM Conference on Recommender Systems*, RecSys '14, pages 105–112, New York, NY, USA, 2014. ACM.

[16] A. L. Maas, A. Y. Hannun, and A. Y. Ng. Rectifier nonlinearities improve neural network acoustic models. In *International Conference on Machine Learning Workshop on Deep Learning for Audio, Speech, and Language Processing*, 2013.

[17] J. McAuley and J. Leskovec. Hidden factors and hidden topics: Understanding rating dimensions with review text. In *Proceedings of the 7th ACM Conference on Recommender Systems*, RecSys '13, pages 165–172, New York, NY, USA, 2013. ACM.

[18] J. Pennington, R. Socher, and C. D. Manning. Glove: Global vectors for word representation. In *Empirical Methods in Natural Language Processing (EMNLP)*, pages 1532–1543, 2014.

[19] S. Purushotham, Y. Liu, and C.-C. J. Kuo. Collaborative topic regression with social matrix factorization for recommendation systems. In *Proceedings of the 29th International Conference on Machine Learning (ICML)*, pages 759–766, 2012.

[20] R. Salakhutdinov and A. Mnih. Probabilistic matrix factorization. In *Advances in Neural Information Processing Systems*, volume 20, 2008.

[21] Y. Shen, X. He, J. Gao, L. Deng, and G. Mesnil. A latent semantic model with convolutional-pooling structure for information retrieval. In *Proceedings of the 23rd ACM International Conference on Conference on Information and Knowledge Management*, CIKM '14, pages 101–110, New York, NY, USA, 2014. ACM.

[22] A. van den Oord, S. Dieleman, and B. Schrauwen. Deep content-based music recommendation. In *Advances in Neural Information Processing Systems 26*, pages 2643–2651. Curran Associates, Inc., 2013.

[23] C. Wang and D. M. Blei. Collaborative topic modeling for recommending scientific articles. In *Proceedings of the 17th ACM SIGKDD International Conference on Knowledge Discovery and Data Mining*, KDD '11, pages 448–456. ACM Press, August 2011.

[24] H. Wang, N. Wang, and D.-Y. Yeung. Collaborative deep learning for recommender systems. In *Proceedings of the 21th ACM SIGKDD International Conference on Knowledge Discovery and Data Mining*, KDD '15, pages 1235–1244, New York, NY, USA, 2015. ACM.

Parallel Recurrent Neural Network Architectures for Feature-rich Session-based Recommendations

Balázs Hidasi
Gravity R&D
Budapest, Hungary
balazs.hidasi@gravityrd.com

Massimo Quadrana *
Politecnico di Milano
Milan, Italy
massimo.quadrana@polimi.it

Alexandros Karatzoglou
Telefonica Research
Barcelona, Spain
alexk@tid.es

Domonkos Tikk
Gravity R&D
Budapest, Hungary
domonkos.tikk@gravityrd.com

ABSTRACT

Real-life recommender systems often face the daunting task of providing recommendations based only on the clicks of a user session. Methods that rely on user profiles – such as matrix factorization – perform very poorly in this setting, thus item-to-item recommendations are used most of the time. However the items typically have rich feature representations such as pictures and text descriptions that can be used to model the sessions. Here we investigate how these features can be exploited in Recurrent Neural Network based session models using deep learning. We show that obvious approaches do not leverage these data sources. We thus introduce a number of parallel RNN (p-RNN) architectures to model sessions based on the clicks and the features (images and text) of the clicked items. We also propose alternative training strategies for p-RNNs that suit them better than standard training. We show that p-RNN architectures with proper training have significant performance improvements over feature-less session models while all session-based models outperform the item-to-item type baseline.

Keywords

deep learning; recurrent neural networks; gated recurrent units; recommender systems; training strategies

1. INTRODUCTION

In traditional recommender systems algorithms it is often assumed that user history logs (e.g. clicks, purchases or views) are available. We show that this assumption does not hold in many real-world recommendation use cases: (1) many e-commerce sites do not require user authentication even for purchase; (2) in video streaming services users also rarely log in; (3) many sites have a small percentage of returning users; (4) or the user intent can change between different sessions, typical for e.g. classified sites. User tracking can partly solve the user identification problem across sessions (e.g. through fingerprinting technology, cookies), but this is often unreliable and also raises privacy concerns. So, in such cases the typical solution is to resort to item-to-item recommendations. Here we investigate how we can exploit session data to improve recommendations.

Given the absence of user profiles, it is vital to draw as much information as possible from the session clicks. Besides the click-stream data of the session (clicked item-IDs), one can also take into account the characteristics of the items that have been clicked. Items often come with rich feature representation such as detailed text description or (thumbnail) image. One can expect that e.g. users shopping for a particular type of item will click on items that have similar text descriptions and similar visual features. Images, text or potentially even richer features such as animated gifs are eventually what the user sees and what will determine the appeal of an item to a user. Features become particularly important in a session modeling setting where historical user specific data is missing or has no importance. Such features should be utilized to aid the session modeling process. Item features are also a very good way to deal with item cold start i.e. when a new item enters the pool of selectable items. The joint modeling of the sequence of clicked item-IDs and item features poses some interesting problems.

The algorithms in this work utilize deep learning techniques both to extract high quality features from visual information and to model the sessions. (We also extract features from text via bag-of-words.) Individual user sessions can be seen as sequence of clicks. We use Recurrent Neural Networks (RNNs) to model the session data. RNNs have been shown to perform excellent in modeling sequence data [15]. We introduce a number of parallel[1] RNN (p-RNN) ar-

*The author worked at Telefonica Research as an intern during the time of this research.

[1]Note that we use the term 'parallel' to indicate that for each aspect/feature of the clicked item (e.g. the item-ID, text description, image features) there is a separate RNN processing the input. 'Parallel' refers to the fact that we have multiple RNNs rather than distributed processing of the data or the algorithm computations. While distributed

RecSys '16, September 15-19, 2016, Boston, MA, USA
© 2016 ACM. ISBN 978-1-4503-4035-9/16/09... $15.00
DOI: http://dx.doi.org/10.1145/2959100.2959167

chitectures to model the session clicks concurrently with the features (text or images) of the clicked items.

Instead of using a single RNN where all the data is used at the input in a concatenated form, we apply parallel architectures because of the very different nature of the data: image features tend to be much denser than the one-hot representation of the item-ID or the bag-of-words representation of text. Parallel training also allows us to fine-tune the individual networks with respect to their hyper-parameters while also maintaining a connection between the networks through shared parameters and optimization. We introduce 3 different architectures of p-RNNs that combine the ID-click data with the features of the clicked items. The architectures vary with regards to the shared model parameters and interactions of the hidden states (Section 3).

We also point out that training p-RNNs is not trivial. Standard simultaneous training can waste the capacity of the network, because different parts of the same network may learn the same relations from the data. Therefore we devise 3 alternative optimization procedures to train p-RNNs. We thoroughly evaluate the proposed p-RNN architectures on (1) video recommendations using the thumbnail and (2) product recommendations using text description on a classified site. We compare against the industry standard session-based solution, that is today the item-kNN.

2. RELATED WORK

Deep neural networks have been employed with tremendous success in image recognition, segmentation and retrieval tasks. Deep learning techniques have been used in tasks such as image and speech recognition [5, 10, 20] where unstructured data is processed through several convolutional and standard layers of (usually rectified linear) units.

Neural models for RecSys. Most of the work on deep models and recommendations focus on the classical collaborative filtering (CF) user–item setting. Restricted Boltzmann Machines (RBM) were one of the first neural networks to be used for classical CF and recommender systems [22]. More recently denoising autoencoders have been used to perform CF in a similar manner [30]. Deep networks have also been used in cross-domain recommendation whereby items are mapped to a joint latent space using deep neural networks [4].

Recurrent Neural Models. RNNs are the deep models of choice when dealing with sequential data (see [15] for a comprehensive review). RNNs have been used in image and video captioning, time series prediction, natural language processing, conversational models, text and music generation, and much more. Long Short-Term Memory (LSTM) [11] networks are a type of RNNs that have been shown to work particularly well, it includes additional gates that regulate when and how much to take the input into account and when to reset the hidden state. This helps with the vanishing gradient problem that often plagues the standard RNN models. Slightly simplified version of LSTM – that still maintains all their properties – are Gated Recurrent Units (GRUs) [2] which we use in this work.

Session-based recommendations. Classical CF methods (e.g. matrix factorization) break down in the session-based setting when no user profile can be constructed from past user behavior. A natural solution to this problem is the item-to-item recommendation approach [24, 14]. In this setting an item-to-item similarity matrix is precomputed from the available session data, items that are often clicked together in sessions are deemed to be similar. These similarities are then used to create recommendations. While simple, this method has been proven to be effective and is widely employed. Though, these methods only take into account the last click of the user, in effect ignoring the information of the previous clicks.

Markov Decision Processes (MDP) [25] are the only other approach that aims to provide recommendations in a session-based manner while taking into account information beyond the last click. MDPs are models of sequential stochastic decision problems. An MDP is defined as a four-tuple $\langle S, A, Rwd, tr \rangle$ where S is the set of states, A is a set of actions Rwd is a reward function and tr is the state-transition function. In recommender systems the set of actions are essentially the recommendations that can be shown. The simplest MPDs boil down to first order Markov chains where the next recommendation can be simply computed through the transition probabilities between items. A major issue with applying Markov chains in the session-based recommendation setting is that the state space quickly becomes unmanageable when trying to include all possible sequences of potential user selections over all items.

The first application of neural models in session-based recommendation used RNNs to model the session data [7]. The recurrent neural network is trained with a ranking loss on a one-hot representation of the session (clicked) item-IDs. The RNN is then used to provide recommendations on new user sessions. This work only focused on the clicked item-IDs while here we aim at modeling a much richer representation of the clicked items.

Feature-rich recommendations. Deep models have been used to extract features from unstructured content such as music or images [3, 26]. In recommender systems these features are then typically used together with more conventional collaborative filtering models. Convolutional deep network have been used to extract features from music files that are then used in a factor model [28]. More recently [29] introduced a more generic approach whereby a deep network is used to extract generic content-features from items, these features are then incorporated in a standard CF model to enhance the recommendation performance. This approach seems to be particularly useful in settings where there is not sufficient user–item interaction information. Image features that have been extracted using convolutional networks have been used in classical matrix factorization-type CF in [6, 16] to enhance the quality of recommendations.

3. P-RNN ARCHITECTURES

In this section we describe the proposed parallel RNN (p-RNN) architectures that utilize item representations (features) for session modeling. A p-RNN consists of multiple RNNs, one for each representation/aspect of the item (e.g. one for ID, one for image and one for text). The hidden states of these networks are merged to produce the score for all items. We also introduce baseline architectures, naive approaches for using the different item representations.

As a basis, we take the best RNN setting from [7]: a single GRU layer without feedforward layers and the TOP1 pairwise loss function along with session-parallel mini-batching. The input of the networks is the item ID of a transaction.

versions of RNNs exist [21] this is not the focus of this work.

The input then translates to either (a) a one-hot ID vector[2]; or (b) a precomputed dense image feature vector; or (c) a sparse unigram + bigram text feature vector. See details on feature extraction in Section 4. The proposed architectures use a subset of the above 3 item representations. The output is a score for every item indicating the likelihood of being the next item in the session. During training scores are compared to a one-hot vector created from the item ID of the next event in the session to compute the loss. In order to reduce computational costs, only the score of the target item and that of a small subset of "negative" items – sampled in each step (see [7]) – are computed during training.

The TOP1 loss is the regularized approximation of the relative rank of the relevant item. The relative rank of the relevant item is given by $\frac{1}{N_S} \cdot \sum_{j=1}^{N_S} I\{\hat{r}_{s,j} > \hat{r}_{s,i}\}$ where N_S is the sample size, $\hat{r}_{s,i}$ is the predicted score of the target item, $\hat{r}_{s,j}$ is the score of negative (other) items in the sample and $I\{\cdot\}$ is approximated with a sigmoid. Optimizing for this loss modifies the parameters so that the score for i is high. This loss though is unstable as some positive items also act as negative examples and so scores tend to become increasingly higher. To avoid this, the scores of the negative examples are pushed towards zero through a regularization term. The loss function thus takes the following form: $L_s = \frac{1}{N_S} \cdot \sum_{j=1}^{N_S} \sigma\left(\hat{r}_{s,j} - \hat{r}_{s,i}\right) + \sigma\left(\hat{r}_{s,j}^2\right)$. Given that a typical item set in recommender systems is in the 100,000s, evaluating this loss over all items is computationally prohibitive. We thus use a sampling procedure whereby the loss is evaluated on a sample of the items. For a given session we use the items in the other sessions of the mini-batch as negative samples. This is computationally cheap and also allows us to get samples from the real distribution of the data.

We devised the following architectures (see Figure 1). Due to limited space, we only present architectures with ID and image features; for text features one can proceed analogously as with image ones. The parallel architectures can also deal with ID, image and text features simultaneously. The architectures can be separated into two groups:

1. Baseline architectures:

ID only: This architecture only uses the one-hot ID vectors and is identical to the one used in [7]. It serves as a baseline in our experiments.

Feature only: The input of this variant is one of the content feature vectors (image or text). Otherwise it works similarly to the previous network.

Concatenated input: The easiest way to combine different item representations is to concatenate them. This network uses the concatenated representations as its input.

2. p-RNN architectures:

Parallel: The first parallel architecture trains one GRU network for each of the representations. Outputs are computed from the concatenation of the hidden layers of the subnets.[3] Training can be done in different ways (see training strategies below).

Parallel shared-W: This architecture differs from the previous one by having a shared hidden to output weight matrix. Scores are not computed for each subnetwork separately. Instead, the weighted sum of the hidden states is multiplied by a single weight matrix to produce the output. Having a shared weight matrix greatly reduces the number of parameters and thus decrease training times and overfitting. This model is also analogous to the pairwise model from context-aware factorization research.[4]

Parallel interaction: In this architecture, the hidden state of the item feature subnet(s) is multiplied by the hidden state of the ID subnet in an element-wise manner before computing the score of the subnet(s). Mixing different aspects of the session to compute item scores is analogous to context-aware preference modeling. For that task [9] found that the *interaction model*, i.e. the sum of the user–item and user–context–item interaction to perform the best. This architecture mimics that model with the ID subnet being promoted to the primary representation of the session. The main difference to the context-aware task is that all of our representations are session representations and not (mostly) independent dimensions. Also note that contrary to the original interaction model, the output weight matrix (item feature matrix) is not shared in our model.

3.1 Training p-RNNs

Training parallel architectures is not trivial. Standard backpropagation across the whole architecture can produce suboptimal results due to different components of the architecture learning the same relations from the data. This can be avoided by pretraining some parts of the network and training the rest afterwards. This cycle can be done several times, motivated by the success of alternating methods like ALS for matrix factorization. Note that while the parameters of fixed networks remain unchanged they still participate in the forward pass and they are only excluded from the backpropagation. We developed the following training strategies for p-RNNs:

Simultaneous: Every parameter of every subnet is trained simultaneously. Serves as the baseline.

Alternating: Subnets are trained in an alternating fashion per epoch. For example, the ID subnet is trained in the first epoch, while the others are fixed; then we fix the ID subnet and train the image subnet for one epoch; and so on. The cycle restarts after each subnet was trained.

Residual: Subnets are trained one after the other, on the residual error of the ensemble of the previously trained subnets. The cycle does not start over, but the individual training of a subnet is longer compared to the alternating method. For example, the ID subnet is trained for 10 epochs, then the image subnet is trained on the residual error of the ID subnet and so on.

Interleaving: Alternating training per mini-batch. For each mini-batch of training examples, the first subnet is trained, the second subnet is trained on the residual error for the current mini-batch and so on. The more frequent alternation allows for a more balanced training across subnets without the drawbacks of the simultaneous training.

4. FEATURE EXTRACTION

In this Section we describe the feature extraction process

[2]Also referred to as 1-of-N encoding. The length of the vector equals to the number of items and only the coordinate corresponding to the ID is 1, the others are 0.

[3]Equivalent to computing output scores separately, weighting them and applying through the final activation function.

[4]The hidden to output matrix is the item feature matrix. The hidden states are different representations of the session, i.e. different context dimensions.

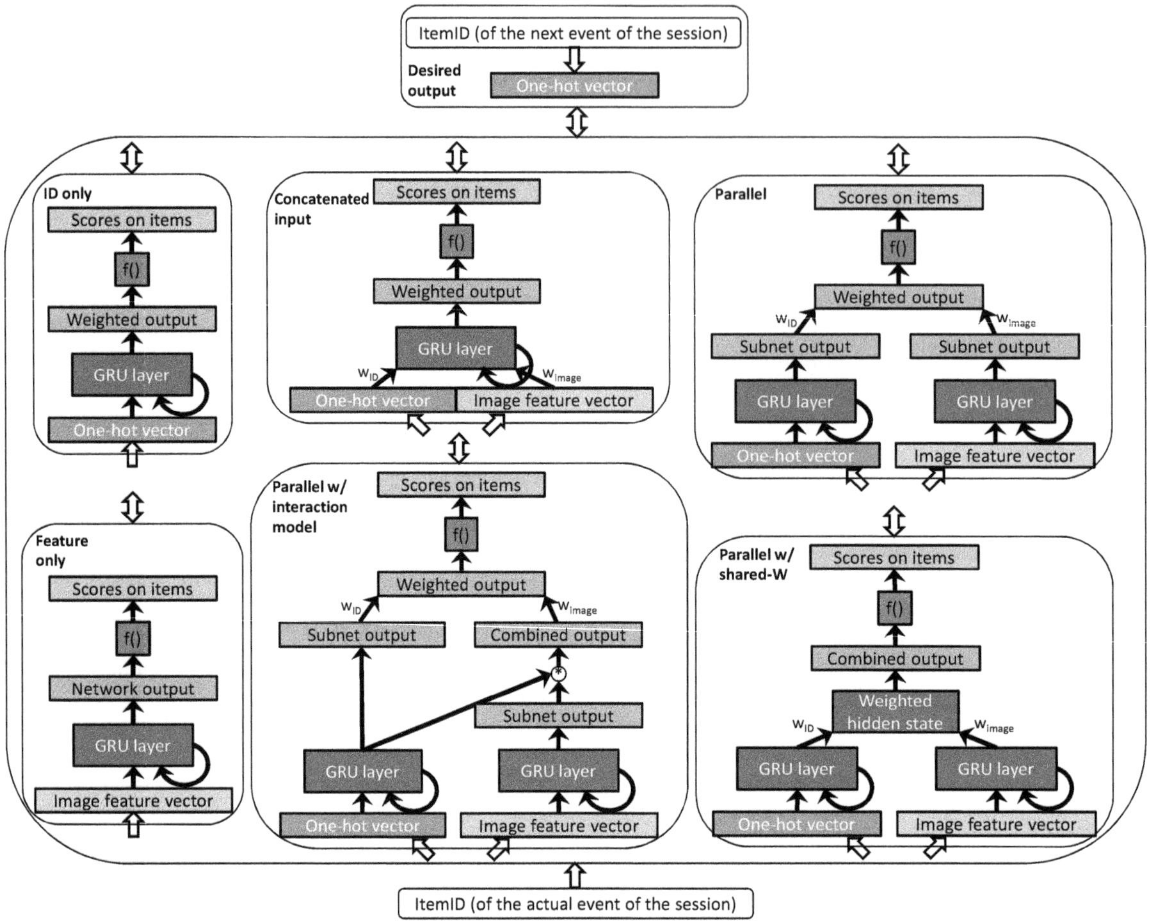

Figure 1: RNN architectures for feature inclusion. Architectures are presented with ID and image features only, but text features can be used in place of the image features as well. The parallel architectures can also be extended to have networks for ID, image and text features simultaneously. f() is the nonlinearity applied to the network output (tanh in our case). ***Top row (left to right):*** **ID only; Concatenated input; Parallel.** ***Bottom row (left to right):*** **Feature only; Parallel with interaction model; Parallel with shared weight matrix.**

used to create item representations from images and text. Image features were extracted from video thumbnails, while text features are based on product descriptions.

Encoding images. Recently, deep learning research on convolutional neural networks (CNNs) achieved breakthroughs in a variety of different image-related tasks, like object recognition, image segmentation, video classification, etc. [12, 13] even surpassing human performance on the task of object recognition [5]. Unlike other approaches, CNNs don't require prior feature extraction, since they are capable of working on the raw image data. CNNs trained on millions of images produce image features that can then be used as input in other algorithms e.g. clustering [3, 26]. These models generalize well and also perform well on images that the CNN has never encountered during training and can thus be used as generic feature extractors. This makes CNNs ideal for extracting high quality image features.

We used the GoogLeNet [27] implementation of the Caffe deep learning framework [12] to extract features from the thumbnails of the videos. The network was pre-trained as an image classifier on the ImageNet ILSVRC 2014 dataset [19] that contains 1.2M images organized into 1000 categories. The video thumbnails first had to be scaled down and cropped in order to fit the input of the network. Features were extracted from the last average pooling layer.[5] The feature vectors were normalized to an $l2$ norm of 1. The image feature representation we end up with is a real-valued vector of length 1024.

Figure 2 demonstrates the feature quality by showing the 3 most similar images to two query images, where similarity is defined as the cosine similarity between the image feature vectors. Given the good quality, we do not plug the CNN directly into the RNN, as it would introduce unnecessary complexity to the training and is also unpractical, because (a) this network would converge much slower as it needs to learn the model on incomplete/changing item representations; (b) the network would not be suitable for datasets with lower number of items, as 10,000s of items are not enough to leverage the full potential of the CNN; (c) retraining would take much longer. Another possibility is to use the pretrained network and fine tune the item representations during the training of the RNN. This did not make much difference in our experiments, therefore we did not use fine tuning.

[5] Extracted as the value of the *pool5_7x7_s1* layer.

Figure 2: Top3 similar images to query images, based on cosine similarity of image feature vectors.

Encoding text. Given the strict limitation on the length of the descriptions imposed by online classified advertisement platforms, advertisers usually provide rather concise text for their items. The main goal of the description is to attract the attention of potentially interested users. Therefore, descriptions often contain only the main characteristics of the item and use syntactically incorrect sentences. Moreover, it is not rare to have descriptions written in multiple languages to capture a broader audience. The majority of descriptions of our dataset used a subset of 3 main languages with a handful of less frequent ones also present.

Given the inherent noise in user generated, unstructured text and multiple languages in our data, we adopted the classical bag-of-words representation to encode product descriptions. First we concatenated the title and the description of the items.[6] We filtered stopwords and extracted unigrams and bigrams from text, and discarded all the entries that appear only once. Finally, the resulting bag-of-words was weighted using TF-IDF [23]. The item representation is a sparse vector of length 1,099,425 with an average of 5.44 non-zero coordinates.

We tried other methods to extract features from unstructured text, e.g. distributed bag-of-words [18] and Language Modeling with RNNs [17]. However the classical bag-of-words with TF-IDF was found to work best with our data. We attribute this to the noisiness of user generated content. The lack of English text and the presence of multiple languages prevented us from using pre-trained word representations, e.g. from word2vec.[7]

Experiments with adding an embedding layer between the features and the network resulted in worse performance, therefore, the classical bag-of-words/TF-IDF features were used as item representations and were used directly as the input of the RNNs.

5. RESULTS

The evaluation was done on two proprietary datasets. The first dataset – coined VIDXL – was collected over a 2-month period from a Youtube-like video site, and contains video watching events having at least a predefined length. During the collection item-to-item recommendations were displayed next to the featured video, generated by a selection of different algorithms. The second dataset consists of product view events of an online classified site. We refer to this dataset as CLASS. The site also had recommendations displayed with different algorithms during the collection period.

During the preprocessing of the raw event streams we filtered out unrealistically long sessions as these are likely due to bot traffic. We removed sessions of one (single click) event because they are not useful for session-based recommendations and also removed items whose support is below five, as items with low support are not ideal for modeling. The sessions of the last day of each dataset are put into the test set. Each session is assigned to either the training or the test set, we do not split the data mid-session. We also filter items from the test dataset if they were not in the training set. This affects only a tiny fraction of the items. The datasets are summarized in Table 1.

Table 1: Properties of the datasets.

Data	Train set		Test set		Items
	Sessions	Events	Sessions	Events	
VIDXL	17,419,964	69,312,698	216,725	921,202	712,824
CLASS	1,173,094	9,011,321	35,741	254,857	339,055

We evaluate wrt. the (sequential) next-event prediction task, i.e. given an event of the session how well can the algorithms predict the next event of the session. The trained model is fed with the events of a session one after another and we check the rank of the selected item of the next event. The hidden state of the network is reset to zero after a session ends.

As recommender systems recommend only a few items at once, the relevant item should be amongst the first few items of the list. Therefore, our first evaluation metric is recall@20 that is the proportion of cases having the desired item amongst the top-20 items of all test cases. Recall does not consider the actual rank of the item as long as it is below 20. This is an accurate model for certain practical scenarios where no recommendation is highlighted and their absolute order does not matter. Recall also usually correlates well with important online KPIs, such as click-through rate (CTR)[8]. The second metric used in the experiments is MRR@20 (Mean Reciprocal Rank). MRR is the average of the reciprocal ranks of the desired items. The reciprocal rank is set to zero if the rank is above 20. MRR takes the rank of the item into account, which is important in cases where the order of recommendations matters (e.g. the lower ranked items are only visible after scrolling).

5.1 Thumbnail based video recommendation

We extracted image features from the thumbnails of the videos, see Section 4 for the details of the feature extraction. We experimented with different architectures and training strategies described in Section 3 to see how image data can contribute to recommendation accuracy.

Similarly to [7], the networks optimize for TOP1 loss using adagrad. The parameters – such as dropout, learning rate, momentum, batch size, etc. – of the ID only and the feature only networks were optimized on a hold out validation set. Then the networks were retrained on the full training set (validation set included) and the final results were measured on the test set. Due to the size of the VIDXL dataset, the more complex networks used the optimal parameters of the ID and image networks in their corresponding subnets. The weights of the subnets were set to be equal as we did not get significantly different results until either of the subnet weights was set to zero.

To speed up evaluation, we computed the rank of the rel-

[6]We explicitly avoided to repeat the title if this was already written at the beginning of the text
[7]https://code.google.com/p/word2vec

evant item compared to the 50,000 most supported items. While this evaluation methodology somewhat overestimates the rank and thus the evaluated metrics are a little bit higher, the comparison of the algorithms remains fair [1].

Table 2 summarizes the results with different architectures and training methods. In this experiment the number of hidden units was set to 100 for the baseline architectures and 100 per subnetwork for p-RNNs. The networks are trained for 10 epochs as there is no significant change in the loss after that. The networks are compared to the item-kNN algorithm, the de-facto solution for item-to-item and item-to-session recommendation tasks in the industry. p-RNNs with 100+100 hidden units can easily outperform the ID only network with 100 units, due to the additional information source and the increase of the overall capacity of the network. Therefore we also measured the accuracy of the ID only network with 200 units. Note that this is a very strong baseline, because having 200 hidden units increases the capacity of the network ~4 times, while having 100+100 only doubles it. Also, the doubled capacity of p-RNN is split between two information sources, therefore it is clearly in disadvantage to even an RNN with doubled capacity. Nevertheless we show that p-RNNs can often beat this strong baseline as well, while they are typically better than the ID only network with 100 units.

Table 2: Results on VIDXL, using image features extracted from thumbnails. The best results are typeset in bold. p-RNNs use 100+100 hidden units, others use 100 unless stated otherwise. Performance gain over item-kNN is shown in parentheses.

Method	Recall@20	MRR@20
Item-kNN	0.6263	0.3740
ID only	0.6831 (+9.07%)	0.3847 (+2.85%)
ID only (200)	0.6963 (+11.17%)	0.3881 (+3.77%)
Feature only	0.5367 (−14.30%)	0.3065 (−18.05%)
Concatenated	0.6766 (+8.03%)	0.3850 (+2.94%)
Parallel (sim)	0.6765 (+8.01%)	0.4014 (+7.34%)
Parallel (alt)	0.6874 (+9.76%)	0.4331 (+15.81%)
Parallel (res)	0.7028 (+12.21%)	**0.4440** (+18.72%)
Parallel (int)	**0.7040** (+12.41%)	0.4361 (+16.60%)
Shared-W (sim)	0.6681 (+6.66%)	0.4007 (+7.13%)
Shared-W (alt)	0.6804 (+8.63%)	0.4035 (+7.88%)
Shared-W (res)	0.6425 (+2.58%)	0.3541 (−5.31%)
Shared-W (int)	0.6658 (+6.31%)	0.3715 (−0.66%)
Int. model (sim)	0.6751 (+7.78%)	0.3998 (+6.90%)
Int. model (alt)	0.6847 (+9.32%)	0.4104 (+9.74%)
Int. model (res)	0.6749 (+7.76%)	0.4098 (+9.56%)
Int. model (int)	0.6843 (+9.25%)	0.4040 (+8.02%)

Similar to [7], the RNN outperforms the item-kNN baseline by a large margin. The recall for the RNN on this task is very high, therefore it is very hard for the more advanced architectures to significantly improve on this result. The network that is trained on the image features only is significantly worse than the ID only network and even worse than the item-kNN, demonstrating that the sequence of item features in and of itself is not enough to model the session well. Feeding the network with the concatenated input of IDs and image features, because the stronger input dominates during the training, thus the performance hardly differs from that of the ID only network. It is hard for a single GRU layer to handle two types of inputs at once, resulting in a performance very similar to that of the ID only network. Adding item features using the naive approach has no observable benefits. Therefore we propose to use p-RNNs instead.

Moving on to the proposed p-RNN architectures, one can see that several configurations perform significantly better than the strong ID only baseline. Due to the originally high recall of the network, these novel architectures mostly increase the MRR, i.e. they don't find more relevant items, but they rank them better. The best performing architecture is the classic parallel one. With the naive simultaneous training it is significantly better than the strong ID only baseline wrt. MRR, but slightly worse wrt. recall. With simultaneous training, different components of the p-RNN learn the same relations from the data, thus the full capacity of the network is not leveraged. Therefore we propose using alternative training strategies.

The best of the alternative training methods is residual training, closely followed by the interleaving one, but the alternating training is also not far behind. The p-RNN with residual training outperforms the strong ID only baseline by 14.07% in MRR, while achieving similar recall. The improvement is even greater over the industry de facto item-kNN solution: 12.21% in recall and 18.72% in MRR.

Table 3: Results on VIDXL, using image features extracted from thumbnails. The best results are typeset in bold. p-RNN architectures use 500+500 hidden units, others use 1000. Performance gain over item-kNN is shown in parentheses.

Network variant	Recall@20	MRR@20
ID only, 10 epochs	**0.7279** (+16.21%)	0.4350 (+16.32%)
ID only, 20 epochs	0.7207 (+15.07%)	0.4287 (+14.63%)
Feature only	0.6479 (+3.45%)	0.4089 (+9.34%)
Concatenated	0.7216 (+15.22%)	0.4291 (+14.72%)
Parallel (sim)	0.7084 (+13.10%)	0.4420 (+18.19%)
Parallel (alt)	0.7142 (+14.03%)	0.4456 (+19.15%)
Parallel (res)	0.7165 (+14.40%)	0.4513 (+20.67%)
Parallel (int)	**0.7262** (+15.59%)	**0.4587** (+22.64%)

By increasing the number of hidden units, the capacity of the RNN increases, thus this parameter has a large effect on performance. However this parameter also obeys the law of diminishing returns. We found that results do not improve significantly above ~1000 hidden units on this problem. We ran experiments with 1000 units on non-parallel and 500+500 units on the best performing p-RNN architecture (i.e. classic parallel) to confirm that adding item features can also benefit session modeling when increasing the network capacity and/or the number of epochs has diminishing returns. Table 3 depicts the results.

With more hidden units, the performance increases and even the feature only network outperforms the item-kNN baseline as the capacity of the network is enough to leverage the information in the image features. But otherwise the relation between the results is similar to that of the previous experiments. This further underpins that p-RNNs with alternative training strategies are vital for efficiently incorporating item features into learning session models. Further increasing the number of hidden units and/or the number of epochs did not increase the performance of any network significantly, but p-RNN architectures significantly outperform the ID only network with more than 2 times larger capacity in terms of MRR (~7% with interleaving training) and have similar recall. This means that the proposed architectures with the proposed training strategies can significantly increase performance, even when increasing the capacity of the network has diminishing returns. In other words, adding additional data sources (item features) can increase the accuracy of recommendations beyond the maximum achievable just from item IDs. However handling multiple sources requires special architectures and training: p-RNNs and alternative training strategies.

5.2 Using product descriptions

We repeated the last experiment – i.e. baseline RNNs had 1000 hidden units; the classic p-RNN had 500 per subnet – on the CLASS dataset with features extracted from product descriptions instead of images. See the detailed feature extraction process in Section 4. The experimental setup was the same as before, except that we opted for ranking all items during evaluation, because it is possible to do the full evaluation within reasonable time due to the significantly smaller size of this dataset (compared to VIDXL).

Table 4: Results on CLASS, using textual features extracted from product descriptions. The best results are typeset in bold. p-RNN architectures use 500+500 hidden units, others use 1000. Performance gain over item-kNN is shown in parentheses.

Training info	Recall@20	MRR@20
Item-kNN baseline	0.2387	0.0839
ID only, 10 epochs	0.2849 (+19.38%)	0.1062 (+26.56%)
ID only, 20 epochs	0.2783 (+16.60%)	0.1051 (+25.26%)
Feature only	0.2397 (+0.47%)	0.0937 (+11.70%)
Conc. input	0.2844 (+19.17%)	0.1029 (+22.64%)
Parallel (sim)	0.2741 (+14.85%)	0.1019 (+21.53%)
Parallel (alt)	0.2877 (+20.97%)	0.1096 (+30.62%)
Parallel (res)	**0.2946** (+23.44%)	**0.1119** (+33.36%)
Parallel (int)	0.2854 (+19.57%)	0.1058 (+26.17%)

The results (see Table 4) concur with that of the earlier experiments with image features. The text only network significantly outperforms the item-kNN baseline in terms of MRR. This confirms that textual features can be effectively exploited to generate better rankings. However it falls short when compared with the ID only network. This suggests that text features alone are not enough. With concatenated input, the network performs similarly to the ID only network analogously to previous experiments.

The proposed alternative training strategies are of crucial importance when training p-RNNs, the simultaneous training is clearly suboptimal wrt. recommendation accuracy. The classic p-RNN with alternative training strategies significantly outperformed both the ID only RNN and item-kNN in *both* recall and MRR. Residual training proved to be the best strategy in this experiment with ~6% improvement in recall and ~6.5% in MRR over the ID only network. Note that further increasing the number of hidden units or number of epochs for the baseline RNNs did not improve the results any further. Thus using text based item features in p-RNNs with proper training can also increase recommendation accuracy beyond what is achievable from IDs only.

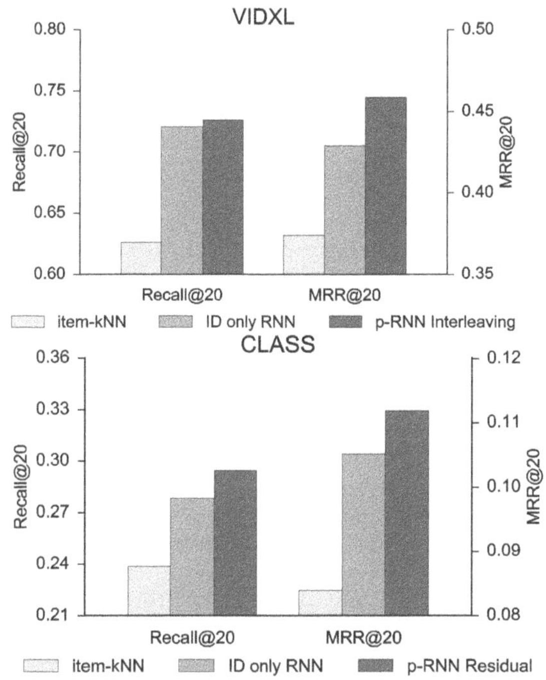

Figure 3: Comparing best performing p-RNN against the ID only RNN and item-kNN.

We demonstrate the power of the proposed solution (500 units per subnet) by comparing it to item-kNN and the ID only network with 1000 hidden units on Figure 3.

6. CONCLUSION

In this paper we examined the use of item features (image data and text) in RNN-based session modeling to improve session-based recommendations. We pointed out that using item features in and of themselves is not enough to properly model the session and combining multiple data sources efficiently (e.g. ID and image) is not trivial. We proposed p-RNN architectures that can leverage the added value of multiple item representations. We devised alternative training strategies (alternating, residual and interleaving training) that fit these architectures better than backpropagating the error through the whole network. The proposed architectures and training methods significantly outperformed both RNNs with ID only input and the industry de facto solution for this problem, item-kNN. Finally, we showed that by using p-RNNs with alternative training, recommendation accuracy can be increased beyond the maximum that is achievable by RNNs with ID only input by increasing their capacity and/or the number of training epochs.

Acknowledgments

The work leading to these results has received funding from the European Union's Seventh Framework Programme (FP7/2007-2013) under CrowdRec Grant Agreement n° 610594.

7. REFERENCES

[1] A. Bellogin, P. Castells, and I. Cantador. Precision-oriented evaluation of recommender systems: An algorithmic comparison. In *RecSys'11: 5th ACM Conf. on Recommender Systems*, pages 333–336, 2011.

[2] K. Cho, B. van Merriënboer, D. Bahdanau, and Y. Bengio. On the properties of neural machine translation: Encoder–decoder approaches. In *SSST-8: 8th Workshop on Syntax, Semantics and Structure in Statistical Translation*, pages 103–111, 2014.

[3] J. Donahue, Y. Jia, O. Vinyals, J. Hoffman, N. Zhang, E. Tzeng, and T. Darrell. DeCAF: A deep convolutional activation feature for generic visual recognition. In *ICML'14: 31st Int. Conf. on Machine Learning*, pages 647–655, 2014.

[4] A. M. Elkahky, Y. Song, and X. He. A multi-view deep learning approach for cross domain user modeling in recommendation systems. In *WWW'15: 24th Int. Conf. on World Wide Web*, pages 278–288, 2015.

[5] K. He, X. Zhang, S. Ren, and J. Sun. Deep residual learning for image recognition. *arXiv preprint arXiv:1512.03385*, 2015.

[6] R. He and J. McAuley. VBPR: Visual Bayesian Personalized Ranking from implicit feedback. *CoRR*, 1510.01784, 2015.

[7] B. Hidasi, A. Karatzoglou, L. Baltrunas, and D. Tikk. Session-based recommendations with recurrent neural networks. *International Conference on Learning Representations*, 2016.

[8] B. Hidasi and D. Tikk. Fast ALS-based tensor factorization for context-aware recommendation from implicit feedback. In *ECML-PKDD'12, Part II*, number 7524 in LNCS, pages 67–82. Springer, 2012.

[9] B. Hidasi and D. Tikk. General factorization framework for context-aware recommendations. *Data Mining and Knowledge Discovery*, 30(2):342–371, 2015.

[10] G. Hinton, L. Deng, D. Yu, G. E. Dahl, A.-R. Mohamed, N. Jaitly, A. Senior, V. Vanhoucke, P. Nguyen, T. N. Sainath, et al. Deep neural networks for acoustic modeling in speech recognition: The shared views of four research groups. *Signal Processing Magazine, IEEE*, 29(6):82–97, 2012.

[11] S. Hochreiter and J. Schmidhuber. Long short-term memory. *Neural computation*, 9(8):1735–1780, 1997.

[12] Y. Jia, E. Shelhamer, J. Donahue, S. Karayev, J. Long, R. Girshick, S. Guadarrama, and T. Darrell. Caffe: Convolutional architecture for fast feature embedding. In *MM'14: 22nd ACM Int. Conf. on Multimedia*, pages 675–678, 2014.

[13] A. Krizhevsky, I. Sutskever, and G. E. Hinton. ImageNet classification with deep convolutional neural networks. In *NISP'12: 26th Annual Conf. on Neural Information Processing Systems 2012*, pages 1106–1114, 2012.

[14] G. Linden, B. Smith, and J. York. Amazon.com recommendations: Item-to-item collaborative filtering. *Internet Computing, IEEE*, 7(1):76–80, 2003.

[15] Z. C. Lipton, J. Berkowitz, and C. Elkan. A critical review of recurrent neural networks for sequence learning. *CoRR*, 1506.00019, 2015.

[16] J. McAuley, C. Targett, Q. Shi, and A. van den Hengel. Image-based recommendations on styles and substitutes. In *SIGIR'15: 38th Int. ACM SIGIR Conf. on Research and Development in Information Retrieval*, pages 43–52, 2015.

[17] T. Mikolov, M. Karafiát, L. Burget, J. Černocký, and S. Khudanpur. Recurrent neural network based language model. In *INTERSPEECH'10: 11th Ann. Conf. of the Int. Speech Communication Association*, pages 1045–1048, 2010.

[18] T. Mikolov, I. Sutskever, K. Chen, G. Corrado, and J. Dean. Distributed representations of words and phrases and their compositionality. *CoRR*, 1310.4546, 2013.

[19] O. Russakovsky, J. Deng, H. Su, J. Krause, S. Satheesh, S. Ma, Z. Huang, A. Karpathy, A. Khosla, M. Bernstein, A. C. Berg, and L. Fei-Fei. ImageNet large scale visual recognition challenge. *Int. Journal of Computer Vision*, 115(3):211–252, 2015.

[20] O. Russakovsky, J. Deng, H. Su, J. Krause, S. Satheesh, S. Ma, Z. Huang, A. Karpathy, A. Khosla, M. S. Bernstein, A. C. Berg, and F. Li. ImageNet large scale visual recognition challenge. *CoRR*, 1409.0575, 2014.

[21] H. Sak, O. Vinyals, G. Heigold, A. Senior, E. McDermott, R. Monga, and M. Mao. Sequence discriminative distributed training of long short-term memory recurrent neural networks. *Entropy*, 15(16):17–18, 2014.

[22] R. Salakhutdinov, A. Mnih, and G. Hinton. Restricted boltzmann machines for collaborative filtering. In *ICML'07: 24th Int. Conf. on Machine Learning*, pages 791–798, 2007.

[23] G. Salton and C. Buckley. Term-weighting approaches in automatic text retrieval. *Inf. Process. Manage.*, 24(5):513–523, Aug. 1988.

[24] B. Sarwar, G. Karypis, J. Konstan, and J. Riedl. Item-based collaborative filtering recommendation algorithms. In *WWW:01: 10th Int. Conf. on World Wide Web*, pages 285–295, 2001.

[25] G. Shani, R. I. Brafman, and D. Heckerman. An MDP-based recommender system. In *UAI'02: 18th Conf. on Uncertainty in Artificial Intelligence*, pages 453–460, 2002.

[26] A. Sharif Razavian, H. Azizpour, J. Sullivan, and S. Carlsson. CNN features off-the-shelf: An astounding baseline for recognition. In *CVPR'14: IEEE Conf. on Computer Vision and Pattern Recognition Workshops*, June 2014.

[27] C. Szegedy, W. Liu, Y. Jia, P. Sermanet, S. E. Reed, D. Anguelov, D. Erhan, V. Vanhoucke, and A. Rabinovich. Going deeper with convolutions. *CoRR*, 1409.4842, 2014.

[28] A. Van den Oord, S. Dieleman, and B. Schrauwen. Deep content-based music recommendation. In *Advances in Neural Information Processing Systems*, pages 2643–2651, 2013.

[29] H. Wang, N. Wang, and D.-Y. Yeung. Collaborative deep learning for recommender systems. In *KDD'15: 21th ACM SIGKDD Int. Conf. on Knowledge Discovery and Data Mining*, pages 1235–1244, 2015.

[30] Y. Wu, C. DuBois, A. X. Zheng, and M. Ester. Collaborative denoising auto-encoders for top-N recommender systems. In *WSDM'16: 9th ACM Int. Conf. on Web Search and Data Mining*, pages 153–162, 2016.

The Contextual Turn: from Context-Aware to Context-Driven Recommender Systems

Roberto Pagano,
Paolo Cremonesi,
Massimo Quadrana
Politecnico Di Milano
Milan, Italy
<name.surname>@polimi.it

Martha Larson
Delft University of Technology
& Radboud University
Delft & Nijmegen, Netherlands
m.a.larson@tudelft.nl

Balázs Hidasi,
Domonkos Tikk
Gravity R&D Inc.
Budapest, Hungary
<name.surname>@gravityrd.com

Alexandros Karatzoglou
Telefonica I+D
Barcelona, Spain
alexandros.karatzoglou@telefonica.com

ABSTRACT

A critical change has occurred in the status of context in recommender systems. In the past, context has been considered 'additional evidence'. This past picture is at odds with many present application domains, where user and item information is scarce. Such domains face continuous cold start conditions and must exploit session rather than user information. In this paper, we describe the 'Contextual Turn': the move towards context-driven recommendation algorithms for which context is critical, rather than additional. We cover application domains, algorithms that promise to address the challenges of context-driven recommendation, and the steps that the community has taken to tackle context-driven problems. Our goal is to point out the commonalities of context-driven problems, and urge the community to address the overarching challenges that context-driven recommendation poses.

Keywords

position paper; context; recommender systems

1. INTRODUCTION

In recent years, the recommender system community has discovered the benefits of context. A common characterization of context-aware recommender systems is that they 'try to incorporate or utilize additional evidence (beyond information about users and items) to estimate user preferences on unseen items' [1]. In this position paper, we declare that it is time for a *Contextual Turn*, which revisits this definition, and acknowledges that being *aware* of context is not always enough. Instead, an increasing number of application domains call for recommender system algorithms that are actually *driven* by context. In contrast to context-aware recommendation, in context-*driven* recommendation users and items take a back seat.

For the philosophically minded, the Contextual Turn is valuable because it overthrows the assumption that personalization in recommender systems involves recommendation for specific individuals. Instead, a context-driven recommender system, 'personalizes' to users' context states. In this way, it introduces a disassociation between users and their historical behavior, giving users room to develop beyond their past needs and preferences. Instead, users receive recommendations based on what is going on around them in the moment (situation) and on what they are trying to accomplish (intent). The Contextual Turn re-envisions the original insight of user-user collaborative filtering by taking the position that people have more in common with other people in the same situation, or with the same goals, than they do with past versions of themselves.

The Contextual Turn is very much a phenomenon of this moment. Until recently, a system whose main driver is context, would not be conceivable. Context-driven recommendation is made possible by a confluence of developments: huge amounts of data generated by users in a wide range of contexts are available, new sources of context-data are provided by sensors (smart phones, Internet of Things), and the computational power to process this data is within our reach. Finally, recent years have seen a rapprochement of recommender systems and information retrieval (IR). In IR, relevance has long been acknowledged as situational, e.g., dynamic, multidimensional, and dependent on user goals and situation [3]. IR also realizes that users themselves fill the gap between the results list and the perfect item, i.e., using diversification of results lists in cases in which the user's information need may not be completely clear [14]. Together, these new resources and new insights make *now* the right moment to launch consolidated effort towards context-driven recommendation.

Conceptually, the Contextual Turn can be seen as a turn away from what we call the *Immutable Preference* paradigm

RecSys '16, September 15 - 19, 2016, Boston , MA, USA

ISBN 978-1-4503-4035-9/16/09...$15.00

DOI: http://dx.doi.org/10.1145/2959100.2959136

(ImP) in recommender systems. ImP assumes that users goals, needs, and tastes do not develop, and that the set of items to be recommended remains relatively static. Current state-of-the-art models try to overcome the ImP assumptions by tweaks to existing models. For example, they introduce decay to prioritize recent preferences over past preferences, they filter the recommendation list to include only currently available items, or they adjust weights to account for seasonality or trends. Recommender systems after the Contextual Turn will reject the assumption of ImP in their algorithmic fabric, rather than as an afterthought.

We do not expect the Contextual Turn to introduce a discontinuity into recommender system research. In fact, the underlying challenges of context-driven recommendation can be seen as more extreme forms of familiar recommender system challenges. The conventional problem of sparse user-item interactions is driven to an extreme, since a context-driven recommender uses a context-state as a target, and may have no user ID whatsoever. Further, for the context-driven recommender systems the cold start challenge is not a start-up challenge, but rather user and item dynamics make the challenge *continuous cold start*.

We anticipate that the Contextual Turn will unify currently disparate strands in the recommender system community. Most obviously, context-aware recommendation is the direct progenitor of context-driven recommendation. However, other areas also have something to add. We mention session-based recommendation, which models context as a series of user interactions carried out within a session. Then, both content-based recommendation and stream-based recommendation also contribute because of their power to tackle cold start and sparse user interactions. The Contextual Turn is in line with the operational requirements for today's commercial recommender systems. Due to the difficulties of session modeling, most online recommenders use item-item recommendations. Although they account for 80% of recommendation traffic only 0.1% of recsys research focuses on this topic [12]. The Contextual Turn puts focus on session modeling and brings research into better alignment with industry needs.

Even though we name the Contextual Turn, we do not claim to have invented it. The notion of *context-driven recommendation* has been in the air for some time. Our concern is that its current state of fragmentation, pursued, as it is, via isolated research efforts under different names, is not particularly productive. Our purpose here is to point out commonalities across a range of application domains that build a unified picture of context-driven recommender system as a domain-overarching challenge for recommender systems. By discussing the potential of existing algorithms, and the challenges that still remain open, we aim to encourage the recommender system community to join forces and develop new breeds of algorithms specifically suited to context-driven recommendation. Section 2 provides a short recap of context-aware recommendation, Section 3 discusses domains which, at present, have emerged as needing context-driven recommendation. Then, Section 4 covers algorithms suitable for context-driven recommendation, and sets the stage for Section 5, discussing the future challenges faced in order to successfully execute the Contextual Turn.

2. PAST: CONTEXT-AWARE RECSYS

Conventionally, context-aware recommender systems fall into three types: *contextual pre-filtering*, where context drives data selection; *contextual post-filtering*, where context is used to filter recommendations once they have been computed using a traditional approach; and *contextual modeling*, where context is integrated directly into the model [1]. An example of contextual pre-filtering is the so-called *user micro-profile*, in which a single user is represented by a hierarchy of possibly overlapping contextual profiles [2]. Post-filtering methods can use traditional approaches and then apply filtering or weighting. In their experimental evaluation, Panniello *et al.* [10] found that the choice of a pre-filtering or post-filtering strategy depends on the particular recommendation problem.

Context-aware recommendation has become increasingly sophisticated, since the first models, which simply considered items to be different items if the context was different, i.e., a restaurant was considered a different restaurant when it was raining that when it was sunny. The Contextual Turn can be considered to represent a return to the idea that the context has a strong determining force on the item.

3. NEW CONTEXT-CENTRIC DOMAINS

The trigger of the Contextual Turn is the rise of new application domains in which the ImP assumptions fail to hold, and which require context-driven recommendation. Here we cover key domains, and mention examples of existing work.

Domains with *seasonality* patterns are strongly context-centric: Linear TV consumption is periodical and strongly dependent on the channel rather than the program itself [16]. E-tourism faces a similar break down of ImP assumptions: touristic items are time-variant and price-sensitive products. For instance, prices and cancellation policies of flight tickets or hotel rooms are dynamic and heavily depend on both absolute time context (e.g., low-season vs high season) and relative time context (e.g., days before booking). Incorporating seasonality as a contextual variable has already been proven to deliver better results [16, 5].

Domains with *availability* patterns cannot assume that all items are always available, but rather are dependent on contextual factors such as the number of users who have 'consumed' items at any moment of time. Examples of *limited availability* of items (or bounded capacity), include e-tourism or online marketplaces. Research has suggested that profile-based approaches traditionally used in e-commerce domains do not necessarily work for e-tourism applications, because of the particular nature of the touristic products [17]. Examples in the e-tourism domain are seats in restaurants, or rooms in hotels. A hotel may become unavailable during high season or when the booking time is close to the desired time of usage. The quality of the offering of items is not constant: as the number of available items decreases, the quality of the remaining ones tends to decrease, because the items that are first sold are typically the "best" ones. In a context-driven setting, the availability of the items can be used as a contextual variable, useful for understanding the conditions (situations) that led the user to choose some product among the available ones.

The *turnover* of the items is related to availability. With turnover items disappear or are replaced, never to return. The turnover (or dynamic catalog) property of the domain can be found in the Linear TV, online marketplaces, news and user generated content recommendation domains. In these domains items are added and removed from the catalog very frequently. This problem can be solved by the context-driven paradigm by considering the joint user-item-context information of previous interactions. Moreover the use of sessions can also address this problem, for example by favoring recent sessions (that therefore use recent and available items).

Finally, we turn to consider the dynamics of users. Here, we first point to *personal development*, the changes that users undergo because they learn or otherwise evolve over time. For example, recommending learning materials or jobs must take into account that users evolve over their lifetimes. A related phenomenon is *taste drift*, which also involves changing preferences for items, but is not necessarily a development pattern.

The *immediate task* of the user is crucial in domains such as music recommendation. The authors of [15] developed a learning-free recommender that was only exploiting contextual signals gathered from smartphone sensors. The system provides, e.g., workout music when the user is exercising at the gym.

Session is another contextual signal that plays a fundamental role in the music domain. Sessions are sequences of user interactions with the online service. A subset of these interactions is relative to the items, such as purchase or view. A session usually has a goal, such as finding a good TV program, watching short clips in a certain topic, or listening to music of a certain style or mood. There is an increasing number of session-aware algorithms that exploit the session for providing recommendation. In the music domain, [4] showed that the sequence of songs the user already listened to is a proxy for the kind of music the user want to listen to *in that particular situation.*

4. PRESENT: USEFUL ALGORITHMS

The notion of context key to context-driven recommendation is the user situation and the user intent. This abstract concept must be translated into concrete algorithmic solutions. We point out that context can still be regarded as either fully observable, partially observable or unobservable [1]. A context-driven recommender uses observable context (e.g., geo-location), directly, and relies on inference to exploit partially observable or unobservable contexts (e.g., activity, physical state, mood, user goal).

The existence of domains in which the ImP assumptions breakdown poses a serious challenge for recommender systems. However, the availability of increasing amounts of data from a variety of sources provides an opportunity to compensate. The challenge is to identify helpful information sources to exploit. The RecSys 2015 best paper [9] is an example of work that opens up new possibilities for exploiting different context-variables (or signals), even when there are no user interactions (continuous cold start situation). We also mention that collecting useful data may mean elicitation of information from users, either actively or by presenting them with opportunities to engage in informative interactions. Here, active learning strategies would offer themselves as helpful.

A context-driven algorithm merges characteristics of collaborative, content, and context-aware (and session-aware) algorithms. Of course it's context-aware, since it exploits contextual variables. It is collaborative, but the collaboration happens among context states rather than among users. It is content-based, since the content of an item can be used to refine the system's understanding of the user context.

Some state-of-the-art algorithms can already be adapted to the context-driven paradigm with some modifications. Here we list some state-of-the art algorithms and their ability to deliver context-driven recommendations.

Decision Trees (and Gradient Boosted Trees and Random Forest in particular) perfectly fit in the context-driven definition, since they usually do not include user and item in their training. In this way the tree can learn the best hierarchy among the contextual features.

General Factorization Framework (GFF) [8] is a powerful context-aware factorization algorithm that makes it possible to experiment with preference models. The preference model is provided to the algorithm as an input. The number and meaning of the input dimensions is arbitrary. Due to its flexibility, this framework already has the ability to deliver context-driven recommendation. For example, it can exclude the user ID from the preference model.

Factorization machines (FM) are another powerful factorization algorithm that can be applied to context-aware data [13]. Similarly to GFF, FMs can (but are not limited to) model pairwise interactions between the input dimensions, which in turn are not constrained to contain the user (or item). For this reason, they can be used in pure context-driven scenarios.

Session-based algorithms deserve special attention, because they are intrinsically *context-driven.* Recurrent neural networks (RNNs) deliver good performance for modeling and generating sequences. RNNs have been demonstrated in [6] to be useful for session-based recommendations, providing recommendations based on items in the active session of the user. Moreover, deep learning is able to exploit item content directly in order to derive semantic representations of the data and model user preferences. Adding other contextual variables as well as the content of the item and removing the user is straightforward and enables the neural network to model preference patterns in different contexts. Finally, the availability of an increasing amount of data and work in this area, makes Deep Learning a promising direction for context-driven recommendation.

5. FUTURE: CONTEXT-DRIVEN RECSYS

We conclude with a discussion of open issues left by algorithms in Section 4 and a discussion of additional benefits.

5.1 Open Challenges for Research

The Contextual Turn requires addressing a number of research challenges.

Continuous context. Factorization methods require discrete input variables. Context, however, is often continuous (time, geo-location). Methods are needed for integrating continuous information or packaging it into categorical form without damaging its value. Initial work in this direction was carried out by [7].

Missing values. With current state-of-the-art methods, each event must have a value for each input dimension, i.e. missing context is not handled. While this is a realistic requirement for e-commerce and online services, it is far less reasonable for sensory data.

Scalability. Since the recommendation depends on the value of contextual variables, there are two choices: compute the recommendation at the moment of request or precompute the recommendations for every possible contextual state. The second option is feasible if the set of contextual states is not large, but becomes challenging when we are dealing with many contextual variables or sessions.

Evaluation In the simplest case, evaluation can be carried out using conventional approaches, but replacing the user with the appropriate contextual variables. However when dealing with sessions, the evaluation must be adapted, in order to take into account the sequential dependency between items. In some domains, recommendations are only useful to users if strict ordering is respected (e.g., app recommendation for a task). In others, a certain amount of flexibility is allowed (e.g., users tolerate, or even welcome, shuffle in their playlists). From the business perspective it is key that clients are able to understand the metrics, and put them to use.

5.2 Benefits of the Contextual Turn

The benefits of the Contextual Turn potentially transcend conventional requirements for recommender systems.

Popping the Bubble Recommenders focusing on context-state rather than on individuals can counter the dangers of hyper-personalization, i.e., the Filter Bubble problem [11]. Of course context gives rise to its own bubble effect. However, people arguably have more control over their context, the situation and goal of the moment (intent), than over their accumulated past history.

Leveling the playing field Issues of *bias* are closely related to the Filter Bubble. Recommendations for jobs, online educational courses, or scientific literature must be blind to user characteristics such as gender, ethnicity, and social economic background. Under context-driven recommendation, the focus of the recommender system is, by design, on situation and intent, and not on demographic group (i.e., something users do not choose themselves).

Protecting privacy Both user requirements for privacy and laws regarding the storage of personal information are in flux, cf. the European General Data Protection Regulation, adopted April 2016. Facing these calls requires algorithms that need as little data as possible, and, in particular, can avoid storing data associated with specific user ID for extended periods. By focusing on effective exploitation of context and not individuals, algorithms will be robust to future evolution of privacy requirements.

Adding transparency Context-driven recommendations can use context variables to explain recommendations to users. Establishing best practices would require a significant amount of additional research, but we point to the potential of context-based explains to be less 'creepy' and more readily understandable for users.

Companies already understood the potential of context for making recommendations. As an example Google Context Awareness API can already exploited to gather high quality contextual data. We hope that this paper will foster a stronger cooperation between academia and industry for better addressing new research paths in recommender systems, e.g., by organizing challenges or providing data for benchmarks.

In closing, we emphasize that we do not expect context-driven recommendation to replace context-aware recommendation or conventional personalization. Instead, our intent is that by explicitly pointing out the ongoing Contextual Turn, we can encourage the recommender system community to look specifically at how context can be exploited as the primary source of information for recommendations.

As a final note, we mention that space constraints have kept our reference list here to a bare minimum. As a resource to the recommender system community we have published an extended bibliography[1].

6. REFERENCES

[1] G. Adomavicius and A. Tuzhilin. *Context-Aware Recommender Systems*, pages 191–226. Springer, 2015.

[2] L. Baltrunas and X. Amatriain. Towards time-dependant recommendation based on implicit feedback. In *CARS Workshop at ACM RecSys 2009.*

[3] P. Borlund. The concept of relevance in IR. *JASIST*, 54(10):913–925, 2003.

[4] A. Condorelli, P. Cremonesi, R. Pagano, M. Quadrana, and R. Turrin. Large scale music recommendation. In *LSRS Workshop at ACM RecSys 2015.*

[5] P. Cremonesi, F. Garzotto, R. Pagano, and M. Quadrana. Recommending without short head. In *ACM WWW 2014 Companion*, pages 245–246.

[6] B. Hidasi, A. Karatzoglou, L. Baltrunas, and D. Tikk. Session-based recommendations with recurrent neural networks. *ICLR*, 2016.

[7] B. Hidasi and D. Tikk. Approximate modeling of continuous context in factorization algorithms. In *ACM Workshop on CARR 2014.*

[8] B. Hidasi and D. Tikk. General factorization framework for context-aware recommendations. *Data Min. Knowl. Disc.*, 30(2):342–371, 2015.

[9] A. Q. Macedo, L. B. Marinho, and R. L. Santos. Context-aware event recommendation in event-based social networks. In *ACM RecSys 2015*, pages 123–130.

[10] U. Panniello, A. Tuzhilin, M. Gorgoglione, C. Palmisano, and A. Pedone. Experimental comparison of pre- vs. post-filtering approaches in context-aware recommender systems. In *ACM RecSys 2009*, pages 265–268.

[11] E. Pariser. *The filter bubble: What the Internet is hiding from you.* Penguin UK, 2011.

[12] I. Pilászy, A. Serény, G. Dózsa, B. Hidasi, A. Sári, and J. Gub. Neighbor methods vs matrix factorization – case studies of real-life recommendations. In *LSRS Workshop at ACM RecSys 2015.*

[13] S. Rendle, Z. Gantner, C. Freudenthaler, and L. Schmidt-Thieme. Fast context-aware recommendations with factorization machines. In *ACM SIGIR 2011*, pages 635–644.

[14] R. L. Santos, C. Macdonald, and I. Ounis. Exploiting query reformulations for web search result diversification. In *ACM WWW 2010*, pages 881–890.

[15] A. Sen and M. Larson. From sensors to songs: A learning-free novel music recommendation system using contextual sensor data. In *LocalRec Workshop at ACM RecSys 2015.*

[16] R. Turrin, A. Condorelli, P. Cremonesi, and R. Pagano. Time-based TV programs prediction. In *RecSysTV Workshop at ACM RecSys 2014.*

[17] H. Werthner and F. Ricci. E-commerce and tourism. *Commun. ACM*, Dec. 2004.

[1] http://www.citeulike.org/groupfunc/20206/home

Discovering What You're Known For: A Contextual Poisson Factorization Approach

Haokai Lu
Texas A&M University
hlu@cse.tamu.edu

James Caverlee
Texas A&M University
caverlee@cse.tamu.edu

Wei Niu
Texas A&M University
Wei@cse.tamu.edu

ABSTRACT

Discovering what people are known for is valuable to many important applications such as recommender systems. Unlike an individual's personal interests, what a user is known for is reflected by the views of others, and is often not easily discerned for a long-tail of the vast majority of users. In this paper, we tackle the problem of discovering what users are known for through a probabilistic model called Bayesian Contextual Poisson Factorization. Moving beyond just modeling user's content, it naturally models and integrates additional contextual factors, concretely, user's geo-spatial footprints and social influence, to overcome noisy online activities and social relations. Through GPS-tagged social media datasets, we find that the proposed method can improve known-for prediction performance by 17.5% in precision and 20.9% in recall on average, and that it can capture the implicit relationships between a user's known-for profile and her content, geo-spatial and social influence.

1. INTRODUCTION

Discovering what people are *known for* is valuable to many important applications, including recommender systems and question-answering sites. For example, item-based recommenders can be augmented to customize recommendations based on what knowledgeable users prefer, rather than relying on all users [2]. While an individual's *personal interests* are often reflected in the media she consumes and generates, what a user is *known for* is reflected by the views of others and is often not easily discerned. A few high-profile people are easily recognized – for example, a researcher may be interested in basketball, biking, and recommender systems, though mainly known for recommender systems. But there is a long-tail of the vast majority of users for whom we have only limited insight into what they are known for.

And yet accurate identification of a user's known-for profile is challenging. First, the content that a user chooses to post on social media is often noisy and ambiguous. What users are truly known for can be buried among posts about daily routines and personal interests. Second, many users post only infrequently, meaning extreme sparsity for the vast majority of all users. Third, while a natural step to overcoming this sparsity is the integration of additional contextual factors (e.g., social links between users), it is not clear how different contextual factors correlate with users' known-for profiles and how we can model these contextual influence and integrate them together.

Hence, in this paper, we tackle the problem of *discovering what users are known for* through a probabilistic factorization model called Bayesian Contextual Poisson Factorization (BCPF). Three of the key features of the proposed BCPF model are: (i) It is jointly learned on a small fraction of users whose known-for profiles are already known and the vast majority of users for whom we have little (or no) information. (ii) Moving beyond just modeling the content a user generates, it naturally models and integrates additional contextual factors that provide implicit linkages between users for improved known-for profile estimation. Concretely, we investigate the impact of geo-spatial footprints and social influence as additional contextual signals. (iii) It inherits the strengths of Bayesian Poisson factorization (BPF), a variant of probabilistic matrix factorization recently proposed in [9, 10], which demonstrates scalable inference for sparse data and outperforms traditional matrix factorization [9].

In summary, this paper makes the following contributions:
– First, we define the problem of discovering user's known-for profile in social media, and propose a probabilistic method called Bayesian Contextual Poisson Factorization. This model can capture the implicit relationships between user's known-for profile and her content, geo-spatial and social influence. We then develop an efficient approximate variational inference to learn the latent parameters of BCPF.
– Second, we evaluate the proposed method over two Twitter datasets and against several alternative baselines. Overall, we see a significant improvement of 17.5% in precision and 20.9% in recall on average over the next-best method.
– Finally, we study the inferred geo-spatial and social influence latent factors, and observe that the geo-spatial factors are able to capture the underlying distributions of user's known-for profile at different locations. We also show that friends have different social influence on users with respect to different topics, and that our model is able to learn this fine-grained social influence.

Problem Formulation. We assume there exist a set of users U in a social network, and a set of tags T used to describe what users are known for with respect to different topics or aspects. The **known-for profile** p_u of a user

RecSys '16, September 15-19, 2016, Boston , MA, USA
© 2016 ACM. ISBN 978-1-4503-4035-9/16/09. . . $15.00
DOI: http://dx.doi.org/10.1145/2959100.2959146

$u \in U$ is defined to be a subset of tags from T which can best describe what this user is *known-for* by others, instead of what u is personally *interested-in*. To give an example: suppose Alice is known by others as a chef and frequently posts many food recipes, but she also posts news and personal related stories now and then as her personal interest. We associate Alice with tags "chef" and "recipe" instead of "news" to best describe her perceived image by others, and treat "chef" and "recipe" as the *known-for* profile for Alice.

With the above definition, we can define the task of discovering user's known-for profile in social media as follows: **User Known-For Profile Discovery.** Given the users U^{old} whose known-for profiles are already known (labeled users), identify the known-for profiles for the rest of the users U^{new} (unlabeled users) based on U^{old}. Equivalently, the task is the same as identifying the top-n tags from T for unlabeled users as their known-for profiles.

However, discovering user's known-for profile is a classic cold-start problem. Since unlabeled users do not have any identified tags in their profile, collaborative filtering techniques fail to infer the profiles of unlabeled users since the corresponding rows of the user-profile matrix are all zeros for unlabeled users. Thus, to overcome the cold-start situation, we propose to leverage a user's contextual information to extract implicit relationships between their profile and the context for the task as described in the following.

2. KNOWN-FOR PROFILE DISCOVERY

As a first pass, we can attack the problem of known-for profile discovery with Bayesian Poisson factorization (BPF), a variant of probabilistic matrix factorization recently proposed in [9, 10] to model implicit feedback for recommendation. Due to the assumption of Poisson distribution instead of traditional Gaussian distribution in modeling the discrete data, BPF can capture the long-tailed distribution of user behavior, enjoy scalable inference for sparse data and outperform traditional matrix factorization [9]. In our setting, since a user's known-for profile is inherently of discrete nature, i.e., either a tag exists in the profile or not, it is a natural choice to adopt a Poisson distribution instead of a Gaussian distribution to model user's contextual influence.

Specifically, given the binary occurrence r_{ut} of tag t in the known-for profile for user u, BPF assumes that r_{ut} is generated according to:

$$r_{ut} \sim Poisson(\theta_u^T \theta_t) \tag{1}$$

where $\theta_u \in \mathbb{R}^K$ is the latent factor of u representing what u is known for in a latent space, and $\theta_t \in \mathbb{R}^K$ is the latent attribute of t. Each component of these latent parameters is drawn according to a Gamma distribution as follows:

$$\theta_{\cdot k} \sim Gamma(\lambda_a, \lambda_b) \tag{2}$$

where λ_a and λ_b are the shape and rate parameter of the Gamma distribution, respectively. Given a binary matrix of known-for profiles, BPF can find each user's latent factors over the tag's latent attributes. These inferred latent factors can be further used to identify other related tags which may fit the user's known-for profile.

2.1 Bayesian Contextual Poisson Factorization

While BPF is able to reveal the latent factors for users whose known-for profiles are already known or partially known, it will fail to infer the known-for profiles of unlabeled users, since these users are "zero rows" in the user-tag matrix. Hence, a natural approach to extend BPF to these missing users is through the integration of additional contextual information that may provide implicit linkages between users.

We refer to this extended framework as **Bayesian Contextual Poisson Factorization** since it inherits the strengths of BPF and is extended to integrate valuable contextual information. Intuitively, BCPF is designed to learn the influence of each contextual feature individually and combine them together for overall representation. Under the assumption of Poisson factorization, since the sum of Poisson random variables is still a Poisson distribution, we can linearly add different contextual influence together without changing the underlying probabilistic assumption.

In the rest of this section, we present how several important contextual factors can be modeled under BCPF – user content, geo-spatial impact, and social influence – and how these factors can be integrated into BCPF. Note that the proposed model is generalizable and other contextual factors could be incorporated as well. Concretely, we model users in a heterogeneous graph $\mathbb{G} = (\mathbb{V}, \mathbb{E})$, consisting of four types of nodes $\mathbb{V} = (U, C, L, P)$. Each user u has a sample of the textual content that she posts online, denoted as $c_u \in C$, and a pair of geographical coordinates $(l_u^{lat}, l_u^{lng}) \in L$ indicating the approximate location of this user's posting activities. The known-for profile of a labeled user from U^{old} is denoted as $p_u \in P$. All of the above relations are directly relevant to users themselves, and can be regarded as user attributes. Furthermore, users may also have social relations with each other. Together, user attributes and social relations constitute all edges $\mathbb{V}$ between different entities.

Content factor. The first baseline factor is a user's content – that is, we assume that a user's known-for profile can be reflected by the usage of words in posts. Let $\mathbf{R^c}$ be a sparse matrix describing the usage of words from all users, where each element r_{uw} is the count of word w adopted by user u. We then choose to model every count r_{uw} using a Poisson distribution, with the intensity parameter factorizing over u's latent factor θ_u and w's latent factor θ_w as follows:

$$r_{uw} \sim Poisson(\theta_u^T \theta_w) \tag{3}$$

where θ_u and θ_w are both K-dimensional non-negative vectors with Gamma priors specified in Equation 2.

Factorizing over the word matrix $\mathbf{R^c}$ gives us an unsupervised version of users' latent preference over words. However, for labeled users U^{old}, θ_u should also reflect their known-for profiles. For instance, if both users are labeled with "sports", it is likely that they may share some common words in their sports-related posts. Thus, to capture this intuition, θ_u should also be constrained by users' known-for profiles. Let $\mathbf{R^p}$ be a binary matrix describing known-for profiles for all users, where each element r_{ut} represents if user u is labeled with tag t. Similarly, we model each binary r_{ut} with a Poisson distribution, with its intensity parameter factorizing over θ_u and t's latent factor θ_t as follows:

$$r_{ut} \sim Poisson(\theta_u^T \theta_t) \tag{4}$$

where θ_t is a K dimensional non-negative vector parametrized with Gamma priors. By sharing user's latent factor for both factorization 3 and 4, the model can not only reflect user's latent preference over common use of words, but also ensure that users with similar profiles have similar θ_u. Note however that a user's posts may be intertwined with other

Figure 1: Geo-spatial distribution of users who are known for "entrepreneur" (left) and "politics" (right).

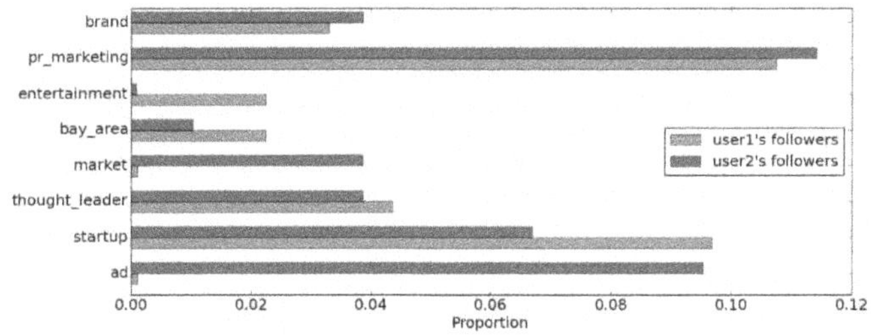

Figure 2: Proportion of followers who have the same tag in their known-for profile as the users. user1: red; user2: blue.

non-revealing texts, and thus can be noisy. To enhance the representation for unlabeled users, we also incorporate each user's geo-spatial footprints and social connections to further refine the model.

Geo-spatial factor. To demonstrate how geo-spatial location may reflect what a user is known for, we first show heat maps of users in US who are known for "entrepreneur" and "politics" in Figure 1 based on a sample of crowd-generated Twitter lists (described more fully in Section 3). As we can observe, for both topics, these well-known users are mostly distributed in a few areas, with a majority focused in San Francisco for "entrepreneur" and in Washington D.C. for "politics". This suggests that (i) for a specific tag, users do not distribute evenly across the entire geo-scope and may concentrate in a few areas; (ii) geo-spatial distributions of well-known users may vary by different topics.

Given the above observations, how can we use geo-spatial coordinates to enhance the representation of users? We notice from Figure 1 that users known for certain topical tags often appear in clusters, i.e., they concentrate in several discrete regions. In light of this, we introduce a region-dependent variable to represent a region's affinity over tags.

Concretely, we assume that the geographical space is partitioned into $\mathcal{I}$ regions. Each user can then be assigned into the region where she belongs, which gives a matrix $\mathbf{R^{ul}}$. Each region corresponds to a K-dimensional location latent factor, denoted θ_l, indicating the region's affinity over tags. If we consider that each r_{ut} in the matrix R^p is only dependent on user's location, then r_{ut} can be generated through the following Poisson distribution:

$$r_{ut} \sim Poisson(\theta_{l_u}^T \theta_t) \tag{5}$$

where l_u represents the region where user u belongs, and the intensity parameter is determined by the inner product of the corresponding location and tag latent factor. Similarly, each component of θ_l has a conjugate Gamma prior as specified in Equation 2. Thus, through the explicit handling of tag's dependence over locations, it is expected that θ_l could indicate which tags are mostly dominant for the corresponding region.

Social influence factor. Homophily in social networks [22] suggests that people tend to connect with others who are similar to themselves. Indeed, there already exists some works [19, 21] exploiting social relations for item recommendations. Here, we would like to explore how social relations may benefit user known-for profile discovery. An immediate problem is that user's social relations are often noisy, i.e., if a friend of a user is known for a tag, it does not necessarily mean that the user is also known for the tag. In Figure 2, we randomly select two Twitter users who are known for eight tags, and examine the proportion of followers who have the same tag in their known-for profiles. We can see that even though user1 is known for "ad", very few followers of the user are also known for "ad". On the contrary, a significant portion of followers of user2 are known for "ad". This indicates that users may have different degree of social influence.

Thus, to capture this observation, we introduce a social influence parameter θ_f for each friend f of all users, indicating the degree of social influence of this friend on any user who follows her. Thus, if we have a total of M friends, the influence parameters constitute a vector of Θ^f with dimension M. Then, given user u's friends $\mathcal{N}_u$, if we consider that each r_{ut} in the matrix $\mathbf{R^p}$ is only dependent on user's friends' known-for profiles, then r_{ut} could be generated through the following Poisson distribution:

$$r_{ut} \sim Poisson(\sum_{f \in \mathcal{N}_u} \theta_f r_{ft}) \tag{6}$$

where r_{ft} is the element in the matrix $\mathbf{R^{ft}}$ indicating if friend f has the tag t. The intensity parameter is obtained by aggregating all of the friends' latent influence for the user.

However, since each friend may be labeled with multiple tags, it is very likely that this friend has different levels of influence for different tags, as shown in Figure 2. In the figure, many people following user2 have the tag "pr marketing" and "ad". Thus, although user2 is also known for "entertainment", it is obvious that this user is more influential on "pr marketing" and "ad". As a result, if a new user starts to follow her, it is very likely that this user follows her because she is also known for "pr marketing" or "ad".

Hence, to capture this intuition, we assume that for each friend f of all users' friends, there is a latent factor θ_{ft} for each tag t. This parameter is used to capture the degree of influence that f has over t. Thus, if we have a total of N tags, the influence parameters constitute a M by N matrix Θ^{ft}. Thus, given user u's friends $\mathcal{N}_u$, similarly as above, r_{ut} can be generated through the following:

$$r_{ut} \sim Poisson(\sum_{f \in \mathcal{N}_u} \theta_{ft} r_{ft}) \tag{7}$$

where the intensity parameter is obtained by aggregating all of the friends' latent influence for this user and the corresponding tag. Consequently, Equation 7 is able to model the above scenario where the new user is more likely to have the tag "pr marketing" or "ad" instead of "entertainment" if she follows user2. Similarly, each nonzero component of Θ^{ft} is put on Gamma priors for inference.

Integrating contextual factors. So far, we can generate independent known-for profiles through user's content, geographical coordinates and social relations. However, it is

Algorithm 1: Generative Process for BCPF

Input: hyper-parameter λ_a^w, λ_b^w, λ_a^u, λ_b^u, λ_a^l, λ_b^l, λ_a^t, λ_b^t, λ_a^{ft}, λ_b^{ft}

for each word w in the vocabulary, draw
  word topic factor $\theta_w \sim$ Gamma(λ_a^w,λ_b^w)
for each user u, draw user content factor
  associated with tags, $\theta_u \sim$ Gamma(λ_a^u,λ_b^u)
for each word w used by user u, draw
  the occurrence count $r_{uw} \sim$ Poisson($\theta_u^T\theta_w$)
for each discretized region l, draw region factor
  associated with tags, $\theta_l \sim$ Gamma(λ_a^l,λ_b^l)
for each friend tag pair (f,t), draw
  friend social influence on t, $\theta_{ft} \sim$ Gamma(λ_a^{ft},λ_b^{ft})
for each tag t, draw tag factor associated with
  user content and region, $\theta_t \sim$ Gamma(λ_a^t,λ_b^t)
for each tag t in user u's known-for profile, draw
  binary $r_{ut} \sim$ Poisson(λ_{ut}), where λ_{ut} is determined
  by Equation 8.

natural to combine all types of contextual influence to form a better representation for users. Since the sum of Poisson distributions is still a Poisson distribution, we can combine the generative process specified by Equation 4, 5 and 7 together to obtain the overall intensity parameter of the sum Poisson distribution as:

$$\lambda_{ut} = \alpha\theta_u^T\theta_t + \beta\theta_{l_u}^T\theta_t + \gamma\sum_{f\in\mathcal{N}_u}\theta_{ft}r_{ft} \tag{8}$$

where α, β and γ are the tradeoff weights for content, geospatial and social contributions, respectively. The entire generative process of BCPF is described in Algorithm 1.

2.2 Prediction

We have specified a Bayesian probabilistic model over the latent parameters Θ^u, Θ^w, Θ^l, Θ^{ft} and Θ^t, and the observed discrete data matrix $\mathbf{R^p}$, $\mathbf{R^c}$, $\mathbf{R^{ul}}$ and $\mathbf{R^{ft}}$. To predict the known-for profiles for new users, we need to estimate the posterior distributions of the latent parameters $p(\Theta^u,\Theta^w,\Theta^l,\Theta^{ft},\Theta^t|\mathbf{R^p},\mathbf{R^c},\mathbf{R^{ul}},\mathbf{R^{ft}})$ given the observed data. Once we have the posterior distributions of the latent factors, we can predict the known-for profiles for new users with the expectation of the sum of weighted Poisson distributions. This leads to computing the expectation of the intensity parameter λ_{ut}, which gives:

$$E(r_{ut}) = \alpha E(\theta_u)^T E(\theta_t) + \beta E(\theta_{l_u})^T E(\theta_t) + \gamma\sum_{f\in\mathcal{N}_u} E(\theta_{ft})r_{ft}$$

where all expectations are with respect to the posterior distributions. By making use of a new user's contextual information, we can predict the ranking of the tags for this user by their expected occurrence.

2.3 Learning with Variational Inference

Since it is not tractable to compute the exact posterior of the latent factors Θ, we propose to use variational methods [15] for approximate inference. Variational inference casts the approximation process as an optimization problem. By defining a freely parameterized family of distributions over latent variables, variational methods seek to fit its parameters so as to minimize the KL-divergence between the defined distribution and the posterior distribution. In our case, variational inference solves the following minimization problem:

$$q^*(\Theta) = argmin_q KL(q(\Theta)||p(\Theta|\mathbf{R^p},\mathbf{R^c},\mathbf{R^{ul}},\mathbf{R^{ft}})) \tag{9}$$

where $q^*(\Theta)$ is the optimized variational distribution that is used as the proxy for the exact posterior. To facilitate the inference, we first introduce several auxiliary latent variables [9] for Equation 3 and 8. Specifically, let's assume $z_{uwk} \sim Poisson(\theta_{uk}\theta_{wk})$, where $\sum_k z_{uwk} = r_{uw}$, and $z_{utk}^c \sim Poisson(\alpha\theta_{uk}\theta_{wk})$, $z_{utk}^l \sim Poisson(\beta\theta_{l_uk}\theta_{tk})$, $z_{utf} \sim Poisson(\gamma\theta_{ft}r_{ft})$, where $\sum_k z_{utk}^c + \sum_k z_{utk}^l + \sum_{f\in\mathcal{N}_u} z_{utf} = r_{ut}$. Since the sum of a set of Poisson random variables is still a Poisson distribution, these auxiliary variables can still preserve the marginal distribution of r_{uw} and r_{ut} when marginalized out. Thus, our latent variables include latent parameters Θ and auxiliary latent variables Z_{uw}, Z_{ut}.

Before solving Equation 9, we need to derive the complete conditionals, i.e., the conditional distributions of a latent variable given all other variables, for each of Θ, Z_{uw} and Z_{ut}. Since each of Θ has conjugate Gamma priors, the complete conditionals for Θ are also Gamma distributions. For auxiliary latent variables, we follow the conclusion from [14] that given a vector Z_{ut} of Poisson distributed count, Z_{ut} is distributed as a multinomial conditioned upon the observed sum r_{ut}. Similarly, Z_{uw} is also a multinomial given r_{uw}. Thus, all complete conditionals can be derived.

Variational inference assumes $q(\Theta, Z_{uw}, Z_{ut})$ is in the same exponential family with the complete conditionals [10]. Thus, we employ the following mean field variational family, where each latent variable is independent with each other and governed by its own variational parameters:

$$q(\Theta^u,\Theta^w,\Theta^l,\Theta^{ft},\Theta^t,Z_{uw},Z_{ut}) = \prod_{u,k} q(\theta_{uk}|\eta_{uk}^a,\eta_{uk}^b)$$
$$\prod_{w,k} q(\theta_{wk}|\eta_{wk}^a,\eta_{wk}^b)\prod_{l,k} q(\theta_{lk}|\eta_{lk}^a,\eta_{lk}^b)\prod_{t,k} q(\theta_{tk}|\eta_{tk}^a,\eta_{tk}^b)$$
$$\prod_{f,t} q(\theta_{ft}|\eta_{ft}^a,\eta_{ft}^b)\prod_{u,w,k} q(z_{uwk}|\phi_{uwk})\prod_{u,t,k} q(z_{utk}^c|\phi_{utk}^c)$$
$$\prod_{u,t,k} q(z_{utk}^l|\phi_{utk}^l)\prod_{u,t,f\in\mathcal{N}_u} q(z_{utk}|\phi_{utf})$$

where $\eta_\cdot^a$ and $\eta_\cdot^b$ are the shape and rate parameter of the variational Gamma distributions; and $\phi_{ut\cdot}$ is the parameter of the variational Multinomial distributions. To obtain optimal values for $\eta_\cdot^a$, $\eta_\cdot^b$, $\phi_{uw\cdot}$ and $\phi_{ut\cdot}$, we need to solve the minimization in Equation 9. Since variational inference requires that the natural parameter of each $q(\cdot)$ is the expectation of the natural parameter of the corresponding complete conditional under $q(\cdot)$ [11], we just need to compute the expectation of the natural parameters of each complete conditional. To give an example, we show how to compute parameter η_{tk}^a and η_{tk}^b. The expectation of the natural parameters on the complete conditional of θ_{tk} gives:

$$\begin{aligned}\eta_{tk}^a &= \lambda_t^a + \sum_u r_{ut}\phi_{utk}^c + \sum_u r_{ut}\phi_{utk}^l \\ \eta_{tk}^b &= \lambda_t^b + \alpha\sum_u \frac{\eta_{uk}^a}{\eta_{uk}^b} + \beta\sum_u \frac{\eta_{l_uk}^a}{\eta_{l_uk}^b}\end{aligned} \tag{10}$$

where we have applied the fact that the expectation of a Gamma random variable is equal to the ratio of the shape parameter over the rate parameter. Similarly, we can derive the formula to compute other latent parameters. For auxiliary latent variable Z_{ut}, the expectation of its natural

Algorithm 2: Variational inference for BCPF

Input: hyper-parameter λ_a^w, λ_b^w, λ_a^u, λ_b^u, λ_a^l, λ_b^l, λ_a^t, λ_b^t, λ_a^{ft}, λ_b^{ft}, data matrix $\mathbf{R^p}$, $\mathbf{R^c}$, $\mathbf{R^{ul}}$, $\mathbf{R^{ft}}$

repeat

Initialize all variational parameters $\eta_\cdot^a$, $\eta_\cdot^b$, $\phi_{ut\cdot}$, $\phi_{uw\cdot}$

for each r_{uw}

Update ϕ_{uwk} for each k with

$\phi_{uwk} \sim \exp(\psi(\eta_{uk}^a) - \ln(\eta_{uk}^b) + \psi(\eta_{wk}^a) - \ln(\eta_{wk}^b))$

Normalize $\phi_{uw\cdot}$

for each r_{ut}

Update ϕ_{utk}^c for each k, ϕ_{utk}^l for each k, and ϕ_{utf} for each $f \in \mathcal{N}_u$ with Equation 11

Normalize $\phi_{ut\cdot}$

for each w, update η_{wk}^a and η_{wk}^b for each k with

$\eta_{wk}^a = \lambda_w^a + \sum_u r_{uw}\phi_{uwk}$, $\eta_{wk}^b = \lambda_w^b + \sum_u \frac{\eta_{uk}^a}{\eta_{uk}^b}$

for each u, update η_{uk}^a and η_{uk}^b for each k with

$\eta_{uk}^a = \lambda_u^a + \sum_w r_{uw}\phi_{uwk} + \sum_t r_{ut}\phi_{utk}^c$

$\eta_{uk}^b = \lambda_u^b + \sum_w \frac{\eta_{wk}^a}{\eta_{wk}^b} + \sum_t \frac{\eta_{tk}^a}{\eta_{tk}^b}$

for each l, update η_{lk}^a and η_{lk}^b for each k with

$\eta_{lk}^a = \lambda_l^a + \sum_t \sum_u I(l_u = l) r_{ut}\phi_{utk}^l$

$\eta_{lk}^b = \lambda_l^b + \sum_t \sum_u I(l_u = l)\frac{\eta_{tk}^a}{\eta_{tk}^b}$

for each t, update η_{tk}^a and η_{tk}^b for each k with Equation 10

for each f and each t, where $r_{ft} > 0$

Update η_{ft}^a and η_{ft}^b with

$\eta_{ft}^a = \lambda_{ft}^a + \sum_u I(f \in \mathcal{N}_u) r_{ut}\phi_{utf}$

$\eta_{ft}^b = \lambda_{ft}^b + \sum_u I(f \in \mathcal{N}_u) r_{ft}$

until Converge

parameter of the complete conditional leads to

$$\begin{aligned}\phi_{utk}^c &\sim \alpha \exp(\psi(\eta_{uk}^a) - \ln(\eta_{uk}^b) + \psi(\eta_{tk}^a) - \ln(\eta_{tk}^b))\\ \phi_{utk}^l &\sim \beta \exp(\psi(\eta_{l_uk}^a) - \ln(\eta_{l_uk}^b) + \psi(\eta_{tk}^a) - \ln(\eta_{tk}^b)) \quad (11)\\ \phi_{utf} &\sim \gamma r_{ft} \exp(\psi(\eta_{ft}^a) - \ln(\eta_{ft}^b))\end{aligned}$$

where $\psi(\cdot)$ is the digamma function; and we have applied the fact that $E(\ln(X)) = \psi(\eta^a) - \ln(\eta^b)$ when $X \sim Gamma(\eta^a, \eta^b)$. Similarly, we could obtain the formula for Z_{uw}. We then use coordinate ascent to update each variational parameter by turns to obtain the locally optimal values. The overall update algorithm is shown in Algorithm 2.

The complexity of Algorithm 2 is largely determined by the product of K and the maximum number of non-zeros of the matrix $\mathbf{R^c}$, $\mathbf{R^p}$ and $\mathbf{R^{ft}}$. Thus, learning is quite efficient for a sparse data matrix. Here, we omit detailed complexity analysis due to the space limit.

3. EXPERIMENTAL EVALUATION

In this section, we conduct several experiments to evaluate the proposed BCPF for user known-for profile discovery.

Data. Our data is based on a sample of about 12 million Twitter lists collected from 2013 to 2014. Twitter lists [3, 8] are crowd-generated, for which a labeler can put a user on a tagged list, if the labeler thinks the user is known for the topic indicated by the tags. Thus, if a user is labeled by different labelers with certain tags, for example, "chef" and "recipe", then we consider this user is known for these topics. In our experiments, we use the threshold of three labelers to determine the existence of a tag in user's known-for profile. In addition, we also filter out infrequent tags with fewer than 20 users to focus on quality tags. We randomly sample two datasets (see Table 1), one in the US and one across the world. We also crawled about 30 recent tweets for each user and sampled her social relations.

Table 1: Geo-tagged Twitter data.

Loc	# of users	# of tweets	# of following links
US	10,552	317,436	24,676
World	19,776	594,929	30,853
Loc	**# of tags**	**# of records**	**sparsity**
US	1,011	85,994	0.81%
World	1,456	136,625	0.47%

Experimental Setup. For evaluation, we randomly partition all users into 60% for training, 30% for testing, and 10% for cross-validation. For the dimension K of the latent factors, we empirically select 100 for all methods. For the tradeoff weights α, β and γ in Equation 8 for BCPF, we set them to 1, 1.2 and 0.2 via cross-validation. To initialize the hyper-parameters of the Gamma priors in BCPF, we follow [10] and set them to 0.3 plus a small random variations on geo-spatial and social latent factors for sparse solutions; for user content and word variational parameters, we adopt LDA [5] and use document topic distribution and topic word distribution to initialize η_{uk} and η_{wk}, respectively. In the modeling of geo-spatial influence, it is assumed that the geographical space is partitioned into discrete regions. Here, we adopt k-means clustering instead of a simple gridding by clustering users' geo-coordinates. We choose a clustering-based approach because the geo-spatial distribution of users exhibits a clustering effect, as shown in Figure 1. For evaluation metrics, we adopt Precision@k (Prec@k) and Recall@k (Rec@k). Prec@k measures the percentage of the correctly identified tags over the top k predicted tags. Rec@k represents what percentage of true tags can emerge in top k predicted tags. Both measures are averaged over all testing users. In our experiments, we select k to be 5 and 10.

Baselines. We compare BCPF with the following baselines:
– *k-Nearest Neighbors.* In this baseline, we extract content features from user's sampled tweets, and apply kNN to find n most similar users to the testing user u. We then compute tag's score according to $s_{ut} = \sum_i^n w_{ui} r_{it}$, where w_{ui} is the similarity between user u and i, and select top k tags for prediction. We use two approaches to compute textual similarity, one with the bag-of-words model (kNN-BoW), another with the topic model (kNN-LDA) [5].
– *One-Vs-Rest multi-label ranking* [4]. We train a One-Vs-Rest multi-label classifier with bag-of-words on user's tweets. Logistic regression is used as the classification method to have a probabilistic output for ranking tags.
– *Wsabie* [29]. Wsabie is an embedding-based model which learns a mapping from a feature space to the joint space with the tags. Here, we train the model with WARP loss on bags-of-words of user's tweets, and use the learned user and tag embeddings for ranking tags.
– *Content-based Poisson Factorization (C-PF).* This is the method where we only keep the content factor in BCPF. It can be considered a form of CTPF proposed in [10] where we treat user's tweets as documents, and user's known-for profiles as binary ratings. We also ignore the topic offsets since the testing users are in complete cold-start situation.
– *Geo-spatial CPF (GC-PF).* This is the method in which

we keep both content and geo-spatial factor in BCPF.

– *Social influenced CPF (SC-PF).* This method keeps both content and social influence factor in BCPF.

3.1 Effectiveness of BCPF

How well does the proposed BCPF perform compared to alternative baselines? In Table 2, we report Prec@k and Rec@k for all methods. Overall, BCPF gives the best results for all metrics and both datasets. Specifically, it gives an average improvement of 17.5% in precision and 20.9% in recall over the best content based method C-PF. This indicates the superiority of BCPF by exploiting geo-spatial and social influence factors other than user's content.

In content-based methods, neighborhood-based methods generally provide the worst performance of all since only local information can be used in prediction. Here, LDA based kNN performs better than BoW based kNN, since LDA can take advantage of the global topic information in users' posts. Supervised methods, however, give relatively better performance than neighborhood methods, as shown by One-Vs-Rest multi-label ranking and Wsabie. Both methods are trained with multiple labeled tags for each user on the BoW features, where Wsabie obtains embeddings for each user and tag. However, One-Vs-Rest clearly outperforms Wsabie, although Wsabie is more efficient and requires less computation time. C-PF, however, gives the best performance of all content-based methods, indicating the superiority of joint modeling by learning labeled users' profiles on content features and unlabeled users' texts.

Furthermore, we can see from the table that both GC-PF and SC-PF provides better performance against only content-based C-PF, respectively. Specifically, GC-PF gives an average improvement of 8.07% in precision and 11.1% in recall, respectively. SC-PF gives an average improvement of 10.9% in precision and 11.2% in recall, respectively. This indicates that geo-spatial features and parameterized social influence can both improve the identification of user's known-for profile. Given the overall improvement of the combination of these features, we can also conclude that these factors are able to complement each other.

3.2 Geo-spatial Factor Analysis

In the modeling of geo-spatial influence on user's known-for profile, we discretize the US/world area into geographical regions, and treat user's location as the region where she belongs. An important question here is how to select the number of regions $\mathcal{I}$. As we can imagine, if $\mathcal{I}$ is too small, the model may not be able to reflect the geo-spatial distribution of user's known-for profile; if it is too large, regions may be too small, thus leads to sparse observations. To that end, we select $\mathcal{I}$ for k-means clustering from 10 to 200, and run GC-PF with each value for ten random initializations of parameters. In Figure 3, we show how precision and recall changes with respect to the number of regions for both datasets. We can see that as $\mathcal{I}$ goes up, precision generally also increases. However, the performance plateaus when it is large. We attribute this to: first, when the number of regions increases, we obtain finer-grained geo-spatial characterization of tags; second, when it is large enough, a finer-grained discretization does not help distinguish tag's local distributions. It may even result in sparse counts in regions and also increases model complexity, thus degrading the final performance. Note that it requires less number of

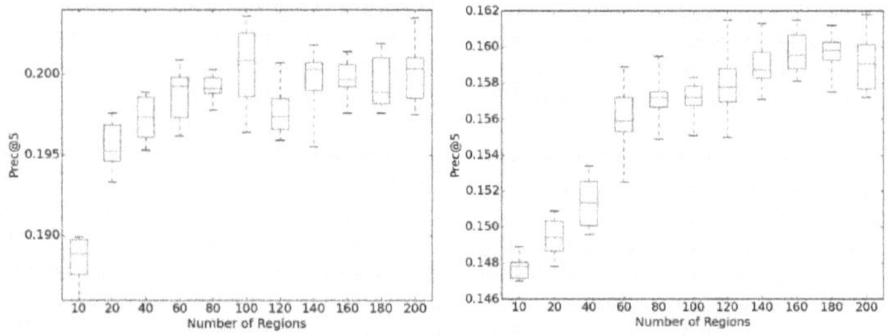

Figure 3: Box plot for precision@5 with respect to the number of regions. Left: US; Right: world.

Table 3: Top ranking tags for different areas obtained from latent location factors and tag factors.

Los Angeles	D.C.	SF	Chicago
la	dc	sf	chicago
celebrity	politics	geek	chi
star	progressive	bay area	illinois
tv	baltimore	dev	pr
artist	us	technology	advertising
actor	conservative	mobile	social media
famous people	government	startup	marketing
entertainment	politico	software	marketer

regions, i.e., larger partition of areas, for the US dataset than world to get to the best average performance. The reason is that the world data may be more diverse in terms of the geo-spatial distribution of user known-for profiles, thus requiring finer-grained geo-segments to reach the best performance.

To further examine the inferred region factors, we show in Table 3 the top ranking tags associated with selected areas. In particular, we compute the affinity score between a location and a tag by taking the expected inner product of the latent factor of the location and the tag, denoted as $E(\theta_l^T \theta_t)$. We can see from the table that, generally, the top ranking tags can reflect the common knowledge of the characteristics of those selected areas. For example, it is very likely that a user from the Washington D.C. area is well known for her political activities/comments. Thus, these inferred region factors are capable of nudging user's known-for profile toward her region characteristics.

3.3 Social Influence Factor Analysis

We have seen from the previous experiments that social influence plays an importance role in representing user's known-for profile by looking at her connections. In order to get a further understanding of how social influence varies for different friends and tags, we consider the following methods using social influence: (i) naive SC-PF (nSC-PF), where we replace θ_f with a single parameter θ_{naive} in Equation 6 for all friends and tags; (ii) user weighted SC-PF (uSC-PF), which models social influence by a vector of dimension M, with each element indicating the level of a friend's social influence for all tags (see Equation 6); and (iii) SC-PF, which models each friend's social influence for every tag of hers by matrix Θ_{ft}. We compare these methods with C-PF to see which method models social influence the best. Note that we also include the content factor as a basic representation for users since not all users have social connections.

Table 2: Comparison of performance with alternative methods. BCPF generally gives the best performance by integrating the contextual influence of textual, geo-spatial and social factors, and these factors are able to complement each other.

Method	US				World			
	Precision		Recall		Precision		Recall	
	@5	@10	@5	@10	@5	@10	@5	@10
kNN-BoW	0.114	0.098	0.120	0.181	0.083	0.072	0.099	0.151
kNN-LDA	0.150	0.127	0.155	0.226	0.120	0.100	0.137	0.200
One-Vs-Rest	0.166	0.140	0.176	0.250	0.136	0.112	0.161	0.227
Wsabie	0.159	0.137	0.169	0.244	0.116	0.101	0.134	0.201
C-PF	0.188	0.160	0.194	0.279	0.147	0.126	0.168	0.246
GC-PF	0.199	0.174	0.212	0.312	0.159	0.138	0.186	0.277
SC-PF	0.209	0.177	0.217	0.309	0.165	0.138	0.189	0.270
BCPF	**0.222**	**0.188**	**0.240**	**0.336**	**0.173**	**0.147**	**0.201**	**0.295**

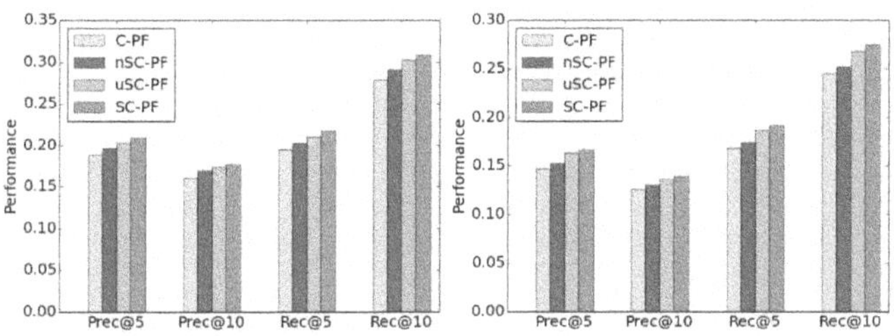

Figure 4: Comparative performance of the methods modeling social influence. SC-PF performs best by making it dependent on both friends and tags. Left: US; Right: world.

Table 4: User's inferred social influence θ_f by uSC-PF and social influence θ_{ft} for top ranking tags by SC-PF.

User	θ_f	top-1/θ_{ft}	top-2/θ_{ft}
@UnderTheBar	0.00290	entrepreneur 0.0230	health 0.0226
@skwigg	0.00425	fit 0.0217	nutrition 0.0190
@mollyblock	0.0143	marketer 0.104	pr 0.0226
@bikehugger	0.210	bicycle 0.435	cycling 0.303

As we can see from Figure 4, overall, social connection is able to improve the performance for predicting user's known-for profile. Specifically, we can make the following two conclusions: (i) it is generally better to differentiate social influence for different friends, rather than treating all friends with the same influence; (ii) it is generally better to differentiate social influence for different tags of each friend, rather than treating all tags of each friend with the same influence.

Table 4 shows the inferred social influence for different users and their top-ranking tags, which further exemplifies the observation that users may have different social influence on their followers with respect to different tags. In particular, user @UnderTheBar shows little influence on his followers' known-for profiles even if he may have tens of thousands of followers. This indicates that users who follow @UnderTheBar are not necessarily also known for "entrepreneur" or "health". On the contrary, @mollyblock has much larger social influence on her followers for her tag "marketer", indicating that users following @mollyblock are more likely to also be known for "marketer", even if @mollyblock has fewer followers than @UnderTheBar. One explanation for this observation is that people connect with others for different reasons on social media, and that popularity itself is not necessarily an indicator of one's social influence.

4. RELATED WORK

User profiling is an important task, with many efforts building user's topic interests for personalized search [7, 24], targeted advertising [1] and social media systems [6, 27, 34]. For example, Dou et al. [7] built user interest profile by predefined topic categories for personalized webpage re-ranking. Ahmed et al. [1] proposed a statistical framework to extract user's dynamic interest profile for behavioral targeting. Chen et al. [6] built topic profiles of users with bag-of-words model to recommend conversations in Twitter. Zhao et al. [34] improved user's topic interest profile by joint factorization of user's topic matrix and behaviors. User profiles are also used to provide recommendations for online activities such as commenting on news stories [25] and mentions in micro-blogging systems [27]. Besides user's topic interest profile, other works [16, 17, 23] focus on inferring user's attribute and demographics profile such as gender and education. For example, Mislove et al. [23] proposed community detection based approaches to infer user's college and major. Li et al. [16] presented a weakly-supervised approach to extract user's job and education. Our work is different from the above works in that we tackle the problem of discovering what users are known for instead of user's topic interests.

Contextual information in social media has been widely used in previous works [10, 13, 19, 21, 26, 28, 31, 33] to learn better user profiles and improve task performance. A seminal work by Singh and Gordon [26] proposed collective matrix factorization to simultaneously factor several matrices encoding contextual information for better prediction of user-movie ratings. Wang and Blei [28] proposed collaborative topic regression to learn latent user preference by modeling both ratings and content. Similarly, Gopalan et al. [10] also modeled both user's ratings and content but with Poisson factorization. Jamal et al. [13] proposed a context dependent factor model to learn general latent factors of entities in social networks for better recommendation. Temporal information has also been used in [31] to learn both user-oriented topics and time-oriented topics. Other contextual information used to learn user preference includes domain-specific communities [33] and social relations [19,

21] which are used to regularize latent factors between socially connected users. In our work, instead of using social regularization for latent factors, we learn both user and tag dependent social influence from the data with Poisson distribution for fine-grained modeling of social relations.

Geographical footprints have also been widely explored in many location-based applications [12, 18, 20, 30, 32, 35]. One of the most popular applications is POI recommendation, where geographical influence is combined with user preference for better performance [18, 30]. Other works have used geographical influence for rating prediction in Yelp [12], activity recommendation with GPS history [35], expert recommendation [20] and event-based group recommendation [32]. In contrast, we are focused on geo-spatial influence for user known-for profile discovery in social media.

5. CONCLUSION

In this paper, we tackled the problem of discovering what users are known for in social media. By integrating user's textual, geo-spatial and social influence, we proposed Bayesian Contextual Poisson Factorization to overcome the noisiness of user's posting activities and social relations. Experimental results showed that BCPF can improve known-for prediction by 17.5% in precision and 20.9% in recall on average. We also showed that user's connections have varying social influence for different topics, confirming our fine-grained modeling of social influence by making it dependent on both users and topics. In our future work, we are interested in exploring the impact of additional contextual signals beyond the textual, geo-spatial and social influence studied here.

Acknowledgment. This work was supported in part by NSF grant IIS-1149383 and Google Research Award. Any opinions, findings and conclusions or recommendations expressed in this material are the author(s) and do not necessarily reflect those of the sponsors.

6. REFERENCES

[1] A. Ahmed, Y. Low, M. Aly, V. Josifovski, and A. J. Smola. Scalable distributed inference of dynamic user interests for behavioral targeting. In *SIGKDD*, 2011.

[2] X. Amatriain, N. Lathia, J. M. Pujol, H. Kwak, and N. Oliver. The wisdom of the few: a collaborative filtering approach based on expert opinions from the web. In *SIGIR*, 2009.

[3] P. Bhattacharya, S. Ghosh, J. Kulshrestha, M. Mondal, M. B. Zafar, N. Ganguly, and K. P. Gummadi. Deep twitter diving: Exploring topical groups in microblogs at scale. In *CSCW*, 2014.

[4] C. M. Bishop. *Pattern Recognition and Machine Learning*. Springer-Verlag New York, Inc., 2006.

[5] D. M. Blei, A. Y. Ng, and M. I. Jordan. Latent dirichlet allocation. *JMLR*, 2003.

[6] J. Chen, R. Nairn, and E. Chi. Speak little and well: recommending conversations in online social streams. In *SIGCHI*, 2011.

[7] Z. Dou, R. Song, and J.-R. Wen. A large-scale evaluation and analysis of personalized search strategies. In *WWW*, 2007.

[8] S. Ghosh, N. Sharma, F. Benevenuto, N. Ganguly, and K. Gummadi. Cognos: crowdsourcing search for topic experts in microblogs. In *SIGIR*, 2012.

[9] P. Gopalan, J. M. Hofman, and D. M. Blei. Scalable recommendation with poisson factorization. *arXiv preprint arXiv:1311.1704*, 2013.

[10] P. K. Gopalan, L. Charlin, and D. Blei. Content-based recommendations with poisson factorization. In *NIPS*, 2014.

[11] M. D. Hoffman, D. M. Blei, C. Wang, and J. Paisley. Stochastic variational inference. *JMLR*, 2013.

[12] L. Hu, A. Sun, and Y. Liu. Your neighbors affect your ratings: on geographical neighborhood influence to rating prediction. In *SIGIR*, 2014.

[13] M. Jamali and L. Lakshmanan. Heteromf: recommendation in heterogeneous information networks using context dependent factor models. In *WWW*, 2013.

[14] N. Johnson, A. Kemp, and S. Kotz. *Univariate Discrete Distributions*. John Wiley and Sons, 2005.

[15] M. I. Jordan, Z. Ghahramani, T. S. Jaakkola, and L. K. Saul. An introduction to variational methods for graphical models. *Machine learning*, 1999.

[16] J. Li, A. Ritter, and E. H. Hovy. Weakly supervised user profile extraction from twitter. In *ACL*, 2014.

[17] R. Li, C. Wang, and K. C.-C. Chang. User profiling in an ego network: co-profiling attributes and relationships. In *WWW*, 2014.

[18] B. Liu, Y. Fu, Z. Yao, and H. Xiong. Learning geographical preferences for point-of-interest recommendation. In *SIGKDD*, 2013.

[19] X. Liu and K. Aberer. Soco: a social network aided context-aware recommender system. In *WWW*, 2013.

[20] H. Lu and J. Caverlee. Exploiting geo-spatial preference for personalized expert recommendation. In *RecSys*, 2015.

[21] H. Ma, H. Yang, M. R. Lyu, and I. King. Sorec: social recommendation using probabilistic matrix factorization. In *CIKM*, 2008.

[22] M. McPherson, L. Smith-Lovin, and J. M. Cook. Birds of a feather: Homophily in social networks. *Annual review of sociology*, pages 415–444, 2001.

[23] A. Mislove, B. Viswanath, K. P. Gummadi, and P. Druschel. You are who you know: inferring user profiles in online social networks. In *WSDM*, 2010.

[24] F. Qiu and J. Cho. Automatic identification of user interest for personalized search. In *WWW*, 2006.

[25] E. Shmueli, A. Kagian, Y. Koren, and R. Lempel. Care to comment?: recommendations for commenting on news stories. In *WWW*, 2012.

[26] A. P. Singh and G. J. Gordon. Relational learning via collective matrix factorization. In *SIGKDD*, 2008.

[27] B. Wang, C. Wang, J. Bu, C. Chen, W. V. Zhang, D. Cai, and X. He. Whom to mention: expand the diffusion of tweets by@ recommendation on micro-blogging systems. In *WWW*, 2013.

[28] C. Wang and D. M. Blei. Collaborative topic modeling for recommending scientific articles. In *SIGKDD*, 2011.

[29] J. Weston, S. Bengio, and N. Usunier. Wsabie: Scaling up to large vocabulary image annotation. In *IJCAI*, 2011.

[30] M. Ye, P. Yin, W.-C. Lee, and D.-L. Lee. Exploiting geographical influence for collaborative point-of-interest recommendation. In *SIGIR*, 2011.

[31] H. Yin, B. Cui, L. Chen, Z. Hu, and Z. Huang. A temporal context-aware model for user behavior modeling in social media systems. In *SIGMOD*, 2014.

[32] W. Zhang, J. Wang, and W. Feng. Combining latent factor model with location features for event-based group recommendation. In *SIGKDD*, 2013.

[33] X. Zhang, J. Cheng, T. Yuan, B. Niu, and H. Lu. Toprec: domain-specific recommendation through community topic mining in social network. In *WWW*, 2013.

[34] Z. Zhao, Z. Cheng, L. Hong, and E. H. Chi. Improving user topic interest profiles by behavior factorization. In *WWW*, 2015.

[35] V. W. Zheng, Y. Zheng, X. Xie, and Q. Yang. Collaborative location and activity recommendations with gps history data. In *WWW*, 2010.

TAPER: A Contextual Tensor-Based Approach for Personalized Expert Recommendation

Hancheng Ge, James Caverlee, Haokai Lu
Department of Computer Science and Engineering
Texas A&M University
{hge,caverlee,hlu}@cse.tamu.com

ABSTRACT

We address the challenge of personalized recommendation of high-quality content producers in social media. While some candidates are easily identifiable (say, by being "favorited" many times), there is a long-tail of potential candidates for whom we have little evidence. Through careful modeling of contextual factors like the geo-spatial, topical, and social preferences of users, we propose a tensor-based personalized expert recommendation framework that integrates these factors for revealing latent connections between homogeneous entities (e.g., users and users) and between heterogeneous entities (e.g., users and experts). Through extensive experiments over geo-tagged Twitter data, we find that the proposed framework can improve the quality of recommendation by over 30% in both precision and recall compared to the state-of-the-art.

1. INTRODUCTION

Recommender systems are a cornerstone of how we engage online – by impacting the media we consume, the friends we connect with, and the products we purchase. A typical assumption in many recommender systems is to focus on *specific items* like movies, songs, or books as the basis of recommendation. In a separate direction, there are efforts to focus on *high-quality content producers* rather than specific items [21, 22]. These content producers – like creators of highly-rated Spotify playlists, Amazon's top reviewers, or media curators on platforms like Tumblr, Facebook, and Twitter – can potentially serve as conduits to high-quality curated items. Indeed, previous research has shown that in some cases item-based recommenders can be improved by biasing the underlying models toward the opinions of these "experts" [2].

While some high-quality content producers are easily identifiable (say, by being "favorited" or starred many times), there is a long-tail of potential candidates for whom we have little evidence. Hence, a natural question is whether we can identify these high-quality content producers – whom we shall refer to as *experts* in the rest of this paper – and recommend them to the right people. Such *personalized expert recommendation* faces a number of key challenges, though. First, many existing works have aimed at uncovering expert users in online systems – e.g., [4, 7, 9, 28, 32] –

RecSys '16, September 15-19, 2016, Boston , MA, USA

DOI: http://dx.doi.org/10.1145/2959100.2959151

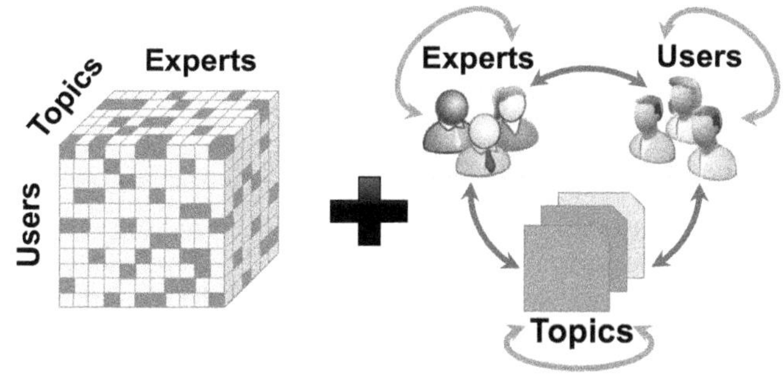

Figure 1: Personalized expert recommendation with contextual factors: augmenting the sparse tensor (left) with contextual factors (right) like the geo-spatial, topical, and social relationships between homogeneous entities (e.g., users and users) and between heterogeneous entities (e.g., users and experts).

but typically without an emphasis on personalized recommendation. That is, these efforts have often attempted to explore general topic experts with broad appeal, e.g., the best doctors in Seattle or the top engineers in a certain field, rather than connecting users with personal experts. Second, personalized expert recommendation faces extreme sparsity since few users provide feedback on the quality of content producers. Third, there are typically complex relationships between users, candidate experts, and topics of interest.

Hence, we aim in this paper to tackle these challenges via a personalized expert recommendation framework called **TAPER** – for **T**ensor-based **A**pproach for **P**ersonalized **E**xpert **R**ecommendation. This proposed approach inherits the advantages of traditional recommender systems by making personalized recommendations based on the history of actions by similar users. In this way, specific personal experts can be recommended to individuals, rather than relying on globally-recognized (and less personalized) ones. While matrix factorization approaches have shown success in mitigating sparsity [15, 18], ultimately they are restricted to two-dimensional data (e.g., a user-expert matrix). In contrast, user preferences for experts may be impacted by many contextual factors including the topic of interest, the location of the user (and possibly of the expert), as well as social connections among users and experts, among many others. As illustrated in Figure 1, these user-expert-topic preferences naturally suggest a tensor-based approach where these multiple and varied relationships may augment the sparse tensor (on the left) by considering the relationships (on the right) between both homogeneous entities (e.g., users and users, experts and experts) and the relationships between heterogeneous entities (e.g., users and experts, topics and experts).

Through the TAPER framework, we explore questions like: What kinds of contextual factors impact preferences for personalized experts? How can these contextual factors be integrated into a tensor-

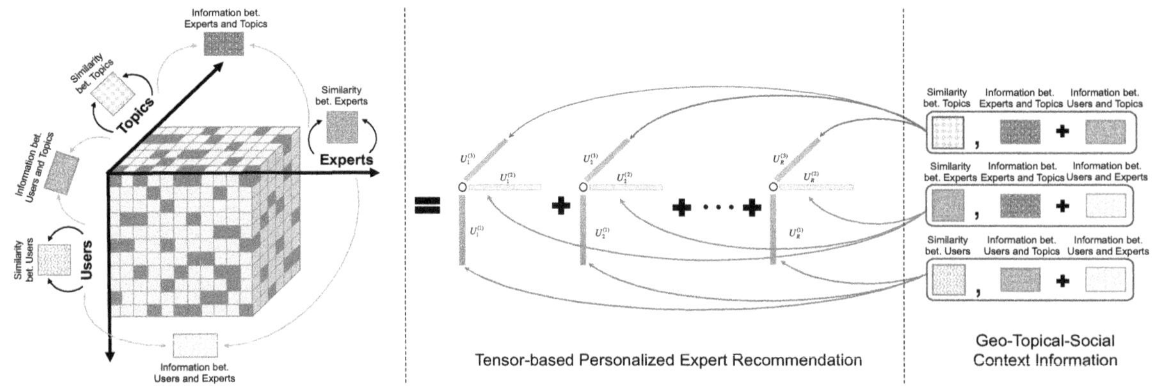

Figure 2: Overview of the proposed tensor-based personalized expert recommendation framework.

based personalized expert recommender? Do these factors result in higher quality recommendations than state-of-the-art methods? And are some contextual factors more important than others?

Related Work. Expert finding has been widely studied for many years. For instance, Weng et al. [28] proposed a PageRank-based approach to identify topic experts by applying both topical similarity between users and social link structure. Ghosh et al. [9] proposed the Cognos system to find topic experts by relying on Twitter lists. Zhang et al. [32] identified top experts in a Java forum by applying link analysis approaches such as PageRank and HITS. Hu et al. [12] proposed a more personalized recommendation by considering network semantic information, in addition to network topological measures for expert recommendation. Of course, there are many other efforts, including [10, 19, 25].

One promising approach for recommenders is to cast the problem as a matrix factorization problem, in which user preferences may be projected into a lower dimensional embedding space [15, 17, 29, 31]. In recent years, tensor factorization models – that are highly suitable for multiway data analysis as in our domain – have been applied in applications like tag recommendation [24], user group detection [16], link prediction [8], and anomaly detection [26]. There are two widely used low-rank decompositions – CANDECOMP/PARAFAC (CP) and the Tucker decomposition [14]. Karatzoglou et al. [13] studied multi-dimensional recommendations by leveraging contextual information to build a User-Item-Context tensor model. Hidasi and Tikk [11] developed an Alternating Least Squares (ALS) based tensor factorization approach for context-aware recommendations. Bhargava et al. [5] applied a tensor factorization-based approach to provide collaborative recommendations for points of interest (POI) involving multi-dimensions such as locations, activities and time. Similarly, Lu et al. [17] introduced a matrix-factorization approach for personalized expert recommendation, but restricted to two-dimensional data (e.g., a user-expert matrix) and only considering user's geo-spatial preferences on experts. In contrast, this work is the first to investigate tensor factorization for personalized expert recommendation by integrating user's preferences on experts from geo-topical-social contexts as well as valuable relationships between users, experts and topics, and to explore the impact of these contexts on such an approach.

2. PROBLEM STATEMENT

Let $\boldsymbol{L} = \{u_1, u_2, \ldots, u_N\}$ be a set of users where N is the total number of users, and $\boldsymbol{E} = \{e_1, e_2, \ldots, e_M\}$ be a set of experts where M is the total number of experts and $\boldsymbol{E} \in \boldsymbol{L}$. An expert e_i may have expertise in multiple topics expressed as $\boldsymbol{T} = \{t_1, t_2, \ldots, t_K\}$ where K is the total number of topics. A user may personally prefer some experts rather than others based upon the user's personal interest in their expertise. For example, Andy may prefer Bella in the topic of "Python programming", but have no opinion on Chris who may be a better Python developer. We denote the personal preferences of users towards experts in topics as a tensor $\boldsymbol{\mathcal{X}} \in \mathbb{R}^{N\times M\times K}$ where element $\boldsymbol{\mathcal{X}}(i,j,k)$ is binary, representing whether a user u_i prefers an expert e_j in a topic t_k.

We define the *personalized expert recommendation problem* as: Given a set of users $\boldsymbol{L}$ with partially observed preferences denoted as a tensor $\boldsymbol{\mathcal{T}}$ on experts $\boldsymbol{E}$ over topics $\boldsymbol{T}$, our goal is to recommend the top-k relevant experts to a user u_i.

Basic Recommendation by Tensor Factorization. As a natural first step, we can tackle this problem with a basic recommendation framework using tensor factorization. Let $U^{(1)} \in \mathbb{R}^{N\times R}$, $U^{(2)} \in \mathbb{R}^{M\times R}$ and $U^{(3)} \in \mathbb{R}^{K\times R}$ be latent factor matrices for users, experts, and topics, respectively, where $R \ll min(N, M, K)$ is the number of latent factors as the rank of a tensor. The basic tensor-based expert recommendation model can be defined as:

$$\begin{aligned} \underset{U^{(n)},\boldsymbol{\mathcal{X}}}{\text{minimize}} \quad & \frac{1}{2}\|\boldsymbol{\mathcal{X}} - [\![U^{(1)}, U^{(2)}, U^{(3)}]\!]\|_F^2 + \frac{\lambda}{2}\sum_{n=1}^{3}\|U^{(n)}\|_F^2, \\ \text{subject to} \quad & \boldsymbol{\Psi} \circ \boldsymbol{\mathcal{X}} = \boldsymbol{\mathcal{T}}, U^{(n)} \geq 0, n = 1,2,3 \end{aligned} \tag{1}$$

where $\boldsymbol{\mathcal{X}}$ denotes the complete preferences of users towards experts across topics, $\boldsymbol{\mathcal{T}}$ denotes the observed user's preferences on experts, $\|U^{(n)}\|_F^2$ is a Tikhonov regularization term used to avoid overfitting and provide a unique solution, $\circ$ is a Hadamard product operator and $\boldsymbol{\Psi}$ is a non-negative weight tensor with the same size as $\boldsymbol{\mathcal{X}}$ with $\boldsymbol{\Psi}(i,j,k) = 1$ indicating that we observe the selection of user u_i on expert e_j in a topic t_k, $\boldsymbol{\Psi}(i,j,k) = 0$ otherwise. This basic model estimates $\hat{\boldsymbol{\mathcal{X}}}$ that approximates the original (unknown) $\boldsymbol{\mathcal{X}}$ via learning optimal latent factor matrices $\{U^{(n)}, n = 1,2,3\}$. For each user and topic of interest, this model can recommend a ranked list of personalized experts.

Research Challenges. While this basic tensor factorization framework provides a first step toward personalized expert recommendation, it leaves open many critical questions:

- First, since the user-expert-topic tensor is necessarily sparse (meaning that even with factorization the underlying latent factors may be of poor quality), can we augment this basic approach with additional contextual preferences for experts by considering the relationships among both homogeneous entities (e.g., users and users, experts and experts) and heterogeneous entities (e.g., users and experts, topics and experts)?
- How can we integrate these contextual preferences into a tensor-based personalized expert recommendation framework?

Table 1: Dataset Summary

Data Type	Total Number of Records
Twitter Lists	11,322
Users (list creators)	10,559
Experts (list members)	8,417
List Relationships	117,187
Sparsity	0.13%

- How effective is the proposed tensor-based framework in comparison with other state-of-the-art baselines? And which contextual preferences have the most significant impact on the quality of personalized expert recommendations?

3. THE TAPER FRAMEWORK

We turn in this section toward constructing the contextual tensor factorization framework, as illustrated in Figure 2.

3.1 Evidence of Geo-Topical-Social Impact

We begin our investigation by examining the impact of three factors – geo-spatial, topical, and social context – on the observed preferences towards experts. Our goals in this section are to assess whether and to what degree these factors do affect how users select experts. Informed by these observations, we turn in the following to integrate them into the tensor-based factorization framework.

Geo-Tagged Twitter Lists. We adopt geo-tagged Twitter lists as evidence of the revealed preferences of users for other users. A Twitter list allows a user u_i to label another user u_j with an annotation (e.g., news, food, technology). In isolation these lists support the curation of an individual user's information stream, but in the aggregate the list labels can encode what a target user is "known-for". Many efforts have demonstrated that these labels can provide a crowdsourced expertise profile of the target user [6, 7, 9, 23]. Concretely, we use a geo-tagged Twitter list dataset containing over 12 million crowd-generated lists and 14 million geo-tagged list relationships between list creators and members. We filter the lists to only keep US-based users in topics: news, music, technology, celebrities, sports, business, politics, food, fashion, art, science, education, marketing, movie, photography, and health. The dataset is summarized in Table 1. Both list creators and list members are associated with GPS coordinates.[1] We shall refer to list creators as *users* and members in the lists as *experts*.

Geo-Spatial Context. We begin by investigating the impact of distance on the experts selected by users. Figure 3(a) shows the cumulative distribution of the average distance between a user and the experts they have labeled, aggregated for eight different cities. In general, we see that users from different cities have different levels of locality. For example, users in San Francisco are more likely to select experts from a wider geographical scope than users based in Chicago. Specifically, almost 40% of users in Chicago have an average distance to their experts within 100 miles. However, only 14% of users in SF have an average distance within 100 miles. In a similar fashion, Figure 3(b) shows the cumulative distribution of the average distance between users and the experts they have labeled for seven different topics. For a fixed distance (e.g., 100 miles), the topic *food* has the largest probability. This implies that users interested in *food* are closer to their chosen experts while users interested in a broad topic like *celebrity* instead select experts with a wider geographical scope. Hence, we can conclude that *the geo-spatial context of users, experts, and topics does indeed affect the preference for experts, and that these factors are impacted to varying degrees based on topic and on the particular locations of both users and experts.*

[1]For those without GPS coordinates, their locations can be estimated with their tweets by an approach previously used for check-ins and geo-tagged images [20]. In order to simplify our study, we only focus on users with GPS coordinates.

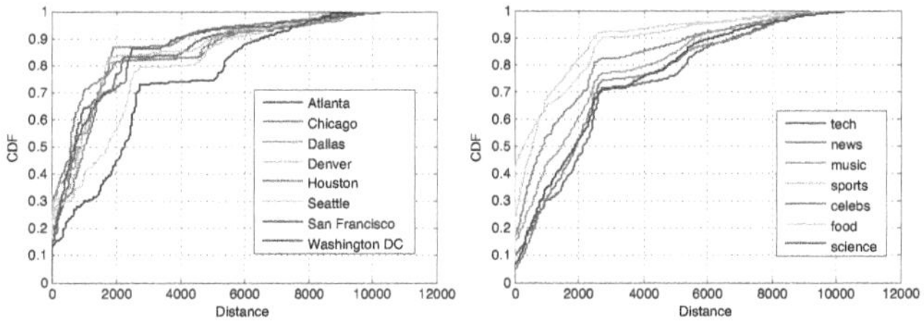

(a) Different Cities (b) Different Topics

Figure 3: The impact of distance on expert preferences by location (a) and by topic (b).

Topical Context. As we observed in Figure 3(b), different topics have different levels of locality. Here, we further investigate the impact of topical context on personalized preferences for experts. We begin by viewing each user as a vector of the experts they have selected, in which the element is 1 when the expert is listed by the user, otherwise 0. We then measure the impact of the number of shared topics between users (e.g., if two users have used three of the same topics in their lists, then we consider the number of shared topics between them to be three) on how similar are the users with respect to the experts they have selected. As we can see in Figure 4(a), users are more likely to select similar experts when they share more common topics. In other words, common topical interest impacts the choice of experts. In a similar fashion, we can view each expert as a vector of all users, in which the element is 1 when the expert is listed by the user, otherwise 0. We then measure the impact of the number of shared topics between experts (e.g., if two experts have been labeled by four of the same topics, then we consider the number of shared topics between them to be four) on how similar are the experts with respect to the users who have selected them. As we can see in Figure 4(b), experts who share more topics are more likely to be preferred by similar users. *We conclude that topical context has a strong impact on user preferences for experts.*

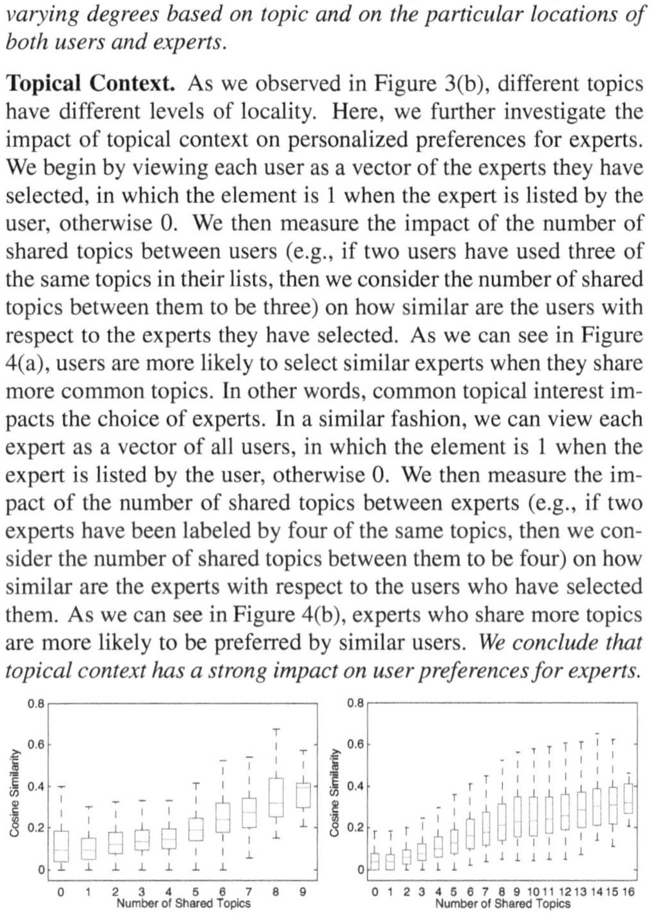

(a) Users-Users (b) Experts-Experts

Figure 4: The relationship between the number of shared topics and the similarity between users (a) and experts (b).

Social Context. Finally, the social connections among users and experts can be a strong indicator of shared topical interests, as well as an implicit signal that two users are more likely to be near each other. Researchers have found that social ties increase the likelihood of two users being near each other [3]. Figure 5 shows the cumulative distributions of the similarity of users and experts, respectively. Using the same approach introduced above, each user is represented as a vector of all experts; each expert is represented as a vector of all users. The cosine similarity is employed to calculate the similarity of users and experts. We can observe that users who follow the other generally have a larger similarity on selecting experts. For experts, we can see a similar pattern that those who follow the other are more likely to be selected by the same users. Through these observations, we can draw the conclusion that *social context strongly affects a user's preferences for experts.*

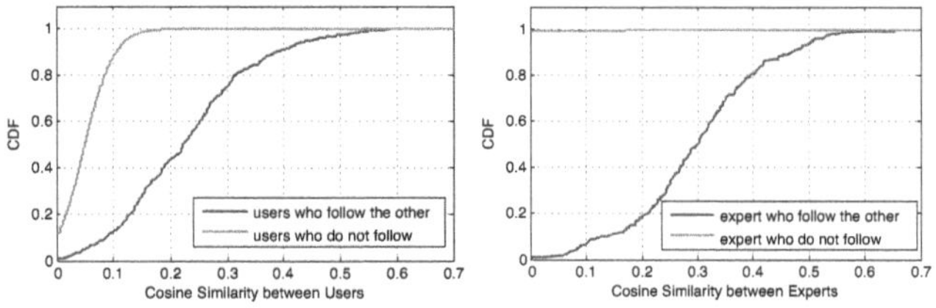

(a) Users-Users (b) Experts-Experts

Figure 5: The impact of social connections on selecting experts for users (a) and being selected for experts (b)

3.2 Integrating Contextual Preferences

Given this evidence of the significance of geo-topical-social context with respect to preferences on experts, a natural approach is to integrate them into the basic tensor-based expert recommendation framework as regularization terms. Intuitively, if two entities are similar, e.g., two users have similar preferences in recognizing experts across topics, the latent representations of these two entities should be similar. Hence, we can regulate latent representations of two similar entities to make them as close as possible. We denote S as a symmetric similarity matrix encoding contextual information between homogeneous entities (e.g., users and users, experts and experts), and then formally minimize the following loss function:

$$
\begin{aligned}
\Theta &= \frac{1}{2}\sum_{i,j} S(i,j)\|U_i^{(n)} - U_j^{(n)}\|^2 \\
&= \sum_{i} U_i^{(n)} D(i,i) U_i^{(n)T} - \sum_{i,j} U_i^{(n)} S(i,j) U_j^{(n)T} \\
&= \mathrm{tr}(U^{(n)T}(D-S)U^{(n)}) \\
&= \mathrm{tr}(U^{(n)T}\mathcal{L}U^{(n)})
\end{aligned}
$$

where $U_i^{(n)}$ is the ith row of the factor matrix $U^{(n)}$ for the nth-mode of a tensor $\boldsymbol{\mathcal{X}}, n \in \{1,2,3\}$, $tr(\cdot)$ is denoted as the matrix trace, D is a diagonal matrix with the element $D(i,i) = \sum_j S(i,j)$, and $\mathcal{L} = D - S$ is the graph Laplacian of the similarity matrix S. For the contextual information between heterogeneous entities (e.g., users and experts, topics and experts), we denote $\boldsymbol{A}, \boldsymbol{B}, \boldsymbol{C}$ as matrices encoding the contextual information between users and experts, users and topics and experts and topics, respectively. We then regulate them by directly adding regularization terms $\|\boldsymbol{A} - U^{(1)}U^{(2)^T}\|_F^2$, $\|\boldsymbol{B} - U^{(1)}U^{(3)^T}\|_F^2$, and $\|\boldsymbol{C} - U^{(2)}U^{(3)^T}\|_F^2$ into the basic framework. In order to simplify the parameter tuning, $\boldsymbol{A}$, $\boldsymbol{B}$ and $\boldsymbol{C}$ are normalized to the same scale.

After integrating all regularization terms into Eq. (1), TAPER aims to solve the following optimization problem [2]:

$$
\begin{aligned}
\underset{U^{(n)},\mathcal{X}}{\text{minimize}} \quad & \frac{1}{2}\|\boldsymbol{\mathcal{X}} - [\![U^{(1)}, U^{(2)}, U^{(3)}]\!]\|_F^2 + \frac{\lambda}{2}\sum_{n=1}^{3}\|U^{(n)}\|_F^2 \\
& + \frac{\gamma}{2}\sum_{n=1}^{3}\mathrm{tr}(Z^{(n)T}\mathcal{L}_n Z^{(n)}) + \frac{\beta}{2}(\|\boldsymbol{A} - U^{(1)}U^{(2)^T}\|_F^2 \\
& + \|\boldsymbol{B} - U^{(1)}U^{(3)^T}\|_F^2 + \|\boldsymbol{C} - U^{(2)}U^{(3)^T}\|_F^2), \\
\text{subject to} \quad & \boldsymbol{\Psi} \circ \boldsymbol{\mathcal{X}} = \mathcal{T}, U^{(n)} = Z^{(n)} \geq 0, n = 1,2,3
\end{aligned} \tag{2}
$$

where γ controls the weight of the contextual information between homogeneous entities (e.g., users and users, experts and experts), and β controls the weight of the contextual information between heterogeneous entities (e.g., users and experts, topics and experts). But how specifically should we model these contextual preferences for integration into the tensor-based framework? In the following, we consider geo-spatial, topical, and social preferences in turn.

3.2.1 *Modeling Geo-Spatial Preferences*

We first aim to model geo-spatial context for integration into the tensor-based factorization approach.

Relationships between Homogeneous Entities: Supported by the data-driven observations of the previous section and following Tobler's First Law of Geography [27] – which asserts that near things are more related than distant things – we propose to model user preferences as a function of distance. Concretely, we consider three graphs over homogeneous entities $\mathcal{G}_G^{uu}$, $\mathcal{G}_G^{ee}$ and $\mathcal{G}_G^{tt}$ for users, experts, and topics, respectively. For each graph, we treat "nearby" nodes as more alike if they are geographically closer. In this way, preferences on experts may be propagated to these nearby nodes in the tensor-based factorization approach.

To begin, consider the user-user graph $\mathcal{G}_G^{uu}$, where nodes are users and edges capture the affinity between users. We can define the adjacency matrix $\boldsymbol{H}_G \in \mathbb{R}^{N\times N}$ as:

$$\boldsymbol{H}_G(u_i, u_j) = exp(-\frac{Dist(u_i, u_j)^2}{2\alpha^2}),$$

where α is a decay constant (which we experimentally set to 20 miles) and $Dist$ is to measure the geographic distance between two users by using the Haversine formula. The affinity $\boldsymbol{H}_G(u_i, u_j)$ approaches one as two users are nearer each other.

Similarly, the expert-expert graph $\mathcal{G}_G^{ee}$ can be constructed, where nodes are experts and here edges represent the spatial similarity of pairs of experts. Rather than purely measuring the geographic nearness of two experts (which does not take into account the recognizability of experts in various locations), we consider how the users who have labeled those experts are distributed. The intuition is that experts who are preferred have higher popularity in the location of a user. Let $l(u_i) \in \mathbb{L}$ be a location of user u_i and $\phi_{e_i}^{l(u_i)}$ as the spatial popularity be the number of users selecting expert e_i in the location of user u_i across topics. The adjacency matrix $\boldsymbol{V}_G \in \mathbb{R}^{M\times M}$ can be defined as:

$$\boldsymbol{V}_G(e_i, e_j) = exp(-\frac{Dist(l(e_i), l(e_j))^2}{2\alpha^2} * \sum_{u_i \in U}(\phi_{e_i}^{l(u_i)} - \phi_{e_j}^{l(u_i)})^2),$$

where the first part in the exponential is to calculate the deviation of geo-spatial preferences between experts (so that experts who are nearby are considered "closer"), the second part is to consider the difference of their spatial popularities over all locations of users (to capture the nearness in terms of who is interested in them).[3]

The third graph – the topic-topic graph $\mathcal{G}_G^{tt}$ – has topics as nodes and edges that represent the geo-spatial correlation between topics. Intuitively, selecting experts could be impacted by the choice of topic. The spatial preference in the topic *food* is much more local than the topic *technology*. We aim to capture the similarity of spatial preference between topics. Let $d_{u_i}^{t_i}$ be the average distance between user u_i and a set of experts $E_{u_i}^{t_i}$ he/she recognizes in a topic t_i. The empirical distribution of spatial preference for a topic t_i can be obtained from calculations $\{d_{u_i}^{t_i}, u_i \in U\}$, which is denoted as Υ_{t_i}. We then apply the Kullback-Leibler divergence $D_{KL}(\cdot\|\cdot)$ to measure the closeness of empirical distributions between topics. Hence, we can define the adjacency matrix $\boldsymbol{W}_G \in \mathbb{R}^{K\times K}$ as:

$$\boldsymbol{W}_G(t_i, t_j) = 1 - D_{KL}(\Upsilon_{t_i}\|\Upsilon_{t_j}),$$

[2] An open question is how can we efficiently estimate the solution to this optimization problem since there is no closed form solution? In the supplementary material [1], we show how to solve this problem based on ADMM (Alternating Direction Method of Multipliers).

[3] In this case, we discretize the continental U.S. surface with a 1° by 1° geodesic grid, so we can map the location of a user (GPS coordinate) to a discrete region.

where $\boldsymbol{W}_G$ will approach to 1 if two topics have similar empirical distributions of spatial preferences.

Relationships between Heterogeneous Entities: In addition to the geo-spatial correlations between users, experts, and topics themselves, we can additionally consider the relationships across heterogeneous entities. Specifically, we consider the relationships between users and experts, as well as between users and topics.

First, we propose to leverage the geo-spatial preferences between users and experts so that users are more likely to select experts who have a high popularity in the location of this user. The intuition is that the local popularity of an expert can be considered as a prior on what a user would prefer. For example, given a new user in Seattle with no expert preferences, we can default to a locally popular expert like Jeff Bezos. Concretely, we propose to improve the learning of latent matrices of users and experts as:

$$\mathcal{F}_{\boldsymbol{A}_G} = \|\boldsymbol{A}_G - U^{(1)}U^{(2)^T}\|_F^2,$$

where $\boldsymbol{A}_G$ is the adjacency matrix in which an element indicates the spatial popularity of an expert in the location of a user. By minimizing $\mathcal{F}_{\boldsymbol{A}_G}$, the recommender will prefer locally popular experts.

Similarly, the geo-spatial preferences between users and topics can also be leveraged so that a user is more likely to select experts on topics that have high popularity in the location of this user. Formally, we have the latent matrices of users and topics as:

$$\mathcal{F}_{\boldsymbol{B}_G} = \|\boldsymbol{B}_G - U^{(1)}U^{(3)^T}\|_F^2,$$

where $\boldsymbol{B}_G$ is the adjacency matrix in which an element indicates the spatial popularity of a topic in the location of a user. Again, by minimizing $\mathcal{F}_{\boldsymbol{B}_G}$, the recommender will prefer experts on topics that are more popular locally.

3.2.2 Modeling Topical Preferences

Beyond geo-spatial preferences, we next turn to models of topical preference. As we have observed in Section 3.1, the topical context can influence a user's preference for experts. Intuitively, users who have similar interests on topics tend to have similar preferences on experts.

Relationships between Homogeneous Entities: We begin by considering two graphs – one for the user-user graph $\mathcal{G}_T^{uu}$ and the other for the expert-expert graph $\mathcal{G}_T^{ee}$ in terms of topical preference.

In this case, the user-user graph $\mathcal{G}_T^{uu}$ has nodes that represent users but now edges represent the similarity between users in terms of topical preferences (rather than in terms of distance as in the geo-spatial case in the previous section). Inspired by the work [5], we define the adjacency matrix $\boldsymbol{H}_T$ as:

$$\boldsymbol{H}_T(u_i, u_j) = \frac{|T_{u_i} \bigcap T_{u_j}|}{|T_{u_i} \bigcup T_{u_j}|} * exp(\sum_{t \in T}(o_{u_i}^t - o_{u_j}^t)P_t),$$

where T_{u_i} is the set of topics a user u_i is interested in by labeling the lists with keywords related to these topics, $o_{u_i}^t$ denotes the number of experts a user u_i labeled in a topic t, and P_t denotes the probability of being interested in a topic t, which can be formally defined as $P_t = (\sum_{u \in U} o_u^t)/(\sum_{t \in T}\sum_{u \in U} o_u^t)$. The first part in $\boldsymbol{H}_T$ is used to measure how common two users share topics; the second part is applied to quantitively evaluate the similarity of their interests across all topics.

For the second graph – the expert-expert graph $\mathcal{G}_T^{ee}$ – we have nodes as experts and edges representing the similarity of experts towards their expertise. The adjacency matrix $\boldsymbol{V}_T$ is defined as:

$$\boldsymbol{V}_T(e_i, e_j) = \frac{|T_{e_i} \bigcap T_{e_j}|}{|T_{e_i} \bigcup T_{e_j}|} * exp(\sum_{t \in T}(\delta_{e_i}^t - \delta_{e_j}^t)P_t),$$

where T_{e_i} is the set of topics in which an expert e_i have expertise labeled by users, and $\delta_{e_i}^t$ is denoted as the number of times an expert e_i labeled by users in a topic t. The first part in $\boldsymbol{V}_T$ is used to measure how common two experts have the same expertise; the second part is applied to quantitively evaluate the similarity of their expertise across all topics.

Relationships between Heterogeneous Entities: In addition to the topical correlations between users and experts, themselves, we additionally consider the relationships across users and topics, as well as across experts and topics. Since each Twitter list is labeled with certain labels, the topic preferences of a user can be revealed by aggregating all of the labels he/she applies in the lists. As a result, we propose to leverage a user's topical preferences to improve the learning of latent matrices of users and topics as follows:

$$\mathcal{F}_{\boldsymbol{B}_T} = \|\boldsymbol{B}_T - U^{(1)}U^{(3)^T}\|_F^2,$$

where $\boldsymbol{B}_T$ is the affinity matrix where an element indicates whether a user is interested in certain topic by applying keywords related to this topic in her lists. Our goal is to minimize $\mathcal{F}_{\boldsymbol{B}_T}$ so that a user is more likely to select experts who have expertise on topics of interest to this user.

Meanwhile, an expert's expertise can be also found by aggregating all of the labels in all the lists this expert appears. Therefore, we leverage the expert's topic preferences to improve the learning of latent matrices of experts and topics as illustrated below:

$$\mathcal{F}_{\boldsymbol{C}_T} = \|\boldsymbol{C}_T - U^{(2)}U^{(3)^T}\|_F^2,$$

where $\boldsymbol{C}_T$ is the affinity matrix in which the element indicates the number of times that an expert has been recognized by users with respect to certain topics. Through minimizing $\mathcal{F}_{\boldsymbol{C}_T}$, an expert who has higher recognition in a topic is more likely to be selected by users who are interested in this topic.

3.2.3 Modeling Social Preferences

Finally, we consider how to model the social preferences of users with respect to personalized expert preferences. Concretely, we consider the social connections among users and experts:

Relationships between Homogeneous Entities: Similar to our previous efforts, we construct a graph $\mathcal{G}_S^{uu}$ in which nodes represent users and edges represent the pairwise similarity of users in terms of their social preferences, and a graph $\mathcal{G}_S^{ee}$ in which nodes represent experts and edges represent the pairwise similarity of experts with respect to their social connections. By applying the Jaccard coefficient, the adjacency matrix $\boldsymbol{H}_S$ for users is defined as:

$$\boldsymbol{H}_S(u_i, u_j) = \frac{|F_{u_i} \bigcap F_{u_j}|}{|F_{u_i} \bigcup F_{u_j}|},$$

where F_{u_i} represents the set of users u_i follows. As a similar fashion, we define the adjacency matrix $\boldsymbol{V}_S$ for experts as:

$$\boldsymbol{V}_S(e_i, e_j) = \frac{|F_{e_i} \bigcap F_{e_j}|}{|F_{e_i} \bigcup F_{e_j}|},$$

where F_{e_i} represents the set of users e_i follows. The intuition behind $\boldsymbol{H}_S$ and $\boldsymbol{V}_S$ is that users/experts who share more friends are more likely have similar behaviors on selecting experts/being selected by users.

Relationships between Heterogeneous Entities: In order to take advantage of the social connections between different entities (e.g., user-expert) into the expert recommendation, we leverage the following social relationships from a user to an expert to improve the learning of latent matrices of users and experts, as shown below:

$$\mathcal{F}_{\boldsymbol{A}_S} = \|\boldsymbol{A}_S - U^{(1)}U^{(2)^T}\|_F^2, \quad (3)$$

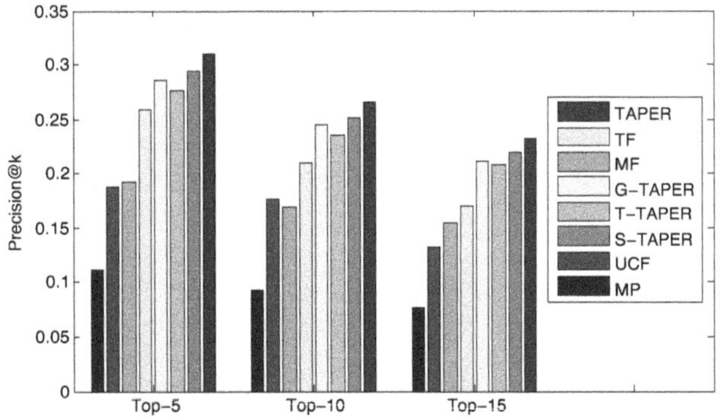

Figure 6: Precision@k: Comparing TAPER versus Alternative Methods.

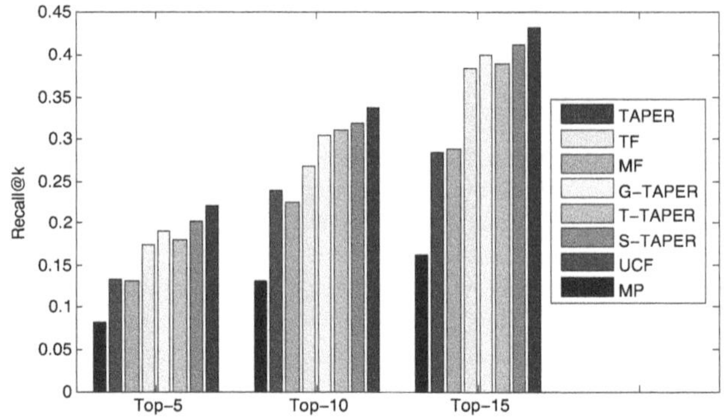

Figure 7: Recall@k: Comparing TAPER versus Alternative Methods.

where $\boldsymbol{A}_S$ is a matrix where the element indicates if a user follows an expert. In this way, the recommender can prefer experts who are followed by this user through minimizing $\mathcal{F}_{\boldsymbol{A}_S}$. Note that this is a very strong signal, and unlikely to be present for most users.

4. EXPERIMENTS

In this section, we investigate (i) the effectiveness of TAPER versus alternatives; (ii) the impact of specific contextual factors (e.g., geo-spatial, topical, and social); (iii) how incorporating evidence of experts for whom a user is *not interested* affects recommendation quality; and (iv) the impact of the amount of training data.

4.1 Experimental Setup

To evaluate the performance of the proposed framework, we randomly split experts for a user into 50% for training and 50% for testing. For latent factor dimension, we empirically choose 20 for all methods after testing various settings {5, 10, 20, 30, 40, 50, 100} for a tradeoff between accuracy and the computational cost. For the number of experts that a user does not pick up in the Twitter lists, we empirically select 350 through all experiments we conducted. The effects of this number will be further discussed in Section 4.3. Three positive parameters are involved in the experiments: λ, γ and β in Eq. (2). λ is the regularization parameter used to avoid overfitting. γ is to control the contribution of contextual information between homogeneous entities. β is to control the contribution of contextual information between heterogeneous entities. As a common way, we employ the cross-validation to tune these parameters.[4] Concretely, we empirically set $\lambda = 0.1$, $\gamma = 0.1$ and $\beta = 0.01$ for general experiments, respectively. Their effects on the performance of the proposed framework is evaluated in [1].

We adopt Precision@k and Recall@k as our evaluation metrics. Precision@k represents the percentage of correctly recommended experts out of the top-k recommendations; Recall@k represents the percentage of experts emerging in the top-k recommendations. Both of them have been widely used to evaluate the quality of recommendation. In our experiments, we test for k at 5, 10, and 15.

4.2 Baselines

We consider seven baselines in addition to the proposed TAPER approach. The first three baseline are classical recommender system approaches:

- *Most Popular (MP)*: This baseline recommends the most listed experts in a topic to all users.
- *User-based Collaborative Filtering (UCF)*: We adopt a user-based recommendation framework [33] to recommend personal experts, which discovers user's implicit preferences towards experts by aggregating similar users.
- *Matrix Factorization (MF)*: This baseline computes a user's preferences on experts for each topic by a pair-wise latent matrix factorization model trained by stochastic gradient descent [17].

The next four baselines are simplified variants of the proposed TAPER approach, all building on tensor factorization:

- *Tensor Factorization (TF)*: In analogy to matrix factorization, tensor factorization computes each user's preferences for experts by considering users, experts, and topics simultaneously. This basic tensor factorization model corresponds to Eq. (1).
- *Geo-based TAPER (**G-TAPER**)*: This model is a variant of the basic tensor factorization model, but only integrates geo-spatial preferences: that is, $\boldsymbol{H}_G$, $\boldsymbol{V}_G$, $\boldsymbol{W}_G$, $\boldsymbol{A}_G$ and $\boldsymbol{B}_G$ in Eq. (2).
- *Topical-based TAPER (**T-TAPER**)*: This model only integrates topical preferences: that is, $\boldsymbol{H}_T$, $\boldsymbol{V}_T$, $\boldsymbol{B}_T$ and $\boldsymbol{C}_T$ in Eq. (2).
- *Social-based TAPER (**S-TAPER**)*: This variant only considers social preferences: that is, $\boldsymbol{H}_S$, $\boldsymbol{V}_S$ and $\boldsymbol{A}_S$ in Eq. (2).

Finally, we consider the proposed TAPER approach:

- *Contextual Personalized Expert Recommendation (**TAPER**)*: This is the proposed framework, incorporating all three types of contextual information among users, experts, and topics in Eq. (2). Specifically, we let $\boldsymbol{H} = \boldsymbol{H}_G * \boldsymbol{H}_T * \boldsymbol{H}_S$, $\boldsymbol{V} = \boldsymbol{V}_G * \boldsymbol{V}_T * \boldsymbol{V}_S$, $\boldsymbol{W} = \boldsymbol{W}_G$, $\boldsymbol{A} = \boldsymbol{A}_G + \boldsymbol{A}_S$, $\boldsymbol{B} = \boldsymbol{B}_G + \boldsymbol{B}_T$ and $\boldsymbol{C} = \boldsymbol{C}_T$.

4.3 Results

We begin by investigating the quality of TAPER versus each of the baselines. We adopt 10-fold cross validation and report the average precision and recall over 10 test runs in Figure 6 and Figure 7. Overall, the proposed personal expert recommendation framework TAPER performs the best among all alternative baseline methods in both precision and recall. From Figures 6 and 7, we can observe that TAPER consistently outperforms the baseline methods MP, UCF, MF, and TF with an average improvement of 42.2% over the best of these four methods in precision and 33.5% in recall. Concretely, TAPER performs better than TF with an average improvement of 14.1% in precision and 17.8% in recall, indicating the superiority of a tensor factorization model integrating rich contextual preferences. Moreover, TAPER has a better performance than MF with an average improvement of 26.6% in precision and 25.8% in recall, which is significantly higher than a related matrix factorization approach in [17].

We observe that MP and UCF perform the worst among all approaches. We attribute the poor performance of the UCF approach to sparseness – the low density of data can lead to poor recommendations, whereas both MF and TF can leverage the low-rank approximation of user preferences towards experts. Overall, we

[4]We find that parameter settings of $\gamma < 1$ and $\beta < 0.1$ lead to fairly stable precision and recall, indicating the stability of TAPER to these regularization parameters.

Table 2: What Impact Does Contextual Preference Have on Each Approach? Here we compare contextual preferences of heterogeneous entities versus homogeneous entities.

Metric	Scenario	G-TAPER-Het	G-TAPER-Hom	T-TAPER-Het	T-TAPER-Hom	S-TAPER-Het	S-TAPER-Hom	TAPER-Het	TAPER-Hom
Precision	Top-5	0.271	0.282	0.262	0.274	0.289	0.278	0.296	0.306
	Top-10	0.234	0.242	0.227	0.232	0.248	0.241	0.254	0.260
	Top-15	0.204	0.208	0.192	0.199	0.214	0.201	0.219	0.229
Recall	Top-5	0.183	0.182	0.177	0.178	0.187	0.180	0.199	0.201
	Top-10	0.286	0.297	0.289	0.304	0.310	0.304	0.313	0.329
	Top-15	0.391	0.388	0.386	0.381	0.402	0.398	0.416	0.411

observe that the best method achieves a precision of around 0.3 and a recall of around 0.4 As Ye et al. [30] have observed, the effectiveness of recommenders with sparse datasets is usually low.

We also observe that adding additional contextual factors improves the basic tensor factorization (TF) approach. Concretely, G-TAPER gives an average improvement of 8.1% in precision and 7.3% in recall over TF. This indicates that the geo-spatial preferences among users, experts, and topics can help identify similar users and distinguish popular experts according to their spatial popularity. T-TAPER performs slightly better than TF with an average improvement of 5.2% in precision and 4.9% in recall, implying that the topical preferences among users and experts can help improve the performance of personalized expert recommendation via tensor factorization. Furthermore, S-TAPER gives an average improvement of 13.2% in precision and 10.6% in recall. This indicates that the social ties of users and experts can help find users with similar behaviors on selecting experts, which provide more significant contributions to the personal expert recommendation than the geo-spatial and topical. Recall that social ties implicitly capture latent geo-spatial and topical preferences.

The Impact of Contextual Preferences. We have seen that geo-spatial, topical, and social preferences can be integrated into tensor factorization for improved personalized expert recommendation. In this section, we aim to dig deeper into the impact of geo-spatial, topical, and social signals on the quality of personalized recommendation. What impact do heterogeneous and homogeneous contextual preferences have? Are these impacts equal across approaches? For this experiment, we add the suffixes *Het* and *Hom* to indicate which variant of the proposed framework is at study. For instance, G-TAPER-Hom represents the model G-TAPER by only leveraging the geo-spatial preferences between homogeneous entities including $\boldsymbol{H}_G$, $\boldsymbol{V}_G$, and $\boldsymbol{W}_G$. Similarly, we consider variations of T-TAPER, S-TAPER, as well as the full TAPER.

As it can be seen in Table 2, TAPER-Hom outperforms TAPER-Het with an average improvement of 3.4% in precision and 1.6% in recall, indicating that in general, the contextual preferences between homogeneous entities plays a more important role than between heterogeneous entities since such information can help identify similar users and further improve the quality of the recommendation. G-TAPER-Hom has a better performance than G-TAPER-Het with an average improvement of 3.0% in precision and 1.6% in recall. T-TAPER-Hom gives an average improvement of 3.5% in precision and 1.9% in recall. These results indicate that the geo-spatial and topical preferences between homogeneous entities contribute more to the proposed framework. However, it is surprising that S-TAPER-Het performs better than S-TAPER-Hom with an average improvement of 4.3% over S-TAPER-Hom in precision and 2.4% in recall. This implies that the following relationships between users and experts are a strong signal, and confirms that if a user is already following this expert, it is very likely that this user will include this expert on the list [17]. In addition, we also observe that the social preferences are more significant in contributing to the proposed framework than other factors.

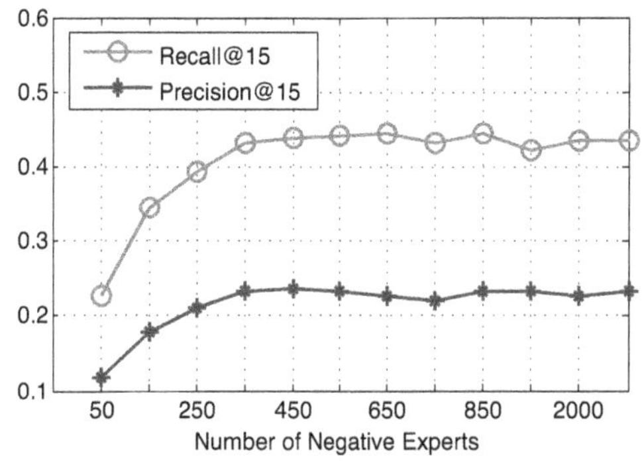

Figure 8: Effect of Number of Negative Experts.

The Impact of Negative Experts. We next turn to the impact of "negative experts", that is, to incorporate evidence of experts for whom a user is *not interested*. We seek to understand if these negative experts can be used as evidence in addition to the positive relationships investigated so far (e.g., by exploiting the geo-spatial preferences of users for experts). For example, knowing that a user is interested in a California Politics expert, but not interested in an expert on US National Politics may convey strong information about the preferences for that user on topics of regional (but not necessarily national) issues. To test the impact of these negative experts, we run the following experiment: first, we take the task of recommending the top-15 experts to users, and then we vary the number of negative experts. We vary the number of negative experts from 50 to 3,000 for each user by randomly selecting experts whom this user do not put in the Twitter list. Figure 8 demonstrates the impact of an increasing number of negative experts on the precision and recall of personalized expert recommendation. First, we observe that both precision and recall increase as the number of negative experts increases. This indicates that this signal of not being interested can provide some additional information beyond the positive relationships exploited so far. Second, we observe that the precision and recall curves flatten once the number of negative experts is larger than 350. Since there are nearly 9,000 experts in the dataset, the probability of false negative samples is small when only selecting a tiny part of them. However, this probability will increase as the number of negative experts grows, further affecting the quality of recommendations.

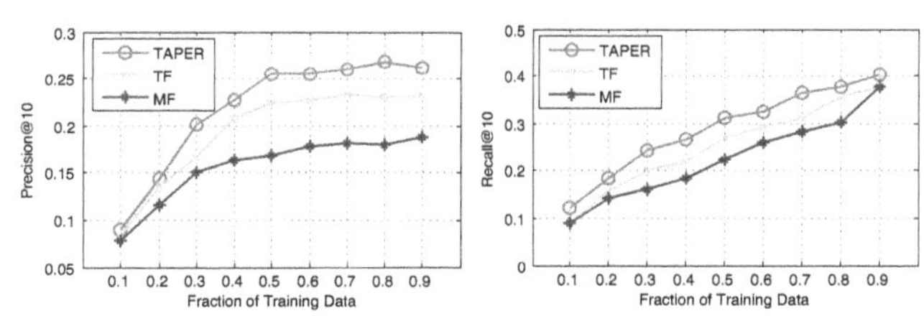

(a) Precison@10 (b) Recall@10

Figure 9: Varying the Amount of Training Data

Varying the Amount of Training Data. For the experiments so far, we have relied on cross-validation over a random split of experts into a training half and a testing half. Here, we explore the impact of varying the amount of training data on the task of personalized expert recommendation. Does the proposed approach still perform better than alternatives even with low amounts of training data? Do precision and recall plateau at some point? We vary the fraction of training data from 10% to 90% and evaluate TAPER versus a baseline tensor factorization method (TF) and a non-negative matrix factorization (MF) method on the task of personalized recommendation of the top-10 experts to each user. As we can see in Figure 9, the proposed framework TAPER consistently outperforms both MF and TF in precision and recall, across all fractions of training data. We also observe that the precision curves for all methods plateaus around 30%, indicating that good results may be achieved with even less training data. Naturally, the recall of all methods consistently increases as the training data increases, since recall is more sensitive to the number of testing samples.

5. CONCLUSION

We have studied the problem of personalized expert recommendation through a tensor-based exploration of geo-spatial, topical, and social context across users, experts and topics. Through a Twitter dataset, we have seen that the proposed framework can improve the quality of the recommendation by over 30% in both precision and recall compared to state-of-the-art baselines. In our continuing work we are interested to integrate additional contextual signals (e.g., are temporal factors important?) and to explore alternative settings (e.g., LinkedIn and Amazon). One promising direction is to evaluate the quality of downstream applications that can be built over these personalized expert models; for example, what impact does integrating these expertise signals into item-based recommenders and under what scenarios do they work well?

6. ACKNOWLEDGEMENTS

This work was supported in part by NSF grant IIS-1149383 and a Google Research Award. Any opinions, findings and conclusions or recommendations expressed in this material are the author(s) and do not necessarily reflect those of the sponsors.

7. REFERENCES

[1] Supplementary material. http://students.cse.tamu.edu/hge/papers/recsys16_expert_supp.pdf.

[2] X. Amatriain, N. Lathia, J. M. Pujol, H. Kwak, and N. Oliver. The wisdom of the few: a collaborative filtering approach based on expert opinions from the web. In *SIGIR*, 2009.

[3] L. Backstrom, E. Sun, and C. Marlow. Find me if you can: improving geographical prediction with social and spatial proximity. In *WWW*, 2010.

[4] K. Balog, L. Azzopardi, and M. De Rijke. Formal models for expert finding in enterprise corpora. In *SIGIR*, 2006.

[5] P. Bhargava, T. Phan, J. Zhou, and J. Lee. Who, what, when, and where: Multi-dimensional collaborative recommendations using tensor factorization on sparse user-generated data. In *WWW*, 2015.

[6] P. Bhattacharya, S. Ghosh, J. Kulshrestha, M. Mondal, M. B. Zafar, N. Ganguly, and K. P. Gummadi. Deep twitter diving: Exploring topical groups in microblogs at scale. In *CSCW*, 2014.

[7] Z. Cheng, J. Caverlee, H. Barthwal, and V. Bachani. Who is the barbecue king of texas?: a geo-spatial approach to finding local experts on twitter. In *SIGIR*, 2014.

[8] D. M. Dunlavy, T. G. Kolda, and E. Acar. Temporal link prediction using matrix and tensor factorizations. *TKDD*, 2011.

[9] S. Ghosh, N. Sharma, F. Benevenuto, N. Ganguly, and K. Gummadi. Cognos: crowdsourcing search for topic experts in microblogs. In *SIGIR*, 2012.

[10] I. Guy, U. Avraham, D. Carmel, S. Ur, M. Jacovi, and I. Ronen. Mining expertise and interests from social media. In *WWW*, 2013.

[11] B. Hidasi and D. Tikk. Fast als-based tensor factorization for context-aware recommendation from implicit feedback. In *MLKDD*. 2012.

[12] D. Hu and J. L. Zhao. Expert recommendation via semantic social networks. *ICIS*, 2008.

[13] A. Karatzoglou, X. Amatriain, L. Baltrunas, and N. Oliver. Multiverse recommendation: n-dimensional tensor factorization for context-aware collaborative filtering. In *RecSys*, 2010.

[14] T. G. Kolda and B. W. Bader. Tensor decompositions and applications. *SIAM*, 2009.

[15] Y. Koren, R. Bell, and C. Volinsky. Matrix factorization techniques for recommender systems. *Computer*, 2009.

[16] Y. Liu, F. Shang, L. Jiao, J. Cheng, and H. Cheng. Trace norm regularized candecomp/parafac decomposition with missing data. *Cybernetics*, 2014.

[17] H. Lu and J. Caverlee. Exploiting geo-spatial preference for personalized expert recommendation. In *RecSys*, 2015.

[18] H. Ma, H. Yang, M. R. Lyu, and I. King. Sorec: social recommendation using probabilistic matrix factorization. In *CIKM*, 2008.

[19] D. W. McDonald and M. S. Ackerman. Expertise recommender: a flexible recommendation system and architecture. In *CSCW*, 2000.

[20] M. Naaman, Y. J. Song, A. Paepcke, and H. Garcia-Molina. Automatic organization for digital photographs with geographic coordinates. In *ICDL*, 2004.

[21] A. Pal, A. Herdagdelen, S. Chatterji, S. Taank, and D. Chakrabarti. Discovery of topical authorities in instagram. In *WWW*, 2016.

[22] S. A. Paul, L. Hong, and E. H. Chi. Who is authoritative? understanding reputation mechanisms in quora. *arXiv preprint arXiv:1204.3724*, 2012.

[23] V. Rakesh, D. Singh, B. Vinzamuri, and C. K. Reddy. Personalized recommendation of twitter lists using content and network information. In *ICWSM*, 2014.

[24] S. Rendle and L. Schmidt-Thieme. Pairwise interaction tensor factorization for personalized tag recommendation. In *WSDM*, 2010.

[25] P. Serdyukov, H. Rode, and D. Hiemstra. Modeling multi-step relevance propagation for expert finding. In *CIKM*, 2008.

[26] J. Sun, D. Tao, and C. Faloutsos. Beyond streams and graphs: dynamic tensor analysis. In *SIGKDD*, 2006.

[27] W. R. Tobler. A computer movie simulating urban growth in the detroit region. *Economic geography*, pages 234–240, 1970.

[28] J. Weng, E.-P. Lim, J. Jiang, and Q. He. Twitterrank: finding topic-sensitive influential twitterers. In *WSDM*, 2010.

[29] B. Yang and S. Manandhar. Tag-based expert recommendation in community question answering. In *ASONAM*, 2014.

[30] M. Ye, X. Liu, and W. Lee. Exploring social influence for recommendation: a generative model approach. In *SIGIR*, 2012.

[31] H.-F. Yu, C.-J. Hsieh, I. Dhillon, et al. Scalable coordinate descent approaches to parallel matrix factorization for recommender systems. In *ICDM*, 2012.

[32] J. Zhang, M. S. Ackerman, and L. Adamic. Expertise networks in online communities: structure and algorithms. In *WWW*, 2007.

[33] D. Zhou, B. Wang, S. M. Rahimi, and X. Wang. A study of recommending locations on location-based social network by collaborative filtering. In *Adv. in Artificial Intelligence*. 2012.

Are You Influenced by Others When Rating? Improve Rating Prediction by Conformity Modeling

Yiming Liu , Xuezhi Cao , Yong Yu
Apex Data and Knowledge Management Lab
Dept. of Computer Science and Engineering
Shanghai Jiao Tong University, Shanghai, China
goblinliu,cxz,yyu@apex.sjtu.edu.cn

ABSTRACT

Conformity has a strong influence to user behaviors, even in online environment. When surfing online, users are usually flooded with others' opinions. These opinions implicitly contribute to the user's ongoing behaviors. However, there is no research work modeling online conformity yet. In this paper, we model user's conformity in online rating sites. We conduct analysis using real data to show the existence and strength of conformity in these scenarios. We propose a matrix-factorization-based conformity modeling technique to improve the accuracy of rating prediction. Experiments show that our model outperforms existing works significantly (with a relative improvement of 11.72% on RMSE). Therefore, we draw the conclusion that conformity modeling is important for understanding user behaviors and can contribute to further improve the online recommender systems.

Keywords

User Behavior, Conformity, Rating Prediction

1. INTRODUCTION

Conformity implicitly shapes people's behaviors to group norms. The phenomenon widely exists in most communities and various scenarios, from political votings to dinner choices. Plenty of psychological researches aim at studying and understanding such behaviors [9]. Experiments also prove the existence and lead to several psychological theories.

Besides traditional real-world experiments, online social networks and services now provide a new opportunity to study and to utilize the social conformity phenomenon. People are flooded with other's opinions when surfing the Internet. When making choices online, users are normally influenced by these just received opinions to some extent. All the opinions and actions are well recorded by the service providers as action logs, providing large-scale valuable data for conformity analysis. However, there are only few research works targeting at analyzing conformity in online environment.

RecSys '16, September 15-19, 2016, Boston , MA, USA
© 2016 ACM. ISBN 978-1-4503-4035-9/16/09... $15.00
DOI: http://dx.doi.org/10.1145/2959100.2959141

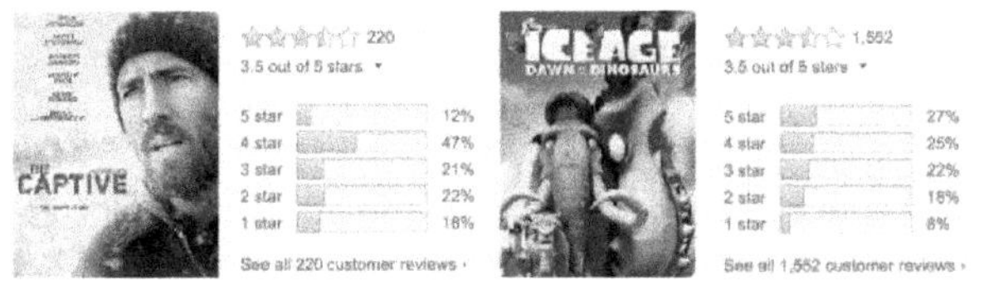

Figure 1: Examples of Public Opinions in Rating Sites

One of the most suitable platforms for analyzing user's online conformity is online rating site. We have various rating sites for different domains, such as e-commerce, movie and restaurant. For most rating sites, users are aware of the public opinion towards the item before rating it. The public opinions are normally highlighted in the item's detail page, including average rating and rating distribution of the item. We show two examples in Figure 1. Such information definitely contributes to the user's rating action to some extent. For example, when user rates a 4-star movie (public opinion), even if he thinks it only worth 2-star (truthful opinion), he might still rate it as 3-star (biased opinion) due to conformity.

The benefit of modeling online conformity is multi-folded. Firstly, it gives us opportunity to better understand the user's online behaviors. Following which, we can undo the effects caused by conformity and recover the user's true preferences towards the items, leading to the improvement of personalized recommender systems. To the best of our knowledge, there is no existing work that models the online conformity jointly with traditional user preference models to improve the quality of recommender systems.

In this paper, we aim at modeling user conformity and improving rating prediction in online rating sites. We first conduct analysis using real data to show the existence of online conformity. We conclude that the conformity do have a strong influence on rating scores. Then we target at improving the accuracy of rating prediction by integrating conformity modeling and matrix factorization techniques. Specifically, we model the strength of conformity by considering the group size, unanimity and cohesion. For analysis and evaluation, we collect and publish a large-scale real data set for this task. Experiments show that our conformity model out-performs existing non-conformity approaches by 11.72% on RMSE and 9.15% on MAE.

2. RELATED WORKS

Rating prediction is one of the core tasks in recommender system. To accurately solve this task, one must model the user's preferences and capture the item's characteristic precisely. Matrix factorization (MF) is the most widely used tool for this task, which represents both users and items in common low-dimension latent factor space [4]. Researchers later extend the traditional MF approach to further employ social relations [2], cross-domain user histories [6] and etc.

Existing user modeling approaches assume user's actions always reflect their preferences truthfully. However, the assumption does not always hold. A study on review-helpfulness voting concludes that users are not always truthful judges. Whether users vote at all, as well as the polarity of their votes, depend highly on the surrounding contents [8]. Krishnan et al. design and conduct a comparative experiment in [5], where users can rate twice before and after being exposed to the public opinions. Results prove the existence of conformity in this setting. However, due to the specialty of the experiment's methodology, we can not directly extend the conclusion to general online scenarios where user actions are more freely conducted comparing to actions in the controlled experiment.

3. DATASET

Due to the special requirement of conformity modeling, there is no public dataset suitable for this task. Besides rating logs, we also need the public opinions users received right before each rating action. As existing datasets only provide action logs over sampled users, the required information can not be accurately recovered.

We collect and publish a large-scale dataset that satisfies the requirement. The dataset can be freely accessed online[1]. We collect the data from Douban[2], one of China's largest movie review sites. We randomly sample 5,000 movies with more than 50 actions, and dump ALL rating actions for these movies. In total, we obtain 17,142,351 rating actions from 1,757,451 users. We recover the public opinions user received right before each rating action, including the number of reviewers, the average rating, and also the rating distribution for the target movie (how many reviewers rates 1-5 stars respectively).

4. CONFORMITY ANALYSIS

In this section, we demonstrate the existence of conformity in online rating sites by statistical analysis.

We show the correlation between the ratings given by users and the public opinions users received according to each movie. For simplicity, we consider only the averaged rating as the public opinion for analysis. We represent each rating log instance k as (r_k, p_k), where r_k is the rating and p_k is the averaged rating right before the action. For each movie, we group its rating logs by similar p_k, and report the average r_k for each group as the indicator of the rating distribution under that specific public opinion. We plot the results for four randomly selected movies in Figure 2. As we can notice, the rating distributions (the mean) clearly correlate with the public opinions users received.

Now we demonstrate the conformity phenomenon widely exists among most movies. Note that we can only conduct

[1]http://dataset.apexlab.org/conformity
[2]http://www.douban.com/

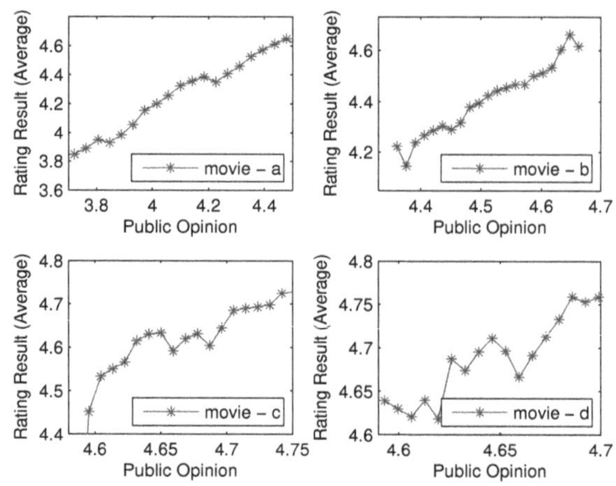

Figure 2: Influence of Public Opinion on User Ratings

the previous analysis in Figure 2 according to each movie separately. Plotting logs for all movies together is meaningless because rating distributions for different movies are not necessarily the same. Instead, we calculate the absolute correlation coefficient between $\{r_k\}$ and $\{p_k\}$ for each movie and plot the coefficient's distribution. The result is depicted in Figure 3, indicating that the correlation exists for a large portion of movies. It may raise concern that the numeric values are rather small. This is because the rating data is highly noisy (users can only rate integer values and are influenced by many other factors), thus perfect correlation is not possible.

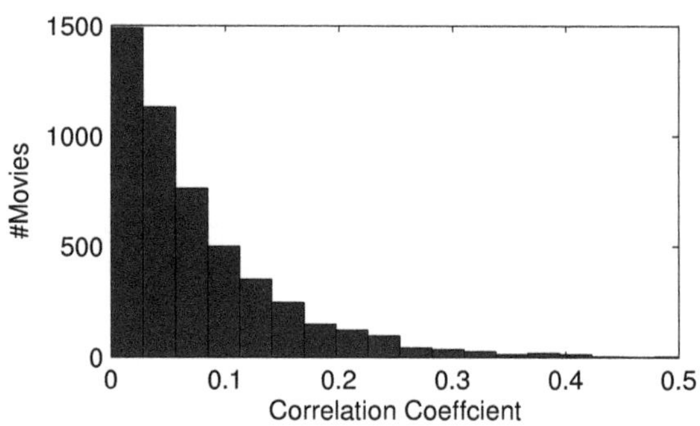

Figure 3: Correlation Coefficient Distribution

5. OUR APPROACH

We base our approach on matrix factorization [4], the most widely used technique for rating prediction. The traditional model captures user preferences and item characteristics with low-dimension latent factors. The rating user u gives to item i is modeled and estimated by:

$$\hat{r}_{ui} = t_{ui} = \mu + b_u + b_i + P_u^T Q_i \quad (1)$$

where μ, b_u, b_i are the global/user/item biases respectively, $P_u, Q_i \in \mathbb{R}^K$ are the latent factors. The loss function is:

$$\mathcal{L}(\Theta_t) = \frac{1}{2}\sum_{u,i}(r_{ui} - \hat{r}_{ui})^2 + \frac{\lambda}{2}||\Theta_t||^2 \quad (2)$$

where Θ_t is the set of parameters. Experiments and online applications both indicate that matrix factorization can successfully capture the users' preferences towards the items.

Instead of using the preference-based estimation directly as the rating modeling ($\hat{r}_{ui} = t_{ui}$), we integrate it with conformity modeling. Specifically, we model the user's final rating as $\hat{r}_{ui} = \mathcal{C}(t_{ui}, p_{ui}, \Theta_{\mathcal{C}})$, where $\mathcal{C}$ is the conformity model, t_{ui} is the prediction of traditional preference-based model, p_{ui} is the public opinion user u receives right before she rates item i, $\Theta_{\mathcal{C}}$ is the set of parameters.

Now we discuss the design of the conformity model $\mathcal{C}$. As conformity is a group phenomenon, factors such as group size, unanimity and cohesion affect the level of conformity an individual displays. Therefore, we first propose the basic conformity model and then extend it for specific aspects in the following subsections.

5.1 Conformity Model - Basic ($\mathcal{C}_B$)

We model the user's biased rating by linear combination of pure preference-based estimation and the influence of public opinion due to conformity. For public opinions, we have $p_{ui} = (c_{ui}, a_{ui}, d_{ui})$, where c_{ui} is the number of ratings for movie i before user u rates it, a_{ui} is the average rating and d_{ui} is the rating distribution. Examples are showed in Figure 1. In the basic model we only consider the average rating a_{ui}. We use a hyper-parameter ω to tune the strength of conformity. The rating prediction model is now:

$$\begin{aligned} \mathcal{C}_B(t_{ui}, p_{ui}) &= (1-\omega) \cdot t_{ui} + \omega \cdot a_{ui} \\ &= (1-\omega) \cdot (\mu + b_u + b_i + P_u^T Q_i) + \omega \cdot a_{ui} \end{aligned} \tag{3}$$

We employ stochastic gradient descent for the parameter learning. The inference of the gradients as well as the loss function are mostly the same as traditional matrix factorization, thus we skip them here.

5.2 Conformity Model - Group Size ($\mathcal{C}_S$)

Group size is an important factor for modeling the conformity strength. Opinions from few people might be considered as coincidence, while the voice of the crowd can not be ignored. In the rating site scenario, the group size is the number of raters for the movie (c_{ui}). For example, knowing that 5 people like the movie might not affect the user a lot. However, when the group size increases to thousands, the conformity strength also boosts.

Therefore, instead of setting conformity strength with constant value as in the basic model, now we model it based on the group size. We model the conformity strength as a function of the group size. Considering the intuitive properties of conformity, we design the function to satisfies the followings: (a) non-linear; (b) monotone increasing; (c) with constrained range; (d) has a 'tipping point' to model the 'threshold' of group size for conformity. For computational convenience, we also require the function to be differentiable. To achieve the requirements, we employ the extended sigmoid function $\omega(x)$ defined as follows:

$$\sigma(x) = 1/(1+e^{-x}),\ \omega(x) = \omega_b + \omega_a \cdot \sigma(\alpha x + \beta) \tag{4}$$

where ω_a, ω_b control the overall scale of conformity strength and α, β control the shape as well as the 'tipping point'. The model is now:

$$\hat{r}_{ui} = \mathcal{C}_S(t_{ui}, p_{ui}) = (1-\omega(c_{ui})) \cdot t_{ui} + \omega(c_{ui}) \cdot a_{ui} \tag{5}$$

The loss function is mostly the same with Eq. (2), with parameter set replaced by $\Theta_{\mathcal{C}_B} = (\Theta_t, \omega_a, \omega_b, \alpha, \beta)$.

We update the parameters for both traditional model and conformity model jointly using stochastic gradient decent. For parameters in traditional model, their gradients are simply the original gradients multiplied by $(1-\omega(c_{ui}))$ for each rating instance (u, i). For the newly introduced parameters, their gradients are as follows (with $e_{ui} = r_{ui} - \hat{r}_{ui}$):

$$\begin{aligned} \frac{\partial \mathcal{L}}{\partial \omega_a} &= \lambda \omega_a - \sum_{u,i} e_{ui}(a_{ui} - t_{ui})\sigma(\alpha c_{ui} + \beta) \\ \frac{\partial \mathcal{L}}{\partial \omega_b} &= \lambda \omega_b - \sum_{u,i} e_{ui}(a_{ui} - t_{ui}) \\ \frac{\partial \mathcal{L}}{\partial \alpha} &= \lambda \alpha - \sum_{u,i} e_{ui}\omega_a(a_{ui} - t_{ui})\sigma(\alpha c_{ui} + \beta)(1-\sigma(\alpha c_{ui} + \beta))c_{ui} \\ \frac{\partial \mathcal{L}}{\partial \beta} &= \lambda \beta - \sum_{u,i} e_{ui}\omega_a(a_{ui} - t_{ui})\sigma(\alpha c_{ui} + \beta)(1-\sigma(\alpha c_{ui} + \beta)) \end{aligned} \tag{6}$$

5.3 Conformity Model - Cohesion ($\mathcal{C}_C$)

Cohesion and unanimity also affect whether and to what extent does conformity influence users. People may follow the majority for no reason when unanimity is reached. And when the cohesion is rather low (the public opinion varies), people tend to express their own opinions instead of following others.

In this scenario, the rating distribution d_{ui} is the indicator of unanimity and cohesion. We give two examples in Figure 1. Although the average ratings are both 3.5-stars, the distribution differs. Intuitively, users are more likely to rate around 4 for (a) comparing to (b) due to cohesion.

We leverage the rating distribution for the conformity model by employing Gradient Boosting Decision Tree (GBDT). GBDT can capture rather complex non-linear correlations, thus suitable for the cohesion modeling. We use XGBoost[1] as the implementation. Specifically:

$$\mathcal{C}_C(t_{ui}, p_{ui}) = xgb(\{\mathcal{C}_B(t_{ui}, p_{ui}), c_{ui}, a_{ui}, d_{ui}\}, \Theta_{xgb}) \tag{7}$$

where the first input for xgb represents the feature set and the second is the parameter set.

We need to split the training data into two disjoint sets for the inner model ($\mathcal{C}_B$) and the GBDT model respectively. If we train them using the same data set, the GBDT model would mostly use the output of the inner model as the final prediction because the inner model is well trained for these data samples. In experiments we use half training data for inner model and the rest for GBDT.

6. EXPERIMENTS

6.1 Experimental Settings

We already described the data set in Section 3, now we explain the evaluation metrics and comparing algorithms.

We employ mean absolute error (MAE) and root mean square error (RMSE) as the main metrics to evaluate the rating prediction models, defined by the following:

$$MAE = \frac{\sum_{u,i} |r_{ui} - \hat{r}_{ui}|}{\#logs},\ RMSE = \sqrt{\frac{\sum_{u,i} (r_{ui} - \hat{r}_{ui})^2}{\#logs}} \tag{8}$$

Table 1: Experimental Results, with 80% Data for Training

Metrics	UserAvg	ItemAvg	PMF	BiasedMF	SVD++	CM-B	CM-S	CM-C
MAE	0.8157	0.7754	0.7577	0.7502	0.7363	0.6798	0.6728	**0.6690**
Improvement	17.99%	13.73%	11.71%	10.83%	9.15%	1.60%	0.57%	
RMSE	1.0429	0.9952	0.9707	0.9752	0.9580	0.8595	0.8530	**0.8457**
Improvement	18.90%	15.02%	12.88%	13.28%	11.72%	1.61%	0.86%	

We evaluate our conformity-based models as well as several state-of-the-art rating prediction models in the experiments. The models are listed as follows:

UserAvg, ItemAvg: Directly predict by user/item's average rating according to training logs.

PMF: Probabilistic matrix factorization proposed in [7].

BiasedMF, SVD++: Original and revised version in [3].

CM-B, CM-S, CM-C: Conformity models proposed in this paper, according to $\mathcal{C}_B, \mathcal{C}_S, \mathcal{C}_C$ in Section 5 respectively.

All dimensions for latent factors are set to 5. Parameters are set by cross validation. We use 80% of data for training set and the rest 20% for testing.

6.2 Results & Analysis

We show the experimental results in Table 1, which indicate the conformity models proposed in this paper out perform the state-of-the-art approaches that depend only on the rating matrix.

Conformity Strength. The parameter ω in the basic conformity model (CM-B) can be viewed as an indicator of conformity strength. $\omega = 0$ degenerates the model to the traditional matrix factorization model (BiasedMF), and $\omega = 1$ indicates users always follow the public opinion. By cross validation, we set ω to 0.9. The value is rather large and indicates strong conformity phenomenon in rating sites.

Conformity vs Group Size. By comparing results of CM-B and CM-S, we conclude the conformity strength does depend on the group size (number of raters for the item). By examining the parameters, we find that the conformity strength ranges over 0.4627 to 0.8868 for only 1 raters and infinite raters respectively.

Conformity vs Cohesion. Result of CM-C indicates the cohesion also contributes to the conformity-behavior. Due to the complexity of the decision trees, we do not depict them here. We notice that there are plenty of nodes in the decision trees use the normalized rating distribution (percentage) as the splitting criteria.

Effect of Training Ratio. We vary the training data ratio from 50% to 80% and show the results in Table 2. As we can notice, the performance of conformity model is rather robust to the training ratio. When training ratio drops from 80% to 50%, the performances of CM-B and CM-C only drop by less than 0.01 for both MAE and RMSE For CM-C, the performance drops slightly increases due to the learning requirement of GBRT (0.0194 and 0.0189 and for the two metrics). Note that the value is still better than traditional approaches. This is because conformity model captures user behaviors in general instead of personalized, thus suffers less from the cold-start problem comparing to traditional approaches.

Table 2: Experimental Results vs Training Ratio

Metric	Model	Training Ratio 50%	60%	70%	80%
MAE	SVD++	0.7650	0.7568	0.7650	0.7363
	CM-B	0.6845	0.6832	0.6812	0.6798
	CM-S	0.6806	0.6774	0.6749	0.6728
	CM-C	0.6883	0.6769	0.6741	0.6690
RMSE	SVD++	0.9784	0.9683	0.9829	0.9580
	CM-B	0.8640	0.8623	0.8586	0.8595
	CM-S	0.8606	0.8576	0.8551	0.8530
	CM-C	0.8645	0.8543	0.8564	0.8457

7. CONCLUSION & FUTURE WORK

In this paper, we model the conformity phenomenon in online rating sites to understand the user behaviors and to improve the rating prediction accuracy. Specifically, we capture key factors for conformity strength including group size, unanimity and cohesion. We further integrate the conformity model with matrix factorization. Analysis and experiments using large-scale real data show the existence of online conformity and prove that it improves the rating prediction accuracy. For future works, we may consider having personalized conformity strength for each user and analyzing what kinds of user groups are more susceptive to public opinions.

8. REFERENCES

[1] T. Chen and C. Guestrin. Xgboost: A scalable tree boosting system. *arXiv:1603.02754*, 2016.

[2] G. Guo, J. Zhang, and N. Yorke-Smith. Trustsvd: Collaborative filtering with both the explicit and implicit influence of user trust and of item ratings. In *AAAI*, pages 123–129, 2015.

[3] Y. Koren. Factorization meets the neighborhood: a multifaceted collaborative filtering model. In *SIGKDD*, pages 426–434. ACM, 2008.

[4] Y. Koren, R. Bell, and C. Volinsky. Matrix factorization techniques for recommender systems. *Computer*, (8):30–37, 2009.

[5] S. Krishnan, J. Patel, M. J. Franklin, and K. Goldberg. A methodology for learning, analyzing, and mitigating social influence bias in recommender systems. In *RecSys*, pages 137–144. ACM, 2014.

[6] B. Li, Q. Yang, and X. Xue. Can movies and books collaborate? cross-domain collaborative filtering for sparsity reduction. In *IJCAI*, volume 9, pages 2052–2057, 2009.

[7] R. Salakhutdinov and A. Mnih. Probabilistic matrix factorization. Citeseer, 2011.

[8] R. Sipos, A. Ghosh, and T. Joachims. Was this review helpful to you?: it depends! context and voting patterns in online content. In *WWW*, pages 337–348. ACM, 2014.

[9] J. W. Thibaut and H. H. Kelley. The social psychology of groups. 1959.

Modelling Contextual Information in Session-Aware Recommender Systems with Neural Networks

Bartłomiej Twardowski
Warsaw University of Technology
Institute of Computer Science
Nowowiejska 15/19, 00-665 Warsaw, Poland
B.Twardowski@ii.pw.edu.pl

ABSTRACT

Preparing recommendations for unknown users or such that correctly respond to the short-term needs of a particular user is one of the fundamental problems for e-commerce. Most of the common Recommender Systems assume that user identification must be explicit. In this paper a Session-Aware Recommender System approach is presented where no straightforward user information is required. The recommendation process is based only on user activity within a single session, defined as a sequence of events. This information is incorporated in the recommendation process by explicit context modeling with factorization methods and a novel approach with Recurrent Neural Network (RNN). Compared to the session modeling approach, RNN directly models the dependency of user observed sequential behavior throughout its recurrent structure. The evaluation discusses the results based on sessions from real-life system with ephemeral items (identified only by the set of their attributes) for the task of top-n best recommendations.

Keywords

recommender system; matrix factorization; recurrent neural network; session-aware recommendations

1. INTRODUCTION

The Session-Aware Recommender System is a type of a Context-Aware Recommender Systems (CARS) where additional information about the user session is incorporated in the prediction process. Such systems can understand user short-term goals and fit better to the changing users behaviour in time. Particularly, in this work, the user is not identified at all, only characterized by the last actions in the current session.

The problem of session-aware recommendations can be even more troublesome, when the recommended items are ephemeral i.e. the item life-cycle is too short or the availability is too dynamic to identify it only by unique id, e.g. news, online auctions. In such settings, the Content-Based filtering is a standard technique. However, neglecting the session information results in loosing lots of information. In this paper novel ways to cope with ephemeral items and to recommend them in the right session context are presented.

The attractiveness of session-aware recommendations for online businesses can be confirmed by the fact that identification of the user can be hard and the same account can be shared among others, e.g. family members. For common e-commerce more than half (57.06%) of all sessions are non-logged users.[1] Only 2.53% of all sessions converts to transaction. Most sessions are *window-shopping* ones, where users are only looking for the product availability, price, and information. The 20.98% of all page views are interactions with the search engine. Out of all sessions, 35.80% used the search engine to find the right offer. User interactions with the search engine is the rich source of their preferences. Yet, the traditional recommender systems do not take this into account directly.

2. RELATED WORK

In most of RS, the information about the time of user actions is omitted (e.g. most of the Collaborative-Filtering algorithms) or is used directly in computing the cost of the model, e.g. in a form of time dependent bias [4]. Different approach is taken in Context-Aware Recommender Systems, where time can be used as a contextual variable. Although, time should be discretized, e.g. to time of a day, day of the week, etc.. Another possibility is to represent time dependencies between actions as a new variables in CARS models, e.g. after viewing particular items, which item was bought/seen next[3].

In work[5] an approach for detecting a topic of the user's session is proposed. The topic is described by the set of item attributes, as in this work. For catching the user's goal (topic of the session) a factored Markov Decision Process is used. In order to train such a model, a strong assumption of attribute independence is being made. This results in efficient optimization of many independent models.

Usage of RNN for session based recommendations was recently proposed in [2]. The GRU units are used to predict the next item in the session. The network input is one-hot-encoded current clicked item id. The output is scoring for fixed number of items. This paper uses similar evaluation

[1]Presented statistics are based on Polish e-marketplace allegro.pl for 3228 M page views sample in January of 2016, where 310 M sessions was identified by HTTP cookie or mobile device hash.

RecSys '16, September 15-19, 2016, Boston , MA, USA
© 2016 ACM. ISBN 978-1-4503-4035-9/16/09... $15.00
DOI: http://dx.doi.org/10.1145/2959100.2959162

methodology, but only considering unseen items as valid recommendations.

3. USER SESSION DATA

User sessions in this work are defined as uninterrupted sequences of activity in the system. The session ends when the user is inactive for more than a predefined number of minutes [1]. This method of setting the session boundary allows to represent all user actions grouped in sessions: $S = \{s_1, \ldots, s_m\}$ where each session is represented as a set of events ordered in time: $s_m = \{e_m^{(1)}, \ldots, e_m^{(t)}\}$, where t is the time of the event occurrence in session m. In turn, each event is described by contextual information: $e_m^{(t)} \in C_1^E \times C_2^E \times \cdots \times C_k^E$, where number of attributes k depends on collected event $e_m^{(t)}$ type.

One of the event context information C_k^E is an association with item $I = \{i_1, \ldots, i_n\}$. Each item is described by a set of defined attributes $i_n \in C_1^I \times C_2^I \times \cdots \times C_p^I$, where the number of all the item attributes is p.

Item and Event Encoding

All methods presented in this work require items and events being represented by real-valued vectors. This is a well-known approach from Content-Base filtering, where every items data before being compared has to be vectorized first. There are two entities to encode items and events. For items, the encoding function $C_1^I \times C_2^I \times \cdots \times C_p^I \rightarrow \mathbf{x}_n$, $\mathbf{x}_n \in \mathbb{R}^{d_I}$ should exist, where d_I is the number of real-values in the encoded item representation. Similarly, the session event $C_1^E \times C_2^E \times \cdots \times C_k^E \rightarrow \mathbf{x}_e$, $\mathbf{x}_e \in \mathbb{R}^{d_E}$, where d_E is the dimension of the encoded event vector.

In this work a unified vectorization method for contextual information is assumed. If the context information is textual or can be treated as a bag-of-words (e.g. offer category path information) the data is one-hot encoded. To constrain the size of the output, the minimum term frequency and maximum vocabulary size are defined. Any categorical information are also one-hot encoded. Numeric attributes are scaled to $[0, 1]$. For events encoding, the encoded contextual information is concatenated with associated encoded item information.

4. SESSION-AWARE RECOMMENDATIONS

4.1 Session Modeling with Matrix Factorization

This method is a simplified version of Factorization Machines[7], where only interactions between variables of the session and the item are allowed for final estimation. The item is represented by the encoded, vectorized representation $\mathbf{x}_i$. The session vector $\mathbf{x_s}$ aggregates variables from all events within it. Due to the fact that some assumptions have to be made about how all events information should be encoded into single session vector this method is considered as an *explicit session modelling.* One solution, which is giving good results and is used in this work, is to aggregate all events data in a time decaying way $\mathbf{x}_s = \sum_{j=1}^{t} \frac{1}{1+t-j} \mathbf{x}_e^{(j)}$, where session vector size $d_S = d_E$ and t event sequence length. The final estimation is:

$$\hat{y}(\mathbf{x_s}, \mathbf{x_I}) = (\mathbf{x_s}\mathbf{Q})(\mathbf{x_I}\mathbf{P})^\intercal + \mathbf{x_s}\mathbf{b_p}^\intercal + \mathbf{x_I}\mathbf{b_q}^\intercal$$

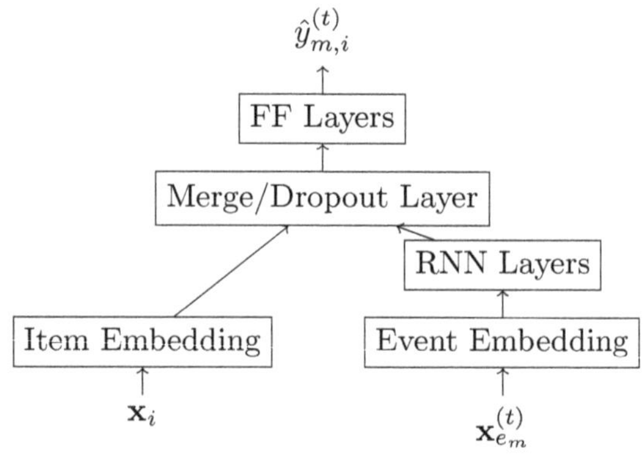

Figure 1: Neural Network Layers Architecture.

where $\mathbf{Q} \in \mathbb{R}^{d_S \times d}$ and $\mathbf{P} \in \mathbb{R}^{d_I \times d}$ are matrices with d-dimensional latent features for session and items variables respectively.

As a loss function the pairwise method is used in form of: Bayesian Personalized Ranking (BPR)[6], TOP-K as defined in work [2] and Weighted Approximated-Ranking Pairwise (WARP)[8] loss.

4.2 Session-Aware Recommendations with a Neural Network

The presented novel method assumes usage of two types of neural networks. Both, Recurrent Neural Network (RNN) and Feed Forward Neural Network (FFNN) are used to predict Top-N recommendations for the session. This combination is the key concept of handling event and item data represented only by their attributes. The RNN is used to capture data dependency between session events in time. It uses hidden state as the memory to handle variable length data. In this case, the sequence of events in session. The FFNN is used as a ranking score estimator. It uses the representation of session context returned by RNN and the new items data as an input. The simplified layer architecture of the network is presented in figure 1.

The input for the network is $\mathbf{x}_{e_m}^{(t)}$, the session event data for the time t and the item data to estimate $\mathbf{x}_i$. Before the input data is passed to next layers, the Embedding Layers map it to continuous, lower-dimensional space. The embedded events data is used in RNN Layers. The session events are passed sequentially. If the session ends, the RNN hidden state is reset for the new session. In RNN Layers different units can be used (Standard RNN, GRU or LSTM). The item data $\mathbf{x}_i$ do not have to be processed by RNN. Thus, after passing the embedding item data is gathered together with a RNN session representation in FFNN Layers. But before that, the dropout is applied as a regularization for the model. The FFNN Layers consists of multilayer perceptrons. It uses the non linear activation function to produce the output $\hat{y}_{m,i}^{(t)}$ - scoring for the current session m at time t of the item i.

In order to learn Top-N recommendation ranking, the pairwise approach for loss function is applied. For every time t the network is minimizing the loss in a form of BPR/TOP-K/WARP. Thus, for every Stochastic Gradient Descent up-

dataset	ALLEGRO	AVITO
items	24360	4374
sessions	20904	31826
events	535871	767550
searches	366874	110204
density %	0.028	0.464
s. len. mean	25.634	24.117
s. len. std	30.282	14.877

Table 1: Dataset statistics

date, a single event $\mathbf{x}_{e,t}$ is passed to calculate RNN Layers output, then multiple (i.e. in BPR/TOP-K method two) positive and negative item examples are passed to estimate $\hat{y}$ and calculate the loss.

5. EXPERIMENTS

5.1 Datasets

In evaluation, two real-life datasets are used: AVITO and ALLEGRO. In both, the session boundary is set by user inactivity for more than 30 minutes. Moreover, additional pre-filtering is made to constraint dataset size (computational purposes). Dataset statistics are shown in Table 1.

The ALLEGRO dataset is based on users' actions in Polish biggest e-marketplace[2]. In this dataset user actions (*search, view, watch/cart add/remove, buy, letter send*) from a single category (beauty products) is taken in a period of two weeks. Only sessions with more than 2 events are taken and events can only be connected with items with more than 10 clicks.

The second dataset, named AVITO, is created from data publicly available on Kaggle platform for context ad click prediction challenge[3]. Only events (*search, view, phone request*) and items from category 43 are used. Pre-filtering includes removing session without search and with less than 4 events. For items, a click cut-off threshold was set to 20.

For further processing, event and items in dataset is encoded. Bag-of-words minimal frequency is set to 10. This results in d_I=473/2710 and d_E=716/5523 and for AVITO/ALLEGRO datasets respectively.

5.2 Experiments Settings and Model Training

For the reference, two baseline methods are used. First, the naive one, always returns the top N most popular (POP) items in the whole dataset. The second method is Content-Based (CB) filtering, where the cosine similarity is being used. The result is a list ordered by the similarity value calculated between items which have positive interactions with the user in the session and those which have not been seen yet.

The matrix factorization (MF) is done with a latent feature dimension set to 100. The L2 regularization is used with rate 0.005 while training the model. The BPR and TOP-K loss functions are applied. Negative examples are sampled uniformly from all items. Two types of the event representations are checked. First, where only the associated item (I) data is encoded and treated as event data. Second, where the item as well as the event context information (IE) are

[2]http://www.allegro.pl/

[3]https://www.kaggle.com/c/avito-context-ad-clicks

	ALLEGRO		AVITO	
	REC@20	MRR@20	REC@20	MRR@20
NN-BPR-IE	**0.4131**±.0051	**0.1328**±.0023	0.1628±.0024	0.0476±.0009
MF-BPR-IE	0.3849±.0031	0.1150±.0003	0.1894±.0008	0.0404±.0001
NN-TOPK-IE	0.3367±.0057	0.0885±.0020	0.1985±.0031	0.0579±.0004
MF-TOPK-IE	0.2862±.0024	0.0773±.0017	**0.2699**±.0018	0.0658±.0005
NN-TOPK-I	0.2863±.0048	0.0709±.0025	0.2003±.0012	0.0579±.0004
MF-BPR-I	0.3080±.0013	0.0864±.0012	0.1883±.0015	0.0408±.0000
MF-TOPK-I	0.2353±.0025	0.0586±.0008	0.2691±.0001	**0.0660**±.0004
CB	0.1858	0.0354	0.1528	0.0243
POP	0.0499	0.0129	0.0193	0.0037

Table 2: Experiment results for Recall and Mean Reciprocal Rank for Top-20 recommendations. A row label describes used algorithm, loss function and contextual information (I - only items data, IE - items and events context). The mean values with 95% CI are given.

encoded and used. In both datasets, besides event type itself, the additional contextual information is delivered from search events. The MF model parameters are learned using adagrad optimization.

In the Neural Network session-aware recommendations the number of hyper-parameters is large: number of RNN/FFNN layers, size of every hidden layer, type of an activation function, dropout, loss function. It is infeasible to perform full hyper-parameters grid search due to computation time over both datasets. Thus, after the first few experiments - best solutions was chosen for the future investigation and precise parameter tuning.

For the RNN Layers - single layer of the Gated Recurrent Unit is used. The FFN Layers consists of MLP with single hidden layer, where for non-linearity *tanh* activation is applied. The first embedding layers are skipped. For both datasets adding embedding to lower dimension is giving worse results. The same is observed in [2]. Nevertheless, this layer may be necessary for bigger datasets (in the meaning of d_E and d_I) and will be subject of future investigations. The GRU hidden dimension is 200 and for MLP 400 (for both the values: 200, 400, 800 was checked). The dropout at level 0.2-0.3 gives the best results.

The network is trained using adagrad optimization with learning rate 0.05 and 128 examples in a single minibatch. The minibatch is created of parallel sessions. If one of the sessions ends, the hidden state of RNN is reset. From the training dataset 3% random sessions are taken as a hold-out set for detecting overfitting. As a loss function BPR and TOP-K, for K=1 was evaluated.

5.3 Results and Discussion

As an evaluation measures Recall@N (REC@N) and Mean Reciprocal Rank (MRR@N) are chosen. The REC@N is used as an indicator for user engagement and the MRR@N as a measure of how good is the ranking. The test dataset was created from 5% of all sessions with latest starting time. Then, the evaluation measures are calculated for the task of predicting the next event for every subsequent events in the test session. This results in 1592/1046 test sessions which generated 291966/121475 event sequences as test cases for AVITO/ALLEGRO dataset.

Evaluation results for REC@20 and MRR@20 are presented in Table 2. For datasets used and two methods proposed in this work (MF and NN), both outperform baseline

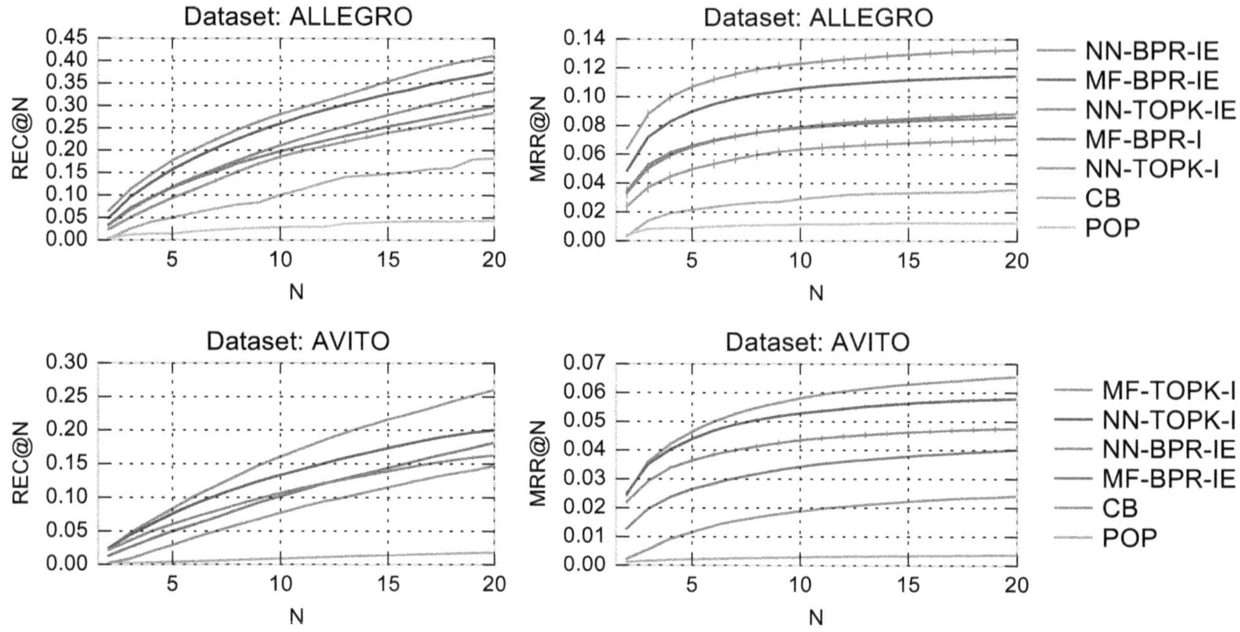

Figure 2: Results in Recall and MRR@Top-N Recommendations (figures share same legends on the right).

methods in the meaning of Recall and MRR. But the more interesting results are presented between the cases where only items data is used (I label suffix) and those where items and events contextual information is used (IE). In every case for the ALLEGRO dataset, where the additional information from event session was incorporated, both methods MF and NN gave better results. The situation is different for the AVITO dataset, where additional event context gives only a slightly better results for MF methods and for NN-TOPK are even lower. On ALLEGRO dataset, the NN significantly outperforms MF methods, while on AVITO, using the same NN configuration results in worst outcome. The difference can be explained by the available attributes of contextual information. The ALLEGRO dataset is rich in terms of items and search contextual information, while AVITO, besides having less items and more events, has less data. After encoding in the same way, both items and events from AVITO dataset have less real-value features than those for ALLEGRO dataset and the same entities. Furthermore, the hyper-parameters setting should be also revised for AVITO, as there is a big space for improvement as the MF-TOPK results present.

Figure 2 presents results of REC@N and MRR@N for N values up to 20. For the sake of readability, only the selected best methods and baselines are presented for each dataset.

6. CONCLUSIONS AND FUTURE WORK

In this paper two new methods for session-aware recommendations are proposed. Methods are presented in the difficult setting, where items are ephemeral (represented only by a set of attributes) and users are not identified between two separate sessions. First method uses matrix factorization technique and explicit session context modeling. The second, applies Recurrent Neural Network to automatic session context modeling. Both outperform significantly baseline approaches in task of top-N recommendations verified by measuring REC@N/MRR@N. However, the usage of RNN is considered more attractive and flexible when no session modeling assumptions is made.

In the future work, more research of using neural network in the field of recommender systems is planed. One research area will involve using RNN to model cross-session/long-term user goals. More experiments over different and bigger datasets are planed. Therefore, the problem of searching the best hyper-parameters and then effective training NN will be investigated.

7. REFERENCES

[1] D. Gayo-Avello. A survey on session detection methods in query logs and a proposal for future evaluation. *Information Sciences*, 179(12), 2009.

[2] B. Hidasi, A. Karatzoglou, L. Baltrunas, and D. Tikk. Session-based Recommendations with Recurrent Neural Networks. *International Conference on Learning Representations*, 2016.

[3] B. Hidasi and D. Tikk. General factorization framework for context-aware recommendations. *Data Mining and Knowledge Discovery*, 30, 2016.

[4] Y. Koren. Collaborative filtering with temporal dynamics. *Proceedings of the 15th ACM SIGKDD international conference on Knowledge discovery and data mining - KDD '09*, 2009.

[5] U. B. Maryam Tavakol. Factored MDPs for detecting topics of user sessions. *Proceedings of the 8th ACM Conference on Recommender systems*, 2014.

[6] S. Rendle, C. Freudenthaler, Z. Gantner, and L. Schmidt-thieme. BPR : Bayesian Personalized Ranking from Implicit Feedback. In *Proceedings of the Twenty-Fifth Conference on Uncertainty in Artificial Intelligence*, 2009.

[7] S. Rendle, Z. Gantner, C. Freudenthaler, and L. Schmidt-Thieme. Fast context-aware recommendations with factorization machines. In *Proceedings of the 34th international ACM SIGIR conference on Research and development in Information*, 2011.

[8] J. Weston, S. Bengio, and N. Usunier. WSABIE: Scaling up to large vocabulary image annotation. *IJCAI International Joint Conference on Artificial Intelligence*, 2011.

Getting the Timing Right: Leveraging Category Inter-purchase Times to Improve Recommender Systems

Denis Vuckovac
ETH Zurich
Weinbergstr. 56-58
8092 Zurich
dvuckovac@ethz.ch

Julia Wamsler
University of Zurich
Plattenstr. 14
8032 Zurich
julia.wamsler@business.uzh.ch

Alexander Ilic
University of St.Gallen
Dufourstr. 40a
9000 St.Gallen
alexander.ilic@unisg.ch

Martin Natter
University of Zurich
Plattenstr. 14
8032 Zurich
martin.natter@business.uzh.ch

ABSTRACT

In the marketing domain, models of grocery buying behavior consider purchase incidence as a key dimension. However, in recommender systems, timing is often subsumed under contextual information and has received little attention yet. For this reason, we analyze the relation between the timing of a recommendation and its acceptance across different product categories. Our study is based on a real-world deployment of an in-store recommendation system in the brick-and-mortar grocery industry. We base our analysis on transaction data of more than 100,000 unique users and more than four million product recommendations. Our findings suggest that the success of a recommendation significantly depends on the inter-purchase time within the respective category. Different sensitivities across product categories further stress the importance of timing and its interplay with category characteristics within the context of recommender systems. The insights gained in this study enable retailers to improve scheduling recommendations and target promotions more efficiently.

CCS Concepts

•**Information systems → Computational advertising;** *Data mining;* Data analytics; •**Applied computing → Online shopping;**

Keywords

inter-purchase times; category; retail; fast moving consumer goods

RecSys '16, September 15 - 19, 2016, Boston , MA, USA

ISBN 978-1-4503-4035-9/16/09...$15.00

DOI: http://dx.doi.org/10.1145/2959100.2959184

1. INTRODUCTION

Customer purchase decisions, both online and in-store, are to a great extent influenced by recommendations. They might be proactively inquired by customers seeking advice or provided by retailers leveraging their customers' past browsing or purchasing behaviors. In the latter scenario, a customer's interest in buying in a particular category at a particular time is not evident and needs to be inferred indirectly, a task often performed by automated recommender systems [2]. Consequently, recommender systems need to solve two questions in order to provide meaningful recommendations: First, whether or not to recommend a product and second, when to recommend it—thus, getting the timing right [12]. In contrast to common retailer promotions, personalized recommendations enable the promotion of specific products based on individual product and time preferences.

In this paper, the success of a recommendation—as indicated by the redemption of personalized in-store price-off promotions—is modeled as a function of category inter-purchase times. We find that inter-purchase times significantly influence the acceptance of recommendations with the effect depending on the respective product category. Particularly, in many fast moving categories, there is an optimal point in time for a product recommendation. Thus, incorporating category inter-purchase times can improve the accuracy of recommendations by up to 6 %[1]. Furthermore, we show that the optimal point in time for a recommendation does not coincide with average category inter-purchase times. Thus, recommendations can influence individual inter-purchase times. Our findings contribute to the efficiency of personalized promotions and their successful implementation within recommendation schedules.

2. RELATED WORK

Traditionally, research on recommender systems has focused on developing distinct approaches for recommending products or services to users. For this reason, content-based [10], collaborative-filtering [8] and hybrid approaches

[1]As measured by the increase of correctly classified redemptions.

[4] have been advanced, incorporating information of the current system user, of similar peers or a combination of both. Yet, independently of the underlying approach, recommender systems have traditionally aimed at answering what to recommend to whom [12]. More recently, research has begun to further leverage context as a multidimensional feature. Such context-aware recommender systems incorporate all kinds of contextual information, depending on the dimension of the respective problem [1]. When a recommender system is used in a commercial context, it should ideally benefit both customers and retailers. While the former improve or facilitate their decision making [8], the latter can improve targeting and exploit cross- and up-selling opportunities [12]. Grocery purchase decisions are usually modeled as consisting of three dimensions, purchase incidence, brand choice and purchase quantity [7, 3]. Hence, customer purchases simultaneously cover the questions when to buy in a certain product category, which brand to buy and how much to buy. First, purchase volumes are assumed to be driven by household size, inventory levels, consumption rates as well as price promotions [7, 3]. The second dimension, brand choice, coincides with the main purpose of recommender systems and thus has been extensively covered in the respective literature [8]. The decision whether or not to buy a certain brand is driven by the entire product attributes including price. Finally, the last dimension describes the timing of a purchase which depends on consumption rates, inventory levels and in-store or price promotions [7, 3]. From a retailer perspective, recommendations are personalized promotions that allow for a precise targeting of single customers and can thus be used in order to influence any of the three dimensions of the customer purchase decision. Retailers can try to influence the timing of a purchase by providing customers with recommendations. The aspired purchase acceleration increases sales if customers do not only engage in stockpiling but adapt their consumption levels accordingly [9]. This is eventually dependent on the underlying product category and its characteristics. Moreover, well-timed promotional recommendations might encourage store switching. Customers would be expected to relocate purchases from competitors' stores to the focus retailer [11]. Thus, the timing of recommendations should receive a greater amount of attention in research on recommender systems, especially in industries where products are regularly re-bought and categories are characterized by distinct purchasing cycles.

3. METHOD AND DATA

To analyze the influence of category-specific inter-purchase times on the success of recommendations, an empirical study of transaction and recommendation data has been conducted at a brick-and-mortar grocery retailer. The results of the empirical analysis address the following questions: (1) Is there a category-specific optimal point in time for a product recommendation? (2) Can recommendations be used to influence individual inter-purchase times? (3) Does incorporating inter-purchase times have a positive effect on the redemption of a recommendation?
The studied in-store recommendation system provides customers with personalized product recommendations in the form of tailored price promotions. Customers can receive these personalized recommendations when they enter the store by scanning their loyalty card at special in-store kiosk terminals. The terminal prints a list of tailored price promotions, in the form of individual discounts on selected products, for every customer. Price promotions are chosen from a specific set of currently active campaigns, which retailers and manufacturers can define to target specific consumers. The specific underlying algorithm is subject to our partner's secrecy. Campaigns are assigned using a dynamic scoring model estimating redemption probabilities based on a similiarty measure between a user's historic shopping baskets, the promoted products and an individual price-off derived from user heterogeneity in price sensitivity. Inter-purchase times are not considered in the scoring algorithm. Campaigns are then assigned to users maximizing total expected revenue constrained to specific campaign goal fulfillment criteria and filters. At the checkout promotions are automatically redeemed when the customer's loyalty card is scanned. As the loyalty program is completely anonymous, no demographics are available. In the following, we analyze transaction data that was collected in 2015 over a period of two months in more than 100 stores in a big European city. Our sample includes more than 100,000 unique users as well as more than four million product recommendations, out of which we analyze more than 500,000. The categorization is provided by a large market research organization. We limit our analysis to the top ten most recommended campaigns in our sample and pick four fast-moving categories which are regularly purchased—namely bread, cola, milk and curd. These are used for an examination of our proposed research questions. This allows us to identify and illustrate different patterns in the adoption and timing of recommendations.

3.1 Category Redemption Rates and Inter-purchase Times

To quantify the impact of inter-purchase times on category level redemptions, we conduct a linear regression of category redemption rates (abbreviated as RR) on the predictor "time since the last category purchase" (subsequently abbreviated as $TSLP$). In order to account for a potentially nonlinear relationship, we add a quadratic and cubic term of our $TSLP$ variable to the regression. We hypothesize that for most categories c there is an optimal point in time for a recommendation that will correspond to the average category inter-purchase time. We expect recommendations made much earlier (low $TSLP$) to be penalized as customers inventory will not be low enough to induce another category purchase. Furthermore, we also expect lower redemption rates for customers that have not made purchases in the respective category for a long time (high $TSLP$). These could either have purchased at a competitor's store or become uninterested in the category itself.

$$RR_c(TSLP) = k_{c,0} + k_{c,1} \cdot TSLP + k_{c,2} \cdot TSLP^2 + k_{c,3} \cdot TSLP^3 \quad (1)$$

Table 1 summarizes the results of the regression described in equation 1 for our four selected categories, while Figure 1 illustrates the corresponding fitted redemption rates. Apart from the category cola, all categories exhibit a characteristic inverse u-shape, indicating the existence of an optimal point in time for a category recommendation. For milk and curd, average inter-purchase times without promotion are higher than the optimal points in time for a recommendation. Thus, in these categories recommendations might trigger purchase acceleration. In the case of the category

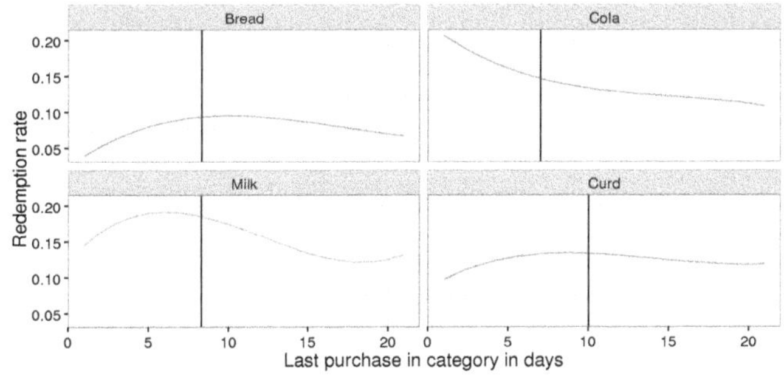

Figure 1: Comparing fitted redemption rates to avg. category inter-purchase times without promotions

cola, this effect might even be so strong that redemptions are highest right after a category purchase.

Table 1: Summary of regression results

	Dependent variable:			
	RR			
	Bread	Cola	Milk	Curd
TSLP	0.016***	−0.017***	0.025***	0.013***
	(0.005)	(0.005)	(0.005)	(0.004)
$TSLP^2$	−0.001**	0.001*	−0.003***	−0.001**
	(0.001)	(0.001)	(0.001)	(0.0004)
$TSLP^3$	0.00002	−0.00002	0.0001***	0.00003*
	(0.00002)	(0.00002)	(0.00002)	(0.00001)
Constant	0.024*	0.223***	0.123***	0.085***
	(0.013)	(0.014)	(0.014)	(0.010)
R^2	0.625	0.843	0.823	0.543
Adjusted R^2	0.559	0.816	0.792	0.462
F Statistic	9.445***	30.540***	26.386***	6.725***
Note:				*p<0.1; **p<0.05; ***p<0.01

3.2 Changes in Individual Inter-purchase Times

In order to determine whether recommendations have an influence on individual category inter-purchase times, we split individual purchases, distinguishing category purchases that are affected by promotions from those that are not. In a first scenario, purchases are only affected by promotions when a promotion is redeemed during that particular purchase. In a second case, we also account for stockpiling, by including the purchase directly following a purchase on promotion into the promotion sample. In this way, we determine average inter-purchase times with and without promotional redemptions, considering only those customers for whom both inter-purchase times can be calculated.[2] Using two-sided Kolmogorov-Smirnov tests (p<0.05), we analyze the average inter-purchase times in both scenarios. In the first case, we find significant differences in average inter-purchase times for all categories. In the second scenario, accounting for stockpiling, we find significant differences in average inter-purchase times for all categories except for curd, where customers might engage in stockpiling when redeeming a promotion.

[2]It should further be noted that purchase volumes are not accounted for as we only focus on purchase incidence.

3.3 Improving Redemption Classification

In order to test the validity of our findings we randomly split our data in an estimation and validation sample (2:1) and then train two different logistic regressions to predict coupon redemptions. First, the standard model only uses the scoring values ($SCORE$) provided by our research partner as a predictor, also accounting for the magnitude of the individual price discount. Second, the extended model additionally includes a variable that indicates the deviation of the $TSLP$ variable from the optimal recommendation time, derived in our previous regression model. We allow the coefficient of this feature to vary depending on whether the recommendation was provided too early (d_{early}) or too late (d_{late}). We analyze whether the incorporation of the optimal recommendation time leads to an improvement in the prediction of coupon redemptions. The standard model, implemented by our research partner, will serve as a baseline.

Table 2: Summary of classification estimation and validation results

	Dependent variable:			
	Redemption			
	Milk		Cola	
	Standard	Extended	Standard	Extended
SCORE	1.440***	1.344***	2.672***	2.476***
	(0.045)	(0.045)	(0.207)	(0.207)
d_{early}		−0.040***		
		(0.011)		
d_{late}		−0.014***		−0.014***
		(0.001)		(0.001)
Constant	−2.116***	−1.825***	−2.401***	−1.953***
	(0.019)	(0.026)	(0.026)	(0.030)
Observations	30,881	30,881	33,032	33,032
LL	−11,770	−11,559	−10,762	−10,471
AIC	23,545	23,126	21,529	20,949
Recall	0.123	0.141	0.035	0.061
		(+14.6 %)		(+74 %)
Precision	0.524	0.540	0.339	0.345
		(+3.1 %)		(+1.8 %)
Prevalence	0.136	0.136	0.090	0.090
Balanced Accuracy	0.553	0.561	0.514	0.524
Note:				*p<0.1; **p<0.05; ***p<0.01

We report the quality of our models on the hidden evaluation set for the two categories with the best model fit in our previous regression analysis: milk and cola. Table 1 summarizes the results of our classification model which will further be discussed with respect to the classification metrics precision and recall.[3] The standard model provides similar results for milk as obtained in previous studies within the retailing industry regarding the classification metrics [6]. The extended model, which incorporates the distance to the optimal recommendation time, improves precision by 3.1 % and recall by 14.6 % compared to the standard model. For the category cola, we can increase recall by 74 %, however, precision can only be marginally increased by 1.8 %. We believe that our extended model can only marginally improve the correct classification in the second category due to the monotonous relationship between $TSLP$ and overall redemption rates as indicated in Figure 1 and Table 1. Furthermore, we get similar precision improvements for the remaining two categories (bread 6.6 % and curd 2.4 %).

4. CONCLUSION AND FUTURE WORK

Purchase incidence is a key pillar of every customer choice decision [7, 3]. Yet, so far it has only received marginal attention in the context of recommender systems. However, as commercial recommendations aim at influencing customer choices [2], purchase incidence should be incorporated when a recommendation is made. For this reason, we have analyzed customer data from an in-store recommendation system at a brick-and-mortar grocery retailer that provides customers with tailored price promotions. Our findings support the view that recommender systems should not only focus on the product or service to recommend but also on the timing of the recommendation [12]. Regarding the first research question we find that in many fast moving categories, there exists an optimal point in time for a recommendation which maximizes its acceptance among customers. In particular, we show that considering this optimum and category-specific individual inter-purchase times, has a positive effect on the success of recommendations, increasing precision by up to 6 %. Thus, answering the third research question, incorporating this additional information improves recommender systems. Moreover, we find that the optimal point in time for a recommendation precedes the average category inter-purchase time for most categories, indicating accelerated category purchases. Finally, regarding the second research question, we find that recommendations can influence individual inter-purchase times.

Altogether, the findings we present in this paper emphasize the importance of incorporating category-specific inter-purchase times when making product recommendations. Yet, the data we have used for our analyses is limited to only four categories and two months. It would be worthwhile to analyze a larger number of categories and to extend the observation period in order to capture seasonality and model dynamic inter-purchase times. Furthermore, as we do not use scanner data but transaction data of a single retailer, we cannot directly account for category purchases at competitors' stores and for inventory building. However, in further analyses deviations from predicted parametric inter-purchase times could help to indicate consumers' shopping at other retailers [5]. This individual risk could be modeled using identifiers based on past purchases and category characteristics. Additionally, it should be noted that in our particular case, recommendations are combined with individual price discounts. Therefore, an analysis of the profitability a recommendation should further consider customers purchase decisions in the absence of a discount. Finally, these opportunities for further research will help to improve the timing of recommendations and design recommender systems that better address the needs of individual customers while leveraging category-specific inter-purchase times.

[3]Precision: Number of instances in which coupon redemption was correctly predicted divided by all instances in which coupon redemption was predicted.
Recall: Number of instances in which coupon redemption was correctly predicted divided by all observed redemptions.

5. ACKNOWLEDGMENTS

We want to thank our research partner, who decided to remain anonymous, for providing us with the data sample.

6. REFERENCES

[1] G. Adomavicius, R. Sankaranarayanan, , S. Sen, and A. Tuzhilin. Incorporating Contextual Information in Recommender Systems Using a Multidimensional Approach. *ACM Transactions on Information Systems*, 23(1):103–145, 2005.

[2] A. V. Bodapati. Recommendation Systems With Purchase Data. *Journal of Marketing Research (JMR)*, 45(1):77–93, 2008.

[3] R. E. Bucklin, S. Gupta, and S. Siddarth. Determining Segmentation in Sales Response across Consumer Purchase Behaviors. *Journal of Marketing Research*, 35(2):189, 1998.

[4] R. Burke. Hybrid Recommender Systems: Survey and Experiments. *User Modeling and UserAdapted Interaction*, 12(4):331–370, 2002.

[5] Y. X. Chen and J. H. Steckel. Modeling Credit Card Share of Wallet: Solving the Incomplete Information Problem. *Journal of Marketing Research*, 49(5):655–669, 2012.

[6] A. Gunawardana and G. Shani. A Survey of Accuracy Evaluation Metrics of Recommendation Tasks. *The Journal of Machine Learning Research*, 10:2935–2962, 2009.

[7] S. Gupta. Impact of Sales Promotions on When, What, and How Much to Buy. *Journal of Marketing Research*, 25(4):342–355, 1988.

[8] J. L. Herlocker, J. A. Konstan, L. G. Terveen, and J. T. Riedl. Evaluating Collaborative Filtering Recommender Systems. *ACM Transactions on Information Systems (TOIS)*, 22(1):5–53, 2004.

[9] S. A. Neslin, C. Henderson, and J. Quelch. Consumer promotions and the acceleration of product purchases. *Marketing Science*, 4(2):147–165, 1985.

[10] R. J. Mooney and L. Roy, R. J. M. Roy, and L. Content-based Book Recommendation Using Learning for Text Categorization. *Proceedings of the Fifth ACM Conference on Digital Libraries*, pages 195–240, 2000.

[11] R. P. L. V. Kumar. Measuring the effect of retail store promotions on brand and store substitution. *Journal of Marketing Research*, 25(2):178–185, 1988.

[12] J. Wang and Y. Zhang. Opportunity Models for E-commerce Recommendation: Right Product , Right Time. *Proc. of the 36th international ACM SIGIR conference on Research and development in information retrieval (SIGIR)*, pages 303–312, 2013.

MAPS: A Multi Aspect Personalized POI Recommender System

Ramesh Baral
School of Computing and Information Sciences
Florida International University, Miami FL, USA
Email: rbara012@fiu.edu

Tao Li
School of Computing and Information Sciences
Florida International University, Miami FL, USA
Email: taoli@cs.fiu.edu

ABSTRACT

The evolution of the World Wide Web (WWW) and the smart-phone technologies have played a key role in the revolution of our daily life. The location-based social networks (LBSN) have emerged and facilitated the users to share the check-in information and multimedia contents. The Point of Interest (POI) recommendation system uses the check-in information to predict the most potential check-in locations. The different aspects of the check-in information, for instance, the *geographical distance*, the *category*, and the *temporal popularity* of a POI; and the *temporal check-in trends*, and the *social* (friendship) information of a user play a crucial role in an efficient recommendation.

In this paper, we propose a fused recommendation model termed **MAPS** (**M**ulti **A**spect Personalized **P**OI Recommender **S**ystem) which will be the first in our knowledge to fuse the categorical, the temporal, the social and the spatial aspects in a single model. The major contribution of this paper are: (i) it realizes the problem as a graph of location nodes with constraints on the category and the distance aspects (i.e. the edge between two locations is constrained by a threshold distance and the category of the locations), (ii) it proposes a multi-aspect fused POI recommendation model, and (iii) it extensively evaluates the model with two real-world data sets.

Keywords

POI Recommendation, Social network analysis

1. INTRODUCTION

The LBSNs, such as, the Facebook[1], the Foursquare[2], the Gowalla[3], and so forth have facilitated the users to share the check-in information of the places of interest. Such check-in information has been the subject of interest to predict the POIs that are most likely to be visited in the future. Albeit, the generic recommendation concept has been used for POI domain (for instance, the Collaborative Filtering (CF) [5], the Content Based Filtering [16], and the Hybrid approaches [13]), its special aspects have motivated the community towards more sophisticated approaches for better results.

The frequency of check-ins varies across different users and places, resulting in the *sparsity* of the *user-location* frequency matrix in comparison to the *user-item* rating matrix in the generic systems. The check-in preference to a near place introduces the *spatial aspect* (the distance to a POI). Though the *social aspect* encourages to incorporate the social tie (*for instance, friendship*), it costs the challenge from the unreliability of check-in information diffusion, as only $\sim$ 96% of people share $<$ 10% of the commonly visited places and $\sim$ 87% of people share nothing at all [14]. The *temporal aspect* depicts the temporal check-in pattern. For instance, the popularity of the *bars* is in the evenings and the nights. Many other relevant factors, such as, (i) the utility of a POI, regardless of the distance, cost, (ii) the popularity of the POI (due to social or other impact), and (iii) the dynamic mobility of a user (trend to visit new places) exist. Although the problem is well explored [1, 4, 11, 15, 17, 18], the incorporation of all the major aspects (*the social, the spatial, the temporal, and the categorical*) is barely explored.

1 www.facebook.com 2 www.foursquare.com 3 www.gowalla.com

RecSys '16, September 15-19, 2016, Boston , MA, USA

© 2016 ACM. ISBN 978-1-4503-4035-9/16/09...$15.00

DOI: http://dx.doi.org/10.1145/2959100.2959187

2. RELATED RESEARCH

2.1 Simple similarity based approaches

Yuan et. al [17] used the Tobler's First Law of Geography [10], (*"everything is related to everything else, but near things are more related than the distant things"*) and proposed a model with the spatial and the temporal aspect. The similarity between any two users was computed using the cosine similarity of their check-in profiles. The recommendation score for a *user-location* pair was computed as the aggregate of visits count on that location across all the users. The temporal similarity was incorporated by assuming the similarity of check-ins that have the same location and the check-in time. The *willingness* of a check-in was claimed to have an inverse relation to the distance. The social, and the categorical aspects were not well defined.

Ye et. al. [15] fused the social and the spatial aspects in their model. Though the *willingness* factor and the weighted cosine similarity measure was used to compare the user profiles for the recommendation, they didn't incorporate the categorical, and the temporal aspects.

2.2 Graphical approaches

Jin et. al [4] used the personalized PageRank [3] to realize the problem as a graph with the users as the nodes, and the following/followers relation as the directed edges. The rank of a user with respect to the location and a time range was defined using the personalized PageRank [3]. The topic sensitive factor for the (*user, location (p), time* (t_1, t_2)) tuple was taken as the ratio of the number of check-ins for the tuple to the number of check-ins for the (*location (p),time* (t_1, t_2)) tuple over all the users. Similarly, the rank of a location within a time interval was defined. This model also ignored the geographical, categorical and the social aspects. Wang et. al. [11] had the users and the locations as the graph nodes, the *user-user* friendship edges, and the *user-location* check-in edges. The friendship similarity was realized by starting from the target user and by ranking all the users (*that form user-user link*). This was followed by the ranking of all the places visited by those users. The places with the highest rank and within a given threshold distance from the past visits were recommended to the user. Their model also ignored the categorical aspect.

3. METHODOLOGY

The PageRank [8] approach used the number and the quality of the links to a web page to estimate its importance. It was extended to the Topic-Sensitive PageRank [3] by introducing some bias to the PageRank vector. It incorporated the set of influential or representative (*or additional context relevant attributes*) topics to address the importance of particular topics. For a given query, it identified the most closely associated/contextual topics and such relevant topic-sensitive (biased) vectors were used to rank the documents satisfying the query. The convergence of PageRank is assured only if the graph is strongly connected and aperiodic [7]. This becomes true if we add the damping constant $(1 - \alpha)$ to the rank propagation which improves the quality of PageRank not only by limiting the effect of the rank sinks [2], but also by assuring the convergence to a unique rank vector [3].

The **MAPS** is based on the Topic-Sensitive PageRank, where the *representative topics* are the spatial and the categorical aspects of the LBSN. The rank of a location (l) in the context of a user (u) and the time (t) is influenced by the check-in history of the user (u) at the time (t). For instance, if a user's check-in history has frequent check-ins in Starbucks coffee shop at 2 pm, then it is more likely that she will visit a coffee shop at that time in future. This temporal aspect should be taken care while recommending some coffee (or relevant category) shops to her. If that coffee shop is inaccessible, the user might not be surprised if a nearby cafe is recommended. Such a dual affinity of the time and the location category has motivated the MAPS to incorporate the categorical and temporal bias in the POI rankings.

Given two candidate POIs, suggesting the near one is more relevant [10]. If the check-in history of a user depicts that the check-ins were made within some distance of other check-ins, then introducing the distance constraint might give better recommendation. MAPS uses such check-in trends to incorporate the spatial bias in the location ranking problem.

In **MAPS**, every location is termed as a node of a graph and the bag of *user, time* tuple is considered as an attribute of the location node. The *location-location* edges exist if they have the same category or are located within some threshold distance. It uses the categorical and the spatial bias in its Topic-Sensitive PageRank model. The terms used in this paper are defined in Table -1. The categorical sensitive PageRank for MAPS is defined as:

$$\Pi^c_{t_1,t_2}(l) = \alpha * \beta_{t_1,t_2}(l) + (1-\alpha) * \sum_{(l'.cat=l.cat)} \Pi^c_{t_1,t_2}(l') \quad (1)$$

where $\beta_{t_1,t_2}(l)$ is the categoric sensitive factor, defined as:

$$\beta_{t_1,t_2}(l) = \tau_1 * \frac{\sum_{u\in U} | V_{u,t_1,t_2}(l) |}{\sum_{u\in U, l.cat=l'.cat} | V_{u,t_1,t_2}(l') |} + \tau_2 * \frac{\sum_{u\in U, l.cat=l'.cat} | V_{u,t_1,t_2}(l') |}{\sum_{p\in L, u\in U} | V_{u,t_1,t_2}(p) |} \quad (2)$$

where τ_1, and τ_2 are constant tuning factors. The relation (1) is somewhat similar to LBSNRank [4] but the equation is specific to our approach.

Terms	Definition
$\Pi^{\mathbf{a}}_{t_1,t_2}(l)$	rank of location l in the time range t_1, t_2 using the aspect **a**
$\beta_{t_1,t_2}(l)$	categoric sensitive factor of location l in the time range t_1, t_2
$\theta_{t_1,t_2}(l)$	distance sensitive factor of location l in the time range t_1, t_2
$P(u, l, t_1, t_2)$	likelihood of checkin by user u to location l in the time range t_1, t_2
$V_{u,t_1,t_2}(l)$	visits by the user u to the location l, within the time interval t_1, t_2
$dist(l_1, l_2)$	distance between locations l_1 and l_2
U	the users in the dataset
L	the locations in the dataset
$l.cat$	category of the location l
ϵ	the threshold distance
α	the damping factor

Table 1: Terms used in the paper

Similarly, the distance sensitive rank of a location is defined using the following relation:

$$\Pi^d_{t_1,t_2}(l) = \alpha * \theta_{t_1,t_2}(l) + (1-\alpha) * \sum_{(l',l)\in E} \Pi^d_{t_1,t_2}(l') \quad (3)$$

where $\theta_{t_1,t_2}(l)$ is the distance sensitive factor, defined as:

$$\theta_{t_1,t_2}(l) = \gamma_1 * \frac{\sum_{u\in U} | V_{u,t_1,t_2}(l) |}{\sum_{u\in U, dist(l,l')\leq\epsilon} | V_{u,t_1,t_2}(l') |} + \gamma_2 * \frac{\sum_{u\in U, dist(l,l')\leq\epsilon} | V_{u,t_1,t_2}(l') |}{\sum_{p\in L, u\in U} | V_{u,t_1,t_2}(p) |} \quad (4)$$

where γ_1, and γ_2 are constant tuning factors. The unified rank is the fusion of the two ranks and is defined as:

$$\Pi_{t_1,t_2}(l) = \xi_1 * \Pi^c_{t_1,t_2}(l) + \xi_2 * \Pi^d_{t_1,t_2}(l) \quad (5)$$

where ξ_1, ξ_2 are tuning parameters for the two aspects. The likelihood of the check-in for the user i at the location l within the time frame t_1,t_2 is defined as:

$$P(u,l,t_1,t_2) = \Pi_{t_1,t_2}(l) * (\psi_d * \sum_{\substack{l' \in L,\\ dist(l,l') \leq \epsilon}} | V_{u,t_1,t_2}(l') |) + \psi_c * \sum_{\substack{l' \in L,\\ l.cat = l'.cat}} | V_{u,t_1,t_2}(l') |) + \psi_s * \sum_{(u',u) \in friend} | V_{u',t_1,t_2}(l) |) \quad (6)$$

The terms ψ_d, ψ_c, and ψ_s are defined using TF-IDF [9, 12] for each user. For a user u,

$$\psi_d = \frac{n_d}{n}.log(1 + \frac{N}{N_d}) \quad (7)$$

where n_d is the number of visits by the user u that are within the threshold distance ϵ, n is the total visits count by u, N is the number of POIs, and N_d is the number of POIs that are within the threshold distance ϵ from the user's check-in history. For the categorial factor, we use the relation:

$$\psi_c = \frac{n_c}{n}.log(1 + \frac{N}{N_c}) \quad (8)$$

where n_c is the number of visits by the user u to the category c, and N_c is the number of POIs with the category c. Similarly,

$$\psi_s = \frac{n_s}{n}.log(1 + \frac{N}{N_s}) \quad (9)$$

, where n_s is the number of visits by the user u in common to her friends, and N_s is the number of visits in common to the friends for all the users $u \in U$.

Based on the aspects we considered, we have analyzed the performance of three different models, the categorical link based model (CLM) (defined in Eqn. (1) and (2)), the spatial link based model (SLM) (defined in Eqn. (3) and (4)), and the fused model MAPS (defined in Eqn. (5)).

4. EVALUATION

4.1 DataSet

We used the Weeplaces and the Gowalla dataset [6], which was collected from the popular LBSNs Gowalla and the Weeplaces. The Weeplaces dataset has 7,658,368 check-ins from 15,799 users over 971,309 different locations. The Gowalla dataset has 36,001,959 check-ins from 319,063 users over 2,844,076 locations. These datasets were well defined and had the attributes relevant to the context of the problem, such as, (i) the location category, (ii) the geospatial co-ordinates, (iii) the friendship information, and (iv) the check-in time. After avoiding incomplete records, the 5 most checked-in categories (and their check-in count) were: (i) Home/Work/Other: Corporate/Office (437,824), (ii) Food: Coffee Shop (267,589), (iii) Nightlife:Bar (248,565), (iv) Shop: Food& Drink:Grocery/Supermarket (161,016), and (v) Travel: Train Station (152,114) for Weeplaces, and (i) Corporate Office (1,750,707), (ii) Coffee Shop (1,063,961), (iii) Mall (958,285), (iv) Grocery (884,557), and (iv) Gas & Automotive (863,199) for the Gowalla dataset. The *work* or *home*-related category (Home/Work/ Other:Corporate/Office) was popular from 6 am to 6 pm, with the highest check-ins (42,019) made at 1 pm. Similarly, the **bars** had highest of 21,806 check-ins at 2 am and the lowest check-ins (15,209) at 5 am. Most of the check-ins were at 12 pm - 6 pm and were either in **Home** or **Work** related categories. The Figure -1 illustrates the inverse relation of the distance to the check-in frequency. It was obtained by plotting the distance between the chronologically sorted consecutive check-ins of each user and the likelihood of the users' check-in in that distance (for ease, the distance was rounded to four decimals). The check-ins centralized within some distance (the dense patches within 0.5 km) illustrate the willingness to near places.

Models	Precision	Recall	F-Score
Weeplaces Dataset			
Ye et. al [15]	0.02417	0.00095	0.00183
LBSNRank [4]	0.08496	0.00063	0.00125
Wang et. al [11]	0.01818	0.00052	0.00101
CLM	0.00428	0.00024	0.00045
SLM	0.09085	0.00799	0.01468
MAPS	0.29769	0.01039	**0.02008***
Gowalla Dataset			
Ye et. al [15]	0.03000	0.00120	0.00230
LBSNRank [4]	0.40900	0.00300	0.00600
Wang et. al [11]	0.10600	0.00200	0.00392
CLM	0.00633	0.00154	0.00247
SLM	0.25350	0.00973	0.01874
MAPS	0.35400	0.03100	**0.05700***

Table 2: Average Performance of MAPS in Weeplaces and Gowalla dataset

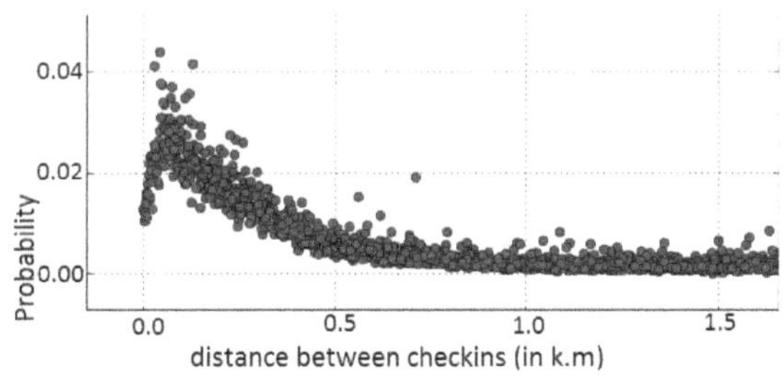

Figure 1: Impact of distance to check-in trend in Weeplaces dataset (*similar trend of Gowalla dataset is not shown due to space constraint*)

4.2 Results

A 5 -fold cross validation with top N (5, 10, 15 and 20) recommendation scores was used for the precision (P), the recall (R) and the F-score (2*P*R/(P+R)) metrics.

We used $\alpha = 0.85$ and the convergence was detected when the rank scores of the nodes were not changing anymore. For each model, the tuning parameters were selected from the random trials conducted with three set of parameters ((0.25:0.75), (0.5:0.5), and (0.75:0.25)). The categoric model performed best when $\tau_1 = 0.75$ and $\tau_2 = 0.25$, and for distance model it was when $\gamma_1 = 0.75$ and $\gamma_2 = 0.25$. Similarly,

Models	Precision@N	Recall@N
Ye et. al [15]	@5= 0.0303 @10= 0.0230 @15= 0.0191	@5= 0.0008 @10= 0.0009 @15= 0.0011
LBSNRank [4]	@5= 0.0853 @10= 0.0848 @15= 0.4090	@5= 0.0006 @10= 0.0006 @15= 0.0030
Wang et. al [11]	@5= 0.0449 @10= 0.0414 @15= 0.1060	@5= 0.0014 @10= 0.0020 @15= 0.0022
MAPS	@5= **0.2440** @10= **0.3050** @15= **0.3360**	@5= **0.0045** @10= **0.0092** @15= **0.0310**

Table 3: Precision@N, Recall@N of MAPS against other studies

among the three set of parameters the unified model performed best with the categorical aspect weight of 0.25. The comparative performance of different models is illustrated in Table -2. The observed difference was statistically significant at 95% confidence level. The Table -3 lists the average metrics across the top 5, 10, and 15 recommendation scores.

5. CONCLUSION AND FUTURE WORK

We analyzed the check-in data based on (a) the categorical, (b) the social, (c) the spatial, and (d) the temporal aspects. This multi-aspect recommendation model with reasonable performance was a significant contribution to the relevant area. Our next task is to analyze the same model against several other contexts, datasets and problem domains.

Acknowledgements

The work was supported in part by the National Science Foundation under grants CNS-1126619, IIS-1213026, and CNS-1461926, the U.S. Department of Homeland Securitys VACCINE Center under Award Number 2009-ST-061-CI0001, and a gift award from Huawei Technologies Co. Ltd.

6. REFERENCES

[1] R. Baral, D. Wang, T. Li, and S. C. Chen. Geotecs: Exploiting geographical, temporal, categorical and social aspects for personalized poi recommendation. In *Information Reuse & Integration, 2016. IRI'16. IEEE International Conference on*, page In Press. IEEE, 2016.

[2] S. Brin, R. Motwani, L. Page, and T. Winograd. What can you do with a web in your pocket? *IEEE Data Eng. Bull.*, 21(2):37–47, 1998.

[3] T. H. Haveliwala. Topic-sensitive pagerank. In *Proceedings of the 11th international conference on World Wide Web*, pages 517–526. ACM, 2002.

[4] Z. Jin, D. Shi, Q. Wu, H. Yan, and H. Fan. Lbsnrank: personalized pagerank on location-based social networks. In *Proceedings of the 2012 ACM Conference on Ubiquitous Computing*, pages 980–987. ACM, 2012.

[5] J. J. Levandoski, M. Sarwat, A. Eldawy, and M. F. Mokbel. Lars: A location-aware recommender system. In *Data Engineering (ICDE), 2012 IEEE 28th International Conference on*, pages 450–461. IEEE, 2012.

[6] X. Liu, Y. Liu, K. Aberer, and C. Miao. Personalized point-of-interest recommendation by mining users' preference transition. In *Proceedings of the 22nd ACM international conference on Conference on information & knowledge management*, pages 733–738. ACM, 2013.

[7] R. Motwani and P. Raghavan. *Randomized algorithms.* Chapman & Hall/CRC, 2010.

[8] L. Page, S. Brin, R. Motwani, and T. Winograd. The pagerank citation ranking: bringing order to the web. 1999.

[9] G. Salton and C. Buckley. Term-weighting approaches in automatic text retrieval. *Information processing & management*, 24(5):513–523, 1988.

[10] W. R. Tobler. A computer movie simulating urban growth in the detroit region. *Economic geography*, pages 234–240, 1970.

[11] H. Wang, M. Terrovitis, and N. Mamoulis. Location recommendation in location-based social networks using user check-in data. In *Proceedings of the 21st ACM SIGSPATIAL International Conference on Advances in Geographic Information Systems*, pages 374–383. ACM, 2013.

[12] H. C. Wu, R. W. P. Luk, K. F. Wong, and K. L. Kwok. Interpreting tf-idf term weights as making relevance decisions. *ACM Transactions on Information Systems (TOIS)*, 26(3):13, 2008.

[13] D. Yang, D. Zhang, Z. Yu, and Z. Wang. A sentiment-enhanced personalized location recommendation system. In *Proceedings of the 24th ACM Conference on Hypertext and Social Media*, pages 119–128. ACM, 2013.

[14] M. Ye, P. Yin, and W. C. Lee. Location recommendation for location-based social networks. In *Proceedings of the 18th SIGSPATIAL International Conference on Advances in Geographic Information Systems*, pages 458–461. ACM, 2010.

[15] M. Ye, P. Yin, W. C. Lee, and D. L. Lee. Exploiting geographical influence for collaborative point-of-interest recommendation. In *Proceedings of the 34th international ACM SIGIR conference on Research and development in Information Retrieval*, pages 325–334. ACM, 2011.

[16] H. Yin, Y. Sun, B. Cui, Z. Hu, and L. Chen. Lcars: a location-content-aware recommender system. In *Proceedings of the 19th ACM SIGKDD international conference on Knowledge discovery and data mining*, pages 221–229. ACM, 2013.

[17] Q. Yuan, G. Cong, Z. Ma, A. Sun, and N. M. Thalmann. Time-aware point-of-interest recommendation. In *Proceedings of the 36th international ACM SIGIR conference on Research and development in information retrieval*, pages 363–372. ACM, 2013.

[18] J. D. Zhang and C. Y. Chow. Geosoca: Exploiting geographical, social and categorical correlations for point-of-interest recommendations. In *Proceedings of the 38th International ACM SIGIR Conference on Research and Development in Information Retrieval*, pages 443–452. ACM, 2015.

Recommending New Items to Ephemeral Groups Using Contextual User Influence

Elisa Quintarelli
Politecnico di Milano – Italy
elisa.quintarelli@polimi.it

Emanuele Rabosio
Politecnico di Milano – Italy
emanuele.rabosio@polimi.it

Letizia Tanca
Politecnico di Milano – Italy
letizia.tanca@polimi.it

ABSTRACT

Group recommender systems help groups of users in finding appropriate items to be enjoyed together. Lots of activities, like watching TV or going to the restaurant, are intrinsically group-based, thus making the group recommendation problem very relevant. In this paper we study ephemeral groups, i.e., groups where the members might be together for the first time. Recent approaches have tackled this issue introducing complex models to be learned offline, making them unable to deal with new items; on the contrary, we propose a group recommender able to manage new items too. In more detail, our technique determines the preference of a group for an item by combining the individual preferences of the group members on the basis of their *contextual influence*, where the contextual influence represents the ability of an individual, in a given situation, to direct the group's decision. We conducted an extensive experimental evaluation on a TV dataset containing a log of viewings performed by real groups, showing how our approach outperforms the comparable techniques from the literature.

Keywords

Group recommendations; influence; context

1. INTRODUCTION

Recommender systems suggest items to users [1], and are fundamental in all the countless scenarios where people need to be helped in choosing something. For instance, the users may need to choose a movie to watch at the cinema, a TV program, a restaurant for a dinner, or a book to read. In addition, it is clear that lots of such activities are inherently social, generally carried out by *groups* of users: indeed, people seldom go to the movies or watch TV on their own, and equally rarely eat out alone. Even the choice of a book may be a group activity, if this book is then to be discussed and analyzed by an (online) community. Last, but not least, touristic activities are often organized for groups, thus group recommendations may provide tour organizers with useful suggestions to compose the daily schedule. Hence the importance of studying *group recommender systems* [27], taking into account the possibility of having multiple users involved in the item choices.

The literature on group recommender systems deals with two different kinds of groups: *persistent* and *ephemeral* [27]. Persistent groups have a significant history of activities together, while ephemeral ones may be constituted by people together for the first time. Since for persistent groups a history of past activities is available, in such a scenario classic recommendation techniques for individual users are employable, treating the whole group as one user. When ephemeral groups are considered, on the contrary, no group history is available, and therefore the group preferences must be computed on the basis of those known for the individual users composing the group. The aim of this work is tackling the more general scenario of ephemeral groups.

To generate ephemeral group recommendations, most approaches propose aggregation functions deriving the preferences of the group by appropriately combining those of the component users, computed exploiting recommendation techniques for individuals. Sometimes this combination is performed using weights based on complex user and item models built from the available feedback provided by the users themselves. The necessity of building these models, however, makes the latter techniques unsuitable for the scenarios characterized by many items which are new in the system, i.e., not associated with past feedback. Since in this work we want to study an approach applicable also to new items, we concentrate on aggregation functions allowing to take them into account. Note that the ability of dealing with new items is essential in several realms, think for instance of the TV domain: many TV programs, e.g. the movies, are often broadcast once and then not any more for a long time, and therefore cannot be associated with past user feedback.

Another interesting point [38] is that, when aggregating the preferences of the members of a group, not all the users should have the same weight: some users might indeed have a greater *influence* in determining the final decision. Consider for instance a family with parents and children in front of the TV: clearly, the parents may be prone to favor the children's wishes in deciding the program to be watched, thus making the children more influential in the decision process.

However, even the latter consideration may be debatable. Indeed, this behavior is likely in the early afternoon, when most children programs are available, while in the late afternoon many other kinds of programs might be chosen and

RecSys '16, September 15-19, 2016, Boston , MA, USA
© 2016 ACM. ISBN 978-1-4503-4035-9/16/09...$15.00
DOI: http://dx.doi.org/10.1145/2959100.2959137

thus the parents should be more influential, in order to exclude those programs that are inappropriate for children.

For this reason, in this work we propose a novel aggregation function, taking influence into account but considering *contextual influence*, because influence weights may vary with respect to the situation, i.e., the context, that the group is currently living.

Running Example.

We consider a running example in the TV domain, with users watching TV programs possibly in groups. There are two possible contexts, i.e., *daytime* and *night*, and four users, i.e., Alice (a), Bob (b), Mark (m) and Susan (s). Alice has a very strong personality, and is willing to watch her favorite programs in any case. On the contrary, Bob is particularly interested in choosing the programs during daytime, but does not like to create problems in the choice during the evening. Finally, Mark and Susan are more permissive.

Paper Structure.

The paper is structured as follows. Section 2 presents the related work, while Section 3 explains our recommendation technique. Section 4 describes the experimental evaluation and, finally, Section 5 concludes the paper.

2. RELATED WORK

The problem of group recommendations has been widely studied in the last years, since the Polylens system [27] was proposed by O'Connor et al. in 2001. Recommendation techniques to groups, as mentioned in the introduction, can be divided into two categories: recommendations to persistent groups and to ephemeral groups. In the former case it is possible to assume the availability of feedback provided by the group as a whole, while in the latter one group feedback is not available and the preferences of a group must be computed on the basis of those of its members.

Chen et al. [8] propose a recommendation technique aggregating the scores of the group members through a weighted average, where the weights are computed exploiting a genetic algorithm; the fitness function of the algorithm relies on known group preferences, so it is implementable only for persistent groups. Vildjiounaite et al. [34] in the TV domain consider the families as fixed groups, and build a classifier for each family. Seko et al. [29] compute the scores for the items to be recommended to a group exploiting the similarities with the items belonging to the group history. Hu et al. [19] devise a complex model based on restricted Boltzmann machines, learned starting from explicit ratings provided by the groups. We do not consider these approaches, because – as stated in the introduction – in this paper we set ourselves in the more general scenario of ephemeral groups.

Recommendations to ephemeral groups are performed composing the preferences of the group members by using aggregation functions, the most famous being *average* and *least misery*. The average [24, 36, 31, 4, 30, 6, 26, 7, 2, 12, 21, 17] is the simplest aggregation function: it computes the group preference for an item just as the arithmetic mean of those of the group members. Least misery [27, 24, 4, 30, 6, 26, 33, 18, 7, 12, 21, 17], on the contrary, does not maximize the average satisfaction, but tries to make everyone happy, choosing the items for which the lowest value among the preferences of the group members is the greatest. Other popular aggregation functions are the *maximum satisfaction* [24, 6, 26, 7, 12, 21], maximizing the greatest preference, and average without misery [24, 32, 12], computing an average but neglecting the items whose preference is below a certain threshold. Works [5, 16, 2] aggregate the group members' preferences through a weighted average, where the weight represents the expertise, computed on the basis of the amount of activity performed by the user in the system. Amer-Yahia et al. [3] introduce an interesting function which, on the one hand, tries to maximize the satisfaction of the group components, but, on the other hand, also tries to minimize the disagreement among them. In the experimental section we carry out comparisons with these techniques. Also the approach of De Campos et al. [11], building a bayesian network and using it to learn both the individual preferences and the aggregation weights, is worth mentioning; this technique, however, needs the construction of a complex model including the items, and therefore cannot be used to recommend new items because these are not part of the model.

The importance of influence in group recommenders has first been noticed by Masthoff and Gatt [25]. They assume the presence of two kinds of influence: *emotional contagion* is the influence of the affective state of a user on the other group members, while *conformity* regards the tendency of a user to adapt to the choices of the others. These factors are incorporated in the group preference, and their values are derived from prior knowledge of the relationships among the group members. Quijano-Sanchez et al. [28] consider *personality* and *trust* to aggregate individual preferences: the personality factor assigns greater weights to the users with stronger personality, while the trust is used to modify the group members' preferences towards those of the users in whom they trust. The personality factor is determined on the basis of psychological tests, while the trust requires social network information. Also Kompan and Bielikova [22] propose a group recommender taking into account the personality, this time represented through a weighted graph indicating how the users influence each other; in this case the computation of the influence values requires the users to undergo psychological tests as well. Christensen and Schiaffino [9] incorporate in their formulas three social factors, named *trust*, *social similarity* and *social centrality*. The first depends on the level of acquaintance between the users and must be declared, while the second and the third rely on the activities in social networks. These approaches exploit social factors, but require to have prior knowledge of their values. On the contrary, our methodology computes influences only on the basis of training data.

Some approaches build complex models of users and items employed to compute both the individual preferences and the influence values to be used in the aggregation. Ye et al. [35] propose a probabilistic model learned with an expectation-maximization procedure, while Liu et al. [23] and Yuan et al. [37] found their methodologies on the latent Dirichlet allocation. Finally, Kim and El Saddik [20] build a graph for each group containing users and items, and use random walks with restarts to compute affinities between users and items, and the influence of the users within the groups. These techniques are not suitable for new items, because they cannot be included in the learned model and thus cannot be recommended.

In this work we propose an aggregation function to compute group preferences starting from individual ones and exploiting the users' influences in a way suitable also for new items. In addition, our influence values are computed relying only on training data, without the need of asking information to the users. Finally, to the best of our knowledge, this is the first proposal defining the influence in a context-aware manner.

3. RECOMMENDATION METHODOLOGY

This section describes our proposed group recommendation methodology. The methodology starts with the individual preferences of the users for the items, and provides techniques to aggregate them to obtain group preferences. We set ourselves in the more general framework of context-aware recommender systems, and so suppose that the preference of a user for an item may vary according to the context. In addition, we suppose to know also regular, context-unaware preferences of the users for the items. Users' contextual preferences can be computed through an existing context-aware recommender system for individual users, while to compute context-unaware preferences a traditional one may be employed. We also suppose to have a log recording the history of the items chosen in the past by groups of users. To be more general, we assume that the set of the available items may change depending on the time instant in which it is requested. This is the case of the TV setting of the running example, but also of other scenarios like event recommendations or recommending movies in theaters now.

PROBLEM STATEMENT. *Let $\mathcal{U}$ be a set of users, $\mathcal{I}$ a set of items, $\mathcal{C}$ a set of contexts. Supposing that the following data are known:*

- *A context-aware scoring function $score\_ctx(u, i, c)$, $u \in \mathcal{U}$, $i \in \mathcal{I}$, $c \in \mathcal{C}$, assigning a score to the items in the various contexts*
- *A context-unaware scoring function $score\_no\_ctx(u, i)$, $u \in \mathcal{U}$, $i \in \mathcal{I}$, assigning a score independent of the context to the items*
- *A log $\mathcal{L}$ recording the history of the items chosen by the groups, in the form of 4-ples $l_j : (t_j, c_j, G_j, i_j)$ with $c_j \in \mathcal{C}$, $G_j \in \wp(\mathcal{U})$ and $i_j \in \mathcal{I}$; t_j is the time instant in which the item has been chosen*

Then, given a target group $G \in \wp(\mathcal{U})$, a context $c \in \mathcal{C}$ and a time instant t, the problem of group recommendation is defined as recommending a list of K items from those in $\mathcal{I}$ which are available at time instant t that users in G may be interested in when in context c.

EXAMPLE 1 (LOG). *Table 1 shows a possible log in our TV running example. Each row indicates the time instant, the context, the composition of the group and the chosen item. Since in our scenario, in a given time instant, only a subset of the items is available, i.e., the programs that are on the air, for convenience each row reports also the items that are available in the corresponding time instant.*

The group preference for an item is determined by aggregating the individual preferences of the group members on the basis of their influence. The influence of a given user u

Table 1: Log in our running example

Time	Context	Group	Chosen item	Available items
t_1	daytime	{a, b, m}	p_1	$\{p_1, p_2, p_3\}$
t_2	daytime	{a, m, s}	p_5	$\{p_4, p_5, p_6\}$
t_3	daytime	{b, s}	p_8	$\{p_7, p_8, p_9\}$
t_4	daytime	{a, m}	p_{11}	$\{p_{10}, p_{11}, p_{12}\}$
t_5	night	{a, b, s}	p_{15}	$\{p_{13}, p_{14}, p_{15}\}$
t_6	night	{b, s}	p_{16}	$\{p_{16}, p_{17}, p_{18}\}$
t_7	night	{a, b}	p_{21}	$\{p_{19}, p_{20}, p_{21}\}$

is derived by comparing the behavior of u when alone represented by his/her individual preferences with his/her behavior when in groups represented by the interactions contained in the log $\mathcal{L}$. In more detail, the influence of u evaluates how many times the groups containing u have selected one of his/her favorite items. Let $TopK(u, c, t)$ be the list of the K preferred items of user u in context c according to the values of $score\_ctx(u, i, c)$ for the various $i \in \mathcal{I}$ available at instant t; in the TV domain of our running example, the $TopK$ at a certain time instant must include just programs on the air at that time instant. The contextual influence is defined as follows:

$$infl\_ctx(u, c) = \frac{|l_j \in \mathcal{L} : c = c_j \wedge u \in G_j \wedge i_j \in TopK(u, c, t_j)|}{|l_j \in \mathcal{L} : c = c_j \wedge u \in G_j|} \tag{1}$$

The value of $infl\_ctx(u, c)$ quantifies the ability of user u to direct the group's decision towards his/her own tastes while in context c.

EXAMPLE 2 (CONTEXTUAL INFLUENCE). *Suppose we compute the influences using K=1 in Equation* (1)*, i.e., using top-1 lists, and suppose that at the time instants of Example 1 the programs preferred by the users are the following:*

- t_1: $a \rightarrow p_2$, $b \rightarrow p_1$, $m \rightarrow p_2$
- t_2: $a \rightarrow p_5$, $m \rightarrow p_5$, $s \rightarrow p_4$
- t_3: $b \rightarrow p_8$, $s \rightarrow p_9$
- t_4: $a \rightarrow p_{11}$, $m \rightarrow p_{10}$
- t_5: $a \rightarrow p_{15}$, $b \rightarrow p_{13}$
- t_6: $b \rightarrow p_{16}$, $s \rightarrow p_{16}$
- t_7: $a \rightarrow p_{21}$, $b \rightarrow p_{20}$

The contextual influence computations for users Alice, Bob and Mark are as follows:
$infl\_ctx(a, daytime) = 2/3 = 0.667$
$infl\_ctx(b, daytime) = 2/2 = 1$
$infl\_ctx(m, daytime) = 1/3 = 0.333$
$infl\_ctx(a, night) = 2/2 = 1$
$infl\_ctx(b, night) = 1/3 = 0.333$
The value of $infl\_ctx(m, night)$ cannot be computed, because Mark provided no feedback in the context night.

The context-unaware influence of a user can be computed as the context-aware one, but considering the whole log instead of the contextual:

$$infl\_no\_ctx(u) = \frac{|l_j \in \mathcal{L} : u \in G_j \wedge i_j \in TopK(u, c_j, t_j)|}{|l_j \in \mathcal{L} : u \in G_j|} \tag{2}$$

EXAMPLE 3 (NON-CONTEXTUAL INFLUENCE). *The non-contextual influence is a single value for each user, and is computed exploiting the whole log:*
$influence\_no\_ctx(a) = 4/5 = 0.8$
$influence\_no\_ctx(b) = 3/5 = 0.6$
$influence\_no\_ctx(m) = 1/3 = 0.333$

Given a group $G \in \wp(\mathcal{U})$, its preference $score\_ctx(G, i, c)$ for $i \in \mathcal{I}$ in the context $c \in \mathcal{C}$ is computed as the mean of the preferences of its members weighted on the basis of each member's influence in context c:

$$score\_ctx(G, i, c) = \frac{\sum_{u \in G} infl\_ctx(u, c) \cdot score\_ctx(u, i, c)}{\sum_{u \in G} infl\_ctx(u, c)} \quad (3)$$

If the number of contexts is high, it may well happen that some users are not associated with feedback in some contexts. In order to deal with such cases, it is possible to compute also a non-contextual score for the items:

$$score\_no\_ctx(G, i) = \frac{\sum_{u \in G} infl\_no\_ctx(u) \cdot score\_no\_ctx(u, i)}{\sum_{u \in G} infl\_no\_ctx(u)} \quad (4)$$

Algorithm 1 summarizes the way we compute the top-K list of items preferred by a certain group G in a context c at time instant t. If all the members of G have provided feedback in context c, then context-aware scores are computed using Equation (3); otherwise, a non-contextual score is obtained using Equation (4).

Note that a first alternative to determine the group preferences for contexts when some of the group members have not provided feedback was to apply Equation (3) anyway, inserting non-contextual values of preference and influence *just for those users for whom the contextual ones are not known*, thus mixing context-aware and context-unaware quantities in the computation. However, this strategy, which "blends" values measured on different subsets of the log, showed a bad behavior in the experiments. We then did a manual check, sampling users from our dataset and controlling how much their influence varies according to context, and how far these values are from their non-contextual influence. Often, non-contextual influence turned out to be quite distant from the contextual one, thus we explain this somehow unexpected behavior with the fact that putting together contextual and non-contextual influences creates a sort of "unbalanced situation" among the members of the group, which reflects reality worse than keeping the weights uniform.

As a consequence, we decided to adopt the technique described in Algorithm 1.[1]

EXAMPLE 4 (SCORE COMPUTATION). *Suppose that at instant t_8, during daytime, a group composed of Bob and Mark is watching TV, and it is needed to recommend one program among the available p_{22}, p_{23} and p_{24}. Note that this group is never recorded in the log: it is the first time that these two users watch TV together without other people. The following individual preference values are given: score_ctx(b, p_{22}, daytime) = 0.8, score_ctx(b, p_{23}, daytime) = 0.2, score_ctx(b, p_{24}, daytime) = 0.3, score_ctx(m, p_{22}, daytime) = 0.2, score_ctx(m, p_{23}, daytime) = 0.5, score_ctx(m, p_{24}, daytime) = 0.9. The group scores for the three available items are computed as weighted averages. Since both the users have provided feedback in the context* daytime *Algorithm 1 prescribes to employ Equation* (3)*, where we use the influence values computed in Example 2:*
$score\_ctx(\{b, m\}, p_{22}, daytime) = \frac{1 \cdot 0.8 + 0.333 \cdot 0.2}{1 + 0.333} = 0.650$
$score\_ctx(\{b, m\}, p_{23}, daytime) = \frac{1 \cdot 0.2 + 0.333 \cdot 0.5}{1 + 0.333} = 0.275$
$score\_ctx(\{b, m\}, p_{24}, daytime) = \frac{1 \cdot 0.3 + 0.333 \cdot 0.9}{1 + 0.333} = 0.450$
Therefore, the system recommends p_{22} to the group. Note that the choice is directed by the heavier influence of Bob.

Suppose now that at instant t_9, in the context night*, a group with Alice, Bob and Mark is watching TV and needs one recommendation, choosing among p_{25}, p_{26} and p_{27}. Note that Mark provided no feedback in the context* night*, and therefore it is not possible to utilize contextual preferences and influences. As described in Algorithm 1, non-contextual preferences and influences are used. The following non-contextual preferences are given: score_no_ctx(a, p_{25})=0.9, score_no_ctx(a, p_{26})=0.1, score_no_ctx(a, p_{27})=0.6, score_no_ctx(b, p_{25})=0.2, score_no_ctx(b, p_{26})= 0.9, score_no_ctx(b, p_{27})=0.3, score_no_ctx(m, p_{25})=0.3, score_no_ctx(m, p_{26})= 0.7, score_no_ctx(m, p_{27})=0.5. The group scores for the three available items are computed using Equation* (4) *and the non-contextual influences of Example 3:*
$score\_no\_ctx(\{a, b, m\}, p_{25}) = \frac{0.8 \cdot 0.9 + 0.6 \cdot 0.2 + 0.333 \cdot 0.3}{0.8 + 0.6 + 0.333} = 0.542$
$score\_no\_ctx(\{a, b, m\}, p_{26}) = \frac{0.8 \cdot 0.1 + 0.6 \cdot 0.9 + 0.333 \cdot 0.7}{0.8 + 0.6 + 0.333} = 0.492$
$score\_no\_ctx(\{a, b, m\}, p_{27}) = \frac{0.8 \cdot 0.6 + 0.6 \cdot 0.3 + 0.333 \cdot 0.5}{0.8 + 0.6 + 0.333} = 0.477$
Therefore, the system recommends program p_{25} to the group.

Algorithm 1 Top-K computation for a group of users

```
function COMPUTETOPK(G ∈ ℘(U), c ∈ C, time instant t)
    if all users in G provided feedback in context c then
        USE_CONTEXT = true
    else
        USE_CONTEXT = false
    end if
    for all i ∈ I do
        if USE_CONTEXT then
            score(G, i, c) = score_ctx(G, i, c)
        else
            score(G, i, c) = score_no_ctx(G, i)
        end if
    end for
    return the K items i ∈ I with the greatest values of
            score(G, i, c), among those available at time t
end function
```

4. EXPERIMENTS

Our methodology was tested using a dataset in the TV domain, containing implicit feedback and context information. The TV scenario is actually a perfect setting for our approach: in fact, watching TV is inherently a group activity. Moreover, many kinds of TV programs – like the movies – are broadcast once and then not anymore for a long time, thus making the new item problem extremely relevant.

We remark that the dataset we employ contains implicit feedback by real groups constituted by people really watching TV together. Several approaches from the literature (e.g., [27, 4]), on the contrary, use datasets containing just individual feedback, like Movielens, and then build groups

[1]Please notice that, in scenarios where efficiency is critical, the online top-K computation, where each item's score is derived aggregating the preferences of the single users, may be executed by using fast algorithms from the literature, like the Threshold Algorithm proposed by Fagin et al. [15]. Such algorithms would derive the top-K by applying Equations (3) and (4) to just a subset of the items.

Table 2: Time slots

Start time	End time	Description
02:00:00	07:00:00	Graveyard slot
07:00:00	09:00:00	Early morning
09:00:00	12:00:00	Morning
12:00:00	15:00:00	Daytime
15:00:00	18:00:00	Early fringe
18:00:00	20:30:00	Prime access
20:30:00	22:30:00	Prime time
22:30:00	02:00:00	Late fringe

artificially. We found two publicly available datasets envisaging feedback by real groups: Meetup, employed in [23], and Plancast, employed in [37]. Unfortunately, both contain just group feedback, and this makes them unsuitable to test our methodology. The influence computation, indeed, is based on a comparison between the behavior of the users when alone and when in groups, and therefore does need group feedback but requires individual feedback as well.

The preference functions adopted to determine the contextual and non-contextual scores of the items for the single users in the TV dataset are those recently proposed in [10], which represents a state-of-the-art technique to generate TV program recommendations for individual users relying on implicit feedback. The recommendation methodology defined in [10] is content-based, thus allowing to compute users' preference values also for new items.

Note that, as underlined in the running example, in this special domain all the recommendation lists are generated, rather than as subsets of the whole set of items (i.e., available TV programs), just as subsets of the programs aired at the time instant in which the recommendation is required.

4.1 Dataset

The employed dataset contains TV viewing information related to 7921 users and 119 channels, broadcast both over the air and by satellite. The dataset is composed of an electronic program guide (EPG) containing the description of 21194 distinct programs, and a log containing both individual and group viewings performed by the users. The attributes available for each program in the EPG are its genre and the channel on which it is transmitted.

The log spans from December 3rd, 2013 to March 1st, 2014 and contains 4968231 entries, among which we retained just the syntonizations longer than three minutes. 3519167 viewings are performed by individual users, and are those used to feed the methodology [10] for the computation of the individual preferences of the group members. The remaining 1449064 viewings envisage more than one person. Each log row specifies the identifier of the user and that of the program he/she watched, along with start time and end time. Start and end times were employed to derive the day of the week and the time slot, which are the context dimensions considered in the experiments; the available values for the time slot are shown in Table 2.

The group viewings were split into a training set, including the syntonizations between December 3rd, 2013 and February 15th, 2014 (1210316 entries), and a test set, containing the remaining ones (238748 entries). The former was used as the log $\mathcal{L}$ in input to the formulas proposed in this paper, while the latter was employed to assess the quality of the recommendations.

4.2 Evaluation Metrics

The performance of our recommendation algorithm was evaluated using *Recall@K*, describing the number of test items included in recommendation lists of length K computed at the instant in which the viewing of the test items started and in the context in which they were watched.

More formally, let v be a program view in the test set, v_t the start time of the view, v_G the group of users that watched the program, v_i the program watched and v_c the context in which the view took place. $TopK(G, c, t)$ indicates the set of top-K items for the group G in context c among those on the air at time instant t, determined using the recommendation methodology to be evaluated. Recall@K is computed as follows:

$$Recall@K = \frac{|v \in \text{Test Set} : v_i \in TopK(v_G, v_c, v_t)|}{|v \in \text{Test Set}|} \quad (5)$$

We executed experiments for K=1, K=2 and K=3.

4.3 Compared Methods

The methodology introduced in this paper, from now on dubbed *CtxInfl*, was compared with several other techniques, among those presented in Section 2 which allow to recommend new items to ephemeral groups:

- Average (AVG)
- Least misery (LM)
- Maximum satisfaction (MS)
- The approach of [3], taking into account the disagreement between the group members (DIS)
- Weighted average using the expertise, where the expertise of a user in our experiments is defined as the number of program viewings which he/she performed (EXP)

In addition, our methodology was compared with a version of itself exploiting only non-contextual influences, i.e., computing influences always using Equation (2); this approach is named *Infl.* Such a comparison is important to verify whether the usage of the context to model the influence may actually provide a performance gain.

Besides the evaluation on the whole the test set, we also executed experiments considering different subsets of the test items on the basis of the group size and heterogeneity. About the group sizes, we measured the recall related to the groups containing two (192378 test items), three (35216 test items), four (9739 test items) and five (1151 test items) members. The heterogeneity of the group was measured using the Spearman's footrule distance with location parameter ℓ [14] between top-K lists[2], employing $K = 3$ and $\ell = K + 1$. The distance was measured between the top-3 lists of favorite items of all the pairs of group members and then averaged. The values of this distance range from 0 if the top-3 lists of the users contain the same items identically ordered, to 12 if the top-3 lists of the users are completely disjoint. We measured the recall related to the groups with average distance h such that $h \leq 4$ (46935 test items), $4 < h \leq 8$ (99333 test items), and $h > 8$ (92480 test items).

[2]The Spearman's footrule distance is the L_1 distance between two permutations of the elements of a domain. The Spearman's footrule distance with location parameter ℓ is a variation allowing to deal with top-K lists, where all the elements of the domain not included in the top-K list are placed by default at position ℓ.

Finally, in Section 3 we have explained that CtxInfl uses non-contextual preferences and influences for the groups containing at least one member whose feedback in the context of interest is unknown. As a consequence, CtxInfl and Infl apply exactly the same formulas on all the test items v such that at least one user in v_G provided no feedback in the context v_c, thus making scarcely significant the comparison of CtxInfl and Infl on these items. Therefore, to better analyze the relevance of the context in influence modeling we compared CtxInfl and Infl also on further restrictions of the test sets listed above, containing just the test items v such that all the users in v_G provided feedback in the context v_c; on these test items, CtxInfl never executes the ELSE branch at Line 10 of Algorithm 1. The test sets obtained through this further restriction contain about 3/4 test items with respect to the original ones.

4.4 Results

In this subsection we present in tabular form the results obtained in the experiments. Tables 3, 4 and 5 show, respectively, Recall@1, Recall@2 and Recall@3, expressed in percentage, measured on the whole test set and on the test sets restricted, as explained above, on the basis of the group size and heterogeneity. Table 6, on the other hand, compares only CtxInfl and Infl showing Recall@1, Recall@2 and Recall@3 on the test sets further restricted by removing the test items v such that at least one user in v_G did not provide feedback in the context v_c. The tables report on the rows the test set composition, and on the columns the employed technique. Our algorithm CtxInfl and its variant Infl were run setting K=1 in Equations (1) and (2), since this is the value achieving the best results.

4.5 Result Analysis

In the following the results reported in the tables are analyzed in detail. Subsection 4.5.1 focuses on the comparison of CtxInfl with the competitors from the literature, while Subsection 4.5.2 examines the differences between CtxInfl and its non-contextual variant.

4.5.1 Comparison with the Competitors from the Literature

The comparison starts with the whole test set, and then considers those derived on the basis of the group size and the group heterogeneity.

Full Test Set.
The measured recall values highlight how our strategy (CtxInfl) dominates its competitors for all the experimented lengths of the recommendation list. It is also possible to notice that, among the other approaches, the best-performing one is EXP, and this suggests the goodness of the strategies relying on a weighted average with respect to plain average, least misery, maximum satisfaction, and also the approach of [3] taking disagreement into account. Another aspect that can be noticed from the results is that the difference between our methodology and the baselines is larger when recommending few items: 2.81% for Recall@1, 2.29% for Recall@2 and 1.81% for Recall@3. This happens because many users watch just a limited number of channels, and therefore even simple strategies are able to identify the proper program in lists containing more items.

Results Varying the Group Size.
In these experiments CtxInfl is also the best one, and its main competitor in most cases remains EXP. It is immediately evident that the advantage obtained by CtxInfl grows when the group size is bigger: considering Recall@1, the difference is 2.43% when the group size is 2, 4.31% when the group size is 3, 4.47% when the group size is 4, and 5.65% when the group size is 5. This result is easily interpreted: when groups are larger social factors are more important.

Results Varying the Group Homogeneity.
Once again, CtxInfl is the leading technique and EXP the second one. The first evidence is that lower heterogeneity corresponds to higher recall; therefore, as it is intuitive, recommending to homogeneous groups is a simpler problem. Moreover, the gain brought by CtxInfl with respect to EXP grows with the heterogeneity of the groups: considering Recall@1, the gain is 1.84% for $h \leq 4$, 2.43% for $4 < h \leq 8$ and 3.68% for $h > 8$. Also this outcome is very intuitive: if the group is homogeneous the members have the same tastes, and therefore it is not important who are the most influencing ones.

4.5.2 Relevance of the Context in Influence Computation

The results clearly show that adding the context to the influence provides performance improvements, for all the experimented test sets and lengths of the recommendation list. The improvements brought by CtxInfl with respect to Infl are more evident in the results shown in Table 6 than on those shown in Tables 3, 4 and 5, because the former consider just the test items on which the two methodologies apply different formulas. In more detail, in Table 6 we observe that the gain seems to be bigger when the recommendation lists are shorter: considering all the test items v such that all the members of v_G provided feedback in the context v_c, the benefit provided by the context is 1.68% for Recall@1, 1.48% for Recall@2 and 1.20% for Recall@3. In addition, the performance improvement grows with group heterogeneity: considering Recall@1, the gain is 0.56% for $h \leq 4$, 1.65% for $4 < h \leq 8$ and 2.26% for $h > 8$.

4.6 Accuracy Improvement Evaluation

To validate the statistical significance of the accuracy improvement provided by our algorithm, we used McNemar's test [13], comparing CtxInfl with the other experimented algorithms. The statistical test aims at verifying that the performance differences between two approaches are significant and not just due to chance.

McNemar's test was executed considering the whole test set for Recall@1, Recall@2 and Recall@3. Table 7 shows the values of the McNemar's test statistic obtained by comparing CtxInfl with its competitors: the greater the value of the statistic, the more significant the results. The measured values are very high, corresponding to p-values extremely close to 0 and thus providing strong evidence for rejecting the hypothesis of no improvement. Note that a p-value of 0.05 corresponds to a value 3.8415 of the test statistic.

4.7 Summary of the Evaluation

The evaluation assessed the quality of the group recommendation technique proposed in this paper using a dataset in the TV domain, a domain particularly suitable to carry

Table 3: Recall@1

Test set	CtxInfl	Infl	AVG	LM	MS	DIS	EXP
All	34.12%	32.85%	30.24%	28.93%	28.95%	30.56%	31.31%
Group size = 2	34.81%	33.66%	31.47%	30.14%	30.30%	31.72%	32.38%
Group size = 3	31.18%	29.39%	25.49%	24.93%	23.95%	26.21%	26.87%
Group size = 4	31.71%	29.98%	23.87%	20.89%	21.30%	24.17%	27.24%
Group size = 5	31.89%	30.58%	26.67%	19.64%	23.81%	27.02%	26.24%
$h \leq 4$	44.44%	44.03%	42.11%	41.57%	41.63%	42.15%	42.60%
$4 < h \leq 8$	36.13%	34.88%	32.50%	32.03%	30.43%	33.04%	33.70%
$h > 8$	26.71%	24.99%	21.78%	19.18%	20.92%	22.01%	23.03%

Table 4: Recall@2

Test set	CtxInfl	Infl	AVG	LM	MS	DIS	EXP
All	51.35%	50.24%	48.47%	45.87%	46.35%	48.77%	49.06%
Group size = 2	52.14%	51.18%	49.92%	47.34%	47.68%	50.21%	50.38%
Group size = 3	48.29%	46.61%	43.11%	40.56%	41.29%	43.37%	43.86%
Group size = 4	47.86%	45.93%	40.55%	37.00%	39.17%	41.00%	43.14%
Group size = 5	47.96%	45.78%	42.66%	42.57%	42.05%	42.75%	43.44%
$h \leq 4$	64.44%	64.27%	63.63%	62.25%	60.46%	63.35%	63.84%
$4 < h \leq 8$	54.17%	53.30%	51.74%	49.15%	49.40%	52.17%	52.50%
$h > 8$	41.68%	39.82%	37.26%	34.03%	35.91%	37.61%	37.87%

Table 5: Recall@3

Test set	CtxInfl	Infl	AVG	LM	MS	DIS	EXP
All	62.48%	61.58%	60.12%	57.35%	58.18%	60.34%	60.67%
Group size = 2	63.36%	62.61%	61.48%	58.71%	59.58%	61.73%	61.90%
Group size = 3	59.25%	57.72%	55.30%	52.25%	52.85%	55.46%	56.11%
Group size = 4	57.88%	56.31%	52.03%	49.83%	50.82%	51.89%	53.84%
Group size = 5	58.91%	56.21%	53.87%	56.21%	54.21%	54.39%	55.52%
$h \leq 4$	75.25%	75.08%	74.48%	72.98%	71.87%	74.53%	74.72%
$4 < h \leq 8$	65.41%	64.84%	63.78%	60.61%	61.57%	63.86%	64.16%
$h > 8$	52.86%	51.21%	48.90%	45.92%	47.59%	49.37%	49.77%

Table 6: Recall measured considering only the test items v such that all the users in v_G provided feedback in the context v_c

Test set	Recall@1		Recall@2		Recall@3	
	CtxInfl	Infl	CtxInfl	Infl	CtxInfl	Infl
All	35.58%	33.90%	53.36%	51.88%	64.60%	63.40%
Group size = 2	36.14%	34.64%	54.02%	52.77%	65.35%	64.38%
Group size = 3	33.27%	30.78%	50.65%	48.30%	61.90%	59.77%
Group size = 4	32.90%	30.41%	50.03%	47.25%	59.44%	57.18%
Group size = 5	31.95%	30.00%	50.39%	47.14%	61.95%	57.92%
$h \leq 4$	47.40%	46.84%	68.33%	68.08%	79.06%	78.83%
$4 < h \leq 8$	37.40%	35.75%	56.12%	54.98%	67.44%	66.70%
$h > 8$	27.85%	25.59%	43.07%	40.62%	54.48%	52.30%

Table 7: Values of the McNemar's test statistic

	Infl	AVG	LM	MS	DIS	EXP
Recall@1	912.3	3870.6	2786.5	4870.5	3001.9	2160.4
Recall@2	868.9	2498.1	2775.6	4201.3	1849.5	1628.6
Recall@3	765.1	1942.4	2601.8	3092.9	1389.5	1221.8

out this evaluation, because we are interested in new items and in such a domain most of the items are new. The experiments proved that our algorithm outperforms the existing approaches in terms of recall and, in more detail, the performance gain grows with the size and the heterogeneity of the group. The experiments showed also the relevance of employing the context in the influence computation. Finally, the significance of the improvements was confirmed through a statistical test.

5. CONCLUSION

This paper has studied a group recommendation methodology for ephemeral groups, able to recommend also items that are new in the system. The proposed approach derives group preferences by aggregating individual ones relying on the contextual influence, that is the ability of a user, in a given situation, to direct the group's decision. The influence values are determined exclusively from log data, without asking information from the users. The effectiveness of the proposed approach has been proven through experiments on a dataset in the TV domain, envisaging real groups.

Interesting developments of the present work regard the analysis of novelty and serendipity problems for group recommendations.

Acknowledgments

This research has been partially supported by the IT2Rail project funded by European Union's Horizon 2020 research and innovation program under grant agreement No: 636078, and by the Italian project SHELL CTN01_00128_111357.

6. REFERENCES

[1] G. Adomavicius and A. Tuzhilin. Toward the next generation of recommender systems: A survey of the state-of-the-art and possible extensions. *IEEE Trans. Knowl. Data Eng.*, 17(6):734–749, 2005.

[2] I. Ali and S. Kim. Group recommendations: Approaches and evaluation. In *Proc. IMCOM*, page 105. ACM, 2014.

[3] S. Amer-Yahia, S. Basu Roy, A. Chawla, G. Das, and C. Yu. Group recommendation: Semantics and efficiency. *PVLDB*, 2(1):754–765, 2009.

[4] L. Baltrunas, T. Makcinskas, and F. Ricci. Group recommendations with rank aggregation and collaborative filtering. In *Proc. RecSys*, pages 119–126. ACM, 2010.

[5] S. Berkovsky and J. Freyne. Group-based recipe recommendations: Analysis of data aggregation strategies. In *Proc. RecSys*, pages 111–118. ACM, 2010.

[6] S. Bourke, K. McCarthy, and B. Smyth. Using social ties in group recommendation. In *Proc. 22nd Irish Conference on Artificial Intelligence and Cognitive Science (AICS)*, 2011.

[7] A. J. Chaney, M. Gartrell, J. M. Hofman, J. Guiver, N. Koenigstein, P. Kohli, and U. Paquet. A large-scale exploration of group viewing patterns. In *Proc. TVX*, pages 31–38. ACM, 2014.

[8] Y. Chen, L. Cheng, and C. Chuang. A group recommendation system with consideration of interactions among group members. *Expert. Syst. Appl.*, 34(3):2082–2090, 2008.

[9] I. A. Christensen and S. N. Schiaffino. Social influence in group recommender systems. *Online Information Review*, 38(4):524–542, 2014.

[10] P. Cremonesi, P. Modica, R. Pagano, E. Rabosio, and L. Tanca. Personalized and context-aware TV program recommendations based on implicit feedback. In *Proc. EC-Web*, pages 57–68. Springer, 2015.

[11] L. M. de Campos, J. M. Fernández-Luna, J. F. Huete, and M. A. Rueda-Morales. Group recommending: A methodological approach based on bayesian networks. In *Proc. ICDE Workshops*, pages 835–844. IEEE, 2007.

[12] T. De Pessemier, S. Dooms, and L. Martens. Comparison of group recommendation algorithms. *Multimedia Tools Appl.*, 72(3):2497–2541, 2014.

[13] T. G. Dietterich. Approximate statistical test for comparing supervised classification learning algorithms. *Neural Computation*, 10(7):1895–1923, 1998.

[14] R. Fagin, R. Kumar, and D. Sivakumar. Comparing top k lists. *SIAM J. Discrete Math.*, 17(1):134–160, 2003.

[15] R. Fagin, A. Lotem, and M. Naor. Optimal aggregation algorithms for middleware. In *Proc. PODS*, pages 102–113. ACM, 2001.

[16] M. Gartrell, X. Xing, Q. Lv, A. Beach, R. Han, S. Mishra, and K. Seada. Enhancing group recommendation by incorporating social relationship interactions. In *Proc. GROUP*, pages 97–106. ACM, 2010.

[17] S. Ghazarian and M. Nematbakhsh. Enhancing memory based collaborative filtering for group recommender systems. *Expert Syst. Appl.*, 42(7):3801–3812, 2015.

[18] J. Gorla, N. Lathia, S. Robertson, and J. Wang. Probabilistic group recommendation via information matching. In *Proc. WWW*, pages 495–504. ACM, 2013.

[19] L. Hu, J. Cao, G. Xu, L. Cao, Z. Gu, and W. Cao. Deep modeling of group preferences for group-based recommendation. In *Proc. AAAI*, pages 1861–1867. AAAI Press, 2014.

[20] H. Kim and A. El-Saddik. A stochastic approach to group recommendations in social media systems. *Inf. Syst.*, 50:76–93, 2015.

[21] N. Kim and J. Lee. Group recommendation system: Focusing on home group user in TV domain. In *Proc. SCIS*, pages 985–988. IEEE, 2014.

[22] M. Kompan and M. Bieliková. Social structure and personality enhanced group recommendation. In *Proc. UMAP Workshops*. CEUR-WS.org, 2014.

[23] X. Liu, Y. Tian, M. Ye, and W. Lee. Exploring personal impact for group recommendation. In *Proc. CIKM*, pages 674–683. ACM, 2012.

[24] J. Masthoff. Group modeling: Selecting a sequence of television items to suit a group of viewers. *User Model. User-Adapt. Int.*, 14(1):37–85, 2004.

[25] J. Masthoff and A. Gatt. In pursuit of satisfaction and the prevention of embarrassment: Affective state in group recommender systems. *User Model. User-Adapt. Int.*, 16(3-4):281–319, 2006.

[26] E. Ntoutsi, K. Stefanidis, K. Nørvåg, and H. Kriegel. Fast group recommendations by applying user clustering. In *Proc. ER*, pages 126–140. Springer, 2012.

[27] M. O'Connor, D. Cosley, J. A. Konstan, and J. Riedl. Polylens: A recommender system for groups of user. In *Proc. ECSCW*, pages 199–218. Kluwer, 2001.

[28] L. Quijano-Sánchez, J. A. Recio-García, B. Díaz-Agudo, and G. Jiménez-Díaz. Social factors in group recommender systems. *ACM TIST*, 4(1):8, 2013.

[29] S. Seko, T. Yagi, M. Motegi, and S. Muto. Group recommendation using feature space representing behavioral tendency and power balance among members. In *Proc. RecSys*, pages 101–108. ACM, 2011.

[30] C. Senot, D. Kostadinov, M. Bouzid, J. Picault, A. Aghasaryan, and C. Bernier. Analysis of strategies for building group profiles. In *Proc. UMAP*, pages 40–51. Springer, 2010.

[31] C. Shin and W. Woo. Socially aware TV program recommender for multiple viewers. *IEEE Trans. Consumer Electronics*, 55(2):927–932, 2009.

[32] R. Sotelo, Y. Blanco-Fernández, M. López-Nores, A. Gil-Solla, and J. J. Pazos-Arias. TV program recommendation for groups based on muldimensional tv-anytime classifications. *IEEE Trans. Consumer Electronics*, 55(1):248–256, 2009.

[33] M. O. van Deventer, J. de Wit, J. Vanattenhoven, and M. Guelbahar. Group recommendation in an hybrid broadcast broadband television context. In *Proc. UMAP Workshops*. CEUR-WS.org, 2013.

[34] E. Vildjiounaite, V. Kyllönen, T. Hannula, and P. Alahuhta. Unobtrusive dynamic modelling of TV programme preferences in a Finnish household. *Multimedia Syst.*, 15(3):143–157, 2009.

[35] M. Ye, X. Liu, and W. Lee. Exploring social influence for recommendation: a generative model approach. In *Proc. SIGIR*, pages 671–680. ACM, 2012.

[36] Z. Yu, X. Zhou, Y. Hao, and J. Gu. TV program recommendation for multiple viewers based on user profile merging. *User Model. User-Adapt. Int.*, 16(1):63–82, 2006.

[37] Q. Yuan, G. Cong, and C. Lin. COM: A generative model for group recommendation. In *Proc. KDD*, pages 163–172. ACM, 2014.

[38] H. Zhu, B. A. Huberman, and Y. Luon. To switch or not to switch: Understanding social influence in online choices. In *Proc. CHI*, pages 2257–2266. ACM, 2012.

Guided Walk: A Scalable Recommendation Algorithm for Complex Heterogeneous Social Networks

Roy Levin
Microsoft
Herzliya, Israel
rolevin@microsoft.com

Hassan Abassi
Technion
Haifa, Israel
hassan@cs.technion.ac.il

Uzi Cohen
IBM Research
Haifa, Israel
uzic@il.ibm.com

ABSTRACT

Online social networks have become predominant in recent years and have grown to encompass massive scales of data. In addition to data scale, these networks can be heterogeneous and contain complex structures between different users, between social entities and various interactions between users and social entities. This is especially true in enterprise social networks where hierarchies explicitly exist between employees as well.

In such networks, producing the best recommendations for each user is a very challenging problem for two main reasons. First, the complex structures in the social network need to be properly mined and exploited by the algorithm. Second, these networks contain millions or even billions of edges making the problem very difficult computationally.

In this paper we present Guided Walk, a supervised graph based algorithm that learns the significance of different network links for each user and then produces entity recommendations based on this learning phase. We compare the algorithm with a set of baseline algorithms using offline evaluation techniques as well as a user survey. The offline results show that the algorithm outperforms the next best algorithm by a factor of 3.6. The user survey further confirms that the recommendation are not only relevant but also rank high in terms of personal relevance for each user.

To deal with large scale social networks, the Guided Walk algorithm is formulated as a Pregel program which allows us to utilize the power of distributed parallel computing. This would allow horizontally scaling the algorithm for larger social networks by simply adding more compute nodes to the cluster.

CCS Concepts

•Human-centered computing → Social recommendation;

RecSys '16, September 15-19, 2016, Boston , MA, USA

© 2016 ACM. ISBN 978-1-4503-4035-9/16/09. . . $15.00

DOI: http://dx.doi.org/10.1145/2959100.2959143

Keywords

Recommendations, Heterogeneous Networks, Social Networks, Apache Spark, GraphX, Pregel

1. INTRODUCTION

In the last decade levels of activity in online social networks has proliferated and is still rapidly growing. Every minute Facebook users share nearly 2.5 million pieces of content [6]. Due to the sheer amount of activity, manually sifting through the content is a complex and Sisyphus task. This problem has given birth to a recommendation system, first introduced by Facebook in 2006 [6], that generates a personalized news-feed for each user. Other social networks such as Twitter, LinkedIn and Google+ have followed suit and have adopted a similar concept.

Recently, such recommendation systems have also been developed for Enterprise Social Networks (ESN) such as Tibbr, Yammer, Jive and IBM Connections. The goal of these systems is also to filter and rank news items according to their usefulness to a specific employee. Rather than reporting other employees' actions in the form of a news-feed, a similar task is recommending specific social entities to an employee [14]. For example, raising the user's awareness about a specific blog post. However, in addition to the actions employees perform on the different social entities ESNs typically also contain complex structural information. For instance, in IBM-Connections [11] hierarchies exist between social entities as well as between employees. A community contains blogs which contains articles which, in turn, can contain comments. An employee's manager may 'like' any of these social entities. This kind of structure is illustrated in Figure 1.

Producing a recommendation for "user 1" in the example from Figure 1 is a difficult task as it requires taking into account (a) the relationships between users, (b) the relationships between entities and (c) the interactions between users (employees) and entities. Such networks form complex heterogeneous networks as they contain various types of relationships between entities and they also encompass complex structures. One common recommendation technique is Collaborative Filtering (CF) [24]. CF makes predictions about user's interests based on preferences of other users. However, CF is generally designed for bipartite graphs which model interactions between users and items hence it cannot be easily applied over complex heterogeneous networks such as in our example.

Recommendations for more complex network structures can be generated based on a similarity search which finds the

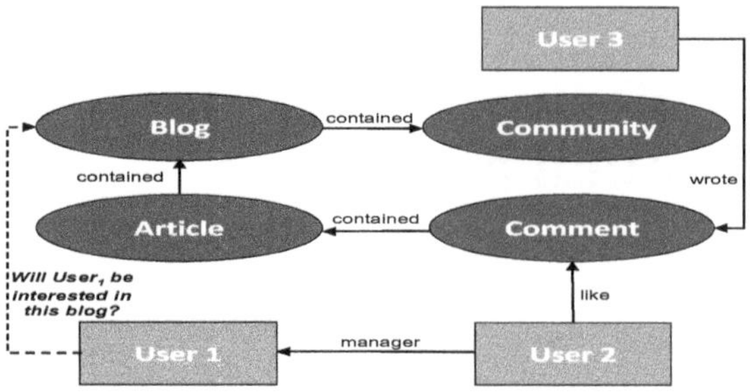

Figure 1: How to recommend entities to an employee taking into account the complex network structure?

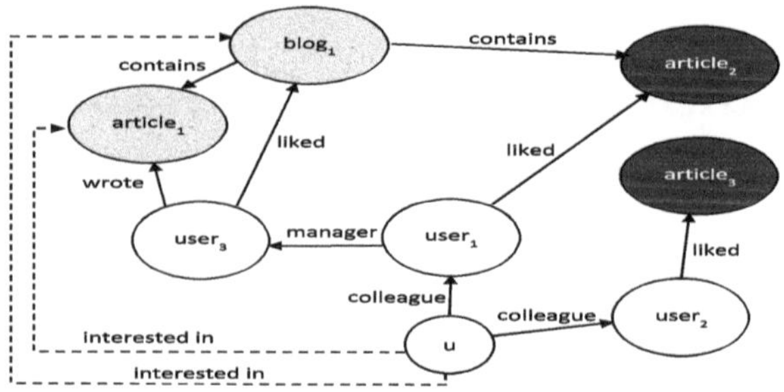

Figure 2: In the example, user u is interested in $article_1$ and $blog_1$. The task is to recommend article-2 or article-3 based on the known user interests and network structure.

most proximate node to a given node. Personalized PageRank [13] and SimRank [12] have been shown to be useful similarity measures to use for this technique. In this paper we propose a novel approach which is a **supervised** version of a Simple Random Walk on a Graph [18] called *Guided Walk* (GW). In the simple and directed case of a random walk all outgoing edges are assumed to have equal probabilities and the probabilities of reaching each vertex in the graph from a given starting point is calculated. This is similar to the Personalized PageRank [13] approach mentioned above. However, in our case, the edges are not assigned uniform probabilities but are rather learned and determined based on the user's actions. Edges in the graph are assigned probabilities based on their likelihood to lead to entities that are known to interest the user. To explain the intuition behind this approach consider the example depicted in Figure 2. In the example, employee u already knows about $article_1$ and $blog_1$ hence the task is to recommend a new entity, i.e., either $article_2$ or $article_3$. Based on the graph in the example it is more likely that the user would be interested in $article_2$ than in $article_3$. The intuition for this is due to the fact that there is a path from user u via $user_1$ to $article_2$ and from $blog_1$ to $article_2$ and we see that other paths from $user_1$ and $blog_1$ lead to items that interest user u. On the other hand, the only path from u to $article_3$ is via $user_2$ which does not lead to any entities that are of interest to u. Hence, it makes sense to assume that $article_2$ is a better recommendation than $article_3$ for user u.

One key challenge in implementing such an approach is in efficiently calculating the edge probabilities. This must be done without enumerating every possible path from the source in a given graph. Furthermore, as social networks nowadays tend to be extremely large, loading the entire graph into main memory and running a sequential process on a single machine is usually not a feasible option. In recent years, data-parallel systems like MapReduce and Spark [4, 34] have been designed to process large amounts of data. These systems achieve horizontal scalability by allowing computations to be distributed over a cluster of machines using various fault-tolerance strategies. However, they are not designed for graph processing thus making it difficult for programmers to express graph processing tasks. Furthermore, it may also lead to suboptimal data processing performance over the cluster which involves too much data shuffling [31]. To cope with this challenge, large-scale distributed graph-parallel frameworks such as Pregel have lately been introduced [20, 31]. These make graph algorithms such as PageRank, Connected Components, Triangle Counting and others relatively easy to express and process efficiently in parallel using the power of distributed computing.

For the purpose of our research we implemented the Guided Walk algorithm as a set of Pregel algorithms. The Pregel algorithms are applied both for the learning phase, during which we learn the edge transition probabilities, and for the the later phase that assigns recommendation scores to entities per-employee. Our graph is modeled as a Resilient Distributed Graph (RDG), and then, using Spark's GraphX [31] layer to apply the set of Pregel algorithms. In addition to scalability, this approach allows us to fully utilize the cluster's RAM for processing the graph.

2. RELATED WORK

For the purpose of mining useful information from networked data, various types of networks have been categorized and studied. From homogeneous networks which have only a single type of object and a single type of link through multi-relational networks which have a single type of object but multiple types of links and finally heterogeneous networks which have both multiple types of objects and of links [26]. Each of these types of networks can be further categorized based on the complexity of the structures formed in the graph. For example bipartite networks are heterogeneous networks which are widely used to construct interactions among two types of objects, such as user-item[33], and document-word [17]. Alternatively in a star-schema network there is a target object that is connected to objects around it which form its attributes [22, 29]. Multiple-hub networks further extend this idea and form star-schema networks around multiple types of target objects [30]. Besides these widely studied network types, many real systems form yet more complex heterogeneous networks which do not natuarully fit into either of these sub-categories [26].

In this paper we study the problem of personalized recommendations of entities in the enterprise social network (ESN). As illustrated in Section 1, an ESN forms a complex heterogeneous information network, having different types of entities with various relationships between them as well as hierarchies among entities and users. Recommendation tasks in complex heterogenous information networks have lately been the focus of several studies [28, 32, 15, 27]. A common approach employed in these works involves three basic steps. First, a "bootstrapping" step is employed in which a set of Meta-Paths are manually selected to be considered by the recommendation algorithm. Each Meta-Path may capture the similarity semantics between two entities connected corresponding paths which are encoded according to the various entity types and relationship types that are included in that path. The next step generally involves measuring the similarity between each pair of entities by exploiting path information using similarity measures such as PathSim [29], HeteSim [25] and PCRW [16]. The final step, performs the actual recommendation based on entity-similarity information. This final recommendation step can be classified into two main types, either Random-Walk based [16] or CF and Matrix-Factorization based [19].

More specifically some research has been focused on the problem of recommending entities in a social network setting [14, 5]. Rather than recommending specific entities to a user some papers have studied the problem of producing a news-feed for the user [23, 9, 1]. A news-feed includes actions performed by other users rather merely the entities themselves. Specific aspects of producing news-feeds in the ESN have also been studied recently [3, 7, 6].

Finally Supervised Random Walks have also been studied (e.g. [2]). There are a few key differences however w.r.t. this work. First, using the algorithm requires domain knowledge since it involves a feature extraction phase for nodes and edges. Next, a supervised random walk is employed to learn their importance. The recommendation itself is then based on these learned features and not on the paths leading to the recommended entity. Second, the algorithm is not designed to run in a distributed environment or on large graphs. In fact, the algorithm is tested on graphs with no more than 175,000 nodes while limiting recommendations to nodes that are no more than 2-hops away from the source. This further reduces the number of candidate recommendations that need be examined.

Compared to previous works, this work is not tailored for a specific domain nor does it require schema knowledge or manual extraction of meta-paths and/or other features. Much like other works, in this work we also utilize a random walk to form a similarity metric between nodes however, in our case, it is preceded by a training phase which learns edge transition probabilities, per-user, based on specific user's preferences as embodied in the relationships. A novel supervised learning algorithm is used to guide the walk based on those preferences. Finally, the algorithm is based on the Pregel paradigm allowing it to run in a distributed environment over many machines, thus enabling it to run on large scale graphs.

3. PROBLEM DEFINITION

In this Section we describe our framework and layout the model for the Guided Walk recommendation method.

3.1 Data Model

Let V denote the set of all social entities and users (e.g., employees, blogs, wikis, articles, etc.) and E be a set of all relationships between them. The relationships may include actions between users and entities, structural information between entities (e.g., a community containing a blog) and relationships between users. Note that some of the relationships may be directed and some may be undirected. For instance, when an employee creates a blog post, it forms a directed relationship from the employee to the blog post, whereas if two employees are colleagues, it forms an undirected relationship.

Let U be a set of users (in our case employees) for which we would like to produce recommendations. For each $u \in U$ let $G_u(V_u, E_u)$ be a *Personalized Graph* such that E_u is a set of directed edges derived from E where each edge represents the relationships from the point of view of user u. Hence, under this definition all the colleagues of u are represented as outgoing edges from u (in our dataset other types of edges remain unchanged). The set of vertices V_u are the vertices in V that are reachable from u via the directed edges in E_u. Figure 2 depicts an example of the Personalized Graph of u. An additional limitation here is that $G_u(V_u, E_u)$ must be a DAG. This limitation is enforced during the construction of the personalized graph for each user from V and E. Note that in the dataset we used (details in Section 5) cycles do not exist. Among the set of social entities V_u we define the subset of entities called *Recommendation Candidates* which may potentially appear in user u's list of recommendations. In our case this is done based on entity types that we wish to focus our recommendations on.

Recall from the description in Section 1 that our goal is to learn edge probabilities based on the actual interests of the user for guiding the recommendation algorithm. For this purpose we take a subset of entities from V_u which are known to be of interest to user u (based on user activities such as 'liked', 'clicked', etc.). We refer to this subset of entities as the *Known User Interests (KUI)* , denoted $K_u \subseteq V_u$. These entities are removed from the Recommendation Candidates to avoid recommending entities the user is already aware of.

3.2 Problem Formulation

We now describe the problem as follows. Given an employee $u \in U$ we generate her personalized graph $G_u(V_u, E_u)$ from V and E and select the user's known interests set KUI K_u. The task is then to generate a ranked list of social entity recommendations for user u such that the entities are ranked based on how likely they are to interest u.

3.3 Guided Walk Problem Formulation

The Guided Walk method involves a two phase process. The first phase is a training phase in which we determine edge weights. These edge weights represent the "importance" of an edge to the user u. This is modeled by estimating the likelihood of a specific edge to be on a path leading from u to an entity that interests u. The second phase is then to produce a list of top-k recommendations based on their expected likelihood based on the edge weights. We next describe these two phases in detail.

3.3.1 Determining Edge Probabilities

We define a *Full Path* between two vertices $v, l \in V_u$ in a given G_u, as an edge path which starts at v, ends at l where l is a leaf, i.e., it has an out-degree of 0. For every $v \in V_u$ let Ψ_v be a set of all Full Paths staring at v. Let $X_v : \Psi_v \to \mathbb{N}$ be a random variable representing a *Full Path Gain (FPG)* defined on a given Full Path $\psi \in \Psi_v$ as the number of vertices in ψ that are also in the KUI set K_u, i.e., $X(\psi) = |K_u \cap \psi|$ (this is a slight abuse of notation as ψ here should be interpreted as the set of vertices spanned by the path of edges). The expected value of the path gain random variable is equal to the FPG multiplied by the probability

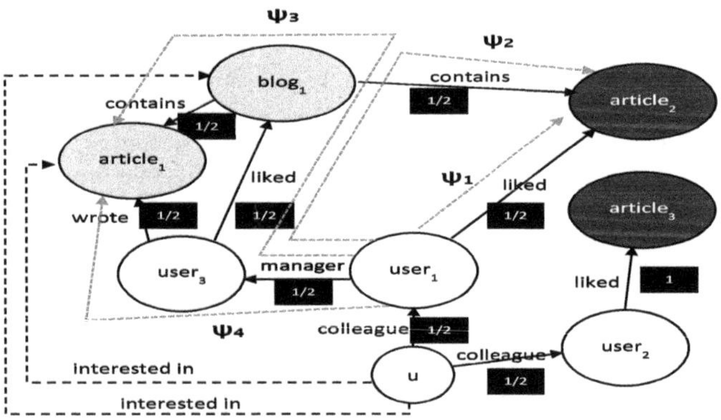

Figure 3: Full path score calculation illustration

of uniformly picking that path out of the set of all possible paths. The expected FPG is given in Equation 1.

$$E[X_v] = \sum_{\psi \in \Psi_v} X(\psi) \cdot p(\psi) \tag{1}$$

In Figure 3 we illustrate an example of how the expected value of the FPG $E[X_{user_1}]$ is calculated. The set of Full Paths $\Psi_{user_1} = \{\psi_1, \psi_2, \psi_3, \psi_4\}$ as well as the edge transition probabilities are depicted for each edge. Based on the figure, the FPGs starting from $user_1$ are as follows:

- $X_{user_1}(\psi_1) \cdot p(\psi_1) = 0 \cdot \frac{1}{2} = 0$
- $X_{user_1}(\psi_2) \cdot p(\psi_2) = 1 \cdot \frac{1}{2} \cdot \frac{1}{2} \cdot \frac{1}{2} = \frac{1}{8}$
- $X_{user_1}(\psi_3) \cdot p(\psi_3) = 2 \cdot \frac{1}{2} \cdot \frac{1}{2} \cdot \frac{1}{2} = \frac{1}{4}$
- $X_{user_1}(\psi_4) \cdot p(\psi_4) = 1 \cdot \frac{1}{2} \cdot \frac{1}{2} = \frac{1}{4}$

Hence, $E[X_{user_1}] = \sum_{i=1}^{4} X_{user_1}(\psi_i) \cdot p(\psi_i) = \frac{5}{8}$ is the expected FPG for $user_1$. Note that in practice calculating the expected FPG for each vertex by iterating over all possible full paths in the graph may be impractical or very inefficient at best. In Section 4 we describe how it can be calculated efficiently and how it can be applied over large scale data by utilizing distributed and parallel computation technologies.

The next step is to determine edge transition probabilities for all the edges based on their target vertex FPG. This will assign higher transition probabilities to edges leading to vertices with higher expected gains. However, before doing so, note that some FPGs may be 0. This happens for vertices which do not have any Full Paths leading from them to entities that are of interest to u. This is a problem since lack of information about the user being interested in some entity does not really indicate that the likelihood of interest to the user is really 0. Treating it as such would be a classic case of over-fitting. To deal with this problem we employ an Additive Smoothing approach in a similar fashion to how its used in Naive Bayes Classifiers [8]. Intuitively, instead of setting edge transition probabilities to 0 they are set to some predefined (small) ε value and the probability function is adjusted for the other edges accordingly. The final transition probabilities for the edges is given in Equation 2.

$$P(e = (v_1, v_2)) = \frac{E[X_{v_2}] + \varepsilon}{\sum_{e' \in E} (E[X_{v_2}] + \varepsilon)} \tag{2}$$

3.3.2 Recommendation Scores

We now describe how we use Equation 2 to calculate the recommendation score for each $v \in V_u$ in the Personalized Graph of user u. The score of a vertex $v \in V_u$ should reflect the probability of reaching it from u using the edge traversal probabilities defined in Equation 2. As a result, a vertex with a higher score generally reflects the fact that full paths leading from u via v to leaves in G_u contain items of interest to u. This is true since ε in Equation 2 is generally kept small. Note that the higher the value assigned to ε the greater the significance given to the number of full paths passing through v in G_u. As a result, the smaller the value assigned to ε the more the Guided Walk will fit the recommendation to the user specifically. At the extreme, setting $\varepsilon = 0$ will over-fit the recommendations to the user giving absolutely no weight to other user actions. Hence, selecting the best value for ε is a matter of tuning (more details in Section 5). Equation 3 formalizes the recommendation score of an entity $v \in V_u$ w.r.t. the user u where Γ represents the set of all edge paths between user u and entity v.

$$s(v) = \sum_{\gamma \in \Gamma} \left(\prod_{e \in \gamma} P(e) \right) \tag{3}$$

Note that this recommendation score function is calculated per-user, i.e., for each G_u separately. Once more, in Section 4 we describe how Equation 3 is computed efficiently and in a scalable manner.

4. THE SOLUTION

In this Section we present our Guided Walk algorithm and explain in detail how it is implemented efficiently and in a scalable manner using the Pregel paradigm [20] over the Apache Spark GraphX framework [34, 31]. In addition we also describe a set of benchmark algorithms used to evaluate our algorithm experimentally as further detailed in Section 5.

4.1 Learning Edge Weights Using Pregel

In Subsection 3.3.1 we formulated the edge traversal probabilities. We now show how they are computed efficiently and in a scalable fashion. We next explain how we calculate the expected FPG for each vertex $v \in V_u$ which is depicted in Equation 1.

We begin with a few definitions and notations. Given a DAG, $G(V, E)$ and a subset of vertices $S \subseteq V$, we define a *Path Count (PC) Function* denoted $\#_{G,S} : V \to \mathbb{N}$ as a function mapping each vertex $v \in V$ to the number of paths starting at any $s \in S$ and leading to v via the edges in E. We use the notation $L(G) \subseteq V$ to denote the leaf vertices of $G(V, E)$ (i.e., all vertices with an out degree of 0). Let G^{rev} denote the the graph G with its edges reversed. Following the definitions above, it is easy to see that for any $v \in V_u$, $\#_{G_u^{rev}, L(G_u)}(v)$ is equivalent to the number of Full Paths in G_u starting at vertex v (since $L(G_u)$ are the roots of G_u^{rev}). Furthermore, the number of Full Paths starting at v but which pass via user u's known interest entities is given by $\sum_{s \in K_u} \#_{G_u^{rev}, L(G_u)}(s) \cdot \#_{G_u^{rev}, \{s\}}(v)$. Since the number of full paths is counted once per entity in K_u it is equivalent to the FPG as defined in Section 3.3.1. Also note that, $\frac{1}{\#_{G_u^{rev}, L(G_u)}(v)}$ is the probability of uniformly selecting a specific full path among all possible full paths starting at

v. Hence, equation 4 is equivalent to the expected FPG as defined in Equation 1 of Section 3.

$$E[X_v] = \frac{\sum_{s \in K_u} \#_{G_u^{rev}, L(G_u)}(s) \cdot \#_{G_u^{rev}, \{s\}}(v)}{\#_{G_u^{rev}, L(G_u)}(v)} \quad (4)$$

However, to compute equation 4 we need the function $\#_{G_u^{rev}, \{s\}}$ for each $s \in K_u$. For users with a lot of activity this would require more computations. An examination of our data reveals that entities in K_u are either leafs or are distant a single edge away from a leaf. We can therefore closely approximate Equation 4 more efficiently as follows.

$$E[X_v] \cong \frac{\#(G_u^{rev}, K_u)(v)}{\#(G_u^{rev}, L(G_u))(v)} \quad (5)$$

It follows then that we can closely approximate the expected FPG $E[X_v]$ by computing $\#_{G_u^{rev}, K_u}$ and $\#_{G_u^{rev}, L(G_u)}$ and combining their values over each vertex as illustrated in Equation 5. We now explain the Pregel algorithm which computes PC Functions. The description is based on Apache Spark's GraphX APIs [1]. In general, the Pregel paradigm is an iterative vertex-centric process. Each iteration a.k.a. super-step has three main steps which it applies (in our case we only explain the directed graph case):

1. **Vertex Program (vprog):** A vertex receives a combined message of all the messages sent to it in the previous super-step (or an initial message if this is the first super-step). A new state is computed based on the current state and the combined message by applying the provided 'vprog'.

2. **Send Messages: (send):** Outgoing edges [2] of vertices that received messages in the current super-step apply the given 'send' message and can optionally send a message via these edge.

3. **Merge Messages:: (merge):** Each vertex that appeared as a destination in the Send Messages step applies a provided 'merge' method on the messages sent to it to combine them into a single unified message.

A Pregel algorithm terminates when the latest super-step does not send any more messages or when a some predefined maximum number of super-steps is reached.

Before applying our Pregel algorithm using GraphX, we first replace the content of the vertices with content that represents a vertex's state in the current super-step. The content of each vertex is a pair containing: (a) the PC updated according to current super-step i and (b) its value before the update took place (i.e., the PC value at super-step $j < i$). The latter is needed to keep track of the change done to the PC in the current super-step by vprog. Initially these values are set to $1, 0$ respectively for vertices in S and $0, 0$ for all other vertices — this represents the starting values, i.e., in super-step 0. An initial message of 0 is sent to all vertices in super-step 1. The algorithm, as well as the types used to represent vertex content, message types and the 3 methods 'vprog', 'send' and 'merge' are detailed in Table 1.

[1]http://spark.apache.org/docs/latest/graphx-programming-guide.html#pregel-api

[2]These are actually triplets (not plain edges) which are edges with embedded vertex content.

Types

ID *description* *notations*	vertex id *(id)*
VD *description* *notations*	vertex content tuple of the form *(new-count, old-count)* (nc, oc)
A *description* *notations*	message containing the *change-count* Δ

Methods

vprog	(ID, VD, A) : VD $(id, (nc, oc), \Delta) \rightarrow$ if $(\Delta > 0)$ then $(nc + \Delta, nc)$ else (nc, oc)	update PC based on changes done in the previous super-step
send	$((ID, VD), (ID, VD)) : (ID, A))$ $((sid, (snc, soc)), (did, (\_, \_))) \rightarrow$ if $(snc - soc > 0)$ then $(did, (snc - soc)))$	if vprog changed value of its PC then send change via outgoing edges
merge	$A^K : A$ $\{\Delta_1, \Delta_2, \ldots, \Delta_K\} \rightarrow \sum_{k=1}^{K} \Delta_k$	combined change in PC is sum of PC changes

Table 1: Pregel program for calculating PCs for each vertex

4.2 Recommendations From Edge Weights

Now that edge weights are available for a given user, recommendation scores can be produced as described in Section 3.3.2. Recall that the recommendation scores produced by the Guided Walk algorithm represent, for each vertex, the expected probability of reaching that vertex from the source user u using the transition probabilities calculated during the training phase. To calculate these recommendation scores we can reuse the Pregel program (defined in Table 1) with some minor changes as follows. First, we apply the algorithm on G_u (not on G_u^{rev}) and we set $S = \{u\}$. Second, since in this phase we compute expectancies rather than plain counts we also need to change the way messages are produced. For this purpose, we multiply the delta count in the send method (see the 'send' method in Table 1) by the transition probability of the edge. That is, the send message method is changed as follows. Let $m = P(sid, did) \cdot (snc - soc)$ and if $(m > 0)$ then (did, m)). When the program completes we produce recommendations for user u and rank the candidate entities in descending order based on the computed recommendation scores.

4.3 Baseline Algorithms

To measure the effectiveness of our Guided Walk algorithm we implemented a set of baseline algorithms for comparison. We next explain each one of these algorithms.

4.3.1 *Simple Directed Random Walk (RW)*

To see if the learning phase produces benefit a good baseline is to create a version of the Guided Walk algorithm that skips the learning phase and assigns edge probabilities uniformly to every outgoing edge of every vertex. To implement this algorithm we reuse the algorithm for producing recommendations from edge weights described in Section 4.2 where all outgoing edges of a vertex v are assigned a probability equal to $\frac{1}{|out(v)|}$.

4.3.2 *Collaborative Filtering (CF)*

Collaborative Filtering is a widely used algorithm for producing personalized recommendations and, as such, is a good baseline for comparison. We used Spark's implicit feedback collaborative filtering implementation [3] implemented according to [10]. In our case an implicit feedback is given whenever a user performs any type of operation on an entity, e.g., "like", "comment", "create", "vote", etc. In other words, any operation that indicates an entity should be in a user's known interests is counted as an implicit feedback by a user on that entity. This is the only input necessary for the algorithm and it produces a ranked list of recommendations for each user based on the implicit feedback of all users. We describe how we choose the parameters for CF in Section 5.

4.3.3 Popular in Neighborhood (PN)

Given a personalized graph G_u, the Popular in Neighborhood (PN) algorithm ranks the candidate entities based on the number of actions all users performed on them within the context of G_u. Hence, the algorithm ranks the candidate entities that appear in G_u based on how popular they are. Recall that G_u only contains vertices and edges reachable from u, therefore this algorithm is still personalized in that it disregards entities outside the reach of u.

5. EXPERIMENTAL EVALUATION

In this Section we describe the experimental setting, our dataset and our evaluation methods. We analyze our results and provide evidence to support the usefulness of our Guided Walk recommendation algorithm for complex heterogeneous social networks.

5.1 Dataset

Our dataset was imported from a deployment of IBM Connections (IC) [11] within a large global enterprise. IC is a social media application suite for the enterprise. We used data collected over a period of 6 month, from October 2015 to March 2016 (inclusive). The data was exported as a textual CSV file whose size is roughly 100GB. The data consists of different types of social media entities which include: Communities, Blogs, Blog-entries, Wikis, Wiki-entries, Comments, Files, Forums, Forum-topics and Microblogs (similar to Tweets). Employees can create. edit, like, add comments and bookmark any of these entities and also add other employees as their colleagues (similar to friending in Facebook), tag them or follow them. Furthermore, hierarchical information about the structure between the entities also exists, e.g., a community can contain blogs that contain blog entries which contains user comments. For further information about IC and the dataset that it exports see [11, 6].

5.2 Environment

We used a shared multi-tenant Hadoop YARN cluster with 11 data/compute nodes with a total of 3.18TB of RAM and 260 virtual cores. The application framework we used is Apache Spark version 1.6.0. The graph based algorithms described in Section 4 were implemented using the GraphX framework and the Collaborative Filtering algorithm was implemented by using the MLlib implementation provided by Apache Spark.

[3]http://spark.apache.org/docs/latest/mllib-collaborative-filtering.html#explicit-vs-implicit-feedback

5.3 Offline Experiments

We selected 1100 of the most active IBM-Connections users within the above time period. We split the dataset into a training set and a test set. For the training set we used 4 months worth of data, from October 2015 to January 2016 (inclusive) and for the test we used the remaining 2 months of data after January 2016. We evaluated the algorithms described in Section 4 by training them on the training data and then having each algorithm produce the top 10, 50 and 100 recommendations for the selected users over the test data. The relevant documents for the information needs of a specific user were determined as any entity the user performed an action on according to the test dataset. The type of actions that were available to us in the dataset were 'like', 'comment', 'edited', 'joined a community', etc. However, one limitation is that we did not have access to passive view data, i.e., which entities users only viewed. To make the comparison between all the algorithms simple we further filtered this list by removing entities that were not present in the training set, e.g., new blogs, wikis, etc. which were not available to the algorithms during their training phase.

5.3.1 Parameter Tuning

We arbitrarily chose 100 of the 1100 users to tune the parameters of each of our tested algorithms by training the algorithm on the training set with different parameters and then examining the Mean Average Precision (MAP) [21] results on the test set for these same 100 users (as described above). Based on these results, we then chose the optimal parameters for each algorithm to produce recommendations for the remaining 1000 users. The parameters we chose for CF are rank = 10, $\alpha = \frac{1}{10000}$, $\lambda = \frac{1}{10000}$ and the number of iterations was set to 100. For GW we chose $\varepsilon = \frac{1}{1000000}$.

5.3.2 Results

To determine the quality of the recommendations produced by the algorithms described in Section 4, we calculated the MAP@10, MAP@50 and MAP@100 results for each algorithm over the 1000 users that were not part of the parameter tuning phase described in Section 5.3.1. The MAP results are reported in Figure 4. We added one more algorithm just to serve as a a minimum baseline for all other algorithms. This baseline algorithm is called Random-Rank (RR) (not to be confused with Random Walk (RW)) and it simply produces a randomly ranked list of recommendations from the training dataset for each user. Its MAP scores are barely noticeable in the figure since they are orders of magnitude lower than the scores of the other algorithms. Based on the figure, when comparing MAP@100 results, GW outperforms CF, PN, RW, RR by the factors of 3.6, 13.7, 16.3 and 7138 respectively. Especially interesting is the comparison between GW and RW since, as described in Section 4.3.1, RW works just like GW only without the learning phase. The fact that MAP results are improved $16 -$ fold provides clear evidence that the learning phase works well.

To find out how diverse the top recommendations produced by each algorithm are, we report the Jaccard Similarity between the top-100 recommendations produced by each algorithm in Table 2. First, from the comparison between all the algorithms to PN we can learn which algorithms tend to recommend entities that are more popular, i.e., entities that are not necessarily tailored to a specific user. It should

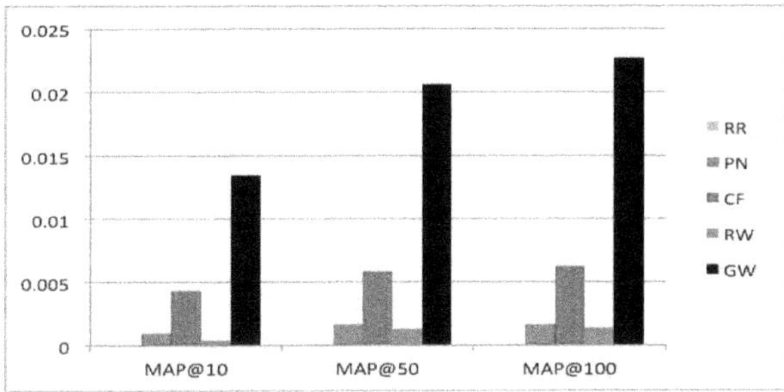

Figure 4: Offline experiments MAP results. The tested algorithms are Guided Walk (GW), Simple Directed Random Walk (RW), Popular in Neighborhood (PN), Alternating Least Squares Collaborative Filtering (CF) and Random-Rank (RR). Note that MAP values for RR are barely noticeable since they are very close to 0.

(PN,CF)	(PN,RW)	(PN,GW)	(CF,RW)	(CF,GW)	(RW,GW)
0.187	0.387	0.230	0.139	0.220	0.132

Table 2: Jaccard similarity ratios between the top-100 entities produced by each pair of algorithms averaged over all users. (0/1 indicates that sets are disjoint/identical).

not be surprising that the similarity between PN and RW is relatively high since entities that many users found interesting also tend to have more paths passing through them (i.e., via those users). Also interesting is that all similarity scores to PN tend to be somewhat high. We can learn from this that all the algorithms gave some natural preference to popular entities. This is a good sign since indeed popular entities tend to be of interest. Finally, notice that similarity between CF and GW is higher than CF and RW or RW and GW since both CF and GW try to better tailor the recommendations personally to the user.

We also tracked the running times of each of the algorithms when running in our environment. Note that the average per-user personalized graph G_u contained around 2 million edges and some vertices contained tens-of-thousands of adjacent edges making them hypernodes. The absolute running times are specific to our setting, however we report them in Table 3 to provide a comparison between the algorithms. To enhance user-recommendations throughput for GW which has a relatively high runtime we further utilized parallelism by splitting the set of 1000 users into 6 disjoint sets and running a Spark job for each of them separately. This allowed us to calculate the MAP values for GW over all 1000 users within less than 2 days. Each job was run on 11 Spark Executors with 2 cores each and 8 GB RAM per Executor.

5.4 User Survey

	GW	CF	RW	PN
Training	670 (per-user)	1590	-	-
Recommending	402	13	294	0.5

Table 3: Average running times in seconds for each algorithm. Note that RW and PN have no training phase and for GW the training phase is applied per-user whereas for CF it is applied once for the entire dataset.

One drawback of the offline experiment is that only entities which the user actually performed actions on during the test period are determined as relevant. Hence some entities may have been incorrectly categorized as irrelevant merely because the user was unaware of their existence. Furthermore, the degree of personal relevance between the entities and the users could not be directly assessed.

To address these problems we ran a user survey. We arbitrary selected 373 highly active IC users and sent each of them a list of recommendations based on their activity in the last two months (March and April 2016). The recommendations were produced by having the algorithms PN, CF, RW and GW each contribute their top-3 recommendations. The final list of recommendations was randomly shuffled. Out of the 373 selected users 94 chose to participate.

We sent the list of shuffled recommendations to each of the participants and asked them to rate the entities based on personal relevance on a scale of 0 to 3 (0 meaning irrelevant and 3 indicates the highest degree of personal relevance). We report the average ratings in Table 4.

	GW	CF	RW	PN
Rating	2.40	2.05	2.11	2.09

Table 4: Survey ratings for each algorithm averaged over all participants. (We ran ANOVA with $\alpha = 0.05$ which yielded an F-Value of 6.78 where the critical point value is 2.61 — this indicates that GW's score is statistically significant).

The results show that all algorithms achieve very high relevance ratings from the participants. Table 4 shows that GW achieves an average rating at least %14 higher than that of every other algorithm. Interestingly, RW in the survey slightly outperforms CF which does not correspond well with the offline experiment MAP results reported in Figure 4. We speculate that this has to do with the fact that RW recommends entities that the user was unaware of (hence the lower MAP values) but are none-the-less relevant to her since there are many paths in the social network from the user to those entities. As CF is oblivious to the social network structure, it is not as effective in finding such entities.

6. CONCLUSION

In this work we studied the problem of social entity recommendation in the context of a complex heterogeneous ESN. We devised a supervised learning algorithm called Guided Walk (GW) which builds on existing similarity based recommendations methods. However, unlike the previous methods its learning phase is fully automated and requires no domain knowledge or manual configuration. Moreover, the algorithm is implemented as a Pregel program allowing it to utilize the power of parallel distributed computing. As a result, the algorithm can cope with ever growing social networks by adding more compute nodes to the the cluster.

To evaluate the quality of recommendations we ran an offline experiment as well as a user survey. We show that GW's MAP scores are better than the other baseline algorithms by a factor of, at least, 3.6. Furthermore, the user survey results also confirm that recommendation are not only relevant but also rank high in terms of personal relevance for each user.

7. REFERENCES

[1] D. Agarwal, B.-C. Chen, R. Gupta, J. Hartman, Q. He, A. Iyer, S. Kolar, Y. Ma, P. Shivaswamy,

A. Singh, et al. Activity ranking in linkedin feed. In *SIGKDD*, pages 1603–1612, 2014.
[2] L. Backstrom and J. Leskovec. Supervised random walks: predicting and recommending links in social networks. In *Proceedings of the fourth ACM international conference on Web search and data mining*, pages 635–644. ACM, 2011.
[3] E. M. Daly, M. J. Muller, L. Gou, and D. R. Millen. Social lens: Personalization around user defined collections for filtering enterprise message streams. In *ICWSM*, 2011.
[4] J. Dean and S. Ghemawat. Mapreduce: simplified data processing on large clusters. *Communications of the ACM*, 51(1):107–113, 2008.
[5] W. Feng and J. Wang. Retweet or not?: personalized tweet re-ranking. In *WSDM*, pages 577–586, 2013.
[6] I. Guy, R. Levin, T. Daniel, and E. Bolshinsky. Islands in the stream: A study of item recommendation within an enterprise social stream. In *SIGIR*, pages 665–674, 2015.
[7] I. Guy, T. Steier, M. Barnea, I. Ronen, and T. Daniel. Finger on the pulse: the value of the activity stream in the enterprise. In *Human-Computer Interaction*, pages 411–428. 2013.
[8] P. Harrington. *Machine learning in action.* 2012.
[9] L. Hong, R. Bekkerman, J. Adler, and B. D. Davison. Learning to rank social update streams. In *SIGIR*, pages 651–660, 2012.
[10] Y. Hu, Y. Koren, and C. Volinsky. Collaborative filtering for implicit feedback datasets. In *ICDM*, 2008.
[11] IBM. Ibm-connections. http://www-03.ibm.com/software/products/en/conn, 2007.
[12] G. Jeh and J. Widom. Simrank: a measure of structural-context similarity. In *SIGKDD*, pages 538–543, 2002.
[13] G. Jeh and J. Widom. Scaling personalized web search. In *WWW*, pages 271–279, 2003.
[14] I. Konstas, V. Stathopoulos, and J. M. Jose. On social networks and collaborative recommendation. In *SIGIR*, pages 195–202, 2009.
[15] P. Kouki, S. Fakhraei, J. Foulds, M. Eirinaki, and L. Getoor. Hyper: A flexible and extensible probabilistic framework for hybrid recommender systems. In *ACM RecSys*, pages 99–106, 2015.
[16] N. Lao and W. W. Cohen. Fast query execution for retrieval models based on path-constrained random walks. In *Proceedings of the 16th ACM SIGKDD international conference on Knowledge discovery and data mining*, pages 881–888, 2010.
[17] B. Long, Z. M. Zhang, and P. S. Yu. Co-clustering by block value decomposition. In *SIGKDD*, pages 635–640, 2005.
[18] L. Lovász et al. Random walks on graphs: A survey. *Combinatorics, Paul Erdos is Eighty*, 2:353–398, 1996.
[19] C. Luo, W. Pang, Z. Wang, and C. Lin. Hete-cf: Social-based collaborative filtering recommendation using heterogeneous relations. In *ICDM*, pages 917–922, 2014.
[20] G. Malewicz, M. H. Austern, A. J. Bik, J. C. Dehnert, I. Horn, N. Leiser, and G. Czajkowski. Pregel: a system for large-scale graph processing. In *Proceedings of the 2010 ACM SIGMOD International Conference on Management of data*, pages 135–146, 2010.
[21] C. D. Manning, P. Raghavan, H. Schütze, et al. *Introduction to information retrieval*, volume 1. 2008.
[22] R. S. Marcus and J. F. Reintjes. A translating computer interface for end-user operation of heterogeneous retrieval systems. ii. evaluations. *Journal of the American Society for Information Science*, 32(4):304–317, 1981.
[23] T. Paek, M. Gamon, S. Counts, D. M. Chickering, and A. Dhesi. Predicting the importance of newsfeed posts and social network friends. In *AAAI*, volume 10, pages 1419–1424, 2010.
[24] F. Ricci, L. Rokach, and B. Shapira. *Introduction to recommender systems handbook.* 2011.
[25] C. Shi, X. Kong, Y. Huang, P. S. Yu, and B. Wu. Hetesim: A general framework for relevance measure in heterogeneous networks. *Knowledge and Data Engineering*, 26(10):2479–2492, 2014.
[26] C. Shi, Y. Li, J. Zhang, Y. Sun, and P. S. Yu. A survey of heterogeneous information network analysis. *TKDE*, 2015.
[27] C. Shi, Z. Zhang, P. Luo, P. S. Yu, Y. Yue, and B. Wu. Semantic path based personalized recommendation on weighted heterogeneous information networks. In *Proceedings of the 24th ACM International on Conference on Information and Knowledge Management*, pages 453–462, 2015.
[28] Y. Sun and J. Han. Meta-path-based search and mining in heterogeneous information networks. *Tsinghua Science and Technology*, 18(4):329–338, 2013.
[29] Y. Sun, J. Han, X. Yan, P. S. Yu, and T. Wu. Pathsim: Meta path-based top-k similarity search in heterogeneous information networks. *VLDB*, 2011.
[30] R. Wang, C. Shi, S. Y. Philip, and B. Wu. Integrating clustering and ranking on hybrid heterogeneous information network. In *SIGKDD*, pages 583–594. 2013.
[31] R. S. Xin, J. E. Gonzalez, M. J. Franklin, and I. Stoica. Graphx: A resilient distributed graph system on spark. In *First International Workshop on Graph Data Management Experiences and Systems*, page 2, 2013.
[32] X. Yu, X. Ren, Y. Sun, Q. Gu, B. Sturt, U. Khandelwal, B. Norick, and J. Han. Personalized entity recommendation: A heterogeneous information network approach. In *WSDM*, pages 283–292, 2014.
[33] X. Yu, X. Ren, Y. Sun, B. Sturt, U. Khandelwal, Q. Gu, B. Norick, and J. Han. Recommendation in heterogeneous information networks with implicit user feedback. In *ACM RecSys*, pages 347–350, 2013.
[34] M. Zaharia, M. Chowdhury, T. Das, A. Dave, J. Ma, M. McCauley, M. J. Franklin, S. Shenker, and I. Stoica. Resilient distributed datasets: A fault-tolerant abstraction for in-memory cluster computing. In *Proceedings of the 9th USENIX conference on Networked Systems Design and Implementation*, pages 2–2, 2012.

STAR: Semiring Trust Inference for Trust-Aware Social Recommenders

Peixin Gao
Institute for Systems Research
University of Maryland
gaopei@umd.edu

Hui Miao
Dept. of Computer Science
University of Maryland
hui@cs.umd.edu

John S. Baras
Institute for Systems Research
University of Maryland
baras@umd.edu

Jennifer Golbeck
College of Information Studies
University of Maryland
jgolbeck@umd.edu

ABSTRACT

Social recommendation takes advantage of the influence of social relationships in decision making and the ready availability of social data through social networking systems. Trust relationships in particular can be exploited in such systems for rating prediction and recommendation, which has been shown to have the potential for improving the quality of the recommender and alleviating the issue of data sparsity, cold start, and adversarial attacks. An appropriate trust inference mechanism is necessary in extending the knowledge base of trust opinions and tackling the issue of limited trust information due to connection sparsity of social networks.

In this work, we offer a new solution to trust inference in social networks to provide a better knowledge base for trust-aware recommender systems. We propose using a semiring framework as a nonlinear way to combine trust evidences for inferring trust, where trust relationship is model as 2-D vector containing both trust and certainty information. The trust propagation and aggregation rules, as the building blocks of our trust inference scheme, are based upon the properties of trust relationships. In our approach, both trust and distrust (i.e., positive and negative trust) are considered, and opinion conflict resolution is supported. We evaluate the proposed approach on real-world datasets, and show that our trust inference framework has high accuracy, and is capable of handling trust relationship in large networks. The inferred trust relationships can enlarge the knowledge base for trust information and improve the quality of trust-aware recommendation.

1. INTRODUCTION

Recommender systems are continuously evolving to take advantage of new sources of information. Social sources in particular can be useful for building better recommendations. The idea of integrating signals from social networks to improve the performance of recommendation algorithms has been well accepted and has attracted an increasing amount of research [2,28].

One type of social recommender system is the trust-aware recommender, where the social connections are annotated with trust relationship information in the recommendation algorithm. A series of trust-aware recommenders have been proposed, such as user-based approaches [12,16,25], and matrix factorization based methods [17,22,24]. With the help of the additional trust information, trust-aware recommenders have been shown useful for improving recommendation quality in terms of accuracy and user experience, as well as addressing challenges of classical recommender system approaches such as cold start and adversarial attacks [12,23].

However, trust-aware recommender systems face several challenges: a) sparse social connections; b) inconsistency and conflicts in trust opinions; c) trust data availability.

To address these challenges, there has been a line of study regarding trust inference in trust-aware recommender systems, which can generally be categorized in two groups. One group conducts theoretical studies on trust metrics and their properties [3, 14, 18, 19, 30]. The other group proposes effective data-driven approaches for inferring trust, such as graph-theoretic models [4, 10–12, 25, 27] and machine learning approaches [20].

Graph-theoretic models generally have good performance in terms of efficiency and reasoning. However, as most work applies linear weighted averaging over trust opinions from neighbors, nonlinearity in human decision making and interaction between trust and distrust may not be fully captured. The path-based design is also sensitive to the connection sparsity in the trust network, since the trust path will not exist if some edges in between are missing. These defects restrain the accuracy of the models. On the other hand, machine learning methods can solve the data sparsity, sometimes with better label prediction accuracy. However, due to the nature of the formulation, machine learning methods are slower in speed and have weak interpretation on how trust is inferred.

It is ideal if there exist a method which addresses most challenges at the same time. In [9], we introduced a theoretical semiring structure for nonlinear trust fusion with distrust considered. It requires that both trust and certainty information are explicitly given. The model proposed

RecSys '16, September 15-19, 2016, Boston , MA, USA
© 2016 ACM. ISBN 978-1-4503-4035-9/16/09...$15.00
DOI: http://dx.doi.org/10.1145/2959100.2959148

in [9] is easy to interpret and runs fast. However,it cannot be applied in real world scenarios, due to lack of certainty models and inference algorithms on the overall network dealing with data sparsities. In order to apply it to trust evaluation for trust-aware recommendation, the original design needs revision and redefinition.

In this work, we propose a trust inference method for trust-aware recommendation. Our technology extends the semiring model proposed in [9]. The basic idea is to build up a nonlinear trust aggregation rule that can handle both trust and distrust information, and offer conflict resolution in the opinion combination process. Apart from the flexibility in modeling, this approach has the advantages of efficiency inherited from graph theoretic models and better accuracy due to an iterative component and optimization over parameters. The evaluated trust can enlarge the knowledge base for recommendation algorithms, and alleviate the issue of the data sparsity and cold start in recommender systems.

The contributions of our work are four-fold:

1. a novel trust metric for trust-aware recommender systems is introduced
2. we introduce two certainty models for semiring-based trust evaluation in our application, and discuss several properties of the evaluation framework
3. we introduce trust iteration, as well as partial reciprocity, in order to further improve the coverage and accuracy of our proposed trust metric
4. we evaluate our model using real-world dataset, and show that our approach can achieve the accuracy to about 95%

Our paper is organized as follows. In Sec. 2, we discuss some preliminaries and related work. Accordingly, we introduce STAR, our semiring nonlinear model for trust inference in a social recommender scenario in Sec. 3, with some extensions for better performance. We evaluate our proposed approach in Sec. 4, and summarize our work in Sec. 5.

2. PRELIMINARIES

2.1 Trust relationships in SNS

The wide application of trust has made it an umbrella term with multiple interpretations in different contexts. In [18], two definitions of trust, *reliability* and *decision* trust, are discussed. In social network scenario, the notion of decision trust can be applied, which links to the extent to which an agent (i.e. the truster) is willing to depend on another one (trustee) in a given situation for decision making, with a feeling of similarity, closeness or security [30].

2.1.1 Trust & distrust

In social network scenario, trust relationship is based on the social connection between truster and trustee. There are various ways to quantitatively represent trust [13,18,30,31]. The trust value domain $\mathcal{T}$ is application dependent. For instance, it can be a set of discrete labels $\{0, 1\}$ or a continuous range like $[0, 1]$. It can have both positive values and negative values, and can even be a multi-dimensional vector space. When $\mathcal{T}$ contains negative trust values, it can be used to differentiate unknown users (i.e. of trust value 0) from ones that are not trusted (e.g. negative trust values). The negative trust relationship is also called distrust. Although recent research [8, 13, 30] shows an emerging interest in modeling the notion of distrust, models that take into account both trust and distrust are still limited. Introducing distrust makes the trust model complex as the non-negativity of trust values no long exists, and the linearity of trust aggregation is hard to argue. This can be especially challenging for many trust inference approaches such as matrix factorization [28]. Additionally, the subjective property of trust makes it even more complicate as conflicts between trust opinions may exist.

2.1.2 Trust networks

We refer to a **Trust Network** as the graph based on the trust relationships in a social network. The trust network can be defined as a directed graph with trust weight on edges, $\mathcal{G}(V, E, t_e)$, where V is the set of users, E is the set of connections denoting the directed trust relationships, and $t_e : E \mapsto \mathcal{T}$ is a mapping from an edge to the trust value placed on the edge. We use $\langle v_i, v_j \rangle_{\text{trust}}$ to denote trust relationship when $e_{ij} \in E$ and $t_{ij} > 0$. For a user $v \in V$, we denote the 1-hop neighbors as **Neighbor Set** $\mathcal{N}_v$. The undirected situation can be seen as having two edges with equal weights on both directions for the pair of vertices.

In the defined trust network, a directed path of length k is a sequence of distinct nodes, $\{v_1, v_2 \cdots, v_{m+1}\}$, such that $(v_i, v_{i+1}) \in E, \forall i \in 1, 2, \cdots, m$. Between two nodes in the network, there might be multiple distinct paths.

2.1.3 Transitivity in trust

The transitivity of trust relationships is the foundation for most trust metrics, it allows the truster to acquire information about the trustee from friends and their friends ("word of mouth") [15]. For example, if node v_1 and v_3 are not directed connected, but if v_1 trusts v_2, and v_2 trusts v_3, then v_1 can use such trust evidence to infer its opinion about v_3 using transitivity.

Formally, transitivity in trust can be defined as:

$$\langle v_i, v_j \rangle_{\text{trust}} \wedge \langle v_j, v_k \rangle_{\text{trust}} \Rightarrow \langle v_i, v_k \rangle_{\text{trust}} \quad \forall v_i, v_j, v_k \in V \quad (1)$$

Based on the assumption of transitivity (may be partial), trust can propagate along the paths between two nodes in the network and their trust relationship can be inferred. When multiple paths exist, a combination scheme is needed to derive the trust value. Due to the subjective nature, conflicts may happen in such occasion and need to be resolved.

Transitivity becomes more complex when considering distrust relationships [7]. For example, the trust relation between node v_1 and v_3 is not obvious if v_1 distrusts v_2 and v_2 distrusts v_3. The conflict resolution is also much more difficult with distrust.

2.1.4 Reciprocity in trust

Trust reciprocity describes the extent of symmetry in directed trust relationships between two users (i.e. nodes) in the social network. Similar to Eq. 1, we can write the following expression for reciprocity.

$$\begin{aligned} &\langle v_i, v_j \rangle_{\text{trust}} \Rightarrow \langle v_j, v_i \rangle_{\text{trust}} && \text{(trust reciprocity)} \\ &\langle v_i, v_j \rangle_{\text{distrust}} \Rightarrow \langle v_j, v_i \rangle_{\text{distrust}} && \text{(distrust reciprocity)} \quad (2) \\ & && \forall v_i, v_j \in V \end{aligned}$$

As shown in [6,10], trust relationships are asymmetric in terms of values (especially magnitude) in social network scenarios, thus most trust evaluation approaches don't consider reciprocity. However, by relaxing the condition in Eq. 2 to only sign agreement of positive trust relationships, **partial**

reciprocity can be defined. As we will show in Sec. 4.1, the partial reciprocity exists in the Epinions trust network dataset. The partial reciprocity between nodes may be useful in inferring indirect trust under some circumstances when data is very sparse (e.g. social recommender).

2.2 Semirings

A semiring is an algebraic structure, consisting of a set **A** and two binary operations, addition ($\oplus$) and multiplication ($\otimes$), with several conditions over the operations.

Definition. A *semiring* is a tuple $\langle \mathbf{A}, \oplus, \otimes, \mathbf{0}, \mathbf{1} \rangle$ such that

- **A** is a nonempty (possibly infinite) set with two special elements $\mathbf{0}, \mathbf{1} \in \mathbf{A}$
- $\oplus$ is the additive operation, which is commutative and associative:
$$a \oplus b = b \oplus a$$
$$a \oplus (b \oplus c) = (a \oplus b) \oplus c \qquad \forall a, b, c \in A$$
with $\mathbf{0}$ as the unit element ($a \oplus \mathbf{0} = a = \mathbf{0} \oplus a$)
- $\otimes$ is the multiplicative operation, which is associative,
$$a \otimes (b \otimes c) = (a \otimes b) \otimes c \qquad \forall a, b, c \in A$$
with $\mathbf{1}$ as the unit element and $\mathbf{0}$ as absorbing element ($a \otimes \mathbf{1} = a = \mathbf{1} \otimes a,\ a \otimes \mathbf{0} = \mathbf{0} = \mathbf{0} \otimes a$)
- $\otimes$ distributes over $\oplus$,
$$a \otimes (b \oplus c) = (a \otimes b) \oplus (a \otimes c)$$

An example of a semiring is the set of nonnegative integers $\mathbb{N}$, with the usual addition ($+$) and multiplication ($\times$).

The operations used in a semiring structure can be seen as a generalization of addition and multiplication which have used in trust inference for social recommendation. These semiring operations, with careful design, are able to capture the nonlinearity in trust evaluation [29].

2.3 Semiring-based trust fusion

The sets **A** in most semiring models only have nonnegative elements (e.g. the range of $[0, 1]$) [5, 29]. Due to the complexity and asymmetry introduced by negativity, the semiring framework needs to be carefully modified. In [9], the possibility of applying semiring for nonlinear trust fusion in online decision making was discussed, and a semiring called a *Distrust Semiring* was introduced. The semiring structure was defined on a 2-dimensional trust opinion model, with both trust and distrust relationships being considered.

2.3.1 Trust opinion vectors

The 2-dimensional trust opinion vector $\tau_{ij} \in \mathcal{T} = [-1, 1] \times [0, 1]$ from truster i to trustee j is defined as

$$\tau_{ij} = (t_{ij}, c_{ij}) \qquad (3)$$

where $t_{ij} \in [-1, 1]$ is the trust level representing how much i trusts (likes)/distrusts (dislikes) the opinions (tastes) of j. By making trust levels take values in the range of $[-1, 1]$, distrust is considered along with trust. $c_{ij} \in [0, 1]$ is the certainty level which shows how much i believes in the integrity of j. Note that certainty is orthogonal to trust value, it denotes the quality and accuracy of the trustee's opinion. While a high trust value may be because of similarity in taste or preference, a high certainty value may be due to direct connection with the truster or large number of connections (i.e. high degree). Certainty determines if the opinion will be considered, and opinions with a high certainty value are more useful in making trust decisions.

As both trust level and certainty level about the trustee are considered in the opinion vector, more complicated situations can be modeled and analyzed.

Based on Sec. 2.1.2 and the definition of trust opinion vector, the trust network can be derived.

Definition. A trust network based on the set $\mathcal{T}$ of trust opinions is a directed and weighted graph $\mathcal{G}(V, E, t_e)$, $t_e : E \mapsto \mathcal{T}$, where V is the set of users. E is the set of trust relationships. For $\forall e_{ij} = (v_i, v_j) \in E$, $v_i, v_j \in V, i \neq j$, t_e associates it with an opinion vector $\tau_{ij} = (t_{ij}, c_{ij}) \in \mathcal{T}$, indicating the trust and certainty that node v_i holds on v_j. Trust links are directed. $N_i = \{v_j | e_{ij} \in E\}$ is the neighbor set of node v_i.

2.3.2 Distrust semirings

A distrust semiring [9] is a 2-dimensional semring defined on the trust opinion set $\mathcal{T}$, such that

- $\mathbf{A} = \mathcal{T} = [-1, 1] \times [0, 1]$ the set of trust opinion vectors, with two special elements $\mathbf{0} = (0, 0), \mathbf{1} = (1, 1)$
- The additive operation $\oplus$ is defined as
$$(t_a, c_a) \oplus (t_b, c_b) = (t, c) \qquad (4)$$
with $c = max\{c_a, c_b\}$, and
$$t = \begin{cases} t_a & c_a > c_b \\ t_b & c_b > c_a \\ sign(t_a + t_b) \cdot max\{|t_a|, |t_b|\} & c_a = c_b \end{cases} \qquad (5)$$
- The multiplicative operation $\otimes$ is defined as
$$(t_a, c_a) \otimes (t_b, c_b) = (t, c) \qquad (6)$$
where $c = c_a c_b$, and
$$t = \begin{cases} 0 & t_a < 0,\ t_b < 0 \\ t_a t_b & \text{otherwise} \end{cases} \qquad (7)$$

For the trust network shown in Fig. 1, there are three paths from node v_1 to v_5. For the left path, when we multiply τ_{12} and τ_{25} using $\otimes$, we have $\tau_1 = \tau_{12} \otimes \tau_{25} = (0.36, 0.56)$. Similarly, the middle path has $\tau_2 = (0.12, 0.25)$ and the right one $\tau_3 = (-0.15, 0.56)$. When combining τ_1, τ_2, τ_3, we can use $\oplus$ defined in distrust semiring and have combined opinion $\tau = \tau_1 \oplus \tau_2 \oplus \tau_3 = (0.36, 0.56)$.

Based its definition in [9], distrust semiring is a promising algebra structure that can be used in designing trust metrics for social recommender systems. However, [9] only proposed the framework with some theoretical analysis, without experiments and evaluation with real datasets. Also, in the work, trust is represented by a 2-D vector with both trust and certainty information, with the assumption that information about both components are explicit and available. However, in social recommender setting, certainty information is generally missing. In order to use the 2-D representation of trust, a model for certainty based on social context is required yet has not been discussed.

3. STAR: SEMIRING TRUST INFERENCE FOR TRUST-AWARE RECOMMENDATION

In this section, we draw connections between distrust semiring and trust inference in trust-aware social recommender systems: a) we first show the distrust semiring definition

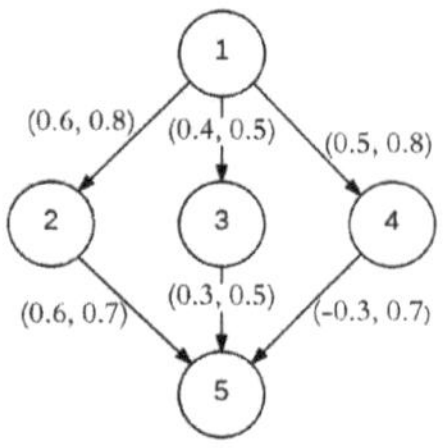

Figure 1: An example trust network

(Eq.4-7) is consistent with the properties for trust propagation and aggregation in Sec. 3.1; b) next in Sec. 3.2, we propose practical certainty models and parameter tuning framework in order to use distrust semiring in practice; c) we then propose the overall **S**emiring trust inference for **T**rust-**A**ware social **R**ecommenders (STAR) framework in Sec. 3.3; d) furthermore, to address the data sparsity and improve accuracy and coverage, we introduce iterative trust evaluation in semiring trust in Sec. 3.4.

3.1 Distrust semiring and trust properties

Trust information diminishes and becomes noisy in the process of propagation, and increases when aggregating neighborhood values. These are basic properties [19] of trust. Distrust semiring essentially defines an algebraic way to calculate trust, thus we first need to show whether the basic operations, addition used in trust aggregation and multiplication used in trust propagation, satisfies the commonsense.

By defining a partial ordering, we show that the semiring framework is intuitive and consistent with requirements for trust propagation and aggregation.

Definition. A partial order relation $\preceq$ can be defined upon two 2-D opinion vectors $\tau_a = (t_a, c_a)$ and $\tau_b = (t_b, c_b)$:

$$\tau_a \preceq \tau_b \tag{8}$$

if and only if

$$c_a \leq c_b, \text{ or } \quad |t_a| \leq |t_b| \text{ and } c_a = c_b \qquad \forall\, \tau_a, \tau_b \in \mathcal{T}$$

Theorem 3.1. The distrust semiring structure satisfies the following two conditions,

1. the multiplication operation is non-increasing:

$$\forall \tau_a, \tau_b \in \mathcal{T}, \quad \tau_a \otimes \tau_b \preceq \tau_a \wedge \tau_a \otimes \tau_b \preceq \tau_b \tag{9}$$

2. the addition operation is non-decreasing

$$\forall \tau_a, \tau_b \in \mathcal{T}, \quad \tau_a \preceq \tau_a \oplus \tau_b \wedge \tau_b \preceq \tau_a \oplus \tau_b \tag{10}$$

Proof. Let $\tau_a \otimes \tau_b = (t, c)$. As $c_a,\ c_b \in [0, 1]$, and $t_a,\ t_b \in [-1, 1]$, based on the definition of the multiplication operation, it is easy to see that $c = c_a c_b \leq c_a$, $c = c_a c_b \leq c_b$. For the trust value, if both t_a and t_b are negative, then $t = 0 < |t_a|, |t_b|$. Otherwise, $|t| = |t_a t_b| = |t_a||t_b| \leq |t_a|$, and $|t| = |t_a t_b| \leq |t_b|$. Thus Eq. 9 holds, and the non-increasing property of the multiplication operation is proved.

The non-decreasing property of trust aggregation can be shown in a similar way. In aggregation, $\tau = (t, c) = \tau_a \oplus \tau_b$. based on definition, $c = \max\{c_a, c_b\} \geq c_a, c_b$. Thus the first condition is satisfied, and the non-decreasing property of the additive operation is proved. □

The non-increasing property of the multiplication operation is in accordance with the requirement for trust propagation process, whereas the non-decreasing property of the addition operation connects to the trust aggregation process. Thus the two operations for a distrust semiring can be applied to modeling trust propagation and aggregation respectively.

3.2 Certainty models

In the context of trust-aware recommenders, though trust data is available, the certainty information is generally implicit and contained in user interactions. Without certainty data, it is infeasible to apply the 2-D semiring model for trust inference. In practice, certainty may be derived by sentiment analysis or other natural language processing pipelines. However, NLP toolboxes are not light-weight and require rich text data in the SNS. In this paper, we consider the situation when only SNS connections and trust data are available. We propose two ways to model certainty. One is based on length of the trust path, the other one is degree-oriented.

3.2.1 Path-based certainty models

Based on the fact that neighbors which are reachable via a longer trust path carry less valuable trust information [12], we come up with a path-based certainty model. We model the certainty value of user v_s about v_t as a function of hops (i.e. the length of the shortest path) between the two.

$$c_{st} = g(\text{dist}_{s,t}) = \alpha^{\text{dist}_{s,t}} \tag{11}$$

where $\alpha \in (0, 1]$ is a hyperparameter and can be seen as the decay factor, and $\text{dist}_{s,t}$ represents the shortest trust path length between v_s and v_t. When $\alpha = 1$, the decay disappears and nodes of all distances are considered equally. Such definition is equivalent to introducing a 1-hop decay of magnitude α at each hop. Instead of calculating c_{st}, we consider the decay at node v_i in the middle:

$$c_i = g(v_i) = \alpha \qquad \text{(the decay factor)} \tag{12}$$

then along path_{st} from v_s to v_t, $c_{st} = \prod_{v_i \in \text{path}_{st}} c_i$. In this simple model, partial order relation between two paths is stable for $\forall \alpha \in (0, 1)$.

3.2.2 Degree-based certainty models

Another way to model certainty in social recommender setting is based on node degree, with the hypothesis that nodes of higher degree are more reliable and their trust opinions have more certainty. The certainty function of a node v_i can be accordingly denoted as

$$c_i = g(v_i) = g(d_i) \tag{13}$$

where d_i is the degree of v_i.

We consider two realizations for $g(d_i)$, a linear model and an exponential model. The linear model can be written as

$$g(d_i) = \min(\beta + \gamma d_i, 1) \tag{14}$$

which is determined by a cut-off degree value Δ, when $d_i > \Delta$, $g(d_i) = 1$.

The exponential model can be described by

$$g(d_i) = 1 - \eta^{d_i} \tag{15}$$

The coefficients β, γ, and η are tunable. Given the trust metric, an optimization problem over the parameters can be formulated accordingly to maximize its performance. The optimization formulation, due to the complexity of network structure and the semiring model we use, is non-convex and hard to solve. However, as there's only very few optimization variables (i.e. model parameters), we can simplify the problem by conducting parameter search schemes, such as greedy search, random search or even annealing approach, and measure its effect on system performance.

3.3 Inferring trust via semiring operators

With the certainty model defined above, the trust between two arbitrary users in the trust network can be inferred via the trust metric developed in this work. The trust metric consists of two components, i.e. trust propagation and aggregation, which can be defined using the distrust-semiring. In STAR, trust aggregation is conducted along different paths first before trust propagation, in order to reduce the noises caused by longer paths.

3.3.1 Trust propagation

In the trust metric, the trust value between two nodes v_s and v_t, who have no direct connection, can be estimated via the multiplicative operation $\otimes$ of trust values on edges along the path between the two nodes. Along each path path_{st},

$$(t_{st}, c_{st}) = \prod_{\otimes, e_{ij} \in \text{path}_{st}} (t_{ij}, c_{ij}) \tag{16}$$

Considering the decay of influence along the path, a maximum hop value λ can be introduced in order to stop early and accelerate the calculation. As shown in Sec. 4, 4-hop semiring calculation already reaches about 95% accuracy.

When multiple paths between two nodes exist, trust opinions reached along all paths should be aggregated together.

3.3.2 Trust aggregation

The trust aggregation component in the trust metric is to combine trust information from different sources (i.e. paths). It can be defined upon a semiring operation as follows:

$$(t, c) = \sum_{\oplus, \{a | \text{path}_a \in P\}} (t_a, c_a) \tag{17}$$

where P is the set of trust paths considered in aggregation, and each (t_a, c_a) with $\text{path}_a \in P$ is the trust vector along that trust path a.

3.3.3 Overall trust inference framework

A trust metric can be developed based on the trust propagation and aggregation rules defined above. Given a pair of users v_s (truster) and v_t (trustee), the proposed trust inference method is a function $f : V \times V \mapsto \mathcal{T}$, such that

$$(t_{st}, c_{st}) = f(v_s, v_t) = \sum_{\oplus, v_j \in N_s} (t_{sj}, c_{sj}) \otimes (t_{jt}, c_{jt}) \tag{18}$$

where N_s is the neighbor set of v_s. In order to save computation resources, a threshold for trust value (σ_t) and certainty value (σ_c) can be introduced. When below the thresholds, the trust opinion will not be considered in aggregation, i.e.

$$(t_{st}, c_{st}) = \sum_{\oplus, v_j \in N_s, (\sigma_t, \sigma_c) \preceq \tau_{sj} \otimes \tau_{jt}} (t_{sj}, c_{sj}) \otimes (t_{jt}, c_{jt}) \tag{19}$$

The way that the trust metric is applied to trust inference is shown in Alg. 1. The algorithm is to evaluate the trust opinion (t_{st}, c_{st}) of v_s (truster) about v_t (trustee), with λ the maximum hop number, σ_t and σ_c the lower bounds for trust and certainty value respectively. One can interpret the algorithm as follows: v_s asks her neighbors for their trust opinions about v_t. Each neighbor $v_i \in N_s$ provides her opinion about v_t (i.e. t_{it} and c_{it}), either directly or estimated using the trust inference algorithm recursively. At each hop forward, λ, the current hop reached, will decrease by 1 until reaching 0. Then v_s aggregates all the evidence and reach (t_{st}, c_{st}) about v_t.

In such a trust inference framework, both trust and distrust (i.e. negative trust) are taken into consideration for trust inference. As paths above the thresholds are all integrated into the calculation, trust information are fully exploited in this approach for better coverage. At each node, the trust information along different paths is first aggregated together and then propagation to the node as a unified trust opinion. Such scheme can reduce the noises caused by long paths. The possible conflicts among opinions are handled in a non-trivial way with the introduction of certainty value and nonlinear addition operation ($\oplus$).

Algorithm 1 STAR algorithm, $f_{star}(v_s, v_t, \lambda, \sigma_t, \sigma_c)$

```
Mark v_s as visited
if t_st exists then
  return (t_st, g(v_t))
end if
t_st ← 0
c_st ← 0
if λ = 0 then
  return (0, 0)
end if
for each v_i ∈ N_s, the neighbor set of node v_s do
  c_si = g(v_i)
  if (v_i visited) or (|t_si| < σ_t) or (c_si < σ_c) then
    continue
  end if
  (t_it, c_it) ← f_star(v_i, v_t, λ − 1, σ_t/|t_si|, σ_c/c_si)
  if (t_si < 0 and t_it < 0) or (t_it = 0) then
    continue
  end if
  (t_st, c_st) ← (t_st, c_st) ⊕ ((t_si, c_si) ⊗ (t_it, c_it))
end for
return (t_st, c_st)
```

3.4 Iterative trust evaluation

Alg. 1 is built on the trust paths between two users. In real world data, the trust data often is sparse, thus the coverage of STAR is limited by the amount of trust data present. In order to address the sparsity, we propose collective method from network analysis. Iterative method is a type of collective approaches in classification problem [21]. Such method is used when the data contains interconnection and correlation between objects, such as webpages and SNS, and has been shown to be very effective over network data [26]. The basic idea is treating the independent inference as a joint inference problem, and use an iterative approach to predict labels; the new label predicted in the previous iterations is used in the following iterations.

In the trust inference problem, trust relationships among users are intercorrelated, we introduce iterative trust evaluation in Alg. 2 to improve the performance. The basic idea of the design is to iteratively evaluate the trust opinions associated with the edges in the test dataset, conditioned on the both ground truth and current predictions. Initially, the knowledge base is the training dataset, and the result set is empty. While running, the "diff" in Alg. 2 is used to measure the difference of results between two iterations. Here the Euclidean norm is used in calculating the difference. The iteration ends when convergence on local predictions is reached or maximum number of iterations has finished.

3.5 Discussions

3.5.1 Exploiting partial reciprocity in trust

As discussed in Sec. 2.1.4, partial reciprocity can be added into the trust inference algorithm to improve both coverage and accuracy. We extend the trust inference algorithm

Algorithm 2 Iterative trust evaluation

```
Let E: set of edges to evaluate
knowledge_base ← known trust relationships
result_set ← ∅
Let K: max number of iterations
for i : 1 to K do
  diff ← 0
  for edge e_j ∈ E do
    knowledge_base ← knowledge_base \ (t_j, c_j)
    calculate trust metric f_star(e_j)
    if ((t_j, c_j) ∉ result_set) then
      diff ← diff + ||f_star(e_j)||
    else
      diff ← diff + ||f_star(e_j) − (t_j, c_j)||
      result_set ← result_set \ (t_j, c_j)
    end if
    (t_j, c_j) ← f_star(e_j)
    result_set ← result_set ∪ (t_j, c_j)
    knowledge_base ← knowledge_base ∪ (t_j, c_j)
  end for
  if (diff < ε) then
    return result_set
  end if
end for
return result_set
```

(Alg. 1) by introducing partial reciprocity in a careful way. Apart from considering trust evidences from neighbors, the truster also treat the direct trust opinion about herself from the trustee as a source of information, as a reflection of partial reciprocity. In order to reduce the error due to asymmetry in trust relationships, we only consider positive reciprocity (i.e. the reciprocity in positive trust relationships), and the certainty value in a trust opinion reached using reciprocity has a smaller magnitude compared the one reached through transitivity-based propagation.

3.5.2 Optimistic vs pessimistic semiring definitions

In Sec. 3.3, the trust metric takes an optimistic definition for trust aggregation, as the binary operation $\oplus$ takes the larger magnitude of the two and its sign as the combined trust value when the certainty levels are the same. We use this to define trust aggregation based on the hypothesis that extreme opinions weigh more than neutral ones [11,12]. In a pessimistic model, when $c_a = c_b$, the addition operation for trust aggregation (Eq. 5) can be modified as

$$t = sign(t_a + t_b) \cdot \min\{|t_a|, |t_b|\} \tag{20}$$

Such definition is "pessimistic", as the aggregated trust value conservatively picks the smaller magnitude between the two incoming trust values. With such model, trust aggregation is not non-decreasing any more, which is against the basic properties of trust as mentioned in Sec. 3.1.

4. EVALUATION

In order to verify the model and evaluate the performance of our semiring-based approach, we conduct experiments on a real world dataset.

We use the Epinions trust network dataset for evaluation [1]. The dataset contains both direct trust connections (with edge weight of +1) and distrust ones (with edge weight of −1), and form the trust network $\mathcal{G}(V, E, t_e)$ where $t_e : E \mapsto \mathcal{T} = \{-1, 1\}$. To the best of our knowledge, it is the largest dataset available online that contains both explicit trust and distrust information marked in a binary (+1 and −1) format. The dataset has 91.053 users with 841,372 edges, 717,667 trust relationships and 123,705 distrust relationships. Notice that the method works on continuous trust value domains as well. However, large-scale public datasets are not available.

4.1 Transitivity and partial reciprocity in data

In order to evaluate our trust metric, we first verify the transitivity and partial reciprocity of trust relationships using the Epinions dataset.

4.1.1 Transitivity

Inspired by previous works, we investigate the transitivity phenomenon. For transitivity, we count the number of triangles represented by triplets (i, j, k) such that

$$v_i, v_j, v_k \in V, \; e_{ij}, e_{jk}, e_{ik} \in E \tag{21}$$

$$\text{and} \qquad t_{ij}t_{jk}t_{ik} > 0 \qquad \text{(structural balance)} \tag{22}$$

Based on this definition, among all 11033232 triangles that satisfy Eq. 21, 10229847 (92.7%) are transitive. We also look at the case when v_i distrusts v_j, v_j distrusts v_k (i.e. $t_{ij} < 0$ and $t_{jk} < 0$), what the relationship between v_i and v_k is. It turns out that $\approx$ 50% situations have $t_{ik} < 0$ with another half having $t_{ik} > 0$, which endorses the setting "the enemy of your enemy is actually unknown" in our trust metric.

4.1.2 Partial reciprocity

We also evaluate the partial reciprocity of trust relationships in Epinions dataset. We consider partial reciprocity of trust relationships as symmetry on signs, i.e. we consider pairs (v_i, v_j) as having partial reciprocal trust relationships when both e_{ij} and e_{ji} exists and $t_{ij}t_{ji} > 0$.

Based on the experimental results, we notice that partial reciprocity commonly exists between nodes in the network. Among all 259,751 pairs of nodes having bi-directional relationships, 254,345 ($\approx$ 98%) are partially reciprocal relationships (both directions are of the same sign, either positive or negative), and 98% of reciprocal ones are of positive connections, which corresponds to the concept of partial reciprocity that we discussed in Sec. 2.1.4.

However, as both trust and distrust relationships are single-valued, the symmetry on magnitude of trust relationships is unable to be evaluated.

4.2 Experimental design

In Epinions dataset, all trust values in the training dataset are in the set $\mathcal{T} = \{-1, 1\}$. Based on the definition of our trust metric model, though certainty value of each predicted edge varies in $[0, 1]$, the set for predicted trust values will be $\mathcal{T}_p = \mathcal{T} \cup \{0\} = \{-1, 0, 1\}$, where the value of $t_{st} = 0$ represents the case when not enough information is available for predicting the trust relationship associated with the edge e_{st}. Unlike linear approach such as [14], no rounding is needed for predicting discrete trust values.

To evaluate the performance of our trust evaluation approach, we measure and compare *accuracy* and *coverage*. Accuracy is the fraction of correctly predicted trust relationships among all nonzero ones in the test data:

$$\text{accuracy} = \frac{\|\{e_{ij} \in S_{\text{test}} \mid t_{ij} = t'_{ij}\}\|}{\|\{e_{ij} \in S_{\text{test}} \mid t_{ij} \neq 0\}\|} \tag{23}$$

where S_{test} is the test edge set, t_{ij} is the trust value reached using our trust inference algorithm, and t'_{ij} is the ground

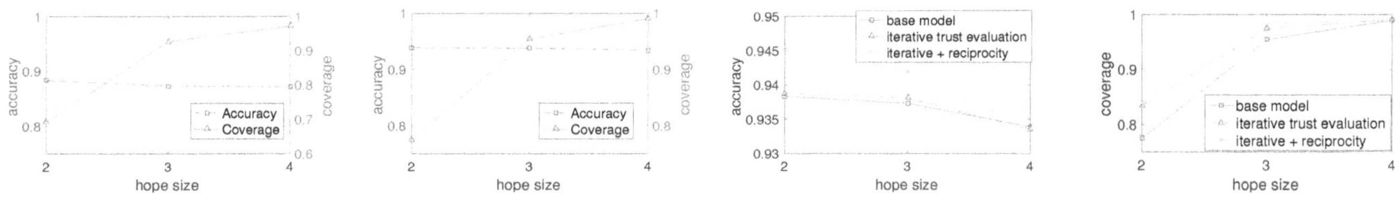

(a) Large test dataset (b) Small test dataset (c) Accuracy (d) Coverage

Figure 2: Evaluation results of the proposed semiring trust inference framework

truth trust value. The denominator in Eq. 23 only take edges that have nonzero predictions.

Coverage is defined as the number of edges predicted over the number of edges predictable in test data:

$$\text{coverage} = \frac{\|\{e_{ij} \in S_{\text{test}} \mid t_{ij} \neq 0\}\|}{\|\{e_{ij} \in S_{\text{test}} \mid \exists k, l \in V \text{ s.t. } e_{ik}, e_{lj} \in S_{\text{train}}\}\|} \quad (24)$$

where an edge is predictable if both of its vertices are present in the training set.

4.2.1 *Test data partitioning*

We partition Epinions dataset into two parts to evaluate STAR. The first part contains all the known trust relationships, i.e. the trust network before inference, while the second part includes a set of edges serving as the ground truth of our evaluation. We evaluate STAR using the known trust information in the first part to predict the trust relationships in the second part. This is a practice used in previous trust inference work and link prediction literatures. On the partition strategy, we examine the time-ordered partition and the random partition. The evaluation results are consistent between the two strategies. All numbers reported here are under the time-ordered partition strategy.

We conduct experiments on datasets of two sizes, we refer the test dataset generated with percentage $\rho = 0.5\%$ as the small dataset, while the one using $\rho = 5\%$ as the large test dataset. The experimental results for the two datasets are shown in Fig. 2(a) and Fig. 2(b) respectively. From the results, we see that the performance of our approach works better on the smaller dataset, in terms of both accuracy and coverage. The major reason is that more trust information is known for the smaller test dataset, which means the trust network used for prediction is more connected and has more trust evidence for prediction. Thus, the performance is positively correlated with the known/test data ratio.

4.2.2 *Experimental results*

Varying trust path length λ: As discussed in previous literature [10, 25], the longer the trust path in graphical trust evaluation models, the more noise may be introduced. While the introduction of distant friends improves the coverage of the social recommendation algorithm, it affects its accuracy. As the average shortest path length in Epinions dataset is about 4, in the experiment, we set the maximum hop length λ as 2, 3 and 4 respectively, and evaluate the performance of our trust metric under different settings.

In Fig. 2(a) and Fig. 2(b) we can see that, the coverage of our approach is better with paths of more hops considered, as more nodes are reachable and used in trust evaluation. However, though the variation is subtler compared to coverage change, the accuracy result is just slightly decreasing with an increasing maximum hop length parameter.

Table 1: Alg.2 using random-ordered test data

random set #	1	2	3	4	5
Accuracy	0.9314	0.9314	0.9328	0.9314	0.9319
Coverage	0.9895	0.9899	0.9895	0.9899	0.9895

Iterative trust evaluation: Apart from data size and maximum hop length, we also compare the base STAR model (Alg. 1) with the model applying collective methods (Alg. 2). As shown in Fig. 2(c)(d), the iterative trust inference method improves the performance in both coverage and accuracy.

When applying iterative approaches in classification problem [21], the ordering of value updates in the iterative trust evaluation may affect the predictive accuracy and convergence rate. Here, in order to investigate the stability in trust iteration over test data, we randomize the order of the node pairs for prediction, and compare the experimental results. We list the results for the 4-hop case in Table 1. According to the results, the application of iterative approach for the trust metric in social recommender system setting is fairly robust to randomized orderings of the test dataset.

Exploiting partial reciprocity: From Fig. 2(c) and Fig. 2(d), by getting trust information based on partial reciprocity for trust evaluation, the coverage and accuracy of the trust inference algorithm are even better. By applying collective methods and partial reciprocity, more trust evidence can be used in the trust metric.

Parameter tuning in certainty: As discussed in Sec. 3.2, we proposed two tunable models for certainty based on degree. Here we vary the values of the parameters and investigate the influence of parameter tuning towards model performance. In the linear model (Eq. 14), there are two parameters, β and γ. β is in the range of $[0, 1]$, and γ is dependent on β and the cut-off degree. The exponential model described in Eq. 15 has one parameter $\eta \in [0, 1]$. In the experiment, we fix maximum degree value used in linear model to be 5, 10 and 15, and let β and η both vary from 0 to 1 with step change to be 0.05. The results are shown in Fig. 3, where Δ represents maximum degree value. From the plots we can see that the linear model leads to lower accuracy and coverage, while the exponential model doesn't change very much with varying parameter values. Using exponential model for certainty with a relatively small η around 0.2 would be a good setting for trust inference.

4.3 Comparison with other approaches

Base on the experimental results discussed in Sec. 4.2, the performance of our method STAR can be as small as 5.8% error rate and as good as 98.3% coverage rate for reachable pairs, As a fair comparison, the graph-theoretic linear approach based on matrix operations [14] has an optimal prediction error rate of 6.4%. The machine learning approach introduced in [20] can reach an accuracy about 0.934

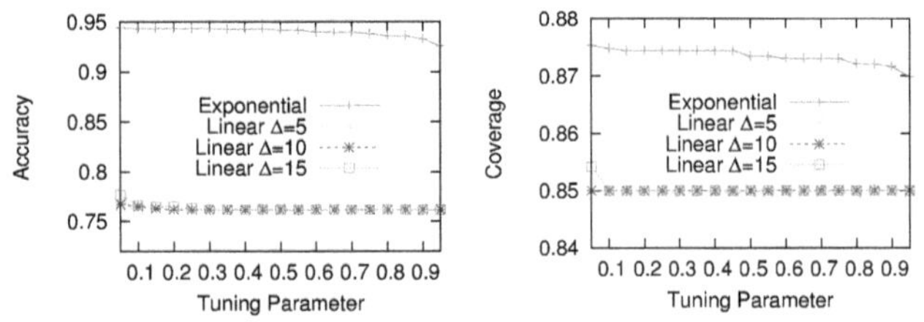

(a) Accuracy (b) Coverage

Figure 3: Performance with parameter tuning

(i.e. $\approx 6.7\%$ error rate). For [7] which used probabilistic confidence models for trust inference, it achieved an accuracy of 89% (11% error rate) using Epinions dataset. From comparison, we can see an improvement on accuracy can be obtained using the STAR approach, not to mention its computation efficiency and interpretability.

4.4 Discussions

Because the trust (and distrust) relationships in the dataset are binary ($+1$ and -1), a lot of nuance and variance in the trust relationships are lost. This prevents us from conducting some evaluations. For example, since the trust values are not continuous in $[-1, 1]$, the deviation of evaluated trust value from ground-truth difficult to measure and analyzed.

The high accuracy of STAR on this dataset shows its flexibility and power in SNS trust-aware recommendation.

5. CONCLUSIONS

In this work, we propose STAR, a novel trust inference method for trust-aware social recommenders. It not only has high accuracy comparing with machine learning methods, but also has the efficiency from graph-theortical models. Our method is based on a 2-D semiring framework reflecting trust propagation and aggregation properties over the trust network. The nonlinearity and inconsistency in human's opinion formulation process are captured in the trust inference algorithm. To address the data sparsity, we introduce collective semiring methods and propose partial reciprocity. In order to validate the model and evaluate the performance of our approach, we conduct a series of experiments using the Epinions dataset. The experimental results show that the approach proposed in this work has advantages in both accuracy and coverage. The trust relationships inferred via our approach can be used to improve the quality of trust-aware recommendations.

6. REFERENCES

[1] Epinions trust network dataset – KONECT, Oct. 2014.

[2] C. C. Aggarwal. Social and trust-centric recommender systems. In *Recommender Systems*. Springer, 2016.

[3] R. Andersen, C. Borgs, J. Chayes, U. Feige, A. Flaxman, A. Kalai, V. Mirrokni, and M. Tennenholtz. Trust-based recommendation systems: an axiomatic approach. In *WWW 2008*.

[4] P. Avesani, P. Massa, and R. Tiella. A trust-enhanced recommender system application: Moleskiing. In *ACM SAC*, 2005.

[5] S. Bistarelli. *Semirings for soft constraint solving and programming*, volume 2962. Springer Science & Business Media, 2004.

[6] C. Castelfranchi and R. Falcone. *Trust theory: A socio-cognitive and computational model*, volume 18. John Wiley & Sons, 2010.

[7] T. DuBois, J. Golbeck, and A. Srinivasan. Predicting trust and distrust in social networks. In *Privacy, Security, Risk and Trust (PASSAT) and IEEE SocialCom*, 2011.

[8] R. Forsati, I. Barjasteh, F. Masrour, A.-H. Esfahanian, and H. Radha. Pushtrust: An efficient recommendation algorithm by leveraging trust and distrust relations. In *ACM RecSys*, 2015.

[9] P. Gao, J. S. Baras, and J. Golbeck. Semiring-based trust evaluation for information fusion in social network services. In *IEEE Fusion*, 2015.

[10] J. Golbeck. *Computing and applying trust in web-based social networks*. PhD thesis, University of Maryland College Park, 2005.

[11] J. Golbeck. Personalizing applications through integration of inferred trust values in semantic web-based social networks. In *Semantic Network Analysis Workshop at ISWC*, 2005.

[12] J. Golbeck. *Generating predictive movie recommendations from trust in social networks*. Springer, 2006.

[13] J. Golbeck. *Computing with social trust*. Springer, 2008.

[14] R. Guha, R. Kumar, P. Raghavan, and A. Tomkins. Propagation of trust and distrust. In *WWW*, 2004.

[15] C. Haydar, A. Roussanaly, and A. Boyer. Local trust versus global trust networks in subjective logic. In *2013 IEEE/WIC/ACM International Joint Conferences on Web Intelligence and Intelligent Agent Technologies*.

[16] M. Jamali and M. Ester. Trustwalker: a random walk model for combining trust-based and item-based recommendation. In *ACM KDD*, 2009.

[17] M. Jamali and M. Ester. A matrix factorization technique with trust propagation for recommendation in social networks. In *ACM RecSys*, 2010.

[18] A. Jøsang, R. Ismail, and C. Boyd. A survey of trust and reputation systems for online service provision. *Decision support systems*, 43(2):618–644, 2007.

[19] A. Jøsang, S. Marsh, and S. Pope. Exploring different types of trust propagation. In *Trust management*, pages 179–192. Springer, 2006.

[20] J. Leskovec, D. Huttenlocher, and J. Kleinberg. Predicting positive and negative links in online social networks. In *WWW*, 2010.

[21] B. London and L. Getoor. Collective classification of network data. *Data Classification: Algorithms and Applications*, 399, 2014.

[22] H. Ma, I. King, and M. R. Lyu. Learning to recommend with social trust ensemble. In *ACM SIGIR*, 2009.

[23] H. Ma, M. R. Lyu, and I. King. Learning to recommend with trust and distrust relationships. In *ACM RecSys*, 2009.

[24] H. Ma, H. Yang, M. R. Lyu, and I. King. Sorec: social recommendation using probabilistic matrix factorization. In *ACM SIGIR*, 2008.

[25] P. Massa and P. Avesani. Trust-aware recommender systems. In *ACM RecSys*, 2007.

[26] J. Neville and D. Jensen. Iterative classification in relational data. In *Proc. AAAI Workshop on Learning Statistical Models from Relational Data*, pages 13–20, 2000.

[27] M. Richardson, R. Agrawal, and P. Domingos. Trust management for the semantic web. In *The Semantic Web-ISWC 2003*, pages 351–368. Springer, 2003.

[28] J. Tang, X. Hu, and H. Liu. Social recommendation: a review. *Social Network Analysis and Mining*, 3(4):1113–1133, 2013.

[29] G. Theodorakopoulos and J. S. Baras. Trust evaluation in ad-hoc networks. In *3rd ACM workshop on Wireless security*, 2004.

[30] P. Victor, C. Cornelis, and M. De Cock. *Trust networks for recommender systems*, volume 4. Springer, 2011.

[31] C.-N. Ziegler and G. Lausen. Propagation models for trust and distrust in social networks. *Information Systems Frontiers*, 7(4-5):337–358, 2005.

Vista: A Visually, Socially, and Temporally-aware Model for Artistic Recommendation

Ruining He
UC San Diego
r4he@cs.ucsd.edu

Chen Fang
Adobe Research
cfang@adobe.com

Zhaowen Wang
Adobe Research
zhawang@adobe.com

Julian McAuley
UC San Diego
jmcauley@cs.ucsd.edu

ABSTRACT

Understanding users' interactions with highly subjective content—like artistic images—is challenging due to the complex semantics that guide our preferences. On the one hand one has to overcome 'standard' recommender systems challenges, such as dealing with large, sparse, and long-tailed datasets. On the other, several new challenges present themselves, such as the need to model content in terms of its visual appearance, or even social dynamics, such as a preference toward a particular artist that is independent of the art they create.

In this paper we build large-scale recommender systems to model the dynamics of a vibrant digital art community, *Behance*, consisting of tens of millions of interactions (clicks and 'appreciates') of users toward digital art. Methodologically, our main contributions are to model (a) rich content, especially in terms of its visual appearance; (b) temporal dynamics, in terms of how users prefer 'visually consistent' content within and across sessions; and (c) social dynamics, in terms of how users exhibit preferences both towards certain art styles, as well as the artists themselves.

Keywords

Recommender Systems; Artistic Preferences; Markov Chains

1. INTRODUCTION

The power of recommender systems lies in their ability to model the complex preferences that people exhibit toward items based on their past interactions and behavior. To extend their expressive power, various works have made use of features such as temporal dynamics [14], social influence [17], or the content of the items themselves [9]. Yet modeling and recommendation still remains challenging in settings where these forces interact in subtle and semantically complex ways.

In this paper, we propose new models for the social art website *Behance*,[1] an online art community with millions of users and artistic images. We seek to model both implicit preferences, such as users navigating between items, as well as explicit preferences, such as users liking or 'appreciating' each other's content. On *Behance* users are both content creators and content evaluators, meaning that there is a need to model who appreciates what, as well as who appreciates whom.

There are several aspects that make modeling this data interesting and challenging. First is the need to model *content*, in particular the visual appearance of items, which are both high-dimensional and semantically complex. Second is the need to model temporal and social dynamics, in terms of users' tendency to interact with consistent content within and across sessions, and their preferences towards individual artists as well as art styles. And third is simply the scale and sparsity of the data involved; with data on the order of millions of users and items, and tens of millions of interactions we must expend considerable effort developing methods that scale; this issue is exacerbated when modeling visual content, due to the high-dimensional representations of the items involved.

Methodologically, our work primarily builds upon two methods, *FPMC* ('factorized personalized markov chains,' [21]) and *VBPR* ('visual bayesian personalized ranking,' [10]). FPMC models the notion of 'smoothness' between subsequent interactions using a Markov chain, an idea that we adapt to capture the fact that users tend to browse art with consistent latent attributes during the course of a browsing session. VBPR is a recently-proposed content-aware recommender system, that models the visual appearance of the items being considered (primarily to recommend clothing). By combining the two models, we can capture individual users' preferences towards particular visual art styles, as well as the tendency to interact with items that are 'visually consistent' during a browsing session. We also make several extensions of these models, e.g. to handle longer memory than simply the previous action.

Another aspect that differentiates our model and data from traditional recommendation scenarios is the need to model the content *creator* in addition to the content itself. Unlike most recommender systems, which model interactions between users and items, in *Behance* the items are created by the same population of users who evaluate them. Thus we need to model the social dynamics that guide users' preferences toward particular artists. For example, a user might follow the creations of particular artists, even when their art differs from the style they normally exhibit preferences toward. Note that this particular type of social dynamics (amongst creators and evaluators) is different from traditional friendship/trust relations (amongst evaluators themselves).

We perform experiments on both implicit (click) and explicit (appreciate) data, where we show that substantial performance improvements can be gained by modeling temporal, social, and visual

[1] https://www.behance.net/

RecSys '16, September 15-19, 2016, Boston, MA, USA

DOI: http://dx.doi.org/10.1145/2959100.2959152

features in concert. Improvements are especially large for newly-uploaded art, where modeling content—or even the identity of the artist—yields improvements of up to 30% in terms of AUC.

Our model, VIsually, Socially, and Temporally-aware Artistic recommendation, or *Vista* for short, is the first to be simultaneously visually, socially, and temporally aware, which proves key to modeling the dynamics of online art communities.

Contributions We summarize our main contributions as follows:

- We build models to capture the large-scale dynamics of artistic preferences. Methodologically we extend recent techniques that model visual appearance for content-aware recommendation, and techniques that model short-term, session-level dynamics, to capture the notion of 'visual consistency' between successive actions. Since users of *Behance* are themselves content creators, we capture both preferences toward particular artists, as well as particular art styles.
- We introduce the *Behance* dataset as a benchmark for modeling visual and artistic preferences. We perform experiments on both click and 'appreciate' data, and while the former is proprietary, we shall release complete 'appreciate' data for benchmarking and evaluation.
- Our experiments reveal that each of the components (social, temporal, visual) are critical to obtaining satisfactory performance on our data, substantially outperforming models that consider each of the factors in isolation. We also use our model to visualize the various art styles that users exhibit preferences toward.

Note in particular that our proposed method can be easily adapted to cope with sequential prediction in other domains by replacing the visual features with other types of item content.

2. RELATED WORK

Visually-aware recommender systems. In recent years, there have been some works that investigate parsing or retrieving visually similar clothing images (e.g. [11, 26, 27]), although they do not focus on learning user preferences. Recent works have introduced visually-aware recommender systems where the visual rating dimensions of users are uncovered on top of the visual signals in the system—product images. Such visual dimensions have been demonstrated to be successful at link prediction tasks useful for recommending alternative (e.g. two similar t-shirts) and complementary (e.g. a t-shirt and a matching pair of pants) items. This thread of work has also extended standard Matrix Factorization with visual dimensions to facilitate item recommendation tasks [8, 10]. A following work [9] further considers the long-term temporal dynamics associated with the visual preference of the communities, i.e., fashion evolution. However, none of above works focuses on predicting session-level user actions, a key recommendation task that requires the ability to model *sequential* data.

Modeling Temporal Dynamics. Apart from the visual domain, in the machine learning community there have also been earlier efforts that investigate temporally-evolving data with algorithms such as SVMs [12], decision trees [25], instance-based learning [1], etc. Similar to ours are Collaborative Filtering models that take into account temporal dynamics. In particular, early works are based on similarity-oriented Collaborative Filtering, where a time weighting scheme can be used to assign previously-rated items with decaying weights when computing similarities (e.g. [5]). In contrast, recent works are mostly based on the well-known Matrix Factorization

Table 1: Notation

Notation	Explanation
$\mathcal{U}, \mathcal{I}$	user set, item set
u, i	a specific user or item (resp.)
$\mathcal{S}^u$	sequential action history $(\mathcal{S}^u_1, \ldots, \mathcal{S}^u_{\lvert\mathcal{S}^u\rvert})$ of u
$\mathcal{S}^u_t$	the item user u interacted with at time step t
o_i	owner/creator of item i, $o_i \in \mathcal{U}$
O_i	owners/creators of item i, $O_i \subseteq \mathcal{U}$
Γ	latent space measuring *user-item* affinity
γ_u	latent preference vector of user u, $\gamma_u \in \Gamma$
γ_i	latent property vector of item i, $\gamma_i \in \Gamma$
Φ	latent space measuring *user-user* similarity
ϕ_u	latent vector of user u, $\phi_u \in \Phi$
Ψ	latent space measuring *item-item* similarity
ψ_i	latent vector of item i, $\psi_i \in \Psi$
f_i	explicit feature vector of item i (e.g. visual features), $f_i \in \mathbb{R}^F$

technique [13]. For instance, Koren [14] showed state-of-the-art results on *Netflix* data using Matrix Factorization to model the underlying temporal dynamics. However, these works do not consider handling the complex semantics of visual and social signals.

Sequential recommendation. Markov chains are a powerful tool to model stochastic transitions between different 'states.' In sequential recommendation domains, Markov chains have been studied by several earlier works, from investigating their strength at uncovering sequential patterns (e.g. [18, 29]), to directly modeling decision processes with Markov transitions [22]. In a more recent paper [21], Rendle *et al.* proposed to combine the strength of Markov chains at modeling the smoothness of subsequent actions and the power of Matrix Factorization at modeling *personal* preferences for sequential recommendation. The resulting model, called FPMC, has shown superior prediction accuracy by benefiting from both simultaneously. Our work extends the basic idea mainly by modeling complex visual and social dynamics and further considering Markov chains with higher orders.

Notably, there is another line of work that employs (personalized) probabilistic Markov embeddings to model sequential data like playlists and POIs (e.g. [3, 4, 6]). These works differ from ours in terms of both the signals being modeled and the types of models. Moreover, none of them has shown to be able to handle datasets on the same scale with *Behance* to the best of our knowledge.

Social recommendation. In the recommender systems literature, there has been a large body of work that models social networks for mitigating cold-start issues in recommender systems, e.g. [2, 7, 16, 17, 28]. The type of social signals they usually benefit from are so-called 'trust' relations amongst different users, which are different from the those we are interested in. In contrast, we focus on modeling the *ownership* signal, i.e., the interactions between a viewer and the creator of an item, which brings a unique set of challenges.

3. THE MARKOV CHAIN MODEL

3.1 Problem Formulation

Formally, let $\mathcal{U} = \{u_1, u_2, \ldots, u_{|\mathcal{U}|}\}$ represent the set of users and $\mathcal{I} = \{i_1, i_2, \ldots, i_{|\mathcal{I}|}\}$ the set of items (i.e., artistic images). Each item $i \in \mathcal{I}$ is created by a certain user $o_i \in \mathcal{U}$ (or in some cases multiple users $O_i \subseteq \mathcal{U}$). For each user u, a sequential action history (e.g. items clicked/appreciated by u) $\mathcal{S}_u$ is known: $\mathcal{S}^u =$

$(\mathcal{S}_1^u, \mathcal{S}_2^u, \dots, \mathcal{S}_{|\mathcal{S}^u|}^u)$ where $\mathcal{S}_k^u \in \mathcal{I}$. The action history of all users is denoted by $\mathcal{S} = \{\mathcal{S}^{u_1}, \mathcal{S}^{u_2}, \dots, \mathcal{S}^{u_{|\mathcal{U}|}}\}$. Additionally, each item i is associated with an explicit feature vector f_i, e.g. in our case visual features extracted from images. Given the above data, our task is to recommend items to each user based on their predicted next action.

Notation to be used throughout the paper is summarized in Table 1. Next, we will build our model incrementally which we detail in each of the following subsections.

3.2 Predicting Sequential Actions

In this paper, we are interested in modeling *binary* actions such as clicks, appreciates, etc. Given the previous action sequence $\mathcal{S}^u$ of user u, the probability that user u will interact with item i in the next action is $P(X_t^u = i \mid \mathcal{S}_{t-1}^u, \mathcal{S}_{t-2}^u, \dots, \mathcal{S}_1^u)$, where random variable X_t^u is the choice u made at time step t and $|\mathcal{S}^u| = t-1$. This probability can be approximated by $P(X_t^u = i | \mathcal{S}_{t-1}^u)$, which is then modeled by factorizing a personalized Markov chain (as in [21]). This follows the intuition that a user's *recent* actions should be more predictive of their future actions than earlier ones.

Intuitively, the transition of user u from item $\mathcal{S}_{t-1}^u$ (at time step $t-1$) to item i (at time step t) can be explained from two aspects: (1) the interaction between user u and item i, which captures the *long-term* preferences of user u; and (2) the interaction between the previous item $\mathcal{S}_{t-1}^u$ and item i, which captures the *short-term* or temporary interest of user u. Following this intuition, we propose to factorize the personalized Markov chain with the following formulation:

$$P(X_t^u = i \mid \mathcal{S}_{t-1}^u) \propto \underbrace{\overbrace{\langle \phi_u, \phi_{o_i} \rangle}^{\text{owner appreciation}} + \overbrace{\langle \gamma_u, \gamma_i \rangle}^{\text{item appreciation}}}_{\text{interaction between } u \text{ and } i \text{ (long-term dynamics)}}$$
$$+ w_u \cdot \underbrace{(\overbrace{\langle \phi_{o_i}, \phi_{o_{\mathcal{S}_{t-1}^u}} \rangle}^{\text{owner similarity}} + \overbrace{\langle \psi_i, \psi_{\mathcal{S}_{t-1}^u} \rangle}^{\text{item similarity}})}_{\text{interaction between } i \text{ and } \mathcal{S}_t^u \text{ (short-term dynamics)}}, \quad (1)$$

where we use three latent spaces to capture the interactions between users and items, users and users, items and items respectively: (1) **Space Γ:** D_1-dimensional vectors γ_u and γ_i are employed to capture user u's latent preferences and item i's latent properties respectively; (2) **Space Φ:** Each user u is associated with a D_2-dimensional vector ϕ_u for measuring affinity/similarity with other users (within Φ); and (3) **Space Ψ:** Each item i is associated with a D_3-dimensional vector ψ_i for measuring affinity/similarity with other items (within Ψ). Inner products of vectors from Γ, Φ, and Ψ measure the corresponding user-item, user-user, and item-item affinity/similarity respectively.

In Eq. 1, the interaction between u and i consists of two parts: how much user u *appreciates*—or is 'similar' to—the creator/owner o_i of i (term one), and how much u likes the *specific* item created by o_i (term two). Likewise, the similarity of i and $\mathcal{S}_{t-1}^u$ comprises two components as well: the similarity between their creators (term three) and the two items themselves (term four). w_u is a parameter to capture the statistical short-term *consistency* of the actions of the specific user u. Intuitively, a bigger value of w_u will favor short-term interests, which means u tends to interact with items similar to those they just interacted with, instead of those that most fit their long-term preferences.

Modeling ownership data and user interactions can help address both *cold user* and *cold item* issues in real-world recommender systems:

1. For a cold (or 'cool') user u who has very few actions in the system, the representation of u (in space Φ, i.e., ϕ_u) can still be learned as long as some users have interacted with items *created by* u. When predicting the actions for u, ϕ_u will help rank items created by similar users higher.

2. For a cold item i with very few interactions in the system, we can still model it reasonably well as long as its creator's representation ϕ_{o_i} can be learned. Fortunately, two sources of signals are available in the system for inferring ϕ_{o_i}: both actions made by o_i (active) and the interactions received by all other items created by o_i (passive). These signals are relatively abundant and unlikely to suffer from sparsity issues.

Handling Multiple Creators. In certain cases an item i may be collaboratively created by multiple users in the system $O_i \subseteq \mathcal{U}$. In such scenarios we take the *average* of their associated vectors as the corresponding vectors (i.e., ϕ_{o_i} and $\phi_{o_{\mathcal{S}_{t-1}^u}}$) in Eq. 1. Note that this will not affect the training efficiency as an owner sampling scheme can be used, which we will detail later.

3.3 Modeling Higher-Order Markov Chains

The formulation in Eq. 1 only models a personalized Markov chain of order 1, with the assumption that a user's next action (at t) is independent of any historical actions if given the most recent one (at $t-1$). However, this suffers from noise and can't capture longer-term consistency (e.g. earlier clicks in a session). This inspires us to address this limitation by modeling Markov chains with higher order.

Due to the large scale and sparsity of real-world data, a light-weight yet expressive model is required. To this end, we model high order personalized Markov chains by extending our first-order formulation with a personalized *decaying* scheme, as shown below. The first part still measures the affinity between a user u and the next item i with long-term memory; while the second part computes the weighted sum of the similarities of item i to each of the previous items:

$$P(X_t^u = i \mid \mathcal{S}_{t-1}^u, \mathcal{S}_{t-2}^u, \dots, \mathcal{S}_{t-K}^u) \propto \underbrace{\langle \phi_u, \phi_{o_i} \rangle + \langle \gamma_u, \gamma_i \rangle}_{\text{interaction between } u \text{ and } i}$$
$$+ \sum_{k=1}^{K} \underbrace{w_u^k}_{\substack{\text{personalized}\\ \text{decaying weight}}} \cdot (\underbrace{\langle \phi_{o_i}, \phi_{o_{\mathcal{S}_{t-k}^u}} \rangle + \langle \psi_i, \psi_{\mathcal{S}_{t-k}^u} \rangle}_{\text{interaction between } i \text{ and the } k\text{-th previous item}}). \quad (2)$$

There are two main intuitions behind the proposed formulation: (1) recent actions should be more correlated with future actions, which is why we employ a decaying term; and (2) different users may differ in behavior so that personalization should be taken into account. We model the personalized decay scheme as follows:

$$w_u^k = \frac{1}{e^{a_u \cdot (k-1) + b_u}}, k = 1, 2, \dots, K, \text{for } u \in \mathcal{U}. \quad (3)$$

Note that the above formulation only introduces two additional parameters (i.e., a_u and b_u) for each user u, which allows us to model users' differing behavior in a light-weight manner.

3.4 Incorporating Content-Based Features

Up to now, our formulation only makes use of the collaborative data, without being aware of the underlying content of the items themselves.[2] Such a formulation may suffer from *cold item* issues where there aren't enough historical observations to learn accurate

[2]Without loss of generality, we take item features as an illustrative example. User features can be handled in a similar manner.

representations of each item. Modeling the content of the items can provide auxiliary signals in cold-start settings and alleviate such issues.

Intuitively, content-based features of items should be informative of the two latent vectors: γ_i and ψ_i. Given the explicit feature vector f_i of item i, embedding techniques have been successful at incorporating (high dimensional) content-based features into the Collaborative Filtering framework (e.g. [9, 10]). In particular, we augment the vector representations of items (i.e., γ_i, ψ_i) as follows:

$$\gamma_i = \gamma_i' + \mathbf{E}_\Gamma f_i, \tag{4}$$

$$\psi_i = \psi_i' + \mathbf{E}_\Psi f_i. \tag{5}$$

Here $\mathbf{E}_\Gamma$ and $\mathbf{E}_\Psi$ are two embedding matrices that project item i into space Γ and Ψ respectively. The new formulation for each vector in the corresponding space (γ_i) now consists of two parts: the base part from the item content ($\mathbf{E}_\Gamma f_i$), and the residue (γ_i'). For warm-start items, the residue part is expressive and can represent the item accurately; for cold-start items, the residue part will be regularized (towards 0) and the base part will still be able to provide reasonably good approximations of the true representations. By substituting the augmented vector representations Eq. 4 and Eq. 5 into Eq. 2, the new formulation will be able to benefit from the content-based features to alleviate *cold item* issues.

Note that the two matrices are shared by all items which means that only a modest number of parameters are added to the model.

3.5 Fitting the Model

Predicting next actions can be viewed as a ranking task where the ground-truth item should be ranked as high as possible among all items. This inspires us to optimize an efficient ranking loss such as sequential Bayesian Personalized Ranking (S-BPR) [21].[3]

3.5.1 Objective Function

Let $>_{u,t}$ denote the total order over the items of user u at time step t, then $i >_{u,t} j$ means item i is ranked higher than item j for user u at t given the action sequence before t. S-BPR optimizes *maximum a posteriori* (MAP) of all the model parameters (denoted by Θ) assuming independence of users and time steps:

$$\arg\max_{\Theta} = \ln \prod_{u \in \mathcal{U}} \prod_{t=2}^{|\mathcal{S}^u|} \prod_{j \neq \mathcal{S}_t^u} P(\mathcal{S}_t^u >_{u,t} j|\Theta)\ P(\Theta), \tag{6}$$

where for each user u and for each time step t, the objective goes through the *pairwise* ranking between the ground-truth $\mathcal{S}_t^u$ and all negative items. The pairwise ranking between a positive (i) and a negative (j) item $P(i >_{u,t} j|\Theta)$ is estimated by a sigmoid function $\sigma(\widehat{p}_{u,t,i} - \widehat{p}_{u,t,j})$ where the difference of the predicted likelihoods are taken as the inputs ($\widehat{p}_{u,t,i}$ is short for the Markov prediction, i.e., Eq. 2). $P(\Theta)$ is a Gaussian prior over the model parameters.

Note that for Markov chains of order K, our formulation (i.e., Eq. 2) can allow t to run from 2 (instead of $K+1$) to the last item in $\mathcal{S}^u$ due to its additive characteristic.

3.5.2 Scaling Up

Stochastic Gradient Descent (SGD) is widely employed for learning in BPR-like optimization frameworks (e.g., [20, 21]). According to SGD, our basic training procedure is as follows. First, a user $u \in \mathcal{U}$ as well as a time step $t \in \{2, 3, \ldots, |\mathcal{S}^u|\}$ are uniformly sampled from the training corpus. Next, a negative item $j \in \mathcal{I}$ ($j \neq \mathcal{S}_t^u$) is uniformly sampled, which forms a training triple (u, t, j). Finally, the optimization procedure updates parameters as follows:

$$\Theta \leftarrow \Theta + \alpha \cdot (\sigma(-\widehat{x}_{u,t,j}) \cdot \frac{\partial \widehat{x}_{u,t,j}}{\partial \Theta} - \lambda_\Theta \Theta), \tag{7}$$

where $\widehat{x}_{u,t,j}$ is a shorthand for $\widehat{p}_{u,t,\mathcal{S}_t^u} - \widehat{p}_{u,t,j}$. α is the learning rate and λ_Θ is a regularization hyperparameter. Note that it is cheap to evaluate the gradient due to the additive characteristic of the proposed method (see Appendix for complexity analysis).

The above procedure is suitable for training on large datasets. However, it is limited when training with the augmented version of our model (with content-based features) as updating the embedding matrices can be time-consuming. To speed up the training procedure, we make the following two observations and employ two modifications accordingly.

Sampling. Matrices $\mathbf{E}_\Gamma$ and $\mathbf{E}_\Psi$ are *global* parameters and only account for a tiny fraction of Θ (e.g. 0.29% for *Behance*). This means that less training data is needed to accurately estimate $\mathbf{E}_\Gamma$ and $\mathbf{E}_\Psi$. In other words, they are updated more often than needed under the above scheme. As such, we lower their updating frequency by flipping a biased coin for each training triple to decide whether or not to update $\mathbf{E}_\Gamma$ and $\mathbf{E}_\Psi$. Likewise, we can also sample a single owner and only update their associated parameters in multiple-owner cases due to the rich user interactions available.

Asynchronous SGD. Notably, only a tiny fraction of parameters will be updated for each training triple (u, t, j), i.e., representations of u and a few *relevant* items, and they are unlikely to overlap.[4] It has been pointed out that in such cases lock-free parallelization of SGD could be employed to achieve fast convergence [19].

Experimentally, this naïve sampling and asynchronous SGD procedure can help finish training on huge datasets within reasonable time on commodity machines without losing prediction accuracy.

4. EXPERIMENTS

We perform comprehensive experiments on *Behance* to evaluate the proposed method. We begin by introducing the dataset we work with, and then we compare against a variety of baselines. Finally, we visualize the learned model and qualitatively analyze the results.

4.1 Dataset

Behance is a popular online community where millions of professional photographers, designers and artists share their work, organized as projects, with others. The contents of these projects vary significantly, ranging from photographs to animation, fashion, interior design, paintings, sculpting, calligraphy, cartoons, culinary arts, etc. Each project is created by a user or a few users and consists of a collection of images (as well as videos in certain cases). The creator/owner of the project selects the most representative image which the website presents to all users as the cover image. On the website, users browse through large numbers of cover images, click through attractive projects, and 'appreciate' those they like.

From *Behance* we collected two large corpora of timestamped user actions: (1) *appreciates* consisting of 373,771 users, 982,002 items (i.e., projects), and 11,807,103 appreciates (i.e., explicit feedback), and (2) *clicks* comprising 381,376 users, 972,181 items, and 48,118,748 clicks (i.e., implicit feedback). 52.7% users have created their own projects, and 2.3% items are created by multiple users. In our experiments, appreciates and clicks are used as two separate datasets to evaluate the efficacy of all methods on explicit and implicit datasets respectively.

[3] S-BPR was originally proposed to optimize sequential *set* data. However, the same idea can also be applied to single-item cases.

[4] The sampling scheme also helps reduce collisions when updating the embedding matrices.

For each item, we extract a 4096-dimensional feature vector from its cover image with a pre-trained VGG neural network [23] as the content-based features f_i. Such features have been shown to generate state-of-the-art results on visually-aware item recommendation tasks [9, 10].

Complete appreciate data and code are available on the first author's webpage.[5]

4.2 Evaluation Metric

We construct a validation set and a test set by selecting the most recent two actions of each user, one for validation and the other for testing. The remainder are used for training. All comparison methods were trained on the training set with hyperparameters tuned with the validation set. Finally, the trained models are used to report corresponding performance on the test set.

Recall that the task is to predict which item a user will interact with given the previous action history, which means that the model in question needs to rank the ground-truth item higher than other items. Therefore for the held-out action, a reasonable evaluation would be calculating how highly the ground-truth item has been ranked for each user.

To this end, we evaluate all methods on the *test* set with the widely used AUC (*Area Under the ROC curve*) measure (e.g., [9, 10, 20]):

$$AUC = \frac{1}{|\mathcal{U}|} \sum_u \frac{1}{|\mathcal{I} \setminus \mathcal{I}_u^+|} \sum_{j \in \mathcal{I} \setminus \mathcal{I}_u^+} \mathbf{1}(\widehat{p}_{u,|\mathcal{S}^u|,g_u} > \widehat{p}_{u,|\mathcal{S}^u|,j}), \quad (8)$$

where $\mathbf{1}(\cdot)$ is the indicator function, and g_u is the ground-truth item of user u at the most recent time step $|\mathcal{S}^u|$.

4.3 Comparison Methods

We compare against a series of state-of-the-art methods, both in the field of item recommendation and sequential data prediction.

Popularity (POP): always recommends popular items in the system at each time step.

Bayesian Personalized Ranking (BPR-MF) [20]: is a state-of-the-art method for personalized item recommendation. It takes standard Matrix Factorization [15] as the underlying predictor.

Visual Bayesian Personalized ranking (VBPR) [10]: is an extension of BPR-MF that models raw visual signals for item recommendation. It captures the visual but not the temporal dynamics of binary action sequences.

Factorized Markov Chain (MC): factorizes the $|\mathcal{I}| \times |\mathcal{I}|$ transition matrix to capture the likelihood that a user transits from one item to another. We used a first order model as higher orders incur a state-space explosion (we have almost one million items) and degrade the performance, especially considering the data sparsity.

Factorized Personalized Markov Chain (FPMC) [21]: is a state-of-the-art personalized Markov chain algorithm to model sequential data. However, FPMC is unable to capture visual and social dynamics and only models first-order Markov chains.

VIsually, Socially, and Temporally-aware Artistic recommendation (*Vista*): is the method proposed by this paper in Eq. 2. Markov chains of different orders will be experimented with and compared against other methods.

***Vista+*:** augments *Vista* with the 4096-dimensional visual features extracted from cover images.

For clarity, the above methods are collated in Table 2 in terms of whether they are 'personalized,' 'temporally-aware,' 'socially-aware,' and 'visually-aware.' The ultimate goal is to evaluate (1) the performance of state-of-the-art item recommendation methods on our task (i.e., BPR-MF); (2) the gains from using raw visual signals especially for cold-start settings (i.e., VBPR); (3) the importance of modeling temporal dynamics (i.e., MC); (4) the effect of modeling personalized temporal dynamics (i.e., FPMC); and (5) the importance of modeling social dynamics (i.e., *Vista*) and further performance enhancements from incorporating content-based features (i.e., *Vista+*).

[5]https://sites.google.com/a/eng.ucsd.edu/ruining-he/

Table 2: Models

Model	Personalized?	Temporally-aware?	Socially-aware?	Visually-aware?
POP	✘	✘	✘	✘
BPR-MF	✔	✘	✘	✘
VBPR	✔	✘	✘	✔
MC	✘	✔	✘	✘
FPMC	✔	✔	✘	✘
Vista	✔	✔	✔	✘
Vista+	✔	✔	✔	✔

We performed all experiments on a single machine with 8 cores and 64GB main memory. Our own most time-consuming method—*Vista+* with a third-order Markov chain—required around 50 hours of training time.

4.4 Performance & Analysis

As analyzed in Section 3.2, the proposed model should be helpful for cold-start settings including both cold user and cold item scenarios. Therefore, we compare all methods in terms of overall accuracy (denoted by 'Full') as well as the two cold settings. Overall accuracy is evaluated with the *full* test set as introduced in Section 4.2. '*Cold User*' is evaluated by a subset of the full test set, consisting of only those cold users with at most 5 actions in the training set; likewise, '*Cold Item*' uses the subset comprising only cold items with at most 5 interactions.

In addition, we also decompose the full test set into subsets according to whether the previous item (at $t-1$) of the action being tested (at t) is created by a different owner (i.e., owner transition), or whether the action is the start of a new session[6] (i.e., session transition). This gives us four settings: 'Owner Trans.' vs. 'Same Owner,' and 'Session Trans.' vs. 'Same Session' to thoroughly evaluate the ability of all models under various transitioning circumstances.

For all methods, we try to use the same number of dimensions: BPR-MF and MC use 20 latent dimensions; VBPR uses 10 latent plus 10 visual dimensions; FPMC uses two 10-d vectors to represent each item and one 10-d vector to represent each user; *Vista* and *Vista+* use 10 dimensions for γ_u, ϕ_u, γ_i, and ψ_i (i.e., $D_1 = D_2 = D_3 = 10$). Using additional dimensions yielded only marginal performance improvement for all methods.

AUC results on the two datasets are shown in Tables 3 and 4. We make a few comparisons and analyze our findings as follows:

BPR-MF vs. MC vs. FPMC. Ultimately, BPR-MF and MC focus on modeling long-term and short-term dynamics respectively. BPR-MF ranks items according to what the given user likes from a long-term perspective, which makes it relatively strong when a user's action differs significantly from the previous one ('Owner

[6]Since no session metadata is available, sessions are obtained by temporally partitioning each user's clicks/appreciates with gaps larger than 1hr.

Table 3: AUC for next-**appreciate** prediction (higher is better). 'Full' evaluates the overall accuracy, '*Cold User*' measures the ability to recommend/rank items for cold users, and '*Cold Item*' examines the ability to recommend cold items correctly. The rest are more detailed settings for evaluation. The best performance for each setting is boldfaced. We test different orders of the Markov chain (i.e., 1, 2, and 3).

Setting	(a) POP	(b) BPR-MF	(c) VBPR	(d) MC	(e) FPMC	(f-1) *Vista*	(f-2) *Vista*	(f-3) *Vista*	(g-1) *Vista+*	(g-2) *Vista+*	(g-3) *Vista+*	improvement ours vs. e	improvement ours vs. best
Full	0.8282	0.8559	0.8802	0.8449	0.8689	0.9199	0.9220	0.9206	0.9203	**0.9270**	0.9203	6.69%	5.32%
Cold User	0.7637	0.8132	0.8500	0.8134	0.8208	0.8994	**0.9008**	0.8979	0.8964	0.8877	0.8958	9.75%	5.98%
Cold Item	0.0562	0.4384	0.5826	0.4559	0.5429	0.7574	0.7644	0.7604	0.7686	**0.7714**	0.7603	42.09%	32.41%
Owner Trans.	0.8470	0.8814	0.8960	0.8600	0.8800	0.9076	0.9115	0.9118	0.9074	**0.9186**	0.9115	4.39%	2.52%
Same Owner	0.7677	0.7388	0.8076	0.7753	0.8176	0.9761	0.9699	0.9609	**0.9795**	0.9657	0.9607	19.80%	19.80%
Session Trans.	0.7876	0.8476	0.8710	0.8289	0.8524	0.9032	0.9057	0.9051	0.9025	**0.9126**	0.9045	7.06%	4.78%
Same Session	0.8545	0.8674	0.8931	0.8672	0.8919	0.9431	0.9445	0.9421	0.9451	**0.9472**	0.9424	6.20%	6.06%

Table 4: AUC for next-**click** prediction (higher is better). The best performance for each setting is boldfaced.

Setting	(a) POP	(b) BPR-MF	(c) VBPR	(d) MC	(e) FPMC	(f-1) *Vista*	(f-2) *Vista*	(f-3) *Vista*	(g-1) *Vista+*	(g-2) *Vista+*	(g-3) *Vista+*	improvement ours vs. e	improvement ours vs. best
Full	0.8116	0.8972	0.8968	0.8954	0.9089	0.9319	**0.9362**	0.9349	0.9330	0.9337	0.9354	3.00%	3.00%
Cold User	0.7555	0.8475	0.8535	0.8708	0.8605	0.9114	**0.9154**	0.9127	0.9121	0.9114	0.9126	6.38%	5.12%
Cold Item	0.1919	0.4284	0.5097	0.5732	0.4828	0.6932	0.7234	0.7290	0.7001	**0.7398**	0.7367	53.23%	27.6%
Owner Trans.	0.8522	0.9021	0.9009	0.8733	0.9018	0.9194	0.9223	0.9231	0.9193	0.9185	**0.9232**	2.37%	2.34%
Same Owner	0.6251	0.8810	0.8834	0.9662	0.9316	0.9763	0.9771	0.9738	0.9770	**0.9825**	0.9747	5.46%	1.69%
Session Trans.	0.8031	0.8651	0.8671	0.8279	0.8641	0.9007	0.9012	0.9012	0.9009	0.8962	**0.9013**	4.31%	4.18%
Same Session	0.8234	0.9179	0.9160	0.9391	0.9379	0.9537	0.9573	0.9579	0.9538	**0.9580**	0.9575	2.14%	2.01%

Trans.' and 'Session Trans.'). In contrast, MC ranks items based on the transition matrix, i.e., 'similarity' of the next item to the previous item. Such short-term awareness makes MC strong in cases where action consistency is maximally demonstrated, i.e., 'Same Owner' and 'Same Session.' Additionally, note that MC seems to suffer less from cold-start issues due to the consistency of sequential actions. FPMC is inherently a combination of BPR-MF and MC, which makes it the strongest among the three, though it is not necessarily the best in all settings.

BPR-MF vs. VBPR. Like BPR-MF, VBPR focuses on long-term dynamics, but benefits from making use of additional visual signals in the system. As expected, it alleviates *cold item* issues and is slightly better than BPR-MF in most other settings as well.

***Vista* vs. FPMC.** *Vista* is able to capture social dynamics by modeling ownership signals as well as gains from a fully personalized Markov chains with higher orders. As such, it beats FPMC in all settings significantly especially in cold-start scenarios. Note that *Vista* improves as much as 47.66% on average for cold item recommendation, which is a major concern when predicting sequential actions (see Section 3.2 for detailed cold-start analysis of *Vista*).

***Vista+* vs. *Vista*.** Further augmenting *Vista* with content-based features, in this case visual signals, is beneficial as *cold item* issues are further mitigated. However, the improvement is comparatively small as such issues have already been alleviated to a large extent by modeling social dynamics (i.e., *Vista*).

Orders of Markov chains. As we increase the order of the Markov chain (from 1 to 3), the performance generally gets better as the next click is related to multiple previous clicks. Using a small order seems to be good enough, presumably since the few most recent actions capture enough information to predict future actions.

Sparse vs. Dense data. Comparing the results of next-appreciate (sparse) and next-click (dense) prediction we can find that *Vista* outperforms other methods more significantly for *sparse* datasets where social and visual dynamics are forced to carry more weight.

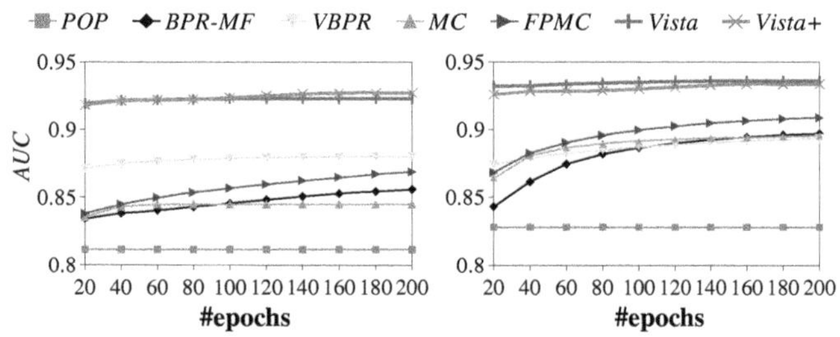

(a) Appreciate Prediction (b) Click Prediction

Figure 1: Performance comparison of different methods with number of training epochs on *Behance* data. All methods are from Section 4.4. *Vista* and *Vista+* use second-order Markov chains.

4.5 Training Efficiency

Next, we demonstrate the accuracy on the full test set (i.e., 'Full' setting) of all comparison methods as the number of training epochs increases.[7] As shown by Figure 1, our proposed methods can converge in a few epochs due to the rich interactions being modeled. Since *appreciate* data is inherently sparser than *click* data, we can find that modeling signals like social dynamics and visual data can help more significantly for appreciate prediction (as shown by the gap between (1) *Vista*/*Vista+* vs. others, and (2) VBPR vs. other baselines). In our experiments, we used a sampling probability of 5% for *Vista+* to update the two embedding matrices. Benefiting from multithreading, each epoch of asynchronous SGD takes around 20 minutes to train our third-order *Vista+* on click data. See Appendix for more details about the time complexity of *Vista+*.

[7]All baselines, except POP, are trained with multiple epochs until convergence or observance of overfitting (on the validation set). Each epoch consists of processing training samples with the size of the whole training corpus.

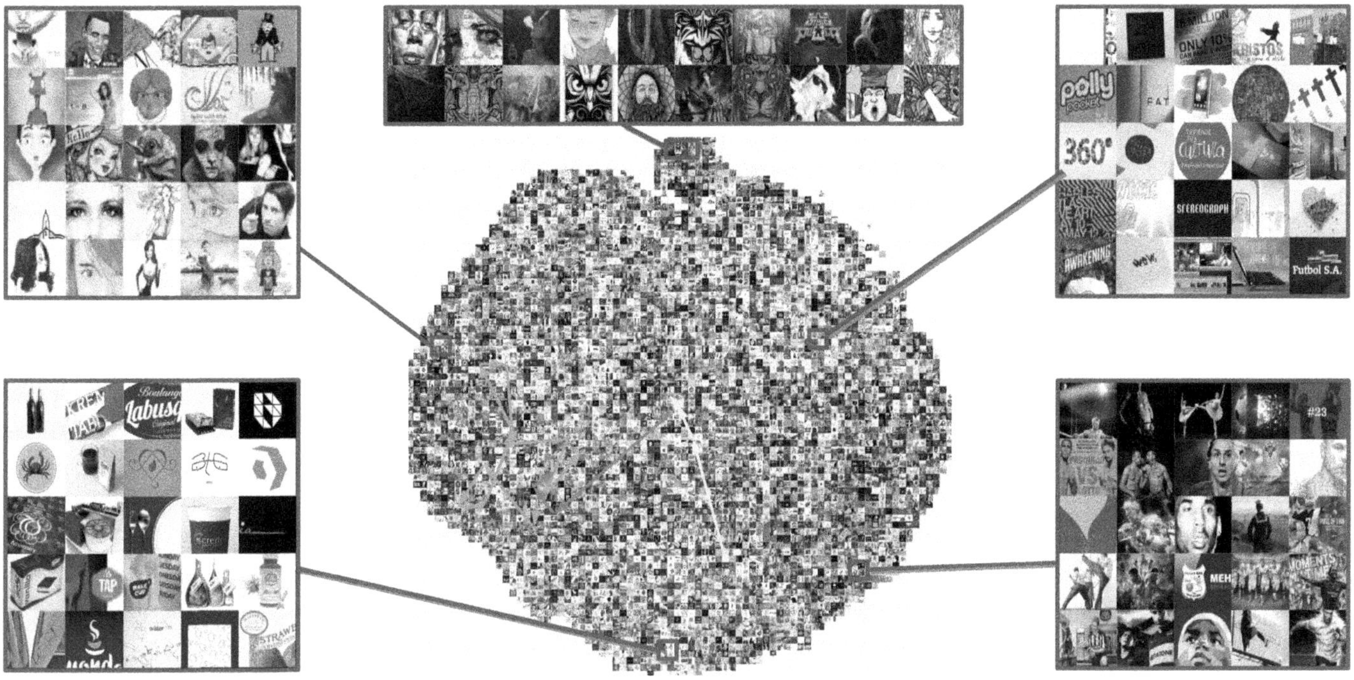

Figure 2: A 2-d visualization of space Ψ with t-SNE [24]. Here the *Vista+* model is trained on *Behance* click data with the same setting as in Table 4. We randomly sample a user and visualize three of their click sessions in the space, denoted by three paths with different colors on the grid view. There is a tendency that clicks are around a specific region in the space (i.e., near the green arrows), which reflects the long-term preference of the user. And each click sequence shows a certain amount of consistency, encoding the transition of short-term interests.

4.6 Latent Space Visualization

We proceed by visualizing the latent space Ψ, which is used to measure the similarity between different items. To this end, we take the *Vista+* trained on *Behance* click data (see Section 4.4) and further use t-SNE [24] to embed the 10-d space into 2-d. Figure 2 demonstrates a grid view of 972,181 items in the 2-d space.[8] From this figure we can see that items with similar contents and styles tend to be neighbors in the latent space, e.g. culinary arts on the lower-left patch, and sports on the lower-right. Notably, items on the same patch may visually deviate from each other significantly.

On the grid view, we also demonstrate a few click sessions of a randomly selected user. The click sequence of each session is represented by a directed path with a unique color (red/yellow/green). We make a few observations as follows. (1) Clicks tend to occur around a specific region in the space, near the green and red arrows. This reflects the long-term preferences of the user as people ultimately tend to explore items that they like. (2) Each click sequence demonstrates consistency to a certain degree (e.g. red and yellow) and encodes the transition of short-term interests (e.g. green). (3) Finally, the choice made at each click is a combination of long- and short-term preferences, due to which there are both long jumps and short jumps. Therefore, it is essential to capture both long- and short-term dynamics simultaneously in order to be successful at addressing our prediction task.

4.7 Visualizing Sessions

Users differ in habitual patterns especially in a dataset as large as ours. For example, for some users their short-term dynamics are more important. This means they tend to click/appreciate items similar to those they just interacted with. In contrast, there are also users whose long-term preferences are more emphasized, demonstrating less short-term consistency during a session. This characteristic is captured by the personalized weighting factor w_u in Eq. 1 (and w_u^k in Eq. 2).

In Figure 3, we show a few sample sessions of the above two types of users, with different session lengths. Sampled sessions of users with the largest w_u (i.e., $\arg\max_u w_u$) are shown above the horizontal dashed line, with each row demonstrating the list of items clicked during the corresponding session. We can see some consistency from these sessions: logo designs, a certain style of cartoon characters, interior designs, and fashion models respectively. On the right of each arrow is the corresponding recommendation with the highest score predicted by the *Vista+* model.

In contrast, below the dashed line we also demonstrate a few sessions from users with the least w_u, i.e., for whom long-term dynamics are more important. As expected, contents in each session demonstrate comparatively larger variance, though the long-term preference towards object designs, logos, cartoons, and characters (respectively) are captured by the *Vista+* model.

5. CONCLUSION

Modeling artistic preferences with complex visual, social, and sequential signals is challenging especially when it comes to the need to scale up to large real-world datasets. In this paper, we address these challenges by building visually and socially-aware Markov chains to model visual appearance and social dynamics simultaneously. Empirically we evaluated our proposed method on two common sequential prediction tasks to test its ability to handle both explicit and implicit artistic preferences of users. Experimental results demonstrated that our proposed methods significantly outperform a series of state-of-the-art baselines for both tasks on large scale datasets collected from a popular social art website, *Behance*.

[8]Each cell randomly selects one image if items overlap.

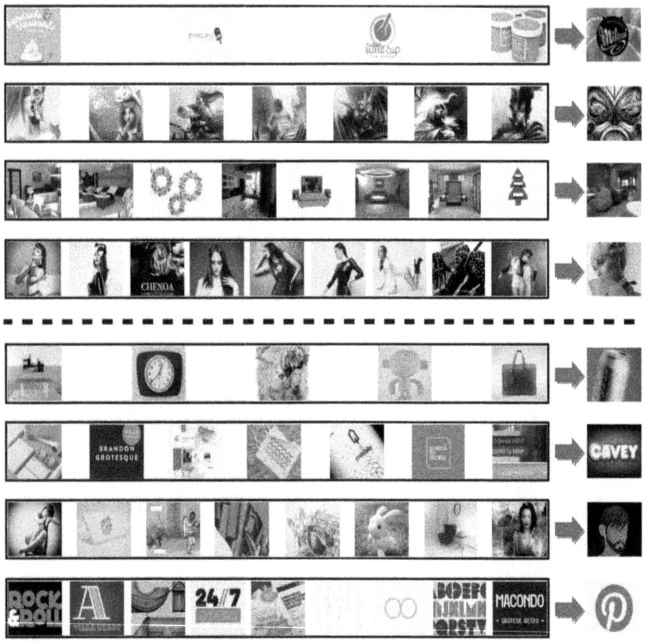

Figure 3: Above the dashed line are four sample sessions of users with the largest w_u (i.e., strong short-term consistency). Below the dashed line are four sample sessions of users with the least w_u (i.e., weak short-term consistency). Items on the right of the arrows are recommendations made by *Vista+*.

APPENDIX

A. SCALABILITY ANALYSIS

We analyze the time complexity of the K-order *Vista+* as follows. Recall that we use a sampling scheme to handle multiple creators (see Section 3.2). For a given user u, time step t, and item i, the prediction $\widehat{p}_{u,t,i}$ takes $O(D_1 * F + D_2)$ to compute the interactions between u and i, and $O(K * (D_2 + D_3 * F))$ for the interactions between i and K previous items. Therefore for each sampled training triple (u, t, j), the calculation of $\widehat{x}_{u,t,j}$ will take $O(D_1 * F + D_2 + K * (D_2 + D_3 * F)) = O(D_1 * F + K * D_2 + K * D_3 * F)$. According to Eq. 7, computing the partial derivatives and updating relevant parameters also have the time complexity of $O(D_1 * F + K * D_2 + K * D_3 * F)$ (when the two embedding matrices are updated). Summing up all above components, it takes $O(D_1 * F + K * D_2 + K * D_3 * F)$ to process each training triple. Using our lock-free asynchronous SGD training procedure with sampling, multiple triples are trained simultaneously.

References

[1] D. W. Aha, D. Kibler, and M. K. Albert. Instance-based learning algorithms. *Machine learning*, 1991.

[2] A. J. Chaney, D. M. Blei, and T. Eliassi-Rad. A probabilistic model for using social networks in personalized item recommendation. In *RecSys*, 2015.

[3] S. Chen, J. L. Moore, D. Turnbull, and T. Joachims. Playlist prediction via metric embedding. In *SIGKDD*, 2012.

[4] S. Chen, J. Xu, and T. Joachims. Multi-space probabilistic sequence modeling. In *SIGKDD*, 2013.

[5] Y. Ding and X. Li. Time weight collaborative filtering. In *CIKM*, 2005.

[6] S. Feng, X. Li, Y. Zeng, G. Cong, Y. M. Chee, and Q. Yuan. Personalized ranking metric embedding for next new poi recommendation. In *IJCAI*, 2015.

[7] G. Guo, J. Zhang, and N. Yorke-Smith. Trustsvd: Collaborative filtering with both the explicit and implicit influence of user trust and of item ratings. In *AAAI*, 2015.

[8] R. He, C. Lin, J. Wang, and J. McAuley. Sherlock: sparse hierarchical embeddings for visually-aware one-class collaborative filtering. In *IJCAI*, 2016.

[9] R. He and J. McAuley. Ups and downs: Modeling the visual evolution of fashion trends with one-class collaborative filtering. In *WWW*, 2016.

[10] R. He and J. McAuley. VBPR: visual bayesian personalized ranking from implicit feedback. In *AAAI*, 2016.

[11] Y. Kalantidis, L. Kennedy, and L.-J. Li. Getting the look: clothing recognition and segmentation for automatic product suggestions in everyday photos. In *ICMR*, 2013.

[12] R. Klinkenberg. Learning drifting concepts: Example selection vs. example weighting. *Intelligent Data Analysis*, 2004.

[13] Y. Koren. Factorization meets the neighborhood: a multifaceted collaborative filtering model. In *SIGKDD*, 2008.

[14] Y. Koren. Collaborative filtering with temporal dynamics. *Communications of the ACM*, 2010.

[15] Y. Koren and R. Bell. Advances in collaborative filtering. In *Recommender Systems Handbook*. Springer, 2011.

[16] H. Ma, I. King, and M. R. Lyu. Learning to recommend with social trust ensemble. In *SIGIR*, 2009.

[17] H. Ma, H. Yang, M. R. Lyu, and I. King. Sorec: social recommendation using probabilistic matrix factorization. In *CIKM*, 2008.

[18] B. Mobasher, H. Dai, T. Luo, and M. Nakagawa. Using sequential and non-sequential patterns in predictive web usage mining tasks. In *ICDM*, 2002.

[19] F. Niu, B. Recht, C. Ré, and S. J. Wright. Hogwild: A lock-free approach to parallelizing stochastic gradient descent. In *NIPS*, 2011.

[20] S. Rendle, C. Freudenthaler, Z. Gantner, and L. Schmidt-Thieme. BPR: bayesian personalized ranking from implicit feedback. In *UAI*, 2009.

[21] S. Rendle, C. Freudenthaler, and L. Schmidt-Thieme. Factorizing personalized markov chains for next-basket recommendation. In *WWW*, 2010.

[22] G. Shani, R. I. Brafman, and D. Heckerman. An mdp-based recommender system. In *UAI*, 2002.

[23] K. Simonyan and A. Zisserman. Very deep convolutional networks for large-scale image recognition. 2015.

[24] L. van der Maaten. Accelerating t-SNE using tree-based algorithms. *JMLR*, 2014.

[25] H. Wang, W. Fan, P. S. Yu, and J. Han. Mining concept-drifting data streams using ensemble classifiers. In *SIGKDD*, 2003.

[26] K. Yamaguchi, M. Kiapour, and T. Berg. Paper doll parsing: Retrieving similar styles to parse clothing items. In *ICCV*, 2013.

[27] W. Yang, P. Luo, and L. Lin. Clothing co-parsing by joint image segmentation and labeling. In *CVPR*, 2014.

[28] T. Zhao, J. McAuley, and I. King. Leveraging social connections to improve personalized ranking for collaborative filtering. In *CIKM*, 2014.

[29] A. Zimdars, D. M. Chickering, and C. Meek. Using temporal data for making recommendations. In *UAI*, 2001.

Representation Learning for Homophilic Preferences

Trong T. Nguyen
School of Information Systems
Singapore Management University
ttnguyen.2014@smu.edu.sg

Hady W. Lauw
School of Information Systems
Singapore Management University
hadywlauw@smu.edu.sg

ABSTRACT

Users express their personal preferences through ratings, adoptions, and other consumption behaviors. We seek to learn latent representations for user preferences from such behavioral data. One representation learning model that has been shown to be effective for large preference datasets is Restricted Boltzmann Machine (RBM). While homophily, or the tendency of friends to share their preferences at some level, is an established notion in sociology, thus far it has not yet been clearly demonstrated on RBM-based preference models. The question lies in how to appropriately incorporate social network into the architecture of RBM-based models for learning representations of preferences. In this paper, we propose two potential architectures: one that models social network among users as additional observations, and another that incorporates social network into the sharing of hidden units among related users. We study the efficacies of these proposed architectures on publicly available, real-life preference datasets with social networks, yielding useful insights.

Keywords

user preferences; homophily; representation learning; social recommendation; restricted Boltzmann machine

1. INTRODUCTION

Representation learning [5] deals with deriving useful latent representations from a large amount of data, so as to enable better learning or prediction. It is an area of active research in diverse fields, including speech recognition [13], computer vision [19], natural language processing, etc., where approaches based on neural networks and deep learning are currently generating a lot of interest.

In this work, we are particularly interested in representation learning for preference data. Users express their preferences in various ways, e.g., when they assign ratings to items, when they tag or bookmark contents they like, when they purchase or re-purchase products, when they watch videos or listen to music. Such behaviors generate a large amount of data that carry a lot of information about what users like and dislike. Our aim is to learn a latent representation for each user's preferences from such behavioral data.

One pioneering work based on undirected graphical model [31] used Restricted Boltzmann Machine (RBM) to model user preferences from ratings. [31] showed that RBM could learn representations for user preferences from large-scale datasets such as Netflix [4], with collaborative filtering performance competitive with matrix factorization's. Moreover, being a basic building block of many deep learning models, RBM could potentially benefit from further development in the currently very active deep learning research.

Many online social media platforms today capture not just users' preferences through their behaviors, but also their social connections with one another through their friendship links. This highlights an important aspect of user preferences that has not yet been factored in by previous RBM-based models, i.e., *homophily*, or the tendency of people with social connections to have shared preferences at some level. Homophily is an established notion in sociology [26], and as we will survey in Section 2, factoring in social network information often helps collaborative filtering algorithms.

Given the preponderance of evidence from the literature on homophily, we hypothesize that social network information could also potentially improve the performance of RBM-based models at learning representations for user preferences. The research questions lie in *how* to do so appropriately. In this paper, we investigate two primary structures.

The first is to model social network links as *observations* that are generated by RBM, in addition to behaviors such as ratings or adoptions. This yields our first proposed model, SocialRBM-*Wing* described in Section 4, which features a dual-wing structure, i.e., two groups of visible units (corresponding to item adoptions and social links respectively) sharing a common layer of hidden units. This has the advantage of simplicity, by learning the social effects from data.

Rather than modeling social links as observations, the second model, SocialRBM-*Deep* described in Section 5, features a deep structure, i.e., a higher layer of *hidden units that are partially shared* among friends, while still maintaining some global sharing across all users. This has the advantage of incorporating the homophily assumption directly into the higher layer of hidden units, so as to allow the original lower layer of hidden units to focus on capturing patterns of item adoptions among all users. Moreover, deeper structures tend to produce more robust features, which are less likely to suffer from noise than shallower structures.

RecSys '16, September 15 - 19, 2016, Boston , MA, USA

ISBN 978-1-4503-4035-9/16/09...$15.00

DOI: http://dx.doi.org/10.1145/2959100.2959157

Contributions. In this work, we make the following contributions:

1. As far as we know, this is the first systematic study of different means for incorporating social network information into RBM-based models for preference data.
2. Towards this objective, we propose two models, namely: SocialRBM-*Wing* in Section 4 and SocialRBM-*Deep* in Section 5, and describe their inferences.
3. To verify the efficacy of the models, we conduct an empirical analysis based on two publicly available real-life datasets: *Delicious* and *Last.fm*, showing promising results in terms of improving the representations learnt by RBM-based models from these datasets.

2. RELATED WORK

A Boltzmann Machine (BM) [1] is a network of stochastic binary units, with one hidden layer and one visible layer. A more popular form with simpler inference is Restricted Boltzmann Machine (RBM) [31], which allows only connections between hidden and visible layers, but not within each layer. Variants of RBM include replacing binary units with Gaussian hidden units [31] or visible units [30] for continuous values, or learning from inequality constraints [35]. RBM can also be extended to have multiple hidden layers, forming a Deep Boltzmann Machine (DBM) [30].

The use of RBM for collaborative filtering was pioneered by [31]. This has been extended in several directions. [8] expanded into two sets of hidden layers: for modeling correlations among users and items respectively. [32] used autoencoder in place of RBM. [7] used autoencoder on ratings to learn representation for initializing an existing matrix factorization [22]. In this work, we build upon the well-established RBM model [31] to further incorporate social networks.

By incorporating social networks into modeling ratings or adoptions, our work is related to multi-modal representation learning. For instance, [17, 39] modeled text and images, [33] modeled audio and video, while [38] modeled text and ratings. We are distinct in two ways. For one, we are modeling a different set of modalities. For another, most of these works treat modalities as observations, whereas we also explore another means for incorporating one modality (social network) into the configuration of shared hidden units.

Previous works in collaborative filtering were mostly based on matrix factorization [2, 16, 18]. It thus follows that past works on incorporating social networks were modifications of matrix factorization [10, 40], e.g., generating social network links [23], regularizing friends' latent vectors [24], or expressing one's ratings [21] or latent vector [15] as a function of those of friends. These and our work essentially follow two different forks of collaborative filtering paradigms: matrix factorization and RBM respectively. The two paradigms are effectively complementary and co-existent. Previous studies showed that ensembles of collaborative filtering paradigms could yield better performance than any one paradigm on its own [3, 4, 14]. In this work, we focus on investigating the effects of homophily on RBM-based preference models.

There are also efforts to factor in social network into other types of models, such as topic modeling [28, 37]. Such works rely heavily on the availability of rich features, such as words. Modeling features is an orthogonal direction to our focus here on the effects of social networks on adoptions.

3. PRELIMINARIES

Restricted Boltzmann Machine (RBM). RBM is a form of Markov Random Field, with the structure of a bipartite graph, connecting two types of binary stochastic units: *visible* units $\mathbf{x} \in \{0,1\}^{\mathcal{N}}$ and *hidden* units $\mathbf{h} \in \{0,1\}^{K}$.

As a member of the family of energy-based models, its energy function is defined as follows:

$$E(\mathbf{x},\mathbf{h}) = -\mathbf{a}^T\mathbf{x} - \mathbf{b}^T\mathbf{h} - \mathbf{x}^T\mathbf{W}\mathbf{h}, \quad (1)$$

where $\mathbf{a}$ and $\mathbf{b}$ are bias vectors for visible and hidden units respectively, and $\mathbf{W}$ is the $\mathcal{N} \times K$ matrix of weights associated with the connections between visible and hidden units.

Based on the energy function, the likelihood $P(\mathbf{x})$ of an observed boolean vector $\mathbf{x}$ is as follows:

$$P(\mathbf{x};\Theta) = \sum_{\mathbf{h}} \frac{\exp(-E(\mathbf{x},\mathbf{h}))}{Z}, \quad (2)$$

where $Z = \sum_{\mathbf{x}',\mathbf{h}'} \exp(-E(\mathbf{x}',\mathbf{h}'))$ is the *partition function* for normalization, while Θ is the set of model parameters.

The two conditional probabilities $P(\mathbf{h}|\mathbf{x})$ and $P(\mathbf{x}|\mathbf{h})$ can be expressed as follows:

$$P(h_k = 1|\mathbf{x}) = \sigma\left(\sum_{i=1}^{\mathcal{N}} W_{ik}x_i + b_k\right), \quad (3)$$

$$P(x_i = 1|\mathbf{h}) = \sigma\left(\sum_{k=1}^{K} W_{ik}h_k + a_i\right), \quad (4)$$

where $\sigma(t) = 1/1 + exp(-t)$ is the logistic function. The conditional distributions indicate that units in one layer are activated independently given activations from the other.

The model can be trained by maximizing the log-likelihood $\log P(\mathbf{x};\Theta)$ using an approximation gradient ascent "contrastive divergence" (CD) introduced by [12].

RBM for Preference Data. Let us denote $\mathcal{U}$ to be the number of users, and $\mathcal{N}$ to be the number of items. For each user, we observe a visible vector $\mathbf{x} \in \{0,1\}^{\mathcal{N}}$, where '1' indicates the user's adoption of an item, and '0' otherwise. Here, for simplicity, we model binary adoptions. For multi-scale ratings, we can use softmax units instead, as in [31].

These observations can be modeled as one RBM instance for each user, with the same number of K hidden units, and all the instances share the same $\mathbf{a}$, $\mathbf{b}$ and $\mathbf{W}$ weights. This way, we can derive a $K-$dimensional latent representation vector $\mathbf{h}$ for each user, within a huge space of combinations resulting from the activations of various binary hidden units.

Incorporating Social Networks. We assume that we are also given a social network graph $\mathcal{G}$, where each edge is a symmetric connection between two users. Our objective is to integrate $\mathcal{G}$ into an RBM model for user preferences, so as to arrive at a better latent representation $\mathbf{h}$ for each user.

In the RBM above, there is no user-specific parameter. Therefore, unlike some non-RBM approaches outlined in Section 2, we cannot simply tie user-specific parameters of friends. Directly employing regularization among hidden layers of RBM would not be applicable either, because the shared weights would lead to optimization on the whole network globally at the same time, rather than just locally among friends. This motivates our approach of placing social constraints to express homophily through the model structure so as to learn personalized representation using the hidden layers. In the next two sections, we describe two RBM-based structures that we find effective for this problem.

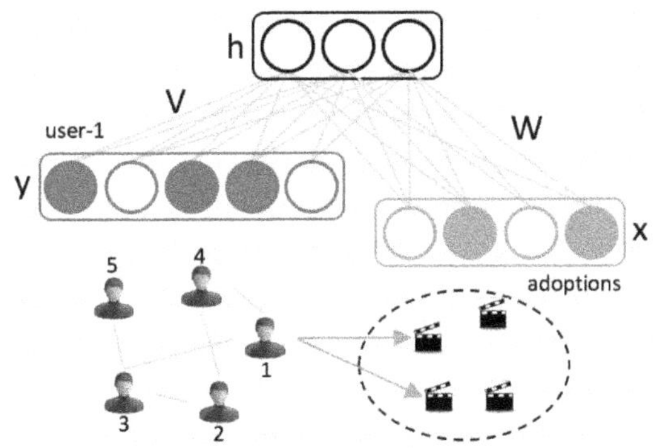

Figure 1: SOCIALRBM-*Wing*: both social connections and ratings/adoptions play a role as observations encoded jointly through a shared hidden layer.

4. SOCIAL NETWORK AS OBSERVATION

Our first model, SOCIALRBM-*Wing*, models item adoptions and social connections as two sets of observations, which are encoded through a shared hidden layer. As shown in Figure 1, the two sets of visible units resemble two "wings" attached to a "body" (the shared hidden layer), thus the name of the model. Our intuition is that if the model can learn co-occurrence patterns across both users' item adoptions and social connections, we would then be able to predict item adoptions given one's social connections.

4.1 Model

Each user is associated with two sets of visible units. The first set, for item adoptions, is $\mathbf{x} \in \{0,1\}^{\mathcal{N}}$, as described in Section 3. The second, for social connections, is $\mathbf{y} \in \{0,1\}^{\mathcal{U}}$, i.e., a binary vector of $\mathcal{U}$ dimensions, where each element y_j in the vector is activated if the user has a connection to user u_j in the social network $\mathcal{G}$. In the following, for simplicity, we describe the model and the learning for an individual user. For the collection of all users, the gradients with respect to the shared weight parameters are averaged over all users.

Figure 1 shows an illustration for one example user *user-1* or u_1, with a social connection to herself as well as to her friends (u_3 and u_4), thus the visible units y_1, y_4 and y_5 are activated (shaded in blue). The user is also observed to have two item adoptions (the second and fourth items), thus the visible units x_2 and x_4 are activated (shaded in green).

The conditional distribution of $\mathbf{x}$ is as shown in Eq. (4). In turn, the conditional distribution of $\mathbf{y}$ is shown in Eq. (5) below, where V_{jk} is the weight parameter (shared among all users) associated with the connection between visible unit y_j and hidden unit h_k.

$$P(y_j = 1|\mathbf{h}) = \sigma\left(\sum_{k=1}^{K} V_{jk}h_k + a_j\right) \quad (5)$$

The conditional distribution over hidden units for encoding both visible layers is given in Eq. (6), while the energy function is given in Eq. (7).

$$P(h_k = 1|\mathbf{x},\mathbf{y}) = \sigma\left(\sum_{j=1}^{\mathcal{U}} V_{jk}y_j + \sum_{i=1}^{\mathcal{N}} W_{ik}x_i + b_k\right) \quad (6)$$

$$E(\mathbf{x},\mathbf{y},\mathbf{h}) = -\sum_{j=1}^{\mathcal{U}}\sum_{k=1}^{K} y_j V_{jk} h_k - \sum_{i=1}^{\mathcal{N}}\sum_{k=1}^{K} x_i W_{ik} h_j - \sum_{k=1}^{K} h_k b_k - \sum_{j=1}^{\mathcal{U}} y_j a_j - \sum_{i=1}^{\mathcal{N}} x_i a_i \quad (7)$$

Learning. From Eq. (7), we can derive the log-likelihood $\mathcal{L}(\mathbf{x},\mathbf{y};\Theta)$ of visible inputs $\mathbf{x}$ and $\mathbf{y}$ for each user:

$$P(\mathbf{x},\mathbf{y};\Theta) = \sum_{\mathbf{h}} \frac{\exp\left(-E(\mathbf{x},\mathbf{y},\mathbf{h})\right)}{Z(\Theta)}, \quad (8)$$

$$\mathcal{L}(\mathbf{x},\mathbf{y};\Theta) = \log\sum_{\mathbf{h}} \exp\left(-E(\mathbf{x},\mathbf{y},\mathbf{h})\right) - \log Z(\Theta), \quad (9)$$

where $Z(\Theta) = \sum_{\mathbf{x}',\mathbf{y}',\mathbf{h}'} \exp\left(-E(\mathbf{x}',\mathbf{y}',\mathbf{h}')\right)$ is the partition function to normalize the probability sum to 1.

Model parameters are learned by contrastive divergence [12] (CD) with n-step sampling (CD-n), as shown in Eq. (10) where P_0, P_n are respectively data distributions at step 0 and n after sampling from conditional distributions. In practice, we use one-step (CD-1) to approximate the gradients, which is commonly used for training RBM [34].

$$\frac{\partial\mathcal{L}(\mathbf{x},\mathbf{y})}{\partial\Theta} = \langle\frac{-\partial E(\mathbf{x},\mathbf{y},\mathbf{h})}{\partial\Theta}\rangle_{P_0} - \langle\frac{-\partial E(\mathbf{x}',\mathbf{y}',\mathbf{h}')}{\partial\Theta}\rangle_{P_n} \quad (10)$$

Regularization. Due to the strong imbalance in data between seen and unseen (missing) items, we find that CD tends to lead to hidden biases increasing over time. If most of the hidden units were activated during the training process, then the model would not differentiate the representations among users. Hence, we incorporate regularization of the expected hidden activations around a desired level of activation τ into the objective function [20]. As shown in Eq. (11), the aggregated gradients are updated at the same time with the direction found in Eq. (10), where $\bar{P}$ is the expected activation of hidden units. λ is a tunable coefficient.

$$\tilde{\mathcal{L}}(\mathbf{x},\mathbf{y};\Theta) = \mathcal{L}(\mathbf{x},\mathbf{y};\Theta) - \lambda\sum_{k=1}^{K} |\ \tau - \bar{P}(h_k|\mathbf{x},\mathbf{y})\ |^2 \quad (11)$$

4.2 Inference

After learning the model parameters, we estimate the latent representation, and predict unseen adoptions by reconstructing the visible layer from the hidden layer, by performing one step of sampling to reconstruct the data as below:

$$\hat{h}_k \leftarrow \sigma\left(\sum_{j=1}^{\mathcal{U}} V_{jk}y_j + \sum_{i=1}^{\mathcal{N}} W_{ik}x_i + b_k\right)$$
$$\hat{r}_i \leftarrow \sigma\left(\sum_{k=1}^{K} W_{ki}\hat{h}_k + a_i\right) \quad (12)$$

Compared to the RBM model for adoptions only, incorporating social network puts more constraints on deciding the user preferences, which will be affected by both global (all users) and local (their friends) patterns. In terms of learning, one more benefit is the potential to reduce overfitting due to cross-modality patterns produced from two sides of observations. In addition, to deal with cold-start users with few or no observed adoptions, the model can make use of the observations from their social connections to infer item adoptions. This is related to the notion of cross-modality in [39] with similar structure, but with different types of stochastic units, targeted for modeling text and images.

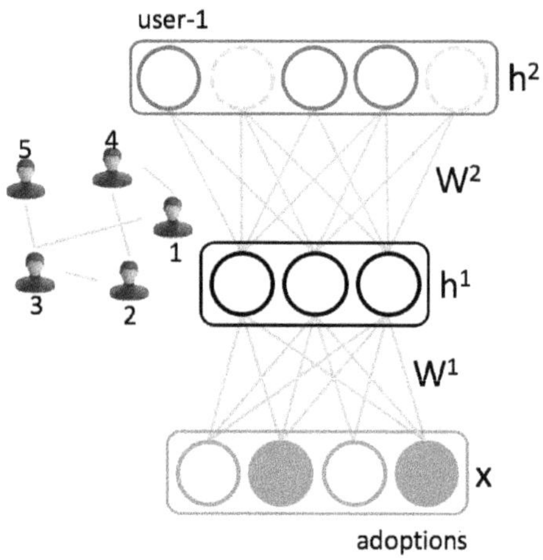

Figure 2: SOCIALRBM-*Deep*: The top layer $\mathbf{h}^2$ has $\mathcal{U}$ hidden units, corresponding to $\mathcal{U}$ users. Each user is represented by a single hidden unit on the top layer with weights shared with their friends. For example, user u_1 has connections to u_3 and u_4, thus the hidden units h_1^2, h_3^2 and h_4^2 are available for encoding u_1's adoptions. The other hidden units h_2^2 and h_5^2 will be unavailable (dashed). All K units in the middle layer $\mathbf{h}^1$ will always be available to all users.

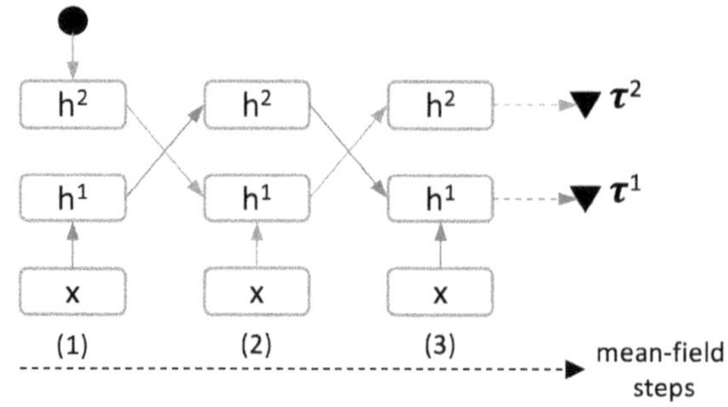

Figure 3: A visual for the sequence of forward steps in the mean-field inference, in which at the first step, hidden units $\mathbf{h}^2$ in the top layer will be randomized for initialization. The errors from both τ^1 vs. τ^2 in the regularization are backpropagated through this sequence for the gradient updates.

5. SOCIAL NETWORK AS SHARING OF HIDDEN UNITS

In this section, we propose an alternative approach that adapts the model architecture to the social network structure. The intuition of SOCIALRBM-*Deep* is that instead of letting social connections bring users and their friends closer through shared observations, we allow friends to affect each other's representations through sharing hidden units.

5.1 Model

In terms of its structure, this model SOCIALRBM-*Deep* is a "flipped" version of SOCIALRBM-*Wing*, with the social network layer now stacked up on top of the item adoption layer. Its role also changes from visible units for observation to hidden units, as illustrated in Figure 2.

The structure of SOCIALRBM-*Deep* is reminiscent of a two-layer Deep Boltzmann Machine (DBM), thus its name. There are two layers of hidden units $\mathbf{h}^1$ (middle layer) and $\mathbf{h}^2$ (top layer). The middle layer is shared across all training instances (users). However, one critical difference from DBM is that our top layer is not shared across *all* instances. Our structure is such that each user is represented at the top layer by a group of hidden units. When learning the representation of a user, only the groups of hidden units corresponding to her own, as well as those of her friends' could be activated. This induces sharing particularly among users with social connections. Without losing generality, in this work we use a group size of one, to keep the number of parameters of SOCIALRBM-*Deep* the same with SOCIALRBM-*Wing*, thus establishing parity for comparison later. In other words, to encode the item adoptions of a user, SOCIALRBM-*Deep* makes use of $(F_u + 1)$ hidden units, where F_u is the number of friends of u. In Figure 2, for user u_1 with two friends, three hidden units are available at the top layer.

The energy function with all connections in the model is shown below:

$$E(\mathbf{x}, \mathbf{h}^1, \mathbf{h}^2) = -\sum_{i=1}^{\mathcal{N}}\sum_{k=1}^{K} x_i W_{ik}^1 h_k^1 - \sum_{k=1}^{K}\sum_{j=1}^{\mathcal{U}} h_k^1 W_{kj}^2 h_j^2 - \sum_{i=1}^{\mathcal{N}} x_i a_i - \sum_{k=1}^{K} h_k^1 b_k - \sum_{j=1}^{\mathcal{U}} h_j^2 a_j, \quad (13)$$

where $\mathbf{h}^1$ and $\mathbf{h}^2$ are the vectors of hidden units at the middle and top layers respectively.

Learning. The parameter updates are similar to Eq. (10), except that $P_0 = P(\mathbf{h}^1, \mathbf{h}^2|\mathbf{x})$ is now approximated by a variational distribution $Q(\mathbf{h}^1, \mathbf{h}^2)$ [30] as described in Section 5.2. For the full distribution, we run n-step Gibbs sampler through following conditional distributions:

$$p(h_k^1 = 1|\mathbf{x}, \mathbf{h}^2) = \sigma\left(\sum_{i=1}^{\mathcal{N}} W_{ik}^1 x_i + \sum_{j=1}^{\mathcal{U}} W_{kj}^2 h_j^2 + b_k\right),$$

$$p(h_j^2 = 1|\mathbf{h}^1) = \sigma\left(\sum_{k=1}^{K} W_{kj}^2 h_k^1 + a_j\right),$$

$$p(x_i = 1|\mathbf{h}^1) = \sigma\left(\sum_{k=1}^{K} W_{ik}^1 h_k^1 + a_i\right).$$

Our model is based on social network to allow sharing in the training process of the top layer. Due to the connectivity across layers, the effect of sharing permeates through all levels of the deep structure. The model is a combination of two kinds of sharing: one is "global" across all users (the first layer); the other is "local" based on the graph structure, whereby users are co-trained only with direct friends or through mutual friends (via overlapping hidden groups). In contrast, the original RBM only explores global patterns.

To better initialize the parameters for mean-field steps, we apply pretraining stage for each layer in the deep network. As discussed in [30], mid-layer hidden units can be activated from both higher and lower layers; thus, the aggregation of posterior over these units could be contributed by halving the weights after learning, or duplicating them in training and keeping its value in the testing process.

Regularization. As in Section 4, we apply regularization to hidden activations. However, due to the use of variational inference for posterior approximation (as discussed in Section 5.2), the gradients could be computed via back-propagation algorithm (illustrated in Figure 3) through n steps of mean-field update as discussed in [29]. The aggregate objective function is as follows:

$$\tilde{\mathcal{L}}(\mathbf{x};\Theta) = -\lambda_1 \sum_{k=1}^{K} \mid \tau_1 - \bar{P}(\mathbf{h^1_k}|\mathbf{x}) \mid^2 - \lambda_2 \sum_{j=1}^{\mathcal{U}} \mid \tau_2 - \bar{P}(\mathbf{h^2_j}|\mathbf{x}) \mid^2 + \mathcal{L}(\mathbf{x};\Theta), \quad (14)$$

where τ_1, τ_2 are the desired levels of hidden unit activations in each of the two respective layers.

5.2 Inference

We apply the mean-field inference [30] to approximate the true posterior by a fully factorized distribution Q. Learning is conducted via minimizing the $KL(Q(\mathbf{h^1}, \mathbf{h^2})||P(\mathbf{h^1}, \mathbf{h^2}|\mathbf{x}))$ or maximizing the lower-bound of likelihood with respect to variational parameters $(\mu_k = Q(h^1_k = 1), \mu_j = Q(h^2_j = 1))$ as shown below:

$$\ln P(\mathbf{x};\Theta) \geq \sum_{i=1}^{\mathcal{N}}\sum_{k=1}^{K} x_i W^1_{ik}\mu_k + \sum_{k=1}^{K}\sum_{j=1}^{\mathcal{U}} \mu_k W^2_{kj}\mu_j - \ln Z(\Theta) + \sum_{k=1}^{K}(\mu_k \ln \mu_k + (1-\mu_k)\ln(1-\mu_k)) + \sum_{j=1}^{\mathcal{U}}(\mu_j \ln \mu_j + (1-\mu_j)\ln(1-\mu_j)) \quad (15)$$

The fixed-point equations are produced below :

$$\mu_k \leftarrow \sigma\left(\sum_{i=1}^{\mathcal{N}} W^1_{ik}x_i + \sum_{j=1}^{\mathcal{U}} W^2_{kj}\mu_j + b_k\right) \quad (16)$$

$$\mu_j \leftarrow \sigma\left(\sum_{j=1}^{\mathcal{U}} W^2_{kj}\mu_k + a_j\right) \quad (17)$$

$$\hat{r}_i \leftarrow \sigma\left(\sum_{k=1}^{K} W^1_{ki}\mu_k + a_i\right) \quad (18)$$

For experiments, we set 15 iterations for updating alternatingly from Eq. (16) and Eq. (17) until convergence. Finally, the probabilities for unseen items are computed via Eq. (18), and ranked in descending order for prediction.

6. EXPERIMENTS

The experimental objective is primarily to investigate the effects of homophily on RBM-based models for learning the representation of user preferences. We pursue this objective by evaluating the performance of comparable RBM-based models on two publicly-available[1] real-life datasets [6].

Datasets. The first dataset, *Delicious*, originally came from an online bookmarking site, whereby a set of users bookmark a set of URL's. These are essentially binary observations of item adoptions. In addition, it is also an online social network, which allows users to indicate friendship links. The second dataset, *LastFM*, originated from an online radio site, where users can tag their favourite artists (items). These are also modeled as binary observations of adoptions. Similarly, it has a social network among users.

[1] http://grouplens.org/datasets/hetrec-2011

	Delicious	LastFM
No. of users	1,867	1,892
No. of items	69,226	17,632
No. of adoptions <user, item>	104,220	92,834
No. of social links <user, user>	15,328	25,434
Adoption density	0.08%	0.27%
Social network density	0.44%	0.71%

Table 1: Dataset Sizes

The statistics for these two datasets are shown in Table 1. While the number of users are similar, *Delicious* is the larger and sparser dataset, with many more items and significantly lower adoption density. This sparsity also implies that it is the more difficult dataset for prediction. Other than their sizes, the two datasets are characteristically quite different. *Delicious*, driven by bookmarks, tends to have a greater level of personalization and expected homophily, whereas *LastFM*, driven by music artists, tends to have greater uniformity due to the presence of popular artists with broad appeal. Experimentation with these two contrasting natures would allow us to derive greater insights.

We focus on binary adoptions, because our main concern here is on the effects of social networks. With some modification, the models could apply to multi-scale ratings, which we will consider for future work. Moreover, we do not use tag information from the datasets, for parity with the original RBM model [31] that does not use such features either.

Comparisons. Because of our objective of studying homophily on RBM-based models, we can demonstrate this most clearly and directly by comparing the two proposed models SOCIALRBM-*Wing* and SOCIALRBM-*Deep* (with social network) to the original RBM model [31] (without social network). To establish parity among the models, we use the same dimensionality for the latent representations, i.e., $K = 100$ hidden units. This setting was also used in in [14, 31]. We will conduct this comparison in Section 6.1.

Although the dimensionality of the representation is the same, the models do not all have the same number of parameters. The two models with social networks SOCIALRBM-*Wing* and SOCIALRBM-*Deep* have an identical number of parameters. Compared to RBM, both have an additional number of $K \times \mathcal{U}$ weight parameters, which are required to connect the social layer and the hidden units. To ensure that the observed effects are not due to these additional parameters alone, in Section 6.2, we conduct another set of experiments comparing the same models (SOCIALRBM-*Wing* or SOCIALRBM-*Deep* respectively), but replacing the social networks with random networks of the same structure.

Finally, in Section 6.3, we briefly explore whether the learnt representations of friends tend to exhibit greater similarity after incorporating social networks during learning.

6.1 Comparison of Various Models

In this section, we conduct a comparison between the two proposed models and the baseline RBM model.

Task. Since one of the main applications of learning representations from preference data is for recommendation, here we evaluate the models on the task of predicting users' item adoptions. The adoption data for each user is ran-

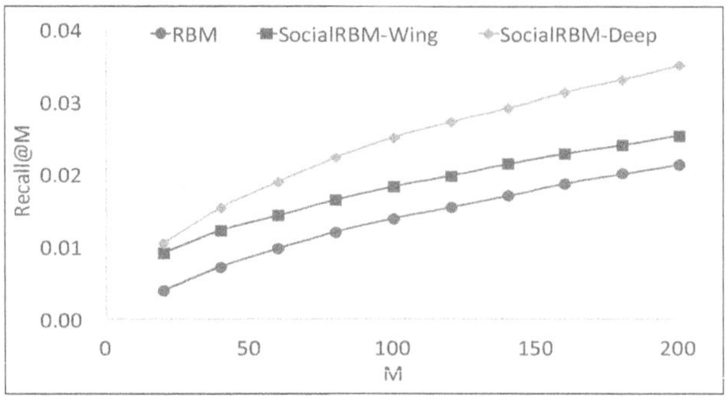

Figure 4: Recall@M for Delicious at various M's.

domly split into 80% for training vs. 20% for testing. For each dataset, we create ten such training/testing splits. For each user, we seek to predict the held-out item adoptions in the testing set. This is done by getting each model to learn from the training set, and output a ranked list of the top M items whose adoptions were not seen in the training set.

In the training stage, each sample data is divided into small batches of 100 instances (users) for each iteration. All models are trained with a learning rate of 0.003 in 1000 iterations util convergence. We also apply a momentum of 0.8 to speed up and a weight-decay of 0.001. For the pretraining stage in SocialRBM-*Deep*, we train each layer in 500 iterations with the similar process discussed in [30].

Metric. There are various ways to evaluate recommendations [11, 27]. For sparse preference datasets such as ours, unseen item adoptions may not necessarily mean that a user dislikes the items; the user might simply have been unaware of them. This makes it difficult to compute precision accurately. However, since the observed item adoptions in the testing sets are known to be true positives, following [28, 36], we focus on measuring recall. The recall of a model's prediction of top M items for a user is defined as follows:

$$recall@M \leftarrow \frac{\text{number of correctly predicted items in top } M}{\text{total number of held-out adopted items}}$$

For comparison across models, we average the recall@M across all the users. We vary the value of M in the range of $[20 \ldots 200]$. Higher recall at lower M indicates a better result, implying that the correct items tend to be among the top-ranked predictions. We average the results across the ten training/testing splits described above. Where appropriate, we present not only the mean, but also the standard deviation, as well as statistical significance test results.

Analysis. First, we look into the *Delicious* dataset. Figure 4 shows the cumulative recall up to top 200. As expected, as M increases, recall generally increases, because the numerator of the recall equation above would increase, while the denominator is stable. Importantly, based on the trend lines in Figure 4, it is evident that both SocialRBM-*Wing* and SocialRBM-*Deep* have higher recall results than the baseline RBM. Between the two models with social networks, SocialRBM-*Deep* has a higher performance than SocialRBM-*Wing*. Interestingly, the former tends to increase faster in recall than the latter as M increases, indicating SocialRBM-*Deep*'s greater effectiveness at placing the ground truth items higher in the prediction ranked lists.

To look into the differences between various models in greater detail, Table 2 shows not just the mean recall values,

M	RBM	SocialRBM-*Wing*	SocialRBM-*Deep*
20	0.0040 ± 0.0007	$0.0092 \pm 0.0007^{\dagger\dagger}$	$\mathbf{0.0105} \pm 0.0008^{\dagger\dagger\S\S}$
40	0.0072 ± 0.0007	$0.0122 \pm 0.0012^{\dagger\dagger}$	$\mathbf{0.0153} \pm 0.0013^{\dagger\dagger\S\S}$
60	0.0097 ± 0.0008	$0.0143 \pm 0.0013^{\dagger\dagger}$	$\mathbf{0.0190} \pm 0.0013^{\dagger\dagger\S\S}$
80	0.0120 ± 0.0004	$0.0164 \pm 0.0014^{\dagger\dagger}$	$\mathbf{0.0224} \pm 0.0014^{\dagger\dagger\S\S}$
100	0.0139 ± 0.0005	$0.0183 \pm 0.0011^{\dagger\dagger}$	$\mathbf{0.0252} \pm 0.0014^{\dagger\dagger\S\S}$
200	0.0214 ± 0.0011	$0.0254 \pm 0.0015^{\dagger\dagger}$	$\mathbf{0.0351} \pm 0.0022^{\dagger\dagger\S\S}$

Table 2: Comparison of Recall@M (mean $\pm$ standard deviation) for Delicious. Best results are in bold. † (0.05 level) and †† (0.01 level) indicate statistically significant improvement over RBM. **§§ (0.01 level) indicates statistically significant improvement over** SocialRBM-***Wing*.**

M	RBM	SocialRBM-*Wing*	SocialRBM-*Deep*
20	0.2298 ± 0.0020	$0.2319 \pm 0.0031^{\dagger}$	$\mathbf{0.2380} \pm 0.0037^{\dagger\dagger\S\S}$
40	0.3109 ± 0.0023	$0.3133 \pm 0.0030^{\dagger\dagger}$	$\mathbf{0.3252} \pm 0.0039^{\dagger\dagger\S\S}$
60	0.3651 ± 0.0027	$0.3677 \pm 0.0031^{\dagger\dagger}$	$\mathbf{0.3809} \pm 0.0033^{\dagger\dagger\S\S}$
80	0.4057 ± 0.0026	$0.4080 \pm 0.0033^{\dagger\dagger}$	$\mathbf{0.4224} \pm 0.0039^{\dagger\dagger\S\S}$
100	0.4369 ± 0.0023	$0.4397 \pm 0.0033^{\dagger}$	$\mathbf{0.4542} \pm 0.0042^{\dagger\dagger\S\S}$
200	0.5317 ± 0.0029	$0.5353 \pm 0.0033^{\dagger\dagger}$	$\mathbf{0.5500} \pm 0.0038^{\dagger\dagger\S\S}$

Table 3: Comparison of Recall@M for LastFM.

but also the standard deviations. We see that SocialRBM-*Deep* is the best (in bold). The standard deviations are also relatively small, implying that the mean values are quite reflective of the relative performances across models. We also conduct paired samples Student's t-test for statistically significant differences, indicating that the outperformance by SocialRBM-*Wing* over RBM, as well as that by SocialRBM-*Deep* over the other two models, are indeed statistically significant.

We reiterate that the key result here is the relative outperformance by the models with social network over the baseline RBM, of which the results here are strongly indicative. Compared to RBM, SocialRBM-*Deep* shows an increase by a factor of 1.5X to 2.5X. The increase by SocialRBM-*Wing* is smaller, but still significant. The absolute values of recall in *Delicious* are low, because it represents a very challenging dataset, especially without using any tag feature. A random predictor would attain a recall@200 of merely 0.0029. Thus, the performance of our models represents an increase by an order of magnitude over a random baseline.

Turning to *LastFM*, we show the corresponding table of results in Table 3. Similar observations as made above for *Delicious* on the relative outperformance by the models incorporating social networks can also be made for *LastFM*.

Comparing the two datasets, in terms of the absolute values, the results on *Delicious* are lower than those on *LastFM*. This can be explained by the disparity in the adoption densities shown in Table 1, i.e., 0.08% for *Delicious* vs. 0.27% for *LastFM*. The lower density indicates greater uncertainty in prediction, thus higher error rate. However, the relative improvements among models on *Delicious* are more significant than on *LastFM*. We hypothesize that this comes from the different characteristics of two datasets. For popular items, such as music artists, even unrelated people may still prefer similar music artists. Conversely, bookmarks are less frequent, and may be more prone to social influence, explaining the greater effects of homophily seen in *Delicious*.

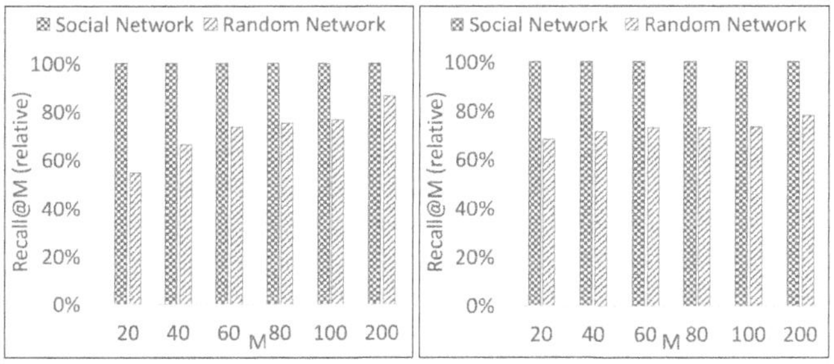

a. SocialRBM-*Wing* b. SocialRBM-*Deep*

Figure 5: Relative Comparison of Social Network vs. Random Network for Delicious.

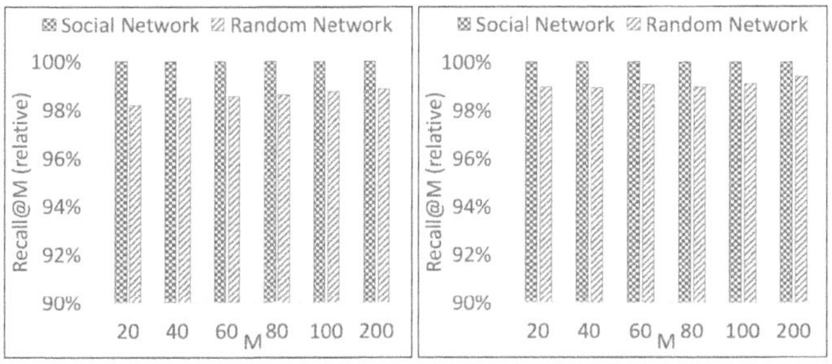

a. SocialRBM-*Wing* b. SocialRBM-*Deep*

Figure 6: Relative Comparison of Social Network vs. Random Network for LastFM.

6.2 Randomization Study

We try to keep the models comparable by using the same dimensionality of latent representation across models. To investigate the effects of the social network itself, in this section we conduct another set of experiments, which attempt to control the effects of the model structure, and isolate the effects of homophily alone. The best way to do so is to compare *within* the same model, but swap the social network graph with a random graph of a similar structure.

Randomization. Ascertaining data mining results via randomization was advocated by [9]. Here, we follow the way they generate random graphs, so as to maintain the structure of the original graph in terms of the degree of each node. Essentially, a random graph is obtained by randomizing the adjacency matrix of the original graph, while keeping the same row and column sums. For each dataset, we generate ten random networks from the original social network, and compare the model run with these random networks with the same model run on the social network.

Analysis. For this study, we still use the recall@M metric described above. However, our focus here is not on the absolute performance, but on whether the same model will produce different levels of performance when run with social network or random network. To present these results clearly, we peg the performance by the model with social network at 100% (the absolute values can be seen in Table 2 and Table 3), and present the relative results by the same model but with random network as a percentage of the former.

For *Delicious*, Figure 5(a) shows the relative comparison of recall by SocialRBM-*Wing*, when social network is replaced by random network. Figure 5(b) shows that of SocialRBM-*Deep*. For both, we witness significant drops in recall for random networks, e.g., recall@20 drops to 55% for SocialRBM-*Wing*, and 65% for SocialRBM-*Deep*.

Figure 6(a) and Figure 6(b) show similar experiments on *LastFM*. They tell a similar story, though the drop is modest, with random networks attaining 98% of the performance of social network. This is another evidence of the relatively weaker effect of homophily on *LastFM* than on *Delicious*, which we trace to the different natures of the items. If the patterns of adopting popular artists are similar among users, changing the network structure would not lead to significant changes in adoptions, thus explaining the smaller drop rates.

For both *Delicious* and *LastFM*, the drops due to random networks are statistically significant at 0.01 level in all cases. This supports the hypothesis of the measurable effects of homophily on the RBM-based models for item adoptions.

Dataset	RBM	SocialRBM-*Wing*	SocialRBM-*Deep*
Delicious	0.0084 ± 0.0004	$0.0250 \pm 0.0008^{\dagger\dagger}$	$0.0210 \pm 0.0031^{\dagger\dagger}$
LastFM	0.0486 ± 0.0015	$0.0629 \pm 0.0121^{\dagger\dagger}$	$0.0821 \pm 0.0024^{\dagger\dagger}$

Table 4: Comparison of MAP for Similarity Ranking of Social Links. †† (0.01 level) indicates statistically significant improvement over RBM.

6.3 Similarity in Latent Representations

So far we learn that improvements arise from the right model architecture, as well as the right network structure. This comes from the intuition built into the models to bring together the representations of socially connected users, either via hidden units (SocialRBM-*Deep*) or visible units (SocialRBM-*Wing*). In this final experiment, we briefly explore this intuition, by using the similarities among the learnt representations of users to rank one's friends.

Task. The user representation is a vector of hidden units inferred from Sections 4 and 5. For each user, we rank other users based on the cosine similarity to their learnt representations. The aim is to see whether the user's friends would be ranked highly in this list, i.e., friends have similar representations. This study is not meant to be predictive, but rather *reflective*, whether the learnt representations may be correlated to the social connections in the training set.

Metric. We borrow a metric from information retrieval: Mean Average Precision or MAP [25]. This is computed as the mean of the average precision across all users, as follows.

$$MAP \leftarrow \frac{1}{\mathcal{U}} \sum_{j=1}^{\mathcal{U}} AvgPrecision_j$$

$AvgPrecision_j$ is computed by averaging the precisions at each of u_j's recall points (the ranks of u_j's friends).

Analysis. The main expectation is that if the proposed models do indeed absorb the social network information well during the learning phase, they would perform better at this task than the baseline RBM. Table 4 shows that on both datasets, SocialRBM-*Wing* and SocialRBM-*Deep* have significantly higher MAP than RBM. For *LastFM*, they increase by a factor of 1.3X to 1.7X. For *Delicious*, they increase by an even larger factor of 2.5X to 3X, supporting the hypothesis of a stronger homophily effect on *Delicious*. Overall, these results support that the learnt representations of friends become more correlated as a result of the homophily assumptions built into our proposed models.

7. CONCLUSION

We study the homophily effect on RBM-based models for preference datasets, proposing two models for incorporating social network. The first, SOCIALRBM-*Wing*, operates by fitting two sets of observations: item adoptions and social network. The second, SOCIALRBM-*Deep*, uses social network as a form of sharing hidden units at the top layer. These models are verified on two publicly available real-life item adoption datasets. The main conclusions are two-fold. First is the importance of the right architecture, as evidenced by SOCIALRBM-*Deep*'s outperformance over SOCIALRBM-*Wing* and RBM. Second is the importance of the right network information, as evidenced by the outperformance by social network over random network for each model. For future work, we plan to investigate enrichments to the proposed models, such as additional modalities.

Acknowledgments

This research is supported by the National Research Foundation, Prime Minister's Office, Singapore under its NRF Fellowship Programme (Award No. NRF-NRFF2016-07).

8. REFERENCES

[1] D. H. Ackley, G. E. Hinton, and T. J. Sejnowski. A learning algorithm for boltzmann machines. *Cognitive Science*, 9(1):147–169, 1985.

[2] G. Adomavicius and A. Tuzhilin. Toward the next generation of recommender systems: A survey of the state-of-the-art and possible extensions. *TKDE*, 17(6):734–749, 2005.

[3] X. Amatriain and J. Basilico. Recommender systems in industry: A netflix case study. In *Recommender Systems Handbook*, pages 385–419. Springer, 2015.

[4] R. M. Bell and Y. Koren. Lessons from the Netflix prize challenge. *ACM SIGKDD Explorations Newsletter*, 9(2):75–79, 2007.

[5] Y. Bengio, A. Courville, and P. Vincent. Representation learning: A review and new perspectives. *TPAMI*, 35(8):1798–1828, 2013.

[6] I. Cantador, P. Brusilovsky, and T. Kuflik. 2nd workshop on information heterogeneity and fusion in recommender systems (HetRec 2011). In *RecSys*, 2011.

[7] S. Deng, L. Huang, G. Xu, X. Wu, and Z. Wu. On deep learning for trust-aware recommendations in social networks. *TNNLS*, (99):1–14, 2016.

[8] K. Georgiev and P. Nakov. A non-iid framework for collaborative filtering with restricted Boltzmann machines. In *ICML*, pages 1148–1156, 2013.

[9] A. Gionis, H. Mannila, T. Mielikäinen, and P. Tsaparas. Assessing data mining results via swap randomization. *TKDD*, 1(3), 2007.

[10] I. Guy. Social recommender systems. In *Recommender Systems Handbook*, pages 511–543. Springer, 2015.

[11] J. L. Herlocker, J. A. Konstan, L. G. Terveen, and J. T. Riedl. Evaluating collaborative filtering recommender systems. *TOIS*, 22(1):5–53, 2004.

[12] G. Hinton. Training products of experts by minimizing contrastive divergence. *Neural Computation*, 14:2002, 2000.

[13] G. Hinton, L. Deng, D. Yu, G. E. Dahl, A.-r. Mohamed, N. Jaitly, A. Senior, V. Vanhoucke, P. Nguyen, T. N. Sainath, et al. Deep neural networks for acoustic modeling in speech recognition: The shared views of four research groups. *Signal Processing Magazine*, 29(6):82–97, 2012.

[14] M. Jahrer and A. Töscher. Collaborative filtering ensemble. In *KDD Cup*, pages 61–74, 2012.

[15] M. Jamali and M. Ester. A matrix factorization technique with trust propagation for recommendation in social networks. In *RecSys*, pages 135–142, 2010.

[16] D. Jannach, M. Zanker, A. Felfernig, and G. Friedrich. *Recommender systems: an introduction*. Cambridge University Press, 2010.

[17] R. Kiros, R. Salakhutdinov, and R. S. Zemel. Unifying visual-semantic embeddings with multimodal neural language models. *TACL*, 2015.

[18] Y. Koren, R. Bell, and C. Volinsky. Matrix factorization techniques for recommender systems. *Computer*, (8):30–37, 2009.

[19] A. Krizhevsky, I. Sutskever, and G. E. Hinton. ImageNet classification with deep convolutional neural networks. In *NIPS*, pages 1097–1105, 2012.

[20] H. Lee, C. Ekanadham, and A. Y. Ng. Sparse deep belief net model for visual area v2. In *NIPS*, pages 873–880, 2008.

[21] H. Ma, I. King, and M. R. Lyu. Learning to recommend with social trust ensemble. In *SIGIR*, pages 203–210, 2009.

[22] H. Ma, I. King, and M. R. Lyu. Learning to recommend with explicit and implicit social relations. *TIST*, 2(3):29, 2011.

[23] H. Ma, H. Yang, M. R. Lyu, and I. King. SoRec: social recommendation using probabilistic matrix factorization. In *CIKM*, pages 931–940, 2008.

[24] H. Ma, D. Zhou, C. Liu, M. R. Lyu, and I. King. Recommender systems with social regularization. In *WSDM*, pages 287–296, 2011.

[25] C. D. Manning, P. Raghavan, and H. Schütze. *Introduction to information retrieval*. Cambridge University Press, 2008.

[26] M. McPherson, L. Smith-Lovin, and J. M. Cook. Birds of a feather: Homophily in social networks. *Annual Review of Sociology*, pages 415–444, 2001.

[27] P. Pu, L. Chen, and R. Hu. A user-centric evaluation framework for recommender systems. In *RecSys*, pages 157–164, 2011.

[28] S. Purushotham, Y. Liu, and C.-c. J. Kuo. Collaborative topic regression with social matrix factorization for recommendation systems. In *ICML*, pages 759–766, 2012.

[29] S. Reed, K. Sohn, Y. Zhang, and H. Lee. Learning to disentangle factors of variation with manifold interaction. In *ICML*, pages 1431–1439, 2014.

[30] R. Salakhutdinov and G. E. Hinton. Deep boltzmann machines. In *AISTATS*, pages 448–455, 2009.

[31] R. Salakhutdinov, A. Mnih, and G. Hinton. Restricted boltzmann machines for collaborative filtering. In *ICML*, pages 791–798, 2007.

[32] S. Sedhain, A. K. Menon, S. Sanner, and L. Xie. AutoRec: Autoencoders meet collaborative filtering. In *WWW*, pages 111–112, 2015.

[33] N. Srivastava and R. R. Salakhutdinov. Multimodal learning with deep Boltzmann machines. In *NIPS*, pages 2222–2230, 2012.

[34] T. Tieleman. Training restricted boltzmann machines using approximations to the likelihood gradient. In *ICML*, pages 1064–1071, 2008.

[35] T. Tran, D. Phung, and S. Venkatesh. Thurstonian Boltzmann machines: Learning from multiple inequalities. In *ICML*, pages 46–54, 2013.

[36] C. Wang and D. M. Blei. Collaborative topic modeling for recommending scientific articles. In *KDD*, pages 448–456, 2011.

[37] H. Wang, B. Chen, and W.-J. Li. Collaborative topic regression with social regularization for tag recommendation. In *IJCAI*, 2013.

[38] H. Wang, N. Wang, and D.-Y. Yeung. Collaborative deep learning for recommender systems. In *KDD*, pages 1235–1244, 2015.

[39] E. P. Xing, R. Yan, and A. G. Hauptmann. Mining associated text and images with dual-wing harmoniums. In *UAI*, 2005.

[40] X. Yang, Y. Guo, Y. Liu, and H. Steck. A survey of collaborative filtering based social recommender systems. *Computer Communications*, 41:1–10, 2014.

Personalized Recommendations using Knowledge Graphs: A Probabilistic Logic Programming Approach

Rose Catherine
Language Technologies Institute
Carnegie Mellon University
Pittsburgh, PA, USA
rosecatherinek@cs.cmu.edu

William Cohen
Machine Learning Department
Carnegie Mellon University
Pittsburgh, PA, USA
wcohen@cs.cmu.edu

ABSTRACT

Improving the performance of recommender systems using knowledge graphs is an important task. There have been many hybrid systems proposed in the past that use a mix of content-based and collaborative filtering techniques to boost the performance. More recently, some work has focused on recommendations that use external knowledge graphs (KGs) to supplement content-based recommendation.

In this paper, we investigate three methods for making KG based recommendations using a general-purpose probabilistic logic system called ProPPR. The simplest of the models, `EntitySim`, uses only the links of the graph. We then extend the model to `TypeSim` that also uses the types of the entities to boost its generalization capabilities. Next, we develop a graph based latent factor model, `GraphLF`, which combines the strengths of latent factorization with graphs. We compare our approaches to a recently proposed state-of-the-art graph recommendation method on two large datasets, Yelp and MovieLens-100K. The experiments illustrate that our approaches can give large performance improvements. Additionally, we demonstrate that knowledge graphs give maximum advantage when the dataset is sparse, and gradually become redundant as more training data becomes available, and hence are most useful in cold-start settings.

Keywords

Knowledge Graph based Recommendations; Probabilistic Logic Programming; Graph based Matrix Factorization

1. INTRODUCTION

Recommendation is usually social or content-based, with social methods best for problems with many users and relatively few items (e.g., movie recommendation for Netflix) and content-based best on cold start or "long tail" settings. An important research problem is how to leverage external knowledge for improving content-based recommendations. Content features are usually available for both users and items. For users, these are typically their demographics. For items like movies, these may include the actors, genre, directors, country of release, etc. and for items like restaurants, these may include the location, cuisine, formal vs. casual, etc. Although many methods have been proposed in the past that use content, not many use the interconnections between the content itself and external knowledge sources, which we refer to as a knowledge graph (KG).

However, in recent work [27], the authors propose a metapath based method to infer users' preferences to items that have not been explicitly rated by them, and showed state-of-the-art results on two large real-world datasets. In this paper, we show how KG recommendations can be performed using a general-purpose probabilistic logic system called ProPPR[26]. We formulate the problem as a probabilistic inference and learning task, and present three approaches for making recommendations. Our formulations are not identical to that proposed in [27], but are similar in spirit. We show that a number of engineering choices, such as the choice of specific metapaths and length of metapaths, can be eliminated in our formalism, and that the formalism allows one to easily explore variants of the metapath approach. Our best methods outperform the latter.

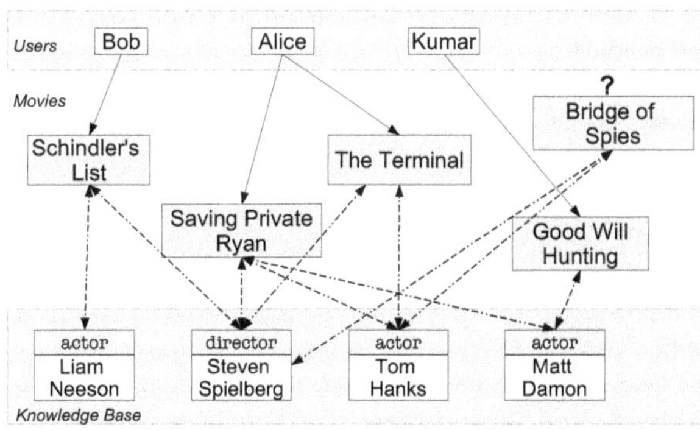

Figure 1: Example of Movie Recommendation

A typical movie recommendation example is depicted in Figure 1 where users watch and/or rate movies, and content about the movies are available in a database. The links in the figure show the content associated with each of the movies as well as the movies that each of the users watched. `EntitySim`, the simplest of the methods proposed in this paper, learns users' preferences over the content, and leverages the link structure of the KG to make predictions. In some cases, it is also possible to obtain a *type* information

RecSys '16, September 15-19, 2016, Boston , MA, USA

DOI: http://dx.doi.org/10.1145/2959100.2959131

about the content. For example, Tom Hanks is of type Actor. TypeSim, the second method, builds on EntitySim but additionally models the type popularities and type similarities. It is closest to the method of [27] in that it uses the type information of the nodes to prioritize certain paths in the graph. GraphLF, the most complex of the models proposed in this paper, is a latent factorization model over the knowledge graph, and is type agnostic i.e. it does not required typed KGs. By comparing our methods to the published results of the state-of-the-art method that uses KGs in generating recommendations [27], we show that our methods are able to achieve a large improvement in performance.

We also study the behavior of the methods with changing dataset densities and show that at higher densities, just the graph link structure suffices to make accurate recommendations and the type information becomes redundant. Additionally, our experiments show that at much larger densities, the knowledge graph itself becomes redundant and simple methods can perform as well or better. However, in sparse datasets with few training examples, the knowledge graph is a valuable source of information.

The rest of the paper is organized as follows: Section 2 discusses the prior relevant work. The approaches proposed in this paper are detailed in Section 3 followed by experiments and a discussion of results in Section 4. In Section 5 we conclude and give future directions of research.

2. RELATED WORK

Recommendation systems have been popular for a long time now and are a well researched topic. However, there has not been much effort directed at using external KGs for improving recommendations.

A recent method [27], called HeteRec_p, proposed the use of KGs for improving the recommender performance. Since this method is the present state-of-the-art against which we compare our approaches, we detail it in Section 2.1. Another link-based method [28] proposed by the same authors precedes [27], and learns a global model of recommendation based on the KG, but does not attempt to personalize the recommendations.

Another recent effort at using multiple sources of information is the HyPER system [16], where the authors show how to recommend using a Probabilistic Soft Logic framework [2]. They formulate rules to simulate collaborative filtering (CF) style recommendation. For instance, in the case of user-based CF, the rule is of the form, $SimilarUsers(u_1, u_2) \wedge Rating(u_1, i) \Rightarrow Rating(u_2, i)$, where $SimilarUsers$ indicate if the users u_1 and u_2 are similar using a k-nearest neighbor algorithm, computed offline using different similarity measures like Cosine, Pearson etc. If the friend-network of users is available, then they leverage it using the rule $Friends(u_1, u_2) \wedge Rating(u_1, i) \Rightarrow Rating(u_2, i)$. If other rating prediction algorithms like Matrix Factorization (MF) are available, then they induce an ensemble recommender using the rules $Rating_{MF}(u, i) \Rightarrow Rating(u, i)$ and $\neg Rating_{MF}(u, i) \Rightarrow \neg Rating(u, i)$. Eventually, during the training phase, they learn a weight per rule using the PSL framework, which is later used for predicting the ratings in the test set. Similar to HyPER is the approach proposed in [11] that uses Markov Logic Networks, and that proposed in [6] that uses Bayesian networks to create a hybrid recommender. Like these methods, we also base our methods on a general-purpose probabilistic reasoning system. However, we differ from these methods in our focus on using external knowledge in recommendations.

Prior research has previously proposed using various kinds of special purpose or domain–specific knowledge-graphs. In [12], the authors proposed to use a trust-network connecting the users especially for making recommendations to the cold-start users. The latter is matched up against the network to locate their most trusted neighbors, whose ratings are then used to generate the predictions. Another popularly used network is the social network of the users. Prior work like [14] and [9] among various other similar approaches use the social connection information of the users to find similar users or "friends" in this case, and use their ratings to generate recommendations for the former.

2.1 HeteRec_p

HeteRec_p [27] aims to find user's affinity to items that they have not rated using *metapaths*. Metapaths describe paths in a graph through which two items may be connected. In the example of Figure 1, an example metapath would be User $\rightarrow$ Movie $\rightarrow$ Actor $\rightarrow$ Movie. Given a graph/network schema $G_T = (A, R)$ of a graph G where A is the set of node types and R is the set of relations between the node types A, then, metapaths are described in the form of $P = A_0 \xrightarrow{R_1} A_1 \xrightarrow{R_2} A_2 \ldots \xrightarrow{R_k} A_k$ and represent a path in G_T, which can be interpreted as a new composite relation $R_1R_2 \ldots R_k$ between node-type A_0 and A_k, where $A_i \in A$ and $R_i \in R$ for $i = 0, \ldots k$, $A_0 = dom(R_1) = dom(P)$, $A_k = range(R_k) = range(P)$ and $A_i = range(R_i) = dom(R_{i+1})$ for $i = 1, \ldots, k-1$. For the specific purpose of recommending on user-item graphs, HeteRec_p uses metapaths of the form $user \rightarrow item \rightarrow * \rightarrow item$. Given a metapath P, they use a variant of PathSim [24] to measure the similarity between user i and item j along paths of the type P, a method the authors refer to as *User Preference Diffusion*. For each P, they use the user preference diffusion to construct the diffused user-item matrix $\tilde{R}_P$. Let $\tilde{R}^{(1)}, \tilde{R}^{(2)}, \ldots \tilde{R}^{(L)}$ be the diffused matrices corresponding to L different metapaths. Each such $\tilde{R}^{(q)}$ is then approximated as $\hat{U}^{(q)} \cdot \hat{V}^{(q)}$ using a low-rank matrix approximation technique. Then, the global recommendation model is expressed as: $r(u_i, v_j) = \sum_{q \in L} \theta_q \; \hat{U}_i^{(q)} \cdot \hat{V}_j^{(q)}$ where, θ_q is a learned weight for the path q. To personalize recommendations, they first cluster the users according to their interests. Then, the recommendation function is defined as: $r^*(u_i, v_j) = \sum_{k \in C} sim(C_k, u_i) \sum_{q \in L} \theta_q^{(k)} \; \hat{U}_i^{(q)} \cdot \hat{V}_j^{(q)}$ where, C represents the user clusters and $sim(C_k, u_i)$ gives a similarity score between the kth cluster center and user i. Note that the θ_q is now learned for each of the clusters. This formulation of the rating prediction function is similar to [5]. Although HeteRec_p performed well on the recommendation tasks, the algorithm needs several hyper-parameters that need to be determined or tuned, like choosing the specific L metapaths from a potentially infinite number of metapaths, and the number of clusters. It also requires a rich KB with types for entities and links.

3. PROPOSED METHOD

3.1 Preliminaries

In this paper, we use the term *entity* as a generic term to denote a word or a phrase that can be mapped onto a knowledge base or an ontology. Since the knowledge bases used in this paper are based on structured data, the mapping is straightforward. However, when using a generic knowledge base like Wikipedia[1], Yago [23] or NELL [21], one might require a wikifier or an entity linker [17].

A Knowledge Graph (KG) is a graph constructed by representing each item, entity and user as nodes, and linking those nodes that interact with each other via edges. In [27], the authors emphasize that their method is tailored to Heterogenous Information Networks (HIN), which are essentially KGs but with type mapping functions for entities and links, where there is more than one type (heterogenous). Otherwise, the network becomes homogenous. This is in contrast to prior works that use graphs or networks of only one type of nodes, like say, a friend network. A KG, as referred to in this paper, is therefore a relaxed version of a HIN where the types of entities and links may or may not be known. We assume that the nodes are typically heterogenous even if their type information is missing. If the types are unknown, then only the two methods `EntitySim` and `GraphMF` are applicable. However, if the knowledge graph is indeed an HIN, then all three methods apply.

Similar to [27], we too use binary user feedback. i.e. the rating matrix entry R_{ij} for user i and item j is 1 if a review or another form of interaction like clicking or liking is available. Otherwise, R_{ij} is 0.

3.2 Running Example

For example, consider a movie recommendation task, similar to that of [27], where we are tracking three users `Bob`, `Alice` and `Kumar`. From historical records, we know that `Alice` has watched `Saving Private Ryan` and `The Terminal`, both of which have `Steven Spielberg` as the `Director` and `Tom Hanks` as an `Actor`, as specified by the knowledge base. The knowledge base may also provide additional content like plot keywords, language and country of release, awards won etc. Similarly, we also know the movies that were watched in the past by `Bob` and `Kumar`. In addition to watching, we could also include user's actions such as "reviewing" or "liking", if available. Given the past viewing history of users, we may want to know the likelihood of them watching a new movie, say `Bridge of Spies`. This scenario is graphically represented in Figure 1. Although in this particular case, the movie-entity graph is bipartite, it is also common to have links between movies themselves like say, `Finding Nemo` and `Finding Dory` where the latter is a sequel to the former, or between entities themselves like for example, `Tom Hanks` and `Best Actor Academy Award`.

3.3 Recommendation as Personalized PageRank

Similar to the Topic Sensitive PageRank proposed in [10] and the weighted association graph walks proposed in [4], imagine a random walker starting at the node `Alice` in the graph of Figure 1 (ignore the direction of the edges). At every step, the walker either moves to one of the neighbors of the current node with probability $1 - \alpha$ or jumps back to the start node (`Alice`) with probability α (the reset parameter). If repeated for a sufficient number of times, this process will eventually give an approximation of the steady-state probability of the walker being in each of the nodes. However, since we need only the ranking of the movies and not the other entities like actors and directors, we consider only those nodes corresponding to the movie nodes being tested, and sort them according to their probability to produce a ranked list of movie recommendations.

[1]https://en.wikipedia.org

In the above method, there is no control over the walk. The final outcome of the walk is determined by the link structure and the start node alone. However, recent research has proposed methods to learn how to walk. Backstrom et. al in [3] showed how a random walker could be trained to walk on a graph. This is done by learning a weight vector w, which given a feature vector ϕ_{uv} for an edge in the graph $u \rightarrow v$, computes the edge strength as $f(w, \phi_{uv})$, a function of the weight and the feature vectors, that is used in the walk. During the training phase, learning w is posed as an optimization problem with the constraint that the PageRank computed for the positive example nodes is greater than that of the negative examples. In our case, the positive examples would be those movies that the user watched, and negative examples would be those that the user did not watch or give an explicit negative feedback.

3.4 Learning to Recommend using ProPPR

ProPPR [26], which stands for **Pro**gramming with **P**ersonalized **P**age**R**ank, is a first-order probabilistic logic system which accepts a *program* similar in structure and semantics to a logic program [18] and a set of *facts*, and outputs a ranked list of entities that *answers* the program with respect to the facts. ProPPR scores possible answers to a query based on a Personalized PageRank process in the proof graph (explained below) for the query. Below, we show how it can be used for the task of learning to recommend.

For the recommendation task, the first step is to find a set of entities that each user is interested in, from their past behaviors. We call this set the `seedset` of the user because it will later seed the random walk for that user. For this, we use the ProPPR program of Figure 2. The first rule states that the entity `E` belongs to the `seedset` of user `U` if `U` has reviewed `M` which is linked to entity `X` and `X` is related to `E`. Further, two entities are defined to be related if they are the same (Rule 2), or if there is a link between `X` and another entity `Z` which is related to `E` (Rule 3). This last rule is recursive. The `link` and the *type* (`isEntity`, `isItem` and `isUser`) information forms the knowledge graph in our case. Sample entries from the knowledge graph in the ProPPR format are shown in Figure 3. To find the seed set for `Alice`, we would issue the query Q = `seedset(Alice, E)` to ProPPR.

```
seedset(U,E) ←reviewed(U,M),link(M,X),related(X,E),
              isEntity(E).                              (1)
related(X,X) ←true.                                     (2)
related(X,E) ←link(X,Z),related(Z,E).                   (3)
```

Figure 2: Seed Set generation

```
link(Bridge of Spies,Tom Hanks)            isEntity(Tom Hanks)
link(Tom Hanks,Saving Private Ryan)        isEntity(Matt Damon)
link(Saving Private Ryan,Matt Damon)       isItem(Bridge of Spies)
```

Figure 3: Example entries from the knowledge graph

ProPPR performs inference as a graph search. Given a program LP like that of Figure 2 and a query Q, ProPPR starts constructing a graph G, called the *proof graph*. Each node in G represents a list of conditions that are yet to be proved. The root vertex v_0 represents Q. Then, it recursively adds nodes and edges to G as follows: let u be a node of the form $[R_1, R_2, ..., R_k]$ where R_* are its predicates. If ProPPR can find a fact in the database that matches R_1, then the corresponding variables become bound and R_1 is removed from the list. Otherwise, ProPPR looks for a rule in LP of the form $S \leftarrow S_1, S_2, ..., S_l$, where S matches R_1. If it finds such a rule, it creates a new node with R_1 replaced with the body of S as, $v = [S_1, S_2, ..., S_l, R_2, ..., R_k]$, and links u and v. In the running example, v_0 is `seedset(Alice, E)` which is then linked to the node v_1 = `[reviewed(Alice,M), link(M,X), related(X,E), isEntity(E)]` obtained using Rule 1. Then, ProPPR would use the training (historical) data for `reviewed` to substitute `Saving Private Ryan` and `The Terminal` for `M` creating two nodes v_2 and v_3 as `[link(Saving Private Ryan,X), related(X,E), isEntity(E)]` and `[ link(The Terminal,X), related(X,E), isEntity(E)]` respectively. ProPPR would proceed by substituting for `X` from the knowledge graph and `related(X,E)` using the rules and so on until it reaches a node whose predicates have all been substituted. These nodes are the answer nodes because they represent a complete proof of the original query. The variable bindings used to arrive at these nodes can be used to answer the query. Examples would be:

$$\texttt{seedSet}(\texttt{Alice}, \texttt{E} = \texttt{TomHanks})$$
$$\texttt{seedSet}(\texttt{Alice}, \texttt{E} = \texttt{StevenSpielberg})$$

Note that such a graph construction could be potentially infinite. Therefore, ProPPR uses an approximate grounding mechanism to construct an approximate graph in time $O(\frac{1}{\alpha\epsilon})$, where ϵ is the approximation error and α is the reset parameter. Once such a graph has been constructed, ProPPR runs a Personalized PageRank algorithm with the start node as v_0 and ranks the answer nodes according to their PageRank scores.

The output of the program of Figure 2 is a ranked list of entities for the user `U` and the first K of these will be stored as `U`'s seed set. Note that the Personalized PageRank scoring will rank high those entities that are reachable from the movies that the user reviewed through multiple short paths, and rank low the entities that are either far and/or do not have multiple paths leading to them.

$$\texttt{reviewed}(\texttt{U}, \texttt{M}) \leftarrow \texttt{seedset}(\texttt{U}, \texttt{E}), \texttt{likesEntity}(\texttt{U}, \texttt{E}),$$
$$\texttt{related}(\texttt{E}, \texttt{X}), \texttt{link}(\texttt{X}, \texttt{M}), \texttt{isApplicable}(\texttt{U}, \texttt{M}). \quad (4)$$
$$\texttt{likesEntity}(\texttt{U}, \texttt{E}) \leftarrow \{\texttt{l}(\texttt{U}, \texttt{E})\}. \quad (5)$$

Figure 4: `EntitySim`: ProPPR program for finding movies that a user may like using similarity measured using the graph links

After generating the seed set for each user, the next step in recommendation is to train a model and then use it to make predictions. As one method, we use the ProPPR program of Figure 4. It states that the user `U` may like a movie `M` if there is an entity `E` belonging to `U`'s seed set, and `U` likes `E`, and `E` is related to another entity `X`, which appears in the movie `M` (Rule 4). The predicate `isApplicable` controls the train and the test information for each user. During training, it lists the positive and negative training examples and during the test phase, that for the test, for each user. The predicate `related` is defined recursively as before. For the definition of the predicate `likesEntity`, note the term `{l(U,E)}`. This corresponds to a feature that is used to annotate the edge in which that rule is used. For example, if the rule is invoked with `U = Alice` and `E = Tom Hanks`, then the feature would be `l(Alice, Tom Hanks)`. In the training phase, ProPPR learns the weight of that feature from the training data. During the prediction phase, ProPPR uses the learned weight of the feature as the weight of the edge. Note that these learned weights for each user-entity pair are not related to the ranking obtained from the seed set generation program of Figure 2, because these weights are specific to the prediction function.

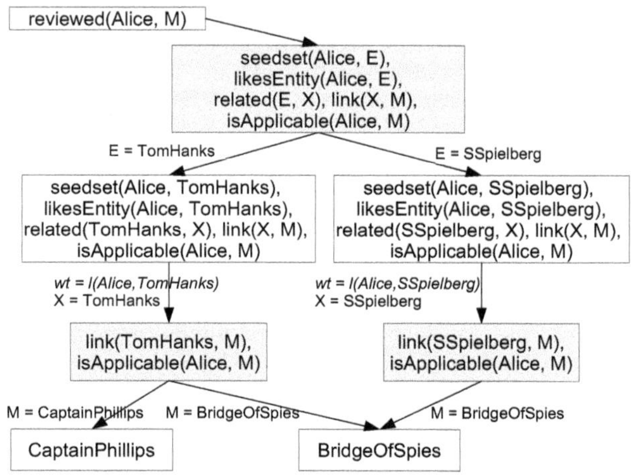

Figure 5: Sample grounding of the `EntitySim` ProPPR program

During the training phase, ProPPR grounds the program similar to that for the seed set generation discussed earlier. A sample grounding for `EntitySim` is depicted in Figure 5 where `Bridge Of Spies` and `Captain Phillips` are in the set of test examples for `Alice`. We may have other test examples for `Alice`, but if they are not provable using the rules (or beyond a certain approximation error), they will not be present in the grounding. ProPPR then follows a procedure similar to that proposed by Backstrom et. al in [3], to train the random walker. This is done by learning a weight vector $\mathbf{w}$, which given a feature vector $\mathbf{\Phi}_{uv}$ for an edge in the graph $u \rightarrow v$, computes the edge strength as $f(\mathbf{w}, \mathbf{\Phi}_{uv})$, a function of the weight and the feature vectors. i.e. the probability of traversing the edge $P(v|u) \propto f(\mathbf{w}, \mathbf{\Phi}_{uv})$. Our method uses $f(\mathbf{w}, \mathbf{\Phi}_{uv}) = e^{\mathbf{w} \cdot \mathbf{\Phi}_{uv}}$.

During the training phase, learning of $\mathbf{w}$ is posed as an optimization problem with the constraint that the PageRank computed for the positive example nodes is greater than that of the negative examples, as below:

$$-\sum_{k=1}^{m} \Big(\sum_{i=1}^{I_m} \log \mathbf{p}[u_i^{k+}] + \sum_{j=1}^{J_m} \log(1 - \mathbf{p}[u_j^{k-}]) \Big) + \mu \|\mathbf{w}\|_2^2 \quad (6)$$

where, $\mathbf{p}$ is the PageRank vector computed with the edge weights obtained with $\mathbf{w}$. The optimization function of Equation 6 used by ProPPR is the standard positive-negative log loss function instead of the pairwise loss function used in [3]. To learn $\mathbf{w}$, we use AdaGrad [8] instead of the quasi-Newton method used in [3] and SGD used in [26]. The initial learning rate used by AdaGrad and the regularization parameter μ are set to 1. For a thorough description of ProPPR, we refer the reader to [26] and [25].

3.5 Approach 2: TypeSim

The `EntitySim` method uses only the knowledge graph links to learn about user's preferences. However, recall that we are in fact using a heterogenous information network where in addition to the link information, we also know the "type" of the entities. For example, we know that `New York City` is of type `City` and `Tom Hanks` is of type `Actor`. To leverage this additional type information, we extend the `EntitySim` method to `TypeSim` method as shown in Figure 6.

$$\begin{aligned}
\texttt{reviewed(U,R)} \leftarrow\ & \texttt{seedset(U,E)}, \texttt{likesEntity(U,E)}, \\
& \texttt{popularEntity(E)}, \texttt{related(E,X)}, \\
& \texttt{link(X,R)}, \texttt{isApplicable(U,R)}. && (7)\\
\texttt{likesEntity(U,E)} \leftarrow\ & \{\texttt{l(U,E)}\}. && (8)\\
\texttt{popularEntity(E)} \leftarrow\ & \texttt{entityOfType(E,T)}, \\
& \texttt{popularType(T)}\{\texttt{p(E)}\}. && (9)\\
\texttt{popularType(T)} \leftarrow\ & \{\texttt{p(T)}\}. && (10)\\
\texttt{typeAssoc(X,Z)} \leftarrow\ & \texttt{entityOfType(X,S)}, \texttt{entityOfType(Z,T)}, \\
& \texttt{typeSim(S,T)}. && (11)\\
\texttt{typeSim(S,T)} \leftarrow\ & \{\texttt{t(S,T)}\}. && (12)
\end{aligned}$$

Figure 6: TypeSim method for recommendations

`TypeSim` models the general popularity of each of the node types in Rule 10 by learning the overall predictability offered by the type of the entity using `p(T)`. For example, nodes of the type `Actor` may offer more insight into users' preferences than those of type `Country`. Note that, the learned weight is not specific to the user and hence its weight is shared by all the users. Similar to Rule 10, in Rule 9, the model learns the overall predictability offered by the entity itself, independent of the user using `p(E)`. For example, it could be that the movies directed by `Steven Spielberg` are more popular than those by other lesser known directors. `TypeSim` also models a general traversal probability between two types using Rules 11 and 12. For example, `Actor` → `Movie` is generally a more predictive traversal on the graph compared to `Country` → `Movie`. These weights are incorporated into the prediction rule of `EntitySim` as shown in Rule 7.

3.6 Approach 3: GraphLF

One of the most successful types of Collaborative Filtering (CF) are the Latent Factor (LF) models [15]. They try to uncover hidden dimensions that characterize each of the objects thus mapping users and items onto the same feature space for an improved recommendation performance. Koren et al. note in [15] that for movies, latent factors might measure obvious dimensions such as comedy versus drama, amount of action, or orientation to children, as well as less well-defined dimensions such as depth of character development, or quirkiness, or even uninterpretable dimensions. For users, each factor measures how much the user likes movies that score high on the corresponding factor. Singular Value Decomposition (SVD) is one of the more popular methods of generating LF models for recommendation. An SVD method assigns users and items with values along each of the hidden dimensions while minimizing a loss function over the predicted and actual rating matrix.

The main attraction of Collaborative Filtering methods is that they do not require any knowledge about the users or items and predict solely based on the rating matrix. Similarly, the main attraction of Latent Factor based CF models is that they develop a general representation of users and items based on the ratings data that are more generalizable and often indiscernible in the raw data.

$$\begin{aligned}
\texttt{reviewed(U,R)} \leftarrow\ & \texttt{related(U,E)}, \texttt{related(E,X)}, \texttt{link(X,R)}, \\
& \texttt{isApplicable(U,R)}. && (13)\\
\texttt{related(U,E)} \leftarrow\ & \texttt{seedset(U,E)}, \texttt{simLF(U,E)}. && (14)\\
\texttt{related(X,X)} \leftarrow\ & . && (15)\\
\texttt{related(X,Y)} \leftarrow\ & \texttt{link(X,Z)}, \texttt{simLF(X,Z)}, \texttt{related(Z,Y)}. && (16)\\
\texttt{simLF(X,Y)} \leftarrow\ & \texttt{isDim(D)}, \texttt{val(X,D)}, \texttt{val(Y,D)}. && (17)\\
\texttt{val(X,D)} \leftarrow\ & \{\texttt{v(X,D)}\}. && (18)
\end{aligned}$$

Figure 7: GraphLF method for recommendations

Given that we have access to a KG that connects the items via different entities, the third approach that we propose in this paper, `GraphLF`, integrates latent factorization and graph-based recommendation. The overall ruleset is defined in Figure 7. Its principal rule is the definition of Latent Factor Similarity `simLF` in Rules (17) and (18). Essentially, `simLF` of two input entities `X` and `Y` is measured by first picking a dimension `D`, and then measuring the values of `X` and `Y` along `D`. If there are many dimensions `D` along which the values of both `X` and `Y` are high, then probabilistically, their similarity scores will also be high. The value of an entity `X` along dimension `D`, `val(X,D)` is learned from the data during the training phase, as defined in Rule (18).

Note how the recursive definition of the relatedness of two entities `related(X,Y)` in Rule (16) has now changed to account for their latent factor similarity in addition to the presence of a link between them. Also, the original prediction rule has changed in Rule (13) to use a new relatedness score between the user and the entity. Essentially, the definition of `related(U,E)` in Rule (14) replaces the earlier predicate `likesEntity(U,E)` with the latent factor similarity `simLF(U,E)`, between the user and an entity belonging to their seedset. Therefore, the model no longer learns a weight for each user-entity pair, and instead learns weights for the users and entities separately along each of the dimensions.

It is also important to note that `GraphLF` is type-agnostic unlike `TypeSim` and `HeteRec_p`. Types are not always available, especially for general-purpose graphs like the Wikipedia. Therefore, being type-agnostic is a desirable property and increases its applicability to a wide range of data domains.

3.7 Model Complexity

Let n be the number of users and m, the items. Let e be the number of distinct entities and t be the types. Then the complexity of the model as characterized by the number of parameters learned for each of the methods proposed in this paper are as below:

- EntitySim - $\mathcal{O}(n)$: In this method, we learn one parameter per user-entity pair. However, by virtue of the rules, we constrain the entities to be chosen from the seedset of that user, which is of a constant size c.
- TypeSim - $\mathcal{O}(n + e + t^2)$: In addition to those parameters learned for EntitySim, it also learns $e + t$ weights for each of the entities and types. Moreover, it also learns the type association between pairs of types leading to an additional t^2 parameters.
- GraphLF - $\mathcal{O}(n+m+e)$: For each of the users, entities and items, we learn a constant d number of weights corresponding to the latent dimensions.

In typical domains, we would expect $t \ll m$. Therefore, EntitySim is the simplest of the models and GraphLF is the more complex of the models proposed in this paper, in terms of the number of parameters.

4. EXPERIMENTS AND RESULTS

4.1 Datasets

To test our proposed methods, we use two well known large datasets:

- **Yelp2013**: This is the 2013 version of the Yelp Dataset Challenge[2] released by Yelp[3], available now at Kaggle[4]. We use this earlier version instead of the latest version from the Yelp Dataset Challenge for the purposes of comparing with the published results of the HeteRec_p algorithm. Similar to [27], we discard users with only 1 review entry.

- **IM100K**: This dataset is built from the MovieLens-100K dataset[5] unified with the content — director, actor, studio, country, genre, tag — parsed out from their corresponding IMDb pages[6]. We could not obtain the dataset used in [27], which we will refer to as IM100K-UIUC. Our dataset IM100K* is a close approximation to it, created from the same MovieLens-100K dataset, but we have recovered the content of 1566 movies of the total 1682 movies compared to 1360 in [27], and have 4.8% more reviews than [27].

For all the datasets, similar to [27], we sort the reviews in the order of their timestamps, and use the older 80% of the reviews as training examples and the newer 20% of the reviews as the test examples. The overall statistics of these datasets, viz. the number of users, the number of items and the total number of reviews/ratings, are listed in Table 1.

4.2 Experimental Setup

We evaluate the performance using the standard metrics, Mean Reciprocal Rank (MRR), and Precision at 1, 5 and 10 (P@1, P@5 and P@10) [19].

In our experiments, we found that any reasonable choice for the seed set size worked well enough. A fixed size serves to constrain the number of parameters learned and hence, the complexity of the model.

Dataset	#Users	#Items	#Ratings
Yelp	43,873	11,537	229,907
IM100K-UIUC	943	1360	89,626
IM100K*	940	1566	93,948

Table 1: Dataset Statistics

In the following sections, we compare our methods to the state-of-the-art method HeteRec_p proposed in [27] on the two datasets. We also compare the performance to a Naïve Bayes (NB) baseline, which represents a recommender system that uses only the content of the item without the knowledge graph and link information, to make predictions. Naïve Bayes classifiers have been previously shown to be as effective as certain computationally intensive algorithms [22]. For each user, the NB system uses the entities of the items in that user's training set as the features to train the model. These are the same entities used by our methods. We use the probabilities output by the classifier to rank the pages. The implementation used is from the Mallet [20] package. Since HeteRec_p was shown to be better than Popularity (which shows the globally popular items to users), Co-Click (which uses the co-click probabilities to find similar items), Non-Negative Matrix Factorization[7] and Hybrid-SVM (which uses a Ranking SVM[13] on metapaths) in [27], we refrain from repeating those comparisons again.

4.3 Performance Comparison on Yelp

The performance of the algorithms proposed in this paper as well as the baselines on the Yelp data are tabulated in Table 2. It can be seen from the results that our methods outperform HeteRec_p by a large margin. For example, GraphLF is 126% better on P@1 and TypeSim is 89% better on MRR.

Also, we can note that using the type information (TypeSim) improves the performance drastically compared to EntitySim. For example, P@1 improves by 118% and MRR by 51%. Similarly, we can note that discovering the latent factors in the data (GraphLF) also improves the performance tremendously compared to its lesser-generalizable counterpart (EntitySim). For example, P@1 improves by 115% and MRR by 37%.

However, there is no clear winner when comparing TypeSim and GraphLF: while the former scores better on MRR, the latter is better on P@1.

The NB baseline's performance is poor, but that was expected since the dataset is extremely sparse.

4.4 Performance Comparison on IM100K

The performance of HeteRec_p on the IM100K-UIUC dataset, and that of the algorithms proposed in this paper and the Naïve Bayes baseline on the IM100K* dataset, are tabulated in Table 3.

As noted in Section 4.1, the IM100K-UIUC dataset and the IM100K* dataset are slightly different from each other. Therefore, we cannot compare the performance of the methods directly; the most that can be said is that the methods appear to be comparable.

A more interesting and surprising result is that the simplest of the methods, NB and EntitySim, perform as well or

[2]https://www.yelp.com/dataset_challenge
[3]http://www.yelp.com/
[4]https://www.kaggle.com/c/yelp-recsys-2013/data
[5]http://grouplens.org/datasets/movielens/
[6]http://www.imdb.com/

Method	P@1	P@5	P@10	MRR	Settings
HeteRec_p	0.0213	0.0171	0.0150	0.0513	*published results*
EntitySim	0.0221	0.0145	0.0216	0.0641	$n = 20$
TypeSim	0.0444	**0.0188** [↑ 10%]	**0.0415** [↑ 176%]	**0.0973** [↑ 89%]	$n = 20$
GraphLF	**0.0482** [↑ 126%]	0.0186	0.0407	0.0966	$n = 20$, $dim = 10$
NB	0	0.0012	0.0013	0.0087	

Table 2: Performance comparison on Yelp: The best score for each metric is highlighted in blue and the lowest score in red. [↑ x%] gives the percent increase compared to the corresponding HeteRec_p score

Method	P@1	P@5	P@10	MRR	Settings
HeteRec_p (on IM100K-UIUC)	0.2121	**0.1932**	0.1681	**0.553**	*published results*
EntitySim	0.3485	0.1206	**0.2124** [↑ 26.3%]	0.501 [↓ −9.4%]	$n = 10$
TypeSim	**0.353** [↑ 66.4%]	0.1207 [↓ −37.5%]	0.2092	0.5053	$n = 10$
GraphLF	0.3248	0.1207 [↓ −37.5%]	0.1999	0.4852	$n = 10$, $dim = 10$
NB	0.312	0.1202	0.1342	0.4069	

Table 3: Performance comparison on IM100K (IM100K-UIUC & IM100K*): The best score for each metric is highlighted in blue and the lowest score in red. [↑ x%] gives the percent increase compared to the corresponding HeteRec_p score and [↓ x%], the percent decrease.

better than the more complex TypeSim and GraphMF. In fact, NB outperforms HeteRec_p on the P@1 metric. This leads us to speculate that when there are enough training examples per user and enough signals per item, simple methods suffice. We explore this conjecture more fully below.

4.5 Effect of Dataset Density on Performance

In the previous two sections, we saw how on the Yelp dataset TypeSim and GraphLF performed extremely well in comparison to the EntitySim method, whereas on the IM100K dataset, the latter was as good as or better than the former two. In this section, we explore this phenomenon further.

An important difference between the two datasets is that Yelp is a complete real world dataset with review frequencies exhibiting a power law distribution, while IM100K is a filtered version of a real world dataset counterpart, as noted by the authors of [27]: in IM100K dataset, each user has rated at least 20 movies.

To quantitatively compare their differences, we define the Density of a dataset as $\frac{\#\texttt{reviews}}{\#\texttt{users} \times \#\texttt{items}}$, which is the ratio of filled entries in the rating matrix to its size. Using this definition, the density of Yelp was found to be only 0.00077 whereas that of IM100K* was 0.06382.

To study this further, we created 4 additional datasets from Yelp by filtering out users and businesses that have less than k reviews, where k =10, 25, 50 and 100. The MRR scores of our methods and the NB baseline with varying k is plotted in Figure 8 (with the left y axis). These are with a seedset of size 20. The graph densities at the different k are also plotted in the same Figure 8 (in green with the right y axis). Note that the density increases to 0.11537 at $k = 100$, which is 148 times higher than the density at $k = 2$.

From the figure, we can see that when the dataset is the least dense ($k = 2$), the more complex methods TypeSim and GraphLF perform much better than the simple EntitySim. However, as the density increases with larger k, we

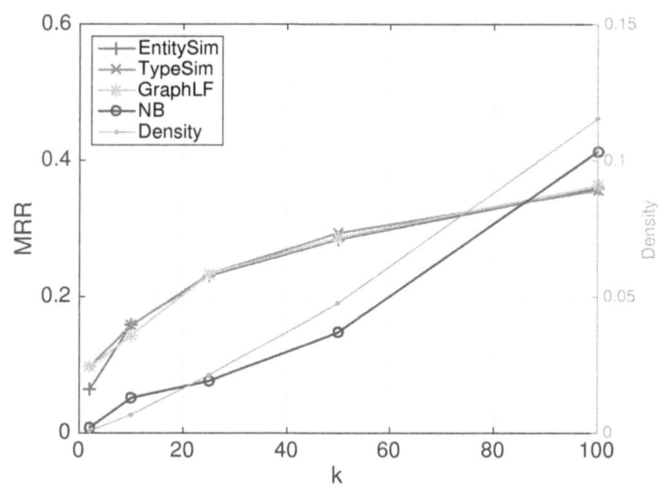

Figure 8: Performance of different methods with varying graph densities on Yelp

can observe that EntitySim eventually equals TypeSim and comes within 1% of that of GraphLF, at $k = 100$. Therefore, we can deduce that, when we have enough training examples and a dense graph connecting them, a simple method like EntitySim that predicts based on just the links in the graph can give good results.

Another observation from Figure 8 is that the NB recommender, whose performance is poor at low graph densities — 633% worse than EntitySim — slowly improves with increasing k to eventually better all the KG based methods at $k = 100$ (14% better than GraphLF). From this, we conjecture that when there are enough training examples per user, we can produce accurate predictions using a simple classifier based recommender like NB. However, at slightly lower densities, like at $k = 50$, the knowledge graph is a valuable source of information for making recommendations, as can be seen from the figure, where NB is 92% below **EntitySim** at $k = 50$.

5. CONCLUSIONS AND FUTURE WORK

Recommender systems are an important area of research. However, not many techniques have been developed in the past that leverage KGs for recommendations, especially in the case of sparse long-tailed datasets. In this paper, we proposed three methods for performing knowledge graph based recommendations using a general-purpose probabilistic logic system called ProPPR. Our methods use the link structure of the knowledge graph as well as type information about the entities to improve predictions. The more complex of the models proposed in this paper combined the strengths of latent factorization with graphs, and is type agnostic. By comparing our methods to the published results of the state-of-the-art method that uses knowledge-graphs in generating recommendations, we showed that our methods were able to achieve a large improvement in performance.

We also studied the behavior of the methods with changing dataset densities and showed that at higher densities, just the graph link structure sufficed to make accurate recommendations and the type information was redundant. In addition, we showed that in sparse datasets, the knowledge graph is a valuable source of information, but its utility diminishes when there are enough training examples per user.

In the future, we plan to use the sentiments expressed in the reviews to improve the recommendations. Extending the approach to account for the temporal dynamics would also be an interesting direction for research.

Acknowledgments

We would like to thank Kathryn Mazaitis for her help with the ProPPR code. This research was supported in part by Yahoo! through the CMU InMind project [1].

6. REFERENCES

[1] A. Azaria and J. Hong. Recommender system with personality. In *Proc. RecSys*, 2016.

[2] S. H. Bach, M. Broecheler, B. Huang, and L. Getoor. Hinge-loss markov random fields and probabilistic soft logic. arXiv:1505.04406 [cs.LG], 2015.

[3] L. Backstrom and J. Leskovec. Supervised random walks: Predicting and recommending links in social networks. In *Proc. WSDM '11*, pages 635–644, 2011.

[4] M. Brand. A random walks perspective on maximizing satisfaction and profit. In *Proc. SDM*, 2005.

[5] A. S. Das, M. Datar, A. Garg, and S. Rajaram. Google news personalization: Scalable online collaborative filtering. In *Proc. WWW '07*, pages 271–280, 2007.

[6] L. de Campos, J. Fernández-Luna, J. Huete, and M. Rueda-Morales. Combining content-based and collaborative recommendations: A hybrid approach based on bayesian networks. *Int. J. Approx. Reasoning*, 2010.

[7] C. Ding, T. Li, and M. Jordan. Convex and semi-nonnegative matrix factorizations. *IEEE TPAMI*, 2010.

[8] J. Duchi, E. Hazan, and Y. Singer. Adaptive subgradient methods for online learning and stochastic optimization. In *JMLR '11*, pages 2121–2159, 2011.

[9] I. Guy, N. Zwerdling, D. Carmel, I. Ronen, E. Uziel, S. Yogev, and S. Ofek-Koifman. Personalized recommendation of social software items based on social relations. In *Proc. RecSys*, 2009.

[10] T. H. Haveliwala. Topic-sensitive pagerank. In *Proc. WWW '02*, pages 517–526, 2002.

[11] J. Hoxha and A. Rettinger. First-order probabilistic model for hybrid recommendations. In *Proc. ICMLA '13*, pages 133–139, 2013.

[12] M. Jamali and M. Ester. Trustwalker: A random walk model for combining trust-based and item-based recommendation. In *Proc. KDD*, 2009.

[13] T. Joachims. Optimizing search engines using clickthrough data. In *Proc. SIGKDD*, 2002.

[14] I. Konstas, V. Stathopoulos, and J. M. Jose. On social networks and collaborative recommendation. In *Proc. SIGIR '09*, pages 195–202, 2009.

[15] Y. Koren. Factorization meets the neighborhood: A multifaceted collaborative filtering model. In *Proc. KDD '08*, pages 426–434, 2008.

[16] P. Kouki, S. Fakhraei, J. Foulds, M. Eirinaki, and L. Getoor. Hyper: A flexible and extensible probabilistic framework for hybrid recommender systems. In *Proc. RecSys '15*, pages 99–106, 2015.

[17] T. Lin, Mausam, and O. Etzioni. Entity linking at web scale. In *Proc. AKBC-WEKEX '12*, pages 84–88, 2012.

[18] J. W. Lloyd. *Foundations of Logic Programming.* Springer-Verlag New York, Inc., 1984.

[19] C. D. Manning, P. Raghavan, and H. Schütze. *Introduction to Information Retrieval.* Cambridge University Press, 2008.

[20] A. K. McCallum. Mallet: A machine learning for language toolkit. http://mallet.cs.umass.edu, 2002.

[21] T. Mitchell, W. Cohen, E. H. Jr., P. Talukdar, J. Betteridge, A. Carlson, B. Mishra, M. Gardner, B. Kisiel, J. Krishnamurthy, N. Lao, K. Mazaitis, T. Mohamed, N. Nakashole, E. Platanios, A. Ritter, M. Samadi, B. Settles, R. Wang, D. Wijaya, A. Gupta, X. Chen, A. Saparov, M. Greaves, and J. Welling. Never-ending learning. In *Proc. AAAI*, 2015.

[22] M. Pazzani and D. Billsus. Learning and revising user profiles: The identification ofinteresting web sites. *Mach. Learn.*, 27(3):313–331, June 1997.

[23] F. M. Suchanek, G. Kasneci, and G. Weikum. Yago: A core of semantic knowledge. In *Proc. WWW*, 2007.

[24] Y. Sun, J. Han, X. Yan, P. S. Yu, and T. Wu. Pathsim: Meta path-based top-k similarity search in heterogeneous information networks. *PVLDB*, 2011.

[25] W. Y. Wang and W. W. Cohen. Joint information extraction and reasoning: A scalable statistical relational learning approach. In *Proc. ACL 2015*, pages 355–364, 2015.

[26] W. Y. Wang, K. Mazaitis, and W. W. Cohen. Programming with personalized pagerank: A locally groundable first-order probabilistic logic. In *Proc. CIKM '13*, pages 2129–2138, 2013.

[27] X. Yu, X. Ren, Y. Sun, Q. Gu, B. Sturt, U. Khandelwal, B. Norick, and J. Han. Personalized entity recommendation: A heterogeneous information network approach. In *Proc. WSDM*, 2014.

[28] X. Yu, X. Ren, Y. Sun, B. Sturt, U. Khandelwal, Q. Gu, B. Norick, and J. Han. Recommendation in heterogeneous information networks with implicit user feedback. In *Proc. RecSys*, 2013.

Efficient Bayesian Methods for Graph-based Recommendation

Ramon Lopes[1,2]
rlopes@ufrb.edu.br

Renato Assunção[2]
assuncao@dcc.ufmg.br

Rodrygo L. T. Santos[2]
rodrygo@dcc.ufmg.br

[1]Exact Sciences and Technology Center
Universidade Federal do Recôncavo da Bahia
Cruz das Almas, BA, Brazil

[2]Department of Computer Science
Universidade Federal de Minas Gerais
Belo Horizonte, MG, Brazil

ABSTRACT

Short-length random walks on the bipartite user-item graph have recently been shown to provide accurate and diverse recommendations. Nonetheless, these approaches suffer from severe time and space requirements, which can be alleviated via random walk sampling, at the cost of reduced recommendation quality. In addition, these approaches ignore users' ratings, which further limits their expressiveness. In this paper, we introduce a computationally efficient graph-based approach for collaborative filtering based on short-path enumeration. Moreover, we propose three scoring functions based on the Bayesian paradigm that effectively exploit distributional aspects of the users' ratings. We experiment with seven publicly available datasets against state-of-the-art graph-based and matrix factorization approaches. Our empirical results demonstrate the effectiveness of the proposed approach, with significant improvements in most settings. Furthermore, analytical results demonstrate its efficiency compared to other graph-based approaches.

CCS Concepts

•**Information systems → Recommender systems;** *Top-k retrieval in databases;*

Keywords

collaborative filtering; item recommendation; Bayesian statistics

1. INTRODUCTION

The main objective of Recommender Systems (RS) is to guide users in a personalized way to interesting products to maximize user satisfaction and improve merchant revenue. These systems have become largely utilized in multiple business niches; the most relevant applications are recommendation of products in online shopping websites like Amazon, movies in video portals like YouTube and friends in social networks like Facebook. RS fundamentally take one of two approaches, namely, Collaborative Filtering (CF) or Content-based Filtering, or show a combination of them. Loosely speaking, Collaborative Filtering uses the preferences of similar users to select items, and Content-based Filtering uses features of items to find similar content.

The representation of users and the choice of a measure of similarity between them are two fundamental questions in the context of CF systems. In memory-based CF approaches, n users are represented as vectors embedded in an m-dimensional vector space where each dimension corresponds to an item, and measures of similarity are often based on operations defined over this vector space. Thus, data are represented as an $n \times m$ user-item matrix where rows correspond to users, columns to items and each entry usually represents a rating. On the one, hand such approaches provide a simple representation, but, on the other hand, it is computationally expensive to compute similarities between all pairs of users as the dataset size increases.

As an attempt to overcome the computational expense previously pointed out, the user-item matrix can be regarded as an adjacency matrix of a user-item undirected bipartite graph, giving rise to so-called graph-based approaches. As a result, measures of similarity between users are based on graph statistics such as commute or hitting time between nodes [4]. For instance, users that possess the same taste will be connected by a large number of short paths [4].

Page et al. [15] propose to treat an entity graph as a Markov chain whose long-term stationary distribution can be used as a global ranking scoring. There exists several works in the literature [1, 3, 4, 5, 9, 20] that make use of random walks in the context of RS. To this end, transition probabilities are defined so that they exploit the user-item graph structure. For instance, the transition probability between two items is proportional to the number of users that rated both items [9]. The authors in [1, 3] take a step further and show that it is possible to improve recommendation quality by obtaining the distribution within three or five steps instead of incurring the computational burden of obtaining the long-term stationary distribution as in [4, 5, 9, 20].

Due to the size of the transition matrix, the methods presented in [1, 3, 4, 5, 9, 20] suffer from memory limitation as the dataset size increases. In addition, these methods are computationally intensive as they require matrix multiplications. To overcome these issues, Christoffel et al. [1] and Cooper et al. [3] propose to approximate the final distribution by a sampling process. The proposed methods are applicable to medium or large size datasets, but recommen-

RecSys '16, September 15–19, 2016, Boston , MA, USA

DOI: http://dx.doi.org/10.1145/2959100.2959132

dation quality depends on the sample size adopted in the sampling process. Thus, we claim that there is a lack of less resource demanding methods in the context of graph-based approaches that do not degrade the quality of recommendations.

As a concrete example, given two items where one has 80 positive out of 100 ratings while the other has 20 positive out of 20 ratings, which item is likely to maximize user satisfaction in face of this information? In this scenario, we believe that the set of ratings given by users to items contains a valuable source of latent information that should be taken into account for recommendation. Thus, in this work we hypothesize that graph-based RS can benefit from the exploitation of the set of ratings for recommendation and then improving user satisfaction. To the best of our knowledge, such hypothesis has not been investigated in the context of graph-based RS. Furthermore, the current state-of-the-art graph-based approaches do not extract any further information from the set of ratings to leverage recommendation. To fulfill this gap, we propose a CF method that not only relies on the user-item bipartite graph, but it also takes advantage of ratings given by the users to make recommendations.

In this work, we propose three scoring functions based on the Bayesian paradigm that are at the core of our recommendation approach. Similar to the works presented in [1, 3], we exploit three-step paths in the user-item bipartite graph starting from the target user with the advantage that we resort neither to matrix multiplications nor sampling processes. Instead, we propose the enumeration of all such paths hence overcoming the computational burden incurred by the allocation and multiplication of transition matrices. We analytically show that the enumeration process is more efficient than the approaches proposed in [1, 3].

We carried out experiments on seven datasets freely available. The results show that our method clearly outperforms the approaches proposed in [1, 3] in all metrics used for comparison. It is common sense in the RS literature that matrix factorization approaches are the state-of-the-art methods for item recommendation in explicit feedback domains. Thus, we compare our method against matrix-factorization approaches, and results show that our method is able to improve their results in some datasets. The contributions of this paper are three-fold: a) we propose a more computationally efficient graph-based approach than those presented in [1, 3]; b) we propose three Bayesian scoring functions that take advantage of the set of ratings for recommendation; c) we present a comprehensive empirical evaluation of our method against state-of-the-art RS approaches across several datasets.

2. RELATED WORKS

Fouss et al. [4, 5] propose a CF approach that relies upon random walks over user-item bipartite graph. They consider four similarity measures, namely, average first passage time, average commute time, Euclidean commute time distance and pseudo inverse of the Laplacian matrix C^+, where $C = B - A$, A represents the adjacency matrix, B is a diagonal matrix where each entry represents vertex degrees associated to the user-item bipartite graph. Computational results show C^+ provided the best results for a movie dataset.

ItemRank [9] is a random walk based scoring algorithm for recommendation. It makes use of an item correlation graph where edge weights represent item correlations. The correlation between two items amounts to the number of users that rated both items. In turn, the transition matrix is given by the normalized correlation matrix of items. Experiments show that ItemRank performs better than the methods proposed by Fouss et al. [4, 5].

Singh et al. [20] propose an approach to CF that combines social relationships and ownership data to make recommendations. To this end, they model user-item relations as a bipartite graph and augment it with user-user social links. The algorithm is based on random walks with absorbing states that induces a distribution per user over all items. A walker begins from a target user from where it may transition to a friend or to an item. Once the walker reaches an item, he cannot be transitioned out of it. The authors evaluate the proposed method using data from an online game service to suggest items the user might buy, and from text corpus to suggest words to papers.

Cooper et al. [3] propose three scoring algorithms called P^3, P^5 and P^3_α, which are based on random walks on the graph representing associations between users and items. Let $G = (U \cup I, E)$ be an undirected bipartite graph of users and items, where U is the set of users, I is the set of items and there exists an edge between user u and item i if u rated i. Define the transition matrix $P = B^{-1}A$, where A is the adjacency matrix associated to G and B is a diagonal matrix where each entry equals the degree of the corresponding vertex. P^3 and P^5 are based on the distribution of random walks of three and five steps, respectively, starting from the target user vertex. In turn, P^3_α generalizes P^3 in the sense that its transition matrix is raised to the power of α. Experiments show that P^3_α provides better results than P^3, which in turn provides better results than P^5. Due to the memory burden of the proposed methods, the authors resort to estimating the distribution per user over all items via random walk sampling. They show that direct simulations of random walks for P^3 and P^5 are more memory efficient when compared to methods based on matrix calculations, so random walking sampling can be applied to larger datasets at the cost of recommendation quality. As a conclusion, the authors show P^3 and P^3_α provide better results than the methods proposed in [4, 5, 9].

Christoffel et al. [1] introduce an algorithm called RP^3_β which is based on P^3 to optimize accuracy and diversity. RP^3_β compensates for the influence of popular items by taking into account item popularity in the ranking given by P^3. Let P^3_{ui} be the original score of item i for target user u as the outcome of P^3. RP^3_β re-weights the score with $\tilde{P}^3_{ui} = P^3_{ui}/b^\beta_{ii}$, where b_{ii} represents the degree of vertex i and $\beta \in \mathbb{R}_+$. Experiments show that RP^3_β increases accuracy and diversity when compared to P^3. Similarly to Cooper et al. [3], due to memory limitations, the authors resort to a sampling approximation of the proposed method where distributions per user over all items are estimated by using 5 million random walks.

A naive implementation of the methods proposed in [1, 3] results in time complexity $\Theta((|I| + |U|)^3)$ and space complexity $\Theta((|I| + |U|)^2)$. Thus, the authors in [3] propose an approach that split the matrices in blocks and compute P^3 by a sequence of multiplications and additions of these blocks which results in time complexity $\Theta(|I|^2 \times |U|^2)$ and space complexity $\Theta(|I| \times |U|)$.

As we move to medium/large size datasets, the methods discussed here have computational limitations since the size of the transition matrix may become too large to fit in memory. As an alternative, Cooper et al. [3] propose approximating transition probabilities by sampling random walks of a fixed length. However, random walk sampling may require a large number of simulations to converge. Thus, there is a lack of a method that provides exact calculations and decreases memory burden without degrading recommendation quality. To fulfil this lack, we also propose a strategy to compute P^3, P^5, P^3_α and RP^3_β without resorting to matrix calculations, so bypassing the memory burden due to matrix allocation.

The methods discussed in this section do not take into account for recommendation any latent information present on the set of ratings. In fact, these graph-based approaches solely make use of the set of user-item pairs to define the structure of the user-item bipartite graph. Thus, the rating system is completely discarded in these approaches. For instance, in these methods, there is no distinction between a scenario where a user gives the maximum possible rating for an item and a scenario where a different user gives the minimum possible rating for the same item.

3. EFFICIENT BAYESIAN SCORING

The Bayesian paradigm provides a principled way of incorporating prior information to data and, then, allows the assignment of non-zero probabilities to unseen events. These probabilities represent our beliefs in those events. For instance, the Bayesian paradigm naturally allows us to answer questions like which item should we buy where one item has 2 up-votes out of 2 ratings while the other has 35 up-votes out of 40 ratings. Thus, the scoring functions we propose relies on the Bayesian paradigm to leverage recommendation.

3.1 Model

Let U be the set of users and I be the set of items. We define the set of evaluations $D = \{(u, i, r_{ui}) | u \in U, i \in I, r_{ui} \in R\}$, where R represents the set of possible rating values. Thus, $(u, i, r_{ui}) \in D$ represents the evaluation made by user u where item i received rating r_{ui}. We assume that $R = \{0, 1\}$, where, given $u \in U, i \in I$, $r_{ui} = 1$ representing a positive assessment while $r_{ui} = 0$ representing a negative assessment. Such assumption is not unrealistic, for instance YouTube adopts a thumbs up/down rating scale so that users can provide explicit feedback. Also, according to the media Netflix[1] and Uber[2] may replace their 5-star rating system.

Given $u \in U$, $I_u = \{i \in I | (u, i, r_{ui}) \in D\}$ represents the set of items evaluated by user u. Let $U_i = \{v \in U | (v, i, r_{vi}) \in D\}$ be the set of users who evaluated item i. Similarly, let $R_j = \{r_{vj} \in R | (v, j, r_{vj}) \in D\}$ be the set of ratings given to item j. Thus, we define the set $R_j^+ = \{r_{vj} \in R_j | r_{vj} = 1\}$ of positive assessments and the set $R_j^- = \{r_{vj} \in R_j | r_{vj} = 0\}$ of negative assessments received by item j.

Let $G = (U \cup I, E)$ be an undirected bipartite graph, where $E = \{(u, i) | (u, i, r_{ui}) \in D\}$, that is, there exists an edge between user u and item i if u rated i. We define $\delta(x) = \{i | (x, i) \in E\}$ as the neigborhood of a vertex x, $\Delta_U = \max_{u \in U} |\delta(u)|$ as the maximum vertex degree in U and Δ_I is defined similarly for I, $\Gamma_U = \frac{\sum_{u \in U} |\delta(u)|}{|U|}$ as the average degree of vertices in U and Γ_I is defined similarly for I. Given $u \in U$, we define $\mathcal{P}_u = \{\langle u, v, w, x \rangle | v \in I_u, w \in U, x \in I, (u, v), (v, w), (w, x) \in E\}$ as the set of all three-step paths starting from vertex $u \in U$. Let $\mathcal{P} = \cup_{u \in U} \mathcal{P}_u$ be the set of all three-step paths in the graph starting from users.

Given $j \in I$, let Y_j be a binary random variable that assumes 1 if j receives a positive assessment and 0 otherwise, where $\mathbb{P}(Y_j = 1) = \theta_j$. We place a Beta distribution as the prior of θ_j, where $\theta_j \sim \text{Beta}(\hat{a}, \hat{b})$. Intuitively, θ_j represents the unknown reliability of item j within the range $(0, 1)$. As $|R_j|$ increases, the Beta distribution shape tends to concentrate around its mean, then such notion of reliability turns out to be more precise. After observing R_j, we update our knowledge about θ_j, so that

$$\theta_j | R_j \sim \text{Beta}(a, b), \tag{1}$$

where $a = \hat{a} + |R_j^+|$ e $b = \hat{b} + |R_j^-|$.

The method we propose in this work makes a recommendation list for a target user $u \in U$ based on $\mathcal{P}_u$. To this end, we define a ranking function $f_u : I \to \mathbb{R}_+$ defined as $f_u(x) = \sum_{\langle u, v, w, x \rangle \in \mathcal{P}_u} s(\langle u, v, w, x \rangle)$, where $s : \mathcal{P} \to \mathbb{R}_+$ is a scoring function. Intuitively, $f_u(x)$ represents the sum of the weights of all three-step paths connecting u and x.

input : $G = (U \cup I, E)$, $u \in U$, scoring function s
output: f_u
1 **for** $v \in \delta(u)$ **do**
2   **for** $w \in \delta(v)$ **do**
3   **for** $x \in \delta(w)$ **do**
4             $f_u(x) := f_u(x) + s(\langle u, v, w, x \rangle)$
5   **end**
6   **end**
7 **end**

Algorithm 1: f_u computation for target user u.

Algorithm 1 illustrates the method we propose in this work. The algorithm receives as input the user-item undirected bipartite graph G, target user u and a scoring function s as previously defined. In lines 1-3, we systematically iterate over each neighbor of the corresponding vertex. Thus, we enumerate all three-step paths starting from u. In line 4 we compute the value function f_u for the final vertex x in the path $\langle u, v, w, x \rangle \in \mathcal{P}$. The algorithm outputs the ranking function f_u. In this work, we propose three scoring functions that are based on the Bayesian paradigm. These scoring functions are discussed next.

3.2 Scoring Functions

Posterior Inequality Scoring. We propose a scoring function dubbed Posterior Inequality Scoring (PIS) where

$$s(\langle u, v, w, x \rangle) = \begin{cases} \mathbb{P}(\theta_x > \theta_v | \mathcal{R}_x, \mathcal{R}_v), & \text{if } v \neq x \\ 0, & \text{otherwise} \end{cases}$$

given $\langle u, v, w, x \rangle \in \mathcal{P}_u$. We can obtain $\mathbb{P}(\theta_i > \theta_j | \mathcal{R}_i, \mathcal{R}_j)$ from (1). Intuitively, PIS represents the probability of the reliability of candidate item x being greater than the reliability of item v in the user history.

Posterior Prediction Scoring We propose a scoring

[1]http://www.businessinsider.com/netflix-wants-to-ditch-5-star-ratings-2016-1

[2]http://qz.com/574033/uber-may-replace-its-five-star-driver-rating-system-with-emoji/

function called Posterior Prediction Scoring (PPS) where

$$s(\langle u,v,w,x\rangle) = \begin{cases} \mathbb{P}(Y_v = 1|R_v) \times \mathbb{P}(Y_x = 1|R_x), & \text{if } v \neq x \\ 0, & \text{otherwise} \end{cases}$$

given $\langle u,v,w,x\rangle \in \mathcal{P}_u$. We can obtain $\mathbb{P}(Y_j = 1|R_j) = \frac{a+1}{a+b+1}$ from (1). Intuitively, PPS represents the probability of both v and x receiving positive assessments where we assume that Y_v and Y_x are independent.

Posterior Odds Ratio Scoring We propose a scoring function denominated Posterior Odds Ratio Scoring (PORS) where

$$s(\langle u,v,w,x\rangle) = \begin{cases} \frac{\psi_x}{\psi_v}, & \text{if } v \neq x \\ 0, & \text{otherwise} \end{cases}$$

given $\langle u,v,w,x\rangle \in \mathcal{P}_u$. We define $\psi_i = \frac{\mathbb{P}(Y_i=1|R_i)}{\mathbb{P}(Y_i=0|R_i)}$ for $i \in I$. Intuitively, PORS represents how large the odds of x receiving a positive assessment is when compared to the odds of v receiving a positive assessment.

The scoring functions we propose are global in the sense that they do not depend on the target user. However, the ranking function f_u is in fact customized for each user since the final result depends on the paths starting from vertex u.

Complexity Analysis. Our method incurs space complexity $\mathcal{O}(|U| \times \Delta_U)$ and time complexity $\mathcal{O}(|U| \times \Delta_I^2 \times \Delta_U)$ at worst case scenario considering the set of target users U. Thus, both space and time complexity of our method is lower than those presented in Section 2.

Implementation Details. We represent G as an adjacency list and obtain $\mathcal{P}_u$ by systematically enumerating according to G all three-step paths starting from vertex u. Thus, our implementation for P^3_α and RP^3_β makes use of such enumeration instead of relying on matrix calculations or sampling as proposed by Christoffel et al. [1] and Cooper et al. [3]. Cook [2] proposes an analytical approach to compute Beta inequalities. However, this approach is computationally expensive since it relies on recursive function calls. Thus, we resort to numerical integration methods to compute $\mathbb{P}(\theta_i > \theta_j|R_i, R_j)$. To this end, we make use of GNU Scientific Library [6] as the numerical integration library for PIS and memoization technique for storing results and, then, avoid recomputing such values. To avoid the occurrence of probabilities equal to zero in the proposed scoring functions, we make use of pseudo counts. For each item, we add one positive and one negative pseudo-assessment as if they both were given by a dummy user. The reason to add one for each end of the scale is to balance out the analysis so we do not induce bias.

4. EXPERIMENTAL SETUP

Our experiments are designed to answer the following questions: i) can we improve the accuracy of recommendations by taking into account the latent information present in the set of ratings by means of the scoring functions we propose in this work? ii) how do our proposed scoring methods compare to one another? To answer these questions we make use of several datasets and baselines in our experiments.

4.1 Datasets

The BookCrossing (BX as an abbreviation) dataset [21] contains data about book lovers that exchange books all around the world. The original dataset contains 278,858 anonymous users providing 1,149,780 ratings about 271,379 books spanning a period of time from August to September 2004. Ratings are given by users in a ten-star rating scale. In our experiments, we removed ratings related to implicit feedback.

The MovieLens datasets [10] are widely used in the Recommender Systems literature and comprise four datasets of increasing sizes. Each dataset consists of users' preferences for movies expressed in a five-star rating scale. In this work we consider the MovieLens 1M (ML 1M for short) dataset that comprises 1 million ratings from 6,000 users on 4,000 movies.

The Amazon dataset [14] contains 142.8 million product reviews spanning May 1996 - July 2014 and product metadata from Amazon. Ratings are given by users in a five-star rating scale. In this work, we select three representative product categories from that dataset, namely, Cds & Vynil (Cds as an abbreviation), Electronics and Kindle.

The FilmTrust dataset [8] contains 35,497 movie ratings crawled in June 2011 from 1,508 users on 2,071 movies. This dataset also provides ratings among users denoting how much a user trusts another in the social network. In turn, the Epinions dataset [13] contains 664,824 product ratings from 49,290 users on 139,738 products.

Since we do not focus on cold start issues, we keep users and items with at least 10 ratings. As a result, the data used for experiments differ from the original datasets and are summarized in Table 1. A common sense in the RS literature is that most users consume a small fraction of the items present in the catalogue and many items have few ratings [16]. One can see that except for MovieLens 1M dataset the maximum and average degree for items and users are significantly less than the corresponding total number in the dataset which turns out to favor our enumeration process.

4.2 Recommendation Baselines

We consider P^3_α, RP^3_β, Most Popular (MP), Bayesian Personalized Ranking Matrix Factorization (BPRMF) [17] and Weighted Regularized Matrix Factorization (WRMF) [11] as recommendation baselines in our investigations. MP sorts items according to their global popularity and so the recommendation list does not depend on the target user. In turn, WRMF and BPRMF are two representative matrix-factorization approaches for recommendation. WRMF extracts latent factors from implicit feedback and introduces regularization to prevent overfitting. BPRMF optimizes a maximum posterior estimator derived from a Bayesian analysis of the problem and learning relies on stochastic gradient descent with bootstrap sampling. In our experiments, we make use of the WRMF and BPRMF implementations provided in the Java port MyMediaLite [7] recommender system framework.[3]

4.3 Evaluation Methodology

The datasets are not compliant with the assumption $R = \{0, 1\}$. For instance, in the Amazon dataset $R = \{1, 2, 3, 4, 5\}$. Given a dataset and user u present on it, we calculate the average $\bar{r}_u$ of all ratings given by u. Assume that item i was graded $\hat{r}_{ui}$ by u. We define r_{ui} equals 1 if $\hat{r}_{ui} \geq \bar{r}_u$ or 0 otherwise. We replace $(u, i, \hat{r}_{ui})$ in D by (u, i, r_{ui}). As a result,

[3] https://github.com/jcnewell/MyMediaLiteJava

Table 1: Datasets properties.

DataSet	$\|D\|$	$\|U\|$	$\|I\|$	Δ_U	Δ_I	Γ_U	Γ_I
BookCrossing	42,137	1,842	2,065	964	225	22.87	20.40
Cds & Vynil	445,412	15,592	16,184	2,069	603	28.56	27.52
Electronics	347,393	20,247	11,589	317	1,376	17.16	29.98
Kindle	367,478	14,356	15,885	664	377	22.60	23.13
MovieLens 1M	998,539	6,040	3,260	2,233	3,428	165.32	306.30
FilmTrust	28,320	949	159	83	848	29.84	178.11
Epinions	300,304	10,706	8,945	525	1,491	28.05	33.57

we make a transformation of the original set of ratings into a dichotomized set where the user bias is taken into account.

We carried out experiments on the datasets described by using 5-fold cross validation. To this end, we randomly partitioned D into 5 subsets, where a subset T is retained for testing, and the remaining 4 subsets are used as training data. We repeated this process 5 times and report the average result across all the test folds in 5 trials.

Given $u \in U$, we define the set $T_u \subset I_u$ of items rated by u and used for testing. We partition $T_u = T_u^+ \cup T_u^-$, where $T_u^+ = \{i \in I_u | (u, i, r_{ui}) \in T, r_{ui} = 1\}$ is the set of items used for testing that u rated positively and T_u^-, in turn, is the set of items used for testing that u rated negatively. To express our lack of information about data we adopt an uninformative prior distribution by setting $\hat{a}$ and $\hat{b}$ to one so that Beta distribution reduces to Uniform distribution.

4.4 Evaluation Criteria

To answer the questions we raised, we make use of metrics largely adopted in the RS literature [18]. The metrics we report are computed by averaging over all the users in testing. Given $u \in U$, let L_u be the recommendation list ordered according to f_u. For a given $N \in \mathbb{N}$, let L_u^N be the recommendation list composed of the N highest scored items according to f_u. Given L_u, $L_u[i]$ represents the item at position i and the same applies for L_u^N. Finally, let A be the set of all $|I|$ length ordered lists composed of items in I where repetition is not allowed.

Precision. Given L_u^N, precision is defined as

$$P@N = \frac{|L_u^N \cap T_u^+|}{N} \tag{2}$$

Mean Average Precision (MAP). Given L_u, Mean Average Precision (MAP) is defined as

$$MAP = \sum_{N:=1}^{|L_u|} \frac{P@N \times \mathbf{1}_{T_u^+}(L_u[N])}{|T_u^+|} \tag{3}$$

where $\mathbf{1}_{T_u^+}$ is an indicator function.

Mean Reciprocal Rank (MRR). In the Information Retrieval literature Mean Reciprocal Rank is defined as the average of the multiplicative inverse of the rank position of the first correct answer for a set of queries. Shi et al. [19] define RR for a given recommendation list of a user by how early the first relevant recommended item is in the list and MRR as the average of the RR across all the recommendation lists for individual users. Thus, given L_u we define

$$\text{RR} = \frac{1}{\text{rank}(L_u)} \tag{4}$$

where $\text{rank} : A \to \mathbb{N}, \text{rank}(L_u) = \min\{i | 1 \le i \le |L_u|, L_u[i] \in T_u^+\}$.

Normalized Discounted Cumulative Gain (NDCG). It is a commonly used measure of the performance of web search engines in Information Retrieval. In the context of RS, NDCG measures the quality of a ranking based on the graded relevance of the recommended entities with respect to an ideal ranking of entities. It is defined as

$$\text{NDCG@}N = \frac{DCG@N}{IDCG@N} \tag{5}$$

$DCG@N$ is defined as

$$DCG@N = \text{rel}(L_u^N[1], T_u) + \sum_{i:=2}^{N} \frac{\text{rel}(L_u^N[i], T_u)}{log_2(i)}$$

where $\text{rel} : I \times \mathcal{P}(I) \setminus \emptyset \to \{0, 1, 2\}$ is a function that indicates the relevance of an item and we define it as

$$\text{rel}(i, T_u) = \begin{cases} 2, & \text{if } i \in T_u^+ \\ 1, & \text{if } i \in T_u^- \\ 0, & \text{otherwise} \end{cases}$$

In turn, $IDCG@N$ is the maximum possible $DCG@N$ where L_u^N is sorted in non-increasing order by item relevance. In this work, we consider items in T_u^+ as highly relevant, items in T_u^- as fairly relevant and those not in T_u as irrelevant items for recommending to a target user u. For further information we refer the reader to [12].

5. EXPERIMENTAL RESULTS

In this section we assess the performance of our approach and the baselines. We use the symbols △ (▽) and ▲ (▼) to denote statistically significant increase (decrease) at $p < 0.05$ and $p < 0.01$ levels, respectively, while the symbol ∘ is used to denote no significant difference according to Student's t-test. Since PPS shows the best results among the scoring functions we propose, as can be seen in Table 2, we present the results for the other methods when compared to PPS.

Table 2 provides the results for the methods and datasets considered in this work. The first columns presents the dataset name. The second column shows the method considered in the experiments. The next two columns give the results for MAP and MRR, respectively. The next two columns present results for P@N respectively for $N = 5$ and $N = 10$. Finally, the last two columns show results for NDCG@N for $N = 5$ and $N = 10$, respectively. Each result entry presents the proper symbol representing the t-test result, metric value and in parenthesis the mean percentage improvement of PPS over the considered method.

In the BX dataset, PPS provides statistically significant increase at the $p < 0.01$ level over the other methods for all metrics. When compared to P^3_α and RP^3_β, all the methods we propose provide better results, where PPS respectively shows results at least 219.8% and 296.5% superior than P^3_α and RP^3_β. When compared to the matrix factorization approaches, PPS respectively shows results at least 140.3% and 13.5% superior than BPRMF and WRMF. Finally, an interesting finding here is that MP provides results better than P^3_α, RP^3_β and even BPRMF in all metrics.

In the Cds dataset, PPS provides statistically significant increase at the $p < 0.01$ level over the other methods for all metrics. When compared to P^3_α and RP^3_β, all the methods we propose provide better results, where PPS respectively shows results at least 280.6% and 626.9% superior than P^3_α and RP^3_β. The matrix factorization approaches provide results inferior when compared to PPS, namely, the latter respectively shows results at least 143.8% and 44.8% better than BPRMF and WRMF.

In the Electronics dataset, PPS provides statistically significant increase at the $p < 0.01$ level over the other methods for all metrics. When compared to P^3_α and RP^3_β, all the methods we propose provide better results, where PPS respectively shows results at least 299.7% and 829% better than P^3_α and RP^3_β. When compared to the matrix factorization approaches, PPS respectively shows results at least 80.4% and 20% superior than BPRMF and WRMF. Finally, MP provides results better than P^3_α, RP^3_β and even BPRMF in all metrics.

In the Kindle dataset, PPS provides statistically significant increase at the $p < 0.01$ level over the other methods for all metrics. When compared to P^3_α and RP^3_β, all the methods we propose provide better results, where PPS respectively shows results at least 284.4% and 441% superior than P^3_α and RP^3_β. The matrix factorization approaches provide results inferior when compared to PPS, namely, the latter respectively shows results at least 291.3% and 209.1% better than BPRMF and WRMF.

In the ML 1M dataset, PPS provides statistically significant increase at the $p < 0.01$ level over MP, P^3_α and RP^3_β for all metrics. When compared to P^3_α and RP^3_β, all the methods we propose provide better results, where PPS respectively shows results at least 50.3% and 492.1% superior than P^3_α and RP^3_β. In turn, MP provide better results than P^3_α and RP^3_β for all metrics. When compared to BPRMF and WRMF, our methods do not show any statistically significant increase. In fact, except to MRR, PPS respectively show results at most 29.4% and 38.8% inferior than BPRMF and WRMF. Even though PPS shows results 4.3% better than BPRMF in MRR, there is no significance difference according to Student's t-test.

In the FilmTrust dataset, PPS provides statistically significant increase at the $p < 0.01$ level over P^3_α and RP^3_β for all metrics. When compared to P^3_α and RP^3_β, all the methods we propose provide better results, where PPS respectively shows results at least 23.3% and 128.8% superior than P^3_α and RP^3_β. When compared to BPRMF and WRMF, PPS provides statistically significant increase at the $p < 0.01$ level for MAP, MRR and $P@5$, but no significance difference for the other metrics. In fact, the most striking improvements are found in MRR, where PPS provides results 103% and 159.1% better than BPRMF and WRMF, respectively. In turn, PPS provides no significance difference for MAP, $P@5$ and $P@10$ when compared to MP. However, MP provides statistically significant increase at the $p < 0.05$ level in $NDCG@5$ and $NDCG@10$ over PPS. Thus, the most interesting finding here is that MP provides results at least as good as PPS except for MRR.

In the Epinions dataset, PPS provides statistically significant increase at the $p < 0.01$ level over BPRMF, MP, P^3_α and RP^3_β for all metrics. PPS respectively provides results at least 54.7%, 270.4% and 635.6% better than BPRMF, P^3_α and RP^3_β. One can see that MP provides better results than P^3_α and RP^3_β for all metrics. When compared to WRMF, PPS provides statistically significant increase at the $p < 0.01$ level for MAP, MRR, $P@5$ and $P@10$, where PPS shows results at most 38.2% superior. However, WRMF provides statistically significant increase at the $p < 0.05$ and the $p < 0.01$ in $NDCG@5$ and $NDCG@10$, respectively, over PPS.

Among the methods we propose in this work, PPS clearly outperforms PIS and PORS in all datasets and metrics, except for $P@10$ in the FilmTrust dataset where there is no statistically significant difference. PIS systematically provides results as good as PORS in all datasets and metrics except for the FilmTrust dataset where the latter outperforms the former. However, PIS is the most computationally demanding method we propose as it makes use of numerical integration.

In summary, PPS provides the best results in the BookCrossing and all Amazon datasets. In the MovieLens dataset, WRMF provides the best results. In the FilmTrust dataset, due to its simplicity, we advocate that MP is the best choice even though PPS provides a significant improvement in MRR. Finally, in the Epinions dataset, PPS provides the best results for all metrics except for $NDCG$.

6. CONCLUSION

In this paper, we studied ranking algorithms for personalized recommendation in the context of explicit feedback. We have presented three scoring methods based on the Bayesian paradigm that take advantage of the set of ratings given by the users. Also, we have proposed a strategy to cope with the memory and computational burden incurred from graph-based approaches in the literature, and analytically showed that our strategy is more efficient. The method we propose exploit three-step paths starting from the target user in the user-item graph to score items by means of the proposed scoring methods.

In our evaluation, we carried out experiments in seven datasets to assess the performance of the recommendation methods. We empirically showed that our PPS method clearly outperforms the graph-based approaches considered in all datasets and metrics. We also compared our methods against two representative matrix factorization methods and the results show that PPS clearly outperforms those methods in four datasets and is competitive with them in the other two; among the methods we propose, PPS clearly outperforms PIS and PORS. Thus, we confirm our hypothesis that graph-based approaches can take advantage of the set of ratings for improving the user satisfaction in recommender systems.

We plan to investigate the relaxation of the assumption $R = \{0, 1\}$, so that our method is able to deal with a multiple scale rating system. In this way, we can have a better idea of how effective our scoring methods are in such contexts and,

Table 2: Performance comparison of our method and baselines on datasets used for evaluation.

		MAP	MRR	P@5	P@10	NDCG@5	NDCG@10
BX	BPRMF	▼ 0.024 (190.1)	▼ 0.042 (140.3)	▼ 0.013 (228.1)	▼ 0.011 (167.2)	▼ 0.013 (237.8)	▼ 0.013 (190.7)
	MP	▼ 0.026 (165.9)	▼ 0.052 (94.5)	▼ 0.014 (185.5)	▼ 0.012 (148.0)	▼ 0.015 (186.9)	▼ 0.014 (162.9)
	P^3_α	▼ 0.021 (226.1)	▼ 0.032 (219.8)	▼ 0.011 (290.1)	▼ 0.008 (261.3)	▼ 0.012 (262.1)	▼ 0.011 (250.1)
	PIS	▼ 0.055 (26.0)	▼ 0.080 (25.4)	▼ 0.033 (24.6)	▼ 0.025 (19.3)	▼ 0.035 (25.8)	▼ 0.030 (22.6)
	PORS	▼ 0.039 (80.1)	▼ 0.055 (81.3)	▼ 0.021 (96.9)	▼ 0.017 (80.3)	▼ 0.022 (104.2)	▼ 0.019 (93.3)
	PPS	0.070	0.100	0.041	0.030	0.044	0.037
	RP^3_β	▼ 0.016 (327.5)	▼ 0.023 (336.9)	▼ 0.009 (363.4)	▼ 0.008 (296.5)	▼ 0.010 (363.9)	▼ 0.009 (322.1)
	WRMF	▼ 0.056 (25.0)	▼ 0.078 (28.4)	▼ 0.034 (20.9)	▼ 0.027 (13.5)	▼ 0.037 (20.0)	▼ 0.032 (14.5)
Cds	BPRMF	▼ 0.018 (202.2)	▼ 0.040 (153.5)	▼ 0.014 (177.0)	▼ 0.012 (143.8)	▼ 0.015 (168.3)	▼ 0.014 (145.4)
	MP	▼ 0.007 (662.4)	▼ 0.017 (482.6)	▼ 0.005 (633.6)	▼ 0.005 (507.2)	▼ 0.005 (641.2)	▼ 0.005 (551.5)
	P^3_α	▼ 0.014 (280.6)	▼ 0.026 (282.6)	▼ 0.009 (361.3)	▼ 0.007 (333.1)	▼ 0.009 (345.3)	▼ 0.008 (328.4)
	PIS	▼ 0.046 (17.4)	▼ 0.086 (16.5)	▼ 0.034 (14.7)	▼ 0.026 (13.9)	▼ 0.035 (15.5)	▼ 0.030 (15.3)
	PORS	▼ 0.028 (89.9)	▼ 0.057 (77.4)	▼ 0.021 (91.2)	▼ 0.017 (77.1)	▼ 0.020 (102.6)	▼ 0.018 (93.7)
	PPS	0.054	0.100	0.039	0.030	0.040	0.034
	RP^3_β	▼ 0.007 (626.9)	▼ 0.013 (670.7)	▼ 0.004 (921.9)	▼ 0.004 (724.2)	▼ 0.004 (934.1)	▼ 0.004 (783.3)
	WRMF	▼ 0.031 (72.4)	▼ 0.060 (67.1)	▼ 0.025 (56.7)	▼ 0.020 (48.0)	▼ 0.027 (50.7)	▼ 0.024 (44.8)
Electronics	BPRMF	▼ 0.014 (92.6)	▼ 0.031 (80.4)	▼ 0.009 (98.1)	▼ 0.007 (95.1)	▼ 0.009 (94.1)	▼ 0.008 (92.5)
	MP	▼ 0.017 (58.9)	▼ 0.037 (54.3)	▼ 0.010 (72.3)	▼ 0.008 (65.7)	▼ 0.010 (69.8)	▼ 0.009 (67.3)
	P^3_α	▼ 0.007 (299.7)	▼ 0.011 (406.0)	▼ 0.003 (480.4)	▼ 0.002 (488.5)	▼ 0.003 (420.7)	▼ 0.003 (435.5)
	PIS	▼ 0.025 (9.8)	▼ 0.052 (10.1)	▼ 0.016 (9.6)	▼ 0.012 (9.5)	▼ 0.015 (10.2)	▼ 0.013 (10.5)
	PORS	▼ 0.022 (24.1)	▼ 0.045 (27.1)	▼ 0.013 (28.1)	▼ 0.011 (23.3)	▼ 0.013 (32.6)	▼ 0.011 (29.3)
	PPS	0.027	0.057	0.017	0.014	0.017	0.015
	RP^3_β	▼ 0.003 (829)	▼ 0.004 (1199)	▼ 0.001 (2349)	▼ 0.001 (1726)	▼ 0.001 (2348)	▼ 0.001 (1896)
	WRMF	▼ 0.022 (23.5)	▼ 0.042 (33.8)	▼ 0.014 (26.2)	▼ 0.011 (23.0)	▼ 0.014 (21.6)	▼ 0.012 (20.0)
Kindle	BPRMF	▼ 0.019 (505.4)	▼ 0.039 (291.3)	▼ 0.013 (519.4)	▼ 0.011 (426.0)	▼ 0.013 (551.2)	▼ 0.012 (479.1)
	MP	▼ 0.006 (1679.1)	▼ 0.016 (870.9)	▼ 0.004 (1984.8)	▼ 0.003 (1694.2)	▼ 0.004 (2001.2)	▼ 0.004 (1787.8)
	P^3_α	▼ 0.027 (312.1)	▼ 0.039 (284.4)	▼ 0.017 (373.5)	▼ 0.013 (360.1)	▼ 0.018 (366.1)	▼ 0.015 (359.2)
	PIS	▼ 0.089 (27.3)	▼ 0.115 (31.2)	▼ 0.065 (25.9)	▼ 0.047 (24.4)	▼ 0.065 (27.5)	▼ 0.054 (26.4)
	PORS	▼ 0.065 (73.2)	▼ 0.087 (72.9)	▼ 0.046 (77.8)	▼ 0.036 (65.2)	▼ 0.044 (88.1)	▼ 0.038 (78.8)
	PPS	0.113	0.151	0.081	0.059	0.083	0.069
	RP^3_β	▼ 0.020 (471.3)	▼ 0.028 (441.0)	▼ 0.012 (568.1)	▼ 0.011 (459.9)	▼ 0.012 (605.4)	▼ 0.011 (523.5)
	WRMF	▼ 0.026 (342.2)	▼ 0.049 (209.1)	▼ 0.018 (350.8)	▼ 0.015 (293.8)	▼ 0.019 (339.0)	▼ 0.017 (303.6)
ML 1M	BPRMF	▲ 0.165 (-29.4)	○ 0.250 (4.3)	▲ 0.250 (-24.1)	▲ 0.213 (-25.2)	▲ 0.253 (-25.9)	▲ 0.236 (-27.2)
	MP	▼ 0.097 (19.2)	▼ 0.207 (25.8)	▼ 0.164 (15.4)	▼ 0.141 (12.9)	▼ 0.164 (14.1)	▼ 0.153 (12.5)
	P^3_α	▼ 0.071 (62.6)	▼ 0.173 (50.3)	▼ 0.114 (66.9)	▼ 0.091 (74.8)	▼ 0.121 (54.8)	▼ 0.108 (59.1)
	PIS	▼ 0.111 (4.5)	▽ 0.243 (7.0)	▼ 0.184 (3.2)	▼ 0.155 (2.5)	▼ 0.181 (3.3)	▼ 0.166 (3.3)
	PORS	▼ 0.096 (20.9)	▼ 0.205 (27.3)	▼ 0.152 (24.8)	▼ 0.136 (17.0)	▼ 0.143 (31.1)	▼ 0.138 (24.6)
	PPS	0.116	0.260	0.189	0.159	0.187	0.172
	RP^3_β	▼ 0.020 (492.1)	▼ 0.018 (1331.2)	▼ 0.003 (6916.0)	▼ 0.004 (4358.3)	▼ 0.004 (4774.6)	▼ 0.005 (3383.9)
	WRMF	▲ 0.190 (-38.8)	○ 0.261 (-0.3)	▲ 0.288 (-34.3)	▲ 0.241 (-34.0)	▲ 0.290 (-35.5)	▲ 0.268 (-35.9)
FilmTrust	BPRMF	▼ 0.439 (3.0)	▼ 0.161 (103.0)	▼ 0.307 (5.6)	○ 0.263 (1.8)	○ 0.362 (0.5)	○ 0.342 (0.6)
	MP	○ 0.449 (0.9)	▼ 0.266 (22.9)	○ 0.320 (1.2)	○ 0.269 (-0.6)	△ 0.370 (-1.8)	△ 0.349 (-1.5)
	P^3_α	▼ 0.349 (30.2)	▼ 0.230 (42.9)	▼ 0.249 (30.8)	▼ 0.182 (48.2)	▼ 0.296 (23.3)	▼ 0.251 (37.3)
	PIS	▼ 0.428 (5.8)	▼ 0.290 (12.5)	▼ 0.309 (4.9)	▽ 0.257 (4.2)	▼ 0.346 (5.2)	▼ 0.326 (5.3)
	PORS	▼ 0.434 (4.2)	▼ 0.290 (12.8)	▽ 0.314 (3.2)	○ 0.263 (1.6)	▼ 0.349 (4.1)	▼ 0.334 (3.0)
	PPS	0.453	0.327	0.324	0.268	0.364	0.344
	RP^3_β	▼ 0.189 (143.2)	▼ 0.113 (198.4)	▼ 0.059 (615.4)	▼ 0.119 (128.8)	▼ 0.066 (639.4)	▼ 0.120 (194.3)
	WRMF	▼ 0.435 (4.0)	▼ 0.126 (159.1)	▼ 0.303 (7.1)	○ 0.263 (1.6)	○ 0.363 (0.1)	○ 0.342 (0.4)
Epinions	BPRMF	▼ 0.018 (100.9)	▼ 0.042 (92.4)	▼ 0.014 (94.3)	▼ 0.013 (71.4)	▼ 0.017 (64.8)	▼ 0.016 (54.7)
	MP	▼ 0.015 (141.7)	▼ 0.034 (136.4)	▼ 0.011 (139.7)	▼ 0.010 (120.4)	▼ 0.015 (88.4)	▼ 0.013 (83.0)
	P^3_α	▼ 0.010 (270.4)	▼ 0.020 (306.0)	▼ 0.006 (350.4)	▼ 0.005 (341.0)	▼ 0.007 (296.8)	▼ 0.006 (295.8)
	PIS	▼ 0.033 (8.7)	▼ 0.074 (10.2)	▽ 0.026 (6.9)	▼ 0.020 (5.3)	▼ 0.026 (8.7)	▼ 0.023 (7.6)
	PORS	▼ 0.022 (65.7)	▼ 0.050 (63.2)	▼ 0.016 (76.3)	▼ 0.014 (53.7)	▼ 0.014 (100.9)	▼ 0.014 (79.9)
	PPS	0.036	0.081	0.027	0.022	0.028	0.025
	RP^3_β	▼ 0.005 (635.6)	▼ 0.008 (902.4)	▼ 0.002 (1073.0)	▼ 0.002 (901.4)	▼ 0.003 (985.4)	▼ 0.002 (892.8)
	WRMF	▼ 0.031 (15.6)	▼ 0.059 (38.2)	▼ 0.025 (11.4)	▼ 0.020 (6.6)	△ 0.030 (-4.8)	▲ 0.027 (-7.3)

eventually, propose further improvements. Also, we plan to carry out experiments to explain why our approach fails in improving results in MovieLens dataset when compared to the matrix factorization methods. Furthermore, we intend to assess how the path length affects the performance of our method. Finally, we are currently investigating the customization of the scoring methods so that probabilities are conditioned on the target user.

Acknowledgments

This work was partially funded by projects InWeb (MCT/CNPq 573871/2008-6) and MASWeb (FAPEMIG/PRONEX APQ-01400-14), and by the authors' individual grants from CNPq and FAPEMIG.

References

[1] F. Christoffel, B. Paudel, C. Newell, and A. Bernstein. Blockbusters and wallflowers: Accurate, diverse, and scalable recommendations with random walks. In *Proceedings of the 9th ACM Conference on Recommender Systems*, pages 163–170, New York, NY, USA, 2015. ACM.

[2] J. Cook. Exact calculation of beta inequalities. Technical report, Department of Biostatistics, November 2005.

[3] C. Cooper, S. H. Lee, T. Radzik, and Y. Siantos. Random walks in recommender systems: Exact computation and simulations. In *Proceedings of the 23rd International Conference on World Wide Web*, pages 811–816, New York, NY, USA, 2014. ACM.

[4] F. Fouss, A. Pirotte, and M. Saerens. A novel way of computing similarities between nodes of a graph, with application to collaborative recommendation. In *Proceedings of the 2005 IEEE/WIC/ACM International Conference on Web Intelligence*, pages 550–556, Washington, DC, USA, 2005. IEEE Computer Society.

[5] F. Fouss, A. Pirotte, J.-m. Renders, and M. Saerens. Random-walk computation of similarities between nodes of a graph with application to collaborative recommendation. *IEEE Transactions on Knowledge and Data Engineering*, 19(3):355–369, 2007.

[6] M. Galassi et al. *GNU Scientific Library Reference Manual*. Network Theory Ltd., 3rd edition, 2009.

[7] Z. Gantner, S. Rendle, C. Freudenthaler, and L. Schmidt-Thieme. Mymedialite: A free recommender system library. In *Proceedings of the Fifth ACM Conference on Recommender Systems*, RecSys '11, pages 305–308, New York, NY, USA, 2011. ACM.

[8] J. Golbeck and J. Hendler. Filmtrust: movie recommendations using trust in web-based social networks. In *Proceedings of Consumer the 3rd IEEE Communications and Networking Conference*, pages 282–286. IEEE, 2006.

[9] M. Gori and A. Pucci. Itemrank: A random-walk based scoring algorithm for recommender engines. In *Proceedings of the 20th International Joint Conference on Artificial Intelligence*, pages 2766–2771, San Francisco, CA, USA, 2007. Morgan Kaufmann Publishers Inc.

[10] F. M. Harper and J. A. Konstan. The movielens datasets: History and context. *ACM Transactions on Interactive Intelligent Systems*, 5(4):19:1–19:19, Dec. 2015.

[11] Y. Hu, Y. Koren, and C. Volinsky. Collaborative filtering for implicit feedback datasets. In *Proceedings of the 2008 Eighth IEEE International Conference on Data Mining*, ICDM '08, pages 263–272, Washington, DC, USA, 2008. IEEE Computer Society.

[12] K. Järvelin and J. Kekäläinen. Cumulated gain-based evaluation of ir techniques. *ACM Transactions on Information Systems*, 20(4):422–446, Oct. 2002.

[13] P. Massa and P. Avesani. Trust-aware recommender systems. In *Proceedings of the 2007 ACM Conference on Recommender Systems*, RecSys '07, pages 17–24, New York, NY, USA, 2007. ACM.

[14] J. McAuley, R. Pandey, and J. Leskovec. Inferring networks of substitutable and complementary products. In *Proceedings of the 21th ACM SIGKDD International Conference on Knowledge Discovery and Data Mining*, pages 785–794. ACM, 2015.

[15] L. Page, S. Brin, R. Motwani, and T. Winograd. The pagerank citation ranking: Bringing order to the web. Technical Report 1999-66, Stanford InfoLab, November 1999.

[16] Y. Park and A. Tuzhilin. The long tail of recommender systems and how to leverage it. In *Proceedings of the 2008 ACM Conference on Recommender Systems*, pages 11–18, New York, NY, USA, 2008. ACM.

[17] S. Rendle, C. Freudenthaler, Z. Gantner, and L. Schmidt-Thieme. Bpr: Bayesian personalized ranking from implicit feedback. In *Proceedings of the Twenty-Fifth Conference on Uncertainty in Artificial Intelligence*, UAI '09, pages 452–461, Arlington, Virginia, United States, 2009. AUAI Press.

[18] G. Shani and A. Gunawardana. *Recommender Systems Handbook*, chapter Evaluating Recommendation Systems, pages 257–297. Springer US, Boston, MA, 2011.

[19] Y. Shi, A. Karatzoglou, L. Baltrunas, M. Larson, N. Oliver, and A. Hanjalic. Climf: Learning to maximize reciprocal rank with collaborative less-is-more filtering. In *Proceedings of the Sixth ACM Conference on Recommender Systems*, RecSys '12, pages 139–146, New York, NY, USA, 2012. ACM.

[20] A. P. Singh, A. Gunawardana, C. Meek, and A. C. Surendran. Recommendations using absorbing random walks. In *North East Student Colloquium on Artificial Intelligence*, 2007.

[21] C. Ziegler, S. M. McNee, J. A. Konstan, and G. Lausen. Improving recommendation lists through topic diversification. In *Proceedings of the 14th International Conference on World Wide Web*, pages 22–32, New York, NY, USA, 2005. ACM.

Using Navigation to Improve Recommendations in Real-Time

Chao-Yuan Wu
Computer Science, UT Austin
cywu@cs.utexas.edu

Alexander J. Smola
CMU, Pittsburgh, PA
alex@smola.org

Christopher V. Alvino
Netflix, Los Gatos, CA
calvino@netflix.com

Justin Basilico
Netflix, Los Gatos, CA
jbasilico@netflix.com

ABSTRACT

Implicit feedback is a key source of information for many recommendation and personalization approaches. However, using it typically requires multiple episodes of interaction and roundtrips to a recommendation engine. This adds latency and neglects the opportunity of immediate personalization for a user *while* the user is navigating recommendations.

We propose a novel strategy to address the above problem in a principled manner. The key insight is that as we observe a user's interactions, it reveals much more information about her desires. We exploit this by inferring the within-session user intent *on-the-fly* based on navigation interactions, since they offer valuable clues into a user's current state of mind. Using navigation patterns and adapting recommendations in real-time creates an opportunity to provide more accurate recommendations. By prefetching a larger amount of content, this can be carried out entirely in the client (such as a browser) without added latency. We define a new Bayesian model with an efficient inference algorithm. We demonstrate significant improvements with this novel approach on a real-world, large-scale dataset from Netflix on the problem of adapting the recommendations on a user's homepage.

1. INTRODUCTION

Recommender systems are particularly important for services with large numbers of items. They rely on the promise that through effective algorithmic use of collected data, they can help the user discover novel content by presenting personalized, relevant items to the user [18]. Recommendation is fundamental to many places, such as news readers [5, 8], blogs [10], homepages [4], search engines [12], and streaming video [11]. Click models are often used to model the viewing behaviors and estimate intrinsic relevance [12, 5].

A key challenge in such approaches is that a user's intention can vary significantly between sessions in ways that cannot be captured by prior knowledge. For instance, movie consumption preferences are context-dependent: whether a viewer watches alone, with friends, with a romantic love interest, or with children. Likewise, they are situation dependent (dedicated viewing vs. background entertainment during a chore), depend on the available time (short episode vs. full movie) and can even depend on mood.

Context-aware recommendation approaches try to address this problem by leveraging supplemental information such as time of day or (geo)location to provide insight about the potential per-session user intent [20, 3]. However, contextual recommendations do not fully address the problem since they only offer a *prior* over the likely attributes using observable context prior to the start of a session. Likewise, the use of multiple viewer profiles such as those offered by Netflix, only captures a small facet of this information.

In short, it is difficult to predict a user's intention when recommendations are typically generated — *before* their session has begun. We argue that the problem of understanding intent is inherent to recommendation, that it is compounded in cold-start situations, and that observable context can only partially mitigate it. We propose a way to overcome this problem by using navigation behavior as instant implicit relevance feedback.

Relevance Feedback in Search

A wide variety of user interaction signals have been considered to understand user intent. For example, [14] studies interactions on touch-enabled devices, [19] studies modeling of mouse cursor movements, and [26] uses text selection events in search. In particular, recent work has studied eye gaze positions and mouse cursor movements, and shows that they are able to indicate user preference or attention [15, 16, 13, 23]. However, all work uses such data to infer *a posteriori* what the user's intent and interests might have been, rather than using it immediately.

In contrast to search systems, understanding the current user intent and using it effectively is even more pertinent in *lean back* recommendation experiences (e.g. Android TV, Playstation, Apple TV, Roku) where the primary mode of interaction is to navigate and select items. In contrast, in search, the user can rewrite queries if the results did not match their current intent, e.g. by specializing "apple" to "apple tree". The analysis of query chains [7] has been used extensively to improve relevance. Augmenting a page of recommendations *on the fly* in the way described in this paper gives the recommender system designer a chance to infer the

RecSys '16 September 15-19, 2016, Boston , MA, USA

ACM ISBN 978-1-4503-4035-9/16/09.
DOI: http://dx.doi.org/10.1145/2959100.2959174

current user intent, and thereby guide them towards items that better match their current desires.

Recently, the search engine Surf Canyon offered an extension that is able to alter the result page dynamically based on user's interaction with the page. Based on clicks in previous search queries, the system is able to alter results for *future* queries in the same session. [17] shows that with the dynamic adaptation users consume more results and spend a longer time searching. This strategy is natural for search engines since people can search multiple times for the same goal, and previous queries thus give valuable information.

We push this strategy to its logical conclusion — rather than waiting for a click to expand and clarify results, we can do this *while* the user is still exploring a page, i.e. we propose to dynamically *modify* the result page, based on a user's behavior on that page.

Context in Recommender Systems

Using context is a popular strategy for recommendation. Factorization-based linear models, for example, are among the most effective and popular recommendation approaches [21, 24]. A rich line of work has been proposed in jointly modeling multiple sources of information to alleviate these problems, such as ratings and item meta-data [1], text features [2], and reviews [9].

On the other hand, joint models of content consumption and navigation signals are still lacking in recommender systems. One challenge is that navigation signals are usually very noisy [23]. The data is also usually not publicly available. By working with a proprietary dataset from Netflix containing a large amount of logged navigation events, we are able to show that updating a page of recommendations based on within-session navigation behavior has the capability to help users find items of interest more effectively. Such updates can be done with negligible latency by computing within a browser *without* a roundtrip to a backend server.

Specifically, we propose to supply additional relevant recommendations by reordering rows of items, since each row typically contains a thematically coherent set of recommended content. Many online services use rows of recommendations to organize content and facilitate user navigation [6], though the technique can be adapted to other displays.

Probabilistic user model. Our model jointly captures navigation and consumption through a latent interest variable for the purpose of generating online recommendations based on the current user intent. To the best of our knowledge, this is the first principled attempt to capture both effects jointly.

Hybrid Inference. The algorithm uses both offline inference to learn static user preferences as well as online inference through Expectation Maximization in order to incorporate user navigational information as it becomes available.

Cold-start Experiments. We provide empirical validation that this approach can be effective for updating user recommendations on-the-fly by augmenting the recommendations on the Netflix homepage with better rows of thematically coherent videos. We also present experiments showing how the method is effective in dealing with user cold-start.

We support the model design through insights we obtained from the datasets in question. They make a clear case for advanced session modeling to improve user satisfaction and engagement. Our contributions are both *conceptual* in the form of instant navigation-based relevance feedback and also *statistical* in the form of a novel user interest model. Both are justified experimentally and can be used individually.

Figure 1: The user interface deployed on the Sony PS3 in the Netflix app in 2015. Note the distinct rows of movies in the UI. Each row is thematically or contextually coherent.

2. USER INTERFACE

Netflix is an online video streaming service that provides (e.g. on its homepage) a personalized collection of videos. In this paper, we consider the problem of optimizing the positions of these videos. The specific user interface (UI) considered is illustrated in Figure 1. A page is composed of a list of rows, each of which is composed of a list of videos. Videos in a row are topically or contextually coherent to ease user navigation (e.g. "TV Comedies" or "Popular on Netflix"). The UI has one row in focus at a time. A user can either scroll vertically to see other rows, scroll horizontally to see more videos in a row, or select a video to play. Depending on the device, typically one or more rows are displayed above or below the current selection.

We assume that we have a base recommender system that selects about 40 rows from all possible rows types, and each of which selects 75 personalized candidate videos from our full catalog. Our goal is to optimize the ranking of the rows and also the ranking of videos within each of them. While users navigate within a page, we want to model the navigation signals and perform real-time adaptation online to further improve the ranking of the rows.

While we conduct experiments on a dataset of homepages generated for a specific device UI, our model is completely general and can be directly applied to homepages on many devices, including websites, tablets, smartphones, and smart TVs. This model can also be applied to other applications that have similar structure to the row layout, such as Google Shopping, Google Express, YouTube, and Amazon.com. Also note that it is *not* our goal to design a novel UI layout but rather to demonstrate that implicit feedback from navigation can be incorporated in a principled fashion within a given, real-world UI.

3. MODEL

We now design a statistical model that addresses many aspects of user interaction with an online content recommendation service: First and foremost we need to predict play probabilities (Section 3.1). This is followed by a per-session user intent model (Section 3.2) and finally the full graphical model (Section 3.3). The ranking procedure is described in Section 3.4. We also discuss some domain-specific user behavior we found (e.g. fatigue) and how to incorporate them for improved accuracy (Section 3.5).

Note that *the choice of the model is largely independent of the function class.* That is, we could use inner product recommenders, factorization machines, deep networks, decision trees or anything else. Instead, *the model is tightly coupled with the UI design*, since we aim to encode the way a user interacts with an application in quantifiable terms. Moreover, the insight of instant implicit feedback can be used in any model where the entire interface does not fit on a single display (e.g. maps, search results, messages) and the model can incorporate navigation data. We use the following symbols below:

Symbol	Definition
t_i	i-th video of a row
r_i	i-th row in a page
ρ_r	Row type of row r
ψ_*	Parameters for play probability model
v_*	Factorization-based parameters for interest model
w_*	Feature-based parameters for interest model
f_t	$\in \mathbb{R}_+^d$, vector of d features of video t
$f_r^{(row)}$	$\in \mathbb{R}_+^d$, vector of d features of row r
$\mathcal{S}$	$\in \{0,1\}$, scroll indicator
$\mathcal{C}$	$\in \{0,1\}$, play indicator
$\mathcal{I}$	$\in \{0,1\}$, interest indicator

3.1 Play Prediction

An accurate estimate of the play probability of each video is essential to optimizing pages full of video recommendations. We begin by considering the problem of estimating play probabilities of videos in one row at a time. Subsequently we generalize this model to incorporate user intent model on multiple rows. Some of our design choices are inspired by the "Fair and Balanced" model of [ ]. That is, we use the notion of submodularity to estimate the relevance of any term, given the previously presented results. Note that a function f defined on a set X is submodular if it satisfies

$$f(X \cup \{A\}) - F(X) \leq f(X' \cup \{A\}) - F(X') \text{ for } X' \subseteq X.$$

In other words, the benefit from adding A to X is less than or equal to when we add it to a subset X'. Whenever equality holds throughout, we call f modular (i.e. linear in the parameters). In the context of movies this means that the added benefit from recommending a movie is not determined in isolation but in terms of how novel it is relative to the previous recommendations. This models typical user browsing behaviors to achieve diversity and personalization at the same time. To convert scores into probabilities we employ a logistic transform $\sigma(x) = \frac{1}{1+e^{-x}}$:

$$\mathbb{P}(\mathcal{C}_i = 1) = \sigma(g(t_{0:i}, \Psi)) \tag{1}$$

$$g(t_{0:i}, \Psi) = \langle \psi, f_{t_i} \rangle + \left\langle \tilde{\psi}, q(t_{0:i}) - q(t_{0:i-1}) \right\rangle \tag{2}$$

Here the coordinates of q are given by

$$[q(t_{0:i})]_j := h\left(\sum_{k=0}^{i} [f_{t_k}]_j\right)$$

where h is a suitably chosen concave function. The vectors ψ and $\tilde{\psi}$ denote modular and submodular parameters respectively. Each q_j is a submodular function of a set of videos that captures the diminishing returns effect of feature j. Intuitively, we assume users become "tired" of a certain feature if they see it in many videos. Taking this into consideration, maximizing play probability leads to a page that has diversity. Each $\tilde{\psi}_j$ models the strength of the diminishing return in each feature j.

Unlike [ ], we have full access to a user's viewing behavior: Since the viewport of our user interface consists of only 5 titles, users can easily glance at all of them. Hence we do not need to model views as latent variables, which can be computationally costly.

For the purpose of personalization and to share statistical strength, we adopt a hierarchical decomposition of parameters: $\psi = \psi_0 + \psi_u + \psi_{\rho,0} + \psi_{\rho,u}$, where the the terms denote shared, user-specific, row-specific, and {row, user}-specific latent factors respectively. We use a similar decomposition for the submodular parameters $\tilde{\psi}$.

3.2 User Intent

While users generally have relatively stable tastes, they often have different intents in different sessions. This unobserved aspect is hard to estimate from general behavior but is much easier once the user interacts with a service. Failing to consider variations in user intent can lead to inaccurate recommendations, even when they match a user's overall taste profile. Here we describe our model that jointly models plays, navigation signals and user intents. A key distinction in this work is the ability to infer and respond to a specific user's preferences without any meaningful penalty in terms of latency and computational cost.

We assume that in each session a user is only interested in some subset of rows. We use $\mathcal{I}_{s,r} \in \{0,1\}$ to indicate a user's interest in row r of session s. As before we use a logistic transform to define a probability:

$$\mathbb{P}(\mathcal{I}_{s,r} = 1 | w, v, v_\rho) = \sigma(g'(r)) \tag{3}$$

$$\text{where } g'(r) = \langle w, f_r \rangle + \langle v, v_\rho \rangle . \tag{4}$$

Here $\langle w, f_r \rangle$ is linear with features f_r and parameters $w_r \in \mathbb{R}^n$, and $\langle v, v_\rho \rangle$ is factorization-based with row-type ρ based latent factors v_ρ and v. This captures latent co-consumption patterns that are not captured by features. Again, we decompose $w = w_0 + w_u + w_s$, where w_0 is shared, w_u is user-specific, and w_s is session-specific parameters, and similarly for $v = v_0 + v_u + v_s$.

We focus on horizontal scrolls as navigation signals. Figure 2 shows the play probability of a row, given different numbers of horizontal scrolls on that row. The fact that the play probability is *increasing* as a function of scrolls within a row suggests that scrolls are a rich source of information about user intent. The fact that the biggest increase occurs between zero and one scroll means that a binary scrolling indicator might suffice to capture most of the information about whether a user is interested in a row. We thus introduce $\mathcal{S}_{s,r} \in \{0,1\}$, which indicates whether a row r was scrolled. As before, we use a logistic transform to connect probabilities to scores:

$$\mathbb{P}(\mathcal{S}_{s,r} = 1 | \mathcal{I}_{s,r} = 1, \delta_{\rho_r}) = \sigma(\delta_{\rho_r}) \tag{5}$$

Note that $\mathbb{P}(\mathcal{S}_{s,r} = 1 | \mathcal{I}_{s,r} = 0, \delta_{\rho_r}) = 0$ by definition since users won't click on something they are not interested in ($\mathcal{I}_{s,r} = 0$). We use ρ_r to denote the row type of r and δ_{ρ_r} governs the likelihood of scrolling on each row type.

Similarly, the play probability of the i-th video of r follows

$$\mathbb{P}(\mathcal{C}_{s,r,i} = 1 | \mathcal{I}_{s,r} = 1, \Psi) = \sigma(g(t_{0:i}, \Psi)) \tag{6}$$

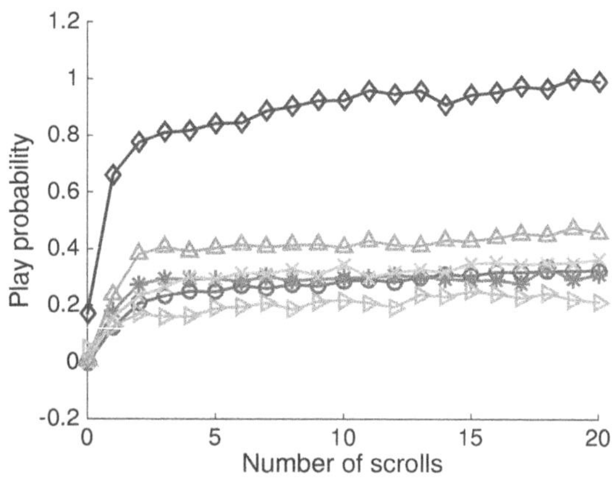

Figure 2: Play probability within a row as a function of videos scrolled to on that row. Each line represents a different row type. Remarkably the conditional play probability *increases* as the user delves into the list. To protect proprietary data we rescaled the numbers [0, 1] so that only the relative magnitudes can be compared.

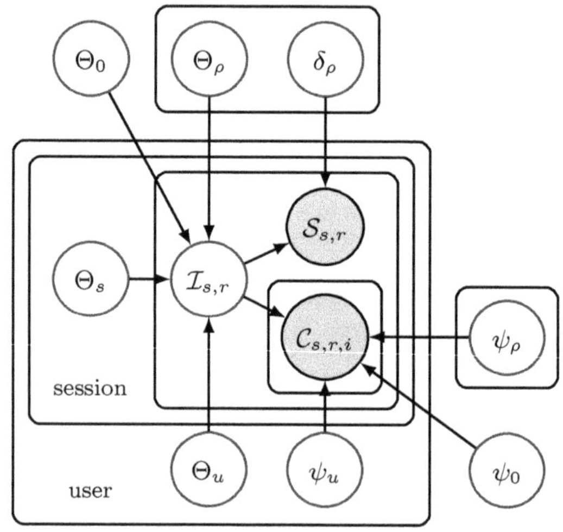

Figure 3: User interaction model. Shaded circles correspond to observed variables, namely play indicators and scroll indicators. For clarity of illustration we omitted the associated hyperparameters from the diagram. Θ models interest and ψ models the play probabilities.

and likewise $\mathbb{P}(\mathcal{C}_{s,r,i} = 1 | \mathcal{I}_{s,r} = 0, \Psi) = 0$. Here $g(t_{0:i}, \Psi)$ is as defined in Equation (2). Again, we assume users only play videos from the rows that they are interested in.

3.3 Graphical Model

Our design choices are best illustrated in the graphical model of Figure 3. Throughout we assume that all the parameters are drawn i.i.d. from normal distributions, since they are merely auxiliary latent variables used to capture the randomness in the observed user behavior. The generative process is as follows:

1. Sample $v_0 \sim \mathcal{N}(0, \lambda_v I)$ and $w_0 \sim \mathcal{N}(0, \lambda_w I)$.
2. For each row type ρ,
   (a) Sample $\delta_\rho \sim \mathcal{N}(0, \lambda_\delta)$.
   (b) Sample $v_\rho \sim \mathcal{N}(0, \lambda_v I)$.
3. For each user u,
   (a) Sample $v_u \sim \mathcal{N}(0, \lambda_v I), w_u \sim \mathcal{N}(0, \lambda_w I)$.
   (b) For each session s of u,
      i. Sample $v_s \sim \mathcal{N}(0, \lambda_v I), w_s \sim \mathcal{N}(0, \lambda_w I)$.
      ii. For each row r with row type ρ:
         A. Sample $\mathcal{I}_{s,r}$ via (3).
         B. Sample $\mathcal{S}_{s,r} | \mathcal{I}_{s,r}$ via (5).
         C. For i-th video in r sample $\mathcal{C}_{s,r,i}$ via (6).

Figure 3 provides the plate notation of this model. For conciseness we set $\Theta_{(*)} := \{v_{(*)}, w_{(*)}\}$. The plates inside a session are understood to be rows, and the plates inside the rows correspond to videos. In other words, we have a principled mapping of the user interface hierarchy directly into a graphical model.

3.4 Online Page Adaptation

Our goal is to optimize both positions of rows on a page and videos within a row such that the user finds interesting content with minimal effort. It follows from (1) that the play probability is maximized when $g(t_{0:i}, \Psi)$ is maximized. Thus, our goal is to find the set of videos that maximizes total gain $\sum_i g(t_{0:i}, \Psi)$. Note that by telescoping with (2), we can see that this sum is a submodular function. Here we use a greedy procedure to optimize this sum:

$$t_i = \operatorname*{argmax}_{t \in \mathcal{T}_r} g(t_{0:i-1} \cap t, \Psi)$$

where $\mathcal{T}_r$ is the set of candidate videos in a row. Properties of submodularity tell us that this greedy procedure guarantees $(1 - \frac{1}{e})$-optimality.[1]

Similarly, to ease navigation we rank the rows according to the probability of play for any of the videos in the row. So the j-th row is selected by

$$r_j = \operatorname*{argmax}_{r \in \mathcal{R}_s, r \notin r_{0:j-1}} \mathbb{P}(\mathcal{I}_r = 1 | v, w) \sum_i \mathbb{P}(\mathcal{C}_{r,t_i} | \mathcal{I}_r = 1). \quad (7)$$

where $\mathcal{R}_s$ is the set of rows preselected for session s.

Since we cannot predict user intent beforehand, we infer it on the fly as we observe navigation signals online to update our estimation of session parameters in real time. That is, we first present the page with Θ_s sampled from prior, and keep updating the posterior as we observe more navigation signals for session s. From (7), we can see this in turn updates $\mathbb{P}(\mathcal{I}_r = 1 | v, w)$ and thus the rank of the rows. A detailed description about updating v_s and w_s is presented in Section 4.2.

Users expect a video to be fixed in a position once they see it. Similar behavior can also be found in the information retrieval literature: [23] shows that change of search results can hinder users finding what they are looking for. *Therefore, to provide a consistent experience to users, we fix a row once it is seen and only rearrange the rows that a user has yet to see.* This still provides great opportunity for improvement since when a user has not played any videos in the observed portion, the user is likely to consume from the unobserved part. Experiments show that already after

[1]Note that the gain is transformed by a logistic function, hence submodularity of click probabilities is not guaranteed. That said, maximizing the total gain is efficient in practice.

observing navigation signals from only 2 rows, online adaptation can improve the result quality considerably.

We believe that dynamic result adaptation is widely applicable. Firstly, the computation tends to be fairly lightweight and can be carried out on a client device. Hence it does not add any meaningful latency caused by another roundtrip to a server. Moreover, the same strategy could be applied to retrieving and presenting search results, or to games, where the environment is being generated dynamically in accordance to the player's interest and abilities.

3.5 Impression fatigue and repeated plays

Beyond a generic relevance and diversity model for recommendation, we also need to take into account impression fatigue and repeated plays. That is, we need to control for the fact that a user might have seen a recommendation previously or watched the movie before on the service.

We observe significant impression fatigue in our dataset, similar to what is described in [ ]. That is, the more a video is presented to a user, generally the less likely the user plays it (when ignoring repeated plays): Repeated display is *not causal* in reducing the play probability, as is evident from the fact that previous plays are a conditioning variable.

As can be seen in Figure 4, most videos have stronger than exponential fatigue effects. It is also worth noting that for less popular videos, e.g. the lowest two curves in Figure 4, repeated impressions initially *do* increase play probability. We conjecture that it is due to "advertisement" effects: as we repeatedly present a less-known video to a user, a user becomes aware of and possibly even interested in the video. For already well-known videos, this effect is relatively minor and dominated by fatigue effects. Also, most curves can be approximated by piecewise linear functions in log-probability space. We thus add the following term to (2):

$$\text{fatigue}(x_t) = \begin{cases} a_t x_t + b_t & \text{if } x_t < k. \\ a_t k + b_t + d_t(x - k) & \text{otherwise} \end{cases} \quad (8)$$

Here $a_t, b_t, d_t \in \mathbb{R}$ control slope, offset and secondary slope of the fatigue function. $k \in \mathbb{Z}^+$ determines the position of the slope change, and x_t is the number of previous impressions. As before we can decompose a_t (similarly for b_t, d_t) into $a_{u,t} + a_{0,t}$ to prevent overfitting.

Also of interest is the high probability of repeated play. This applies to both episodic content (e.g. TV shows), for which many users continue watching subsequent episodes after watching some of them *and*, quite surprisingly, to standalone videos (e.g. movies). See Figure 5 for details.

Nonetheless, the curves clearly form two groups, one for episodic videos (with a higher repeated-play probability) and one for standalone ones. The curves within each group are very similar. This suggests that binary indicators of previous play and episodic videos are sufficient (see Section 5.4).

4. INFERENCE

Given this rather complex statistical model, we need to design efficient inference algorithms for both offline and online adaptation of the model. In particular, the online updates need to be very lightweight to run on consumer devices.

We choose the negative log-posterior of the data such that we can obtain a maximum-a-posteriori (MAP) estimate.

$$L := -\log \mathbb{P}(\mathcal{S}, \mathcal{C}|\text{rest}) + \Omega(\Theta, \Psi, \delta), \quad (9)$$

Here the first term maximizes the likelihood while the second term is a regularizer that penalizes complex models.

$$\log \mathbb{P}(\mathcal{S}, \mathcal{C}|\text{rest}) = \sum_s \sum_r \log \mathbb{P}(\mathcal{S}_{s,r}, \mathcal{C}_{s,r,:}|\text{rest}) \quad (10)$$

$$\mathbb{P}(\mathcal{S}_{s,r}, \mathcal{C}_{s,r,:}|\text{rest}) = \sum_{j\in\{0,1\}} \mathbb{P}(\mathcal{I}_{s,r} = j|\Theta)\mathbb{P}(\mathcal{S}_{s,r}|\mathcal{I}_{s,r} = j, \delta) \prod_i \mathbb{P}(\mathcal{C}_{s,r,i}|\mathcal{I}_{s,r} = j, \Psi) \quad (11)$$

Unfortunately the summation over inspection states is inside the logarithm, rendering the problem non-convex. For tractability, we design an efficient EM procedure using variational inference.

4.1 Offline training

The key to offline training is that if $\mathcal{I}_{s,r}$ is known then the full model decomposes nicely. Thus, we propose a stochastic EM algorithm to efficiently solve this inference problem. In the E-step we estimate $\mathcal{I}_{s,r}$ with all other parameters fixed, and in the M-step we optimize all parameters with $\mathcal{I}_{s,r}$ fixed.

E-step Here we estimate the posterior probability of $\mathcal{I}$ with fixed $\{\Phi, \Theta, \delta\}$. We define

$$\begin{aligned} Q(\mathcal{I}_{s,r})_j :=& \mathbb{P}(\mathcal{I}_{s,r} = j|\mathcal{S}_{s,r}, \mathcal{C}_{s,r,:}) \\ \propto& \prod_i \mathbb{P}(\mathcal{C}_{s,r,i}|\mathcal{I}_{s,r} = j, \Psi)\mathbb{P}(\mathcal{S}_{s,r}|\mathcal{I}_{s,r} = j, \delta) \\ & \mathbb{P}(\mathcal{I}_{s,r} = j|\Theta) \end{aligned} \quad (12)$$

M-step Next we optimize Ψ, Θ, and δ with $\mathcal{I}_{s,r}$ weighted by the posterior $Q(\mathcal{I}_{s,r})_j$. Define

$$J(Q, \Psi, \Theta, \delta) := \sum_{j\in\{0,1\}} Q(\mathcal{I}_{s,r})_j \log \frac{\mathbb{P}(\mathcal{I}_{s,r} = j, \mathcal{S}_{s,r}, \mathcal{C}_{s,r,:})}{Q(\mathcal{I}_{s,r})_j}$$

$$\{\Psi, \Theta, \delta\} = \operatorname*{argmin}_{\Psi,\Theta,\delta} -J(Q, \Psi, \Theta, \delta) + \lambda \left\|(\Psi, \Theta, \delta)\right\|_2^2$$

In experiments we use stochastic gradient descent for offline inference. It randomly picks a session from training set and performs a gradient step with gradient

$$\partial_\Psi J = \partial_\Psi \sum_{j\in\{0,1\}} Q(\mathcal{I}_{s,r})_j \log \mathbb{P}(\mathcal{C}_{s,r,:}|\mathcal{I}_{s,r} = j, \Psi)$$

$$\partial_\delta J = \partial_\delta \sum_{j\in\{0,1\}} Q(\mathcal{I}_{s,r})_j \log \mathbb{P}(\mathcal{S}_{s,r}|\mathcal{I}_{s,r} = j, \delta)$$

$$\partial_\Theta J = \partial_\Theta \sum_{j\in\{0,1\}} Q(\mathcal{I}_{s,r})_j \log \mathbb{P}(\mathcal{I}_{s,r} = j|\Theta)$$

We can view the updates with regard to Ψ as videos being weighted by $Q(\mathcal{I}_{s,r})_j$. This matches intuition: a play/non-play decision made on videos from a row that a user is interested in should be more important than a decision made on other rows. For example, when a user is looking for an exciting movie, we should not penalize a video from "Kids' Movies" too much when it is not played. Experiments show that by modeling interests, we are able to obtain a more accurate estimates of play probabilities.

4.2 Online Updates

We now proceed to describe the updates in a per-session context. Note that online does not refer to online learning in the traditional sense but rather to an online response and parameter update due to user behavior in the current

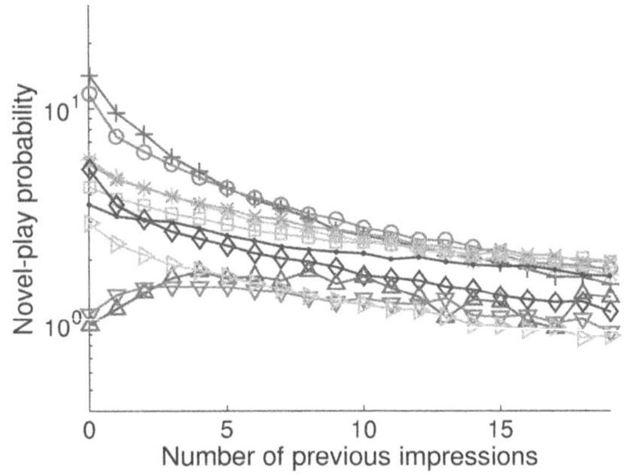

Figure 4: Novel-play probability as a function of non-play impressions for 10 videos. With exception of some rather unpopular videos the log-popularity decreases piecewise linearly. We renormalize them to provide relative magnitudes (the absolute numbers are proprietary).

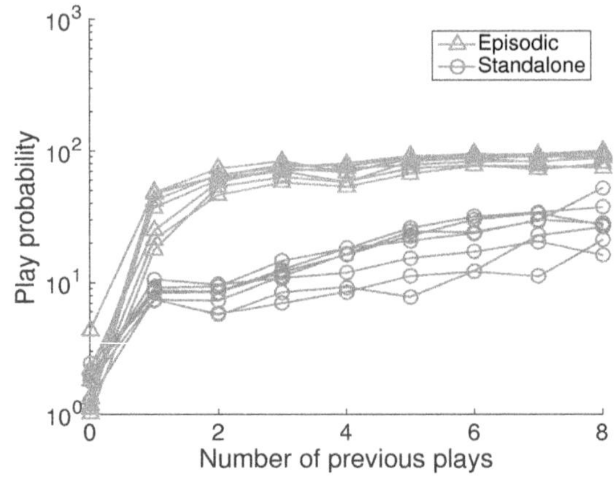

Figure 5: Play probability as function of number of previous plays. *Episodic* refers to content with multiple episodes, *Standalone* defaults to a single video (or movie). As before, probabilities are renormalized to protect proprietary information.

session. When a user scrolls or skips to the next row without scrolling we update the MAP estimate of Θ_s accordingly:

$$\mathbb{P}(\Theta_s|\text{rest}) \propto \prod_{r\in R_{\text{seen}}} \sum_{j\in\{0,1\}} \mathbb{P}(\mathcal{S}_{s,r}|\mathcal{I}_{s,r}=j,\delta) \qquad (13)$$
$$\mathbb{P}(\mathcal{I}_{s,r}=j|v_s,w_s,\text{rest})\mathcal{N}(v_s|\lambda_v)\mathcal{N}(w_s|\lambda_w).$$

Here R_{seen} is the set of displayed rows. We adopt a similar EM strategy. The E-step remains unchanged, while in the M-step we make an update with gradient

$$\partial_{\Theta_s} J(Q,\Psi,\Theta,\delta) = \partial_{\Theta_s} \sum_{j\in\{0,1\}} Q(\mathcal{I}_{s,r})_j \log \mathbb{P}(\mathcal{I}_{s,r}=j|\Theta)$$

Once we update our estimation on Θ_s and in turn $\mathcal{I}_{s,r}$, we can then adapt the page. This is computationally inexpensive because we only need to reorder a small (typically $<$ 40) subset of rows. This is easily feasible by most modern browsers and devices. Most of the terms in (12) and (13) can be precomputed, and computing (and updating) $\mathbb{P}(I_{s,r})$ only involves a logarithm and an inner product of sparse feature vectors.

5. EXPERIMENT

We use a real-world dataset from Netflix and show that:

1. Online adaptation improves recommendations at a row level in both mean reciprocal rank (MRR) and Precision@5. (Section 5.2)
2. Our model is able to address cold-start. Even for users with *no* previous data and using *no* context, our model provides personalized recommendations. (Section 5.3)
3. Modeling impression fatigue and repeated play behaviors significantly improves recommendations in both MRR and Precision@5 (Section 5.4).

Comparing the performance with other production systems or other sophisticated models is out of the scope of this paper, since after all, our goal is to investigate the possibility of real-time online updates and to explore new methods to jointly model plays and navigation signals.

5.1 Dataset

The dataset consists of homepage sessions, collected by Netflix for a particular type of playback device from 57,386 distinct profiles pre-computed for members from a single country. For each video on the page, the dataset also contains an indicator about whether the video was displayed to the user, and whether it was played. The dataset consisted of sessions collected over a three-month period in 2015. Sessions from April and May are used for training, while those from June are split into validation (for hyperparameter tuning) and test sets (to report performance).

We are interested in cases where users are navigating the page to discover new content to watch instead of continuing to watch previously watched shows. We thus filter out sessions where users choose from *Continue Watching*, *Recently Watched* or *My List* rows. This leaves approximately 294k training and 59k testing sessions.

Each homepage in the dataset consists of 40 rows that were chosen according to a production personalized recommender system that selects and orders the rows in a personalized fashion for each profile. Thus, for this dataset, the method in this paper already has the space of rows filtered down to a set that are deemed to be relevant. Each row consists of up to 75 videos placed horizontally in the row. The videos are placed in what appears to be a two-dimensional grid, but, in fact, a page is a series of rows on which the user has the ability to scroll individually in a horizontal fashion. When a row comes into the viewport, five videos appear horizontally. In light of this, we only consider a row to be *scrolled on* when a user has viewed more than five videos horizontally in that row.

While a comparison using publicly available datasets would be ideal, there are no such datasets available that form a page of recommendations that are comparable to the one described above. Instead, the purpose of this paper is to present a novel method and show the improvement in relevance metrics with the online adaptation strategy.

5.2 Online Updates

We examine the contribution of the online adaptation

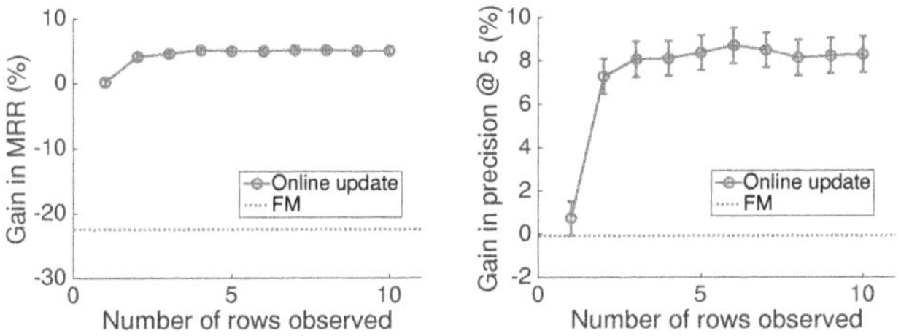

Figure 6: Gains in MRR (left) and Precision@5 (right) as a function of the number of rows visited. We see a clear improvement even just after 2 rows. The Factorization Machine baseline is provided for reference.

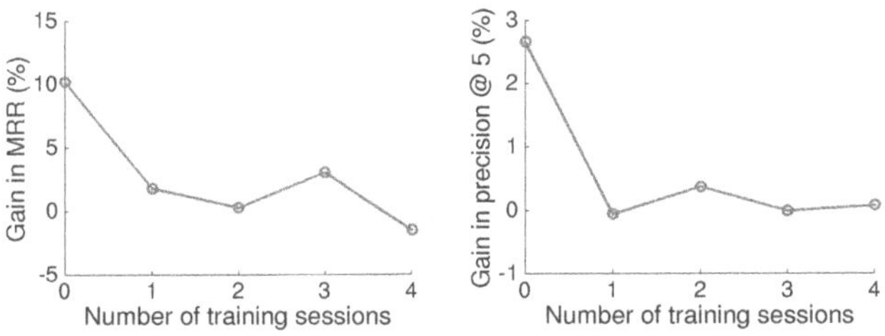

Figure 7: Gain in MRR (left) and Precision@5 (right) compared to offline-only model. For users with few training sessions, the benefit gained from online update is the greatest.

strategy. We first generate pages with the model trained using only previous sessions. During testing, we simulate the online adaptation procedure by looking at one row at a time, and update the page according to navigation signals (scroll or no scroll). To control the causal effects, we must use navigation signals from rows in the order from the original page instead of the reordered page. We thus evaluate using the following procedure: only use navigation signals up to a certain row (the 10th row in experiments) on a page, and only reorder the rows below that row. We then compare the adapted pages with the pages without adaptation.

We evaluate performance by two standard metrics: mean reciprocal rank (MRR) and precision at 5 (P@5). MRR measures how early we place the relevant (played) rows on a page. P@5 measures the fraction of relevant rows in the next 5 rows. Figure 6 shows MRR and P@5 vs. number of rows observed. We see on both metrics that online adaptation provides a significant improvement over non-adapted pages. Not surprisingly, as we observe more rows, online adaptation provides greater improvements. We already see improvements with only 2 rows. This means users only need to scroll 2 rows to have a benefit from this strategy, which is often the case when users are exploring for new videos.

Without a known row ordering baseline, we compared against ordering the rows on the page via Factorization Machines (FMs) using libFM [22]. The FM was trained and tested on the same data as our model. For features we used: user ID and row type identifier; we sampled played rows as positives and unplayed rows within one row of the played rows as negatives. The best FM model was trained with MCMC optimization and latent dimension 15. We show relative MRR and P@5 metrics in Figure 6.

5.3 Coldstart

The coldstart problem is the bane of many recommender systems. It occurs whenever a new user or a new video comes to the service. In such cases, we have relatively little data to infer the preferences of the user or the properties of the video: For new users we often only have basic context information such as device type and location. This makes recommending an initial set of videos exceedingly difficult, yet it is this first impression that matters a lot when it comes to convincing a new user to continue using a service.

Our online adaptation strategy helps alleviate the user coldstart problem. Figure 7 shows MRR and P@5 scores as a function of the number of training sessions available. We see that users with fewer training sessions (coldstart users) benefit most from online adaption. Quite remarkably, it works well even for users with no previous sessions. This opens a new avenue to address the coldstart problem: even when there is *no* previous data and using *no* context information, with online modeling navigation signals, we are able to personalize recommendations within the first page. We are effectively observing the user in a live environment and adjusting recommendations to reduce the amount of navigation needed to find something interesting to watch.

5.4 Fatigue

We discussed the importance of impression fatigue and repeated viewing in Section 3.5. To illustrate the effect we examine the horizontal MRR and P@5 within a row to evaluate the play probability estimates. Relative improvements compared to the model without them are shown in Figure 8. We can see that each provides clear improvement and using a combination is best. This gain is achieved by only using a small number of model parameters.

6. CONCLUSION AND FUTURE WORK

We proposed inferring user intent through in-session navigation information and then updating pages of recommendations based on that intent. To accomplish this, we defined a probabilistic model capable of incorporating current session navigational information as well as logged navigation and consumption data. The model infers interest in candidate rows of recommended items based on homepage navigation to a certain point on the page, and can populate the remaining rows on the page with more relevant content that reflects the current likely intent as predicted by the model.

This is the first work of its kind that performs online updating of recommendations based on user navigation within a single page. Thus, it is the intention of this paper to demonstrate feasibility of such a method, which we do on real-world dataset from Netflix. The model not only improves the relevancy of future recommendations on the page, but also helps to alleviate the user coldstart problem by using navigation information, yielding improved recommendations even within the first page. For users without any offline training sessions, i.e. with online navigation signal alone, we are able to provide personalized recommendations. We argue that this approach addresses the coldstart problem in a more effective manner than traditional approaches, though could be combined with them as well.

This work opens a new avenue for future work on online page adaptation. While we use binary horizontal scrolls in experiments, the online adaptation strategy is completely general. We can easily change the emission function of navigation signals to fit navigation signals in many domains, such as mouse hover, section expansion, or text selection.

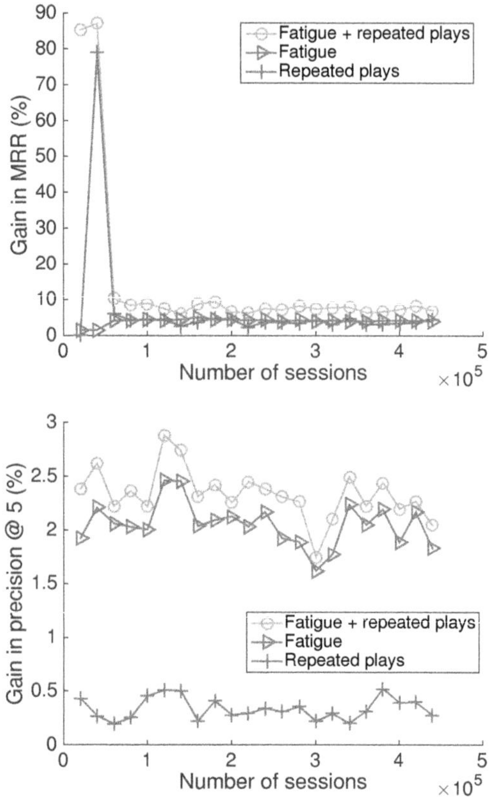

Figure 8: Gain in MRR (Top) and Precision@5 (Bottom) obtained by modeling impression fatigue and repeated plays. Performance compared to the model without modeling impression fatigue and repeated plays.

Extending it to model multiple sources of signals is also straightforward. Also, while we focus on reranking rows, a similar model could also be applied to reranking items within each row. It can likewise be adapted to model other UI designs.

7. REFERENCES

[1] D. Agarwal and B.-C. Chen. Regression-based latent factor models. In *KDD*, pages 19–28. ACM, 2009.

[2] D. Agarwal and B.-C. Chen. FLDA: matrix factorization through latent Dirichlet allocation. In *WSDM*, pages 91–100. ACM, 2010.

[3] D. Agarwal, B.-C. Chen and P. Elango. Spatio-temporal models for estimating click-through rate. In *WWW*, pages 21–30. ACM, 2009.

[4] D. Agarwal, B.-C. Chen, P. Elango, N. Motgi, S.-T. Park, R. Ramakrishnan, S. Roy, and J. Zachariah. Online models for content optimization. In *NIPS*, pages 17–24, 2009.

[5] A. Ahmed, C.-H. Teo, S.V.N. Vishwanathan, and A. J. Smola. Fair and balanced: Learning to present news stories. In *WSDM*, pages 333–342, 2012. ACM.

[6] C. Alvino and J. Basilico. Netflix tech blog: Learning a personalized homepage. http://techblog.netflix.com/2015/04/learning-personalized-homepage.html.

[7] P. Boldi, F. Bonchi, C. Castillo, D. Donato, A. Gionis, and S. Vigna. The query-flow graph: model and applications. In *CIKM*, pages 609–618. ACM, 2008.

[8] A. Das, M. Datar, A. Garg, and S. Rajaram. Google news personalization: scalable online collaborative filtering. In *WWW*, pages 271–280. ACM, 2007.

[9] Q. Diao, M. Qiu, C.-Y. Wu, A.J. Smola, J. Jiang, and C. Wang. Jointly modeling aspects, ratings and sentiments for movie recommendation (JMARS). In *KDD*, pages 193–202. ACM, 2014.

[10] K. El-Arini, G. Veda, D. Shahaf, and C. Guestrin. Turning down the noise in the blogosphere. In *KDD*, pages 289–298. ACM, 2009.

[11] C.A. Gomez-Uribe and N. Hunt. The Netflix recommender system: Algorithms, business value, and innovation. *ACM TMIS*, 6(4), 2015.

[12] F. Guo, C. Liu, A. Kannan, T. Minka, M. Taylor, Y.-M. Wang, and C. Faloutsos. Click chain model in web search. In *WWW*, pages 11–20. ACM, 2009.

[13] Q. Guo and E. Agichtein. Beyond dwell time: estimating document relevance from cursor movements and other post-click searcher behavior. In *WWW*, pages 569–578. ACM, 2012.

[14] Qi Guo, H. Jin, D. Lagun, S. Yuan, and E. Agichtein. Mining touch interaction data on mobile devices to predict web search result relevance. In *SIGIR*, pages 153–162. ACM, 2013.

[15] J. Huang, R. White, and G. Buscher. User see, user point: gaze and cursor alignment in web search. In *SIGCHI*, pages 1341–1350. ACM, 2012.

[16] J. Huang, R. White, and S. Dumais. No clicks, no problem: using cursor movements to understand and improve search. In *SIGCHI*, pages 1225–1234, 2011.

[17] J.Y. Kim, M. Cramer, J. Teevan, and D. Lagun. Understanding how people interact with web search results that change in real-time using implicit feedback. In *CIKM*, pages 2321–2326. ACM, 2013.

[18] J.A. Konstan and J. Riedl. Recommender systems: from algorithms to user experience. *User Model. User-Adapt. Interact.*, 22(1-2):101–123, 2012.

[19] D. Lagun, M. Ageev, Q. Guo, and E. Agichtein. Discovering common motifs in cursor movement data for improving web search. *WSDM*, pg. 183–192, 2014.

[20] H. Lieberman and T. Selker. Out of context: Computer systems that adapt to, and learn from, context. *IBM Systems Journal*, 39:617–632, 2000.

[21] S. Rendle. Factorization machines. In *ICDM*, pages 995–1000. IEEE, 2010.

[22] S. Rendle. Factorization Machines with libFM. *Trans. Intell. Syst. Technol.*, 3(3), pages 57:1–22. ACM, 2012.

[23] K. Rodden, X. Fu, A. Aula, and I. Spiro. Eye-mouse coordination patterns on web search results pages. In *CHI*, pages 2997–3002. ACM, 2008.

[24] R. Salakhutdinov and A. Mnih. Bayesian probabilistic matrix factorization using markov chain monte carlo. In *ICML*, pages 880–887. ACM, 2008.

[25] J. Teevan, E. Adar, R. Jones, and M.A. Potts. Information re-retrieval: repeat queries in yahoo's logs. In *SIGIR*, pages 151–158. ACM, 2007.

[26] R.W. White and G. Buscher. Text selections as implicit relevance feedback. In *SIGIR*, pages 1151–1152. ACM, 2012.

Bayesian Low-Rank Determinantal Point Processes

Mike Gartrell
Microsoft
mike.gartrell@acm.org

Ulrich Paquet*
Microsoft
ulripa@microsoft.com

Noam Koenigstein
Microsoft
noamko@microsoft.com

ABSTRACT

Determinantal point processes (DPPs) are an emerging model for encoding probabilities over subsets, such as shopping baskets, selected from a ground set, such as an item catalog. They have recently proved to be appealing models for a number of machine learning tasks, including product recommendation. DPPs are parametrized by a positive semi-definite kernel matrix. Prior work has shown that using a low-rank factorization of this kernel provides scalability improvements that open the door to training on large-scale datasets and computing online recommendations, both of which are infeasible with standard DPP models that use a full-rank kernel. A low-rank DPP model can be trained using an optimization-based method, such as stochastic gradient ascent, to find a point estimate of the kernel parameters, which can be performed efficiently on large-scale datasets. However, this approach requires careful tuning of regularization parameters to prevent overfitting and provide good predictive performance, which can be computationally expensive. In this paper we present a Bayesian method for learning a low-rank factorization of this kernel, which provides automatic control of regularization. We show that our Bayesian low-rank DPP model can be trained efficiently using stochastic gradient Hamiltonian Monte Carlo (SGHMC). Our Bayesian model generally provides better predictive performance on several real-world product recommendation datasets than optimization-based low-rank DPP models trained using stochastic gradient ascent, and better performance than several state-of-the art recommendation methods in many cases.

1. INTRODUCTION

Online shopping revenue has grown significantly in recent years. Central to the online retail experience is the recommendation task of "basket completion", where we seek to compute predictions for the next item that should be added to a shopping basket, given a set of items already present in the basket. Determinantal point processes (DPPs) offer an attractive model for basket completion, since they jointly model *set diversity* and item *quality* or *popularity*. DPPs also offer a compact parameterization and efficient algorithms for performing inference.

A distribution over sets that models diversity is of particular interest when recommendations are complementary. For example, consider a shopping basket that contains a smartphone and a SIM card. A collaborative filtering method based on user and item similarities, such as a matrix factorization model [27], would tend to provide recommendations that are similar to the items already present in the basket but not necessarily complementary. In this example, matrix factorization might recommend other similar smartphones to complete this basket, which may not be appropriate since the basket already contains a smartphone. In contrast, a complementary recommendation for this basket might be a smartphone case, rather than another smartphone. In this setting, DPPs would be used to learn the inherent item diversity present within the observed sets (baskets) that users purchase, and hence can provide such complementary recommendations.

DPPs have been used for a variety of machine learning tasks [16, 18, 19]. DPPs can be parameterized by a $M \times M$ positive semi-definite $\mathbf{L}$ matrix, where M is the size of the item catalog. There has been some work focused on learning DPPs from observed data consisting of example subsets [1, 10, 12, 17, 24], which is a challenging learning task that is conjectured to be NP-hard [18]. Some of this recent work has involved learning a nonparametric full-rank $\mathbf{L}$ matrix [12, 24] that does not constrain $\mathbf{L}$ to take a particular parametric form, while other recent work has involved learning a low-rank factorization of this nonparametric $\mathbf{L}$ matrix [10]. A low-rank factorization of $\mathbf{L}$ enables substantial improvements in runtime performance compared to a full-rank DPP model during training and when computing predictions, on the order of 10-20x or more, with predictive performance that is equivalent to or better than a full-rank model.

The low-rank DPP model presented in [10] uses stochastic gradient ascent to maximize an objective function defined in terms of a low-rank factorization of $\mathbf{L}$. While this approach for model learning is efficient on large-scale data, it has some drawbacks. Careful tuning of regularization hyperparameters is required to prevent overfitting and provide good predictive performance. This tuning can be performed using a line search over the range of possible regularization settings. This procedure is expensive since it entails train-

*Currently at Google DeepMind.

RecSys '16, September 15 - 19, 2016, Boston , MA, USA

ISBN 978-1-4503-4035-9/16/09...$15.00

DOI: http://dx.doi.org/10.1145/2959100.2959178

ing a separate model for each regularization setting and then selecting the model that performs best. The optimization-based approach also provides a point estimate that commits to a single most probable setting for each learned parameter, which can be problematic in that it does not consider uncertainty. In contrast to this approach, we present a Bayesian low-rank DPP model that provides better predictive performance and robust regularization, without the need for expensive hyperparameter tuning.

Our work makes the following contributions:

1. We present a Bayesian low-rank DPP model, which uses an efficient stochastic gradient Hamiltonian Monte Carlo (SGHMC) algorithm for learning from observed data.

2. The Bayesian low-rank DPP model does not require expensive hyperparameter tuning and provides robust regularization, in contrast to prior work on an optimization-based learning algorithm for low-rank DPPs.

3. A detailed experimental evaluation on several real-world datasets shows that our Bayesian model provides better predictive performance than existing low-rank DPP models. Our model also provides significantly better predictive performance than several other recommendation methods in many cases.

2. MODEL

DPPs originated in statistical mechanics [23], where they were used to model distributions of fermions. Fermions are particles that obey the Pauli exclusion principle, which indicates that no two fermions can occupy the same quantum state. As a result, systems of fermions exhibit a repulsion or "anti-bunching" effect, which is described by a DPP. This repulsive behavior is a key characteristic of DPPs, which makes them a capable model for diversity. We now proceed with some details of DPPs, including how they are defined and a method for efficient learning.

2.1 Background

A point process is a distribution over configurations of points selected from a ground set $\mathcal{Y}$, which are finite subsets of $\mathcal{Y}$. In this paper we deal only with discrete DPPs, which describe a distribution over subsets of a discrete ground set of items $\mathcal{Y} = 1, 2, \ldots, M$, which we also call the item catalog. A discrete DPP on $\mathcal{Y}$ is a probability measure $\mathcal{P}$ on $2^{\mathcal{Y}}$ (the power set or set of all subsets of $\mathcal{Y}$), such that for any $A \subseteq \mathcal{Y}$, the probability $\mathcal{P}(A)$ is specified by $\mathcal{P}(A) \propto \det(\mathbf{L}_A)$. In the context of basket completion, $\mathcal{Y}$ is the item catalog (inventory of items on sale), and Y is the subset of items in a user's basket; there are $2^{|\mathcal{Y}|}$ possible baskets. The notation $\mathbf{L}_Y$ denotes the principal submatrix of the DPP kernel $\mathbf{L}$ indexed by the items in Y, which is the restriction of $\mathbf{L}$ to the rows and columns indexed by the elements of Y: $\mathbf{L}_A \equiv [\mathbf{L}_{ij}]_{i,j \in A}$. Intuitively, the diagonal entry L_{ii} of the kernel matrix $\mathbf{L}$ captures the importance or quality of item i, while the off-diagonal entry $L_{ij} = L_{ji}$ measures the similarity between items i and j.

The normalization constant for $\mathcal{P}$ follows from the observation that $\sum_{A' \subseteq \mathcal{Y}} \det(\mathbf{L}_{A'}) = \det(\mathbf{L} + \mathbf{I})$. The value $\det(\mathbf{L}_A)$ associates a "volume" to basket A from a geometric viewpoint, and its probability is normalized by the volumes of all possible baskets $A' \subseteq \mathcal{Y}$. Therefore, we have

$$\mathcal{P}(A) = \frac{\det(\mathbf{L}_A)}{\det(\mathbf{L} + \mathbf{I})} . \tag{1}$$

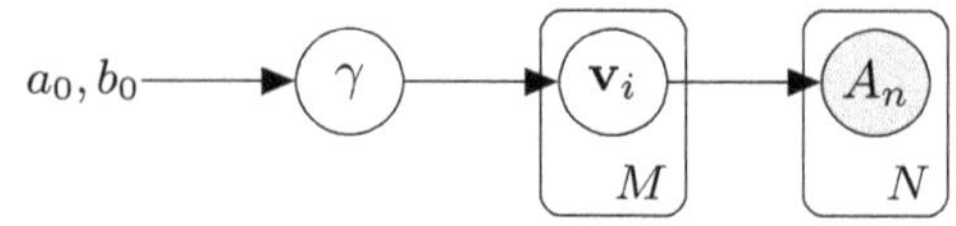

Figure 1: A graphical model for the low-rank DPP model.

We use a low-rank factorization of the $M \times M$ $\mathbf{L}$ matrix,

$$\mathbf{L} = \mathbf{V}\mathbf{V}^T , \tag{2}$$

for the $M \times K$ matrix $\mathbf{V}$, where M is the number of items in the item catalog and K is the number of latent trait dimensions. This low-rank factorization of $\mathbf{L}$ leads to significant efficiency improvements compared to a model that uses a full-rank $\mathbf{L}$ matrix when it comes to model learning and computing predictions [10]. This also places an implicit constraint on the space of subsets of $\mathcal{Y}$, since the model is restricted to place zero probability mass on subsets with more than K items (all eigenvalues of $\mathbf{L}$ beyond K are zero). We see this from the observation that a sample from a DPP will not be larger than the rank of $\mathbf{L}$ [11].

2.2 Model Specification

Our learning task is to fit a DPP kernel $\mathbf{L}$ based on a collection of N observed subsets $\mathcal{A} = \{A_1, \ldots, A_N\}$, where each subset A_n is composed of items from the item catalog $\mathcal{Y}$. These observed subsets in $\mathcal{A}$ constitute our training data, and our task is to infer $\mathbf{L}$ from $\mathcal{A}$. The log-likelihood for seeing $\mathcal{A}$ is

$$f(\mathbf{V}) = \log \mathcal{P}(\mathcal{A}|\mathbf{V}) = \sum_{n=1}^{N} \log \mathcal{P}(A_n|\mathbf{V}) \tag{3}$$

$$= \sum_{n=1}^{N} \log\det(\mathbf{L}_{[n]}) - N \log\det(\mathbf{L} + \mathbf{I}) \tag{4}$$

where $[n]$ indexes the observations or objects in $\mathcal{A}$. Recall from (2) that $\mathbf{L} = \mathbf{V}\mathbf{V}^T$.

Figure 1 shows the graphical model for our Bayesian low-rank DPP model. We place a multivariate Gaussian prior on each item in our model. Our prior distribution on $\mathbf{V}$ is given by

$$p(\mathbf{V}|\gamma) = \prod_{i=1}^{M} \mathcal{N}(\mathbf{v}_i; \mathbf{0}, \gamma^{-1}\mathbf{I}) \tag{5}$$

where $\mathbf{v}_i$ is the row vector from $\mathbf{V}$ for item i, and all items i share the same precision γ. We furthermore place a conjugate gamma prior on γ: $p(\gamma|a_0, b_0) = \text{Gamma}(\gamma; a_0, b_0)$. The joint distribution over $\mathcal{A}$, $\mathbf{V}$ and γ, as depicted in Figure 1, is

$$p(\mathcal{A}, \mathbf{V}, \gamma|a_0, b_0) = \mathcal{P}(\mathcal{A}|\mathbf{V})\, p(\mathbf{V}|\gamma)\, p(\gamma|a_0, b_0) . \tag{6}$$

To draw samples from the posterior $p(\mathbf{V}, \gamma|\mathcal{A}, a_0, b_0)$ we alternately Gibbs-sample from $p(\gamma|\mathbf{V}, a_0, b_0)$ and $p(\mathbf{V}|\mathcal{A}, \gamma)$. The first conditional distribution is

$$\gamma|\mathbf{V}, a_0, b_0 \sim \text{Gamma}(\gamma; a, b)$$
$$a = a_0 + \frac{MK}{2}$$
$$b = b_0 + \frac{1}{2}\sum_i \|\mathbf{v}_i\|^2 , \tag{7}$$

and is sampled in Line 4 in Algorithm 1.

The second conditional distribution $p(\mathbf{V}|\mathcal{A},\gamma)$ does not have the same simple form, and is:

$$p(\mathbf{V}|\mathcal{A},\gamma) \propto \exp\left(f(\mathbf{V})\right) \prod_{i=1}^{M} \mathcal{N}(\mathbf{v}_i|\mathbf{0},\gamma^{-1}\mathbf{I}) \ , \tag{8}$$

$$\log p(\mathbf{V}|\mathcal{A},\gamma) = f(\mathbf{V}) + \frac{\gamma}{2}\sum_{i=1}^{M} \mathbf{v}_i^T\mathbf{v}_i + \mathsf{const} \ , \tag{9}$$

where const indicates an additive constant independent of $\mathbf{V}$. In the following section, we consider sampling from $p(\mathbf{V}|\mathcal{A},\gamma)$.

2.3 Learning Algorithm

We estimate the conditional distribution $p(\mathbf{V}|\mathcal{A},\gamma)$ using stochastic gradient Hamiltonian Monte Carlo (SGHMC) [7]. Hamiltonian Monte Carlo (HMC) [9, 26] is a Markov chain Monte Carlo (MCMC) method that uses the gradient of the log-density of the target distribution to efficiently explore the state space of the target. HMC defines a Hamiltonian function, an idea borrowed from physics, in terms of the target distribution that we wish to sample from. The Hamiltonian function has a potential energy term, corresponding to the target distribution, and a kinetic energy term, defined in terms of auxiliary momentum variables. By updating the momentum variables using the gradient of the log-density of the target distribution, we simulate a Hamiltonian dynamical system that enables proposals of distant states, thus allowing HMC to move rapidly through the state space of the target. We cannot simulate directly from the continuous Hamiltonian dynamics, so HMC uses a discretization of this continuous system composed of a number of "leapfrog steps".

HMC requires computation of the gradient of the log-density of the target distribution over all training instances with each iteration of the algorithm, which is expensive or infeasible for large datasets or a complex target. SGHMC addresses this issue by using stochastic gradients that are computed on minibatches, where each minibatch is composed of training instances sampled uniformly at random from the full training set. SGHMC adds a friction term to the momentum update, which counteracts the effects of noise from the stochastic gradients. The estimates computed by SGHMC samples are not unbiased any more (notice that there is no accept-reject step in Algorithm 1, and the distribution that is sampled from is different from the true posterior), but due to the effectively faster mixing, we are able to efficiently train our Bayesian low-rank DPP model on large-scale datasets.

Since we learn $p(\mathbf{V}|\mathcal{A},\gamma)$ by SGHMC, we need to efficiently compute the gradient of the log-density for this distribution. We begin by computing the gradient of log-likelihood, $\partial f/\partial \mathbf{V}$, which will be a $M \times K$ matrix. For $i \in 1,\ldots,M$ and $k \in 1,\ldots,K$, we need a matrix of scalar derivatives, $\{\frac{\partial f}{\partial \mathbf{V}}\}_{ik} = \frac{\partial f}{\partial v_{ik}}$. Taking the derivative of each term of the log-likelihood, we have

$$\begin{aligned}\frac{\partial f}{\partial v_{ik}} &= \sum_{n:i\in[n]} \frac{\partial}{\partial v_{ik}}\left(\log\det(\mathbf{L}_{[n]})\right) - N\frac{\partial}{\partial v_{ik}}\left(\log\det(\mathbf{L}+\mathbf{I})\right) \\ &= \sum_{n:i\in[n]} \mathsf{tr}\left(\mathbf{L}_{[n]}^{-1}\frac{\partial \mathbf{L}_{[n]}}{\partial v_{ik}}\right) - N\,\mathsf{tr}\left((\mathbf{L}+\mathbf{I})^{-1}\frac{\partial(\mathbf{L}+\mathbf{I})}{\partial v_{ik}}\right) .\end{aligned} \tag{10}$$

Algorithm 1 Sampling algorithm for learning $p(\mathbf{V}|\mathcal{A},\gamma)$

```
initialize V randomly, W = 0
samples := {}
repeat
   sample γ|V, a_0, b_0 according to (7)
   // approximately sample V|A, γ:
   for leapfrogSteps j = 1, ..., L do
      W := η∇Ũ(V) − αW + N(0, 2(α − β̂)η)
      V := V + W
   end for
   samples := {samples, V}
until sufficient samples have been taken
```

Examining the first term of the derivative, we see that

$$\mathsf{tr}\left(\mathbf{L}_{[n]}^{-1}\frac{\partial \mathbf{L}_{[n]}}{\partial v_{ik}}\right) = \mathbf{a}_i \cdot \mathbf{v}_k + \sum_{j=1}^{M} a_{ji}v_{jk} \ , \tag{11}$$

where $\mathbf{a}_i$ denotes row i of the matrix $\mathbf{A} = \mathbf{L}_{[n]}^{-1}$ and $\mathbf{v}_k$ denotes column k of $\mathbf{V}_{[n]}$. Note that $\mathbf{L}_{[n]} = \mathbf{V}_{[n]}\mathbf{V}_{[n]}^T$. Computing $\mathbf{A}$ is a relatively inexpensive operation, since the number of items in each training instance A_n is generally small for many recommendation applications.

For the second term of the derivative, we see that

$$\mathsf{tr}\left((\mathbf{L}+\mathbf{I})^{-1}\frac{\partial(\mathbf{L}+\mathbf{I})}{\partial v_{ik}}\right) = \mathbf{b}_i \cdot \mathbf{v}_k + \sum_{j=1}^{M} b_{ji}v_{jk} \tag{12}$$

where $\mathbf{b}_i$ denotes row i of the matrix $\mathbf{B} = \mathbf{I}_m - \mathbf{V}(\mathbf{I}_k + \mathbf{V}^T\mathbf{V})^{-1}\mathbf{V}^T$. Computing $\mathbf{B}$ is a relatively inexpensive operation, since we are inverting a $K \times K$ matrix with cost $O(K^3)$, and K (the number of latent trait dimensions) is usually set to a small value.

We now proceed with computing the gradient of the log-density for $p(\mathbf{V}|\mathcal{A},\gamma)$ shown in Equation 9. Looking at one component of this gradient, we have:

$$\frac{\partial \log p(\mathbf{V}|\mathcal{A},\gamma)}{\partial v_{ik}} = \gamma v_{ik} + \frac{\partial f}{\partial v_{ik}} \tag{13}$$

Our SGHMC algorithm is shown in Algorithm 1. In this algorithm, $\nabla\tilde{U}(\mathbf{V})$ is a noisy estimate of the log-density gradient of $p(\mathbf{V}|\mathcal{A},\gamma)$ computed for a minibatch, $\eta > 0$ is the learning rate, $\alpha \in [0,1]$ is the momentum coefficient, and $\mathbf{W}$ is the auxiliary momentum variable. $\hat{\boldsymbol{\beta}}$ is an estimate of the noise from the gradient, which we ignore by setting $\hat{\boldsymbol{\beta}} = 0$ and relying on small η, as explained in [7]. We find that setting $\alpha = 0.01$ and $\eta = 1.0 \times 10^{-5}$ or $\eta = 1.0 \times 10^{-6}$, with a minibatch size of 1000 instances, works well for the datasets we tested.

2.4 Predictions

We compute singleton next-item predictions, given a set of observed items. An example of this class of problem is "basket completion", where we seek to compute predictions for the next item that should be added to shopping basket, given a set of items already present in the basket.

We use a k-DPP to compute next-item predictions. A k-DPP is a distribution over all subsets $A \in \mathcal{Y}$ with cardinality k, where $\mathcal{Y}$ is the ground set, or the set of all items in the item catalog. Next item predictions are done via a conditional density. We compute the probability of the observed basket A, consisting of k items. For each possible item to be recommended, given the basket, the basket is enlarged with the new item to $k+1$ items. For the new item, we determine the probability of the new set of $k+1$ items, given that k items are already in the basket, using a Monte Carlo estimate from the samples. Ignoring burn-in samples, and letting s index the S remaining $\mathbf{V}^{(s)}$ samples in samples,

$$p(A_{+1}|A, \mathcal{A}, a_0, b_0) = \int \mathcal{P}(A_{+1}|A, \mathbf{V})\, p(\mathbf{V}|\mathcal{A}, a_0, b_0)\, d\mathbf{V}$$

$$\approx \frac{1}{S}\sum_{s=1}^{S} \mathcal{P}(A_{+1}|A, \mathbf{V}^{(s)}) \quad (14)$$

where A_{+1} indicates set A enlarged to contain a new item b from the catalog $\mathcal{Y}$. The samples in $\mathbf{V}$ implicitly marginalize out γ from the posterior density. We run the sampler to generate 2,000 samples, and discard the first 1,800 samples as burn-in. From [10], we see that the conditional probability for an item b in the singleton set B, given the appearance of items in A, is

$$\mathcal{P}(A_{+1} = A \cup B|A) = \frac{L^A_{bb}}{e_1(\lambda^A_1, \lambda^A_2, \ldots, \lambda^A_N)} \quad (15)$$

where L^A_{bb} denotes diagonal elément bb from the k-DPP kernel matrix conditioned on A, $\mathbf{L}^A$; $\lambda^A_1, \lambda^A_2, \ldots, \lambda^A_N$ are the eigenvalues of $\mathbf{L}^A$; and $e_1(\lambda^A_1, \lambda^A_2, \ldots, \lambda^A_N)$ is the first elementary symmetric polynomial on these eigenvalues. See [10] for full details on how to efficiently compute conditional densities for a k-DPP given an observed basket.

3. EVALUATION

In this section we evaluate the performance of Bayesian low-rank DPP model on on the task of basket completion for several real-world datasets. We compare to several competing recommendation methods, including an optimization-based low-rank DPP [10] and two matrix factorization models [13, 27], and find that our approach provides better predictive performance in many cases.

We formulate the basket-completion task as follows. Let $A_{\texttt{test}}$ be a subset of $n \geq 2$ co-purchased items (i.e, a basket) from the test-set. In order to evaluate the basket completion task, we pick an item $i \in A_{\texttt{test}}$ at random and remove it from $A_{\texttt{test}}$. We denote the remaining set as $A_{\texttt{test}-1}$. Formally, $A_{\texttt{test}-1} = A_{\texttt{test}} \setminus \{i\}$. Given a ground set of possible items $\mathcal{Y} = 1, 2, ..., M$, we define the candidates set $\mathcal{C}$ as the set of all items except those already in $A_{\texttt{test}-1}$; i.e., $\mathcal{C} = \mathcal{Y} \setminus A_{\texttt{test}-1}$. Our goal is to identify the missing item i from all other items in $\mathcal{C}$.

3.1 Datasets

Our experiments are based on several datasets:

1. **Amazon Baby Registries -** Amazon[1] is one of the world's leading online retail stores. The Amazon Baby Registries dataset [12] is a public dataset consisting of 111,006 registries or "baskets" of baby products. The choice of this dataset was motivated by the fact that it has been used by several prominent DPP studies [10, 12, 24]. The registries are collected from 15 different categories (such as "feeding", "diapers", "toys", etc.), and the items in each category are disjoint. We maintain consistency with prior work by evaluating each of its categories separately using a random split of 70% of the data for training and 30% for testing. The low-rank DPP models trained on this dataset were built with $K = 30$ trait dimensions.

In addition to the above evaluation, we also constructed a dataset composing of the concatenation of the three most popular categories: apparel, diaper, and feeding. This three-category dataset allows us to simulate data that could be observed for department stores that offer a wide range of items in different product categories. Its construction is deliberate, and concatenates three disjoint subgraphs of basket-item purchase patterns. This dataset serves to highlight differences between DPPs and models based on matrix factorization (MF). Collaborative filtering-based MF models – which model each basket and item with a latent vector – will perform poorly for this dataset, as the latent trait vectors of baskets and items in one subgraph could be arbitrarily rotated, without affecting the likelihood or predictive error in any of the other subgraphs. MF models are invariant to global rotations of the embedded trait vectors. However, for the concatenated dataset, these models are also invariant to arbitrary rotations of vectors in each disjoint subgraph, as there are no shared observations between the three categories. A global ranking based on inner products could then be arbitrarily affected by the basket and item embeddings arising from each subgraph.

2. **MS Store -** This dataset is based on data from Microsoft's web-based store [2]. The dataset is composed of 243,147 baskets consisting of commonly purchased items from a catalog of 2097 different hardware and software products. We randomly sampled of 80% of the data for training and kept the remaining 20% for testing. Recall from Section 2.1 that a low-rank DPP places zero probability mass on subsets with more than K items, where K is the number of trait dimensions in $\mathbf{V}$ or the rank of $\mathbf{L}$. With this constraint in mind, we use $K = 15$ trait dimensions for the low-rank DPP models trained on this data, since the largest observed basket in this dataset is composed of 15 items.

3. **Belgian Retail Supermarket -** This public dataset includes 88,163 baskets consisting of 16,470 unique supermarket items. It was collected in a Belgian retail supermarket over three non-consecutive time periods, as described in [3, 4]. Again, we randomly sampled 80% of the data for training and kept the remaining 20% for testing. We use $K = 76$ trait dimensions for the low-rank DPP model trained on this data, since the largest observed basket in this dataset is composed of 76 items.

Since we are interested in the basket completion task, which requires baskets containing at least two items, we remove all baskets containing only one item from each dataset before splitting the data into training and test sets.

3.2 Competing Methods

We evaluate against several baselines:

1. **Full-rank DPP -** This DPP model is parameterized by a full-rank $\mathbf{L}$ matrix, and uses a fixed-point optimization algorithm called Picard iteration [24] for learning $\mathbf{L}$. As described in [10], a full-rank DPP does not scale well to datasets containing large item catalogs during training or when computing predictions.

[1] www.amazon.com

[2] microsoftstore.com

2. **Low-rank DPP trained using stochastic gradient ascent (SGA) -** This DPP model is parameterized by a low-rank $\mathbf{L}$ matrix that is factorized using a $\mathbf{V}$ matrix composed of latent item trait vectors, and has a likelihood function identical to our Bayesian low-rank DPP. In contrast to our Bayesian approach, this optimization-based model is trained using stochastic gradient ascent, and uses regularization based on item popularity. We selected the regularization hyperparameter for this model using a line search performed with the training set.

3. **Poisson Factorization (PF) -** Poisson factorization (PF) is a prominent variant of matrix factorization designed specifically for implicit ratings [13]. The likelihood of the PF model is based on the Poisson distribution, which is useful with implicit datasets (e.g. datasets based on click or purchase events). The evaluations in this paper are based on the publicly available implementation[3] from [5]. In PF, Gamma priors are placed on the trait vectors. Following [6, 13], we set the Gamma shape and rate hyperparameters to 0.3.

4. **Reco Matrix Factorization (RecoMF) -** RecoMF is a matrix factorization model powering the Xbox Live recommendation system [27]. The likelihood term of RecoMF uses a sigmoid function to model the odds of a user liking or disliking an item in the dataset. Unlike PF, RecoMF requires the generation of synthetic negative training instances, and uses a scheme for sampling negatives based on popularity. RecoMF places Gaussian priors on the trait vectors, and gamma hyperpriors on each. We use the hyperparameter settings described in [27], which have been found to provide good performance for implicit recommendation data.

5. **Associative Classifier (AC) -** Since association rules are often used for market basket analysis [2, 15], we consider an associative classifier as a competing method. We use the publicly available implementation [8] of the Classification Based on Associations (CBA) algorithm [22]. We set minimum support and minimum confidence thresholds of 1.0% and 20.0%, respectively.

We use a flexible prior in our Bayesian low-rank DPP model by setting $a_0 = \sqrt{K}$ and $b_0 = 1$, and find that the model is not sensitive to these settings.

The matrix-factorization models are parameterized in terms of users and items. Since we have no explicit users in our data, we construct "virtual" users from the contents of each basket for the purposes of our evaluation, where a new user u_m is constructed for each basket b_m. Therefore, the set of items that u_m has purchased is simply the contents of b_m. Additionally, we use $K = 40$ trait dimensions for the matrix-factorization models.

3.3 Metrics

In the following evaluation we consider three measures:

1. **Mean Percentile Rank (MPR) -** Computing the Percentile Rank of an item requires the ability to rank the item j against all other items in $\mathcal{C}$. Therefore, the MPR evaluation results don't include the AC model, which ranks only those items for which an association rule was found. For other models we ranked the items according to their probabilities of completing the missing set Y_{n-1}. Namely, given an item i from the candidates set $\mathcal{C}$, we denote by p_i the probability $P(Y_n \cup \{i\} | Y_{n-1})$. The Percentile Rank (PR) of the missing item j is defined by

$$\mathrm{PR}_j = \frac{\sum_{j' \in \mathcal{C}} \mathbb{I}(p_j \geq p_{j'})}{|\mathcal{C}|} \times 100\%$$

where $\mathbb{I}(\cdot)$ is an indicator function and $|\mathcal{C}|$ is the number of items in the candidates set. The Mean Percentile Rank (MPR) is the average PR of all the instances in the test-set:

$$\mathrm{MPR} = \frac{\sum_{t \in \mathcal{T}} \mathrm{PR}_t}{|\mathcal{T}|}$$

where $\mathcal{T}$ is the set of test instances. MPR is a recall-oriented metric commonly used in studies that involve implicit recommendation data [14, 21]. MPR = 100 always places the held-out item for the test instance at the head of the ranked list of predictions, while MPR = 50 is equivalent to random selection.

2. **Precision@k -** We define precision@k as

$$\mathrm{precision@}k = \frac{\sum_{t \in \mathcal{T}} \mathbb{I}[\mathrm{rank}_t \leq k]}{|\mathcal{T}|}$$

where rank_t is the predicted rank of the held-out item for test instance t. In other words, precision@k is the fraction of instances in the test set for which the predicted rank of the held-out item falls within the top k predictions.

3. **Popularity-weighted precision@k -** Datasets used to evaluate recommendation systems typically contain a popularity bias [28], where users are more likely to provide feedback on popular items. Due to this popularity bias, conventional metrics such as MPR and precision@k are typically biased toward popular items. Using ideas from [28], we define popularity-weighted precision@k:

$$\text{popularity-weighted precision@}k = \frac{\sum_{t \in \mathcal{T}} w_t \mathbb{I}[\mathrm{rank}_t \leq k]}{\sum_{t \in \mathcal{T}} w_t}$$

where w_t is the weight assigned to the held-out item for test instance t, defined as $w_t \propto \frac{1}{C(t)^\beta}$,where $C(t)$ is the number of occurrences of the held-out item for test instance t in the training data, and $\beta \in [0, 1]$. The weights are normalized, so that $\sum_{j \in \mathcal{Y}} w_j = 1$. This popularity-weighted precision@k measure assumes that item popularity follows a power-law. By assigning more weight to less popular items, for $\beta > 0$, this measure serves to bias precision@k towards less popular items. For $\beta = 0$, we obtain the conventional precision@k measure. We set $\beta = 0.5$ in our evaluation.

Figures 2, 3, and 4 show the performance of each method and dataset for our evaluation measures. Our Bayesian low-rank DPP model is denoted as "SGHMC low-rank DPP" in these figures, in reference to its learning algorithm. Note that we could not feasibly train the full-rank DPP or AC models on the Belgian dataset, since these models do not scale to datasets with large item catalogs. The Bayesian SGHMC low-rank DPP generally outperforms the optimization-based SGA low-rank DPP by a moderate amount on most metrics and datasets, which illustrates the advantage

[3]Note that [5] is actually an implementation of PF with a social component, which was disabled in the course of our evaluations since the data does not include a social graph.

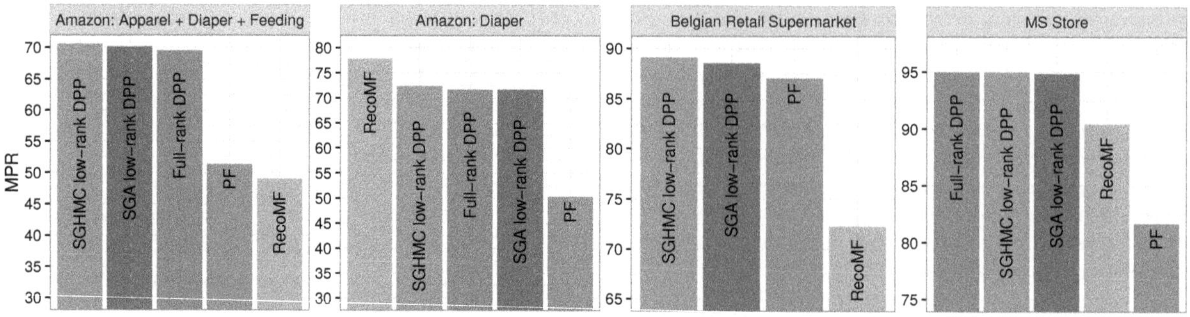

Figure 2: Mean Percentile Rank (MPR)

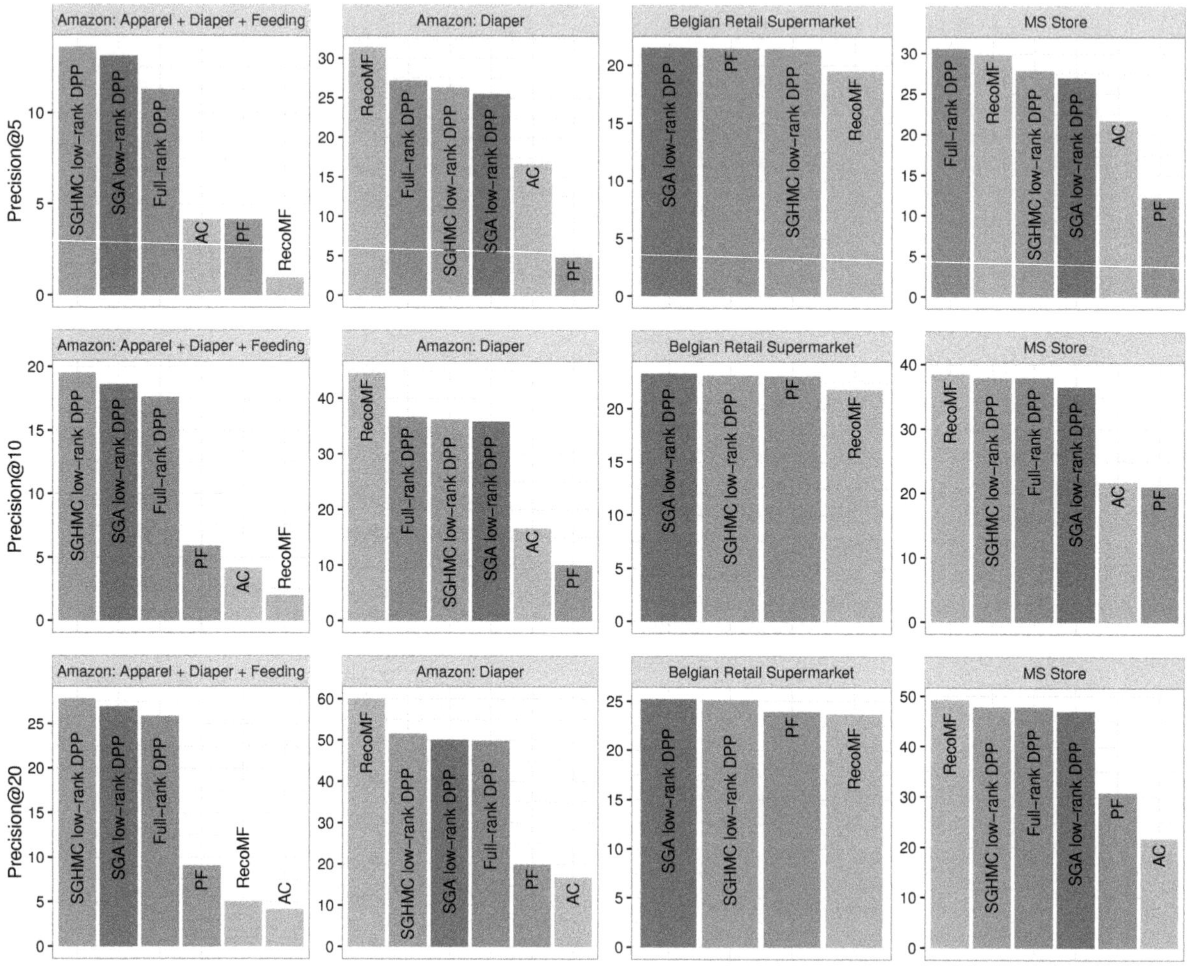

Figure 3: Precision@k

of our Bayesian approach. We attribute this improvement to the more robust regularization provided by a Bayesian model. By averaging over all settings of the parameters that are compatible with both the observed data and the prior, our Bayesian low-rank DPP model deals with uncertainty more effectively than the SGA low-rank DPP model, which commits to a single most probable setting for each parameter. An additional advantage of our Bayesian approach is that it provides a predictive distribution instead of just a single point estimate, which enables the confidence in the prediction to be estimated according to its variance. We can therefore make use of this predictive confidence when making recommendations.

We see that the RecoMF model outperforms all other models on all metrics for the Amazon Diaper dataset. For all other datasets, the Bayesian low-rank DPP model outperforms non-DPP models on MPR by a sizeable margin, and provides consistently provide high MPR across all datasets. For the precision@k metrics, the Bayesian low-rank DPP often leads or provides good performance that is close to the leader.

Limitations. The popularity-weighted precision@k results in Figure 4 highlight a limitation of the DPP models. For this metric RecoMF generally provides the best performance, with the DPP models in second place. This behavior may result from the scheme for sampling negatives by popu-

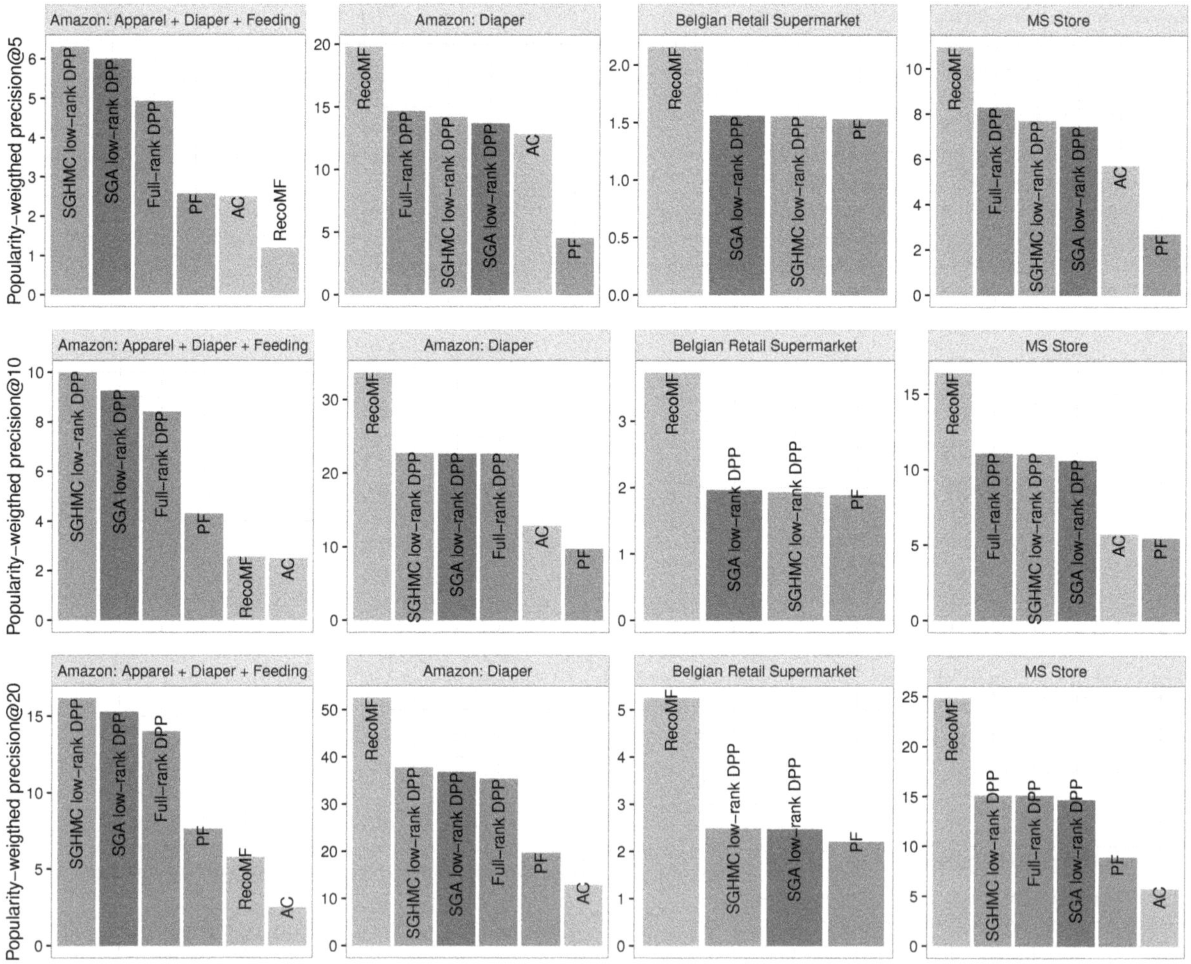

Figure 4: Popularity-weighted precision@k. These results show a limitation of the DPP models. Since this metric biases precision@k towards less popular items, we see that the RecoMF model generally provides better predictive performance for less popular items.

larity in RecoMF, which tends to improve recommendations for less popular items [27]. We conjecture that a different choice of prior for our Bayesian low-rank DPP model may improve our performance on this metric. It is also important to note the limitations of this metric, including the assumption that item popularity follows a power-law, and the power-law exponent β setting of 0.5 used when computing the metric for each dataset. Due to these limitations, the popularity-weighted precision@k results we present here may not fully reflect the empirical popularity bias actually present in the data.

4. RELATED WORK

Several algorithms for learning the DPP kernel matrix from observed data have been proposed. Ref. [12] presented one of the first methods for learning a non-parametric form of the full-rank kernel matrix, which involves an expectation-maximization (EM) algorithm. This work also considers using projected gradient ascent on the DPP log-likelihood function, but finds that this is not a viable approach since it usually results in degenerate estimates due to the projection step. In [24], a fixed-point optimization algorithm for full-rank DPP learning is described, called Picard iteration. Picard iteration has the advantage of being simple to implement and performing much faster than EM during training. Ref. [10] shows that a low-rank DPP model can be trained far more quickly than Picard iteration and therefore EM, while enabling much faster computation of predictions than is possible with any full-rank DPP model.

Ref. [1] presented Bayesian methods for learning a DPP kernel, with particular parametric forms for the similarity and quality components of the kernel. Markov chain Monte Carlo (MCMC) methods are used for sampling from the posterior distribution over kernel parameters. Furthermore, [1] uses a full-rank DPP kernel and thus shares the scalability issues common to any full-rank DPP model. In contrast to this work, and similar to [10, 12, 24], our approach uses a non-parametric form of the kernel and therefore does not assume any particular parametrization.

A method for partially learning the DPP kernel is studied in [17]. The similarity component of the DPP kernel is fixed, and a parametric from of the function for the quality component of the kernel is learned. This is a convex optimization problem, unlike the task of learning the full kernel, which is a more challenging non-convex optimization problem.

A number of approaches to the basket completion problem that we focus on in this paper have been proposed. Ref. [25] describes a user-neighborhood-based collaborative filtering method, which uses rating data in the form of binary purchases to compute the similarity between users, and then generates a purchase prediction for a user and item by computing a weighted average of the binary ratings for that item. A technique that uses logistic regression to predict if a user will purchase an item based on binary purchase scores obtained from market basket data is described in [20]. Additionally, other collaborative filtering approaches could be applied to the basket completion problem, such as the one-class matrix factorization model in [27] and Poisson factorization [13], as we illustrate in this paper.

5. CONCLUSIONS

We have presented a Bayesian method for learning a low-rank factorization of the DPP kernel from observed data. Previous low-rank DPP approaches have focused on learning a point estimate of kernel using an optimization method, which requires expensive tuning of regularization hyperparameters to prevent overfitting and provide good predictive performance. We have shown that our Bayesian low-rank DPP model generally provides better predictive performance than an optimization-based low-rank DPP model without the need for hyperparameter tuning. Our experimental evaluation using several real-world datasets in the domain of recommendations for shopping baskets also shows that in many cases our model provides better predictive performance than competing methods, including two state-of-the-art models based on matrix factorization.

6. ACKNOWLEDGEMENTS

We thank Gal Lavee and Shay Ben Elazar for many helpful discussions. We thank Nir Nice for supporting this work.

7. REFERENCES

[1] R. H. Affandi, E. Fox, R. Adams, and B. Taskar. Learning the parameters of determinantal point process kernels. In *ICML*, pages 1224–1232, 2014.

[2] R. Agrawal, T. Imieliński, and A. Swami. Mining association rules between sets of items in large databases. In *Proc. of SIGMOD 1993*, pages 207–216, 1993.

[3] T. Brijs. Retail market basket data set. In *Workshop on Frequent Itemset Mining Implementations (FIMI'03)*, 2003.

[4] T. Brijs, G. Swinnen, K. Vanhoof, and G. Wets. Using association rules for product assortment decisions: A case study. In *KDD*, pages 254–260, 1999.

[5] A. J. Chaney. Social Poisson factorization (SPF). https://github.com/ajbc/spf, 2015.

[6] A. J. Chaney, D. M. Blei, and T. Eliassi-Rad. A probabilistic model for using social networks in personalized item recommendation. In *RecSys*, pages 43–50, 2015.

[7] T. Chen, E. Fox, and C. Guestrin. Stochastic gradient hamiltonian monte carlo. In *ICML*, pages 1683–1691, 2014.

[8] F. Coenen. TLUCS KDD implementation of CBA (classification based on associations). http://www.csc.liv.ac.uk/~frans/KDD/Software/CMAR/cba.html, 2004. Department of Computer Science, The University of Liverpool, UK.

[9] S. Duane, A. D. Kennedy, B. J. Pendleton, and D. Roweth. Hybrid monte carlo. *Physics letters B*, 195(2):216–222, 1987.

[10] M. Gartrell, U. Paquet, and N. Koenigstein. Low-rank factorization of determinantal point processes for recommendation. *arXiv preprint arXiv:1602.05436*, 2016.

[11] J. Gillenwater. *Approximate inference for determinantal point processes.* PhD thesis, University of Pennsylvania, 2014.

[12] J. A. Gillenwater, A. Kulesza, E. Fox, and B. Taskar. Expectation-maximization for learning determinantal point processes. In *NIPS*, pages 3149–3157, 2014.

[13] P. Gopalan, J. M. Hofman, and D. M. Blei. Scalable recommendation with hierarchical Poisson factorization. In *UAI*, 2015.

[14] Y. Hu, Y. Koren, and C. Volinsky. Collaborative filtering for implicit feedback datasets. In *ICDM*, pages 263–272, 2008.

[15] S. Kotsiantis and D. Kanellopoulos. Association rules mining: A recent overview. *GESTS International Transactions on Computer Science and Engineering*, 32(1):71–82, 2006.

[16] A. Kulesza and B. Taskar. Structured determinantal point processes. In *NIPS*, pages 1171–1179, 2010.

[17] A. Kulesza and B. Taskar. Learning determinantal point processes. In *UAI*, 2011.

[18] A. Kulesza and B. Taskar. Determinantal point processes for machine learning. *Foundations and Trends in Machine Learning*, 5(2-3):123–286, 2012.

[19] J. T. Kwok and R. P. Adams. Priors for diversity in generative latent variable models. In *NIPS*, pages 2996–3004, 2012.

[20] J.-S. Lee, C.-H. Jun, J. Lee, and S. Kim. Classification-based collaborative filtering using market basket data. *Expert Systems with Applications*, 29(3):700–704, 2005.

[21] Y. Li, J. Hu, C. Zhai, and Y. Chen. Improving one-class collaborative filtering by incorporating rich user information. In *CIKM*, pages 959–968, 2010.

[22] B. Liu, W. Hsu, and Y. Ma. Integrating classification and association rule mining. In *KDD*, 1998.

[23] O. Macchi. The coincidence approach to stochastic point processes. *Advances in Applied Probability*, pages 83–122, 1975.

[24] Z. Mariet and S. Sra. Fixed-point algorithms for learning determinantal point processes. In *ICML*, pages 2389–2397, 2015.

[25] A. Mild and T. Reutterer. An improved collaborative filtering approach for predicting cross-category purchases based on binary market basket data. *Journal of Retailing and Consumer Services*, 10(3):123–133, 2003.

[26] R. M. Neal. Mcmc using hamiltonian dynamics. *Handbook of Markov Chain Monte Carlo*, 2:113–162, 2011.

[27] U. Paquet and N. Koenigstein. One-class collaborative filtering with random graphs. In *WWW*, pages 999–1008, 2013.

[28] H. Steck. Item popularity and recommendation accuracy. In *RecSys*, pages 125–132, 2011.

Recommending Repeat Purchases using Product Segment Statistics

Suvodip Dey
Dept. of Computer Science
Indian Institute of Technology,Kharagpur
Kharagpur 721302, India
suvodip15@gmail.com

Pabitra Mitra
Dept. of Computer Science
Indian Institute of Technology,Kharagpur
Kharagpur 721302, India
pabitra@cse.iitkgp.ernet.in

Kratika Gupta
SW Development Engineer
Flipkart Internet Private Limited
Bangalore 560034, India
kratika.gupta@flipkart.com

ABSTRACT

Repeat Purchases have become increasingly important in measuring customer's satisfaction and loyalty to e-commerce websites in regard to online shopping. In this paper, we first propose a model for estimating repeat purchase frequency in a given time period from a given product category using Poisson/Gamma model. Second, we estimate the purchase probabilities of different product types in a product category for each customer using Dirichlet model. Experimental results on data collected by a real-world e-commerce website show that it can predict a user's average repeat purchase frequency along with their product types with decent accuracy. We also argue that the output of our models can be used as prior information to enhance the performance of time-sensitive recommendation.

Keywords

Repeat purchase, Poisson/Gamma model, Dirichlet model

1. INTRODUCTION

Repeat Purchase is a common phenomenon in online shopping which can depict a customer's satisfaction and loyalty to an e-commerce website. In this work we describe a model for predicting the number of repeat purchases along with their product types from a given product category, in a given time period, for a given customer. We also show that these predictions can guide existing systems for better time-sensitive recommendation.

Repeat purchases are generally predicted using time sensitive recommender system. Several studies have been done in the field of time-sensitive recommendation. Work in [3] represented the problem of recommending the right product at right time with the help of Hazards model in survival analysis. Work in [4] clusters user-product into groups having similar purchase behaviour using topic model and then filters out products from each cluster based on purchase time interval. Work in [1] addresses the problem with the help of self-exciting temporal point process(Hawkes process) where each point represents a purchase event.

There are several challenges in predicting repeat purchase events. The major hindrance is irregular purchases by customers. Model described in [3] works well when a customer purchases consistently from the e-commerce website. But real life scenarios are different. It has been observed that some customers are active for only a short time period and remains inactive for rest of the year. On the other hand frequency of purchases for majority of the customers are extremely low whereas for some customers it is uncharacteristically high. Another issue for predicting repeat purchase is data sparsity. In [1], parameters are estimated for each user-product pair. A low rank Hawkes process has been proposed as a solution and ample data is required to get a good estimate. Work in [4] tries to compute average purchase interval for each pair of products which not only increases the computational cost but also suffers from data sparsity.

One common assumption in all the existing time sensitive recommendation is that the current purchase is dependent on previous purchase/purchases. In context of repeat purchase, this assumption must hold true in ideal case. But analysis of real purchase data shows that this dependency assumption holds true for only a few customers. For the rest of the customers, it would be better to assume that purchases over a longer time periods(several weeks or months) are independent. These observations and repeat buying theory of Ehrenberg [2] serves as the motivation of our work.

For predicting number of repeat purchases along with their product types, we use a two stage top down procedure. The first stage predicts the number of repeat purchases for a given product category and time period. In the second stage, the model matches predicted repeat purchases with possible product types. If shampoo is a product category, then a group of shampoos with similar features form a product type. The model only provides a broad estimate about repeat purchases over a longer duration of time with decent accuracy. Thus it should not be used as a standalone recommendation system for predicting repeat purchase. Instead it can be used as a supporting system in parallel with existing recommendation system where the predicted information about repeat purchases and product types can be used as prior knowledge.

2. PROPOSED APPROACH

We propose a two stage top down method to achieve our

RecSys '16, September 15-19, 2016, Boston , MA, USA
© 2016 ACM. ISBN 978-1-4503-4035-9/16/09. . . $15.00
DOI: http://dx.doi.org/10.1145/2959100.2959145

goal. The first stage predicts the number of repeat purchases from a given product category in a given time period for a given user. The second stage matches the predicted repeat purchases with possible product types. We also show how this model can be used to enhance the performance of existing time-sensitive recommendation system.

2.1 Predicting Number of Repeat Purchases

In this stage we predict the number of repeat purchases. We build a Poisson/Gamma model to estimate the average purchase frequency of each customer for a given time period and product category. Here time period is longer - several weeks or months.

Before further detail, we state three assumptions behind the model. First, repeat purchases in one product category is independent of other product categories. Repeat purchases can be dependent across several product categories but we are restricting our scope to this independent assumption. Second, purchase frequency of each customer is independent. This assumption is pretty straightforward and can be verified from purchase data. The third and the most important assumption is that the successive purchases of a customer behave as if random over a longer duration of time. A closer observation on the purchase data clearly shows that the purchase frequency of a customer is very irregular over longer time period(several weeks or months). That is why the successive purchases in a single time period tends to be effectively independent and can be regarded as if random. Moreover, we observe a very low correlation between the average purchase frequency of different time periods. So we also assume that the average purchase frequency of different time periods are independent.

Now we describe our model for estimating average purchase frequency. The occurrence of a purchase event can be viewed as arrival of a customer to purchase a product. Then our objective can be represented as the prediction of number of times a customer will arrive/purchase in a given time period. As this is a count data problem, we assume that the purchase frequency of each customer follows a Poisson distribution for a given time period. Then according to our assumption, purchase instances of all the customers in a given time period are independent and sampled from Poisson distribution. We assume that mean of the Poisson distributions of all the customers in a given time period is sampled from a gamma prior. The basic model has been described in Figure 1. We build a separate version of the same model for different time period and product category.

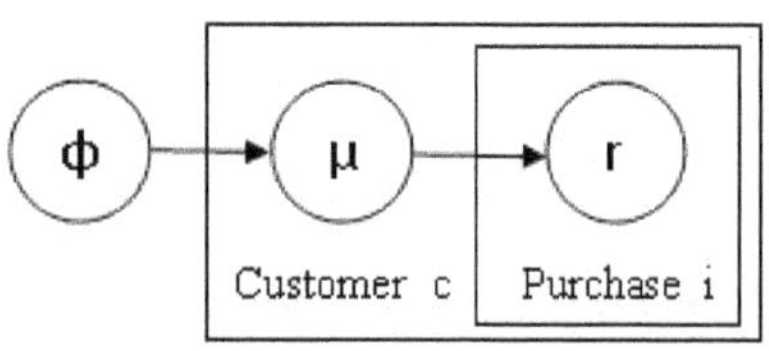

Figure 1: Distribution of each customer c in a given time period t and product category m, share information through prior ϕ. $r_{c,i}$ is the total number of purchases in the ith observation by customer c in time period t from product category m. Average purchase frequency μ_c is the mean of the Poisson distribution for customer c in time period t for product category m. μ_c of all the customers are sampled from prior $\phi = Gamma(k, a)$ where k and a are shape and scale parameter respectively.

We use maximum likelihood estimate to infer the model parameters μ_c and ϕ or $\{k, a\}$ for each time period t and product category m.

Let D be the observed purchase frequency of all the customers for a given time period and product category. From our assumption, $r_{c,i} \sim Poisson(\mu_c)$ and $\mu_c \sim Gamma(k, a)$. Then we can write the likelihood function as

$$p(D|\phi) = \prod_c \frac{e^{-n_c\mu_c}\mu_c^{\sum_{i=1}^{n_c} r_{c,i}}}{\prod_{i=1}^{n_c} r_{c,i}!} \frac{\mu_c{}^{k-1}e^{-\frac{\mu_c}{a}}}{\Gamma(k)a^k}, \quad (1)$$

where n_c is the number of observations for customer c.

The posterior distribution(θ_c) of μ_c given D follows a Gamma distribution.

$$p(\theta_c) = p(\mu_c|D) = Gamma(k', a'), \quad (2)$$

where $k' = \sum_{i=1}^{n_c} r_{c,i} + k$ and $a' = \frac{a}{1+n_c a}$.

Maximizing the likelihood in Equation 1 is equivalent to maximizing the log likelihood $L(\phi)$.

$$L(\phi) = \ln p(D|\phi)$$
$$= \sum_c -(n_c + \frac{1}{a})\mu_c + (\sum_{i=1}^{n_c} r_{c,i} + k - 1)\mu_c - \ln\Gamma(k) - k\ln(a) \quad (3)$$

We use Expectation Maximization algorithm to estimate the parameters. The process to infer parameters using EM algorithm is to iterate between the following E-step and M-step until convergence.

In the E-step, we infer μ_c as the expectation of the posterior distribution.

$$\mu_c = E[\theta_c] = k'a' \quad (4)$$

In M-step, we infer ϕ or $\{k, a\}$ that maximizes the log likelihood $L(\phi)$ in equation 3.

2.2 Predicting Product Types

The objective of this stage is to predict the product types given the number of repeat purchases. Ideally the goal was to predict products from a given product category. As the number of products in a product category can be large and dynamic, we only predict product types. Generation of product types within a product category has been discussed later. The assumptions for this stage are - (1) Each customer's choices among the available product types follow a Multinomial distribution, (2) These choice probabilities follow a Dirichlet distribution across different customers.

Let $p_{c,j}$ denote the probability of purchasing product type j by customer c for a given product category. Let $x_{c,j}$ denote the number of purchases from product type j by customer c and $\sum_{j=1}^{k} x_{c,j} = m_c$. Then the probability mass function for the Multinomial distribution of customer c can be written as

$$p(x_{c,1}, ...x_{c,k}|p_{c,1}, ...p_{c,k}, m_c) = \frac{m_c!}{\prod_{j=1}^{k} x_{c,j}!} \prod_{j=1}^{k} p_{c,j}{}^{x_{c,j}}, \quad (5)$$

where $\sum_{j=1}^{k} p_{c,j} = 1$.

The probability distribution of the choice probabilities of a customer c given prior $\alpha = \{\alpha_1, ..., \alpha_k\}$ can be written as

$$p(p_{c,1},...,p_{c,k}|\alpha_1,\alpha_1,...,\alpha_k) = \frac{\Gamma(S)}{\prod_{j=1}^{k}\Gamma(\alpha_j)}\prod_{j=1}^{k} p_{c,j}{}^{\alpha_j-1}, \quad (6)$$

where $S = \sum_{j=1}^{k} \alpha_j$.

Let D be the observed data of purchased product types by all customers. Then we can write the likelihood function as

$$p(D|\alpha_1,\alpha_2,...,\alpha_k) = \prod_c \left\{ \frac{m_c!}{\prod_{j=1}^{k} x_{c,j}!} \prod_{j=1}^{k} p_{c,j}{}^{x_{c,j}} \frac{\Gamma(S)}{\prod_{j=1}^{k}\Gamma(\alpha_j)} \prod_{j=1}^{k} p_{c,j}{}^{\alpha_j-1} \right\} \quad (7)$$

Posterior distribution(θ_c) of choice probabilities given D follows a Dirichlet distribution.

$$p(\theta_c|D) = Dirichlet(\alpha_1{}',\alpha_1{}',...,\alpha_k{}') \quad (8)$$

where $\alpha_j{}' = \alpha_j + \sum_{x_{c,j}{}^{(i)} \in D} x_{c,j}{}^{(i)}$.

Here we have to estimate the choice probabilities $p_{c,j}$ and prior α for each product category. Again we use Expectation Maximization algorithm in a similar fashion.

In the E-step we infer the choice probabilities from posterior distribution of each customer.

$$p_{c,j} = E[\theta_c] = \frac{\alpha_j{}'}{\sum_{i=1}^{k} \alpha_i{}'} \quad (9)$$

In M-step, we infer α that maximizes the log likelihood of equation 7.

A product type is a group of similar products within a single product category. In this work we used k-means clustering algorithm to generate product types. We used product price and brand equity as clustering features as they held good partitioning attribute for the products of our dataset. Let x be total number of sales in a particular brand b. Let y be the total number of purchases by the users of brand b from the entire product category of b. Then we can denote brand equity as $(y-x)/x$ where a lower value indicates higher brand equity and vice versa.

2.3 Application of the model

In this section we discuss how our model can be used to enhance the performance of existing time-sensitive recommendation system. Predicted product types can help reducing the search space of the recommendation. On the other hand, predicted number of repeat purchases can be used in various ways for guiding the time-sensitive recommendation. Here we discuss one such application in detail.

Let a recommender system is recommending a product at time t for customer c and estimates the probability of purchase as q. Let t belongs to time period T. For example, if we assume time period of one month and t is some date of January, then time period T is the entire January month. Let the category of this product be m. Let y_c be the number of products already purchased in T by customer c from category m. Let μ_c be the average purchase frequency of this customer in category m and time period T. Then the probability of purchasing $(y_c+1)^{th}$ product given μ_c can be written as

$$p((y_c+1)|\mu_c) = \begin{cases} e^{-\frac{(y_c+1)-\mu_c}{\sigma}}, & \text{if } (y_c+1) > \mu_c \\ 1, & \text{otherwise} \end{cases} \quad (10)$$

We can now use q and $p((y_c+1)|\mu_c)$ to get the updated purchase probability as

$$q' = q * p((y_c+1)|\mu_c) \quad (11)$$

The basic idea is to penalize the probability score when the number of purchase exceeds average purchase frequency. Here we have used an exponential kernel for this task.

Evaluation of this part requires data regarding actual recommendations along with their time. We could not run our evaluation due to lack of this ground data. Instead we give a theoretical justification about the possible impact on time-sensitive recommendation. Let a user has already purchased 3 diapers in a given time period. Let the average purchase frequency for this user in the given time period be 2. Now let a recommender system recommend another diaper to this user in the same time period. Surveys show that this type of scenario is frequent in real-world e-commerce websites which also hurts customer satisfaction with the recommender system. Thus, prior information regarding average purchase frequency can certainly help to tackle this type of situations. Penalizing the probability score is one such solution to avoid over optimistic recommendation. It can also be used in dealing with situations where number of recommendations are lesser than average purchase frequency.

3. EXPERIMENTAL RESULTS

3.1 Dataset

We have used purchase data collected on a real-world e-commerce website as our dataset. Training data contained purchase history from 2014-01-01 to 2014-12-31. Duration of test data was from 2015-01-01 to 2015-12-31. Analysis of the raw data suggested that repeat purchases in FMCG(fast-moving-consumer-goods) products are more frequent than other products. That is why we used sales data and product details of some popular FMCG products(Shampoo,Soap,Diaper and Deodorant) as our data source.

3.2 Evaluation Methodology and Result

We used two different methods to evaluate our two models as described next.

3.2.1 Evaluation of predicted repeat purchase

For evaluating the prediction of repeat purchase, we analyze the standard deviation of test data from the estimated average purchase frequency. Let μ_c and x_c be the estimated and actual purchase frequency respectively of a customer c for product category m and time period t. Then we use the following equation to calculate the standard deviation of our model(σ_{Model}) for time period t and product category m

$$\sigma_{Model} = \sqrt{\frac{1}{N}\sum_{c=1}^{N}(x_c-\mu_c)^2} \quad (12)$$

Let σ_{Mean} denotes the standard deviation of test data when average purchase frequency for each customer is estimated as the sample mean. We compute σ_{Model} and σ_{Mean}

for different time period and product category. Results has been shown in Table 1 and 2.

Table 1: **Std Deviation for Time Period of 2 months**

Period	Exp Type	Diaper	Deo	Shampoo	Soap
Jan-Feb	σ_{Model}	1.067	0.916	0.642	0.964
	σ_{Mean}	1.293	1.110	0.804	1.147
Mar-Apr	σ_{Model}	0.821	0.913	0.673	0.951
	σ_{Mean}	1.066	1.130	0.871	1.128
May-Jun	σ_{Model}	0.662	0.902	0.641	0.978
	σ_{Mean}	0.909	1.113	0.816	1.201
Jul-Aug	σ_{Model}	0.817	0.852	0.554	0.909
	σ_{Mean}	0.924	0.901	0.772	0.941
Sep-Oct	σ_{Model}	0.815	0.764	0.584	1.017
	σ_{Mean}	0.941	0.803	0.846	1.155
Nov-Dec	σ_{Model}	0.786	0.728	0.582	0.938
	σ_{Mean}	0.879	0.859	0.788	1.014

Table 2: **Std Deviation for Time Period of 3 months**

Period	Exp Type	Diaper	Deo	Shampoo	Soap
Jan-Mar	σ_{Model}	1.372	1.148	0.842	1.208
	σ_{Mean}	1.653	1.402	1.039	1.421
Apr-Jun	σ_{Model}	0.934	1.155	0.831	1.246
	σ_{Mean}	1.247	1.415	1.038	1.489
Jul-Sep	σ_{Model}	1.072	0.971	0.656	1.085
	σ_{Mean}	1.301	1.318	0.989	1.228
Oct-Dec	σ_{Model}	1.013	0.913	0.705	1.213
	σ_{Mean}	1.269	1.245	0.954	1.343

Comparison shows that the value of σ_{Model} is less than σ_{Mean} for all the cases. Therefore our model gives better prediction of average purchase frequency in comparison to simply using sample mean for the same task. We performed the evaluation taking different time periods. Results for time period 2 and 3 months has been shown in Table 1 and 2 respectively. We observe same trend in results for different time periods which show that our model works better even if the time period is variable.

3.2.2 Evaluation of predicted product types

For evaluating this section, we compute conversion rate of products using estimated purchase probability of product types. Here conversion rate is the ratio between number of products correctly recommended and number of products actually purchased. We compare the result with conversion rate using highest selling product types in a product category.

Let T_c be the total number of purchases from product category m by customer c. Let P_c be the list of top k product types based on estimated purchase probabilities for a given customer c and product category m. Let S_c be the total number of purchases from product types enlisted in P_c by customer c. Let f_m denote the average conversion rate of product types using P_c. Then f_m can be written as

$$f_m = \frac{1}{N} \sum_{c=1}^{N} \frac{S_c}{T_c}, \tag{13}$$

where N is total number of customers in test data.

Let Q be the list of top k highest selling product types from product category m common to all users. Let $S_c{}'$ be the total number of purchases from product types enlisted in Q by customer c. Let g_m denote the average conversion rate of product types using Q. Then g_m can be written as

$$g_m = \frac{1}{N} \sum_{c=1}^{N} \frac{S_c{}'}{T_c} \tag{14}$$

The results of f_m and g_m has been compared in Table 3. We performed this evaluation for different values of k where each product category had 20 product types.

Table 3: **Evaluation of conversion rates**

top k	Exp Type	Diaper	Deo	Shampoo	Soap
k=1	f_m	0.618	0.338	0.434	0.411
	g_m	0.482	0.217	0.256	0.255
k=2	f_m	0.816	0.497	0.598	0.564
	g_m	0.814	0.352	0.335	0.412
k=3	f_m	0.892	0.621	0.708	0.656
	g_m	0.853	0.471	0.493	0.631
k=4	f_m	0.931	0.724	0.791	0.749
	g_m	0.891	0.652	0.547	0.704
k=5	f_m	0.951	0.801	0.832	0.814
	g_m	0.917	0.726	0.765	0.731

Comparison shows that usage of estimated purchase probabilities results in better performance than using highest selling product types. Conversion rate of our model is dependent on the clustering of products. A more sophisticated clustering algorithm can be used for better accuracy.

4. CONCLUSION

In this paper, we developed two models for predicting number of repeat purchases and product types respectively. We used Poisson/Gamma model for estimating average purchase frequency whereas Dirichlet model for estimating purchase probability of a product type. We also argued that the output of our models can guide existing system for better time-sensitive recommendation. In the future, we want to explore the dependency of repeat purchases across different product categories.

5. REFERENCES

[1] N. Du, Y. Wang, N. He, J. Sun, and L. Song. Time-sensitive recommendation from recurrent user activities. In C. Cortes, N. D. Lawrence, D. D. Lee, M. Sugiyama, and R. Garnett, editors, *Advances in Neural Information Processing Systems 28*, pages 3474–3482. Curran Associates, Inc., 2015.

[2] A. Ehrenberg. *Repeat-buying: Facts, Theory, and Applications*. Charles Griffin Book. Griffin, 1988.

[3] J. Wang and Y. Zhang. Opportunity model for e-commerce recommendation: Right product; right time. In *Proceedings of the 36th International ACM SIGIR Conference on Research and Development in Information Retrieval*, SIGIR '13, pages 303–312, New York, NY, USA, 2013. ACM.

[4] G. Zhao, M. L. Lee, and H. Wynne. Utilizing purchase intervals in latent clusters for product recommendation. In *Proceedings of the 8th Workshop on Social Network Mining and Analysis*, SNAKDD'14, pages 4:1–4:9, New York, NY, USA, 2014. ACM.

Bayesian Personalized Ranking with Multi-Channel User Feedback

Babak Loni[1], Roberto Pagano[1,2], Martha Larson[1,3], Alan Hanjalic[1]
[1]Delft University of Technology, Netherlands
[2]Politecnico di Milano, Italy
[3]Radboud University Nijmegen, Netherlands
{b.loni, m.a.larson, a.hanjalic}@tudelft.nl, roberto.pagano@polimi.it

ABSTRACT

Pairwise learning-to-rank algorithms have been shown to allow recommender systems to leverage unary user feedback. We propose Multi-feedback Bayesian Personalized Ranking (MF-BPR), a pairwise method that exploits different types of feedback with an extended sampling method. The feedback types are drawn from different "channels", in which users interact with items (e.g., clicks, likes, listens, follows, and purchases). We build on the insight that different kinds of feedback, e.g., a click versus a like, reflect different levels of commitment or preference. Our approach differs from previous work in that it exploits multiple sources of feedback simultaneously during the training process. The novelty of MF-BPR is an extended sampling method that equates feedback sources with "levels" that reflect the expected contribution of the signal. We demonstrate the effectiveness of our approach with a series of experiments carried out on three datasets containing multiple types of feedback. Our experimental results demonstrate that with a right sampling method, MF-BPR outperforms BPR in terms of accuracy. We find that the advantage of MF-BPR lies in its ability to leverage level information when sampling negative items.

1. INTRODUCTION

In many domains, users provide unary feedback via a number of different 'channels'. For example, online marketplaces collect view, add-to-cart and buy signals, and music platforms log listen, favorite and add-to-playlist events. Bayesian Personalized Ranking [8], a pair-wise learning-to-rank method that learns the preferences of the users by sampling pairs, allows recommender systems to learn effectively from unary feedback. However, current instantiations of BPR fall short of taking full advantage of the entire range of different types of feedback that are available in certain domains.

In this paper, we propose an approach called Multi-Feedback Bayesian Personalized Ranking (MF-BPR). The innovation of MF-BRP is a sampling method designed to simultaneously exploit unary feedback from multiple channels during training. New sampling methods have proven effective in improving BPR [7]. However, previous attempts to leverage different sources of unary feedback have focused on channels individually, e.g., [5].

RecSys '16, September 15-19, 2016, Boston , MA, USA
© 2016 ACM. ISBN 978-1-4503-4035-9/16/09. . . $15.00
DOI: http://dx.doi.org/10.1145/2959100.2959163

The key to our approach is to map different feedback channels to different 'levels' that reflect the contribution that each type of feedback can have in the training phase. BPR samples pairs such that the first item in the pair is preferred to the second item. The levels of MF-BPR help to automatically direct sampling to focus on the most informative pairs. The appeal of the approach is that it takes advantage of the available information consistently with the intuition that some user feedback signals are more reliable or meaningful than others.

The paper is organized as follows. In the next section, we cover relevant related work. Then, we present MF-BPR in detail, and introduce the three data sets on which we test it. Next, we report experimental results, which demonstrate the ability of MF-BPR to improve over BPR. Finally, we close with a discussion of the results, which sheds light on improvement delivered by judicious sampling of the 'negative' item of the item pair.

2. RELATED WORK

Since the BPR was introduced [8], many improvements have been proposed. MF-BPR belongs to that class of approaches that propose sampling refinements. The initial contribution in this direction was made by [3] who weights item sampling by popularity. Recently, [7] has proposed adaptive sampling, which over-samples informative pairs based on the current model. MF-BPR is similar to this approach in its focus on informative pairs, but its sampling is driven by feedback channels. In the remainder of this section, we cover a selection of the various techniques that have been proposed to exploit feedback from different sources, providing key examples of each, and noting the differences with MF-BPR.

Matrix factorization approaches have attempted to simultaneously factorize multiple matrices. The authors of [11] take into account different signals from social networks (comment, re-share, or create-post) with separate factorizations, which are used to make predictions that are subsequently combined. The work of [4] exploits multiple types of relations, and is directed at the cold start problem. In contrast, the 'multi' of MF-BPR refers to multiple types of feedback reflecting the same user-item relation.

Other approaches have leveraged the fact that ratings represent different levels of user feedback. A list-wise optimization criterion is proposed in [9], which allowed learning-to-rank to take advantage of graded feedback. Most closely related to our work is [5], which modified the BPR algorithm using graded implicit feedback derived from ratings and interaction counts, and also explores the contribution of temporal information. The outlook of the paper points out the promise of hybrid approaches. Our MF-BPR can be considered hybrid, since it simultaneously uses different sources of feedback. However, it differs from [5] in that it avoids hand-chosen weights, and, more significantly, uses multiple feedback channels simultaneously.

3. MULTI-FEEDBACK BPR

BPR-MF is based on the insight that user feedback collected via various channels reflects different strengths of user preference, and the sampling method of BPR can exploit these differences. In short, we allow BPR to learn from the fact that, e.g., a click represents a different level of commitment or preference than a 'like'.

For a given training set S consisting of user-item pairs (u, i), standard BPR creates tuples (u, i, j) by sampling an observed feedback pair (u, i) from S and a negative item j not observed with u. For each sampled tuple, the BPR algorithm updates the parameters with Stochastic Gradient Descent in such a way that i is ranked higher than j. MF-BPR maps different types of feedback onto *levels*, which allow us to constrain sampling to reflect the preference strengths that we associate with the feedback types. Figure 1 compares the standard BPR sampling method (A) with the extended sampling method used by MF-BPR (B), which imposes an order on the types of positive feedback, that makes finer-grained differences between feedback available during the learning phase.

We now express formally how MF-BPR takes advantage of feedback levels. Let $\mathbb{L} = (L_1, \ldots, L_p)$ represent a given ordered set of levels in a dataset such that a feedback in L_i is a stronger signal of interest compared to a feedback in L_{i+1}, that is $L_i \succ L_{i+1}$. For generality, the unobserved feedback is also considered to belong to a level L_{uo} such that for each positive feedback level L_i and negative feedback level L_j, $L_i \succ L_{uo}$ and $L_{uo} \succ L_j$. The set of training feedback in level L is denoted by S_L. We further define $\mathbb{L}^+$ and $\mathbb{L}^-$ as positive and negative feedback levels. In the standard BPR, $|\mathbb{L}| = 2$, $|\mathbb{L}^+| = 1$ and $|\mathbb{L}^-| = 0$ since there is only one level for positive and one level for unobserved feedback and there is no explicit negative feedback. We also define $I_{L,u}$ as the items in level L that user u interacted with and I_u as all items that u interacted with (in all levels). The set of all combinations of preferences in Multi-feedback BPR D_{MF} can be defined as:

$$D_{MF} = \{(u, i, j) | i \in I_{L,u} \wedge j \in I_{N,u} \wedge L \in \mathbb{L}^+ \wedge L \succ N\} \quad (1)$$

In the standard BPR the tuples (u, i, j) are sampled uniformly but in MF-BPR we introduce a non-uniform sampler that takes into account the level (importance) of the feedback channel. To use multiple levels, MF-BPR requires sampling L and N from $\mathbb{L}$, and then the tuples (u, i, j) can be sampled with respect to the given levels. The positive item is sampled by sampling an observed feedback from S using sampling distribution $p(u, i, L)$, which also samples the positive level L. The probability distribution $p(u, i, L)$ can be further expanded as $p(u, i, L) = p(u, i|L)p(L)$ such that $p(u, i|L)$ is a uniform distribution over S_L and $p(L)$ is the sampling distribution of level L. A trivial choice for $p(L)$ would be a uniform distribution over all levels. However, with a uniform distribution, levels with small cardinality will be oversampled, which can result in being a poor sampling. We propose a non-uniform distribution for $p(L)$ where the cardinality of feedback as well as the importance of a level is taken into account with a weight factor. The probability distribution $p(L)$ is defined by:

$$p(L) = \frac{w_L |S_L|}{\sum_{Q \in \mathbb{L}^+} w_Q |S_Q|} \quad (2)$$

where w_L is the weight of level L. With equal weights, positive items are sampled uniformly from all levels. This would be equivalent to the positive sampler of standard BPR. The weight values can be defined non-uniformly to reflect the importance of levels. The weight parameters can be influenced by the available context or other properties of the levels. In our experiments, we found that the inverse rank of positive levels are good candidates for weights (i.e., $w_1 = 1, w_2 = \frac{1}{2}, \ldots$). If the order of levels is not known a priori (for example whether a like should be considered more important that a share or vice versa), the optimal weights can be approximated by using a hyper-parameter search algorithm.

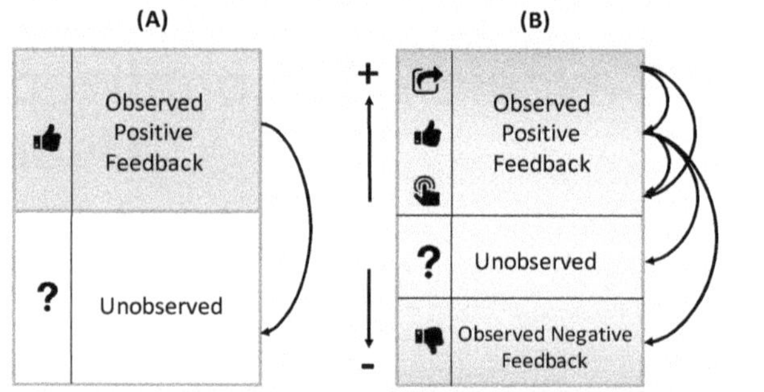

Figure 1: Sampling item pairs in BPR(A) and MF-BPR (B). The arrows show preferences. In MF-BPR any item at the higher level is preferred over all items in the lower levels. In the standard BPR, the only way of sampling item pairs is to sample from observed positive feedback and unobserved feedback.

To sample negative item j, the level of the positive item should be given so that the sampler samples an item from one of the levels below it. Given the positive level L and a positive user-item pair (u, i), we denote $p(j, N|u, L)$ as the sampling distribution of and negative sample j and its corresponding level N. Similar to the positive sampler, the negative sampler can be expanded as $p(j, N|u, L) = p(j|u, L, N)p(N|u, L)$ where $p(j|u, L, N)$ is the negative item sampler and $p(N|u, L)$ is the conditional negative level sampler. We also propose a non-uniform negative item sampler, similar to (2), that takes into account the cardinality and the weights of the levels. The negative level sampler $p(N|u, L)$ is defined as:

$$p(N|u, L) = \begin{cases} \frac{(1-\beta) w_N |S_N|}{\sum_{Q \prec L} w_Q |S_Q|} & N \neq L_{uo} \\ \beta & N = L_{uo} \end{cases} \quad (3)$$

such that $0 \leq \beta \leq 1$ is a parameter that controls the ratio of unobserved feedback in the sampling. For the standard BPR $\beta = 1$, as all negative items are sampled from the unobserved feedback. The right value for β can be found experimentally. In our experiments, we found that with high values of β the model is more accurate. Our observation about the right value of β is discussed in more detail in Section 4.

Similar to the standard BPR, the negative sampler $p(j|u, L, N)$ can sample negative item uniformly from $I_{N,u}$ if $N \neq L_{uo}$ or from $I \backslash I_u$ if $N = L_{uo}$. We denote $p_{uni}(j|u, L, N)$ as the *uniform* negative item sampler which can be defined as:

$$p_{uni}(j|u, L, N) = \begin{cases} \frac{1}{|I_{N,u}|} & N \neq L_{uo} \wedge j \in I_{N,u} \\ \frac{1}{|I \backslash I_u|} & N = L_{uo} \wedge j \in I \backslash I_u \\ 0 & \text{otherwise} \end{cases} \quad (4)$$

In addition, we also propose a *multi-level* item sampler with a non-uniform sampler when N is the unobserved level L_{uo}. We define the multi-level negative item sampler $p_{ml}(j|u, L, N)$ as:

$$p_{ml}(j|u, L, N) = \begin{cases} \frac{1}{|I_{N,u}|} & N \neq L_{uo} \wedge j \in I_{N,u} \\ p(j, u', L'|u) & N = L_{uo} \wedge j \in I \backslash I_u \\ 0 & \text{otherwise} \end{cases} \quad (5)$$

where $u' \neq u$ and $L' \in \mathbb{L}^+$. Here, if the given level L is an observed level, the negative item is sampled uniformly the same as the uniform-item sampler. However, if the the given level $N =$

```
procedure LEARN MF-BPR(S, β, W, 𝕃)
    initialize Θ
    repeat
        draw (u, i, L) from p(u, i, L)
        draw N from p(N|u, L)
        draw j from p(j|u, L, N)
        update Θ with BPR update rule [8]
    until convergence
    return Θ
end procedure
```

Figure 2: Learning MF-BPR with Stochastic Gradient Descent.

L_{uo}, the negative item is sampled non-uniformly with respect to $p(j, u', L'|u)$. Here the probability of sampling a negative item depends on its feedback from other users. Items that are more popular and have enjoyed user interactions from stronger levels, have a higher chance of being sampled. In other words, if $N = L_{uo}$ the sampler selects feedback by sampling a tuple (u', j, L') for which an interaction between u and j is not observed. Note that u' and L' for the tuple are subsequently discarded.

By sampling the tuple (u, i, j) the parameters of the model can be updated via Stochastic Gradient Descent (SGD) similarly to standard BPR. Note that here the parameters β, the weights of the levels W and the order of levels in $\mathbb{L}$ are given a priori. Figure 2 lists the learning algorithm of BPR with Multi-feedback sampler.

4. DATASET AND EXPERIMENTS

The MF-BPR is evaluated on three datasets and its performance is compared with different methods using 4-fold cross validation. The ground truth and relevant recommendations however, are different in the three datasets depending on the problem. The datasets, the splitting strategy and the feedback signals of the datasets are described bellow. Dataset statistics are presented in Table 1.

Kollekt.fm Kollekt.fm is an online music discovery platform. For Kollekt.fm the recommender task is to recommend playlists to users. Kollekt.fm is interested in increasing the number of followers for their playlists, so we predict follows. This dataset contains three different levels of feedback relevant to playlists: `follows`, which is considered the highest level of feedback. `listening` which refers to the ratio of the listening time to a playlist to the total time a user listened to any playlist. `favorites` is the ratio of the songs in a playlist which are favorited to the total number of songs in the playlist. For both listening and favorites we used only the occurrences with a value greater than a specific threshold. Due to space constraints, we report results setting both thresholds to 0.1.

XING XING[1] is a social network and a job discovery framework. This dataset is related to the job postings of in XING. This is the data used for the RecSys 2016 challenge. It contains four different levels of feedback: `click`, `bookmark`, `reply` and `remove`. To be compliant with XING's needs, we used 'click', 'bookmark' and 'reply' as positive feedback for both training and ground truth and 'remove' as negative. Adopting XING's own valuation of user feedback, we used reply as the highest level, then bookmark and click as the lowest level of positive feedback. In order to reduce data sparsity and the size of the dataset we filtered out all the users and jobs that have less than five instances of feedback.

MovieLens-1M For the sake of completeness, we also report the results for the MovieLens dataset [2], containing movie ratings on a 1-5 scale. We considered each discrete rating as a different level of feedback. For each user, we took the levels above the user's average rating as positive feedback, both for training and ground truth, and the ones below as negative. We consider a recommendation relevant if user has rated it above his average.

[1]http://xing.com/

[2]http://grouplens.org/datasets/movielens/

Table 1: The statistics of the datasets used in this work.

Dataset	#user	#item	#feedback	%density	#levels
Kollect	15972	34910	195k	0.0350	3
ML1M	6040	3706	1000k	4.4684	5
XING	11324	9857	569k	0.5097	4

The experiments are implemented with an open source toolkit developed by the authors and available online [6]. To measure performance we calculated Mean Reciprocal Rank (MRR), recall, precision, all at 10, as well as and mean average precision and nDCG. For calculating these metrics, we applied the approach known as *One-plus-random* [2, 1]. Here we report MRR@10. In the interest of space, we simply state that the other metrics were comparable.

The three datasets are evaluated with four different algorithms:

MF-BPR-UNI This is Multi-Feedback BPR with uniform item sampling. The positive item is sampled with the level-based sampler and the negative item is sampled according to (4).

MF-BPR-ML This is another variation of Multi-Feedback BPR with multi-level negative feedback sampler where negative feedback are sampled non-uniformly according to (5).

BPR This is the standard BPR [7] where all positive feedback are assumed to be equally strong.

BPR-Dynamic This is BPR with dynamic sampling method [7]. The items are re-scored after every few iterations and they are sampled proportional to their current score.

We also compared our results with random and popularity baseline. The popularity baseline exploits the positive feedback from all channels without differentiating levels. In all our experiments, we used 50 latent features and 100 iterations. For the SGD algorithm, learning-rate is set to 0.05 and the regularization parameter λ is set to 0.002 for all the four algorithms.

Figure 3 compares the performance of the two sampling models of MF-BPR with previous BPR methods. We report on the y-axis MRR@10 and on the x-axis the ratio of unobserved sampled items (i.e., parameter β), to see the influence of β on performance of MF-BPR. As we can see from the figure, increasing β improves the accuracy of the model. This observation implies that a combination of an observed and an unobserved item in a pair is a better candidate to train the model. This validates the 'missing not at random' hypothesis which is highlighted by [10]. That is, the missing (unobserved) items are most likely missed as negative items. Another implication is that the presence of feedback in lower levels indicates that all positive levels contribute in defining what is preferred by the user w.r.t to the unobserved feedback.

The performance improvement of MF-BPR-ML can be attributed to the fact that it selects unobserved feedback as negative samples using a non-uniform sampling strategy that is sensitive to the strength of the feedback given by other users. However an interesting observation is that the MF-BPR-ML method performs better than the standard BPR and MF-BPR-UNI in the XING and Kollect.fm datasets, while it performs worse in the Movielens dataset. This can be explained by the fact that MovieLens is rather a dense dataset and a uniform-item sampler can sample a good enough representative of items.

Another interesting result is that in the Kollekt.fm dataset the popularity-based method outperforms BPR. An explanation can be found in Figure 4 where the popularity-skewness of the three datasets

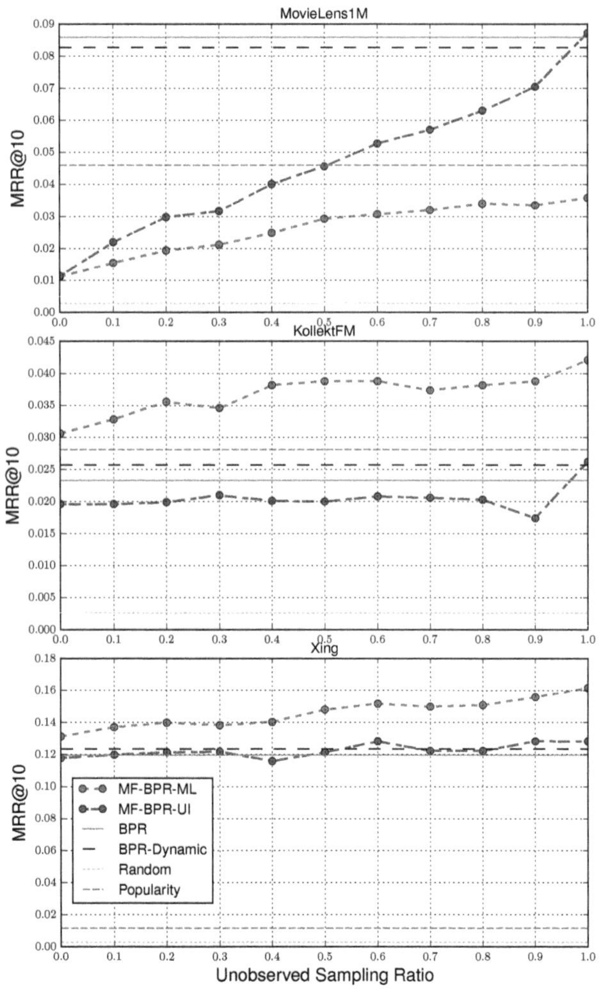

Figure 3: Comparison of results for our multi-level methods and the original and dynamic BPR algorithm. The horizontal axis represents the unobserved sampling ratio (β).

are plotted. The y axis represents the ratio of interactions for a given ratio of items on the x axis, sorted by decreasing popularity. Kollekt.fm is the most *popularity skewed* dataset, where 1% of the items accounts for 40% of the interactions. A consistent behavior of the popularity baseline can be found in the other datasets: the less the dataset is popularity skewed, i.e. the feedback is well distributed among the items, the worst are the popularity-based performances.

5. CONCLUSION

In this work we introduced MF-BPR, an extension to BPR that can be used when multiple types of feedback are available. MF-BPR extends the standard BPR sampling model by exploiting the difference in strength among user feedback 'channels'. From our experiments we can draw two insights. The first is that the data is 'not missing at random', but rather the missing data can be regarded as negative feedback. This supports the underlying assumptions in the BPR model and it is further validated by the fact that sampling negative items from the lower levels of observed feedback decrease the overall quality of the recommendation algorithm. Second, we showed that sampling the negative item with a level-based method has a substantial impact on the quality of recommendations. In future work, we will learn the optimal relative ordering of the levels automatically, and also explore the contribution of additional context information.

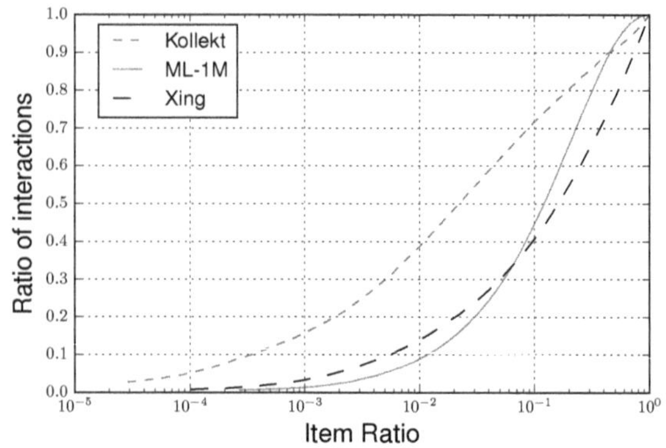

Figure 4: Popularity skewness of the datasets

Acknowledgment

This research is supported by an EU-FP7 project under grant agreements no. 610594 (CrowdRec), and Dutch national e-infrastructure with the support of SURF Cooperative.

References

[1] Alejandro Bellogin, Pablo Castells, and Ivan Cantador. Precision-oriented evaluation of recommender systems: An algorithmic comparison. In *RecSys '11*, 2011.

[2] Paolo Cremonesi, Yehuda Koren, and Roberto Turrin. Performance of recommender algorithms on top-n recommendation tasks. In *ACM RecSys '10*, 2010.

[3] Zeno Gantner, Lucas Drumond, Christoph Freudenthaler, and Lars Schmidt-Thieme. Bayesian personalized ranking for non-uniformly sampled items. *JMLR W&CP, Jan*, 2012.

[4] Artus Krohn-Grimberghe, Lucas Drumond, Christoph Freudenthaler, and Lars Schmidt-Thieme. Multi-relational matrix factorization using bayesian personalized ranking for social network data. In *WSDM '12*, pages 173–182, 2012.

[5] Lukas Lerche and Dietmar Jannach. Using graded implicit feedback for bayesian personalized ranking. In *ACM RecSys '14*, pages 353–356, 2014.

[6] Babak Loni and Alan Said. Wraprec: An easy extension of recommender system libraries. In *Proceedings of ACM RecSys 2014*, RecSys '14, 2014.

[7] Steffen Rendle and Christoph Freudenthaler. Improving pairwise learning for item recommendation from implicit feedback. In *WSDM '14*, pages 273–282, 2014.

[8] Steffen Rendle, Christoph Freudenthaler, Zeno Gantner, and Lars Schmidt-Thieme. BPR: Bayesian personalized ranking from implicit feedback. In *UAI '09*, pages 452–461, 2009.

[9] Yue Shi, Alexandros Karatzoglou, Linas Baltrunas, Martha Larson, and Alan Hanjalic. xCLiMF: optimizing expected reciprocal rank for data with multiple levels of relevance. In *ACM RecSys '13*, pages 431–434, 2013.

[10] Harald Steck. Training and testing of recommender systems on data missing not at random. In *KDD '10*, pages 713–722, 2010.

[11] Zhe Zhao, Zhiyuan Cheng, Lichan Hong, and Ed H Chi. Improving user topic interest profiles by behavior factorization. In *WWW '15*, pages 1406–1416, 2015.

Mendeley: Recommendations for Researchers

Saúl Vargas, Maya Hristakeva and Kris Jack
Mendeley Ltd.
{firstname.lastname}@mendeley.com

Abstract

For a researcher, keeping up with what is going on in their research field can be a difficult and time-consuming task. For example, a fresh PhD student may want to know what are the relevant papers matching their research interests. An assistant professor may like to be up-to-date with what their colleagues are publishing. A professor might want to be notified about funding opportunities relevant to the work done in their research group. Since the volume of published research and research activity is constantly growing, it is becoming increasingly more difficult for researchers to be able to manage and filter through the research information flow.

In this challenging context, Mendeley's mission is to become the world's "research operating system". We do this not only by providing our well-know reference management system, but also by providing discovery capabilities for researchers on different kinds of entities, such as articles and profiles. In our talk, we will share Mendeley's experiences with building our article and profile recommendation systems, the challenges that we have faced and the solutions that we have put in place. We will discuss how we address different users' needs with our data and algorithm infrastructure to achieve good user experience.

Keywords

research article recommendation; people recommendation

RecSys '16 September 15-19, 2016, Boston , MA, USA

ACM ISBN 978-1-4503-4035-9/16/09.

DOI: http://dx.doi.org/10.1145/2959100.2959116

Bio

Saúl Vargas is a Senior Data Scientist at Mendeley and Elsevier, where he is working on a variety of tools and products powering recommendations for researchers. Before that, he was working as a postdoc at the University of Glasgow doing research in the area of Social Media Analysis. He has a PhD in the area of recommender systems from the Autonomous University of Madrid under the supervision of Prof. Pablo Castells.

Maya Hristakeva is a Lead Data Scientist at Mendeley and Elsevier working on building tools to help researchers connect to their research and to collaborators. Her research interests are in the areas of machine learning, recommender systems and optimization algorithms. She is also interested in building end-to-end data products: from algorithms to good user experience. Prior to Mendeley, Maya worked as a Researcher at startups focused on behavioural targeting and recommendations as well as on non-invasive glucose measurement in humans.

Kris Jack is the Chief Data Scientist at Mendeley and Head of Data Science at Elsevier. He is passionate about making software that helps people to understand and communicate complex information as well as make new discoveries. His main research interests lie in the fields of Recommendation Systems, Information Retrieval, Information Extraction, Machine Learning, and Artificial Intelligence. He is also passionate about transforming technology into useful products for real users and the team dynamics involved in getting stuff done.

When Recommendation Systems Go Bad

Evan Estola

Meetup

evan@meetup.com

ABSTRACT

Machine learning and recommendations systems have changed the way we interact with not just the internet, but some of the basic services that we use to organize and run our life. As the people that build these systems, we have a social responsibility to consider how these systems affect people, and furthermore, we should do whatever we can to prevent these models from perpetuating some of the prejudice and bias that exist in our society today. This talk will cover some of the recommendation systems that have gone wrong across various industries, and attempt to provide some solutions for raising awareness and prevention. Approaches that will be explored include using interpretable models, using ensemble models to separate features that shouldn't interact, and designing test data sets for capturing accidental bias.

RecSys'16, September 15–19, 2016, Boston, MA, USA.

ACM ISBN 978-1-4503-4035-9/16/09.

DOI: http://dx.doi.org/10.1145/2959100.2959117

Short CV of the Presenter

Evan is a Lead Machine Learning Engineer working on the Data Team at Meetup. Combining product design, machine learning research and software engineering, Evan builds systems that help Meetup's members find the best thing in the world: real local community. Before Meetup, Evan worked on hotel recommendations at Orbitz Worldwide, and he began his career in the Information Retrieval Lab at the Illinois Institute of Technology.

News Recommendations at scale at Bloomberg Media: Challenges and Approaches

Dhaval Shah
Engineering Manager
Bloomberg L.P
dshah100@bloomberg.net

Pramod Koneru
Software Engineer
Bloomberg L.P
pkoneru@bloomberg.net

Parth Shah
Senior Software Engineer
Bloomberg L.P
pshah229@bloomberg.net

Rohit Parimi
Software Engineer
Bloomberg L.P
rparimi@bloomberg.net

ABSTRACT

In the past decade, news consumption through traditional channels such as print has been on the decline while online and digital news consumption has been steadily growing. Bloomberg, renowned for its products in the financial world, has a very strong presence in the news and media industry. Bloomberg Media, on an average, publishes 400-500 stories and videos per day and we have close to 30 million unique visitors on our websites and mobile applications every month consuming this content. At such a scale it is very important to recommend relevant information for a good user experience. Recommendations in the News and Media domain bring a unique set of challenges due to the dynamic nature of the data as well as unique consumption patterns.

The biggest challenge with building recommendation systems in the News domain is the dynamic nature of the domain itself; new content is published every few minutes and majority of the content has a short shelf life, i.e., the news is not relevant to users after a certain time span and the time span is generally of the order of hours rather than days, making it important to deliver relevant content in a timely manner. Moreover, our users consume content differently based on time of day. For example, some users whose focus is market news and market data during the day consume more long form and generic articles and videos in the evening. User preferences, along with being cyclical in nature, tend to change over time, so algorithms need to adapt to the changing taste of the user. In addition, we need to ensure that the users do get their share of important/trending news and are not put into a filter bubble.

In this talk, we will present some novel techniques we have applied to popular approaches in the field of Recommender Systems to be able to address the unique challenges which the news domain presents.

RecSys '16 September 15-19, 2016, Boston , MA, USA

ACM ISBN 978-1-4503-4035-9/16/09.

DOI: http://dx.doi.org/10.1145/2959100.2959118

CCS Concepts

•**Information systems → Collaborative filtering; Personalization;** *Web log analysis;* RESTful web services;

Keywords

Recommender Systems; Collaborative Filtering; Real-time

Bios

Dhaval Shah

Dhaval Shah is an Engineering Manager at Bloomberg, overseeing all Machine Learning and Big Data related activities for Bloomberg Media. Dhaval's team has been applying Machine Learning and Big Data techniques to build Recommender Systems for Bloomberg Media's websites and native applications, including the flagship Bloomberg.com website, since 2011. Dhaval's team is also responsible for building automated tagging systems for Bloomberg's News articles as well as systems for personalizing push notifications for Bloomberg's iOS and Android applications.

Pramod Koneru

Pramod Koneru is a Software Engineer at Bloomberg, since 2013. He is part of the Machine Learning and Big Data team at Bloomberg Media and works primarily on recommender and tagging systems for news content, used across the web and mobile platforms. He has a BS from DA-IICT, India.

Parth Shah

Parth Shah is a Senior Software Engineer at Bloomberg, since 2012. He is part of the Machine Learning and Big Data team at Bloomberg Media and works primarily on recommender and tagging systems for news content, used across the web and mobile platforms. He has a MS from University Of Southern California, with focus on NLP.

Rohit Parimi

Rohit Parimi is a Software Engineer at Bloomberg, since 2015. He is part of the Machine Learning and Big Data team at Bloomberg Media and works primarily on recommender and tagging systems for news content. He has a PhD from Kansas State University, focused on cross-domain recommender systems.

Marsbot: Building a Personal Assistant

Max Sklar
Foursquare Labs
max@foursquare.com

ABSTRACT

Foursquare recently launched Marsbot, an SMS-based app for local recommendations. Marsbot is an intelligent friend that lives in your pocket and learns about you through the places you go in the real world. While this product is aligned with Foursquare's long-standing mission to find the best places, it represents a new era in the way people interact with recommendation engines. The promise of the latest crop of personal assistants is get us information more quickly and seamlessly, but building them comes with many challenges. In this talk, we discuss why we built Marsbot and some of the many lessons learned along the way.

Short CV of the Presenter

Max Sklar is a data scientist and engineer at Foursquare and frequent contributor to RecSys. As part of the engineering team, Max has focused on using both machine learning and heuristics to build new features into the apps Foursquare and Swarm. His contributions include work on early versions of the recommendation algorithm, venue ratings, and the natural language processing stack. Most recently, Max pulled out all stops in the organization to launch of Marsbot, the topic of his talk. He has presented at a variety of conferences, including the 2015 Workshop on Urban Data Science at Cambridge University, and is a frequent guest speaker at meetups and university courses. He holds an M.S. in Information Systems from NYU, and a B.S. in Computer Science from Yale.

RecSys'16, September 15–19, 2016, Boston, MA, USA.

ACM ISBN 978-1-4503-4035-9/16/09.

DOI: http://dx.doi.org/10.1145/2959100.2959119

Music Personalization at Spotify

[Abstract for Industrial Session]

Kurt Jacobson
Spotify
48 Grove St Suite 306
Somerville, MA 02144
kurtj@spotify.com

Vidhya Murali
Spotify
45 W 18th st
NY, NY 10011
vidhya@spotify.com

Edward Newett
Spotify
45 W 18th st
NY, NY 10011
enewett@spotify.com

Brian Whitman
Spotify
45 W 18th st
NY, NY 10011
bwhitman@spotify.com

Romain Yon
Spotify
45 W 18th st
NY, NY 10011
romain@spotify.com

ABSTRACT

Spotify is the world's largest on-demand music streaming company, with over 75 million active listeners choosing what to listen to among tens of millions songs. Discovery and personalization is a key part of the experience and critical to the success of the creator and consumer ecosystem. In this talk, we'll discuss the state of our current discovery approaches, such as the Discover Weekly playlist that has already streamed billions of new discoveries and Fresh Finds, a scalable platform for brand new music that focuses suggestions on the long end of the popularity tail. We'll discuss the technologies at scale necessary to distill the information about music from our listeners and the world at large we collect outside of Spotify – with the massive amounts of user-item activity data we collect every day to create highly personalized music experiences.

Entire teams at Spotify focus on understanding both the creator and listener through collaborative filtering, machine learning, DSP and NLP approaches – we crawl the web for artist information, scan each note in every one of our millions of songs for acoustic signals, and model users' taste through a cluster analysis and in a latent space based on their historical and real-time listening patterns. The data generated by these analyses have ensured our discovery products are precise and help our users enjoy music and media across our entire catalog.

We'll dive deep into the workings of Discover Weekly, our marquee personalized playlist which updates weekly and reached 1 billion streams within the first 10 weeks from its release. The technology behind Discover Weekly is powered by a scalable factor analysis of Spotify's over two billion user-generated playlists matched to each user's current listening behavior. We'll discuss its innovative genesis and the challenges and opportunities the system faces a year after its launch. We'll also discuss Spotify's home page, seen by each of our users, currently undergoing vast efforts around personalization to ensure each listener gets a targeted list of playlists, shows and music to select throughout their day. We'll discuss the various similarity metrics, ranking approaches and user modeling we're working on to increase precision and optimize for our users' happiness.

RecSys '16 September 15-19, 2016, Boston , MA, USA

ACM ISBN 978-1-4503-4035-9/16/09. . . $15.00

DOI: http://dx.doi.org/10.1145/2959100.2959120

1. PRESENTER BIO

1.1 Vidhya Murali

Vidhya is an engineer at Spotify's Music Recommendations team. With domain interests in big data and machine learning and a passion for building products, Vidhya works on music recommendations and personalization at Spotify. She works on building scalable data pipelines and machine learning models to power users discover their next favorite music. She received her Masters in Computer Science from the University of Wisconsin-Madison and Bachelors from BITS Pilani, India. She has presented at various conferences including the GHC, WiML and DataEngConf.

Recommending for the World

Justin Basilico
Netflix, Inc.
121 Albright Way
Los Gatos, CA 95032
jbasilico@netflix.com

Yves Raimond
Netflix, Inc.
121 Albright Way
Los Gatos, CA 95032
yraimond@netflix.com

ABSTRACT

The Netflix experience is driven by a number of recommendation algorithms: personalized ranking, page generation, similarity, ratings, search, etc. On the January 6th, 2016 we simultaneously launched Netflix in 130 new countries around the world, which brought the total to over 190 countries. Preparing for such a rapid expansion while ensuring each algorithm was ready to work seamlessly created new challenges for our recommendation and search teams. In this talk, we will highlight the four most interesting challenges we encountered in making our algorithms operate globally and how this improved our ability to connect members worldwide with stories they'll love.

In particular, we will dive into the problems of uneven availability across catalogs, balancing personal and cultural tastes, handling language, and tracking quality of recommendations. Uneven catalog availability is a challenge because many recommendation algorithms assume that people could interact with any item and then use the absence of interaction implicitly or explicitly as negative information in the model. However, this assumption does not hold globally and across time where item availability differs. Running algorithms globally means needing a notion of location so that we can handle local variations in taste while also providing a good basis for personalization. Language is another challenge in recommending video content because people can typically only enjoy content that has assets (audio, subtitles) in languages they understand. The preferences for how people enjoy such content also vary between people and depend on their familiarity with a language. Also, while would like our recommendations to work well for every one of our members, tracking quality becomes difficult because with so many members in so many countries speaking so many languages, it can be hard to determine when an algorithm or system is performing sub-optimally for some subset of them. Thus, to support this global launch, we examined each and every algorithm that is part of our service and began to address these challenges.

RecSys '16 September 15-19, 2016, Boston , MA, USA

ACM ISBN 978-1-4503-4035-9/16/09.

DOI: http://dx.doi.org/10.1145/2959100.2959121

Keywords

Recommender Systems; Search; Internationalization; Netflix

BIOS

Justin Basilico is a Research/Engineering Manager for Page Algorithms Engineering at Netflix. He leads an applied research team focused on developing the next generation of algorithms used to generate the Netflix homepage through machine learning, ranking, recommendation, and large-scale software engineering. He has also developed machine learning approaches that yielded significant improvements in the personalized ranking algorithms that drive the Netflix recommendation system. Prior to Netflix, he worked on machine learning in the Cognitive Systems group at Sandia National Laboratories. He is also the co-creator of the Cognitive Foundry, an open-source software library for building machine learning algorithms and applications. He grew up in Boston, did his undergrad at Pomona College, and started doing research in Recommender Systems in 2002 while in graduate school at Brown University.

Yves Raimond is a Research Manager at Netflix, where he leads the Search & Recommendation Algorithm Engineering team: a mixed team of researchers and engineers building the next generation of Machine Learning algorithms used to drive the Netflix experience. Before that, he was a Lead Research Engineer in BBC R&D, working on information extraction from Multimedia content. He holds a PhD from Queen Mary, University of London.

The Exploit-Explore Dilemma in Music Recommendation

Òscar Celma
Pandora Media
2100 Franklin St. Oakland, CA (USA)
ocelma@pandora.com

ABSTRACT

Were The Rolling Stones right when they said, *"You can't always get what you want; but if you try sometime you get what you need"*? Recommendation systems are the crystal ball of the Internet: predicting user intentions, making sense of big data, and delivering what people are looking for before they even know they want it.

Pandora radio is best known for the *Music Genome Project*; the most unique and richly labeled music catalog of 1.5 million+ tracks. While this content-based approach to music recommendation is extremely effective and still used today as the foundation to the leading online radio service, Pandora has also collected more than a decade of contextual listener feedback in the form of more than 65 billion thumbs from 79M+ monthly active users who have created more than 10 billion stations. This session will look at how the interdisciplinary team at Pandora goes about making sense of these massive data sets to successfully make large scale music recommendations to our listeners.

As opposed to more traditional recommender systems which need only to recommend a single item or set of items, Pandora's recommenders must provide an evolving set of sequential items, which constantly keep the experience new and exciting. The talk will present an overview of recommendation at Pandora, followed by a deep dive into the challenges of recommending content in the long tail. A mixture of experts based system will be discussed as well as the many data resources required to bring small stations to life for both new and indie artists.

Furthermore, in this talk I will present a dynamic ensemble learning system that combines musicological data and machine learning models to provide a truly personalized experience. This approach allows us to switch from a lean back experience (exploitation) to a more exploration mode to discover new music tailored specifically to users individual tastes.

Following this session the audience will have an in-depth understanding of how Pandora uses science to determine the perfect balance of familiarity, discovery, repetition and relevance for each individual listener, measures and evaluates user satisfaction, and how our online and offline architecture stack plays a critical role in our success.

Keywords

Ensemble learning; exploit-explore dilemma; content-based recommendation; machine listening; A/B online testing; offline evaluation; thumbprint radio

Short CV of the Presenter

Dr. Òscar Celma is currently Director of Research at Pandora, where he leads a team of 60 scientists and musicologists to provide the best personalized online radio experience.
From 2011 till 2014 Òscar was Senior Research Scientist at Gracenote. His work focused on music and video recommendation and discovery. Before that he was co-founder and Chief Innovation Officer at Barcelona Music and Audio Technologies (BMAT).
Òscar published a book named *"Music Recommendation and Discovery: The Long Tail, Long Fail, and Long Play in the Digital Music Space"* (Springer, 2010). In 2008, Òscar obtained his Ph.D. in Computer Science and Digital Communication, in the Pompeu Fabra University (Barcelona, Spain). He holds a few patents from his work on music recommendation and discovery as well as on Vocaloid, a singing voice synthesizer bought by Yamaha in 2004.

RecSys'16, September 15–19, 2016, Boston, MA, USA.

ACM ISBN 978-1-4503-4035-9/16/09.

DOI: http://dx.doi.org/10.1145/2959100.2959122

Feature Selection For Human Recommenders

Katherine A. Livins
Stitch Fix, Inc.
1 Montgomery St, Ste 1200
San Francisco, CA 94104
1-415-882-7765
klivins@stitchfix.com

ABSTRACT

Recommendation systems struggle to incorporate rich features, such as those derived from natural language and images. While humans can readily process this sort of information, they cannot not scale in the same way that statistical/ML models can. As a result, hybrid-algorithms that make recommendations based on the outputs of both computers and humans are becoming increasingly popular. This talk will explore novel methods for determining what features the human side of these systems should be processing. It will outline how experimental methods (borrowed from the behavioral sciences) can be used to this end, along with how the human recommendations may be improved as a result.

CCS Concepts

• Human-centered computing • Collaborative and social computing systems and tools • Empirical studies in collaborative and social computing

Keywords

Human Computation

RecSys '16, September 15-19, 2016, Boston , MA, USA
ACM 978-1-4503-4035-9/16/09.
http://dx.doi.org/10.1145/2959100.2959120

REFERENCES

[1] Doran, H., Bates, D., Bliese, P., & Dowling, M. 2007. Estimating the Multilevel Rasch Model: With the lme4 package. *Journal of Statistical Software.* 20, 2 (April 2007), 1-18).

[2] Duchowski, A.T. 2002. A breadth-first survey of eye tracking applications. *Behavior Research Methods, Instruments, and Computers.* 34, 4 (Nov, 2002), 455-470. DOI=10.3758/BF03195475

[3] Law, E., and von Ahn, L. 2011. *Human Computation.* Morgan & Claypool Publishers.

[4] Martin, J.B, Colson, E., and Klingenberg, B., 2015. Feature selection and validation for human classifiers. *HCOMP 2015* (San Diego, USA November 08-11, 2015).

[5] Nickles III, G., M., Melloy, B.J., and Grampopadhye, A.K. 2003. A comparison of three levels of training designed to promote systematic search behavior in visual inspection. *International Journal of Industrial Ergonomics*, 32, 331-339. DOI=10.1016/S0169-8141

Considering Supplier Relations and Monetization in Designing Recommendation Systems

Jan Krasnodebski
Director of Revenue Optimization, Expedia
Geneva, Switzerland
+41 22 580 1871
jkrasnodebski@expedia.com

Dr. John Dines
Data Scientist, Expedia
Geneva, Switzerland
+41 22 580 1897
jdines@expedia.com

ABSTRACT
E-commerce merchants need to optimize their recommendations and sort listings on multiple dimensions beyond product attributes to include supplier considerations, long-term customer experience and the value of the sale to achieve long term success. Product recommendations for optimizing customer conversion can be modeled effectively with predictive analytic methodologies. However, supplier and customer experience elements are not easily modeled in the same manner. This paper outlines an algorithmic approach for these considerations from Expedia's experiences.

Keywords
Recommender systems; E-commerce; Metrics; Evaluation.

1. INTRODUCTION
Expedia is the world's largest Online Travel Agency and provides millions of travelers hotel recommendations every day from a plethora of diverse choices at different price and quality levels. Expedia relies on thousands of hotel partners for its inventory and earns a commission from the partner when a customer makes a purchase on its site. Techniques such as boosted decision trees and factorization machines are used to determine which offers are most interesting to customers using relevance metrics such as click-through and conversion [1], [2]. While maximizing short-term results, this does not take into consideration a number of behavior-driven elements, such as having the best product and price from suppliers to offer customers in the future, ensuring good customer experiences, and stable compensation, which are all measured post conversion. Ebay outlines their considerations without reference to how they work [3]. This paper outlines how Expedia's recommendation algorithm was restructured to allow for these elements and still show high-converting offers.

2. STRUCTURE OF SUPPLIER AND MONETIZATION CONSIDERATIONS
The approach was to (1) outline the main non-conversion oriented business requirements (2) formulate separate mathematical expressions for each requirement (3) scale the terms to ensure consistency amongst themselves (4) simulate their effect on the overall recommendation algorithm to determine the appropriate system parameters, then (5) AB test on live traffic.

RecSys '16, September 15-19, 2016, Boston , MA, USA
ACM 978-1-4503-4035-9/16/09.
http://dx.doi.org/10.1145/2959100.2959124

The starting point was a linear combination of three separate scores. The first is the most important and focuses solely on providing the best offers for specific customers; the second incentivizes suppliers to provide the best product and customer experiences, and the third is compensation considerations. While not optimal from a pure modeling perspective, this was the best compromise because of the following:

- Trying to model for all elements at once is too complex and likely to lead to a suboptimal (and non-understandable) final result as per Bottou [4]. Initial attempts using pairwise comparisons for compensation and supplier elements supported this.
- Addition of separate scores provides the most flexibility for changing the influence of the different elements and adding or removing factors. It is also easier to manage outlying business cases.
- The second and third components are related to supplier behavior. For these to be effective, communicating their significance and operation is critical. Suppliers will only respond to what they can readily and quickly see and understand. Keeping the factors separate facilitates this communication.

2.1 Supplier Considerations
A key element is to ensure partners provide a robust supply of competitively-priced products. When they do not, the overall value proposition to the customer suffers. This should be disincentivized. Balancing short and longer term objectives can be modelled as a combined behavioral and game theory problem. It was found the over-riding element was incentivizing positive supplier behavior while not affecting short-term conversion, giving rise to a supplier quality score with the following features:

- All customer-unfriendly transgressions (restricting product, uncompetitive prices, poor customer experiences, etc.) are translated into a common score using the customer viewpoint.
- Thresholds and circuit-breakers were included to ensure a high level of confidence ("beyond reasonable doubt"), as much of the information is based on automatically collected data.
- Significant automatic communication was put in place to suppliers alerting them of their status and transgressions.

- The supplier's ranking in recommendations is affected over a significant period of time, decaying only once issues are resolved. This was critical to obtain supplier attention and prevent future issues.

The final form of the equation was a sigmoidal whose magnitude builds on transgressions and decays linearly once the supplier has rectified their issues. Choices of coefficients were guided to promote (1) the consumer experience (2) supplier understandability and reaction, and AB tested to ensure they did not affect the overall quality of product offers. Since most suppliers have positive behavior, reacting to those who do not was relatively innocuous.

2.2 Monetization

General theory suggests a compensation format such as expected revenue equals probability of conversion multiplied by expected revenue per transaction. However, this was found to be too limiting in AB testing. It was best to first outline the business criteria in terms of which situations and to what level should compensation be important, and then choose curves that best fit these requirements. Smooth functions such as sigmoids and natural logs were the best performing in AB tests. It was also best to decompose the compensation to its base elements, i.e. to the percentage commission and product price. These could then be compared and recombined with the other components of the overall sort equation.

The combined sigmoid-log was structured so compensation could be the distinguishing factor amongst similar offers, react more strongly to below-average outliers but have a capped effect so the underlying product offer would always dominate. It was essential to carefully balance the importance of the price of the recommended product with the other product attributes. The highest compensation is achieved by the most expensive high-margin product, but customers' budgets need to be respected. With this approach there was no significant impact to customer conversion in AB tests and a significant increase in profit.

The result of the combined algorithms gives rise to the Expedia Marketplace, where customer satisfaction is the primary goal, but product placement will judiciously shift for revenue and supplier considerations.

2.3 Refinement

Once the base equations were established the supplier and compensation components were refined to have a weaker effect in cases they could impact customer recommendations too strongly, such as when there are fewer product options. Linear decay below product-relevant thresholds performed as well as any other approaches in AB testing and were the simplest to implement.

2.4 Scaling

To make the results consistent across searches, markets and pricing environments, the three components had to be standardized. The best approach was to scale the supplier and compensation factors with respect to the distribution of the customer conversion score, as opposed to normalizing them. This proved simpler to implement and helped avoid mistakes, with other stakeholders having to adjust less to normalised scores. The chosen scaling method, Sn (median of median absolute deviation between scores), was similar to IQR and is described in references [5] and [6]. Sn has the advantage of being less sensitive to outliers, which is an important consideration as scores are often not normally distributed.

3. REPORTING

A key element to successfully including supplier metrics is having them be easily understood. To that end, reporting was developed to communicate the impact of suppliers' actions to them.

4. CONCLUSION

By combining separate mathematical expressions such as sigmoids and natural logs, it was possible to include supplier and compensation elements in recommendations without significantly affecting conversion. A key was to identify the cases where the non-product offer terms would not affect the quality of recommendations and provide the most leverage.

5. ACKNOWLEDGMENTS

We would like to thank our colleagues Adam Woznica, Phong Nguyen, Jun Wang, Phil Christenson, Fokko Beekhof, Marc Dakin, Jing Xi, Sean Downes and Dan Friedman, who were instrumental in the development of the base and supplier-management algorithms.

6. REFERENCES

[1] Fuchs M. and Zanker M. 2012 Multi-criteria ratings for recommender systems: An empirical analysis in the tourism domain. In C. Huemer and P. Lops, editors, *E-Commerce and Web Technologies, volume 123 of Lecture Notes in Business Information Processing*, pages 100-111. Springer Berlin Heidelberg.

[2] Joachims, T. 2002 Optimizing search engines using click-through data. *Proceedings of the eighth ACM SIGKDD international conference on knowledge discovery and data mining*, pages 133-142. ACM, NY.

[3] Ebay, http://pages.ebay.com/help/sell/searchstanding.html

[4] Bottou, L. Large Scale Machine Learning in the Real World, Part 1 – Paid Search. Big Data, *Large Scale Machine Learning Course, CILVR Lab, New York University,* Spring 2013.

[5] Rousseeuw P. and Croux C. Alternatives to the Median Absolute Deviation, *Journal of the American Statistical Association*, December 1993, Vol. 88, No. 424, Theory and Methods.

[6] Rousseeuw P. and Croux C. 1992 Time-efficient algorithms for two highly robust estimators of scale. *Proceedings of the 10th Symposium on Computational Statistics*, pages 411-428. Dodge Y. and Whittaker J., Springer-Verlag.

A Cross-Industry Machine Learning Framework with Explicit Representations

Denise Ichinco
Nara Logics, Inc
215 First St
Cambridge, MA 02142
denise@naralogics.com

Sahil Zubair
Nara Logics, Inc
215 First St
Cambridge, MA 02142
sahil@naralogics.com

Jana Eggers
Nara Logics, Inc
215 First St
Cambridge, MA 02142
jana@naralogics.com

Nathan Wilson
Nara Logics, Inc
215 First St
Cambridge, MA 02142
nw@naralogics.com

ABSTRACT

At Nara Logics, we provide recommendations for ecommerce, supply chain, financial services, travel & hospitality, operations and more for the Global 200. We've learned that for machine intelligence to be accepted, it must interact seamlessly with humans, expose its reasoning to humans, and even incorporate human feedback in real time into its decision making. Just as you take your friends' recommendations more seriously when you can probe their mental model of your likes and dislikes, machine recommendations are more appealing when users understand how they were generated and can provide feedback to those recommendations. These aspects are necessary as commercial interfaces increasingly leverage recommendations alongside statistical analysis.

In this talk, I will discuss a new general purpose framework, "synaptic intelligence", for learning and maintaining explicit representations in real-time. This framework can be used both to make recommendations and to explain why each recommendation was made to meet the objectives outlined. We will also discuss how we extend our technology to enable users to have meaningful interactions where they're able to find what they're looking for. We believe in developing recommendation technology that facilitates a conversation with the user. The examples we showcase will demonstrate how we are able to leverage an explicit representation to make this possible.

One key to unlocking this type of interaction is in building and maintaining an explicit representation of relevant aspects of the items considered for recommendation and their features. We have integrated an explicit representation into our model which allows our clients (and customers of our clients) to interact with our recommendations in a way that they otherwise wouldn't have been able to do. While content-based recommenders and other explicit models have fallen out of favor due to their inability to perform competitively against models that use latent features, we provide additional motivation for the inclusion of content metadata through hybrid recommenders.

By maintaining explicit representations, we are able to introspect: to explain why those items and not other items are at the top of the list. This is a fundamental feature that enables users to make decisions with confidence. This feature is particularly helpful when trying to understand the behavior of models that are trained with different or new data. Using data contained in explicit representations, we can ensure that the results are grounded in facts and observations that are relevant for a particular domain. We can even provide new recommendations with feedback from the user on the "whys".

Explicit representations also give users the ability to adjust their priorities dynamically. For instance, a user searching for a restaurant might see that their recommendations tend toward one particular cuisine. An explicit representation allows them to say: "I'm feeling adventurous tonight! Give me recommendations where cuisine isn't a factor." This can also form the basis for natural conversational recommender systems. Unlike a typical conversational recommender system, which is essentially a rote preference elicitation mechanism and/or a tree-based rules engine, this conversational recommender system allows users to react to the specific reasons we produced recommendations and audit our representation of their preferences.

This talk will demonstrate that maintaining an explicit representation bestows benefits on a recommendation system beyond accuracy: explicit representations are what will make the system accessible to users.

Keywords

recommendations; synaptic intelligence; explicit representation

RecSys '16, September 15-19, 2016, Boston, MA, USA
ACM 978-1-4503-4035-9/16/09.

DOI: http://dx.doi.org/10.1145/2959100.2959125

Leveraging a Graph-Powered, Real-Time Recommendation Engine to Create Rapid Business Value

Adam Anthony
GraphSQL Inc.
adam@graphsql.com

Yu-Keng Shih
GraphSQL Inc.
yu-keng.shih@graphsql.com

Ruoming Jin
GraphSQL Inc.
ruoming@graphsql.com

Yang Xiang
GraphSQL Inc.
yang.xiang@graphsql.com

Keywords

Graph Databases; Real Time Recommendation; Recommendation Analysis

1. ABSTRACT

Deployment of open source recommendation systems has been shown to be an effective way to increase sale conversions on a variety of e-commerce sites. However, there remains a large gap between deploying the core algorithm provided by these systems and delivering an application-quality recommendation system, specifically tailored to address complex and dynamically changing business needs.

We will present a real-time recommendation engine built on our graph data platform that provides the following extensions to a basic recommendation model:

1. **True real-time recommendation algorithms**: We provide a simple framework for customers to author and deploy real-time recommendation algorithms with no pre-computation required.
2. **Streaming updates of user behavior and product information**: As quickly as data are generated, the recommendation engine applies the updates and can serve updated results.
3. **Support for offline recommendation algorithms**: Users with existing investment in a quality recommendation program can import their pre-computed results into the graph database for efficient, unified service of results.
4. **Tools for Business-centric requirements**: The engine offers a range of weighting, sorting, and filtering options to tailor recommendation algorithms to business needs. For example, the engine can eliminate products that are out of stock or favor products that are known to perform well in different real-time contexts.
5. **Multiple algorithm ensemble support**: There is rarely a case where one algorithm is sufficient to identify the best items to recommend to a user. Integrating points 1 through 4, the engine provides intuitive methods for specifying and combining the results of multiple recommendation algorithms to achieve the highest-performing results.
6. **Recommendation feedback tools**: Pre- and Post-analysis tools, built around a business' logic, are used to generate reports to assess the value of both potential and currently deployed algorithms.

Of particular interest to RecSys attendees, we will discuss the technical aspects of a graph-based implementation of the recommendation engine and how it facilitates the rapid design and deployment of an efficient real-time recommendation system under a single service. We will briefly discuss the architecture of our graph database system to show how it can efficiently serve a large user base even from a single server shared-memory architecture. Attendees will also learn about graph-based data modeling and how viewing data from this perspective can lead to new types of business insights and applications that are not easily implemented using traditional relational and/or NoSQL platforms. We will conclude with a brief demonstration of a real deployed application UI to demonstrate the ease by which recommendation systems can be implemented and deployed using the engine.

2. ABOUT THE AUTHORS

Dr. Adam Anthony received his Ph.D. in computer science from the University of Maryland Baltimore County in 2009. His expertise is in data clustering, pattern recognition and computing similarity in graphs. He has been working at GraphSQL for three years, one of 7 early members. GraphSQL is developing a next-generation graph database and parallel processing architecture that has been shown to be capable of real-time storage and querying of hundreds of millions of vertices and billions of edges on a single server architecture. His primary contribution at GraphSQL has been the development of novel parallel graph algorithms within a map-reduce style computational framework for graph data.

RecSys '16 September 15-19, 2016, Boston , MA, USA

ACM ISBN 978-1-4503-4035-9/16/09.

DOI: http://dx.doi.org/10.1145/2959100.2959126

His primary role is in the direction and development of a flexible, graph-based recommendation engine with an emphasis on real-time recommendation with business-centric optimization. The recommendation engine is currently used in production systems, delivering revenue-boosting recommendation systems with minimal developer effort.

Dr. Yu-Keng Shih received his Ph.D. in computer science and engineering from The Ohio State University in 2013. His expertise is in graph algorithms, especially in graph clustering, path searching and graph matching. His most recent research was in developing graph clustering algorithms for different applications, especially social networks and biological networks. He has been working at GraphSQL for one year. His primary contribution is utilizing GraphSQL's graph computation platform to develop features on real-time recommendation systems for increasing accuracy and efficiency.

Dr. Ruoming Jin is Founder and CEO of GraphSQL. He was the founding CTO of GraphSQL. Dr. Jin received his Ph.D. in Computer Science and Engineering from the Ohio State University in 2005. Dr. Jin is on long-term academic leave from Kent State University where he is an associate professor (tenured). Dr. Jin is considered a leading expert in Graph Analytics and BigData. He has published almost 100 technical papers in these areas and many of his papers have appeared in leading data mining and database conferences and journals, including SIGMOD, PVLDB, SIGKDD, ICDM, TODS, and TKDE. He has served at numerous program committees including SIGMOD, KDD, PVLDB, ICDM, and served as associate editors of TKDE. Dr. Jin is also a recipient of the prestigious NSF CAREER award.

Yang Xiang received the PhD degree in Computer Science from Kent State University in 2009. In 2010, he received the Computing Innovation Fellow (CIFellow) Award from the US National Science Foundation (NSF)/CRA/CCC. In 2012, he was appointed research assistant professor in the Department of Biomedical Informatics, The Ohio State University. In 2015, he joined GraphSQL as a Senior Research Scientist and Solution Architect. He research expertise includes graph algorithms, graph databases, data mining, and biomedical informatics. He is a senior member of the ACM and a senior member of the IEEE.

Hypothesis Testing: How to Eliminate Ideas as Soon as Possible

Roman Zykov
Retail Rocket, Chief Data Scientist
Moscow, Russia
+7 499 702-36-88
rzykov@retailrocket.ru

ABSTRACT

Retail Rocket helps web shoppers make better shopping decisions by providing personalized real-time recommendations through multiple channels with over 100MM unique monthly users and 1000+ retail partners.

The rapid improvement of the product is important to win on the high-concurrency market of real-time personalization platforms. The necessity of introducing constant innovations and improvements of algorithms for recommendation systems requires correct tools and a process of rapid testing of hypotheses. It`s not a secret that 9 out of 10 hypotheses actually do not improve the performance at least. We had the task stated as follows: How to detect and eliminate the idea that doesn`t improve as early as possible, to spend a minimum of resources on that process.

In the report we will talk about:

- How we make our process of hypotheses testing faster.
- One programming language for R&D.
- Enmity and friendship of offline and online metrics.
- Why it is difficult to predict the impact of changing diversity of algorithms.
- What is the benefit of AA/BB online tests.
- Bayesian statistics for the evaluation of online tests.

Roman Zykov is the Chief Data Scientist at the Retail Rocket. In Retail Rocket is responsible for algorithms of personalized and non-personalized recommendations. Previous to Retail Rocket, Roman was the Head of analytics at the biggest e-commerce companies for almost ten years. He received Ms.Sc. in applied mathematics and physics from the MIPhT in 2004.

Keywords

recommender systems, A/B testing, AA/BB testing, hypotheses testing, diversification, Bayesian statistics, evaluation

RecSys '16, September 15-19, 2016, Boston , MA, USA
ACM 978-1-4503-4035-9/16/09.
DOI: http://dx.doi.org/10.1145/2959100.2959127

Recommending the World's Knowledge: Application of Recommender Systems at Quora

Lei Yang, Xavier Amatriain
Quora Inc.
650 Castro St.
Mountain View, CA, USA
lei, xavier@quora.com

ABSTRACT

At Quora, our mission is to share and grow the world's knowledge. Recommender systems are at the core of this mission: we need to recommend the most important questions to people most likely to write great answers, and recommend the best answers to people interested in reading them. Driven by the above mission statement, we have a variety of interesting and challenging recommendation problems and a large, rich data set that we can work with to build novel solutions for them. In this talk, we will describe several of these recommendation problems and present our approaches solving them.

Keywords

Recommender systems; ranking; collaborative filtering; machine learning; personalization

1. RECOMMEND THE HOME FEED

The Quora feed is the homepage that a user sees when logged into the product. On that page, we select and recommend the most "interesting" stories for a given user at a given time. This problem is challenging because we need to meet a number of requirements: (1) we need to recommend stories that are topically relevant to the user, (2) we need to recommend stories that are socially relevant to the user because there are explicit connections between users on Quora, (3) we need to recommend stories that are "timely" and sometimes relate to ongoing trending events, (4) we need to both engage users to read interesting content and present questions to users who can write good content for, and (5) we need to make our recommendations responsive to real-time user actions and impressions. To meet the above requirements, we use a personalized learning-to-rank approach and build a multi-stage system where different candidates are selected and ranked in advance before the final recommendation is actually performed.

2. RECOMMEND DIGEST ANSWERS

The popular Quora digest email includes a collection of personalized answers that are selected and recommended for users. Our recommender system first tries to identify a set of candidate answers that pass certain quality bar and other requirements, and then uses a learning-to-rank model that is optimized for a different objective function than the home feed recommendation problem. Specifically, the model tries to predict the likelihood that the user will click on the answer shown in the digest email. It's worth noting that we also train separate collaborative filtering models to add as features in the above model and expand the candidate pool by introducing answers from topics that the user doesn't explicitly follow.

3. RECOMMEND WRITERS TO ANSWER

Ask To Answer (A2A) is a feature on Quora that recommends experts best qualified to answer questions and enables users to route their questions to such experts. In addition to generating great answers, A2A also adds a unique social element to Quora by allowing users to interact and engage with others through these requests. The recommendations of expert users are generated by a supervised machine learning model. Using the set of historical A2A data from recommendations shown in the past to generate features and labels, the model predicts the label on new incoming data and the top scoring candidates are recommended. Some of the important features are the answers that a user has written on a given topic and the upvotes, downvotes, or views the user has received on those answers, as well as the "endorsements" the user has on the topic, which is an explicit acknowledgement on someone's expertise coming from other users.

4. RECOMMEND RELATED QUESTIONS

Another type of recommendations is presenting users questions that are somewhat related to the current one. Related question is particularly effective in creating engagement of logged-out users when they visit the question page from an external search engine, and that is one of the reasons why currently this recommendation model is un-personalized. Note that what makes a good recommendation is decided not only by how similar the target item is to the source, but also the "interestingness" of the target. At Quora, related questions are determined by using an machine learned model that takes into account different features such as textual similarity, user co-visit data, topics of the question, or popularity or quality of the question.

5. EFFICIENT MACHINE LEARNING PLATFORM FOR RECOMMENDATIONS

We will also share our experiences building a flexible and efficient platform to quickly experiment with different machine learning models for recommender systems. Specifically, we have built a framework to simplify machine learning workflows on Quora's infrastructure, supporting collaborative filtering algorithms commonly used in recommender systems such as weighted average least squares (WALS) and Bayesian personalized ranking (BPR). It provides efficient C++ implementations for the algorithms to allow seamless integration with our infrastructure, through a simple Python API that is intuitive and easy to use for developers.

RecSys '16, September 15-19, 2016, Boston , MA, USA
ACM 978-1-4503-4035-9/16/09.
http://dx.doi.org/10.1145/2959100.2959128

Multi-corpus Personalized Recommendations on Google Play

Levent Koc
Google Inc.
Mountain View, CA USA
lkoc@google.com

Cyrus Master
Google Inc.
Mountain View, CA USA
lkoc@google.com

ABSTRACT

Google Play is a seamless approach to digital entertainment on all of your devices. It gives you one place to find, enjoy and share your favorite entertainment, from apps to movies, music, books and more, on the web or any device. With more than 1 billion active users in 190+ countries around the world, Play is an important distribution platform for developers to build a global audience. More than 50 billion apps have been downloaded from Google Play.

However, generating personalized recommendations for different kind of content is a complex technical and product problem. Each of Play verticals (apps, games, books, movies, music) has different business goals, metrics to optimize, and user behavior. In this talk, we'll present an overview of how Play recommendations work across these verticals, how we evaluate our results, and the impact of deep neural networks in improving recommendations.

CCS Concepts

•**Computing methodologies** → **Machine learning;** *Neural networks; Supervised learning;* •**Information systems** → *Recommender systems;*

Keywords

Recommender Systems; Google Play; Machine Learning

RecSys '16 September 15-19, 2016, Boston , MA, USA

ACM ISBN 978-1-4503-4035-9/16/09.

DOI: http://dx.doi.org/10.1145/2959100.2959129

Item-to-item Recommendations at Pinterest

Stephanie Rogers
Pinterest
San Francisco, California
srogers@pinterest.com

ABSTRACT

This talk presents Pinterest Related Pins, an item-to-item recommendation system that combines collaborative filtering with content-based ranking to drive a quarter of the total engagement on Pinterest. Signals derived from user curation, the activity of users organizing content, are highly effective when used in conjunction with content based ranking. This will be an in-depth dive into the end-to-end system of Related Pins, a real-world implementation of an item-to-item hybrid recommendation system.

RecSys '16, September 15-19, 2016, Boston , MA, USA
ACM 978-1-4503-4035-9/16/09.
http://dx.doi.org/10.1145/2959100.2959130

Candidate Generation

Pinterest is a user-powered content curation service as content is collected and grouped into boards, creating a rich set of metadata associated with Pins' images. User curation reveals relations among images: we observed that images of Pins on the same board are semantically and often visually similar to each other. Therefore, if enough users save these two Pins together, there is a high likelihood that another user may also find them to be related.

Using board co-occurrence as an estimate of how similar two pins are, we can narrow down the set of pins we believe to be related. This form of collaborative filtering allows us to generate an initial, smaller set of image candidates, making it possible and more feasible to do content-based reranking.

Reranking

After generating a set of candidates for each pin, we rerank the results using a machine learned model based on various features. These features are a combination of pin features, both from the query and candidate pins, and user context features to personalize the results. We have explored various modeling techniques from linear modeling to gradient boosted decision trees.

Challenges

Along the way we have been presented with a ton of challenges including: personalization, the tradeoff of relevance vs. diversity, infrastructure stability and pipeline productionization, collecting unbiased training data, and more. Many of these challenges will be presented in the talk.

A Recommender System to tackle Enterprise Collaboration

Gabriel de Souza P. Moreira
ITA – Brazilian Aeronautics Institute of Technology
CI&T, Brazil
gabrielpm@ciandt.com

Gilmar Souza
CI&T, Brazil
gilmarj@ciandt.com

ABSTRACT

In order to survive, companies depend on their capacity to generate and manage knowledge while promoting alignment among its employees. To tackle this problem, it was developed an enterprise collaboration platform named Smart Canvas, a service whose goal is to leverage companies' knowledge and tear down silos by connecting people, teams, and content. These connections are suggested by a Recommender System, using techniques like Topic Modeling, Content-Based Filtering and Graph traversing.

Smart Canvas is a multi-tenant Software as a Service, featuring a scalable cloud-based Recommender System architecture, including tools like Spark and Titan Graph Database, deployed on Google Cloud Platform.

Keywords

Recommender system; corporate collaboration; content-based filtering; topic modeling; recommendations explanations.

1. INTRODUCTION

Any organization with more than a couple of dozen employees will eventually and surely create silos of knowledge. By breaking those silos they can ignite innovation potential. Collaboration platforms have been available for many years, but they struggle to overcome what is known as the collaboration paradox [1]: people want all the benefits provided by such tools, but they won't invest their times without some sort of immediate gain. To tackle this problem we have created Smart Canvas [1], a service that allows people to create and curate content relevant to their organization. You can find a video demo at this link [2].

Smart Canvas is powered by a recommender system which:

- Suggests relevant content, explaining to the users which of his topics of interest have generated each recommendation (Figure 1).

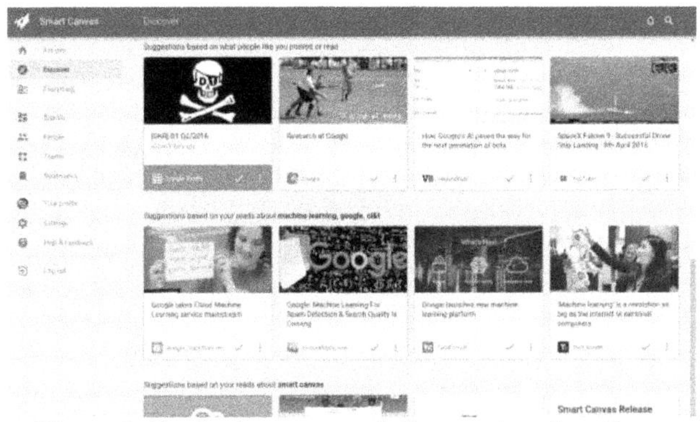

Figure 1. Content recommendations and explanations.

- Associates tags to users' profiles based on topics discovered from content they have contributed (Figure 2). These expertise and interests tags are searchable (Figure 3).

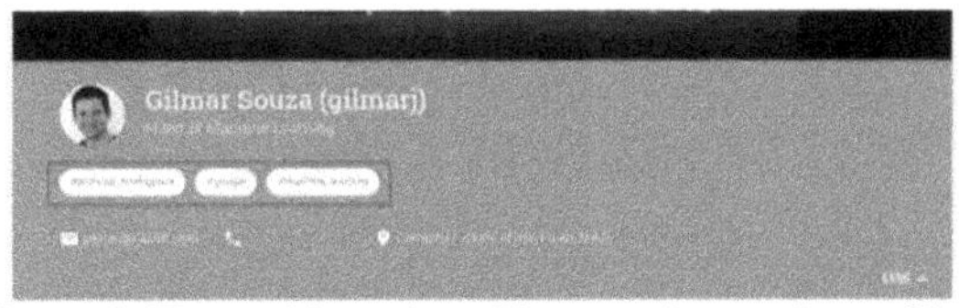

Figure 2. Tags with topics of interest in user's profiles.

Figure 3. People are searchable by their expertise or interests.

- Recommends people with similar interests, explaining which topics brings them together (Figure 4).
- Suggests for curator users some boards (content groups) related to a post, to help them in knowledge organization.

2. SYSTEM OVERVIEW

Smart Canvas uses Topic Modeling techniques for better representation of users diverse interests. This makes it possible to improve the accuracy of content-based recommendations. It also allows the explanation of recommendations in the user interface, increasing their transparency and promoting trust and satisfaction.

1 http://www.smartcanvas.com

1 http://youtu.be/msWy6BMSQVE

RecSys '16, September 15-19, 2016, Boston , MA, USA
ACM 978-1-4503-4035-9/16/09.
http://dx.doi.org/10.1145/2959100.2959115

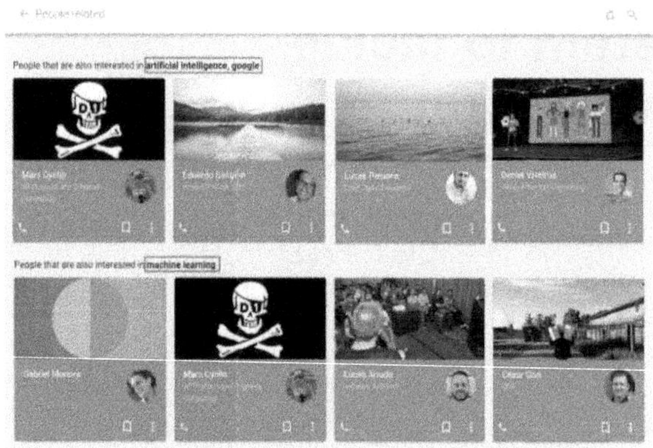

Figure 4. Recommends people with similar interests, explaining which topics are shared

Our typical data pipeline includes the ingestion millions of user events (using Google PubSub and BigQuery), the batch processing of the models (with PySpark and Scikit-learn), and the online recommendations (with Google App Engine, Titan Graph Database and Elasticsearch).
An overview of the RecSys batch processing can be seen in Figure 5, where Spark jobs run for each of our clients (tenants).

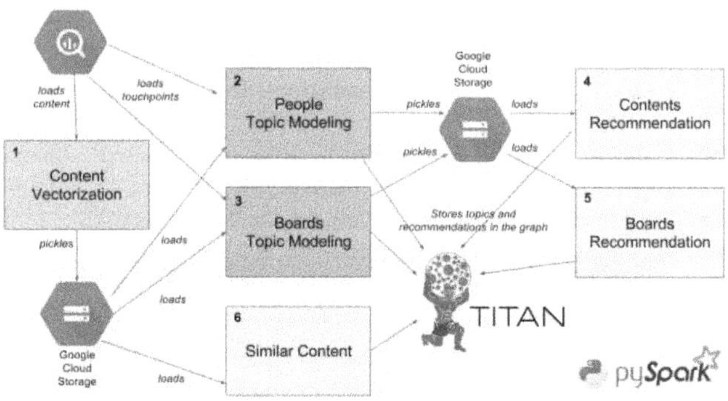

Figure 5. Batch recommendation jobs pipeline.

Job #1 retrieves from BigQuery all published content, vectorizes them using TF-IDF, and persists the vocabulary and the sparse matrix for further usage.
For each user, Job #2 process a corpus formed by the posts user has interacted more recently, using Non-Negative Matrix Factorization (NMF) to model the topics of interest, with some semantic heuristics to define the best number of topics (k). Then, topics relevance is weighted by the count of each interaction type (i.e. views, likes, comments), decayed by the age of the interactions to boost recent user interests.
Job #3 makes an analogous process to discover topics of boards (content groups), based on the posts pinned on them by users.
Job #4 recommends content for each of users topics using cosine similarity. With individual Bloom Filters, posts that users have already seen are efficiently ignored. Job #5 does the same for boards topics recommendations.
Job #6 process related posts recommendations, calculating similarity with vectors under pivoted unique normalization [2] to balance short and long posts.
All recommendations are persisted as edges in Titan Graph Database, as shown in Figure 6, where they can be efficiently retrieved and presented to the users.

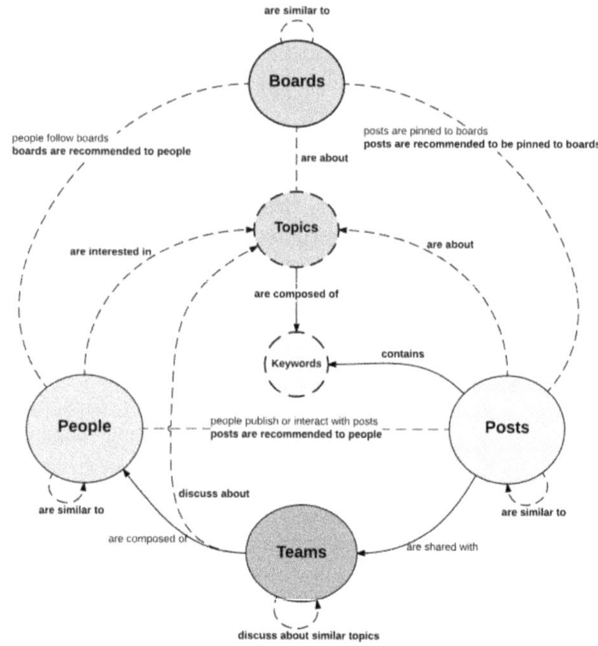

Figure 6. Graph Model, with recommendations represented as dashed lines and bold labels.

As the stream of created and shared posts flows in the system, online recommendations are generated for people and boards. This online process involves vectorizing the posts with TF-IDF, persisting the top 50 relevant keywords (tokens) as vertices in Titan Graph Database, and running graph traversals which implements an approximate cosine similarity between posts keywords and people and boards topics.

3. CONCLUSIONS

This demo paper presented a functional and architectural overview of Smart Canvas Recommender System, a scalable multi-tenant SaaS solution featuring web and mobile clients.
We expect to provide with this demo a compelling use case where a recommender system is used in the context of a corporate collaboration platform.

4. ACKNOWLEDGMENTS

We would like to thank CI&T and D1 team, which developed Smart Canvas and allowed us to share its internals to the academic community. We also would like to thank ITA for providing the research environment

5. REFERENCES

[1] Nigel Fenwick, 2015. Resolving *The Collaboration Paradox. Forrester Reports* (Jun. 2015). Available in https://www.forrester.com/report/Resolving+The+Collaboration+Paradox/-/E-RES119837

[2] Singhal, A., Buckley, C., & Mitra, M. 1996. *Pivoted document length normalization*. In Proceedings of the 19th annual international ACM SIGIR conference on Research and development in information retrieval (pp. 21-29). ACM

Conversational Recommendation System with Unsupervised Learning

Yueming Sun, Yi Zhang
University of California, Santa Cruz
{yueming,yiz}@soe.ucsc.edu

Yunfei Chen, Roger Jin
Rulai Inc., Sunnyvale, California, USA
{yunfei,roger}@rulai.io

ABSTRACT

We will demonstrate a conversational products recommendation agent. This system shows how we combine research in personalized recommendation systems with research in dialogue systems to build a virtual sales agent. Based on new deep learning technologies we developed, the virtual agent is capable of learning how to interact with users, how to answer user questions, what is the next question to ask, and what to recommend when chatting with a human user.

Normally a descent conversational agent for a particular domain requires tens of thousands of hand labeled conversational data or hand written rules. This is a major barrier when launching a conversation agent for a new domain. We will explore and demonstrate the effectiveness of the learning solution even when there is no hand written rules or hand labeled training data.

CCS Concepts

•Information systems → Recommender systems;

Keywords

Dialogue systems, recommendation systems, personal assistant, chat bot

1. INTRODUCTION

Recommendation systems have achieved much commercial success and are becoming increasingly popular in a wide variety of online stores. Current recommendation systems provided ranked lists or images of items for a given user. Virtual sales agent with the capabilities of personalized recommendation have been imagined for years. With the ever increasing popularity of smart phones, mobile devices and virtual reality systems, this becomes a very important problem that could be a huge impact in the near future.

Research in recommendation systems field has enjoyed wide success, largely because the techniques are not restricted on a particular domain and can be adapted to many domains and business. To launch a recommendation system to a new domain, researchers and engineers normally only need to use the domain's existing user click or transaction data to train the recommendation model, without requiring too much manually labeled data.

However, dialogue system technologies behind virtual agents, such as Apple's "Siri", are usually developed for a particular domain. The major elements of the agents include a language understanding component that converts user input (text or speech or multi-modal) into abstract representation, an internal state update component that updates the memory about the conversation, a policy component that determines the next system acts, and a natural language generation component for generating response to the user. Each component can be rule based, machine learning based or using a hybrid approach. For example, in order to predict user intention and update the memory, a learning based system usually learns from many hand labeled data points that look like this [1]:

"I don't mind, but it should serve Japanese food."

$$Label : \{act = inform, slots : [food = Japanese]\}$$

This is a major barrier when launching a dialogue system to a new domain/system, because much efforts are needed to either collect hundreds of thousands of hand labeled training data for machine learning algorithm to learn or hire people to write many rules.

Due to the limitation of existing dialogue system technologies, how to build a personalized conversational recommendation agent that can be easily adapted to many different domains or systems is a big challenge. This demo will demonstrate how we tackle this challenge and our efforts on developing such a general purpose conversational recommendation system Rul.ai. This system learns from unlabeled user conversations and delayed user actions, thus it can be adapted to a new domain or business with descent performance. A video of the system in action is available at https://youtu.be/V_7G3wYt0mw.

2. SYSTEM IMPLEMENTATION

Our system has several major components, as shown in Figure 1. Most of the components are similar to a typical dialogue system, except that a personalized recommendation engine is added and used by the policy component to influence machine actions.

RecSys '16 September 15-19, 2016, Boston , MA, USA

ACM ISBN 978-1-4503-4035-9/16/09.

DOI: http://dx.doi.org/10.1145/2959100.2959114

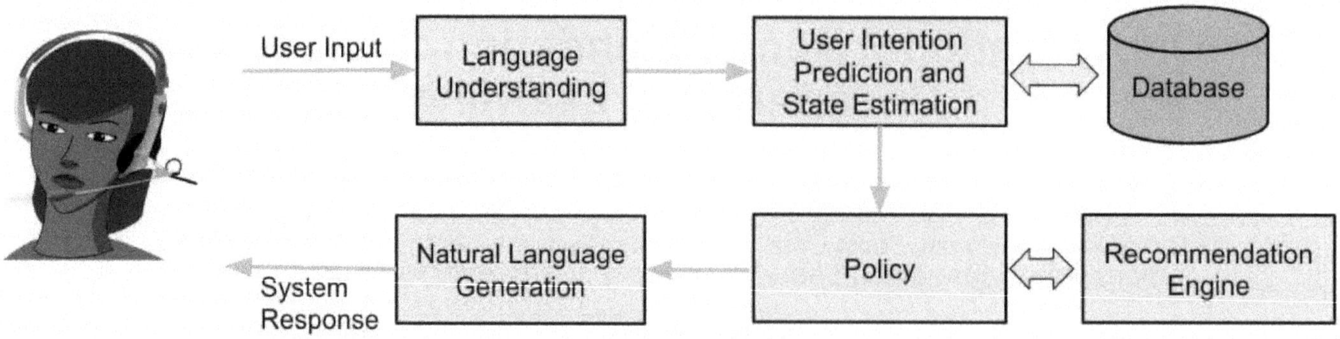

Figure 1: System Architecture

2.1 User Intention Prediction and State Tracking

The goal of a conversational recommendation agent is to finalize a purchasing order for the user at the end of the conversation. In order to achieve this goal, the users need to provide values for meta data needed for the agent to place the order. These information are also known as slot-value pairs [1]. For example, a pair [$type$ = $latte$] denotes the type of coffee ordered by user is "latte". After each user utterance, the user intention prediction and state tracking component needs to predict the current user's intention precisely and to update which state she/he is at. The state includes all slot-value pairs the agent has from the user so far, such as [$food = Japanese, location = 95070$]. Without requiring hand labeled data for each user utterance, we developed a new unsupervised learning method to train models used by this component. Our approach is to train a deep learning model [2] that learns from delayed rewards, which are the orders at the end of each conversation. These delayed rewards are collected by e-commercial companies in their normal business.

2.2 Personalized recommendation and learning

Recommendation in conversation is an open area for research. Besides user transaction history and user demographic information that are normally used in traditional recommendation engines, our engine also has a rich set of additional information about the user needs, such as possible user initial request (i.e. a user query) or supplemental information collected while talking with the user. To better serve users in our system, we have a recommendation system that's capable of using those information to rank products, generate recommendations, get user feedback to update memory and actively solicit additional user feedback.

2.3 Machine utterance generation

We will demonstrate two machine utterance generation mechanisms inside our system. One is a template based model with a statistical learning method to select a template and automatically fill the missing components in the selected template for each machine utterance generation request. The second solution is based on a deep learning model (i.e. a sequence to sequence language generation model).

3. DATA

We trained the model with unlabeled data collected by a mobile app, which provides personal assistance services to thousands of daily active users. The data set contains natural language chats between many users and real human agents (i.e. assistant). In a successful chat session, a real human agent guides a user through the processes to fulfill a purchasing order.

4. A DIALOGUE EXAMPLE

Figure 2: Demo Screenshot

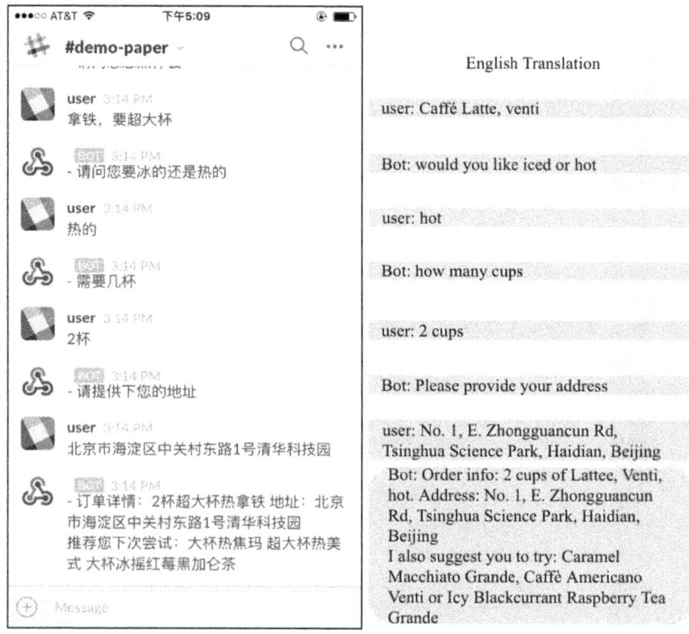

Both English and Chinese versions will be used for demo.

5. REFERENCES

[1] Jason Williams, Antoine Raux, Deepak Ramachadran, and Alan Black, "The Dialog State Tracking Challenge", *Proceedings of the SIGDIAL 2013 Conference,* Metz, France, August 2013

[2] LeCun, Yann, Yoshua Bengio, and Geoffrey Hinton, "Deep learning", *Nature* 521, no. 7553 (2015): 436-444.

Powering Content Discovery through Scalable, Realtime Profiling of Users' Content Preferences

Ido Tamir
Outbrain
Netanya, Israel
itamir@outbrain.com

Roy Bass
Outbrain
Netanya, Israel
rbass@outbrain.com

Guy Kobrinsky
Outbrain
Netanya, Israel
gkobrinsky@outbrain.com

Baruch Brutman
Outbrain
Netanya, Israel
bbrutman@outbrain.com

Ronny Lempel
Outbrain
Netanya, Israel
rlempel@outbrain.com

Yoram Dayagi
Outbrain
Netanya, Israel
ydayagi@outbrain.com

ABSTRACT

Outbrain is the Web's leading content discovery service, recommending billions of stories daily to a global audience across many of the world's most prestigious and respected publishers. Outbrain's recommendation technology combines contextual cues with personalization, where the personalization aspects are a combination of content-based and collaborative filtering techniques.

This paper, and the accompanying demo, offer a behind-the-scenes view of the content-based aspects of Outbrain's personalization technology. We detail the types of features we extract from content, as well as the attributes we keep in each user's content-affinity profile. We then describe and demonstrate how we update each user's profile, in real time, as the user consumes content while browsing the Web.

CCS Concepts

•Information systems → Personalization; Recommender systems;

Keywords

User Profile; Content-Based Recommendation Systems; Personalization

1. INTRODUCTION

The vast supply of items available to consume or buy online has given rise to the proliferation of recommendation systems [?]. Pioneered in the pre-Web days by the Tapestry system [?], recommender systems in the early days of the Internet were mostly found on e-commerce sites [?]. Today, advanced recommender systems also recommend music and videos, games and movies (e.g. by Pandora, YouTube, Xbox and NetFlix); suggest friends and connections on social networks; and – in the case of Outbrain – assist users in discovering content as they are reading stories of online publishers.

Indeed, Outbrain is the Web's leading content discovery service, recommending billions of stories daily to a global audience of well over half a billion unique monthly users, across many of the world's most prestigious and respected publishers. Outbrain's recommendation technology combines contextual cues with personalization, where the personalization aspect is a combination of content-based [?] as well as collaborative filtering techniques [?]. In order to deliver personalized content-based recommendations, Outbrain represents the content affinity exhibited by each user in a *profile*, which is updated every time we observe the user interacting with online content. Our production infrastructure for updating user profiles, which today sustains up to 800,000 updates per minute across several data centers, is the focus of this demo.

2. THE FEATURES BEHIND OUTBRAIN'S RECOMMENDATIONS

Outbrain computes recommendations by leveraging several feature families:

1. **Contextual features:** the context in which the request for recommendations is made, while disregarding the user. Namely, the story in which the request is made from, the publisher and the section in which the story is published, the type of device making the request, etc.

2. **Popularity and performance features:** Outbrain tracks the number of page views each story attracts, as well as the breakdown of page views by referrer type (traffic from within the publisher, from outside the publisher, from social networks, etc.). Furthermore, we also have the performance that each story delivers when served as a recommendation (e.g., its click through rate), and we further segment performance by the context in which the recommendation was made.

3. **Personal features:** we track users' affinity to content in order to power content-based personalized recommendations, as well as the "collaborative filtering

RecSys '16 September 15-19, 2016, Boston , MA, USA

ACM ISBN 978-1-4503-4035-9/16/09.

DOI: http://dx.doi.org/10.1145/2959100.2959111

persona" of the user[1] in order to surface personalized recommendations stemming from co-consumption patterns that arise from the data.

3. OUTBRAIN'S RECIPE FOR CONTENT-BASED RECOMMENDATIONS

At a high level, Outbrain employs a standard three-step recipe [?] for producing the content-based aspect of our recommendations:

Content understanding. We extract metadata and semantic features from each story we encounter. Metadata includes attributes like the publisher and section in which the story was published, the publish date, etc. Semantic features are derived, and include features such as categories that the story is associated with; latent topics [?] that are present in the story; and prominent named entities that the story is about. This results in each story being represented by several - say k - vectors (e.g. category vector, latent topic vector, entities vector, etc).

Profile Aggregation. As users consume stories on the Outbrain network of publishers, we aggregate the features of the stories each user consumes into a profile representing the content affinity of the user. The aggregation process is sequential, where each story the user consumes strengthens the user's affinity to that story's attributes, and causes some decay to the other affinities. In this manner, persistent interests of the user will stand out while temporary interests will eventually fade. This results in users also being represented by k feature vectors. Unlike the sparse vectors that represent each story, user vectors are typically more dense.

Matching. Since users are represented by aggregation of story features, both users and stories are represented in the same feature space, namely k feature vectors. This allows for similarity scoring between users and stories. At its simplest form, one can derive, per feature vector, a similarity score such as cosine measure, as is standard in Information Retrieval [?], and then learn a predictive model over the k similarity scores.

4. DEMO OUTLINE

We will demonstrate how user browsing actions are reflected in the user profile, and how the user profile is leveraged when producing personalized recommendations. Specifically, the demo we will show is comprised of the following steps:

1. Open a new incognito browser window, to generate a new user with an empty profile.

2. Browse a few stories on publishers in the Outbrain network, and visualize how the profile changes upon each page view.

3. Make a request for recommendations, and observe how the served recommendations reflect the profile built so far.

4. Repeat steps 2-3 again, to observe how the recommendations have changed as the profile matures.

5. CONCLUSIONS

We demonstrate three components of Outbrain's personalization stack:

1. A user profile visualization tool, showing how we represent users' affinity to content and how the representation is updated in real time, as users browse the Web.

2. A personalized content discovery experience, whose recommendations to a user reflect the user's profile.

3. Introspective explanations that tie the profile to the served recommendations.

The first and third components above have proven to be extremely valuable to the process of developing and reasoning about Outbrain's personalization technology. Investing in them in parallel to the obvious scale and quality aspects of the personalization system has been well worth the effort.

6. REFERENCES

[1] D. M. Blei, A. Y. Ng, and M. I. Jordan. Latent dirichlet allocation. *J. Mach. Learn. Res.*, 3:993–1022, Mar. 2003.

[2] D. Goldberg, D. Nichols, B. M. Oki, and D. Terry. Using collaborative filtering to weave an information tapestry. *Commun. ACM*, 35(12):61–70, Dec. 1992.

[3] J. Herlocker, J. Konstan, and J. Riedl. An empirical analysis of design choices in neighborhood-based collaborative filtering algorithms. *Information Retrieval*, 5(4):287–310, 2002.

[4] P. B. Kantor, F. Ricci, L. Rokach, and B. Shapira. *Recommender Systems Handbook*. Springer, Dordrecht, 2011.

[5] Y. Koren, R. M. Bell, and C. Volinsky. Matrix factorization techniques for recommender systems. *Computer, IEEE*, 42(8):30–37, 2009.

[6] C. D. Manning, P. Raghavan, H. Schütze, et al. *Introduction to information retrieval*, volume 1. Cambridge university press Cambridge, 2008.

[7] M. Pazzani and D. Billsus. Content-based recommendation systems. In P. Brusilovsky, A. Kobsa, and W. Nejdl, editors, *The Adaptive Web*, volume 4321 of *Lecture Notes in Computer Science*, pages 325–341. Springer Berlin Heidelberg, 2007.

[8] J. B. Schafer, J. Konstan, and J. Riedl. Recommender systems in e-commerce. In *Proceedings of the 1st ACM Conference on Electronic Commerce*, EC '99, pages 158–166, New York, NY, USA, 1999. ACM.

[1] By "collaborative filtering persona" we mean the data required to compute collaborative filtering recommendations for the user. This can be a list of users exhibiting similar consumption patterns in user neighbourhood models [?], or the user's latent vector in matrix factorization schemes [?].

RecExp: A Semantic Recommender System with Explanation Based on Heterogeneous Information Network

Jiawei Hu
Beijing University of Posts and Telecommunications
Beijing, China
hujiawei@bupt.edu.cn

Zhiqiang Zhang
Ant Financial Services Group
Hangzhou, Zhejiang Province, China
lingyao.zzq@alipay.com

Jian Liu
Beijing University of Posts and Telecommunications
Beijing, China
fullback@yeah.net

Chuan Shi
Beijing University of Posts and Telecommunications
Beijing, China
shichuan@bupt.edu.cn

Philip S. Yu
University of Illinois at Chicago
IL,USA
psyu@cs.uic.edu

Bai Wang
Beijing University of Posts and Telecommunications
Beijing, China
wangbai@bupt.edu.cn

ABSTRACT

In recent years, there is a surge of research on recommender system to alleviate the information overload. Many recommendation techniques have been proposed and they have achieved great successes in many applications. However, the explanation of recommendation results is an important but seldom addressed problem. In this paper, we organize the objects and relations in a recommender system with a heterogeneous information network, which integrates more informations and contains rich semantics. Then we employ a semantic meta path based personalized recommendation model and design a recommender system with explanation, called RecExp. The RecExp system has two unique features. (1) Semantic recommendation. RecExp provides different recommendation models to comply with users' requirements through setting of meta paths. (2) Interpretive recommendation. Under a hybrid recommendation model, RecExp provides the explanations for the recommendation results.

Keywords

Recommender Systems; Heterogeneous information network; Recommendation explanation

1. INTRODUCTION

Recently, recommender systems have attracted much attention from multiple disciplines, and many techniques have been proposed to build recommender systems. However, these techniques only focus on the accuracy metrics, they seldom care about the explanation of recommendation results. As we all known,good explanations could help inspire user trust and loyalty, and increase satisfaction. Recommendation explanation makes it quicker and easier for users to find what they want, and persuade them to try or purchase a recommended item [4].

RecSys '16 September 15-19, 2016, Boston , MA, USA

ACM ISBN 978-1-4503-4035-9/16/09.
DOI: http://dx.doi.org/10.1145/2959100.2959112

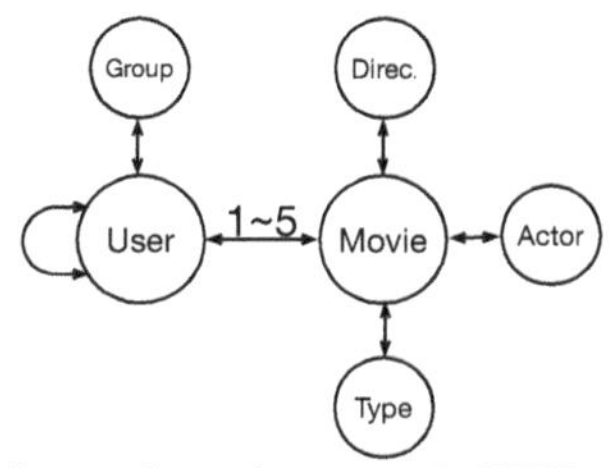

Figure 1: Network schema of HIN constituted by douban movie recommendation.

In this paper, we develop a **Rec**ommender system with **Exp**lanation (called RecExp). Inspired by the recent surge of heterogeneous information network (HIN) [1], we organized the objects and relations in a recommender system as a HIN. Fig. 1 shows such an example in movie recommendation. The HIN not only contains different types of objects in movie recommendation (e.g., users and movies) but also illustrates all kinds of relations among objects, such as viewing information, social relations, and attribute information. Moreover, two objects in a HIN can be connected via different paths, called meta path [3], and different meta paths have different meanings. So we can find the similar users of a user through different meta paths connecting these two users, and then we can combine the recommendation results of different similar users under different meta paths. Based on this idea, we design the semantic recommender system, RecExp, with explanation, which has the following two significant features:

- Semantic recommendation. Utilizing different meta paths, RecExp can find different similar users, and thus generate different recommendation results according to these similar users. Moreover, these meta paths correspond to different recommendation models, so RecExp can realize semantic recommendation through selecting proper meta paths.
- Recommendation explanation. RecExp utilizes semantics and weights of meta paths to present personalized recommendation explanation, which can reveal user preferences and make explanation more persuasive.

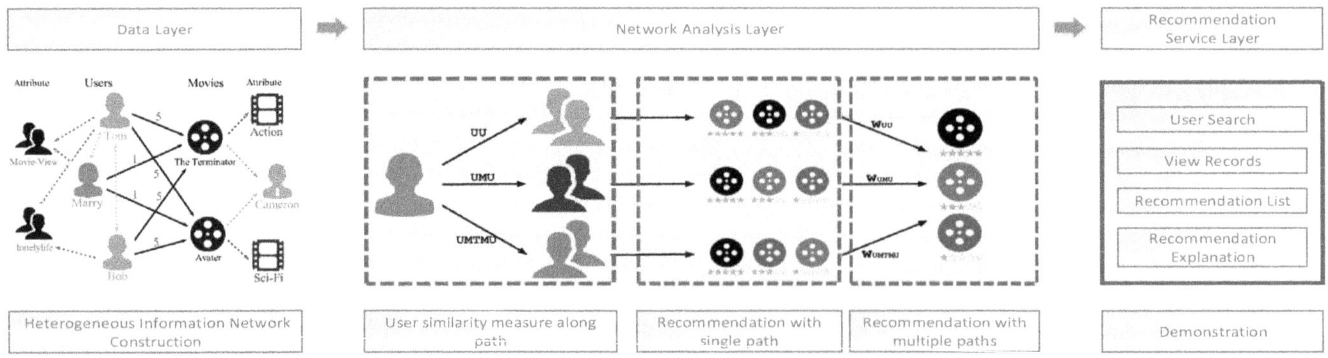

Figure 2: The architecture of *RecExp* system.

2. SYSTEM FRAMEWORK

Fig. 2 shows the system architecture. The three main components are detailed as follows.

- Data layer: it extracts data from different data sources (e.g., database and web) to construct a HIN.
- Network analysis layer: it analyzes the HIN and provides the recommendation services. It first computes the similarities between users along different meta paths, such as "User-Movie-User". And then, based on similarity of users, we find the similar users of a target user under a given path, and the predicted rating score of the target user on a movie can be inferred from the rating scores of these similar users on the movie. Under different meta paths, there are different predicted rating scores. Through the weight learning method, we assign each meta path with a preference weight for each user, and the final predicted rating under all meta paths can be the weighted average of predicted rating under each meta path. More technique details can be found in our work[2].
- Recommendation service layer: it provides the succinct and friendly web interface of recommendation services. The recommendation services include five kinds of semantic recommendations , hybrid recommendation with explanation, and the view record for the searched user.

3. DEMONSTRATION

In this part, we will show the two major components of the *RecExp* system. For more details, please visit our introduction video at https://youtu.be/-AjdS7vedAI.

- Recommendation functions: there are six recommendation function buttons in Fig. 3. Each function button represents a typical recommendation model through selecting a meta path. For example, the collaborative filtering corresponds to the UMU path. The description of the selected recommendation model is detailed under the button box. For example, if you press the "Hybrid recommendation" button, the below panel will show "Recommendation based on hybrid information, such as movie content and social relation".
- Recommendation explanation: the function will be invoked when the "Hybrid recommendation" function is selected. Fig. 4 shows the details of the explanation. Since the hybrid recommendation generates the results through multiple meta paths, the fan chart shows the weights of each meta path which can represent the user preference on these paths. The larger the weight is, the more the user prefers to get recommendation from the corresponding meta path. On the right of the fan chart, it shows three most important meta paths and corresponding explanations. In each explanation, we display the three most similar users with the target user based on corresponding meta path.

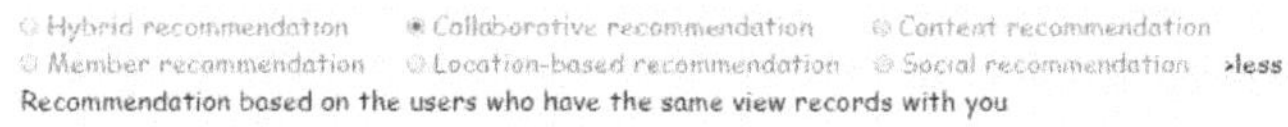

Figure 3: Recommendation Functions.

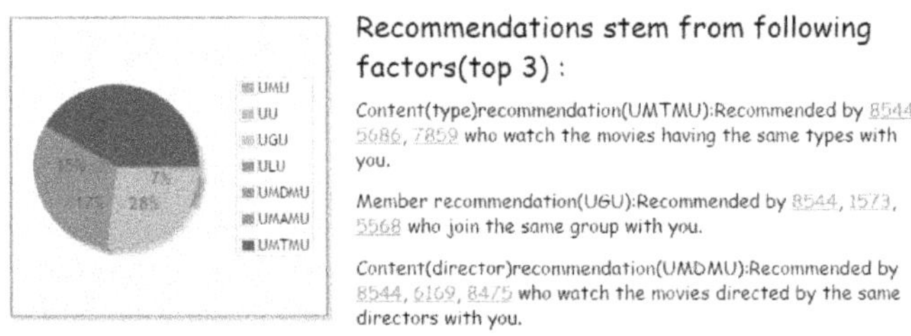

Figure 4: Recommendation Explanation.

4. CONCLUSION

Based on the heterogeneous network, we designed a novel recommendation system: *RecExp*. The *RecExp* system has two unique properties: semantic recommendation and interpretable recommendation. The demonstration on the real-world movie data set validates its effectiveness.

5. ACKNOWLEDGMENTS

This work is supported in part by National Key Basic Research and Department (973) Program of China (No. 2013CB329606), and the National Natural Science Foundation of China (No. 61375058), and the Co-construction Project of Beijing Municipal Commission of Education, and the CCF-Tencent Open Fund.

6. REFERENCES

[1] C. Shi, Y. Li, J. Zhang, Y. Sun, and P. S. Yu. A survey of heterogeneous information network analysis. *arXiv preprint arXiv:1511.04854*, 2015.

[2] C. Shi, Z. Zhang, P. Luo, P. S. Yu, Y. Yue, and B. Wu. Semantic path based personalized recommendation on weighted heterogeneous information networks. In *CIKM*, 2015.

[3] Y. Sun, J. Han, X. Yan, P. S. Yu, and T. Wu. Pathsim: Meta path-based top-k similarity search in heterogeneous information networks. *VLDBq́r11*, 2011.

[4] N. Tintarev and J. Masthoff. A survey of explanations in recommender systems. In *WPRSIUI*, 2007.

Topical Semantic Recommendations for Auteur Films

Christian Rakow, Andreas Lommatzsch, and Till Plumbaum
Technische Universität Berlin – DAI-Labor
Ernst-Reuter-Platz 7, D-10587 Berlin, Germany
{Christian.Rakow, Andreas.Lommatzsch, Till.Plumbaum}@dai-labor.de

ABSTRACT

With the ubiquity of fast internet connections and the growing availability of Video-On-Demand (VOD) services powerful recommender systems are needed. Traditionally, movie recommender systems apply user-based collaborative filtering providing high quality recommendations if users maintain user profiles describing preferences and movie ratings. The shortcomings of Collaborative Filtering are that comprehensive user profiles are required and users tend to get recommendations very similar to the user profile ("filter bubble"). In addition, CF-based recommenders neither consider current trends nor the context. In order to overcome these weaknesses, we develop a system identifying interesting events in the stream of current news and deploying this information for computing recommendations. Our system gathers topics of interest from TWITTER and RSS-Feeds, extracts relevant Named Entities, and uses semantic relations for recommending movies closely related to these topics. We explain the used algorithms and show that our system provides highly relevant recommendations.

Keywords

movie recommendations; semantic graphs; named entities

1. INTRODUCTION

Movie recommendation systems have been a widely studied topic for many years. The most frequently used approach is Collaborative Filtering (CF) based on the assumption that users who showed similar preferences in the past will like the similar movies in the future. CF-based algorithms deliver high quality results if a sufficient number of ratings for all movies is available and user profiles contain a sufficient number of preferences. Known weaknesses of CF-based approaches are: The bias towards popular movies, the "cold-start problem", and the missing consideration of the user's context as well as currents trends. These shortcomings make CF-based approaches inappropriate for niche markets characterized by limited number of ratings and specific user preferences. In this paper we present a system tailored to the needs of a VOD portal specialized on auteur films. In contrast to the main stream VOD companies, the film catalog focuses on the genres art house, independent, and documentaries. Specific challenges (when developing a recommender for this portal) are the limited user feedback, documentaries (having features differing from regular movies), and the specific interest of the target group.

RecSys '16 September 15-19, 2016, Boston , MA, USA

ACM ISBN 978-1-4503-4035-9/16/09.
DOI: http://dx.doi.org/10.1145/2959100.2959110

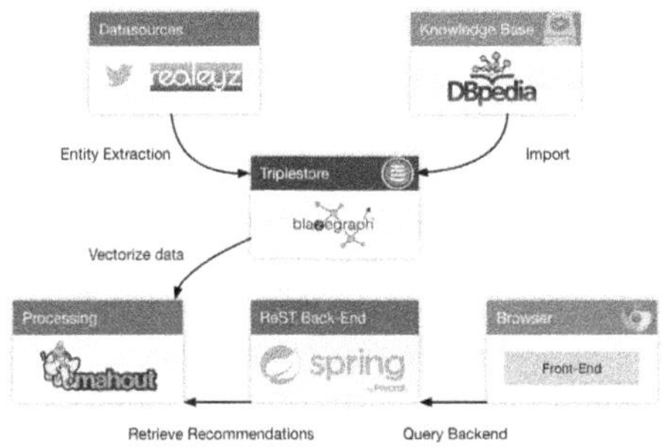

Figure 1: The figure visualizes the main components of our recommender system.

In order to provide highly relevant recommendations and to overcome the shortcomings of CF, we decided to develop a recommender strategy that analyzes news streams (relevant for the target group) and identifies the events suitable for computing topical recommendations. For each event we recognize related Named Entities and compute the films semantically connected with these entities.

We present our system for providing film recommendations based on the analysis of current news and TWITTER messages. We explain the architecture of the system and discuss the used algorithms in detail (Sec. 2). A description of the recommender service and a preliminary evaluation are given in Sec. 3. Finally, Sec. 4 gives a conclusion and an outlook on future work.

2. SYSTEM OVERVIEW

The system is built of components visualized in Fig. 1. We discuss the components tailored for crawling relevant documents, identifying relevant Named Entities, and computing recommendations in the next Section.

News Retrieval and Semantic Knowledge Bases

We collect news relevant for the target group of the recommender system. For this purpose we consider three different sources: (1) TWITTER messages published by an expert-

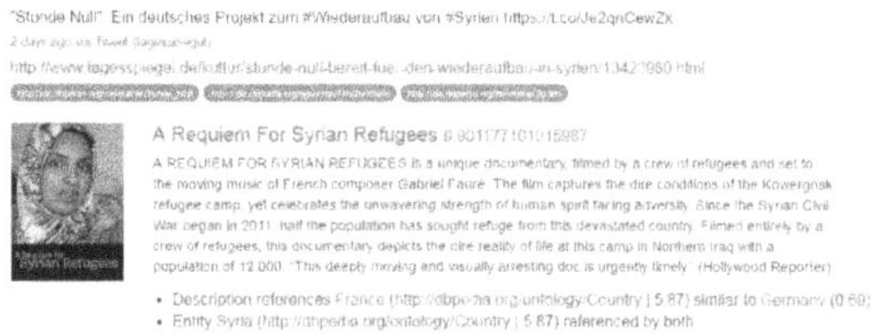

Figure 2: The figure shows a example recommendation. Based on the Named Entites recognized in a Twitter message, a movie is recommended. The semantic connections between the film and the Named Entites are provided as an explanation.

defined set of users, (2) **RSS** feeds created by portals relevant for our target group, and (3) general news headlines published on TWITTER. We continuously update our news database ensuring the news collection is always up to date.

The catalog of available films is imported as a semantically represented data collection. The film data set provides detailed text-based descriptions, including a summary of the plot, the list of related persons (actors, directors, etc.) as well as festivals and awards. In addition to the film catalog we import DBPEDIA (http://wiki.dbpedia.org/). We use DBPEDIA SPOTLIGHTfor identifying Named Entities in the film descriptions and linking them with their matching DBPEDIA entity. The results are stored in a semantic store (BLAZEGRAPH, https://www.blazegraph.com/).

Processing and Computing Recommendations

The continuously collected news is periodically processed. In the first step we recognize and disambiguate Named Entities in the texts/messages. Subsequently we compute the co-occurrence vectors of each entity using the most recent news documents. The vectors are clustered using the DBSCAN algorithm [3] in order to obtain clusters representing the topics dominant in the news. The vector processing and clustering is implemented in the APACHE MAHOUT framework (http://mahout.apache.org/). The computed topics are ranked by the number of retweets and references in order to give popular news a bigger weight.

Based on the most popular topics we recommend movies that are closely related. Every entity in a topic is compared to each entity extracted from the film descriptions or the meta-data. The relatedness of films to a topic is computed by the number of entities directly connected to both. In addition, we considered the similarity between linked entities, which is computed based on their attributes by using a vector-space-model (as explained in [2]). In general, the similarity between two entities is the bigger the more they share common subjects (based on DBPEDIA edges type `skos:subject`). The recommendation result is built from the films containing the Names Entities recognized in the news or entities similar to these entities.

Front End

The recommendations are provided as a ReSTful web service. For visualizing the results we built a web application allowing us testing different parameter sets and collecting feedback from users for the computed recommendations. Fig. 2 shows an example: Based on the Named Entities recognized in a tweet, a movie about a Syrian woman is recommended. One can see how the detected entities contribute to the relevance score.

3. EVALUATION AND SYSTEM DEMO

The implemented web application allows us testing the recommendations and discussing the suggestions.

In the system demonstration we show the recommendations based on live news data. Users can select the sources used for identifying topics. In addition, we demonstrate the effect of different methods used for clustering and computing the similarity between topics and films. The explanations provided for the recommendations help users to understand why a movie is related to the identified topics and why the movie is recommended.

A preliminary evaluation of the recommendation results shows that the implemented recommender approach provides relevant suggestions. The use of topics extracted from politics-related news delivers good recommendations for documentaries and film strongly related to certain regions and crises. News retracted from arthouse-related tweets and RSS feeds are well-situated for detecting artist-related events (e.g. anniversaries and festivals). Entities-based (semantic) similarity measures outperform term-based similarity measures. The weights of the considered semantic edge types must be tuned for the scenario in order to ensure high-quality recommendations.

4. CONCLUSIONS

We presented a novel approach combining topics extraction and linked open data for computing topical recommendations. The preliminary evaluation shows that the recommender delivers highly relevant results. Events detected in the recent news are accepted by users as helpful explanations. As future work, we plan extended user studies. Furthermore, we plan to apply the approach in different domains. The adaption for new domains does not require much effort, since the approach only requires a stream of documents (allowing us identifying Named Entities). When applying the algorithm to new domains the set of considered entities and the similarity measure must be adapted accordingly.

5. REFERENCES

[1] J. Daiber, M. Jakob, C. Hokamp, and P. N. Mendes. Improving efficiency and accuracy in multilingual entity extraction. In *Procs. of the 9th Intl. Conf. on Semantic Systems (I-Semantics)*, 2013.

[2] T. Di Noia, R. Mirizzi, V. C. Ostuni, D. Romito, and M. Zanker. Linked open data to support content-based recommender systems. In *8th Intl. Conf. on Semantic Systems - I-SEMANTICS '12*, NY, USA, 2012. ACM.

[3] M. Ester, H.-P. Kriegel, J. Sander, and X. Xu. A density-based algorithm for discovering clusters in large spatial databases with noise. In *Procs. of KDD-96*, pages 226–231. AAAI, 1996.

Acknowledgments

The work has been partially done in the EEGoF project supported by the German Federal Ministry for Economic Affairs and Energy. The research leading to these results was performed in the CrowdRec project, which has received funding (or partial funding) from the EU 7th Framework Programme FP7/2007-2013 under grant agreement No. 610594.

T-RecS: a Framework for a Temporal Semantic Analysis of the ACM Recommender Systems Conference

Fedelucio Narducci Pierpaolo Basile Pasquale Lops
Marco De Gemmis Giovanni Semeraro

Dept. of Computer Science - University of Bari 'Aldo Moro - Italy
name.surname@uniba.it

ABSTRACT

This paper presents T-RecS (Temporal analysis of Recommender Systems conference proceedings), a framework that supplies services to analyze the Recommender Systems Conference proceedings from the first edition, held in 2007, to the last one, held in 2015, under a temporal point of view. The idea behind T-RecS is to identify linguistic phenomena that reflect some interesting variations for the research community, such as topic drift, or how the correlation between two terms changed over time, or how similarity between two authors evolved over time. The implemented framework can be easily adapted for the analysis of different corpora and domains.

1. INTRODUCTION

Several authors tried to perform a computational history of science by analyzing corpora of scholarly papers [1, 2]. Those works are particularly focused on the identification of topics and their evolution over time. These analyses are useful for mining trends of research topics and to discover how science is evolving over time. T-RecS provides a set of services with a twofold purpose: first, to perform an author-centered analysis of the topics characterizing the RecSys conference series, similarly to the work proposed in [3]; second, to examine how semantics of topics has evolved over time. The correlation between authors and topics is computed by exploiting two different techniques inspired respectively to the Google Books N-gram Viewer[1] and to the Explicit Semantic Analysis [4]. The topic semantics is studied by means of a framework named Temporal Random Indexing [5] able to outline the evolution in the usage of a particular term over time. T-RecS is implemented as a web application and empowers users who want to know, for example, the authors who studied a given topic in a specific time interval, the most used recommendation paradigm in a given period, the evolution of the semantics of a specific topic, how a given problem has been addressed over time, and so on.

The rest of the paper is organized as follows. Section 2 provides an overview of the implemented techniques, and Section 3 reports a demonstration summary of the web application. Finally, conclusions and future applications are drawn in Section 4.

[1]https://books.google.com/ngrams

RecSys '16 September 15-19, 2016, Boston , MA, USA

ACM ISBN 978-1-4503-4035-9/16/09.
DOI: http://dx.doi.org/10.1145/2959100.2959113

2. DESCRIPTION OF THE SYSTEM

Figure 1 shows the general architecture of T-RecS, consisting of three main components: the *N-gram Analyzer*, the *ESA Analyzer*, the *TRI Analyzer*. Details for each component are reported in the following subsections.

2.1 N-gram Analyzer

The N-gram Analyzer counts the occurrences of n-grams ($n = 1, ..., 5$) in the documents of a corpus. We analyzed the RecSys proceedings corpus in the time interval from 2007 to 2015. We set parameters in order to count n-grams grouped by author and year. In that way it is possible to show the percentage of n-grams in the corpus for each year, and to split this value by author. This component is inspired to the Google Books N-gram Viewer [6], a web application for culturomics that displays in a chart the counting of 1-grams, 2-grams, 3-grams, 4-grams, and 5-grams from the Google corpus of over 15 million books. The goal of this component is to discover the evolution of topics represented by n-grams through the analysis of their occurrences in the corpus.

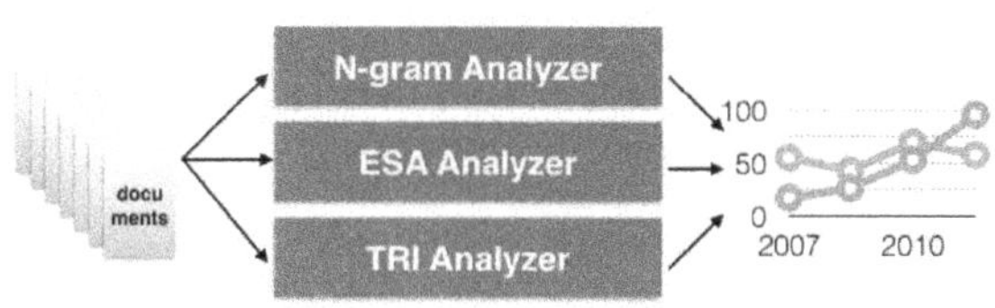

Figure 1: General Architecture of T-RecS

2.2 TRI Analyzer

The Temporal Random Indexing (TRI) Analyzer extends a Distributional Semantic Model technique called Random Indexing (RI) to allow the analysis of semantic changes of words over time [5]. The semantic vector for a word in a given time period is the result of its co-occurrences with other words in the *same* time interval, but the usage of RI for building the word representations over different times guarantees their comparability along the timeline. A *WordSpace* is built by taking into account words co-occurrences, according to the distributional hypothesis [7] which states that words sharing the same linguistic contexts are related in meaning. In our case the linguistic context is defined as the words that co-occur in the same time period with the target (*temporal*) word, i.e. the word under the temporal analysis. In our implementation, we adopted the open source version of Temporal RI available on github[2].

2.3 ESA Analyzer

The Explicit Semantic Analysis (ESA) Analyzer is inspired to the ESA technique [4] proposed by Gabrilovich and Markovitch, which establishes a correlation between terms in a vocabulary and semantic concepts extracted from Wikipedia. In T-RecS, this component builds a matrix for each edition of the conference proceedings, in which rows are the terms occurring in the proceedings and columns are the authors. Given a term, it is possible to compare the most related authors by extracting from the matrix the row vector of that term. It is also possible to extract the most related authors for a text fragment consisting of different terms. In that case, the system computes the centroid vector of the row vectors of the terms composing the text fragment. The column vectors of the matrix are used for computing similarity scores between authors. Indeed, the column vectors are bags of words related to specific authors, with a weight associated to each term. In order to define the similarity between two authors, ESA Analyzer computes the cosine similarity between their column vectors.

3. DEMONSTRATION SUMMARY

The GUI of T-RecS consists of the following components: a text box to formulate a query, an *analysis* menu that allows the user to select the analysis she desires to perform, a list of retrieved authors that allows to draw a chart tailored on a specific person[3]. The first interaction step is the selection of the analysis to be performed by the corresponding menu. Next, the user selects the time interval for the analysis, and finally she sets the following analysis-dependent parameters:

Topic-Author Correlation. The Topic-Author correlation is powered by the ESA Analyzer. The *author sorting* parameter has two options: total (the ranking considers years with 0 correlation score), and relative (the ranking does not consider years with 0 correlation score).

The *authors list* is shown on the right side of the GUI and contains authors relevant with respect to the query. The user can then select one or more authors and the system shows their contribution on that topic (i.e., the query) for each year.

N-gram Analyzer. The user indicates the n-grams to be searched, separated by commas. The number of n-grams to be retrieved are limited by the *Result Size* parameter. The user can select one or more authors from the *authors list* and the corresponding chart is drawn. For each author, the number of times and the number of papers the input n-grams occur in are reported in brackets. The *with smoothing of* parameter allows the smoothing of the chart by choosing a value from the corresponding menu.

Topic Semantics. The only input required to the user for this analysis is a list of topics (query) whose semantics will be analyzed. Topics must be separated by comma. For each topic (e.g., LDA), the chart shows how its semantics has changed over the years.

TRI Similarity. The input is a pair of topics (query) whose semantic correlation will be analyzed. Topics must be separated by comma (e.g., matrix factorization, collaborative filtering). The query may consist of two or more pairs, sequentially written and separated by commas.

Author Similarities. The user indicates the author name (e.g., Jill Freyne) as query and the system retrieves the most similar authors for each year. This analysis requires to set the neighborhood size, namely the number of similar authors to retrieve, and a flag that allows to exclude co-authors from the computation.

[2]https://github.com/pippokill/tri

[3]The web application is available at http://193.204.187.192/recsys/, and a video demo is available at https://www.dropbox.com/s/3pyy2ur3lmdkci0/TRecS.mp4?dl=0

4. CONCLUSIONS AND FUTURE APPLICATIONS

In this work we presented T-RecS, a web application that implements several computational linguistic techniques for analyzing the corpus of the RecSys conference proceedings. T-RecS is a tool that may be useful to validate assumptions on the evolution of a topic, the application of a solution for a specific problem, and so on. The proposed techniques might turn out to be exploitable in different tasks, such as recommendation of reviewers, of program committee members, of special tracks and challenges, analysis of trending topics, literature reviews. The framework is not tailored to the specific corpus of the RecSys conference proceedings, thus it can be exploited for analyzing different corpora and domains.

5. REFERENCES

[1] T. L. Griffiths and M. Steyvers, "Finding scientific topics," *Proceedings of the National Academy of Sciences*, vol. 101, no. suppl 1, pp. 5228–5235, 2004.

[2] D. Hall, D. Jurafsky, and C. D. Manning, "Studying the history of ideas using topic models," in *Proceedings of the conference on Empirical Methods in Natural Language Processing*. Association for Computational Linguistics, 2008, pp. 363–371.

[3] A. Anderson, D. McFarland, and D. Jurafsky, "Towards a computational history of the ACL: 1980-2008," in *Proceedings of the ACL-2012 Special Workshop on Rediscovering 50 Years of Discoveries*. Association for Computational Linguistics, 2012, pp. 13–21.

[4] E. Gabrilovich and S. Markovitch, "Wikipedia-based semantic interpretation for natural language processing," *Journal of Artificial Intelligence Research*, pp. 443–498, 2009.

[5] D. Jurgens and K. Stevens, "Event Detection in Blogs using Temporal Random Indexing," in *Proceedings of the Workshop on Events in Emerging Text Types*. Association for Computational Linguistics, 2009, pp. 9–16.

[6] J.-B. Michel, Y. K. Shen, A. P. Aiden, A. Veres, M. K. Gray, T. G. B. Team, J. P. Pickett, D. Hoiberg, D. Clancy, P. Norvig, J. Orwant, S. Pinker, M. A. Nowak, and E. L. Aiden, "Quantitative analysis of culture using millions of digitized books," *Science*, vol. 331, no. 6014, pp. 176–182, 2011.

[7] Z. S. Harris, *Mathematical Structures of Language*. New York: Interscience, 1968.

4th Workshop on Emotions and Personality in Personalized Systems (EMPIRE)

Marko Tkalčič
Free University of Bolzano
Piazza Domenicani 1
39100 Bolzano, Italy
marko.tkalcic@unibz.it

Berardina DeCarolis
Marco de Gemmis
University of Bari Aldo Moro
Italy
nadja@di.uniba.it
marco.degemmis@uniba.it

Andrej Košir
University of Ljubljana
Faculty of Electrical Engineering
Slovenia
andrej.kosir@fe.uni-lj.si

ABSTRACT

The 4th Workshop on Emotions and Personality in Personalized Systems (EMPIRE) is taking place in Boston on September 16th, 2016 in conjunction with the ACM RecSys 2016 conference. The workshop focuses on the acquisition and usage of emotions and personality as user-centric aspects of personalization.

CCS Concepts

•**Information systems** → *Information systems applications;* •**Human-centered computing** → *Human computer interaction (HCI);* •**Computing methodologies** → *Machine learning;*

Keywords

Emotions; Personality; Recommender Systems

1. INTRODUCTION

The workshop will be held in conjunction with the ACM RecSys 2016 conference in Boston (MA) on Friday, 16. September, 2016. It will take place at the Massachusetts Institute of Technology (MIT) and the IBM Research campuses.

2. DESCRIPTION

The RecSys research community has done a tremendous job in the last decade on exploiting various data sources to improve recommendations through sophisticated algorithms. The workshop complements these core RecSys activities by pushing the agenda of taking into account user-centric aspects, such as emotions and personality, into the RecSys framework. In fact, personality and emotions shape our daily lives by having a strong influence on our preferences, decisions and behaviour in general. In recent years, emotions and personality have shown to play an important role in various aspects of recommender systems, such as implicit feedback, contextual information, affective content labeling, cold-start problem, diversity, cross-domain recommendations, group recommendations etc. With the development of robust techniques for the unobtrusive acquisition of emotions (e.g. from various modalities, such as video or physiological sensors) and personality (e.g. from social media) the time is right to take advantage of these possibilities to collect massive datasets and improve recommender systems.

RecSys '16 September 15-19, 2016, Boston , MA, USA

ACM ISBN 978-1-4503-4035-9/16/09.

DOI: http://dx.doi.org/10.1145/2959100.2959201

3. TOPICS

The topics include but are not limited to:

- usage of affect to improve personalized systems
- usage of personality to improve personalized systems
- implicit detection of affect for personalized systems
- implicit detection of personality for personalized systems
- computational models of emotion and personality
- affect and personality as contextual factors
- affect as implicit feedback
- affect and personality in cross domain recommenders
- affect and personality as user/item similarities
- affect and personality-based evaluation methods
- affect and personality in applications (e.g. movie recommenders, music recommenders, e-learning, people-to-people recommenders etc.)
- affect and personality with human decision making
- affect and personality in group recommenders
- affect and personality for the cold-start problem
- privacy aspects of the usage of affect and personality in personalized systems
- affect and personality in connection to social media

Engendering Health with Recommender Systems

Workshop abstract

David Elsweiler
I:IMSK University of Regensburg Germany
david.elsweiler@ur.de

Bernd Ludwig
I:IMSK University of Regensburg Germany
bernd.ludwg@ur.de

Alan Said
University of Skövde Sweden
alansaid@acm.org

Hanna Schäfer
RG: Social Computing TU Munich Germany
hanna.schaefer@tum.de

Christoph Trattner
Know-Center Graz Austria
ctrattner@know-center.at

ABSTRACT

The first Workshop on Engendering Health with Recommender Systems was organized in conjunction with ACM RecSys 2016. The focus of the workshop was on bringing together researchers and practitioners from diverse areas of health, well-being, decision support, and behavioral change. Health-related issues in recommender systems have been a growing research topic in the recent years and this was a initial attempt at bringing together academics and practitioners to share their experiences on working on related issues.

CCS Concepts

•**Information systems** → **Information systems applications; Information retrieval;** *Web mining;* •**Applied computing** → **Health informatics;** *Health care information systems;* •**Human-centered computing** → *Human computer interaction (HCI);*

Keywords

Health-aware computing; Health-aware information systems; Recommender Systems; Well-being; Accessibility;

1. INTRODUCTION

Busy lifestyles, abundant options, lack of knowledge; there are many reasons why people make poor decisions relating to their health [1, 2]. Yet these poor decisions are leading to epidemics, which represent some of the greatest challenges we face as a society today. Noncommunicable Diseases (NCDs), which include cardiovascular diseases, cancer, chronic respiratory diseases and diabetes, account for ~60% of total deaths worldwide. These diseases share the same four behavioral risk factors: tobacco use, unhealthy diet, physical inactivity and harmful consumption of alcohol and can be prevented and sometimes even reversed with simple lifestyle changes. Eating more healthily, exercising more appropriately, sleeping and relaxing more, as well as simply being more aware of one's state of health are all things that would lead to improved health. Yet knowing exactly what to change and how, implementing changes and maintaining changes over long time periods are all things people find challenging. These are also problems, for which we believe recommender systems can provide assistance by offering specific, tailored suggestions for behavioral change. In recent years recommender systems for health has become a popular topic within the RecSys community and a selection of empirical contributions and demo systems have been published. Efforts to date, however have been sporadic and lack coordination. We lack shared infrastructure such as datasets, appropriate cross-disciplinary knowledge, even agreed upon goals. The aim of this workshop was to use is as a vehicle to:

- Establish the problem as a prominent RecSys topic
- Create a community of researchers who will determine a concrete research agenda for health in RecSys
- Attract scientists from other domains to RecSys: health (e.g. sports, nutrition, medicine), psychology, signal processing, wearables, HCI, etc.
- Create new ideas for collaboration, particularly cross-domain collaborations
- Establish shared infrastructure (datasets and tools)

The topics of specific interest to the workshop were:

- Motivation - increasing motivation, understanding motivation, utilizing psychological models, gamification
- Algorithms for Health Recommendations
- Interfaces - Explanations/Presentation, Feedback, Usability
- Persuasive Design
- Sensors - e.g. activity tracking, context detection, quantified self, motivation by self assessment
- Mobile devices

RecSys '16 September 15-19, 2016, Boston, MA, USA

ACM ISBN 978-1-4503-4035-9/16/09.

DOI: http://dx.doi.org/10.1145/2959100.2959203

- Gamification - e.g. Making exercise or diet fun
- Social Motivation - Inclusion of Social Context, Coactivity and Group Recommenders
- Knowledge representation - Transfer of domain knowledge to digital systems
- Ethics - Gap between recommendations and medical advice
- Ease of use - embedding systems into everyday life Learning about health
- User modelling, behavioral analytics and behavioral change

2. ACCEPTED PAPERS

In total 5 papers were accepted to the workshop.

- *Palakorn Achananuparp and Ingmar Weber.* Extracting Food Substitutes From Food Diary via Distributional Similarity
- *Jennifer Ekstrand and Michael Ekstrand.* First Do No Harm: Considering and Minimizing Harm in Recommender Systems Designed for Engendering Health
- *Santiago Hors-Fraile, Francisco J NÃžÃśez Benjumea, Laura Carrasco HernÃąndez, Francisco Ortega Ruiz and Luis Fernandez-Luque.* Design of two combined health recommender systems for tailoring messages in a smoking cessation app
- *Emmanuel Agu and Mark Claypool.* Cypress: A Cyber-Physical Recommender System to Discover SmartPhone Exergame Enjoyment
- *Ulrich Reimer, Edith Maier and Tom Ulmer.* Automatic User Adaptation for Behavior Change Support

3. ACKNOWLEDGMENTS

We thank the RecSys 2016 organizing committee for giving us the opportunity to host this workshop in conjunction with RecSys 2016 in Boston, MA, USA. We would also like to thank the authors, presenters, and reviewers, whose efforts made the workshop possible. The organizers are supported in part by the Enable Cluster (BMBF, Funding number: 01EA1409H) and the Know-Center. The KnowCenter is funded within the Austrian COMET Program - managed by the Austrian Research Promotion Agency (FFG).

4. REFERENCES

[1] S. Abbar, Y. Mejova, and I. Weber. You tweet what you eat: Studying food consumption through twitter. In B. Begole, J. Kim, K. Inkpen, and W. Woo, editors, *Proceedings of the 33rd Annual ACM Conference on Human Factors in Computing Systems, CHI 2015, Seoul, Republic of Korea, April 18-23, 2015*, pages 3197–3206. ACM, 2015.

[2] M. D. Choudhury, S. S. Sharma, and E. Kiciman. Characterizing dietary choices, nutrition, and language in food deserts via social media. In D. Gergle, M. R. Morris, P. Bjørn, and J. A. Konstan, editors, *Proceedings of the 19th ACM Conference on Computer-Supported Cooperative Work & Social Computing, CSCW 2016, San Francisco, CA, USA, February 27 - March 2, 2016*, pages 1155–1168. ACM, 2016.

RecProfile '16: Workshop on Profiling User Preferences for Dynamic, Online, and Real-Time recommendations

Rani Nelken
Outbrain Inc.
39 W 13th Street
New York, NY 10011 USA
rani@outbrain.com

ABSTRACT

This paper summarizes RecProfile '16, the first workshop on profiling user preferences for dynamic, online, and real-time recommendations, held in conjunction with RecSys '16, the 10th ACM conference on recommender systems. We describe the main themes arising in the workshop's papers.

Keywords

User profiling; user preferences; dynamic user profiling; graph algorithms; recommendation systems; dynamic community detection; matrix factorization; collaborative filtering; content-based recommender systems

1. INTRODUCTION

Constructing user preference profiles is obviously crucial for effective and accurate predictions in recommendation systems across diverse domains. For many traditional recommendation services, creating user profiles is well understood, either through explicit user preference elicitation or through tracking implicit user actions. The growing prevalence of dynamic online recommendation services, however, raises interesting challenges for maintaining and updating user profiles.

First, effectively representing user preferences in dynamic settings requires novel modeling techniques, for instance using latent factorization to allow dynamic updates and to alleviate cold start issues. Second, it might be infeasible to aggregate all the observed user profile signals in a sufficiently time-efficient and space-efficient manner, when the range of possible user options is large. Instead, one may need to resort to algorithms that balance accuracy with scalability, for instance using streaming or sketching algorithms. Third, there are significant engineering architecture challenges in maintaining, updating, and retrieving large volumes of user profiles in real-time and combining those profiles with other real-time signals to rank recommendations in milliseconds.

This topic is of considerable interest to both industrial and academic recommender systems researchers, since it is important for many state-of-the-art practical recommendation services, and opens up many interesting theoretical research questions of a more algorithmic nature.

The half-day workshop's program consisted of two invited talks and four accepted submissions all addressing these topics.

- Laurent Charlin (Invited). Modeling User Preferences.
- Jonathan Siddharth (Invited). Building User Interest Profiles in Real-time for a Content Recommender System.
- Takuya Kitazawa, Incremental Factorization Machines for Persistently Cold-starting Online Item Recommendation.
- Jorge Díez, David Martínez-Rego, Amparo Alonso-Betanzos, Oscar Luaces and Antonio Bahamonde. Metrical Representation of Readers and Articles in a Digital Newspaper.
- Ido Tamir, Roy Bass, Baruch Brutman, Yoram Dayagi, Guy Kobrinsky and Ronny Lempel. Powering Content Discovery through Scalable, Realtime Profiling of Users' Content Preferences.
- Megan Bingham-Walker and Richard Searle. Personalized User Profiling for Time-Dependent Recommendation of Structured Products.

These papers describe domains that are inherently dynamic and therefore force novel solutions that handle the change in user preferences. This is obviously true for news recommendations, which is a focus of the invited talk by Siddharth, the papers by Díez *et al.* and Tamir *et al.* A novel domain of dynamic recommendations is structured financial products as described by Bingham-Walker and Searle. The trend of highly dynamic recommendation applications can safely be expected to continue in coming years in an increasing number of domains.

Successfully dealing with the online nature of the recommendations and the dynamic changes in user preferences requires novel algorithmic solutions, both for collaborative filtering approaches and for content-based approaches.

Charlin's talk focuses on several extensions of collaborative filtering that add explicit modeling power to user profiles. In [1], Charlin *et al.* propose a dynamic extension of Poisson Factorization [2], which explicitly models changes in the latent factors representing user taste, as well as those representing items, allowing for more accurate prediction in

RecSys '16, September 15-19, 2016, Boston , MA, USA

ACM ISBN 978-1-4503-4035-9/16/09.
DOI: http://dx.doi.org/10.1145/2959100.2959204

dynamic contexts. In [3], the authors incorporate user exposure to items as part of the model. The model tries to distinguish between items that a user did not select due to genuine lack of interest vs. items that the user was not exposed to. This distinction allows for better balance between positive and negative training examples.

Kitazawa proposes an interactive version of Factorization Machines [4], which are usually applied in a batch setting. Meanwhile, Díez *et al.* encode the problem of predicting user trajectories algebraically, where each item is encoded as a vector, and then learn a transition matrix predicting the online trajectory of users along a session path.

Bingham-Walker and Searle avoid explicit matrix factorization, opting instead for a dynamic community-detection based approach on the full graph of users, items, and their attributes.

Finally, both Siddharth and Tamir *et al.* adopt a content-based approach, whereby they track the implicit content-based features of articles that users interact with, and aggregate them into a user profile. They then drive recommendations by finding articles that are contextually similar to the profile. The dynamic nature of user tastes require balancing users' short term and longer term interests within the profiles.

In summary, the workshop's submitted papers and invited talks covered multiple aspects of enhancing user profiles to handle dynamic, online, and real-time recommendations. We expect these topics to continue to be at the forefront of many recommender design problems in multiple domains.

2. ACKNOWLEDGMENTS

Special thanks to the workshop's co-organizer, Marko Grobelnik, and to the members of the program committee, Ronny Lempel, Mike Gartrell, Jan Neumann, Gal Lavee and Lior Rokach.

3. REFERENCES

[1] L. Charlin, R. Ranganath, J. McInerney, and D. M. Blei. Dynamic poisson factorization. In *Proceedings of the 9th ACM Conference on Recommender Systems*, pages 155–162. ACM, 2015.

[2] P. K. Gopalan, L. Charlin, and D. Blei. Content-based recommendations with poisson factorization. In *Advances in Neural Information Processing Systems*, pages 3176–3184, 2014.

[3] D. Liang, L. Charlin, J. McInerney, and D. M. Blei. Modeling user exposure in recommendation. In *Proceedings of the 25th International Conference on World Wide Web*, pages 951–961. International World Wide Web Conferences Steering Committee, 2016.

[4] S. Rendle. Factorization machines with libfm. *ACM Transactions on Intelligent Systems and Technology (TIST)*, 3(3):57, 2012.

RecSys'16 Joint Workshop on Interfaces and Human Decision Making for Recommender Systems

Peter Brusilovsky
School of Information Sciences
University of Pittsburgh
USA
peterb@pitt.edu

Alexander Felfernig
Institute for Software Technology
Graz University of Technology
Austria
afelfernig@ist.tugraz.at

Pasquale Lops
Department of Computer Science
University of Bari
Italy
pasquale.lops@uniba.it

John O'Donovan
Department of Computer Science
University of California
USA
jod@cs.ucsb.edu

Giovanni Semeraro
Department of Computer Science
University of Bari
Italy
semeraro@di.uniba.it

Nava Tintarev
Department of Computer Science
Bournemouth University
UK
ntintarev@bournemouth.ac.uk

ABSTRACT

As intelligent interactive systems, recommender systems focus on determining predictions that fit the wishes and needs of users. Still, a large majority of recommender systems research focuses on accuracy criteria and much less attention is paid to how users interact with the system, and in which way the user interface has an influence on the selection behavior of the users. Consequently, it is important to look beyond algorithms. The main goals of the IntRS workshop are to analyze the impact of user interfaces and interaction design, and to explore human interaction with recommender systems. Methodologies for evaluating these aspects are also within the scope of the workshop.

CCS Concepts

•Information systems → Decision support systems; Information retrieval; •Human-centered computing → User interface design;

Keywords

Recommender Systems, Human Decision Making, User Interfaces, Human Computer Interaction, Evaluation Methods, Decision Biases

1. INTRODUCTION

The complexity of decision tasks, limited cognitive resources of recommender systems users, and a tendency to keep decision efforts as low as possible are related to the phenomenon of bounded rationality [12], i.e., users tend to employ decision heuristics rather than exhaustive search for optimal decisions. Furthermore, preferences of users are typically constructed within, and often changed throughout a recommendation session [1].

Decision making under bounded rationality is a door opener for different types of influences on decision outcomes. There exist different psychological theories that describe settings that can lead to suboptimal decisions. The manner in which alternatives are presented via a user interface, including accompanying information, can have an impact on the decision outcome.

Recently, these issues have gained some attention in the recommender systems community [4, 8]. Cosely et al. [6] show that user ratings can be manipulated by the predictions shown by the system. Chang et al. [3] show that preference elicitation can be completed more efficiently if the interface does not support initial personalization by letting users express their preferences on individual items but rather on groups of items. Stettinger et al. [10] analyze anchoring effects in the preference acquisition phase of group decision scenarios. The earlier the preferences of other group members are visible the lower is the standard deviation of individual user ratings. The later preferences are disclosed, the higher is the satisfaction with the final group decision and the perceived degree of decision support. Teppan and Felfernig [13] analyze the impact of decoy effects in recommendation scenarios where disliked items as part of a result set can have an impact on the selection behavior of the user. Chen and Pu [5] and O'Donovan et al. [11] show the positive impact of explanations on the trustworthiness of recommender systems. For an overview of different explanation approaches in recommender systems see e.g., [14]. Bollen et al. [2] show that larger recommendation sets that contain solely good items do not necessarily trigger higher choice satisfaction since increased difficulty in selection choice counteracts the attractiveness of the recommendation set. Finally, Tkalcic et al. provide an overview of the role of emotions in recommender systems. Specifically, they discuss models and acquisition methods for emotions and personality [15]. For further related discussions see e.g., [8, 9].

IntRS aims to bring together researchers and practitioners

RecSys '16 September 15-19, 2016, Boston, MA, USA

ACM ISBN 978-1-4503-4035-9/16/09...$15.00

DOI: http://dx.doi.org/10.1145/2959100.2959199

focusing on topics of designing and developing novel intelligent interfaces and evaluating their impact in terms of different dimensions such as usability, perceived recommendation quality, time needed to take a decision, decision quality and degree of subjective well-being [7]. A primary goal of the workshop is to foster a community with a strong focus on recommendation-related decision making and user interface design issues.

2. TOPICS AND CONTRIBUTIONS

The workshop covers *three interrelated themes*: (1) *user interfaces* (e.g., visual interfaces, explanation interfaces, natural language interfaces, trust-aware and social interfaces, context-aware interfaces, ubiquitous and mobile interfaces, and decision making interfaces), (2) *interaction mechanisms, user modeling, and decision making* (e.g., cognitive modeling for recommender systems, human - recommender interaction, controllability, decision theories, preference construction, interfaces that take into account the role of emotions, argumentation and persuasive recommendation, cultural differences, approaches to high-quality group decision making, and the detection and avoidance of decision biases), and (3) *evaluation* (e.g., case studies, empirical studies, new interfaces and interaction designs, and evaluation methods).

Topics of *contributions* submitted to this year's workshop are matchmaking for decision support, explanation interfaces, cross-cultural aspects of recommender user interfaces, decision biases triggered by recommender user interfaces, effects of user interfaces on the perceived recommendation quality, and novel applications.

3. WORKSHOP FORMAT

The *3rd Joint Workshop on Interfaces and Human Decision Making for Recommender Systems (IntRS'16)* is a result of merging two original RecSys workshops: *Human Decision Making and Recommender Systems (Decisions@RecSys – 2010–2013)* and *Interfaces for Recommender Systems (InterfaceRS'12)*. The idea of merging the two workshops was motivated by the strong interrelationship between user interface and human decision making topics. The combination of these two aspects seems to be highly attractive, for example, the IntRS'15 workshop in Vienna had 60 participants. The list of accepted IntRS'16 papers and the workshop schedule can be found at: *intrs16.wordpress.com*.

4. CONCLUSIONS

IntRS aims to bring together researchers and practitioners from areas related to users interfaces and decision making in recommender systems. This year's contributions are high quality and are expected to attract a large audience.

5. ADDITIONAL AUTHORS

Martijn Willemsen (School of Innovation Sciences, Eindhoven University of Technology, The Netherlands, email: `M.C.Willemsen@tue.nl`).

6. REFERENCES

[1] R. Bettman, M. Luce, and J. Payne. Constructive consumer choice processes. *Journal of Consumer Research*, 25:187–217, 1998.

[2] D. Bollen, B. Knijnenburg, M. Willemsen, and M. Graus. Understanding choice overload in recommender systems. In *4th ACM Conference on Recommender Systems*, pages 63–70, Barcelona, Spain, 2010.

[3] S. Chang, F. Harper, and L. Terveen. Using groups of items for preference elicitation in recommender systems. In *18th ACM Conference on Computer Supported Cooperative Work & Social Computing*, pages 1258 – 1269, 2015.

[4] L. Chen, M. deGemmis, A. Felfernig, P. Lops, F. Ricci, and G. Semeraro. Human decision making and recommender systems. *ACM Transactions on Interactive Intelligent Systems*, 3(3):17, 2013.

[5] L. Chen and P. Pu. Trust building in recommender agents. In *International Workshop on Web Personalization, Recommender Systems and Intelligent User Interfaces (WPRSIUI'05)*, pages 135–145, Reading, UK, 2005.

[6] D. Cosley, S. Lam, I. Albert, J. Konstan, and J. Riedl. Is seeing believing? how recommender interfaces affect users' opinions. In *Conference on Human Factors in Computing Systems*, pages 585–592, 2003.

[7] E. Diener. The science of happiness and a proposal for a national index. *Am. Psychol.*, 55(1):34–43, 2000.

[8] A. Jameson, M. Willemsen, A. Felfernig, M. de Gemmis, P. Lops, G. Semeraro, and L. Chen. Human decision making and recommender systems. *Recommender Systems Handbook*, pages 619–655, 2015.

[9] B. Knijnenburg, M. Willemsen, Z. Gantner, H. Soncu, and C. Newell. Explaining the user experience of recommender systems. *User Modeling and User-Adapted Interaction (UMUAI)*, pages 441–504, 2012.

[10] G. L. M. Stettinger, A. Felfernig and S. Reiterer. Counteracting anchoring effects in group decision making. In *23rd Conference on User Modeling, Adaptation, and Personalization*, pages 118–130, Dublin, Ireland, 2015.

[11] J. O'Donovan, B. Smyth, B. Gretarsson, S. Bostandjiev, and T. Höllerer. Peerchooser: Visual interactive recommendation. In *Proceedings of the SIGCHI Conference on Human Factors in Computing Systems*, CHI '08, pages 1085–1088, New York, NY, USA, 2008. ACM.

[12] H. Simon. A behavioural model of choice. *Quarterly Journal of Economics*, 69(1):99–118, 1955.

[13] E. Teppan and A. Felfernig. Minimization of decoy effects in recommender result sets. *Web Intelligence and Agent Systems*, 1(4):385–395, 2012.

[14] N. Tintarev and J. Masthoff. Explaining recommendations: Design and evaluation. In *Recommender Systems Handbook*, pages 353–382. Springer, 2015.

[15] M. Tkalcic, M. deGemmis, and G. Semeraro. Personality and emotions in decision making and recommender systems. In *1st International Workshop on Decision Making and Recommender Systems*, pages 14–18, Bolzano, Italy, 2014.

RecSys'16 Workshop on Deep Learning for Recommender Systems (DLRS)

Alexandros Karatzoglou
Telefonica Research
Barcelona, Spain
alexk@tid.es

Balázs Hidasi
Gravity R&D
Budapest, Hungary
balazs.hidasi@gravityrd.com

Domonkos Tikk
Gravity R&D
Budapest, Hungary
domonkos.tikk@gravityrd.com

Oren Sar-Shalom
IBM Research
Haifa, Israel
orensr@il.ibm.com

Haggai Roitman
IBM Research
Haifa, Israel
haggai@il.ibm.com

Bracha Shapira
Ben-Gurion University
Beersheba, Israel
bshapira@bgu.ac.il

ABSTRACT

We believe that Deep Learning is one of the next big things in Recommendation Systems technology. The past few years have seen the tremendous success of deep neural networks in a number of complex tasks such as computer vision, natural language processing and speech recognition. Despite this, only little work has been published on Deep Learning methods for Recommender Systems. Notable recent application areas are music recommendation, news recommendation, and session-based recommendation. The aim of the workshop is to encourage the application of Deep Learning techniques in Recommender Systems, to promote research in deep learning methods for Recommender Systems, and to bring together researchers from the Recommender Systems and Deep Learning communities.

Keywords

deep learning; neural networks; recommender systems

1. INTRODUCTION

The past few years have seen the tremendous success of deep neural networks in a number of complex tasks such as computer vision, natural language processing and speech recognition. Therefore it is one of the hottest topics in the machine learning community recently. Deep learning is a class of algorithms where data is passed through a cascade of nonlinear processing layers organized in complex architectures where each layer learns latent representations of the data.

Despite this yet relatively limited uptake of the technology in the recsys community, we believe that deep learning is one of the next big things in recommendation systems technology due to several reasons:

(1) Deep learning is capable of capturing complex dependencies and nonlinearities in large sets of data that other algorithms can't, thus it can bring a new and deeper modelling of user preferences encoded into the algorithmic layer, without the necessity to understand the exact nature of patterns contributing to the prediction.

(2) Deep learning techniques can integrate additional data sources (the content itself, text, images, music, video, etc.) to enrich the preference models of recommender algorithms by extracting high quality feature representations. Previously recommender systems have focused on utilizing the transactions and/or the descriptors of the content (i.e. metadata). However, the visual information users see about the product (i.e. an image of the product) makes a large contribution to user decisions (e.g. if they will click or not on the recommendations). Deep learning methods allow for a better and more accurate modeling of the content features of the item, particularly visual features such as images, textual features such as the description of the item or the audio signal of a song.

(3) Deep learning has the potential to allow for direct modeling of user preferences, with enough data on user preferences it is conceivable that user models of product preferences could be derived based on the content features of the items alone. For example one could potentially fine-tune a generic convolutional image classification model to recognize items that a user will like e.g. a particular pair of shoes or sportswear or even a potential partner (reciprocal recommendation). This will allow for user preference models that do not depend on collaborative filtering and thus the collection and modeling of large amounts of preference data on a single server.

(4) Finally deep learning methods provide a rich toolkit for key recommendation problems e.g. session-based recommendation with recurrent neural networks. The uptake of machine learning methods in the recommendation community is relatively limited to a small set of methods e.g. matrix factorization, LDA. Deep learning methods can and have been used in collaborative filtering models e.g. denoising autoencoders, Restricted Boltzmann Machines etc. We expect to see more research on how to use deep learning methods in a collaborative filtering setting with models that take into account content and context. Deep learning methods have the potential to expand upon this set of methods and to enhance existing ones.

The aim of DLRS 2016 is to help introduce and speed-

RecSys '16 September 15-19, 2016, Boston , MA, USA

ACM ISBN 978-1-4503-4035-9/16/09.

DOI: http://dx.doi.org/10.1145/2959100.2959202

up the use of deep learning in the RecSys Community by bringing together researchers from the Recommender Systems and Deep Learning communities.

2. DEEP LEARNING IN RECSYS

Most of the work on deep models and recommendations focus on the classical collaborative filtering (CF) user–item setting. Restricted Boltzmann Machines (RBM) were one of the first neural networks to be used for classical CF and recommender systems [5]. More recently denoising autoencoders have been used to perform CF in a similar manner [8]. Deep networks have also been used in cross-domain recommendation whereby items are mapped to a joint latent space using deep neural networks [1].

Including automatically generated content features in the recommender is one of the most exciting imminent research paths with deep learning. Prior work typically used these features together with more conventional collaborative filtering models. Convolutional deep networks have been used to extract features from music files that are then used in a factor model [6]. More recently [7] introduced a more generic approach whereby a deep network is used to extract generic content-features from items, these features are then incorporated in a standard CF model to enhance the recommendation performance. This approach seems to be particularly useful in settings where there is not sufficient user–item interaction information. Image features that have been extracted using convolutional networks have been used in classical matrix factorization-type CF in [2, 4] to enhance the quality of recommendations. Deep learning can also address novel recommendation problems. For example [3] used a custom recurrent neural network to model click-session data to provide session-based recommendations.

3. THE POTENTIAL OF DEEP LEARNING

We outline four major broad research topics, which have huge potential to significantly improve recommender algorithms.

Content modeling: Incorporating unstructured data sources such as text, audio, video or image into recommendation algorithms is one of the more trivial ways of applying deep learning. As we argued earlier, the inclusion of the content instead of its metadata makes more sense and expected to give better recommendations. True content based methods can help recommenders with long standing issues like the item cold-start, while simultaneously recommending relevant content.

User and session modeling: Traditional collaborative filtering is largely focused on creating static user models, which are good for domains where tastes are expected to change slowly and item relevance is preference-based rather than necessity based (e.g. movies as opposed to household appliances). Some domains require more dynamic behavior modeling. In others, it is important to find the balance between using long-term and short-term user histories. Modeling intent is also important for knowing what the user really wants and recommending accordingly. Last, but not least, using sessions rather than user histories is important in situations where the permanent user cold-start problem is present. All of the aforementioned problems can be potentially addressed by the proper use of deep learning's sequence modeling (e.g. recurrent neural networks).

Situation modeling: Surrounding ourselves with more and more sensors allows recommenders to get more data about the situation that we are in and recommend accordingly. Moving towards this situation based (or context-driven) recommendation will be one of the main shifts in the next few years. Understanding the situation from a large amount of sensory data requires powerful pattern recognition methods, such as deep neural networks.

Adapting deep learning: Even though deep neural networks have great potential, their application in the field of recommender systems should be done with care. Practical considerations – e.g. training time, response time and scalability – must be taken into account when developing novel methods. Therefore neural models should be adapted to fit the recommendation task.

4. SUMMARY

Deep learning achieved tremendous success on tasks, considered to be hard for computers. We believe it is time to apply them in the RecSys domain as well. Deep learning has the potential to be the core of the next generation of recommender systems. DLRS 2016 aims to speed up the spread and acceptance of these methods in the RecSys Community.

Acknowledgments

The organizers are supported in part by European Community's Seventh Framework Programme (FP7/2007-2013) under grant agreement n° 610594 known as the CrowdRec project http://crowdrec.eu/.

5. ADDITIONAL AUTHORS

Additional authors: Lior Rokach (Ben-Gurion University, email: liorrk@bgu.ac.il).

6. REFERENCES

[1] A. M. Elkahky, Y. Song, and X. He. A multi-view deep learning approach for cross domain user modeling in recommendation systems. In *WWW'15: 24th Int. Conf. on World Wide Web*, pages 278–288, 2015.

[2] R. He and J. McAuley. VBPR: Visual Bayesian Personalized Ranking from implicit feedback. *CoRR*, 1510.01784, 2015.

[3] B. Hidasi, A. Karatzoglou, L. Baltrunas, and D. Tikk. Session-based recommendations with recurrent neural networks. *International Conference on Learning Representations*, 2016.

[4] J. McAuley, C. Targett, Q. Shi, and A. van den Hengel. Image-based recommendations on styles and substitutes. In *SIGIR'15: 38th Int. ACM SIGIR Conf. on Research and Development in Information Retrieval*, pages 43–52, 2015.

[5] R. Salakhutdinov, A. Mnih, and G. Hinton. Restricted boltzmann machines for collaborative filtering. In *ICML'07: 24th Int. Conf. on Machine Learning*, pages 791–798, 2007.

[6] A. Van den Oord, S. Dieleman, and B. Schrauwen. Deep content-based music recommendation. In *Advances in Neural Information Processing Systems*, pages 2643–2651, 2013.

[7] H. Wang, N. Wang, and D.-Y. Yeung. Collaborative deep learning for recommender systems. In *KDD'15: 21th ACM SIGKDD Int. Conf. on Knowledge Discovery and Data Mining*, pages 1235–1244, 2015.

[8] Y. Wu, C. DuBois, A. X. Zheng, and M. Ester. Collaborative denoising auto-encoders for top-N recommender systems. In *WSDM'16: 9th ACM Int. Conf. on Web Search and Data Mining*, pages 153–162, 2016.

RecTour 2016: Workshop on Recommenders in Tourism

Daniel R Fesenmaier
University of Florida
Gainesville, FL, USA
drfez@ufl.edu

Tsvi Kuflik
The University of Haifa
Haifa, Israel
tsvikak@is.haifa.ac.il

Julia Neidhardt
E-Commerce Group, TU Wien
Vienna, Austria
julia.neidhardt@ec.tuwien.ac.at

ABSTRACT
In this paper, we summarize RecTour 2016 – a workshop on recommenders in tourism co-located with RecSys 2016. There was a great variety of submissions, i.e., research papers, demo papers and position papers, addressing fundamental challenges of recommender systems in the tourism domain. The main topics included group recommendations, context-aware recommenders, choice-based recommenders and event recommendations.

CCS Concepts
• **Information systems→Recommender Systems.**

Keywords
Tourism recommenders; decision context; on-the-go decisions; discrete choice models, mobile systems; group decisions.

1. INTRODUCTION
RecTour 2016 focuses on a variety of challenges specific to recommender systems within the tourism domain. In this domain, there are considerably more complicated scenarios than finding the best product for a user. Planning a vacation usually involves searching for a set of products that are interconnected (e.g. means of transportation, lodging, attractions etc.), with a rather limited availability, and where contextual aspects may have a major impact (spatiotemporal context, social context, environmental context). In addition and most importantly, products are emotionally "loaded" and experientially based; therefore, decision taking is not based solely on rational and objective criteria (i.e., system 2 thinking) [15]. As such, providing the right information to visitors of a tourism site at the right time about the site itself and various services nearby is challenging. Additionally, and in contrast to many other domains, information providers are normally small - medium enterprises (SMEs) that do not have full information about available opportunities. Moreover, there is no single, standard format to house this information. Last, much of the tourism experience is co-produced; that is, it occurs during the consumption of the product and therefore, the context of the recommendation is extremely important [8]. Thus, given this diversity, building effective recommender systems within the tourism domain is extremely challenging.

The rapid development of information and communication technologies (ICT) in general and the Web has transformed the tourism domain whereby most travelers rely little on travel agents/agencies [14]. Indeed, recent studies indicate that travelers are now active in searching for information and composing their vacation packages according to their specific preferences. When onsite, they search for freely available information about the site itself rather than renting a visitor guide that may be available, but considered to be expensive and sometimes outdated. However, like in many other cases, the blessing of the web comes with a curse, the curse of information overload. Recommender systems have been suggested as a practical tool for overcoming this information overload. However, the tourism domain is substantially more complicated, and as such, creates huge challenges for those designing tourism-focused recommenders.

This workshop aims at bringing together researchers and practitioners working in the tourism recommendation domain in order to look at the challenges from the point of view of the user interactions as well as from the perspective of service providers as well as from additional stakeholders (i.e., destination management organizations for instance). Further, the workshop aims at attracting presentations of novel ideas for addressing these challenges with the goal to advance the current state of the art in this field by providing a forum for researchers and practitioners from different fields, e.g., tourism, recommender systems, user modelling, user interaction, mobile, ubiquitous and ambient technologies, artificial intelligence and web information systems, to explore various practical use cases of applications of these technologies in tourist recommender systems of the future. The overall goal of the workshop is to identify and discuss in depth various user groups, tasks and roles needed to achieve personalization, as to further enhance recommendations for tourism applications. Further details and a link to the workshop proceedings can be found at the website of the workshop.[1]

2. WORKSHOP PROGRAM
The workshop starts with a keynote presentation by Prof. Hannes Werthner, head of the E-Commerce Group and dean of the Faculty of Informatics at TU Wien, Austria, who is one of the leading researchers and a distinct expert in the area of e-tourism. In his talk he addresses specific challenges in the context of recommenders and tourism and discusses novels way to implicitly elicit user preferences for tourism products such as the picture-based approach [10]. The following summarizes the various papers presented at the workshop.

2.1 Group Recommendations
Group recommender systems have become an important focus as social media support social systems wherein many activities are typically done within groups. This is particularly true for travel,

RecSys '16, September 15-19, 2016, Boston , MA, USA
ACM 978-1-4503-4035-9/16/09.
http://dx.doi.org/10.1145/2959100.2959205

[1] http://www.ec.tuwien.ac.at/rectour2016

which is often a social activity. Delic et al. [2] discuss challenges of performing group research to understand the dynamics of group decisions and their integration into group recommenders. A user study is presented that examines the group decision process and the benefits and potential shortcomings of such studies are addressed and the implications on the design of group recommender systems are outlined.

2.2 Context-Aware Recommenders

One of the most important research issues on recommender systems deals with the question of how to incorporate user context when delivering recommendations, in order to improve the results. In this context, the location of the user is taken into account as one important contextual aspect, due to the increasing availability of geo-tagged data. Hiesel et al. [6] present an approach for integrating different data sources with check-in information for POIs in order to obtain estimates about the popularity of these POIs in general on the one hand and their popularity conditioned on different time and weather conditions on the other hand. Trattner et al. [12] consider weather conditions as a contextual aspect for POI recommendation. In the presented work they show that taking weather data into account clearly improves the state-of-the-art Rank-GeoFM algorithm. Kaya and Bridge [7] present an approach for recommending photo-taking locations which improves existing algorithms wherein they integrate map locations of geo-tagged photos and a grid using a geo-hashing algorithm based on the assumption that users prefer locations that are close to current photo-taking locations. Vakeel and Ray [13], on the other hand, define motivation as a contextual factor that can be used to explain the delivered recommendation to the user. They distinguish seven motivations of users for checking-in at different POIs as a basis for a post-filtering approach.

2.3 Choice-Based Recommenders

Sanchez Vila [11] proposes a recommender approach based on choice and utility theory in order to overcome some limitations of rating-based approaches, i.e., these approaches are mainly based on heuristic models rather than decision-making theories and rely on post-experience utilities, i.e., ratings, rather than pre-experience utilities. The introduced models are evaluated with the help of gastronomy datasets and improve the prediction accuracy of state-of-the-art rating-based methods.

2.4 Event Recommendations

Providing recommendations for events is particularly challenging as events usually have a limited duration and previous ratings and behaviors of users might not be relevant for new events. In the workshop, two mobile applications are demonstrated that aim to overcome certain problems in this context. Donohue et al. [3] present an application that aims at dealing with the cold-start problem for event recommendations. The idea is to allow the user to set-up their preferences in a fast and non-intrusive way to receive interesting recommendations immediately. MacLachlan et al. [9] showcase a mobile application that allows users to access recommendations in different ways, i.e., searching, browsing categories, following, and finally, obtaining recommendations in a traditional manner, which acknowledges the fact that users have different information needs and preferences at different times.

2.5 Further Research Challenges

The workshop concludes with a panel discussion based upon three position papers [1], [4], [5] which identify and discuss a range of challenges for the development of recommender systems in tourism and outlining important future research directions.

3. CONCLUSIONS

The papers and discussion at RecTour 2016 highlight many fundamental challenges for tourism-related recommender systems. They offer thoughtful and useful approaches for addressing these challenges and therefore, provide a substantial foundation for future research.

4. REFERENCES

[1] Dareddy, M.R., 2016. Challenges in Recommender Systems for Tourism. In *Proceedings of RecTour 2016.*

[2] Delic, A., Neidhardt, J., Nguyen, T.N., and F. Ricci, 2016. Research Methods for Group Recommender Systems. In *Proceedings of RecTour 2016.*

[3] Donohue, S., Dragovic, N., and Pera, M.S., 2016. Anything Fun Going On? A Simple Wizard to Avoid the Cold-Start Problem for Event Recommenders. In *Proceedings of RecTour 2016.*

[4] Ehmke, J.F., Mattfeld, D.C., and Albrecht, L., 2016. Combining Mobility Services by Customer-Induced Orchestration. In *Proceedings of RecTour 2016.*

[5] Herzog, D. and Wörndl, W., 2016. Exploiting Item Dependencies to Improve Tourist Trip Recommendations. In *Proceedings of RecTour 2016.*

[6] Hiesel, P., Braunhofer, M., and Wörndl, W. 2016. Learning the Popularity of Items for Mobile Tourist Guides. In *Proceedings of RecTour 2016.*

[7] Kaya, M., and Bridge, D. 2016. Improved Recommendation of Photo-Taking Locations using Virtual Ratings. In *Proceedings of RecTour 2016.*

[8] Lamsfus, C., Wang, D., Alzua-Sorzabal, A., and Xiang, Z., 2015. Going mobile defining context for on-the-go travelers. *Journal of Travel Research*, 54(6), 691-701.

[9] MacLachlan, S., Dragovic, N., Donohue, S., and Pera, M.S., 2016. "One Size Doesn't Fit All": Helping Users Find Events from Multiple Perspectives. In *Proceedings of RecTour 2016.*

[10] Neidhardt, J., Schuster, R., Seyfang, L., and Werthner, H., 2014. Eliciting the users' unknown preferences. In *Proceedings of the 8th ACM RecSys Conference*, 309-312.

[11] Sanchez Vila, E., 2016. Choice-based recommender system. In *Proceedings of RecTour 2016.*

[12] Trattner, C., Oberegger, A., Eberhard, L., Parra, D., and Marinho, L.B., 2016. Understanding the Impact of Weather for POI Recommendations. In *Proceedings of RecTour 2016.*

[13] Vakeel, K., and Ray, S., 2016. A Motivation-Aware Approach for Point of Interest Recommendations. In *Proceedings of RecTour 2016.*

[14] Werthner, H., Alzua-Sorzabal, A., Cantoni, L., Dickinger, A., Gretzel, U., Jannach, D., Neidhardt, J., Pröll, B., Ricci, F., Scaglione, M., Stangl, B., Stock, O., and Zanker, M., 2015. Future research issues in IT and tourism. *Journal of IT & Tourism*, 15(1):1-15.

[15] Werthner H., and Ricci, F., 2004. E-commerce and tourism. *Communications of the ACM*, 47(12), 101-105.

Third Workshop on New Trends in Content-based Recommender Systems (CBRecSys 2016)

Toine Bogers
Department of Communication and Psychology
Aalborg University
Copenhagen
toine@hum.aau.dk

Marijn Koolen
Dutch Institute of Sound and Vision
Hilversum, The Netherlands
mkoolen@beeldengeluid.nl

Cataldo Musto
cataldo.musto@uniba.it

Pasquale Lops
pasquale.lops@uniba.it

Giovanni Semeraro
giovanni.semeraro@uniba.it

University of Bari "Aldo Moro"
Bari, Italy

ABSTRACT

While content-based recommendation has been applied successfully in many different domains, it has not seen the same level of attention as collaborative filtering techniques have. However, there are many recommendation domains and applications where content and metadata play a key role, either *in addition to* or *instead of* ratings and implicit usage data. For some domains, such as movies, the relationship between content and usage data has seen thorough investigation already, but for many other domains, such as books, news, scientific articles, and Web pages we still do not know *if* and *how* these data sources should be combined to provided the best recommendation performance. The *CBRecSys 2016* workshop provides a dedicated venue for papers dedicated to all aspects of content-based recommendation.

1. INTRODUCTION

Content-based recommendation has been applied successfully in many different domains [9, 7], yet it has not seen the same level of attention as collaborative filtering techniques have. In the past decade, competitions like the Netflix Prize[1], CAMRA[2], and the Yahoo! Music KDD Cup 2011 [8] have spurred on advances in collaborative filtering and how to utilize ratings and usage data. However, there are many recommendation domains and applications where content and metadata play a key role, either *in addition to* or *instead of* ratings and implicit usage data. For some domains, such as movies, the relationship between content and usage data has seen thorough investigation already (e.g. [10]), but for many other domains, such as books, news, scientific articles, and Web pages we still do not know *if* and *how* these data sources should be combined to provided the best recommendation performance. Only recently have we seen the introduction of competitions that include content-based information in the recommendation process, such as CLEF NewsReel[3]

[1] http://www.netflixprize.com/
[2] http://www.dai-labor.de/camra2010/

RecSys '16 September 15-19, 2016, Boston, MA, USA

ACM ISBN 978-1-4503-4035-9/16/09.
DOI: http://dx.doi.org/10.1145/2959100.2959200

2. FORMAT, AUDIENCE AND TOPICS

The *CBRecSys 2016* workshop is the follow-up to the successful first two editions of the workshop in Silicon Valley in 2014 [4, 5] and Vienna in 2015 [1, 3], which featured interesting and high-quality programs.

CBRecSys 2016 will be organized as a full-day workshop. After the opening keynote, the late morning session is reserved for general submissions dedicated to content-based recommendation, organized by theme with the accepted papers presented as 15-minute talks with 5 minutes for discussion. The afternoon program continues the accepted paper talks and concludes the afternoon session with a panel on the future challenges and trends of content-based recommendation with speakers from both academia and industry to make for a lively and applied discussion.

The CBRecSys 2016 workshop aims to address this by providing a venue for papers dedicated to all aspects and new trends of content-based recommendation. This would include both recommendation in domains where textual content is abundant (e.g. books, news, scientific articles, jobs, educational resources, and Web pages) as well as dedicated comparisons and combinations of content-based techniques with collaborative filtering approaches.

2.1 Topics of Interest

Relevant topics of the workshop include:

- Processing and Representing Content
  - Estimating (implicit) ratings associated with text reviews
  - Opinion mining and sentiment analysis of text reviews to support content-based recommendation
  - Multilingual Content representation
  - Exploiting Deep Learning approaches for content representation

[3] http://www.clef-newsreel.org/

- Exploiting semantic technologies for processing and representing content
- Extracting user personality traits and factors from text reviews for recommendation

- Exploiting user generated contents
  - Social tag-based recommender systems
  - Mining microblogging data in content-based recommender systems
  - Exploiting Semantic Web and Linked Open Data in content-based recommender systems
  - User Profiling based on Big, Social and Linked Data
- Mining contextual data from content
  - Extraction of contextual signals from text contents for recommendation
  - Considering the time dimension in content-based recommendation
  - Mood-based recommender systems
- Addressing limitations of recommender system
  - Addressing the cold-start problem with content-based recommendation approaches
  - Increasing diversity in content-based recommendations
  - Providing novelty in content-based recommendations
- Developing novel recommendation approaches
  - Hybrid strategies combining content-based and collaborative filtering recommendations
  - Content-based approaches to cross-system and cross-domain recommendation
  - Latent factor models for content-based and hybrid recommendation

3. SUBMISSIONS

A total of 14 papers were submitted to the workshop, which were all reviewed by a program committee of international experts in the field.

Nine of these papers were accepted for presentation at the workshop for an acceptance rate of 64%. Several papers focus on using machine learning approaches for content-based recommendation, such as deep learning and learning-to-rank. Other papers present hybrid systems combining collaborative filtering and content-based recommendation, as well as a variety of different features, such as sentiment, temporal, and visual features. Like in previous years, some of the accepted papers focus on using semantic resources such as Linked Open Data to improve the effectiveness of content-based recommender algorithms. The nine accepted papers span a breadth of different domains, such as movies, Linked Open Data, news articles, research papers, e-commerce.

4. WEBSITE AND PROCEEDINGS

The workshop material (list of accepted papers, invited talk, and the workshop schedule) can be found on the CBRecSys 2016 workshop website at `http://cbrecsys2016.aau.dk`. The proceedings are published as a CEUR Workshop Proceedings volume, a link to which can be found on the workshop website. Similar to last years' workshops [2, 6], we will also look into publishing a summary of the workshop in venues like the SIGIR Forum, to increase cross-disciplinary awareness of recommender systems research.

5. REFERENCES

[1] T. Bogers and M. Koolen, editors. *Proceedings of the 2nd Workshop on New Trends in Content-based Recommender Systems, co-located with the 9th ACM Conference on Recommender Systems, CBRecSys@RecSys 2015, Vienna, Austria, September 20, 2015*, volume 1448 of *CEUR Workshop Proceedings*. CEUR-WS.org, 2015.

[2] T. Bogers and M. Koolen. Report on RecSys 2015 Workshop on New Trends in Content-Based Recommender Systems. *ACM SIGIR Forum*, 49(2):141–146, December 2015.

[3] T. Bogers and M. Koolen. Second Workshop on New Trends in Content-based Recommender Systems: (CBRecSys 2015). In *Ninth ACM Conference on Recommender Systems, RecSys '15, Vienna, Austria - September 16 - 20, 2015*, pages 339–340, 2015.

[4] T. Bogers, M. Koolen, and I. Cantador, editors. *Proceedings of the 1st Workshop on New Trends in Content-based Recommender Systems, co-located with the 8th ACM Conference on Recommender Systems, CBRecSys@RecSys 2014, Foster City, Silicon Valley, California, USA, October 6, 2014*, volume 1245 of *CEUR Workshop Proceedings*. CEUR-WS.org, 2014.

[5] T. Bogers, M. Koolen, and I. Cantador. Workshop on New Trends in Content-based Recommender Systems: (CBRecSys 2014). In *Eighth ACM Conference on Recommender Systems, RecSys '14, Foster City, Silicon Valley, CA, USA - October 06 - 10, 2014*, pages 379–380, 2014.

[6] T. Bogers, M. Koolen, and I. Cantador. Report on RecSys 2014 Workshop on New Trends in Content-Based Recommender Systems. *ACM SIGIR Forum*, 49(1):20–26, June 2015.

[7] M. de Gemmis, P. Lops, C. Musto, F. Narducci, and G. Semeraro. Semantics-aware Content-based Recommender Systems. In *Recommender Systems Handbook*, pages 119–159. Springer, 2015.

[8] G. Dror, N. Koenigstein, Y. Koren, and M. Weimer. The Yahoo! Music Dataset and KDD-Cup '11. In *JMLR Workshop and Conference Proceedings*, volume 18 of *Proceedings of KDD Cup 2011*, pages 3–18. Springer, 2012.

[9] P. Lops, M. de Gemmis, and G. Semeraro. Content-based Recommender Systems: State of the Art and Trends. In *Recommender Systems Handbook*, pages 73–105. Springer, 2011.

[10] I. Pilászy and D. Tikk. Recommending New Movies: Even a Few Ratings Are More Valuable Than Metadata. In *RecSys '09: Proceedings of the Third ACM Conference on Recommender Systems*, pages 93–100. ACM, 2009.

LSRS'16: Workshop on Large-Scale Recommender Systems

Tao Ye
Pandora Inc.
2101 Webster St., Suite 700
Oakland, CA 94612
(+1) 510-451-4100
tye@pandora.com

Danny Bickson
Turi Inc.
936 North 34th St.,
Seattle, WA 98195
(+1) 347-514-7650
bickson@turi.com

Denis Parra
Pontificia Universidad Católica de Chile (PUC Chile)
Vicuña Mackenna 4860
Santiago, Chile
(+56) 2-2354-4442
dparra@ing.puc.cl

ABSTRACT

With the increase of data collected and computation power available, modern recommender systems are ever facing new challenges. While complex models are developed in academia, industry practice seems to focus on relatively simple techniques that can deal with the magnitude of data and the need to distribute the computation. The workshop on large-scale recommender systems (LSRS) is a meeting place for industry and academia to discuss the current and future challenges of applied large-scale recommender systems.

Categories and Subject Descriptors
H.2.8 [Database Management]: Database Applications – *data mining*. H.3.4 [Database Management]: System and Software – *distributed systems*.

Keywords
Recommendation systems; big data; scalability; machine learning

1. BACKGROUND AND MOTIVATION

Modern Recommender Systems face greatly increased data volume and complexities. Previous computational models and experience on small data may not hold today, thus, how to build an efficient and robust system has become an important issue for many practitioners. Meanwhile, there is an increasing gap between academia research of recommendation systems focusing on complex models, and industry practice focusing on solving problems at large scale using relatively simple techniques. Evaluation of models have diverged as well. While most publications focus on fixed datasets and offline ranking measures, industry practitioners tend to use long term engagement metrics to make final judgements.

The motivation of this workshop is to bring together researchers and practitioners working on large-scale recommender systems in order to: (1) share experience, techniques and methodologies used to develop effective large-scale recommenders, from architecture, algorithms, programming model, to evaluation (2) challenge conventional wisdom (3) identify key challenges and promising trends in the area, and (4) identify collaboration opportunities among participants.

2. OBJECTIVES

This workshop aims to foster discussions in several fields that are of interest to our growing community of recommendation system builders. On the practical side, we would like to encourage sharing of architecture best practices in large-scale recommender systems as they are practiced in industry, as well as particular challenges and pain points. We hope this will guide future research that is system aware. On the research side, we focus on bringing in ideas and evaluations on scaling beyond the current generation of big data systems, with improved recommendation metrics. We believe the brightest minds from both sides will mutually benefit from the discussions and accelerate problem solving.

3. TOPICS OF INTEREST

We solicited submissions from industrial level recommendation system practitioners in either a short paper or slides format on large scale system practice, as well as from recommendation systems researchers on their new research related to system aspect of recommendation with Big Data.

We focused on the following topics:

Systems of Large-scale RS:

- Architecture
- Programming Model
- Distributed systems
- Real-time recommendation
- Online learning for recommendation
- Scalability and Robustness

Data & Algorithms in Large-scale RS:

RecSys '16, September 15-19, 2016, Boston , MA, USA
ACM 978-1-4503-4035-9/16/09.
http://dx.doi.org/10.1145/2959100.2959206

- Big data processing in offline/near-line/online modules
- Streaming data for recommendation
- Data platforms for recommendation
- Large, unstructured and social data for recommendation
- Heterogeneous data fusion
- Sampling techniques
- Parallel algorithms
- Incremental algorithms
- Algorithm validation and correctness checking

Evaluation of Large-scale RS:

- Offline optimization and online measurement consistency
- Evaluation metrics alignment with product/project goal
- Large data and privacy issue
- Large user studies
- Visualization

4. PROGRAM COMMITTEE

We are grateful for the help of our program committee to review submissions:

Anders Arpteg, Spotify
Linas Baltrunas, Netflix
Leandro Balby Marinho, Federal University of Campina Grande
Steve Bourke, Schibsted Media Group
Michael Ekstrand, Texas State University
Gianmarco De Francisci Morales, Qatar Computing Research Institute
Andreas Lommatzsch, Technische Universität Berlin
Vito Ostuni, Pandora
Guy Rapaport, Turi
Srikrishna Sridhar, Turi
Christoph Trattner, Know-Center, TU-Graz
Andy Twigg, InsideSales.com
David Zibriczky, ImpressTV

5. WORKSHOP FORMAT

The workshop will feature one keynote and three presentation sessions. We expect a mix of peer reviewed contributions one presentation session to be 3-4 peer reviewed papers and the other two shorter sessions to be invited talks.

6. ACKNOWLEDGMENTS

We thank the RecSys 2016 organizing committee for giving us the opportunity to host this workshop in conjunction with RecSys 2016 in Boston, USA.

3rd Workshop on Recommendation Systems for Television and Online Video (RecSysTV 2016)

Jan Neumann
Comcast Labs
1110 Vermont Ave NW
Washington, DC 20005
jan_neumann@cable.comcast.com

John Hannon
Zalando IE
Dublin, Ireland
john.hannon@zalando.ie

Claudio Riefolo
Moviri S.p.A. - ContentWise R&D
Via Schiaffino, 11- Milan, Italy
Claudio.Riefolo@moviri.com

Hassan Sayyadi
Comcast Labs
1110 Vermont Ave NW
Washington, DC 20005
hassan.sayyadi@cable.comcast.com

ABSTRACT

For many households the television is the central entertainment hub in their home, and the average TV viewer spends about half of their leisure time in front of a TV. At any given moment, a costumer has hundreds to thousands of entertainment choices available, which makes some sort of automatic, personalized recommendations desirable to help consumers deal with the often overwhelming number of choices they face. The 3rd Workshop on Recommendation Systems for Television and Online Video aims to offer a place to present and discuss the latest academic and industrial research on recommendation systems for this challenging and exciting application domain.

Keywords

Recommendations; big data; television; movies; video-on-demand.

1. BACKGROUND AND MOTIVATION

For many households the television is still the central entertainment hub in their home and the average TV viewer spends about half of their leisure time in front of a TV (3-5 hours/day).

The choice of what to watch becomes more overwhelming though because the entertainment options are scattered across various channels, such as on-demand video, digital recorders (on premise or in the cloud) and the traditional linear TV. In addition, consumers can also access the content not just on the big screen, but also on their computers, phones, and tablet devices.

Recommendation systems provide TV users with suggestions about both online video-on-demand and broadcast content and help them to search and browse intelligently for content that is relevant to them. While many open questions in video-on-demand recommendations have already been solved, recommendation systems for broadcast content (e.g., linear channels and catch-up TV) still experience a number of unique challenges due to the peculiarity of such domain. For example, the content available on linear channels is constantly changing and often only available once which leads to severe cold start problems and we often consume TV in groups of varying compositions (household vs individual) which makes building taste profiles and modeling consumer behavior very challenging.

Finally, recommendation systems have to address a number of very different consumption patterns, such as actively browsing through a list of personalized Video on Demand choices that match our current mood, compared to enjoying a "lean back experience" where a recommendation systems playlists a stream of TV shows from our favorite channels for us.

The unique challenges and wide-ranging applications of recommender systems in this domain motivated us to organize this workshop to bring together researchers from industry and academy in order to identify and share the key challenges, approaches and solutions of the field.

2. OBJECTIVES

The objective of this workshop is to encourage discussions among the researchers in the field, disseminate the latest approaches and encourage future collaboration among the participants. We believe that all participants will mutually benefit from the workshop activities and hopefully this will accelerate progress towards creating better recommendation systems for television and online video in the future.

3. TOPICS OF INTEREST

We solicited contributions from industrial and academic researchers on novel approaches to challenges found in the TV and online video recommendations space. Authors submitted both long and short papers focused on the following topics:

RecSys '16, September 15-19, 2016, Boston , MA, USA
ACM 978-1-4503-4035-9/16/09.
http://dx.doi.org/10.1145/2959100.2959198

Context-aware TV and online video recommendations

- Leveraging contextual viewing behavior, e.g. device specific recommendations
- Mood based recommendations
- Group recommendations

User modeling & leveraging user viewing and interaction behavior

- How can social media improve TV recommendations
- Cross-domain recommendation algorithms (linear TV, video on demand, DVR, gaming consoles)
- Multi-viewer profile separation
- Evaluation metrics for TV and online video recommendations

Content-based TV and online video recommendations

- Analysis techniques for video recommendations based on video, audio, or closed caption signals
- Utilization of external data sources (movie reviews, ratings, plot summaries) for recommendations

Other topics related to TV and online video recommendations

- Video play listing
- Linear TV usage and box office success prediction
- Catch-up TV recommendations
- Personalized advertisement recommendations
- Recommendations of 2nd screen web content
- Recommendations of short form videos (previews, trailers, music videos)

4. PROGRAM COMMITTEE

We thank the program committee for their help with reviewing the submissions:

Balázs Hidasi, GravityR&D

Justin Basilico, Netflix

Craig Carmichael, Rovi

Emanuele Coviello, Keevio

Humberto Corona, Zalando

Paolo Cremonesi, Politecnico di Milano

Joaquin Delgado, OnCue TV (Verizon)

Diana Hu, OnCue TV (Verizon)

Brendan Kitts, Adap.tv (AOL)

Gert Lanckriet, UC San Diego

Rani Nelken, Outbrain

Royi Ronen, Microsoft

Barry Smyth, Insight Centre for Data Analytics

Esti Widder, Viaccess-Orca

Dávid Zibriczky, ImpressTV

5. WORKSHOP FORMAT

The workshop will consist of several key note and presentation sessions with contributions from both academic and industrial researchers. We will also have an industrial demo session to demonstrate the latest state of the art systems in the area of TV and online video recommendations.

6. ACKNOWLEDGEMENTS

We thank the RecSys 2016 organizing committee for giving us the opportunity to host this workshop in conjunction with RecSys 2016 and our companies Comcast, Moviri and Zalando for supporting this event.

RecSys Challenge 2016: Job Recommendations

Fabian Abel
XING AG
Hamburg, Germany
fabian.abel@xing.com

András Benczúr
Hungarian Academy of Sciences
Budapest, Hungary
benczur@sztaki.hu

Daniel Kohlsdorf
XING AG
Hamburg, Germany
daniel.kohlsdorf@xing.com

Martha Larson
TU Delft
Radboud University Nijmegen
Netherlands
m.a.larson@tudelft.nl

Róbert Pálovics
Hungarian Academy of Sciences
Budapest, Hungary
palovics@sztaki.hu

ABSTRACT

The 2016 ACM Recommender Systems Challenge focused on the problem of job recommendations. Given a large dataset from XING that consisted of anonymized user profiles, job postings, and interactions between them, the participating teams had to predict postings that a user will interact with.

The challenge ran for four months with 366 registered teams. 119 of those teams actively participated and submitted together 4,232 solutions yielding in an impressive neck-and-neck race that was decided within the last days of the challenge.

CCS Concepts

•**Information systems → Recommender systems;** *Data mining; Test collections;*

Keywords

Recommender Systems; Data Mining Challenge; XING

1. INTRODUCTION

The ACM RecSys Challenge allows researchers and engineers around the world to jointly work on real-world recommender system problems in various domains such as social media [3] or product recommendations [2]. In 2016 the challenge was dedicated to the problem of job recommendation[1] [1]. We released a dataset from XING[2]—a business-oriented social network with around 18 Million users worldwide and more than 10 Million users in Germany.

XING supports people in discovering career opportunities. Job recommendations are therefore an essential part of the XING platform and its mobile apps. Those recommendations aim to satisfy the demands of both the job seekers who have certain preferences concerning their next career step and the recruiters who aim to hire the most appropriate candidate for a given job. In this challenge, we focused on the demands of the job seekers by defining the following task: *Given a XING user, the recommender had to predict those job postings that a user will positively interact with by clicking on it or bookmarking it.*

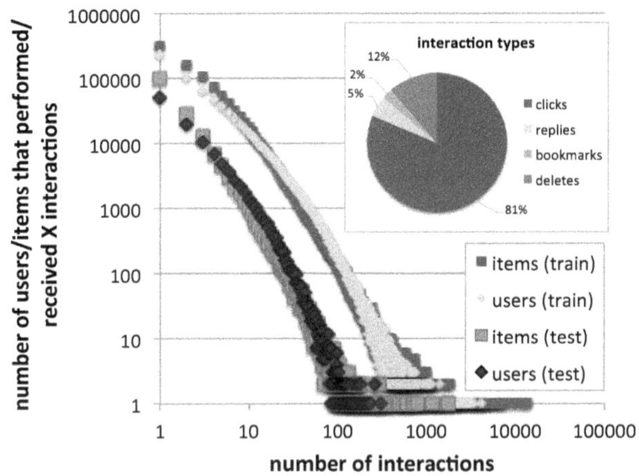

Figure 1: Number of interactions per user and item. 328,618 items (24.2%) and 582,370 users (42.9%) remained without interactions during the training period. More than 80% of the interactions are clicks, followed by deletes, replies and bookmarks. The distributions for training data and test data (ground truth) follow similar characteristics.

2. DATASET

We provided a training dataset featuring user profiles, job postings, and interactions that users performed on job posts. The dataset also incorporated user-item *impressions*, i.e. information about job postings that were shown to users. The training data[3] contained 1,367,057 users and 1,358,098 items. Users and items were described by several similar attributes such as job categories, career level, industry, lo-

[1]http://2016.recsyschallenge.com
[2]http://xing.com
[3]https://github.com/recsyschallenge/2016/#data

RecSys '16 September 15-19, 2016, Boston , MA, USA

ACM ISBN 978-1-4503-4035-9/16/09.
DOI: http://dx.doi.org/10.1145/2959100.2959207

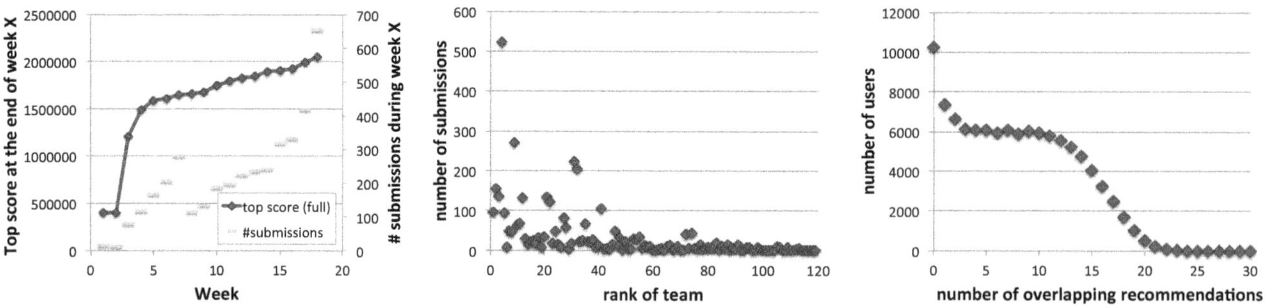

(a) Top score over time and number of submissions during each week of the challenge.

(b) Number of submissions per team (ordered by final rank of the team).

(c) Overlap between top solution and recommendations generated by XING's job recommender.

Figure 2: Submission statistics.

cation, etc. In addition, the educational background and details about work experience were given for the users.

Around 12 weeks of interaction data between the users and the items was released for training including including (1) *clicks* on job postings, (2) *bookmarks*, (3) *replies* indicating that users intended to apply for the job and (4) *deletes* which corresponds to removing an item that the user no longer wants to see. Figure 1 describes the characteristics of the different interactions. Two weeks of interactions for a set of 150,000 *target users* were used as test data in order to evaluate the submitted solutions. Figure 1 also shows the distribution of that ground truth dataset.

2.1 Anonymization

Anonymization of the training dataset was carried out with an iterative protector/attacker procedure. We took a simple and straightforward approach to threat modeling: The attacker profile was implicit the choice of a highly experienced Data Science team that attempted to de-anonymize the data. At each step the dataset was further bleached, and additional synthetic users were added. Then, tests were carried out to check if the dataset could be de-anonymized by the attacker and also if the dataset supported training a recommender system algorithm effective on a plain-text test set. This procedure ensured that enough information was left in the data to make this to be a useful data set for solving the problem on the actual plain-text data, while at the same time protecting the privacy of XING users.

The bleaching procedure involved replacing named entities with IDs, removing a selection of user attribute values, and removing a selection of interactions. The relative ordering of the interactions was maintained. Synthetic users were created by clustering real users. Further protections included the obvious measure of including only a fraction of XING's users and job postings in the dataset, and also protecting the dataset legally with a user agreement that explicitly prohibits attempts to de-anonymize the dataset, share it, or use it for non-academic purposes.

3. CHALLENGE SETUP AND RESULTS

We used a scoring function as evaluation measure that combines precision@k and recall@k[4]. This evaluation measure was based on the key performance indicators that XING is using to monitor the quality of the job recommender system. Each team was allowed to submit 5 solutions per day and solution files were allowed to feature at most 30 recommendations per user. A public leaderboard that was based on 30% of the ground truth data immediately informed the teams about the performance of their algorithms after their submissions.

The participating teams came from more than 30 different countries such as USA (25%), Germany (11%), China (9%), France (7%) or Hungary (4%). Teams came both from academia (~25%) and industry (~75%, most common: *Internet & IT*), e.g. from larger companies such as Yandex or Amazon as well as from smaller start-up companies.

The evolution of the top full score—based on the entire ground truth—is depicted in Figure 2a together with the number of submissions that were performed during that week. The top score thus increased from week to week. In fact, the highest score of the challenge was achieved just 30 minutes before the official submission deadline. Figure 2b reveals that not only the top teams very highly active in submitting solutions, but also many teams that finally ended up at rank 30 and above submitted a high number of solutions.

The top solution achieved a score of 2,052,185 points that is 24.1% of the best possible score. Figure 2c also shows that the top solution managed to include items that XING's system does not recommended. Hence, algorithms developed during the challenge seem to complement XING's recommender ensemble and are likely to have a significant impact on XING's future job recommendations.

Acknowledgments. The work leading to these results has received funding from the EU's Seventh Framework Programme (FP7/2007-2013) under CrowdRec Grant Agreement no. 610594.

4. REFERENCES

[1] F. Abel. We know where you should work next summer: Job recommendations. In *Proceedings of ACM RecSys 2015*, pages 230–230, 2015. ACM.

[2] D. Ben-Shimon, A. Tsikinovsky, M. Friedmann, B. Shapira, L. Rokach, and J. Hoerle. RecSys Challenge 2015 and the YOOCHOOSE Dataset. In *Proceedings of ACM RecSys 2015*, pages 357–358, 2015. ACM.

[3] A. Said, S. Dooms, B. Loni, and D. Tikk. Recommender Systems Challenge 2014. In *Proceedings of ACM RecSys 2014*, pages 387–388, 2014. ACM.

[4] https://github.com/recsyschallenge/2016/#evaluation

Group Recommender Systems*

Ludovico Boratto
Dipartimento di Matematica e Informatica
Università di Cagliari
Via Ospedale 72
09124 Cagliari - Italy
ludovico.boratto@acm.org

ABSTRACT

Group recommender systems provide suggestions in contexts in which people operate in groups. The goal of this tutorial is to provide the RecSys audience with an overview on group recommendation. We will first formally introduce the problem of producing recommendations to groups, then present a survey based on the tasks performed by these systems. We will also analyze challenging topics like their evaluation, and present emerging aspects and techniques in this area. The tutorial will end with a summary that highlights open issues and research challenges.

CCS Concepts

•**Information systems → Recommender systems;**

Keywords

Group Recommendation; Algorithms; Research Challenges

1. INTRODUCTION

While recommender systems suggest items that the individual users might like, *group recommender systems* are designed to operate in contexts in which more than one person is involved in the recommendation process [7]. The goal of this tutorial is to provide the RecSys audience with an overview on group recommendation, by analyzing the aspects that characterize these systems, the evaluation methods (evaluating the accuracy for a group is not trivial [10]), the emerging aspects, and the current challenges.

2. TUTORIAL OUTLINE

In detail, the outline of the tutorial is the following.

1. **Group recommendation introduction**
   - *Definition and application domains*
   - *Problem statement*
2. **Tasks and state of the art survey**
   - *Types of groups.* In [2], we highlighted that the type of group handled by a system is one of the characterizing aspects of a group recommender system and we provided a classification of the different types of groups.
   - *Preference acquisition.* A group recommender system might acquire the preferences by considering only those expressed by the individual users, or by allowing the groups to express them.
   - *Group modeling* [9] is the process adopted to combine the individual preferences in a unique model that represents the group.
   - *Rating prediction* is the most characterizing aspect in all the types of recommender systems, and also plays an important role when working with groups, since the ratings might be predicted for the individual users or specifically for the groups [7].
   - *Help the members to achieve consensus.* This task is adopted in order to find an agreement on what should be proposed to the group.
   - *Explanation of the recommendations*, i.e., the task performed by some of the systems to justify why an item has been suggested to the group.
3. **Evaluation methods**
   - *Offline methods*, which evaluate a system on existing datasets.
   - *User surveys* that test the effectiveness of a system by asking users to answer questionnaires.
   - *Live systems* that work in real-world domains, like the social networks.
4. **Emerging aspects and techniques**
   - *Advanced recommendation techniques applied to group recommendation.* The last advances in recommendation techniques, such as matrix factorization and graph-based techniques, have recently been employed in group recommender systems too [8, 11].

*This work is partially funded by Regione Sardegna under project NOMAD (Next generation Open Mobile Apps Development), through PIA - Pacchetti Integrati di Agevolazione "Industria Artigianato e Servizi" (annualità 2013).

RecSys '16 September 15-19, 2016, Boston , MA, USA

ACM ISBN 978-1-4503-4035-9/16/09...$15.00
DOI: http://dx.doi.org/10.1145/2959100.2959197

- *Temporal aspects in group recommendation.* Recently, the temporal factor has been considered in the recommendation process [1, 5].
- *Social group recommender systems.* The widespread relevance of social media has recently had an impact also on this research area [6, 8].
- *Group recommendation with automatic detection of groups.* There are scenarios in which groups do not exist, but the recommendations have to be proposed to groups because of limitations on the number of recommendation lists that can be produced (i.e., it is not possible to suggest a different list of items to each user), so a clustering of the users specifically designed for recommendation purposes has to be performed [3].

5. **Summary**
   - *Open issues*
   - *Research challenges*

3. PRESENTER

Ludovico Boratto is a research assistant at the University of Cagliari (Italy). His main research area are Recommender Systems, with special focus on those that work with groups of users and in social environments. In 2010 and 2014, he spent 10 months at the Yahoo! Lab in Barcelona as a visiting researcher.

4. REFERENCES

[1] S. Amer-Yahia, B. Omidvar-Tehrani, S. Basu Roy, and N. Shabib. Group recommendation with temporal affinities. In *Proc. 18th International Conference on Extending Database Technology (EDBT)*, pages 421–432. OpenProceedings.org, 2015.

[2] L. Boratto and S. Carta. State-of-the-art in group recommendation and new approaches for automatic identification of groups. In *Information Retrieval and Mining in Distributed Environments*, volume 324 of *Studies in Computational Intelligence*, pages 1–20. Springer Berlin Heidelberg, 2011.

[3] L. Boratto and S. Carta. Using collaborative filtering to overcome the curse of dimensionality when clustering users in a group recommender system. In *ICEIS 2014 - Proceedings of the 16th International Conference on Enterprise Information Systems, Volume 2*, pages 564–572. SciTePress, 2014.

[4] L. A. M. Carvalho and H. T. Macedo. Generation of coalition structures to provide proper groups' formation in group recommender systems. In *Proceedings of the 22Nd International Conference on World Wide Web Companion*, pages 945–950. International World Wide Web Conferences Steering Committee, 2013.

[5] J. Chen, Y. Liu, and D. Li. Dynamic group recommendation with modified collaborative filtering and temporal factor. *The International Arab Journal of Information Technology (IAJIT)*, 2014.

[6] I. A. Christensen and S. Schiaffino. Social influence in group recommender systems. *Online Information Review*, 38(4):524–542, 2014.

[7] A. Jameson and B. Smyth. Recommendation to groups. In *The Adaptive Web, Methods and Strategies of Web Personalization*, volume 4321 of *Lecture Notes in Computer Science*, pages 596–627. Springer, Berlin, 2007.

[8] H.-N. Kim and A. E. Saddik. A stochastic approach to group recommendations in social media systems. *Information Systems*, 50(0):76 – 93, 2015.

[9] J. Masthoff. Group recommender systems: Combining individual models. In *Recommender Systems Handbook*, pages 677–702. Springer, 2011.

[10] F. Ricci. Recommender systems: Models and techniques. In *Encyclopedia of Social Network Analysis and Mining*, pages 1511–1522. Springer New York, 2014.

[11] Q. Yuan, G. Cong, and C.-Y. Lin. Com: A generative model for group recommendation. In *Proceedings of the 20th ACM SIGKDD International Conference on Knowledge Discovery and Data Mining*, KDD '14, pages 163–172. ACM, 2014.

Matrix and Tensor Decomposition in Recommender Systems

Panagiotis Symeonidis
Department of Informatics
Aristotle University
Thessaloniki, 54124, Greece
psymeon@gmail.com

ABSTRACT

This turorial offers a rich blend of theory and practice regarding dimensionality reduction methods, to address the information overload problem in recommender systems. This problem affects our everyday experience while searching for knowledge on a topic. Naive Collaborative Filtering cannot deal with challenging issues such as scalability, noise, and sparsity. We can deal with all the aforementioned challenges by applying matrix and tensor decomposition methods. These methods have been proven to be the most accurate (i.e., Netflix prize) and efficient for handling big data. For each method (SVD, SVD++, timeSVD++, HOSVD, CUR, etc.) we will provide a detailed theoretical mathematical background and a step-by-step analysis, by using an integrated toy example, which runs throughout all parts of the tutorial, helping the audience to understand clearly the differences among factorisation methods.

1. INTRODUCTION

Representing data in lower dimensional spaces has been extensively used in many disciplines such as natural language and image processing, data mining and information retrieval. Recommender systems deal with challenging issues such as scalability, noise, and sparsity and thus, matrix and tensor factorization techniques appear as an interesting tool to be exploited [2, 4]. That is, we can deal with all the aforementioned challenges by applying matrix and tensor decomposition methods (also known as factorization methods).

The rest of this paper is organized as follows. Section 2 provides a detailed outline of the tutorial for matrix decomposition techniques. Section 3 provides a detailed outline of the tutorial for tensor decomposition. Finally, Section 4 concludes this paper.

2. MATRIX DECOMPOSITION

Matrix Factorization denotes a process, where a matrix is factorized into a product of matrices. Its importance relies on the exploitation of the latent associations that exist in data among the participating entities (e.g. between users and items). In a trivial form, the matrix factorization method uses two matrices, which hold the information of correlation between the user-feature and item-feature factors, respectively.

Figure 1 shows an example of the latent factors, which could be revealed after performing matrix decomposition. As shown, the X'X axis divides both people and movies according sex (e.g., male or female). When a movie is closer to the female part of X'X axis, it means that this movie is most popular in women rather than in men. The Y'Y axis divides people and movies as "war-like" and "romantic". A "war-like" viewer is assumed to prefer movies showing blood and deaths. In contrast, a "romantic" viewer chooses movies that present love and passion.

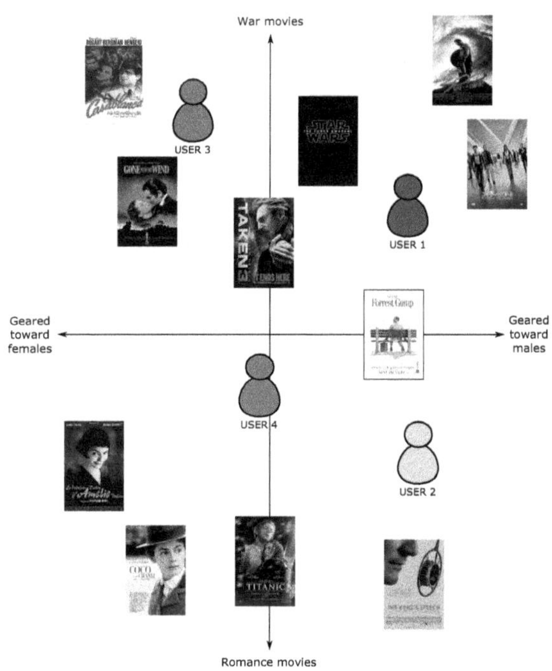

Figure 1: Visual representation of users and movies using two axes — male versus female and war-like versus romantic.

RecSys '16 September 15-19, 2016, Boston , MA, USA

ACM ISBN 978-1-4503-4035-9/16/09.
DOI: http://dx.doi.org/10.1145/2959100.2959195

To predict a user's rating over a movie, we can compute the dot product of the movie's and user's [x,y] coordinates on the graph. In addition, Figure 1 shows where movies and users might fall on the basic two dimensions. For example, we would expect *User 3* to love *"Casablanca"*, to hate *"The King's Speech"*, and to rate *"Amelie"* about average. Note that some movies (i.e. *"Taken 3"*) and users (i.e. *User 4*) would be characterised as fairly neutral on these two dimensions.

In this tutorial, we provide the related work of basic matrix decomposition methods. The first method that we discuss is known as Eigenvalue Decomposition, which decomposes the initial matrix into a canonical form. A second method is the Non-Negative Matrix Factorization (NMF), which factorizes the initial matrix into two smaller matrices with the constraint that each element of the factorized matrices should be non-negative. A third method is the Probabilistic Matrix Factorization (PMF), which scales well to large datasets. PMF mathod performs well on very sparse and imbalanced datasets using spherical Gaussian priors. The last but one method is Probabilistic Latent Semantic Analysis (PLSA) which is based on a mixture decomposition derived from a latent class model. The last method is CUR Decomposition, which confronts the problem of density in the factorized matrices (a problem that is faced on SVD method). Moreover, we describe Singular Value Decomposition (SVD) and UV-Decomposition in details. We minimise an objective function, which captures the error between the predicted and the real value of a user's rating. Moreover, an additional constraint of friendship is added in the objective function to leverage the quality of recommendations [1].

Finally, we study the performance of the described SVD and UV-decomposition algorithms, against an improved version of the original item-based CF algorithm combined with SVD.

3. TENSOR DECOMPOSITION

Because of the ternary relational nature of data in many cases (e.g., Social Tagging Systems (STSs), Location-based social network (LBSNs) etc.), many recommendation algorithms originally designed to operate on matrices cannot be applied. Higher order problems put forward new challenges and opportunities for recommender systems. For example, the ternary relation of STSs can be represented as a third-order tensor $\mathcal{A} = (a_{u,i,t}) \in \mathbb{R}^{|U|\times|I|\times|T|}$. Symeonidis et al. [3], for example, proposed to interpret the user assignment of a tag on an item, as a binary tensor where 1 indicates observed tag assignments and 0 missing values (see Figure 2):

$$a_{u,i,t} := \begin{cases} 1, & \text{if user } u \text{ assign on item } i \text{ tag } t \\ 0, & \text{otherwise} \end{cases}$$

Tensor factorization techniques can be employed in order to exploit the underlying latent semantic structure in tensor $\mathcal{A}$. The basic idea is to transform the recommendation problem as a third-order tensor completion problem, by trying to predict the non-observed entries in $\mathcal{A}$.

In this tutorial, we provide the related work on tensor decomposition methods. The first method that is discussed is the Tucker Decomposition method (TD), which is the underlying tensor factorization model of HOSVD. TD decomposes a tensor into a set of matrices and one small core tensor. The

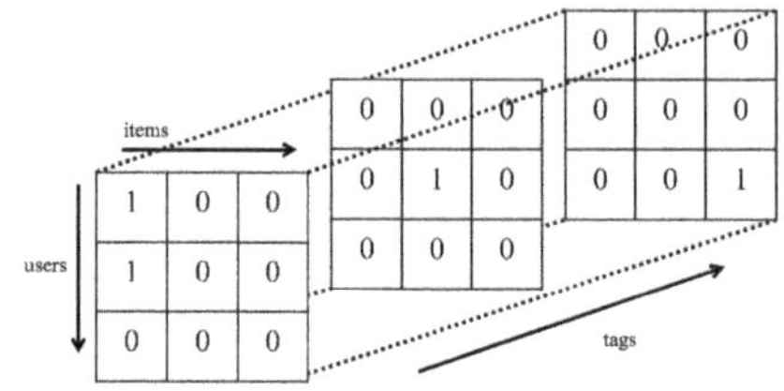

Figure 2: Tensor representation of a STS where positive feedback is interpreted as 1 (i.e., $a_{utr} := 1$) and the rest as 0 (i.e., $a_{utr} := 0$).

second one is PARAFAC method (PARAllel FACtor analysis), which is the same as TD method with the restriction that core tensor should be diagonal. The third method is the PITF method (Pairwise Interaction Tensor Factorization), which is a special case of TD method with linear runtime both for learning and prediction. The last method that is analyzed is the Low-order Tensor Decomposition (LOTD) method.

The main factorization method that will be presented in this tutorial is Higher Order SVD (HOSVD), which is an extended version of the SVD method. In particular, we will present a step-by-step implementation of HOSVD in a toy example. Then, we will present how we can update HOSVD when a new user is registered in our recommender system. We will also discuss how HOSVD can be combined with other methods for leveraging the quality of recommendations. Finally, we will provide experimental results of tensor decomposition methods on real datasets in STSs. Moreover, we will discuss about the metrics that we will use (i.e., Precision, Recall, RMSE, etc.). Our goal is to present the main factors that influence the effectiveness of algorithms.

4. CONCLUSIONS

In this tutorial, we discuss the advantages and limitations of each matrix and tensor decomposition algorithm for recommender systems, and provide future research directions.

References

[1] Yehuda Koren. Factorization meets the neighborhood: A multifaceted collaborative filtering model. In *Proceedings of the 14th ACM SIGKDD International Conference on Knowledge Discovery and Data Mining*, KDD '08, pages 426–434, New York, NY, USA, 2008. ACM.

[2] Yehuda Koren, Robert Bell, and Chris Volinsky. Matrix factorization techniques for recommender systems. *Computer*, 42(8):30–37, August 2009.

[3] Panagiotis Symeonidis, Alexandros Nanopoulos, and Yannis Manolopoulos. Tag recommendations based on tensor dimensionality reduction. In *RecSys '08: Proceedings of the 2008 ACM conference on Recommender systems*, pages 43–50. ACM, 2008.

[4] Gábor Takács, István Pilászy, Bottyán Németh, and Domonkos Tikk. Matrix factorization and neighbor based algorithms for the netflix prize problem. RecSys '08, pages 267–274, New York, NY, USA, 2008. ACM.

People Recommendation Tutorial

Ido Guy
Yahoo Research, Israel
Ben-Gurion University of the Negev, Israel
idoguy@acm.org

Luiz Pizzato
Commonwealth Bank of Australia, Australia
luiz@pizzato.cc

ABSTRACT

People recommenders have become a rich research area within the broad recommender systems community and social recommender systems in particular. From "people you may know" and "who to follow" widgets, through people introduction at conferences, job recommendations and job-candidate search, to dating partner matchmakers, people recommendations proliferate. This tutorial will present an overview of the people recommender systems domain. We will present the different types and use cases of people recommendations, the special techniques used to recommend people to themselves, key research work, and open challenges.

Keywords: people recommenders; reciprocal recommendations; recommending people; social recommender systems.

1. INTRODUCTION

In the past decade, people recommender systems have emerged as a prominent field within the recommender systems domain, and social recommender systems in particular. Recommending people to themselves has inherent reciprocity, which bears unique characteristics compared to traditional item recommendation. Factors such as trust, reputation, privacy, and interpersonal attraction, play a more significant role in people recommenders than in traditional recommenders.

In this tutorial, we will discuss the key motivations driving people recommendation and review the fundamental recommendation approaches. We will present the key types of people recommendations, based on the nature and time-span of the relationship between the user and the recommended individual. Each recommendation type will be demonstrated with principal case studies from the literature. We will then review evaluation techniques, with emphasis on the pros and cons of each method. Finally, we will summarize by discussion of open issues and challenges in the field.

The tutorial is intended for the broad RecSys audience and requires no prior knowledge.

RecSys '16 September 15-19, 2016, Boston , MA, USA

ACM ISBN 978-1-4503-4035-9/16/09.

DOI: http://dx.doi.org/10.1145/2959100.2959196

2. TUTORIAL OUTLINE

1. Introduction to People Recommendation
    - Social Matching
    - Reciprocal Recommendation
    - People Recommendation on Social Media
2. Main Recommendation Methods
    - Content-based Methods
    - Graph-based Methods
    - Interaction-based Methods
3. Relationship Types
    - Familiarity
    - Similarity
    - Interest
4. Network Effects
5. Ad-hoc People Recommendation
    - Recommending Familiar People
    - Recommending Similar People
    - Recommending Interesting People
6. Evaluation Methods
    - Offline Methods
    - User Surveys
    - Live Systems
7. Emerging Domains
    - Healthcare
    - Smart TVs
    - Wearable Technologies
8. Directions for Future Work
    - Group Recommendation
    - Privacy
    - Interactivity

3. INSTRUCTORS

Ido Guy is a Principal Research Engineer at Yahoo Research, where he focuses on data science for Yahoo products in search, social media, and email. Prior to joining Yahoo Research, Ido was a senior technical staff member (STSM) and manager of the Social Technologies group, an area that he established and managed in 2007-2014, as part of the IBM Haifa Research Lab. He has published over 50 scientific papers in the fields of Data Mining, Human-Computer Interaction, Computer-Supported Cooperative Work, Information and Knowledge Management, Information Retrieval, and Recommender Systems. In recent years, Ido has been particularly active in the area of Social Recommender Systems and published key papers on people recommendation [1, 2, 7, 10, 13] and related areas, including people search and expertise location [6, 14, 23], reputation [11, 15, 17], social stream analysis [8, 9, 12], and web search [5, 16]. Ido has served as co-chair of the Workshop on Social Recommender Systems (2010-2015) and RecSys workshop on Recommender Systems and the Social Web (2011-2014). He is author of the chapter on Social Recommender Systems at the Recommender Systems Handbook [4] and the chapter on People Recommendation on Social Media at the Social Information Access book (to appear). Ido has also served as the program co-chair of RecSys 2012.

Luiz Pizzato is a Data Scientist, an Educator and an Entrepreneur. He works as a data scientist for the Commonwealth Bank of Australia, and a data science instructor for General Assembly. Luiz is also a co-founder and researcher for Octosocial Labs and provides independent data science consultancy. Luiz was previously a senior data scientist at 1-Page, working on a number of problems including finding the set of potential candidates for a job position. Luiz also worked as a Research Fellow at the University of Sydney and was involved in a number of people recommender research including the development, deployment and testing of online dating recommendations for one of the large online dating companies in Australia. Luiz has published over two dozens research papers in recommender systems and natural language processing, including a number of papers about reciprocal recommenders in online dating [18, 19]. Luiz has organized a number of workshops at top-tier conferences and has been part of a large number of reviewing and program committees.

Ido gave a tutorial on Social recommender systems at WWW 2011 (with David Carmel), WWW 2014, and RecSys 2014 (with Werner Geyer). Luiz gave a tutorial named "Beyond Friendship: The Art, Science and Applications of Recommending People to People in Social Networks" at RecSys 2013 (with Amnol Basin). That tutorial focused on reciprocal recommenders and people recommenders as implemented on LinkedIn and on Online Dating companies. The scope of this tutorial is broader, and encompasses all types of people recommenders, including recent developments, such as recommendation of people to mention [3, 21], suggesting activity partners [20], and lifestyle-based recommendation [22].

4. REFERENCES

[1] J. Chen, W. Geyer, C. Dugan, M. Muller, and I. Guy. Make new friends, but keep the old: recommending people on social networking sites. In *PROC. CHI*, pages 201–210, 2009.

[2] J. Freyne, M. Jacovi, I. Guy, and W. Geyer. Increasing engagement through early recommender intervention. In *Proc. RecSys*, pages 85–92, 2009.

[3] Y. Gong, Q. Zhang, X. Sun, and X. Huang. Who will you "@"? In *Proc. CIKM*, pages 533–542, 2015.

[4] I. Guy. *Recommender Systems Handbook*, chapter Social Recommender Systems, pages 511–543. Springer US, Boston, MA, 2015.

[5] I. Guy. Searching by talking: Analysis of voice queries on mobile web search. In *Proc. SIGIR*, pages 35–44, 2016.

[6] I. Guy, U. Avraham, D. Carmel, S. Ur, M. Jacovi, and I. Ronen. Mining expertise and interests from social media. In *Proc. WWW*, pages 515–526, 2013.

[7] I. Guy, M. Jacovi, A. Perer, I. Ronen, and E. Uziel. Same places, same things, same people?: mining user similarity on social media. In *Proc. CSCW*, pages 41–50. ACM, 2010.

[8] I. Guy, R. Levin, T. Daniel, and E. Bolshinsky. Islands in the stream: A study of item recommendation within an enterprise social stream. In *Proc. SIGIR*, pages 665–674, 2015.

[9] I. Guy, I. Ronen, and A. Raviv. Personalized activity streams: Sifting through the "river of news". In *Proc. RecSys*, pages 181–188, 2011.

[10] I. Guy, I. Ronen, and E. Wilcox. Do you know?: Recommending people to invite into your social network. In *Proc. IUI*, pages 77–86, 2009.

[11] I. Guy, I. Ronen, N. Zwerdling, I. Zuyev-Grabovitch, and M. Jacovi. What is your organization âĂŸlikeâĂŹ? a study of liking activity in the enterprise. In *Proc. CHI*, pages 3025–3037, 2016.

[12] I. Guy, T. Steier, M. Barnea, I. Ronen, and T. Daniel. Swimming against the streamz: Search and analytics over the enterprise activity stream. In *Proc. CIKM*, pages 1587–1591, 2012.

[13] I. Guy, S. Ur, I. Ronen, A. Perer, and M. Jacovi. Do you want to know?: recommending strangers in the enterprise. In *Proc. CSCW*, pages 285–294. ACM, 2011.

[14] I. Guy, S. Ur, I. Ronen, S. Weber, and T. Oral. Best faces forward: A large-scale study of people search in the enterprise. In *Proc. CHI*, pages 1775–1784, 2012.

[15] M. Jacovi, I. Guy, S. Kremer-Davidson, S. Porat, and N. Aizenbud-Reshef. The perception of others: Inferring reputation from social media in the enterprise. In *Proc. CSCW*, pages 756–766, 2014.

[16] E. Kravi, E. Agichtein, I. Guy, Y. Kanza, A. Mejer, and D. Pelleg. Searcher in a strange land: Understanding web search from familiar and unfamiliar locations. In *Proc. SIGIR*, pages 855–858, 2015.

[17] G. Mark, I. Guy, S. Kremer-Davidson, and M. Jacovi. Most liked, fewest friends: Patterns of enterprise social media use. In *Proc. CSCW*, pages 393–404, 2014.

[18] L. Pizzato, T. Rej, J. Akehurst, I. Koprinska, K. Yacef, and J. Kay. Recommending people to people: the nature of reciprocal recommenders with a case study in online dating. *User Modeling and User-Adapted Interaction*, 23(5):447–488, 2012.

[19] L. Pizzato, T. Rej, T. Chung, I. Koprinska, and J. Kay. Recon: A reciprocal recommender for online dating. In *Proc. RecSys*, pages 207–214. ACM, 2010.

[20] W. Tu, D. Cheung, N. Mamoulis, M. Yang, and Z. Lu. Activity-partner recommendation. In *Advances in Knowledge Discovery and Data Mining*, volume 9077, pages 591–604. Springer International Publishing, 2015.

[21] B. Wang, C. Wang, J. Bu, C. Chen, W. V. Zhang, D. Cai, and X. He. Whom to mention: Expand the diffusion of tweets by @ recommendation on micro-blogging systems. In *Proc. WWW*, pages 1331–1340, 2013.

[22] Z. Wang, J. Liao, Q. Cao, H. Qi, and Z. Wang. Friendbook: A semantic-based friend recommendation system for social networks. *Mobile Computing, IEEE Transactions on*, 14(3):538–551, March 2015.

[23] A. Yogev, I. Guy, I. Ronen, N. Zwerdling, and M. Barnea. Social media-based expertise evidence. In *Proc. ECSCW*, pages 63–82, 2015.

Tutorial: Lessons learned from building real-life recommender systems

Xavier Amatriain
Quora
650 Castro St. #450
Mountain View, CA 94041, USA
xavier@quora.com

Deepak Agarwal
LinkedIn
2029 Stierlin Court
Mountain View, CA 94043, USA
dagarwal@linkedin.com

ABSTRACT

In 2006, Netflix announced a $1M prize competition to advance recommendation algorithms. The recommendation problem was simplified as the accuracy in predicting a user rating measured by the Root Mean Squared Error. While that formulation helped get the attention of the research community, it put the focus on the wrong approach and metric while leaving many important factors out.

In this tutorial we will describe the advances in Recommender Systems in the last 10 years from an industry perspective based on the instructors' personal experience at companies like Quora, LinkedIn, Netflix, or Yahoo!. We will do so in the form of different lessons learned through the years.

Some of those lessons will describe the different components of modern recommender systems such as: personalized ranking, similarity, explanations, context-awareness, or multi-armed bandits. Others will also review the usage of novel algorithmic approaches such as Factorization Machines, Restricted Boltzmann Machines, SimRank, Deep Neural Networks, or Listwise Learning-to-rank. Others will dive into details of the importance of gathering the right data or using the correct optimization metric.

But, most importantly, we will give many examples of prototypical industrial-scale recommender systems with special focus on those unsolved challenges that should define the future of the recommender systems area.

Related Publications

- Recommender Systems in Industry: A Netflix Case Study. X Amatriain, J Basilico, Recommender Systems Handbook, 385-419
- Personalizing LinkedIn Feed. Deepak Agarwal et al.. KDD 2015
- Data Mining Methods for Recommender Systems. X Amatriain, JM Pujol, Recommender Systems Handbook, 227-262
- Mining large streams of user data for personalized recommendations. X Amatriain, ACM SIGKDD Explorations Newsletter 14 (2), 37-48
- Recommending items to users: an explore/exploit perspective. Deepak Agarwal UEO@CIKM 2013: 1-2
- Multiverse recommendation: n-dimensional tensor factorization for context-aware collaborative filtering. A Karatzoglou, X Amatriain, L Baltrunas, N Oliver. Proceedings of the fourth ACM conference on Recommender systems, 79-86
- Temporal diversity in recommender systems. N Lathia, S Hailes, L Capra, X Amatriain. Proceedings of the 33rd international ACM SIGIR conference
- The wisdom of the few: a collaborative filtering approach based on expert opinions from the web. X Amatriain, N Lathia, JM Pujol, H Kwak, N Oliver. Proceedings of the 32nd international ACM SIGIR conference
- I like it... i like it not: Evaluating user ratings noise in recommender systems. X Amatriain, JM Pujol, N Oliver. User modeling, adaptation, and personalization, 247-258
- Movie Recommender: Semantically Enriched Unified Relevance Model for Rating Prediction in Collaborative Filtering. Yashar Moshfeghi, Deepak Agarwal, Benjamin Piwowarski, Joemon M. Jose: ECIR 2009: 54-65

RecSys '16 September 15-19, 2016, Boston , MA, USA

ACM ISBN 978-1-4503-4035-9/16/09.
DOI: http://dx.doi.org/10.1145/2959100.2959194

Context-Based IDE Command Recommender System

Marko Gasparic
Free University of Bozen-Bolzano
Piazza Domenicani, 3, I-39100 Bozen-Bolzano, Italy
marko.gasparic@stud-inf.unibz.it

ABSTRACT

Software developer's working process could benefit from the support of an active help system that is able to recommend applicable and useful integrated development environment (IDE) commands. While previous work focused on prediction methods that can identify what developers will eventually discover autonomously, and without taking into account the characteristics of their working tasks, we want to build a system that recommends only commands that lead to better work performance. Since we cannot expect that developers are willing to invest a significant effort to use our recommender system (RS), we are developing a context-aware multi-criteria RS based on implicit feedback.

We already created and evaluated context and user models. We also acquired a data set with more than 100,000 command executions. Currently, we are developing RS algorithm for predicting the scores of performance and effort expectancy and developer's intention to use a specific command. We are also developing a user interface, that has to be persuasive, effective, and efficient. To date, a user interface for IDE command RS has not been developed.

Keywords

integrated development environment; command; recommendation; context

1. INTRODUCTION AND MOTIVATION

Modern integrated development environments (IDEs) bring together multiple tools to create and manipulate software project artifacts. Professional software developers spend most of their time working in an IDE and to effectively use it, they have to know a large number of commands that could be relevant for the task at hand, such as Generate Getters and Setters, Open Resource, and Navigate to Type Definition, amongst others. Previous research shows that developers use IDEs sub-optimally [10], thus, their learning and working process could benefit from the support of an active help system that is able to recommend applicable and useful commands.

RecSys '16, September 15 - 19, 2016, Boston , MA, USA

ISBN 978-1-4503-4035-9/16/09...$15.00

DOI: http://dx.doi.org/10.1145/2959100.2959106

Recommender systems (RSs) are personalized information search and filtering tools that suggest useful items [12]. Murphy-Hill et al. [11] showed that it is feasible to automatically recommend novel and useful IDE commands, even when simple RS algorithms are used. Nevertheless, in our opinion, if the goal of a RS is to recommend an item with the largest utility for the developer, current scientific work in IDE command recommendations suffers from several deficiencies. First, state-of-the-art algorithms focus on accurately predicting the next command that the developer will autonomously discover, which is generating redundant and not only novel command recommendations, as the online evaluation in [11] indicates. Second, such an approach recommends commands without considering their relevance to the developer's work, which may lead to better IDE knowledge, but not necessarily to better work performance of the developer. And third, to the best of our knowledge, a standalone IDE command RS has not yet been implemented: Zolaktaf and Murphy [16] performed only offline evaluations, while Murphy-Hill et al. [11], who performed an online evaluation, presented the recommendations to the study participants *in-person*, instead of developing a user interface or its mock-up to decrease the effect of presenter's persuasiveness on the perceived quality of the recommendations.

While previous work focused on prediction methods that can identify what developers will eventually discover autonomously, and without taking into account the characteristics of their working tasks, we aim at developing an IDE command RS that can improve developer's use of an IDE, which, ultimately, has to result in a better work performance, since developers are not interested in becoming IDE experts, but only want to complete their tasks as quick and as good as possible. Consequently, we have to create an algorithm that is capable of identifying commands that the developer can and will use during the work and we have to devise a user interface through which the acceptance of useful recommendations can be attained. We seek to answer the following research questions:

- RQ1: How to generate valuable work-related IDE command recommendations?
- RQ2: How to present IDE command recommendations?

We already created context and user models that enable the detection of different situations in which certain (different) developers are using certain (different) commands. Now we are developing a RS algorithm based on implicit feedback and context that can predict the scores of *performance* and *effort expectancy* and developer's *intention to use* a specific command; and we are developing a user interface that has to be *persuasive*, *effective*, and *efficient*.

2. RELATED WORK

Matejka et al. [9] apply collaborative filtering algorithms and domain knowledge to provide command recommendations in AutoCAD. Murphy-Hill et al. [11] apply the same algorithms as [9] and four new algorithms to recommend commands in Eclipse,[1] namely, "most widely used", "collaborative filtering with discovery", "advanced discovery", and "most popular discovery" algorithms. The first algorithm is a special version of the "most popular" algorithm, while other three are based on sequential pattern mining, which is used to model the process of discovery of new commands. When the most successful algorithms were used in an online study, experts evaluated 26% of commands as novel, while novices evaluated 80% of commands as such, and experts evaluated 80% of commands as useful, while novices evaluated 100%.

Zolaktaf and Murphy [16] suggest a new algorithm for command recommendations that is based on the command discovery patterns and co-occurrence of command executions in the session. The offline evaluations show that this algorithm outperforms other existing algorithms, according to the accuracy of predicting the next command that will be discovered by the developer.

We are developing a context-aware multi-criteria RS based on implicit feedback that aims at convincing software developers to learn new IDE commands. By the RSs community, the command recommendation as such has not been addressed yet, however, there exists a large body of work in the domains that are related to our problem. Adomavicius et al. [2] define the context-aware RSs (CARSs): the overview of recent developments is provided by Adomavicius and Tuzhilin [3]. Adomavicius and Kwon [1] present the field of multi-criteria RSs. Hu et al. [7], in their seminal work, describe the properties of implicit feedback and propose some techniques for generating recommendations. Jameson et al. [8] describe everyday human decision making approaches that are relevant also in the context of RSs. Tintarev and Masthoff [13] discuss the role, the design, and the evaluation techniques for recommendation explanations.

3. RECOMMENDATION GENERATION AND PRESENTATION

In this section, we present more in detail the IDE command recommendation approach that we have designed and plan to implement. We assume that the Unified Theory of Acceptance and Use of Technology [14] (UTAUT) can help us to understand the drivers of command acceptance. According to Venkatesh et al. [14], three determinants directly affect the intention to use a new system—in our case, a new IDE command:

- Performance expectancy: strength of belief that the usage of the new command will improve job performance;
- Effort expectancy: user's perception of simplicity of use of the new command;
- Social influence: opinions of important others.

The first two aspects (performance and effort expectancy) of IDE command can be highly influenced by recommendation generation and presentation, while the third aspect (social influence) is less impacted by them [6]. We want to develop and implement an algorithm that will be able to assess the individual criteria (performance expectancy and effort expectancy) and properly integrate these evaluations into a prediction of the intention of a specific developer to use a specific command, if it was recommended.

Generally, the work performance of a software developer is improved if the process or the product under development are improved; however, it is hard to explicitly define how useful an IDE command is, since the perception of the quality and the value of saving time varies between developers, teams, and organizations. For instance, even if it seems unnecessary and inefficient to use some refactoring commands in a certain moment, they may lead to better readability of the source code, which can decrease long-term maintenance costs, or to less bugs, which can increase customer satisfaction. Since we cannot assume that developers are willing to change their working process or to invest a significant effort to use our RS, we have to rely on implicit feedback—the execution of a command—and the observations of the context—*"any information that can be used to characterize the situation of an entity"* [5], which is in our case the situation of a developer using an IDE—that do not require repetitive or substantial manual effort. We posit that the estimation of the performance can be based on models that are not only learned from the data and explicit input but are based on general principles, i.e., heuristics. We assume that the performance of a command can be defined implicitly: the command is more useful if the target developer finds herself more often in the situations in which the command is executed more often. These situations can be identified using the context model described in Section 4.

The effort required to use an IDE command consists of the learning effort and the command execution effort. Since the effort required to execute a command is negligible,[2] we conjecture that the overall effort strongly correlates with the effort required to understand why and how the command should be used, which depends on the complexity of the command and developer's knowledge. We assume that the complexity of a command is a characteristic of a command that is independent of developers and context. We plan to estimate the complexity of commands using their description text complexity metrics. Nevertheless, developers with more experience, who are more familiar with IDE concepts and its interface, will likely need less effort to comprehend the meaning of the recommended command. Thus, we plan to personalize the recommendations by integrating a user model in the RS algorithm as well.

We assume that the perception of the scores (i.e., ratings) of the individual criteria is correlated to the true (i.e., experienced) value of these criteria. However, it can be largely affected by the recommendation presentation as well. Thus, the goal of the user interface design should be to present the recommendations in a way that developers' perception of criteria is as close as possible to the true value of it.

[1] http://www.eclipse.org

[2] To execute a command in a high-functionality application, the user has to select a menu button or press a certain key sequence.

To increase the likelihood of recommendation acceptance, the system has to be *persuasive*. In our case, it means that the commands have to be presented in such a way that the *performance expectancy* is high and *effort expectancy* is low. At the same time, since we are aiming at the long term usage of a RS and we do not want to risk loosing trust by tricking the users, the gap between the expected and experienced values should be small; thus, the command presentation and the recommendation explanation have to be *effective* [13].

The third criterion we want to satisfy in designing the user interface is the *efficiency*. Unless the developer is explicitly learning how to use an IDE, we cannot expect that she will be willing to invest a lot of time and effort in the interaction with a RS or simply into reading the explanations of recommendations. Moreover, efficient recommendations decrease the required effort, which directly improves the persuasiveness of the RS as well.

To accurately predict the *performance expectancy*, *effort expectancy*, and *intention to use* an IDE command related to a specific developer, and to satisfy the criteria related to the user interface—*persuasiveness*, *effectiveness*, and *efficiency*—we need information about the context and the user. For instance, recommending a version control command for resolving merging conflicts to a developer who does not know or use version control will lead to low *performance* and high *effort expectancy*, which will result in a low *intention to use*, thus, such a command should not be recommended. On the other hand, recommending an editing command to an experienced developer will require low effort from her and can significantly improve the performance, but the presentation and the explanation will have to be convincing to persuade her to change the old development style. We present our context and user models in the next section.

4. MODELS FOR IDE USAGE

In our previous work, we devised a context model for characterizing the situations of a developer using an IDE and a user model for characterizing the developers. They can be used to improve the accuracy of recommendations and to provide the information about the context of command usage, which can be used as a rationale for the recommendations. In this section, we briefly describe the models, which we plan to incorporate in our IDE command RS.

To date, in software development applications, contextual factors—variables with precise domains of possible values that are used to identify the context—have typically been limited to project artifacts, such as source code [6]. We propose a new context model that consists of eleven contextual factors, which we grouped into three categories:

- *What* – to capture the information about what developers are doing with an IDE and which project artifacts they are using; it includes *current* and *previous activity*, and *type*, *length*, and *complexity of the artifact under development* contextual factors;
- *When* – to capture the information about temporal aspects of developer's interaction with an IDE; it includes *time of the day* and *day of the week* contextual factors;
- *Where* – to capture the information about the IDE environment with which a developer is interacting; it includes *IDE instance*, *active perspective*, *opened user interface elements* and *user interface element with focus* contextual factors.

We also propose a user model that consists of three factors:

- *Who* – to capture the information about the developer who is interacting with an IDE; it includes *developer unique identifier*, *general experience*, and *IDE experience* contextual factors.

The inclusion of factors is based on the previous literature and our own experience. To evaluate the relevance of the factors for describing the IDE usage, we examined the correlations between different situations—as described by the proposed factors—and IDE command usage. We gathered data about which commands in an IDE were used by eight Eclipse users working in either academia or a medium-sized company for ten weeks; together they executed more than 100,000 commands. The factors included in the model statistically correlate with the usage of at least some commands; in particular, when the values of the factors change, different developers—as individuals and as a group—use commands differently, according to Pearson's χ^2 and Fisher–Freeman–Halton tests. Table 1 displays the results of the tests.

Table 1: The results of the statistical tests. The values are the numbers of used commands that correlate with the factors.

Developer	A	B	C	D	E	F	G	H	All
Num. of used commands	60	93	85	66	81	70	60	15	193
Current activity	41	77	62	39	53	47	37	4	130
Previous activity	30	48	40	36	45	40	19	2	101
Artifact type	22	61	37	33	48	26	26	4	103
Artifact length	/	/	31	20	34	20	5	/	83
Artifact complexity	/	/	35	24	38	26	5	/	86
Time of the day	20	32	11	22	14	12	10	0	72
Day of the week	29	40	24	24	43	25	20	5	84
IDE instance	/	/	/	/	/	20	23	/	136
Active perspective	24	41	10	19	/	18	0	5	122
Opened UI elements	20	66	36	39	43	36	18	4	130
UI element with focus	35	65	50	45	48	44	24	0	126
Developer ID	/	/	/	/	/	/	/	/	137
Developer general exp.	/	/	/	/	/	/	/	/	118
Developer IDE exp.	/	/	/	/	/	/	/	/	10

/ – the detection failed or the values did not change

By observing the entire sample, we can see that the contextual factor for which the usage of the most commands changes is *developer unique identifier*; this indicates that the systems supporting users in their interaction with an IDE should be personalized, because users behave differently, even if we observe only a small set of users working in a similar environment. Almost the same result is achieved by *IDE instance*; probably because only three participants changed it during the case study and consequently it strongly reflects *developer unique identifier*. On the third place, we find *current activity* and *opened views and editors*. The first could be expected since commands are strictly connected to the *current activity*: a developer who executed Delete Line command is currently editing and the one who executed Resume Debug is debugging, for example. The second is rather unexpected; we assume that *opened views and editors* indicates the change in usage of so many commands because the domain of the factor is so large: it contains 372 different values, which is more than all other factors combined; consequently, we conclude that more fine-grained observations lead to higher accuracy, however, the generalizability of the situations may suffer. The only factor that performs very poorly on our data set is *developer IDE experience*. This is probably due to the size of the set of participants and their characteristics, since we only classified participant H as a "novice" and he only executed 15 different commands.

The set of executable commands and the visualization of menu bars in Eclipse depends mainly on the *user interface element with focus* and *type of the artifact under development*. These two factors are outperformed by several other factors that are not taken into account by the IDE. If we knew more about the situations in which commands are useful, we could compare them with the situations in which specific developers often find themselves. Hence, an IDE command RS would be able to identify the recommendations that are more suited to developer's work. Such knowledge may be used also for generating explanations of recommendations. We discuss the directions of this research next.

5. CURRENT AND FUTURE WORK

We are currently designing a RS algorithm that will incorporate contextual information according to the *contextual modeling* paradigm [2].[3] We are testing our ideas offline, using the data set we acquired during the context model evaluation. We are also designing the RS user interface. We assume that visualizing the command name or key sequence of the shortcut, if it exists, is not sufficient to reach developer's understanding of what the RS is recommending nor to convince her to accept the recommendation. We are currently designing different user interfaces, focusing on maximizing their *persuasiveness*, *effectiveness*, and *efficiency*. We are also exploring the possibilities for generating *context recommendations*[4] for a specific command, which can then be included in the explanations: when the command should be executed; or can be used for calculating the best timing for different recommendations: when should RS suggest developers to learn and start using a new IDE command.

In the future, we plan to perform the evaluations of user interface mock-ups with a survey and in a laboratory setting. Then we will integrate the best performing user interface in our IDE command RS. And at the end, we plan to conduct a case study to evaluate and compare our RS algorithm with the state-of-the-art IDE command RSs and algorithms generally used in CARSs.

[3] *Contextual modeling* or *contextualization of recommendation function* refers to a direct usage of the context in the modeling technique as part of the rating estimation. [2]

[4] Baltrunas et al. [4] introduce the *best context* concept for defining the conditions most suited for a particular item—in their case, it is a music track. Zheng [15] presents the latest achievements in this field. We are trying to identify the *best context* for IDE command.

6. REFERENCES

[1] G. Adomavicius and Y. Kwon. Multi-criteria recommender systems. In *Recommender Systems Handbook*, pages 847–880. Springer, 2015.

[2] G. Adomavicius, B. Mobasher, F. Ricci, and A. Tuzhilin. Context-aware recommender systems. *AI Magazine*, pages 67–80, 2011.

[3] G. Adomavicius and A. Tuzhilin. Context-aware recommender systems. In *Recommender Systems Handbook*, pages 191–226. Springer, 2015.

[4] L. Baltrunas, L. Rokach, M. Kaminskas, B. Shapira, F. Ricci, and K.-H. Luke. Best usage context prediction for music tracks. In *Workshop on Context Aware Recommender Systems*, 2010.

[5] A. K. Dey. Understanding and using context. *Personal and Ubiquitous Computing*, pages 4–7, 2001.

[6] M. Gasparic and A. Janes. What recommendation systems for software engineering recommend: A systematic literature review. *Journal of Systems and Software*, pages 101–113, 2016.

[7] Y. Hu, Y. Koren, and C. Volinsky. Collaborative filtering for implicit feedback datasets. In *IEEE International Conference on Data Mining*, 2008.

[8] A. Jameson, M. C. Willemsen, A. Felfernig, M. Gemmis, P. Lops, G. Semeraro, and L. Chen. Human decision making and recommender systems. In *Recommender Systems Handbook*, pages 611–648. Springer, 2015.

[9] J. Matejka, W. Li, T. Grossman, and G. Fitzmaurice. CommunityCommands: Command recommendations for software applications. In *ACM Symposium on User Interface Software and Technology*, 2009.

[10] E. Murphy-Hill. Continuous social screencasting to facilitate software tool discovery. In *International Conference on Software Engineering*, 2012.

[11] E. Murphy-Hill, R. Jiresal, and G. C. Murphy. Improving software developers' fluency by recommending development environment commands. In *ACM SIGSOFT International Symposium on the Foundations of Software Engineering*, 2012.

[12] F. Ricci. Recommender systems: Models and techniques. In *Encyclopedia of Social Network Analysis and Mining*, pages 1511–1522. Springer, 2014.

[13] N. Tintarev and J. Masthoff. Explaining recommendations: Design and evaluation. In *Recommender Systems Handbook*, pages 353–382. Springer, 2015.

[14] V. Venkatesh, M. G. Morris, G. B. Davis, and F. D. Davis. User acceptance of information technology: Toward a unified view. *MIS Quarterly*, pages 425–478, 2003.

[15] Y. Zheng. Context suggestion: Solutions and challenges. In *IEEE International Conference on Data Mining Workshop*, 2015.

[16] S. Zolaktaf and G. C. Murphy. What to learn next: Recommending commands in a feature-rich environment. In *International Conference on Machine Learning and Applications*, 2015.

Generating Pseudotransactions for Improving Sparse Matrix Factorization

Wibowo, Agung T.*
University of Aberdeen
r01atw15@abdn.ac.uk

ABSTRACT

Recent research on Recommender Systems, specifically Collaborative Filtering, has focussed on Matrix Factorization (MF) methods, which have been shown to provide good solutions to the cold start problem. However, typically the same settings are used for Matrix factorization regardless of the density of the matrix. In our experiments, we found that for MF, Root Mean Square Error (RMSE) for recommendations increases (i.e. performance drops) for sparse matrices. We propose a Two Stage MF approach so MF is run twice over the whole matrix; the first stage uses MF to generate a small percentage of pseudotransactions that are added to the original matrix to increase its density, and the second stage re-runs MF over this denser matrix to predict the user-item transactions in the testing set. We show using data from Movielens that such methods can improve on the performance of MF for sparse matrices.

Keywords

Matrix Factorization; Sparse Matrices; Two Stage Matrix Factorization; Pseudotransactions;

1. INTRODUCTION

Recommender systems has been developed by many researchers using different approaches [2], such as content based [14, 19], collaborative [5], model based [19], and hybrid method [19, 3]. Many open data in various domains (movie: MovieLens[7], Netflix [10]; music: Yahoo Music [9]; joke: Jaster [6], etc.) has been published to accelerate recommender systems research. The first winner [10] of the Netflix prize[1] reported that Matrix factorization has many benefits for overcoming problems in recommender systems such as data sparsity and cold start [21].

*Computing Science PhD Student at University of Aberdeen, UK, Lecturer at Telkom University, Indonesia, email : agungtoto@telkomunivesity.ac.id

[1]https://en.wikipedia.org/wiki/Netflix_Prize

RecSys '16, September 15-19, 2016, Boston , MA, USA

DOI: http://dx.doi.org/10.1145/2959100.2959107

Matrix factorization (MF) can be defined as producing two factor matrices, lets say $W = [w_{ij}] \in \mathbb{R}^{m\times k}$ and $H = [h_{ij}] \in \mathbb{R}^{k\times n}$ from one known matrix $V = [w_{ij}] \in \mathbb{R}^{m\times n}$, so that the product of W and H is (approximately) equal to V:

$$V \approx WH \tag{1}$$

where each cell is computed as:

$$v_{xy} \approx \sum_{i=1}^{k} w_{xi}h_{iy} \tag{2}$$

There are many algorithms for MF, such as Multiplicative [11, 12], Gradient descent [4, 1], Alternating Least Square [4, 1], and more. These algorithms aim to minimize the difference between the known matrix V and its multiplicative form WH (the cost function) through an iterative process, where in each iteration the cells in W and H are varied to try to reduce the cost function. Researchers in recommendation systems have typically used MF with around 40 to 110 iterations [10]. Many cost functions have been developed, but most common used is the Forbenius distance [4, 8], as formulated in equation (3):

$$f(W,H) = \frac{1}{2} \parallel V - WH \parallel_F^2 \tag{3}$$

The goal of Recommender Systems is to, given a matrix of user-item transactions (or ratings), estimate the missing cells; i.e. to predict the rating a user would give to a rated item. MF has been adapted to provide a solution to this problem. By defining a cost function that only minimises the difference between populated cells in the known matrix V and its multiplicative form WH, MF algorithms return a matrix WH which has populated empty cells in V, even while minimizing changes to cells already populated in V. These *predictions* for previously missing cells have been found to make good recommendations.

Typically the same algorithms are used for Matrix factorization regardless of the density of the matrix. In our experiments, however, we found that for MF, Root Mean Square Error (RMSE) for recommendations increases (i.e. performance drops) for sparse matrices. Our goals in this paper are to adapt standard algorithms for MF to improve their performance on sparse matrices. We propose a two-stage MF approach (§2.2) so that MF is performed twice over the whole matrix, the first stage to generate a small percentage of pseudotransactions that are added to the original matrix to increase its density, before re-running MF on this denser matrix. We show using data from Movielens [7] that such methods can decrease RMSE compared to the standard single stage MF (§4), before finishing with a discussion of how our method relates to previous work, and potential directions for future work (§5).

2. METHOD

2.1 RMSE and Matrix Density

To investigate the performance of MF as a function of matrix density, we ran experiments using a subset of the MovieLens 20M dataset [7] that involved the most active users (interactions frequency $\geq$ 1,750) and most active items (interactions frequency $\geq$ 5,000). Using those criteria, we obtained a matrix of 361 users, 1,005 items, and 362,805 transactions. 10% of the populated cells were held back as a test dataset. The remaining training matrix was subsampled to provide 19 smaller training sets by with different levels of density. We applied MF (gradient descent [20] [2] with 100 iterations) with different values of k (10, 15, 20) and the results are plotted in Figure 1.

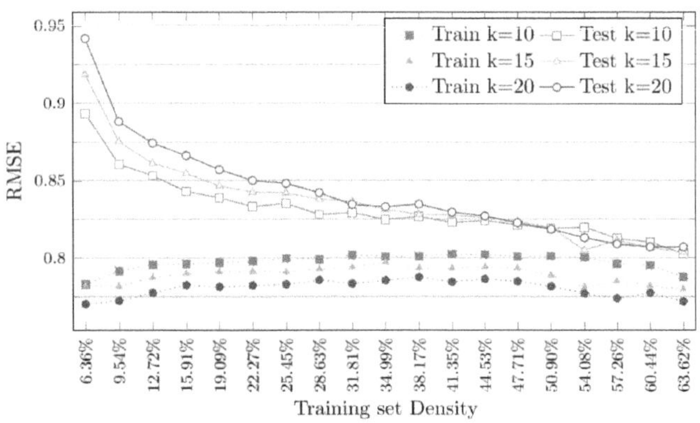

Figure 1: RMSE performance by matrix density.

In general, Figure 1 shows that the RMSE on unseen test data increases (i.e. performance decreases) when the matrix gets sparcer. The increase in RMSE begins to get steeper when density is below around 30%. This observation leads us to the hypothesis that we can attempt to reduce the RMSE by modifying the MF algorithm to operate in two stages. The first stage is geared towards adding pseudotransactions to increase the density of the matrix to around 30%. The second stage applies MF to the known matrix with added pseudotransactions. We explore one method of generating the pseudotransactions in this paper; there are potentially others, and the strength of the paper is that this idea can be generalised to incorporate numerous other methods, as discussed in §5.

2.2 A Two-Stage Matrix Factorization

Many Recommender Systems operate on sparse matrices (for instance, the density of the transaction matrix for Netflix Prize is 1.18% dense [10]; MovieLens 10M is 1.31% dense [7]; MovieLens 20M is 0.53% dense [7]; EachMovie is 2.37% dense). From §2.1, we can see MF makes better test set predictions when operating on a more dense matrix. The two stage MF proposed here tries to adopt this finding by generating a more dense matrix through the introduction of pseudotransactions.

In the first stage, MF is run over the known matrix (after removing the test data cells) V in m iterations. This stage produces factors W and H, from which a full pseudotransactions matrix is computed as WH. We add a proportion p of values from WH to the known matrix V, to give us a denser matrix V'. In the second stage, we re-run MF over this denser matrix V' in n iterations to give us factors W' and H'. The product matrix $W'H'$ is then used to predict the user-item transactions in the testing set. In this paper we explore both the effect of p, the proportion of pseudotransactions added, and the effect of m, the number of iterations used to generate pseudotransactions.

[2] http://www.quuxlabs.com/blog/2010/09/matrix-factorization-a-simple-tutorial-and-implementation-in-python/

3. EXPERIMENTAL SETTINGS

3.1 Datasets

For our experimets, we followed the methodology in §2.1 to sample a matrix from the Movielens 20M dataset by selecting most active users and items, this time filtered by interaction frequency $\geq$ 1,000 for both users and items to give us a larger dataset (3,159 users; 1,894 items; 2,033,580 transactions). Again 10% of the populated transactions are held as test dataset, while the remaining was subsampled to provide 5 training dataset. These data are described in Table 1.

Table 1: Training Set Density Level

Dataset	#Transactions	Density
Training set 1 (TS-1)	184,871	3.090%
Training set 2 (TS-2)	369,742	6.180%
Training set 3 (TS-3)	554,613	9.270%
Training set 4 (TS-4)	739,484	12.359%
Training set 5 (TS-5)	924,355	15.449%
Test set	184,870	

3.2 Evaluation Setting

In this experiment, we applied our two-stage strategy by varying two parameters: p, the proportion of pseudotransactions used, and m the number of iterations used in matrix factorisation. For a fair comparison, we kept constant the total number of iterations performed in each stage; i.e $m+n = 100$, and also report the performance of single stage MF with 100 iterations.

As seen in Figure 1, the RMSE begins to rise more steeply when the matrix density is below around 30%. Based on this, we ran experiments using three proportions ($p = 20\%$, 25%, 30%) of pseudotransactions. We also varied the value of m, the number of iterations used for the first stage, in increments of 5. for each run the number of iterations used for the second stage was $n = 100 - m$. In the experiment we also compare our strategy to original Matrix Factorization with Gradient Descent with 100 iterations (which can be thought of as $m = 0$ and $n = 100$).

4. RESULTS

Table 2 shows the RMSE for the testing set for different values of m and n, the number of iterations, and p, the proportion of pseudotransactions used. The blue cells in these tables are the Testing set RMSE using the standard one stage MF. These tables show that the two stage MF outperforms the single stage MF for a wide variety of parameter settings (marked as yellow cells), but only on more sparse training sets (TS-1, TS-2, and TS-3). The Best RMSE improvement around 0.01 is achieved in TS-1 (most sparse matrix) with 25% additional pseudo transactions. It appears from the tables that lower values of p perform better.

5. DISCUSSION AND FUTURE WORKS

Our results show that the proposed two stage MF works better for most combinations of m and n, and that the increase in performance is greater for sparser matrices. Our experiments have only sampled matrices with density of 3% to 15%. In the recommendation system domain, matrices are often more sparse (Netflix Prize is 1.18% dense [10]; MovieLens 10M is 1.31% dense [7]; MovieLens 20M is 0.53% dense [7]; EachMovie is 2.37% dense), and the two stage methods should be explored for even sparcer matrices than used in this study. In this report we used MF using the Gradient Descent algorithm. We have no reason to believe the two-stage method will not work for other algorithms (such as Multiplicative [11, 12], Alternating Least Square [4, 1], and more), but this needs to be verified in future work.

In this paper we have explored only one method of generating pseudotransactions. There are related methods that have been reported in the literature, that for instance use hybrid methods by for example using memory based collaborative filtering to add pseudotransactions. Sharaifi et. al. [18] report an RMSE of 1.9346 over the Movielens 100K dataset for MF with a cost funcion over all cells and report lower RMSE for the method by replacing all zero-cells with item median (RMSE 1.1292), user median (RMSE 1.0234) and total median rating (RMSE 0.9973) before applying MF. This cannot be directly compared to ours because they use MF methods that calculate a cost function over all cells (not just known (i.e. non-zero) cells in the data, as we do, which gives better RMSE results for MF). Others explore inputting the missing value using combinations of attribute selection and local learning to optimize the recommendation process [16] or using external resources to identify similarities between users or items (e.g. Facebook pages [17] or demographic data [13]).

There are other multi-stage methods we are keen to explore that restrict themselves to using MF. One example is to use a divide and conquer strategy. If we sort the rows (users) and columns (items) of the matrix by the transaction frequency, the top left of the matrix is most dense, and the bottom right least dense. Various divide and conquer approaches can be applied to leverage the denser part of the matrix. Figures 2 shows one of many methods of applying MF iteratively on sub-matrices of different sizes starting from denser matrices at the top or the left, before finally applying MF to the full matrix. Yellow boxes are the target matrices to populate in the current iteration, red boxes are already completed matrices, while thick boxes are the submatrices that we apply MF to in the current iteration. Divide and conquer strategies have in the past been used to speed up MF [15] for the purpose of improving time performance and should be investigated further for possible RMSE reduction.

We also wish to investigate combining MF with clustering or content based filtering to generate hybrid methods. When

Table 2: Testing set RMSE Performance varying number of iterations in each stage (m and n)

Proportion of pseudotransactions used: $p = 20\%$

Iterations		Learning Set				
m	n	TS-1	TS-2	TS-3	TS-4	TS-5
One Stage MF		0.8451	0.8322	0.8248	0.8150	0.8062
15	85	0.8714	0.8347	0.8252	0.8217	0.8171
20	80	0.8559	0.8300	0.8245	0.8214	0.8186
25	75	0.8463	0.8287	0.8238	0.8213	0.8180
30	70	0.8418	0.8269	0.8233	0.8210	0.8189
35	65	0.8399	0.8269	0.8227	0.8207	0.8191
40	60	0.8371	0.8265	0.8229	0.8209	0.8186
45	55	0.8364	0.8264	0.8223	0.8211	0.8191
50	50	0.8358	0.8261	0.8229	0.8210	0.8199
55	45	0.8353	0.8257	0.8229	0.8208	0.8199
60	40	0.8352	0.8268	0.8237	0.8216	0.8203
65	35	0.8358	0.8271	0.8237	0.8221	0.8208
70	30	0.8367	0.8280	0.8251	0.8223	0.8205
75	25	0.8375	0.8290	0.8255	0.8232	0.8208
80	20	0.8394	0.8305	0.8268	0.8245	0.8236
85	15	0.8410	0.8331	0.8293	0.8260	0.8236
90	10	0.8449	0.8363	0.8328	0.8300	0.8285
95	5	0.8515	0.8420	0.8390	0.8353	0.8322

Proportion of pseudotransactions used: $p = 25\%$

Iterations		Learning Set				
m	n	TS-1	TS-2	TS-3	TS-4	TS-5
One Stage MF		0.8451	0.8322	0.8248	0.8150	0.8062
15	85	0.8749	0.8358	0.8278	0.8230	0.8210
20	80	0.8572	0.8314	0.8254	0.8230	0.8203
25	75	0.8489	0.8288	0.8242	0.8209	0.8190
30	70	0.8430	0.8274	0.8235	0.8214	0.8191
35	65	0.8397	0.8270	0.8233	0.8213	0.8197
40	60	0.8381	0.8266	0.8233	0.8209	0.8191
45	55	0.8364	0.8266	0.8228	0.8206	0.8200
50	50	0.8362	0.8264	0.8230	0.8212	0.8194
55	45	0.8352	0.8266	0.8225	0.8210	0.8200
60	40	0.8355	0.8269	0.8231	0.8207	0.8199
65	35	0.8351	0.8270	0.8231	0.8215	0.8203
70	30	0.8365	0.8273	0.8240	0.8218	0.8198
75	25	0.8366	0.8279	0.8248	0.8222	0.8204
80	20	0.8381	0.8299	0.8262	0.8237	0.8222
85	15	0.8401	0.8313	0.8278	0.8251	0.8225
90	10	0.8435	0.8349	0.8306	0.8285	0.8252
95	5	0.8484	0.8393	0.8361	0.8345	0.8296

Proportion of pseudotransactions used: $p = 30\%$

Iterations		Learning Set				
m	n	TS-1	TS-2	TS-3	TS-4	TS-5
One Stage MF		0.8451	0.8322	0.8248	0.8150	0.8062
15	85	0.8776	0.8381	0.8285	0.8237	0.8204
20	80	0.8587	0.8323	0.8261	0.8234	0.8208
25	75	0.8487	0.8298	0.8245	0.8223	0.8200
30	70	0.8435	0.8289	0.8239	0.8217	0.8196
35	65	0.8407	0.8276	0.8236	0.8215	0.8187
40	60	0.8386	0.8272	0.8236	0.8209	0.8201
45	55	0.8369	0.8268	0.8231	0.8210	0.8199
50	50	0.8368	0.8267	0.8234	0.8209	0.8200
55	45	0.8360	0.8267	0.8232	0.8212	0.8192
60	40	0.8357	0.8270	0.8230	0.8209	0.8200
65	35	0.8359	0.8268	0.8234	0.8210	0.8195
70	30	0.8356	0.8270	0.8235	0.8217	0.8195
75	25	0.8363	0.8278	0.8240	0.8217	0.8192
80	20	0.8377	0.8291	0.8250	0.8226	0.8199
85	15	0.8394	0.8308	0.8268	0.8240	0.8201
90	10	0.8422	0.8333	0.8295	0.8273	0.8234
95	5	0.8475	0.8391	0.8361	0.8326	0.8263

clustering or content based filtering is used as a first stage, we can create many small subsets of users and items to create pseudotransactions matrices, before then applying MF in the second stage.

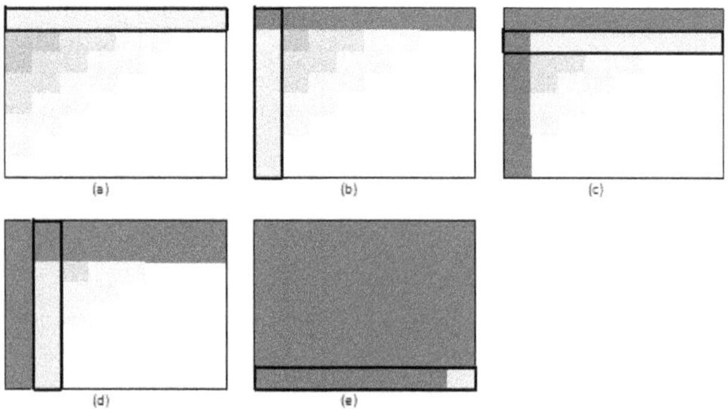

Figure 2: Possible Divide and Conquer Strategy.

6. ACKNOWLEDGEMENTS

I would like to thank Lembaga Pengelola Dana Pendidikan (LPDP), Departemen Keuangan Indonesia in awarding a scholarship to support my financial studies at the University of Aberdeen. I also would like to thank my supervisors, Advaith Siddharthan, Chenghua Lin, and Judith Masthoff, for their patient guidance, encouragement and advice to enhance my works.

7. REFERENCES

[1] M. W. Berry, M. Browne, A. N. Langville, V. P. Pauca, and R. J. Plemmons. Algorithms and applications for approximate nonnegative matrix factorization. *Computational statistics & data analysis*, 52(1):155–173, 2007.

[2] J. Bobadilla, F. Ortega, A. Hernando, and A. GutiÃl'rrez. Recommender systems survey. *Knowledge-Based Systems*, 46:109–132, 7 2013.

[3] R. Burke. Hybrid recommender systems: Survey and experiments. *User modeling and user-adapted interaction*, 12(4):331–370, 2002.

[4] M. Chu, F. Diele, R. Plemmons, and S. Ragni. Optimality, computation, and interpretation of nonnegative matrix factorizations. In *SIAM Journal on Matrix Analysis*. Citeseer, 2004.

[5] C. Desrosiers and G. Karypis. A comprehensive survey of neighborhood-based recommendation methods. In *Recommender systems handbook*, pages 107–144. Springer, 2011.

[6] D. Gupta, M. Digiovanni, H. Narita, and K. Goldberg. Jester 2.0 (poster abstract): evaluation of an new linear time collaborative filtering algorithm. In *Proceedings of the 22nd annual international ACM SIGIR conference on Research and development in information retrieval*, pages 291–292. ACM, 1999.

[7] F. M. Harper and J. A. Konstan. The movielens datasets: History and context. *ACM Transactions on Interactive Intelligent Systems (TiiS)*, 5(4):19, 2015.

[8] H. Kim and H. Park. Nonnegative matrix factorization based on alternating nonnegativity constrained least squares and active set method. *SIAM Journal on Matrix Analysis and Applications*, 30(2):713–730, 2008.

[9] N. Koenigstein, G. Dror, and Y. Koren. Yahoo! music recommendations: Modeling music ratings with temporal dynamics and item taxonomy. In *Proceedings of the Fifth ACM Conference on Recommender Systems*, RecSys '11, pages 165–172, New York, NY, USA, 2011. ACM.

[10] Y. Koren. The bellkor solution to the netflix grand prize. *Netflix prize documentation*, 81, 2009.

[11] D. D. Lee and H. S. Seung. Learning the parts of objects by non-negative matrix factorization. *Nature*, 401(6755):788–791, 1999.

[12] D. D. Lee and H. S. Seung. Algorithms for non-negative matrix factorization. 2001.

[13] B. Lika, K. Kolomvatsos, and S. Hadjiefthymiades. Facing the cold start problem in recommender systems. *Expert Systems with Applications*, 41(4):2065–2073, 2014.

[14] P. Lops, M. Gemmis, and G. Semeraro. Recommender systems handbook. (Content-based Recommender Systems: State of the Art and Trends):73–105, 2011.

[15] L. MacKey, A. Talwalkar, and M. b. Jordan. Divide-and-conquer matrix factorization. 2011.

[16] U. Ocepek, J. Rugelj, and Z. BosniÄĞ. Improving matrix factorization recommendations for examples in cold start. *Expert Systems with Applications*, 42(19):6784–6794, 2015.

[17] A. N. Rosli, T. You, I. Ha, K.-Y. Chung, and G.-S. Jo. Alleviating the cold-start problem by incorporating movies facebook pages. *Cluster Computing*, 18(1):187–197, 2015.

[18] Z. Sharifi, M. Rezghi, and M. Nasiri. A new algorithm for solving data sparsity problem based-on non negative matrix factorization in recommender systems. pages 56–61, 2014.

[19] X. Su and T. M. Khoshgoftaar. A survey of collaborative filtering techniques. *Adv.in Artif.Intell.*, 2009:4:2–4:2, jan 2009.

[20] G. Takács, I. Pilászy, B. Németh, and D. Tikk. Matrix factorization and neighbor based algorithms for the netflix prize problem. In *Proceedings of the 2008 ACM Conference on Recommender Systems*, RecSys '08, pages 267–274, New York, NY, USA, 2008. ACM.

[21] K. Zhou, S.-H. Yang, and H. Zha. Functional matrix factorizations for cold-start recommendation. In *Proceedings of the 34th International ACM SIGIR Conference on Research and Development in Information Retrieval*, SIGIR '11, pages 315–324, New York, NY, USA, 2011. ACM.

Gray Sheep, Influential Users, User Modeling and Recommender System Adoption by Startups

Abhishek Srivastava
Indian Institute of Management Ranchi
Suchna Bhawan, Meurs Road
Ranchi, Jharkhand, India
+91-9454248508
abhishek.srivastava13fpm@iimranchi.ac.in

ABSTRACT

This proposed thesis work explores two research areas in the domain of Recommender Systems [RS] , algorithms and their real world applications. First is related to identification of Gray Sheep [GS] users and Influential Users [IU] in any system using different personality models and also creating psychographic profile of such users. The second part of this work is an empirical study to find out the determinant of RS adoption in Start-ups context of developing nations, by using diffusion of innovation (DOI) theory and Technology–Organization-Environment (TOE) frameworks.

Keywords

Gray Sheep Problem; Social Network Analysis; Big Five; Basic Human Values; Human Needs; User Modeling; Recommender System; Collaborative Filtering ; Diffusion of Innovation; Technology – Organization-Environment framework ; Startups

1. INTRODUCTION

Since the past one and a half decade, there has been tremendous rise in the number of studies related to the realm of RS. Recurrent reports on how some of the most successful commercial organizations of the world like Amazon, Google and Netflix etc. have effectively used RS to boost their efficiency , has made RS a popular constituent of IT and digital marketing strategy.

However the focus of academic community still continues to be primarily on increasing the prediction efficiency of the algorithms used by RS, as compared to the user experience and RS acceptance issues. The algorithms too usually focuses on entire system as a whole and relatively lesser attention has been paid in identifying and creating psychographic profiles of special category of users like GS and IU.

To the best of our knowledge this thesis explores in a novel way both of the above mentioned dimensions of RS and the findings of this work will have both academic and managerial implications in designing and implementing of RS algorithms and digital marketing strategies.

RecSys '16, September 15-19, 2016, Boston , MA, USA
 ISBN 978-1-4503-4035-9/16/09…$15.00
DOI: http://dx.doi.org/10.1145/2959100.2959103

The rest of the paper is structured as follows. In section 2.1 we present the existing work done in the area of GS and IU and then in 2.2 we showcase our proposed model along with result of some preliminary empirical work. In section 3.1 we present different theories and framework used in adoption of new technologies in the existing literature apart from formal definition of startups in Indian context. In section 3.2 we present our proposed hypothesis and methodology followed by conclusion in section 4 and references in section 5.

2. GRAY SHEEP, INFLUENTIAL USERS AND USER MODELING

2.1 Literature review

The traditional Collaborative Filtering algorithm does not work with similar efficiency for all the users [1],and it has been found that there exist two kinds of users in the system, White Sheep [WS] and GS. WS are those users who have high correlation value with many other users and GS are the users who partially agree/disagree with other users and have low correlation coefficient with almost all users [2][3]. While these GS users themselves do not benefit much from the system but their presence also diminishes the quality of the recommendations made to the rest of the users in the system [2]. To Identify the GS users in system, clustering based approaches [2][4] or social network approach [5] , has been suggested.

In the context of RS , influence is defined as the amount of effect a user has over others via the predictions they receive [6] . Looking from social network perspective social network, there might be a set of users who help a large number of other users to receive recommendations. These users are known as most influential users [6][7]. One way to observe this effect is to exclude a user and measure the net changes in predictions caused by the removal. This formed the base of algorithm independent approach to find IU [6].Identification of IU is important to prevent shilling attack on RS [8] and also in promotional campaigns [9]

However, as all the previously mentioned approaches to find GS and IU uses only the ratings (which are usually sparse) given by the users, to measure the similarity between the users, they are unable to capture the entire difference in taste and preferences of users. Relying solely on ratings ignores the implicit tastes of each user that gets reflected in the reviews and opinion, and ignoring this rich source of information is a major shortcoming of existing work on RS [10].

2.2 Proposed Model and methodology

As user's taste and preferences is manifestation of their personality [11], in order to more effectively identify the different kind of users based on their taste and preferences, we propose the usage of the psychographic constructs based user models to specifically identify these GS and IU . We have chosen three frameworks from psychology, marketing and Information science literature - Costa and Norman's Five Factor Model (Big Five) [12][11], Schwartz's Basic Human Values [13][14] and Human Needs Model based on Kotler's and Ford's work in marketing [15]. Big Five model describes how a person engages with the world through these five factors– Openness, Conscientiousness, Extraversion, Agreeableness, Neuroticism [12]. Basic human Values are "desirable, transsituational goals, varying in importance, that serve as guiding principles in people's lives" and it can be measured using following five dimensions - Conservation, Openness to change, Hedonism, Self Enhancement, Self-transcendence [13][14] . Human Needs are characterized by these twelve categories which describes at a high level what aspect of a product are likely to resonate with the person - Excitement, Harmony, Curiosity, Ideal, Closeness, Self-expression, Liberty, Love, Practicality, Stability, Challenge, and Structure [15].

As part of preliminary study we have verified our proposed model to identify GS users. We used the Amazon movie reviews data set which has been shared at Stanford Large Network Dataset Collection as part of Stanford Network Analysis Platform (SNAP) of Stanford university [1][16]. For our preliminary experimental purpose we have extracted the reviews for top 1000 rated movies by 95 users. The ratings are in the scale of 1 to 5. The Sparsity level of the data set used in this experimentation is 90%.

After the extraction of reviews, the text was cleaned of html formatting tags and junk characters. Then user modeling services of IBM Watson personality insight service was used by creating a IBM's cloud based solution bluemix's instance to extract the values of each parameters of the three personality frameworks. To extract the Big Five personality characteristic ,Basic Human Value dimensions and Human Needs Model parameters, Watson uses the latest work done in the area of linguistic analytics [17][18][19]. We used SNA approach to find threshold for GS identification so as to benchmark it with existing work [5] and results have been encouraging for Big Five and Basic Human Values as shown in Fig 1(a) and (b).

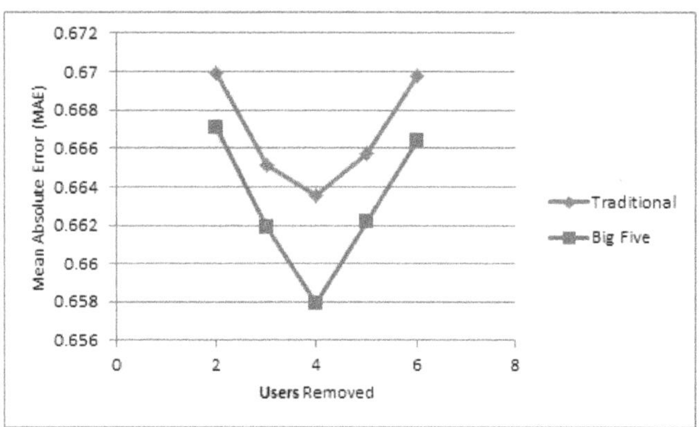

Fig.1(a) Threshold calculation using Big Five Model

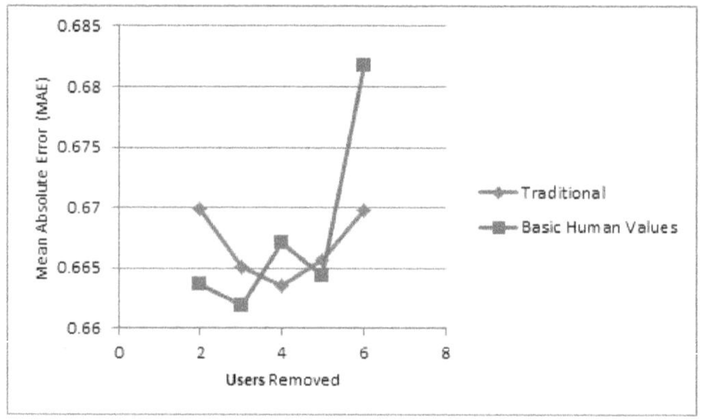

Fig.1(b) Threshold calculation using Basic Human Values

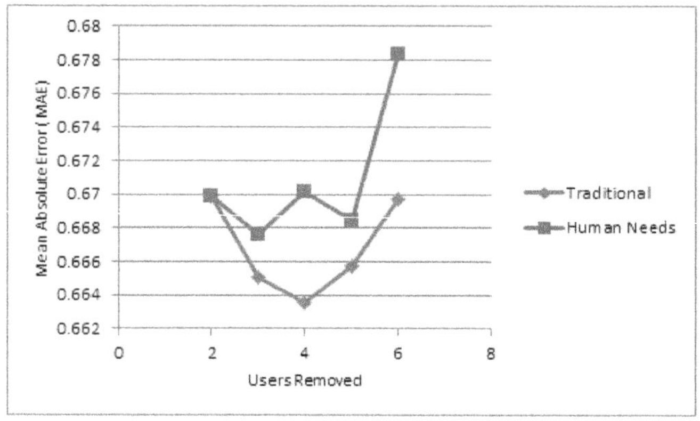

Fig.1(c) Threshold calculation using Human Needs

Similarly we intend to use these models for identification of IU and for GS too on other data sets from different product domains and at different sparsity levels. Constructs of these different models can also be combined together to see if they collectively perform better to identify GS and IU. Apart from merely using an iterative process to find the optimum threshold for GS and IU identification, for each product domain we also intend to do an in-depth study to explore if there are certain common psychological characteristics that increases the likelihood of users becoming a GS or IU in the systems through clustering based on those user models. In further works, we also intend to explore if behavior of GS and IU remains consistent across Cross Domain RS and Context Aware RS systems or not. One more experiment that we propose to do is to explore if for content based algorithms too, rest of the conditions remaining same, does there exist some users for whom the algorithm consistently works poor. If yes, then are there any specific psychographic profiles of such users too.

3. RS adoption and Indian Startups

3.1 Literature review

Most of the work elucidating the success of RS adoption in business world covers mostly big organizations like Amazon , Google or Netflix etc. from developed economies [20] [21] . While there have been some studies on RS adoption in developing economies [22] but that too has focused on big retail chains and financial institution. Some of the commonly used model used to study adoption of new and emerging technologies in scholarly research literature are technology acceptance model (TAM) [23] [24], theory of planned behavior (TPB) [25] , decomposed theory of planned behavior (DTPB) unified theory of acceptance and use of technology (UTAUT) [26], diffusion of innovation (DOI) theory [27],Technology – organization-environment (TOE)

[1] http://snap.stanford.edu/data/web-Amazon.html

framework [28]. TAM, DTPB and UTAUT models primarily pertain to measurement individual's choices rather than organizational comportment. In organizational context DOI and TOE are the models of choice and have been widely used to study adoption of new and emerging technologies [29]. In Indian context Startups are formally defined by Department of Industrial Policy and Promotion , Ministry of Commerce and Industry , as entity with following characteristics [30]

a) Up to five years from the date of its incorporation/registration,

b) If its turnover for any of the financial years has not exceeded Indian National Rupees 25 crore, and

c) It is working towards innovation, development, deployment or commercialization of new products, processes or services driven by technology or intellectual property.

3.2 Proposed Model and methodology

Using TOE context to strengthen the DOI is a well-defined technique [31][32] and we propose the following constructs and hypothesis based on them -

Relative advantage is the ''degree to which an innovation is perceived as being better than its precursor''[33] . Innovations that have strategic advantage have far better chances of adoption by firms [34]–[36]. Thus

H1: Relative advantage will positively influence RS adoption.

Complexity is the ''degree to which an innovation is perceived to be relatively difficult to understand and use''[33] . The easier it is to integrate the technology into business operations, the greater the chance of its adoption. RS technology may require entirely new professionals or intensive training of IT professionals. Thus,

H2: Complexity will negatively influence RS adoption.

Rogers [33] defines compatibility as ''the degree to which the innovation fits with the potential adopter's existing values, previous practices, and current needs". An organization that finds the suitability of RS with its existing practices may adopt this technology and vice-versa. Thus,

H3: Compatibility will positively influence RS adoption.

Technology infrastructure and support are an important component for adoption of a technology, and it has been widely studied in various works related to IS adoption [37], [38]. Hence, RS also requires technology readiness as an important component. Hence,

H4: Technological readiness will positively influence RS adoption.

Top management support plays an important role in RS adoption because it guides the organisation towards a rather new technology like other information technology adoption [31], [37], [39].Top management that recognizes the benefits of RS is likely to allocate the necessary resources for its adoption and influence the organization's members to implement the change. Thus,

H5: Top management support will positively influence RS adoption.

The environment context is the setting in which a firm conducts its business and is influenced by the nature of the industry. Internal as well as external environment from competitors form a peer pressure to adopt a new technology [31], [37]. Adoption of newer technology may help organization to compete with their peers by impacting the value chain. Hence,

H6: Competitive pressure will positively influence RS adoption.

The impact of regulatory support helps a firm to abide by a set of regulations which form a level playing field for all organization in industry [31], [40] . If a regulator supports the best technology to be carried out in an industry, it helps the adoption process. Thus,

H7: Regulatory support will positively influence RS adoption.

In order to reach startups for data collection, a web based survey will be floated with sample frame being statrups currently being incubated by NASSCOM 10k startup initiative.[2]. It is a government backed initiative to promote and support startup ecosystem in India. Scales used to measure the constructs have been adopted from existing works [29] . Depending on the number of data samples collected, we intend to adopt the method of logistic regression [41] if number is small or Structure Equation Modelling [29] if the number is adequate enough for SEM for testing our hypothesis.

4. CONCLUSION

Apart from providing an alternate and possibly more efficient method for GS and IU identification, this work will also study and provide psychographic profile of these GS and IU , and that information can be used by marketing manager to take more informed decision on how to meet the requirements of such users. Identification of factors that impact the adoption of RS by Indian Startups will help in designing and implementing of IT and digital marketing strategies in smaller firms. In the future we also propose a comparative study of RS adoption on large and small firms from similar and different geographies to find if there are any cultural factors too that impact RS adoption.

5. REFERENCES

[1] M. Claypool, T. Miranda, A. Gokhale, P. Murnikov, D. Netes, and M. Sartin, "Combining content-based and collaborative filters in an online newspaper," Proceedings of Recommender Systems Workshop at ACM SIGIR, pp. 40–48, 1999.

[2] M. A. Ghazanfar and A. Prügel-Bennett, "Leveraging clustering approaches to solve the gray-sheep users problem in recommender systems," Expert Systems with Applications, vol. 41, no. 7, pp. 3261–3272, 2014.

[3] R. Burke, "Hybrid recommender systems: Survey and experiments," User modeling and user-adapted interaction, 2002.

[4] M. Ghazanfar and A. Prugel-Bennett, "'Fulfilling the Needs of Gray-Sheep Users in Recommender Systems, A Clustering Solution.'" 21-Jan-2011.

[5] M. Kim and I. Im, "Resolving the 'Gray sheep' Problem Using Social Network Analysis (SNA) in Collaborative Filtering (CF) Recommender Systems," J Intell Inform Syst, vol. 20, no. 2, p. 137~148, 2014.

[6] A. Rashid, G. Karypis, and J. Riedl, "Influence in Ratings-Based Recommender Systems: An Algorithm-Independent Approach," in Proceedings of the 2005 SIAM International Conference on Data Mining, Society for Industrial and Applied Mathematics, 2005, pp. 556–560.

[7] M. a Morid, M. Shajari, and a. H. Golpayegani, "Who are the Most Influential Users in a Recommender System?"

[8] P. Chirita, W. Nejdl, and C. Zamfir, "Preventing Shilling Attacks in Online Recommender Systems," in WIDM'05, November 5, 2005, Bremen, Germany., pp. 67–74.

[2] 10000startups.com

[9] P. Domingos and M. Richardson, "Mining the Network Value of Customers," Proceedings of the Seventh {ACM} {SIGKDD} International Conference on Knowledge Discovery and Data Mining, pp. 57–66, 2001.

[10] J. McAuley and J. Leskovec, "Hidden factors and hidden topics: understanding rating dimensions with review text," Proceedings of the 7th ACM conference on Recommender systems - RecSys '13, pp. 165–172, 2013.

[11] R. Hu and P. Pu, "Enhancing collaborative filtering systems with personality information," Proceedings of the fifth ACM conference on Recommender systems - RecSys '11, p. 197, 2011.

[12] P. Costa and R. McCrae, "Influence of extraversion and neuroticism on subjective well-being: happy and unhappy people.," Journal of personality and social …, 1980.

[13] S. . Schwartz, "Value priorities and behaviour: Applying a theory of integrated value systems," The psychology of values, vol. 8, pp. 1–24, 1996.

[14] S. Schwartz, "Are There Universal Aspects in the Structure and," Journal of social issues, 1994.

[15] J. Ford, Brands laid bare: Using market research for evidence-based brand management. 2005.

[16] J. McAuley and C. Targett, "Image-based recommendations on styles and substitutes," Proceedings of the 38th …, 2015.

[17] T. Yarkoni, "Personality in 100,000 words: A large-scale analysis of personality and word use among bloggers," Journal of research in personality, 2010.

[18] J. Chen, G. Hsieh, J. U. Mahmud, and J. Nichols, "Understanding individuals' personal values from social media word use," Proceedings of the 17th ACM conference on Computer supported cooperative work & social computing - CSCW '14, pp. 405–414, 2014.

[19] H. Yang and Y. Li, "Identifying user needs from social media," IBM Research Division, San Jose, 2013.

[20] K. Hosanagar and D. Fleder, "Will the global village fracture into tribes? Recommender systems and their effects on consumer fragmentation," Management Science, 2013.

[21] A. Das, M. Datar, a Garg, and S. Rajaram, "Google news personalization: scalable online collaborative filtering," Proceedings of the 16th international conference on, pp. 271–280, 2007.

[22] A. Asosheh, S. Bagherpour, N. Yahyapour, and a Asosheha, "Extended Acceptance Models for Recommender System Adaption, Case of Retail and Banking Service in Iran," WSEAS Transactions on Business and Economics, vol. 5, no. 5, pp. 189–200, 2008.

[23] F. D. Jr, "A technology acceptance model for empirically testing new end-user information systems: Theory and results," 1986.

[24] F. D. Davis, "Perceived usefulness, perceived ease of use, and user acceptance of information technology," MIS quarterly, pp. 319–340, 1989.

[25] I. Ajzen, "The theory of planned behavior," Organizational behavior and human decision …, 1991.

[26] V. Venkatesh, M. Morris, G. Davis, and F. Davis, "User acceptance of information technology: Toward a unified view," MIS quarterly, 2003.

[27] E. Rogers, "Di/" fusion of innovations (Sth ed.)," 2003.

[28] L. Tornatzky, M. Fleischer, and A. Chakrabarti, "Processes of technological innovation," 1990.

[29] T. Oliveira, M. Thomas, and M. Espadanal, "Assessing the determinants of cloud computing adoption: An analysis of the manufacturing and services sectors," Information & Management, vol. 51, no. 5, pp. 497–510, 2014.

[30] "Definition of Startup." [Online]. Available: http://dipp.nic.in/English/Investor/startupindia/Definition_Startup_GazetteNotification.pdf.

[31] T. Oliveira and M. F. Martins, "Information technology adoption models at firm level: review of literature," in European Conference on Information Management and Evaluation, 2010, p. 312.

[32] Y. Wu, C. G. Cegielski, B. T. Hazen, and D. J. Hall, "Cloud computing in support of supply chain information system infrastructure: understanding when to go to the cloud," Journal of Supply Chain Management, vol. 49, no. 3, pp. 25–41, 2013.

[33] E. M. Rogers, Diffusion of innovations. Simon and Schuster, 2010.

[34] M. J. Tippins and R. S. Sohi, "IT competency and firm performance: Is organizational learning a missing link?," Strategic Management Journal, vol. 24, no. 8, pp. 745–761, 2003.

[35] D. J. Teece, "Business models, business strategy and innovation," Long Range Planning, vol. 43, no. 2–3, pp. 172–194, 2010.

[36] E. Almirall and R. Casadesus-Masanell, "Open Versus Closed Innovation: a Model of Discovery and Divergence," Academy of Management Review, vol. 35, no. 1, pp. 27–47, 2010.

[37] C. Low, Y. Chen, and M. Wu, "Understanding the determinants of cloud computing adoption," Industrial management & data systems, vol. 111, no. 7, pp. 1006–1023, 2011.

[38] K. Zhu, K. L. Kraemer, and S. Xu, "The Process of Innovation Assimilation by Firms in Different Countries: A Technology Diffusion Perspective on E-Business," Management Science, vol. 52, no. 10, pp. 1557–1576, 2006.

[39] J. Baker, "The technology–organization–environment framework," in Information systems theory, Springer, 2012, pp. 231–245.

[40] H. P. Borgman, B. Bahli, H. Heier, and F. Schewski, "Cloudrise: exploring cloud computing adoption and governance with the TOE framework," in System Sciences (HICSS), 2013 46th Hawaii International Conference on, 2013, pp. 4425–4435.

[41] R. R. Dholakia and N. Kshetri, "Factors Impacting the Adoption of the Internet among SMEs Authors (s): Ruby Roy Dholakia and Nir Kshetri Published by : Springer Stable URL : http://www.jstor.org/stable/40229367 Accessed : 25-03-2016 08 : 43 UTC Factors Impacting the Adoption of the In," Small Business Economice, vol. 23, no. 4, pp. 311–322, 2004.

Increasing the Trustworthiness of Recommendations by Exploiting Social Media Sources

Catalin-Mihai Barbu
University of Duisburg-Essen
Interactive Systems Group
Duisburg, Germany
catalin.barbu@uni-due.de

ABSTRACT

Current recommender systems mostly do not take into account as well as they might the wealth of information available in social media, thus preventing the user from obtaining a broad and reliable overview of different opinions and ratings on a product. Furthermore, there is a lack of user control over the recommendation process—which is mostly fully automated and does not allow the user to influence the sources and mechanisms by which recommendations are produced—as well as over the presentation of recommended items. Consequently, recommendations are often not transparent to the user, are considered to be less trustworthy, or do not meet the user's situational needs. This work will investigate the theoretical foundations for user-controllable, interactive methods of recommending, will develop techniques that exploit social media data in conjunction with other sources, and will validate the research empirically in the area of e-commerce product recommendations. The methods developed are intended to be applicable in a wide range of recommending and decision support scenarios.

Keywords

Recommender Systems; Interactive Recommending; User Interfaces; Trust.

1. INTRODUCTION AND MOTIVATION

For many years, recommender systems (RS) research has mostly focused on improving the algorithms used to generate recommendations, with aspects such as user control and the presentation of results receiving relatively little attention by comparison [9]. While the accuracy of RS has increased as a result of the introduction of more complex models and heuristics, users are finding it difficult to understand and influence the process through which recommendations are computed. The lack of transparency and minimal control have a detrimental effect on the perceived trustworthiness of such systems [5]. Against this background, further optimizing the already quite mature recommender algorithms alone is unlikely to yield significant additional benefits for the user. Instead, more user-oriented approaches to recommending are needed [9].

RecSys '16, September 15 - 19, 2016, Boston, MA, USA

ACM 978-1-4503-4035-9/16/09…$15.00
DOI: http://dx.doi.org/10.1145/2959100.2959104

Furthermore, current RS mostly do not take full advantage of the wealth of information that is available through social media channels. Collaborative filtering (CF) techniques have traditionally relied on user ratings to generate predictions. Other kinds of user-generated content that CF does not usually take into account, in particular textual contributions, tags, as well as user-user and user-item relationships, permeate the Web and can offer consumers a better overview of different opinions and ratings on a given product or service—potentially influencing the decisions that people make online. Since users tend to rely on the opinions of peers [4], it is reasonable to assume that they would also consider recommendations more trustworthy if the underlying RS were to augment them with information extracted from social media.

The aim of this thesis is to increase the trustworthiness of recommendations by developing more interactive approaches to recommending that enhance existing algorithms and methods with trust-related information extracted from social media sources. Furthermore, new methods for personalizing the presentation of recommended items with social media data will be produced to meet users' situational needs better. The research goals can be summarized as follows:

- Investigate and model users' decision making behavior with recommendations;
- Extract trust-related information from social media sources;
- Develop methods for providing users with trust-related information;
- Provide users with adaptive techniques for exploring trust information in social media and semantic data.

The remainder of this paper is structured as follows: Section 2 describes the state of the art with respect to the trustworthiness of recommendations, the personalization of the way in which these predictions are presented, and the relevant choice and decision support strategies that are being considered for RS. Section 3 details the proposed methods that will be applied in this research and in Section 4 the research plan is introduced. Section 5 concludes the paper by summarizing the expected contributions and next steps.

2. RELATED WORK

Trustworthiness of recommendations: There have been several studies on how humans build trust in RS. Herlocker et al. [7] found that providing explanations helps users understand the reasons that led the system to recommend certain items. By increasing transparency, the perceived trustworthiness of recommendations also increases. More recently, Pu et al. [13] proposed a trust model for RS that aims to raise the perceived trustworthiness of predictions by explaining the advantages and tradeoffs of each recommended item. Harman et al. [5] observed that people reacted more strongly to inaccurate predictions when these were personalized: Their trust in the RS decreased more strongly and they were more dissatisfied with the results in comparison with the case where personalization was not used. Transparency and user control are often cited as having a significant effect on the perceived trust of RS and on the users' overall satisfaction with the technology (see, e.g., [9], [6], and [15]). This work will build upon these findings by investigating the effects that social media data has on recommendations.

Besides the factors that influence users' trust in RS, a separate line of research studies how trust in *other users* can be leveraged to improve the accuracy of CF techniques [10]. Such approaches typically rely on people marking other social network users as being trustworthy (or not). As it will be shown in the next section, this kind of information might be unavailable in the type of scenarios that this research proposes to address. In principle, however, it could be possible to extract trust measurements from social media interactions.

Personalizing the presentation of recommendations: Aspects such as what information to present, how to present it and when, and how much of it to present for any given prediction are important when discussing interactivity in RS. Prior work has, for instance, explored the effects of using different types of result lists and combinations of text with images on the persuasiveness of recommendations [12]. Other researchers suggested a model for timing recommendations [1] or determined the number of results that leads to high choice satisfaction without increasing choice difficulty [2]. However, most of this work does not focus specifically on interactive RS. Some interactive approaches to visualizing recommendations have been proposed, such as those implemented in TasteWeights [3] and TalkExplorer [17]. These systems afford a certain degree of control over the recommendation process to elicit feedback and preferences as well as to increase transparency. Personalizing the presentation of recommendations is typically achieved through explanations ([16], [14]). The proposed research will advance the state of the art in two ways. First, integrating social media data more tightly into the presentation of the recommended items will open up novel interaction possibilities for users. Second, the effect that such an enriched presentation has on the user's perceived trustworthiness of the recommendations will be evaluated empirically.

Choice and decision support for RS: Recent research suggests that novel approaches in RS can also stem from understanding how people make choices. Jameson et al. [8] performed a comprehensive analysis of this topic and proposed several ways in which recommender technology can be applied to support the human processes of choice and decision making. By giving users more control, they become involved in the decision-making process. Thus, recommendations also become a form of choice support. The authors note that typical support strategies for RS are "advise about processing" (i.e. recommending a particular course of action) and "evaluate on behalf of the chooser" (i.e. recommending an item or set of items). This work aims to investigate other choice support strategies that are not specifically related to recommendation technologies, such as "combine and compute" (i.e. performing complex calculations in order to present more relevant information) and "design the domain" (i.e. adapting the interface to make it easier for the user to choose between several options). To the author's knowledge, these aspects have not yet been explored in detail.

The specific research questions that will be addressed are:

- RQ1: What methods can be used to extract trust-related information from social media sources?
- RQ2: What measures for user similarity can be defined, taking into account factors such as social relationships, rating behavior, or elicited preferences?
- RQ3: How can the presentation of recommendations be adapted and personalized to increase users' trust?

3. PROPOSED METHODS

In order to explore the research questions, one specific domain was chosen in which the trustworthiness of recommendations is especially important, namely hotel booking. The reasons for selecting this domain are threefold: 1) There is a higher degree of risk associated with such choices (in comparison with, e.g., the frequently used domain of movie recommendations); 2) the items have a reasonable set of attributes that have to be taken into account; and 3) there is a large body of user-generated content, in the form of reviews, photos, tags, and ratings.

While analyzing the output of several online accommodation booking websites, it already became apparent that there is a lot of room for improving the way in which recommendations are presented to users. For instance, although most websites allow users to specify whether they are traveling for business or leisure, the effect of this choice on the presentation of individual recommendations is typically minimal. The argument put forth here is that the choices that people make during their search—destination, number of nights, desired amenities, purpose of travel, etc.—should influence the presentation of the output. Specifically, the presentation could be personalized not only in terms of the recommended items, but also tailored precisely to support each user's needs. To give an example, stating a preference for "fitness center" could lead to information such as opening hours, available machines, and pricing information being displayed more prominently.

When booking accommodation, each person has a number of expectations about what the ideal place ought to be like. Some are precise (e.g., the room must have soft beds), while others may be vaguer (e.g., the hotel should be close to public transport). Still others may apply only in specific situations, such as when a person travels for work (e.g., there must be a writing desk in the room). Expectations often evolve as the user becomes more experienced at traveling, or her social status changes over time. The proposed argument is that recommendations that satisfy users' expectations and are presented in a personalized fashion shall be considered more trustworthy. For a RS to achieve this, it must first be able to infer expectations from information available in user profiles, such as user ratings, reviews, tags (i.e. explicit feedback), interaction behavior (i.e. implicit feedback), and user relationships (from social media). Reviews, especially, can be a very rich source of information about what a user liked or disliked about a specific stay in a hotel. Such information can allow the system to learn more about the person who wrote them, in addition to its being a resource for other users. After returning from a trip, those who leave reviews will often highlight amenities that influenced—either positively or negatively—their stay in the hotel. (As a result, some online booking websites also made it possible for users to give separate ratings to frequently-mentioned hotel characteristics such as Wi-Fi quality.) Furthermore, reviews will often contain references to amenities that are not available as filters when selecting the hotel ("soft bed" being a good example).

By applying methods such as text mining and text analysis, an algorithm will be developed that extracts hotel attributes mentioned in reviews, calculates the user's degree of (dis)satisfaction based on her statements, and builds basic expectations that can be exploited by the RS during the generation and presentation of recommendations (Figure 1). Implicit feedback, such as discarded recommendations, could also be exploited to identify "deal breakers", namely attributes (or combinations thereof) that the user wants to avoid.

Extending the above procedure to an entire user base will allow RS to personalize and adapt the output by showing more relevant details about recommended items. To illustrate this point, consider someone who is interested in venues that offer good Wi-Fi connectivity. When browsing recommendations, she might find it useful to read reviews that specifically mention aspects such as connection speed and signal strength or those that give an overall quality assessment. To facilitate comparison, this information could, for example, be presented in the form of a graphical scale that shows the proportion of people who rated the internet connection positively versus those who rated it negatively. By taking into account expectations, a RS will be able to identify attributes that are most important to users and subsequently enhance the recommendations with such personalized summaries, thereby increasing their trustworthiness.

In addition to summarizing information related to user expectations, perhaps equally important is to make people aware of potential deal breakers they might not be aware of (Figure 2). If a significant proportion of guests have mentioned in their reviews that, e.g., the breakfast buffet was modest, this information could be passed along to the user in the form of advice [8]. Moreover, by allowing users to give feedback on these summaries, the RS could refine the user models and improve the presentation of the recommendations.

By mining past bookings and reviews, a complex network consisting of users, hotels, and hotel attributes can be created. This will allow to identify, with greater accuracy, which items a user is likely to find attractive based on the attributes mentioned in her reviews as well as in reviews of similar users [11]. At the same time, the system could extract and present, for each recommended item, the experiences of other people who are interested in the same combination of attributes as the current user. Such a network, which might be referred to as "co-staying in hotels", will further facilitate the discovery of users with similar expectations and who have already stayed in the same hotel or in hotels with similar characteristics to the one that a person is considering. It is expected that this could thus introduce novel ways of interacting with RS. For example, someone who has a strong preference for soft beds will be able to explore the opinions of others who share this preference. Taking this a step further, the user might then ask herself, "What *other* preferences do such people have?" Personalizing the presentation to facilitate the exploration of similar people's expectations could allow the user to discover new preferences that she would not have considered otherwise.

Giving users more control over the recommendation process and over the way in which these recommendations are presented also offers opportunities to experiment with learning by choosing, as proposed by Jameson et al. [8]. There is an attractive relationship between these two aspects. If a user already has fixed preferences, then user control means enabling her to put these preferences into practice (e.g., set the parameters for determining the relative weights of hotel attributes). But if she does not, it is a matter of enabling her to experiment to find out in the first place what she likes (as well as to put the results into practice subsequently). The types of appropriate support are different in the two cases; however, the second case is less well understood. This research will provide

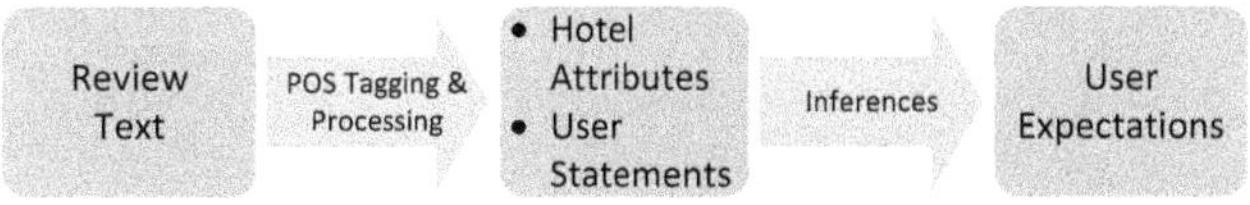

Figure 1 – Extracting expectations from reviews

the basis for studying novel interaction techniques that help users learn while making choices about the recommendations.

An initial model showing the interactions between the three components that have been discussed throughout this section, namely user profiles, hotel attributes, and hotels, is depicted in Figure 3: Information stored in a user's profile is exploited to identify individual expectations and similar users. These, in turn, help the system to select the appropriate hotel attributes. Hotel recommendations generated from these attributes are refined and reordered based on the reviews produced by similar users. Finally, the personalized recommendations are presented to the user.

4. RESEARCH PLAN

In order to implement, refine, and evaluate the methods proposed in the previous section, an adequate dataset is needed. For the hotel booking scenario, this translates into: 1) A sufficiently large number of hotels, ideally covering several major European cities; and 2) a diverse set of reviews contributed by people travelling for different purposes. The first requirement ensures a representative and interesting subset of hotels, covering as many types of amenities as possible. The second requirement is intended to maximize the variety of user opinions and arguments, thereby increasing the range of possible user expectations. Since most datasets available online do not contain user-generated data such as reviews, ratings, and tags, it was necessary to build a custom crawler for collecting this information into a database. The online booking website Booking.com was chosen as the data source because it only allows verified hotel guests to submit reviews. The collected dataset comprises 576,506 reviews, written by 219,699 users who have stayed in at least one of the 10,154 establishments in 5 major European cities[1]. This should provide an adequate testbed for developing algorithms to mine reviews and user profiles necessary for extracting trust-related information (cf. RQ1).

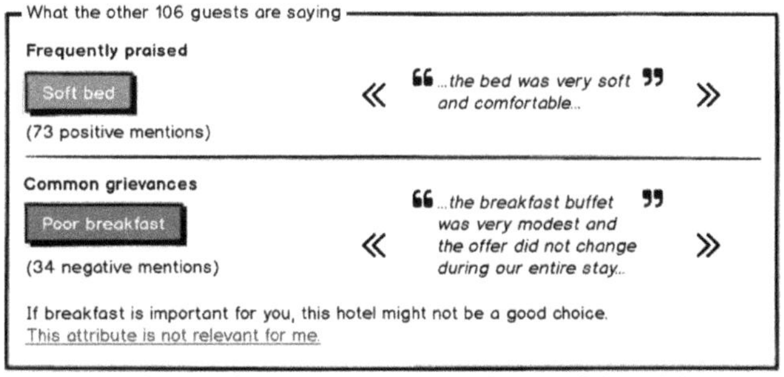

Figure 2 - Making the user aware of potential problems

Given that similar users play an important role in the model introduced in the previous section, developing accurate algorithms for identifying and ranking them is critical for success of the proposed approach. Existing metrics for computing user similarity, which typically consider rating behaviors, will be extended by taking into account user expectations, attributes mentioned in reviews, and co-staying (cf. RQ2).

In parallel to building the knowledge base, use cases for the hotel booking scenario are being prepared, which will serve as the basis

[1] Barcelona, Berlin, Brussels, London, and Rome

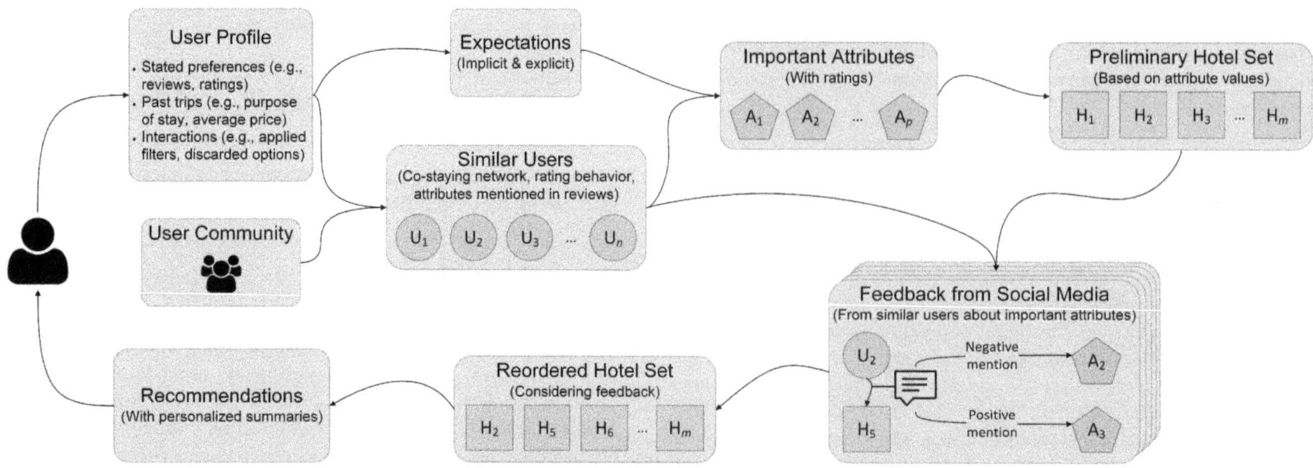

Figure 3 - Initial model for enhancing recommendations by exploiting social media data

for the initial user interface mockups. The purpose of the mockups is to decide what adapted information will be presented, what interaction possibilities (i.e. to related information) will be available, and the interactive mechanisms through which they will be achieved. Once finished, the mockups will be evaluated in a user study to identify usability problems and to further refine the above-mentioned model. Subsequent implementations and iterative testing of the recommendation technology will investigate the theoretical foundations for user-controllable, interactive methods of recommending, will develop techniques to exploit social media data to increase the trustworthiness of recommendations, and will validate the research empirically (cf. RQ3).

5. CONCLUDING REMARKS

This paper proposes several methods through which current RS could be improved further by 1) leveraging the growing corpus of user-generated content to extract relevant information, and 2) personalizing the presentation of the recommended items so that they are perceived by users as more trustworthy. The next steps will focus on methods for extracting relevant information from the mined reviews and on improving existing user similarity measures.

6. ACKNOWLEDGEMENTS

This work is supported by the German Research Foundation (DFG) under grant No. GRK 2167, Research Training Group "User-Centred Social Media".

7. REFERENCES

[1] Betzalel, N. D., Shapira, B., & Rokach, L. "Please, not now!" A model for timing recommendations. In *Proc. RecSys '15*, ACM (2015), 297–300.

[2] Bollen, D., Knijnenburg, B. P., Willemsen, M. C., & Graus, M. Understanding choice overload in recommender systems. In *Proc. RecSys '10*, ACM (2010), 63–70.

[3] Bostandjiev, S., O'Donovan, J., & Höllerer, T. Tasteweights: a visual interactive hybrid recommender system. In *Proc. RecSys '12*, ACM (2012), 35–42.

[4] Flanagin, A. J., & Metzger, M. J. Trusting expert-versus user-generated ratings online: The role of information volume, valence, and consumer characteristics. *Computers in Human Behavior*, *29*(4), 1626–1634.

[5] Harman, J. L., O'Donovan, J., Abdelzaher, T., & Gonzalez, C. Dynamics of human trust in recommender systems. In *Proc. RecSys '14*, ACM (2014), 305–308.

[6] Harper, F. M., Xu, F., Kaur, H., Condiff, K., Chang, S., & Terveen, L. Putting users in control of their recommendations. In *Proc. RecSys '15*, ACM (2015), 3–10.

[7] Herlocker, J. L., Konstan, J. A., & Riedl, J. Explaining collaborative filtering recommendations. In *Proc. CSCW '00*, ACM (2000), 241–250.

[8] Jameson, A., Willemsen, M. C., Felfernig, A., Gemmis, M. de, Lops, P., Semeraro, G., & Chen, L. Human Decision Making and Recommender Systems. *Recommender Systems Handbook*, Springer US (2015), 611–648.

[9] Konstan, J. A., & Riedl, J. Recommender systems: From algorithms to user experience. *User Mod. and User-Adapted Interaction 22*, 1-2 (2012), 101–123.

[10] Massa, P., & and Avesani, P. 2007. Trust-aware recommender systems. In *Proc. RecSys '07*. ACM (2007), 17–24.

[11] McAuley, J., & Leskovec, J. Hidden factors and hidden topics: Understanding rating dimensions with review text. In *Proc. RecSys '13*, ACM (2013), 165–172.

[12] Nanou, T., Lekakos, G., & Fouskas, K. The effects of recommendations' presentation on persuasion and satisfaction in a movie recommender system. *Multimedia Systems 16*, 4-5 (2010), 219–230.

[13] Pu, P., Chen, L., & Hu, R. Evaluating recommender systems from the users' perspective: Survey of the state of the art. *User Mod. and User-Adapted Interaction 22*, 4-5 (2012), 317–355.

[14] Pu, P., & Chen, L. Trust-inspiring explanation interfaces for recommender systems. *Knowledge-Based Systems*, *20*(6) (2007), 542–556.

[15] Sinha, R., & Swearingen, K. The Role of Transparency in Recommender Systems. In *Proc. CHI EA '02*, ACM (2002), 830–831.

[16] Tintarev, N., & and Masthoff, J. Designing and evaluating explanations for recommender systems. *Recommender Systems Handbook*. Springer US (2011), 479–510.

[17] Verbert, K., Parra, D., Brusilovsky, P., & Duval, E. Visualizing recommendations to support exploration, transparency and controllability. In *Proc. IUI '13*, ACM (2013), 351–362.

Mining Information for the Cold-Item Problem

Fatemeh Pourgholamali
Dept. of Computer Engineering
Ferdowsi University of Mashhad, Mashhad, Iran
fatemehjfg@gmail.com

ABSTRACT

One of the strong points of E-commerce websites is that they are often abundant with product reviews from consumers who experienced the products and testify to the usefulness of the products or otherwise. These reviews are helpful for consumers to optimize their purchasing decisions. However, while popular products receive many reviews, many other products do not have an adequate number of reviews leading to the cold item problem. In this proposal, we propose a solution outline for the cold item problem by automatically generating reviews and predicting ratings for the cold products from available reviews of similar products in e-commerce websites as well as users' opinion shared in the microblogging platforms such as Twitter. We propose a framework to build a formal semantic representation of products from unstructured product descriptions, user reviews as well as user ratings. Such presentations assist us to measure product similarity and relatedness in a accurate and cost-effective way. Besides, we propose a model to generate additional reviews for a cold product by mining users' posts shared on medium such as Twitter and transfer them to the e-commerce website. Preliminary experiments show promising results in finding products similar to the cold products.

1. INTRODUCTION

With the growing popularity of online services, many commercial websites have provided user feedback section as one of their most important services which allows users to express their opinions about products and services and rate them. On the one hand, users' opinions can help others to make an informed purchase decision, and on the other hand, they help providers to improve the quality of their services and products. Recommender systems can also benefit from users opinions to improve their recommendations through *collaborative filtering*.

However, various studies have shown that in commercial websites such as Amazon.com and Epinions.com, there are not adequate number of reviews and ratings for different products: more than 90% of products have less than 10 reviews, leading to so-called cold items problem [7]. The problem of data sparsity and cold start is particularly challenging in recommender systems as recommendation performance in a cold start situation degrades dramatically.

There are various earlier works that address the problem of cold start and cold item in recommender systems [3, 7, 8, 10]. Some works use content information to bridge the gap between existing and new items by inferring similarities among them and combine them with collaborative algorithms in various ways [1, 10]. Some works exploit additional external taxonomies or ontologies [2, 3]. The main issue of these works is that they rely on an external ontology which is non-generalizable and hard to scale. There are other works that don't need the taxonomy but work with product category information that is inherently structured [1, 8]. The problem with this approach is it will limit the extraction of information to one or potentially few websites. In this proposal, we go beyond these approaches and mine information about a product from anywhere on the Web, specifically microblogging platforms and any unstructured description about products. We aim to propose a framework to address cold item problem by finding a unique representation of items using description texts of products and exploiting this representation to find further information on microblogging platforms which are rich in information.Our main contributions can be enumerated as follows:

1- As a first step of our work, we propose a technique to extract product representations. We are interested in finding a suitable formal representation of products that can be mined from unstructured product descriptions, user reviews as well as user ratings. Such representation would need to enable us to measure product similarity and relatedness in an accurate and cost-efficient way. We are interested in exploring methods proposed in Word Embedding literature [5, 9] for producing vector representation for e-commerce products.

2- Given the formal vector representation of products, we will explore a *review selection model* to select ratings and reviews of non-cold products with similar vector representation to the cold start product; and then transfer a subset of them as a potential review for the cold product. Note that, selected reviews should satisfy different metrics, which will be discussed in Section 3.

3- To collect more reviews for cold products, we aim to exploit some auxiliary and rich sources such as microblogging platforms (e.g., Twitter), in order to find users feedback related to the cold start product. We then generate reviews

RecSys '16, September 15-19, 2016, Boston , MA, USA
© 2016 ACM. ISBN 978-1-4503-4035-9/16/09...$15.00
DOI: http://dx.doi.org/10.1145/2959100.2959102

from users' feedback; predict users' ratings and finally transfer them to e-commerce website.

2. RELATED WORK

In recent years, common approaches to mitigate the cold start problem rely on exploiting external contents in addition to users ratings and combine them with collaborative filtering approaches. Examples of external content include item taxonomies, product categories and external knowledge bases which are adopted by several researchers [2, 3].

Leung et.al [3] integrate item taxonomy information within the collaborative filtering model. To do so, they proposed Cross-Level Association RulEs (CLARE) based on item taxonomies to infer rating for the cold start item. However, since building item taxonomies for different types of product is not a trivial-task, this approach might not be easily scalable for different domains.

Barjasteh et al. [1] propose a matrix factorization approach which constructs a similarity matrix based on structured contents of items available on different websites. First, they filter out cold items from the original matrix and then fill in the missing values of the non-cold items. Afterwards, they transduct the information from non-cold items to cold items by applying spectral clustering on similarity matrix. However, the functionality of this approach depends on products' structured information which limits the extraction of product information to few websites.

Park et al. [8] propose to retrieve relevant opinion sentences from the reviews of other products using specifications of a new product. Their key idea is that opinions on similar products may be applicable to the product that lacks reviews. They computed similarity between products based on the structured product specifications which are available in the some review websites. They further introduce a probabilistic approach to generate a set of review sentences from similar product for the cold start product. However, this approach can only perform on the structured content and is not applicable on unstructured description of products, which limit its capability in product modeling and presentation.

Our proposed work borrow from the same principals as Park et al. but does not limit itself to structured product specifications. In our research, we propose an approach to address the limitations of existing works in dealing with the cold item problem. Our approach is generalizable in that it does not rely on any external structured information such as product taxonomies or ontologies. Rather, we propose to mine product information from unstructured data anywhere on the Web and create a formal representation for products. We further exploit microblogging platforms such as Twitter to identify users' feedback about the cold product to be transferred onto the e-commerce website.

3. RESEARCH CONTRIBUTIONS

In this section, we present our proposed framework for addressing cold item problem. Our framework consists of three components: 1) Product representation model and the associated method for extracting it, which will produce domain-independent representation of products; 2) Review selection model to find suitable reviews from similar products to be assigned to the cold product; and 3) Review transferring approach to enrich the reviews of cold products by exploiting auxiliary information from source such as Twitter.

In the following, we describe each component of our framework in more details.

3.1 Semantic Product Representation (SPR)

The idea of producing product representations for the purpose of product similarity, clustering and recommendation has already been widely explored in the literature [8]. There have also been approaches that build product representations to address the cold start problem [1]. However, the majority, if not all, of these approaches build the product representation from structured specifications provided by e-commerce websites. For instance product categories, tags, and property/values are used for generating the product representation; therefore, limiting their applicability to the applicability of the extracted representation to the source from which the representation was extracted.

We are interested in learning product representations that can be transferable across multiple domains. To this end, we will consider *Word Embedding* techniques in our work. Word Embedding techniques have been applied by some researchers for the purpose of semantic text annotation, content disambiguation and entity linking. The work in [13] applies the Skipgram model [5] to produce continuous real valued vectors for each word from entity name (surface words) and takes an average of the vectors to represent the entity. We propose that the same strategy that has been used for entity and concept representation can be extended for learning product representations. However, we argue that building vectors based on the surface words is limiting, as the meaning of the composing words can be different from the meaning of the entity as a whole. Our proposed approach in product representation addresses these limitations.

The basic idea of our proposed work for SPR is to extract products descriptive contents available on the Web, which are mainly unstructured, and semantically represent them based on the Word Embedding approaches. In SPR, we will consider an unstructured text about the product, e.g., the description of a product in the website, review texts of the product, wikipedia pages, among other, as an input and exploit Word Embedding methods such as Skipgram, CBOW, [5] and GloVe [9] to represent the product as vector of features. The reason that we are interested in Word Embeddings is that they are distributional representations of words which give collective meaning to the words which are used in similar contexts. So, by exploiting this technique and using descriptive contents available on the Web, we can potentially bring products into a semantic representation space which preserve distance and geometric properties, which is desirable for the sake of review transfer in the later stages of our work. This representation of products opens up many possibilities such as product mention identification, product similarity calculation, product categorization and clustering, just to name a few.

We formalize the product representation model as follows:

Given a product p and its associate descriptive text, we first pre-process the text to remove stopwords and also stem the words. We then replace any mentions of the target product with a unique token, rather than treating it as just union of words. The reason for this action is that the meanings of the exact words are different from the meaning of the product as a whole. For example, we cannot reach a proper representation for product *"Apple iPhone 6s Plus"* by simply composing the meanings of {*Apple, iPhone, 6s, Plus*}. Alternatively, we should consider all these words as one token e.g., {*Apple-iPhone-6s-Plus*}, and then represents it as a vector. Now we introduce interleave function:

$$interleave(t, w, k) = t[1..k] + w + t[k+1..2*k] + w + ... \quad (1)$$

Where t is a text, w is a word, k is a constant integer, and $t[1..k]$ denotes the substring of t containing the first k words of t. The operator $+$ here represents the strings concatenation operation. we obtain final text $t\prime$ as follows:

$$t\prime = interleave(t, ut, ilf) \quad (2)$$

Where t is the descriptive text, ut represents a unique token for p, and ilf is an interleaving factor that defines the distance between two product tokens in the final text. The goal of interleaving is to place ut in every ilf words of t. We interleave to make sure that all relevant words for a product are placed in a visible context for the Word Embedding technique. Given numerous Word Embedding techniques [5, 9] in the literature, we apply different Word Embedding method such as Skipgram and GloVe on $t\prime$ to produce a model that contains feature vectors for each word in $t\prime$.

$$model = Skipgram(t\prime) \quad (3)$$

Where $model$ contains the set of all word vectors in the $t\prime$. The generated vector of the p is presented as:

$$v_p = model[ut] \quad (4)$$

v_p is the vector in the model which corresponds to ut.

3.2 Review Selection Model

Park et al. [8] have already argued that an effective approach for fixing the cold item problem is to transfer ratings and reviews from similar products. We adopt a similar strategy and are interested in identifying transferable reviews and ratings from similar products. Unlike the work by Park et al. that identifies similar products based on structured product information, we will use our own SPR model to mine product specifications. We will use various vector similarity measurement techniques to identify similar products. The reviews and ratings of warm products that are highly similar to the cold products can then be transferred to the cold products. However, the review selection mechanism is a non-trivial task and there are several issues that need to be properly addressed: 1) the number of selected reviews: finding an optimal number of reviews that would be transferred is challenging. On the one hand, a small number of reviews would contain only a limited set of information and would not be able to address the cold products problem. On the other hand, a large set of reviews could potentially carry irrelevant information and may confuse users. We are interested in applying the work in microblog summarization techniques [12] for determining an optimal number of reviews or ratings that would be transferred 2) review coverage: it is most probable that reviews only cover one or few aspects of the product. We need to identify major aspects of the products and then select those covering reviews that address the majority of them. This would need to be addressed in concert with the problem of identifying the number of reviews. We will consider the literature on mining product review aspects [6] for the purpose of determining the most important aspects of a product that have been mentioned in reviews or social microblogging platforms 3) review centrality: It is important that the selected reviews should reflect the central opinion of users [8]. That is, the selected reviews should include the orientation distribution of users' reviews. For example, if there are more reviews that contains a "poor screen display" than a value "high quality display" for a certain feature, it is more desired to select those review with a higher observation frequency.

3.3 Transferring Reviews from Twitter

In the third step of our work, we intend to enrich the products reviews by collecting more information about them from some auxiliary and rich sources. For our purpose, we choose Twitter, one of the most popular microblogging platforms, which allows users to freely share their feelings and opinions in a real-time manner. We propose a review transferring approach to retrieve those tweets that express users feedback about cold product, and then transfer them to the e-commerce website. There are already work that perform sentiment mining for certain brands or products from microblogging platforms [11], but to the extent of our knowledge, none have considered the idea of generating reviews and transferring them for the cold item problem. Our proposed model consists of three steps:

1) *tweet selection*: Our objective is to find a representation that would be able to detect Related Products (RP) that are not necessarily the exact product that we are looking for but have sufficiently similar characteristics for their reviews and comments to be transferable to the product of interest.

2) *rating prediction from tweets*: Since in Twitter users share their feeling and opinion about products, we employ sentiment analysis techniques on RP's tweets. The overall rating of the tweets would be transferred to the e-commerce website in the form of summarized ranking for the cold item.

3) *review generation*: A subset of RP's tweets which are compliant with the characteristics described earlier such as review centrality, coverage and size are selected and considered to be used for generating reviews. Our hypothesis will be that tweets about products could potentially be viewed as product reviews that have been posted on Twitter as opposed to an e-commerce website. We will summarize the set of tweets to serve as the generated reviews for a cold product and would be transferred to the e-commerce website. It is important to note that, selecting tweets relevant to specific products is non-trivial for two reasons: 1) structured descriptive content that are available for products are not necessarily present in the microblog posts; and 2) entity linking techniques identify the mention of a device but not its brand, make and other details; therefore, making it harder to identify close matches. Our SPR model that relies on Word Embedding techniques can help in this respect as such techniques have already been used for entity linking on Twitter [14].

4. EVALUATION STRATEGY

4.1 Data set

In order to evaluate our proposed approach, we need to first collect a dataset of real-world users reviews and ratings associated with products which is available in e-commerce websites such as Amazon.com, BestBuy.com, and CNET.com. Among them, we chose CNET.com because it has reasonable number of products and review information and rela-

Table 1: Pediction Error (RMSE) of KNN on SPR features

	ilf:1	ilf:5	ilf:20
Skipgram	0.881	0.9846	0.985
GloVe	1.104	1.259	1.236

tively large descriptions. We have crawled CNET.com and extracted related information about products such as their descriptive content, their associated reviews and ratings as well as the users' information.

4.2 Evaluation Plan

The goal of the proposed approach is to generate reviews and predict their associated ratings for the cold products. We plan to incorporate different Word Embedding techniques such as Glove, Skipgram and LDA in SPR; and choose the one which yields the best possible results in review generation and rating prediction.

For evaluating the performance of the review generation approach, using standard retrieval measures do not seem appropriate. Instead, we select a set of non-cold products and we apply our review generation approach on such products. Then we measure the proximity between the generated reviews and their actual reviews. Since the generated reviews can be considered as summarization task, as indicated in [8] we then employ summarization evaluation methods such as ROUGE [4], which is a standard evaluation system for multiple document summarization, and evaluate the quality of an automatically generated reviews by comparing them with the actual reviews of non-cold products. Furthermore, to evaluate the performance of rating prediction approach, the common approach is to measure how much the predicted ratings are close to the actual ratings. Metrics such as MSE, RMSE and MAE would be adopted for this purpose.

4.3 Preliminary Results

As a preliminary step for our work, we crawled the phone category in CNET.com website which contains 4,848 phone products, 6,215 reviews; and ratings within a range of [0,5] from 867 users. We extracted the description of products that are available on the website as the input for SPR, described in Section 3.1. We then experimented three different interleaving factors: 1, 5, 20 and used Skipgram and GloVe methods to make the model with window size of 5 and vector dimension of 200. We applied K-nearest neighbor (KNN) algorithm on feature vectors of products. We then evaluate rating prediction error of the model using RMSE metric. Experimental results are shown in Table 1 and indicate that the prediction error of KNN based on PRS model is minimum when $ilf = 1$, as well as skipgram outperforms GloVe in rating prediction with similar settings.

5. CONCLUSIONS

In this research, we propose to address cold item problem in e-commerce website. Our approach is generalizable as there is no need for structured information like external taxonomies or ontologies or structured specifications of products. Our proposed approach enables us to mine information about products from anywhere on the Web, specifically microblogging platforms and any unstructured description about products. Our contributions are three-folds: 1) we introduce an algorithm to build a formal representation of products using unstructured content; 2) we propose a review and rating selection model to find similar products and transfer their reviews to the cold start products; and 3) to benefit from the abundance of information on Twitter, we propose mechanisms to analyse those tweets related to a cold product; and then transfer them as reviews to e-commerce websites.

6. REFERENCES

[1] I. Barjasteh, R. Forsati, D. Ross, A. Esfahanian, and H.Radha. Cold-start recommendation with provable guarantees: A decoupled approach. *Knowledge and Data Engineering, IEEE Transactions on*, 2016.

[2] C. Kim and J. Kim. A recommendation algorithm using multilevel association rules. In *Proceedings of International Conference on Web Intelligence*, 2003.

[3] C. Leung, S. Chan, and F. Chung. An empirical study of a cross level association rule mining approach to cold start recommendations. *Knowledge Based Systems*, 21:515–529, 2008.

[4] C. Y. Lin. Rouge: A package for automatic evaluation of summaries. In *Text Summarization Branches Out:Proceedings of the ACL Workshop*, pages 74–81, 2004.

[5] T. Mikolov, K. Chen, G. Corrado, and J. Dean. Efficient estimation of word representations in vector space. In *ICLR Workshop Papers*, 2013.

[6] S. Moghaddam and M. Ester. On the design of lda models for aspect based opinion mining. In *CIKM'12*, 2012.

[7] S. Moghaddam and M. Ester. The flda model for aspect based opinion mining: Addressing the cold start problem. In *WWW'13*, 2013.

[8] D. H. Park, H. D. Kim, C. Zhai, and L. Guo. Retrieval of relevant opinion sentences for new products. In *international ACM SIGIR conference on Research and development in information retrieval.* ACM, 2015.

[9] J. Pennington, R. Socher, and C. Manning. Glove: global vectors for word representation. In *Proceedings EMNLP'14*, pages 1532–1543, 2014.

[10] A. L. V. Pereira and E. R. Hruschka. Simultaneous co-clustering and learning to address the cold start problem in recommender systems. *Knowledge Based Systems*, 42(19):6784–6794, November 2015.

[11] H. Saif, Y. He, and H. Alani. Semantic sentiment analysis of twitter. In *The Semantic Web ISWC*, 2012.

[12] B. Sharifi, M. Anthony, and J. Kalita. Summarizing microblogs automatically. In *Proceeding HLT '10 Human Language Technologies.* ACM, 2010.

[13] Y. Sun, L. Lin, D. Tang, N. Yang, Z. Ji, and X. Wang. Modeling mention, context and entity with neural networks for entity disambiguation. In *Proceedings of IJCAI'15.* Springer, 2015.

[14] E. S. Yang and Y. S. Kim. Named entity recognition on twitter with induced word representation. In *ACL-IJCNLP*, 2012.

Personalized Support for Healthy Nutrition Decisions

Hanna Schäfer
Technical University of Munich
Arcisstraße 21
D-80333 Munich, Germany
hanna.schaefer@tum.de

ABSTRACT

Despite their high priority, healthy nutrition, physical activity and other preventive health factors are rarely adopted over a long term. Traditional nutrition support systems lack of practical everyday knowledge, social support and motivation as well the consideration of the personal context. We address these impediments with a holistic decision support system that empowers people to change their lifestyle successfully. We aim at analyzing previous approaches from various disciplines and integrating them into one concept for nutrition support giving personalized context aware recommendations to each user while presenting and teaching practical information about healthy nutrition. Additionally, we consider the ease of usage of such an application by automating necessary burdens and motivating participants with social incentives. The decision support system is tested in a 6-month intervention study using regression analysis on usage patterns and matrix factorial designs for interacting features. The social and interactive components are observed in a 1-year field study, utilizing a realistic environment.

CCS Concepts

•Information systems → Expert systems; •Human-centered computing → Social recommendation; *User models; User centered design;* **•Applied computing → Health informatics;** *Interactive learning environments;*

Keywords

Nutrition; Health; Personalization; Knowledge based Recommender Systems; Decision Support

1. INTRODUCTION

According to the World Health Organization (WHO), about 38 million people (60% of deaths) annually die due to Non-communicable Diseases (NCDs) [21]. Those diseases share the same four behavioral risk factors: tobacco use, unhealthy diet, physical inactivity and harmful consume of alcohol [21]. Changing any of those requires substantial support for critical targets, such as those with obesity or prediabetes. Currently such cases are treated with different interventions such as psychotherapy or medical treatment [14]. Less severe cases might only require stronger consciousness consequences of their own behavior and the means and motivation to change it. Part of the consciousness might be provided by self-quantification through gadgets. Part of the motivational aspects is given by social support. To address the full range nutritional behavior changes, developing a system that seamlessly integrates different nutrition support variants into people's everyday life is essential. In order to reach this goal, such a system needs to integrate the following aspects:

- Formalized knowledge on nutrition/physical science that is usable and accessible in digital contexts
- Delivery and presentation of relevant information in everyday situations of the user
- Intrinsic motivation through e.g. self-quantification and gamification
- Extrinsic motivation through e.g. groups and social feedback mechanisms

This paper is organized as follows. After giving the motivation for this research projects, the second chapter gives an overview of related work on different aspects of the topic. In the third chapter the collected aspects are summarized into a system proposal from which key research questions are deduced. Finally, in chapter 4 the future study designs and evaluation techniques are presented.

2. RELATED WORK

Previous work has been conducted on several different aspects of nutrition support. Thus this related work section covers each major aspect in turn. First the traditional nutrition support done by experts and facilities is compared with modern socio-technical systems. Secondly different approaches for the integration and modelling of domain knowledge are presented. We then consider various approaches of user context and the personalization of nutrition support. Finally, we compare approaches of automation and interaction principles that could be utilized inside a nutrition support system.

RecSys '16, September 15-19, 2016, Boston , MA, USA
© 2016 ACM. ISBN 978-1-4503-4035-9/16/09...$15.00
DOI: http://dx.doi.org/10.1145/2959100.2959105

2.1 Traditional Nutrition Interventions

In traditional nutritional interventions patients are guided by in-person consultation and stationary or session based medical interventions. Disadvantages of those interventions are e.g. the lack adherence to sessions [3] or the maintenance of changes after returning to everyday life [14]. A first step that has been taken to counteract those problems is the integration of technology into the reporting methods. [17] compared 27 nutritional interventions using technological support for diet tracking and concluded that a combination with self-monitoring, counselling, group support and an individually tailored program promise even better results.

2.2 Domain knowledge transfer

The easiest way to improve nutrition is to reduce the daily energy intake which depends on metrics such as age and gender and the level of physical activity. By determining the physical activity level the recommender system can adapt the recommended calorie intake to the current user state concerning energy consumption. In addition, to the pure energy intake the source of energy, e.g. fat or carbohydrates, influences the healthiness of a meal. Different definitions of optimal consumption ratios between food groups are given by rule based guidelines such as the Healthy Eating Index [7] or the 10 rules of the DGE [12]. Those guidelines can be modelled for example by Food Pyramids or Decision Trees [5]. Also nutrients such as vitamins and minerals are of high relevance to preventive healthcare. One well-known concept in nutrition science is called diet optimization. It optimizes the nutrients intake while changing the habitual nutrition as little as possible in order to support easy adoption by using Fuzzy Expert Systems [9]. Another approach to judging the healthiness of food is to let users rate their meals. Research shows that the accumulated health ratings of a crowd based on meal pictures come close to the health estimate that experts would give the same food [20].

2.3 Context aware personalization

There are different levels of context and personalization to be considered. From the medical point of view, the context of previous nutritional intake, previous physical activity and in some cases even medical states such as blood values and history of illnesses [5] are a necessary personalization for providing accurate feedback. From the convenience and user experience perspective contexts such as food availability, weather, user preferences and time [16] are deciding factors for the adherence to recommendations. On a third level of abstraction, the social environment on a long term basis such as in a family or within the current situation such as a work meeting have a strong influence on the long term behavior and on habit building. For example, [8] researched the effect of familiarity and similarity of social relations to improve the adoption rate of recommended items and [2] [1] analyzed health related recommendations for families. All of these different contexts should be considered in order to improve the adherence to nutrition advice in everyday situations.

2.4 Automation and interaction models

In addition to modelling personalized domain knowledge, the motivation and adherence of users to presented recommendations strongly depends on the interface between user and system. How can the user insert data about his state and context? How can the system present its results in an understandable way? The point of system input interfaces is answered in a lot of automation concepts for mobile application such as image recognition [15], augmented reality [4] or wearables for motion tracking. Also gamification has been suggested for unburdening tedious tasks especially for younger people [13]. On the output perspective several approaches for information representation and for incentivizing the given recommendations, e.g. visualization [11] and explanations [19], have been studied.

3. PROBLEM STATEMENT AND RESEARCH QUESTIONS

There are multiple approaches from different disciplines to support healthy nutrition and lifestyle changes in general. The focus of this PHD thesis will be to evaluate different support components and to combine and integrate those approaches in a way, that supports synergetic interaction effects. To design such a system, we defined major research questions for each research field:

- Decision Support System Research Questions:
  1. Can crowd based health knowledge collected by multidimensional ratings compete with expert knowledge?
  2. To what degree are different contexts motivating or improving adherence?
  3. How does transparent advice/explanations/persuasion improve knowledge and adherence?
  4. How can of diet optimization (nutrition science) be combined with current recommender approaches?
- Socio-Technical System Research Questions:
  1. How can feedback by ratings of other users influence self-awareness and acceptance of health advice?
  2. Which social interactions (communication, games, group dinner, group sports) motivate adolescents to change and maintain their health attitude?
  3. How can health recommendations best be adapted to the group level (group dinner, group activity)?
  4. How can social circles and their interaction be designed to enhance motivational effects within a group environment?
- Human Computer Interaction Research Questions:
  1. Which input methods offer the optimal user experience for tracking the dietary intake in different settings (e.g. Restaurant dinner, self-cooked meal)?
  2. Which input methods offer the optimal accuracy for food mass and food types in different settings (e.g. Restaurant dinner, self-cooked meal)?
  3. How can a realistic user avatar enhance motivation and self-quantification in a serious games platform?
  4. Gamification and automation of content and size estimation from meal pictures by utilizing a combination of image recognition and augmented reality?

4. METHODOLOGY OF EVALUATION

At the current stage only smaller pre-tests have been conducted. One study concerns motion tracking with smartphones for school children. Another study tests advantages of different versions of a dietary diary. Nevertheless, the study design for the final holistic intervention shall be presented in the following sections.

4.1 Decision Support System

A in depth description of this study on decision support systems can be found in [18]. We plan an intervention of 6 moth, with a follow up after additional 3 months. The core of this intervention is to offer participants different versions of one decision support system, that helps change their nutritional behavior by offering: (1) automated on-demand generation of personalized recommendations on a mobile device, (2) easy or automated digital input of contextual information such as dietary intake and physical activity (PA), (3) motivation by integration of gadgets and blood characteristics, as well as (4) clear communication of the given advice by visualization and explanation. The main target group of the study are people with an BMI higher than 25. People with a normal BMI are usually already quite health aware. The System is targeting German speaking people living in Germany. In addition to German language, also the recipe and food selection will be German based. Due to lack of medical allowance of the system, people with serious diseases are excluded.
The results of the interventions will be measures on a quantifiable medical level, as well as with qualitative measures on usage patterns. We decided on the following quantifiable variables:

- Healthy Eating Index: Average value in Germany 84.8 ± 9.8 should be changed by 5-7%
- Body Mass Index: Participants have a BMI larger than 25. There should be a change of about $1kg/m^2$
- Nutrients: Improvement towards optimal levels
- Blood Values: Triglycerides, Cholesterol, Iron, Homocysteine, Vitamin D, Phospholipids (ω-3/ω-6)
- Waist-To-Hip-Ratio

The second level are the qualitative measures of sustainable application usage. Those are defined as follows:

- Durability of usage by dropout rate
- Frequency of usage
- Frequency of data input
- Acceptance of recommendations

The study is split into two interconnected interventions. The first intervention consists of 330 initial participants, with an expected drop-out of 50%. In this group blood measures are taken in order to personalize the recommendations to the biological factors of participants. Besides the blood personalization all participants in the first intervention group receive a decision support application with the full range of functionalities. Those include: Food type based recommendations [5], recipe based recommendations [6][10], 7-day-recall food-frequency-questionnaire, daily dietary diary, motion tracking using the smartphone or wearables, feedback by visualization and feedback with explanations. Since all functionalities are openly available to the users, the usage patterns will be analyzed by a regression analysis to determine which combination of application features had which impact on the outcome measurements. Additionally, surveys will be conducted after 3, 6 and 9 months to gain insight on the perception of the application.
The second intervention uses no blood measurements and is designed as a matrix factorial design with 5 factors of the following 2-3 levels:

- Recommendation: Food based, recipe based, both
- Intake tracking: 7-day recall, diary, both
- Movement tracking: Sensor data, Questionnaire
- Visualization: Yes, No
- Explanations: Yes, No

Within the matrix factorial study, we want to measure the main effects and interaction effects of all combinations of the given factors using an ANOVA analysis.
The interconnection between both interventions is given by the fully functional part of the matrix design, which covers the exact same application elements, as the first intervention. By comparing those effects, we can determine whether personalization based on blood values improves the behavioral change.

4.2 Socio-Technical System

For the analysis of social effects in a nutrition assistance system, an application with multidimensional rating based recommendation of meals, social network integration and group recommendations is being tested. In contrast to the decision support system analysis, we decided to evaluate this system in a field study, since the restricted environment of an intervention study might bias the results of social networks. In this field study, we measure the following qualitative outcome measurements:

- Durability of usage by dropout rate
- Frequency of (group) interactions
- Adherence to (group) recommendations
- Improvement of nutrition measured by received ratings
- Quality of crowd ratings compared to expert ratings

The field study is designed to last 1 year during which users may join or leave at will.

4.3 Human Computer Interaction

The evaluation of interaction principles is split into two categories. The evaluation of automated input methods, such as image recognition and augmented reality will not only show which methods have higher accuracies but also conduct usability testing to show which are faster for the users to apply.
The second evaluation will focus on the serious games platform and its motivational and educational effects on younger participants. On concept that will be the focus of this observation is, how participant interact with their avatar in each environment of the serious games platform. These concepts will be assessed during a field study of 1 year with various in-app questionnaires and interviews.

5. CONCLUSIONS

In summary this PHD project covers a nutritional decision making system, that engages users with easy in- and output functionalities, such as gamified/ automated data insertion and intrigues him with avatar-based self-quantification or explanations. It also motivates users by personalizing on specific user needs and applying social pressure to ensure long term habit development. Finally, the system provides both crowd based and expert based recommendations, as well as hybrid recommendations tailored to the users needs and contexts.

As future work, we will conduct the described field studies and interventions. Secondly, further automation and recommender techniques proposed in the researched literature will be investigated on their improvements on the system. Finally, all optimal features will be included into one mobile system so that we can measure the maximal effects on behavior change.

6. ACKNOWLEDGMENTS

I thank my advisor, Georg Groh, for his support and guidance. This thesis is supported by the interdisciplinary enable cluster about nutrition research funded by the Federal Ministry of Education and Research (BMBF, Funding number: 01EA1409H).

7. REFERENCES

[1] N. Baghaei, S. Kimani, J. Freyne, E. Brindal, S. Berkovsky, and G. Smith. Engaging Families in Lifestyle Changes Through Social Networking. *International Journal of Human-Computer Interaction*, 27(10):971–990, 2011.

[2] S. Berkovsky, J. Freyne, M. Coombe, D. Bhandari, and N. Baghaei. Physical activity motivating games: you can play, mate! *Proceedings of the 21st Annual Conference of the Australian Computer-Human Interaction Special Interest Group: Design: Open 24/7*, pages 273–276, 2009.

[3] S. U. Dombrowski, F. F. Sniehotta, M. Johnston, I. Broom, U. Kulkarni, J. Brown, L. Murray, and V. Araújo-Soares. Optimizing acceptability and feasibility of an evidence-based behavioral intervention for obese adults with obesity-related co-morbidities or additional risk factors for co-morbidities: an open-pilot intervention study in secondary care. *Patient education and counseling*, 87(1):108–119, 2012.

[4] M. Domhardt, R. Dinic, T. Stütz, and S. Ginzinger. Evaluation der Interaktion mit einer AR - basierten Smartphone - App. pages 165–174, 2014.

[5] P. M. Gibney and D. M. Walsh. Personalised Nutrition : paving a way to better population health A White Paper from the Food4Me project. (March):100, 2015.

[6] T. Greupner. *Development of Food-based Dietary Recommendations for Personalized Nutrition Advice on the Basis of the Food4Me Study*. PhD thesis, 2015.

[7] P. M. Guenther, K. O. Casavale, J. Reedy, S. I. Kirkpatrick, H. a. B. Hiza, K. J. Kuczynski, L. L. Kahle, and S. M. Krebs-Smith. Update of the Healthy Eating Index: HEI-2010. *Journal of the Academy of Nutrition and Dietetics*, 113(4):569–580, 2013.

[8] I. Guy, N. Zwerdling, D. Carmel, I. Ronen, E. Uziel, S. Yogev, and S. Ofek-Koifman. Personalized Recommendation of Social Software Items Based on Social Relations. *Proceedings of the RecSys'09*, pages 53–60, 2009.

[9] P. Heinonen, M. Mannelin, H. Iskala, A. Sorsa, E. Juuso, and F.-t. Oy. Development of a Fuzzy Expert System for a Nutritional Guidance Application. pages 1685–1690, 2009.

[10] R. Hektor. *Personalized Food Recommender Systems.* PhD thesis, 2015.

[11] D. Huang, M. Tory, B. A. Aseniero, L. Bartram, S. Bateman, S. Carpendale, A. Tang, and R. Woodbury. Personal visualization and personal visual analytics. *Visualization and Computer Graphics, IEEE Transactions on*, 21(3):420–433, 2015.

[12] A. Jungvogel, I. Wendt, K. Schäbethal, E. Leschik-Bonnet, and H. Oberritter. Überarbeitet: Die 10 regeln der dge. *Ernährungs Umschau*, 11:M644–M645, 2013.

[13] S. McCallum. Gamification and serious games for personalized health. *Studies in Health Technology and Informatics*, 177:85–96, 2012.

[14] S. Meister, S. Becker, and U. Simson. Digitale gesundheit - unterstützung der adipositastherapie durch digitale technologien? *Adipositas - Ursachen, Folgeerkrankungen, Therapie*, 10:38–42, 2016.

[15] A. Myers, N. Johnston, V. Rathod, A. Korattikara, A. Gorban, N. Silberman, S. Guadarrama, G. Papandreou, J. Huang, and K. Murphy. Im2Calories : towards an automated mobile vision food diary. (December):1233–1241, 2016.

[16] M.-H. Park, J.-H. Hong, and S.-B. Cho. Location-Based Recommendation System Using Bayesian User's Preference Model in Mobile Devices. *Ubiquitous Intelligence and Computing*, 4611:1130–1139, 2007.

[17] L. C. Raaijmakers, S. Pouwels, K. A. Berghuis, and S. W. Nienhuijs. Technology-based interventions in the treatment of overweight and obesity: A systematic review. *Appetite*, 95:138–151, 2015.

[18] N. Sahinagic, N. Leipold, H. Schäfer, M. Madenach, M. Böhm, G. Groh, K. Gedrich, and H. Krcmar. Can an automated personalized nutrition assistance system successfully change nutrition behavior? - study design. *2016 International Conference on Information Systems (ICIS 2016)*, 2016.

[19] N. Tintarev and J. Masthoff. A survey of explanations in recommender systems. *Proceedings - International Conference on Data Engineering*, pages 801–810, 2007.

[20] G. M. Turner-McGrievy, E. E. Helander, K. Kaipainen, J. M. Perez-Macias, and I. Korhonen. The use of crowdsourcing for dietary self-monitoring: crowdsourced ratings of food pictures are comparable to ratings by trained observers. *Journal of the American Medical Informatics Association : JAMIA*, pages 1–6, 2014.

[21] WHO. Global status report on noncommunicable diseases 2014. *World Health*, page 176, 2014.

Proactive Recommendation Delivery

Adem Sabic
Alpen-Adria-Universitaet
Klagenfurt, Austria
ademsabic@gmail.com

ABSTRACT

The main purpose of Recommender Systems is to minimize the effects of information/choice overload. Recommendations are usually prepared based on the estimation of what would be useful or interesting to users. Thus, it is important that they are relevant to users, whether to their information needs, current activity or emotional state. This requires deep understanding of users' context but also the knowledge of the history of previous users' interactions within the system (e.g. clicks, views, etc.). But even when the recommendations are highly relevant, their delivery to users can be very problematic. Many existing systems require active user participation (explicit interaction with the recommender system) and attention. Or, on other side of spectrum, there are RS that handle recommendation delivery without any consideration for users' preferences of when, where or how the recommendations are being delivered. Proactive Recommender Systems promise a more autonomous approach for recommendation delivery, by anticipating information needs in advance and acting on users' behalf with minimal efforts and without disturbance. This paper describes our work and interest in identifying and analyzing the factors that can influence acceptance and use of proactively delivered recommendations.

Keywords

Proactive Recommendation Delivery, Recommender Systems, Content Relevance, Timing, Modality

1. INTRODUCTION & MOTIVATION

Recommender Systems (RS) are a well-proven and effective approach to minimize choice overload, whether the user is faced with abundance of content, goods, applications and services, etc. In ideal scenario, users receive highly relevant and interesting recommendations (items), while organizations (system providers) benefit from increased user engagement (e.g. more videos watched, books read, items bought etc.). On a more practical level, relevancy, interestingness and other metrics are determined by the accuracy of the algorithms, or by optimizing for very specific metrics.

RecSys '16, September 15 - 19, 2016, Boston , MA, USA

ISBN 978-1-4503-4035-9/16/09... $15.00

DOI: http://dx.doi.org/10.1145/2959100.2959108

Many existing RS require active user participation and attention (i.e. request from the system when you need something). Or, on other side of spectrum, there are RS that handle recommendation delivery without any consideration for users' preferences of when, where or how the recommendations are being delivered. With abundance of applications/services there is also ongoing competition for user attention. Human attention is generally considered as a scarce resource, especially in the recent times where organizations try to increase user engagement by delivering unsolicited content without basic understanding of users' current context/situation. This intrusive approach can lead to frustration and disturbance of users. These unwanted interruptions can have negative effects on work performance [3], emotional state [1], etc. Preliminary studies on time, location and modality (user interface) of interruptions, showed promising results in easing the negative effects of information delivery that was not explicitly requested.

Contrary to existing approaches, Proactive Systems (PS) want to avoid any requirement of user participation and effort. PS promise to anticipate user needs in advance and then to take appropriate actions on their behalf. Actions are usually related to delivery of relevant content at the right time, place, etc. [5]. Consequently, Proactive Recommender Systems (PRS) should deliver relevant recommendations when needed, without disturbing users in any possible way. Finding relevant content and identifying opportune moments, places, modalities for recommendation delivery is, at least for now, mostly unchartered research area.

In the next sections you can read about: related work, proposed research model and methodology for this thesis, progress to date and ongoing work, and finally about some closing thoughts and outlook on future work.

2. RELATED WORK

Since research in this domain is still at a very nascent stage, for the theoretical foundations we must look at the existing work in Proactive Computing (PC), (context-aware) RS, information delivery, interruption and notification management research areas.

The majority of research is focused on the theoretical foundations and potential of PS [11]. Experimental work is scarce, but what exists is usually related to tourism domain. More prominent work includes RS with proactive delivery of recommendations for POI[1] [4], gas-stations [17],

[1]Points of Interest

and restaurants [14]. Additionally, there are efforts to bring proactiveness to RS for writing tasks [9], personalized news, [19], and e-learning systems [7].

On more theoretical level, we can find user studies that investigate user attitudes towards PS. Key insights from these studies can be summarized as follows [12, 13]: a) PS can create highly engaging experiences, in which such they can assist and enhance user experience and bring convenience and help when needed; b) in general users show strong interest and willingness to adopt and follow proactive recommendations; c) practical implementations need to be handled with care, given that some users are afraid of growing too reliant on these systems, whereas others, still, refrain from using them due to unnecessary interruptions and the frustration they cause.

The present work was designed with insights on interruption management work in mind, as wrong interruptions seem to be possibly the biggest challenge for successful implementation of PRS. Interruption management studies focus on aspects like timing, location, modality, user feedback, etc. which are similar/complementary to previously mentioned principles of Proactive Recommendation Delivery (PRD). Finding optimal timing seems to be very challenging. Preliminary studies argue that good time for interruptions/information delivery could be after successful end of some primary task [6]. Location and Modality also seem to play major role for information delivery. Depending on the location, users seem to be more or less open to receive relevant notifications [8]. Modality (how information is presented), on the other hand, can affect trust, understandability, transparency, accessibility of system that manages information delivery [10].

To summarize, PRS should follow core principles of PC paradigm, by offering relevant recommendations to users only at appropriate situations (right time, location, modality, etc.). Thus, we want to investigate them, their relations and effects on actual acceptance and use of proactively delivered recommendations.

3. RESEARCH MODEL & METHODOLOGY

In this section we present research questions for this thesis. Their scope ranges from user attitudes towards PRS; importance and effects of the mentioned factors on their acceptance and actual use; but also how to incorporate user feedback and what measures to use to for their evaluation. Concretely, we want to find out what are the perspectives, key factors to focus on when going for practical implementations and how to use user feedback and evaluation measures to continuously improve existing systems.

3.1 Attitudes

How users perceive PRS?
Are they open to share their personal information?
Is there an economic perspective for commercial implementations?

Although the questions are self-explanatory to what is goal of our research, we would add that these questions (e.g. economic perspective, access to user data, etc.) are probable concerns for any organizations willing to discuss any kind of practical implementation in this area.

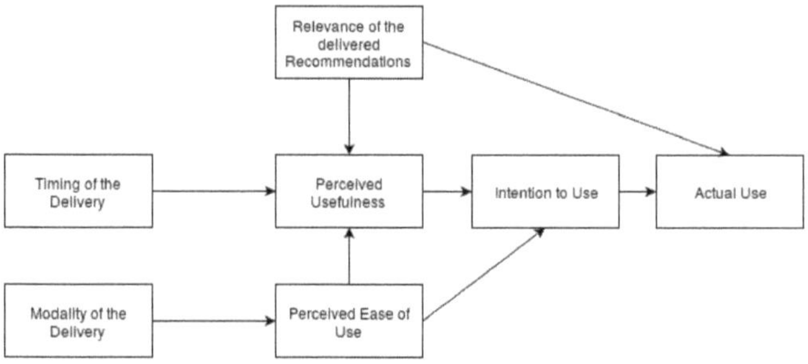

Figure 1: Adapted TAM for PRS

3.2 Acceptance & Use

What are the effects of relevancy of recommendations, timing and modality of their delivery, on acceptance and use of PRS?

Let's start with some basic understanding of the mentioned terms. Relevance can be defined as a subjective and contextual judgment of information/content [15]. It is a complex concept that can be explained by five-factor model: topicality, novelty, reliability, understandability, and scope [18]. Some of these factors have higher level of importance on relevance (e.g. topicality). Specifically, situational/contextual relevance refers to utility of information to particular situation, task, or problem at hand [16]. Factors that define tasks could be importance, urgency, and complexity [2]. For further investigation of these research questions, we want to execute task-driven user studies with between-subjects design recommendations relevance, timing and modality of the delivery as manipulated variables.

Acceptance and Usage are well-known TAM[2] concepts. Relevance of Recommendations with Timing and Modality of the delivery, were incorporated into adapted version of TAM presented on Figure 1.

This represents the most complex and important part of this thesis, and thus majority of attention in our future user studies and experiments will be on investigating relations from this model.

3.3 User Feedback & Evaluation

How to elicit and incorporate user feedback?
How to evaluate proactive recommendation deliveries?

User Feedback is very important since it can allow organizations to improve PRS. It is necessary to investigate whether the users are willing to provide feedback at all, and in which form/modality. We plan to investigate jointly with research studies on appropriate modality for PRD.

Evaluation is another important factor for organizations that want to continuously improve their systems. We believe that concepts like Responsiveness (i.e. time until user responds to delivered content), Attentiveness (i.e. whether and how user interacts with delivered content) and Receptivity (i.e. whether user accepts delivered content) from interruptions / notifications management literature, can be

[2]Technology Acceptance Model

reused to create unique set of measures adapted to evaluation of PRS.

4. PROGRESS TO DATE & ONGOING WORK

In this section we want to present more details about our research progress to date and ongoing work.

4.1 Economic and Privacy perspective

Since practical implementations are very scarce and generally not available to academic community, we wanted to start first with analysis of user attitudes towards these kind of systems. We looked at relationships between factors that would most probably impact the perception and adoption of proactive systems. Specifically, we were for instance looking at the relationships between information needs, attitudes towards making personal data available to a system, willingness to pay for proactive systems and the characteristics of a user's personality. Information needs are important because main purpose of PRS should be information delivery. Attitudes towards making personal data available to a system and the willingness to pay for proactive systems are also important, because user data collection and monetization are logical challenges/concerns for organizations willing to consider any kind of practical implementation.

In our exploratory study [12], we used Structural Equation Model technique with Maximum Likelihood Estimation to explore models for the economic and the privacy perspective. The economic perspective seems to be highly influenced by users' tolerance towards interruptions from certain types of events (which is influenced by users' trust) and attitude towards providing feedback. Analysis shows that lower the satisfaction with current solutions the brighter the economic perspective of proactive system would be. We concluded that in order to precisely quantify this perspective (economic model) it is necessary to find a proper strategy for measuring these concepts in an additional field study. A second model was related to information needs and users' openness to allow system to exploit data for the purposes of providing better services. Personal belief of Self-Efficacy (based on General Self-Efficacy scale) and Technology Use (i.e. the availability of different technical devices to the participant) seemed to influence the information needs and users' openness to share their personal data. Based on this, for practical system development the sensitivity towards privacy concerns of users has to be high and an appropriate strategy for asking users to share their personal data is required. This will be partially investigated with our future studies on how to acquire user feedback from users and preferred modality for interaction with system.

4.2 Influence of Content Relevancy on Acceptance and Use

We are interested in analysis of factors which influence acceptance and actual use of proactively delivered recommendations. Specifically in: content relevancy, timing and modality of the delivery. So far, we have investigated only the content relevance and the preliminary results (not yet published) are presented in this section.

We conducted an online experiment among graduate students participating in a large statistics course at a university in the Netherlands. Participants were invited to take part in a multi-stage study (involving a pre-survey, the application challenge, and a post-survey). The pre-survey assessed demographics, which were combined with a participant's responses from Application Challenge (AC). The post-challenge survey assessed manipulation checks and participants' experience with the recommendations inside the application and application behavior itself. The AC was the most technically complicated and time-consuming part of the study. In the AC, participants were given two tasks to work on using mobile applications either on iOS or Android platforms. The two tasks involved the planning of a hypothetical trip to London for attendance at royal wedding (T). Each task required submission of an open-ended answer with necessary information (cost, type, etc.). The tasks were identical for all participants and distributed in the same order (i.e., sequentially). In order to complete these two tasks, participants needed to search for information exclusively via in-application browser.

The most important functionality of the AC was to allow participants to work on tasks and to proactively deliver recommendations – even when they didn't anticipate such recommendations. The AC employed a between-subjects design for the recommendations, and participants were randomly split to two experimental groups / conditions (CND). The first group received recommendations that were immediately relevant to the current task (CND = 1). For example, for the first task, participants received 5 recommendations in the form of links to websites that could help participants to find a mode of transportation (e.g. bus, train, plane, etc.) from their city to London. For the second task, they received 5 recommended links that could help them find an accommodation (e.g. hotel, hostel, etc.) in London. For the second group of participants, recommendations were related to the general topic of "traveling to London", but were, nonetheless, irrelevant to the specific task (CND = 2). For example, for the first task, participants received recommendations related to web travel guides for London (e.g. Fodors, LonelyPlanet, etc.) and for the second task, these recommendations were related to websites that offered general information on London's transportation modes (e.g. metro, taxi, etc.) and gastronomical places (e.g. Yelp guide, etc.). The first group's recommendations (CND = 1) thus were directly relevant to task at hand, while the second group's recommendations (CND = 2) were somewhat relevant (tourism, city of destination), but too generic to solving the task at hand. Recommendations were delivered exactly 60 seconds after the start of each of the tasks, independently of platform or CND. The recommendations were delivered inside view – that is, on top of any application or UI that the participant was at the time working with it.

We manipulated the immediate relevance of recommendations and tested for differences in our dependent variables, that are *how useful the participants perceived the received recommendations* and *if they actually used them.* The analysis showed empirical evidence that the immediate relevance of proactively recommended content is well perceived by its recipients and led to its actual use. We furthermore also detected relations between relevance and the exact time when participants consumed the content, i.e. if the content is highly relevant to the task at hand it will be consumed immediately. We plan to reuse existing dataset and deploy new modified versions of the study setup to further investigate remaining factors.

5. CONCLUSIONS & FUTURE WORK

In this paper we discuss relatively novel concepts like PRS/PRD. Our motivation for research is driven by their promising nature and existing efficiency of RS. Proposed research model in this paper is based on theoretical foundations of PC, (context-aware) RS, information delivery, interruption and notification management. From there we reuse concepts and principles to determine key research questions. They are grouped in three specific sections: *Attitudes* towards PRS, *Acceptance & Use* and *User Feedback & Evaluation* of PRS. Factors affecting acceptance and use represent the main focus of this thesis. For that specific set of questions we created an adapted version of TAM. Preliminary results are promising. Specifically, we identified factors that influence the economic perspective but also users' willingness to share data. Also, we determined that contextual relevance of content influences perceived usefulness and usage of proactively determined recommendations.

For our future work, we plan to continue to analyze the influence of other factors on acceptance and use of PRS. For this purpose it will be necessary to modify the initial study design and find more ways for users to provide feedback, but also to put more attention on analysis of contextual information during the actual delivery of recommendations.

6. ACKNOWLEDGEMENTS

Special gratitude to Dr. Laurens Rook and Dr. Markus Zanker for their support, guidance and valuable feedback.

7. REFERENCES

[1] P. D. Adamczyk and B. P. Bailey. If not now, when?: the effects of interruption at different moments within task execution. In *Proceedings of the SIGCHI conference on Human factors in computing systems*, pages 271–278. ACM, 2004.

[2] N. K. Agarwal, Y. C. Xu, and D. C. Poo. A context-based investigation into source use by information seekers. *Journal of the American Society for Information Science and Technology*, 62(6):1087–1104, 2011.

[3] B. P. Bailey and J. A. Konstan. On the need for attention-aware systems: Measuring effects of interruption on task performance, error rate, and affective state. *Computers in human behavior*, 22(4):685–708, 2006.

[4] M. Braunhofer, F. Ricci, B. Lamche, and W. Wörndl. A context-aware model for proactive recommender systems in the tourism domain. In *Proceedings of the 17th International Conference on Human-Computer Interaction with Mobile Devices and Services Adjunct*, pages 1070–1075. ACM, 2015.

[5] G. Fischer. Context-aware systems: the'right'information, at the'right'time, in the'right'place, in the'right'way, to the'right'person. In *Proceedings of the International Working Conference on Advanced Visual Interfaces*, pages 287–294. ACM, 2012.

[6] J. E. Fischer, C. Greenhalgh, and S. Benford. Investigating episodes of mobile phone activity as indicators of opportune moments to deliver notifications. In *Proceedings of the 13th International Conference on Human Computer Interaction with Mobile Devices and Services*, pages 181–190. ACM, 2011.

[7] D. Gallego, E. Barra, A. Gordillo, and G. Huecas. Enhanced recommendations for e-learning authoring tools based on a proactive context-aware recommender. In *Frontiers in Education Conference, 2013 IEEE*, pages 1393–1395. IEEE, 2013.

[8] A. Hinze and A. Voisard. Location-and time-based information delivery in tourism. In *Advances in Spatial and Temporal Databases*, pages 489–507. Springer, 2003.

[9] M. C. P. Melguizo, L. Boves, and O. M. Ramos. A proactive recommendation system for writing: Helping without disrupting. *International Journal of Industrial Ergonomics*, 39(3):516–523, 2009.

[10] E. Murphy-Hill and G. C. Murphy. Recommendation delivery. In *Recommendation Systems in Software Engineering*, pages 223–242. Springer, 2014.

[11] F. Ricci. Mobile recommender systems. *Information Technology & Tourism*, 12(3):205–231, 2010.

[12] A. Sabic and M. Zanker. Investigating user's information needs and attitudes towards proactivity in mobile tourist guides. In I. Tussyadiah and A. Inversini, editors, *Information and Communication Technologies in Tourism 2015*, pages 493–505. Springer International Publishing, 2015.

[13] I. P. Tussyadiah and D. Wang. Tourists? attitudes toward proactive smartphone systems. *Journal of Travel Research*, page 0047287514563168, 2014.

[14] D. G. Vico, W. Woerndl, and R. Bader. A study on proactive delivery of restaurant recommendations for android smartphones. In *ACM RecSys Workshop on Personalization in Mobile Applications, Chicago, USA*, 2011.

[15] X. Wang, Z. Hong, Y. C. Xu, C. Zhang, and H. Ling. Relevance judgments of mobile commercial information. *Journal of the Association for Information Science and Technology*, 65(7):1335–1348, 2014.

[16] P. Wilson. Situational relevance. *Information storage and retrieval*, 9(8):457–471, 1973.

[17] W. Woerndl, J. Huebner, R. Bader, and D. Gallego-Vico. A model for proactivity in mobile, context-aware recommender systems. In *Proceedings of the fifth ACM conference on Recommender systems*, pages 273–276. ACM, 2011.

[18] Y. C. Xu and Z. Chen. Relevance judgment: What do information users consider beyond topicality? *Journal of the American Society for Information Science and Technology*, 57(7):961–973, 2006.

[19] K. F. Yeung and Y. Yang. A proactive personalized mobile news recommendation system. In *Developments in E-systems Engineering (DESE), 2010*, pages 207–212. IEEE, 2010.

Recommender Systems from an Industrial and Ethical Perspective

Dimitris Paraschakis
Dept. of Computer Science
Malmö University
SE-205 06 Malmö, Sweden
dimitris.paraschakis@mah.se

ABSTRACT

Over the recent years, a plethora of recommender systems (RS) have been proposed by academics. The degree of adoptability of these algorithms by *industrial* e-commerce platforms remains unclear. To get an insight into real-world recommendation engines, we survey more than 30 existing shopping cart solutions and compare the performance of popular recommendation algorithms on proprietary e-commerce datasets. Our results show that deployed systems rarely go beyond trivial "best seller" lists or very basic personalized recommendation algorithms, which nevertheless exhibit superior performance to more elaborate techniques both in our experiments and other related studies. We also perform chronological dataset splits to demonstrate the importance of preserving the sequence of events during evaluation, and the recency of events during training. The second part of our research is still ongoing and focuses on various *ethical* challenges that complicate the design of recommender systems. We believe that this direction of research remains mostly neglected despite its increasing impact on RS' quality and safety.

Keywords

industrial recommender systems; recommendation ethics; Netflix Prize; ethical recommendation framework; e-commerce; recommender systems survey

1. INTRODUCTION: ECHOES FROM THE NETFLIX PRIZE

Recommender systems emerged as an independent research area of machine learning in mid-1990s and received a great deal of attention after the announcement of the Netflix Prize[1] in 2006. The contest was set to crowdsource recommendation algorithms from the large research community, whose goal was to surpass Netflix' own algorithm by 10% in terms of accuracy (measured in RMSE). After 10 years, the Netflix Prize still teaches us lessons. One of them is the fact that the prize-winning algorithm was never put to real use: Netflix concluded that the measured accuracy gains "did not seem to justify the engineering effort needed to bring them into a production environment" [1]. This motivates the investigation of the receptiveness of *e-commerce* platforms to recent academic advances in the field of recommender systems. We trust that the high *practical* value of recommender systems in e-commerce ought to be the reason why this research field exists in the first place. As Pradel *et al.* [13] note, "case-studies are necessary to better understand the specificities of purchase datasets and the factors that impact recommender systems for retailers". The first part of our work is such a case study. The specificity of purchase datasets has to do with the absence of explicit feedback (such as movie ratings) and the extreme sparsity of data (because of the severe long-tail effect). As a result, the majority of algorithms designed for *rating* datasets cannot be directly applied to *purchase* data. Furthermore, many e-commerce domains (e.g. fashion, travel, etc.) exhibit more profound seasonality effects in comparison to movie rating datasets. Therefore, we argue that the realistic offline evaluation of recommendation algorithms in industrial contexts has to be done on time-based dataset splits, as we explain in Section 2. We also present the results of the survey and our comparative study of several recommendation algorithms.

Aside from the apparent research shift towards explicit feedback RS, the comparably smaller amount of research on e-commerce RS may also be attributed to the lack of publicly available retail datasets. In our experience, many retailers are reluctant to release their sensitive purchase data because of the *failure of anonymization* [10]. This is where another motivating lesson from the Netflix Prize comes in. This time, we learn the lesson of ethics: two years after its public release, the Netflix dataset was de-anonymized via a linking attack [8], putting the privacy of 500,000 users at risk. This resulted in a lawsuit and put an end to the planned Netflix Prize sequel [7]. The problems of ethics in recommender systems certainly go far beyond anonymization and relate to areas such as data collection and filtering, algorithmic opacity and biases, behaviour manipulation, A/B testing, etc. According to the recent study by Tang & Winoto [14], there exist only two publications (apart from [14]) that specifically address the problem of ethical recommendations. Therefore, this research direction deserves further attention. We discuss ethical issues briefly in Section 3. We conclude the paper and outline our future work in Section 4.

[1] http://www.netflixprize.com/

RecSys '16, September 15 - 19, 2016, Boston , MA, USA

ISBN 978-1-4503-4035-9/16/09...$15.00

DOI: http://dx.doi.org/10.1145/2959100.2959101

2. E-COMMERCE RECOMMENDER SYSTEMS: AN INDUSTRIAL PERSPECTIVE

2.1 Methodology

Our study[2] employs mixed methodology to meet its goals. First, we conduct offline experiments to compare the performance of algorithms from three families of collaborative filtering (CF):

- MF-based CF: *Weighted Regularized Matrix Factorization (**WRMF**)*, *Bayesian Personalized Ranking Matrix Factorization (**BPRMF**)*
- Memory-based CF: *User-user K-nearest neighbours (**UserKNN**)*
- Data mining: *Association Rules Miner (**ARM**)*

Most popular and ***random*** product recommendations are used as baselines. The accuracy of algorithms is measured in terms of *MAP*, *F1@5*, and *R-precision.* The optimal parameters for algorithms are estimated via golden section search. We refer the reader to [11] for the technical details of the above algorithms and evaluation metrics. The evaluation is performed both on *random* and *chronological* dataset splits. The datasets come from two real e-commerce retailers: a fashion store (denoted as D1) and a book store (denoted as D2). The summary of the two datasets is given in Table 1. The results of the experiments are presented in Section 2.3.1.

Table 1: Summary for datasets D1 and D2

	D1	**D2**
Domain	Fashion	Books
Timespan	9 months 26 days	3 months 10 days
Customers	26,091	505,136
Products	4706	210,455
Events	78,449	1,623,576
Sparsity	99.936%	99.998%

Second, we run an online survey[3] to assess recommendation engines of existing e-commerce platforms on three criteria: a) *properties of recommendations*, b) *data utilized for recommendations*, and c) *recommendation techniques.* The selection of these techniques is based on the classification by Amatriain *et al.* [2] (with the addition of several extra techniques). The survey results are given in Section 2.3.2.

2.2 Evaluation

In our experiments, we follow two data splitting strategies:

1. **Traditional approach (random split)**. As it is often practised in the RS literature, we discard *cold-start users* (having less than 10 purchases in our case) and then split user profiles into training and test sets using random sampling (50/50 ratio in our case). Finally, we divide users into 5 folds for cross-validation.

2. **Proposed approach (chronological split)**. To attempt a more realistic evaluation, we keep *cold-start users*[4] in the dataset and divide it using time-based split points. In particular, we propose an *expanding time window* approach, where after setting the temporal split point, the recommender is trained on increasing portions of the training set, starting from the most recent events and ending with the full history.

[2]published in full in [11]

[3]http://goo.gl/forms/zFEfLLlFHO

[4]those with at least 2 events to allow per-user splitting

The motive for attempting both approaches was to determine whether the commonly used random splits can reliably reproduce the ranking of algorithms coming from more realistic temporal, cold-start splits.

2.3 Results

2.3.1 Experiments

The performance of algorithms in *random* mode is given in Tables 2 and 3. It can be seen that UserKNN and ARM outperform MF-based methods on all metrics. This is particularly evident in case of D2, where BPRMF performs on the same level as the recommender of most popular items. This finding is in line with those reported in [13].

In *chronological* mode, the temporal dataset partitioning resulted in the following splits:

- D1: test set containing the last month of data and 9 training sets of increasing length from 1 to 9 months;
- D2: test set containing the last 2 weeks of data and 6 training sets of increasing length from 2 to 12 weeks;

From observing the accuracy measurements of algorithms for each training set[5], we can see that the optimal training history for D1 amounts to the last 3 months of data, which appears reasonable for a fashion store. Likewise, the trend of favouring recent events was observed in D2. It was also evident that the *best seller* list's accuracy peaked when it was trained on the most recent and smallest chunk of data. After averaging accuracy scores over all training sets (Tables 4 and 5), we noticed that the relative ranking of algorithms was very similar to that of the random split, with UserKNN and ARM being on top. In absolute terms, however, the accuracy scores dropped down significantly in the chronological mode. Whereas this can be attributed to the presence of cold-start users, in our additional experiments (not reported here) we show empirically that the random splitting itself can significantly overestimate the accuracy of algorithms.

In terms of running times, MF-based methods were either (fairly) accurate or fast, but never both. The accuracy-speed trade-off of these models is adjusted by balancing between the number of iterations and the number of factors. The best accuracy-speed ratio was achieved by ARM, which also required no parameter tuning.

2.3.2 Survey

20 commercial and 11 open-source e-commerce platforms participated in the survey, whose responses are summarized in Figure 1.

We can see that *transactional data* is used by more than 80% of respondents, which points to the clear dominance of CF over content-based filtering. Surprisingly, *temporal data* is mostly neglected by industrial RS, which contrasts to our empirical findings. It seems that commercial platforms tend to put more effort in *personalization* than their open-source rivals. We observe that *neighborhood-based CF* and *association rules mining* are the most popular personalized recommenders, which is totally in line with our experimental results. Recommending *best sellers* is the preferred approach for most platforms. Indeed, our experiments show that outperforming best-seller lists can be a challenging task even for personalized recommenders. Moreover, trivial *random* and *manual* recommenders appear more widespread than state-of-the-art techniques, such as MF-based algorithms.

[5]the performance charts are omitted due to limited space

Table 2: Scores for the random split on D1

Recommender	*MAP*	*F1@5*	*R-prec*	*Running Time*
WRMF	0.0927	0.1013	0.1036	00:05:21
BPRMF	0.0650	0.0676	0.0698	00:00:32
UserKNN	0.1000	0.1078	0.1073	00:00:05
ARM	**0.1100**	**0.1162**	**0.1155**	00:00:01
Most Popular	0.0523	0.0458	0.0468	00:00:00
Random	0.0028	0.0000	0.0010	00:00:00

Table 3: Scores for the random split on D2

Recommender	*MAP*	*F1@5*	*R-prec*	*Running Time*
WRMF	0.1293	0.1322	0.1363	07:10:10
BPRMF	0.0188	0.0148	0.0187	00:12:46
UserKNN	**0.1796**	**0.1859**	**0.1854**	00:56:21
ARM	0.1774	0.1813	0.1825	00:16:24
Most Popular	0.0139	0.0149	0.0156	00:07:02
Random	0.0002	0.0001	0.0001	00:09:09

Table 4: Average scores for the chronological split on D1

Recommender	*MAP*	*F1@5*	*R-prec*	*Running Time*
WRMF	0.0244	0.0188	0.0147	00:05:27
BPRMF	0.0214	0.0121	0.0095	00:00:06
UserKNN	0.0312	**0.0229**	0.0222	00:00:06
ARM	**0.0334**	0.0214	**0.0225**	00:00:01
Most Popular	0.0206	0.0113	0.0080	00:00:00
Random	0.0037	0.0014	0.0009	00:00:00

Table 5: Average scores for the chronological split on D2

Recommender	*MAP*	*F1@5*	*R-prec*	*Running Time*
WRMF	0.0351	0.0260	0.0224	02:27:10
BPRMF	0.0160	0.0130	0.0114	00:18:37
UserKNN	0.0469	0.0363	**0.0352**	00:50:14
ARM	**0.0488**	**0.0377**	0.0346	00:20:35
Most Popular	0.0150	0.0114	0.0094	00:10:24
Random	0.0001	0.0000	0.0000	00:14:42

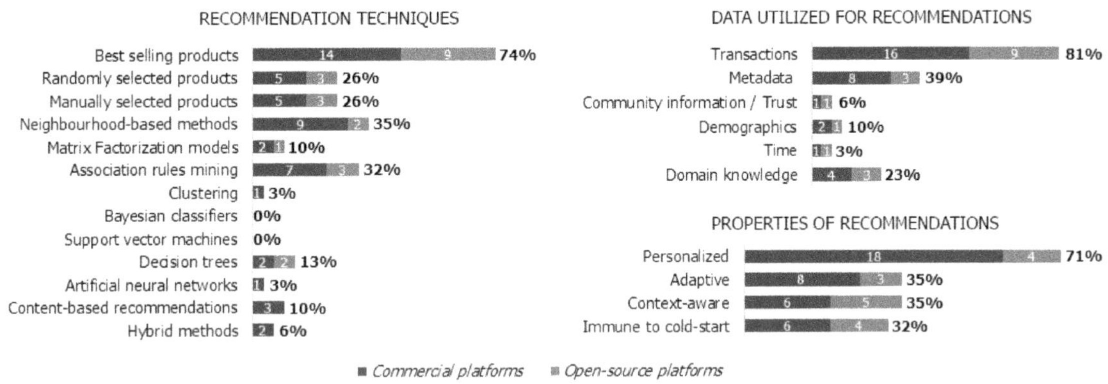

Figure 1: Survey responses from 31 e-commerce platforms

3. TOWARDS ETHICAL RECOMMENDER SYSTEMS

Our ongoing work focuses on another rather overlooked aspect of recommender systems, which is the problem of *ethics*. This problem is multifaceted and relates to many broader areas of data science. In this section, we give a brief overview of some ethical challenges in and around recommender systems.

Data collection. The lack of *transparency* and *informed consent* is what explains the great demand in "do not track" tools that would help users gain control over the data collection process. Furthermore, enriching user profiles by means of tracking cookies, linked open data, social networks, and even data brokers increase the risk of user privacy breaches.

User profiling. User behaviour profiles built for serving personalized recommendations may as well be utilised for malicious purposes, such as *phishing* or *social engineering* [7]. Moreover, disclosed user profiles may reveal sensitive private information. *Profile injection* is another possible attack that uses fake profiles to promote or demote recommendations of certain items [3], e.g. by artificially influencing their ratings. A number of *privacy preserving collaborative filtering* (PPCF) algorithms have been proposed in RS literature (e.g. [15]) to protect user profiles from leakage. The major challenge in such systems is to preserve recommendation accuracy.

Data publishing. The massive research on RS would not be possible without publicly released datasets (MovieLens, Netflix, etc.), which have positive impact on both research and practice [5]. Because a *public* dataset typically contains *private* data, releasing a myriad of user records is a serious and responsible moral act. The naive assumption that the dataset remains safe as long as *personally identifiable information* has been disguised has long ceased to hold. Many examples of user re-identification in anonymized datasets (e.g. [9]) have been reported in the literature (recall the Netflix case). The existence of quasi-identifiers and rich "outside" information makes de-anonymization of public datasets a persistent threat. On the other hand, an attempt of aggressive anonymization can render the dataset useless for a RS.

Data filtering. With very few exceptions (e.g. [14]), contemporary RS do not employ any moral filtering of their output. This raises an issue of content censorship with all its consequent implications. As noted in [14], what is *algorithmically* appropriate is not necessarily *ethically* appropriate. Should the RS be held liable for serving offensive or hazardous content? How to balance between commercial and moral values in a RS? The ethical appropriateness of candidate items can be established by mapping potentially harmful elements in media content (drug use, nudity, etc.) to a user's persona (gender, age, etc.), as explained in [14]. Authors suggest that moral values are incorporated in system requirements, with users having control over the filtering process.

Algorithmic opacity. A typical RS operates as a "black box", with its *output* being the only part that is visible to a user. Collecting data and processing it into recommendations is done completely behind the scenes. What are the ethical implications of not knowing the *algorithm* that rules recommendations? Apparently, this opacity makes it hard to reason about the political, economic, and cultural agendas behind these suggestions [12]. From the corporate ethics perspective, however, the intentional secrecy is needed to retain company's competitive advantage. Even when an algorithm is not kept in secrecy, explaining it to a user might be hardly possible because of its inherent mathematical complexity.

Biases and behaviour manipulation. In their interaction with RS, how can users be certain that their interests are respected and prioritized? What if the users' behaviour is being algorithmically manipulated to meet RS's own objectives (e.g. selling expensive / overstocked / nearly expired products)? One example of an unethical algorithmic bias is *price discrimination*, i.e. charging customers different prices based on their perceived willingness to pay [4]. How to ensure that the RS is unbiased? One way to aid transparency is to implement an *explanation interface* [6] for recommendations.

A/B testing. Many industrial RS resort to *A/B testing* to assess the effects of tweaking their algorithms. In most cases, visitors are silently dragged into these experiments without their knowledge, let alone consent. Should an e-commerce interface allow users to opt out of A/B testing? Is it their moral right to demand interacting with the "real" recommender system instead of the one being put to test?

4. CONCLUSIONS AND FUTURE WORK

In this paper, we have taken a closer look at *industrial* recommender systems in e-commerce and have touched upon certain *ethical* implications that affect the design and implementation of these systems.

After experimenting on retail data and surveying existing e-commerce platforms, we conclude that their adoption of sophisticated RS that have been proposed by the research community over the years is rather slow. Whether it has to do with the unjustifiable "engineering efforts" that had stopped Netflix from implementing a better algorithm, or strict real-time performance requirements of industrial shopping cart solutions, the suitability of these models to the realities of the e-commerce realm requires further investigation.

Our experiments also illustrate the importance of *time-aware* evaluation, where dataset splits are done chronologically and the sequence of events in user profiles is preserved. Without this property, the analysis of a retail dataset is prone to significant overestimation of the algorithm performance due to capturing erroneous shopping patterns. We also show that training on all available history is in most cases suboptimal. The proposed *expanding time window* method can be used to establish the optimal timespan of the training set, thus improving recommendation accuracy and speed.

Finally, we observe that multiple moral dilemmas of varied severity emerge on virtually every stage of RS design. We plan to continue our work on identifying their impact and possible solutions in hope to outline an ethical framework for RS designers.

5. REFERENCES

[1] X. Amatriain and J. Basilico. Netflix recommendations: Beyond the 5 stars. Online: http://techblog.netflix.com/2012/04/netflix-recommendations-beyond-5-stars.html/, Apr. 2012. Accessed: 2015-03-12.

[2] X. Amatriain, A. Jaimes, N. Oliver, and J. Pujol. Data mining methods for recommender systems. In F. Ricci, L. Rokach, B. Shapira, and P. B. Kantor, editors, *Recommender Systems Handbook*, chapter 2, pages 257–297. Springer-Verlag New York, Inc., 2010.

[3] R. Burke, M. O'Mahony, and N. Hurley. Robust collaborative recommendation. In F. Ricci, L. Rokach, B. Shapira, and P. B. Kantor, editors, *Recommender Systems Handbook*, chapter 25, pages 805–835. Springer-Verlag New York, Inc., 2010.

[4] N. Diakopoulos. Algorithmic accountability reporting: On the investigation of black boxes. *Tow Center for Digital Journalism A Tow/Knight Brief*, 2014.

[5] F. M. Harper and J. A. Konstan. The movielens datasets: History and context. *ACM Trans. Interact. Intell. Syst.*, 5:19:1–19:19, Dec. 2015.

[6] J. L. Herlocker, J. A. Konstan, and J. Riedl. Explaining collaborative filtering recommendations. In *Proceedings of the ACM Conference on Computer Supported Cooperative Work*, pages 241–250. ACM, 2000.

[7] A. Koene, E. Perez, C. J. Carter, R. Statache, S. Adolphs, C. O'Malley, T. Rodden, and D. McAuley. Ethics of personalized information filtering. In *Second International Conference on Internet Science, INSCI*, pages 123–132, 2015.

[8] A. Narayanan and V. Shmatikov. Robust de-anonymization of large sparse datasets. In *Proceedings of the 2008 IEEE Symposium on Security and Privacy*, pages 111–125, 2008.

[9] A. Narayanan and V. Shmatikov. De-anonymizing social networks. In *30th IEEE Symposium on Security and Privacy*, pages 173–187. IEEE, 2009.

[10] P. Ohm. Broken promises of privacy: Responding to the surprising failure of anonymization. *UCLA Law Review*, 57:1701, 2009.

[11] D. Paraschakis, B. J. Nilsson, and J. Holländer. Comparative evaluation of top-n recommenders in e-commerce: An industrial perspective. In *14th International Conference on Machine Learning and Applications (ICMLA)*, pages 1024 – 1031. IEEE, 2015.

[12] F. Pasquale. The black box society. the secret algorithms that control money and information. Harvard University Press, 2015.

[13] B. Pradel, S. Sean, J. Delporte, S. Guérif, C. Rouveirol, N. Usunier, F. Fogelman-Soulié, and F. Dufau-Joel. A case study in a recommender system based on purchase data. In *Proceedings of the 17th ACM SIGKDD International Conference on Knowledge Discovery and Data Mining*, KDD '11, pages 377–385, 2011.

[14] T. Tang and P. Winoto. I should not recommend it to you even if you will like it: the ethics of recommender systems. *New Review of Hypermedia and Multimedia*, 19:111–138, 2016.

[15] J. Zhan, C.-L. Hsieh, I.-C. Wang, T.-S. Hsu, C.-J. Liau, and D.-W. Wang. Privacy-preserving collaborative recommender systems. *Trans. Sys. Man Cyber Part C*, 40:472–476, July 2010.

Author Index

www.ingramcontent.com/pod-product-compliance
Ingram Content Group UK Ltd.
Pitfield, Milton Keynes, MK11 3LW, UK
UKHW051414290926
15471UKWH00009B/1593

9 781450 346818